The Gun Digest Book of

ASSAULT WEAPONS

5TH EDITION

Jack Lewis & David E. Steele

Published by

 krause
publications

700 E. State Street • Iola, WI 54990-0001
Telephone: 715/445-2214

Please call or write for our free catalog or visit our website.
Our toll-free number to place an order or obtain a free catalog is 800-258-0929
or please use our regular business telephone 715-445-2214
for editorial comment and further information.
www.krause.com

Library of Congress: 85-73744
ISBN: 0-87341-778-X

Printed in the United States of America

Introduction

FIRST, YOU WILL note that this edition of *The Gun Digest Book of Assault Weapons* carries a double byline. That means that some of the material was written by Jack Lewis and other parts by David E. Steele. In the beginning, the two of us worked together, then suddenly we were nearly 3000 miles apart. That made it difficult to use the editorial "we." The ultimate answer was to write the text in third person narrative, identifying each of the authors in that manner.We feel it will appear to be a more honest effort on our part(s) and will help the reader to know who is doing what. We hope it works for you.

This is the fifth edition of this book. It has been approximately 13 years since the first edition appeared. In reviewing that original book and the other editions published in the interim, it becomes obvious that some things seem not to change. The Cold War ended years ago to be replaced by a series of brush wars that sap our national wealth and military strength. And one of the first things we noted in our review is the fact that the so-called "weapons race" did not end with the tearing down of the Berlin Wall. It is still going on!

Of particular interest to many readers, we feel, will be the final section of this volume that deals with the types of weapons and accessories military types will be using – and facing – near the start of the new millennium.

There was a time when military tacticians felt it was better to wound a man than to kill him in combat. In that era, it took four men to carry the woundee to an aid station. That took five men total out of battle for each wounding.

But somewhere the theory has changed. Today, military small arms are becoming more deadly with each new generation. The object now seems to be to put the enemy soldier out of the game – and out of existence – for keeps! Nuclear weapons to mass destruction may be on hold, at least for the moment, but the weaponry being built now to arm front line troops in future engagements is far more destructive than were the M-1 rifle, the M-16, the hand grenade and a host of other weapons used from World War I through Vietnam. These examples now are found primarily in military museums or in the hands of a few collectors.

The computer sciences have had much to do with the development of today's super-sophisticated weaponry, which seems to do everything but think for itself ... and that possibility may not be far away.

For the most part, the weaponry discussed in this book is based upon present-day use by police and military forces. That is what they are: weapons. They should not be construed as being toys. In some cases, true, sporting firearms have found a practical use in military situations, but invariably, further changes are ordered to make the particular firearm a lot less sporting and a good deal more deadly.

Also, the military assualt once was considered a close-quarters exercise involving bayonets, rifle butts, trench knives and even fists. Today, assaults are launched in armored vehicles with weaponry that brings death and destruction upon an enemy at ranges of thousands of yards.

Many would like to think such armament is a deterrent against nations becoming involved in full-scale wars such as those of the past. But what we must remember above all else is that other nations – including those not our friends – are following the same path, developing sophisticated weaponry that kills at long range, is controlled largely by computers and is totally impersonal. One thing military tacticians – and more importantly, the world's politicians – should keep in mind is that a computer does not have a conscience!

Jack Lewis,
Kehena Beach, Pahoa, Hawaii

David F. Steele,
Los Angeles, California

About the Authors

JACK LEWIS was editor/publisher of *GUN WORLD* magazine for 37 years, and has lost track of the number of books he and his staff produced over that period. He also has lost track of the number of full-auto weapons he has fired in his research efforts.

Over the years, he has managed to combine two careers—journalism and the military—with uncommon success. He is the author of nearly 6000 published magazine articles. He also wrote and produced the first four editions of this particular book and now resides in Hawaii, where he writes magazine articles and novels.

A veteran of World War II, Korea and Vietnam, he is a decorated and now-retired lieutenant colonel of the Marine Corps Reserve. His fascination with selective-fire weaponry dates back more than a half-century to his days as a private first class machine gunner.

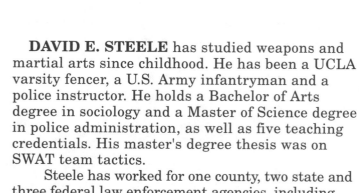

DAVID E. STEELE has studied weapons and martial arts since childhood. He has been a UCLA varsity fencer, a U.S. Army infantryman and a police instructor. He holds a Bachelor of Arts degree in sociology and a Master of Science degree in police administration, as well as five teaching credentials. His master's degree thesis was on SWAT team tactics.

Steele has worked for one county, two state and three federal law enforcement agencies, including U.S. Customs. He was supervisor of the Police Weapons Center project in Washington, D.C., testing police equipment and writing tech manuals. For the past decade, he has been a criminal investigator for the state of California. He has authored two books and more than 500 published articles on firearms, knives and self-defense subjects.

Acknowledgements

WITH VIRTUALLY ANY book of a technical nature that finds its way into print, the authors have to turn to a great number of people for help. Equipment has to be obtained for study and evaluation, references and histories must be located, tech manuals are an obvious requirement and there is a need for plenty of advice based upon the experiences of those "who have been there."

This book is no different. Other than those individuals listed on the title page, we owe a great deal to a host of individuals, who were happy to cooperate in this effort. As has been the case with past editions of The Gun Digest Book of Assault Weapons, we could not have completed it—at least, not by deadline time—without the aid and understanding of C. Reed Knight, Jr., major domo of Knight's Armament Co. in Vero Beach, Florida. He not only gave us a key to his museum and let us tote valuable weaponry to and from shooting sites, but also allowed us access to what has to be one of the best firearms libraries in the world. If you need an answer about automatic weapons, Reed either has it or can find it!

Bill McClure, vice-president of Knight's Armament, also was of great help to the authors. We had hoped to include a full-scale review of the Knight SR-50 semi-automatic 50-caliber rifle in this edition, but said biggie is not yet in production as we approach our publishing deadline.

Others whose contributions cannot be ignored include Master Sergeant Ron Appling of Marine Base Hawaii, who followed through on arrangements for us to fire the M19 40mm machine gun; retired Marine Master Sergeant Ralph J. Austin, who picked up his combat camera once again to photograph the Hughes-developed chain gun; Robert K. Brown of Soldier of Fortune magazine, who helped with the chapter on new Russian weaponry; George Ealovega, who worked with us on the story concerning his new Parker-Hale mini submachine gun; Mossberg's Bud Fini, who worked far into the night to see that we received on time two shotguns we needed for testing; Dan Fitzgerald for backing up David Steele on needed photos; and Travis Hall of U.S. Repeating Arms Co., for prompt loan of the Winchester Model 1200 Defender.

Robert Joseph, who aided us with chapters on shooting schools, is no less deserving of recognition than are Paul Johnston for his photo support for Chapter 9; Mike Jordan of Winchester/Olin for tech advice; Tom Nelson, a noted arms authority and honcho of Collector's Armory, Limited; First Lieutenant Joe Peters, U.S. Army, for help in developing the chapter on the M-4 Carbine; Walt Rausch, peace officer extraordinaire for backup photos used with the H&K G96 chapter; Robbie Robison of L.A.R. Manufacturing, makers of the 50 BMG single-shot; Jim Schmidt of Arizona Ammunition, who handloaded the 50 BMG ammo; Colonel Bill White of the Marine Corps Association for editorial input in developing the section regarding infantry small arms and accessories of the future, and to Rueselle Lewis for endless hours devoted to keeping this project on track!

We hope you enjoy their efforts and ours. If we have inadvertently neglected to include some worthy individual in the list above, we apologize here and now.

Assault Weapons, 5th Edition
Table of Contents

Page 217

Page 124

Page 138

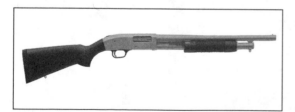

Page 182

Page 140

Page 107

About our Covers....

On the Front:

The new Colt M4 Carbine is shown in a close-up photograph of the receiver area and, as well, full-length. This derivation of the M16 has been under development for a number of years. It is intended to replace a variety of current small arms, to include certain submachine guns, M-9 pistols and some M16 rifle assignments. It is possible the M4 will fully replace the M16A2 rifle.

On the Back:

Above, the SACO M19 Machine Gun fires 40mm grenades; shown here on a special operations vehicle. Below is an artist's illustration of the internal workings of the versatile Heckler & Koch G36 E Assault Rifle.

Page 178

Section I
Then & Now

CHAPTER 1

A SPECIAL KIND OF GUN CONTROL

Parker-Hale's New Individual Defense Weapon Brings A Whole New Concept To Muzzle Control For Full-Auto Fire

GEORGE D. EALOVEGA'S FIRST love is wildlife photography and his second is shooting and firearms; on second thought, that order of interests just possibly may be the other way around.

The last time we saw him, he had been hanging out on Florida's Merritt Island just off the coast from the NASA space launch site. He had decided he could create what's known as a coffee table book based upon the wild creatures that still thrive on this island in spite of all of the space business going on only a few miles away. The morning we talked, he had been on the island and had been crawling along an overhung trail on his belly, when he came face to face with the creator of said trail: a 12-foot alligator.

"What did you do?" was the obvious question.

"I shot three quick shots of his nostrils and got the hell out!" was the less than obvious answer. This had happened as he was waiting for contracts to be completed for the manufacture of a mini-submachine gun he had designed and built. At that time, it was called the Ealovega IDW (for Individual Defense Weapon). The contracts have since been signed and the novel firearm is in production in England as the Parker-Hale IDW. There will be a model number, but it had not been determined at the time of this writing.

The gun's designer, George Ealovega, is a graduate of Wayne State University in Detroit, where he pursued a double major—fine arts

and engineering. He became an advertising photographer and ultimately was earning as much as $5,000 a day for his product photos. In 1969, he migrated to England, where he lived while working all over Europe, Japan, Australia and even

Africa. Before he returned to the United States in 1991, he experienced one of the more unusual misadventures of his life.

"I had photographed what are called dangerous game animals all over Africa—lions, elephants, Cape buffalo and the rest— and never suffered any harm, although there were a few close calls. It was in London that I was hired to do an advertising shot with what was supposedly a tame lion.

"I had the camera set up and was trying to shoot when the animal suddenly went berserk and charged me from across the studio. He did a good job of chewing before they got him off me." Ealovega still carries scars from that encounter. He never did mention to us whether he got the photograph.

At the unlikely age of 13, Ealovega built his first firearm with the aid of his grandfather. This was a cap-and-ball single-shot rifle. He later became a lifelong hunting enthusiast, but most of the guns he has used have been muzzleloaders which he built. It's a far cry from muzzleloaders to submachine guns, but Ealovega tends to blame his old shooting partner, Peter

The Picketinny rail atop the gun allows for a variety of sighting equipment to be mounted and eye relief adjusted for benefit of the shooter.

West, for this particular interest. West was a military armorer for the British Army.

"It was Pete West who educated me in the matter of military firearms," the designer admits. "He exposed me to all sorts of gunsmithing and maintenance problems, then taught me how to solve those problems."

One of the subjects often discussed was recoil of full-auto weaponry and the tendency for the muzzle to climb. The two of them—West and Ealovega—spent a lot of time on ranges, trying to learn the best cyclic rate of fire for the optimum return in accuracy.

"In the beginning, it was all trial and error," Ealovega explains, "and we burned up a lot of ammunition before eventually determining that the best compromise was a rate of 400 rounds

The Parker-Hale 9mm IDW is compared with a SIG 9mm handgun to offer an idea of the subgun's compact size.

per minute." The average full-auto military weapon fires at between 600 to 1200 rounds per minute. Excessive rate of fire has been a continuing problem with submachine guns and has been remedied in various ways over the past 50-plus years. The German Schmeisser, for instance, used a heavy bolt that was supposed to slow down movement of the action. All of this called for a heavier receiver, as well.

A Finnish gun designer named Aimo Johanssen Lahti came up with a rate reducer that was created by vacuum. The device was positioned at the rear of the receiver and delayed the forward movement of the bolt. Problem was that it did not reduce the rate enough to gain any serious manufacturing attention.

The Czechoslovakian ZK 383 submachine gun was built so that the bolt carried a removable weight. If one wanted the gun to fire more rapidly, the weight was removed, allowing the bolt to move with greater speed. This, of course, translated to more shots per minute.

The Spanish came up with a rate control device for their Star subgun

that slowed the bolt slightly, and the Japanese Nambu subgun originally was outfitted with a pneumatic rate reducer. It was unsuccessful enough that it soon was dropped.

George Ealovega decided that if he was going to solve the problem, he would have to take a different approach. He designed a mini-submachine gun and called it the Mark I, then he and his mentor, Peter West, devised an electrical system that allowed for varying rates of fire.

The Mark I was displayed and demonstrated at the British Army Equipment Exposition in 1990. "It was a phenomenal success," Ealovega recalls. "In fact, we had immediate

interest for 5500 guns, but we just couldn't deliver them. We had given no thought to marketing, much less production. Everything to that point had been engineering, and there was research and development still to do."

Finances, further test work and engineering caused the project to drag on. Ealovega had hoped to interest the U.S. government in the project, but it was rejected because of the gun's dependency on batteries to operate the electrical system. Some of the mechanical systems listed earlier were considered and rejected. Eleovega returned to the U.S. in 1991 to continue development work, and it was then that he hit upon the idea of using a hydraulic system to control the rate of fire.

The Parker-Hale submachine gun has a two-stage stock that folds against the action to give a thin profile.

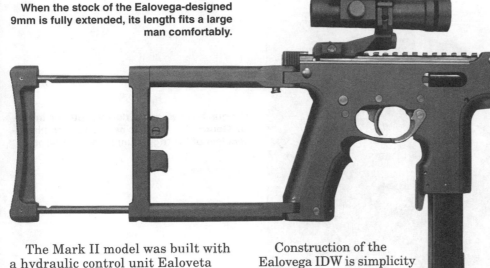

When the stock of the Ealovega-designed 9mm is fully extended, its length fits a large man comfortably.

The Mark II model was built with a hydraulic control unit Ealoveta designed to fit compactly into the grip of the gun. Experimentation and testing called for some additional work and another version was designed and designated as the IDW Mark III.

With this third concept, Ealovega, living and carrying on his development work in Florida by this time, approached Knight's Armament Co. in Vero Beach, Florida, and Reed Knight, Jr., agreed to help. The designer contracted with Knight for the use of his battery of engineering-geared computers on which he then finalized the ultimate IDW design. The contract also allowed for the use of the Knight range facilities.

During this time, Ealovega also designed and built three M-4 carbines and one M-16 prototype with the IDW rate control system to prove the design would work successfully in any full-auto weapon. It did.

The Rheinlander Instrument Corp. of Fort Pierce, Florida, produced the actual production-ready prototypes—four of them. With these in hand, Ealovega set up shop on the Knight Armament range and began to check out the likely longevity of his brainchildren. At this writing, one of the prototype guns has had 22,000 rounds of 9mm ammo fired through it without a problem and continues to be totally functional, even though Ealovega has put it in semi-retired status. Three other prototype guns each have had some 6000 rounds fired through their workings. Treatment of the guns during these tests was unique. Each evening, the designer would run a brush through the bore and wipe the gun off with a clean cloth. After 6000 rounds, each gun was field stripped, cleaned and examined.

Construction of the Ealovega IDW is simplicity personified, yet probably can be classified as a new generation of submachine gun. There are three moving parts in the trigger system and two parts in the rate control system. Five metal pins hold the gun together, and they can be removed without tools in order to disassemble the piece.

The IDW fires from the open bolt, but George Ealovega contends the gun "has both the fast lock time and first-shot accuracy that, until now, has been credited to much more complicated and sensitive closed-bolt models. This is because the IDW's rate-control system now allows firing by means of an extremely lightweight bolt with short travel.

"Being open-bolt, one doesn't have to worry about accidental discharges due to cook-off as is the case with closed-bolt guns," the designer adds. "And, in testing, I haven't had the split groupings suffered with many closed-bolt subguns, their first round printing in one spot and the balance of the groups printing elsewhere on—or off—the target."

Reliability is a major factor in any firearm and with this go both ease and efficiency of care. The IDW can be disassembled by taking out five pins, allowing removal of the trigger group and the hydraulic rate-control system. The control unit itself can be removed by pushing out only two pins. Thus the unit can be exchanged almost instantly for one offering a different rate of fire.

"We feel this can be useful in training those unfamiliar with full-auto weaponry," Ealovega states. "A unit allowing an exceedingly slow rate of fire can be installed for early training and familiarization."

The gun has built-in rails to guide the bolt. As a result, the bolt touches nothing else in the gun's innards during operation. The bolt weighs only eight ounces and travels only two inches in firing the submachine gun.

Weight of the gun without the stock is 4.7 pounds and 5.7 pounds with it. The design of the stock, according to Ealovega, was no afterthought. It was designed as an integral component of the design. Whether folded or deployed, this stock locks into rigid position, offering one the feeling of a fixed stock.

With the stock extended, it provides 14.3 inches of distance from the butt to the trigger, an advantage for precise aimed shots. With it in the folded position, Ealovega feels it is ideal for room clearing, allowing the shooter to hold the gun close to the chest and fire from that position. The stock also is easily removed by slipping out two metal pins, making it a machine pistol. The inventor made the point that two of his guns can be fitted into the same slim-line briefcase.

With the stock folded, overall length of the IDW 9mm is 11.6 inches. Height, without the magazine is 6.7 inches and 10.25 inches with a 30-round, double-stack magazine in the well. Width of the gun is 1.17

Viewed from the top, the 9mm IDW presents a thin image. Note that the rail runs the full length of the receiver.

The gun has two safety devices, but the inventor, George Ealovega, is careful to keep his finger clear of the trigger until ready to shoot.

inches. If the stock is folded, this adds half an inch to the width.

The barrel of this little blaster measures only 4.0 inches and it is easily changed. The cocking handle is the standard military-oriented M-16 variety. And speaking of the M-16, Ealovega used one of these and the more recently issued M-4A1 carbine in some of his development experiments. He outfitted both of them with the hydraulic rate control unit and brought them down to 400 rounds per minute.

A notched accessory rail machined directly into the upper receiver extends almost full length atop the gun's frame, allowing a variety of scopes and other sighting devices to be added. It also offers a rigid, compact mounting system for any of these sights. If one wants low profile,

the Bushnell Holosight retains the compactness of the overall package. If one needs a higher sight, he simply switches the mount. It's the user who makes the choice.

During development and testing, the designer favored a red-dot sight that allows him to fire 25 rounds in the full-auto mode to print a 12-inch group at 25 yards. Using the same sighting system, he can reduce this to about seven inches when firing the same number of rounds in two- and three-round bursts. Off a rest or bipod, a 25-round burst can be held in a six-inch circle at 25 yards. Jack Lewis can and does testify that this also is one subgun that can be fired pistol fashion without climbing off the target.

"Experienced automated weapons users are painfully aware of the fact that compactness and lightness always

result in increased rates of fire—and a higher rate of fire only serves to increase weapon-climb off the target," the designer points out. "This is the reason so many submachine guns and assault rifles in the field today actually are never used in the full-auto mode. That's also the reason designers have come to incorporate a two- or three-round burst mechanism. Anything after the second or third round usually is off-target."

The IDW has no provision for semi-automatic fire or three-round bursts, but Ealovega insists there is no need for either. With the 400-round-per-minute cyclic rate going for him, he demonstrated that he could fire single rounds—or three-round bursts—strictly by means of finger control on the trigger.

Co-author Jack Lewis met Ealovega several years ago on the

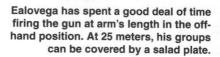

Ealovega has spent a good deal of time firing the gun at arm's length in the off-hand position. At 25 meters, his groups can be covered by a salad plate.

For serious shooting, the designer fires the gun from the shoulder. He expended more than 22,000 rounds through one prototype.

Knight Armament range where the author was checking out some of Reed Knight's gun collection and the inventor was conducting tests on his own gun.

Lewis was immediately intrigued by the compactness and accuracy of the IDW prototype and had a chance to fire it there. He found, after several minutes of concentration, that he also could get the count down to a single round or—in more instances—no more than two rounds per finger twitch.

After this discussion of firing, it seems logical we should talk a bit about the IDW's safety system. The designer didn't forget that facet, either. In fact, one might think he has gone to extremes. The IDW employs not one but two positive though independent safety systems.

What Ealovega has come up with is a double-key system; both safety systems must be off before the gun can be either cocked or fired. Being independent of each other, either system on its own prevents movement of any of the trigger components, including the bolt, and renders them totally safe.

The first safety system is made up of a pair of levers, one positioned on each side of the receiver. Whether left or right-handed, the shooter is in charge, since the levers are situated so they are operated by the trigger finger. At the same time, there is no need to alter the position of the hand or the weapon from its aimed, ready-to-fire position. The levers also block access to the trigger, thus making the shooter aware of the position of the safety levers by feel, if it is dark or he

Author Jack Lewis looks over the Parker-Hale IDW, noting some of its features.

Jack Lewis found the little subgun was easy to use accurately at 25 meters with the stock fully extended. The 400-rounds-per-minute rate of fire results in little barrel climb, making the gun easy to hold on the target.

does not want to interrupt his concentration on the target.

The second system chosen by Ealovega is a grip safety that is positioned under the trigger guard and in front of the grip. This safety is deactivated automatically when the shooting hand grasps the grip. When the hold on the grip is released, the safety is reactivated instantly. Should the subgun be dropped, even if the safety levers are in their off positions, the gun still cannot be discharged.

"With that system, the IDW can be carried safely while cocked and loaded, even with the safety levers in the off position," the designer points out. "That makes it easy to operate the gun without ever taking the sights off the target."

All of this is the culmination of more than a decade of research and development, coupled with large doses of frustration and, at times, even rank despair, but there is no doubt in our minds that George Ealovega has ushered in a new era of submachine gun technology and design. In fact, there are those who feel his work could have an effect upon all future automatic weapons design!

Although the gun's most controllable rate of fire was determined through an extended series of range tests to be 400 rounds per minute, the technology used in the design will allow it to be fired at any other rate, if desired. All that is required is installation of a different hydraulic unit.

When the M-14 rifle was introduced to the military, it was discovered quickly that full-auto

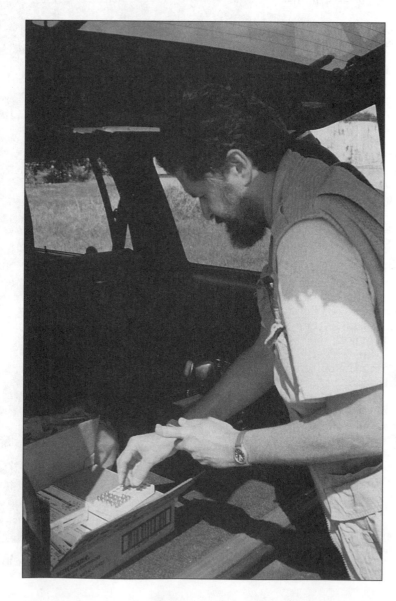

During his series of torture tests for the gun, George Ealovega used the trunk of his car as an office and mobile supply point.

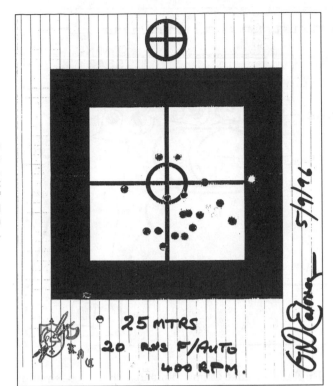

This target, fired by George Ealovega on the Knight's Armament range in Florida, tells its own story. It was shot during torture tests of one of the prototype guns that fired some 22,000 rounds of 9mm ammunition.

25 MTRS
20 RDS F/AUTO
400 RPM.

capability for the average soldier is an enemy of fire discipline. It did not take long for military leaders to see what was happening and the fire control lever was removed from the gun, making it a semi-automatic-only rifle. Then came the M-16, which did not have this limiting option as such. America once was known as a nation of riflemen, but in Vietnam we became a nation of sprayers! The three-round burst control was incorporated in the M-16A2, of course, but by that time, the war in the rice paddies was over. The only winners were the ammunition manufacturers.

With the type of weapon this artist-turned-inventor has developed—one tuned for maximum control—there are numerous advantages. First, there will continue to be "sprayers" in the midst of our ground forces. It's a situation born of fear and adrenaline, but chances are, with the ability to hold the gun on target, this individual's chances of hitting an enemy target are decidedly better.

The individual responsible for bringing the gun to the point of production is David John Cockayne, founder and chief executive of an English-based organization called Modular Industries, Limited.

Young David Cockayne left school at the age of 16 to begin an apprenticeship with England's GEC Limited, winning an Apprentice of the Year award for his achievements. Upon graduation, he gained some valuable sales experience before returning to the company as an engineer. In 1975, he started his own business. In the two-plus decades since, Modular Industries has become a business giant, buying other companies and dovetailing their activities with Cockayne's business goals.

In 1997, Cockayne acquired the assets of Birmingham Gunmakers, using that entity as the basis for founding the Bremmer Arms Company, Limited. Here he oversaw development of an innovative tactical shotgun for police and military use. Other Bremmer products include a remake of the Model 1903 Springfield rifle series and a 22-caliber semi-automatic clone of the AR-15.

In 1998, David Cockayne and his Modular Industries acquired Parker-Hale, Limited, a firm respected for more than a century for its quality sporting firearms and accessories. It is there that the headquarters for Modular Industries are being established and it is in this factory that the Ealovega-designed Parker-Hale IDW submachine gun is being built.

It seems fitting that a gun that may change the concept of future small arms development should be produced in a factory that once was the proof house testing site for the

Specifications

Name:	Parker-Hale Individual Defense Weapon (IDW).
Type:	Submachine gun.
Caliber:	9mm Parabellum.
Operation:	Recoil-operated; fires from open bolt; hydraulic rate control.
Cyclic Rate:	380 to 400 rounds per minute; variable by change of hydraulic rate control unit.
Weight:	4.7 pounds, without stock; 5.7 pounds, with stock.
Length:	11.6 inches (stock folded).
Barrel:	4.0 inches; 1:10" twist.
Magazine:	10-, 20- and 30-shot; double-stacked type; welded sheet metal.
Stock:	Folding, with extension on twin cylindrical rails.
Finish:	Anodized on aluminum frame, stock.
Maker:	Parker-Hale, Limited Golden Hillock Road Birmingham, B11 2PZ England

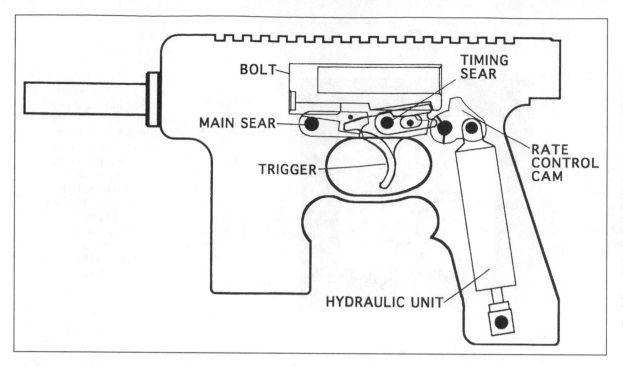

BOLT

TIMING SEAR

MAIN SEAR

TRIGGER

RATE CONTROL CAM

HYDRAULIC UNIT

Parker-Hale engineers prepared this drawing to show how the IDW's inner workings operate. The trigger is shown in the pulled position, having operated the main sear. The bolt is shown in the timed position after the initial shot, where it has been arrested by the timing sear. The returning rate control cam is about to release the timing sear, causing the next round to be fired after a controlled delay. The hydraulic unit is concealed in the grip.

many gunmakers who were once in great profusion in Birmingham.

It was in 1880 that an avid rifle marksman, A.G. Parker, began manufacturing and marketing a line of shooting aids. At the turn of the century, he took in a partner, T.C. Hale. The company continued to make accessories and shooter needs such as cleaning gear.

During World War I, the company turned its attention to serving British military needs, and developed a technique for relining the barrels of worn-out big-bore rifles with 22 rimfire tubes. At the outbreak of World War II, Parker-Hale Limited again plunged into defense work, turning out thousands of 22-caliber training rifles, as well as several types of anti-tank projectiles.

After the war, Parker-Hale set about expanding its markets and became the world leader in the remanufacture of military rifles to sporting configurations. This was followed by development of a line of Mauser centerfire rifles. The company also produced a 7.62mm sniper rifle which was accepted by several nations for their armed forces.

In 1971, the company became aware of the growing interest in blackpowder, muzzle-loading rifles. The result was reintroduction of the early Enfield rifles used by both sides in our Civil War. Other Enfield designs also were resurrected for manufacture

In 1982, Parker-Hale won a contract to produce a large quantity of 7.62mm NATO target rifles for

England's Cadet Corps, replacing the old 303 No. 4 rifle. The company also marketed a line of sporting shotguns and pistols, mostly for export. Parker-Hale has come a long way since A.G. Parker started production some 120 years ago, but the traditions of craftsmanship are still evident in the products manufactured.

"By combining new manufacturing technology with its 'quality' culture, Parker-Hale has established an international reputation for large-scale production and supply of superior firearms," Cockayne points out. Unstated is the fact that in a unique blend of culture, Modular Industries and Parker-Hale bring together almost 150 years of manufacturing experience. The company is involved currently with special contracts, and recent products include new generation bolt-action target rifles and an enhanced version of the famed Parker-Hale rifle bipod. The firm also is entering the ammunition business.

Production of the new subgun obviously is going to be no problem, but then comes the matter of sales. A good deal of thought has been given to that factor by both the corporate officers and George Ealovega. The latter still recalls the initial unveiling of the first prototype and the 5500 orders—and no means of making the guns. He sees availability from Parker-Hale as a definite plus.

The diminutive size of the IDW is a definite advantage in some military situations. Over the years, there have

been efforts to come up with a practical weapon for tank crews, helicopter crews, drivers, officers, commando-type units, SWAT teams and other law enforcement personnel. At one point, the Garand M-1 rifle of World War II was being cut down to be handier in a tank; the Air Force went for the tiny AR-7 as a survival weapon; the 45-caliber M-3 Grease Gun of WWII served some of these purposes in the past.

One cannot forget that Parker-Hale began its existence by supplying accessories to shooters. That still is an important part of the business and is being carried over in the introduction of the 9mm IDW. Factory options include additional barrels in lengths of 6, 10, 12 and 14 inches; a red dot sight system; spare magazines; a flashlight and mount; sound suppressor; spare firing rate regulators; slings; a holster; and the Parker-Hale bipod with telescoping legs.

"I gave a good deal of thought to possible uses for the IDW," David Cockayne told us. "When an assault rifle is too big and inconvenient, in a situation where a conventional submachine gun is too uncontrollable, and a handgun doesn't offer realistic firepower, I think this gun could be the weapon of choice, based upon concealment and hit probability alone."

And for George Ealovega, photographer/engineer extraordinaire, his IDW might not be a bad backup to have along with his camera when crawling around the Florida swamps, seeking 12-foot alligators!   ●

CHAPTER 2

DEMISE OF THE BATTLE RIFLE

Old Arms Don't Disappear; They Get Recycled!

AROUND **THE TURN** of the century, the great poseurs moved from blackpowder to smokeless for infantry rifles. This not only meant the battlefield was clear of the vast pall of smoke that characterized Civil War engagements, but it also meant decreased fouling and increased velocity. Smokeless powder also gave improved reliability, particularly when rifle ammo was used in machine guns.

Bullets could be reduced in size and even copper-jacketed without sacrificing wounding power. Now, instead of a 45- to 69-caliber soft lead bullet, the soldier's rifle used a 25- to 30-caliber hardball round. Wounds were still serious, but the limb-destroying characteristics of Civil War 58-caliber loads, and those of the British India 45-caliber Dum-Dum cartridge were avoided. Of course, lest anyone think war was made more humane by the 1905 Hague Accords,

the development of fragmentation and full-auto weapons far exceeded the levels of 19th century warfare.

By World War I, single shot and lever-action rifles had been replaced by bolt actions, an outgrowth of the

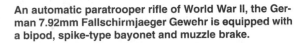

An automatic paratrooper rifle of World War II, the German 7.92mm Fallschirmjaeger Gewehr is equipped with a bipod, spike-type bayonet and muzzle brake.

Franco-Prussian War of 1870. America entered the Great War with the U.S. Springfield M1903, the British P-14 and the Canadian Ross rifles. After the war, only the Model 1903 remained in U.S. service. It served between the wars and at the beginning of World War II, soldiering on as a sniper rifle through the Korean War.

The 30-06 cartridge used in the Model 1903 was also used in the Model 1918 Browning Automatic Rifle (BAR), the Model 1917 Browning water-cooled machine gun, the Model 1919 Browning air-cooled machine gun, and the M-1 Garand semi-automatic rifle. The 30-06 round also proved itself in the hunting fields on medium and big game. Though it is not used today by any major

armies, it is still likely to appear anywhere in the Third World.

Around 1957, the U.S. Army sought to replace the M-1 rifle—what Patton called the finest fighting instrument ever designed—plus the M-1/M-2 carbines, the M-3A1 and Thompson submachine guns and the Model 1918 Browning Automatic Rifle (BAR) with the M-14/M-15 rifle "system."

A system approach had become the buzzword for complex weapons, such as those mounted in aircraft. However, this approach did not work well in the low tech world of infantry combat, where standardization had to compete with matching weapons to highly different missions and climates. Ammunition interchangeability was the most worthwhile goal of this project, but the 308 Winchester (7.62mm NATO) cartridge did not possess much flexibility.

The 308 was shorter and easier to carry than the 30-06, and didn't give up much in power or accuracy. It suited the 20-round magazines developed for the M-14 rifle. In fact, the M-14 was essentially an updated M-1, with a box magazine instead of eight-round clips, as well as a flash hider and a few other modifications.

The M-14/15 project got off to a rocky start. The M-15 heavy barrel version proved too light and inaccurate to adequately replace the BAR as a squad support weapon. A select-fire M-14A2 version with dual handles and modified gas system was an improvement over the M-15, but most soldiers could not control it with three-round bursts (dispersion was too great with more than two) for it to be popular, especially as a replacement for the legendary BAR.

The original M-14 was designed for select-fire, but almost immediately the button mechanisms were

Germans in World War II developed the assault rifle. The soldier on the left is carrying the StG43 7.92 Kurz assault rifle, with magazine carriers on his belt. Other soldiers are armed with K98 Mausers.

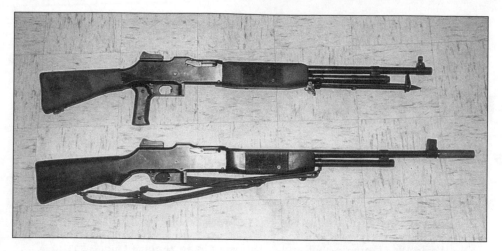

Variations of the venerable 30-06 Browning Automatic Rifle, popularly termed the BAR. The design was used by the Army and Marine Corps in World War I, World War II and Korea, as well as a lot of Banana Wars in between.

removed, making it semi-auto only. The recoil of the 7.62mm NATO cartridge made full-auto a waste of ammo for most troops. A few SEAL and sniper M-14s in Vietnam retained full-auto capability in order to break contact from an ambush.

The sniper M-14 used in Vietnam eventually was renumbered as the M-21. It had a Sionics suppressor to eliminate muzzle flash and noise, though the bullet itself still made a supersonic crack through the air. A Leatherwood ART ranging scope allowed hits out to 1000 yards. The basic rifle was specially selected and issued with match ammo. Experienced hunters and competitive shooters were chosen from available infantry to attend a special three-week sniper school "in country." The scout/sniper specialty was not taught in the States during the Vietnam Conflict, since "McNamara's band" still was looking at the "Big Picture," preparing for the expected Soviet confrontation, instead of changing Basic and Advanced infantry training for the hot war in Vietnam. Today's army is more flexible in training and mission, though underfunded.

The M-14 was the standard training rifle in the U.S. Army through the late 1960s. Most soldiers destined for Vietnam got an M-16 when they arrived in-country. Marines in 1965 still carried their M-14s in 'Nam. Army troops stationed Stateside, in Germany, or in Korea continued with the M-14, which was considered superior to the M-16 outside of jungle combat.

Our author, David Steele, was one of the soldiers saddled with the M-14. Except for special training at Fort Benning, which included the M-14A2, M-16, 45 Colt pistol, M-79 grenade launcher, M-72 LAW, M-60 LMG, M-2HB 50 MG, and various grenades, recoilless rifles, and rocket launchers, the M-14 was his only weapon. "When I left Benning in 1968 I was in a batch of 70 infantrymen. Those whose last names began from A to L were sent to Vietnam. The rest of us went to Korea, considered a hot area after the North Korean capture of the spy ship *U.S.S. Pueblo*. The build-up probably did avert a war there, even though the North Koreans pushed again in 1969, shooting down an EC-121 spy plane, which extended my tour an extra month."

Because of his security clearance, Steele was assigned to guard a Maximum Security Area. This is where the tactical nuclear weapons were stored. South Korean contract guards with shotguns patrolled other parts of the camp, but not the MSA. At the same time as the *Pueblo* capture, a North Korean commando team was sent south to assassinate President Park Chung Hee and to commit various acts of sabotage. Fortunately, local villagers spotted

them, and they were all apprehended or killed. One of them was carrying a map targeting the MSA where Steele worked.

Because of this incident, guards went from carrying a mere 20 rounds for the M-14s to carrying 100 rounds, plus four fragmentation grenades and four CS grenades in the towers. Of course, this was still just the first line of defense: 50-caliber machine guns were placed on nearby hillsides, and quick reaction forces were geared to bring in support weapons.

"For this type of work I found the M-14 to be clumsy in the extreme. Slung, it was hard to get up through the trapdoor of the tower. While sleeping in the standby hut, it was hard to store the M-14 out of the way. A couple of times mine hit the cement floor, which significantly moved the front sight in its dovetail. The sling strap could not be rigged for assault fire, and its retaining clip could come loose, spilling the rifle (into another soldier's meal tray on one occasion).

"The flash hider could fill with dirt, that could freeze in place in cold weather. Since the M-14 is 44.14 inches long, if it is slung upside down, for instance in the rain, it does not take much of a stumble to put the muzzle in the ground. Keep in mind that adequate cleaning, repair and re-zeroing are not simple matters in field situations, unlike on a civilian range. Also, we were short of cleaning supplies, even patches, because the lion's share went to Vietnam," Steele recalls.

Some of the problems might have been cured by issue of the Type III folding stock developed for the M-14 without wood or synthetic stock. For accuracy or hand-to-hand combat the full stock is best, but overall length is excessive. Recently, La France Specialties has produced a select-fire,

There are numerous versions of the 7.62x51mm FN FAL. The model with the heavier barrel and bipod has been set up as a squad automatic weapon.

Portuguese troops carried the German G3 battle rifle in Mozambique in the 1960s. It then was being made under license in Portugal and designated at the 7.62mm NATO rifle, M961.

short-barrel, modified-gas-system version of the M-14 that works better.

The Main Battle Rifle is designed to produce grazing fire out to about 600 yards, not quite the 1000 yards of a 19th century infantry rifle, but substantial. However, the modern battlefield, especially for First World armies, is filled with support weapons that obviate the need for an infantryman rifle to be effective beyond 300 yards. Instead, the soldier is expected to place "suppressive" fire on the enemy in the last phase of an attack, the assault. Instead of traditional, British-style aimed fire, the emphasis is on Soviet-style spray fire. Lighter ammo, like the 7.62x39mm Russian or 5.56mm NATO, is easier to carry and easier to control in full-auto. Combine this with a lighter, easier to carry rifle, and it

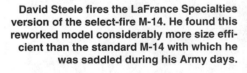

David Steele fires the LaFrance Specialties version of the select-fire M-14. He found this reworked model considerably more size efficient than the standard M-14 with which he was saddled during his Army days.

should be no surprise that the 5.56mm M-16 rifle went from being an Air Force police and Army Special Forces weapon in Vietnam to U.S. Army and Allied country standard.

However, this progression did not come easily, The first assault rifle was developed in Germany in 1943, mislabeled an MP (Maschinen Pistole), later StG (Sturmgewehr) 43/44, because of Hitler's early objection to the 7.92mm intermediate cartridge He felt the huge stocks of full-power 7.92mm ammo, some left from World War I, should be used in a weapon like the FG (Fallschirm-Jaeger Gewehr) 42 designed for Luftwaffe paratroops.

The Soviets got a full dose of the StG 44, and took its technology back to Moscow after the war. A tank sergeant named Kalashnikov developed the PPSh 41 submachine gun for the Red

Army. The 7.62x39mm intermediate cartridge gave far more accuracy and penetration than the 7.62mm TT pistol round. The AK and its successors proved to be the most reliable and prolific design of the post-war era.

Probably the most successful battle rifles issued since World War II are the Belgian FN and the German G3. Originally developed for the German 7.92mm PP43 intermediate cartridge, the FN FAL is best known for its 7.62mm NATO version, developed after Britain and Canada adopted the U.S. 308-caliber round, originally designated the caliber .30 T65E3 in testing.

The FN (Fabrique Nationale) FAL (*Fusil Automatique Legere*) light automatic rifle gained fame from Northern Ireland to the Sinai. It was issued in two dozen countries, from

The Heckler & Koch MP5 submachine gun is closely related to the German G3 military rifle, with some interchangeable parts. Here it is fired by a Marine from a reconnaissance unit. This subgun currently is standard with such units as well as Marine Corps anti-terrorist teams.

Ed Arthur, a two-tour veteran of Vietnam, advisor to Cuban exile groups and general soldier of fortune, carries the CETME during a field operation. It is the predecessor of the German G3.

Australia to Venezuela. Probably the most rigorous use of the FAL was by Israeli troops in the 1967 Six-Day War, although some troops found it sand-sensitive.

The FAL also was used by both British and Argentine troops in the 1982 Falklands campaign. Now, the FN has been scaled down to a 5.56mm version, called the "CAL." However, it may have more competition in this caliber, from guns like the M-16A2 and the Galil.

After World War II, German designers went to Spain and developed a roller-locked, delayed-blowback, 7.92mm rifle known as the CETME (*Centro De Estudios Tecnicos De Matereiles Especiales, Madrid*). Both Spain and Portugal used this weapon in 7.62mm NATO. The West German army showed interest in the weapon, moving development to Heckler & Koch, who designed the G3, which was to replace the FAL in Bundeswehr service. H&K was to use the G3 as a base for an entire weapons system, from the MP5 submachine gun to the HK 21 GPMG, with substantial parts overlap, in calibers from 9mm Parabellum to 7.62mm NATO. The MP5 and the G3 rifle have been the most successful members of the system on the world market.

While the battle rifle has been superseded by the assault rifle in First World armies, variations are still found in brushfire wars around the world. For example, Christian Phalangist fighters in 1980s Beirut often employed the FAL, using an unusual assault fire position. They would wrap its extra-long sling around the neck, then position the buttplate into the groin. Using the body to index the weapon, three-round bursts could be triggered accurately to 100 meters, faster than aimed fire.

It seems modern freedom fighters always manage to squeeze new life out of super-power discards. •

When Marines first arrived in Vietnam, they were carrying the M-14 7.62 NATO rifle. Reconnaissance units such as this were the first to be issued the new M-16 rifle in 5.56mm. Other units soon were similarly armed.

CHAPTER 3

OLD UZI, NEW UZI

"THOUGH I ALWAYS was fascinated by submachine guns, because they were so rare in the United States, the first one I ever fired was an original, wood-stocked Uzi. Just after I finished my Army service in Korea," co-author David Steele recalls, "I lived for a time on a kibbutz in the Negev desert on the border with the Gaza Strip. There were Israeli army reservists on the kibbutz, who set up ambushes in the fields every night, killing a terrorist one evening that I recall. Their duties included checking the fields every morning for land mines before we began work."

One of the Israeli paratroopers there showed Steele how to field-strip the Uzi FSMG, which turned out to be a relatively simple matter. Later, Steele got the kibbutznik assigned to oversee the Druse guards to allow him to shoot the guard's Uzi on the farm's 22 rimfire range.

"The Druse, incidentally, make up an Arab minority group loyal to the State of Israel. In Druse culture, I learned, an adult male is most manly if he has a mustache and carries a gun for a living. The Druse are often hired as night watchmen by kibbutzim to allow the kibbutz members more time for farm work and administration."

At that time, 1969, the Uzi served in front-line units of the Israeli Army as a supplement to the FN-made FAL, the main battle rifle. The 9mm Uzi also was used as a sidearm by auxiliary troops and civilians in hazardous areas. They were far more common than pistols, but they all belonged to the government, this being a socialist state. Today, in Israel, private ownership of handguns is not unusual, especially those models considered appropriate for self-defense in urban areas. Uzis are still common as well, but even when hitchhiking, front-line troops carry M-16s or Galils, as a deterrent to terrorism. When Steele eventually returned to the States, he wrote an article on the Uzi, his first published work, appearing in *Ordnance*

magazine. One of the photos used was of him with the Druse gun on the practice range.

This little article had some surprising results. More than any other qualification, it landed Steele the job as supervisor of the fledgling Police Weapons Center research project at the International Association of Chiefs of Police, headquartered in Washington D.C. "In addition,

Today's standard Uzi differs little from the one fired by David Steele in 1969, except the wooden stock has been replaced by a folding unit.

20 years later I was trying to interest the editor of *Visier*, a firearms magazine in Germany, in some manuscripts. I was somewhat amazed to find that he not only knew who I was, but he verbally reviewed my Uzi/ *Ordnance* article in detail. Perhaps, this is how the Germans got their reputation for thoroughness and scholarship. The editor not only knew his subject and the view of German shooters, but he was multilingual and intimately familiar with American and other authors."

Note should be made of some Uzi tactics used by Israeli paratroops at that time. The most notable was a penchant for hip-shooting. The first and every other cartridge in the

This photo was taken in Chad in the 1960s. The French Foreign Legionnaire with his back to camera holds a French-issue MAT-49 sub-gun. The man at his left is holding an Israeli-made Uzi.

David Steele fired the Israeli-issue Uzi 9mm submachine gun on a kibbutz range in 1969. Note the padded shoulder sling which is set up for assault-position underarm shooting.

magazine was a tracer, so rounds could be "walked" on target. The idea was to assault aggressively, shooting on the run, keeping the enemies' heads down, finishing them with grenades and in hand-to-hand combat. Commonly, two magazines were wired together in an "L" shape to facilitate quick change and allow the shooter to keep up the firepower.

The Uzi was designed by Major Uziel Gal of the Israeli Defense Forces, (TSAHAL), and was admittedly based on the Czech ZK476. Czechoslovakia was one of the few countries then willing to supply arms to the Israelis during their 1948 War of Independence. This was fortuitous, as Czechoslovakia was always the premier small arms designer in what then was the Soviet Bloc.

The later Czech Models 23 and 25 have the following features in common with the Uzi: (1) the magazine well is in the pistol grip; (2) short overall length compared to barrel length made it possible for the gun's hollow bolt to telescope over the barrel; (3) the ejection port is closed to dirt intrusion prior to cocking; and (4) disassembly and reassemble were extremely simple.

The original 1950s-era Uzi is a 9mm Parabellum, blowback weapon fired from the open-bolt position. It

weighs 8.9 pounds, and 25- or 32-round magazines are available. Overall length is 25.2 inches with the wood stock in place. Barrel length is 10.2 inches. The front sight is a truncated cone with protecting ears. The rear folding-leaf sight has apertures for 100- and 200-meter firing. Cyclic rate of fire is 650 rounds per minute.

Today's production guns were for a time marketed in this country by Mossberg, and what Israeli Military Industries lists as the Original Uzi has some minor differences. First, there are two models, one firing from the open bolt, the other from a closed bolt. Overall length is 2/10-inch longer than that of the 1950s version, and

today's barrel length is 1/10-inch shorter. The wooden stock has been replaced by a metal folding stock.

The gun has a grip safety, as well as a manual safety on the left side of the receiver. A single selector button has positions for full auto, semi-auto fire, and safety. The cocking handle is on top of the receiver and is made in two sizes: small, below the line of sight, and large, with a slit for line of sight. There is some advantage to the latter for fast action. The sling is on the left side, and is designed to fit over the shoulder in the assault-ready position.

In the earlier versions produced for the Israeli Army, both a long and short wooden

The authors prefer the size and performance of the Mini-Uzi, which is four inches shorter than the standard model with the stock folded.

Steele shoots the Mini-Uzi made by Israeli Military Industries and once marketed in the U.S. by Mossberg. He favors this model over the other two.

The latest offering in the Uzi production line is the Micro-Uzi, which has a side-folding stock and a vertical foregrip. When we fired this one, we found it difficult to hold with any accuracy beyond about 10 feet.

stock were produced. Both stocks were detachable by a single button. Unfortunately, some troops had the notion of detaching the stock for ease of off-duty carry, which made the gun inaccurate beyond 10 yards. For paratroops, there was a folding stock of simple design that could be opened by pulling down and rearward; it can be refolded quickly and easily by pressure on two locking joints. This is the stock marketed on the guns being imported into this country today.

To disassemble the Uzi, the barrel is removed by depressing a lever and unscrewing the barrel ring. The receiver cover is removed by releasing another button. The bolt is pushed to the rear and upward, which releases the bolt, its recoil spring and guide in one unit. The pistol grip assembly can be removed for complete stripping by pressing out a single pin, using the fingers or a cartridge.

As history readily shows, the Uzi proved itself in the Israeli campaigns of 1956, 1967 and 1973, as well as in brush fire wars from Asia to Africa to Latin America. By 1982, the period of the Lebanon Incursion, front-line Israeli units had converted to 5.56mm Galil and U.S. M-16 assault rifles. These provided more range, accuracy and penetration than the 9mm Uzi. They also offered greater firepower with less weight than did the FN rifle. The Uzi was relegated to auxiliary units and border police. Counter-terrorist units, like the commandos who raided Entebbe airport in 1976 to rescue hostages, continued to rely

on the Uzi, especially with the suppressor attached.

As even Third World countries moved to assault rifles—often supplied by the United States or what then was the Soviet Union—submachine guns became the primary arms of SWAT and counter-terrorist units. Around 1967, the U.S. Secret Service adopted the Uzi for carrying in specially rigged attache cases or special plastic shoulder holsters. The holsters were made by Seventrees Ltd. in New York.

The Secret Service found the Uzi to be compact and reliable, a capable backup weapon where shotguns and rifles could not be carried. It was prominent in the defense of Henry Kissinger and Ronald Reagan, among others. The California State Police also adopted the Uzi for the governor's protection detail.

When Interarms first imported the Uzi around 1970, we had the opportunity to fire several of them, comparing them to the Heckler & Koch MP5, among other guns. At that time, the standard military Uzi was the only one available. Given its reputation in brush fire wars and its adoption by the Secret Service, it should have had the inside track for adoption by U.S. SWAT teams, the first of which was organized by the Los Angles Police Department in 1967.

However, 1970s-era police were not ready for "European-style" support weapons and seemed content with their shotguns and rifles. It also should be pointed out that they did not have the discretionary funds later provided by drug asset forfeiture laws. Further, the Uzi, firing from open bolt, did not have the semi-auto accuracy of the MP5, a feature required by police teams.

The authors feel the continuing trend toward miniaturization did not benefit the Micro-Uzi, which measures only 11 inches in length with the stock folded. This one has a side-folding stock and can be equipped with a vertical foregrip.

The Israeli-made Galil 5.56 MAR assault rifle is replacing submachine guns in front-line Israeli army units. This model, like others in the Galil line, is based upon the familiar Kalashnikov action.

Being marketed as an Uzi product is a line of pistols also made by Israeli Military Industries. This one is equipped with a laser sight.

Around 1980, after the famous hostage-saving operation by Britain's Special Air Service (SAS) at the Iranian Embassy in London, American SWAT teams moved to the submachine gun and they chose the German-made MP5. In 1970, Heckler & Koch already had geared the gun to the paramilitary police role, and at this writing, they have continued to produce accessories and equipment to keep them number one in U.S. police sales.

Still, Israel Military Industries has continued to produce the Uzi, but with variations suited to police, SWAT, counter-terrorist and protective teams in different parts of the world. The emphasis has been on smaller guns with optional closed-bolt design.

To keep the record straight, through its export branch TAAS-Israel Industries Ltd., Israeli Military Industries no longer delivers the Uzi line, along with the Galil automatic rifle, and the Jericho pistol to the United States through Mossberg Firearms. In addition to the standard or what Mossberg advertised as the Original Uzi with its folding stock, there is the Mini-Uzi in open-bolt and closed-bolt variations, the Micro-Uzi in closed-bolt configuration only, and the closed-bolt Uzi pistol.

In the Uzi line, the caliber remains 9mm Parabellum, with magazines of 20-, 25- and 32-round capacity. Having used all these models, we tend to favor the Mini-Uzi in open-bolt configuration. This version would appear to offer optimum balance of compactness, accuracy and reliability for the protective/concealment role and as a SWAT

entry gun. IMI produces a sound suppressor for this gun to assist in room-to-room combat situations. Wilson Arms in Brunswick, Georgia, and a couple other American specialists also make and market suppressors for this model.

For paramilitary use, the original Uzi, it would appear, has been superseded by the more compact Mini-Uzi. Today, the 5.56mm Galil assault rifle has been reduced in length to virtually the size of the first Uzi. In fact, IMI's recently introduced Galil MAR (Mini Automatic Rifle) is even lighter than the Uzi David Steele used in 1969.

While the Heckler & Koch MP5 will continue to dominate American SWAT teams for the foreseeable future, we believe the Uzi has a future, especially with bodyguard teams, whose members would find it easier to conceal these guns with their magazines positioned forward of the trigger guard. •

Specifications

Name:	Micro Uzi (Model 83202)
Type:	Submachine gun.
Caliber:	9mm Parabellum.
Action:	Blowback; fires from closed bolt.
Length:	19 inches (stock extended); 11.0 inches (stock folded).
Stock:	Side-folding metal type; vertical foregrip.

Specifications

Name:	Original Uzi (Models 82101, 82102)
Type:	Submachine gun.
Caliber:	9mm Parabellum.
Operation:	Blowback; Model 82101 fires from open bolt; Model 82102 fires from closed bolt; selective fire.
Length:	25.4 inches (stock extended); 18.3 inches (stock folded).
Barrel:	10.1 inches
Stock:	Metal; folds under the gun in sections.

Specifications

Name:	Mini Uzi (Models 82201, 82202)
Type:	Submachine gun.
Caliber:	9mm Parabellum.
Operation:	Blowback; Model 82201 fires from open bolt; Model 82202 fires from closed bolt; selective fire.
Length:	23.4 inches (stock extended); 14.0 inches (stock folded).
Barrel:	7.7 inches
Stock:	Metal; folds under the gun in sections.

CHAPTER 4

LIFESAVER SIXGUN

THE UNITED STATES Air Force has long had a problem of sorts where air base security is concerned. In areas where aircraft are parked, there are guards and sentries who have been armed with the general issue M-16A2 rifle, which fires the 5.56mm round. In the days before the Korean War, these planes were guarded with the larger-caliber M-14 rifles carrying the 7.62 NATO cartridge in its magazine.

The fear was that if a saboteur should get among the aircraft and be spotted, it would be logical to try to shoot him. The downside of all this is that the 7.62 cartridge can make an interesting and even devastating hole in an aircraft and probably would wreck interior electronics and control mechanisms.

One of the considerations, we feel certain, for the Air Force's adoption of the Armalite-made AR-15 rifle for security forces was the fact that it made a smaller hole, at least on entry! The AR-15, of course, was championed by Air Force Chief of Staff General Curtis LeMay in those days and became the M-16, when adopted by the Pentagon for all U.S. forces. That all happened more than 30 years ago.

In more recent times, an outfit in Michigan called Sage International— through its subsidiary, Sage Control

Ordnance, Inc.—has been dealing with security products and came up with a device called the Less-Lethal Launched Ammunition and Ordnance System. For the sake of brevity, this has come to be called the L3AOS.

We had heard of this firearm, which can be termed that since an explosive charge is required to launch the load, but we had never seen one. Finally came the day that a retired Marine colonel out of co-editor Jack Lewis' military past made contact and reported he was representing the makers of the L3AOS. Would we like to check it out?

This device comes in several configurations, but the one we tested in our parking lot was described by Colonel W. Robert Young—more familiarly known as Bob—as a "multi-role projectile launcher." At first glance, it bears great exterior similarities to the South African-made 12-gauge shotgun known universally as Street Sweeper. This gun, of course, no longer is legal for the average citizen in this country to acquire. And Bob Young is quick to admit that one is not likely to find any edition of the L3AOS in civilian gun racks at this point in history. But, in addition to its planned military role, it does have great promise as a law enforcement

instrument for less-lethal riot control and similar situations.

According to Bob Young's sales pitch, "It can be used for neutralizing such threats as a knife-wielding, mentally deranged person; it can be used to introduce chemical agents into a rioting crowd, forcing them to disperse, and it can be used to deliver tear gas to roust a barricaded gunman such as a bank robber. These are all less-lethal alternatives to deadly force."

He also mentioned that when the projectile was used against the hull of an obsolete Air Force plane in tests, it left a dent in the metal, but did not penetrate the metal skin. Sage Industries' honchos feel that "having an accurate multiple-shot system that can deliver blunt, trauma-inducing projectiles, chemical agents and even barricade-penetrating projectiles could simplify law enforcement confrontations."

The model we tested in our parking lot was designated as the SL-6. The over-sized cylinder, with its six chambers, handles 37mm ammunition that is available from Sage Control Ordnance. The device also will fire British-made ARWEN ammunition.

The device's drum resembles the cylinder of an Old West six-gun and breaks open for loading the chambers

Colonel Bob Young explains the sighting system on the Less-Lethal Ordnance and Ammunition System LS-6 to Jack Lewis during a parking lot demonstration and test of the device.

The 44 Magnum blackpowder charge makes its presence known during firing. Smoke from the powder seeps from the rear of the giant six-round cylinder.

The blackpowder smoke does not obscure the gun's sights nor the target, which is a square of corrugated cardboard backed by lightweight cloth.

Lewis and Young inspect damage to the target by the former and other shooters who wanted to try the less-lethal concept.

with the various types of ammunition that can be accommodated. This ammo drum features a unique spring-motor magazine drive with mechanical stops that ensure proper indexing of the chambers.

Jack Lewis, assigned to fire the test series, soon found that two safety features made this launcher both user friendly and safe. Behind the trigger is a push-button-type safety that blocks the trigger when the safety is on. A second patented feature adding safety to operation is an out-of-line firing system that prevents the SL-6 from being fired, until the trigger has been fully cycled to bring the chamber in line with the barrel. This final pull on the trigger makes it ready to fire, but should the gun be dropped prior to that final move, the gun cannot be discharged.

The test was conducted at 25 yards across the parking lot. With vehicles moved out of the way the area suddenly had become a shooting range. The backstop was a concrete block wall. It was in front of this wall that the retired colonel set up a quick-assembly portable target unit he had devised. To this was attached a square of ordinary corrugated cardboard and behind that, a square of free-hanging lightweight cloth.

Target circles had been drawn on the cardboard with a blue marking pen, each measuring six inches in diameter. It was a typical California winter day along the Pacific Coast, and there had been heavy fog sweeping in from the ocean earlier. That had been dispersed by a fast rain storm that passed through. The weather still was overcast and hardly conducive to a good sight picture.

With Young at his elbow, offering advice and instruction, Lewis triggered off three rounds in rapid succession. Two of them hit one of the six-inch circles, but as he fired the third round, he called it as a miss. He had pulled it off-target and the projectile struck the wood of the target frame. He later admitted he had not been able to see the blue circles in the rainy-day light and had simply been firing for group in the standing offhand position. His later shots were fired more slowly and grouped better in the circles, which had been redrawn.

It should be noted that a number of the projectiles (batons) did pass through the corrugated cardboard, but they were stopped by the loose-hung cloth. Each baton was inspected after the shoot. None suffered any damage and could be reused, according to Bob Young. None of the projectiles had gotten through the cloth to hit the block wall behind. That was just as well, since it wasn't our wall!

The propelling force for the L3AOS is nothing more than a 44 Magnum cartridge case loaded with a charge of blackpowder and a standard primer. Each round, specially loaded, was priced at something under $3, but Young had found that they can be reloaded up to 15 times, thus bringing operational and training costs down considerably.

The type of ammunition we were firing—the KO1—is referred to as a baton and is the one that would be used to put down an opponent, hopefully without serious injury. The use of plastic and even wooden baton-type ammo for controlling an individual or even a rioting crowd is not new, of course. The limiting factors

In cases where the baton penetrated the cardboard, it was stopped by the loose flap of light-weight cloth behind. There was no damage to the block wall behind the target.

The front sight is a flip-up type that has three apertures for various ranges. Maximum effective range for the gun is 100 meters, according to Young.

with these materials always has been lethality and a lack of accuracy.

The KO1 baton-type impact ammunition has a projectile of polyurethane and a cartridge case of aluminum that, like the 44 propellant cartridge, is reloadable. Reloading equipment that can be mounted on RCBS presses also is available from Sage Control Ordnance, as well as new cartridge cases, batons and propelling charges.

The SL-6 has deliberately not been called a non-lethal weapon, but a LESS-lethal device. Reason for this is the fact that it is possible to kill with the system under certain circumstances. On record is one instance in which an individual downed by a baton suffered an immediate heart attack that led to his death. At extremely close range, the force of the baton can fracture ribs, which in turn may puncture the lungs. A close-range shot in the vicinity of

the heart also may do damage of a lethal nature.

The other type of ammunition perfected for use in the L3AOS six-gun is listed as BPSCS and is a 37mm barricade penetrator. This round utilizes what Bob Young calls a "cookie cutter," a penetrator ring of hard plastic that cuts its way through wooden doors and glass windows. Upon impact and target penetration, the potent payload of 75.1 grains of high-concentration, micronized CS dust (tear gas) is disseminated and becomes airborne. Since the BPSCS round is non-pyrotechnic and non-metallic, it can be used in areas where

The plastic cylinder atop the stock serves as a cheek rest, making sighting easier. Note the flip-up single-aperture rear sight.

The gun breaks open to load the cylinders with whatever type ammo is to be used. Visible are the 44 Magnum blank cartridges that serve as the propellant for the batons.

The K01 round carries a baton and is powered by a 44 Magnum blank loaded with blackpowder. At left is the standard round; in center is a cut-away used in instruction and to show how the baton is fitted in the case. At right is the baton after it has been fired. It can be reloaded.

Rounds for the SL-6 are easily reloaded. The only tool needed is a press available from RCBS, but other reloading needs are furnished by Sage International, who markets the unit.

flammable substances are stored. This round, incidentally, is not reloadable. Tests have shown that the BPSCS will penetrate 5/16-inch glass at 87 yards; a hollow-core interior door at 65 yards; 1/2-inch plywood at 44 yards and a slanted auto windshield at 22 yards.

The effective range of the L3AOS, according to Young, is 100 meters. Its accuracy with both baton-type ammunition and the barricade penetrator results from the unit's rifled barrel, which measures 10.5 inches and has five deep-cut grooves. Rate of twist is one turn in 38 inches. Aiding in accuracy is a calibrated sighting system and an assortment of ammunition designed for specific missions.

Sage International and its subsidiary have been marketing one other less-lethal projectile launcher, a single-shot listed as the SL-1. This has the same general specs as the SL-6, except it does not have the six-round drum. Like the SL-6, it has a rifled barrel and calibrated sighting; it also can handle the same array of ammunition as the steroided six-gun. Like the LS-6, length of its barrel is 10.5 inches with the same rate of twist for its five grooves.

Going a step beyond, the same outfit has the PL-36, actually a conversion kit, which can be used to convert such tear gas launching receivers as those from Smith & Wesson, Def-Tech and Federal Laboratories with a precision-rifled 37mm barrel. Included is a flip-up ladder-type front sight, a flip-up rear sight and a raised cheekpiece as on the other two models. The conversion can fire all of the ammunition variations supplied by Sage Industries, as well as the ARWEN ammo marketed by Britain's Royal Ordnance, PLC.

If an armory or police department has an on-hand supply of standard 37mm tear gas munitions, the launcher can be converted back to fire conventional loads simply by removing the Sage Control Ordnance PL-37 rifled barrel and installing the original smooth-bore barrel.

We have no current count on the number of L3AOS LS-6 guns that have been sold, but at the time we fired the gun, more than 60 law enforcement agencies across the nation had purchased from one to 11 of the devices. Both the U.S. Army and the Air Force have been doing extensive testing, too.

Bob Young had to show us the collection of newspaper clippings that have touted the less-lethal gun. Regarding the L3AOS, one police lieutenant, David Frisby, had some interesting observations:

"In most cases, if the suspect had a firearm and was shooting lead bullets, this device would not be appropriate," he feels. "There may be a window of opportunity to use it in such a case, but if it doesn't take out the suspect, it would make the situation worse, because the subject is going to become even more angry.

"However," the lieutenant adds, "the less-lethal type weapon is going to be an emerging field in law enforcement, especially regarding people who are suicidal. We would rather stun or disorient a suspect. A dozen years ago, that might not have been what would have happened."

In Tallahassee, Florida, a man armed with a machete charged the police during a confrontation. Police Sergeant John Parsons fired a baton from the L3AOS to put the man down. This allowed members of the city's apprehension and control team to put him in handcuffs without further violence.

A year later, in the same city, a baton was fired at a 14-year-old boy from one of the LS-6 launchers. He had been caught in the act of burglarizing a golf shop and was armed with a handgun.

The teenager was wearing a heavy coat, which protected him from the first baton fired at him. The shot have relatively little effect, if any, according to Police Sergeant Kelly Burke, who was on the scene.

But the second baton hit below the coat, striking the would-be burglar on the thigh. He immediately surrendered and was returned to the psychiatric facility from which he had escaped. •

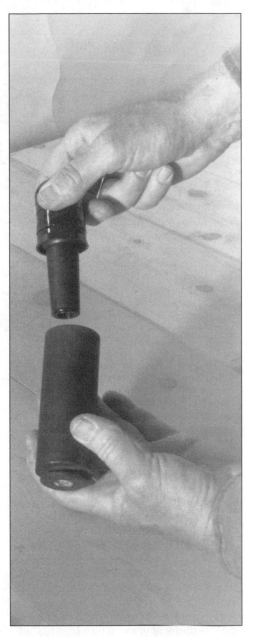

The baton fits closely into the aluminum case. The designer kept the ammunition simple, making it easy to reload after once being used.

The SL-6 is field-stripped for cleaning with little effort. Assembly and disassembly is a matter of only a few seconds, plus a bit of know-how.

Specifications

Name:	Less-Lethal Ammunition and Ordnance System (L3AOS) LS-6.
Caliber:	37mm.
Operation:	Revolver-type spring motor drive magazine; mechanically operated magazine stops.
Weight:	10.6 pounds.
Length:	33 inches.
Barrel:	10.5 inches; rifled with five grooves; 1:38-inch twist.
Capacity:	6 rounds
Sights:	Flip-up front with ballistic ladder to 100 meters in 20-meter increments; flip-up rear with aperture.
Ammunition:	All types from Sage Control Ordnance and Royal Ordnance ARWEN type.
Maker:	Sage Industries, Inc. 630 Oakland Ave. Pontiac, Michigan 48342.

CHAPTER 5

GLOBAL STUDIES IN SUBMACHINE GUNS

BACK IN 1970, an outfit called Security Arms Company, located in Arlington, Virginia, imported several guns that had been made by Heckler & Koch in what then was West Germany. SACO was run by one John S. (Jack) Wood, Jr., a retired Army colonel with special operations

The Heckler & Koch MP5A2 has an optional three-round burst feature. David Steele calls this the best MP5 variation for general usage by SWAT teams.

experience dating back to the OSS Jedburg teams in occupied France. It should be noted that Wood was importing Heckler & Koch firearms before the German company set up its own U.S. import operation.

Among the new weapons was a pair of 9mm MP5 submachine guns. One was the MP5A2 with fixed stock, the other an MP5A3 with a sliding stock. David Steele was one of the first to test these guns, as part of a research project he was running for a major law enforcement agency. When he finished his work, his manual, "Submachine Guns in Police Work," listed the MP5 as the best choice for police teams. This recommendation was made in spite of the gun having no track record on U.S. soil, the Uzi being the choice of the Secret Service. History, we feel, has confirmed Steele's original judgment.

A few SWAT teams like the Los Angeles Special Enforcement Bureau adopted the MP5 in the 1970s. However, the real landslide occurred sometime after 22 Special Air Service troops used their "Knocklers" in the May 5, 1980, raid to recover London's Iranian Embassy from a splinter gang of Arab terrorists.

The SAS troops were photographed carrying the MP5A3s, with the stocks retracted, the guns suspended from their Heckler & Koch three-way slings. The subguns were backed up by Browning L9 (P35) 9mm pistols in strapped-down thigh holsters.

The Special Air Service counter-terrorist kit was perfected in Ulster, during operations against the Irish Republican Army. Those assigned wore a black, flame retardant uniform without visible insignia. Each SAS trooper also carried the standard British Army gas mask, an anti-flash hood, body armor, North Island gloves and low boots with rubber soles. At that time, leather rather than nylon still was used for the thigh holster with carriers for two additional 9mm pistol magazines. A three-magazine carrier for the submachine gun was positioned on the left thigh. On the upper right side of the vest was a British-issue utility knife with one fixed blade for cutting snagged rope. This later was replaced by a folding knife.

When not using the gas mask, British SAS troops often wear a balaclava (ski mask) to cover their faces. This, it is reported, is meant to reduce the likelihood of retaliation against the individual, his family or his unit by terrorists, particularly the Irish Republican Army. Like the unmarked uniforms, this custom was adopted by some U.S. SWAT teams without thought to the differences between an elite Army counter-

revolutionary warfare unit and civilian police in a democratic setting.

"Unless working undercover, police should not conceal their faces," co-author Steele contends. "Further, unmarked police uniforms can create an identification problem for other officers, as well as suspects during a dynamic entry. Administrators also should consider potential public relations problems with issuing of the 'Nazi-style' Kevlar helmets now used by American military troops."

Britain's Special Air Service also pioneered the so-called flash/bang for counter-terrorist use. While the concussion grenade actually dates back to World War I, its first modern employment was in October, 1977, when West Germany's GSG-9— *Grenzschutzgruppe 9*, part of the *Bundesgrenschutz* border patrol— stormed a Lufthansa Boeing 737 plane on the tarmac at Mogadishu, Somalia.

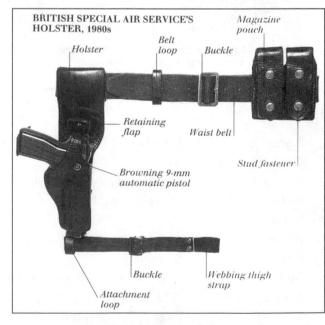

BRITISH SPECIAL AIR SERVICE'S HOLSTER, 1980s

Holster · Belt loop · Buckle · Magazine pouch · Retaining flap · Waist belt · Stud fastener · Browning 9-mm automatic pistol · Buckle · Webbing thigh strap · Attachment loop

During the 1980s, this rig was worn by British SAS troops. Today, leather has been replaced by nylon. Note the Old West leg tie-down for the holster.

This is the rig that members of the British Special Air Service wore in hostage rescue work in the 1980s. Design has changed little from that day. Note the folded sheath knife positioned on the upper right section of the load-bearing vest.

When the airliner first was captured by terrorists of the Red Army faction, GSG-9 requested SAS assistance. The British supplied this in the persons of Captain Alastair Morrison and Sergeant Barry Davies. At the moment of truth, the SAS men tossed in their magnesium flash/bangs, which were followed the GSG's 30-man entry team and the subsequent demise of the terrorists.

The flash/bang has progressed considerably since the first disposable SAS models were put to use. Current U.S. SWAT teams are likely to use recyclable cases like the DEF-TEC M25. A non-fragmenting metal body with vents, the M25 can be reloaded a couple of dozen times. It produces the required 175 decibel shock wave that disorients more by blast than by dazzling light.

The first modern SWAT team was formed by the Los Angeles Police Department in 1967, in the aftermath of the 1965 Watts Riot and the 1996 Texas Tower sniper incident in Austin. Anti-robbery units such as the Flying Squads active in Shanghai, China, in the 1930s, and the 1950s Hat Squad of the LAPD were active much earlier,

of course, but SWAT has been better trained and equipped for counter-sniper and barricaded suspect situations. The early emphasis was on the "sling rifle" terminating a hostage-holder, firing from a distance.

However, after the Vietnam War and civil rights disturbances, the Los Angeles SWAT contingent felt it needed a continuing challenge to retain a professionally sharp edge. Personnel were turned to serving high-risk search warrants on behalf of the narcotics squad and other investigative units. Some of these efforts turned into massive fire fights, including LAPD's warrant service by SWAT on Black Panther headquarters in 1969 and service of an FBI warrant on a safe house of the Simbeonese Liberation Army in South Central Los Angeles in 1974.

Gradually, though, such episodes faded into the past, as SWAT started using new technology and experience gained by well-funded military counter-terrorist units. Teams like the SAS, GSG-9, Delta Force and SEAL Team 6 spend most of their time in training. These military teams have had some spectacular successes at such sites as Entebbe in 1975 and Mogadishu the following year, not to mention the Peruvian Army's 1997 recovery of the Japanese Embassy from Tupac Amaru terrorists. Still, since the military mission is to kill rather than to arrest terrorists, the overlap between military and police SWAT training is less than perfect.

Thankfully, normal warrant service in a city environment does not require Delta Force or SEAL operators. The typical police "dynamic entry" is directed primarily at drug dealers, who may have a few guns to protect their stash from pirates. Officers operating as a team, armed with pistols and submachine guns, usually are more than enough to overcome any resistance.

Sniper rifles, carbines, assault rifles and shotguns usually are kept outside but on the perimeter during such an operation. The entry team needs short, easily maneuvered and easily protected weapons like pistols and subguns. Occasionally, a semi-automatic, 14-inch-barreled shotgun such as the Benelli entry gun or a short assault rifle like the Heckler & Koch HK53 is chosen for extra stopping power. The MP5—in MP5A2, MP5A3, MP5K and MP5SD variations—is the preferred submachine gun, backed up by high-capacity 9mm pistols such as the Glock 17, the SIG P226 and the Beretta M92F.

David Steele has used and recommended the MP5 since it was imported initially in 1970. Here he is testing the Wilson Arms sound suppressor on the MP5A3.

SEAL veteran Harry Humphries checks gear on a student entry team. Note the Sure-Fire flashlight mounted on the forearm of the MP5.

Steele demonstrates the weapon retention guard technique used by the first man through the door in a forced entry. The left elbow is forward, the left hand braced on the chest. The right hand holds the pistol or submachine gun outboard at the hip.

Law enforcement has its fashion trends, if that can be considered the proper term, and smaller agencies tend to copy larger, better known entities. Typically, a SWAT team will wear black or Navy blue coveralls, though military camouflage still is common in some areas. Vietnam-style boots have given way to those made by Danner and other specialty footwear manufacturers. Goggles usually are made by Oakley or Bolle.

Since police work seldom involves a shrapnel threat for which the military helmet was designed, many teams do not wear them at all; other teams insist a helmet makes members more recognizable, since hardly any dope dealers wear helmets. They also can be protective against thrown objects or blunt instruments.

Other gear may include the balaclava, a gas mask, flame-resistant Nomex aviator gloves, a tactical two-way radio, a load-bearing vest, plus an armored vest with its trauma plate, a utility knife, handcuffs, pepper spray and a police-type baton. Pistols and magazines usually are carried in nylon rigs, with at least three extra magazines for the subgun and three for the pistol.

Specialized gear can include anything—and everything—from rappelling ropes to sledge hammers. However, other than Kevlar body armor, the most important gear for the modern SWAT unit is the flash/bang, also known as a "crash" in SEAL terminology. A DEF-TEC 25 can provide a level of safety unknown to early SWAT personnel.

In addition to better gear, the modern entry team has access to better training. For instance the Yavapai County sheriff's SWAT team in Arizona trains regularly at nearby Gunsite, the commercial training installation that is internationally known. There, they not only go through the firearms courses, but also operate as a team in live-fire exercises. On occasion, this unit also plays the bad guys in such events as the National Tactical Invitational meet. In such meets, they may use Simunitions—fired projectiles that leave a dye mark on whatever they hit. It's been compared to "serious paint-ball competition."

In California, the Bell Gardens Police Department sent its entry team to a five-day curriculum with Global Studies Group, Inc. (Box 1006, Huntington Beach, CA 92605). Included in the schedule was a

Weapon retention with the MP5 submachine gun involves falling backwards, kicking the attacker in the crotch, then throwing him over if he continues to hang on.

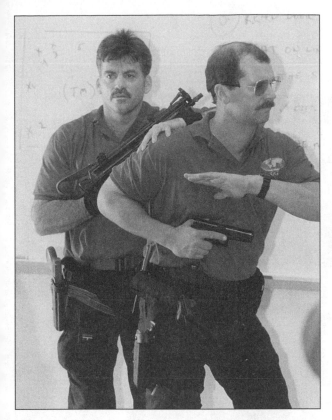

GSGI instructors Bill Murphy (foreground) and Dennis Chalker demonstrate proper positioning of weapons for a SEAL-type entry. Both are former Navy SEALs.

California's Bell Gardens Police Department's SWAT team prepares the "conga line"—also called the "stack"—for a practice entry in the Fun House at the San Diego Naval Training Center.

two-day entry course for police employment of the MP5 subgun.

Among the GSGI staff are Harry Humphries and Denny Chalker, both veteran SEALs who have seen combat, as well as Bill Murphy, a working police officer and firearms instructor. Training for the Bell Gardens contingent was held at the firing range of the now closed San Diego Naval Training Center, which features a live-fire Fun House.

The first day of training was devoted to lectures and endless dry-fire rehearsals of two-, four-, six- and eight-man room entries, including a variety of close-quarter combat techniques. The second was devoted first to live-fire pistol and submachine gun techniques on the range, then live-fire entries at the Fun House.

Two of the most notable GSGI methods involve elbow weapons retention and the sling shooting positions. The first man entering a room does so with his weak-side to prevent a sudden assault by an unarmed attacker. Meanwhile, his subgun or pistol is kept close to the right hip.

The second distinctive technique is the sling-fire or SAS assault method. At close range, the user of the MP5 keeps the stock folded and shoots as soon as the sling reaches full extension and he sees the front sight. This is different from the technique

taught at Gunsite, where instructors recommend firing from the shoulder.

In the so-called conga line, the weapon is over the left forearm, with the left hand on the preceding man's shoulder. In order to engage safely, the shooter must push the weapon up over his buddy's head, then down toward the target. Unless the shooters train continually as a team, we feel this technique is not as safe as the method wherein the gun is held down and to the right.

The GSGI style does have some advantage in speed, and should an opponent grab the muzzle, just pushing down on the barrel with the

left hand should cause release.

"Also, the sling must be adjusted to the individual for the sling-fire method to work well even at five yards," opines David Steele. "Further, if the shoulder weapon is anything but an MP5A3, the technique will have to be modified."

Since World War II, the submachine gun has gone from front-line infantry weapon to the policeman's entry tool. With the wide array of models and accessories, coupled with the accuracy of the semi-auto, the Heckler & Koch MP5 has become the premier submachine gun. Elite teams from around the world have come to rely on the MP5, as have training schools such as the Gunsite Training Center and the Global Studies Group. •

In this dry-fire simulation, the entry team moves in, guns at the ready. The first man opens the door and tosses in a flash/bang grenade.

CHAPTER 6

TOOLS FOR ARMED ENTRY

How They Are Used May Be More Important Than The Arms!

MODERN ENTRY GUNS for narcs, SWAT and counter-terrorist teams are becoming increasingly sophisticated. However, sophisticated weapons do not make a sophisticated team.

For example, Egypt had the usual lineup of ComBloc and Free World weapons for its fledgling counter-terrorist unit, along with some advice from U.S. Navy SEAL advisors. But Egyptian Rangers lacked certain essentials of modern armies, such as education among the troops and leadership within the officer corps. Enlistees were peasants, officers were princes with political clout. Even the "elite" troops lacked the marksmanship, physical conditioning and unit cohesion expected of modern special ops teams. This became obvious in 1985 when Egyptian "commandos" assaulted a hijacked Egyptair plane in Malta, killing 57 passengers and destroying the plane in the process.

In contrast, Israeli Unit 269 has conducted a number of successful hostage rescue operations, but tends to rely on training and unit cohesion rather than sophisticated weaponry. In past operations, the most common weapons were the Uzi submachine gun backed up by the Browning P35, both loaded with 9mm NATO ball ammo.

Accidental discharges are not unknown even in the best trained units. Counter-terrorist teams not only use firearms more than conventional units, but their training involves "pushing the envelope," by doing live fire exercises with shorter time constraints.

This Marine aboard ship in port carries a riot gun with an extended magazine, heavy medicine for thieves or saboteurs. He wears the new issue Kevlar helmet and carrys a gas mask.

For example, shortly after the formation of Navy SEAL Team 6, a 90-man unit dedicated to counter-terrorism like the Army's Delta Force, troopers were firing 2500 rounds a week through various weapons. During one room-clearing, hostage-rescue exercise, the team had just switched from running the drill with their stainless S&W M66 revolvers to their Beretta M9s. The revolvers always were used double-action, the autos always single-action. After shifting to the Beretta, one trooper stumbled going through the doorway and put a bullet through his partner's back.

The carry condition of any entry firearm is of serious concern. Quick reaction to enemy targets has to be balanced against what may be the greater hazard of accidental

discharge. Given the loss of fine motor control that accompanies stress, it should be no surprise that double-action revolvers and pistols have a better record than single-action autos. A well-honed double-action revolver would be about as fast as a single-action auto, but safer. If double-action-only autos ever become as smooth as a K-frame Smith, & Wesson, there will be little need for double-action/single-action autos.

Most police SWAT and narcotics teams mandate that officers present their pistols double-action with finger off the trigger. The round in the chamber can be fired quickly, but there is little risk of an accidental discharge.

The pistol is highly evolved as a "threat management tool" for safely holding suspects at gunpoint. It may have a DA trigger, manual safety, firing pin safety, magazine safety, etc. In fact, the move to handguns for home defense in this country is probably the biggest reason for a lower accident rate than in Depression days when the hunting rifle or shotgun had to serve.

This Remington 870 has been modified as the Model 90100 by Scattergun Technologies, Inc. It has an 18-inch barrel, ghost ring sights, a 7-round magazine and an 11,000 candlepower flashlight attached to the foregrip.

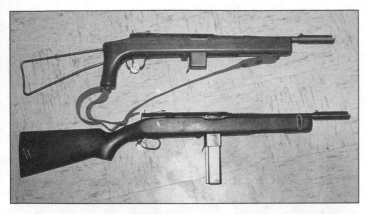

The paratroop and standard Reising 45 ACP submachine guns were issued to Marines in World War II. They still are used by several police departments, including the Los Angeles County Sheriff. A semi-auto version also was produced.

Sporting long guns have not been designed with police work in mind.

The shotgun is routinely carried by patrol and narcotics units for room clearing. However, the typical pump gun not only has a single-action trigger, but it has no firing pin safety. The run-of-the-mill riot gun can go off if dropped or struck against a hard object. In one Los Angeles Sheriffs incident, a deputy cranked a round into the chamber on a burglary call, then he and his female partner had to get back in the car to go to a second reported location of the suspect.

Once there, his partner got out of the vehicle first. As the deputy got out, the shotgun's stock hit the dashboard, setting off a buckshot round into his partner's back, killing her. Subsequent departmental tests showed loaded issue riot guns would discharge about 50 percent of the time when the stock was hit.

Keeping in mind that the cross-bolt safety on a riot gun only blocks the trigger, the very safest way to carry a shotgun is chamber empty, firing pin cocked, safety on. Unfortunately, chambering and shooting from this condition requires four separate moves: press the slide release; pump the handle; release the

The short barrel of the Scattergun Technologies Model 90121 makes the piece highly maneuverable. The ghost ring sights make it accurate. It is built around the Remington Model 870.

safety; pull the trigger. This is too slow for unknown risk or high risk warrant service. One option is carrying the weapon uncocked, safety off, chamber empty. A chamber-empty shotgun works just as well for threat management as one that is loaded. To get it into action requires only the

gross motor movement of pumping the slide, which may have an added psychological benefit. Some authorities like Massad Ayoob recommend only chamber-loaded, safety on for searches, which most would agree is reasonable in known high risk entry situations (e.g., violent suspects), in spite of the danger, especially since it might have to be fired one-handed.

Keeping the finger off the trigger is the most important safety procedure. W.E. Fairbairn of the Shanghai Municipal Police did not believe in any manual safety. He felt chamber-empty carry was the only safe way to carry a pistol. The Israelis have adopted his method for routine carry of pistols, submachine guns and assault rifles. Cross-border commandos carry the Uzi with the chamber empty, bolt forward; and the pistol is carried chamber empty, hammer down. The submachine gun may be cocked just before action, with finger off the trigger, selector set on semi-auto, but the pistol remains with the chamber empty until called on to replace a malfunctioning or empty subgun. At this time, the subgun is slung or discarded, the pistol is drawn from its right side holster, grasped by the slide in a left-handed pinch grip, then thrust forward, chambering a round, and turned into firing position. Tactically, this carry has not decreased Israeli efficiency.

David Steele tries out the standard Benelli M1 Super 90 12-gauge autoloader, with standard barrel and stock. Note the ghost ring sights.

The Mossberg 500 12-gauge pump gun is increasingly common as a search warrant entry gun, and is often issued to military guards. Here David Steele demonstrates the hip shooting technique.

The pistol grip 12-gauge can be used effectively from eye level with buckshot, as demonstrated with this Mossberg 500. Note the tactical sling for packing the gun while searching a location after entry and securing.

In America the subgun is rarely carried, except by SWAT and specialized federal agents. The shotgun, a carry-over from the Old West, is the only routine backup weapon for patrol and narcs. Aside from its safety problems, the riot gun also has other drawbacks, like its weight, length, limited range, slow loading, low shell capacity, minimal accuracy and heavy recoil. In its favor, the shotgun has multi-hit capability, great stopping power, low cost and great intimidation power. Because of the shotgun's standard length, entry guns are often shortened fore and aft.

"Sometimes I've packed an 18-inch Mossberg 500 with pistol grip as an entry gun, sufficient for the usual five-yard apartment width, and definitely intimidating, but far less accurate than I would prefer," reports our David Steele.

In a typical entry situation there will be occasions where other officers or innocent bystanders cross in front of the detective. It is common practice to enter with the weapon downward. Officers trained in this way typically point their muzzle down whenever a "non-threat" passes in front of it. However, the Los Angeles Sheriff's

Department has found that when the officer suddenly comes across the suspect in a closet or behind furniture, he may automatically lower the muzzle or back up. One Sheriff's Special Enforcement Bureau agent

told me he now keeps his Beretta M92F pointed straight ahead, Weaver stance, finger off the trigger, no matter what. If he comes across the suspect unexpectedly his body language and weapon are in line for business.

Dan Fitzgerald tries out the Calico 9mm submachine gun. It has a fixed stock, 50-round magazine and a brass catcher. This is a useful entry gun for those police departments that authorize it.

Prime entry guns for the Los Angeles County Sheriff's Special Enforcement Bureau are the Heckler & Koch MP5 submachine gun and the Beretta M92F pistol. Both are chambered for the 9mm Parabellum round.

The Heckler & Koch MP5, the most common SWAT subgun, can be carried in the underarm position, muzzle pointed straight ahead, finger off the

trigger, even with the chamber loaded and the selector set to semi-auto. The MP5 trigger is heavy enough to resist accidental discharges, as is the striker safety.

The MP5 fires from closed bolt, an accuracy advantage over the typical Uzi. In fact, the MP5 has become so refined for counter-terrorist, hostage-rescue use that British SAS, German GSG-9, Navy SEAL Team 6 and FBI hostage teams, among other units, have adopted it.

Currently, the Los Angeles Sheriff's Department Special Enforcement Bureau uses only the double-action pistol, usually a Beretta M92F, and the MP5 subgun for entry. Shotguns remain on the perimeter. The pistol and MP5 are compact and precise. Incidentally, LASD was one of the first units in this country to adopt the MP5. Like other departments, there was some resistance at first, since SMGs tend to be considered "unAmerican" and expensive. When

SEAL 6 adopted the MP5, they rejected the one available U.S.-made product that met their needs, the MAC-10 (which we feel really cannot compete with the HK except in the quality of its sound suppressor).

Jim Cirillo, who killed a dozen armed robbers while serving with the New York Police Department Stakeout Unit, used to say that Jeff Cooper was correct about combat shooting being a matter of accuracy, power and speed, but the greatest of these was accuracy. In most of his encounters he used either a four-inch S&W Model 10 38 Special or a cut-down Ithaca Model 37 12-gauge.

The Stake Out Unit's Ithaca had a shortened stock and tube, but accuracy was retained by using rifle sights and a slug barrel. A nylon hand guard was attached to the slide to keep the pump hand from slipping in front of the muzzle.

Although distances were usually short, accuracy was still critical. A store robbery lookout could be shooting from as far away as 60 feet. That is why the SOU Ithaca kept its stock.

"A pistol-grip shotgun, like my Mossberg 500, is usually more for visual deterrence. I call it my the universal translator, since it gets attention and compliance even from non-English speakers, but its accurate range is less than 10 yards," reports David Steele.

"Compared to the standard or pistol-grip riot gun, the handgun and SMG are capable of excellent close range accuracy. Putting two or three 9mms into a subject's upper chest, without endangering nearby hostages, is the way to go."

Just how accurate these weapons are depends on the practice and training of volunteers. As mentioned, SEAL 6 used 2500 to 3000 rounds a week per man, eventually straining the slide rails on their Berettas, causing a move to the SIG-Sauer P226. SEAL 6 increased practice time by informal betting on pistol contests, pasting 3x5 cards to the silhouette to represent the kill zone, only hits on the card would count.

Cirillo of NYPD/SOU would color-code silhouettes, then call out which target was to be a hostage, which was a robber, which robber was wearing body armor (requiring a head shot) just before giving the command to fire. This sort of training called for judgment, speed and accuracy.

Once shooting skills have been developed, teams must design better, more realistic test scenarios. At one

This MP5 subgun with integral sound suppressor is a common choice for the counter-terrorist operations of SEAL Team 6, as well as for police SWAT teams. It is useful for taking out guard dogs as well as bad guys.

extreme is a combined GSG-9/SEAL 6 exercise in the North Sea on an oil rig. Climbing the ice-covered stanchions almost cost one SEAL his life. Once aboard the rig, GSG-9 used the HK P7

The SOCOM pistol in 45 ACP was designed by Heckler & Koch for the U.S. Special Operations Command's Offensive Handgun Weapons System.

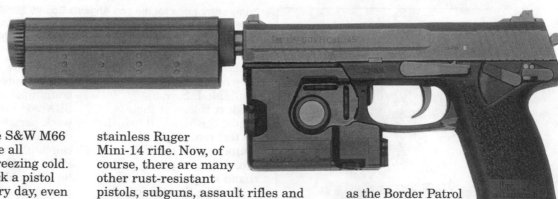

The H&K SOCOM 45 ACP pistol carries a suppressor as well as a flashlight and visible and invisible laser beams. It was designed for used by hostage rescue teams such as Delta Force and SEAL Team 6.

9mm and SEALs used the S&W M66 357 Magnum to neutralize all terrorists in spite of the freezing cold.

SEAL 6 also had to pack a pistol and other contraband every day, even through airport security, without attracting notice. In order to defeat terrorists SEAL 6 had to think like them, except better. Most police entry teams do not have to carry their equipment clandestinely.

European teams usually are restricted to Geneva Convention-approved ball ammo. American teams can use specialized ammo whenever conventional military targets are not involved. The load developed for SEAL use against sentry dogs in Vietnam was the 147-grain 9mm subsonic hollow-point, still used by military and police teams for taking out guard dogs with suppressed pistols, like the "Hush Puppy" Beretta M92F and subguns like the HK MP5SD.

SEAL 6 also experimented with stainless steel for use in weapons that might get dunked, starting with the S&W M66 revolver and the stainless Ruger Mini-14 rifle. Now, of course, there are many other rust-resistant pistols, subguns, assault rifles and shotguns on the market.

For police entry teams not permitted SMGs or assault rifles, the carbine is a better choice than the shotgun for search warrant service or hostage rescue. Some police departments have used the M-1 Carbine with success, as well as the Mini-14, the Marlin Camp Gun in 45 ACP or 9mm, the old semi-auto Reising, the semi-auto versions of the Uzi, MP5, and Colt Commando.

For those entry teams limited to pistols and shotguns, we would recommend pistols with a consistent, fairly heavy trigger, like the Smith K-frame revolver and the Beretta or SIG-Sauer double-action-only models. Shotgun choices include semi-autos like the Benelli M1 Super 90 entry gun and the Beretta 1200. Pump shotguns should be modified along the lines originated by NYPD/SOU. Some of the best are modified Remington 870s sold as the Border Patrol Model by Scattergun Technologies Inc. in Nashville, Tennessee. This firm's BP Model #90121-NW is a totally reworked Remington 870 with 14-inch barrel, ghost ring sights, action sling, and other goodies. This gun is so good the only additional change we would recommend for entry use is shortening the stock another inch or two. SGT Inc. also produces several pistol-grip, shortened 870s for concealed or entry gun purposes.

The best entry teams train constantly, with full logistics support and the latest weapons. The team training is the most important factor. Even most police SWAT teams have other assignments between call-outs. Full-time training is left to military teams like GSG-9, SAS, Delta and SEAL Team 6.

Constant training of international teams also requires a political and

The Heckler Koch P7 is the most common entry pistol used by members of the German GSG-9 hostage rescue teams.

Jim Cirillo, a veteran of shootouts while assigned to the New York Police Department's Stake Out Unit, shows that marksmanship, even with a simple K-frame revolver, is the answer to close combat with armed criminals.

command structure that understands special warfare. Delta and SEAL 6 may be as good as Great Britain's Special Air Service and Unit 269, but they cannot count on a military support structure or a political system which will underwrite preemptive counter-terrorist strikes, such as those conducted by SAS in Northern Ireland or Israeli commandos in border territories and Lebanon.

The Desert One disaster in the 1980 attempt to rescue U.S. Embassy hostages in Iran was just the most obvious example of high-ranking lack of imagination and moral courage. SpecWar expertise has been in the U.S. military since the Vietnam era—along with sabotage by careerist flag rank officers, congressmen and presidents. Even in World War II, Britain was using its Commandos for deep penetration raids, while the comparable US/ Canadian First Special Service Force was misused as spearhead infantry in the Italian meat grinder.

Moving down the chain from elite military counter-terrorist teams, we come to city "heavy weapons" units like Munich's SEK or Los Angeles' SWAT. These teams train together and practice tactics on search warrants and high risk arrests.

Finally, there are improvised entry teams made up of line officers or detectives. The obvious example is narcotics raids. The team may or may not have trained or performed together before. More than one agency may be involved.

"I have organized search warrant teams of as many as three agencies," David Steele recalls. "I delegated jobs based on agency expertise and my intuitive assessment of each person's ability. I got to the assembly site and found 18 people: two federal, three state, plus 13 from a local police department, including patrolmen and three types of detectives.

"I gave everybody jobs, but for the entry team; I chose one patrolman (so occupants couldn't claim we were just a bunch of guys in loud jackets), three narcs (one spoke Spanish; all had kicked doors together), and me (Mossberg in hand). Most of the action took place in a narrow hallway, funneling a total of 15 illegal Mexicans out to the arrest team."

Whether you are improvising with a "pickup team" or "on selection" for Special Air Service, the rules are the same. Use what is available to get in, dominate the scene and kill or capture the occupants. ●

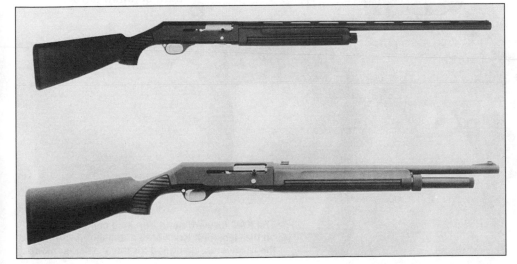

At top is the field version of Beretta's 1200F semi-auto 12-gauge, which is built for bird hunting. Beneath is the Model 1200FP combat version made specifically for law enforcement agencies. It has a 20-inch Improved Cylinder barrel, a seven-round magazine and rifle sights.

CHAPTER 7

THE KNIGHT IS NO PAWN

C. Reed Knight's Firearms Accessories Business Tells A Story Of It Own.

ON THE EAST coast of southern Florida sprawls the city of Vero Beach, a community that plays host to baseball teams for spring training, plus hordes of tourists who come to watch the teams or to visit the nearby Kennedy Space Center. The area also is home to thousands of retirees who like the relaxed way of life and the generally pleasant weather.

Inland, beyond the beaches and the city proper, lie thousands of acres of citrus trees: oranges, grapefruit and tangerines. And in the middle of one of these grapefruit groves is a compound that houses Knight's Manufacturing Company—and a little-publicized subsidiary called Knight's Armament. This enterprise, to which C. Reed Knight, Jr. has devoted most of his adult life, is perhaps best described as a combination think tank and armament design facility.

Reed Knight, Jr., was a long-time associate of the late Gene Stoner, noted for his development of the AR-15 selective-fire rifle that later became the M-16 adopted by U.S. military forces and some of our more friendly allies. A number of other Stoner projects, including the 308-caliber SR-25 sniper rifle, have been cycled through this structure and the adjoining test range. Other developments originated by the arms genius prior to his death in mid-decade still are in the works; weapons that have created great military interest and helped to establish the world class reputation of the enterprise. Included is a silenced revolver that was designed at a U.S. government agency's behest specifically for clandestine operations. The Colt 2000 autoloading pistol was another project that originated in

Knight's shops, with a design hand from Gene Stoner. The noted designer's last two guns, the 5.56mm Stoner light machine gun and his 50-caliber SR-50 sniper rifle also have seen the light of existence in the Knight's Armament machine shops.

This M-4 carbine is equipped with Knight's Armament Rail Adapter System which allows the addition of all sorts of accessories, including the forward hand grip and the scope. The sound suppressor also is a Knight product.

Knight has succeeded in his defense-oriented pursuits where many others have failed. Stoner, in fact, had his own military armament development company in Ohio for several years, but finally had to fold it with the end of the Cold War and the parallel arms race.

Unlike some others who have attempted to build such enterprises, we feel, Knight's success is based largely upon the fact that he is a businessman secondly and a dreamer first. He gained his initial business experience early in life. On his 15th birthday, his

parents gifted him with his own grapefruit grove. The deal was that the grove was his, but he would have to work it, develop it and learn to market the fruit. From this early experience, he learned a great deal about basic economics, not to mention developing a sense of judgment about mankind.

Some of the groves he developed around that initial beginning are still there; in fact, his shooting range is hidden away in one of them. However, Knight is much more interested in arms development today than he is in the best technique for fertilizing a citrus tree.

The soft-spoken Florida native is not one to insist on formality. He is much more at home in his office wearing a soft-finished, open-collar shirt, a pair of khaki pants and a pair of sturdy walking shoes than he would be in a Brooks Brothers suit and $200 hand-made Italian brogans. This lack of formality has been passed on to his staff of administrators,

The KAC forward hand grip also can be installed on the Heckler & Koch MP5 submachine gun, using the rail system designed for this particular model.

Several types of illumination devices also may be installed on weapons by use of the Knight-produced rail system and specially designed mounts.

technicians, machinists and computer whizzes, most of whom follow his lead regarding office attire.

"We figure we get more done if our folks are comfortable and happy. It's tough to be happy in a suit and necktie, when the weather outside is about 100 degrees and the humidity is almost that bad," says Bill McClure, the company vice-president and Knight's right-hand man. McClure also functions as president of another Knight enterprise, a company that supplies professional equipment to city police officers and other law enforcement personnel throughout the Southeast.

Reportedly, the company's owner once commented that he was interested in development, not manufacturing. His seeming goal was to pioneer various pieces of armament or the hardware to go with them, then sell the products to those better suited to manufacturing and marketing. He also actively sought contracts from the Pentagon to develop various pieces of equipment. More recently, he has begun to fill orders for small numbers of guns that his firm has developed. You'll learn more of this in other chapters in this book devoted to Stoner- and Knight-developed arms.

Knight, however, tends to look beyond the immediate, and somewhere in his crystal ball he saw the need for a supplier of accessories that would make official-issue arms easier to handle, more accurate and generally more effective in the hands of military personnel and law enforcement agents. This has led to yet another facet of development and production. This particular enterprise is known as the KAC Modular Weapon System. There are several variations for rifles, carbines and submachine guns.

Over the years, a part of Knight's development program has involved the design and manufacture of smaller but better sound suppressors for a variety of military and law enforcement weapons. More recently, he took a long look at the armament now being issued to this nation's front-line military troops and apparently decided to concentrate on practical accessories for the M-16 series of rifles and the M-4-type carbines, all of which fire the 5.56mm NATO cartridge. In addition, both weapons are built around the original Gene Stoner design and have a large number of interchangeable parts.

"The baseline modular weapon combines a standard rifle or carbine with a non-permanent but innovative rail assembly called the Rail Interface System or simply RIS," Knight explains. "The modular weapons have recently expanded to include the Rail Adapter System (RAS). A beefed-up version includes a model for the M-16A2 and M-16A4 rifles The RAS has been adopted by the U.S. Army."

Replacing the standard handguard on the listed long arms, the RIS is composed of four parallel accessory-mounting rails which are positioned in quadrants at 90 degrees around the weapon's barrel. Once mounted, the RIS provides precise indexing points for the mounting of a broad spectrum of what are best listed as "tactical accessories."

Military-oriented accessories currently available include both standard and flip-up iron sights, telescopic sights, reflex sights, starlight telescopic sights, small state-of-the art night vision devices and visible as well as infrared laser aim lights. Other accessories that may be mounted on the RIS include a vertical pistol grip, a quick-detachable mounting bracket for the M203 grenade launcher, a quick-detachable sound suppressor and visible and infra-red illuminators.

To some who have had the opportunity to test the setup and its various options, the *piece de resistance* may be the KAC Masterkey breaching weapon, which is an adaptation of the familiar Remington Model 870 slide-action shotgun. A lock-buster slug from this instrument usually will take out a door's dead bolt or even the hinges with little difficulty—a definite plus especially for law enforcement agencies.

At first, the problem of mounting the various accessories appears to approach the challenge of a

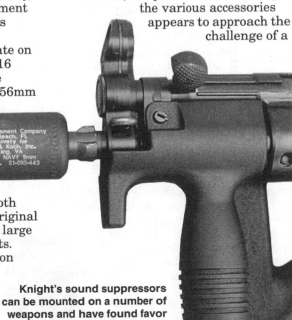

Knight's sound suppressors can be mounted on a number of weapons and have found favor with large segments of the law enforcement community.

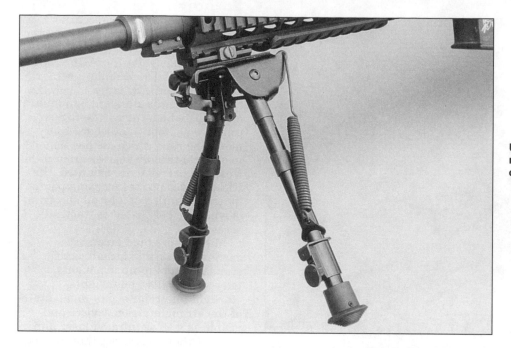

Using the Knight RAS or RIS rail system and mount, the Harris bipod can be installed in only a matter or seconds.

Using Knight-developed systems, the Model 870 shotgun can be mounted beneath the barrel of the M-4A1 carbine and M-16 variations. The M203 grenade launcher also can be installed, but it and the shotgun cannot both be installed at the same time.

jigsaw puzzle with half the pieces missing. However, Knight and his staff have gone to some lengths to simplify this likelihood. It's sort of like being told to "follow the directions printed on the back of the box."

"The individual rails of the RIS and RAS carry several precise recoil grooves along their lengths," Bill McClure explained, as we eyed the RIS-equipped M-16A2 and the collection of accessories. "The numbers on the top rail have a T prefix, while those on the bottom rail are prefixed with the letter B" He didn't explain, but it stood to reason that the T stood for top and the B for bottom. What followed made this seem even more logical.

"Additionally," our erstwhile lecturer explained, "the numbers on the rail to the shooter's left are prefixed with the letter L and the numbers on the rail to his right are marked with the letter R. The numbers and prefixes are provided as a memory aid that is meant to assist the shooter in remounting an accessory in the same position and to provide an alpha/numerical address for every position on the system."

The mount for installing the Aimpoint 5000 and other sighting devices is a Knight product, which attaches to the rail atop the rifle.

We had to agree with Bill McClure's contention that providing such an address system was useful in explaining to the user precisely where he should mount certain accessories, at the same time indicating which addresses are not compatible with other accessory combinations.

Illustrating the fact that a lot of serious thought went into development of the Rail Interface System is the fact that each rail is threaded with three 1/4-20 TPI holes. These are the standard camera adapter size and are threaded into the recoil grooves along the length of the rail. According to McClure, these are provided so standard camera or video gear may be attached. Another suggestion, which we took with a feeling of far more practicality, was the fact that an RIS or RAS-equipped M-4A1 Carbine with a night vision device can be mounted on a standard photo tripod for support and

As pictured here, using the Rail Adapter System, the grenade launcher is slung beneath the barrel of this weapon by means of heavy-duty attachments.

easier night viewing.

Not all of the accessories we inspected were made by Knight's Armament Co., but the mounts that attached the accessories, KAC-developed or not, to the host weapons were developed and tested in the Vero Beach compound.

The upper and lower halves of the RIS or RAS replace the factory handguards and are attached to the host weapon in the same manner. Normally, no tools are required, but in the case of the M-4A1 carbine, if the shooter wants optimum performance, it is necessary to tighten a single screw with a medium flat-tip screwdriver. According to Bill McClure, tightening this screw clamps the upper section of the IRS or RAS assembly to the carbine's front handguard retaining cap.

In one test designed by the U.S. Army to compare RIS-equipped carbines with those carrying the standard carbine handguards, the RIS and RAS "reportedly provided superior thermal protection to the shooter's hand and superior barrel cooling." Several other tests have come up with the same general findings.

The KAC-created system has other advantages, too, according to Knight, who told us, "As accessories are added or repositioned, battle sight zero of reflex sights and aim lights may be confirmed without firing. Zero confirmation of reflex sights is achieved by adjusting the point of aim of the optic to that of the pre-zeroed flip-up rear sight, while simultaneously sighting through both. Zero confirmation of aim lights is achieved by sighting through the pre-zeroed flip-up rear sight and adjusting the point of aim."

It appears fairly obvious that the variety of accessories and the possible combinations should enhance the tactical flexibility and, resultantly, the capabilities of the baseline weapons discussed—not to mention the abilities of the marksmen. "Tactical flexibility can be achieved by allowing the user to custom tailor his assigned weapon to his individual preferences to handle changing situations and combat environments," says C. Reed Knight, Jr. "A key addition to this tactical flexibility of the Modular Weapons System is the addition of small state-of-the-art night vision devices that can enhance low light level performance of daylight sighting systems." An example would be the ITT Pocketscope night vision device mounted behind the Aimpoint 5000 reflex sight.

"The Modular Weapons Systems also offer the military and other users the versatility needed to postpone the obsolescence of current service weapons well into the next century," Knight concludes. That possibility, of course, should be of continuing interest to the Pentagon bean counters who are charged with getting the most bang out of a buck!

Not considered a part of the Modular Weapons System as such, but items that could add further versatility and performance to modular weapons, are two Knight's Armament Company-developed two-stage trigger groups. These are designated as the semi-automatic Target Model and the selective-fire Government Model . The latter can replace the trigger groups of the standard M-16, M-16A1, M-16A2, M-16A4 and the military AR-15. The semi-auto Target version can replace the civilian AR-15's trigger mechanism.

"The standard single-stage trigger mechanism releases the hammer,

The Remington Model 870 pump-action shotgun is attached to the M-4 carbine or M-16 rifle by means of the KAC mounting system. It differs from the unit used to mount the M203 grenade launcher.

firing the weapon, after a steady squeeze on the trigger by the trigger finger," Knight explains. "This trigger squeeze requires steadily increased pressure to overcome the sear spring and other mechanical resistance.

"The creep inherent in the factory single-stage trigger requires that the shooter take time to 'walk' through the trigger pull and find the let-off point in order to achieve accurate fire."

In the semi-auto mode, the Knight's Armament two-stage trigger mechanisms release the hammer, firing the weapon after "two distinct amounts of spring and mechanical resistance are overcome by the trigger finger," Knight explains.

"The initial stage of resistance encountered with this design feels light and, at about 1/8-inch, is relatively long. The second stage of resistance feels noticeably greater but is of only short duration. The result is an extremely predictable, consistent and crisp trigger pull. Because initial resistance of the first stage is overcome quickly and the second stage is crisp and predictable, semi-automatic fire is both quicker and more accurate."

The KAC Government Model selective-fire trigger group provides the same sort of two-stage trigger pull in the semi-automatic mode, but in full-automatic, there is a

The forward hand grip, another KAC product, is designed to be installed on the same maker's rail system, offering added stability to the weapon.

familiar-feeling single-stage trigger pull that alerts the shooter to the selector setting.

As indicated earlier, these two-stage trigger groups are available in both semi-automatic-only and selective-fire configurations. In addition to the arms listed, the semi-auto two-stage trigger can be installed in the civilian-marketed pre-1989 Colt semi-auto-only AR-15s, as well as the non-Colt semi-auto versions of the same rifle. Still

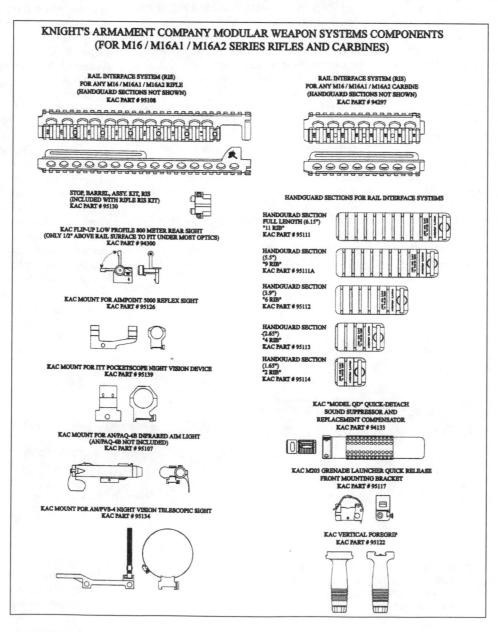

KNIGHT'S ARMAMENT COMPANY MODULAR WEAPON SYSTEMS COMPONENTS
(FOR M16 / M16A1 / M16A2 SERIES RIFLES AND CARBINES)

RAIL INTERFACE SYSTEM (RIS)
FOR ANY M16 / M16A1 / M16A2 RIFLE
(HANDGUARD SECTIONS NOT SHOWN)
KAC PART # 95108

RAIL INTERFACE SYSTEM (RIS)
FOR ANY M16 / M16A1 / M16A2 CARBINE
(HANDGUARD SECTIONS NOT SHOWN)
KAC PART # 94297

STOP, BARREL, ASSY. KIT, RIS
(INCLUDED WITH RIFLE RIS KIT)
KAC PART # 95130

HANDGUARD SECTIONS FOR RAIL INTERFACE SYSTEMS

HANDGURAD SECTION
FULL LENGTH (6.15")
"11 RIB"
KAC PART # 95111

KAC FLIP-UP LOW PROFILE 800 METER REAR SIGHT
(ONLY 1/2" ABOVE RAIL SURFACE TO FIT UNDER MOST OPTICS)
KAC PART # 94300

HANDGURAD SECTION
(5.5")
"9 RIB"
KAC PART # 95111A

HANDGUARD SECTION
(3.9")
"6 RIB"
KAC PART # 95112

KAC MOUNT FOR AIMPOINT 5000 REFLEX SIGHT
KAC PART # 95126

HANDGUARD SECTION
(2.65")
"4 RIB"
KAC PART # 95113

HANDGUARD SECTION
(1.65")
"2 RIB"
KAC PART # 95114

KAC MOUNT FOR ITT POCKETSCOPE NIGHT VISION DEVICE
KAC PART # 95139

KAC "MODEL QD" QUICK-DETACH
SOUND SUPPRESSOR AND
REPLACEMENT COMPENSATOR
KAC PART # 94133

KAC MOUNT FOR AN/PAQ-4B INFRARED AIM LIGHT
(AN/PAQ-4B NOT INCLUDED)
KAC PART # 95107

KAC M203 GRENADE LAUNCHER QUICK RELEASE
FRONT MOUNTING BRACKET
KAC PART # 95117

KAC MOUNT FOR AN/PVS-4 NIGHT VISION TELESCOPIC SIGHT
KAC PART # 95134

KAC VERTICAL FOREGRIP
KAC PART # 95122

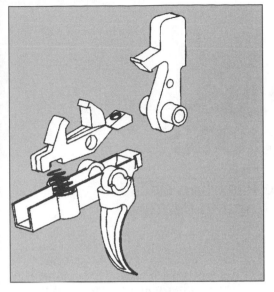

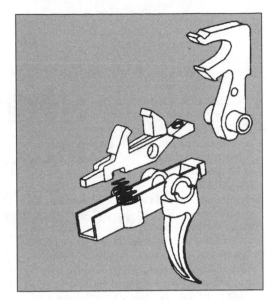

At left is the KAC semi-automatic two-stage Target trigger group, which is available for M-16 variations as well as pre-1989 AR-15s. This is KAC Part #94KTSA. At right is the KAC Government Model selective-fire, two-stage trigger group listed as KAC Part #94KTAU. At present, neither unit is available to civilian shooters due to rulings by the BATF.

in development is a special two-stage semi-automatic trigger group kit for installation in the post-1989 Colt AR-15s, using larger .170-inch diameter pins.

As an update module for the M-16A2 rifle and the M-4 carbine series that fire the three-round burst, Reed Knight and his staff have developed a two-stage trigger group that consists of only three unique KAC parts: the hammer, a front hook and a rear hook. According to Knight, these parts take the place of the standard hammer, burst cam, clutch spring, burst disconnect and semi-auto disconnect. With installation of the selective-fire trigger group kit, the three-round-burst weapons are upgraded to full-automatic fire.

Knight points out, however, that although the installation of the KAC selective-fire two-stage trigger group and other selective-fire parts will not convert semi-automatic-only rifles and carbines to full-automatic fire, the U.S. Bureau of Alcohol, Tobacco and Firearms has chosen to consider these firearms illegal contraband. Thus, the knowledge outlined in these last few paragraphs is offered strictly for informational purposes.

As we understand it, the late Gene Stoner was involved in the development of some of the accessories listed here. This, as one might expect, leads to a story.

One of the M-16 rifles, a firearm Stoner originally developed, had

been brought into the assembly area of the Knight enterprise and all of the accessories discussed here were attached to it. Stoner surveyed the results which appeared to have some relationship to what is featured in today's space combat movies, then shook his head.

"I don't understand it," he mused thoughtfully. "I spent years trying to come up with a five-pound combat rifle, but when we add all of these accessories to make it better and more combat competitive, it weighs 20 pounds!"

He was joking, of course, and aware of the fact that other than the RIS unit, most of the accessories would be mounted only when needed and most often as individual additions. ●

The infantryman must wear night vision goggles to take full advantage of an M-16-series rifle that is outfitted with the AN/PAQ-4B infrared laser aim light attached with a KAC mount. This rifle also carries the KAC flip-up rear sight and the same maker's Model QD quick-detach sound suppressor.

CHAPTER 8

SPECIAL TEAMS, SPECIAL WEAPONS

The Hard Law Enforcement Lessons Of The Past Two Decades Have Set The Equipment Trend For The Coming Century.

IF LIFE FOLLOWS fiction, as some claim, we saw an excellent example in Los Angeles several years ago. A pair of heavily armed bank robbers held trained officers at bay, until well-armed police reinforcement arrived and carried the day. One of the Los Angeles Police Department's first officers on the scene was a Vietnam veteran. He recognized the distinctive sound of the AK-47 rifle. For him, it was back to combat! The rifle that finally took the bad guys down was a much improved version of the original M-16 that first served in Vietnam.

The City of Angels experiences over 1000 bank robberies during the course of the average year. It was heavily armed neighborhood gangs such as the Simbianese Liberation Army, the Black Panthers and the Weather Underground groups that led to formation and training of the original Special Weapons and Tactics groups in the LAPD. In later years, various groups have taken hostages during botched burglaries or holdups, and drug dealers have been found to be increasingly well armed.

LAPD's experience points out that while hardware is important, it is the human element that is most critical. Human beings are very much individuals and there are good and bad examples among every profession.

"But I was proud of the LAPD in this operation," declares R.K. Campbell, a working South Carolina police officer and one of our geographical contacts on law enforcement. "Not one officer failed to

show courage and determination. Outgunned but not outfought, they kept the bad guys ducking, avoiding a civilian bloodbath. They held the fort until the cavalry arrived!

"Some of us may find ourselves in a kind of culture shock as cops are

This Olympic Arms copy of the AR-15 is chambered for 223 Remington and offers police officers an advantage in desperate situations.

forced into duties resembling paramilitary units. When I visited France a few years ago, we observed troops with slung submachine guns at nearly every intersection. The general assembly was in session and security was high. I had visited Italy during the time of Aldo Moro's murder and police were a heavily armed presence on every street in Rome.

"In America, people want their local gendarmes to be approachable and friendly. The local police should know local families, good and bad, and

have the skills of the social worker tempered with an understanding of the rougher man's way of life. But police officers are more in danger than ever before from felons willing to shoot it out. These men have little fear of punishment. The bad guys in the LA shootout had spent three months in jail after conviction on a previous weapons charge!

"Today's officers must be community policemen, be computer literate and even politically correct. Training budgets are limited, but expectations of officer performance are high. Despite a multi-million dollar crime bill, the only concrete effort from Washington, D.C., seems to be a concerted effort to lower police officer qualifications. Ignored is the wisdom that if you hire from the bottom of the barrel, you will have corresponding problems," Officer Campbell contends. "Fortunately, law enforcement has not reached that point. Americans have been lucky to have had better law enforcement than they were willing to pay for during most of this century.

This shortened 5.56mm carbine is from Olympic Arms, a Washington-state company that produces variations on the AR-15 rifle, as well as other weapons.

The Heckler & Koch HK53 chambered for 223 is a proven light rifle and a premium support weapon.

"Most peace officers value liberty and freedom and some of us feel distinctly uncomfortable with the action of some of the black-suited 'ninja teams.' There is no question that ill-trained and perhaps ill-chosen teams have broken the law on more than one occasion. Other teams have done excellent work. New York's Emergency Services Division and the various LAPD units have performed dozens of rescues, as have many large and small units across the country. Having worn a shiny target to the left of my heart for a significant part of the past 20 years, I am well aware of the dual trust and suspicion citizens have for peace officers."

However well trained, peace officers cannot be compared to military units. Military contingents have tremendous support, should be well led, and must expect high casualties. Peace officers have different objectives and the only acceptable casualty rate is Zero for both police and civilians. Peace officers must rely upon individual initiative. Nonetheless, modern criminals are becoming increasingly well armed and bold. We must meet them on an even footing.

A few generations ago the biggest man on the department was relied upon to kick the door down on raids, and the top deer hunter in the department was the first called out to handle a sniper. Today fewer recruits are familiar with firearms and size doesn't necessarily mean the most during such confrontations. Today's officers must devote a significant amount of time to training that prepares for felony raids and other uproars. The cost of such training and equipment may be a shock to city fathers. But the needs of the people must be met.

The threat may come from armed gangs or individuals. For instance, Campbell was called out a few weeks ago to guard a government officer who had received death threats. There had been two murders the previous day, lending a heightened sense of urgency to the death threats. The suspect was armed with some type of auto-loading 223-caliber rifle. As is true in most cases, there was no further bloodshed, but a heavily armed police presence may have been a deterrent.

There are two basic categories of police firearms in current use. These are the pistol and the long gun.

Among the long guns, the categories are the rifle, carbine, submachine gun and the pistol-caliber carbine.

"Pistols probably receive more attention than they merit. The most powerful pistols are only fractionally as powerful as long guns. The so-called tactical pistol can be a formidable weapon at close range if it is well handled. The caliber should be either 40 Smith & Wesson or 45 ACP," Campbell feels. That being said, there are a lot of special response teams relying upon the 9mm Parabellum pistols. Usually these teams are using the weapon their parent agency issues. "This is not altogether a bad idea, since officers issued the 9mm pistol probably will come to rely upon the long gun instead!"

New York Emergency Services has done good work with the Model 92 Beretta 9mm, which sometimes is loaded with the Glaser Safety Slug.

Officer R.K. Campbell, a South Carolina policeman, tests most of the new weapons for his department. In this case, it is SIG's P220 chambered for the 38 Super cartridge.

There are several philosophies that have been extended to sidearm issue. Some use the pistol as a precise, short-range hostage rescue gun. This pistol might be characterized by the tuned Browning 9mm Hi Power model. A number of these pistols will group into four inches at 50 yards in good hands, but the power of any pistol is severely degraded as range increases. Penetration falls off rapidly as any simple test reflects

The other philosophy followed by the special team is to consider the sidearm a last-ditch, close-range weapon. The Colt 1911s originally issued to Los Angeles police officers were modified to feed the Speer 200-grain hollow-point bullet. This hard-hitting round has earned an enviable reputation for both accuracy and effect.

The move in modern units is toward simpler pistols. When an anti-terrorist pistol first was envisioned in Germany, it was the SIG P220 that emerged from the competition. This weapon has no safety; only safety features.

The Glock pistol is a simple, rugged gun well suited to the rigors of special duties. The 40-caliber Glock Model 22 is an excellent duty pistol, and paired with Pro-Load 180-grain ammunition as issued by Southern California's Burbank Police Department is an excellent choice for every task.

"We should avoid over-specialization and dependence upon the pistol," Campbell insists. "Because of my personal deep distrust of the 9mm cartridge, I will stay with the proven 45 auto. With an excellent reputation as a trench fighter, as well as for bunker emptying and as an urban defense weapon without peer, the 45 is soldiering on into our next century."

There are several distinct categories of long guns. There is a significant difference between the entry weapon and the general-use carbine. Surprisingly, a number of weapons are useful as entry weapons, for general use and for sniper suppression. Fortunately, the well-trained lawless sniper is rarely encountered, but a madman with the family hunting rifle has paralyzed police departments on several occasions.

We have seen this happen when the sniper or barricaded suspect has only a lowly 22 rimfire The pistol is helpless in these situations in most hands. An exception was a valiant federal agent in Oklahoma who suppressed a madman's rifle fire at 80 yards, using a handgun

There is much to be said for the general issue of patrol rifles to deal with these circumstances. The trend in progressive agencies now appears to be toward the patrol carbine.

Dynamic entries often are executed when serving "no knock" warrants. Either the threat to officer safety or the likelihood of the destruction of evidence is so great the issuing judge will validate such a warrant.

In some situations, even after giving the suspects proper warning, there still is a need to take the doors down and rush into harm's way. These movements can be confusing and the preservation of life demands practiced tactics. We are aware of a raid in which the point man went down with a bullet in the rear panel of his Second Chance vest. His backup man had stumbled and clutched his Glock in mid-step. Fortunately, a well-trained team did not open up in reaction to the lead man falling, as has happened in several instances of such cop/criminal interaction.

The shotgun remains a capable and effective entry weapon. Few of us can forget television's Joe Friday reverently checking out an Ithaca Model 37 12-gauge as he and partner Bill Gannon proceeded to kick in a door and bust a dangerous individual. It was somewhat spectacular on the TV screen then, but single officers, posses and teams have been using the shotgun for such duty for at least a hundred years. From the New York Police Department's double-barrel

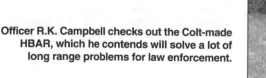

Officer R.K. Campbell checks out the Colt-made HBAR, which he contends will solve a lot of long range problems for law enforcement.

Some law enforcement jobs call for special equipment such as this bomb squad knife made by Chuck Stapels, and the stainless steel Smith & Wesson 9mm pistol.

shotguns to the Los Angeles department's trademark Ithacas, the shotgun has saved the lives of many officers. The FBI has favored Browning autoloaders.

Experienced teams often use an extremely short-barreled shotgun. This makes much more sense than a pistol-grip shotgun. Many professionals feel a pistol-grip shotgun is a liability. The full-stocked, short-barreled shotgun is fast and capable in confined quarters, and all shotguns are great stoppers. Few felons will stay on their feet even with body armor after taking a pair of hits from a 12-gauge slug. The shotgun also is versatile. Reduced loads, magnum buckshot, full-power slugs, door-breaching rounds, flash/bang distraction rounds and flechettes are just a few of the options available with the shotgun. "The combat shotgun is probably underrated. The weapon doesn't have to be babied and probably works better if it isn't coddled. With a good barrel and a premium slug such as the Remington or Brenneke, the shotgun is an option out to 50 yards. The shotgun is not impressive, however, against car glass or light cover if loaded with buckshot," Officer Campbell has learned from personal experience.

The submachine gun is an expensive instrument, demanding intense training. Figure-eight and

shoot-through tactics are expensive to master in terms of taxpayer-supported man-hours and ammunition. Weekly practice is demanded of the subgun-armed officer. The SMG has a high hit probability in trained hands and more range than the shotgun. However, there are drawbacks as well. The SMG is typically chambered for pistol cartridges.

"I am aware of one instance in which a burst of 9mm SMG fire failed to penetrate a car windshield adequately. The felon was struck by only one bullet which had partially expanded. The bullet merely flattened against the felon's skull," Campbell reports.

An option for special teams is the sound-suppressed submachine gun. There is no such thing as a silenced weapon, but the suppressed gun has a muzzle signature reduced from 120 decibels to less than 100 decibels. Damage to the eardrums begins at about 100 dcb. By suppressing the SMG, it is possible to reduce the muzzle signature to about the sound level of a 22 rimfire rifle. Commands and movements can be heard at this level, the principal advantage, officers' hearing being preserved as well.

"The weapons are ideal under certain circumstances, but they are controversial, expensive and extremely specialized," Campbell is quick to point out. "A significant

Due to the blunt design and deep cavity, this Speer 45 ACP cartridge has come to be known as the Flying Ashtray. It is highly effective as a man-stopper.

An on-going tactical concern for officers is the matter of penetration. The bullets fired into the door of this junked police vehicle did not penetrate the door.

problem is that the suppressor reduces pistol ammunition velocity. The Heckler & Koch MP5SD2, for instance, has 30 ports on its 5.73-inch barrel. This dissipates propellant gas. One of the few loads that retains over 90 percent of its velocity in suppressed weapons is the Pro Load 147-grain 9mm round." Many of today's officers have found the 9mm cartridge isn't much without solid, multiple strikes. Many 9mm loads are reduced to the 380 ACP level, when fired from suppressed weapons.

We feel that the submachine gun is a viable tool for highly trained, select-budget teams, but this weapon should not be adopted without top-grade training support.

The anti-sniper/police sniper rifle is an individualistic instrument. The scope's eye relief and contours of the stock are particularly important. Calibers of special team weapons run from the 223 Remington to the 300 Winchester Magnum. These rifles are capable of shots well past 300 yards, but virtually all engagements involving police snipers take place at much closer ranges. The two most widely used calibers at this time are the 223 Remington and the 308 Winchester. The 223 rifle is usually a semi-automatic such as the Colt AR-15 or the Olympic Arms version of that model. The 223 may not be reliable against light cover and glass, while the 308 rifle exhibits good penetration and extreme accuracy. Even with heavy bullet loads, the 223 cannot equal the 30-caliber rifle.

Still, the most useful single weapon in the special team arsenal, in Campbell's opinion, is the 223 carbine. Admittedly, this weapon has far more power and light cover penetration than the submachine gun or pistol caliber carbine, but it's little if any harder to control in rapid fire.

"The standard rifle has a 20-inch barrel while the carbine has a 16-inch barrel. Often the carbine will have a shortened stock as well. The AR-15 is considered to be user-friendly and fast handling, and the controls well located.

"This is one of the fastest of all rifles to reload in a tactical situation. Accuracy is good—even the carbines—out to nearly 300 yards. The 223 cartridge is a proven stopper, far more effective than any pistol. Despite its light cover penetration capability, the 223 usually will not pass through the human body. Even military ball ammo

Officer Bob Campbell contends that the shotgun is a low-tech weapon that deserves more respect from police officers than it usually gets. At the other extreme, it garners great respect from the average suspect!

A common challenge confronted by law enforcement is the drug dealer's guard dog. This target, used in planning drug raids, is marketed by Law Enforcement Targets.

will break up in tissue. The nose will fragment and the rear of the bullet will sometimes break into larger fragments," our South Carolina observer contends. "However, this excellent performance is seriously eroded at longer ranges. The 223 becomes erratic in performance past 100 yards, but this is a fire mission for the 308 at that range."

There are many variations of the AR-15 rifle. Only the Colt 1911 pistol has been modified as often. One of the more interesting options is a 7.25-inch barreled entry weapon, but with a barrel this short ammunition velocity is lowered from 3000 fps to 2500 fps. That is a significant loss in a weapon that relies upon velocity for effect. However, tests have shown that the penetration of the 55-grain bullet is affected only slightly by this velocity loss. In this lightweight weapon, the recoil spring is eliminated by use of a buffer spring. The pistonless gas system is modified to a straight gas tube in most variations. A reinforced handguard is used for better gripping and control. A number of weapons such as the ZM LR 300 have true folding stocks. "These weapons are effective, but they do not come cheap," Officer Campbell is quick to point out. "A number of these model variations cost well over $2,500 each.

"The 223 carbines are very fast and easy to handle with minimal instruction. A good man can perform surprising feats with such a capable tool. As entry weapons, fighting rifles and for anti-sniper work, these are the most versatile of police armanent".

Even as we enter the next century, the man behind the gun always will matter, but these highly developed weapons, proven in hundreds of operations, still will be at the forefront of law enforcement. ●

Popular calibers favored by SWAT units are (from left) the 45 ACP, 9mm Parabellum and the 223 or 5.56mm. The 7.62mm (308 Winchester) round also is popular for specific problems and is in most police armories.

GUNS THAT DIDN'T MAKE IT

Patent Office Files And Proof Rooms Around The Globe Are Full Of Excellent But Unmade Gun Designs

AMONG OUR NATION'S shooting enthusiasts are thousands upon thousands of individuals— would-be firearms designers all—who are convinced they can or have invented the better mouse trap and the world should be beating a path to their respective doors.

Some of these individuals are in the arms business and make a living from perfecting designs or doing cosmetic things to old weaponry with the idea of giving it new life. What most of them really want is to design their own gun and see it go into production.

Others are teenagers with mechanical aptitude who like tinkering in machine shops to see what can be produced. The late and still revered John M. Browning was one of those. Gene Stoner, an aircraft engineer, was another. His first firearm of his own design was a hunting rifle he built, because he didn't have the loose cash to buy a new Remington or Winchester. From the post-World War II period until his death in 1996, Stoner probably had more arms patents issued in his name than any other American.

And there was Marsh Williams, a Southern moonshiner, who was allowed to tinker with an idea for a firearm while he was in a federal prison, thus satisfying a boyhood interest which he had not had the spare time to pursue. He later became famous as Carbine Williams, the creator of the M-1 Carbine of World War II. He continued to dabble with firearms design following his release from prison and employment by Winchester, but none of his other efforts came close to approaching the fame and respect accorded his little 30-caliber combat carbine.

This last is mentioned to point out that even the best known of our nation's gun designers—and those of other nations, as well—do not bat 100

Outfitted with a stock that resembled that of a medieval dueling pistol, this is the way L.E. Lisk thought the subgun should be finished. Note the angle of the grip, making it easier to fire from the hip.

percent. They all have had their failures. The first prototype of the AR-10, ancestor of today's M-16, that Gene Stoner unveiled for the military blew up during official tests on a government rifle range.

In short, there probably are a lot more good firearms designs that did not make the cut, shot down by politics, financing or bureaucracy, than ever make it to the production line. Here are just a few of them.

The Williams/Lisk 22 Rimfire

Unfortunately, your authors have not be able to assemble a great deal of material on the background of L.E. Lisk beyond what appears in this chapter.

The 22 rimfire rifle and handgun should be familiar to everyone who shoots and a lot of the people who don't. There was a time when every farm boy received a single-shot 22 rifle on his 12th birthday. In the rural Midwest, where co-author Lewis spent most of his teen years, this was almost as traditional as the Mossberg pump-action shotgun kept behind the kitchen door.

In those days of innocence, before World War II, that rifle was used to take wild rabbits for the pot, kill animals caught in the youngsters' traps, and to knock disease-spreading pigeons off the top of the barn. Anyone who talked about a 22 rimfire machine gun would have been considered fair prey for the people with the nets.

However, there were such things back then. It was during World War II that the Marine Corps reworked a number of 30-caliber Browning water-cooled machine guns to handle the diminutive rimfire round. Lewis recalls using one during officers' training at Quantico, Virginia, in the early 1940s. They were set up on

This is the original prototype of the subgun designed by Carbine Williams and is the one used in the field tests discussed here.

Not exactly a firearm for rabbit hunting, the Williams/Lisk submachine gun could be employed advantageously in the hands of special mission military units or guerrilla forces.

a short range measuring no more than 50 feet, as he recalls, and belted 22 rounds were fed through them as an inexpensive way to teach officer candidates the basics of machine gunnery. Once they were properly clued in, they went on to fire the "real" guns with the original 30-06 bores.

Specifications

Name:	Williams/Lisk 22 Rimfire Submachine Gun.
Caliber:	22 Long Rifle.
Operation:	Gas-operated; belt-fed; fires from open bolt.
Cyclic Rate:	1500 to 2700 rounds per minute.
Weight:	12 pounds, unloaded; 22 pounds with 1000-round belt.
Length:	26 inches.
Stock:	None; has two aluminum hand grips.
Maker:	Marsh (Carbine) Williams and L.E. Lisk; final disposition of prototypes undetermined.

"We had an old master sergeant who could hardly speak English, but he knew machine guns. He had been a gunner in the German Army in World War I, then served with the French Foreign Legion in North Africa. Somehow he made his way to the United States and enlisted in our own Army. He finally ended up in the Marine Corps where he intended to stay," Lewis recalls. "If you were doing something wrong, he would beat on top of your steel helmet with a brass-tipped swagger stick to get your attention."

We checked on whether this 22-caliber indoctrination still goes on and got a definite negative. In fact, no one in today's Marine Corps remembers such a Quantico setup. Instead, they use electronic targets and guns that are rigged to fire compressed air-driven bullets. All of this can be done in a darkened room with the specially rigged guns, a computer and a screen.

There also have been recurring tales of the use of 22 rimfire machine guns in the hands of South American troops fighting revolutionaries in their own countries. One source declares that a particular nation made a practice of coating the 22 bullets with arsenic for greater death potential. We cannot verify this, however.

But a 22 rimfire machine gun was designed and several prototypes produced by the earlier mentioned Marsh "Carbine" Williams. As Jim Schultz, a Vietnam-era Green Beret, devoted researcher and a working gun writer, put it, "This weapon was a magnificent creation of mechanical wizardry and superb craftsmanship." This description certainly would dovetail with the reputation derived from the work of Carbine Williams.

Sometime during the post-World War II years, Williams took on one J.L. Lisk as a partner in this particular enterprise. Unfortunately, your authors have not been able to assemble a great deal of information concerning Lisk's background. However, it was in 1956 that Lisk began to assist with the development of this gun. At least three different prototypes were developed

prior to Williams' death. When the inventor's will was read, Lisk reportedly was surprised to learn that his mentor and partner had left him total ownership of the 22 machine gun.

During the 15 years following Lisk's first connection with the gun, many modifications were made, some by him and others by Williams before his death. From what we have been able to learn, the design was simple, thus facilitating performance and maintenance. And in spite of its diminutive bore and the small working parts necessary to handle the small cartridge, the gun was reputed to be strong and reliable.

In 1977, L.E. Lisk reportedly packed up his gun and took it to Aberdeen Proving Grounds, where members of the U.S. Army Infantry Board were gathered to review promising weaponry. The little machine gun performed flawlessly in all of the tests demanded of it. In addition to the Army experts, a number of media representatives were on hand and reportedly were greatly impressed by the gun's performance and potential.

Lisk was asked to turn over the weapon to the Army board for further tests and review, but he refused to do so without a written agreement that met his demands.

L.E. Lisk (left) passes the gun to an unidentified observer to inspect and shoot.

This is the late Carbine Williams' idea of how the finished gun should look. Note that he has included a wire stock that can be drawn to the rear for shoulder firing.

The opposite side of the prototype used in informal testing is shown. The knob at the rear was used to adjust the cyclic rate of fire.

The earlier mentioned Jim Schultz, who did much of the research on this gun, reports, "It is felt by every inventor with whom I have talked that government weapons people are not above appropriating the ideas of others. For that reason, inventors are not willing to turn over their work for evaluation."

However, at that point, Lisk did offer to sell the weapon to the U.S. government for further development and use by our military forces. He left the Maryland test site with the promise that he would be contacted within two weeks, and would be asked to return to the Aberdeen Proving Grounds for more tests and possible negotiations.

It was more than three years before Lisk again was contacted by an Army representative who wanted to conduct more testing at the Aberdeen range— and to examine the gun in detail. Again, Lisk refused to let the gun out of his own hands.

It is in this time frame that the history of the gun becomes somewhat murky. Lisk indicated to a captain assigned to a Midwestern National Guard unit, William Roberts, that several foreign countries had shown interest in the gun. Lisk, however, wanted the gun to be in our own nation's military arsenal. He told Captain Roberts that "it is hard to believe the United States does not not seem interested, while another country has offered $10 million."

The original prototype developed by Carbine Williams had a cyclic rate of fire of 2200 rounds per minute. Further, Williams and Lisk later proclaimed that their brainchild could be adapted with ease to fire 5000 rounds per minute! This would require reworking the gun to use only one feed belt that would run through duplex feed and firing systems equipped with twin barrels.

"It doesn't take much imagination to realize that even the 22 Long Rifle

From top are the final prototype with wooden grip and forearm as developed by L.E. Lisk. Center is the original designed and built by Carbine Williams; bottom is the version that Williams felt would be the one that would sell. His death interfered with further progress.

Some idea of the workings of the Williams/Lisk gun may be gained from inspecting this top view of the piece. Williams built the gun in 22 LR to save money in testing. He planned for bigger things!

This photo was taken under poor light conditions and indicates that there was some recoil as the subgun was fired from the hip.

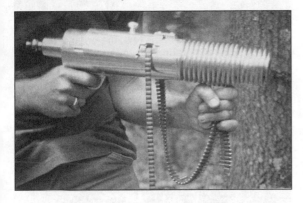

Here the shooter has looped the ammo belt between his fingers so there will be less drag as the rounds pass through the action. The length of the empty belt could present a problem, however.

The gun at right is the one used in tests discussed here. The other gun was what Lisk considered to be the final version. Note that the lines are slimmer and weight has been reduced.

bullet for which the gun was chambered could prove devastating at ranges under 200 yards, with a cyclic rate of fire of 5000 rounds per minute," Jim Schultz opines. According to comments by Lisk, the weapon was developed in 22 rimfire originally to reduce the expense of ammunition during testing. It was Carbine Williams' aim to go on to bigger and better calibers before he submitted it to possible manufacturers. However, with the potential volume of fire as a 22-caliber, it could be an ideal weapon for special military forces and guerrillas, particularly if a silencer should be added.

Captain Roberts had the opportunity to fire the little machine gun in the early 1980s and reported that the prototype he handled had seen more than 100,000 rounds pass through its barrel over a period of more than 15 years, yet the gun appeared to be almost new. There appeared to be no wear on any internal parts.

Test reports show that the rate of fire could be adjusted from 1500 rounds per minute to 2700 by using a round knob that was positioned at the rear of the gun. When the gun was fired continuously for 60 seconds, the captain later reported, "I was able to grasp the barrel cooling fins with my bare hands and experience no discomfort from barrel heat. In addition, the gun's muzzle could be touched directly without discomfort."

This participant in tests seems somewhat puzzled by the size of the gun and the weight combined with that of 1000 rounds of 22 Long Rifle ammo.

The weapon, of course, was fully automatic and had no provision for semi-auto fire. Designed to be fired from the hip, it had neither a stock nor sights. In his tests, Captain Roberts fired approximately 2500 rounds and reported that recoil under sustained fire was negligible. There also was no barrel climb.

Actually, there were three different versions of this particular firearm produced as prototypes, according to all of the information we have been able to assemble. The first looked like a plumber's nightmare and consisted of a tube with a knob at its rear for adjusting the rate of fire. There were two hand grips, one at the rear of the trigger guard, the other mounted on the cooling fins a few inches back of the muzzle. It was this gun with which Captain Roberts conducted his tests.

Loading of the belt of ammo is similar to the systems used on other belt-fed guns of larger caliber.

This photo suggests that a loose belt carrying 1000 rounds of ammo could offer a management problem.

For a gun so small, its 12-pound weight seems a bit out of proportion. A belt with 1000 rounds of 22 Long Rifle ammunition weighs another 10 pounds. However, it was always Lisk's claim that the weight could be reduced to four pounds and size of the gun could approximate the dimensions of the Model 1911Al service automatic pistol. So far as we know, however, no further efforts ever were made toward such miniaturization.

One particular note relative to operation is the fact that no oil or other lubricants are used with the gun. In fact, according to information offered by Lisk at the Aberdeen Proving Ground tests, the introduction of lubricants could lead to malfunctions!

While large quantities of ammunition could be carried—one foot of belt holds 47 rounds of 22 LR ammo—the belt itself could present a problem: A 1000-round belt dragging in one's wake could tend to trip one up or become entangled in brush. A belt that disintegrated every foot or so would prove an advantage. As for disintegrating metal links, they probably would be too small and weak to hold so small a cartridge and would not prove to be a practical answer.

All of this conjecture would appear to be after the fact, since we have not been able to track down the disposition of the three prototypes. A rumor circulated several years ago that they and the production blueprints had been sold to a Saudi Arabian millionaire. If so, none of the guns have been produced and introduced where they can be seen. This may well become one of the great mysteries of gundom! •

In the tests discussed in the text, the original prototype and some 2500 rounds of ammunition were used. The gun reportedly did not heat up when 60-second bursts were fired.

One observer felt that, with 47 rounds per running foot of belt, it would be simple to build a 1000-round drum for the Williams/Lisk gun.

The subgun was designed to be fired from the hip and at relatively close range. Williams and Lisk included no stock and no sights.

L.E. Lisk holds the final prototype, which he favored. It had a wooden hand grip and forearm, perhaps leading to a more stable hold.

THE RSG-12 SNIPER RIFLE

Better Mousetraps Don't Always Sell!

THERE IS NO doubt Randy Fritz knows just about all there is to know about rifles. In his lifetime, he has seen and, in most cases, worked with virtually every bore size from the 58-caliber blackpowder reproductions to the military's 5mm fletchette. The problem would appear to be that he doesn't know the path through the bureaucracy of law enforcement bean-counters who tend to buy from the lowest bid. They don't seem concerned with whether a specific weapon will best do a specific job against the bad guys of the world.

Fritz runs Tar-Hunt Custom Rifles, Inc. And for nearly a decade, he spent his spare moments developing what he felt would be the ultimate in law enforcement entry weapons: a 12-gauge sniper rifle he called the RSG-12.

When you hear members of a SWAT unit talking tactics, they invariably are discussing the head shot to take out a hostage-holder or other felon as the permanent solution. This, of course, should be the most likely approach, but a head shot does not always present itself. If it should appear that the felon is about to shoot a hostage, there is a need to put him down any way possible. In this case, such law

enforcement veterans as Gary Paul Johnson contend that a center body shot is the next best option. Such a shot, he admits, even with a 30-caliber rifle, may not put the felon down, often requiring a second shot.

Randy Fritz saw his RSG-12 as the obvious solution to the problem, and in 1990, he put together a custom-built 12-gauge bolt-action rifle that featured a specially rifled barrel for handling shotgun slugs. This initial prototype was built around an existing commercially produced bolt-action 12-gauge shotgun. The idea then was taken to the McMillan Machine Co. in Phoenix, Arizona, where Rock McMillan looked it over and admitted he was impressed. In fact, he was so impressed that he personally designed a special action for the Tar-Hunt that was heavier and stronger than the one Fritz used in his model.

McMillan built this new prototype receiver to which Randy Fritz fitted a custom rifled barrel. The barreled action assembly then was snugly mounted in a stock that had been made, then modified by McMillan Fiberglass Stocks, another Phoenix outfit. The hybrid was put through some demanding tests and minor

changes resulted. The addition of a scope seemed logical. Then, with a little buffing here and bit of polish there, the prototype was ready to be revealed to the public.

Our Jack Lewis first saw the gun at the 1991 Shooting, Hunting & Outdoor Trade show held in Dallas, Texas. For want of a better name, Randy Fritz had named his brainchild the Rifled Slug Gun-12; less officially, it was to be marketed as the RSG-12.

"I was impressed with what I saw," Lewis recalls. "Other gun writers were swarming around the booth and we all wanted to take it out to a Dallas range and try it out immediately."

That didn't happen. Fritz needed the gun in the booth for display; a number of law enforcement agencies were expressing interest. As a result of comments made during the show, the gunsmith also wanted to make some minor changes in the design.

Eventually, several of the completed guns were sent around the nation to firearms writers who wanted to wring them out. The one aimed at the law enforcement trade had been designated as the RSG-12 Sniper and that was the one in which we were interested.

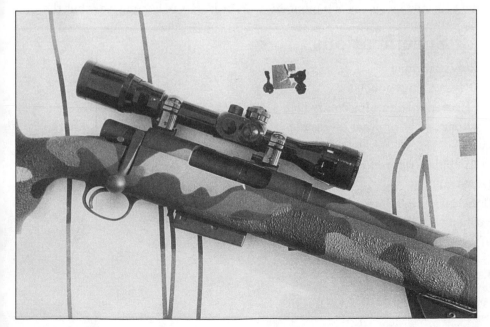

Randy Fritz furnished this Shepherd scope for testing of his 12-gauge rifle. It was an excellent choice. The action for the gun was created by McMillan Machine Co., with an eye to smoothness and strength.

Tests have been conducted by law enforcement agencies under all sorts of conditions, including the darkness of night. Equipped with the proper accessories, the RSG-12 can be as effective as in full sunlight.

The actions built by Rock McMillan's outfit each featured a bolt with two heavy-duty locking lugs that bore some resemblence to those of the Remington Model 788 rifle. Result of the care Rock McMillan had shown was, we found, a smooth-operating action.

The gun had a positive safety mounted on the right side and it was drilled and tapped for mounting a scope. A two-round detachable box magazine was included with the rifle, although Fritz said plans were in the mill to produce a magazine that probably would hold a greater number of rounds. That seemed to be what the law enforcement community wanted. This Sniper model for SWAT use also featured a heavy barrel. The barrel measured 21.5 inches and the gun's overall length was 41.5 inches. Without scope or our Harris Engineering bipod, it weighed 12 pounds.

"With that amount of weight, if one were going to hump it around the tulles for any length of time, it could get to be heavy. A box or two of slugs added to the equipment would make the load even heavier," Lewis felt, but he also realized that this was a special-purpose weapon that would be brought up to the site where it would be used, then operated from a well chosen position.

The custom barrel was built by E.R. Shaw Small Arms Manufacturing Co., of Bridgeville, Pennsylvania, and featured a right-hand twist of one turn in 36 inches. In his own tests, Fritz said, minute of angle groups had been fired consistently at 100 yards with the Shaw-made barrel. He also had taken recoil into consideration and a combo muzzle brake/flash suppressor had been provided by means of a number

of holes bored through the barrel near the gun's muzzle. This, incidentally, would be an optional feature.

Fritz also had arranged for Robar Companies, Inc., also of Phoenix, to provide what they called their SWAT Urban Warfare camouflage pattern on the stock. This was an effective mixture of black and gray.

Gary Paul Johnson, a former co-worker with Jack Lewis, told him that he had taken the opportunity to discuss with Fritz the tactical employment of the RGS-12 Sniper version.

"Being an advocate of gas guns, I asked him why he hadn't simply installed a rifled barrel on a semi-automatic shotgun," Johnson recounts. Fritz pointed out that this might be good enough for close-in shots, but such a gun would not produce pin-point accuracy out to 100 yards. His reasoning was that the

Specifications

Name:	Rifled Slug Gun-12 (Sniper).
Caliber:	12-gauge, 2-3/4-inch slugs or sabots.
Operation:	Bolt-action repeater, with two-lug rotary bolt.
Weight:	12 pounds, without scope or other accessories.
Length:	41.5 inches.
Barrel:	21.5 inches, 1:36-inch, right-hand twist.
Magazine:	Two-shot; removable.
Stock:	McMillan Fiberglass M85 Sniper model; Pachmayr Decelerator rubber butt pad.
Sights:	None. Furnished with Weaver-type rail mounted on receiver.
Other Features:	Positive safety; single-stage; adjustable trigger; matte black finish.
Maker:	No longer in production. Tar-Hunt Custom Rifles R.R. 3, Box 572 Bloomsburg, PA 17815.

The RSG-12, a rifle that fires a 12-gauge slug, is a formidable weapon in the hands of an expert marksman. Tests have shown that a trained shot can take out a dead bolt lock at 200 yards with this law enforcement instrument.

barrel of a semi-auto shotgun is not tightly mated to the receiver and the necessary play would make precision accuracy impossible."

Randy Fritz favored the Shepherd telescopic sight and the Harris bipod and shipped these items with test guns sent out to gun scribes for their evaluations. The scope mounted on the RSG Sniper we fired had a simple and quick zeroing system. The reticle also is marked with hold-over gradations for shots you might have to take beyond 100 yards. We found that this particular scope worked well with the rest of the rig, helping to put slugs where we wanted them.

Randy Fritz had told us earlier that the RSG-12 would work well with virtually any brand of 2-3/4-inch 12-gauge slug, but he had found the BRI sabot round to offer outstanding accuracy at 100 yards and even out to 200. Even better, he felt, were the Lightfield Hybred Sabot Slugs which are manufactured in Hungary and now are imported by the Lightfield Corp. of Freehold, New Jersey.

The Lightfield slug weighs 1.25 ounces and is designed to expand upon contact with the target. We tried some of these and soon found that they probably were more accurate than some of us who fired them. The top rifle shooters on our test team managed minute-of-angle shots at 125 yards without difficulty. Since the slug will drop a little over four inches at

that particular range, it is necessary to make some scope adjustments in order to get on target.

These slugs come packed five to a box and we only had 30 rounds with which to play, so some of our shooting was done with Federal 12-gauge saboted ammo, which has a muzzle velocity of 1500 feet per second. These sabots grouped at 1.5 to two inches for three rounds. In most cases, at least two of the rounds were touching. With a shotgun, even though it has become a rifle, this sort of accuracy at 125 yards seemed unusual to us, but Randy Fritz told us of a law enforcement seminar conducted at the Los Angeles Police Department range in the mid-1990s. He took one of his guns to the shoot and gave all sorts of representatives a chance to shoot it at a 50-yard target.

"There were a lot of people there who were not into serious shooting," Fritz said. "They amazed themselves when they sat down at the bench, sighted in with the scope and squeezed off three rounds. This included female Coast Guard personnel, some police administrative types and a number of gun writers. As I recall now, everyone who shot was able to build a three-round pattern in which all of the holes were touching. Frankly, it was a lot better than I expected and it brought the RSG-12 to the attention of a lot of agencies."

Fritz has had shooters who could have used his weapon to knock the

dead bolt out of a heavy door at 200 yards, but the point has been made that the average rifle shot by a SWAT sniper usually is no more than 30 yards. In discussing this with Gary Paul Johnson, he observed that "over the past 15 years, the longest reported shot by a New York City SWAT sniper was 41 yards."

That brings us back to the center body shot for which the duty sniper may have to settle when he is unable get a killing shot to the head. A 12-gauge slug traveling at the advertised 1500 feet per second is going to spread a lot more shock trauma in the upper body than would a 30-caliber rifle bullet.

We did not have the opportunity to test any of the slugs against angled glass such as that used in auto windshields, nor did we have the chance to knock a dead bolt out of a door at 200 yards, but there was no doubt that the gun did have advantages that a service-issued 30-caliber rifle would not.

In spite of all the interest in the RSG-12, Randy Fritz has retired it from the sales wars. When Jack Lewis talked to him several months ago, Fritz stated that from a public relations viewpoint, the gun had been a total success and all of the SWAT teams who tried it across the country were urging the police brass to buy one for their units.

The problem was the bean-counters. His gun would have to sell

for a price in the neighborhood of $1,600 and no matter how badly the SWAT troopers wanted the gun, the answer that usually came down was: "But you can buy a Mossberg Model 625 for a fifth of that cost!" The fiscal gurus appear not to be interested in long-range accuracy for a sabot!

"The Federal Bureau of Investigation was interested in the gun," Fritz told Lewis. "They borrowed one and put it through all sorts of paces. Upon returning it to Fritz, the FBI contact told him that the gun was considered too high priced even for them."

The unnamed FBI agent also stated, according to Fritz, that if a

Viewed in its entirety, the RSG-12 appears to be an interesting and efficient piece of law enforcement gear. However, the price structure worked against its success.

situation should occur in which they needed to use the RSG-12 for a mission no other firearm could handle, the gun then would become a shoo-in for acceptance. Sometime later, there was such an incident, and the FBI called for the gun. Fritz shipped it out by priority air express. By the time the RSG-12 arrived, however, the felon had released his hostage and surrendered. The gun was shipped back to Fritz without the bore being dirtied.

The only RSG that actually has been purchased by a law enforcement agency went to one in Dade County, Florida. The sale apparently was funded by money seized in drug raids and allotted to improving the department's armament.

"And so far as I have heard, they never have had an opportunity to use the gun in a real-life situation," Fritz reports.

When your authors wanted to borrow one of the 12-gauge sniper models with the idea of collecting additional information for this chapter, Randy Fritz said that he no longer planned to make the gun and didn't want to answer a lot of mail about it.

This is a classic case of an excellent law enforcement weapon that might possibly save lives being sacrificed on the altar of finance. •

CHAPTER 9-C

THE MYSTERIOUS SM-9

An Obscure Little Gun With Shady Roots.

THERE IS ALWAYS something intriguing about the loner who comes out of nowhere and goes into action. That has been the theme of countless novels and movies such as Zane Grey's "Riders of the Purple Sage."

Equally intriguing to many of us is to learn of a firearm that also seems to have come out of nowhere. That is the situation with a submachine gun known as the SM-9—or the SM-90. Guns of the same general design have appeared primarily in several Latin America countries under other designations.

The gun first appeared in early 1977 and was offered for sale by a company based in Guatemala. At that time, the designers of the gun were alleged to be two individuals then known in firearms design circles, Kenneth Dunn and Vito Cellini.

According to Tom Nelson, author of *Submachine Guns of the World*, when the little subgun was designed, the prototype was produced from stainless steel. However, further investigations

have shown that the guns later offered for sale were produced from standard ordnance steels.

The little subgun might best be qualified as a full-auto pistol, except that it measures 12 inches in overall length and has a forward hand grip as well as a pistol grip. The barrel is ported near the muzzle to allow escape of gases and cut down on recoil and muzzle torque. With a sound suppressor of the seller's choice, overall length became 22 inches. In 1978, a Brazilian arms manufacturer introduced what was called the Alpha GP-1 submachine gun. Both it and the SM-9 are designed to carry a spare loaded magazine in the front hand grip. This grip can be rotated so it extends either horizontally or vertically from the gun.

Although there is no concrete evidence regarding the gun's country of origin, the Guatemalan marketers claimed that the little shooter surpassed all other mini-subguns in manufacturing costs.

Further claims were made regarding the SM-9's simplicity, reliability and lack of weight.

The simplicity claim is reflected in the fact that the little gun reportedly has fewer than 25 parts. The Guatemalans' claim was that the gun used only 40 percent of the parts necessary to make other modern submachine guns functional, yet suffered no loss of standard subgun features. The claim that costs of production were greatly reduced was of interest, but if any actual manufacturing costs ever were listed, they have been lost in the two decades since introduction.

Of particular interest to students of firearms is the fact that the SM-9 was designed in such manner that at least 10 of the 25 parts serve two functions. For example, the barrel also serves as a guide for the gun's slide and a stop for the sear. The barrel nut serves as a stop for the main sear and as a retainer for the index button governing the positioning of the front hand grip.

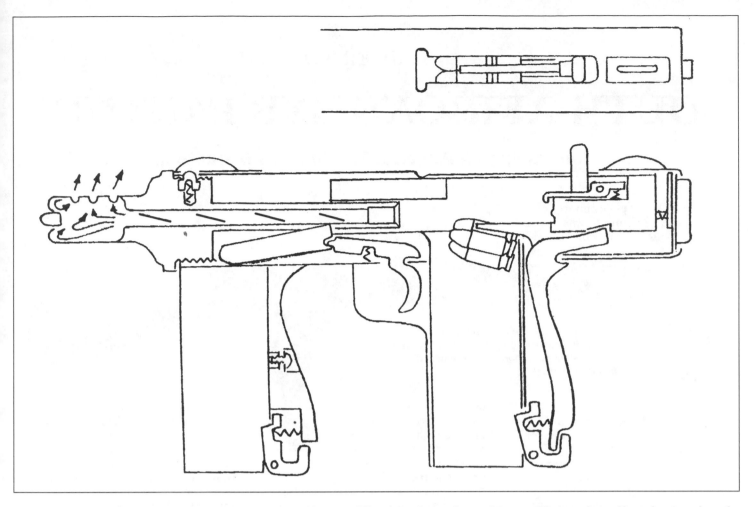

This designer's drawing of the Dunn-Cellini SM-9 submachine gun differs from those of some later modified versions. Above is a top view of the rear section of the gun.

In addition to simply ejecting the spent cartridge case, the ejector also aids in guiding the slide and the cartridges. The gun's slide handle becomes a heavy-duty extractor when a misfire takes place due to faulty ammo. The slide handle also becomes a wide-view rear sight, if needed, while the trigger doubles in locating the sear both laterally and lengthwise.

The main hand grip also carries the magazine catch, the hand grip safety and the feedway ramp. The hand grip safety becomes a secondary sear, if the main sear malfunctions. It also is a magazine lock for full-auto firing. Even the sling cap has an important additional duty. It is used to retain the main slide spring assembly and ejector.

The gun's magazine catch limits the hand grip's safety stroke and houses a spring that is common to both. Finally, the front magazine catch also can be used as a spare for the main hand grip.

A positive safety is installed in the rear hand grip and renders the gun safe the instant the hand grip is released. We find it a bit difficult to believe, but one of the early selling points was the claim that this subgun would function, firing in the full-auto mode, without the trigger, the sear, the front hand grip and the bolt handle. Inspection of exploded drawings leave much doubt regarding this particular capability.

The Dunn-Cellini design—if they truly were the designers—boasted several features that allegedly were patented in Latin American countries. Among these was the push-button indexing of the front hand grip that allowed it to be positioned at different angles. Of particular interest to us is the fact that both the trigger and the safety were held in place without any type of pins. The extractor, which also is the bolt operating handle, is held in place without pins.

Another feature is called "instinctive fire control" and allows automatic switching between the safe mode, semi-automatic fire and full-auto. The gun also included what the Guatemalan sales force of the Seventies called a V-block, which was designed to feed the 9mm cartridge into the chamber.

After its debut in 1978, the gun underwent a number of design changes by various would-be makers, but over the 20-plus years that have passed since its introduction, the SM-9 appears to have disappeared from the manufacturing scene. The few known guns in the United States seem to be in the hands of collectors. •

Specifications

Name:	SM-9 (or SM-90).
Type:	Submachine gun.
Caliber:	9mm Parabellum.
Operation:	Blowback, firing from open bolt; selective fire.
Cyclic Rate:	750 rounds per minute.
Weight:	3.7 pounds unloaded.
Length:	12 inches; with sound suppressor, 22 inches.
Barrel:	5.7 inches.
Magazine:	33 rounds stamped, welded sheet metal box.
Maker:	Undetermined.

SOUTH AFRICA'S BXP PANTHER

Politics Plays A Powerful Part In Arms Marketing.

DUE TO ITS policy on racism, South Africa, as a nation, was not on speaking terms with much of the rest of the world in the 1970s and early '80s. The resultant punishment was to cut off the African nation from a vast majority of imports; this was particularly true of arms and munitions. Even the professional hunters who organized and led hunting safaris were in a dire state when it came to equipping themselves, their staffs and their clients.

The embargo cut deep and affected blacks as well as whites, history now shows. For example, one U.S. company had established a school that was

With the folding stock extended, the South African BXP measures only 23.9 inches. However, with this sound suppressor attached, it is considerably longer.

The gun's ejection port is rather large, but when the bolt is closed, the port is covered, keeping out dirt and dust. The sights are simple and effective.

exclusively aimed at educating the children of black employees. When the embargo went into full effect, the company was unable to conduct business in South Africa and closed down its operations there. The school was closed and stood empty and the black employees were out of work. There were numerous repetitions of this situation.

The result was that the South Africans were forced to get into the business of firearms manufacturing. A government-owned firm called Armscor was organized originally for the purpose of designing and building arms for the beleaguered nation's army. A small arms factory, Lyttelton Engineering Works in Pretoria, began producing the Armscor-developed armament.

In the beginning, there was a great deal of secrecy about the guns being developed by Armscor. Ultimately, however, a 9mm submachine gun designated as the BXP was unveiled and issued to the South African Defense Force. Then, in 1983, the then governing powers announced that they planned on selling arms and electronics products developed by Armscor on the international market.

The subgun probably is best described as a conventional blowback, selective-fire weapon that has been built primarily from stainless steel stampings, steel tubing and precision castings. Introduced in the early 1980s, it chambers the 9x19mm Parabellum cartridge. The original guns had a cyclic rate of fire of 1000 to 1200 rounds per minute. At the time of that introduction, it was acknowledged by military experts as being "a simple but effective" weapon. An exterior view shows great similarities to the U.S.-developed Ingram subguns. The stock folds beneath the gun, resulting in a balance factor that allows it to be fired with one hand as a pistol.

The bolt of the BXP is a telescoping type designed to envelope the rear end of the 8.2-inch barrel. This approach allows overall length to be short; the gun measures only 15.2 inches with the stock folded and 23.9 inches with the stock extended. This design also is an aid to keeping the gun's center of gravity over the pistol grip, with the added design advantage of reducing oscillations normally caused by the bolt's rapid movement during full-auto fire. Thought also has been given to the matter of cleanliness, and when the bolt is in its forward position, all of the apertures are closed, avoiding the possibility of dust or dirt getting into the receiver.

The cocking handle—actually a square knob—is on top of the receiver where it is easily accessible in the manner of the Thompson submachine gun and several other models. In spite of the handle's positioning, it does not interfere with the sights. The rear sight is best described as a

combination, since it incorporates both an aperture and a notch. Working with the gun on the range, we found that the aperture is meant for firing at 100 yards or so, while the notch is meant for 200-yard fire—an unlikely situation with a subgun! Both front and rear sights are protected by heavy-duty wings.

Located on both sides of the receiver behind the trigger guard is the ambidextrous change lever/safety switch. When the catch is in the horizontal position—marked by a green dot—the gun is in its safe mode; the trigger, sear and bolt all are locked. The bolt is locked whether in the forward position or to the rear when the gun is cocked!

When the gunner moves the catch to the red dot, the submachine gun can be fired either single shot or on full-automatic.

Requirement for single shot, actually semi-automatic, is to pull the trigger and release it. For full-auto, the shooter pulls past the one-round pull, feeling heavier pressure on the trigger. Continuing the pull and holding the trigger back will result in full-auto fire.

Of particular interest, we found, was that the designers have incorporated an extra sear notch on the bolt. The purpose of this is to prevent accidental discharge should the weapon be dropped on the butt, the shooter's hand slip during cocking, or in the event that a weak cartridge is fired and plugs the barrel.

The barrel carries six grooves with a right-hand turn. The barrel nut is threaded externally for installation of a barrel protector/compensator unit or a sound suppressor, which can be used in firing either standard or subsonic 9mm ammo.

The gun Jack Lewis fired at Knight's Armament in Vero Beach, Florida, was equipped with a Knight-made suppressor which was almost as long as the gun itself when its stock is folded. The combination was effective, though, for the only real sound seemed to be the rapid

The barrel retaining nut is threaded to accept a sound suppressor or a flash hider. When the stock is folded the buttpad serves as a forward hand grip.

Specifications

Name:	South African BXP (also marketed as the Panther).
Type:	Submachine gun.
Caliber:	9x19mm Parabellum.
Operation:	Selective-fire; blowback system.
Cyclic Rate:	Original version, 1000 to 1200 rounds per minute; later version, 750 to 800 rounds per minute.
Weight:	5.5 pounds.
Length:	15.2 inches (stock folded); 23.9 inches (stock extended).
Barrel:	8.2 inches; six grooves, right-hand twist.
Magazines:	22- or 32-round; detachable box.
Stock:	Folding.
Maker:	Armscor Private Bag X337 Pretoria Republic of South Africa 0001.

The South African firm of Armscor designed the gun for use by the nation's Defense Force. It is made primarily of stainless steel stampings and precision castings.

slamming of the bolt in its back and forth travel.

This particular BXP, which is part of Reed Knight's museum collection, is in excellent condition. Knight credits the condition to a teflon-like coating that creates a rust-resistant finish, also serving as a permanent dry-film lubricant for the weapon.

The folding shoulder stock is of a type incorporated on several other maker's subguns, but that does nothing to degrade its effectiveness. When the stock is not used, it folds neatly under the receiver, and the buttplate can be used as a hand grip in firing from the hip. The unit also serves to deflect heat away from the shooter's hand.

Armscor furnished 22- and 32-round magazines with the gun, either one fitting snugly into the well in the extended pistol grip.

As mentioned, the original guns were scaled for fire 1000 to 1200

rounds per minute, but when Armscor brought the gun to the U.S. in the mid-1980s, the rate of fire had been reduced to 750 to 800 round per minute. Muzzle velocity was approximately 1200 feet per second. At that time, the importer tried to sell the gun to U.S. military and law enforcement agencies as the Panther model, but the change of name did little to change the national feelings regarding apartheid; sales in this country did not thrive and importation soon was dropped. A plus, perhaps, was that someone had decided the 1000 per minute-plus cyclic rate of fire was too high for effective shooting.

From our view, the BXP is a nice little gun that would serve well in any number of roles. Its compactness definitely is in its favor, but there are many other subguns that can do the same jobs. •

The BXP trigger guard is large, giving easy access to the trigger. The safety control is directly behind the trigger.

SACO'S MODEL 683 SUBMACHINE GUN

Once Again, Political Factors Play Havoc With Arms Production.

Although made primarily of steel tubing, castings, heavy-duty synthetics and screw-machine parts are incorporated in the gun's design.

IF WE READ recent history or perhaps bother to check out the Congressional inquires and investigations of the 1980s, it becomes reasonably obvious that our Counter Intelligence Agency, abetted by other governmental entities, was furnishing weapons to rebel groups in several countries. This was done reportedly in the spirit of democracy and a will to see these nations enter the political sphere of the Western world.

While many of these weapons were U.S. military surplus, there were those who felt we needed "special weapons" for dissident groups; guns that could be mass produced cheaply and air dropped to these outfits, just as we did with the various anti-Nazi underground units during World War II.

Up in the pristine state of Maine is an organization known as Saco Defense Systems. This firm has been a supplier of U.S. military arms to our own services and to various friendly countries for decades. The company's most spectacular product has been the Mark 19 40mm machine gun, which is discussed at length elsewhere in this volume. While the M-60 7.62mm machine gun was being phased out of our armed services in favor of the FN-produced M240, Saco made a good thing out of updating the earlier design to the M-60E for supply largely to friendly nations approved by our State Department and the Department of Defense. For these same customers, Saco resurrected the Browning 50-caliber air-cooled machine gun. In more recent annums, however, this gun, now designated as the E2, has become a favorite of ground troops for long range sniping. It reportedly saw useful service during Desert Storm, taking out Iraqi vehicles and the supply compounds of Saddam's Republican Guards.

At the time this nation allegedly was juggling petro dollars and arms in the Middle East to finance guerrilla troops in Latin America, the decision at Saco Defense Industries was to

Specifications

Name:	Saco Model 683.
Type:	Submachine gun.
Caliber:	9mm Parabellum.
Operation:	Blowback; selective fire.
Cyclic Rate:	650 rounds per minute.
Weight:	7.3 pounds (empty).
Length:	20.6 inches (stock folded); 27.5 inches (stock extended).
Barrel:	8 inches.
Magazine:	25 and 32 rounds.
Maker:	Defense Systems Division Maremont Corporation 291 North Street Saco, Maine 04072.

Co-author Jack Lewis checks out the tube sight on one of the two existing prototypes of the Saco Model 683 submachine gun. The gun was designed to be built at little expense, yet Lewis found it well made and easy to handle.

With the tubular stock extended, the gun measures a fraction over 20 inches. It would handle the maker's 25- or 32-round magazines. The latter is in place in this prototype now owned by Reed Knight, Jr.

The magazine well also functions as a forward grip, if desired. The tube sight carries no optics, only a set of crosshairs.

prototype the Model 683 in 9mm Parabellum and see what happened.

The Model 683 prototypes—only two are known to have been produced—was a conventional blowback design. The majority of the parts were of stamped steel, although inspection shows that castings, plastic mouldings and screw-machine parts also were included in the construction. The buttstock was a novel tubular telescoping design that since has been copied by other arms makers. In the Saco design, the tube slides over the receiver when the stock is in the retracted mode.

Perhaps the most unusual feature of the little gun is the combining of a tubular sight and the carrying handle. If that sounds complicated, it is not. The tube is mounted over the receiver and contains no optics. Instead, simple crosshairs are installed in the forward end of the unsealed tube. Apparently, the marketing theory was this sight would work well for those not familiar with more sophisticated sighting arrangements.

At the time the Model 683 was listed in the authoritative British-published Jane's directory of the world's military arms industries, it was stated that the gun was in production. That, however, appears to have been a matter of overly positive thinking on the part of the Saco marketing department. It was during this period that an aircraft loaded with weapons was downed in Latin America.

One of the individuals aboard admitted he was a mercenary paid to make the delivery. That opened a can of worms that turned out to be the Iran-Contra investigation by Congress.

From all of the available evidence, it appears that the simplistic Saco Model 683 was designed to be a submachine gun that could be

For those who think the Model 683 was poorly constructed, this view shows that parts were made and machining done with care. The materials, however, tended to hold down the final price of the gun.

The selective-fire Model 683 carries the firing selector on the right side above the trigger guard. The guard is large enough to accept gloved hands.

manufactured in Third World countries, which are typically without sophisticated manufacturing or metal working facilities.

Whatever the reasons, Reed Knight, Jr., who now is in possession of the two prototype guns, insists these are the only two ever produced. Jack Lewis has worked with both of the prototypes and has come to feel that this was an excellent, low-cost subgun that was built to meet a specific need. The problem for the manufacturer was the fact that suddenly the need no longer existed.

"The balance of the little gun is excellent," Lewis reports, "and the short length makes it ideal for close combat situations. The unusual sighting tube gives one the picture needed to put rounds on a close target."

The fact that the need for such a gun vanished does not take away from the gun's usefulness, and it's a pity the gun was never made in larger quantities.

Section II
The Rifles

THREE DECADES OF THE 5.56

The Caliber Remains The Same; All Else Seems To Have Changed!

HISTORIANS AGREE THAT the assault rifle was invented by the Germans. The Sturmgewehr (StG) 43/44 used the 7.92mm Kurz cartridge, intermediate in power between the 9mm Parabellum pistol round meant then for the MP 38/40 submachine gun, and the full-size 7.92mm rifle round used in the Mauser K-98k carbine. The Kurz round gave greater range and penetration than the 9mm and more controllability in full-auto fire than the 7.92 rifle cartridge.

In 1945, after sweeping over great portions of the former Third Reich, the victorious Soviet Army took the German assault rifle plans back to Mother Russia—along with every other piece of Teutonic technology not too big to move. However, it was up to a tank sergeant named Mikhail Kalashnikov and a crew of "people's designers" to simplify and modernize the assault rifle concept that became the Avtomat Kalashnikova (AK) 47 in 7.62x39mm. While not in common use until the early 1950s, it became the communist tool of oppression in their own countries, and of revolution in other countries until recent days.

Probably learning from the American experience in the Vietnam War, the Soviets eventually converted to a smaller caliber. While one of our authors, David Steele, was working in Washington, D.C., in 1970, one Army researcher showed him what he called a ".221 Russian" round. However, to the best of our knowledge, the North Vietnamese—as proxies of the USSR—never used anything but 7.62x39mm AKs. Some ancient French arms were found among the Viet Cong, undoubtedly taken from the Foreign Legion before they left the country in the Fifties. The AK47s may have been an advantage in Southeast Asian terrain, since 30-caliber barrels are less likely to experience "capillary action" problems when dunked in water than do 22-caliber barrels.

Eventually, though, the Soviets issued the AKS-74 in 5.45mm to elite units, and it was widely employed in Afghanistan during the communist nation's ill-fated efforts there. A carbine model, called the AKSU-74, now is used by bodyguards in the former Eastern bloc, in addition to army and police units.

As the number one partner and supplier in NATO, the United States military apparently felt it could dictate calibers. In the late 1950s, when America went from the 30-06 rifle round to the 308 (later called 7.62x51mm NATO), Europe did likewise, but not with a great deal of enthusiasm. So, when the U.S. Army went to the M-14 rifle, Britain and other Commonwealth countries adopted the FN Self-Loading Rifle (SLR). West Germany, likewise, picked the FN, then replaced it with their own G3, also chambered for the 7.62x51mm NATO cartridge.

Meanwhile, events were under way that were to change the direction of caliber development. In 1958, the Army tested the 5.56mm AR-15 rifle created by the late Gene Stoner and marketed first by Armalite, then by Colt, which

Members of Special Forces Team A-334 carried the M-16A1 rifle in Long Le Chon, Vietnam in 1969. The team leader, second from left, was Robert K. Brown, now editor/publisher of *Soldier of Fortune* magazine.

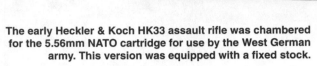

The early Heckler & Koch HK33 assault rifle was chambered for the 5.56mm NATO cartridge for use by the West German army. This version was equipped with a fixed stock.

had purchased manufacturing rights. This was going on during development of the SPIW (Special Purpose Individual Weapon), which was anticipated for 1965. Meanwhile, the U.S. Air Force tested the AR-15 and, on May 22, 1961, ordered quantities to replace M1/M2 Carbines for use by air crews and security police. In January, 1962, the AR-15 was classified as the USAF "standard" M-16, and a contract was let

handling surplus U.S. M-1 Garands and Browning automatic rifles. In-country testing, including limited combat operations, showed the AR-15 was easier for the South Vietnamese soldiers to use than the 30-06 weapons. The testing also showed that the AR-15 provided more range and power than either the M1 Carbine or

result, the Stoner-designed rifle was redesignated as the M-16 and was adopted as Army "limited standard" for Vietnam issue. However, the army insisted on five product improvements, which quickly changed the model designation to the M-16A1.

The first and certainly the most expensive change was the addition of a manual-assist bolt closure device. Although most soldiers who used the

The Armalite AR-10, ancestor of today's M-16 series, is at top. It is chambered for the 7.62x51mm cartridge. The other rifle is the German 7.92 Stg44 assault rifle issued late in World War II. Both now are a part of the BATF reference collection in Washington, D.C.

to Colt. General Curtis LeMay, at that time Chief of Staff of the U.S. Air Force, was a believer in this smallbore weapon.

As early as 1961, U.S. Army Special Forces were operating in South Vietnam as advisors to the Republic of Vietnam Armed Forces (RVNAF). The typical ARVN soldier stood only five feet tall and weighed about 90 pounds. Thus, it is no small wonder that these diminutive soldiers had difficulty in

Thompson submachine gun.

The AR-15 was recommended for Army use in August, 1962, by favorable report from a Department of Defense task force holding forth in Vietnam. In October, 1962, the Secretary of the Army directed a test, which was held through December, 1962, and into January, 1963. As a

rifle in Vietnam came to believe this was to "jam home a faulty round into a dirty chamber," to the best of our knowledge, the bolt assist was added simply because a high ranking U.S. Army officer insisted on it. He never had known of an Army rifle in history which did not have some type of bolt closure system.

This version of the Heckler & Koch-made HK33 assault rifle featured a telescoping metal stock. It also was chambered for the 5.56mm round.

These Chinese mercenaries of Recon Team Mississippi had just returned from a mission against the North Vietnamese Army and Pathet Lao forces when this photo was taken. Note the M-16 and Colt Commando assault rifle with which they are armed.

The Air Force and Marine Corps both objected to the device as unnecessary, since the design of the weapon had eliminated all of the mechanical linkage that could be subject to binding during adverse operating conditions.

The second modification was the lightening of the firing pin to prevent premature firing should the rifle be dropped. Then there was the widening of the charging handle to permit operation with mittens in cold weather. Oddly, this feature became useful during winter operations in the Vietnamese highlands. The fourth change was a revision in the rifling twist from 1:14 inches to 1:12 inches for better bullet stability. The fifth was a change in stock color from olive drab to black. It was this M-16A1 "black rifle" which soldiered on through escalation of the Vietnam War. It was the M-16A1, with the above listed improvements, which was approved officially by the Army. This, incidentally, is contrary to the popular notion that the bolt assist was added after the Army adopted the M-16.

When regular U.S. Army troops were sent to Vietnam in 1965, they were issued the M-16A1, although the Marines continued to lug around the M-14 in early operations. GIs newly equipped with the M-16A1 were expected to carry over their M-14 maintenance procedures from basic training without formal retraining. Also, Armalite had advertised its

David Steele fires the MAR, the recent mini-version of the Galil assault rifle. It also is chambered for the 5.56mm military cartridge.

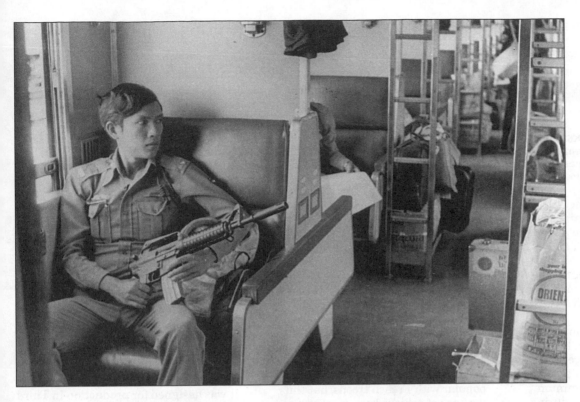

This Thai police officer is armed with a Colt Commando, while protecting a train from communist guerrilla forces along the Malay border. Photo was taken in 1975.

original 7.62mm AR-10 as able to "operate dry," something that certainly did not apply to the M-16A1.

Manuals and cleaning equipment both were in short supply in Vietnam, so it should be no surprise that many weapons soon were discovered to be in bad condition, fouled by rust, dirt and carbon deposits. The most common malfunction was the failure to extract, which, of course, prevented the gun from firing another round and turned the gun into a lightweight club.

Allegations of the M-16A1's failing in combat were investigated in 1967 by a Special Committee of the U.S. Congress headed by Congressman Ichord. The Ichord Committee report was published

in July, 1967. This report was critical of the U.S. Army for not making certain product improvements to the M-16A1 prior to its combat use in Vietnam. However, as of 1966, the Project Manager, Rifles, of the U.S. Army Materiel Command, had added two product improvements: First, he had called for redesign of the buffer to reduce the rate of fire from about 850 to 650 rounds per minute. This was done to strengthen the buffer, as well as to counteract the problem created by ball powder residue build-up in the gas chamber, affecting the rate of fire. The second improvement was chroming of the chamber to facilitate the extraction

of stuck rounds.

The 55-grain M193 bullet used in the M-16A1 traveled at 1005 meters per second. That round and the M196 tracer certainly were effective at Vietnam distances mostly under 50 meters. However, snipers continued to pursue their missions with the 7.62x51mm in the M21 and the Remington-made Model 700 bolt-action rifles.

Wound stories about M193 performance ran the gamut from "just punches neat holes" to "rips huge cavities" to "kills instantly," depending on a variety of factors, like range, yaw, bone strikes or hits in the extremities.

After the Vietnam War, NATO forces went to the 5.56x45mm, but

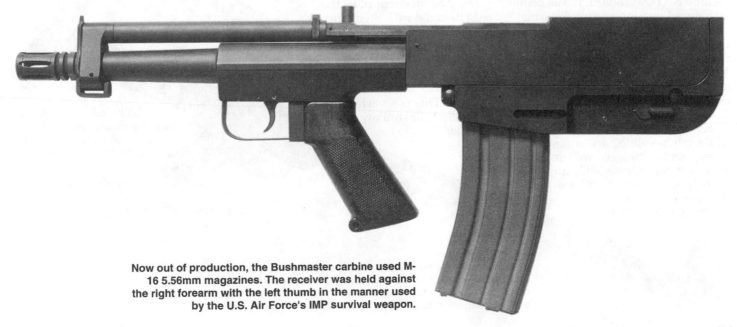

Now out of production, the Bushmaster carbine used M-16 5.56mm magazines. The receiver was held against the right forearm with the left thumb in the manner used by the U.S. Air Force's IMP survival weapon.

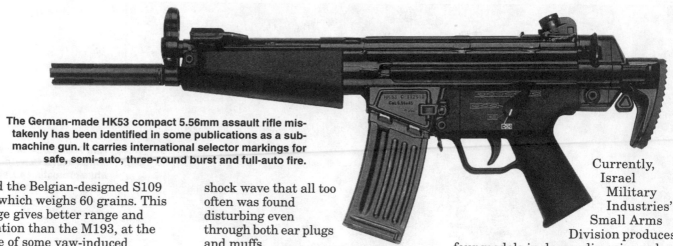

The German-made HK53 compact 5.56mm assault rifle mistakenly has been identified in some publications as a submachine gun. It carries international selector markings for safe, semi-auto, three-round burst and full-auto fire.

adopted the Belgian-designed S109 bullet, which weighs 60 grains. This cartridge gives better range and penetration than the M193, at the sacrifice of some yaw-induced wounding effect. The current issue M-16A2, which now has a 1:7-inch barrel twist, can fire the heavier NATO round without problem.

The M-16A2 also has an improved, impact-resistant handguard, buttstock and pistol grip. The more recent round, ribbed handguard is made of a polymer composite material with aluminum liner inserts to dissipate heat during prolonged firing sequences. One CIA agent, who ran a Special Operations team in Vietnam, insisted he once put so many magazines though an M-16A1, seeking to break contact from an enemy ambush, that he later found his fingers had printed into the melted handguard.

In Vietnam, a shortened M-16A1, officially called the XM177E1, but most often termed the Colt Commando, was issued to some elite units. A short barrel, long flash hider and a telescoping stock were its salient characteristics. Colt currently makes both the M720/M723 Carbine and M733/M735 Commando versions of the M-16A2 for military and police customers.

Even before the 5.56mm cartridge became NATO standard, it was being introduced into interesting firearms designs besides the AR-15/M16 series. In the 1970s, one American company put out the Bushmaster, a semi-auto "pistol" using M-16 magazines and ammo. It was based on the USAF/Colt IMP survival weapon, which used the 221 Fireball cartridge. The rotating receiver was held to the forearm by the off thumb, providing an "organic" stock. The IMP worked well enough, but never was adopted officially. The short Bushmaster worked, too, but the heavier 5.56mm cartridge produced a

shock wave that all too often was found disturbing even through both ear plugs and muffs.

Today, the 5.56mm Ruger Mini-14 is probably the most popular survivor of the "assault weapon" ban. It has been widely used in American law enforcement.

France adopted the FAMAS bullpup rifle in 5.56mm. Nicknamed "the bugle" for its unusual shape, it appears popular with French troops, but thus far has not achieved much sales success on the world arms market.

The German firm of Heckler & Koch has added 5.56mm versions of the G3, namely the HK33 and HK53. The HK33 is a bit overweight for the caliber, compared to the M-16A2, but the shorty HK53 has found some popularity among U.S. SWAT teams.

The U.S. government has sponsored or promoted various 5.56mm research projects. One of these was the Low Maintenance Rifle (LMR) manufactured at TRW Systems, which used the M7 bayonet, M-16A1 magazines, M-60 light machine gun trigger group and other overlapping technologies. Such a weapon could be used to arm indigenous forces, and could be air-dropped as the British did with Sten guns to the French Underground in World War II.

Among the real contenders in the 5.56mm market is the IMI Galil, designed by I. Galil. This is a variation on the Kalashnikov action.

Currently, Israel Military Industries' Small Arms Division produces four models in descending size order: ARM; AR; SAR; and the MAR. The shorty MAR would seem to have a future with SWAT and protective teams.

At Armalite, Eugene Stoner developed another rifle beside the AR-15, the AR-18. With conventional operation and sheet metal stampings, it was designed for production in Third World client states that might not have the sophisticated factories to produce the M-16. It had a solid stock which folded to the left. A short version with a 10.25-inch barrel, called the AR-18S, was developed for use by security troops and dog handlers. At this late date, there is no way of knowing how many of these were sold.

A semi-auto version, the AR-180, was introduced by Armalite on the civilian and police market. After a checkered history, including temporary production in Japan, the AR-18/AR-180 expired. Its most famous use appears to have been with the irregulars of the Irish Republican Army, who even

included "Armalite" in their freedom songs, along with words like "gelignite" and "Thompson gun."

Of course, this is in the Irish tradition, where "all their wars are merry, and their songs are sad." ●

In the early 1970s, TRW Systems produced this experimental Low Maintenance Rifle (LMR). Costs of manufacture were held down by utilization of the trigger group from the M-60 machine gun and the standard M-16 5.56mm magazine. It was fitted to take the issue M7 bayonet.

FROM BURP GUN TO ASSAULT RIFLE

It's Been A Century Of Progress!

IN 1896 MAUSER introduced its so-called Broomhandle pistol chambered for a 7.63mm (30-caliber) bottleneck cartridge. Winston Churchill carried one of these guns at the Battle of Omdurman in 1898; it was a worldwide commercial success, particularly in China.

The 7.63mm cartridge was not noted for its stopping power, compared to the 9mm Parabellum or the 45 ACP, but, with an 86-grain, metal-case bullet moving at 1420 feet per second, it had good accuracy and range, and penetration sufficient to pierce helmets and light body armor.

In 1930, the Soviets replaced their aging 1895 Nagant revolvers with a semi-auto pistol of simplified Colt/Browning design. Named for its inventor, Fedor V. Tokarev, it was known as the Tulas Tokarev—TT, the M1930 (early production), M1933 or TT33. Its 7.62mm Type P cartridge was almost identical with the 7.63mm Mauser and functionally interchangeable. This was to be the most powerful pistol cartridge ever developed by a Communist regime; the Czechs even loaded it up to 1600 fps for their CZ52 pistol. When Russia

decided on a submachine gun, the TT cartridge proved more than adequate.

For that buzz gun, their principal influence was the Finnish Suomi, designed by Aimo Johannes Lahti. The Suomi Model 1926 in 7.65mm Parabellum went through several modifications. Its more developed Model 1931 still had a "first generation" wood stock, but was more modern in construction. The banana-style magazine was dropped in favor of optional stick or drum magazines. This gun was a mainstay of Finns fighting Soviet conscripts in the nearly forgotten Winter War of 1939.

Designed by V.A. Degtyarov, but based partially on the Suomi and the Schmeisser MP2911, the Soviet PPD-

The original wood-stocked AK-47 (top) is compared to its simplified successor, the AKM, which boasted a folding metal stock.

1934/38 was introduced in 1934. Produced at the Sestrorjetsh and Tula Arsenals, this weapon remained in service until 1940. It had a full wood stock and a 71-round drum magazine based on that of the Suomi.

The PPD-1940 was a simplified PPD-1934/38, with, among other things, a short, detachable, wood forearm attached with a screw to the underside of the barrel jacket. This forearm was noticeably absent from its wartime replacement.

The Soviet PPSh-41, designed by George S. Shpagin, replaced the PPD series in World War II. Officially adopted in 1941, and put into large scale production in 1942, over 5,000,000 were produced in Soviet arsenals by the late 1940s, not including the copies produced in communist bloc countries.

The PPSh was more accurate than the PPD series, though it was simpler and had a higher cyclic rate. The entire receiver and barrel jacket assembly is made of heavy-gauge sheet metal stampings, typical of second generation subguns.

While crude in appearance when compared to the second generation German MP40, the PPSh-41 was respected, even admired, by Wehrmacht soldiers who were on the

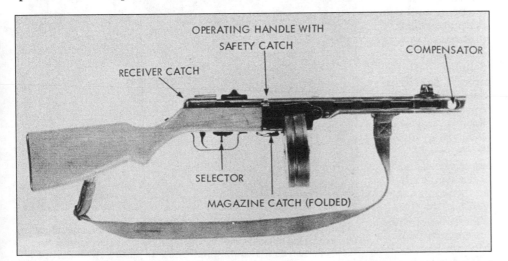

OPERATING HANDLE WITH
SAFETY CATCH
COMPENSATOR
RECEIVER CATCH
SELECTOR
MAGAZINE CATCH (FOLDED)

The Soviet PPSh4I subgun was used extensively in World War II. It was cheap and fast to manufacture and effective. The drum magazine holds 71 rounds of 7.62 pistol ammunition.

At top is the Hungarian AMD, that country's version of the Soviet AKM. It has the distinctive vertical foregrip. (Center) The Czech Vz58P has a folding stock, plus bayonet. It is chambered for the 7.62x39mm Soviet cartridge, the same as the AKM. The two guns have a limited parts/design overlap. (Bottom) The Soviet AK-47 is the gun that started the copycat program among the communist nations.

receiving end of a gun that fired faster (900 vs. 500 rpm) from a larger magazine (71 versus 32 rounds) than theirs. Some Waffen SS soldiers are said to have used captured Shpagins, just as some GIs in Vietnam used captured AK-47s, especially when the M-16A1 developed problems in the early days.

The PPSh-41 was 33.1 inches long with a 10.6-inch barrel and a loaded weight of 12 pounds. It fired 7.62mm Russian ammo at 1600 fps, with a cyclic rate of 900 rpm. It was open-bolt, blowback operated, with selective semi- or full-auto fire. The selector is in the trigger guard; push forward for full-auto, push to the rear for semi. This is in contrast to prettier guns like the German MP40 or the U.S. M-3A1, which fired full-auto only. The PPSh-41 could use 35-round box or 71-round drum magazines. Originally issued with a tangent rear sight, later models had a flip sight for 100 and 200 meters.

The PPSh-41 was rugged and reliable. It required little training, and its rate of fire gave confidence to green troops. As commonly issued as the Mosin-Nagant service rifle, it was particularly effective in house-to-house fighting, as in the battle of Stalingrad. Since it was cheap to

produce, and Stalin had no concern for casualties, the PPSh-41 was the perfect gun for issue to expendable shock troops and partisans. It is said to have been given to housewives to defend their particular doorsteps and hopefully slow up the Nazi advance in street fighting. Since atheistic, international socialism gives no protected status to women, this cynical use of female cannon fodder is not difficult to believe.

The PPSh-41 was produced as the Type 50 in Red China and the Type 49 in North Korea. The Korean version was made from 1950 to 1955, and was used against American and Allied troops throughout the 1950-1953 Korean War. The close-range, fire superiority tactics developed by the Soviets, North Korean and Red Chinese forces were later adapted to the Kalashnikov assault rifle and its ComBloc copies.

The assault rifle, like many other military innovations, including jet aircraft, the "Fritz"-style helmet and camouflage clothing, was a German invention. The Soviets experienced the first assault rifle, the Sturmgewehr (StG) 43/44, from the receiving end. This weapon and its 7.92mm Kurz cartridge was brought back to

Moscow for examination. However, the StG 43/44, as finely engineered as Teutonic craftsmanship could make it, did not serve as a direct model for the Soviet rifle.

The intermediate cartridge was designed to give greater power, range and penetration than the SMG/pistol cartridge, but greater burst fire controllability with lighter weight than the battle rifle cartridge. The Russians developed their own intermediate cartridge, the M43 7.62x39mm, first for the semi-automatic SKS carbine.

A senior tank corps sergeant named Mikhail Kalashnikov is given credit for development of the Soviet assault rifle. He received a cash award and title as a Hero of Socialist Labor. However, like other projects under Stalin, the full details and identities of members of the design team were kept secret. Credit for significant inventions depended as much on Communist political correctness as brilliance. Be that as it may, the Avtomat Kalishnikova was to become the most significant rifle of the late 20th century, in part because of its incredible production numbers, with close to 40,000,000 made.

Kalashnikov's model of 1947, the AK-47, came into service in 1951, supplanting the Simonov SKS

In this 1951 photo, Army Major General Floyd L. Parks displays two examples of the Soviet PPSh41 submachine gun, more commonly known as the "burp gun." One was picked up on Europe's Eastern front in 1945 during World War II. The other was captured from North Korean communist troops early in the Korean War.

Note the differences in the frame and forearm designs of the Romanian-built AKM (top) and the AK-47 produced in Bulgaria.

carbine. The AK-47 was 34.35 inches long, with a 16.34-inch barrel. It had a tangent sight graduated to 800 meters. It fired the M43 round at 2330 fps. When its distinctive, right-side selector lever—neither notably ergonomic nor quiet, but effective—was placed in the full-auto position, it could fire at a rate of 600 rounds per minute from 30-round, detachable magazines ("banana clips" in media parlance).

In 1959, Kalashnikov streamlined his design, simplifying manufacture, and gave it a straight-line stock for better full-auto controllability. The tangent sight was now graduated to 1000 meters, and weight was reduced slightly from 10.58 pounds to 10.24 pounds. This was the AKM, which remained standard in Soviet and client forces until introduction of the AKS-74 5.45mm in the mid-1970s.

The AKM is part of a small arms system that includes the RPK light machine gun, PK general purpose machine gun, PKS medium machine gun and the PKT tank machine gun. Such a successful small arms *system* has yet to be developed in the United States.

The standards by which the Soviet Army judged small arms were simplicity, ease of manufacture, reliability, wounding power and firepower. Weapons had to be simple because of the large number of illiterate and foreign (non-Russian) troops in the Soviet army, not to mention Third World revolutionaries equipped by Moscow.

Small arms must be easy to manufacture so that plants can be set up in rural areas or underdeveloped countries that do not have access to the highest technology. Making guns easy to produce also makes them cheaper and allows the government to make more of them. In any case, the high technology used in American and European assault rifles has not made them more effective than the AK, only more expensive.

Reliability is of great importance to all military weapons, particularly in the former Soviet Union where the climate is cold and harsh. Firepower was also important to Soviet army doctrine, starting in 1939 with spray fire from the submachine gun to achieve fire superiority. The Red Army also found that burst fire had a heartening effect on troops who were poorly trained in marksmanship, something their modern counterparts found useful in advising communist guerillas in Asia and Africa.

The AKM was the revolutionary weapon of the 1960s and '70s, used by everyone from the Viet Cong to the Palestine Liberation fighters. Its comparatively short length and light weight made war more available to Third World women and children, probably not an advance for civilization. Just as the machine gun changed the nature of conventional combat in World War I, the assault rifle, notably the AKM, changed the nature of conflict after World War II, giving serious firepower to every communist proxy army and terrorist cell.

Wounding power has become important, because post-World War II research shows that at 300 meters—the maximum effective range of assault rifles—60 percent of hits are in the extremities. This, combined with increasing use of body armor, means that a modern bullet must incapacitate with a hit to the arm or leg.

Small caliber weapons allow extremely high velocity, greater probability of bullet upset on impact, flatter trajectory, easier burst control, less felt recoil, faster training, and greater ammo capacity both in the gun and in carrying pouches. The cartridge adopted for the AKS-74 was 5.45x39mm.

The 5.45mm round used by Soviet elite troops in Afghanistan had a lacquered steel cartridge case, 22.3 grains of ball powder, and a 53.5-grain bullet. Muzzle velocity was 2956 feet per second with a muzzle energy of 1007 foot-pounds. The bullet has a mild steel core, with a lead filler and forward air space. The balance was toward the rear, which, along with the long, thin shape, gave

The East German MPiK (top) is compared to the Polish PMK. There are few differences in the designs that are visible to the eye.

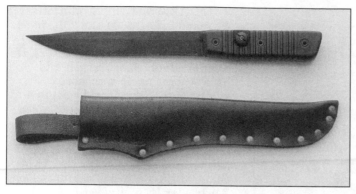

This *puuko*-style bayonet for the Finnish-made Valmet M62 assault rifle is a simple but effective design. The M62 is an update of the Soviet AKM.

good accuracy. The air space behind the solid nose caused both mushrooming and terminal upset. However, since it does not have an exposed lead core, it does not violate international accords.

Basically, the AKS-74 is an AKM with a larger, slightly modified magazine, muzzle brake/flash hider, and internal parts modified to the caliber. A folding stock version was issued, as was a "shorty" model, the AKSU-74, with an eight-inch barrel and side-folding stock. This weapon, capable of a cyclic rate of 800 rounds per minute, has become prominent in security and bodyguard operations lately. Since the collapse of the Soviet Union and with great poverty in the ranks, all of these weapons have appeared on the black market and in the hands of the Russian mafia.

The AK-47 and AKM spawned similar weapons throughout the communist world. All client states had to use the M43 cartridge and, with the

exception of the Czech VZ58, virtually all were direct copies of the Kalishnikov. There were variations made in Bulgaria (PMKM), Poland (PMK), East Germany (MPiK), Hungary (AMD), Romania and Yugoslavia (M70). The Red Chinese Type 56 and the North Korean Types 58 and 68 were well known to Vietnam-based GIs.

Accessories for these AK variations were also based on the Soviet model. For example, the Romanian AK-47 wire-cutting, survival bayonet was quite similar to the Soviet version. It even appeared in Vietnam, though simpler folding bayonets, as on the Chinese Type 56, were more common. This wire-cutting bayonet served as the model for the development of the U.S. M9 multi-purpose bayonet in the 1980s.

The AK design also has been produced in several Free World countries. Finland's version is the Valmet, with models M60, M62, M71 and M76. It was made in both 7.62x39mm and 5.56mm NATO. The M62 *puuko*-style bayonet, David Steele believes, is superior to any communist country versions, as a field and combat knife. The *puuko* has long been a symbol of Finnish warrior ideals. In the 1939 Winter War, many a Soviet conscript "woke up dead" courtesy of a Finnish *puuko*.

The South African R4 is essentially an

Israeli Galil made under license. The Galil, named for its designer, Israel Galil, is now produced by Israeli Military Industries in four variations chambered for the 5.56mm NATO cartridge. The ARM is a squad automatic weapon with folding metal stock, bipod, and carrying handle. The AR assault rifle is the same, minus bipod and carrying handle. The SAR short assault rifle has a shorter barrel. The MAR mini-assault rifle has a shorter barrel still, and is designed for the police role. Generally, all versions have a cyclic rate of 650 rounds per minute, and magazines carrying 35 or 50 rounds. Front-line units in the Israeli Defense Force now carry the Galil, while reservists are issued American-supplied M-16A1s.

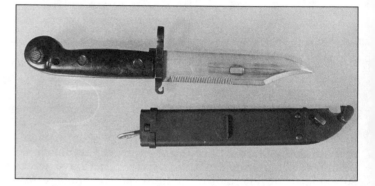

This Romanian AKM bayonet was captured from a North Vietnam soldier near Khe Sanh in April, 1968. The blade is eight inches, and overall length is 13 inches. This design led to development of the M9 multi-purpose bayonet now issued with the M-16A3 rifle.

In order to obtain hard currency, former Soviet and ComBloc states have been selling Kalashnikovs on the open market. However, for the U.S. police market, only the Galil appears to have a future, communist-made guns being associated with terrorism, guerrilla war and subversion for the last 50 years.

Interestingly, the Kalashnikov itself proved to be subversive to American freedoms when large numbers of semi-auto Chinese rifles were brought in under an ill-advised Most Favored Nations import policy. Expensive Swiss and German military-style rifles were virtually unknown in crime, but Chinese-made "AK" copies were not only cheap, but looked evil and were associated with America's enemies. A few notorious crimes later, our socialist politicians were moving for another gun ban.

Although unplanned, this would have to be a victory for communist China, since it makes our government more like theirs, where guns are controlled totally by the power elite!

The MAR, manufactured and marketed by Israeli Military Industries, is the mini-assault version of the familiar 5.56mm Galil rifle. It is being marketed in the U.S. to police and other law enforcement agencies.

CHAPTER 11

SCHOOLS FOR RIFLEMEN

The Long Gun Is An Efficient Tool For Military And Law Enforcement, But It Requires Training To Use It Well.

A FEW YEARS ago, Jack Lewis was involved in writing a book on mercenaries, those military types who tend to fight for whoever is paying the highest buck. In fact, right after World War II, our co-author was propositioned by a doctor in Des Moines, Iowa, about signing on with what he called the Irish Battalion of the infant Israeli Army. For all practical purposes, this was a mercenary organization that had been hired to fight. Lewis, then newly married, was tempted, but his then wife was not. End of story, but not of this chapter.

While researching this book, Lewis met with long-time friend, Bill Askins, who had been a helicopter pilot in Vietnam, then had joined the CIA. He served again in Vietnam as leader of a group of Chinese mercenaries, later being posted to Latin America. He and Lewis were discussing the making of a mercenary, and Askins came up with what seemed a logical explanation.

"After every war, we have a group of people who have learned the soldiering trade. They find little market for this knowledge and training in the normal civilian world, but all they have to do is look at a map and watch CNN to learn there is a demand for their talents somewhere in the world."

In fact, there is even a clearing house for such expertise. A certain American Legion post in the Southwest is made up primarily of absentee solder of fortune members. It is through this mail drop that jobs are heard about and contacts made. Needless to say, perhaps, but the national headquarters of our foremost veterans organization will—and does—deny that there is any such post with any such membership. But it's there, believe us.

At the other extreme, there are those individuals who have tired of foreign travel and the chance to sleep in the mud and get shot at. They look for a means of putting their military knowledge to good use in a situation where they can have dinner at home most nights and play with their kids.

As a result of this thinking, a number of privately run schools have sprung up across the country. These enterprises sell all sorts of courses for the veteran who wants to keep his talents sharp, for active duty military who will take leave to learn a special skill at their own rather than government expense, and for police officers who have come to realize that special talents and special weapons are going to be the future in fighting terrorism. There also are civilian shooters who may suffer from a tinge of Walter Mittyism and want to find out what this is all about, how good at it they can be and are willing to pay to learn.

Still other schools have been set up strictly for the further education of law enforcement personnel. These often are profit-seeking operations, but are taught by highly experienced police

The most popular rifle used in the sniper school was the Remington Model 700 BDL, although scopes and stock designs varied.

officers, either retired or using their vacation days.

These efforts don't always work out as continuing operations, because there is a limited clientele. One old acquaintance of our authors is a retired Marine major, who had been involved in weapons training throughout his career. With retirement, he went back to his old home in Idaho and opened up a shooting range and school to train police officers in marksmanship.

"It was great for about two years," he recalls, "but I eventually ran out of clients. The people I had trained for police departments had gone back and

Wearing the white shirt, John Gnagy coaches students—all law enforcement officers—in the beginning phases of his sniper course.

Armed with a Springfield Armory 308 Winchester semi-automatic rifle, camouflaged Deputy Sheriff Marty Shifflet zeroes in on a target during sniper training. The scope is Leupold's VARI X III 3.5-10x variable.

were training the other members of their department. That meant I didn't get a crack at them."

This individual's problem was solved by signing a contract—approved by our State Department, of course—with the government of Saudi Arabia. He was one of a four-man team of Leatherneck retirees recruited for the purpose of training the Royal Saudi Marine Corps!

There are far too many types of rifle training to cover them all in this book, so we'll look at a couple of courses. One encompasses tactical rifle training and is presented by Max Joseph and his Tactical Firearms Training Team, which is headquartered at 16835 Algonquin Street, #120, Huntington Beach, California 92649. The other course at which we'll take an in-depth look is for law enforcement snipers. It has been taught to police officers and other agents of the law in the Midwest by John Gnagy, a deputy chief of the police department in Champaign, Illinois.

Gnagy is quick to point out that the role of a sniper is more involved than simply taking out a baddie without harming anyone else. "Their value as gatherers of intelligence is as important as their talents as marksmen," he declares. "In both

police and military work, the sniper can be a reliable tool in relaying information from the front line to the command post.

"Snipers are a special breed," the veteran officer adds. "They are trained to get into places undetected and to serve as observers for hours, often under adverse conditions. They must have an uncanny patience many people lack."

Such patience can pay off in different ways. By the time police snipers are deployed, matters usually have escalated to what is considered a dangerous level. The bad guy may surrender, he may go down in a SWAT raid or he may be downed by the sniper's bullet. But until this point is reached, the sniper often is the eyes and ears of the tactical command center.

The primary sniper course which John Gnagy teaches is meant to build the basics of becoming a good shot. Students learn a variety of things about shooting and sniping. For instance, they learn how, in police and military situations, the use of snipers has evolved over the years. In Gnagy's advanced sniper course, students build on what they have learned and put into play complicated problems.

In the wooded hills of central Illinois, where Gnagy conducts some of his training sessions, students are taught the art of personal camouflage, they are introduced to techniques for evaluating terrain and how to use it to their advantage and they learn that weather can have negative effects on the bullets they send downrange.

In the course we covered, there were six students, all law enforcement types. They were made to understand that shooting was paramount, with range exercises and classes on ballistics taking up most of the first two days of the four-day course. They were taught to use mathematics and conversion tables to handle moving targets and inclement weather, but the watchword throughout the course is, "one shot, one kill."

In keeping with this, the goal of this training is for each student to be able to shoot—with consistency—a five-round group into a

All of the sniper training was conducted at a maximum range of 250 yards. This open field is hardly a good position for a sniper, of course, but at this point, the interest was accuracy, not camouflage.

one-inch square that is marked on the reproduced human face of the bad guy. The square is situated in a triangular area on the target that encompasses the paper baddie's eyes and the bridge of his nose.

This exercise with five rounds may not be in keeping with the "one shot, one kill" goal taught at the school, but it shows consistency. As Gnagy puts it, "The only way a sniper can achieve an acceptable level of proficiency is

One student brought along his Heckler & Koch HK91 in 308 Winchester. This semi-auto rifle carried a military-type bipod and Bushnell's Scope Chief VI 3-12x scope.

One of the problems encountered in the two-day course was that of finding a good position for sniping and observation; one that would not automatically make the sniper the target.

through practice. I teach them that repetition, continuity and consistency are the building blocks of becoming a good sniper."

This instructor and veteran sniper feels that the weapon used should be the choice of the sniper who is going to do the shooting. "He must be comfortable with his weapon. When he finds the rifle and scope with which he works best, he should stay with that combination. In my own police department, snipers and their rifles are all but married!"

Gnagy also suggests that every law enforcement agency should record in each sniper's shooting log the serial numbers of the assigned rifle and scope. With this system, each time a specific sniper is called into a situation, he will have the same equipment he always has used and with which he has become totally familiar during training. With numerous variables between one situation and another, the same rifle being carried by the same sniper adds a degree of stability, thus eliminating at least some of the things that can go wrong in a serious live-fire operation.

In Gnagy's experience, the caliber most of his students choose is the 308 Winchester. In many cases, the police officers are military veterans with deep experience with the 7.62mm NATO round. The two calibers are virtually the same. The actual shooting tool varies in make and model, but the preferred model seems to be the Remington 700 BDL Police Special with varying degrees of modification.

One of the students at the session we covered was Michael Paulus, who has more than a half-dozen years of SWAT experience with the police

department in Champaign, Illinois. To the basic Remington package, he has substituted a camouflaged and adjustable McMillan stock and an adjustable Timney trigger. Additions include a Trijicon 3-9x scope and a Harris Model BR tripod.

Mark Medlyn, with more than 15 years of SWAT service, opted for the standard Remington package, with the addition of a Redfield variable 6-18x scope. Sergeant Nick Ficarello of Illinois' Will County Sheriff's Department brought his Heckler & Koch HK91 semi-automatic, carrying a military-style bipod and Model VI 3-13x Bushnell Scope Chief. Deputy Marty Shifflet of the same sheriff's department was firing a Springfield Armory M-1A1, also a

semi-auto, with a Leupold Vari-XII 3.5-10x scope.

It's obvious that experienced police officers armed with such equipment should be able to make telling shots at extremely long ranges. Military snipers are trained to destroy targets out to 1000 yards or more, but John Gnagy conducted all of his training at ranges of 250 yards or less.

"The closer the better," the instructor explained to his students. "Snipers are trained to get as close to the suspect as they possibly can. Distance reduces accuracy by introducing adverse effects on both the marksman and the round. Developing the ability to get close is among the reasons we work at teaching camouflage and movement. These are essential skills for police snipers."

Unlike most military sniper operations, police riflemen often are involved in situations wherein the baddie is holding one or more hostages. This is a situation that requires patience and judgment as well as a keen eye and steady hand. When the sniper gets the command to shoot—and this usually is when a hostage is in extreme danger—his shot must be as precise as the scalpel cut in the hands of a master surgeon. Due to emphasis on camouflage and movement in training, most sniper shots involving a hostage are made at less than 50 yards.

This need was emphasized in the course taught by John Gnagy, a Vietnam-era Marine sniper. For one live-fire exercise each of the students loaded their rifles with only three rounds. Then, fully camouflaged,

On the firing line, the Remington Model 700 BDL was most prominent, but an array of other rifles favored by individual police departments or officers also made an appearance.

Fred Osborne (right) and Nick Ficarello both are members of Illinois' Will County Sheriff's Department. Sergeant Ficarello trained with his department's Heckler & Koch 308 semi-auto, while Osborne was armed with the Remington Model BDL Police Special.

they were sent out in two-man teams, to crawl through thick brush until they could spot a trio of targets. The purpose of this particular mission was to determine whether any, some or all of the six students could fire a single round into each of the three targets before being detected by the teaching team.

Gnagy believes in tough training, contending it will pay off in the field. This exercise was designed to be as competitive and difficult as he could make it, considering the local environment. This meant that nine targets were tacked up, each of them carrying a penciled number. The teams were numbered one through three as were the targets, but the corresponding numbers were not grouped together. Each of the two-man teams had to get close enough—undetected—to the posted targets to see the numbers and identify the assigned three targets.

During this, Gnagy and an aide were positioned atop a nearby hill, sweeping the area with binoculars. If the sniper was spotted or fired on the wrong target, he lost points in scoring. They were required to complete the exercise in 45 minutes or sacrifice still more points.

The usual prize for the winning team was a case of cold beer, which most were willing to share with the less expert students at the end of the training day.

"Our objective is to make this training as tough as possible so the individual students can go back to their departments and know full well

what they may be facing in the field," Gnagy explains. "We're always looking for the impossible in testing these teams. If they don't win the competition, it doesn't matter, so long as they have learned something!"

One of the impossible missions laid out by the instructor and his staff involved maneuvering through a movement course during hours of darkness. The ultimate in this exercise is the demand for each team to drop a series of poorly illuminated steel targets. Illumination carried by the students can range from emergency flares down to a small pocket penlight.

The teams are called upon to approach the Shooting House, where much of the training in other courses is carried out. The sniper team has to approach and open a window, then illuminate—and shoot—a steel silhouette hunkered inside the room.

At the end of their training, their deputy police chief instructor invariably has the opportunity to congratulate them on the imagination and ingenuity utilized in accomplishing their assigned training missions. But he also is quick to point out to them that this training has covered only a few days and is no more than a building block on which they can build, using the lessons learned.

"It takes continuous training for these individuals to maintain the proper edge," John Gnagy states. "If they learn nothing else here, I want them to stress concentration, trigger control and patience in all of their future training. That's what duty as a sniper is all about."

The Tactical Firearms Training Team, the operation run by Max F. Joseph out of his headquarters in Huntington Beach, California, offers courses on a number of subjects. He trains not only law enforcement and military personnel, but also civilians who are interested in the means of self-defense that could be needed by the individual in this uncertain day and age.

In addition to the California facility, TFTT also operates an identical curriculum out of an Eastern Division headquartered in Memphis, Tennessee. More recently, the

Students make final preparations for an exercise in which they are required to move undetected and fire on multiple specified targets. Both of the rifles seen here are Remingtons.

As the student sniper checks for a telling shot during final phases of training, his backup is ready with his own rifle in case of a miss or unforeseen trouble.

company has been setting up what are termed Mobile Training Units or MTUs. These are teams that move into locations around the nation to teach the same courses taught at the Eastern and Western headquarters. One such MTU is headquartered in Dallas, Texas, while another is established in South America. The latter unit specializes in VIP protection, hostage rescue, close quarters shooting and special operations sniping.

Joseph lists his standard courses in an interesting brochure. Course titles are: Advanced Tactical Handgun, Combat Shotgun, Tactical Rifle, Two-Man Team Tactics, and a course called TFTT Optical Rifle, which deals with long-range shooting, and VIP Protection. A special program is listed as the Three-Gun Training Camp.

"This is a special program we structured for professionals who do not want to focus their training on just one weapon," Max Joseph explains. "We have taken the highlights from our rifle, handgun and shotgun programs and developed a concentrated block of non-stop instruction."

Joseph adds, "Some of the most popular courses TFTT conducts are not found on our published schedule. These are courses we structure on request for interested departments or units. Oftentimes, these units require

more diversified subject matter, as opposed to focusing solely upon weapons skills for three or four days." One element being trained on a continuing basis in the VIP Protection Course is security personnel of Boeing Aircraft.

After a bit of discussion, our authors agreed that covering the whole curriculum offered by Joseph's outfit would fill at least one book and possibly several. Therefore, it was decided to concentrate on the Tactical Rifle Course.

"In the hands of a competent operator, the rifle is without a doubt the most formidable weapon available," Joseph tells new classes, explaining that the program on which they are about to embark covers both long-range and close-quarter rifle work. The classroom instruction is in-depth and students are presented with a wide variety of live-fire drills and scenarios.

Some of the initial teachings such as zeroing the rifle may already be familiar exercises for some shooters, along with estimating range or even calling the wind. But such course segments as engaging multiple targets, speed reloading, stoppage drills, weapons retention and structure clearing are included in the students' learning.

For those who might wonder about Max Joseph's qualifications to teach or direct his staff in regard to all of the listed subjects, we wanted to know

Firing from the offhand position, two students concentrate on downrange targets during one of many shooting drills in the Tactical Rifle Course run by California's Tactical Firearms Training Team.

more about the gent. Here are some of the things we learned:

Joseph is the product of a warrior family. His father served in World War II, his grandfather in World War I. Thus, he was raised in a family that

As their varied positions make apparent, these students are in different stages of the rifle-to-pistol transition drill.

The Tactical Firearms Training Team has taught students from 11 countries, as well as domestic applicants. It is run by Max Joseph, a former Marine Corps reconnaissance instructor. He also has instruction teams in Memphis, Dallas and Latin America.

thought in terms of self-reliance and skill with firearms.

He entered the Marine Corps in 1983, volunteering for reconnaissance duty. He was graduated from a 10-week recon school on Okinawa and spent the next seven years pursuing that career. During that period, he was involved in missions in the Philippines and throughout Central America, later serving as a recon instructor.

He honed his talents by going through such service schools as the Marine Scout/ Sniper Instructor School, an anti-terrorist driving school, the Army Ranger's Airborne Course and a Navy school that covered survival, evasion, resistance and escape.

Following discharge in 1990, Max Joseph joined a team of bodyguards for a wealthy California citizen. As the team's training officer, he oversaw 30 armed security agents, insisting that each of them fire no less than 1000 rounds of ammunition per month as a means of staying sharp.

Alan Brosnan had been discharged from the New Zealand Special Air Service and joined Joseph's team. They soon formed their own training unit and taught other protective units, branching out to include police departments, SWAT teams and others interested in first-rank firearms training. Since 1990, Joseph and his staff have instructed several thousand law enforcement officers, including those from the Los Angeles Police Department, the Los Angeles County Sheriff's Department, the San Diego Police Department, the U.S. Marshal's Service and the Customs Service, as well as individuals from Army Special Forces, the Air Force's Special Response Teams and the FBI. He also has trained personnel from 11 different nations over the past decade.

Initial firing for sight zeroing purposes was conducted at 25 yards on small targets. Once this was established, fine tuning was done at 100 meters.

His Tactical Firearms Training Team also arranges specialized training for military and SWAT units, most of them conducted at the Memphis facility. Such special subjects include close quarter battle, hostage rescue, explosives breaching, ballistic shield training, diversionary device employment, as well as raids and interdictions. Soon after the M-4 carbine was introduced to the Army, replacing the special-mission MP5 submachine gun, Joseph's team was

Max Joseph gives his students their introduction to the Fun House, where they learn about house clearing. The mockup is designed so that numerous scenarios can be introduced.

Instructor Troy Tolmack, another former recon Marine, times a student on the first day on what he calls an "adrenaline drill."

called upon to train one of that service's Special Response Teams in close combat techniques.

Firearms writer Paul Hantke decided he needed to brush up his rifle marksmanship talents and made arrangements to go through TFTT's two-day Tactical Rifle Course.

"Joseph and assistant instructor Troy Tolmack, another former recon Marine who had served with Joseph, took the student class through a curriculum that covered all of the pertinent points in use of the tactical rifle," Hantke reports. "They do this at a no-nonsense pace, Joseph telling us several times that he would prefer to teach this as a two-week, not two-day, course."

The class with which Hantke trained was made up of himself and six other individuals, all of whom had taken other TFTT courses. Of the group, he noted, only one was likely to put his knowledge to practical use, as he worked in the security field. The others were young men who enjoyed honing their skills with the rifle and had found someone to teach them.

The course begins with classroom lectures on firearm safety as Joseph demands it be practiced throughout the two days of training. He also impressed upon the students that he expected them to ask questions, as there was a reason for everything they would be taught. The first physical event of the day dealt with zeroing the rifle on a 25-yard course. This was preceded, though, by instruction on proper shooting positions, trigger control and sight alignment.

With the rough zero determined on the short range, the students settled in on the 100-yard line of TFTT's range, fine-tuning a proper battle zero for their rifles. Hantke found that "the proper battle zero setting for a tactical rifle is roughly the same as a point blank setting on a hunting rifle."

Joseph impressed upon his students that they needed to keep a data book, and that they should learn a technique wherein elevation and windage adjustments are backed off the sights in such manner that settings can be duplicated without actually firing the rifle. During this instruction, Hantke noted that the rifle being used by the students was

Safety is considered the most important part of the training program and Joseph (left) and Tolmack stand behind their students during early training phases to spot any unsafe habits.

The Krieg sling is a simple loop attached to the rifle's rear sling swivel. Using it is fast, yet the rifle is secure. It is the method TFTT instructors favor and teach.

some version of the AR-15, ancestor of the military M-16.

In a two-man drill, one man fired while the other spotted for him. This exercise called for engaging steel-backed silhouette targets at ranges varying from 100 to 325 yards. Each student had a range card and targets were identified by range and sector of fire. Using this system, instructors called out specific target designations. The spotter called hits or misses, giving clock-reading and distance off target to the shooter, allowing him to make sight adjustments that would bring him into the black. However, first-hit ratio was in the low 80 percent bracket, so the exercise moved along rapidly.

"A rifle without a sling is worse than a pistol without a holster," Max Joseph told his students, then pointed out that when carrying the rifle American military style, the muzzle up, this will interfere with access to the backup handgun on the same strong side. He demonstrated what he called the African style, rifle slung on the weak side and muzzle down to protect the bore against tropical downpours. It was obvious this method would be faster in getting the rifle into action

and would not interfere with the handgun. This system was used by servicemen in Vietnam's monsoons.

What Joseph insisted is the most versatile is called the Krieg sling. This is a loop attached to the rear sling swivel, then it is slung over the head and under the arm on the strong side. This was the system used in the balance of the TFTT training.

The next exercise was a timed event in which all of the students held their rifles in the patrol ready position, moving downrange 20 yards to a marker, where each fired offhand, seeking to hit a pair of eight-inch steel plates positioned some 30 yards away. Shooters then moved another 25 yards under cover to take on another pair of steel plates, then fired five rounds on a paper bullseye set 75 yards away. The final challenge was to knock down a steel popper target; if hit, it stopped the timer. Each student also was timed with a stopwatch by one of the instructors.

Emphasis on patrol techniques followed, beginning with a walk-and-fire drill. A good deal of ammo was burned up before Joseph and his staff were satisfied with student performance. That led to a standing turn-and-fire drill to be climaxed by a move-and-turn exercise while moving. More speed drills finished the working day, with Joseph critiquing the day, then discussing the effects on a bullet's flight by elevation, wind and weather. Students agreed that this facet of instruction could constitute a week-long course in itself.

At the end of the first day, Joseph also discussed methods of range estimation and what to look for as target indicators, while not revealing one's self as a potential target.

The second day at the Huntington Beach training ground was a post-sunrise review of what had been learned on the first day, followed immediately with more work with the Krieg sling, learning to get the long gun to the shoulder, then transitioning to the handgun. These exercises were repeated a number of times with unloaded weapons, then it was off to the live-fire range.

With the rifle slung across his back, Joseph has drawn his pistol and engaged his target. This practice would be used if there was a stoppage with the rifle.

Max Joseph demonstrates how quickly the rifle can be slung over the back and out of the way if necessary. It goes over the weak-side shoulder so the strong-side hand can be used with the handgun.

As rangemaster for the house-clearing segment, Troy Tolmack addresses a target during his orientation run-through for the students. The whole scenario changed when it was the students' turn.

According to Paul Hantke, "The live-fire efforts took a good deal of time, but by the time we were done, everyone had cut his getting-into-action time by half. Then it was off to what Max called the Fun House."

Those of us who have been through structure clearing assignments—real or otherwise—realize that this is the route to harm's way, with stress tending to interfere with the fact that one has to think in terms of muzzle control, shoot/no-shoot identification, cover that can be used, moving around corners, ad infinitum.

The Fun House on the TFTT "campus" features all sorts of setups that can be changed to alter the problems. The structure has a long hallway with rooms leading off the thoroughfare.

Members of the student team were given a specific mission, which was followed by a review of the muzzle control and safety measures that Joseph and Tolmack expected. The latter instructor went through the house to illustrate

what he expected, then sent the students to sit in the shade for a few minutes, while he changed everything in the Fun House to present a whole new problem. All students went through the house-clearing exercise twice, the instructors demanding safe gun handling as they coached their charges.

One might think such an exercise would mark the end of the training cycle, but that's not the way Joseph and staff work it. Instead, it is back to additional reaction drills. The first one called for each student to walk away from the target, and on command, turn 180 degrees and fire at a 12-inch metal gong. This was a timed event. Later came more unsling, aim and fire practice followed by transition drills, that require slinging the rifle and going to the handgun. Each training segment started with unloaded practice, and was followed by live fire efforts.

On film and television we've all seen the Bruce Lees, the Jackie Chans and Chuck Norrises go into their ballet-like movements to keep an opponent from disarming them. Max Joseph is quick to state that

trained martial arts followers undoubtedly have talents the rest of us lack, but he has his own approach to weapons retention.

It was pointed out that a rifle is not designed to be a short-range weapon, yet there are circumstances such as the Fun House escapade in which it is used at short ranges. This means the user has to think about someone grabbing his rifle and using it on him.

Joseph and Tolmack offered several situations in which one would attempt to disarm the other. In each instance, there was an answer to the problem. The students spent time practicing the various weapon-retaining techniques, interspersing this facet of training with more live-fire drills. The graduation ceremony was another run through the Fun House, which had been rearranged with all new challenges.

The day ended with a critique and debriefing by Joseph and Tolmack before sending the students and their rifles homeward bound. One point we found interesting was that the techniques taught by the Tactical Firearms Training Team can be as valuable in the field, hunting various types of game, as they would be in actual armed conflict!

●

The final segment of the two-day course was devoted to weapon retention, with Joseph (left) and Tolmack demonstrating techniques.

CHAPTER 12

A RIFLE CALLED ERMA

The SR 100 Sniper Rifle And The 338 Lapua Magnum Make An Excellent Combo.

THERE WAS A day when the term *sniper* was a dirty word in the American lexicon. In the last decade, there was a rash of sniper slayings by individuals suffering severe mental problems.

In more recent years, with political terrorists, the mentally disturbed and the usual array of hardened criminals taking hostages and carrying out such outrages as the Los Angeles bank robbery in which the bad guys were much better armed than the police, the professional sniper and his equipment have come to be recognized as a legitimate law enforcement and military need as well as a fact of modern-day life. Our own nation's special operations around the world, facing challenges never experienced before, have caused us to focus on highly refined weaponry meant to perform specific tasks by the individual expert.

As a result of such thinking and acceptance, both the police and military have become increasingly interested in new and better sniper rifles as well as improvements in the ammunition needed for such missions.

Robin Sharpless, vice president of New England Firearms and H&R 1871, Inc., was quick to note the growing interest in precision shooting tools, and his firm began to seek out a sniper rifle they could feel was the

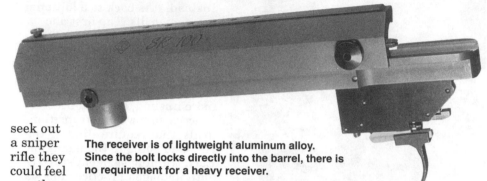

The receiver is of lightweight aluminum alloy. Since the bolt locks directly into the barrel, there is no requirement for a heavy receiver.

ultimate in accuracy, efficiency and plain old strength.

Sharpless' choice narrowed down to the German-made Erma SR 100 sniper rifle, which is chambered for the 338 Lapua Magnum cartridge. Fired through the SR 100, this combination can send a 250-grain bullet downrange at some 3000 feet per second.

Steve Comus, one of the first to test this rifle, points out, "There are faster loads and there are more powerful ones, as well. But what the 338 Lapua Magnum cartridge does as well or better than anything else is to offer snipers a perfect compromise between the performance of the 7.62x51mm NATO cartridge (sold commercially as the 308 Winchester) and the behemoth 50 Browning Machine Gun round."

Testing has shown that—depending upon the intended target, of course—the streamlined, low-drag 338 Lapua Magnum is ideal for shots that are too distant to be made with any predictability by lesser rounds. For example, the 243 Winchester is considered a 400-yard round; the 308 Winchester cartridge is thought of as boasting 500-yard accuracy, while the 300 Winchester Magnum and 7mm Remington Magnum are 1200-yard shooters in the right hands and with the right rifle.

The Browning Machine Gun bullet is considered to be accurate at 1500 yards. The truth of this was seen during Desert Storm, when Army and Marine snipers were knocking out enemy fuel supplies and motor transport at that range. With its efficient bullet design, the more manageable 338 Lapua Magnum performs beautifully at 1400 yards, according to Robin Sharpless, who had witnessed such tests. We went a step beyond.

There will be few needs for shots at such ranges, of course, and the SR 100/338 Lapua Magnum more often will be called upon to perform their accuracy out at considerably shorter distances.

The round, incidentally, didn't just happen nor was it the product of a big-bore wildcatter. It was developed with the interest and blessing of U.S. military forces, who were calling for a rifle that could be used against materiel targets. The 50 BMG guns used in Desert Storm invariably were single shots and awkward to handle or transport. The desire was to find a rifle that looked like a rifle, could handle more than a single round at a time and could be used to destroy enemy supplies and transportation.

The SR 100 can hold five rounds of 338. This cartridge is built on what originally was a shortened 416 Rigby case necked down to 33-caliber. During testing, however, the engineers determined that the Lapua case needed a more beefy web than was found on the standard Rigby offering. As a result, the design crew

Steve Comus sights through the 4-16x scope as he prepares to squeeze off a 338 Lapua Magnum round from the Erma SR 100 sniper rifle. His shooting partner, Blaine Huling, waits to spot the shot through a target scope.

created their own heavy-duty cartridge case that maintained the same outer dimensions as the original version.

At the time we wanted to test the rifle, factory-loaded 338 Lapua ammunition was hard to find, so Steve Comus volunteered to handload for the Erma rifle. To check accuracy and conduct further testing, only one loading was used. This consisted of the Lapua case, Federal's 215 primer, 103 grains of Hodgdon's H870 powder and the Lapua B-408 250-grain bullet. This combination resulted in cartridges that measured 3.6 inches in overall length.

Once set up on a private ranch in the Southern California mountains, the velocity was checked with an Oehler 35P chronograph with the

Specifications

Name:	Erma SR 100.
Type:	Sniper rifle.
Caliber:	338 Lapua Magnum.
Operation:	Bolt-action.
Weight:	17.2 pounds, with scope and magazine.
Length:	52.9 inches, with muzzle brake.
Barrel:	29.5 inches, with muzzle brake; six grooves, 1:10-inch twist.
Magazine:	5-round capacity, box type of stamped and welded steel.
Stock:	Black synthetic; fully adjustable ergonomic design.
Sights:	None furnished; optional fixed sights or detachable scope mounts.
Importer:	H&R 1871, Inc. Industrial Rowe Gardner, Massachusetts 01440

screens placed 20 feet from the muzzle. Firing a half-dozen of Comus' reloads, the highest velocity recorded was 2895 feet per second; the slowest to come out of the muzzle traveled at 2884 feet per second.

Comus feels that the Erma/Lapua combo should be loaded for performance of 3000 fps, using the 250-grain bullet. We tend to agree, but rather than hotrodding this cartridge, we were interested in producing a cartridge that was easy to load and offered consistent results on target.

The bolt lock-up has much to do with the rifle's accuracy. The three squared-off lugs fit solidly into the barrel itself. The bolt handle has a large plastic knob that is easy to find in the dark and offers positive leverage when reloading the gun.

That goal was achieved.

Since he had concocted the load with his shooting buddy, Blaine Huling, Comus reserved the right to be the first to fire the rifle from a weathered picnic bench we found in our chosen test area. Actually, the area is part of a ranch owned by Huling's family with the San Gabriel Mountains as an excellent backstop.

"The combination of weight and design translates into a powerful, long-range rig for which one would have to put the felt recoil in the category of the 257 Roberts," Comus contends. That may seem a bit far-fetched, but the rest of us found it an incredibly comfortable rifle to shoot. No one else who tried the rifle tended to argued with Comus' summation.

Firing from the old picnic table that had been chosen for benchrest use, we soon found that the stock was an important part of shooting comfort. Space Age synthetics have been used in building the rifle and the buttstock has been designed to be "all things to all men." That probably includes women shooters, too.

The thumbhole stock is fashioned so that it is equally adaptable to either left- or right-hand use. Aluminum rails are present for installation of a carrying/shooting sling or a bipod, while the buttplate is adjustable for both length and height. On top of the stock is an adjustable cheekpiece. And extending from the bottom of the stock is an adjustable rack-and-pinion "third leg" system for use with a bipod. In our testing, a Harris bipod was used with excellent results.

Shooting at a measured 100 yards, the best test group measured 0.130-inch, center-to-center. However, none of the shooters involved had

any difficulty holding groups to 0.20-inch or less.

That point of accuracy established, it was time to move on to a real-life scenario. Silhouette targets were set up at measured ranges of 750 and 1000 yards. Four different shooters began exercising the Erma rifle on the closer target. All of Comus' reloads were in the kill zone for each of our shooters.

Somewhat bored with such consistency, our riflemen took on the 1000-yard target with similar results. Any of the four armed with this rifle/ammo combination would be eligible for the sniper spot in almost any SWAT team! In reality, of course, SWAT snipers seldom, if ever, are called upon for such long-range shots. Military snipers are.

Shooting was done on a bright California morning during that time when even normal breezes die for an hour or two, thus there was no appreciable wind to require interpretation.

New targets were set up at 1500 yards as measured by a range finder, and adjustments were made in the 4-6x B. Nickel scope that had been furnished with the test rifle.

The targets used in this test were, divided into two zones, one approximately 18 inches across,

The Harris bipod supported the rifle for shots made from an old picnic table found in the San Gabriel Mountains. Initial range was at 100 yards, but eventually telling shots were being made with the rifle/ammo combo out to 1500 yards.

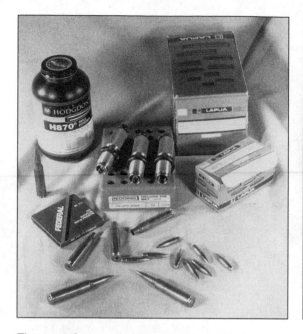

These are the components and dies used to turn out the 338 Lapua Magnum ammunition used in testing the German-made Erma SR 100 rifle.

The three handloaded cartridges all point to a single ragged hole that comprises the group for three other rounds. Accuracy of the rifle was termed awesome by those involved in the testing.

while the inner area—the kill zone—was nine inches. With the rifle rested solidly, using the Harris bipod and the third-leg system beneath the butt, the kill zone was hit with respectable consistency.

Considering the fact that this rifle has a takedown barrel, the shooters were amazed at the accuracy some of them initially had felt to be impossible. For the Erma SR 100, however, the secret lies in the fact that the bolt locks directly into the barrel by means of three sturdy locking lugs. These close-fitting lugs fit precisely and in total alignment with the rifle's bore. Thus, if the barrel is removed, then replaced or a new barrel is introduced, the shooter need not worry about differing tensions on the threads.

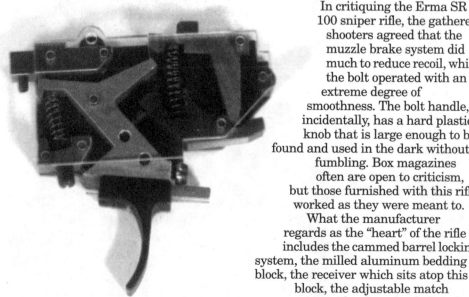

The receiver of the SR 100 sits atop a milled aluminum block. The extension from the bottom of the block is the well for the magazine.

This cut-away view of the adjustable trigger shows how the trigger pull can be adjusted from 500 to as much as 3000 grams to suit individual preference.

In critiquing the Erma SR 100 sniper rifle, the gathered shooters agreed that the muzzle brake system did much to reduce recoil, while the bolt operated with an extreme degree of smoothness. The bolt handle, incidentally, has a hard plastic knob that is large enough to be found and used in the dark without fumbling. Box magazines often are open to criticism, but those furnished with this rifle worked as they were meant to.

What the manufacturer regards as the "heart" of the rifle includes the cammed barrel locking system, the milled aluminum bedding block, the receiver which sits atop this block, the adjustable match trigger, the three-lug bolt and the double-row magazine.

Late in 1996, the Erma-made rifle was adopted by the GSG9, Germany's noted counter-terrorist force. The order was for rifles to be chambered for the 338 Lapua Magnum cartridge. The initial order was for 20 rifles with an adjunct that the order could be increased, if other government agencies, including the German army, chose to adopt it for sniper use.

Meanwhile, Robin Sharpless has established H&R 1871, Inc. as the U.S. importer for the rifle. He reports that the rifle has been tested by the Delta Force headquartered at Fort Bragg, North Carolina. Some months later, they have asked that the rifle be returned with the Army paying all costs associated with the test. In addition to the 338 Lapua Magnum, the rifle also is being manufactured in 308 Winchester and 300 Winchester Magnum calibers. Also, calibers can be changed to either of these configurations by replacing the barrel, bolt and magazine

As accessories, the manufacturer also offers a diopter peep sight, a night vision scope, a mirage deflector, a transport case and a cleaning kit. ●

CHAPTER 13

GALIL'S 7.62 NATO SNIPER MODEL RIFLE

As A Full-Auto Assault Rifle, This Israeli Product Has A Mid-East History. Now It Has An All-New Role.

READERS OF THE first four editions of this book undoubtedly have come to realize that our authors, Jack Lewis and David Steele, dearly love testing selective-fire, military-oriented weaponry. And they are quick to admit that the bang-bang fun is multiplied several fold in those instances wherein the manufacturer is paying for the ammunition.

This is one of the reasons why we found ourselves on the Police Training Range in Burbank, California, checking out the various Galil and Uzi arms being produced by Israeli Military Industries.

The occasion for this shoot was the fact that the weapons being fired were considered too powerful for the limited facilities of the Los Angeles Police Range near Griffith Park. The demonstration of the various weapons, ranging from full-auto assault rifles and submachine guns to 45-caliber pistols, was part of a larger program that had brought law enforcement types from around the state to learn what is new in weapons and tactics.

This part of the show was strictly in the hands of representatives of

Israeli Military Industries. On site to demonstrate the various firearms and to offer advice and help for the lawmen wanting to try the guns for themselves were a gent named Efraim Yaarl. This individual heads up the maker's firearms lab in Israel and had been flown to the U.S. especially for this presentation. With him was Nisim Zusman, marketing manager for Israeli Military Industries in this country. As might be suspected, Zusman maintains his U.S. headquarters offices in Chevy Chase, Maryland, close enough to the Pentagon for frequent sales pitches.

The training range for the Burbank Police Department is located in a narrow canyon high in the mountains behind the city itself. This is an ideal location, since it offers natural backstops for ricochets and errant rounds. Running the range is a retired Marine ordnance type we have known for just this side of forever. The range he oversees has several different venues that include 100-yard targets consisting of steel plates strung on cables across the canyon, and a variety of closer targets that move, spin and

frustrate and do everything but fire back at shooters who don't pay strict attention to what they are doing.

"Both David Steele and I had fired a number of the weapons that were

Specifications

Name:	Galil 7.62mm NATO Sniper Model.
Type:	Semi-automatic sniper model.
Operation:	Gas-operated; rotating bolt; magazine-fed; Kalashnikov type.
Weight:	11.2 pounds, empty.
Length:	40.5 inches.
Barrel:	20 inches; 1:12-inch right-hand twist; four groves.
Magazine:	25 rounds; detachable box type.
Maker:	Israeli Military Industries. P.O. Box 1044 Romat Haharoh Isreal

The Galil Sniper Model introduced at a law enforcement shooting symposium boasted a fixed buttstock and handguard of redwood. The rifle also is available with a metal folding stock.

Efraim Yaarl, who heads the firearms development laboratory for Israel Military Industries, demonstrated the effectiveness of his sniper rifle in sitting and prone positions.

laid out on a picnic table for perusal and I sort of passed them by," Jack Lewis reports. "The two firearms that truly intrigued me were the Micro Galil, which is best described, I guess, as a miniature assault carbine. The other Galil I found even more intriguing was what may best be described as a somewhat disguised semi-auto version of the famed Galil assault rifle that has been reworked strictly for sniper work. A version that was not present has a folding stock and I probably would have taken a pass on that one. I come from a background that always has favored bolt-action rifles with full walnut stocks as precision sniper instruments."

Fact of the matter is that it has taken a bit of basic firearms reeducation for our co-author to accept the fact that several currently made, folding-stocked semi-auto models just might double for sniper work.

Efraim Yaarl, the grizzled but relatively quiet gent who has made armament design and development for the Israeli Army his life's work, checked Lewis out on the Galil Sniper Model with its wooden stock and hand guard, explaining that "only a few of these sniper rifles are built each year.

Each rifle is unique in that it is hand-assembled and tuned to embody the extraordinary level of refinement and precision required to deliver exact shot placement in the most demanding tactical situations." Uttered with a charming Israeli accent, his words sounded like a paragraph from a sales pitch and probably were, but nevertheless, his explanation seemed to fit the situation.

Like the other semi-auto Galil models, this sniper version is a relatively lightweight, air-cooled, gas-operated, magazine-fed, shoulder-fired piece of work. Contributing to the light weight of the piece are that wooden buttstock and matching hand guard. They appear sturdy enough to withstand some rough treatment in the field, yet do not add greatly to the carrying weight.

"At first, I thought the wood might be from the olive tree which I know grows in profusion in the Middle East," Lewis reports, "but closer inspection indicated the material was not nearly so dense or hard as the seasoned wood of an olive tree." Later, it was determined that the stock and forearm both had been fashioned from California redwood!

Lewis is left-handed, but always has shot from the right shoulder, his right eye being the dominant orb. However, Jim Benson, editor of *American Survival Guide*, was on hand for the test shoot, and it was noted he was firing with the gun held to his left shoulder.

"It may be that the Israelis have a large contingent of southpaws among their troops," Lewis suggested, "because some serious design thought had been given to the development of a rifle that has a cocking handle, safety catch lever and magazine catch, all of which can be operated from either side of the weapon."

Efraim Yaarl showed us that only six parts need to be stripped from the rifle to break it down for cleaning, and no tools are required. A quick look at the assembled parts left a strong suggestion that the Galil designers had borrowed liberally from the familiar Kalashnikov design.

The 20-inch air-cooled barrel assembly carries an L-type flip sight that Yaarl told us is set for 300 and 500 yards. The folding night sight is upgraded with the addition of three white reference spots of titanium, while at the front of the barrel is installed a simple, ring-protected post sight.

When field stripped, the sniper rifle consists of only a few parts, all of them hand-honed and fitted. Only a few hundred of these precision machines are being made each year.

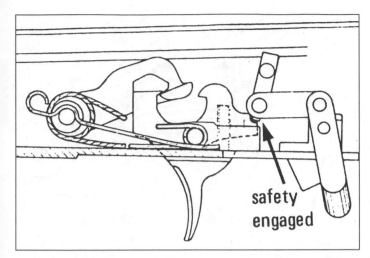

In this illustration, the hammer is cocked and the safety catch is in the safe "S" position.

Mention of the sights is somewhat after-the-fact, since this test rifle was equipped with a Nimrod 6x40 scope that we found to provide excellent light-gathering qualities. Weight of the basic rifle without the scope and without a loaded magazine in place is approximately 11.2 pounds. Add the scope and ammo, however, and the rifle suddenly begins to enter the realm of one of those things the average soldier doesn't want to lug around all day!

"Actually, this is the type of shooting tool that purposely sacrifices handiness for accuracy," Lewis opines. "This one is good for hunkering down in a likely spot and displaying its accuracy on an enemy soldier or perhaps a dangerous felon. There is no doubt that it would be a good choice for a hostage situation, where accuracy is paramount."

When inserting the loaded magazine into what the Israelis refer to as the magazine opening, there is a bit of a trick. Efraim Yaarl explained that the simplest way is to hold the pistol grip in the right hand, tilting the rifle upward about 60 degrees. The magazine, held in

the left hand, is angled about 60 degrees toward the rifle and inserted into the magazine opening. This tilt is an aid in guiding the magazine into the opening. The magazine then is rotated rearward with the left hand until it snaps into place. Incidentally, the rifle's safety catch lever should be on the "S" marking (for safe) while one goes through this exercise.

If one wants to remove the magazine, simply hold the magazine with four fingers of the left hand wrapped around the front side of the box, then press the magazine catch forward, at the same time pulling the magazine in a forward and downward swing. At the other extreme, if you happen to be left-handed, all of these moves can be made without problem with a bit of practice.

But let's assume we have not removed the magazine and want to fire the weapon. While still holding the pistol grip of the rifle, loaded magazine in place, the trigger finger of the right hand moves the safety catch lever to "F" for semi-automatic fire. One then draws the cocking handle all the way to the rear and releases it. This should cause a cartridge to be stripped from the magazine and guided into the chamber. The safety catch should be returned to the safe position, unless you are involved in a hot firefight.

While David Steele was checking out the latest in the

Uzi line, Lewis continued his investigations of the Galil Sniper Model following the firing session. Under the expert lecturing of Efraim Yaarl, he learned that the bolt carrier, which locks and unlocks the bolt, travels in the upper part of the receiver, accommodating the return spring. When the safety catch lever is in the safe position, this blocks the trigger and covers the slot in the cover in which the cocking handle travels. This serves a two-fold purpose: It prevents cocking of the rifle and blocks the entrance of dirt into the mechanism.

For field stripping, one first removes the magazine and pushes the safety catch lever to the "F" position. If the rifle is loaded, remove the cartridge from the chamber, then work the action a couple of times to be certain there is not a cartridge hung up somewhere in the innards.

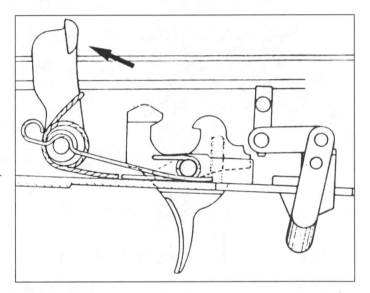

With the trigger and hammer released, the safety catch now is in the firing position.

One then can press the cover catch and lift the rear end of the cover to remove it from the rifle. To remove the return spring assembly and the bolt carrier group, hold the pistol grip with the left hand, then press the cover catch inward with the right thumb. This allows one to pull out the return spring before the bolt carrier is pulled fully to the rear. One then can pull the bolt carrier to the rear and remove it from the receiver. Rotate the bolt counter-clockwise and lift it free of the bolt carrier.

The final step in field stripping is to remove the rifle's gas cylinder. This is accomplished by holding the rear end of this cylinder, pulling it back, then lifting it out. Reassembly, of course, is conducted in the opposite sequence and is no great problem.

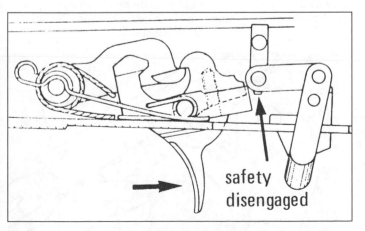

With the safety catch in the "F" or firing position, the trigger is pulled.

There also is a sequence for disassembling the magazine. It is the authors' collective judgment, based upon long experience, that this is best done by a qualified gunsmith or armorer. All too often, when a magazine is taken apart, it will not feed properly when fitted back into the magazine well. The delicate lips can be bent or the spring damaged in some way. This certainly is not the magazine any of us would want to use in a life and death situation.

Meantime, back on the Burbank Police Range, Efraim Yaarl held the Galil Sniper Model, while Nisim Zusman poured a handful of sand and dirt into the rifle's action. Yaarl then threw the rifle to his shoulder and proceeded to squeeze off a half-dozen rounds. He the handed the rifle to Lewis, nodding his head to indicate our co-author should do the same. Aiming downrange at a large white rock that seemed to be clinging to the canyon

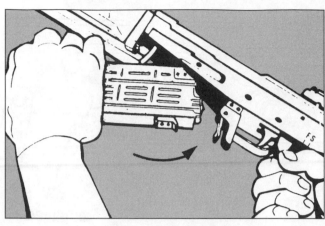

The magazine is inserted in the rifle by holding it at a 60-degree angle to the magazine opening.

still intrigues Lewis. However, he didn't become curious about the type of wood used until after Yaarl had left the country. Also, we were unable to locate Zusman in his Maryland digs.

"Eventually, I came to the conclusion that wood from the olive tree would not be used for buttstocks

That was what had been used to stock this Galil rifle and we can only assume all of this comes under the heading of showmanship. Both the butt and forearm were a bright, almost garish yellow that would stand out in a battle situation. If taken into a combat situation as-is, that brightness just might get the sniper sniped!

We assume that future rifles will have muted or even camouflaged woodwork before being sent out to the field for use in real-life sniping situations. Other than that, we can find anything critical to say about the 7.62 NATO Galil Sniper Model!

However, a safety warning issued by the Israeli manufacturer is worth repeating here: "Use only clean, dry, original high-quality currently commercially manufactured 7.62mm ammunition in good condition. The ammunition must meet industry standards (ANSI/SAAMI Z 229.4-1981). Reloaded or remanufactured ammunition should not be used. Use of this type of ammunition will void all warranties. Never handle ammunition with oily fingers."

On that note, we add that if you still favor the standard folding metal stock and synthetic handguard, the Galil Sniper is available in that configuration, too. The inner workings get the same attention as those in the Show Business Model we have been discussing! •

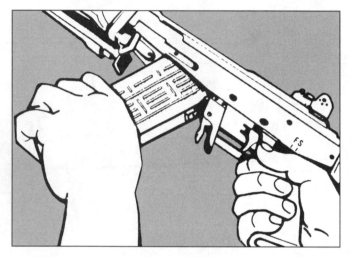

The next step is to insert the magazine in the opening and draw it to the rear in a rotating motion.

wall, Lewis triggered seven rounds, finally dislodging the rock and watching it tumble down the face of the steep cliff.

There was not a stutter from the action, which seemed to be loose enough that it simply ground up the dirt and spit it out through the ejection port with the fired cases.

Next, Yaarl seated himself at the picnic table that was being used to display the various Galil and Uzi models. Without benefit of a sling, he picked out a target at 100 yards and fired five rounds that we found formed a nice little inch-wide rosette of perforations. He urged other onlookers to try their hand at duplicating his performance, but all passed.

"I knew I could not equal the accuracy he had displayed with his rifle," Our Man in Burbank recalls. "Rather than make a fool of myself, I was content to take notes on what I had just witnessed."

The redwood stock which incorporated an adjustable cheekpiece

and handguards, because it is somewhat dense and brittle, Lewis advises "But there was one thing about the Galil sniper's woodwork that bothered me. Anyone who has done any building with redwood recognizes the fact that not all of such wood is red. It comes in a range of shades, much of it an almost bright yellow."

To remove the magazine from the Galil rifle, the magazine catch is pressed forward with the thumb, and the magazine is pulled down and forward. It is almost impossible to remove the magazine with the right hand.

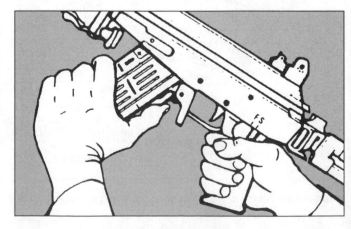

FROM RUSSIA'S ARMS MILLS

The End Of The Cold War Did Not Mark The End Of Arms Development In This European Nation.

WITH THE WRECKING of the Berlin Wall, East and West Germany rejoining to become a single democratic state, and the break-up of the Soviet Union, most Americans came to believe that Russia, as a world power, had lost its initiative and has been in a constant state of turmoil.

In political circles that is somewhat true, but the negatives have been blown totally out of proportion by the news media, and even some of the

political science experts who "look at the Big Picture."

The fact remains that the so-called Big Picture is made up of any number of little pictures which can have their own effect in shaping policy and the future. Russia may have accepted MacDonald's hamburgers, and Levi's faded denim jeans have become a favorite mode of dress, but that does not mean the citizens of Moscow or the less likely hinterlands have become totally

Americanized. The old government-run Soviet small arms factories still are in existence, and now are operating as private companies.

One of these companies is Izemash, reportedly having more than 50,000 employees. This enterprise is located in the Ural Mountains in Izhevak, a metropolis that was a closed city until 1992. Secret development projects were the order of the day there with workers not being allowed to discuss the type of work they were doing.

The AN-94 Assault Rifle

It is within the walls of Izhmash that Gennadly Nickolayevich Nikonov has served more than 20 years as an engineer in what has been described as "a design bureau." Actually, this bureau was involved in small arms development. According to verified reports, Nikonov was appointed as the top engineer in a team that was assigned to produce what then was a top secret military weapon. That was in the 1980s.

With the breakup of the Soviet Union, a great deal of the secrecy that had been the trademark of the communist nation seemed to dissolve in the cauldron of capitalistic expansion. With this mantle of secrecy lowered, Gennadly Nikonov, now 49 years old, has become a well-recognized firearms designer. It was his team that had developed a battle rifle that was touted as being far superior to the faithful old AK-47 and its later variations produced around the world. At this point, Nikonov's new rifle

was known only as the Abakan ASM assault rifle. More recently, it has been redesignated by the Russians as the Automat Nikonova, Model 1994. In general use, that mouthful has been reduced to AN-94.

According to word coming out of Russia, until late 1993, this new rifle had been shown only to high-ranking government officials and to the nation's armament experts, who were involved in testing, evaluation and

possible improvement of the assault rifle. A number of American arms publishers had heard of the gun and tried to get full details, but the top-secret classification imposed by the Russian military frustrated those efforts.

In time, details on the AN-94 design began to leak out of the laboratories where the rifle had been perfected. Perhaps most notable was the fact that Russia seemed to have entered its own Age of Plastics. Earlier arms were made of ordnance steel, metal stampings and wood. Here, with the AN-94, man-made synthetics were being used as never before. According to those who have had an opportunity to inspect the rifle closely and are familiar with synthetics, polyamide, which has been reinforced with fiberglass, is used for the two-piece stock that extends from the butt to the forward hand grip. The stock is hinged and the buttstock can be removed or simply folded forward and held in place by a snap arrangement for close-quarters work.

The Russian-made AN-94 (officially known as the Automat Nikonov, Model 1994,) has been designed to replace the venerable Kalashnikov assault rifle. It uses some design features of the latter rifle, but generally speaking is a departure from designs favored by the now defunct Soviet Union.

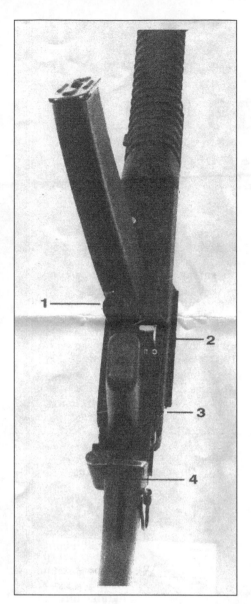

On the underside of the rifle, (1) the magazine latch is easily accessible; (2) the safety shift lever is marked for safe and fire only; (3) the firing-mode selector determines the rate of fire; (4) an integral cleaning rod goes with the rifle, but there also is a separate and complete cleaning kit with each gun.

Slung beneath the barrel is what is termed a stock-extension rod with an under-the-barrel mount for a grenade launcher. A stud is mounted roughly half way down the length of the barrel to carry out a necessary function.

In early tests, it was discovered that in full-auto fire, this extension rod and even the barrel tend to oscillate, resulting in a bounce that invariably is disturbing to the shooter and to accuracy. Some serious experimentation was involved before it was decided to mount the stud in its chosen position on the rod, thus breaking up the frequency of oscillation.

The stud also has a secondary use. When being used to fire from the port of an armored vehicle, the AN-94 can be locked into firing position by means of a specially designed lock. In order to inhibit the barrel of the gun from sliding back and forth in this lock, the stud on the extension rod keeps the barrel in place.

While the AN-94 bears little exterior similarity to the venerable Kalashnikov AK-47, at least five parts have been borrowed from the older model. First is the hinge and release knob for the folding butt. Others are the design of the pistol grip and the magazine, as well as the cleaning kit and the optical sight base. The magazine is the box-type, single-column unit that holds 30 rounds of 5.45x39mm ammo; acceptance of the fact, I guess, that the 22-caliber cartridge family is the thing for warfare these days.

The buttstock of the AN-94 folds to the right, unlike several other models in the Russian ordnance inventory. The designer felt, rightly so, that this positioning allows the butt to unfold more easily and can be brought into firing mode more quickly.

In order to remove the top cover and the handguard, one must pivot downward a lever which is positioned on the front right side of the stock. With this top cover removed, one then pulls the firing unit until it is freed of the guide rails built into the stock extension rod and the stock itself. To strip the trigger unit from the stock, one must depress the folding buttstock's release lock knob as far as it will go, then turn downward a small lever situated above the pistol grip.

The AN-94 has a buffer positioned above the fore grip in the interior of the stock. This is meant to absorb some of the recoil when the firing unit is in its rearmost position. This buffer also is designed to speed the firing unit's return travel. To increase travel of the bolt carrier, a shock absorber is positioned in the rear of the receiver.

On top of the synthetic stock, toward its rear, is a rotary-type diopter sight that has peep holes at differing elevations to accommodate specific ranges. Incorporated is a holder for a tritium bead, which can be installed for work under poor light conditions. This, of course, must be matched up with the post-type front

Features of the AN-94 include: (1) a heavy-duty hinge for the folding buttstock; (2) the rotary diopter-type rear sight; (3) a buttstock lock-release button; and (4) the lever for trigger mechanism release.

Specifications

Name: AN-94 (Automat Nikonova, Model 1994.

Type: Selective-fire assault rifle.

Caliber: 5.45 x 39mm.

Operation: Gas-operated; fires from closed bolt.

Cyclic rate: Variable: 1800 rounds per minute, first two rounds; 600 rounds per minute following.

Weight: 8.4 pounds empty.

Length: 37.1 inches (stock extended); 28.6 inches (stock folded).

Barrel: 15.9 inches; 1:7.6-inch twist; chrome-plated bore, chamber.

Magazine: 30-round detachable box-type; black fiberglass-reinforced polyamide.

Stock: Black fiberglass-reinforced polyamide buttstock, pistol grip.

Finish: Black phosphate.

Sights: Post-type front adjustable for windage and elevation; rotary diopter rear with apertures at five positions for varying elevations; both sights mount tritium beads for night firing.

Accessories: Sling, bayonet, cleaning kit, optical sight, night vision sight, underbarrel grenade launcher.

Maker: Izhmash Joint Stock Company
3 Derjabin Street
426006, Izhevek, Russia

---

sight to which another tritium bead can be affixed. This front sight, incidentally, is adjustable for both elevation and windage.

A feature which some gun experts consider overkill is the variable rate of fire. The cyclic rate may be adjusted from as low as 600 rounds per minute to as high as 1800 rpm! Actually, the first two rounds are fired at the higher rate of fire, then the cyclic rate reverts to the 600 rpm level. The mechanism for this rate change is somewhat complicated and will not be explained here, except to state that the rifle has a sliding type hammer with a special addition that cuts the time between the first two shots.

As one might suspect, this model also comes equipped with a muzzle brake, a unique two-chamber design which is unlike any such device previously used in Russian small arms. Another unusual feature is a side-mounted bayonet that is mounted to the right of the barrel. It does not interfere in any way with the underbarrel grenade launcher that can be attached.

Of course, the ultimate questions regarding such a rifle are simple: How accurate is it at various ranges? How reliable is it in a combat environment?

In May, 1997, the wraps were taken off the until-then top secret weapon. The event took place at a testing range the Russian army maintains near St. Petersburg. An officer displayed one of the early Nikonov-designed prototypes, insisting some 40,000 rounds had been fired through

it without any kind of stoppage. It stands to reason that, during that firing period, there had to be a change of barrels several times, but no mention was made of this possibility.

As with the older AK-47 and some of the subsequent models, the design of the AN-94 is rather simple. The Russians apparently understand that the more parts a gun has, the more there are to go wrong!

Operation is based upon the unoriginal concept of gases from the exploded propellant being diverted from the bore to the gas cylinder. The AN-94 utilizes the BBSP principle, which translates to "blowback shifted pulse." All of this adds up to a delay of the shock of the firing unit in rearmost position, thus allowing time for two bullets to leave the barrel at the rate of 1800 rpm. The shooter feels the recoil from the two bullets as a single shove against his shoulder. They already are well downrange before the recoil is felt by the shooter, thus improving the accuracy potential.

In the full-auto mode, the selector moves the trigger plate in such fashion that an interrupter comes in contact with the shoulder of this plate. The shooter then draws the bolt carrier's operating handle to the rear, thus feeding a round from the magazine. Each repeated movement of the bolt carrier to the rear results in another round being fed into the chamber.

A mark cut into the heavy-duty plastic of the receiver is the numeral

2. When the selector switch is moved to this setting, the rifle fires a two-round burst at the higher rate of fire.

In operation, the bolt carrier shoves the hammer into position for firing and the sear holds it there. The bolt directs the round into the chamber, this action powered by the rifle's shock absorber and the return spring. With the round in the chamber, the barrel is locked into the barrel extension by a pair of heavy locking lugs on the bolt. When the shooter pulls the trigger, the trigger plate is activated to move the sear and thus release the hammer. Driven by the main spring, the hammer falls to hit the firing pin.

The firing element slides within the carrier/stock, thus compressing the buffer spring. When the bullet speeds past the gas port in the barrel, sufficient gas is redirected through the port and against the gas cylinder. The action of the gas on the cylinder forces the piston to act upon the bolt carrier extension; in turn, this pushes the bolt carrier and the hammer to the rear. As one might expect, this series of actions results in the bolt being made to rotate, thus unlocking. The fired cartridge case is extracted, then ejected.

With the bolt carrier and hammer in their most rearward positions, the return spring and shock absorber combine their efforts to shove them forward. At this point, the sear is out of service for the moment, and the next cycle gets under way. The hammer, uninfluenced by the sear at this point, keeps moving, resulting

When field-stripped, the AN-94 pistol grip holds the safety lever, the firing-mode selector, the magazine latch and the trigger group.

in the 1800 rpm firing rate of those first two rounds.

After that second round has headed downrange, the sear and the interrupter return to their positions, the hammer now being retained by the sear. The bolt, guided by the bolt carrier, forces the next round into the chamber, resuming lower firing rate of 600 rounds per minute.

The rate of fire will continue until the trigger is released. When it is pulled again, the first two rounds fire at the high rate of fire, then the action returns to the 600 rpm mode.

This article would be incomplete without further mention of Gennadly Nikolayevich Nikonov. He was born in August, 1950, just as the Korean War was getting into full swing. Both of his parents were employed by Izhmash, the company where Nikonov is now a senior executive charged with design.

In 1968, Nikonov graduated from a technical school, where he had built a reputation for his interest in underwater small arms. He received recognition for his design of the trigger mechanism for an underwater rifle. Based upon this achievement, he soon became an employee of Izhmash as a technician on the staff of the arms plant's chief arms designer. The fact that the young man not only carried out his factory chores but spent most of his evenings in

classrooms at a local technical institute did not go unnoticed by those charged with shaping his future.

It was in 1976 that Nikonov, at the age of 26, was graduated from the Ishevak Mechanical Institute with a degree as an engineer. It was not long before he was assigned to develop a continuing number of arms, including a line of air-operated rifles. His work at that point was devoted to sporting arms, but this interim was only a stepping stone to larger and greater things.

In this early assignment, working with diverse theories and mechanisms, the young engineer demonstrated that he had an excellent grasp of the engineering needs for such work. He also appears to have been considered a good team leader, for he soon became a senior project manager whose assignment was to oversee the development of sniper-type, bolt-action, single-shot rifles, then a variety of full-auto military weapons.

The genius that Nikonov displayed in solving any number of serious engineering problems did not go unobserved by senior executives in the arms factory. The fact that the young engineer began to build an impressive portfolio of patents covering firearms mechanisms was bolstered by the fact that he had more than 40 copyrights in his own name.

The Soviet Union had great interest in the Olympic Games and an equal interest in winning for propaganda purposes abroad and for morale building at home. One of the projects to which Nikonov and his staff of engineers were assigned had to do with design of a straight-pull bolt for a rifle that would be used by Soviet athletes in the Biathlon segment of the winter games. In 1975, Nikonov embarked upon a post-graduate course of study that ultimately resulted in his being awarded a Ph.D.

In the 1980-85 period, before the Soviet Union began to disintegrate, Doctor Nikonov was assigned to a number of projects which were commissioned by the Soviet Ministry for Defense Industry. The AN-94 became one of those and he was awarded the title of Best Designer of the Ministry.

Even though the Soviet Union is defunct and Russia has become a more or less democratic nation, Doctor Nikonov has continued to work for the same organization, now a private enterprise known as the Izhmash Joint Stock Company. His pace is somewhat slower than in past years, for he suffered a serious heart attack several years ago. According to reports coming out of Eastern Europe, the attack was blamed upon overwork. ●

THE GEPARD MODULAR SUBMACHINE GUN

IN RUSSIA'S ANCIENT city of Saint Petersburg stands a factory that once housed the Institute of Military Mechanics. Today, this old Soviet institution is the seat of a capitalist-inspired armament-building firm, the Rex Firearms Company, Limited.

In such a democratic environment, military weapons are being designed and tested with much more efficiency than in the so-called Old Days, when bureaucrat after bureaucrat was involved in second guessing the experts in an effort to gain his own degree of credit for the final product.

One of the recent developments to come out of the Russian company's think tank is a submachine gun that is modular in design. Modular means that it can be one of several things simply by adding accessories or by substituting internal parts for a specific purpose. The Gepard—which translates from the Russian as Cheetah—was developed by a cooperative program between the Rex Firearms staff and Russia's Army Central Shooting Range,

which is headquartered near the town of Rzhevsk.

Managing director of Rex is Evegeniy B. Korotkov, who explains that the company was organized with the aid of what now is Baltic State Technical University (formerly that same old Institute for Military Mechanics!) According to him and his staff, the idea for the Gepard was to provide the shooter with a totally compact and versatile lightweight shooting machine. Without the magazine, weight of the new gun is approximately 4.4 pounds. With the steel buttstock fully extended, length of the Gepard is 25.1 inches; with the stock folded, length is reduced to only 16.5 inces. Width of the gun is only 38mm, which is slightly more than the width of the film you use in your favorite reflex camera. The standard magazine for the Gepard carries 22 rounds of 9mm ammo. With the magazine inserted into the gun, height of the gun is just 7.8 inches. There also is available a 40-shot magazine. Both are double-column designs stamped from sheet metal and detachable.

If you're familiar with Russian weaponry and look closely, you'll see that this new design bears great similarities to the Kalashnikov AKS-74U. The receiver appears to have been shortened and a different stock has been substituted, but some 65 percent of the parts in the new subgun interchange with those of the AKS-74U. In short, the old master still has his hand in!

As one might suspect, this design has been chambered for the Russian 9x18mm Makarov cartridge, but it doesn't end there. Without a change of barrels, the same gun will handle a new Russian 9x30mm cartridge, as well as the more familiar 9x21mm, the 9x19mm Parabellum and Browning's 9x17mm rounds.

According to Eveganiy Korotkov, the gun has been engineered so that the magazine is positioned at the Gepard's center of gravity. This, he contends, is an advantage in controlling the weapon when firing full-auto.

The Gepard's magazine follower features a specially designed spring rest that allows interchangeability of the various 9mm ammunition listed earlier. It should be noted that a change in dimensions of the 9mm cartridge to be fired does not require a change of barrels. Instead of barrels, the chambers are switched by means of a pair of screw-in inserts which fit into a threaded barrel extension.

One researcher, Valery N. Shilin, had the opportunity to fire the Gepard on the Russian Army Central Shooting Range. He found that one of the sleeves will handle rounds ranging from 9x17mm to 9x21mm. The second sleeve is designed specifically for the recently perfected 9x30mm cartridge.

In firing a mixture of 9x19 Parabellum and 9x19 RG-057 ammunition, Shilin found that the two rounds functioned without problems in spite of the differences in bullet lengths and shapes.

According to those who have fired the new subgun, it can penetrate the protective flak jacket currently being issued to Russian troops; it is equally damaging on steel plate and

With silencer attached and stock extended, this shooter finds the 4.4-pound basic weight of the Gepard submachine gun easy to handle. With 9x30mm Russian-made Grom ammo, it's said to have an effective range of 400 meters.

on a hardened titanium plate of 1.25mm thickness. These rounds—all of them reportedly the new 9x30 Grom cartridge with a hard alloy core—were fired at 400 meters, and the resulting groups showed that the gun has excellent control characteristics. Incidentally, the word Grom translates to mean Thunder and the cartridge was developed in the laboratories of the Rex Firearms Company. It can be loaded with either the hard-alloy-core bullet or with the familiar full metal jacket configuration.

According to Alexander Shevchenko, a test engineer at Rex Firearms and one of the designers of the Gepard, the subgun can be fired from a number of positions without undue discomfort. While best accuracy is achieved with the buttstock firmly pressed into the shoulder, the gun is light enough that it can be fired—stock folded, of course—with one hand or when held in a two-handed grip. It is suggested that the carrying sling be looped over the shoulder, offering added stability for such gymnastic efforts

The sights of the Gepard—or Cheetah, as some of us would prefer to call it—are not at all unusual. As one observer stated, "They are vintage Kalashnikov." That makes them no less effective, however, as hordes of Vietnam veterans probably would be quick to testify.

The rear sight, attached to the top of the gun's bolt cover, is the familiar flip-up type boasting a pair of open square notches. One notch is for the 100-meter range, the other for 200 meters. The mechanism is protected by a pair of heavy-duty ears. The front sight is positioned on the gun's gas chamber and is of the familiar post design. It is adjustable for both elevation and windage.

The barrel, which measures only 9.25 inches, is cut with four grooves with a right-hand twist of one turn in 13.7 inches. Both the bore and the chamber are chrome-plated.

The rear of the receiver, a basic Kalashnikov design, has been shortened to accept the hinge for the folding stock. The trigger mechanism shows no differences from that of the AKS-74U, and the stamped-out selector lever is positioned in the familiar location on the receiver's right side, above the trigger. This selector lever governs whether the gun is on safe, or is ready to fire in the semi-auto or full-auto mode. With the lever at its top position, the trigger is blocked and the gun is safe; lever in the low position, one is ready for semi-auto fire. With the lever in its center setting, marked AB for "automaticheski," the shooter is ready to fire full-auto at the rate of 600 to 750 rounds per minute.

Unique is the fact that the Gepard can be made to utilize three varying modes of operation: unlocked free blowback; locked, semi-free blowback, or with a locked breech, it becomes gas-operated. More about that later.

In operation, upon firing, the gun's bolt is forced to the rear, the extractor removing the empty case from the chamber and the ejector sending it through the ejection port located on the right side of the top cover.

As the bolt carrier continues to the rear, the recoil spring is compressed, the hammer is cocked, engaging with an auto-safety cocking cam. The cycle completed, the bolt group then is driven forward by the return spring. A new round is stripped out of the magazine to enter the chamber, and the bolt carrier, in turn, releases the hammer from the safety sear. The Gepard then is ready to fire.

When the trigger is released, the trigger extension moves forward to be held by the sear. When the trigger is drawn back for firing, the trigger extension hook disengages it from what is termed the hammer-cocking cam. Powered by the mainspring, the hammer pivots as it moves forward to hit the firing pin. Naturally, the firing pin is driven forward to strike the cartridge primer and fire the gun.

If firing in the full-auto mode, the sear is deactivated, making it impossible to retain the hammer. In virtually the same fashion as the Kalashnikov, the auto-safety sear is designed to hold back the hammer until the forward-moving bolt carrier releases it for the firing of the next round. It should be noted, incidentally, that this subgun has an additional safety feature, which is positioned on the trigger.

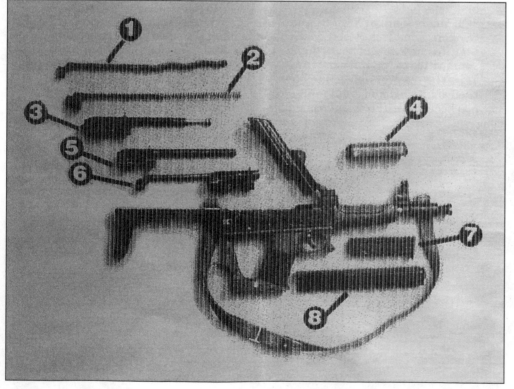

Field-stripped, the Gepard shows great similarities to the venerable Kalashnikov. Actually, 65 percent of parts are interchangeable. (1) return spring mechanism for 9x30mm Grom round; (2) return spring assembly with buffer; (3) bolt carrier and rotary-type bolt for 9x30 Grom cartridge; (4) upper handguard carrying gas chamber; (5) free blowback bolt, bolt carrier, two weights; (6) semi-free blowback bolt group; 22-round double-column magazine; (8) 40-round double-column magazine.

Specifications

Name: Gepard 9mm Submachine Gun.

Caliber: By means of modular chamber inserts, can fire 9 x 18 mm Makarov, 9 x 19 mm Parabellum FMJ, 9 x 19 RG-057, 9 x 21 RG-052, 9 x 21 RG-054, 9 x 30mm Grom.

Operation: With change of modular parts, can be fired by means of several different systems ranging from free blowback to gas-operated.

Cyclic rate: 600 to 750 rounds per minute, depending upon type of ammo and modular parts incorporated for special mission use.

Weight: 4.41 pounds without magazine.

Length: 25.1 inches (stock extended); 16.5 inches (stock collapsed).

Barrel: 9.25 inches; four right-hand grooves; 1:13.7-inch twist..

Magazine: 22- and 40-round capacities; double-column; welded of stamped sheet metal; follower has special spring rest allowing use of various types of 9mm ammo.

Stock: Metal, telescoping type.

Sights: Flip-up rear with square notches for 100 and 200 meters, protective ears; post front mounted on gas cylinder, with protective ears; adjustable for windage and elevation.

Maker: Rex Firearms Co.
1st Krasnoarmeyskaya Street
House 1
198005 St. Petersburg, Russia

As part of the modular planning for versatility, the engineers also have produced a set of bolt blocks that are meant to ensure several types of automatic action. Included are free blowback, free blowback with a pair of weights and gas-assisted blowback with the two weights and a heavier piston. An option is semi-free blowback in the listed combinations. Another option is gas operation with a rotary locking bolt.

In keeping with the modular approach to the design, in any of the firing modes additional weights and other balancing devices can be attached to the gun to improve its handling capabilities. For example, for Makarov High-Impulse ammo, a return spring mechanism with a fiberglass-reinforced buffer pad can be installed. There also is an auxiliary shock-absorbing spring that can be fitted on the guide rod. Or a counter-balanced return rod may be substituted for the gun's standard return spring assembly.

Pursuing the modular concept, there are several muzzle attachments that have been developed to meet special mission needs. Included are muzzle brakes, silencers, flash hiders and recoil-reducing compensators.

Interestingly, the Russians claim the Gepard can be fired with accuracy to a range of 400 yards, using the new 9x30mm Grom round. This is not the usual range suggested for submachine gun use, but if this boast is true, it brings a new dimension to use of this type of armament.

For the sake of comparison, we should report that when several types of 9mm ammo were fired through the Gepard at the Russian army range, velocities ranged from a low of 1082 fps for the venerable 9x18mm Makarov round to approximately 1968 fps for the 9x30mm Grom cartridge. The engineers claim that special construction used in the barrel of the Gepard is responsible for an increase in velocities of nearly 20 percent over conventional barrel designs.

The staff at the Rex Firearms Company, of course, is interested in selling guns and suggestions have been made that our own police and Armed Forces take a long look at the Gepard. Rest assured that at least one of these subguns has found its way to Fort Benning and probably some of our nation's firearms think tanks for a long, hard look. ●

These are the 9mm cartridges that can be fired in the Gepard subgun. From left are two 9x30mm Groms with differing bullet styles; 9x21mm RG-054; 9x21mm RG-052; 9x18 blank cartridge; 9x19mm Parabellum; 9x19mm RG-057; 9x18 High Impulse Makarov; 9x18 standard Makarov; 9x17mm Browning. The 9x30 requires special chamber inserts for firing.

CHAPTER 15

THE NEW STURMGEWEHR: HECKLER & KOCH'S G36

Here Is Germany's Effort To Keep Up With Nato's Current Armament Standards!

THE INTRODUCTION OF a new military rifle by an industrialized nation is not a small event. Unlike sporting arms, military small arms suffer unusually long gestation periods and many, more often than not, suffer a painless death during the embryonic stage. A law of small arms existence seems to be once a design takes hold—and is issued to the troops—it becomes a life unto itself.

The M4 Carbine currently being issued to American forces is a classic example, because it is nothing more than an abbreviated and enhanced version of the M-16 that was dates back to the mid-1960s; a statement to the M-16's longevity.

Therefore, it was a news event of major proportions when the German military placed an order for a substantial number of new rifles built by Heckler & Koch GmbH of Oberndorf, Germany. This new weapon is the H&K G36. It is, like the M4, chambered for the 5.56x45mm NATO round, and like the previously mentioned M-16, employs similar operating principles.

"However, it would be a mistake to create the impression that this latest

The G36 E assault rifle features an 18.9-inch barrel and modular construction. The select-fire weapon has a receiver made of reinforce polymer. Ambidextrous controls include the safety/selector lever, magazine release, cocking lever and bolt catch.

Teutonic wonder from the land of Krupp steel is nothing more than what we have already seen, even if dressed in different furniture, because it does offer features that are a first in a military small arm," reports Frank W. James, an acknowledged expert on Heckler & Koch products. He is author of the classic volume, *Project 64: The MP5 Submachine Gun Story,* published several years ago. Due to his familiarity, we assigned him to check out Heckler & Koch's latest entry.

"When the subject is military small arms, all the experts and commentators watch the German munitions manufacturers closely. Besides being the instigators of two world wars, the Germans always have been at the forefront of military small arms evolution. They were the first to develop the pistol-caliber submachine gun in the closing stages of World War I. Then, between the two world wars, they pioneered the general-purpose, belt-fed machine gun, first with the MG34 and later with the MG42. The MG42, in various forms and calibers, still is being used by a significant number of NATO ground forces," James points out.

A Heckler & Koch training instructor demonstrates advantages of a rifle that can be equipped with two different sighting systems. One sight, a red dot reflex type, can be utilized for close range work, while the second sight can be zeroed for long distance shooting.

The Heckler & Koch G36 is a true military assault rifle. A new design capable of select fire, it features modular construction and offers advantages not currently available with any competitive design.

"The Germans also developed the second-generation submachine gun with the introduction of the MP-38, only to be followed by the easier-to-manufacture MP-40, but the most significant German achievement in the field of the military small arms was the introduction of the *Sturmgewehr*, or assault rifle."

The first assault rifle almost died in its embryonic stages, because Adolf Hitler didn't understand the need for a new category of small arms. However, the designers and military authorities hid it from him by first labeling the gun a "machine pistol," the German designation for what the rest of the world calls a submachine gun.

The assault rifle increased the firepower of the individual foot soldier exponentially, because it was capable of full-auto aimed fire with a round more powerful than the submachine gun's typical pistol cartridge, but one that was less powerful than those used in the full-size battle rifle.

A Russian sergeant by the name of Kalashnikov subsequently designed an improved version of the assault rifle, but the AK-47 and its follow-on variations remain strikingly similar in size and shape to the original MKb42(42), MKb42(H) and the eventual MP43/1.

"For general purpose usage, the assault rifle outclasses every category of military small arm in existence. This is the reason they remain the standard service arm of every major and many minor nations of the world except one—Germany!" Frank James points out.

"The people who created the first assault rifle have not until now equipped their military forces with a true assault rifle. The German Bundeswehr has used the H&K-manufactured G3 since the mid-1950s, but this particular model is what is commonly classified as a battle rifle. Unlike the typical assault rifle that is shorter and lighter, the G3 fires the full-power 7.62x51mm NATO (308 Winchester) cartridge.

With an empty weight of 7.28 pounds, the H&K G36 is not tiring in close quarters battle (CQB) drills. This offers an immense advantage during hours upon hours of waiting for the signal for an assault by military and law enforcement special teams.

A member of the Finnish Army undergoes training with the H&K G36 KE, the carbine version of the basic weapon. The gun, although light in weight, is easy to control in full-auto fire as this soldier demonstrates on close-range targets.

"The G3 battle rifle is a well-made gun and it has a great reputation for reliability, but the fact remains that by today's standards, it is heavy, unwieldy and hard to maneuver in tight spaces. The latter is a vital consideration for any modern military small arm."

What the German small arms planners tried to do two decades ago was jump a category and create, yet again, a new category of military small arm, because Heckler & Koch developed a new class of military small arm in the G-11.

The G-11 used caseless ammunition launching a 4.5mm projectile. It was a strange looking weapon, appearing to be more like a trombone case with an optical sight attached on top. Dynamit-Nobel developed the caseless technology and it was neither an easy nor an inexpensive proposition. "In fact, if one phrase can be used to describe the entire G-11 project, it would be that it wasn't cheap," James opines.

The Heckler & Koch G36 KE carbine has a 12.5-inch barrel. This barrel produces muzzle velocities of nearly 2800 feet per second with standard military ammunition.

The G-11 firing mechanism was complicated, very involved, and once removed from the synthetic outer case, it resembled the guts of a clock. The developers claimed that at the project's end, they had solved all the problems experienced during testing.

To give you a hint as to the difficulties suffered by those testing the G-11 in the prototype stages, it soon earned the label "the self-firing Black Forest Cuckoo Clock." Unfortunately, a "catastrophe" struck the German military and the G-11 procurement budgets before production began: Peace broke out!

European communism threw in the towel, the Berlin Wall fell and suddenly rich West Germany was forced to provide and care for all their destitute relatives in the former East Germany.

Virtually over night, there was no money left in the treasury for the orphaned G-11. The Bundeswehr was forced to make do with their increasingly obsolete G3 rifles, while at the same time being obliged to figure out what they were going to do with the millions of Kalashnikov rifles they inherited from their cousins to the east who had just adopted the latest model, the AK-74.

"Another threatening and dangerous problem was the Russian-designed ammunition for the AK-74, which by West German standards was extremely toxic and harmful to the firer, not just the firee. The AK-74 muzzle device was designed in such a way that it blew highly toxic heavy metals from the priming compound of the ammunition back onto the AK-74 shooter's face and thereby poisoned

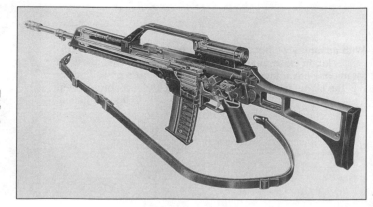

This cut-away view of the G36 E assault rifle shows the gas-actuated piston and bolt carrier with cocking lever. The bolt carrier controls the cam-operated six-lug bolt that locks into the barrel bushing.

the shooter," James' research shows. The German military also discovered they had a mammoth surplus of AK-74 bayonets which quickly became a design requirement on the new G36.

The failure of the Federal German armed forces to order the actual production of the G-11 was a nightmare come true for Heckler & Koch. The company had invested heavy resources into this new technology and without an actual sale they were facing insolvency and bankruptcy. However, British Aerospace purchased H&K and that brought about an infusion of much needed cash, as well as a number of un-German-like lay-offs from the facility at Oberndorf.

"Yet, the German Bundeswehr still needed a modern combat rifle. The situation was made even more critical when Germany committed troops to be part of the NATO Rapid Reaction Force, and everyone suddenly realized that every other member of this force was armed with rifles chambering the 5.56x45mm NATO round. The result was the H&K-designed G36.

"It is not a radical design like the caseless ammo G-11, but it is a design that the makers contend offers a significant number of advantages over competitive rifles," Frank James tells us.

The G36 is a gas-operated, select-fire, folding-stock rifle. In appearance, it combines elements of the past H&K designs (namely the use of polymer and modular assembly), a detachable carrying handle that more or less resembles a really radically stretched out M-16 suitcase handle and a SIG-550-type polymer magazine, complete with locking studs.

The G36 employs a high-strength, carbon fiber-reinforced polymer receiver, carrying handle, grip and folding buttstock. The gas-operated system uses a short-stroke piston and this stands in stark contrast to the direct action gas operation—sometimes called the "Ljungman System"—of the Stoner-designed M-16. The use of a short-stroke piston keeps the internal mechanism cleaner than the direct action system. In their promotional material, Heckler & Koch says that it can go 5000 rounds before cleaning. "This design aspect, if proven true in the field, will be a precedent of its own merit for modern military small arms," James feels.

The G36 is a modular small arm. According to reports, it can easily be converted in the field by a soldier with minimal training into any of three variants: the G36K is the version with the shortest barrel (12.5 inches); the G36 is the standard version infantry weapon and features a barrel of 18.9 inches; and the third version is the MG36 which features a heavier 18.9-inch barrel for sustained fire.

A close cousin of these is the MG36 E light machine gun, which is identical to the MG36 rifle, except is marketed with a bipod and, in addition to the 30-round magazines, there is a 100-round drum-type magazine.

The G36 design is completely ambidextrous. The selector levers copy those seen previously on H&K designs, only these are located more toward the grip and are easier to grasp. There is no need for the shooter to break his grasp of the pistol grip in order to operate the selector. The selector positions are safe, semi-, two-round burst and fully-automatic. The firing positions are highlighted in red paint, while the safe position is a white "S".

In one respect, the G36 mimics the design characteristics of previous H&K military-style rifles. The big difference here, however, is the

Specifications

Name:	Heckler & Koch G36 E.
Caliber:	5.56 x 45mm NATO.
Operation:	Select fire, gas-operated, short-stroke piston mechanism; an optional two-round burst is available.
Weight:	7.28 pounds (G36 E); 7.72 pounds (MG36 E); 6.62 pounds (G36 KE); carbon fiber, reinforced polymer receiver.
Length:	39.29 inches (stock extended, G36 E, MG36 E); 29.84 inches (stock folded); inches (stock extended, G36 KE); 24.21 inches (stock folded).
Barrel:	18.90 inches (G36 E, MG36 E); 12.52 inches (G36 KE); 1:7-inch twist.
Magazine:	30-rounds; polymer, see-through; 100-round for Light support version.
Sights:	1.5x optical; 3x optical, red dot optional.
Maker:	Heckler & Kock GmbH P.O. Box 1329 78722 Oberndorf, Neckar, Germany
Importer:	Heckler & Koch, Inc. 21480 Pacific Blvd. Sterling, VA 20166-8903

The MG36 E is a light machine gun version of the standard rifle with a heavier barrel for sustained full-auto fire. This same weapon can be converted to the short-barrel carbine by change of barrels. Here it is outfitted with the optional dual sight and the 100-round drum magazine.

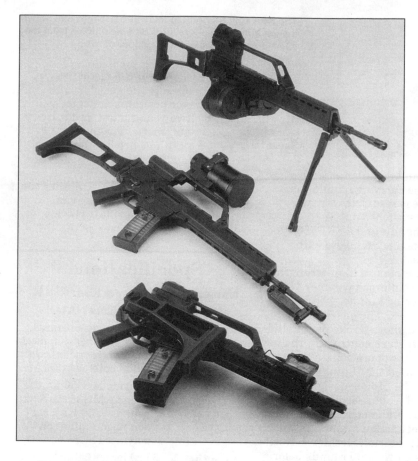

The G36 actually is a family of weapons sharing the same basic design, making it easily convertible. From top are the MG36 E light machine gun, the G36 E assault rifle and the G36K carbine.

receiver to which the barrel is affixed is made entirely of a high-strength fiber-reinforced plastic.

The polymer receiver contains the bolt assembly. The bolt assembly consists of the bolt head carrier, the cocking lever, the bolt head, the control bolt, a cross pin and the firing pin. The bolt head is powered into position by the recoil spring guide rod assembly that is fastened to the back plate. The back plate is retained in the polymer receiver by a lug and a locking pin which also is used to hold the pistol grip trigger mechanism to the receiver.

The unit that combines the pistol grip and the trigger mechanism is worth a few words of discussion. The pistol grip, which is attached to the receiver by means of two locking pins, contains the trigger mechanism and the bolt catch. At the front of the trigger guard is the bolt catch slide, which is used for holding the bolt open in case there is no empty magazine inserted.

Operation of the cocking lever, located on top of the receiver but under the carrying handle, is completely ambidextrous. It's a flat lever that swivels either right or left, whatever the shooter requires. If the magazine is removed and the bolt has been pulled to the rear, the operator is trained to push upward on the bolt catch, which is located inside the trigger guard at the forward upward corner, to engage the bolt lock. This will lock the bolt carrier in the open position. After insertion of a loaded magazine, all the operator has to do to release the bolt is swivel the cocking lever out and pull to the rear.

If the weapon is dirty or fouled, this swiveling cocking lever can be used as

The H&K G36 is completely ambidextrous and can be used easily by both right and left-handed operators. Here, the training instructor loads a full magazine into the weapon.

H&K G36 Optical Sight Reticle Pattern

1. Lead mark for firing at targets moving from left to right at a speed of approx. 15 km/h at a range of 200 m.

2. Point of aim at 200 m range.

3. Circular reticle (interior diameter = 1.75 m man size at 400 m range)

4. Lead mark for targets moving from right to left at a speed of approx. 15 km/h at 200 m range.

5. Horizontal line to find out whether the weapon is canted.

6. Point of aim for firing at approx 400 m range.

7. Point of aim for firing at 600 m range.

8. Point of aim for firing at 800 m range.

9. Man size of 1.75 m at ranges X.

(0-200 m.)

(400 m.)

(600 m.)

(800 m.)

8 6 4 2

---

a forward-assist device. To accomplish this, the cocking lever is swiveled out, then pushed in against the bolt. The bolt carrier can now be pushed closed until it locks fully. Once the bolt is locked, the cocking lever should be pulled away from the bolt carrier and allowed to swivel back to its position of rest. This technique also can be used when there is a need for low-noise loading of the weapon.

The curved box magazine of the G36 holds 30 rounds. It is made of an impact-resistant plastic that is translucent, so it is easy to check the rounds loaded in any magazine. On the outside of the right sidewall of the magazine tube are two female couplings that mate with two male couplings positioned on the left outside wall of a corresponding magazine. This allows the user to connect together a series of magazines without need of tape or metal clamps.

"Perhaps, the most distinctive feature of the HK G36 is the sighting system," James feels." The gun comes standard with a 1.5x optical sight mounted inside the carrying handle, but the carrying handle is detachable and in its place a second sighting arrangement can be installed. This second carrying handle houses two sights: a 3x telescopic sight and a 1x reflex sight."

The reflex sight has an illuminated red dot reticle and is designed for quick reaction shots at ranges out to 200 meters. It's powered by a daylight

collector and the brightness of the red dot adjusts automatically to the ambient lighting conditions. In the event there is insufficient light for activating the red dot, a battery may be used to generate the necessary power. The 3x telescopic sight is intended for target engagement at longer ranges.

The optical sight has a reticle with gradations from 200 to 800 meters in increments of 200 meters. The outer lateral surfaces of the circular reticle serve simultaneously as lead marks for aiming at laterally moving targets, which are traveling at a speed of 15 kilometers per hour at a

range of 200 meters. The interior diameter of the circular reticle corresponds to the height of a man at a range of 400 meters. The range marks at the bottom left, which help to find and set the range at 200, 400 and 800 meters, also are based on a man-size target of about six feet. In similar manner, the heights of the cross-marks at 600 and 800 meters correspond to the height of a man standing at those respective ranges.

For operations during low-light or night conditions, Zeiss has built a night sight attachment, the NSA 80, that incorporates the principle of

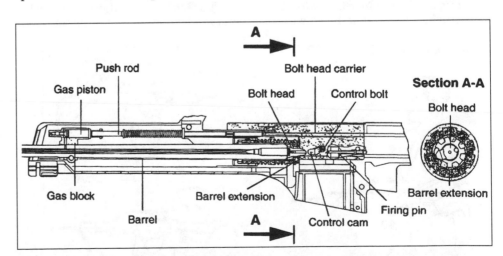

In this artist's illustration, the bolt of the G36 E rifle is locked. In this condition, the bolt head is in the foremost position. The locking lugs of the bolt head engage in the corresponding locking recesses of the barrel extension.

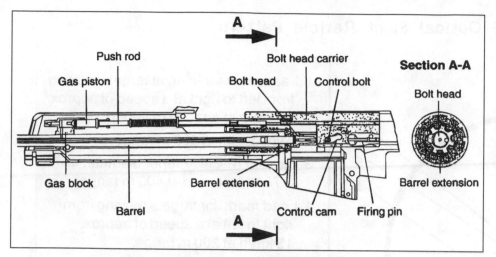

Section A-A

With the bullet fired, gases push the bolt head carrier via the gas piston and the pushrod at the rear. The control bolt and the control cam in the bolt head carrier rotate, thus unlocking the bolt head.

residual light intensification. The NSA 80 is a second-generation night vision device, but an enhanced version is also available that operates at third-generation night vision device levels. The NSA 80 is an optical device with 1x magnification and is powered by a Mignon alkaline manganese battery.

"The big advantage of the optional carrying handle and two daylight sighting systems lies in the fact that each sight can be sighted in for a different zero and thereby provide the end-user with the ability to have a weapon zeroed for both long range precision shooting and close-range, room-length engagements." James points out.

The G36 barrel boasts a rifling twist ratio of 1:7 inches. As such, it is designed to be used with the heavier 62- and 69-grain 5.56mm bullets. "There are a number of differences between the H&K G36 and the M-16 family of weapons, which in North America, at least, will be its major competitor," Frank James points out. "The first noticeable difference is that the burst mode on the G36 has no memory, unlike the M-16, because the G36 provides a complete burst with

Carrying Modes

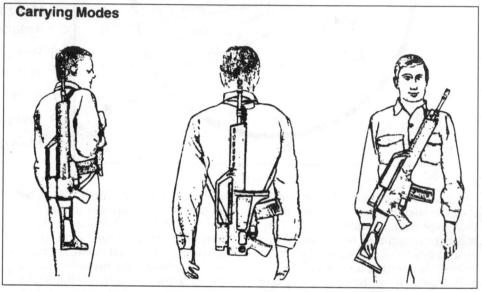

every pull of the trigger. Due to the design of its gas system, the G36 should prove to be a cleaner gun, and even though the G36 magazine is of polymer construction, it is a durable design with several inherent and superior design features when compared to other magazines."

The G36 is a modular military rifle and more versatile than competitive designs. The same basic rifle can be either a carbine-style entry team weapon for law enforcement, a regular length rifle for the military, or with the appropriate changes a squad automatic weapon. This type of versatility is sure to make this weapon a success in any application.

The G36 E version also may be used to fire rifle grenades that do not exceed a weight of 13 ounces. For this, one can utilize either propellant cartridges or ball ammunition, James discovered in checking out the rifle. For firing, the rifle grenade is slid onto the rifle grenade guide over the flash hider.

The grenade then can be fired off the shoulder, with the shooter standing or kneeling. This choice of positions allows for aimed and accurate fire. At the opposite extreme, the grenade can be fired from the hip, but this shot is usually inaccurate.

"The Germans have always demonstrated the ingenuity and the technology which has proven to be the cutting edge in small arms development. The G36 from H&K is only the latest example of this continuing evolution," James concludes.

Firing Positions

CHAPTER 16

THE AR-15 IN POLICE WORK

Here's A Working Street Cop's Evaluation Of This Popular Rifle Based Upon Experience.

THE MODERN M-16A2 military rifle has earned an excellent reputation. Yet, when the rifle was first issued many looked at the high-grade plastics being used and derisively referred to the M-16 as the rifle from Mattel Toys! Designed by Eugene Stoner and initially manufactured and promoted by the Armalite Corporation, the Colt-produced M-16 was an important step in military weapons development. It almost didn't make it.

Pushed by Air Force chief of staff General Curtis E. LeMay, the M-16 was intended to be issued to Air Force security personnel in Vietnam. The architect of American victory in the air against both Germany and Japan and an avid shooter, General LeMay knew his small arms. The M-16 came at a time of transition in the world's military armament. Lighter battle rifles were being designed, partly to allow the individual soldier to carry additional equipment in the form of light anti-tank weapons, as well as mortars and communication equipment. Infantry no longer needed full-power rifles capable of plunging fire or 500-yard accuracy, according to military theory.

The first M-16s did, in fact, prove to be effective. The AK-47 was by no means universal issue among Viet Cong or North Vietnamese Army troops. The Russian-made SKS and even the old Mosin Nagant bolt-action rifles were common in the early days of the conflict. The M-16 would prove far more capable than these and in most ways superior to the AK-47. The M-16 was shown to need maintenance more often than the AK, but eventually it won the respect of most UN troops armed with it. This admiration was based upon the virtues of light weight, fast handling and equally fast reloading.

The original 5.56mm loading was highly destructive against personnel, but somehow the Army would manage to change the original specifications of the load to reduce effectiveness and reliability. It was found that powder clogged the rifle's gas port. Eventually the problem would be solved and the rifle steadily was improved through the M-16A1 and A2 modifications, and more recently, the A3 version. Heavy lubrication and frequent cleaning no longer are quite so imperative. Today's rifles do demand maintenance, of course, and many match shooters have found that the clean M-16 is much more accurate.

The rifle once got the curled lip treatment among U.S. service personnel, but the M-16 is now the envy of several major foreign forces. The French have issued the FAMAS, a bullpup model that fires from an unlocked breech. Reliability is questionable. The British regard the defects of their SA80 as a scandal, and the rifle is despised by many members of the British Army. The veterans of Ireland's Ulster and Belfast battles longed for the M-16. The bullpup SA80 wasn't suitable for firing around walls and the optical sight has proved to be less than perfect for close range affrays.

"It was inevitable that the M-16 would find it's way into American police work," says veteran police officer Robert K. Campbell. "A few of these rifles are full-auto weapons, but most are the semi-auto civilian-available version.

The AR-15 HBAR model features a 20-inch heavy barrel and was introduced by Colt in 1991. It has become a standby of some law enforcement organizations.

The flip-type sight on the AR-15 HBAR has a large aperture for picking up close targets, but simple thumb pressure turns it over.

Model, which was introduced in 1995. In addition to the 223 Remington (5.56mm) round fired by these models, still another version listed as the Colt Match Target Lightweight is being advertised; it is chambered for the familiar 9mm Parabellum cartridge. Needless to say, perhaps, there may be some question concerning the need for a 9mm rifle in competition circles.

Getting back to specifics and calling a rifle what it actually is, the AR-15 HBAR is a gas-operated semi-automatic rifle, with an overall length of 39-5/8 inches and a 20-inch barrel. Rate of barrel twist is 1:7 inches, with a right-hand twist and six grooves handling the work. The civilian version is sold with a five-round box magazine, but law enforcement agencies can order magazines capable of loading either 20 or 30 rounds. The rifle has a windage and elevation-adjustable rear sight that can worked with finger pressure; the front sight is a post type. The stock, grip and forend are of a man-made composition. The rifle has a military black matte finish and a bolt forward assist feature that helps to seat a stubborn cartridge, if necessary. Sans ammunition, weight is 7.5 pounds.

Firing the 5.56mm cartridge, this rifle has a maximum range of 1000 meters and a practical range of 550 meters, according to Colt sources. When the weapon is fired, gas is bled off into a tube which actuates the action, blowing back the strong rotary bolt. The upper and lower

"To some degree, peace officers always have relied upon rifles from early mounted ranger units to the modern state trooper. The handgun is neither powerful nor accurate compared to the rifle. The handgun's main virtue is portability. Whenever we can, we should face danger with a long gun in hand.

"Rifles are useful against barricaded felons or those in vehicles. With the existence of heavily armed gangs and the universal use of automobiles in crime, the patrol rifle has an important role to play. Many officers have prior military service and are familiar with the workings and capabilities of the AR-15, the basis of the M-16. Anyone can be trained to use this rifle well in short order."

Based on his own experience and that of others of his close acquaintance, Campbell urges, "Avoid aftermarket magazines like the plague. Use only factory Colt or military contract magazines for duty. We attempted to use a plastic aftermarket magazine during our evaluations, but it cracked on the second reloading! Experience with off-brand metal mags is little better."

He also feels "there is little reason for a department to adopt the full-auto AR-15 version. Fast semi-auto fire should accomplish anything we need to do. Mastering full-auto techniques such as the figure eight and shoot-through tactics are demanding of time, training and ammunition. In hostage rescue work,

accuracy will be keynoted. In times of war, civilian casualties are accepted. Firepower is everything. At the opposite extreme, in police work, accuracy is everything. Innocent casualties are unacceptable."

At the moment, the Colt Manufacturing Company of Hartford, Connecticut does not list the AR-15 among its offerings, calling it, instead, the "Colt Match Target HBAR Rifle." There are several variations, including the HBAR II Competition

The smaller aperture on the sight is meant for zeroing in on targets at longer ranges.

Sights on the HBAR model are finger adjustable and, according to R.K. Campbell, quite precise. Standard sights require a cartridge nose for adjustment.

Further disassembly is not recommended by other than the department armorer.

"Cleaning and lubrication is the key to AR-15 reliability," Bob Campbell has found. "Remember to allow solvent to dry after cleaning, because solvent will attack grease and oil. Carbon deposits must be removed from the bolt and extractor. The chamber should be clean but not lubed. Locking lugs and the bolt ring should receive a few small drops of oil. Break-Free is the traditional AR-15 lubricant in our police department.

"We have seen fouling collect in the lower receiver during hard use. If enough of it accumulates, it will affect the trigger pull. Keep the AR-15 clean!"

This South Carolina officer has found that the combination of a last shot hold-open device and a well-situated magazine release along with a magazine that is fast to insert make the AR-15 the easiest of battle rifles to keep in action. "To make the AR-15 ready, simply insert a loaded magazine, pull the cocking handle, then put the weapon on safe. For ready storage in the home or vehicle the rifle is best left chamber-empty. We have found the 20-round magazine to be the best choice for our needs, but should be held to 18 for reliability.

"My personal AR-15 is the HBAR version. This rifle is deadly accurate. The sighting equipment consists of a fully adjustable peep in the rear and an adjustable post front sight. The rear peep flips to a small aperture long range sight or large aperture short range sight. Our department's

receiver are of high-tensile-strength aluminum. Steel parts are finished flat black. The bore and chamber are chrome-lined, considered a good feature when firing high-intensity ammunition. The carrying handle is located above the slide on the standard model, but with the HBAR version, the handle may be removed for easy optical sight mounting. The safety is located on the left side of the receiver and is actuated easily without shifting the firing grip. The magazine release is on the right side

of the receiver. The AR-15 can be reloaded quickly, the effort hastened by dropping the empty magazine, with the trigger finger pressuring the release button.

Field-stripping is simple. Making certain the rifle is unloaded, release the magazine. Firmly press to the right the takedown pin which is above the rear hand grip. Pull the upper receiver upward; it is hinged and will fold downward. Then pull the cocking handle to the rear. This removes the bolt carrier assembly.

The knurled button is the forward assist, which will help seat a cartridge that is not chambered completely.

Heavy knurling on the forward assist button, as well as other controls on the rifle, make it relatively idiot-proof.

enthuses. "It is hard to believe it was introduced 40 years ago!"

There are three criteria that must be met by combat ammunition. Reliability is foremost, followed by accuracy and ballistic effect. Campbell feels Black Hills loads meet or exceed every reasonable criterion. "We found generic ball ammunition was excellent for practice, while some foreign loads were terrible."

Modern AR-15 rifles have a tight barrel twist of 1:7 inches, suitable for heavy bullets weighing up to 69 grains. Original M-16 barrels had a 1:14-inch twist, while the M-16A1 rifling was 1:12 inches. "Bullets heavier than 55 grains may not prove accurate in older tubes," Campbell has found, adding, "Even the 40-grain bullets can be highly accurate in the new-type barrels.

"The military 55-grain FMJ load breaks 3200 feet per second. This load fragments in flesh, the only military jacketed load to do so, although some break in half. The SS109 62-grain Penetrator is not suitable for general police use. A superior load for all-round use is the 55-grain JSP. For best results we should carry a premium softpoint. The 55-grain softpoint is very destructive with little chance of perforating the body, given good shot placement.

"The 5.56mm rifle is used in the hostage rescue role with good results. In the anti-sniper role, it can perform admirably. The virtues of low penetration and instant effectiveness make it a good choice. Even the 69-grain load is more readily deflected by glass than any 30-caliber rifle load.

"The 5.56mm is at its best when used against gangs and as a hostage rescue tool. It is far superior to any

issue AR-15 has been fitted with Innovative Weaponry night sights. The IWI sight is a peep type, instead of the usual bar-dot or three-dot self-luminous arrangement. This combination seems to hang in the air in darkness, a circle with a post in the center. For the serious urban rifle, this is a must-have option."

Campbell and members of his North Carolina department have found the AR-15 an easy rifle to shoot well. Like every instrument, practice is required for real proficiency. If the sights are set to print a 55-grain bullet four inches high at 15 meters, the bullet will be practically dead on to 300 meters. "This meets every requirement we can foresee," Campbell reports. This officer also has found the AR-15 to be a formidable small game rifle, coupling flat shooting, gilt-edged accuracy and an instant second shot.

"The AR-15's forte is rapid fire at medium distances. Using the rear

peep, we were able to rapidly acquire and strike man-size targets consistently and rapidly at from 15 to 100 yards. If one must adjust the sights on the standard model, a bullet nose is all that is required for the click adjustable rear sight. The front sight has a plunger that must be depressed. The HBAR's sights may be moved with the fingers."

Campbell considers the AR-15 a phenomenon for a rifle that is not bedded in the conventional sense. Even field-stripping does not affect the rifle's zero. He terms accuracy as superb with a variety of ammunition.

Settling into a prone position during one session, he fired several one-inch, 100-yard groups with Black Hills 52-grain Match loads. Head shots from a hasty rest at 50 yards were not difficult. The forward assist was never used. Function was perfect with over 750 rounds of ammunition. "The AR-15 is among the finest battle rifles in the world," this officer

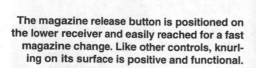

The magazine release button is positioned on the lower receiver and easily reached for a fast magazine change. Like other controls, knurling on its surface is positive and functional.

The HBAR version of the AR-15 was introduced by Colt as a competition gun, but law enforcement quickly saw the advantages of the upgraded model.

pistol-caliber carbine. The 40-grain load is often touted as an urban option for the 5.56mm rifle, but function was sluggish in my personal rifle. Fired cases were not thrown as far in ejection and the bolt did not hold open on the last shot. There are questions concerning adequate penetration and even of bullets disintegrating before they reach the target. Conduct your own tests and I believe you will reach the conclusions I have."

Evan Marshall is a respected compiler of shooting histories. He warns that some of the figures for the 5.56mm seem high, since they were created by trained snipers. All 5.56mm loads were well over 90 percent effective. In nine out of 10 instances, the 5.56mm was instantly effective. The 9mm hardball is rated as a one-in-four stopper by the Police Marksman Association. The very best handgun loads approach 90 percent after multiple shots have been factored out.

"It is easy to understand that the rifle is at least twice as effective as any handgun. Remember that most rifle histories were taken from long range affairs. The handgun battles studied by Evan Marshall most often took place at conversational distances," Campbell points out.

"Marshall warns that 5.56mm performance falls off rapidly past 100 yards, but the AR-15 gives officers and armed civilians an offensive weapon for use in extreme circumstance. In many ways, the Colt AR-15 is better suited to police work than to military service." ●

Average Accuracy Colt AR-15 100 Yards, 5-shot Groups	
Ammunition Bullet Wgt. (grs.)/Style	Group Size (ins.)
Black Hills	
52 Match	.95
55 Softpoint	1.2
60 Softpoint	1.1
68 Match	1.0
Winchester	
55 USA	1.3
55 Softpoint	1.1
64 Softpoint	1.05
Norinco	
55 ball	2.75
Federal	
55 American Eagle FMJ	1.4
55 Softpoint	.95
Hornady	
55 V MAX	.95
40 V MAX	1.25

The flash suppressor not only shields muzzle flash but prevents telltale grass and dirt from being disturbed at the muzzle when firing from the prone position

Section III

Submachine Guns

CHAPTER 17

THE FAMILY OF FIFTIES

Like A Lot Of Other Military Hardware, The 50 Browning Machine Gun Cartridge Has Found New Life In Today's World.

A FEW YEARS ago, the 50 Browning Machine Gun cartridge had come to be considered more or less obsolete for modern warfare. It was being phased out of military Tables of Equipment, along with the late Mr. Browning's equipment for firing said round.

However, in 1985, a group of dedicated civilian shooters established the Fifty Caliber Shooters' Association, Incorporated, better known among members simply as the FCSA, for the specific purpose of advancing the sporting uses of the 50 BMG cartridge. The organization was incorporated in the state of Tennessee, but currently is headquartered at FCSA, P.O. Box 5109, Riverside, CA 92517-5109.

The primary sport of the organization at this time is 1000-yard shooting competitions, with a mission to advance long-range accuracy shooting with 50-caliber rifles. At this writing, the FCSA has over 1600 members and is growing steadily. The organization now is sponsoring about 10 organized 1000-yard matches each year in various locations across the continental United States.

According to retired Army Major John Plaster, author of the *Ultimate Sniper*, "Most of today's 50-caliber military rifles were developed without one single dollar of government money. To give credit where credit is due, it has been the private sector perfectionists of the Fifty Caliber Shooters' Association who have led the way in developing 50-caliber cartridges, rifles and 1000-plus-yard shooting know-how."

Organizational statistics show that only seven percent of the members are military or law enforcement. Sixty-five percent are salaried professionals or business owners and 60 percent have annual incomes in excess of

U.S. military personnel zero their Barrett M82A1 50 BMG rifles during Desert Storm operations in 1990. All of our services now use this as their Special Application Scoped Rifle. In this role it is used for destroying vehicles, ammo dumps, minefields and enemy emplacements.

The 50 BMG rifle was developed and promoted originally in the 1980s by sportsmen, without any federal money involved. The military became interested later.

$50,000. With the price of 50 BMG rifles ranging from $2,500 to more than $7,000 each, and custom-loaded rounds costing upward from four dollars apiece, a healthy recreation budget would appear to be a necessity.

It was in the late 1980s that the military began to think about the need for a big-bore rifle. Desert Storm created an unexpected demand for 50 BMG guns and the ammunition, since such long-range firepower can become a virtual necessity in the vastness of a Middle Eastern desert. The guns that became highly important were those that could be shoulder-fired with the same cartridge, one man handling the chore, if necessary, rather than requiring a crew-served weapon.

The Marine Corps was the first to begin testing such rifles seriously and settled on the Barrett Light 50 semi-automatic as the gun that would meet the qualifications for what came to be came termed a Special Application Scoped Rifle.

The gun was designed by Ronnie Barrett, once a professional photographer in Murfreesboro, Tennessee, where his factory now is located. Other designers and manufacturers soon followed in their efforts to come up with a competing

Don Camario sights in on the wrecked car 200 yards away. He is firearms instructor for the Island of Hawaii Police Department and was highly interested in the gun's capabilities and possibilities.

The Stoner 50 is currently under development and ultimately will be aimed at the military market. Like others, it fires the 50 Browning Machine Gun cartridge.

For our test of the L.A.R. Grizzly 50 Big Boar single-shot rifle, a wrecked car was used as the target. A bulldozer was used to move it into position.

semi-auto and perhaps capture a piece of the military market, while others began turning out single-shots, mostly on a special order basis.

Barrett's Model 82A-1 semi-auto was introduced in 1985. Other self-loading models meeting with little success have been the Pauza 50, one by now defunct Peregrine Industries, as well as guns from Steyr-Mannlicher, Israel Military Industries and McMillan.

A gas-operated semi-auto called the Stoner SR-50 Long Range Precision Rifle has been listed in the *Gun Digest* since 1996, but it still is not in production as of this writing. It's a product of Knight's Armament Company, and we had hoped to include a full-scale test chapter on it. Unfortunately, this 10-shot, 31.5-pounder will have to wait for another edition. For the record, its barrel is 35.5 inches in length and the gun measures 58.37 inches overall, with a tubular steel stock and scope mounts. It has an M-16-type safety lever, and an easily removable barrel. At such time as this model gets into production, the expected price will be something over $7,000.

The Barrett Model 82A-1 also has a 10-round magazine but is a bit lighter at 29 pounds. It is recoil-operated with a recoiling barrel and a self-leveling bipod. It also is priced in the neighborhood of $7,000 per copy.

Ronnie Barrett has another gun, the Model 95 bolt action, that also is built for the 50 BMG cartridge. This one has a five-round magazine and weighs 22 pounds. It was introduced in 1995 and still is being evaluated by the military. Price on it is less than $5,000 at this writing.

All of our military services now are using the Barrett semi-auto, although the Navy was the last holdout. For years they favored a single-shot model chambering the 50 BMG.

The only company currently building a single-shot 50 BMG on a production basis is L.A.R. Manufacturing, Inc., of West Jordan, Utah. This firm made its name originally with design and manufacture of big-bore handguns, but Robbie Robison, the honcho, feels there is a future in the 50-caliber recreational shooting market, as well as in the law enforcement market.

As one observer put it to us, "Start talking about a seven grand rifle to the bean-counters in a small to medium-sized police department and you'll end up talking to yourself. Maybe the big cities can afford such a firearm. Most others feel they can't."

By comparison with the semi-autos or even the bolt-action repeater, L.A.R.'s Grizzly 50 Big Boar is a deal by comparative monetary standards. Retail price on this one is in the neighborhood of $2,600. We suspect that law enforcement

Holes punctured in the doors of the car body were round and neat in appearance.

The shot on the vehicle's wheel not only penetrated both sides of the rim, but passed through the entire body to exit through this inner wall behind the tire on the off side. Note the jagged rollback of the metal.

agencies could do even better with a bit of serious bartering, and the big bore would serve the same purpose in law enforcement as it does with the military in its role as a Special Application Scoped Rifle. For example, it can take down getaway cars with a single shot through the engine block, or can be used to literally destroy brick and cinder block walls that might hide either baddies or contraband.

Jack Lewis' only objection to the gun is its weight. It has a 46-inch barrel, measures 45.5 inches overall and weighs 28.4 pounds before the scope is added. A heavy-duty scope mount that can withstand the recoil is included in the price.

"There is a positive in the weight factor, though," Lewis opines. The Grizzly 50 features all-steel construction. The receiver is of 4140 alloy steel heat-treated to 42 on the Rockwell scale. The bolt is machined from 4340 steel and is heat-treated to a hardness of 46 Rockwell.

Utilizing the bullpup design, the rifle has a trigger block safety and a ventilated rubber recoil pad. An additional pad with Velcro fasteners to fit over the standard pad is shipped with the gun, along with a high-grade padlock that can be used to secure the bolt so it cannot be inserted into the receiver.

When the bolt is opened and pulled to the rear, the whole integrated unit is withdrawn. With the trigger block in the safe position, a 50-caliber round is loaded, inserting the head of the cartridge into the shell holder. Thus attached, the cartridge is loaded into the chamber, then the bolt

is closed. When the safety is moved to the fire position, the gun is ready to fire.

In making preparations to test the gun, Lewis called his shooting partner, "Ace" Kaminski, to ask, "Where can we get an old car body to use as a target? And where can we find enough room to fire this thing without knocking down a mountain?"

"I'll figure out something," Kaminski promised. "I'll get back to you."

Meantime, there was the matter of ammunition. Lewis contacted Larry McGhee of PMC Ammunition in Boulder City, Nevada.

"The last I knew, you were turning out 50 Browning machine gun ammo," Lewis stated after the usual pleasantries had been exchanged. "I'm trying to come up with a few rounds for a test."

"We used to make it," McGhee offered, "but it was made strictly for machine guns and was a bit too hot for the average recreational shooter. We do still make the brass for a number of people. Arizona Ammunition is one of them."

Lewis soon was on the phone to Jim Schmidt, who runs the operation in Phoenix. It only took a few moments for Our Man to learn this was not a pack'em and ship'em

Custom-loaded ammunition for the L.A.R. rifle test was furnished by Arizona Ammunition, a firm that caters to the big-bore 1000-yard shooting fraternity.

operation. Arizona Ammunition caters to a wide audience of 50-caliber fanciers across the nation, and ammunition is loaded to order for whatever purpose it will serve.

"At what range will you be shooting?" Schmidt wanted to know across more than 3000 miles of separation by oceans and mountains.

"Well, the gun's bore-sighted for 200, according to Robbie Robison," Lewis told him. "We'll probably start there and work it back to 500 if we can find that much flat area that's open to shooting."

"How about 700 yards?" the ammo specialist asked.

"Maybe." Lewis' tone was dubious. "We have a lot of lava mountains around here that can get in the way."

Four days later, 25 rounds of 50 BMG ammunition arrived via United Parcel Service. Lewis unwrapped the box to find a heavy-duty plastic case holding the rounds in their own foam nests. On the lid of the case was a printed card stating the cartridges had been loaded specifically for him.

Investigation showed that the contents were high-velocity, Ultra Lube cartridges. The cases were some of Larry McGee's new PMC brass products, loaded with 750-grain Hornady A-MAX bullets. A printed legend stated: "Specifically designed for L.A.R. 50 BMG rifles. Do not use this ammo in any other kind of rifle."

Ace Kaminski checked in, asking Lewis, "You don't mind shooting at a Japanese-made car, do you?"

Lewis, who has a self-admitted Made-in-America fetish, replied, "It'll

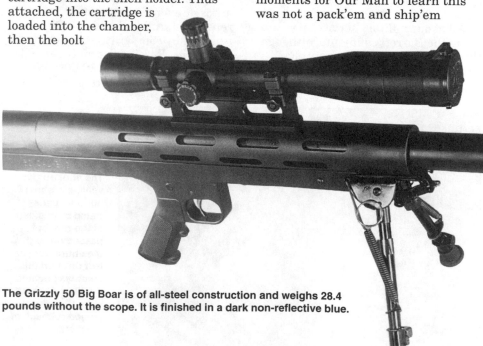

The Grizzly 50 Big Boar is of all-steel construction and weighs 28.4 pounds without the scope. It is finished in a dark non-reflective blue.

The compensator attached to the end of the barrel is meant to reduce recoil.

be a pleasure."

"That's what I thought. Let's go for Sunday morning. We'll be in a quarry that's closed down for the weekend, and we're far enough back in the lava field that there won't be any neighbors to be disturbed."

"We'll have some other people who want to shoot the gun," Lewis warned. "I just wish we had more ammo."

When Lewis arrived in the quarry at 9 a.m. with wife, Rueselle, who was going to photograph the event, Kaminski already was there with a wrecked Honda Civic on a trailer. He also had the keys to a huge bulldozer and moments later was offloading the battered vehicle. Meantime, Lewis had paced off an approximate 200 yards on the crushed lava road, marking the spot where the wreck should be deposited. That was where Kaminski dropped the sorry looking vehicle sideways in the road and backed the bulldozer away.

Back at the starting point, a folding table was set up in the middle of the roadway and furnished with a plastic chair. The table was covered with a thick mat and the L.A.R. Grizzly 50 placed on it. Meantime, Kaminski and the Lewis pair had been joined by Keith Prinz, a neighbor, and his son, 15-year-old Kristoffer, an ardent shooter. Arriving as Lewis settled into the chair for the first shot was Don Canario, marksmanship instructor for the Island of Hawaii Police Department.

Sitting on the edge of the plastic chair, Lewis checked that the rifle was on Safe, then drew out the bolt and the attached recoil pad. He selected one of the 50 BMG custom loads from the supply and carefully slid the head into the bolt's shell holder. Then, with great care, he slipped the cartridge and bolt unit back into the receiver, locking down the bolt. He then fitted the accessory recoil pad over the butt and tucked the arrangement into his shoulder. Bending forward, he looked through the scope, holding the crosshairs on the rear door of the wreck.

"Rear door," he called and took up the slack in the trigger—only there was no slack. Lewis, familiar plugs of yellow foam seated in his ears, experienced the recoil and bellow of the weapon that shoved him several inches back into the chair.

"Rear door," Kaminski confirmed, squinting through a spotting scope mounted on the hood of his truck.

"Front wheel," Lewis called, and began to reload, more assured than he had been on the first shot. He fired again, turning to look at Kaminski,

Specifications

Name:	Grizzly 50 Big Boar.
Caliber:	50 BMG.
Operation:	Single shot.
Weight:	28.4 pounds.
Length:	45.5 inches.
Barrel:	36 inches.
Stock:	Integral; ventilated rubber recoil pad; bullpup design.
Finish:	Non-reflective dark blue.
Sights:	None furnished; scope mount included.
Maker:	L.A.R. Manufacturing Incorporated 4122 West Farm Road (8540 South) West Jordan, UT 84088.

The L.A.R. rifle is loaded by fitting the 50-caliber round into the shell holder, which is part of the bolt/stock. The unit, with cartridge, then is inserted into the receiver.

When the 50-caliber Hornady bullets exited the other side of the car body, they tore jagged holes such as this in the metal. The motor of the vehicle had been removed, so there was no opportunity to try the bullets on such bulky metal.

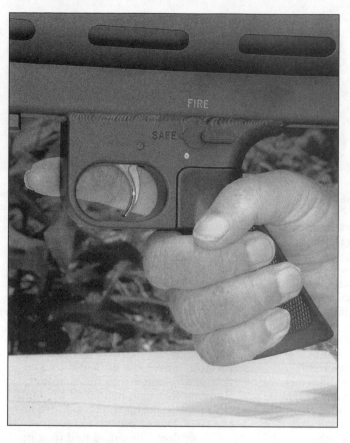

The controls for the rifle are simple. There are two markings for the safety lever: safe and fire. The lever can be switched by the thumb.

who shook his head.

"I don't know. Let's take a look."

The two of them hoofed it the 200 yards up a slight incline to inspect. Lewis' first scored shot turned out to be a rust spot on the door and there was no damage to the front wheel. As he searched in vain for bullet holes, Kaminski went behind the car and inspected the roadway. He found where the two rounds had landed, each some six feet high.

"So much for bore-sighting," Lewis muttered.

Returning to the makeshift shooting bench, he calculated the required change in the scope setting and cranked it down by what he figured as being six feet at that range. Then he rose from the chair and motioned to Kaminski.

"Your turn."

The elevation problem apparently had been solved, for Kaminski promptly put two rounds into one of the doors, an act verified by young Kristoffer, now manning the spotting scope. For good measure, Kaminski put more rounds through the metal.

Keith Prinz was next up, settling in behind the gun as though he'd been doing it for years. With the adjusted scope, he quickly put several rounds into the front door of the car, just under the window.

The old pro, Don Canario took over the chair and concentrated on the rear door handle. His first shot was a trifle low and he laid down the rifle, settled back in the chair and closed his eyes for a moment. Whether that constituted some sort of ancient Hawaiian yoga exercise we'll never know.

Then he reloaded the gun with one of Arizona Ammunition's offerings and settled into it again, snugging the recoil pad into his shoulder. Again, he fired at the rear door handle. He failed to hit it, but his shot was close enough that the 50-caliber bullet took out the handle on the opposite side of the junked vehicle, sending it spinning up the road.

Canario obviously was enjoying himself, trying to remove the rear bumper next. When he finally was down to two rounds, he looked around.

"Anyone else?" he wanted to know. Lewis stepped forward, pointing out that his only two shots had been used for scope adjustment. Replacing the firearms instructor in the chair, he went through the required exercises of checking the safety, loading the gun, then finding the target in the scope's crosshairs. Again, it was the front wheel he was after.

The L.A.R. roared as Lewis pressed the trigger, and that sound was echoed by the clash of metal on metal

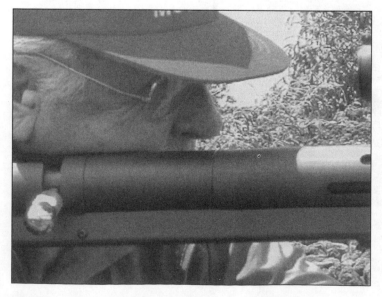

As the first shooter of the L.A.R. 50, Jack Lewis found the target through the scope.

down range. The last remaining cartridge was used in an unsuccessful attempt to tear off the same bumper on which Canario had been working. A hit, yes, but no cigar!

With the ammo expended, the shooters tromped up the hill to see what they had accomplished. Canario, firing the most shots, had done the really telling damage, while Lewis, in the end, had punctured the metal front wheel. The hole was about double the size of the cartridge, but on the other side of the vehicle, the bullet had come through the body, leaving a wound surrounded by twisted metal that was about half the size of a man's hand!

Everyone seemed in agreement that such a single-shot possibly could earn its original cost in reducing risks simply by its appearance. One shot toward a barricaded offender probably would convince him that jail was safer than being hit by the flying rubble of his disintegrating cover!

Lewis asked Kaminski if he needed help in removing the used up car from the scene.

"Nope," was the grinning reply. "I'll just haul it back to the same dump where I found it!" •

Ace Kaminski, Lewis' shooting partner, found the length of the stock adequate for his sizable frame.

In shooting through the wheel of the car, the bullet tore its way through the thick metal of the rim, then perforated the inner flange of the rim as well, continuing on.

Don Camario settles his cap on his brow after his initial shot. He was trying a difficult shot at the door handle on the car some 200 yards away.

CHAPTER 18

THE POLICE SUBGUN

... And How It Has Evolved For Law Enforcement Use.

A SUBMACHINE GUN is defined as a weapon capable of firing more than one round of pistol ammunition for each pull of the trigger. The first one was the Italian Villar Perosa, which saw limited use in World War I, either being fired from the shoulder or in pairs mounted on biplanes. The cartridge was found too anemic for aerial use, but as a close-range "trench gun," the submachine gun had a definite future.

The United States got into the subgun game too late for the Great War—the one that was supposed to end all wars! A 30-caliber semi-automatic conversion kit called the Pedersen Device was developed for the Springfield M1903 rifle, but the first, and perhaps last, great American submachine gun was the Thompson.

General John Thompson's gun was sold first in 1921. However, the market seemed limited at that time to Texas Rangers, the occasional police flying squad, Chicago bootleggers and the Irish Republican Army. Thompson had intended to see this gun employed only by the forces of law

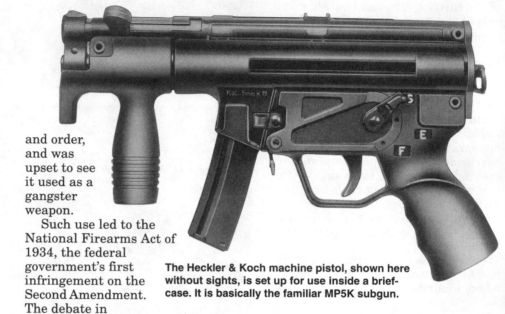

and order, and was upset to see it used as a gangster weapon.

Such use led to the National Firearms Act of 1934, the federal government's first infringement on the Second Amendment. The debate in Congress sounded very much like those of the "assault weapons" debate of 60 years later. John Thompson died, and his Auto-Ordnance company went bankrupt before the United States entered World War II. During that conflict, massive quantities of M-1A1 Thompson guns, a simplified M1921, were used in all theaters of operations.

The Heckler & Koch machine pistol, shown here without sights, is set up for use inside a briefcase. It is basically the familiar MP5K subgun.

In the 1920s and 1930s, American police used the Thompson to take down bank robbers in an era before two-way radios and SWAT teams. The New York City police even mounted a Model 1921 with a 100-round drum on a motorcycle sidecar for use against fleeing desperadoes. Thompsons of that era were well made, remaining in police department inventory through the 1970s. Chicago police used them on raids against Black Panther strongholds in the late 1960s.

Still, by the 1950s, the consensus in American police work was that democratic law enforcement

was a matter for 38-caliber revolvers and 12-gauge pump shotguns. The thinking was that semi-automatic pistols and submachine guns were for the authoritarian regimes in Europe. However, by the 1970s, this view had begun to change. In 1967, the Illinois State Police adopted a 9mm autoloading pistol, the Smith & Wesson Model 39, and since the 1980s, most police departments have switched to the semi-auto pistol. Most popular are those made by Glock, S&W, SIG-Sauer, and Beretta. Also, beginning in the 1960s, starting with the U.S. Secret Service, American law enforcement began using SMGs for executive protection details and SWAT teams.

One of your authors, David Steele, watched this change of thinking first hand, starting in the 1970s as a weapons researcher in Washington, D.C.

At the time, police chiefs, who were mainly of the Depression and World War II eras, were faced with the student unrest, anti-Vietnam War protests, ghetto riots and urban guerrilla warfare of the late 1960s and the early 1970s. It is a credit to them that they were able to handle these situations with 19th century weapons such as "chair leg" batons, revolvers

A low profile attache case such as this has been used by German SWAT teams, mounting the MP5K inside for protection missions.

These Thai police on their way to a student riot in 1975 were armed with a typical Third World hodgepodge of weapons. Included are a Remington riot gun, M-1 Carbines, a Thompson submachine gun and a MAC-10. The last was probably the most modern in the group.

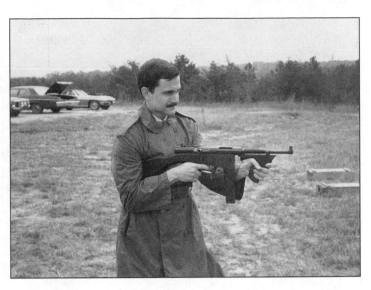

In 1970, David Steele tested this Ingram Model 6. Designed just after World War II, it resembled the Thompson, but was less expensive to produce. It failed to find a market in the law enforcement community.

and pump shotguns, plus some use of tear gas, an invention of World War I!

While high-tech weapons manufacturers were anxious for the police market, administrators were reluctant to spend scarce public funds on new hardware. For example, in 1971, David Steele brought back three telescoping metal batons made by Professor Ni at the Central Police College in Taipei, Taiwan. He loaned a couple to Security Arms Company in Virginia to test market. There was virtually no police interest, purchasing authorities being content with 50-cent straight batons. Now, of course, this sort of telescoping baton, made by ASP Inc. in Appleton, Wisconsin, is state of the art for the Federal Bureau of Investigation, the Drug

Enforcement Agency and other plainclothes agencies, as well as some uniformed departments.

Submachine guns then were viewed as unnecessary or even fascist weapons. Yet, less than 30 years later, we find subguns to be popular among SWAT teams, federal agents and even some anti-gang units. What happened? First, the old guard among police administrators retired. Second, some law enforcement agents realized that the bad guys were literally outgunning the police. Third, the federal government, through an interesting interpretation of the so-called Commerce Clause of the statutes, was looking to extend its power and influence. Fourth, the federal drug war and its attendant statutes and exceptions to the Posse Comitatus rule produced more search warrants, larger

operations and more money from asset forfeiture proceedings.

While this is not the place to discuss the social disruptions of the last 30 years, it is enough to say that if an agency wants submachine guns, they can probably get them through seized asset money. Due to competing priorities, the SMG is still not a standard backup gun, as it is among paramilitary police forces in Europe, but local SWAT teams, the FBI, DEA, Secret Service, BAFT and other agencies have made them more familiar than before.

The big winners in the drug war arms buildup were the pistol makers, particularly Glock, S&W, Beretta and SIG-Sauer. A change-over meant a new gun on every officer's hip in the department. Changes in SWAT teams and federal agencies gave a new

The FAMAE 9mm submachine gun designed and produced in Chile has a fixed stock. It currently is for sale to police agencies.

This MP5A3 with folding stock is wearing a Wilson Arms sound suppressor, as David Steele tries it out. He still wears ear protection.

Members of a SWAT team practice shooting on the move with the Heckler & Koch MP5A2 subgun. It is chambered for 9mm Parabellum.

The Austrian-made Steyr 9mm MP169 submachine gun with a Single-point sight was tried out by this Virginia police officer in the 1970s. This model also failed to score in the police market.

market to subgun manufacturers and importers. Here the top dogs were Heckler & Koch, Colt and Israel Military Industries.

Partly through purchase and partly through confiscations, police armories tended to acquire a number of subguns over the years. Thompsons have become so old and so valuable to collectors, they are being traded to dealers for modern guns. Military subguns like the U.S. M-3, the British Sten or German MP38 are likely to be destroyed, given to museums, or placed in reference collections like the BATF vault in Washington, D.C.

The Colt Model 633 compact subgun was reliable and accurate, but the magazines were difficult to load. Marine recon units used it for a time.

After World War II, Gordon Ingram designed an interesting submachine gun called the Model 6, which looked like a Thompson, but was without the Tommy gun's expensive refinements. Because of its full-size wood stock, it fit in what came to be termed the First Generation of subguns, which included the Thompson, the Bergmann and the Reising. The Model 6 never found a police market, but its designer did not give up. He went on to design the notorious M-10 and M-11 SMGs marketed in the 1970s.

The M-10—also called the MAC-10 for Military Armament Corporation, its producer in Powder Spring, Georgia—was made in 9mm and 45 ACP. The M-11 (MAC-11) was chambered for 380 ACP, an interesting weapon if only for its small size. Mitch WerBell, then the president of MAC, used to demonstrate his product by shooting it into phone books in potential clients' offices. The sound suppressor, originally called Sionics, was the best thing about the gun. The poor placement of the fire selector and safety, the high cyclic rate, open-bolt operation, crude sights and a wobbly folding stock made it a poor choice for police work. If it was suited to anything, it was to jungle ambushes and sentry assassination, but it became best known as the tool of Miami drug dealers and a prop for Hollywood "body count" films.

The number one gun for American SWAT has been the Heckler & Koch MP5. Its semi-auto accuracy, easy burst control, range of accessories and quality of manufacture gave it a substantial edge. Its widespread adoption, however, came after major agencies like the FBI acquired it, and particularly after the

British Special Air Service used it in 1980 to retake the Iranian Embassy in London from terrorists. The SAS troops used the MP5A3, a standard model with folding stock.

This gun is easy to maneuver in the "British-target shooting techniques," but the solid stock MP5A2 is more accurate from a wider variety of shooting distance and positions. The compact MP5K is used without stock for protection details; it is made more useful by the addition of a folding stock in the Personal Defense Weapon (PDW) variation. The MP5SD is the suppressed version, particularly useful

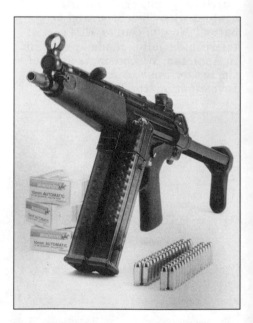

This H&K MP5 is chambered for the 10mm cartridge, an attempt to coordinate with the Federal Bureau of Investigation's move to the 10mm pistol. It has a substantial power advantage over the 9m Parabellum round. The gun also is being chambered to handle the 40 Smith & Wesson cartridge.

The Heckler & Koch VP70 machine pistol was another interesting concept, but it was years ahead of its time in the U.S. police market.

for indoor firefights to avoid shooter disorientation, though the suppressor adds maintenance problems beyond those of a general duty gun.

The only serious American-made competition to the MP5 has been the Colt subgun, based on their M-16 and CAR-15 designs. The 9mm Colt Model 635 fires from the closed bolt, as does the MP5, a feature most departments want. It has a straight-line stock, which extends to the rear for accurate shoulder fire.

Field-stripping is similar to that of the M-16A2. Magazines carry 20 or 30 rounds, though they are best underloaded a round or two for reliability. Full magazines are difficult to insert into the gun when the bolt is closed. Also, the magazines are difficult, though not impossible, to load by hand.

The Colt M635 has been adopted by the DEA. Colt makes an even shorter model, the M633, with folding front sight. Having fired 2000 rounds through one of these, without cleaning, David Steele is quick to say that the gun is quite reliable and surprisingly accurate.

The Israeli Uzi should have had the inside track on the American market since it was adopted by the Secret Service in the late 1960s. However, this superb combat SMG fired from the open-bolt mode, which is more reliable in an adverse military environment, but is not accurate enough for SWAT operations. Also, the original Uzi was a little overweight for easy carrying on protection details.

In 1970, Interarms imported the Uzi and the Walther MPK, competing with the recently imported H&K MP5. By the time police agencies started buying submachine guns in the 1980s, the MP5 was the clear front runner. Marine Corps reconnaissance people first were armed with the Colt subgun, then the H&K MP5. Recent word is that the later subgun will be replaced by the M-4 Carbine. Some police departments also are taking a hard look at the M-4A1 Carbine.

Israel Military Industries then introduced a lighter Uzi, the Mini, which is produced in closed-bolt as well as open-bolt versions. The California governor's protection detail carries the Uzi, as do some other agencies around the country. In keeping with the suddenly popular theory that smaller is better, the Israelis went a step beyond in 1997 by introducing a still smaller version called the Micro Uzi. The original Uzi has an overall length of 25.4 inches with the stock extended and a barrel length of 10.1 inches. The Mini Uzi is two inches shorter in overall length and has a 7.7-inch barrel. The Micro version measures only 19 inches overall with extended stock. Its barrel length is 5.2 inches.

We found the Micro difficult to handle for proper bullet placement and have serious doubts as to its place in law enforcement missions.

Experimental and test quantities of other subguns have been checked out from time to time. The Heckler & Koch VP70 was an excellent machine pistol that pioneered the injection-moulded frame, double-action-only trigger, plastic holster stock, double-stack magazine and burst control ideas that were well ahead of the market. The Walther MPK, an excellent SMG, was

used in Munich, among other European departments, but never took off here. Steyr once brought the MNP169 in from Austria; recently, it has tried to market the "TMP" tactical machine pistol. Various other guns are brought in periodically by the Foreign Science & Technology Branch of the Army for research. Also, we have seen the State Department's Security Branch testing satchels of foreign SMGs, like the Italian Beretta M12 and the Swedish M45, for embassy protection overseas.

Chile recently brought their FAMAE 9mm submachine gun to this country, demonstrating it at the TREXPO show for SWAT teams. In style, it appears to borrow elements from both Steyr and H&K. We found it to be accurate and reliable, but would be surprised if it found much favor on the American market. There also are those watching to see how Ruger's MP-9 subgun will fare around the globe.

Another American contender is the Calico 9mm submachine gun. If the best feature about the MAC-10 was its suppressor, the best feature about the Calico is its staggered, helical-feed, 50- and 100-round magazines. Unlike the old Thompson drum magazines, these are light and reliable. Unfortunately, their very capacity puts their semi-auto civilian versions at odds with our country's leaders and their "10-round rule." Be that as it may, Calico's M-951, M-955, M-950, M-60 and M-961 submachine gun variations should find some share of the police and military markets.

Even in countries where the submachine gun is a standard support weapon—Italy, Germany, France or Israel—there usually are only one or two models in common use. The size and diversity of American law enforcement agencies allow more competition, but it isn't likely the submachine gun ever will be purchased in anything like the numbers of pistols and shotguns bought by those same organizations charged with maintaining law and order. •

The Calico M-960-AS 9mm light mini-subgun has a 50-round helical magazine and a brass catcher. It has created some interest and garnered some sales in U.S. law enforcement circles.

CHAPTER 19

TODAY'S SUBGUN TRAINING

IN THE PAST, American police departments – if they had submachine guns at all – would have some variation of the Thompson. A few Reisings were around; a Los Angeles Sheriff's deputy friend of ours was issued one in 1965 during the Watts Riot, though, as a former Marine, he was aware of the Reising's unreliable reputation and traded it for a Remington 870, then an M-1 Carbine, after he broke the shotgun's stock on a rioter's jaw. A few post-war police departments had Ingram M6s, captured Schmeissers or war surplus M-3 Grease guns in their armories.

New York and Chicago detectives used Tommy guns during raids on militant locations in the 1960s, though real police department acceptance of the SMG did not come until the 1980s. A few federal agencies had adopted special purpose buzz guns.

In the late 1960s, the Secret Service adopted the Israeli Uzi for carry in attache cases and in special shoulder holsters. The State Department Security Branch acquired Beretta M12s, Swedish M45s and other subguns for embassy protection details overseas. However, local SWAT teams, first begun in 1967 in Los Angeles, did not adopt the subgun until about 1980, after Britain's

Special Air Service retook the Iranian Embassy in London via Heckler & Koch MP5s.

Originally organized around infantry scout/sniper tactics, SWAT teams eventually went toward a counter-terrorism model like that pioneered by the British Special Air Service, German GSG-9, Israeli

The Heckler & Koch MP5K PDW 9mm submachine gun can be outfitted with a detachable sound suppressor. The PDW in the designation stands for Personal Defense Weapon.

Commandos, SEAL Team 6 and Delta Force. Most of these units chose the best equipment and small arms from around the world, rather than simply accepting Army issue, thus giving them the edge. In the 1980 embassy operation telecast around the world, the SAS used the HK MP5A3 as its primary weapon, backed up by the FN P35 pistol. The Army-issue Sterling L2A3 submachine gun could not compete in compactness or ergonomics with the German-made MP5.

Although the MP5 had been imported to the United States since 1970, it was several years before trend-setting departments, like the

Los Angeles Sheriff's Special Enforcement Bureau, picked it up. The SAS's 1980 incident set off its current popularity. Now, every local SWAT team has to have one, not to mention controversial agencies like the Bureau of Alcohol, Tobacco and Firearms. The FBI issues a semi-auto MP5A2 to its line agents, reserving full-auto versions for "SWATTERS." Meanwhile, DEA has stayed with the 9mm Colt Commando for its agents. Federal agencies buy what they want, without need for standardization.

Smaller machine pistols, like the Ingram M10 and M11 and the HK VP70, didn't have much chance in the American police market, because they were not accurate enough for urban law enforcement. They had, in fact, been designed for insurgency warfare in the jungles of Vietnam.

The Calico helical-feed, 50- and 100-round subguns have made some inroads. The Uzi in various configurations has been used by the Secret Service and California State Police protective details. However, if there is anything resembling a "standard" police submachine gun in America, it would be the HK MP5.

"In 1970, when I was supervisor of the Police Weapons Center project in Washington, I tested myriad models in order to write the tech manual, *Submachine Guns In Police Work*," David Steele recalls. "Included were antique Thompson, Reising and M-3 guns removed from the Quantico Marine Corps museum for my benefit, a Czech Skorpion VZ61, a Steyr MPi69, the British Sterling L2A3 and the L34A1 suppressed variation, the Walther MPK, several Uzis, a number

The H&K MP5K PDW was designed to give air crew members a weapon specially designed for survival, escape and evasion should their aircraft be shot down.

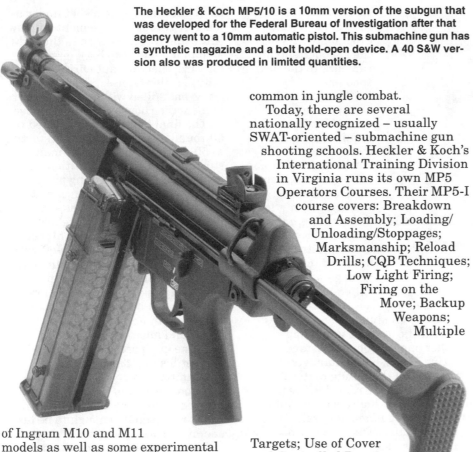

The Heckler & Koch MP5/10 is a 10mm version of the subgun that was developed for the Federal Bureau of Investigation after that agency went to a 10mm automatic pistol. This submachine gun has a synthetic magazine and a bolt hold-open device. A 40 S&W version also was produced in limited quantities.

of Ingram M10 and M11 models as well as some experimental prototypes.

"When advantages and disadvantages for police work were added up, it seemed to me that the most potential was in a gun imported by Security Arms Company of Arlington, Virginia, the MP5. This was prior to the development of their own Virginia-based import company by Heckler & Koch."

At that time the only MP5s imported were the standard fixed- and folding-stock models. These had been developed from West Germany's G3 rifle stystem in the early 1960s and had a number of interchangeable parts.

By 1966, the MP5 had become standard for German city police and border police forces. In common with the G3 rifle, the MP5 fires from the closed bolt and utilizes a refined rotary rear sight. The roller locking system is both unique and reliable.

While a closed bolt system might have drawbacks in mass warfare, since it is more complicated and expensive than an open-bolt mechanism like the Uzi or Sterling. Any closed-bolt system has a theoretical "cook off" problem (only theoretical in 9mm), but it has a sizeable advantage in police work where semi-auto and short-burst fire are the rule. In police use, single point (individual bad guy) targets are the only ones acceptable, not like the area targets or suppressive fire needed and

common in jungle combat.

Today, there are several nationally recognized – usually SWAT-oriented – submachine gun shooting schools. Heckler & Koch's International Training Division in Virginia runs its own MP5 Operators Courses. Their MP5-I course covers: Breakdown and Assembly; Loading/ Unloading/Stoppages; Marksmanship; Reload Drills; CQB Techniques; Low Light Firing; Firing on the Move; Backup Weapons; Multiple Targets; Use of Cover and Controlled Bursts. The MP5-II course adds tactical exercises, covering Firing on the Move; Live Fire Entries; Hostage Rescue; Emergency Evacuation; Lateral Movement; Support Side Firing; Low Light Shooting; Tactical Runs; Weapon Retention; Standard Drills; CQB and Gas Mask Exercises. In addition to these two MP5 Operators Courses, H&K teaches a five-day Tactical Submachine Gun Course geared to high-risk warranty entry teams.

However, America's best known private shooting school, Gunsite Training Center located in Paulden, Arizona, has added an on-site submachine gun course to its curriculum. This course is taught by Peter Kokalis, who writes for *Soldier Of Fortune* magazine, as

well as other well known and highly qualified instructors.

The five-and-a-half-day course breaks down to the following:

The first day is devoted to registration, SMG history, nomenclature, safety, marksmanship, care/cleaning, failure drills and position shooting. Students can obtain guns for the course through Gunsite, which is an authorized Colt distributor.

"I used their Colt Model 633 Compact for the course," David Steele says. "It was accurate and reliable, though the magazines tended to be hard to lock into the well, and full magazines will dump their loads if dropped on the ground." This weapon, in the longer M635 form, is issued to agents of the Drug Enforcement Agency.

The second day covers MP5 history, mechanics and use. The afternoon is devoted to semi- and full-auto drills on paper silhouettes, as well as man-on-man contests, clearing pepper-poppers with two-round bursts, followed by "transition" drills with the pistol.

The third day included an MP5 accessory lecture, followed by prone, sitting and kneeling drills on the range. In the afternoon, there were more semi-auto drills at 50 and 75 yards, then more full-auto-plus-pistol tradition drills at close range. Two-man teams fired a clearing exercise at what is called the Firebox.

"Finally, there was another man-on-man competition, with dual

For the sake of comparison, the H&K MP5K Personal Defense Weapon, with stock folded, is shown with the M9 Beretta pistol issued to U.S. military forces. Both are chambered for the 9mm pistol cartridge.

David Steele had the opportunity to try out the 10mm MP5A3 at the police range in Burbank, California. For the Gunsite school, he chose a subgun made by Colt.

pepper-poppers surrounding a hostage popper. We were to shoot while advancing in the crouch, taking out bad guys with two two-round bursts, then putting the SMG on safe, and transitioning to the pistol for a falling plate target. The day concluded with Kokalis' wound ballistics lecture." Steele reports.

"On the fourth day, we had semi-auto and full-auto drills, including advancing in the assault. A staff demonstration showed us that front sight accuracy with both SMG and pistol can be accomplished on the move. All shooting, except for weapon retention at point blank distance from underarm, is conducted with the stock held into the shoulder pocket. Gunsite does not recommend the Singleton/SAS/HK stock-folded, sling fire technique. Accuracy and control do seem to be increased by shoulder fire and speed does not appear to be affected. Sheriff's SWAT officers from Riverside, California, might have benefited from this technique in their November 1995 operation against a "dusted" suspect holding hostages at a Rubidoux halfway house where he thought he could assassinate ex-LAPD Sergeant Stacey Koon. When the suspect used his pistol, deputies fired long bursts with their Colt 9mm SMGs with the stock held at least two inches from the shoulder. At very close range, any well-practiced technique will work, including shooting from the hip, but the Gunsite technique does appear to be more efficient for a wider array of circumstances."

From notes taken during this schooling, David Steele reports, "After this short-range practice, we went back to 50- and 75-yard position shooting, following the Gunsite pattern of alternating speed with accuracy drills. Following, we had an exercise calling for each of us to run, drop to prone, shoot the silhouette, then run back to the next shooter.

"Then we had the even messier Scrambler. This requires hitting a metal silhouette at 100-yard range from various 'hides,' using the fork of a tree, squatting over a log fence, through the window of a cabin mockup, sitting in a brushy ditch, prone through a dirty sniper hole and, as a finale, shooting from a tree limb reached by climbing."

Later, the student group had another pepper-popper, hostage-clearing exercise with handgun transition on the falling plate. This one added a speed reload to the pistol exercise. Following was a full-auto exercise on dual, moving, rail-mounted plates. This was repeated as a night exercise, combining the subgun with mounted light or field expedient Surefire 6P. Interspersed with the other exercises was a back-lying supine exercise, shooting around and over a barrel with the pistol at metal plates. There was also a two-man house-clearing exercise at what is called the Playhouse, where hostage targets are interspersed in diabolical ways.

"On the fifth day, we spent the morning on semi- and full-auto exercises, including clearance drills and transition to the pistol. At contact distance we practiced moving from the Gunsite Low Ready to the underarm weapon retention position. After this SMG retention drill, we did pectoral level, one-hand pistol shooting. This is done with the left hand up, simulation of an empty-hand strike, then two rounds from the "pec" position, followed by an angled drop back to one knee and a two-hand shot to the target's head."

In the afternoon, the class had low sideways prone exercises simulating a shot under a fence or through a basement window. After this was more step to the right, step to the left, step back or step forward, then full-auto firing and failure drill exercises, followed by a gully walk filled with pepper-poppers and another house clearing exercise.

The final half-day was devoted to a 60-round qualification course starting at 50 yards, then a man-on-man subgun and pistol competition on pepper-poppers and falling plates. The winner got an extra certificate at the commencement ceremonies immediately following the shoot.

We've all seen him, that film or television gangster in a face-off with the cops, a small machine gun held firmly in hand, its banana clip menacingly slammed home before the bolt is drawn back. Or that hero of heroes, John Rambo, decked out in sweat and muscles with an M-60 machine gun perched one-handed against his hip, bandoleers of ammunition draped across his chest and another belt of ammo held with his free hand as he blasts whatever fool is unfortunate enough to be his enemy this day.

These are the images the public has of automatic weapons, courtesy of Hollywood script writers and special effects, but these are not the techniques taught at the Gunsite school or at Heckler & Koch's course. Nor are they taught in any of the other schools scattered around the country that teach submachine gun use.

Michael Paulus reminds his students that submachine guns are weapons to be deployed as safely and as efficiently as any firearm used by police officers. In fact, this instructor who frequently teaches a two-day

In the 1950s, the 45 ACP Reising gun had been abandoned by the Marine Corps. This Leatherneck shooter is demonstrating it on the range at Quantico, Virginia. A number of police departments across the nation still have this model in their inventory.

The Calico helical-feed 9mm submachine gun is making inroads in some police markets. Note the brass-catcher bag suspended beneath the gun.

At the Gunsite Training Center, Peter Kokalis and Jack Farr coach a member of an Arizona SWAT team in subgunning technique with the MP5.

course to law enforcement agents in the Midwest, makes sure his students receive heavy doses of firearms basics along with practice in tactical applications of these automatic weapons.

Paulus is a master firearms instructor for the police department in Champaign, Illinois. He has a Master Firearms Instructor's Certificate from the Police Training Institute in Champaign and serves as a patrol officer and member of his department's Special Weapons And Tactics Team.

We had Bill Rowe, a law enforcement and firearms writer, who lives in Illinois, talk with Paulus and learn about his techniques. Here are some of the things he learned.

"My first objective is to get rid of the idea that the subgun is supposed to be used in a Rambo fashion," Paulus says, referring to the movie hero's tendency to blow away his enemies through an excruciatingly long burst of fire instead of placing accurate shots on his targets. "Just because it's an automatic weapon, a guy can't go in and unload whole magazines on the bad guys. It takes the same control and discipline as any other weapon. But the movies have glamorized submachine guns to the point that the basics can be overlooked."

Hollywood has done such a good job of this glamorization that when the police department in Elk Grove Village, Illinois, went shopping for automatic weapons to supplement their armory, the arguably most famous of all submachine guns, the Uzi, wasn't even considered.

"We didn't look at the Uzi, because it has been associated with

so many negative events by the media and the motion picture industry," says Elk Grove Village firearms instructor Vince Lopez. "We discussed the possibilities of different weapons and we wanted to avoid the whole mystique of police officers carrying Uzis."

Lopez's fellow firearms instructor, John Watts, echoed his partner's sentiments, though he was impressed with the Uzi he fired at one of Mike Paulus' two-day schools.

"the Uzi is a nice, well balanced weapon," Watts admits, "but when we were looking for automatic weapons to supplement our Emergency Response Team, we simply didn't want the department and the Uzi to be connected."

Both officers were quick to point out that as far as they were concerned, the Israeli-made Uzi has earned its reputation as a fine submachine gun. One police officer blames the ignorance of many reporters who cover violent incidents on the bad rap the Uzi has received.

"It doesn't matter whether a criminal or a police officer employs a Beretta, an M-16, an AK-47 or an Uzi, it seems that whenever the press sees an automatic weapon used in a violent way, they call it an 'Uzi assault rifle.' It's not fair to the weapon, its manufacturer or even the police. But

that's the press for you," the officer said.

Of the five automatic weapons Mike Paulus used for this course reviewed by Bill Rowe, three were Uzis. Two were 9mm Uzis and the other was chambered for the 45 ACP cartridge. The other two guns were Beretta Model 12S 9mm submachine guns carried by Watts and Lopez.

Whether the mystique of the submachine gun is good or bad, the reality of the weapon, regardless of manufacture, is that it can be used as an effective tool in law enforcement.

"Submachine guns have a place in proper situations," Paulus feels. "Sometimes, though, these weapons are deployed improperly and used when they shouldn't be used."

An example of poor submachine gun deployment recently happened in the state of Washington, according to Andy Casavant, another instructor.

This is the Swedish M45 submachine gun used by U.S. Army Special Forces and the security branch of our State Department.

This Colt Model 633 Compact subgun was the one that David Steele chose to use for the Gunsite submachine gun course.

"Two officers shot a guy from a range of three or four feet," Casavant reports. "He was hit something like 18 times, and took 10 rounds from one burst. Now that tells me these officers had awfully poor trigger control. Then, to add to the situation, 12 to 14 rounds passed through the suspect, went through a wall and wounded officers in a different room.

"I believe they were armed with H&K MP5s, one of the nicest weapons made for controllability and ease of shooting. But it looks like these guys went overboard, and I feel that my 45-caliber pistol would have done a more effective job in this type of situation. At least the bullets would have stopped and not injured the other officers."

Paulus contends that submachine guns are most useful when officers expect to encounter multiple armed suspects in close quarters. Narcotics raids and barricaded gunmen situations are two scenarios Paulus feels warrant the use of subguns. But he strongly advises officers not to use the weapons when hostages are involved, explaining that when so many rounds are sent downrange, the wrong people could get hurt.

Paulus also lectures that a shooter has to remember that these guns are not magic weapons. Simply because they have a high rate of fire does not make them the answer to all problems in sticky situations.

"You have to remember you're firing a pistol round through these subguns," Paulus cautions. "The fact that they are shoulder-mounted allows for more accuracy than a handgun, but they are still pistol rounds and not the high-velocity rounds one would shoot through rifles chambered for heavier calibers."

Paulus agrees with the philosophy of calling for the biggest rounds available when choosing police sidearms, such as the 45 ACP or 10mm. When it comes to submachine guns, he chooses to arm himself with a 45-caliber model.

"For use as a tactical weapon, the 9mm subgun is probably more accurate than the 45 over a long distance and has a greater magazine capacity," Paulus admits, adding, "But I prefer a larger caliber round than the 9mm."

To balance the big round preference and the need for more bullets and better accuracy, this instructor recommends that officers use 147-grain hollowpoint rounds in the 9mm weapons.

"The 147-grain sub-sonic hollowpoints provide better penetration and expansion than lighter, faster 9mm rounds," Paulus explains. "The lighter bullets have a velocity of about 1100 to 1200 feet per second. This causes them to travel too fast through the target and not get the expansion to stop the felon.

Instructor Peter Kokalis (center) poses with the Sheriff's SWAT team from Yavapai, Arizona. In taking the Gunsite course, they all preferred to use the Heckler & Koch MP5 with the fixed stock.

"With the 147-grain sub-sonic rounds, we're talking about a velocity of 900 to 950 feet per second, which allows the bullets to expand quickly upon penetration and take out an organ or whatever they hit."

Paulus' philosophy is that it is better to shoot the bad guys with a cannon ball than with a BB, but most important of all is to make sure you hit the target. Thus the focus on marksmanship basics, even with automatic weapons. He teaches that trigger control is the biggest thing to learn in his course, and that control has its roots in the basics of pistol marksmanship.

"There is really nothing new to learn about the subguns that isn't taught in basic marksmanship courses, other than differences in trigger control," Paulus teaches. "The basics stay the same with automatic weapons. It's better to be a good shot than to be fast and miss, even with a submachine gun.

"In combat handgun tactics, we use a method called two-rounds-and-assess," Paulus explains. "What that means is that an officer fires two quick rounds at center mass, assesses the situation, then either holsters his weapon or fires more rounds as the situation dictates. With submachine guns, it's the same, except it's two trigger squeezes – or double-tap – and assess. Same idea, more rounds."

Malfunctions are the collective curse inherent to automatic weapons, a curse that can pose a serious threat to the officer's chance of survival. It is

The gun rack at the Gunsite loading shed holds the weapons of students who are collecting their ammo for the SMG course. Included are the Colt Model 635, Colt's Model 633, a pair of H&K MP5s and a customized MAC-10.

obviously a high priority for an officer to know what to do in case of a misfire, especially in a combat situation in which his and possibly other lives count on his ability to perform.

"Shoot first, clear later," Paulus told an officer on the firing line as he tried to clear a misfire. "When the subgun stops shooting, pull your pistol, down the target, then clear the weapon. Shoot the bad guy first. That's number one."

Paulus uses two methods to simulate misfires. On the range, he has his students place the magazines in their guns' magazine wells, but not seat them. When the weapon fails to fire, the officers are required to draw their sidearms, fire at the target, then clear the submachine guns.

For combat drills inside the shooting house, in this case, a seven-room "ballisticized" building, Paulus sabotages the magazines with plastic rounds which cause the weapons to malfunction.

The point of the sabotage is to get the student officers comfortable with reacting quickly to a situation over which they have no control. On the range, when they failed to seat their magazines, the officers knew the weapon would not fire and were ready to react. In the shooting house the misfire is inevitable, yet timing is unpredictable. The trainees know Mike Paulus mixed the plastic dummies with good ammo in their magazines. They simply don't know exactly where the dummies are in the magazine. This increases the tension already brought about by the fact that there are both good guy and bad guy targets situated throughout the house. It is up to the trainees to select the proper targets to pop with their submachine guns without harming any of the good guys.

Another tactic practiced inside the house involves movement with a shoulder-mounted weapon. Unlike handguns, which the officers use daily, the comparatively long submachine guns require different handling skills, especially when moving from room to room in a house filled with potentially dangerous suspects.

"We give them semi-realistic situations for deployment of the subguns," the veteran instructor explains. "From malfunction drills on the range to clearing the shooting house, they become more familiar with their capabilities – both their own and those of the weapon."

Paulus states the deployment of submachine guns always should be determined on a case-by-case basis. He feels that well trained units familiar with what these weapons will do are the ones that will use them most effectively.

This Beretta 12 is another of the subguns used by Mike Paulus' students in learning proper handling and firing of full-auto weapons in a law enforcement role.

Gunsite instructors Walt Jordan (rear) and Jack Furr (front) coach SWAT team members in the submachine gun course in the Arizona desert.

Most submachine gun schools offer night training, which can include the use of flashlights or even lasers attached to the guns by means of special brackets which do not interfere with sighting or operation.

"Subguns should be used to supplement handguns," Paulus cautions. "I believe that if a team of officers has to raid a building, two of them armed with subguns is sufficient. But then those on the scene are the ones responsible for the operation, and deployment of these weapons has to be determined by the facts of each situation. They could need only one or they could need several."

Submachine guns have tactical disadvantages as well as advantages. Besides the possibility of a malfunction in the weapon, another disadvantage is what to do with the weapon under certain circumstances. It is more difficult to "holster" a submachine gun than a pistol if hand-to-hand combat becomes the most efficient means to subdue a suspect.

"I'd hate to be carrying a subgun if I had to grapple with someone," John Casavant said. "Even when slung over your shoulder, they're in your way. They should be used as cover weapons, maybe a couple officers covering the situation while the rest of a team is armed with pistols."

The bottom line, according to both Casavant and Paulus, is that regardless of what an officer learns in training, a successful operation begins between the ears of guys on the front line, the officers who face and evaluate the facts of the situation, then take the action necessary to solve the problem as quickly and as safely as possible.

"I don't teach these guys anything new about firearms that they haven't learned somewhere along the line," Paulus says, "If a person knows how to fire a shoulder-mounted weapon, he knows how to fire a submachine gun. What these students learn, though, is that there are a few more decisions to

make when they use a subgun. There are decisions about which mode of fire to select and trigger control."

Casavant believes that the only advantage the submachine gun has over a pistol is that it can deliver a larger number of rounds more accurately in single-fire mode.

"You have to remember that automatic weapons were designed for military use," Casavant says. "The reason they were developed was to quickly deliver lots of rounds into a specified area. Because of that, I think it's a limited tactical weapon for police officers. When you fire one, you realize they are more versatile and accurate when you don't use the

full-auto firing mode. That's also why we end the course with the Mad Minute. When these guys get to blow through a whole magazine with their weapons on full-auto, they see that controlled bursts or single shots are more accurate and the weapon is easier to control."

Paulus agrees that the mode of fire selection is one of his primary concerns when deploying submachine guns. To stress his point, he related the story about the Washington hostage situation. Two officers armed with automatic weapons went into a bank in which an armed suspect was holding a hostage. The two officers were able to maneuver close enough to

For the law enforcement-only subgun schools run in the Midwest by Michael Paulus, the students usually bring whatever submachine gun is in the departmental armory. This early Uzi has seen better days. The folding stock, weakened during an operation, has a metal sleeve riveted to it for strength.

Firing from various positions has been part of the training in the Midwestern school. The prone position was found to be highly effective, but not of great use in clearing a house.

Concentrated drills were conducted on reacting to a stoppage or other malfunction. The standard operational procedure is to move the subgun to the weaker hand or, if there is a carrying strap, to sling it. In the same motion, the duty handgun is drawn and firing on the target continues. This student is left-handed and fires the Uzi from his left shoulder, firing his pistol with the same hand.

the suspect to take him out without harming the hostage. Though it was a successful operation in that respect, Paulus has a problem with how the automatic weapons were employed.

"Both officers had their weapons on full-auto," Paulus said. "The first one to fire hit the suspect with something like eight rounds. The second officer hit the guy with three or four more rounds. I wasn't there, and I hate to second-guess people, but 11 or 12 rounds sounds like too many. An incident like this reinforces my belief that we need to carefully assess each situation and make decisions based on the

intelligence gathered before going in with guns blazing."

"And then it happened," Bill Rowe tells us. "It wasn't the fault of anyone, really, just one of those things that happens to a person when the mystique of an automatic weapon takes hold. Each student loaded rounds into four magazines and stood on-line about 10 feet from their targets. They slid the magazines into their weapons, seated them with a smack and charged the bolts with a threatening series of clanks. None were outwardly grinning about what was to happen, but each was obviously excited."

Paulus checked the firing line and the shooters leveled their weapons at the targets. When Paulus gave the order, the rounds flew, the empty cartridge cases bounced, and the cops emptied their magazines with one pull of the trigger as their bodies jiggled from the rapid sequence of recoils.

"Their pleasure was more obvious as they reloaded and charged their weapons for the next burst. Maybe their groups weren't as tight as they should be. And so what if the recoil carried the rounds outside center mass? It was their Mad-Minute, and this time they fired from the hip, like Rambo: Hollywood style," Bill Rowe concludes.

In subgun training, as in other live-fire courses, ear protection is a must. Ear plugs help a great deal, but a good set of ear muffs such as those worn here offer better protection against gunshot noise. Shown is a Beretta Model 12.

CHAPTER 20

THE BUSINESSMAN'S SUBGUN

This Executive Self-Protector Has An Interesting Backround.

WE HAVE BEEN waiting to hear from Russia's Ministry of Internal Affairs for six months. At this point, it is beginning to appear that whoever is in charge may not want to become involved in what could well be an embarrassing exchange of information. More specifically, we have been attempting to reach the ministry's Scientific and Industrial Association of the Research Institute for Special Equipment. Success has been negative.

All of this concerns a four-color catalog that advertises what is heralded to be the Kleinmaschinenpistole PP-90. This catalog, incidentally, is printed in English as well as in German. We would assume there is a Russian language version somewhere, unless the ministry folks don't want the Russian people to know what is being manufactured in their arms factories these days. Much of the catalog's contents appear to be meant for defense—or offense, if you will—against rioters and other insurrectionists.

For example, there is the Hochleistungsgasgranate Siren 12. In the catalog's English subtitle, this is described as a "Special Tear-Gas Grenade, Siren-12, With Special Capacity."

In addition to three different types of full-auto machine pistols, several revolvers and autoloading pistols and a rifle, the organization also markets two types of what they call blinding-noise grenades. One is stationary and the other is hand-thrown. According to the catalog text, they "serve to produce blinding and sound effects on criminals. They are used during special operations intended to capture armed criminals, to stop mass disturbances. They also can be used within a security signaling system of perimeter protection." Both styles are stated as being "non-fragmentation and fire-proof grenades."

That should give us some sort of idea of the catalog's contents.

But the PP-90 mentioned earlier is listed as the Small-Size Submachine Gun PP-90. The printed English copy states:

"This submachine gun is designed for armed units of Ministry of Internal Affairs to use against organized crime. The submachine gun features shock-free operation of automatic parts in extreme positions."

There is no date on this catalog to indicate when it was printed, but a wild guess—based on the PP-90 designation—is that the gun itself was introduced in 1990.

All of this brings us into some sort of conflict with information co-author Jack Lewis has had in his files for several years. A 9mm folding subgun that is almost a dead ringer for the Russian offering was patented by Gene Stoner in the early 1980s. At that time, Stoner was heading up Ares, Inc., a Midwestern development agency that had been designing and perfecting armament for the Pentagon and for this country's military friends—both real and temporary—around the globe.

During his tenure at Ares, Stoner had developed any number of military weapons, including a 90mm cannon that the Shah of Iran wanted to install on his cadre of battle tanks. The gun was a success, but the shah was deposed and driven out of his country before more than the prototype could be made and tested. The tank and the gun, incidentally, now repose in the arms museum of Knight's Armament Co. in Florida.

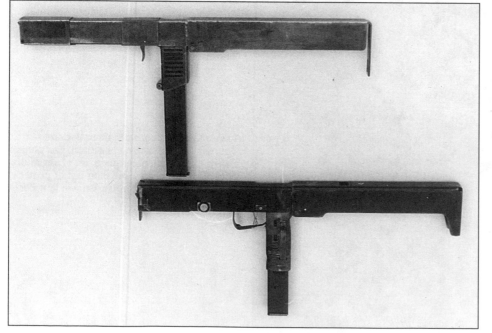

Of the two prototypes of the folding subma-chine gun designed by Gene Stoner, the one at top was made of stainless steel, while the one below is of ordnance steel with a blued finish. Note the slight differences in design. The stainless gun probably was the first produced.

Here the stainless steel gun is fully folded, while the blued steel version is positioned to illustrate means by which it becomes a gun. It is turned into a small but lethal 9mm package.

For the uninitiated, the late Gene Stoner was the creator of the AR-15 rifle, which ultimately became our military M-16. Rumor has it that he received $1 for every M-16 purchased by the military. Apparently, he did not pass on a poor man!

As for the folding submachine gun, Ares, Inc., apparently attempted to market this as the Executive's Protector. The first prototype folded up into what looked like a block of stainless steel and, in this mode, was about half the size of a cigar box. Resting on an executive's desk, it could have been a paperweight.

According to some of Stoner's co-workers at the Ares operation, the designer referred to the creation as the Executive Submachine Gun. That was in the 1970s, during the latter days of the Cold War, when high-ranking politicians, wealthy individuals and even religious leaders were being kidnapped primarily in eastern Europe and some South American countries. In some cases, these kidnappings were for ransom; in other instances, the terrorists were attempting to make a political statement and eventually assassinated their captives, often video-taping the atrocities. A number of American businessmen operating in the areas nations were among the victims.

As the result of long personal study, Stoner came to feel that while bodyguards can be effective up to a point, it becomes the responsibility of the individual at risk to protect himself against such kidnapping efforts. This, the gun designer felt, called for proper armament. His invention was his answer to the need.

On the executive's desk, the gun might look like a small metal box for storage of pens, pencils or even paper clips, but when picked up, the simple depression of a small button set in one corner of the block activated the mechanism. Pressure against the spring-loaded button caused the compact little box to literally unfold and become a fully functional 9mm submachine gun. When the front and rear elements snapped into position, there already was a 30-round magazine of 9mm ammo in place.

Lewis and Stoner had known each other since the middle 1960s, about the time Colt was buying manufacturing rights from Armalite, Inc., for the rifle that would become our military's M-16. Stoner had been chief engineer and designer for the California-based company during the period of invention and development.

"Over the next 25 years or so, Gene and I met from time to time, often discussing some of his designs and plans for the future. To the best of my recollection, though, he never mentioned this little subgun in any of those get-togethers," Lewis reports.

Some months before Stoner's death, Lewis met with him in Florida, where he was attempting to design a new personal defense weapon, although he knew he was suffering from an inoperable brain tumor. Since their last meeting, Lewis had spotted the two prototypes of the Executive Model in the museum at Knight's

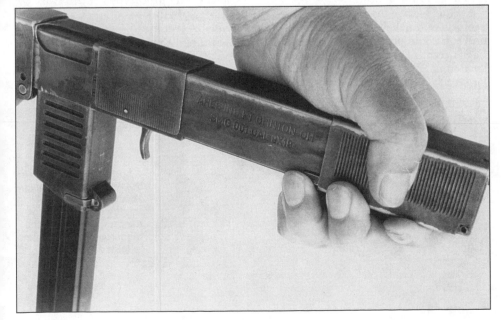

The stainless steel subgun has a metal hand grip on its forward end. The gun was not likely to fire enough rounds for this area to get hot.

The trigger guard on the blued gun is hinged and can be opened for trigger access by a heavily gloved hand. Perforations in the hand grip may have been to reduce weight of the gun.

Armament in Vero Beach. The workings of the little gun intrigued him and he had to know more. When he asked Stoner about this particular design, the inventor seemed puzzled for an instant, then laughed.

"I thought it was a great idea at the time," Stoner said, "but I couldn't interest anyone else. Just the thought of needing an instantly available gun in their own offices here in corporate America even seemed to shock some of them. The general attitude seemed to be that it just couldn't happen here!"

According to Lewis, if there was any bitterness in Stoner's tone, he did not detect it. Instead, the inventor spoke matter-of-factly, passing along pertinent information.

"A lot of bodyguards probably felt my gun might put them out of business," Stoner added at the time, "but the big problem was one I had not considered in proper depth. The fact remained that this was a machine gun and every executive or other individual who bought one would have to spend valuable time learning to handle and shoot the gun properly, then each of them would have to apply for a Federal license simply to own the gun. The more I thought about it, the more complicated the buyer's responsibilities seemed to become. Eventually, I just dropped it."

That was the last discussion Lewis ever had with Gene Stoner. Several times, while in Florida, he tried to contact the inventor, but was told he was too ill to talk with anyone. However, C. Reed Knight, Jr., a close friend and business associate of Stoner's, allowed Lewis to draw both of the Executive Submachine Gun prototypes from the Knight Armament museum for closer study. He also was granted permission to try one of the guns, using the company's outdoor test range. This, of course, was under the supervision of one of Knight's staff.

"During a perfunctory inspection of the two prototype guns, I found that the inner workings appeared to be identical," Lewis reports. "On the exterior, the most obvious difference lay in the fact that one gun was encased in stainless steel, the other in standard ordnance steel. There also was a slight difference in the size of the trigger guards. I can't vouch for Gene Stoner's thinking processes at this point, of course, but it would appear that he felt any use of this gun would be at extremely close quarters, for he had included no sights of any kind."

Lewis questioned Reed Knight as to whether there was any kind of operator's manual for the guns and got a shake of the head.

"Gene was involved in a lot of things at that time," Knight explained. "After the initial negative reaction to the gun, I think he lost interest in it and wouldn't waste time and spend more money in producing a manual for what appeared to be a loser. He may have printed up a one-page sales sheet, but if he did, I've never seen it." So much for backup information.

"While discussing the two prototypes, I asked my host how he had come into possession of the pair," Lewis recalls. The Ares outfit was located in Port Clinton, Ohio, and Knight Engineering Co. was in Florida,

almost a nation apart. In spite of this, Knight's staff of gunsmiths, machinists and arms technicians—not to mention the computer-designing technology available in the Vero Beach establishment—had been called upon to do a great deal of prototype and testing work for Stoner's ever-increasing number of armament ideas.

The destruction of the Berlin Wall, of course, marked the beginning of the end of the Cold War. It also marked the resulting reduction in the number of arms development contracts being let by the various branches of the armed services with the approval of Congress. The result was that Ares, Inc., eventually fell on hard times.

According to the few firearms writers who managed to get inside the high fences and guarded gates of the Ares compound, gaining access had to be more difficult than getting into the president's Oval Office for a social visit. Gary Paul Johnston, a friend and former co-worker with Jack Lewis, told him that Top Secret was the key term used to describe this armament think-tank and that it could be difficult even to determine that Gene Stoner was involved in the enterprise!

Lewis was given to understand that when Ares eventually ceased to operate—but before the last employees left, locking the gates behind them—quite a bill for work done had built up with Knight Engineering. Stoner and Knight had been close friends for years and a friendly arrangement was made whereby the Knight was given the run of the prototype vaults, selecting what he wanted as a means of settling the bill. The Shah of Iran's tank with Stoner's cannon was one of the items chosen. The prototypes of the two folding subguns were among other trade-off trophies.

Stoner's Executive Subgun weighs about five pounds, before being loaded with a magazine holding 30 rounds of 9mm ammo. Unfolded and ready to

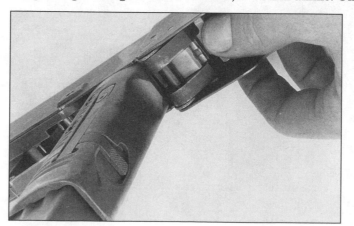

A spring-loaded catch at the rear of the grip/magazine well controls the folding or unfolding of the gun. Above it is the hinge on which the gun is folded.

Specifications

Name:	No official name or model number; popularly called the Executive Submachine Gun.
Caliber:	9mm Parabellum.
Operation:	Unlocked breech mechanism.
Cyclic Rate:	Estimated at 500 to 600 rounds per minute.
Weight:	4.6 pounds, empty.
Length:	10.6 inches (folded); 19.29 inches (unfolded and operational).
Magazine:	30 rounds.
Sights:	None.
Maker:	Ares, Inc. Port Clinton, Ohio (no longer in business)

fire, it measures 19.75 inches overall. Thickness, top to bottom in this mode is 3.25 inches; folded into what appears to be a metal cigar box, width becomes 6.5 inches. The width is a thin but efficient 1.56 inches.

When the metal "cigar box" is picked up, the spring-loaded button in a corner of the metal block is pressed inward. At this point, one portion of the metal case swings to the rear to become a thin buttstock that probably would work best from the hip position rather than shoulder-mounted, which would take more time. The lack of sights might also present a problem for someone used to seeing them atop a gun barrel. When the rear section is aligned with the front section carrying the barrel, the two sections snap together.

On Knight Armament's outdoor test range, the Knight technician loaded the magazine as Lewis watched. He snapped it into the well and asked at what range they should do our firing.

"We were standing at an open-ended metal structure that marks the 100-meter mark, but I motioned toward the dirt backstop that is located farther down the property," Lewis recalls. "I had inspected the area earlier that morning and spotted a number of splintered bowling pins lying against the dirt berm. The pins had been pretty well shot up in other tests, but would do for our purposes."

The first magazine of ammo was expended at about 25 yards with no great marksmanship displayed, even though Lewis fired the gun from the shoulder and simply sighted down the top surface of the barrel. Several of the bowling pins were hit, but it was not a performance that would pay off in what Lewis tends to refer to as "a Close Encounter of the Worst Kind."

The corporate coach reloaded the magazine and the two of them moved down to what they paced off to be in the close vicinity of seven yards. "I reasoned that seven yards—maybe 20 feet—would be the distance from an executive's seat behind his desk and the door an assailant or terrorist would have to come through," Lewis explains. "We didn't have an executive desk around for the sake of realism, so my erstwhile instructor showed me how the square of metal could be drawn from a hip pocket, quickly brought into action and fired. He fired from the shoulder, putting several of the badly used bowling pins out of their misery."

At this point, the Knight technician unrolled what turned out to be a standard silhouette target he had been carrying. The dirt berm was almost vertical, so he was able to place the target against it, then use broken twigs from nearby citrus trees to pin it in place.

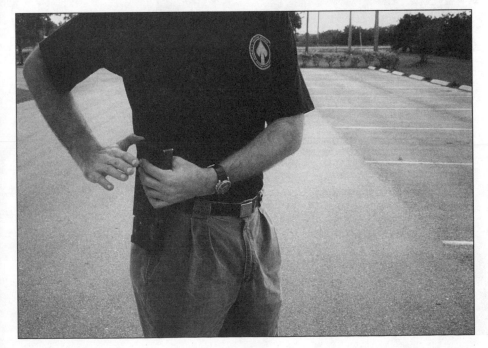

The folded subgun is drawn from the deep pocket of a pair of shorts. It looks like a tool case or other small parcel at this point.

Pressing on the button on one corner of the metal "box" results in the submachine gun unfolding. The loaded magazine is contained within the folded gun.

"The subgun was folded into its innocent configuration and I stuffed it into the right rear pocket of my Levis. We weren't timing this event, so I didn't hurry getting the package out of my pocket. That was easy. And when I pressed the steel button, the gun acted as it should, literally falling into its fully operational mode. I fired from the hip, expending the entire available 9mm supply.

"I won't lie," Lewis admits. "There were rounds kicking up dust all over that berm, but about half of my bullets were in the kill zone on the silhouette. I like to think those were the first rounds and the dust-makers came later."

The ammo Lewis was shooting that bright winter morning was Winchester's 9mm 115-grain Silvertip hollowpoints. Mike Jordan, the information guru for Winchester Ammunition, told us later that this particular load has a velocity of approximately 1095 feet per second at 50 yards. At that distance, the bullet is creating some 300 foot-pounds of energy. Hollowpoints are not considered good fodder for full-auto weaponry, but these loads performed flawlessly.

"I neglected to ask Mike about the length of the barrel in which the test had been made," Lewis says, "but at most, we were firing at 25 yards from the Stoner gun, so I would judge the ballistics we experienced compared somewhat favorably with Winchester's."

There are no documents or guidance to suggest what the little subgun's cyclic rate of fire may be,

but Lewis reports that the gun's lack of recoil and barrel torque was unusual. Using the ease of control as a gauge, he judges the rate of fire to be somewhere between 500 and 600 rounds per minute

Lewis was back home evaluating the material he had assembled on the so-called Executive Subgun during his Florida trip, when a shooting acquaintance showed up in his office, offering what could only be interpreted as a knowing grin.

"You remember that folding submachine gun you've been telling me about?" he wanted to know.

The spring-loaded snap does its thing and the parts become a service-able 9mm subgun.

"Sure," Lewis said. "I just had the pictures printed. Look here." Lewis fanned the 5x7-inch prints out across the top of his desk. These were some of the photos he had taken in Florida. This particular set was of the Executive Submachine Gun.

The visitor eyed the black-and-white photos for a long moment, then reached over Lewis' shoulder to drop what appeared to be a color-printed pamphlet on top of the pictures.

"Well, you may have made a big discovery in Florida, but it's a gun the Russians are making now!" The full-color catalog was folded to a specific page. As Lewis stared down at it, two photos of what appeared to the same gun shown in his own photos stared back at him. With minor exceptions, they appeared to be the same gun. The Russian-built gun advertised in the catalog appeared to be made totally of blued steel. It also appeared to have fold-down front and rear sights, as well as a slightly larger trigger guard than was installed on either of the Stoner prototypes.

Printed in German and English as it was, the catalog obviously had been meant to target the countries familiar with these two languages, even if it was not the native tongue. The last page of the catalog carried a Moscow address for Russia's Research Institute for Special Equipment of the Ministry of Public Affairs. Also listed were the gun's specifications.

As suggested by Reed Knight, Jr., there probably never had been a spec sheet for the Stoner product, since marketing plans never had developed to that point. But as soon as Lewis was

The folding subgun, designed for threatened businessmen, diplomats and such is a truly surprise weapon and dangerous at close ranges.

able to con his friend into leaving the catalog on loan, then send him on his triumphant, self-satisfied way, our co-author began to compare the Russian's specification chart with the pencil-scrawled notes he had taken at Knight's Armament a couple of weeks before.

Measurements of the Stoner folding subgun had been taken with an ordinary steel tape marked off in feet and inches. Those printed by the Russians for their PP-90 were in the metric system. "The Russian figures had more decimal points than mine," Lewis reports, "but the measurements I made in Florida were too close to those listed for the Russian gun for it to be simple coincidence!" The only major disparity lay in the fact that the Russians allegedly had tested the gun with what they stated was a 61-grain 9mm bullet for a muzzle velocity that translated to be 1050 feet per second.

The Russian catalog also stated that one of the maker's test staff had fired the gun in the unsupported offhand position at 25 meters and had put all 30 rounds into a square measuring abut 17 inches in diameter. These figures, incidentally, again were interpolated from the metric by Lewis' pocket calculator.

Thinking that he had happened upon a case of international copyright piracy, Lewis called Reed Knight, Jr., to discuss what he had learned.

"There's nothing really that unusual about the design," Knight admitted, "and it's possible some other people could have had the same idea. We know similar guns have been introduced right here in the United States. In fact, one gunsmith produced about 100 of them a few years back and was able to market them."

"But where did he get the plans?" Lewis wanted to know. "How close was his design to Stoner's?"

"They were almost identical," Knight admitted, "but there were some minor design differences, and this guy insisted he was working from his own blueprints."

"So what about the Russians?" Lewis asked. It turned out Knight had not seen the Russian catalog, but he added that at least one other gun designer had come up with a folding subgun that bore great resemblance to the two prototypes in the Knight collection.

"I'd contact the Russians and ask who designed the gun?" was Reed Knight's suggestion.

Lewis did that some six months ago, addressing his letter to the designated agency of the Ministry of Internal Affairs, which has an address on Lubianka, not far from headquarters of the old KGB, the now disbanded Soviet Secret Police.

Lewis admits that the island on which he now lives in Hawaii has to be America's last communications frontier. Mail, telephone calls and faxes do not always reach their planned destinations. The international mail service could be at fault, either coming or going, he admits, but in the six months prior to this writing, he had heard nothing from the Russians. His remaining clue is in the name the Russians gave the subgun, calling it the PP-90.

"If the Russian gunmakers follow the example of some other countries, it is likely that the PP-90 designation indicates that the Russian gun was produced in 1990," he points out. "If so, this only confuses matters even more." •

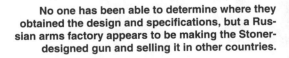

No one has been able to determine where they obtained the design and specifications, but a Russian arms factory appears to be making the Stoner-designed gun and selling it in other countries.

CHAPTER 21

SECOND-GENERATION SUBGUN

The HM-3 9mm Submachine Gun Has Been A Father-To-Son Production.

RAPHAEL MENDOZA, considered the father of Mexico's modern firearms industry, was working at the Mexican National Arms factory in 1930 when he developed a gas-operated light machine gun that came to be designated as the Model C-1934. This became the standard light machine gun of the Mexican army in that period.

Early in World War II, a modified version of the C-1934 was produced, this one chambered for the 7mm cartridge. This particular weapon was not adopted by the Mexican army, although it was designed for military use as a light machine gun on a bipod, and when mounted on a tripod, a heavy machine gun.

Rafael Mendoza formed his own company and designed a number of other automatic weapons, including a light machine gun chambered for the 30-06 round. A number of his guns went into limited production, several of them using the Mendoza idea of a reversible firing pin. If a pin broke, it was simple to remove it, reverse the ends and continue to fire. This, of course, has been copied by numerous designers since.

It was in the 1950s that the younger Mendoza came up with designs for several lightweight submachine guns. These saw limited use by the Mexican military and the country's law enforcement agencies. The only one that Jack Lewis has seen was in a police station in Juarez sometime in the early 1960s. Apparently this gun was not a success and is reported to be one of the things that tended to irk Rafael Mendoza.

But there seems to have been some sort of like father, like son syndrome working, for it was Hector Mendoza, Rafael's son, who took over operation of his father's company, Productos Mendoza, S.A., located in Mexico City. The younger Mendoza also had a thing about producing a successful submachine gun and the record shows that patent applications relative to the HM-3 submachine gun were filed in Mexico City in 1973. Patent applications also were filed in the United States in 1974 and 1975, all in the name of Hector Mendoza Orozco.

Hector Mendoza could hardly be called a simple man, since he was

Without its stock unfolded, the Mendoza HM-3 is a compact 9mm that is more simple than the subgun designed by Hector Mendoza's father.

smart enough to keep the design of his little subgun relatively simple. As the designer of the HM-3, he announced a number of objectives in the gun's development which he intended to achieve.

First, he insisted upon a simple stock that would be ready to use, causing no delay in the gunner moving the gun to the firing position. He had designed the gun with an exposed bolt, which he felt would be easy to wipe off if it collected dirt, and he wanted a simple means of guiding the bolt to the rear during recoil.

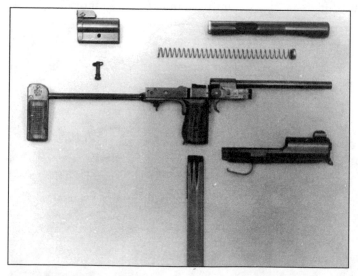

When field-stripped, the Mendoza HM-3 submachine gun consists of seven assemblies. Cleaning and maintenance require only a few minutes.

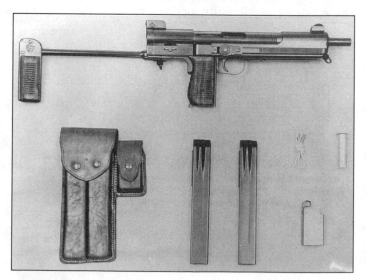

As marketed, the Mendoza HM-3 has been supplied with accessories that include a sling (not shown), a pouch to hold the two furnished magazines, a magazine filler and cleaning accessories.

With the stock swiveled into position, what has been the front hand grip becomes the buttstock. This was a bit of brilliant engineering by young Mendoza.

He included in the designs his father's innovation, the double-ended firing pin, and a grip safety.

It has been our observation that most Latin American arms designers tend to follow old patterns to a great degree, often having bulk and weight in their inventions, when they could easily be improved with modern streamlining and lightweight materials.

Hector Mendoza was one of those who had heeded the need for modernization and that effort shows in the external configuration of the HM-3. Among other design factors, the magazine is housed in the gun's grip; it is out of the way, but totally functional. More important, perhaps, as a design function is the fact that the bolt is literally wrapped around the gun's barrel. The bolt functions much like the slide found in some straight blowback pistols such as several of the Browning models.

Investigation shows that there is no upper receiver as such, but there is a small housing at the upper rear of the gun; the bolt recoils into this recess. According to Tom Nelson, author of *Submachine Guns of the World*, "Without this housing, the bolt might strike the shooter, when the gun is used for aimed fire." The front sight guard is designed to act as a charging handle by which the bolt can be pulled back to the firing position.

In keeping with the younger Mendoza's effort to maintain simplicity in the design, the bolt meets that need, but tests show that it also has several limitations. Should the gunner happen to grip the barrel during the heat of a firefight,

movement of the slide-like bolt could cause a badly damaged hand. The shooter must concentrate on using the horizontal foregrip positioned beneath the barrel. The recoil spring, incidentally, encircles the barrel.

Hector Mendoza's HM-3 fires from the open bolt—or open slide, if you will. The fire selector/safety lever is positioned above the trigger guard on the gun's left side.

When the fire selector is turned to the upward vertical position, the gun is ready for semi-automatic fire. When the lever is horizontal, pointing to the rear, full-automatic is the mode and the gun will fire at a cyclic rate of about 600 rounds per minute. For the safe position, this combo lever is turned downward vertically. This blocks the sear and the bolt cannot be released. The magazine release is situated at the base of the firing grip.

A definite design plus is the fact that when the bolt is in its forward

Specifications

Name:	Mendoza HM-3 Sub-machine Gun.
Caliber:	9mm Parabellum.
Operation:	Blowback; fires from open-bolt, for semi-auto or full-auto fire.
Cyclic Rate:	600 rounds per minute.
Weight:	5.93 pounds (empty).
Length:	23.3 inches.
Barrel:	9.25 inches.
Magazine:	32 rounds; single stack.
Maker:	Productos Mendoza Mexico City, Mexico

position, the grip safety must be squeezed before the bolt can be drawn to the rear. A bit of a negative, perhaps, is the fact that the safety is activated the minute the grip is squeezed and released, but it is effective only when the bolt is in the closed position.

Disassembly of the gun for cleaning or repair is in keeping with Hector Mendoza's simplification efforts. For elementary field-stripping, the instructions are:

1. First, remove the magazine and ascertain there is no cartridge in the chamber. If the bolt/slide is not in the forward position at this point, one should ease it forward before continuing.

2. Pull down on the rear of the spring-held trigger guard, then slide the horizontal foregrip forward and off the end of the muzzle.

3. Next, locate the T-headed detent pin that holds the recoil housing to the rear of the gun's grip frame. This detent must be pressed into line with the shaft of the pin, then the recoil housing may be removed.

4. The housing removed, lift the rear of the bolt/slide unit above the rear of the barrel. The bolt/slide then can be moved forward to the barrel muzzle and removed.

5. The recoil spring and the attached barrel bushing now must be moved to the muzzle and removed.

Hector Mendoza has boasted, incidentally, that the entire field-stripping sequence can be accomplished in as little as 13 seconds. In spite of this, the HM-3 has met with no major successes in the arms market. Several Latin American countries have purchased guns for testing, with an eye to including the HM-3 in their military armories. It also has been reported that several below-the-border police agencies have purchased guns for local use. ●

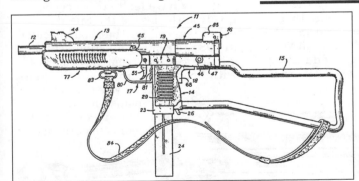

This document from the U.S. Patent Office illustrates the original concept for the Mendoza HM-3. Note that the forend and the skeleton stock are different than on the production model.

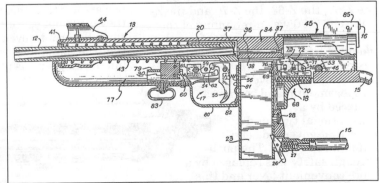

This patent drawing illustrates the working parts of the originally registered gun. This interior design remained basically the same.

CHAPTER 22

STAR'S Z-84: A SUBGUN FOR DIVERS?

The Last Full-Auto Weapon From Star Had A Future With Recon People And Underwater Demolition Specialists.

TODAY, SOMEWHERE IN Spain, there must be an unlikely weapon of war that is waiting to be rediscovered. This is the Star Z-84, the last of a continuing line of submachine guns that started with the maker's Z-45, adopted from the German MP40 during World War II.

The Spanish gun makers acquired the blueprints of the gun in 1942, and after modifying the design a bit, put it into production in 1944. The Spanish army adopted the weapon, as did several other countries, including Portugal and some nations of the Middle East.

Unusual about the Z-45 was the fact that it was one of the first subguns to use a fluted chamber. The gun was designed to fire the 9x23mm submachine gun cartridge, considerably more potent than the standard 9mm Parabellum pistol round. The fluted chamber was designed to make extraction of the cartridge case easier. The military version of the Z-45 had a folding stock. The barrel was enclosed in a perforated metal jacket that was held in place—as was the 7.75-inch barrel—by a muzzle compensator.

After this came periodic updates with newer models being labeled as the Z-62, the Z-63, the Z-70 and the Z-70B. The Z-70 was a renaming of the Z-62 and had two interesting features: a double trigger and a hammer firing system. The trigger, which controlled the rate of fire, proved to be temperamental and soon was replaced by a conventional type and a lever that governed semi-auto and full-auto. The push-through safety was replaced by a more convenient lever and this

gun became the Z-70B, which was accepted by the Spanish army in 1971. In the early 1980s, Jack Lewis had the opportunity to tour Spain's Astra arms factory, a Star competitor. One thing he found odd was that members of the Civil Guardia who protected the Astra factory against espionage and possible corporate piracy all were armed with the Star 70B subgun.

With the possible danger of adding more confusion regarding this family of weapons produced by Star Bonifacio Echeverria S.A., at their plant in Eibar, it should be pointed out that the Z-62 had been chambered originally for the 9mm Largo round. When the chambering was changed to 9mm Parabellum, it became the Z-63; later, this same gun became the Z-70. The Z-70B fired the 9mmP from conception.

Somewhere along the way, the powers at Star came to realize that they could not continue to revamp the same firearm forever. The result was that the company's board of directors junked all previous plans and policies,

Unlike previous Z-series subguns made by Star, the Z-84 stock folds on top of the gun, but does not interfere with the sighting system.

and decided on a new beginning for their submachine gun. The result was the Star Z-84, which was introduced in 1985.

What was produced was a compact subgun that was both light in weight and efficient. The company was in poor financial shape at the time and it was hoped the Spanish army would adopt the gun. This happened only on a limited basis, small quantities of the Z-84 being purchased to equip special mission units. It also became the standard for the country's paramilitary Civil Guardia and was supplied to a number of other countries, including Angola. Word is that negotiations were under way with several Latin American countries at the time Star closed its doors in 1996. One factor that may have led to this decision involved the loss of the Spanish police market, for that body decided in 1988 to replace all submachine guns in law enforcement armories with Franchi pump-action shotguns.

The gun was of interest to the Spanish navy, which purchased a number of the guns to outfit scuba

Unfolded, the stock is sturdy and practical. Construction is heavy enough that it will take a great deal of punishment in the field.

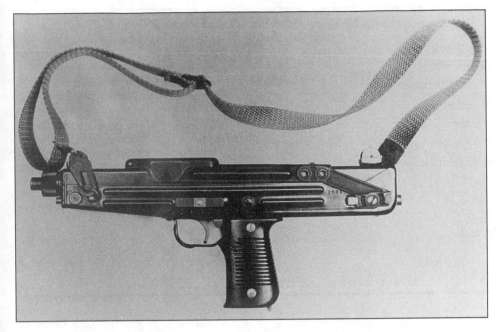

The receiver of the Z-84 is of stamped metal, although the inner workings are precision machined parts. This design was a total departure from previous Z-series guns.

teams involved in underwater operations. A fact that was much publicized at the time of the gun's introduction was its capability for firing underwater without any adverse effect on the mechanism.

This capability was somewhat ignored in later sales efforts, for Star officials had to admit that if fired in an underwater situation, the effective range was no more than five meters! In addition, both the Germans and Russians have developed dart-launching armament that proved to be more effective at far greater ranges.

The gun's chief role for Spanish navy scuba divers did not lie in any scenario that would seem like a bad script for a television segment. Instead, the gun's worth lay in the fact that submersion did not affect it and it could be fired as soon as the divers surfaced or were on their way ashore. A plus, whether submerged or ashore, is the fact that the gun has a thick finish coating its exterior surfaces as well as all interior parts. This finish is impervious to saltwater damage and the gun requires no special lubricants or other preservatives.

Beneath Star's special finish, it's obvious the gun is manufactured from precision castings and steel stampings. According to the manufacturer's early promotional info, special attention had been paid to the feeding system, which was alleged to feed standard military-issue 9mm ammo, half-jacketed rounds and even softpoints with equal degrees of efficiency.

Like earlier guns in the Star Z series, this 84 model is blowback-

operated and fires from an open bolt. As an aid to retaining the compact design, the bolt telescopes around the rear end of the six-groove, right-hand twist barrel which measures only 8.46 inches; a 10.6-inch barrel also was available.

The gun features a fluted chamber, unusual in a blowback-operated firearm, and we're not convinced that it provides any special advantage—or disadvantage in firing. The center of gravity also was given considerable thought by the designers and is situated directly above the pistol grip. The grip also serves as the magazine well for the 25- or 30-round box magazines.

The gun has a removable folding stock that when extended, gives the gun an overall length of 24.2 inches. On other guns in the Star Z series, the stocks have folded under the gun, the butt pad becoming a forward

hand grip. On the Z-84, the stock folds in the opposite direction, the pad lying flat against the top of the receiver, but not interfering with the sights. With the stock folded or removed, the length is shortened to 16.1 inches. This compact size and the center of balance over the grip make for relatively accurate one-handed fire, we found. We use the word relative in consideration of the fact that sans magazine, the gun weighs 6.6 pounds!

Loops for a sling are positioned at the right rear and left front of the gun. Both front and rear sights are protected by heavy-duty steel ears. The front sight can be adjusted both for windage and elevation, while the rear sight is a flip-type aperture with settings for 100 and 200 meters. Using a steel tape, we found that the sight radius is a fraction over 13 inches.

The Z-63 was a fore-runner of the Z-84. Other versions appeared in the years between, but changes were only minor.

Specifications

Name:	Star Z-84 Submachine Gun.
Caliber:	9 x 19mm Parabellum.
Operation:	Blowback; fires from open-bolt.
Cyclic Rate:	600 rounds per minute.
Weight:	6.6 pounds (empty).
Length:	24.2 inches (stock extended); 15.1 inches (stock folded).
Barrel:	8.4 inches (standard); 10.1 inches optional.
Magazine:	25 or 30 rounds; staggered column.
Stock:	Folding metal.
Maker:	Star Bonifacio Echeverria, S.A. Apartado 3 48300 Guernica, Spain (now owned by Astra Sport, S.A.)

The Z-84 is chambered for the familiar 9x19mm Parabellum cartridge and has a cyclic rate of fire of 600 rounds per minute. Muzzle velocity is in the vicinity of 1300 rounds per second.

In operation, the gun's breechblock assembly, which includes the bolt, travels on two full-length rails that are part of the breechblock housing, but the design leaves ample room in this relationship that dirt or other debris are not likely to interfere with proper firing. On the inner rear front face of the breechblock is the cartridge seat with what the manual describes as "a pointed protuberance" —the firing pin—that strikes the primer. The lower rear end of the breechblock is opened in order to pass over the magazine. On the lower left side of the breechblock are several teeth cut into the metal. The foremost of these holds the breechblock in its full-cocked position; those cuts milled at the center are safety teeth in case of incomplete cocking. In other words,

should your hand slip off the cocking handle while drawing it to the rear, the gun will not be fired; an excellent safety touch.

Pulling the cocking handle all the way to the rear, the breechblock overrides the last cocking safety and is locked in the fully cocked position by the sear. Viewed through the ejection port, a red signal is visible on the front of the breechblock. When the cocking handle is released, once the breechblock is cocked, the handle snaps forward to its original position where it remains during firing.

The safety is a sliding button inside the trigger guard and there also is an automatic inertia safety that is designed to lock the bolt in the closed position. This safety is overridden when the cocking handle is pulled to the rear and remains disconnected while the gun is being fired. The selector for single shot or full-auto also is a sliding mechanism located on the gun's left side just above the trigger guard.

Field-stripping of the Z-84 takes only seconds. For this, the stock must be in the extended position. The cross-bolt located at the forward end of the lower receiver is pushed out, thus freeing the upper receiver casing. This allows the breechblock containing the bolt, recoil spring and guide rod to be removed. To remove the barrel, one simply depresses the locking catch for the barrel nut, unscrews the nut and pulls out the barrel.

When we test-fired the Spanish-built subgun, it was done with the stock extended and the butt pad mounted in the shoulder pocket. The left hand was positioned on the bottom of the lower receiver near its forward end. We learned quickly that care was necessary here to be certain the hand wrapped around the gun did not stray forward to feel the effects of a heated barrel!

The gun features top ejection, but fired cases are thrown to the shooter's right and present no problem other than a possible

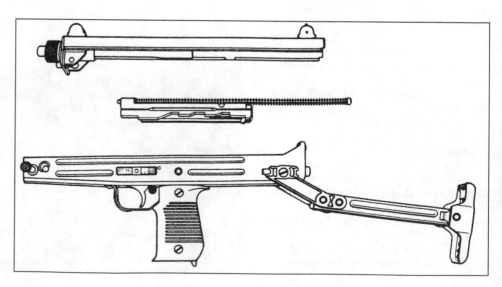

Field-stripping of the Z-84 illustrates the simplicity of design. At the time of its introduction, much was made of the fact that it could be fired underwater.

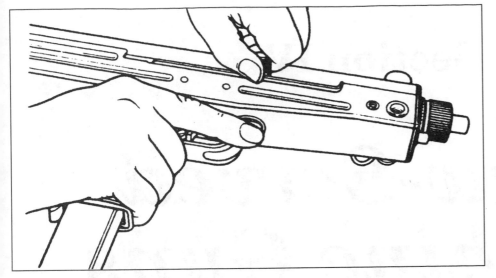

The cocking knob is situated on the right-hand side of the gun, which can be awkward, requiring the left hand to cross over the top of the gun in order to cock it.

distraction during full-auto fire. When the gun is cocked, a sliding cover protects the ejection port.

We found the trigger pull to be lighter than either of us liked and Lewis suggested that the pistol grip could have been slimmed down for more positive holding. However, the fact that this grip holds the magazine possibly negated this modification. At both the 100- and 200-meter ranges, the sights were okay, although we used some Kentucky windage for correction rather than take the time to adjust the front sight for elevation. This is easy to do with a subgun; it's sort of like directing fire on the target by walking fired rounds across the ground until they are on the objective. Trying this technique in organized instruction, of course, will drive most range coaches up a tree.

Rather than an established range with paper targets, we tested the gun in an old quarry, firing across the floor of this man-made abyss at white rocks and other natural objects that might be termed targets of opportunity. It is understood that the Belgian Army tested the gun back in the late 1980s and gave it good marks for accuracy at 50 meters. The ranges at which we were shooting were slightly over 100 meters. This called for use of the sight with the smaller aperture.

As is usually the case with open-bolt guns, maintaining accuracy during full-auto fire was less than successful, and Lewis complained that the gun tended to climb at about the same rate as the old Thompson submachine gun. It turned out that our co-author had not fired a Thompson in about two decades, so that may be an unfair comparison. At the 100-meter range, this could have been a display of the shooters' inadequacies rather than those of the gun. Others will be quick to point out

that the subgun is not designed for effective fire at 100 yards; it is a tool for close-in work in caves, tunnels, room clearing and the like.

We are quick to agree with this mission identification, but one must remember that we tended to make this a fun shoot as well as a scientific investigation. In addition, we had a good supply of Yugoslavian-made ammo that had been imported by Hansen & Co. before the nation exploded in revolutionary violence.

Today's firearms business is a changing world of its own. Many manufacturers throughout the Western world have disappeared or been absorbed by former competitors. Economics and increasingly harsh anti-gun legislation have changed the arms industry.

That was the case with Star Bonifacio Echeverria, S.A. For many years, gun dealers in the United States were among their most important customers, but by the early 1990s, they were down to one major U.S. outlet, Interarms, located in northern Virginia.

"Interarms was importing thousands and thousands of Star-made handguns and selling them," recalls Tom Nelson, a one-time Interarms vice-president, who now operates Collectors Armory, Limited. "Then, about 1994, our laws changed for the worse and any number of handguns that had been imported from Star suddenly were outlawed. This meant that Interarms had to cancel most of its orders, and this was the death knell for Star."

Astra, the former competitor, was a long-established family business, but had been sold to a new owner. This same individual bought the equipment, patents and remaining stock of the Star enterprise when the company went out of business.

Of the last 100 or so Star employees, some of them were absorbed by the Astra operation.

Meantime, it's our feeling that the Star Z-84 never really had an opportunity to display its potential, on land or under the seas. Today, it probably still offers good potential for some enterprising entrepreneur. ●

The grip of the gun holds the magazine, an aid in bringing the balance to the center of the piece. Rate of fire is about 600 rounds per minute.

Section IV
Crew-Served Machine Guns

CHAPTER 23

MACHINE GUNS: FROM LIGHT TO HEAVY

Technology Gives Us Faster Fire And Larger Projectiles.

AMERICAN WAS ONE of the first places to adopt automation and labor-saving devices. Combined with this was the lack of an aristocratic, traditional warrior class. Therefore, it should come as no surprise that the weapon that made death a wholesale affair and eliminated most of the glory from war should be invented in the United States.

The first successful machine gun was invented by Richard Jordan Gatling in 1862. He correctly saw that the generals in the Civil War had adopted tactics of attrition, i.e., decimation and slaughter. Though the songs and propaganda of the era were of brave, personal combat, the reality was impersonal destruction.

Gatling's invention was adopted too late to make a significant difference in that war, though it was used later in the Indian Wars and the Spanish-American War. Its hand-cranked action made it outmoded by the 1880s, but its multi-barrel concept has been adapted to the most modern aerial machine guns.

The next major advance in machine gun development came with another American, Hiram Maxim. He was the first to harness the power of the cartridge propellant to cycle the action of the gun—particularly important in conjunction with the development of

smokeless powder by the French. Maxim patented his gun in 1883. It was first used in action by the British in Gambia in 1888.

The Maxim gun was not accepted immediately by the U.S. military, which is why its inventor had to sell it in Europe. Great Britain gave it a

What amounts to the family of 22-caliber bullets is the current military vogue. The Belgian-made FN Minimi, chambered for 5.56mm, was reworked to become our force's M249 assault weapon. In this instance, a rifle magazine rather than an ammo belt is in place.

test in Asia and Africa in the closing years of the 19th century. The Maxim gun gave the small British expeditionary force a substantial advantage over vast numbers of primitively armed tribesmen. In spite of Winston Churchill's brilliant prose about the heroism of the light cavalry at Omdurman in 1898 in the Sudan, it was a Maxim gun that created most of the casualties and

set the Dervishes to running. The Maxim also figured heavily in the Boer War of 1899-1902.

However, the British officer class could not foresee the influence of the machine gun in European warfare. Although the Maxim was nice for blowing away Dervishes, and Fuzzy-Wuzzies, it was not a weapon for use against men who understood Christian charity, military glory and elan.

By the time of World War I, all the major powers—Britain, France, Germany, Russia and Japan—had the Maxim gun, but none could imagine how it would alter tactics, at least not until 10,000,000 young men were dead. By that time, the bright uniforms were gone, along with the bayonet charges. Men wore mud-colored uniforms and hid behind tanks.

By modern standards the Maxim—called the Vickers gun in England—was a medium machine gun. It weighed about 150 pounds and was operated for decades in second-line communist armies, transported on sledges or wheeled carriages. The problem was to make full automatic firepower more portable so it could advance with the infantry.

For their own army, the Spanish developed the CETME light machine gun. This version is chambered for 5.56mm for squad support. Note the similarities to the classic German MG42.

The U.S. M-60 light machine gun, seen here with bipod, is chambered for 7.62mm NATO and was the mainstay of the ground war in Vietnam. It was considered both powerful and reliable by soldiers and Marines. It is still in the military inventory, but has been replaced in the field by the M240.

Toward the end of World War I, the American forces adopted the Browning Automatic Rifle (BAR). This 16-pound weapon could fire 30-06 bullets at a rate of 350 to 550 rounds per minute from a 20-round box magazine. This weapon served throughout World War II and Korea. A similar gun, the BREN (Brno-Enfield, a joint Czech/British development) was adopted by the British Commonwealth between the wars and served throughout World War II.

Also during World War I, another American inventor, Colonel Isaac N. Lewis, produced a light machine gun that was named after him. The 26-pound Lewis Gun was mounted on biplanes and carried by infantry. It was distinguished by the large aluminum radiator that surrounded the barrel, a device that was found to be almost useless, and the pan-type magazine atop the gun. In spite of its drawbacks, this gun had a long career, with extensive service through the late 1940s in such out-of-the-way places as Palestine.

Too late to jump on the Maxim bandwagon of the World War I, America turned to inventor John M. Browning to design its standard medium and light machine guns. The Browning M1917A1 medium machine gun had a large barrel jacket for water cooling. It fed from a 250-round fabric belt, later changed to one of disintegrating metal links. It fired the standard 30-06 rifle cartridge at a cyclic rate of 450-600 rounds per minute.

Length was 38.5 inches, and weight was 41 pounds. Its special tripod mount weighed 13.15 pounds.

Browning also designed an air-cooled light machine gun, the M1919A4. This 30-caliber weapon fired at 400-450 rpm. As with the M1917A1, it used a cloth belt, later replaced by disintegrating metal links. The gun was 41 inches overall, and had a 24-inch barrel. Weight was 31 pounds for the gun and 14 pounds for the M2 tripod. A more portable version of this gun was produced as the M1919A6, adding a shoulder stock, carrying handle and bipod, modifications now considered

This Thai soldier has come up with a novel means of feeding the ammo belt for his M-60 machine gun. Photo was taken at a border outpost in northeast Thailand.

The Japanese 7.7mm Type 92 aircraft machine gun was used by that country's navy during World War II. It was a close copy of the Lewis gun, but the sights and drum magazine have been removed. Beneath is the Japanese "knee" mortar. Actually, it had to be held on the ground for firing.

In background is an American armored car captured by these German soldiers in 1944. The machine was equipped with a 50-caliber heavy machine gun.

be triggered by an experienced gunner. Standard tactical burst length is six rounds.

The M-60 has a shoulder stock, carrying handle, bipod, quick-change barrel, and an optional M122 tripod. Overall length is 43.75 inches with a barred length of 25.6 inches. Weight is 23.05 pounds plus a 15-pound tripod. Vietnam infantry generally carried it with only the bipod for patrols and in the assault. The tripod usually was reserved for fixed, defensive positions. It was also mounted on jeeps, armored personnel carriers, tanks, patrol boats and helicopters.

Concurrent with the development of the M-60 for the infantry, aircraft-mounted machine guns became heavier and faster. The Gatling principle was combined with modern metallurgy and electric operation. A 7.62mm infantry support weapon was called the Mini-gun, used from the doorway of a converted C47 transport plane. A more powerful Gatling used on jet aircraft was the 20mm Vulcan.

An even more powerful seven-barrel 30mm GAU-8/A Avenger cannon was mounted on the Fairchild A-10, an Air Force ground support aircraft. The Avenger is 21 feet long with a 93.1-inch barrel system. It carries 1350 rounds and fires them at either 2100 or 4200 rpm. It fires 6600-grain HEI (High Explosive Incendiary) projectiles for use against personnel, fuel dumps and

standard on light machine guns.

Finally, Browning produced a 50-caliber machine gun for anti-vehicle and anti-aircraft use and was the standard protection for bombers in World War II. A heavy-barrel version of this gun, the M2HB, was designed in 1933. This particular weapon is still being produced by Saco Defense Industries and is in use, mounted on armored vehicles or on the M3 tripod. Although it cannot penetrate modern tank armor, it is useful to strike personnel in trucks or hiding behind light cover. Tripod-mounted 50s have been used extensively on observation posts in South Korea, with others mounted on armored personnel carriers for quick reaction forces in the Demilitarized Zone between North and South Korea. The M2HB is 65.1 inches overall with a 45-inch barrel. The cyclic rate is 450-550 rounds per minute. Weight is 84 pounds for the gun, plus 44 pounds for the M3 tripod. This puts it well into the heavy machine gun class. Considering that this weapon has served for over 60 years, it must be considered another of Browning's most successful designs and one of the best HMGs ever produced anywhere.

The Vietnam-era successor to the 30-caliber Browning machine guns

was the M-60 7.62x51mm General Purpose Machine Gun. This weapon utilizes the belt feed mechanism of the MG42 and the operating mechanism of the FG42, both German machine guns of World War II. The M-60 fires full automatic only, but its cyclic rate is only 600 rpm, so single rounds can

David Steele test fires a Browning M2HB 50-caliber machine gun in the hills of South Korea in 1958. Updated models are still being used by our armed forces.

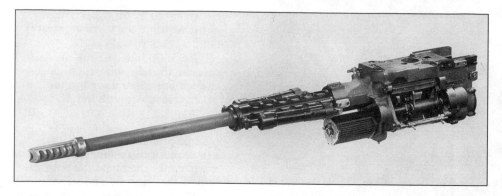

The Hughes XM230E1 30mm Chain Gun was designed to be used in helicopters or armored vehicles for suppressive fire. It has been made in several different chamberings and still is in use with the Marines in 25mm.

light vehicles. It also fires API (Armor Piercing Incendiary) projectiles with depleted uranium cores for use against tanks. The A-10 Thunderbolt is probably the most successful tank-killer in the world. In addition to its Avenger gun, it carries a mix of rockets, bombs and electronic gear. Though it proved the best ground support aircraft in the Persian Gulf War, the Air Force has announced its intention to scrap it in favor of more high-tech aircraft.

Perhaps the most sophisticated Gatling of all is the HIVAP (High Velocity All Purpose) machine gun designed by Don Stoner and developed by TRW Ordance Systems. This weapon utilizes the open-chamber principle invented by David Dardick for his famous pistol in 1950. The HIVAP also employs a dual-feed system with linkless mechanism. A sub-caliber flechette enclosed in a plastic "round" is the ammunition. This weapon fires at an incredible 30,000 rounds per minute, and it has the potential to fire faster.

One of the more interesting machine gun designs, developed by Hughes Helicopters in the 1970s, was the Hughes Chain Gun. The 30mm gun mounted on the Apache attack helicopter, also made by Hughes, was designed in the company's Ordnance Systems Division. Technically called the XM230E1, it was known by the trademark "Chain Gun." This referred to a specific family of weapons, all powered by a unique, but simple and reliable, chain drive. It included 7.62mm, 30mm and 25mm versions. The first two could be mounted on the 500MD, AH-64A or other helicopters, while the 25mm gun was designed for use by armored vehicles, notably the M2 and M3 Bradley fighting vehicles.

Work on the Chain Gun family began back in 1972 with an experimental 20mm version. This prototype was used to develop the 30mm XM230E1, which would be more appropriate for use on the AH-64A Apache being developed at the other end of the Culver City plant.

The XM230E1 was 64.5 inches overall with a weight of 123 pounds, and a cyclic rate of 625 rounds per minute. It was ground and air tested with over 300,000 rounds of ammo, including Honeywell M789 HEDP (High Explosive Dual Purpose), M799 HEI (High Explosive Incendiary), and M7BB TP (Target Practice) rounds, as well as British ADEN and French DEFA ammunition.

The Chain Gun system was designed to provide a weapon that was comparatively inexpensive to produce, while offering such features as a quick change barrel, outward (overboard) ejection, low gas build-up, light weight, hangfire and double feed protection, reliability and minimum maintenance. Its overall size approaches that of self-powered guns, while retaining the greater reliability of what are usually electrically powered ones.

The smallest member of the Chain Gun family was the EX-34 machine gun. Originally designed as a coaxially mounted tank gun, it also has been adapted for helicopter use. It utilized linked belts (the 25mm M242 and the 30mm XM230E1 are linkless feed) of 7.62 NATO rifle ammunition. It ran 37 inches overall, weighed only 30.2 pounds, and had a cyclic rate of 570 rpm.

Machine guns today can run the gamut from 5.56mm Squad Automatic Weapons like the FN-made M249 to the 30mm GAU-8/A automatic cannon. However, most fit into the categories of Light Machine Gun (LMG), General Purpose Machine Gun (GPMG), Medium Machine Gun (MMG) and Heavy Machine Gun (HMG),in American calibers or 30- to 50-caliber. In this configuration, it has been the most common infantry support weapon of the 20th century, which, in 1914, changed the face of warfare. ●

Using the technology of the hand-cranked Gatling gun of the late 1800s, TRW Systems has developed this multi-barreled gun called the HIVAP. It utilizes an external power source to lay down an incredible rate of fire.

CHAPTER 24

CAN BIGGER BE BETTER?

The 40mm Mark 19 Machine Gun Puts A Different Face On Warfare!

"WHEN MOST OF us in my age bracket hear the word, 'assault,' we tend to recall pictures, paintings and even old combat motion pictures of World War I doughboys coming out of the trenches and charging across No-Mans-Land in an effort to dislodge the enemy from their strongholds.

"That picture, of course, is reinforced by photos of Marines charging ashore at Tarawa, seeking to establish a beachhead, and by troops in Korea going over the seawall at Inchon, rifles and bayonets at the ready," recalls Jack Lewis.

"But today, the assault is less of a bayonet-on-bayonet encounter than at any time in history. For the most part, the greater distances involved in the assault phase of an attack call for armored vehicles transporting troops as close to the enemy as is feasible, while long-range automatic weapons make an effort to worry and confuse those we're fighting and cause them to keep their heads down. This is the ideal situation, but it doesn't always work quite that way."

In the winter of 1998, the 13th Marine Expeditionary Unit stopped over at Marine Base Hawaii on the Island of Oahu for some intensive training before going on to the Far East, where officers and men of the unit would be relieving another unit that had been pursuing the continuing peace-keeping mission.

There was supposed to be an amphibious landing on Hale Koa Beach, part of the Marine Base, but high winter surf made it impractical to beach the air-cushioned landing craft that would carry Marine infantry and the mobile equipment that support them. Instead, the landing exercise was canceled and the ships carrying the 13th MEU sailed around the island to anchor at Pearl Harbor.

It also was deemed impractical to attempt to move tanks, light armored vehicles and amphibious assault vehicles across the freeways of the island to the training grounds. Instead, troops and their issue weapons were transported by bus

with trucks bringing M240 7.62 NATO and 50-caliber Browning-designed machine guns, the 40mm Mark 19 and ammo for all.

The original plan had been to mount the 50-calibers and the 40mm M19s in armored vehicles and fire them from turrets. Our Jack Lewis had been trying to put this type of shoot together for eight months so it could be included in this volume, and he was unfazed when it was announced that the troops would be firing from tripods rather than from the vehicles as the training plan stated.

Many people—some even in the military—tend to think of the M19 40mm as a new weapon, but this probably is due to the fact that it has received little publicity since it originally was used in the Vietnam unpleasantness. At that time, the "brown water" Navy was covering inland waterways of the Mekong Delta in motorized launches, seeking to destroy Viet Cong supply lines. The M19 was considered a valuable piece

The Mark 19 Model 3 machine gun is a crew-served weapon for which the assistant gunner observes the impact area, calling shots for the gunner. The big gun fires 40mm high explosive and armor-piercing grenades, with a maximum effective range of 1500 meters. The gun weighs 75.6 pounds.

The Mark 64 cradle that holds the 40mm machine gun mounts on either an M3 ground tripod or the M4 pedestal mount when installed in vehicles. The cradle weighs 12 pounds.

of equipment aboard each of these vessels. When firing high-explosive ammunition, the round has a kill radius of five meters and a wound radius of 15 meters. It also could be fired to sink Viet Cong shipping and to destroy supplies.

The M19 later was adopted by both the Army and Marines. The former service used the big-bore gun to advantage in Somalia, firing anti-sniper missions and taking out other selected targets with great success.

In 1992, then Captain Charles P. Ferry was ordered to bring forward a HMMWV armed with an M19. The mission would be to help a company that was pinned down by sniper fire. The vehicle involved is known to the troops as the "humvee," the acronym standing for High Mobility Multi-purpose Wheeled Vehicle. It replaced the Jeep, which had been a military fixture for well over a half-century!

Writing later in the October/November 1994 issue of *Infantry* magazine, the captain reported, "Three or four blocks back through the company, on National Street, I found a M19 HMMWV near the front of the column, the squad leader coolly directing the fire of his M19 gunner. I told him we needed his firepower and to inform his platoon leader I was taking him."

Enemy fire was still intense and there was still heavy friendly fire all along National Street where the battalion TAC, the anti-armor platoon and the scouts were, according to Ferry's report. "We worked our way back through the company with the Mark 19 HMMWV following me. I had to ground guide it several times.

"We finally reached the front of the company where the lead armored personnel carrier was stopped and learned that the fire was coming from the large hotel on the left side of the street, about 50 meters in front of the lead platoon. I guided the Mark 19 HMMWV up onto a steep sidewalk so the gunner could get an effective shot, and told him to watch my M-16 tracer rounds and to work the building from top to bottom."

Captain Ferry fired tracers into the hotel and the gunner fired a spotting round into one of the windows on the top story, then switched the 40mm machine gun to full-auto. Working from top to bottom, he took out every window in the hotel.

"The effects were devastating," Captain Ferry reported. "Concrete fragments flew everywhere, and two Somalis fell out of the building!"

When the gunner ceased fire, the captain learned from the company point man that enemy fire also had been coming from another building on the right side of the road. The M19 gunner was directed to fire into the building about 40 meters away and the infantry squads began moving forward, the armored personnel carriers following.

In another Somalia incident, an Army Blackhawk helicopter had been shot down and troops were attempting to extricate the body of the dead pilot without great success. Finally, a cable was brought to the scene and hooked to the M19-mounted HMMWV. No firing was conducted during this operation, but the gunner was on

Assembling the M19 is a two-man job handled by the gunner and his assistant gunner. However, setup takes only minutes and the gun can be disassembled quickly for a tactical move.

The M64 gun cradle has been installed on the tripod and the gun is being set into it. Grooves on each side of the gun slide into lugs on the cradle, then it is held in place by a pin inserted at the rear of the cradle.

constant alert as the helicopter was literally torn apart by means of the cable and the heavy-duty vehicle. Thus, the pilot's body was not left for the Somalis to mutilate as had been done with others. Presence of the M19 no doubt discouraged enemy fire during the rescue.

Jack Lewis had never fired the M19, although he had been able to a take close look at several of the guns aboard the Navy vessels patrolling the Mekong Delta in 1970. Even then, the gun intrigued him. He noted that there have been several minor exterior upgrades in the 29-plus years since he made his unofficial inspection.

The current model, designated as the Mark 19 Model 3, operates on an air-cooled, belt-fed, blowback system, firing from an open bolt. Involved also is something called advanced primer ignition. Overall length from muzzle to hand grips is 43.1 inches and the gun weighs 75.6 pounds, meaning it is a crew-served weapon with the people to carry it and the ammo when needed.

Cyclic rate of fire is 375 rounds per minute, although three-round bursts tend to allow one to judge the result of his shooting better than attempting to run an entire belt of 32 or 48 rounds. Muzzle velocity is reported by the maker, Saco Defense Industries, as being 795 feet per second. In firing the gun, Lewis found he was actually able to see his first round leave the muzzle. Firing two- and three-round bursts, he did not try to follow the grenade-type rounds after that. He was too busy watching the high explosive rounds take apart a volcanic ridge an estimated 1000 meters away. Following the coaching by the lance corporal assigned as his assistant gunner, he held the twin grips at arms' length and leaned back to fire. He did not have to use the sights, since the gun already had

been zeroed for him. As for the position, his comment was, "Uncomfortable but effective."

For this effort, the lieutenant in charge of training insisted that Lewis wear the Kevlar helmet now being issued U.S. service personnel, as well as a flak vest. Later, in reading the manual covering operation of the gun, our author learned the reason for such precautions. The manual warned, "Don't let the bolt slam forward as you open the top cover. Serious injury could result." The next paragraph read, "Do not fire high explosive ammunition at targets less than 200 meters away during training or 75 meters away during combat. Fragmentation can reach the gunner position at distances less than 200 meters."

The Mark 19 Model 3 is composed of five major elements. The receiver assembly holds the other four assemblies, ammo being fed into the feeder on the left side. The second unit is the feed slide assembly and tray, which hold the rounds in the feeder and index the ammo into firing position. The top cover assembly holds

the feed slide assembly and tray. It is opened by means of a latch on the left side for loading or to clean and inspect the feeder mechanism.

The gun's receiver assembly holds the receiver sear. When the action releases the sear, it allows the bolt to go forward. The safety is attached to the sear assembly. The final assembly is the bolt and backplate unit. The bolt fires the round when the sear is depressed by trigger action. The recoil springs drive the bolt forward on the receiver rails, the guide rods holding the springs in position. The trigger and hand grips are located on this backplate assembly.

The M19 is designed with two vertical hand grips with the trigger between them. Instead of the usual trigger design, this is a piece of flat metal that is shaped like the letter Y. The two wings of the Y are pointed toward the shooter. Gripping the twin grips with his fingers, the shooter's thumbs are free and one is placed on each extended wing of the trigger, pushing down hard and holding as long as one wants to fire. The trigger is relatively foolproof, since it takes quite a bit of pressure to activate the gun. The safety switch is immediately beneath the Y-split trigger and is rectangular in shape. A solid block of metal, it must be pushed to the left to put the gun on safe, shoved to the right when ready to fire.

Before working the safety, though, the gun has to be loaded and charged. On each side of the receiver is a large handle. The gunner, with a hand on each of these handles, pulls them to the rear, drawing the bolt back. Then, the handles are carefully moved forward and folded out of the way.

In many respects, the M19 is no different than other machine guns. For example, there have been incidents

Co-author Jack Lewis checks out the setup of the M19 on the range at Marine Base Hawaii, where the 13th Marine Expeditionary Unit paused to train before continuing to the Far East.

Wearing a borrowed camouflage helmet and armored vest over his civilian duds, World War II machine gunner Jack Lewis prepares to fire his first round from the Mark 19 40mm machine gun. He was a good deal more confident, he says, than were some of the Marines offering him guidance. He was impressed with the big bore's potential. The test took place at Marine Corps Base Hawaii, where Lewis was stationed in the 1950s. In that era, it was home of the 1st Provisional Marine Air-Ground Task Force.

Specifications

Name: Mark 19 Model 3 Heavy Machine Gun.

Caliber: 40mm.

Operation: Blowback; belt fed; fires from open bolt with advanced primer ignition.

Cyclic Rate: 375 rounds per minute.

Weight: 75.6 pounds.

Length: 43.1 inches.

Barrel: NA.

Magazine: NA.

Sights: Post front; ladder-type rear; fully adjustable.

Mounts: Can be fired from the M64 gun cradle, M3 tripod, M31C pedestal, M4 pedestal, Mark 16 stand standard ring mounts, HMMWV weapons platform and the 40/50 turret.

Ammo: M430 dual-purpose high explosive round, M383 high explosive, M918 flash-bang practice round and M385 practice round.

Maker: Saco Defense Industries 291 North Street Saco, ME 04072

involving runaway guns. With the standard machine gun, the usual cure for this is to twist the belt and thus stop the cartridges from feeding.

That is not the case with this 40mm gun. In fact, there are warnings never to try to twist the M19 ammo belt with the hands, for serious injury could result. The answer, instead, is for the gunner to keep the gun pointed at the target and to press one charger hand lock, then lower one of the charging handles. This, according to the manufacturer, will stop the gun.

"It used to be possible to predict what kind of weapons and supplies would be necessary, since the majority of battles were fought in what might be termed populated, civilized areas," Jack Lewis points out. "That has not been necessarily true, however, since the early days of World War II. In the decades since, U.S. troops have been called upon to battle in jungles and rain forests, deserts and sand dunes, frigid zones with snow, ice and sub-zero temperatures. As a result of some of the lessons learned in the African deserts and the Pacific jungles of World War II, then in the ice and snow of North Korea, more attention has been given to weather-proofing weapons"

Later campaigns in Vietnam and Desert Storm reinforced that need.

The Saco Defense Mark 19 Model 3 is one gun that has been tested in various climes and appears to have passed those tests.

In conditions of hot, wet salt air or sea spray, M19 crews are cautioned to inspect their guns more frequently for

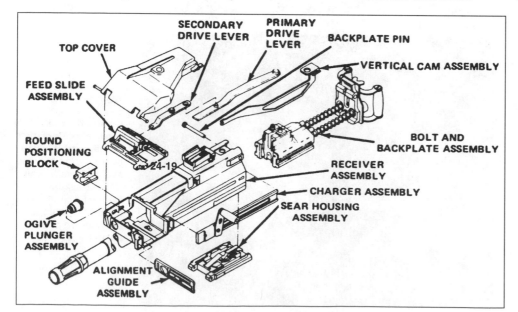

This illustration shows the degree to which the M19 is field-stripped for normal cleaning and maintenance. Only the parts shown should be removed by the user; further break-down requires an armorer.

Rounds for the gun are fed through the rectangular opening just below the feed cover. Because of the explosive nature of the rounds, extreme care is taken in loading and unloading.

signs of rust and to keep the gun as moisture-free as possible. The gun should be field stripped, cleaned and lubed more often to preserve the metal, using a generous second coat of lubricant for extra protection.

In hot, dry areas with great amounts of blowing sand and dust, the weapon also should be stripped down and cleaned more often than normal. As might be expected, extreme heat such as that experienced in Desert Storm dries lubricants rapidly. In addition to the usual application of lubricants, field experience with the gun has shown that more lube should be packed into several areas, one being between the round positioning block and the right-hand wall of the receiver. Extra grease

should be packed between the alignment guide assembly and the forward receiver wall, too.

The extra-lube treatment should continue with application under the primary pawl, under the charger handle locks and between the charger housing and the receiver. Additional lube should be spread inside the feed tray, and after the ammo has been loaded, the tray should be lubed heavily before firing. More lubricant should be packed inside the sear assembly, under the sear and inside the housing.

For frigid weather, including ice and snow, there are some different rules. First, if the gun is to be left outside, it should be covered. If brought inside, the gun should be

kept away from direct heat. If the metal sweats, it should be dried and the parts lubed with a special cold weather grease developed by the Department of Defense. However, before using this formula, the old grease should be removed. The two of them do not mix, according to DOD directives.

Since it fires a high explosive projectile, scattering shrapnel on the target, some are inclined to call the Mark 19 Model 3 a cannon, but it is carried on military equipment tables as a heavy machine gun.

In spite of this, the manufacturer is quick to declare that "with its range, accuracy and rate of fire, the Mark 19 not only performs the role of a heavy machine gun but many of

Two hand grips are centered by a Y-shaped piece of metal that is the gun's trigger. It takes both thumbs to activate the trigger; simple but effective.

The handles used to hold the gun on target are at bottom of the photo; on the action just ahead of the handles is the highly effective battle sight. The cocking handles protrude from each side of the action forward of the sight.

A flash suppressor is attached to the muzzle of the barrel. It also serves to a minor degree as a recoil reducer. Since no tracers are involved with this weapon, it is difficult for an enemy to locate the gun in a combat situation.

the functions of a light cannon, small mortar and portable anti-armor weapon."

Tests have shown that the M19's primary ammo, the M430 high explosive dual-purpose round, can punch through two inches of rolled armor to take out most infantry fighting vehicles and armored personnel carriers. Add to that the large blast and fragmentation coverage and you have a highly effective round against dismounted infantry, trucks and crew-served weapons.

As indicated earlier, the low recoil and comparatively light weight of the M19 allow it to be fired from a variety of tripods on the ground. In addition to the Navy SEALs' installation on small boats and fast attack vehicles, and the Marines using them in the turrets of their amphibious tractors, the Army is mounting the big-bore gun in their HMMWVs and M113 armored personnel carriers.

The manufacturer makes claim that the M19 "can outshoot and outrange any weapon in its size and weight class. That, combined with its lack of smoke and muzzle blast, makes it a major asset that is difficult to find and suppress.

"The M19 fires from an open bolt, the firing cycle beginning and ending with the bolt locked in the rearward position and no round in the chamber. This eliminates the danger of cook-off and enhances cooling between bursts, permitting virtually unrestricted sustained fire." A facet called advanced primer ignition absorbs much of the force of recoil.

I asked the Marines at the Hawaii shooting range about these claims and found no one from the platoon leader down who would dispute any of them,

so there may really be such a thing as truth in advertising!

The Ordnance Systems Division of Georgia-based Martin Marietta designed and holds the patents on ammunition for the M19, and claims that "the unique high-low propulsion design of the 40mm ammunition is a significant contributor to the simplicity and reasonable weight of the gun.

"Ordinarily, the force necessary to propel a 40mm grenade beyond 2000 meters would require a massive receiver, recoil system and mount, making the weapon unacceptably heavy."

This 40mm ammo overcomes the problem by means of a two-stage propulsion system. When the gun is fired, the primer detonates a small high-pressure charge that vents into a larger

low pressure chamber built into the cartridge case. This approach produces a more gradual acceleration of the projectile and lower gas temperatures than would be achieved by exploding the propellant in a single chamber.

As a result, the projectile leaves the muzzle of the M19 at about 795 feet per second, but there is only moderate loading of the gun components and virtually no erosion to the barrel in achieving this velocity.

Since the gun has been around for some three decades, there has been plenty of opportunity to evaluate it. The U.S. Army has listed the service life of the Mark 19 Model 3 as being 25,000 rounds, but there are guns in the military inventory that have exceeded 80,000 rounds and still perform as they should.

Fresh 40mm ammunition was kept clear of the M19 as a safety measure. The range at Marine Corps Base Hawaii is flanked by the Pacific Ocean.

The polished metal section of the gun's feed cover is part of the ammunition feeding mechanism.

The M19 can be field-stripped without tools, and because the ammo produces low gas pressure and temperatures, there is no need to change hot barrels, carry an extra barrel or remember sustained firing rates and other restrictions as with most other machine guns. The current model has been manufactured in its Maine plant by Saco Defense Industries since 1984. This firm also has an ongoing contract to produce the venerable M2HB 50-caliber machine gun and the M-60 7.62mm machine gun, which still are being used in special mission operations and by many of our allies.

The ammunition is currently turned out at the Milan Army Ammunition Plant. This operation has produced more than 192 million rounds of 40mm high velocity grenade ammo, with a quarter of that total being loaded specifically for the M19.

Lewis had absorbed a great deal of this information before joining up with the troops of the 13th Expeditionary Unit. He felt he would be able to surprise the young Marines by telling them things about their gun and its ammo they didn't know. This effort was wasted, since he quickly discovered that training on the gun and its capabilities have given each of these young men as much or more knowledge than he had been able to assemble. So much for one-upmanship!

Lewis was joined in this excursion by Master Sergeant Ron Appling as his escort. At one point during the shoot across the Kaneohe canyon, the M19 jammed. It turned out an unfired round was stuck in the chamber. As the young Marines set about righting the problem, Lewis noted that Top Appling was moving beyond the advertised 15-meter burst radius. Our man quickly followed him.

"I was about to tell you looking over their shoulders was not a smart idea," the master sergeant explained. "Then I saw that you had figured this out for yourself."

Using a metal cleaning rod as a pry—a technique we have not been

During the Desert Storm campaign in Iraq, the M19 was mounted on a variety of vehicles, including those that had their design concept based upon the familiar recreational dune buggy.

Senior Marines check out the M19 after an unfired round had been removed to the chamber and moved to a dud disposal revetment. Note that all personnel wear helmets and flak jackets.

The gunner leans back from the gun as he fires. The target is on the right side of the most distant ridge, although the resultant dust cloud marking hits is not visible in this photo.

able to find outlined in the training manual for the gun—the faulty round was removed and carefully moved to a concrete revetment to be detonated later by the unit's engineers.

Then the troops got on with the shooting. After all, that was what they were there to do!

In reviewing then comparing the manufacturer's manual to the official publication issued to troops, Lewis found they were practically identical. The folks at Saco Defense Industries had not attempted to guild their lily and their version of the manual contained a healthy passage on

troubleshooting the gun. Of particular interest to Lewis was the fact that most of the problems listed have two solutions, one for peacetime training, the other for combat situations. The publication bluntly warns: "Do not use combat misfire procedures during peacetime or

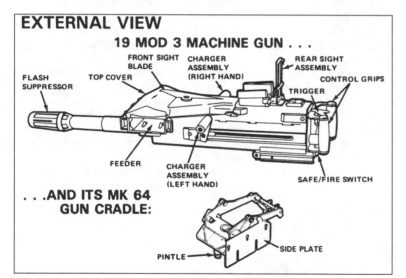

EXTERNAL VIEW

19 MOD 3 MACHINE GUN . . .

FRONT SIGHT BLADE
CHARGER ASSEMBLY (RIGHT HAND)
REAR SIGHT ASSEMBLY
TOP COVER
CONTROL GRIPS
FLASH SUPPRESSOR
TRIGGER
FEEDER
CHARGER ASSEMBLY (LEFT HAND)
SAFE/FIRE SWITCH

. . .AND ITS MK 64 GUN CRADLE:

PINTLE
SIDE PLATE

This drawing shows the positioning of the Mark 19 Model 3 40mm machine gun's interacting assemblies. Below is the Mark 64 gun cradle on which the gun rests when ready for action.

This exploded view of the M19 shows the various assembles. Numbered in sequence, they are: (1) the receiver assembly; (2) the feed slide assembly and tray; (3) the top cover assembly; (4) the sear assembly; and (5) the bolt and backplate assembly.

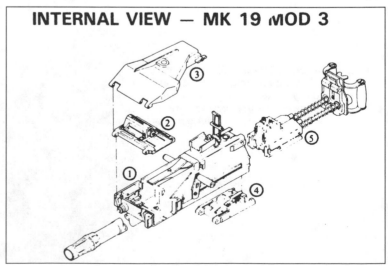

INTERNAL VIEW — MK 19 MOD 3

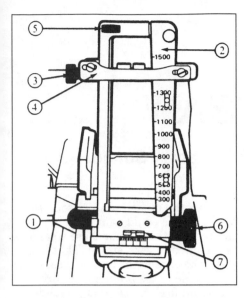

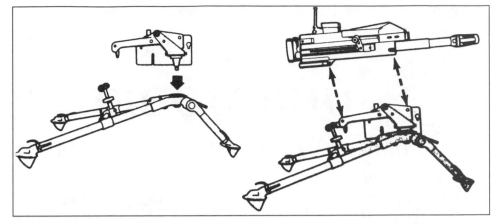

With the gun cradle in place on the tripod, the gun is lowered and its front grooves are slid onto the cradle. The holes at the rear of the gun and cradle are aligned and a locking pin is inserted.

The ladder-type rear sight of the M19 follows the concept of numerous other combat weapons and is simple to adjust. Shown are (1) the plunger that releases (2) the sight frame; the retainer lock (3) must be loosened to raise or lower (4) the aperture carrier. The elevation wheel (5) is turned to adjust degrees of elevation; the windage screw (6) must be moved to the right to move sight to the right, counter-clockwise for movement to the left. When the sight is down, the battle sight (7) allows the gunner to aim down the front sight blade. The AN/TVS-5 night vision sight also may be mounted on the gun.

training. Serious injury can result if safety precautions are not observed."

Another warning in the manual made a lot of sense to our new M19 gunner. It read: "When firing high-explosive or inert ammunition, be alert to these three danger signals: (1) a muffled report from the gun; (2) smoke and debris from the bottom of the receiver; or (3) failure of the warhead to leave the muzzle. Any of these three symptoms mean a bore obstruction. Do not attempt to clear a bore obstruction."

Emergency action in this situation is to place the gun on safe, clear the area of personnel and ammo and to call the range officer. The barrel should be allowed to cool for at least 30 minutes, thus preventing injury in case a lodged round is exploded by a hot barrel. After that, the armorer takes over.

During the firing session in which Lewis was given his indoctrination, one wooden case of the wrong ammunition had been sent. As soon as the case was opened, the Marines realized it was meant for the M203 grenade launcher that attaches beneath the barrel of the M-16 rifle. The box was

quickly repacked and sealed.

"That wouldn't work in the M19 if it was belted?" Lewis wanted to know.

"I don't think so." The gunnery sergeant who had been overseeing the reboxing, pointed to a line in the training manual printed in boldface type. The warning reads: "Remember, using the wrong ammo could blow your head off—so use only authorized ammo." Enough said!

The M19 is built to handle five different types of ammo. The M383 round was in the other wooden cases and that was what we were firing that day. This is a high-explosive grenade designed to inflict personnel casualties. It is packed in a linked, 48-round belt and has a blast radius of 15 meters. Arming distance on this one is 18 to 36 meters and it is identified easily by its yellow ogive and the white markings on an olive drab background.

The M385 TP is an inert training practice round that carries only a propelling charge and has a maximum range of 2200 meters. It is identified by a blue ogive and white markings on a blue background. The M918 is a flash-

bang practice round. The M922 is a dummy round that is totally inert and is used to check gun functioning and for gun crew training. It is issued only to armorers.

The big boomer of the lot is the M430 HEPD, which carries a high-explosive, dual-purpose grenade. With the same yellow ogive as the M383, it has white identity marks on a blue background and is designed to penetrate two-inch armor and to inflict personnel casualties. It has a kill radius of five meters and a wound radius of 15 meters. Arming distance is 18 to 30 meters.

"As with any firearm, there can be problems, but most of those experienced with even the older M19s are relatively simple to cure," is the opinion of Jack Lewis, who adds that he would have been willing to give up Christmas permanently, if someone had issued him such a gun during World War II or Korea.

For a man who tends to be a traditionalist, he now admits that "progress isn't all bad!" That is an admission worth considering in evaluating military equipment! •

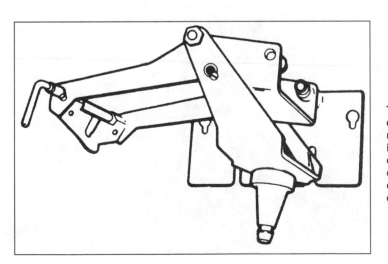

The Mark 64 gun cradle component requires periodic inspection and lubrication, especially during field exercises or in a combat environment.

CHAPTER 25

OUR MODEL 249 SAW

This Machine Gun Is The Base Of Fire For Today's Infantry Squad.

WHEN IT COMES to military acronyms, this is a field that is fraught with room for error. All of those capital letters strung together have to mean something, but sometimes the users can't give you an explanation.

Co-author Jack Lewis recalls the time he was escorting a young newspaper reporter with no military experience. Lewis kept referring to a Battalion Landing Team as a BLT. The reporter finally admitted his puzzlement by commenting, "In my life, a BLT is a bacon, lettuce and tomato sandwich."

But the problem extends beyond reporters and civilians. There is a classic story of a brigadier general who was lecturing before a group of students in a high-level military school. He insisted upon using acronyms and the lecture went along well, until a young captain raised his hand and asked, "General, what does that acronym really mean?"

The general glared at the younger soldier to snarl, "Captain, if you don't

know, you probably don't belong in this school." As it turned out later, the general didn't know the translation of the collected capital letters, either.

Here we are discussing the Model 249 SAW, which in these softer days of political correctness translates to "Squad Automatic Weapon." Originally, the three letters stood for "Squad Assault Weapon," at least among the troops who had to carry one. They knew the true purpose.

Lewis' early military experience had been as a Marine Corps machine gunner. After being commissioned, he ran a machine gun platoon. That was in World War II, as he puts it, "The last war we were allowed to win."

Thus, Lewis had long been retired when the Marine Corps introduced the FN-built M249 machine gun into its four amphibious divisions, but we went to Camp Pendleton, California, and its School of Infantry to learn about it. It is there that young Marines barely out of basic training are taught about this gun and a lot others.

From the term Squad Automatic Weapon, one could gain the impression that one of these weapons is assigned to each squad. That is not quite the case with the Marines. Each 12-man squad is broken into three four-man fire teams, plus a squad leader. And each of these fire teams has one man armed with the M249 machine gun, while another Marine armed with the traditional M-16A2 rifle carries additional ammunition for the gunner.

All of this is designed to provide a lot of covering firepower, while the individual fire teams are leapfrogging forward against an enemy. It is the M249 man who utilizes his bullet output to cause the enemy to keep their heads down while other fire teams are advancing on them.

In theory, this practice works well, but enemy leaders are less than stupid and know what is coming off. Some do not keep their heads down and attempt to discourage the advance with their own small arms, including machine guns.

Co-author Jack Lewis tries his hand with the M249 squad automatic weapon during a training session at Camp Pendleton, California. His range coach feeds a short length of link-belted ammunition into the gun.

A non-commissioned officer shows a newly graduated recruit the proper stance for off-hand fire with the M249. The weapon can be fired from the standing, sitting, kneeling or prone positions. The last, with a bipod, offers the most promise to the average shooter.

But we came to Camp Pendleton to look at the M249 rather than to lecture on tactics. This gun is classified as a light machine gun, a concept that was pioneered by the Germans in World War II. Today, virtually every nation of the globe has its own light machine guns, however employed.

From an open bolt, the M249 fires the NATO-accepted 5.56mm cartridge. Belt-fed with disintegrating metal links, it is gas-operated and air-cooled.

As mentioned, the gun is made by the Belgian armsmaker Fabrique Nationale under a Department of Defense contract for all of our U.S. armed forces. However, the gun is not made in Belgium, as one might naturally expect. It is turned out in a plant in South Carolina. This approach has aided in downgrading the protests of certain Congressmen, who deplore the fact that our nation is dependent upon foreign gun makers for our armament. They already have

noted, of course, that Italy's Beretta is the manufacturer of the M9 handgun, and that FN also produces the 7.62 light machine gun, both staples of U.S. forces' arms inventory. The 81mm mortar is of British origin and some of our amphibious vehicles have come out of Canadian factories.

In situations wherein the M249 is to be used as a light machine gun, it is best mounted on a substantial tripod, although the weapon can be fired by the individual from the standing, sitting

The M249 has a cyclic rate of fire of 850 rounds per minute, but this isn't likely in the offhand mode. Such a rate of fire also requires a barrel change every minute!

The M249 can be utilized as either a light machine gun or as a squad assault weapon. It is of Belgian design, but is being made in the U.S. in an FN-owned factory in South Carolina. The gun has replaced the venerable 1918A1 Browning Automatic Rifle as the squad automatic weapon.

and prone positions. We observed one young first lieutenant who was firing on a standard silhouette target at 100 yards, standing erect and holding the M249 as he would a handgun in his right hand. Firing three-round bursts, he was making hits in the kill zone marked on the target. A bit of questioning revealed that he is assigned as a range officer for the School of Infantry and has had plenty of opportunity to perfect this technique.

The young Marines, fresh from San Diego's boot camp, had no previous experience with the FN-made gun. They had been subjected only to classroom lectures and demonstrations prior to this particular day. A purpose of this range firing was to allow each of the new Marines the opportunity to familiarize himself with the personality and particular quirks of the gun before it would be taken into Camp Pendleton's hilly areas specifically set aside for simulated combat training.

The problem was that all along the line there were frequent stoppages and jams, the instructors patiently helping their young charges to clear the guns and get on with the shooting.

We asked a gunnery sergeant about the stoppages and he stated that the guns being used there for training had been subjected to hundreds of thousands of rounds—

and some, he said, probably had fired more than a million 5.56mm cartridges over the years of training. As a result, parts were worn and needed replacing, but the training schedule did not allow for taking them off the line and sending them to an ordnance repair facility for rework.

He added that the training staff was expecting the aging guns to be replaced shortly, but as this book goes to press, new guns are going to the Marine task forces that seem to be in constant protective action somewhere in the world. This problem, of course, is not specifically Marine Corps. Shortages of funds for training and equipment continue, while the money that normally would be applied to those problems goes toward operations in Bosnia, Haiti, Somolia, ad infinitum.

The currently issued quick-change barrels are air-cooled and each has fixed headspace. Page 1 of the Army/Marine Corps field manual states, however: "Do not interchange barrel assemblies or bolt assemblies from one weapon to another without checking headspace."

The bolt for the M249 is a multiple-lug type that will lock into the barrel extension immediately prior to firing. Gas is collected from the barrel to act on a piston affixed to the bolt carrier.

"The gas pressure on the old-style

barrel was based on the gas exhaust system and was controlled by a two-position regulator—one for normal conditions, the other delivering additional power for adverse conditions," one of the instructors, 1st Lieutenant Eric O. Atkins, explained.

He added that "the new-style barrel has a pre-set gas orifice and rotation of the regulator has no effect on its operation."

Something about this didn't sound all that promising, so our Jack Lewis began looking over one of the guns that had been field-stripped for cleaning. An older model, the gun had a fixed carrying handle, while newer guns have a folding handle. The original gun issued to Marines had a flash suppressor, but the gun has a compensator instead, which is designed not only cut down muzzle flash but also to reduce muzzle climb.

Those sound like worthy changes, but when we come to the gas collar, which is a part of the barrel assembly, we find the original had a two-position control to change the cyclic rate of fire. The newer barrel has only one cyclic rate of fire, and the only function of the gas collar is to lock the gas regulator into the barrel assembly. Printed instructions on the gun mention that, with the original version, if in combat or any other situation in which frequent cleaning of the gun is not possible, and functioning becomes sluggish or stops, the gas

The 1918A1 Browning Automatic Rifle fired the 30-06 cartridge and was the basic automatic weapon for infantry troops in World War II and the Korean War. A popular statement was that it required "three men and a boy to carry the ammunition for it."

Specifications

Name:	Machine Gun, 5.56mm, M249.
Caliber:	5.56mm.
Operation:	Gas-operated.
Cyclic Rate:	850 rounds per minute.
Weight:	17 pounds, unloaded; with bipod.
Length:	40.75 inches.
Barrel:	20.5 inches; 1:7-inch twist.
Magazine:	200-round belt; weighs 6.92 pounds.
Stock:	Moulded composition with internal hydraulic buffer.
Sights:	Hooded post front; aperture rear; fully adjustable.
Finish:	Matte black on plastic; metal parts black anodized or blued.
Maker:	FN Herstal Vole de Liege 33 Herstal 4040, Belgium

regulator may be switched to deliver more power to the weapon. When this conditions starts, the gas collar was to be rotated 180 degrees to the right to properly align the larger gas port with the gas cylinder.

In the newer versions of the gun, this second option is not available. Thus, when the gun becomes sluggish or quits, there could be a big, big problem in any combat situation, whether in the assault or in a defensive position. There just isn't time in such instances to tear down a machine gun and clean it! For our money, this change probably was made at the insistence of the Department of Defense or Government Accounting Office bean counters as a means of saving a few dollars. The option not to spend those dollars could easily result in spending a lot of American lives, in our opinions! A highly unofficial tome known as Murphy's Laws of Combat states: "Never forget that the weapon you take into combat was made by the lowest bidder."

We leafed through the field manual for the M249 and found the section on troubleshooting procedures.

"In my days as a machine gunner—admittedly, more than a half-century ago—we had a program called 'immediate action' which constituted the moves necessary to put a balky or inoperative weapon back into immediate service," Lewis recalls.

The troubleshooting pages of the official manual suggest that, if operation becomes sluggish, any of three different problems might possibly be the cause. First listed was a dirty receiver, the remedy being to clean and lubricate it. The second possible cause is listed as a lack of lubrication; the answer, of course, is to lubricate. And the third cause brings us back to the matter of carbon build-up in the gas system. Your authors agree that with no option for a larger gas port, this would be the first thing we would check.

According to the field manual, if the problem is carbon build-up in the gun's gas system, it should be dismantled and the gas regulator, piston and cylinder cleaned.

For all of this, a tool called a scraper is necessary for proper cleaning the regulator body, which can become heavily coated with hardened carbon. Usually, the regulator sleeve can be cleaned with almost any type of clean cloth, but the hole constituting the gas vent requires the use of the scraper tool. In a true combat situation, a more simple solution might be to grab the gun of someone who already has been put out of action!

The manual we reviewed at Camp Pendleton was published in 1991. If there have been changes since then, they are not included in the field manual being used by the Marines. This manual, incidentally, warns, "Do not modify components, use repair parts or interchange components other than those authorized by this Training Manual. This includes other models of machine guns or foreign versions of this weapon." This would seem to establish the fact that many of the parts are not interchangeable, leading to the fact that inoperative guns probably cannot be cannibalized for parts in the usual supply crunch inevitably found in a true combat environment.

The currently issued M249 is composed of 19 distinct assemblies. These are the: (1) barrel assembly; (2) receiver assembly; (3) head shield; (4) rear sight assembly; (5) cover/feed mechanism; (6) feed pawl assembly; (7) feed tray; (8) cocking handle assembly; (9) buttstock and buffer; (10) bolt assembly; (11) slide; (12) piston; (13) helical compression spring; and (14) the return rod and transfer bare assembly. Completing this list are: (15) the trigger mechanism assembly; (16) handguard assembly; (17) sling and snap hook assembly; (18) gas cylinder assembly; and (19) the bipod.

Proving that perhaps new truly can be better than old is the buttstock. When the first M249s were issued to the troops, the buttstock was a tubular affair that had a piece of webbed plastic

Students at the Marine Corps' School of Infantry await their turn on the firing line, as others become acquainted with the idiosyncrasies of the M249.

The M249 requires frequent cleaning, which could be a problem in a combat environment. A cleaning kit comes with each gun. Included is a scraper for removing carbon from the gas system. It hardly qualifies as "immediate action."

lowered his aging bulk to the prone position. The bipod was affixed to the forward area of the barrel and he had no difficulty in aligning the sights. He had noted earlier that the rear sight had one knob for adjusting elevation and a second one for shifting elevation. Both knobs are positioned on the right side of the sight. This bothered our shooter a mite. He shoots right-handed, because his right eye is dominant. But he is left-handed and tends to adjust things better with the fingers of that hand.

With the safety released at the order to begin firing, he touched the trigger for what he expected to be a three-round burst, but the machine gun recoiled against his shoulder five times, as that many bullets went downrange.

"It took me several bursts to get the correct touch on the trigger for a bonafide three-round burst," he recalls. A larger problem was that he was firing into the clay berm some 10 inches beneath the silhouette target.

During a lull in the firing sequence, as new gunners were taking over along the line, the instructor who had been observing Lewis' shots knelt beside him, saying, "Looks like we need to adjust your sights."

"No need, " the instructor was told. "I'll just raise my aiming point."

The instructor cast him a dubious glance, but the signals were being called for another round of target crunching. The silhouette targets were low and squat, representing the figure of a rifleman in the prone position, paper rifle aimed at the shooter.

"Recalling as best I could where my sights had been aimed during the first string, I simply raised the gun so

as a buttplate. There was no type of buffer to absorb recoil. The buttstock currently attached to the M249 is of solid moulded plastic. Hidden in the interior is a hydraulic-type buffer. Reports from the field have been that this addition, offering the shooter less reason to flinch, has increased shooter accuracy to an interesting degree.

Jack Lewis sat through an on-range lecture concerning the idiosyncrasies of the M249, with warnings to call one of the non-commissioned officers patrolling behind the firing line for help if special attention was needed. Then it was time to fire.

There was no shooting mat, just a hard clay berm onto which Lewis

As for the number of parts, when field-stripped, the gun appears to be relatively simple. The authors, however, feel there are some problems with the basic design.

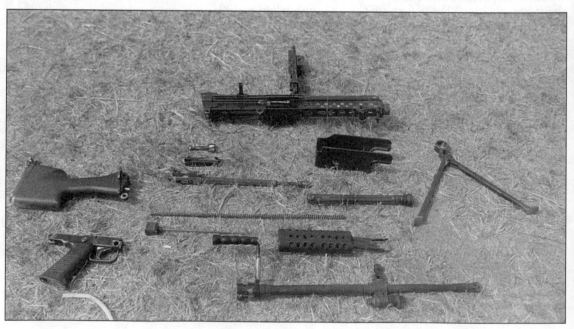

The carrying handle is attached directly to the barrel and used to remove the barrel for replacement. The rear sight is protected by perforated wings. The wings put light on the sight instead of shading it.

that the front sight was centered in the aperture of the rear sight, but roughly 18 inches on the target," our shooter reports. Settling in on this spot, he triggered a three-round burst, then another.

"You're on," the instructor shouted over the noise of the other firing guns. Lewis proceeded to empty the rest of the 20-round belt that had been threaded into the mechanism.

As firing died, the sergeant instructor, still in a kneeling position, bent close to say softly, "I hope no one heard you say you'd use Kentucky windage." He shook his head. "That's a real no-no out here!"

"Sorry about that," was the self-satisfied reply from the offender.

"But how did you do that?" the sergeant wanted to know.

"I spent my first years in the Marine Corps in machine gun outfits," was the reply. "In those days we had

NCOs who were more interested in results than in technique. They tended to teach a lot of things the brass wouldn't understand."

That reply brought a wry grin to the sergeant's face.

Although the shooters along the line were shooting belts of ammo that were limited to 20 rounds, the standard belt carries 200 rounds of 5.56mm in disintegrating metal links. Asked why the shooters were limited to 20 rounds, the sergeant replied that this saved ammo during training and it also was a safeguard against the possibility of a runaway gun. The training manual, incidentally, makes a number of references to this problem and the necessary precautions and actions to be taken in such a situation. The manual points out, too, that if one should remove the trigger assembly from a loaded gun, the result would be a runaway!

The gun will fire four different types of ammunition: the A059 linked ball type; the A064 linked tracer, which has a burnout range of 900 meters; an A060 linked dummy round; and the APR5 linked blank cartridge. This last requires that the same blank-firing attachment used on the M-16 be affixed to the machine gun.

Maximum range of the cartridge fired in the M249 is considered to be 3000 meters, with suppression fire to 1000 yards; the gun can be used on point targets to 600 yards and area targets to 800 yards.

Reviewing the early days of the four-man fire team concept mentioned earlier, this was developed early in World War II, with the 30-06 Browning Automatic Rifle serving as the base of fire. This behemoth weighed 19.4 pounds unloaded. Not only did the BAR man have to carry

The stock of the M249 is a moulded synthetic as opposed to the original stock which used a piece of webbed plastic as a buttplate. This stock also holds a buffer mechanism for reducing recoil.

With the exception of the barrel, most of the metal parts in the M249 are of aluminum alloy, a material that is easier to work than steel and considerably lighter in weight.

The front sight of the squad automatic weapon is of the post type with a ring-type hood. In testing the gun, Jack Lewis found the sights adequate at 200 yards and felt they would serve well, with proper adjustment, at greater ranges.

several cumbersome cloth bandoleers of ammunition, but the rifleman assigned as the assistant BAR man also was loaded down with BAR magazines of ammo, as well as the required combat issue for his own M-1 rifle. As the assistant, he was charged with taking over the gun should the BAR man be killed or wounded.

In the current military environment, the M249 replaces the venerable BAR, although the assistant gunner still carries ammo not only for the machine gun, but for his own M-16. An advantage, of course, is the fact that the 5.56mm cartridge is considerably lighter than U.S. military rounds of the past. On the other hand, some of the veteran troops consider it all part of a plot to allow them to carry more ammo or to make up the difference in pack weight with rolls of razor wire or some other front-line needs.

The BAR of yore fired the same round, of course, as the Model 1903 Springfield rifle and its successor, the M-1 Garand semi-automatic, creating a logistical advantage. The M249 enjoys the same advantage, since it not only feeds the same cartridge as the M-16, but in situations where belted ammo has run out or there is a special need, M-16 magazines can be loaded through an appropriate magazine well. A disadvantage—minor in a combat environment—is the fact that the magazines become bent when used in the M249 and cannot be reloaded and used in the M-16.

Sometime after the Korean War, the Pentagon powers began to worry about what they termed The Soldier's Load. This was based upon a study meant to determine how much weight a soldier can pack into battle and still be able to conduct his assigned mission. Those of us who have been there, of course, realize

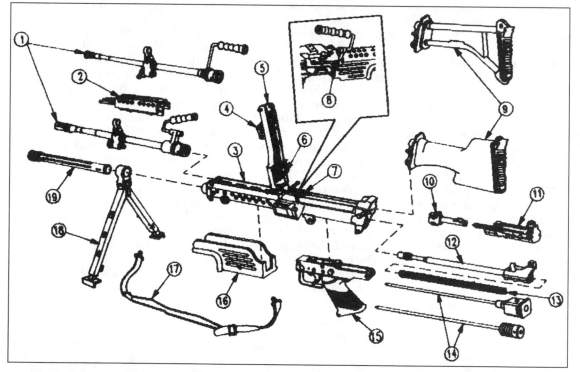

The major components of the M249 machine gun are (1) both the old and new versions of the barrel; (2) the heat shield to protect the shooter's hand from barrel heat; (3) the receiver assembly houses the action and controls functioning; (4) adjustable rear sight assembly; (5) the cover and feed mechanism support the rear sight and offer access to the feed tray; this mechanism feeds linked belt ammo and holds cartridges in position; (6) the feed pawl assembly feeds cartridges, also holding them for stripping, feeding and chambering; (7) the feed tray guides cartridges into position and assists in chambering; (8) the cocking handle moves in a guide rail to pull the moving parts to the rear; (9) buttstock/buffer assembly offers support for aiming, firing; contains a folding shoulder rest and a hydraulic buffer; (10) the bolt assembly handles stripping, chambering, firing and extraction; (11) the slide assembly holds the bolt unit, firing pin and roller assembly, camming the bolt assembly to lock and unlock; (12) the piston assembly transfers gases to the bolt and slide to move recoiling parts to the rear; (13) the helical compression spring provides power to the piston for moving the slide and bolt assemblies forward during functioning; (14) the operating rod absorbs recoil at the end of the recoil movement, transferring recoil to the buffer in the buttstock; (15) the trigger mechanism houses the trigger, sear and safety, controlling firing; (16) the handguard provides thermal insulation to the shooter's hand and also stores cleaning equipment; (17) the sling and snap-hook assembly provide a means of carrying the weapon; (18) the bipod supports the M249 in the sitting or prone position; legs telescope for leveling the gun; (19) the gas cylinder assembly locks the bipod onto the receiver and provides passage for operating gases.

that the soldier often tends to make his own choices. In Korea and even Vietnam, when gas masks were issued, the pouches for carrying them usually were retained, but they were filled with extra cans of C-rations. After all, the average grunt Marine or dogface soldier didn't offer much consideration to the likelihood of nuclear, chemical or biological warfare. Desert Storm, though, changed some of that thinking.

But it was those earlier concerns that brought about the ongoing development of lighter armament, using aluminum alloys and synthetic materials. This worry about The Soldier's Load also led to military acceptance of the smaller and lighter-in-weight 5.56mm cartridge.

The same thinking has been introduced into more than simply the rifle, and the M249 is a good example. Lightweight alloys rather than steel have been used in many of the machine gun's parts, and the buttstock and handguard are cast from heavy-duty plastics.

The M249 has been described as "an interim squad automatic weapon." That indicates that something supposedly better is somewhere in the mill or, at least, under consideration by the military. These decisions usually are not made without all of the armed services getting involved and wanting their own recommendations for a new weapon adopted. Then one has to get the money out of Congress to develop and eventually manufacture such machinery of war.

In short, we might as well learn to live with and love the M249. It's going to be our primary squad assault weapon for untold years to come. By the time a new weapon is decided upon and produced, it probably will fire lasers!

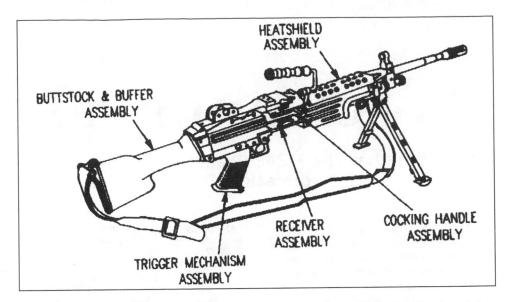

In this drawing, the new type of buttstock and its included buffer assembly are shown. Originally, a piece of plastic webbing served as the buttplate and there was no buffer.

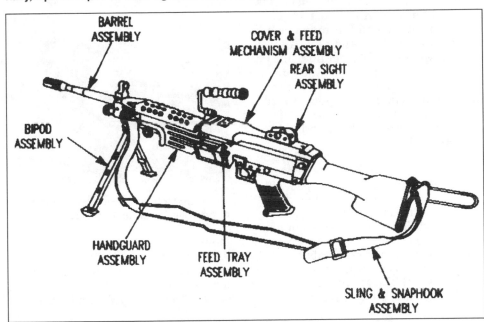

The handguard assembly also has been improved over the original introduced by FN. This one protects the hand against barrel heating.

In this comparison drawing, the old-style M249 barrel has a fixed carrying handle, flash suppressor and a two-position gas collar that can be adjusted to change the cyclic rate of fire. The new-style barrel has a carrying handle that can be folded in three positions and a compensator minimizes muzzle flash, at the same time reducing muzzle climb. The gas collar's only function is to lock the gas regulator into the barrel assembly.

CHAPTER 26

CHAIN OF VIOLENCE

Whether The M242 Chain Gun Is An Assault Weapon Is A Matter Of Interpretation, But That's Not Important In Battle.

THERE WAS A modicum of disagreement between our co-authors as to whether the M242 chain gun should be included in this book. With the barrel alone weighing 92 pounds, it is not something even a heavy weapons company is likely to lug around the battlefield. Obviously, it is not an infantryman's weapon.

On the other hand, it may fire a 25mm cannon shell and have a total system weight of 247 pounds, but it does operate in true machine gun style. There are three firing modes: single-shot, 100 rounds per minute and 200 rounds per minute. Maximum range of this gun is 11,150 yards.

In an assault, as used these days by Marine Expeditionary Units, these guns are mounted in the Corps' light armored vehicles lovingly known simply as the LAV by the troops. This vehicle, which carries a two-man gun crew in the turret, has room for the rest of the crew and six combat infantrymen. The vehicle also is equipped with the M240 7.62mm NATO machine gun, which is

This is the Light Armored Vehicle-25 (LAV) with the M242 chain gun. This unusual weapon fires a 25mm shell at accurate and extended ranges. It is part of today's Marine Expeditionary Unit.

mounted coaxially to the main gun. Ammunition aboard in a combat-ready situation is 210 ready rounds for the chain gun and 420 rounds stored. The M240 7.62mm ammo

supply amounts to 400 ready rounds and 1200 rounds stored. The vehicle is fully amphibious and has a top speed of six miles per hour while afloat, as opposed to 62 miles per hour on land. Loaded with ammo and Marines, it weighs 28,200 pounds!

So much for the way the chain gun is transported into combat. Jack Lewis had a special reason for being intrigued with the M242. Several years ago, he was assigned by *Leatherneck Magazine* to do an article on the LAV. He located the training cadre at the School of Infantry at Camp Pendleton, California, and spent several days with the teaching crew and the students. During his investigations, he had an opportunity to ride in the turret with the commander and to fire the big-bore gun!

"At that time, I was more interested in the overall workings of the LAV and those who manned them than I was in just the guns," Lewis now admits. He took what he refers to as "countless" photos, including those of the 25mm gun both installed and removed from the armored vehicle for

Marine Lance Corporal Pedro Cerda twists and locks the barrel of the M242 25mm gun into place during a maintenance session at the School of Infantry at Camp Pendleton, California.

maintenance. He had preserved the lesson plans and tech information he assembled during his few days at the school, but when it came time to do this chapter, most of the photos had disappeared!

Not far from Camp Pendleton resides a retired master sergeant, Ralph J. Austin. Not only was Austin one of the Corps' top combat photographers in his three-war career, but he and Lewis had served together in the 1950s in various rice paddy settings.

Lewis had particular faith in Austin's photo abilities, because "he's tenacious. He'll do anything—including risking life and limb—for a good shot." Lewis recalls that in Korea he sent Austin, then a staff sergeant, out to film movies of an air strike. According to the plan, a flight of four propeller-driven Marine Corsairs were to dive on an enemy position, bombing and strafing it into what hopefully would be oblivion.

According to witnesses, Austin toured the area of the front where the action would take place, looking for a good position. Finally, he spotted a tall tree and decided that would do nicely.

He was in the tree, awaiting the action, when the North Koreans discovered his presence and began firing at him with rifles, then machine guns. At that point, the planes were coming in and Austin was following their actions through his viewfinder. That was when the mortar shells began to fall around the base of the tree, but his camera kept grinding. Finally, either a large mortar shell or an artillery shell hit the base of the

The size of the 25mm round is obvious when compared with the helmet worn by members of the LAV crew. This one has a blue projectile, indicating that it is a practice round with the same ballistics as the high-explosive round.

tree, knocking it down. Legend is that Staff Sergeant Austin was still filming the air strike as his position became part of the terrain. He was awarded the Bronze Star for this bit of dedicated idiocy.

It might help to understand Austin's dedication, if we explain that he was in the Navy during World War II and volunteered for underwater demolitions training. He was into the sixth week of training before one of the instructors discovered Austin could only swim underwater. On the surface, he had trouble keeping from drowning. That was when the Navy sent him to photo school!

Brother Austin, claiming to be fully retired and a man of extreme leisure, was somewhat reluctant to take on the chain gun assignment, but once he reached Camp Pendleton and found himself among a few old friends, he became downright enthusiastic. The photos in this chapter are his work.

What now is officially designated as the M242 chain gun is almost as convoluted in history as Austin's military career. Originally, it was known as the Hughes Chain Gun and allegedly was invented and perfected by the Military Armament Division of Hughes Helicopters. It is known that the gun has been made in several different calibers, ranging from 7.62mm NATO to 30mm. According to old-timers at Hughes Aircraft, the gun originally was designed to be used in the Apache helicopter, which they built and supplied to the U.S. Army. However, the helicopter entity of the Hughes empire ultimately was

Attaching the 25mm barrel to the main gun assembly is a two-man job.

sold to McDonnell-Douglas. It was then that the design was reworked to handle rifle calibers for mounting on armored vehicles. The design also was licensed to Great Britain's Royal Ordnance Factory in Nottingham, England. There the British manufactured the guns to be mounted on that nation's Challenger tanks.

When Lewis first heard of the gun at the School of Infantry several years ago, he thought that the name was derived from the fact that the gun could deliver a "chain of fire." It took a bit of formal military instruction before he came to realize the name apparently was born of the fact that the big gun utilizes a roller chain in an endless loop to drive the gun's bolt. The chain is powered by a conventional electric motor and a shoe that is part of the chain engages the bolt and carries the big cartridge to the chamber. The shoe holds the bolt closed as the round of 25mm ammo is fired, then the bolt moves rearward to extract and discard the spent metal case. Built-in cams serve to rotate the bolt head, thus locking it to the barrel. This action also activates the firing pin.

The Hughes design involves a brake on the electric motor; this provides insurance that when the trigger is released, the bolt will stop in the open position and thus avoid the possibility of accidental cook-off of a live round.

The belt feed of the M242 also is driven by the same electric motor.

Marine Lance Corporal Pedro Cerda (left) waits for help to insert the barrel of the M242 chain gun. This is a two-man job, since the barrel weighs 92 pounds.

This action is independent of operation of the bolt, but is synchronized with it, according to Sergeant Matt Benack, a member of the instruction team at the School of Infantry. We neglected to learn the horsepower of the electric motor, but it is sufficient that it can handle the

functions outlined above and still have the added power required to feed long belts through the gun.

Mounted in the LAV, the gun has a gauge known as the bolt position indicator, which makes one complete revolution for each round fired. This gauge normally starts and stops at what is marked as the SEAR position. If it stops in the area marked MISFIRE, this means the round still in the chamber did not fire. According to Sergeant Benack, if the gauge stops any place else, the gun is jammed.

The sear assembly for the M242 engages the master link and holds the chain in position to begin the firing sequence. If firing in the single-shot mode, the bolt remains in sear until the signal is transmitted from the trigger. Firing at 100 rounds per minute, the bolt remains in sear until the signal is received from a unit known as "the logic." In firing at 200 rounds per minute—slightly over three rounds per second—the gun is in free-run status and the firing rate is set by the speed of the driving motor.

In feeding ammunition, the master link moves from left to right across the gun's carrier slide path, providing time for a fresh round to be positioned in the bolt face and the spent case is moved in front of the ejector. The feed rotor then sweeps the spent case from

The Hughes-created chain gun, here with the barrel removed, appears to be a complex piece of warfare equipment. The chain that drives the action is visible at upper left.

A number of small but important parts become evident when the M242 is field-stripped. The gun is powered by an electric motor.

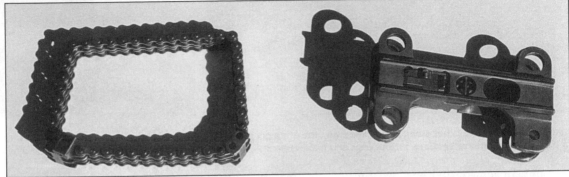

At left is the endless chain that drives the bolt and thus operates the M242. Beside it is the track assembly on which the chain runs.

the bolt and positions the fresh round in the bolt face. The carrier assembly then moves forward, the new round being inserted in the chamber, the spent case ejected.

The bolt is rotated 15 degrees counter-clockwise by the locking cam in the carrier assembly. This rotation locks the bolt into the barrel. After the bolt is locked in position, the firing pin is cocked, then released. The master link moves from right to left, creating dwell time to allow the hot gases to escape through the gun's bore and not into the interior of the vehicle. Unlike most of today's automatic weapons, escaping gasses have no part in operating this gun.

In the event the round fails to fire, the safety link engages the sear assembly to stop the chain's movement. This is designed purposely to keep the unfired shell in the chamber and the bolt in the locked mode.

To resume firing, according to the School of Infantry instructor, the gunner must press what is labeled as the MISFIRE RESET switch and pull the trigger once more.

"To guard against an open-bolt explosion of a hang-fire, the misfire reset circuit has a 2-1/2-second delay before the trigger becomes effective," Lewis recalls from the notes of his earlier exposure. "In the single-shot mode, after a misfire, the first squeeze of the trigger returns the bolt to sear position and the trigger must be released and squeezed once more to resume firing."

He didn't see it happen, but he was told that "after a misfire in either the 100- or 200-round per minute mode, the first trigger squeeze causes the gun to resume firing at the selected rate." That, at least, is the school answer. If the gun still fails to function properly, it is obviously time to call in the experts!

But when the gun is working properly, as the bolt starts to the rear, the locking cam rotates the bolt to unlock it from the breech lugs. The bolt continues its rearward travel and extracts the spent case.

That's a lot of words to outline what happens in split seconds, but it does describe the firing cycle fully.

The M242 chain gun also is versatile as to the types of ammunition it can use. Actually, there are five different 25mm rounds, each of which has a specific purpose.

The first, the M791 round, is armor-piercing with tracer and has a discarding sabot. A fixed-type percussion-primed round, it consists of a sabot-encapsulated projectile that is crimped into a penetrator of solid tungsten alloy. There also are pressed-in tracer pellets. Muzzle velocity for this round is approximately 1345 feet per second, the sabot being discarded as the projectile leaves the barrel.

Maximum effective range is 1700 meters based upon the fact that this range is burn-out for the tracer

The LAV-25 also is armed with automatic weapons firing the 7.62mm NATO round at right. It looks insignificant when seen with the 25mm round.

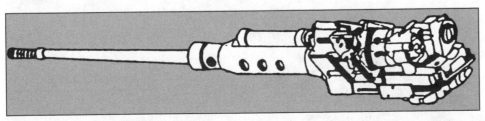

This artist's drawing of the M242 chain gun gives some idea of the complexity of the weapon. Introduced in the late 1960s for Navy service in Vietnam, it has gone through some design upgrades.

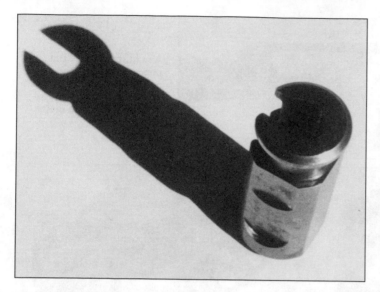

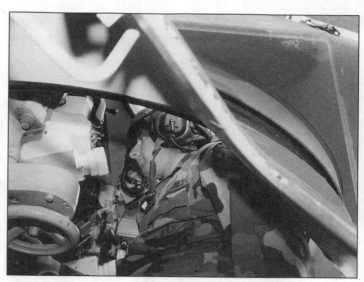

Like the firing pin and other small parts in the gun, the firing pin sleeve is a machined item that requires proper care and maintenance.

With all of the equipment crammed into the LAV's gunnery turret, there is little extra room as demonstrated by Sergeant Matthew Benack.

element. In some situations, greater range can be fired, the gunner or turret commander judging the effectiveness by the impact. However, beyond 2200 meters, accuracy decreases rapidly.

The M919 is another percussion-primed round that is armor-piercing, fin-stabilized and sabot-discarding. This one also consists of a sabot-encapsulated projectile crimped to a steel cartridge case. The body of the projectile consists of a depleted uranium penetrator, screw-on fins and pressed-in tracer pellets. The discarding sabot is of moulded, segmented nylon. There also is a polyethylene nose cap.

Muzzle velocity is about 1420 feet per second, with an effective range of 1700 meters, with increased penetration and increased tracer burning time. According to school personnel, it is designed for use against unarmored vehicles and helicopters, as well as to suppress anti-tank guided missile positions, crew served weapons, dismounted infantry and likely enemy positions at distances up to 3000 meters.

The M792 is described as a high-explosive incendiary with tracer. It consists of a one-piece, high explosive-filled body crimped to the standard steel case. The body of the steel projectile is hollow and holds an M-758 fuse, 32 grams of high explosive mix and pressed-in tracers.

Maximum effective range of this shell is 3000 meters. In fact, if the shell has not impacted at that range, the mechanical fuse will self-detonate the round. Tracer burn-out is at about 2000 meters, but the impact can be observed beyond that range. According to instructors at the Camp Pendleton infantry school, accuracy drops rapidly beyond 1600 meters, but the five-meter bursting radius and rate of fire allow point and area targets to be engaged at distances greater than 3000 meters.

On a somewhat less lethal level, the M910 is a target practice round, with the now familiar discarding sabot and tracer pellets. Ballistically, this round is matched to the M791, but has a maximum range of 8000 meters rather than 11,000-plus. The projectile body is of steel rather than the tungsten alloy of the M910. Burn-out is at 2000 meters, but because it replaces the M910 in practice, it is launched at targets only up to 1700 meters.

Final ammunition entry for the M242 is the M793, a target practice round. Its ballistics are matched to those of the M792 high-explosive round, and all interactions upon being fired are the same.

Again, tracer burn-out is at 2000 meters, but maximum effective range

The firing pin for the M242 chain gun appears to be a relatively simple device despite the complexity of the gun overall.

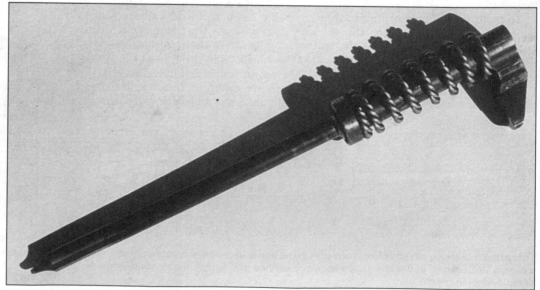

has been found to be about 1600 meters. Training with this round beyond tracer burn-out is conducted only to simulate high-explosive target engagement, and only as long as the impact area is visible.

Students currently are learning about the latest model of the light armored vehicle, the LAV-25, and its armament. They are told that on future battlefields, "the tempo will be such that the LAV-25 crew must be prepared to move and to rapidly engage multiple targets. Platoons will be operating within irregular battle lines, and depending on the tactical situation and the area of operations, threat targets will be intermixed with friendly and civilian vehicles.

"The speed and mobility of the LAV-25 force, coupled with battle doctrine, further enhances the likelihood of opposing and allied forces becoming intermingled during combat operations. Survival in these situations depends on the crew's ability to effectively search for, detect, locate, identify, classify, confirm and rapidly engage threat targets. LAV-25 crews must take advantage of the tactical situation and fire first when required or necessary. Speed and accuracy of an engagement are dependent upon the degree of crew proficiency in both target acquisition techniques and gunnery procedures."

In keeping with this statement, all members of the crew observe

The feeder assembly for the M242 chain gun bears little resemblance to such units for other automatic weapons in our armed forces inventory.

continually, whether in the offense or defense, when the vehicle is moving or when it is stationary. It is drilled into each student that "effective target acquisition for an LAV-25 crew

requires the combined effort of each crew member in the target acquisition process."

Each crew member is assigned a specific sector of observation by the

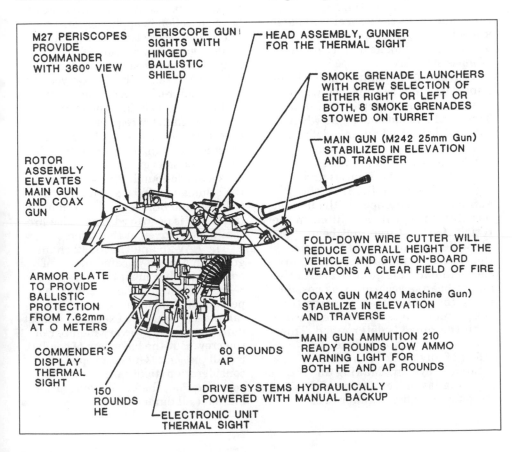

M27 PERISCOPES PROVIDE COMMANDER WITH 360° VIEW

PERISCOPE GUN SIGHTS WITH HINGED BALLISTIC SHIELD

HEAD ASSEMBLY, GUNNER FOR THE THERMAL SIGHT

SMOKE GRENADE LAUNCHERS WITH CREW SELECTION OF EITHER RIGHT OR LEFT OR BOTH, 8 SMOKE GRENADES STOWED ON TURRET

MAIN GUN (M242 25mm Gun) STABILIZED IN ELEVATION AND TRANSFER

ROTOR ASSEMBLY ELEVATES MAIN GUN AND COAX GUN

FOLD-DOWN WIRE CUTTER WILL REDUCE OVERALL HEIGHT OF THE VEHICLE AND GIVE ON-BOARD WEAPONS A CLEAR FIELD OF FIRE

ARMOR PLATE TO PROVIDE BALLISTIC PROTECTION FROM 7.62mm AT O METERS

COAX GUN (M240 Machine Gun) STABILIZE IN ELEVATION AND TRAVERSE

COMMENDER'S DISPLAY THERMAL SIGHT

60 ROUNDS AP

MAIN GUN AMMUITION 210 READY ROUNDS LOW AMMO WARNING LIGHT FOR BOTH HE AND AP ROUNDS

150 ROUNDS HE

DRIVE SYSTEMS HYDRAULICALLY POWERED WITH MANUAL BACKUP

ELECTRONIC UNIT THERMAL SIGHT

This line drawing illustrates the gun turret that later is inserted into the hull of the amphibious armored vehicle. The terms HE and AP stand for high explosive and anti-personnel.,

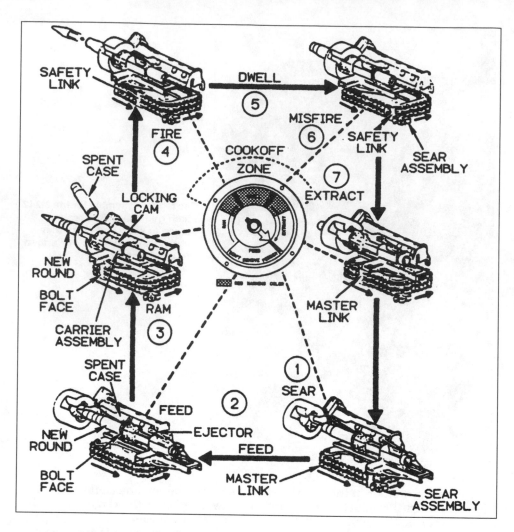

Starting with the circled number 1 and following the numbers clockwise, this chart shows the progress of the firing cycle as seen by the gunner on the dial in the center. This instrument tells him exactly what is happening within the gun.

vehicle commander, who has a 360-degree responsibility, including observation overhead. When operating in platoon strength, each LAV's all-round coverage creates overlapping fields of observation.

To engage this target with the M242 25mm gun, there are two methods, battlesight and precision gunnery. The battlesight technique is the quicker method, but it is less accurate than precision gunnery. At the other extreme, the latter method takes more time. It is the vehicle commander who must determine which method of engaging the enemy will be most advantageous.

Battlesight gunnery is preferable when quick target engagement is necessary—and when the target is within battlesight range. Compiled battle statistics show that the gun that fires first inevitably will be the victor in a duel. Veteran LAV gunners insist that battlesight gunnery reduces engagement time to a great degree, increasing probability for first burst hits.

If the vehicle commander changes from the battlesight mode to precision

gunnery, he includes the appropriate ammunition in his initial fire command. Thus the gunner is made to know he must range the target accurately and make a precise center-of-mass sight lay.

Students are taught that precision gunnery should be employed when there is sufficient preparation time. This would include moments when the vehicle is at a halt, in a defensive position, or the target is beyond battlesight range.

There are various optics and sighting devices in the LAV, the gunner being equipped with one that has stadia range lines printed on the reticle. Once a target has been identified as enemy and fair game, the vehicle commander issues a fire command and his gunner brings the gun to bear as accurately as possible using the stadia lines. In doing this, the gunner moves the reticle upward until the range is determined. This movement actually reduces the effect of any slack in the fire command system. Making an exacting lay on the center of the target's mass, the gunner fires.

"If the target is moving and you need to lead it, the last reticle movement will be in deflection to apply the correct initial lead before firing at the target," student gunners are told. "If the stadia range lines are used properly for ranging, the range should give you the proper center-of-mass aiming point."

To put hot steel into the enemy, precision gunnery requires concentration. The rate of fire control is set at 200 rounds per minute. When the command is given, the gunner first fires a single round. If it is on target, the command will be given and three-to five-round bursts will be fired until the target is destroyed. The cease-fire command is given at that time.

The LAV-25 and the M242 chain gun both are complicated pieces of equipment that must be operated by responsible, well-indoctrinated personnel. Judgment is one of the talents that must be exercised almost daily in combat by every member of the crew. But the basic law of combat is still present: "Give it proper consideration, take care in making your decision, then issue your order—but do it all damned fast!" ●

CHAPTER 27

THE STONER 96 LIGHT MACHINE GUN

It Looks Like This Third-Generation Gun May Be A Winner!

WHEN IT COMES to the unproductive passage of time, the Hollywood film factories and the military-oriented arms industry have a lot in common. Both can be slow to the point of madness.

Here's an example: In 1941, Budd Schulberg published his first novel, *What Makes Sammy Run.* For those interested, it was about a guy who came to Hollywood, got in the picture business and shafted everyone near and dear until he reached the zenith. Once on top of the heap, he discovered he had nothing of value.

So much for plotting. The point is that it was not until late 1998 that it finally was announced the book would be made into a movie. Similarly, a few years back, when the late John Huston made a film of *The Man Who Would Be King*, an advertisement touting the film appeared in *The Hollywood Reporter.* On the next page was a nostalgia column of what had happened in Hollywood 10, 20 and 30 years earlier. The column stated in its 30-years-old news that John Huston was trying to team Clark Gable and

Humphrey Bogart in the same film. It took three whole decades for the late producer to put the deal together. By that time, Gable and Bogart both were long gone from this earth.

Now you're asking what all that has to do with weapons and gunmaking? The answer is little, except for the comparison of time lapse. The late Gene Stoner immediately comes to mind.

If you've read this far in this book, you have to be aware that Stoner was the most prolific gun designer of this century—and possibly of firearms history—but there were no overnight successes. His greatest claim to fame, of course,

The Stoner 96 light machine gun has a much different look from its ancestoral systems. A new stock has been added and a multi-rail forend allows the installation of a forward hand grip among other accessories. This gun is rigged to fire link-belted rounds from a 200-round magazine made for the M249 machine gun.

was development of what now is our military's M-16 rifle. Yet, it was more than 10 years in development before

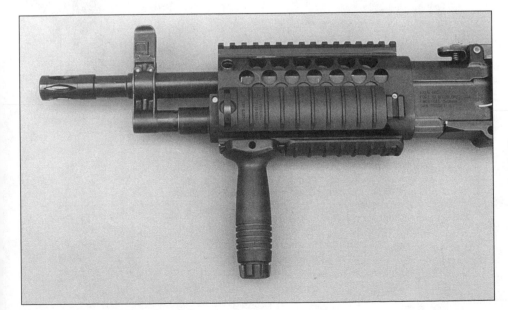

The synthetic hand grip attaches to the multi-rail forend. The grip also can be used as a unipod to support the front end of the gun when firing prone. Both the hand grip and multi-rail are products of Knight's Armament.

The Stoner 96 action allows installation of a variety of scopes and fire control devices. With the installation of a special unit, it also will fire 5.56mm ammo from standard M-16 magazines.

our armed services finally adopted it.

Stoner's desire was to come up with a light machine gun to back up the rifle. He first effort was the Stoner 63, a system that could be converted into several different weapons by the simple means of adding or subtracting various, pins, keys or parts. If you wanted a light machine gun, that was easy. Not much more difficult was the job of turning the weapon into a rifle or even a carbine. The rub was that you had to have the right parts and they tended to become lost or separated from the gun in a combat environment.

Nonetheless, there was great interest in the Stoner 63 system and at least one of our armed services wanted the gun. A few were even purchased for tests and for use by special units.

Stoner took a hard look at his brainchild and decided without prompting from anyone that the concept had too many parts. So it was back to the old drawing board.

Some 20 years later, he came up with the Stoner 86. This, again, was a 5.56mm NATO light machine gun and was a greatly simplified version of the Stoner 63. This new approach had approximately 100 parts; when field stripped, it involved only 15 parts. This, of course, resulted in simple maintenance.

The internal parts of this gun were enclosed in the forged aircraft alloy receiver. The result, of course, is a receiver that is rugged and light in weight.

Co-author Jack Lewis had the opportunity to fire one of the prototypes of this gun when he was writing the fourth edition of *The Gun Digest Book of Assault Weapons*.

Gene Stoner had made most of the changes to create what amounted to a new gun (the S-86) by the time the Department of the Army issued a "Material Need for a Squad Automatic Weapon, Light Machine Gun," in March 1972. The problem was that the Army decided the new gun should be in a new caliber—6.0x45mm— which put it somewhere between the 5.56mm and 7.62mm NATO cartridges already standard in the North Atlantic Treaty Organization.

According to one authority on the era, "Our Department of Defense had literally forced the other member nations to adopt both the 5.56mm and 7.62mm as the official NATO rounds, while we were willing to accept the 9mm as the pistol and submachine gun round. But all of this had not been without a good deal of protest and pressure dealing from our allies."

In the SAW program, more than 1000 different cartridge dimensions had been tried and found lacking, until the 6.0x45mm had been developed. This round fired a 105-grain bullet—nearly double the weight of the M-16 projectile—at 2450 feet per second.

The reason for all of this was the fact that research and development engineers at the U.S. Army's Rock Island Arsenal in Illinois wanted the heavier projectile so they could produce a new and better tracer round. Being called for was a tracer that would be clearly visible out to

The buttstock of the Stoner 96 bears resemblance to that of the M4 carbine in current use. Note the integral carrying strap loop on top.

The integral rail on top of the machine gun's receiver will accept a wide variety of sighting equipment. Note the battle sight beneath the rear of the scope. This is standard equipment with the gun.

800 meters in bright sunlight. Also, the Army's ball ammo program demanded helmet penetration at 800 yards.

Two contracts were awarded for development of prototype guns. One went to the Maremont Corp. for a prototype designated as the XM233. The second contract went to what now is the Ford Aerospace and Communications Corp.; in that era, it was known as Philco-Ford. Their entry was dubbed the XM234. Then the Rodman Laboratories, a government development operation, decided to enter its own prototype, dutifully labeled as the XM235.

In late 1974, engineering and user tests were conducted, with three additional entries showing up. One was the 5.56mm Heckler & Koch HK21, another was the Fabrique Nationale 5.56x45mm Minimi. The third was a heavy-barreled M-16 submitted by Colt Firearms.

The standard M-16 was the weapon against which the six entries were tested. The HK21 was the first dropped, because it did not pass the safety tests. The heavy-barreled M-16 also was dropped, because it could not handle the required belt of 200 rounds of ammo, depending instead upon a 30-round magazine.

The FN Minimi had a major strike against it in the fact that the 5.56x45mm cartridge was not interchangeable with the round for the M-16, nor was the gun chambered for the 6.0x34mm cartridge. The key factor, though, was reliability and the gun proved as good as the guns offered by Maramont, Philco-Ford and Rodman Laboratories, all three of which were chambered for the momentarily favored 6mm.

According to a conversation Jack Lewis held with Gene Stoner several months before the latter's death, the inventor, disgusted with the amount of time involved and the desire for a 6mm machine gun, had not even bothered to enter the competition.

"Considering the problems the Pentagon and State Department had experienced in getting other NATO nations to go along with our 5.56mm and 7.62mm cartridges, I couldn't accept the fact that they would let us cram still a third bastardized cartridge down their throats," Stoner told Lewis.

According to reports, the Secretary of the Army felt the same way. When the Army brass handed him the recommendation for the 6mm cartridge, that worthy virtually threw them out of his office. His edict was that we didn't need a third cartridge that the rest of the world wouldn't want!

This high-level thinking immediately brought military considerations back to the 5.56mm NATO round. In October, 1978, the Army's Material Development and Readiness Command issued a new set of requirements for the to-be 5.56mm Squad Automatic Weapon. This list called for one-man operation, a maximum weight of 21 pounds, the reliability of the M-60 machine gun, a rate of fire that would match its machine gun role and a range out to 800 meters on point and area targets.

The Army assigned Philco-Ford to build 18 prototypes of the XM235 weapon, but a cut in the 1978 military budget left no money to pay for this program. Meantime, the Infantry Center at Fort Benning, Georgia, had been taking a hard look at the FN Minimi and liked what they saw.

A part of the XM235 development was an ammunition improvement program that called for "improvement

Specifications

Name:	Stoner 96 Light Machine Gun.
Caliber:	5.56mm NATO.
Operation:	Gas-operated.
Cyclic Rate:	600 rounds per minute.
Weight:	9.36 pounds (without bipod or buttstock); 16.07 pounds with bipod, loaded 200-round magazine.
Length:	26 inches (without buttstock); 32.5 inches (with buttstock).
Barrel:	15.63 inches; quick-change capability without head space adjustment; 1:7-inch twist.
Magazine:	Linked-round 200-round M249 box magazines or M-16 rifle magazines, with adapter unit.
Sights:	Aperture rear, protected-blade front; integral sight rail for optical sights, other fire control systems.
Maker:	Knight's Armament Company 7750 Ninth St. Vero Beach, FL 32968

A quick breakdown of the Stoner 96 light machine gun illustrates how it has been simplified over previous prototypes.

in hard target effectiveness without a reduction in its effectiveness against unprotected targets; improved daylight tracer range; and maintenance of ammunition commonalty with the M-16 rifle." As Gene Stoner expected, this new approach sounded the death knell for the 6.0x45mm program.

History has shown, of course, that the Belgian-made Minimi was the Squad Automatic Weapon ultimately chosen by the Pentagon, following a number of changes. Meantime, Stoner continued to labor on the rework of his own light machine gun.

At the rear of the receiver, Stoner mounted a long rail which was capable of mounting any number of sighting devices, including all the night vision and optical devices included in the NATO Standardization Agreement. Mounted at the rear of the receiver was a standard long-range aperture sight.

While the machine gun was designed to be belt-fed with metal-linked ammunition, Stoner offered an option. By the installation of a handy magazine well that fits in the side of the gun, standard M-16 magazines can be used to feed the gun's healthy appetite.

In the year or so before his death, Gene Stoner utilized most of the technology and design of his Stoner 86 to perfect today's Stoner 96, as some workers at Knight's Armament have come to call it. Most of the specifications for the S-96 are the same as those as the earlier gun. Rate of fire is 600 rounds per minute, firing NATO's 5.56mm M885/M856

ammunition; and it will feed either from a 100-round ammo pouch or the M249 200-round box magazine. With the adapter unit in place, the latest version also will operate with a standard M-16 magazine. Like the S-86, the newer gun also has a quick-change barrel for which no head space adjustment is required. However, the carrying handle of the S-86 has been deleted for the S-96.

The integral sight rail of the S-86 also has been retained, but Stoner, working with Reed Knight, Jr., of Knight's Armament Co., added a multi-rail forend that offers increased tactical flexibility with the addition of other accessories. The new gun is chambered for the NATO-approved 5.56x45mm cartridge and a new, sleeker buttstock resembling that of the M4 carbine has been substituted for the original.

Without the buttstock or tripod the Stoner 96 weighs 9.36 pounds. With the gun combat ready with a loaded 200-round magazine, weight is 16.07 pounds. Rifled to handle M855 ammo, the barrel's grooves make one right-hand turn in every seven inches.

Overall length of the gun without the buttstock is 26 inches; with the stock, 32.5 inches. The assault-length barrel is 15.63 inches. A 21.69-inch barrel also is available. According to members of the Knight staff, several internal changes also have been made to improve the overall capabilities of the weapon. The bolt has been reworked as has the extractor mechanism.

Following the earlier design, the S-96 is cocked by means of a cocking handle

positioned on the right side, which is similar to that of the old Browning Automatic Rifle of nearly forgotten wars. The operating slide and the gas piston are positioned beneath the barrel. The trigger frame is rather ordinary in appearance, holding the safety and the entire trigger mechanism.

Positioned atop the receiver, this light machine gun's feed system is somewhat unique, the components consisting only of the feed tray and the cover. The latter carries the holding and stop arms, but is without the expected feed pawl machinery. Instead, the feed pawls are a part of the feed arm that is located on the receiver's left side below the tray. This arm is actuated by bolt movement and its own driving spring, but the feed arm also is the ejector. As the gun fires only full-auto, the safety is the safeguard and is positioned in the trigger guard in the same manner as that of the Garand M-1 rifle.

As indicated earlier, a special feed mechanism is included with the gun. Should it become necessary to fire from M-16 magazines rather than the metal-linked belt, the belt feed mechanism can be removed quickly simply by pushing out a single pin. The feed pawl rack then is pulled up and removed from the feed arm. A magazine well resembling that of the M-16 is used to replace the belt feed tray and the cover. This unit is locked into place and is ready to accept M-16 magazines. All of this can be accomplished in less than 15 seconds, but in our opinion, should belted ammo become in such short supply that this substitution becomes necessary, the battle probably already is lost!

KMC MODULAR WEAPON SYSTEM
RAIL INTERFACE SYSTEM AND ACCESSORIES

RAIL INTERFACE SYSTEM (RIS)
FOR ANY M16 / M16A1 / M16A2 CARBINE
(HANDGUARD SECTIONS NOT SHOWN)
KAC PART # 94297

KAC MOUNT ASSY.
FOR AIMPOINT 5000
REFLEX SIGHT
KAC PART # 94303

KAC MOUNT FOR ITT
POCKETSCOPE NIGHT
VISION DEVICE
KAC PART # 95139

HANDGUARD SECTIONS FOR RAIL INTERFACE SYSTEMS

HANDGUARD SECTION
FULL LENGTH (6.15")
"11 RIB"
KAC PART   95047

HANDGUARD SECTION
(5.5")
"9 RIB"
KAC PART   97169

HANDGUARD SECTION
(3.9")
"6 RIB"
KAC PART   97168

HANDGUARD SECTION
(2.65")
"4 RIB"
KAC PART   97166

HANDGUARD SECTION
(1.65")
"2 RIB"
KAC PART   97164

KAC VERTICAL FOREGRIP (BASIC)
KAC PART   97098A

This series of illlustrations shows some of the accessories that can be used on the Stoner 96 to make it more battle efficient. The accessories all are from Knight's Armament Co.

Cleaning of the Stoner 96 is a simple matter, for the entire gun can be field-stripped in less than a minute. It can be reassembled in roughly the same amount of time.

A number of years ago, Gene Stoner designed a unique accessory that combines a muzzle brake with a flash suppressor. This particular unit has been used on a number of Stoner-designed weapons, including the earlier Stoner 86. It appears again on the Stoner 96.

The design is unusual, for the unit carries an internal muzzle brake that bleeds gases off into a somewhat larger cylinder that bears resemblance to a sound suppressor. There are a number of small holes in this cylinder, however, which allow the expanding gases to pass through, dissipating the usual flash. We have seen the gun in use and find that this combination unit works well.

Those who used the Browning water-cooled and air-cooled machine guns of World War II and Korea, as well as the M-60 of later conflicts undoubtedly feel the weight of these guns had much to do with their stability and controllability. Their weight caused them to hug the ground and fire where they were pointed.

The new Stoner gun, weighing only a trifle over 16 pounds, would seem a candidate for sporadic accuracy,

depending largely upon the muscular condition of the shooter. That, however, is not the case. The lack of weight makes the gun highly maneuverable, while the exclusive muzzle brake/flash suppressor makes it relatively easy for the gunner to keep his sights on the target.

Prior to his death from a brain tumor in 1996, Stoner and C. Reed Knight, Jr., devoted a great deal of time to developing the S-96 from Stoner's past designs. One of the items that makes the gun totally original is the choice of a dozen or more different accessories created by Knight and his staff that can be added to the gun.

In the original Stoner 63, the gun could be used in a half-dozen different configurations by adding or subtracting parts. In the updated, Stoner 86, this choice of configurations had been largely forgotten, settling for a quality light machine gun. Now, with development of the Stoner 96, the capabilities of the original concept have been achieved to a great degree by the addition of synthetic rails that allow various mission-oriented tools to be added or subtracted as needed.

Reed Knight Jr., and Gene Stoner enjoyed a long relationship—both business and personal—and Knight was chosen to carry on the work the designer was developing at the time of his death. There are several items that

will see the light of day over the next few years, according to our sources.

Limited production is under way for the Stoner 96 machine gun. The Netherlands government has ordered several hundred of these guns, and several other nations are soon to begin testing for their own armies.

The M249 Squad Automatic Weapon, derived from the 5.56mm FN Minimi, has become the issue weapon for our own ground forces, but it is listed only as an "interim weapon." That means the Pentagon gurus still are looking for the ultimate in light machine guns for the SAW mission. If the gods, the politicians and the times eventually meet on some sort of equal plane, the Stoner 96 could well be their choice for the next few generations of fighting men.

This brings us back to the analogy concerning the length of time it sometimes takes from idea to the showing of a motion picture on the nation's screens. Changes in time, personnel, the public's appetites and other circumstances can all play important parts. It would appear that our nation's military and political leaders are impressed by similar sets of facts and circumstances.

If the time has come for the S-96 to be our nation's light machine gun, the decision would gladden Gene Stoner's heart, for that had been his goal for the last 40 years of his life!

CHAPTER 28

MACHINE PISTOLS

Are They The Logical Solution To The Sidearms Problem?

THE GERMAN TERM, *Maschinen Pistole* (MP), can refer to any submachine gun, i.e., any hand-portable weapon firing pistol ammunition in full-auto operation. However, Americans usually make a distinction between conventional submachine guns, which require two hands to operate like a carbine or rifle, and a burst-fire sidearm called a machine pistol.

When the main battle rifle was standard for infantry, with a 30-caliber bore and full-size stock, officers and support troops generally carried a pistol, submachine gun or a carbine. This allowed the sidearm to be holstered or slung, with both hands free to use the radio, map, binoculars or maneuver some crew-served weapon. In Vietnam, however, infantry officers customarily carried the same lightweight M-16A1 rifles as their men; this was partly because pistols tended to attract the attention of enemy snipers and partly because the rifle was no clumsier than an SMG or carbine.

Without doubt, the pistol is the most convenient but least effective sidearm. To increase its combat hit potential, various modifications have been tried. The first and most obvious method is to increase firepower. With single-shot pistols, this could be done only by carrying multiple guns. Black Beard, the pirate, is always pictured with a half-dozen "cannon-barreled" boarding pistols in his sash.

At this point, it would seem worth noting that in the days of single-shot pistols, edged weapons often were added as backup or carried by themselves as sidearms. Most European and American officers and cavalry troopers carried sabers as well as pistols. Napoleonic artillerymen were issued short swords in the Roman style for self-defense should they be overrun. In the Revolutionary War, non-commissioned officers carried bayonets, hunting swords called hangers, or halberds as a badge of rank and to keep order in the lines.

The hit probability of single-shot pistols can be increased by using more than one projectile. Essentially a one-handed shotgun, this pistol style can be effective at close range, as on the pitching deck of a sailing ship. Such weapons still are made in the form of the 410-bore version of the Thompson/Center Contender as but one example. The 20-gauge Ithaca Auto-Burglar, a double-barrel no longer produced, uses the same principle.

Another way to increase firepower is to add to the number of barrels, or to add a turning cylinder to the pistol. Neither method was considered practical, however, until the development of the percussion cap. Even with percussion revolvers, it was common for cavalrymen to carry four or more such weapons, all loaded and ready, when available. This simplified matters, since reloading in the saddle was often impossible during battle. This was the tactic used by Mosby's Rangers and Quantrill's Raiders during the American Civil War.

Once metallic cartridge revolvers were available, notably the 1873 Colt Army Model, reloading was faster and could be done on the move. Officers and cavalry rarely carried more than two, and outside of the American Plains army, where Custer and others had matched pairs of personal sidearms, the soldier was generally limited to one.

Probably the fastest combat revolver during the cavalry era was the British Webley. Serving from the late 19th century through World War II, the Webley provided a double-action trigger and a top-break action with automatic ejection. The model made in the greatest numbers, and which set

British Commando officer carries a German Luger with snail drum magazine. The soldier behind him is armed with a Thompson M1921 submachine gun with a 100-round magazine.

CARRIER FOR FOUR MAGAZINES

HOLSTER STOCK CATCH

This Soviet Stechkin (APS) pistol is considered obsolete, but still is used in Russia for special mission purposes. It fires the 9mm Makarov cartridge from a 20-round magazine. It is shown with its combination holster and stock.

the standard in reliability and stopping power, was the Webley Mark VI in 455-caliber, introduced in 1915.

Reloading could be accomplished even more rapidly by the use of half- or full-moon clips. The Smith & Wesson Model 1917, 45-caliber revolver, is the best known example. In fact, the clip idea is still being explored in competition revolver shooting and has been found both faster and more reliable than speed loaders.

Still, firepower from the revolver is limited by the number of rounds in the cylinder, usually between five and eight. In 1893, Hugo Borchardt developed a successful 7.63mm semi-automatic pistol, which later was to serve as the design basis for the famed P'08 Luger. The magazines on semi-autos could be internal, as with the 1896 Mauser, but more commonly, were detachable. The detachable magazine could be made larger and could be charged more quickly. The capacity of the magazine could be increased by extending it, widening it or adding a drum. Drum magazines are rare, expensive and have been proven to be less reliable than conventional straight magazines. Probably the most famous is the 32-round snail drum magazine on the equally rare German World War I Artillery Luger. These days, extended magazines are usually additions to wide-body staggered magazines. An

example is the 20-round magazine for the SIG-Sauer P226. These usually require a side-mounted "American" magazine release button. However, on some guns a standard-length, staggered magazine can hold up to 18 rounds with a "European" butt-mounted release, as on the HK VP70Z.

Hit probability, especially in low light, also can be increased by night sights, laser modules and even attached flashlights. This is the principle behind the Heckler & Koch pistol developed for SOCOM. Additionally, sound suppressors can reduce the chances of return fire during assassination, sentry neutralization or ambush operations. The Special Operations Command pistols now use American suppressor technology, which has come to be considered the best in the world. However, suppressors have been used extensively since World War II, by OSS Jedburgh teams in France, CIA U-2 pilots flying over Russia, Army tunnel rats operations in Vietnam and others. Hi-Standard, Ruger, and Colt 22-caliber auto pistols have been utilized in this way more than any other guns or calibers, though 380, 9mm and 45 pistols as well as submachine guns have been used as well.

Another way to increase hit probability is to add a shoulder stock. At least since flintlock days, detachable wood stocks have been made for pistols. Colt made them for various percussion and cartridge revolvers during the 19th century.

By 1896, the wood or wood-and-leather holster stock had been developed for the semi-auto pistol. The most famous example is the 7.63mm Model 1896 Mauser. This gun had a detachable wood holster stock, a

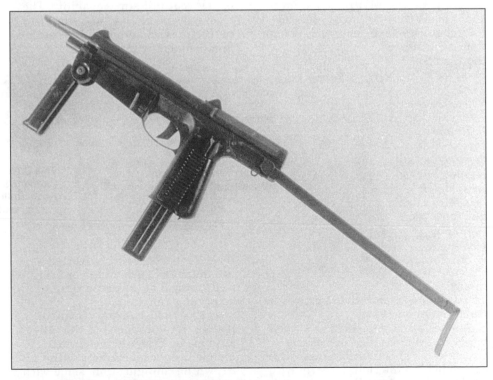

The Polish PM 63 machine pistol fires the 9x18mm Makarov cartridge. In this photo, the stock is extended and the forward grip has been unfolded.

Vietnam sniper Burt Waldron tries the MAC-11 with an experimental wood stock. Photo was taken at Military Armament's range near Powder Springs, Georgia.

firms to produce copies of the Mauser *Schnellfeuerpistole* for the Chinese military market. For some reason, the 1896 Mauser in its full-auto version had become a favorite of the KMT Army, Mao's guerrillas, and Green Gang triads. It could be used as an officer's pistol or a substantial substitute for a submachine gun. Turned on its side, it was used for traversing fire in close combat. A red tassel sometimes was strung from the butt for decoration; this was especially true in communist propaganda performances. Eventually, the Red Chinese government produced its own modernized Mauser called the Type 80.

Also in the 1930s, some Colt Model 1911 45s were converted to be capable of full-auto fire, sometimes with extended magazine and the vertical foregrip designed for the Thompson subgun. One of these was owned by the era's outlaw and bank robber, John Dillinger. Obviously, this would be an intimidating weapon for bank robbery, but accuracy would have been of the "phone booth" variety, and it wouldn't take more than one burst to create a jam or run out of ammo.

Effective, controllable machine pistols are best designed from the ground up for selective fire, with a suitable caliber-to-weight ratio, recoil buffer, burst control, foregrip and a shoulder stock. One of the best examples is the superb Czech VZ61. Although

wood and leather holster stock or detachable wood or wire shoulder stock. These provided greater accuracy and controllability, especially in later models capable of selective fire.

While the 1896 Mauser was the most famous, many other pistols were outfitted with shoulder stocks in the early part of this century. The list includes the 45-caliber Colt M1905, Spanish Astra M900 in 7.63mm, 22 Long Rifle Colt Woodsman, 8mm Japanese Nambu M1904, Finnish Lahti L35 9mm, FN P35 9mm, 7.65mm Luger M1900, the Soviet Stechkin in 9mm Makarov, and even the little Mauser M1910 25 ACP.

Probably the most highly developed holster stock was the one made of high impact plastic for the Heckler & Koch VP70. This *Volkspistole* —translating to People's Pistol—was designed as a hamlet defense weapon for brushfire wars like those then raging in Southeast Asia. When the stock was in place, the VP70 offered semi-auto fire as well as three-round bursts.

A stock also could serve as a wrist brace. The short wire stock on the Czech VZ61 32-caliber machine pistol can be held to the right forearm with the left thumb, as well as conventionally against the shoulder.

A forearm brace "stockless stock" was designed by Dale Davis and produced by Colt for the U.S. Air Force's IMP, which was the accepted acronym for the Individual Multi-Purpose Weapon project. The rotating receiver could be held to the shooting arm by the opposite thumb. A bullpup design, the IMP was produced only in experimental quantities in 221 Fireball caliber. Mack Gwinn, Jr. picked up the patent and produced a 5.56mm commercial version called the Bushmaster "pistol."

However, the main method for increasing firepower and hit probability in the pistol-size sidearm is to give it full-auto capability. The most obvious method was simply to convert a semi-auto pistol to select fire. Still, many pistols' light

This Offensive Handgun Weapons System was developed for the U.S. Special Operations Command by Heckler & Koch. Built around a 45 ACP pistol, it has a sound suppressor, a flashlight and visible/invisible laser sight.

recoiling parts, when converted to full-auto, had such a high cyclic rate, that a single burst would simply empty the gun.

In the 1930s, various Spanish pistols were produced in the full-auto mode. Star produced such pistols in several calibers with Colt/Browning configuration, some with extended magazines and wood holster stocks. Astra was one of the

made in heavier calibers, its most common export variation was in 32 ACP. Easily controlled in short burst, this gun was a favorite of female terrorists with the Italian Red Brigades, who used it to murder the former premier Aldo Moro. This model also was carried as a sidearm, in its leather flap holster, by Ugandan dictator Idi Amin.

The VZ61 Skorpion model fired from a closed bolt and had a good trigger,

A Virginia police officer tries out the Heckler & Koch VP70 machine pistol in this 1970 photo. The gun was far ahead of typical police armament of the era, boasting an 18-round magazine, double-action-only trigger, injection-moulded frame and three-round burst capability.

affording what was considered good semi-auto accuracy. It was equipped with a butt-mounted recoil buffer, a wire stock and a sling. There also was an optional sound suppressor.

Another modern machine pistol, Heckler & Koch's 9mm VP70, was probably ahead of its time. Its injection-moulded frame predated that of the Glock. Its double-action-only trigger predated the police use of 9mm double-action-only service pistols. Its double-stack magazine provided 18 rounds. The plastic holster stock would neither rust, warp nor break; when mounted to the gun, its selector lever provided

three-round bursts, but the selector is frame-mounted, and the metal stock does not have to be in place or extended. A folding vertical foregrip is provided in front of the trigger guard. Fifteen- and 20-round magazines are available, along with a muzzle compensator.

A recent 9mm machine pistol without stock or burst control is the Glock 18. Essentially an oversize Glock service pistol with 33-round, extended, double-stack magazine, the Glock trigger system is refined enough to finger off two-round bursts. However, whether this can be done under combat stress is another matter. A few West

Coast SWAT teams have adopted the Glock 18 as an entry weapon. Distances on room entry are rarely over five yards. Still, most teams have stayed with the heavier Heckler & Koch MP5 subgun to back up their conventional service pistols.

Two-handed submachine guns have been reduced in size to compete with the machine pistol as sidearm. Examples are the MP5K, the Ingram MAC-11 and the Micro-Uzi. The Kurz version of the MP5 is simply shortened, with the stock removed. The MAC-11 was the 380 ACP version of the larger M-10 9mm and 45 ACP subguns. This particular version suffered from a heavy trigger pull, open-bolt operation, poor selector and safety placement, a wobbly wire stock and crude sights. Except as a close-range assassination weapon with "snuffer can" in place, we have come to the conclusion that this gun had little use.

The Micro-Uzi is a shortened, closed-bolt version of the original Uzi. It is easy to carry and conceal for VIP protection teams. With the stock in place and the selector on semi-auto, it is capable of greater accuracy than a service pistol of equal size.

As armies go to assault rifles, submachine guns have to become smaller to compete in the pistol/sidearm market. An example of this design merger is the Polish WZ63 designed around the Makarov cartridge. With muzzle compensator, folding foregrip, extended magazine, folding metal stock and selective fire, it combines most of the elements of a modern military sidearm. •

The Czech-made VZ61 Skorpion, chambered for the 32 ACP round, was carried as a sidearm by Ugandan dictator Idi Amin. It also was favored by female terrorists of Italy's Red Brigade during the 1970s.

The MAC-11 from Military Armament Corporation is a 380 ACP subgun. In this photo, it carries a 32-round magazine, nylon foregrip and a Sionics sound suppressor, as well as a wire stock. It fires from the open bolt, unlike most machine pistols of comparable size.

CHAPTER 29

KEEPING THEIR HEADS DOWN

Well Directed Firepower Is Essential To The Attack.

IN MODERN COMBAT there is no "bullet with your name on it." They all say, "To whom it may concern." Whether you or the guy next to you gets hit is largely a matter of chance.

To decrease the element of chance, armies use the principle of probability. In the 19th century, hit probability was increased by the use of rifled small arms and aimed fire. In the 20th century, quick-firing weapons and multiple projectile/fragmenting ammunition increased hit probability. The army most likely to win the day is the army laying down the greatest amount of firepower in the shortest time at the enemy's weakest point.

In Napoleonic times, when entire regiments marched shoulder to shoulder, heavy firepower in the form of muzzle-loading cannons was widely separated from the line of advance. This continued until World War I when the infantryman acquired the modern hand grenade and the Browning Automatic Rifle. This was the beginning of small unit firepower. Today, with platoons moving rapidly into combat via helicopter, the need for really portable firepower is greater than ever.

Modern hand-held, direct-fire weapons are almost invariably capable of full-automatic fire. This is the era of the assault rifle. To supplement these weapons, there are new fragmentation indirect fire weapons.

In Vietnam, the last time U.S. troops were engaged in large-scale ground combat, infantry units sustained about 80 percent of total casualties. This is understandable, if only because the only physical protection a soldier had was Mother

The M-79 grenade launcher was replaced by the M203, which fit under the barrel of the M-16A1 rifle.

Earth. Still, increased training could have reduced casualty rates. Even late in the Vietnam conflict, Stateside basic infantry training was geared to a war in Europe that Allied commanders had expected since 1945. Training does not come in a vacuum. The politics and prejudices of commanders influence training, as well as the education and overall quality of the recruits.

A modern First World Army evaluates its available manpower pool, selects the best physical and mental specimens, then tests them on paper and in training courses, putting them into appropriate specialties.

The Mossberg 500 is typical of the 12-gauge pump guns carried by point men on patrols in Vietnam. The shotgun was proven for counter-ambushes in jungle conditions.

Some skills must be taught from scratch, others presume related pre-training from civilian life. For instance, U.S. military marksmanship training presupposes no previous exposure to firearms. The era of the country-bred sharpshooter like Alvin York or Audie Murphy is assumed to be over. However, grenade-toss training is abbreviated, building on presumed football and baseball experience of the teenage American male. Likewise, vehicle training presumes some civilian experience in driving a car. In other countries, like Vietnam, for example, teenagers can

be presumed to have no experience throwing a ball or driving a car.

Recruiters and trainers also must evaluate the psychological readiness of recruits. The Army's typical volunteer is a teenager, often from some minority group. As often as not, he is no stranger to drugs. Of course, this situation also exists for European armies, and even the Israeli army has a hashish problem. Russian officers complain of troops draining engine coolant alcohol from their battle tanks when vodka supplies run low.

The typical American recruit also has no concept of the nature of modern war. He does not read books, and the World War II movies he watches show only a fraction of the firepower available on the modern battlefield, as well as giving a distorted picture of how much control an infantryman can exert over his environment. Most Vietnam vets describe the war there as "insane," in part because the media had provided them no way to integrate their experiences with reality.

In the past 40 years, the number of automatic weapons on the battlefield has increased five times. Every American soldier and Marine has his M-16, and he can expect to face an opponent armed with a Kalashnikov or some variation. Multiply this by support weapons ranging from machine guns to helicopter gunships, and it is easy to

The M-3A1 45 ACP Grease Gun provided close range firepower for U.S. infantry in World War II and Korea.

see that battles between two modern armies would have the psychological impact of one continuous car wreck.

Precision marksmanship, as with any other highly developed skill or sport, requires years, not weeks of training. Superior riflery is the subject of historical anomaly, not normality. Berdan's Sharpshooters in the Civil War, the British BEF in the

opening days of World War I, Marine snipers in Vietnam—these are the exception, not the rule.

While the U.S. Marine Corps has attempted to keep rifle training at a high level, even during the manpower requirements of the Vietnam "meatgrinder," the Army began taking shortcuts in the 1960s. Bullseye and known-distance training were out. Silhouettes and Quick Kill were in.

Weapons giving greater hit probability were given priority.

In the 50-yard infantry war in Vietnam, the lack of precision marksmanship did not seem to be critical. If a major ground war had broken out in Europe or Korea, the deficiencies of a 223-caliber rifle and "spray and pray" tactics might have led to more intense emphasis on rifle fundamentals. Meanwhile, fire

The M-79 grenade launcher used in Vietnam is shown with the 40mm high explosive grenade the gun fires. A shotgun round with pellets or flechettes, also was made in that era.

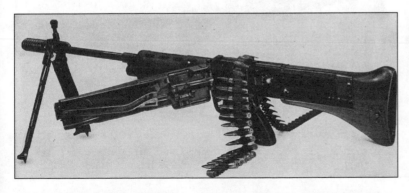

Designated as the U.S. T44 light machine gun, this was an experimental model based on the World War II German FG42 and MG42 machine guns. It had no takers at the Pentagon.

The Ingram Model 6 was developed after World War II as a possible successor to the Thompson subgun. The Ingram, despite its appearance, was much simpler and less expensive to produce.

The Thompson M1A1 submachine gun is a simplified version of the original Thompson M1928. It was issued in World War II and during the Korean War, and still was popular with Special Forces troops in Vietnam.

superiority now depends on "hit probability" weapons as much as trained men.

Pistols produce only a tiny percentage of the casualties in modern war. They are retained for personal defense by military police, officers, tank crews, mortarmen and others with unique needs.

The lowest level of serious infantry firepower is the submachine gun. Developed in World War I, the full-auto subgun fired pistol ammunition. Early versions were configured like machine guns (e.g., the ill-fated Villar Perosa, mounted on biplanes), rifles (e.g., Bergmann, Thompson), or pistols (e.g., Mauser *Schnellfeuer*). In World War II, older guns like the Thompson were simplified to ease production costs. Newer guns, like the British Sten, were designed around stampings and simple machining processes. More recent versions, like the Uzi and MAC-10/11, reduced overall size by using a telescoping bolt and pistol grip feed.

Currently, the submachine gun has been relegated to special operations or police duty in First World armies, sometimes being used with sound suppressors for ambush or assassination. For front-line infantry, the assault rifle is king, with its greater range, accuracy, penetration and wounding power.

Because of its multi-projectile hit probability, the shotgun has received new interest from the military. While there is much to say for improved,

combat-reliable full-auto and semi-auto 12-gauges with box magazines, it is still unlikely that the shotgun will replace the assault rifle for most troops, even in jungle warfare.

Still, the "riot gun" has proven itself as a special purpose weapon. British and Commonwealth troops used the semi-auto Browning Auto 5 and other shotguns during the Malayan Emergency of 1948-60. With its mixed load of BB and buckshot, it was shown to be the most effective counter-ambush weapon available for jungle fighting, when compared to the battle rifle, submachine gun and light

machine gun. It managed to keep communist heads down, so the ambushed patrol could mount a counterattack.

The pump-action 12-gauge has been used by American troops since the turn of the century, when they fought Moros in the Philippines. The gun of choice was the Winchester 1897, as it was in World War I. The pump gun, with its reputation for reliability, was still in service in Vietnam, with short-barreled police models being made by Savage, Winchester, Remington, Ithaca, High Standard and Mossberg.

The shotgun was used extensively in Vietnam, probably more so than at any time since World War I. It often was carried by the point man on patrols, by guards on military vehicles and by indigenous troops for hamlet defense. During the same period in Korea, U.S. military installations were guarded by professional Korean guards armed with pump shotguns.

Due to the inaccuracy, unpredictability and short range of the hand grenade, various shoulder-fired launchers have been developed to assist it. The first serious American grenade launcher was the M-7 developed for the M-1 Garand rifle. The Mark 2 "pineapple" grenade could be fitted into an adaptor unit, then fired by means of a special blank cartridge. Accuracy and speed with this unit were not impressive.

During the Vietnam War, the world's first anti-personnel grenade launcher built from the ground up was issued. This was the famous M-79, which fired a special 40mm grenade. This launcher, shaped like a short

The CETME was perhaps the first light assault machine gun, working on a blowback action and the same roller system as the CETME rifle. It is chambered for 5.56mm ammo and has been adopted by the Spanish and Mexican armies.

The Heckler & Koch MP5 is useful at short ranges and can be used to keep their heads down, but other calibers and weapons do it better.

single-barrel shotgun, probably owed its origin to the tear gas grenade launchers made by Federal and Lake Erie since the 1930s. To the men who carried the M-79, it was like having a 60mm mortar at squad level.

The M-79 could be used from the shoulder or like a "knee mortar" with the toe of the stock resting on the ground. GIs trusted the M-79, in spite of the fairly high dud rate due to the moist climate of Vietnam. Also, the M406 "blooper" fragmentation grenade requires 30 yards to arm the fuse, and it could hit a tree and bounce back to blow away some friendlies.

The main problem with the M-79 was its single-round capacity. Unless the gunner carried a 45-caliber sidearm, he had little protection against an enemy less than 30 yards away if he had a blooper grenade in the spout. To increase its versatility a 12-gauge adaptor was developed, but this kept a 40mm grenade from being inserted in the chamber. Later a 40mm sabot round was perfected to replace the adaptor, but this shell fired only 27 #4 buckshot, which made it no more effective than a single-barrel 12-gauge.

Besides the frag and buckshot rounds, there were special purpose projectiles made for the M-79. Practice and marking rounds were available. A CS tear gas round was used by National Guard units to quell riots and by combat soldiers to smoke VC out of spider holes.

To increase the firepower of the grenade launcher more barrels were mounted experimentally on the M-79. However, this idea was discarded in favor of a launcher mounted underneath the barrel of the M-16A1 service rifle. This was still a single-shot, but the M-16 provided protection for the grenadier between shots. This M203 launcher eventually replaced the M-79 in front line service.

At the time it was being tested, the 5.56mm Minimi was equipped with a 200-round see-through ammo box made from heavy-duty plastic.

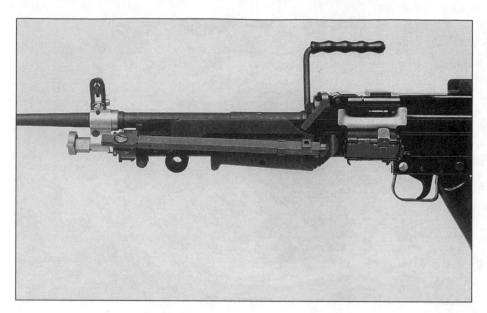

It could operate from belts or from M-16 magazines.

Because of its range, accuracy and penetration limitations, the 5.56mm cartridge is not suitable to support weapons heavier than the Minimi. The 7.62x51mm NATO cartridge is still more appropriate to general purpose machine guns and those mounted on vehicles and helicopters. For example, this is the round used in the so-called Chain Gun, a weapon system that does not depend on gas bleed-off for cycling like the traditional Browning designs. Originally designed as a coaxially mounted tank gun, the EX-34 also has been adapted for use on the Hughes-designed 500MD and other helicopters. It measures 37 inches overall, weighs 30.2 pounds and feeds 7.62mm ammo from linkless belts at

Later, the XM174 12-round automatic 40mm launcher was developed. This device was lighter but similar to the automatic 40mm guns mounted on river patrol boats in Vietnam. This device appears to have a future, at least for fixed base defense.

The selective-fire, intermediate-caliber rifle is now the standard infantry weapon of First World armies. It is usually called an "assault rifle," because it was designed to provide fire superiority in the last phase of an attack usually termed the assault phase.

Intermediate calibers like the 7.92mm Kurz, 7.62x39mm, and 5.56mm were found to have more controllable recoil dispersion than traditional battle rifle calibers like the 303, 308 or 30-06. Also, an infantryman could carry many more rounds. Grunts in Vietnam commonly carried 600 to 900 rounds of 5.56mm ammo in magazines, as well as bandoliers of 7.62mm ammo for the M-60 light machine gun.

The M-60 was the standard support weapon for GIs in Vietnam. It was comparatively reliable, having been developed from World War II German designs. However, it was not light, and its belt-feed design could jam when the ammunition was dirty, as was commonly the case when bandoliers were carried uncovered.

The M240 7.62mm NATO has proved to be an excellent support weapon, laying down accurate fire during an assault. It now is the standard with NATO infantry companies.

Since that time, various 5.56mm squad automatic weapons have been developed, which give greater accuracy and firepower than the standard M-16A2, but which are lighter and easier

This is the Belgian-made XM249 Minimi, which was reworked to become the M249, the current squad automatic weapon for U.S. forces.

to carry than the M-60. The Fabrique Nationale Minimi, first designated XM249, was one of these.

a cyclic rate of 570 rounds per minute. While the U.S. infantryman now has available TOW and Dragon systems, as well as a variety of rocket launchers and recoilless rifles not mentioned here, the average soldier probably will have to face the next brushfire war with variations of the light weapons discussed. The M-16A2 assault rifle will remain the baseline of squad firepower well into the next century. ●

Section V

Combat Shotguns

HANDLING THE COMBAT SHOTGUN

Proper Technique Is A Necessity If This Weapon Is To Be Used To Its Best Advantage.

"**THE MOST CAPABLE** weapon in my battery is the most neglected. I have concentrated on handgun practice, firing my shotgun only seldom," admits R.K. Campbell, a working police officer in Una, South Carolina.

"There are reasons for this neglect, which actually are just excuses. The handgun is always with us, because it is light and easily concealed. Relatively powerful handguns may be worn in hidden comfort. The handgun has evolved far beyond its original limitations of range and power. But if we have any warning of an upcoming fight, we should arm ourselves with a long gun"

Campbell agrees with the preponderance of the nation's street cops that the most appropriate weapon would be the pump-action 12-gauge shotgun. The shotgun is the most effective short-range fighting tool in the law enforcement arsenal.

Simple to use, effective with training and useful against both hard and soft targets, the shotgun is versatile. Today, police shotguns can be loaded with special door-breaching slugs or gas-carrying delivery units.

"Recently I embarked upon a crash course of education concerning the shotgun. I emerged with a deeper respect for this particular piece of equipment. Many of us neglect shotgun practice partly because we feel the weapon is so capable we don't need a lot of practice. Even if this were true, we are selling the weapon and ourselves short by not understanding all of its capabilities," Campbell states.

Shotgun techniques center upon learning to control recoil. For one with little experience, the recoil of the 12-gauge shotgun can be brutal, inflicting bruises and jarring bones. But a well-placed charge of buckshot will prove highly potent on the other end! "We

can't buy skill, of course, with the shotgun or any other weapon, but we all can learn such skill with time and practice," Campbell feels.

Reviewing his own self-training program, the first step was to learn to control recoil. This officer soon found that with each shot, he needed to lean into the gun and have the buttstock firmly pressed into his shoulder. Leaning forward with the shoulders ahead of the hips, he also quickly learned that the weak-side foot should be forward in the firing stance.

"This will provide an excellent platform for firing a strong recoiling weapon. I prefer the pump shotgun, because as the weapon recoils, I can use this energy to work the action and bring the barrel back to level," this police officer explains. "One has to bring the slide handle sharply to the rear, as less than positive action may result in a short cycle. Then forcefully drive the slide handle back to the

Officer R.K. Campbell illustrates what he considers good shotgun-handling stance. The gun is a Model 870 Remington 12-gauge.

The kneeling position should be practiced. It presents a smaller target and provides a degree of stability in holding on the target.

front, bringing the barrel back on target as you do so. I have found that really fast aimed fire can be accomplished with this method."

Campbell makes it a point to fire the shotgun from the kneeling positions and from behind barricades in his own training cycle. He feels he is in as much danger of being shot while using the shotgun as the handgun. An adversary may realize he is in more danger against a shotgun than a handgun, so the scattergun-armed officer should not neglect to use basic survival skills. Find and use cover is one of the first rules!

As a part of his overall program, Officer Campbell has found that trigger discipline is vital. "Keep the finger outside of the trigger guard until you have made the decision to fire," he warns. "In fact, I leave the chamber empty until action is imminent. The shotgun cannot be considered safe if the chamber is loaded. In addition, simply racking the slide to load the chamber has been known to be enough of a threat to bring an end to hostilities—but nothing can be counted on in potentially deadly encounters."

Campbell practices firing from the standing, kneeling and prone positions. In the beginning, he suggests the use of light birdshot loads for developmental training. "This will build experience," he contends, "without the expense and bruises of buckshot. That comes later! Birdshot is easier on target frames, as well."

The shotgun has a limited magazine capacity, so it becomes important to keep the magazine

loaded if the shootout lasts past one or two rounds. Having an ammo belt or, better, a carrier on the weapon will give access to spare ammunition. Campbell suggests we practice reloading without taking our eyes off the target. One has simply to draw the shotshell from the carrier and use the thumb and forefinger to guide it into the magazine until it is seated properly.

There are three acknowledged

Rounding a corner can be a fatal decision. Careful consideration should be given this move before making the decision.

ranges for the shotgun: short, medium and long. In law enforcement circles, these usually are held to be 7, 15 and 25 yards respectively. Individual weapons and loads may alter this equation. Short range is the distance at which the pellet charge impacts together virtually as a single projectile. The spread may be as little as two inches or less. Careful aiming is needed.

At medium range, the pattern has opened a bit. Benefits of the shotgun are seen at this range, as buckshot hits usually result in most of the charge finding the target.

At long range, the shot pattern has spread so much that effectiveness usually is lost. Individual pellets lack the energy to produce stops. It is the striking together of pellets as a mass that produces stops. At longer range, slugs invariably are used.

It is up to the individual user to fire and pattern his shotgun, inspect the patterning targets, then carefully consider the capabilities of his service shotgun—and his own range limitations.

A number of experienced field officers of Campbell's acquaintance feel that the slug load is the best for all-round law enforcement work. This contingent is quick to point out that buckshot is superior only to the middle range of 15 yards. "They have convinced me," Campbell admits, "and

The low ready position is good for movement when you don't think the bad guys are only a few steps away. Note the flashlight mounted on the gun's barrel.

In the low ready, the shotgun is held at belt level. This is still fast for getting into action, but not as uncomfortable as the high ready.

The indoor ready is used for moving or for clearing a building. The gun is held with the butt pressed into the shoulder, muzzle down and pointed toward the ground ahead of the shooter's weak foot.

In spite of the use of the semi-automatic shotgun by SEAL teams and other highly experienced and trained units found mostly in the military, Campbell, like most of his contemporaries, is convinced that the pump-action shotgun remains the best choice as the most reliable design thus far created.

"This is especially true in the matter of maintenance. The pump-action shotgun can be left in the trunk of the patrol car for months on end and come out shooting," he insists. "This isn't an ideal level of maintenance, but it is the treatment most of these weapons receive!"

In the damp, humid South, where he follows his law enforcement career, R.K. Campbell has learned a few other things about maintenance of the pump-action shotgun. "I've found that today's modern plastic shotshells tend to scrape away lubricant as they are chambered," he

I'll stick with conventional wisdom and reserve buckshot only for the shorter ranges."

Veteran law enforcement shotgun handlers have come up with another recommendation that Campbell believes in: It is an excellent tactic to keep the shotgun's tube magazine downloaded by one shell at all times. This not only puts less strain on the spring, but it allows quick insertion of a slug, if the situation calls for such action. This, of course, can be done during a gunfight by loading the slug, hitting the bolt release, then racking the slug into the chamber.

"If you have not committed this technique to muscle memory," says this officer, "you could fumble this drill while on the move.

"I sometimes show students videos of themselves taped on the range during combat training. Those who have practiced the moves do well. Others decide they had better learn. Actually, the mind is a powerful computer, and some of us are surprised at how much we can absorb in our so-called gray matter."

In the sequence that Campbell now teaches to other officers, he impresses them with the fact that ready positions are learned for fast combat presentations, but also can be utilized in avoiding obstacles as well.

"Never lead with the barrel of the shotgun as you enter a building or turn a corner. The muzzle may get grabbed or obstructed. In a severe instance, one is likely to become an instant fatalist, when he finds

himself looking down the barrel of the gun that was just taken away from him!"

The positions for shotgun carry that Campbell teaches break down to the high ready for exterior or stalking use, the low ready when the gun is likely to be carried for an extended period, and the indoor ready for cramped quarters.

In the high ready position, the shotgun butt is pressed into the shoulder and held at eye level. With this, the shooter is ready and alert for any problem and he can get a round off fast!

Officer Bob Campbell has found this to be an excellent firing position in a short-range situation.

notes. A light coat of rust inhibitor such as Sentry Solutions in the chamber is recommended.

"The double slide rails are treated best with a light coat of grease," he adds, "and Tuf Glide dry lubricant is useful in all weather conditions."

Getting back to the shooting end of this essay, Campbell points out that "00 buckshot is considered our best proven anti-personnel load. However, there are those who prefer #1 buckshot, considering it a good compromise between 00 and #4s wider dispersal."

The best loads found in Campbell's own tests tend to follow Evan Marshall's shotgun load ratings, which recommend the reduced or tactical buckshot loads. These are offered by Remington, Federal and Winchester.

Remington currently offers an interesting eight-pellet load they claim offers 20 percent less recoil than standard loads while giving tighter patterns at close range. "Actual shooting results have shown them to be better than standard buckshot," Campbell acknowledges. Incidentally, #4 buckshot is about 10 percent less effective than 00 loads, according to field reports.

In his own shotgun work, the South Carolinian has found that "slugs are impressive; even more effective than the best pellet loads." The one-ounce slug is driven at 1200 to 1300 feet per second, and the 78-caliber projectile typically expands to a diameter of well over an inch when fired into 14 inches of ballistic gelatin.

One should practice reloading the tube magazine without taking his eyes off the target. Here, the shell is about to be directed into the tube.

"It becomes obvious that the slug does not tend to over-penetrate as much as we might think," Campbell opines. "The reduced recoil slug Remington is offering provides good accuracy at well beyond 50 yards, but it will drop faster than standard slugs."

Officer Campbell joins those who consider the shotgun the ultimate short-range weapon. If one needs convincing, look at history. From the jungles of Malaysia to the streets of our cities, the shotgun has proved itself in armed battle!

His personal choice as a duty

shotgun is the rifle-sighted Remington Police Magnum and he tends to avoid pistol grips and folding stocks at all costs. "I prefer a standard stock and forend, although I have seen specially trained officers use the pistol grip shotgun with skill. I guess it's a case of my being brought up with a standard shotgun for quail and waterfowl and that's the type of gun I handle best."

But, as with other weapons, there are a number of organized schools that conduct training in police or military use of the shotgun. One such school is the Tactical Firearms Training Team, which also conducts courses listed as Advanced Tactical Handgun, Tactical Rifle, Two-Man Team Tactics, Optical Rifle and VIP Protection. If you don't see the course you need, they will tailor one to your needs—if you are willing to pay for such special attention. Civilians are welcome in all of these courses.

As mentioned elsewhere in this book, the school is operated by Max F. Joseph, a former reconnaissance Marine, who knows his trade and, more important, knows how to teach it to others.

The scene with which we are familiar is in Huntington Beach, California, and immediate environs. However, Joseph now has a similar school in Memphis, Tennessee, with what he calls Mobile Training Units operating in Texas and South America.

Joseph obviously is agreeing with Officer Bob Campbell when he states, "The shotgun is one of the most often called upon, but least understood weapons in the police inventory." He

The thumb of the weak hand is used to push the shell home when reloading. In this photo the shooter's finger is on the trigger. It shouldn't be.

The U.S. military and many police departments tend to favor the Mossberg 500 pump gun. In testing it, Campbell has found that it offers good results.

Joseph reloads the shotgun he uses in demonstrations, as one of his students observes the technique.

says that his program is designed for either pump-action or semi-auto models and is meant for police departments or individuals who wish to increase their skills and confidence with the shotgun. Others have described it as "training for the worst-case scenarios."

Included in the schedule is a study of ammunition coupled with shot patterning, plus what is termed surgical shooting. There also are presentation drills, structure clearing, close-quarter shooting, weapons retention and transition drills.

As a starter, Joseph hands out printed material with detailed illustrations, then launches into a brief lecture on the missions, capabilities and limitations of the shotgun. He also is quick to point out the strengths and weaknesses of both the pump gun and the semi-auto.

In the course, the first live-fire exercise involves establishing a zero for 12-gauge slugs. Needless to say, such a workout quickly reveals the fact that the guns have radically different points of aim and points of impact. Here, a gun with adjustable sights can make the course a lot easier.

In looking over the trainees and their guns during one course, it became obvious that most of the pump-actions were equipped with simple bead sights. Joseph's initial demand was for shooters firing slugs to score head shots on a silhouette target set at 30 yards. With a bit of practice, all of the shooters without sights were able to use Kentucky

The Tactical Firearms Training Team in California offers combat shotgun training to military personnel, police officers and interested civilians. Both semi-auto and pump-action shotguns are used.

A TFTT instructor critiques a student's approach to the Fun House where structure-clearing exercises are conducted. Every move by students is recorded and discussed following such training.

Max Joseph, director of TFTT, poses behind the gun rack where an array of scatter guns almost as individualized as his students stands ready for the beginning of the training session.

Joseph impresses upon his students that accuracy is better than speed, but he offers both, hitting four targets at 10 yards in less than two seconds.

windage for shots that satisfied the instructor. For the students who had little prior experience with slugs, there was surprise at the accuracy that could be attained.

Next came the chore of patterning each of the guns with 00 buckshot from 10, 15 and 25 yards. The point was made that so—called surgical fire-cutting it close-can be accomplished with buckshot if the shooter is fully aware of how his gun patterns at a given range

During all this, Joseph continually emphasized that what you use in the way of a gun and ammo is not nearly as important as the way you use it. This comment was brought on by the fact that there were both autoloaders and pump guns in the class.

Joseph, himself, uses an aging Winchester Model 1200 in his live-fire demonstrations. At 10 yards, he is able to drop four targets in less than

two seconds! This pretty well proves that in the right hands, the pump gun can be as efficient as the autoloader.

The training sequences that students seem to enjoy the most are the tactical drills on structure clearing. The so-called Fun House in the TFTT setup can be configured to almost any imaginable scenario. It is laid out in totally realistic fashion, with furniture and other household needs such as a stove and refrigerator.

While Joseph and his staff are quick to point out that a single man cannot efficiently clear a structure, there are individuals such as homeowners who may have to make such a move. Instruction was offered with basic rules of keeping a distance from corners, using peripheral vision and staying out of doorways. Emphasized throughout the course is the fact that a 00 buckshot round

contains nine pellets and the shooters must be sure they are going to hit the target, not spread 00 shot to become a hazard downrange.

In the structure-clearing segment, all of the skills learned on the range and information gained through lectures are brought into play. Target identifications are emphasized throughout training, with rapid target identification drills. Students are observed by Joseph and his staff during the clearing operations and an after-action critique is conducted in depth, giving each student a rundown on his performance.

Max Joseph and his staff, all former military types, have offered such shotgun instruction to police officers, military men and civilians seeking to learn more about home protection. They know what they are doing and teach it well! •

THE 12-GAUGE TRANSLATOR

Sometimes Simple Language Isn't Enough!

A LAW ENFORCEMENT agent who worked with the New York Police Department in the 1960s once stopped a suspicious car on a lonely road. The driver got out and said, "No habla Ingles, senor." The officer said, "Wait right here. I have a translator in my car."

The officer went back to his squad car and took the shotgun out of its rack. He put the muzzle at lip level and cranked the slide. Miraculously, the suspect immediately regained his command of the English language.

"I remembered this story a few years later when I was organizing a search warrant on a two-story house in a Los Angeles suburb. The principal suspect had done time for drug dealing and had been deported twice to Mexico under different names," recalls David Steele.

"I had surveilled the house, had seen four people about, all of them of Hispanic appearance. Although I had seen only these four, I knew such a house easily could hold up to 20 Mexicans. Fifteen was the number actually found there.

"Thus, in addition to the few investigators my agency could provide, I got a couple from the Immigration & Naturalization Service, and since the house was in their area, I notified LAPD. The Los Angeles Police Department assigned an amazing 13 patrolmen and investigators, including detectives from Organized Crime, Anti-Terrorism and the Narcotics Divisions."

To keep this controllable, Steele told most of the officers that they would be securing the perimeter and suspects prior to the search. He decided the actual entry would be made by five people. Those would be himself; a patrolman, so suspects inside could not say later that they thought "they were being attacked by a bunch of guys in loud jackets; and the three narcs, who were used to getting into places where they were not wanted."

A Spanish-speaking narc and Steele went to the door and demanded entry. When a woman opened it, the two rushed to the top of a narrow stairway and into a hallway. Steele carried a 12-gauge Mossberg 500 shotgun with pistol grip in his left hand.

"Without a shoulder stock, it was not accurate beyond five yards," Steele admits, "but it was far more visually impressive than the expensive 9mm pistols everyone else held. Mexicans of all ages and sexes came pouring out of the bedrooms. The narc and I pulled them by their wrists toward the stairwell, at the bottom of which other officers handcuffed them."

Few of the captives spoke English, and several went with the immigration officers for deportation. The team did not capture their main suspect, but found several false identification documents with pictures of his face. This allowed them to get an arrest warrant for this individual.

"I also arrested the suspect's father, who claimed ownership of a stolen Glock 10mm pistol we found under a bed," Steele reports. "It was considered a successful operation, but considering the number of non-English speakers involved, the orderly control of suspects on entry was assisted by Mossberg's Universal Translator."

He put the shotgun back in his car, along with his armored vest and raid jacket, then began interviewing suspects in a more benign atmosphere.

Contrary to their movie and television images,

This Remington Model 870 bird gun has had the barrel cut back to police length. It would be effective in a firefight.

detectives are rarely "lethal weapons." In fact, most investigators are chosen for their mental skills, not their martial capabilities. This, Steele feels, is particularly true outside of local police agencies, where detectives are selected from those who already have passed through the crucible of patrol and jail work.

"Thanks to urbanization, a volunteer army and psychological testing for police recruits, it is a wonder that any of today's recruits have any shooting skills," our co-author contends. "One applicant told me of a qualification test that asked whether he liked guns or flowers. An avid gun collector, he felt that admission of his interest in firearms would hurt his employment chances. He chose flowers as the answer."

These days, investigative agencies not part of police departments tend to recruit detectives for skills other than going toe to toe with crooks. A detective"s main job is writing readable reports for prosecutors. When the detective has to make an arrest, he usually can gather a team from his own or other agencies.

When lawyers and politicians demanded a greater representation for women in law enforcement agencies, they insisted that the department provide job-specific, statistical justification for the

Mossberg's M835 Regal pump-action field gun is used by Southern guards on chain gang detail. Long barrels are not inconvenient out of doors and provide accuracy as well as visible deterrence.

Shooting the 12-gauge Mossberg Persuader with its pistol grip stock is done easily from the hip, but when using this system don't expect accuracy beyond five yards.

height, weight and strength standards required of recruits

Choosing a number, an investigator's monthly time line might involve only a few minutes of face-to-face confrontation with bad guys. Thus, his "hazard time" might be only .01 percent of the total. Using added agency and uniformed manpower, the risk factor possibly could be reduced to as little as .001 or even .0001 percent.

Under this theory, agencies tend to hire both male and female candidates whose defensive skills are only "two on a scale of ten." The problem rears its head when this .0001 percent of the agent's time makes him or her disabled or even 100 percent dead!

There are those who contend that some agencies supply only as much expensive training as is necessary to avoid civil liability. Meanwhile, some officers not chosen for their athletic abilities, aggressiveness or martial skills tend to avoid any training for which they are not paid or are not specifically ordered to attend! Result is that it is up to a comparatively few firearms and defensive tactics instructors to bring the troops along as best they can. In keeping with this

task, they must choose weapons and equipment that can be used, concealed and maintained by the recruits our courts and politicos allow to be hired.

"Today, most detectives doing

criminal investigations carry handguns and have access to shotguns for backup. Rifles, carbines and submachine guns are extremely rare in plainclothes work," David Steele has found.

The Benelli semi-automatic shotgun, with a 14-inch barrel (not legal for civilian ownership) is a powerful and maneuverable entry gun.

David Steele is about to pull the Mossberg Persuader from what is called the Mozambique carry. It can be brought into action quickly with little effort.

As discussed earlier, the standard police support weapon is the 12-gauge pump action shotgun with a barrel of 20 inches or less. Currently, the most widely used is the Remington Model 870, sometimes in modified form like the Scattergun Technologies models. The military also stocks short-barreled shotguns for some missions and continues to look for the model they consider the ultimate for their type of work.

Other common pump guns favored for law enforcement work are the Ithaca Model 37, Winchester Model 1200, Savage Model 69 and several discontinued models made originally by High Standard. Seen occasionally in the field as backup weapons are such semi-automatic models as the Benelli Super 90, as well as the

This technique, with the stock tucked under the arm, is fine for weapon retention, but there is little accuracy beyond about five yards.

Remington Model 1100 and the same maker's 11-87. Until only recently, the double-barreled Stevens 311 still was being used by detectives of the New York Police Department. "This one apparently was thought to be simple enough for city boys to use without forgetting to unload it," one observer offers.

"My experience with police training is that shotgun familiarization is repeated so rarely for detectives that unless an investigator owns his own scattergun, he is likely to forget even the simplest things, like where the slide release is located," contends David Steele

For serving high risk or unknown risk search warrants in urban areas, Steele has found that investigators are increasingly turning to local SWAT units to make the entry.

"This allows extra-realistic training for the SWAT members, as well as distributing the legal risk of shooting to team and department policy, rather than that decision falling entirely on the shoulders of an individual officer. The downside of using the SWAT team is that it may not be available, and their protocols for searching may turn a 10-minute search by patrolmen into a four-hour ordeal, involving cordoned-off areas, surveillance gear, explosive entry, et cetera."

Currently, we have found, the shotgun is out of fashion with special weapons units. The high tech Heckler & Koch MP5 submachine gun has been the weapon of choice for entry teams such as Los Angeles' Special Enforcement Bureau. Shotguns thus are kept in reserve on the perimeter. However, for patrol and narcotics teams, the shotgun is still the backup weapon of choice for economic reasons

The Mozambique carry also can be used with full-stocked shotguns such as this Remington 870. The gun is carried on the left shoulder, leaving the right had free to reach a belted pistol if necessary.

David Steele has found that Mossberg's 12-gauge pump gun is an accurate combination when outfitted with a Vang Comp barrel.

if no other. The pump-action shotgun is simple, cheap, reliable and holds a century or more of public acceptance.

In the era of realism before the introduction of political correctness, the New York Police Department had a Stakeout Unit. In operation from 1967 until 1971, the idea was for officers to hide in likely businesses and confront robbers in the act. Small neighborhood grocery stores had complained to the mayor and this had brought some action. Since New York's Sullivan Law prevented most storeowners from having their own pistols, they could only request police assistance.

It was this Stakeout Unit that pioneered some of the SWAT tactics in use today. Unlike modern teams, however, this unit developed some individual "stars", who ran up gunfight records that surely would get them transferred to desk jobs or jail duty in modern departments. One of these stars was a gent named Jim Cirillo, who was involved in 17 gunfights, terminating the careers of a dozen armed robbers in the process.

Cirillo did not believe in going into a situation underarmed. He carried two Smith & Wesson Model 10s in 38 caliber, a Colt Cobra with a two-inch

barrel as his backup, and a cut-down Ithaca 12-gauge Model 37. The shotgun was shortened on both ends, and had rifle sights and a hand sling on the pump handle. This officer had access to M-1 Carbines and softpoint ammunition, but he preferred his 12-gauge. For night action, he used 00 buckshot, but when the light was adequate, he favored the more reliable manstopper slug loads. He felt the advantage of the slug was its greater penetration and shock value.

On one of his stakeouts, Cirillo was behind a curtain at the back of a store with his cut-down Ithaca and his partner. In this instance, there was no available cover; just concealment. A robber entered the store armed with a revolver, and as he passed, Cirillo's partner made a slight noise. The robber whirled, pointing his revolver at the curtain. With no cover and no time to shout a warning command, the officer fired from a distance of 18 inches. The slug entered the robber's brain, killing him instantly.

"With SWAT unavailable or inappropriate—and hiring standards providing less than adequate gunfighters—the investigator organizing a search warrant entry should hand-pick his personnel whenever possible," Steele suggests. "It is no great trick to see who does well on periodic roqualifications, as well as in defensive tactics and baton training.

This Remington Model 870 was modified for David Steele by Scattergun Technologies. Added were a polymer stock, a sling, the extended magazine and rifle sights.

The Scattergun Technologies 870 conversion features a peep sight and a jumbo crossbolt safety.

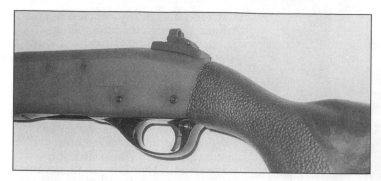

The pebble-grain finish on the grip of the 870 conversion makes for more positive holding in any type of weather.

A nylon sling such as this one installed on the Scattergun Technologies Border Patrol conversion makes it easy to transition to the pistol. In this instance, the gun is slung around the neck.

"A friend who has a black belt in jujitsu and is a London Bobby by profession usually is the first man picked for invading drug dealer flats in London. A device called a spreader is used to push the door jamb outward, allowing silent entry upon the sleeping occupants. Once inside, this martial arts expert can throw or control the most dangerous ones before the other Bobbies are endangered."

Steele's observations have taught him that professional police officers, as opposed to "paycheck policemen," train on their own time and invariably at their own expense. "I have attended three police academies, as well as the FBI firearms instructor course," he says, "but the best introduction to fighting shotguns I have seen was at the Gunsite Training Center in Paulden, Arizona."

This outfit conducts both on-site and off-site classes. On-site, they teach their Tactical Shotgun course, as well as one called Shotgun Advanced Tactical Problems. Off-site, the staff teaches a shorter, weekend tactical shotgun course at California's Huntington Beach police range. It is taught by a local police officer, Bill Murphy.

The Gunsite shotgun course provides a variety of exercises to get the student to respond instantly from the high ready or low ready positions, firing on single or multiple targets first with birdshot, then buckshot and slugs. In addition, students undergo transition drills for situations in which the shotgun malfunctions or runs dry. In this drill, the student secures the long arm and moves to the holstered pistol.

"Instructors frown upon clearing a shotgun during this exercise, and dropping it on the ground receives even less approval," David Steele recalls. "One of the simplest techniques is to tuck the shotgun under the left arm—if you shoot right-handed—then draw and shoot the pistol one-handed. If the shotgun has a sling, it can be strung over the neck or the left shoulder in a variety of quick methods, allowing both hands to hold the handgun."

Scattergun Technologies, Inc. of Nashville, Tennessee converted a used Remington Model 870 for Steele, turning it into what they call their Border Patrol model. This rework has an 18-inch barrel, extended magazine,

This squatting position is known as the "rice paddy prone" among Vietnam veterans. Steele feels it is a valuable tactic with the 870 Border Patrol shotgun.

The standard military-style kneeling position offers stability with any long gun, as demonstrated with the SGT Border Patrol conversion.

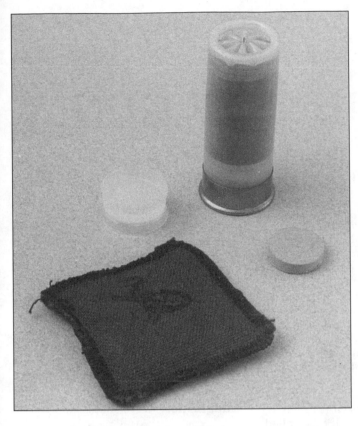

MK Ballistic Systems' Flexible Baton-12 is a stunbag round that can be fired in any 12-gauge riot gun, delivering a non-lethal blackjack-type blow at considerable range.

luminescent follower, three-inch chamber and a jumbo safety. The stock and pump handle now are of synthetic, and there is a tritium front sight with a ghost ring rear, as well as a three-way sling.

"With these simple modifications, I found I could shoot the Gunsite Training Center course with ease," Steele states. "This included four-second runs on the five-silhouette Dozier drill from the low ready. Pumping the slide as the gun came down from recoil allowed times as fast as with the semi-auto Benelli Super M90 M1.

"When I conduct shotgun qualification courses, I let all investigators use my SGT 870. Invariably, they exceed their scores with the conventional Model 870, but all would benefit from extra training. There are only a couple I would pick to carry the riot gun on a search warrant entry."

Social scientists and linguists say that 70 percent of all communication is nonverbal. The tone and intensity of conversation is at least as important as the content. In stress situations, suspects may not understand their own language, must less a foreign tongue. This is particularly true if they are under the influence of drugs or alcohol or there is a great deal of ambient noise.

"An entering officer must communicate and control in the least time possible," Steele points out. "This can be facilitated by the sight of a weapon that brooks no discussion; only total attention. Most people realize that the shotgun is more accurate and less survivable than the handgun.

"However, the officer assigned the shotgun must be totally familiar with it. He must be unafraid of its recoil, as well as aware of its increased potential for accidental discharge. Given these conditions, the modern officer can shoot, move and communicate with it as well as any old-time sheriff or Texas Ranger!" ●

J.H. Cuadros (left) of MK Ballistic Systems shows David Steele some of the Flexible Baton beanbags that are used in 12-gauge riot control shells. This is another step toward non-lethal ammunition.

CHAPTER 31

MOSSBERG'S JUNGLE GUN

Developed At Government Request, This 12-Gauge Meets A Special Need For The Military And Law Enforcement.

WELL OVER A decade back, our Department of Defense, through an agency known as the Joint Services Small Arms Program, issued a call for what they termed an "autoloading, military-specification shotgun." A number of gun makers, foreign and domestic, took a hard look at the core requirements for this combat instrument, and some dropped out of the race before it started. Others investigated the requirements and at least one manufacturer stated privately, "If all of the requirements are met, the gun probably will not function!"

The published requirements called for a maximum length of 41.75 inches but the gun should be no shorter than 35 inches. It should have low-light sights, and chamber 2-3/4- and three-inch shells without any adjustments; it should have interchangeable modules and parts and weigh a maximum of 8.5 pounds. Simple enough? Right. But that was only the beginning of the DOD demands.

The gun should be constructed of non-corrosive materials and finishes, making it resistant also to fungus and chemicals; carry a mounting rail; have a bayonet adaptor, sling and swivels; and feature either a pistol grip and/or a folding stock. The gun should have a trigger pull of between four and eight pounds.

In what the Joint Services Small Arms Program-known as JSSAF-called the Human Factors Category, the requirements called for an ambidextrous safety, the gun should be operable with "special gloves," should allow reloading of six rounds in no more than 15 seconds and the operator should be able to field-strip it in 60 seconds without tools of any type.

Specifications

Name:	Mossberg Model 9200A1 Jungle Gun.
Gauge:	12, 2-3/4-inch chamber.
Weight:	7 pounds.
Length:	30.5 inches.
Barrel:	18.5 inches; fixed Cylinder choke.
Magazine:	Five shots.
Stock:	Black synthetic.
Finish:	Parkerized.
Sights:	Bead front.
Maker:	O.F. Mossberg & Sons 7 Grasso Ave. North Haven, CT 06473

Officer Don Canario looks over the Mossberg 12-gauge Jungle Gun as Ace Kaminski looks on. Canario is small arms instructor for the police department of the Island of Hawaii.

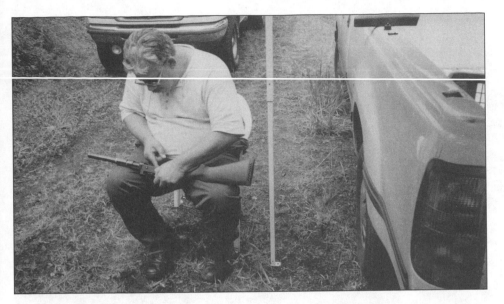

Don Canario checks out the Jungle Gun in an attempt to determine why it would not feed in the initial effort to conduct the test. Investigation showed that Jack Lewis had left out a necessary part when assembling the gun.

There also was a listed requirement that the gun not be hazardous to the shooter or maintainer.

In the matter of accuracy, in firing 00 buckshot at 40 meters, five of the shell's nine pellets should be inside the "E" silhouette target 50 percent of the time. At 100 meters, 50 percent of the slugs fired should fall within a 30-inch circle.

In the matter of reliability, the prototype shotguns submitted for tests should have a durability factor of 10,000 rounds and the entire gun should be proofed to current standards of the Sporting Arms and Ammunition Manufacturers Institute. In completing a 50-round mission, the guns submitted for consideration should show a minimum of 85 percent reliability. It also was demanded that any shotgun submitted for consideration function properly at 125 degrees Fahrenheit and at 40 degrees below zero.

Regarding maintainability, the demand was that preventive maintenance must be accomplished in 20 minutes and that maintenance level repairs be made in two hours. Intermediate repairs should require no more than four hours and the gun should use no lubricants that are not in the DOD supply chain.

In California, the makers of the Calico submachine gun made a stab at producing a prototype and quickly abandoned the project. According to information available to us, they were thinking of using the same general configuration that made their guns unique, with a spiral-type magazine atop the gun.

According to a government document listed as DAAE-9-T-1255, the "shotguns will be used in jungle and anti-narcotics maneuvers."

The result was what Mossberg states is, "the first auto-loading shotgun developed expressly for the U.S. military" and "capable of winning military contract DAAE 2006-P-0363." This, however, is not the winner of the JSSAF-sponsored Combat Shotgun Sweepstakes. There was no winner, because the program as such ultimately was abandoned.

Cynics in the gun business frequently claim that there is nothing really new in gun design; that everything has been done and new efforts are only reworks or combinations of what has gone before. Mossberg, of course, makes no bones over the fact that their M9200A1 Jungle Gun is a rework of the more familiar Model 9200 series of sporting shotguns that include the Crown Grade version; one called the Viking; another that is a Crown Grade, but is custom-engraved with "United States Shooting Team" on the receiver and is called the Model 9200 USST. There also is a Special Hunter model in the line. All of these guns have three-inch chambers, whereas the Jungle Gun has a 2-3/4-inch chamber. It also has a Cylinder-bore choke and is designed, we are told, to function best with 00 buck loads.

The Jungle Gun has a barrel measuring only 18.5 inches and overall length is a compact 38.5 inches overall. Instead of the magazine that could be reloaded with six rounds in 15 seconds as demanded in the ill-fated JSSAP approach, this gun has a five-shot magazine.

According to Bud Fini of Mossberg, this gas-operated autoloader "had to survive the same brutal 3000-round military specifications test used for pump guns.

"To assure this capability, Mossberg engineers simplified the gas system by designing a one-piece piston with no loose seals or rings. In addition, the system's recoil spring is

The test of the Jungle Gun took on some aspects of a major event. Tents were erected and there was catered food and beverage.

With the gun properly assembled, Ace Kaminski ran through the course to be certain the movable targets worked properly. It was time to get on with the test.

mounted forward on the magazine tube to allow the use of a folding stock or pistol grip for maximum compactness and portability."

The Jungle Gun is available with a left-hand folding stock or a fixed butt stock, both of a black synthetic. The forend on either configuration is the same and is of the same man-made material. The receiver is hardcoat anodized and the other metal parts are Parkerized. According to Fini, the trigger housing is of military-quality metal and the heavy-wall barrel meets military specs. The ambidextrous safety is positioned on the tang where it is within each reach of the shooter's thumb. Pushed forward, the gun is ready to fire; no fuss, no muss!

The Jungle Gun is equipped with a bead front sight, which is sufficient for the close range, fast-action, instant triggering for which the gun was designed. Unloaded, the gun weighs approximately seven pounds. It is equipped with sling studs for easier carry with addition of quick detachable swivels and a sling.

When we first tried to lay hands on one of these guns, we were told that it was going to be tough, as they were being sold as rapidly as they could come off the line. After a couple of false starts, however, FedEx ultimately delivered one of the standard-stocked models to Jack Lewis.

Our Man in Hawaii was tired and suffering from the flu (they have it even in Paradise) when he initially

attempted to assemble the gun. He thought it had gone together okay. The next morning, he called a friend, Mark "Ace" Kaminiski, who had agreed to help with the project.

Since this is termed the Jungle Gun and allegedly was designed for such use, it was decided to test it in the jungle environment of Hawaii's Big Island. In a privately owned tract some 25 miles south of Hilo, a semi-abandoned trail once used by local marijuana growers was located by Kaminski. Island police and the Hawaii National Guard, however, have made a continuing project of putting Hawaii pot growers out of business, so the trail was pretty well overgrown, showing only evidence of use by wild pig hunters. Kaminski

Ace Kaminski looks over the gun with Don Canaro and an interested onlooker who happened by the head of the jungle trail where the test was conducted.

Kaminski, who erected the course of fire, followed Dan Elvenia as the latter moves along the overgrown trail once used by local marijuana growers.

made arrangements to use the property for the Jungle Gun tests.

Kaminski, with Lewis at his heels, surveyed the trail and the two of them laid out a rough course, with the idea that they would use swinging silhouette targets as a surprise element. They would be hidden initially in the brush, but would swing out to challenge the shooters, as they happened into the "ambush."

As a state of Hawaii law enforcement agent and a former Big Island police officer, Kaminski has numerous friends in the police community. Thus, it was he who rounded up Officer Don Canario to help with the initial test firing and to see how the course of fire would work out. This individual is a 22 year veteran of the Hawaii Island Police Department and heads up the department's firearms training program.

On the designated morning, Lewis arrived half an hour earlier than the officers were supposed to show up. In addition to Ace Kaminski, there was an entourage on hand. And a tent, with food and drink! Audreen Kaminski, who does Hawaiian catering, explained that one of her customers had canceled after she already had bought the food and started preparation. She had simply finished the job and moved it to our site! This, Lewis insists, goes along with the Hawaiian philosophy that any gathering of more than three people is an excuse for a luau. Kurt Kaminski, Ace's brother, had come to help with the tent and setting up the course.

Ace Kaminski, eager to show off his handiwork, led Lewis along the overhung trail. Just beyond a point

Kaminski pulls one of the cords that causes one of the hidden targets to swing into view for the shooter.

As the targets swing into position, Dan Elvenia begins firing. He found the course a challenge and called it "fun," declaring that police firearms training could use some of the imagination shown.

where each shooter would have to duck beneath an overhanging tree branch was the first silhouette, stationary and waiting. The minute the shooter blasted at this first target, Kaminski, a few feet to the rear, would pull on a series of heavy-duty cords hidden in the high grass. The cords would, in turn, activate the other three targets. Meanwhile, at the sound of the first shot, Mrs. Kaminski, in the shelter of the tent, would start timing with a stop watch. Each shooter would have four rounds with which to take out the silhouettes.

After each shooter made his play, the targets would be removed, rolled up and the shooter's name written on the roll, the holes to be counted later. Scores would be determined by the number of 00 buckshot holes in each shooter's targets divided by the number of seconds it took him to take out the "bad guys."

According to plan, new targets were to be quickly installed, the target frames moved back to their hidden positions and a new shooter taken through the ritual.

Don Canario arrived and donned his blue coveralls with the word Police emblazoned across the back. He was briefed by Lewis on the shotgun and given a short history on how and why the Model 9200A1 had been created. The veteran officer listened through this patiently, but it was obvious he was hot to get on with the shooting.

Lewis briefed him on the fact that there would be four targets and how the event would be timed. No mention was made of the fact that three of the

targets would be hidden, being swung to face him after the first shot. Kaminski had laughingly stated earlier that he had thrown in a challenge. The shooter was right-handed, but only the first target would be on the right. The other three would swing out of the jungle brush from the left.

The initial effort with the course was a rousing failure. As he ducked under an overhanging branch, the island police officer did a good job of taking out the vitals of the first target that seemed about to attack him. On the second target, the gun jammed.

He attempted to eject the shell, but it was hung up.

After half an hour of unsuccessful tinkering, Lewis dug out the Mossberg owner's manual and began leafing through it. Somewhat lamely, he had to admit he had goofed in assembling the shotgun. The manual explained that the Model 9200A1 Jungle Gun's construction differed in one respect from the parent Model 9200. On the former, a heavy-duty nylon spacer had to be installed over the gun's cylindrical magazine, thus holding the barrel extension in proper position during firing and the recycling that followed.

The problem was that Lewis had no recollection of having seen any such spacer. Time out was called and everyone went home for the day, each participant and observer somewhat disgusted at the turn of events.

Lewis searched the carton and the other corrugated packing in which the Jungle Gun had been delivered to him. He was aware that the gun had been assembled in a hurry for delivery to him. Could it be that someone had forgotten to pack the missing ring of nylon?

Feeling somewhat shame-faced, Lewis faxed Bud Fini at Mossberg, asking for another nylon insert, explaining that he didn't know what had happened to the original, but he did know that the gun didn't function properly without it. Three days later, FedEx delivered the familiar red, white and blue package to Lewis' office. On the same day, a local cleaning service scoured the office. They came up with the original

Elvenia appears elated over his performance on the jungle course, as he and Kaminski collect the targets for evaluation.

Darryel Talentino fired the jungle course not only with the Mossberg 12-gauge, but also with his own custom-rigged 12-gauge. He scored better with the Mossberg.

spacer, which apparently had come out of the packing unseen and rolled behind Lewis' desk.

Instead of installing the original spacer, Lewis stuck it in his desk drawer. Being a bit on the superstitious side, he figured the item was jinxed. Instead, he broke down the shotgun, installed the newer nylon ring, then made for a deserted strip of beach where he triggered off four rounds to be certain the gun now worked properly. (Incidentally, Hawaii's so-called Big Island is probably the last of this particular chain of islands where one is likely to find that kind of deserted beach.)

Satisfied that all was well, Lewis called Kaminski and asked if he could get the original shooter and a couple of other working law enforcement types back into the jungle to complete the test. Calls were made and contacts completed, but there suddenly was another complication. It was early March. The normal rainy season in Hawaii extends from December through March.

In most instances, no one pays much attention to the rain. They work in it and they play in it; golfers tend to revel in what they refer to as "liquid sunshine." However, the area in which the target frames had been left standing is one of the wettest areas on the face of the earth. It gets some 180 inches of rain-more than six feet!-helping the jungle to expand in breadth and thickness.

This brought on Lewis' oft spoken words that may become immortal in time: "I don't need any rehearsal to be miserable. I know how." The other participants agreed, so continued testing of the Jungle Gun was put on hold until the skies opened to the sun and there were only two or three showers a day!

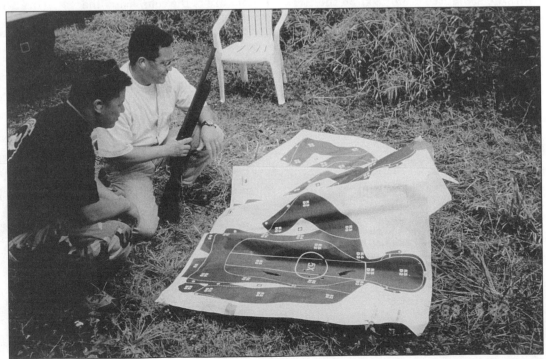

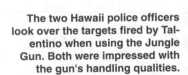
The two Hawaii police officers look over the targets fired by Talentino when using the Jungle Gun. Both were impressed with the gun's handling qualities.

Audreen Kaminski not only oversaw the food and beverage tent, but also served as the official timer for the test series. The stopwatch was activated at the sound of the first shot, stopped at the sound of the fourth.

It was a bright, sunny morning that would leave the Hawaii Visitors Bureau ecstatic, when Kaminski again met Lewis at the end of the jungle trail that faced a dirt road leading to a quarry. It turned out that the former had left the target frames in place after the original test effort. He had arrived early and rigged the targets so they again would swing into place properly when activated. This required cutting some of the grass and brush that had grown up in the trail, but the overhanging branches seemed to have grown in size and thickness during the lay-off. It was agreed this would add greater challenge to the test.

There was another glitch at this point. The original shooter, Don Canario, contacted Kaminski on the latter's cell phone, explaining he was ill and could not make the scene. However, his patrol partner, Officer Daniel Elvenia, and another working policeman, Darryel Talentino, were enroute!

Talentino, we learned, is a veteran of seven years with the island police department. He joined after discharge from the Army, in which he had served as a long range reconnaissance expert. Elvenia has only one year with the department, having joined after six years in the Marine Corps in which he was trained as a transport helicopter mechanic.

Audreen Kaminski, the original timer, sent along cupcakes and coffee, but she had not arrived yet. As her delicacies were washed down with the hot brew, sea stories were passed back and forth. Finally, Lewis glanced at the sun, pointing out that it was approaching noon. Time to get at it before the customary afternoon shower.

The nature of the course and the requirements were explained to the two officers, then Darryel Talentino was handed the Jungle Gun and a pack of five rounds of Winchester 00 buckshot. Each of the 2-3/4-inch shells was loaded with the standard nine

spheres of unplated lead shot. He loaded four rounds as he had been instructed and handed the extra shell to Kaminski.

Dan Elvenia was given the stop watch and told he was to start timing when he heard the first shot, then stop it when he heard the report of the fourth shell.

At a signal, Talentino started up the trail, hunkering low with the Mossberg shotgun at the ready, as though after an actual felon. On the right side of trail, a few paces behind him was Kaminski, who would activate the swinging targets. To his left was Lewis, who was photographing the event for this book - and possible posterity.

Ducking beneath an overhanging branch, the shooter was confronted by the first target, which was stationary on the right. He was no more than five feet from it, when he fired his first round.

No sooner had the shot echoed through the jungle than Ace Kaminski,

Metal parts of the Jungle Gun carry a non-glare Park-erized black finish. Synthetic stock and forearm also are designed to be non-reflective.

The Mossberg Jungle Gun is a variation of the company's Model 9200 sporting shotgun. This gun is marked to fire only 00 buck-shot shells.

Island officers Darryel Talentino (left) and Daniel Elvenia flank Jack Lewis, as he explains the workings of the shotgun and how the test will be conducted. Talentino is a veteran of seven years in police work, while Elvenia has been an officer for a year.

already kneeling, pulled the cords that turned the other three targets toward the officer. There were three more fast shots, as each of the targets was fired.

As Lewis gathered up the four targets, he noted that the last shot, taken at a range of about 20 yards, had been low, only a few of the pellets tearing paper in the target's silhouette area. Meantime, Kaminski was cautioning the shooter not to tell Dan Elvenia how the course was laid out. Talentino's time on the four targets was five seconds.

In a matter of minutes, the target frames fashioned from one-inch PVC had new targets taped to them and the three swinging targets were tucked away, out of sight amid the greenery. It was Elvenia's turn, with Talentino taking over as the timer.

The new shooter locked and loaded, then hoisted the shotgun a couple of times, expressing satisfaction with its balance. At a signal from Kaminski, he started down the trail, taking advantage of his military and law enforcement training should he meet the threat in a real life situation.

The first shot rang out, Lewis clicked his camera several times, then Kaminski activated the swinging targets. There were three fast shots, followed by Elvenia's troubled cry, "I missed the last one!"

As it turned out, he had not missed that most distant target. As had been the case for Talentino, he fired low, piercing the silhouette in both thighs and one hand. His time was six seconds. "Where were you aiming when you fired on that last target," Lewis asked him. The shooter shook his head.

"I didn't aim," Elvenia admitted, "I just swung until I saw black and pulled the trigger!"

As before, the targets were gathered and marked with the shooter's name, then rolled for later counting of shot holes.

"This is fun," Elvenia declared. "Can we try it some more?"

"Until we run out of targets or run out of ammo," he was told.

New targets were taped to the frames and Elvenia made his stalk down the trail. He fired a better score

than his original target, but admitted that this time he knew what to expect.

Darryel Talentino had brought his personal, customized Remington Model 870 12-gauge and wanted to try it on the course. Followed closely by Kaminski, he moved down the trail, firing the required four rounds. He came back minutes later, shaking his head. He had done better with the Mossberg test gun than with his own weapon.

"I did considerably better with the Jungle Gun," he announced, hefting his personal shotgun. "This one's so heavy that when I swing, it's tough to stop on the target."

With the owner's permission, Lewis picked up the gun and looked it over. It was equipped with an after-market black synthetic stock that had a rear hand grip, a heat shield had been installed over the barrel, a flashlight holder and light added to the forward end, and a magazine extension brought its length to the end of the barrel. Lewis judged the gun to weigh in the vicinity of 12 pounds, although the owner had never weighed it.

Stud extending from the magazine cap is drilled to accept a quick-detachable sling swivel. The other stud is attached to the synthetic buttstock.

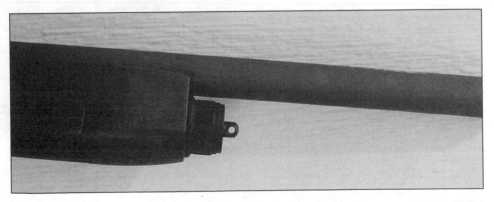

This nylon ring, which helps hold the barrel extension in proper position, was not included in initial assembly of the Jungle Gun. Once it was installed, there was no problem.

"And I think I'm going to take that flashlight off," the owner stated. "I've finally figured out it gives a bad guy out there in the dark something to shoot at. A visible target." Nobody argued his point.

Mrs. Kaminski arrived with more goodies and the crew dug into them, exchanging thoughts and ideas between bites of food and sips of coffee or soda.

Pocket calculator in hand, Jack Lewis set about counting holes in targets, starting with Talentino's four. In the X-marked "kill zone" for four shots, he had 14 holes with a weight of five points each. In the zone offering four points each, he had 13 holes, none in the three-point zone, and with the low shot, two pellets in the two-point zone - the upper legs - and two in the one-point area. This came to a total of 128 points. Divided by his time of five seconds, this gave him a score of 25.6.

In checking the four targets fired by Dan Elvenia, it became obvious that for some reason he was firing on the right side of each target. Opinion was that he may have been canting the gun. Whatever the reason, he only had three holes in the kill zone for a total of 15 points, none in the four-point zone, five in the three-point areas and 15 in the two-point sector at the bottom of the target. This was the target he thought he had missed completely, but he had more points on this most distant target than did Talentino. His total points added up to 60. Divided by his clocked time of six seconds for the four shots, his score was 10. If all of the pellets from the four rounds were in the five-point kill zone, that would add up to 180 possible. As an example, using the average of the times scored by the two shooters', 5.5, this would make the score 32.5.

"Actually," Lewis was quick to admit, "these scores don't really mean anything. The method I used simply gives us some basis for comparison. Even the one slug in each leg probably would put a felon down."

During the after-shoot bull session, it was agreed by all who had fired the Mossberg Jungle Gun that it lived up to its billing. The light weight, the balance and the ease of pointing all were mentioned. One of the shooters admitted the fact that the shoot had been fun and might well have colored their thinking.

"In our own training," this officer explained, "we only fire the shotgun once a year and that's at three targets, firing from the shoulder at relatively close range, then three more targets are fired from the hip at the same range. We could use something like this."

"Actually, I think we've pioneered some kind of new shooting game here," Kaminski ventured. "It doesn't take much in the way of equipment and all that's needed is the space - and your own available jungle!" ●

The nylon ring fits over the magazine tube in a rather loose fit, but when the synthetic forend is installed, the ring does its job.

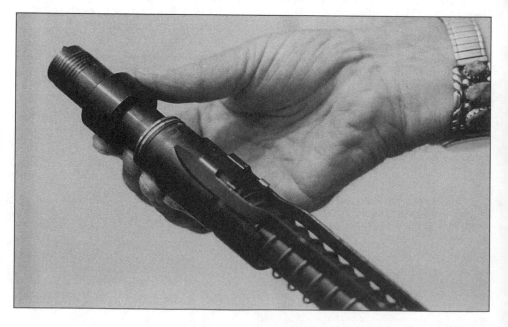

CHAPTER 32

THE WINCHESTER MODEL 1300 DEFENDER

This Venerable Pump-Action Comes From A Long Line Of Successful Combat Shotguns.

DURING THE WINTER of 1977, Winchester invited a group of gun writers to a snow-covered game preserve on New York's Long Island for the purpose of introducing the then brand new Model 1300 sporting shotgun. "That outing was a bit of a fiasco, for several of the guns didn't work at all well," as Jack Lewis recalls. "At this late date, I recall that most of the problem had to do with extraction and ejection.

"Winchester's sales manager, the late, great Bill Talley, was red-faced and apologetic. He allowed as how he had attempted to introduce the gun prematurely for the sake of what he hoped would be a publicity plus. Instead, it was back to the drawing board for a few months, while the kinks were worked out."

In those days, Winchester firearms were made by Winchester/Olin in their Connecticut plant.

Later, the name—for arms production only—and the Connecticut factory were sold to U.S. Repeating Arms and business continued in the same vein. Eventually, Browning took over the Winchester line and USRA. Many of the models both rifle and shotgun of 30 years ago have been abandoned or the manufacturing rights passed on to other gunmaking companies. Still made in the old Connecticut factory, the Model 1300 is alive and well in several configurations, including that once troublesome but now totally functional walnut-stocked bird-hunting version of three decades back.

That early problem, however, has little to do with a current descendant of that original Model 1300. The gun under discussion here is the Winchester Model 1300 Defender, a pump gun designed specifically for combat and police use. That does not mean, however, that the individual cannot buy a Defender. The model certainly is available for home protection. In fact, there is also the Model 1300 Lady Defender, chambered for 20-gauge shells. More about this one later.

Today's standard Defender is available in either 12- or 20-gauge and is chambered for three-inch shells. It has an 18-inch Cylinder-choked barrel, and magazines are available for either five - or eight - round capacity. This particular model measures 38.62 inches overall, and weighs approximately 6.75 pounds.

One has a choice of furniture: There is a stock and forend of walnut-finished hardwood; synthetic full stock; and a pistol grip for close-in police work. As

Specifications

Name:	Winchester Model 1300 Defender.
Operation:	Slide action; twin action bars; front-locking rotarty bolt.
Gauge:	12; three-inch chamber.
Weight:	6.75 pounds.
Length:	38.65 inches.
Barrel:	10 inches; Cylinder bore.
Magazine:	Eight rounds (2-3/4-inch).
Stock:	Black synthetic; black rubber butt pad.
Sights:	Translucent green all-weather front sight; no rear.
Maker:	U.S. Repeating Arms 275 Winchester Ave. Morgan, Utah 04050

The Winchester Model 1300 Defender is descended from the Model 1300 sporting shotgun that has been made by Winchester and successors for more than 30 years. In the tests conducted for this book, Winchester 00 buck and Federal 000 Magnum buckshot were fired.

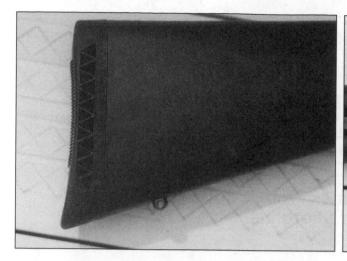

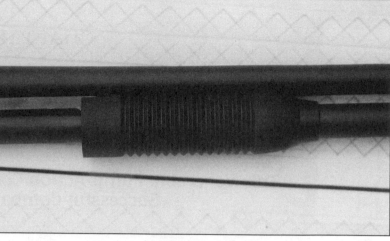

The heavy-duty synthetic stock has a black rubber recoil pad. Note the sling swivel stud extending from the stock.

The slide handle is formed with deep indentations for a firm hold regardless of the weather or other environmental situations.

with past models, the gun features a cross-bolt safety, front-locking rotary bolt and twin action slide bars. Both of our authors like the idea of the parallel slide bars, since they offer assurance that this pairing should pretty much avoid any kinking or bending that would tend to lock up the slide action. The black synthetic slide grip has deep grooves cast into it for firm and positive gripping.

A black rubber butt pad blends nicely with the black synthetic-stocked law enforcement version we chose to check out. Available metal finishes include matte black, standard blue, bright blue or bead-blasting. The gun we received for testing carried the black matte finish.

We noted that the 1999 edition of the *Gun Digest* states the gun is equipped with a standard metal bead front sight. That still was the case, sort of, with the gun sent to us out of USRA's current headquarters in Morgan, Utah. This example carries the metal bead, but it is hidden by a sight that literally surrounds it with a carrier that holds a round section of green plastic. This bit of translucent plastic measures 2.5 inches in length and is less than 1/8-inch in diameter.

"Intrigued with this approach, I tried the sight out on a dark, moonless night only minutes after I unpacked the gun," Lewis reports. "It seems to pick up whatever light is available; even starlight. It glows in the dark so that one doesn't need to use the so-called handkerchief treatment. If you can see the target at all, even in silhouette or vague outline, this Winchester sight should put you on it."

For those who wonder, the so-called "handkerchief treatment" supposedly was created by the late Colonel Charles Askins before World

War II, when he was serving with the U.S. Border Patrol. If this particular patrolman was likely to be involved in a firefight on a dark, moonless night, he would tie a white handkerchief on the forward end of his shotgun barrel so he would be able to see where the sight should be. The same technique also was used on rifles and carbines in that era, Askins told us many years ago.

The Model 1300 Defender arrived at Jack Lewis' office in Hawaii fully assembled, so there was no need to make a detailed search of the carton for small parts. A fast read of the owner's manual assured him that the gun would handle both 2-3/4- and three-inch shells without any mechanical changes.

When the forend is in the forward and locked position, nothing moves. It definitely is locked, with none of the

loose play of the forend and action bar(s) often found on some similarly designed shotguns.

We found the slide release, a small, rounded steel button, positioned on the underside of the receiver, where it nestles behind the trigger. It is small and unobtrusive and Lewis expected it to be difficult to operate. That proved not to be the case at all. A light touch of the finger and the slide was released.

The push-through safety is positioned at the front of the trigger guard, a location familiar to users of a number of shotgun models, but particularly the Winchester pump actions manufactured down through the decades. This, of course, is the usual cross-bolt safety design that can be pushed to the safe position only when the gun is in the cocked mode. The safety is simple enough to

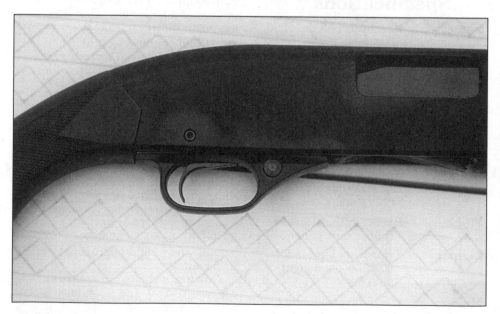

The action of the Defender carries a matte black finish that blends well with the synthetic stock and slide handle.

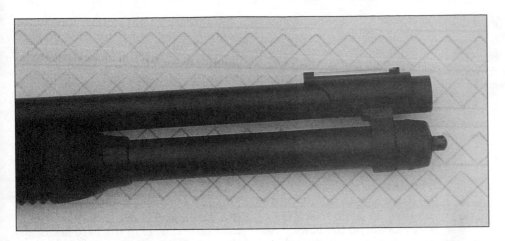

The tubular magazine extends to the end of the barrel and carries eight rounds of 2-3/4-inch 12-gauge ammunition. Note the translucent front sight.

release, but requires that the shooter release his firing grip on the stock to do so. A left-handed shooter is going to find this a bit more of an exercise.

All of the Model 1300 Winchesters, the Defender configuration included, feature a unique front-locking, high-speed rotary bolt. Due to the manner in which the bolt locks into the barrel, the forces of recoil aid in unlocking the bolt and driving it to the rear when the gun is fired. When he first fired the gun, Lewis found this a trifle disconcerting. When he racked the slide to the rear to pick up another shell, he found it was already nearly to the rear due to the forces involved. All he had to do was draw the slide handle a bit farther to the rear to eject the fired hull, then slam it forward for an instant reload.

The magazine tube extends the full length of the 18-inch barrel, thus allowing for a capacity of eight rounds. The magazine tube also carries the forward sling stud for quick-detachable swivels, while the rear stud is situated on the buttstock.

Lewis had decided he wanted to test both 00 buckshot and 000 buck at ranges of seven, 15 and 25 yards, so he called his shooting partner, Ace Kaminski, to ask if he could help. A state law enforcement type, Kaminski currently works a night shift, so he was available during the day.

For the test of the Mossberg Jungle Gun, Kaminski had fashioned target frames made from white PVC pipe. The result was a frame that was relatively strong, lightweight and easy to transport. Another advantage lay in the fact that if a round went through the frame to shatter it, another piece of PVC could be installed quickly to repair the frame.

Kaminski already had staked out a location in a quarry that deals in lava rock in various grades, colors and sizes ranging from gravel to boulders.

He selected an area that had been worked over, leaving a relatively flat and level surface for nearly 100 yards, with a red lava cliff perhaps 50 feet high as the backstop.

Lewis had a supply of Winchester 00 buckshot and was able to buy several five-round packets of Federal 000 buck from a sporting goods shop in Hilo, the island of Hawaii's county seat. Thus outfitted, the two met in the quarry at 9:30 on a rainy Hawaiian morning. Kaminski brought along a number of steel stakes that were driven into the brittle lava, then the legs of the target frames wired to them for support.

Rather than standard targets, Kaminski came up with several pieces of corrugated cardboard that measured approximately 33 by 36 inches. In the center of each of these, he used a black marker to make an aiming spot of about two inches in diameter. These targets were attached

to the frames with two-inch duct tape, as a gentle rain began to diffuse the scene a bit. Lewis and Kaminski called time out and moved to one of their trucks to wait for the offending cloud to pass.

In typical Island fashion, the sun was shining only minutes later and the Model 1300 Defender was broken out of its carrying case and readied for action.

The statisticians have proclaimed that seven yards is the average distance for a firearms face-off, so that was used as the minimum range for testing. Fifteen yards was chosen as an intermediate range and the 25-yard target was set at what is considered by some to be a marginally effective range for buckshot loads.

As most readers probably know, the 2-3/4-inch Winchester Super X 00 buckshot load carries nine lead pellets of approximately 33-caliber. The standard 000 buck load carries eight pellets of 36-caliber. However, we chose to use the three-inch magnum Federal Premium load for these tests. The pellets measure the same, but there are 10 of them packed into each hull rather than eight. All in all, this shell has considerable more shock value than the old 00 standby, considering size of the pellets and the number.

Lewis already had explained the plan to his partner. To begin, he would fire one round of 00 buckshot on each of the three targets, which had been planted at their assigned distances. The resulting holes then would be marked with the black marker for identification. Kaminski then would get his turn to do the same.

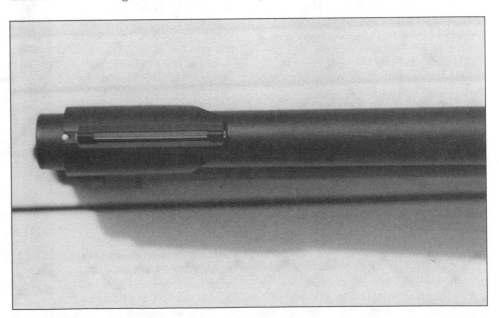

Seen from the top, the length and width of the front sight give some idea as to why the testing staff was intrigued with it.

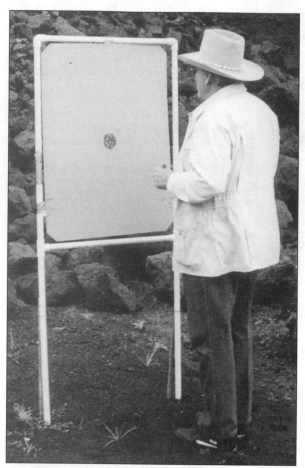

Jack Lewis checks out one of the pattern boards Ace Kaminski erected for the test. They shot both 00 and 000 buckshot.

shot also had been high, one pellet fracturing the top of the frame.

After inspecting his own pattern at 25 yards, Lewis was dissatisfied, feeling that perhaps he had pulled the shot, since most of the shots had gone over the top of the cardboard. He marked the holes from that shot with a series of Xs rather than circles.

Returning to the 25-yard marker, he again took a six o'clock hold on the black aiming spot, pushed off the safety and pulled the trigger. Gun still in hand, he returned to the target to take another look. Not much had changed. Again, the shot printed high, several of the pellets failing to show on the cardboard.

The three targets were stripped off the frames and stored in Lewis' truck against further water damage. Another shower interrupted the proceedings for a few minutes, then Kaminski put up new, clean rectangles of corrugated board, with their own aiming spots. It was time to check out the 000 loads for the sake of comparison.

It should be noted that there was no effort to draw the usual 30-inch circles on the boards to determine patterning. Lewis was interested only in how the loads grouped in relation to the point of aim.

Standing at the firing line, Lewis shouldered the gun, racked a round into the chamber and carefully took his six o'clock hold. For each target, he brought the highly visible round green sight to the bottom of the black aiming spot. He fired each of the three targets using that same hold on each. At least, he thought he did.

The target check that followed showed that the 000 buckshot, with its load of 10 pellets, offered a slightly tighter group than had the 00 loads, but, again, all of the groups were high, printing above the aiming point.

Kaminski did his Polish army routine again, firing the three targets in rapid succession, thus offering a study between Lewis' pseudo-scientific approach and his shooting partner's practical law enforcement actions. Interesting, though, was the fact that while Kaminski's aim had been in the lower half of each target as before, some of his pellets still were high. One of his 25-yard pellets shattered the side of the shooting frame. With the piece Lewis had damaged earlier, an entire corner of the frame was hanging only by the duct tape that held the cardboard to the plastic frame.

Again, the targets were carefully removed and stored for future inspection and thought. Lewis and Kaminski picked up the fired hulls, loaded the target frames in Kaminski's truck and pulled the steel stakes to which the frames had been attached. During all of this, they discussed the obvious fact that the gun shot high. Or maybe the ammunition shot high.

"With a shotgun slug, there is a definite arc in which the slug rises above the straight line of flight, then

Lewis checks out his first group fired at seven yards. It is somewhat high, but still in what would be the kill zone on a standard silhouette target.

Lewis' part of the exercise was completed with each shot being carefully aimed in offhand rifle style at the black aiming spot with a six o'clock hold. And each of the shots printed its pellets unexpectedly high.

"Where did you hold?" Kaminski wanted to know, as he took the Defender and pushed three more rounds of 00 into the tube, then racked one into the chamber.

"At six o'clock on the spot," Lewis stated. Kaminski's reply was a knowing nod, as he stepped to the measured-off firing line and raised the shotgun.

"I'm doing this Polish army style," he announced and fired three fast rounds, one on each target. Even from the firing line, they were able to see that Kaminski's pellets grouped closer to the black spot than those fired more carefully by Lewis.

Lewis shook his head beneath his rain-specked sombrero. "I don't understand it." Kaminski's answer came with a smug smile.

"I cheated," he said. "I fired for the navel area like I always do. I fired a few inches below the black spots." Not particularly scientific, but nonetheless effective. However, with the round fired at the 25-yard range, Kaminski's

With a red lava embankment as a backstop, Jack Lewis takes aim at the first of the three targets. One shot was made on each, first with 00 buck and, after the pellet holes were marked, the same board was fired on with 000 buckshot for the sake of comparison.

In this photo, Lewis appears to be firing uphill. However, the photo was taken at the sound of the shot and shows the gun in full recoil.

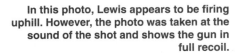

This is the photo in which it was noted that the gun barrel was angled upward. The shooter did not have his cheek properly seated on the synthetic stock.

Ace Kaminski goes into his Polish army act, firing all three targets in rapid succession. He came up with better results than Lewis did.

comes lower when it is downrange," Lewis said, voicing his ponderings. "I don't know whether the same happens with buckshot, but I think it's time to talk to Mike Jordan at Winchester ammunition. He knows about these things."

"There's one other possibility," Ace Kaminski ventured. "It's pretty well accepted that in a firefight, most soldiers and police officers tend to shoot low. The manufacturer may have taken this into account, automatically raising the point of impact as a compensation."

That's where the subject was left for the time being, with Lewis

promising to call Jordan in East Alton, Illinois, where the Winchester Specialty Ammunition works are located. At that moment, he was in a hurry to got the photos processed.

That evening, Lewis was looking over his notes, telling his wife and dearest critic, Rueselle, of the problem. She, at that moment, was looking at his photos she had volunteered to pick up from the processor.

"You don't need to call Mike Jordan," she declared, tapping one of the photos on the edge of Lewis' desk. "You've been shooting so many full-auto weapons that you've forgotten what shotgunning is all about!"

"Huh?" But he already was staring at the photo she had thrust in front of him. Taken by Kaminski, it pictured Lewis leveling the shotgun at one of the targets. Only the gun wasn't level. The barrel appeared to be angled slightly upward. Using a ruler to follow the line of the top of the barrel to the target, it showed he was aiming at the upper edge of the cardboard.

"I didn't have my head down on the gun," Lewis acknowledged. "I must have been too busy admiring that new front sight!"

In spite of these findings, he called Mike Jordan at Winchester Specialty Ammunition and outlined the problem.

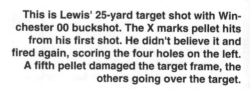

This is Lewis' 25-yard target shot with Winchester 00 buckshot. The X marks pellet hits from his first shot. He didn't believe it and fired again, scoring the four holes on the left. A fifth pellet damaged the target frame, the others going over the target.

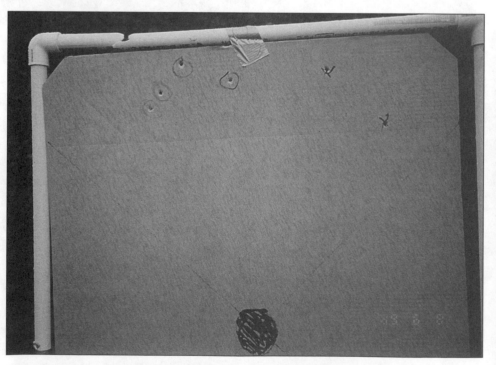

On the 15-yard board, Kaminski checks his own pellet holes against those fired by Lewis with 00 buckshot. Again, his pellets hit lower.

"There's no way the buckshot should be shooting high. Like you said, you may have had your head off the stock, which would cause your aim to be high, or the gun barrel is off," Jordan announced. "That can happen, too."

It became obvious to Lewis that what he had termed a "pseudo-scientific experiment" had become more pseudo than scientific, but he returned to the quarry, set up the targets and took another hack at the black dot in the center of the piece of cardboard. Kaminski was standing by to tell him his head was down on the stock where it belonged and the gun was not pointed at the sky.

As before, Lewis held the fluorescent green plastic sight at six o'clock on the black blob, triggering off a round of 00 buckshot at the seven-yard range. This time, the shot surrounded the black dot in a relatively tight pattern. That much learned, the entire sequence was repeated.

This time, all of the 00 pellets remained on the boards at all three distances, but five of the nine definitely were out of the kill zone at 25 yards. The 000 buckshot, with its 10 pellets, reacted much the

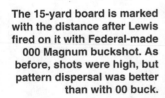

The 15-yard board is marked with the distance after Lewis fired on it with Federal-made 000 Magnum buckshot. As before, shots were high, but pattern dispersal was better than with 00 buck.

Kaminski judges how much PVC pipe he will need to repair the target frame, after pellets hit it in two sections, blowing them away. Spare pipe and glue were included in the test gear and frames were repaired quickly.

same, but grouping a bit tighter than the 00 buck. On the 25-yard target, seven of these pellets were in the kill zone.

Unlike the initial test, part of which had been conducted in the rain, this second outing took place on a bright, sunshine-loaded morning, fleecy tropical clouds passing overhead. It was a pleasant respite to what had come to seem a long, drawn-out endeavor.

Added Note: While the Model 1300 Defender is made in 20-gauge as well as 12, a new version known as the Model 1300 Lady Defender was introduced in 1997 by U.S. Repeating Arms. It is made in 20-gauge only and weighs 6.25 pounds. This one is available with a synthetic full stock or with a synthetic pistol grip. The market aim here, of course, is home defense if the lady of the house is there alone. ●

Like every respectable shooter, Kaminski cleans up his expended hulls after shooting. The test crew left the scene as they found it, except for some pellets probably embedded in the red lava.

CHAPTER 33

THE UNIVERSAL PASS KEY

Law Enforcement Officers Refer To The Shotgun Slug As The Key That Opens Any Door!

FACING A LOCKED door in an effort to serve a warrant upon a dangerous individual usually means this person has nothing positive to say to the servers, and doesn't intend to communicate, let alone be served with a legal document that could be the first step in his going to jail.

In recent years, some law enforcement agencies have come up with custom battering rams and even mechanized units that may take down a door—or the whole house—with little effort. However, in the average police department, be it metropolitan or back country, the shotgun slug tends to fill this bill. Among law enforcement agents, the slug is known as the "universal pass key." It will open virtually any door lock.

We were getting close to deadline time for this edition, when Bud Fini at Mossberg shipped Jack Lewis one of the company's Model 695 Slugster slug guns. By definition, this is a bolt-action shotgun, but in reality, it is a big-bore rifle and looks the part.

The Model 695 is 12-gauge, of course, but has a 22-inch rifled barrel that has nine factory-drilled ports just behind the front sight and three more on each side of the barrel. These, of course, are aimed at reducing recoil. The ramped front sight carries a small white bead that looks as though it should work well against a darker target. The rear sight on this particular gun is a Williams product that's adjustable for windage and elevation. With the aid of the proper screwdriver, there should be no problem with zeroing the gun. This sighting combo, coupled with the configuration of the black synthetic stock, makes this firearm look much like a big game hunter's dangerous game rifle. The gun is drilled and tapped for scope mounts and a pair of Weaver mounts are included

His shooting partner, Ace Kaminski, was there when Lewis took the Model 695 out of the box and threw it up to his shoulder, checking out the sights.

Mossberg's Model 625 Slugster has the general appearance of a heavy-barreled, dangerous game rifle. Firing 12-gauge slugs—or buckshot, if called upon—it has a rifled barrel, rifle-type sights and is drilled and tapped for scope mounting.

"I remember a Cape buffalo in Zimbabwe that should have met this gem," Lewis commented. "I'd have been better off than with the 375 I had!"

The firearm measures 42.5 inches overall and feels and looks like a rifle.

"It'll handle buckshot, too, won't it?" Kaminski wanted to know. Lewis nodded an affirmative.

"But why? Everybody has a gun for buckshot. This is what amounts to a special purpose weapon!" He

The schnabel-type tip of the one-piece synthetic stock reminds one of the work done in wood by European stockmakers. The forward sling stud is firmly seated.

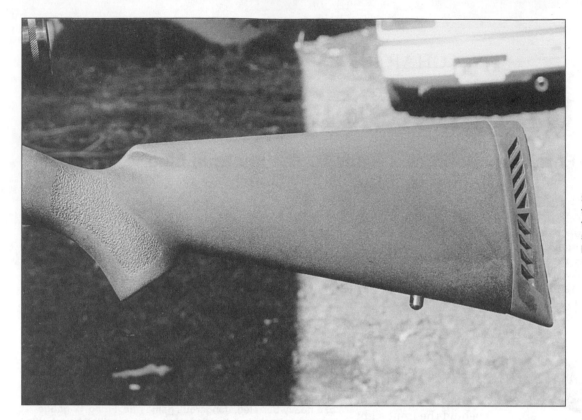

Stippling on the pistol grip, plus the thick black recoil pad make the Mossberg Model 625 Slugster a comfortable gun to shoot, but there is a bit of recoil.

handed the 695 to Kaminski, who began to inspect it closely.

"What range do you want to shoot with it?" was the question.

"We ought to group it at 75 yards just to see what it does. When it comes down to the serious shooting, 50 yards, I think, would be a more practical law enforcement range."

Kaminski nodded in agreement. "I like the sights, but I think we better mount a scope on it."

He volunteered that he had a vintage 2.5-7x33 Western Field scope

that should top off the slug gun adequately. Then there was discussion as to how the gun should be tested. It was agreed that it first should be zeroed in on paper targets or some of the corrugated cardboard rectangles of the type that had been used in other testing.

"Since the idea is to knock the lock out of a door at an extended range, maybe we need to get a couple of old doors, put dead bolts on them and use the locks as our targets," Lewis said slowly, working out the details in his

mind. "Maybe Kevin has some damaged doors."

Kevin Wibberly, a building contractor headquartered in Pahoa, Hawaii, is an avid shooter as well as a friend of our two plotters. He had helped out the pair in other gun-oriented situations.

"I'll check it out," Ace Kaminski promised. "Give you a call."

Lewis had a supply of Winchester's Supreme Hi-Impact hollowpoint sabot slugs. A bit of research showed that each of these rounds was 2-3/4 inches

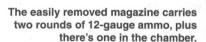

The easily removed magazine carries two rounds of 12-gauge ammo, plus there's one in the chamber.

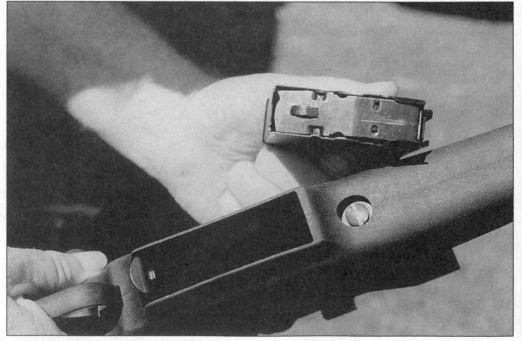

Not visible in this photo is the dead bolt lock that is roughly two inches in diameter. Kaminski has just fired his first round.

The top of the hole from the first round fired was less than a quarter-inch below the metal of the lock.

Kaminski zeroed the gun at both 75 and 50 yards to learn its potential. This group is an example of what can be done with the Slugster.

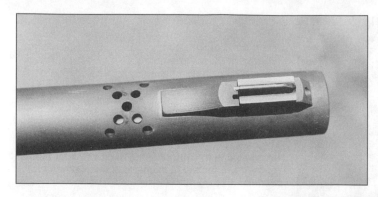

One set of ports meant to bleed off gases behind the bullet form an X just behind the Mossberg's front sight.

in length and carried a once-ounce slug. Within the confines of the sabot, the actual slug measured 50-caliber in cross-section. Velocity of this ammo was listed at 1450 feet per second. This supply had been sent by Mike Jordan of Winchester/Olin, in East Alton, Illinois, at Lewis' request. He was waiting in the Midwest for a report on how the ammo worked.

The rest of the week was taken up by a series of tropical rainstorms, so little was accomplished other than mounting the scope. During one morning of in-and-out sunlight, Kaminski managed to shoot the gun at 75 yards. He had drawn a cross on the target and used this in bringing the scope into line so it was shooting a three-shot group of less than two inches.

Also received had been 30 rounds of what are called Lightfield Hybred Sabot Expanding Slugs. This ammunition is made in Hungary and is being marketed in this country by the an outfit called The Slug Group, which headquarters in New Paris, Pennsylvania. The four-color, five-round packaging indicates that the cartridges are manufactured by Nitrokemia-Fiocchi, Limited. Fiocchi, of course, is an old name in European shotshell production. The packaging also indicates that it contains five rounds with expanding noses and that the ammo is "of Superior Breed."

There also is a warning stating that the ammo should not be used in guns with 3-1/2-inch chambers, adding that "for greater accuracy, use in a rifled barrel tube. In smoothbore guns, use cylinder and improved cylinder bore only."

The Lightfield slug is heavier than that of the Winchester offering, weighing 1.25 ounces. The manufacturer claims that this sabot has a velocity of 1400 feet per second with a muzzle energy of 2323 foot/pounds.

Ace Kaminski installed this 2.5-7x scope, a vintage Western Field model. It worked quite well on the Mossberg gun. Note the heavy-duty, no-nonsense bolt, which is in its open position.

Specifications

Name: Mossberg Model 695 Slugster.

Type: Bolt action; rotating rifle-type thumb safety.

Gauge: 12; three-inch chamber.

Weight: 7.5 pounds, unloaded.

Barrel: 22 inches; rifled and ported.

Magazine: Detachable two-round.

Stock: Black synthetic; equipped with black rubber recoil pad, sling swivel studs.

Finish: Matte black finish on all metal parts.

Sights: Ramped blade front, Williams V-notch rear; furnished with Weaver scope mount; fiber optics sights available at additional cost.

Maker: Mossberg Firearms
7 Grasso Ave.
North Haven, CT 06473.

As for the gray-hulled Winchester hollowpoint, this consists of an angled, five-sided hole in the nose of each slug. This depression measures just under 1/4-inch at its widest, but angles downward into the lead about 1/8-inch and measures about 1/8-inch in diameter at its bottom.

The Lightfield hull is a bright royal blue in color and the diameter of the slug is reduced for a fraction of an inch at its forward end. It would seem that this has been done so the slug will not contact the rolled end of the hull as it starts down the barrel.

The face of the slug proper also has an indentation leading to expansion. The visible face of the slug measures 1/8-inch with clearance from the hull all the way around. The shallow depression in the face appears to be cast in the metal and measures about 1/2-inch across at its widest point.

Lewis called The Slug Group in Pennsylvania and was told marketing was being handled by the Lightfield Corporation in Freehold, New Jersey. He finally ran down a phone number for Lightfield and was prompted to leave a voice mail message. He requested full ballistics information on the Hungarian-made round. A few days later, all he received was a one-page flier repeating the info he had managed to glean from the five-round box.

The weather finally cleared, delivering only the normal shower or two a day. It was time to see what Mossberg's Model 695 Slugster could do in a realistic situation.

Kaminski had gotten two slightly damaged doors from Wibberly and bought new dead bolts at a local hardware, installing one of them in a door. The doors were not the solid type one normally would find at the main entrance to a house. Instead they were the hollow doors used in home or office interiors. The frame in which Kaminski had set the deadbolt was solid, however. These rejects would serve their purpose.

The shoot was taking place in the abandoned arm of a quarry where Kaminski had received permission to

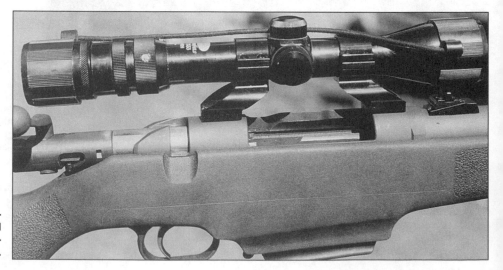

shoot. He and his wife, Audreen, had set up a folding table on the 50-yard marker, as well as a pair of lawn chairs. Ace covered the table with a heavy pad, then stacked a couple of lengths of 6x6-inch timber on it. This arrangement then was covered by a rectangle of camouflage cloth.

"You zeroed it in," Lewis pointed out. "How was it?"

"Well, it took a couple of sessions," Kaminski answered, "and about 15 rounds." He reached up to touch his right shoulder gently, offering a grimace. "I felt it the next morning."

"That brings us to a problem," Lewis informed him. "I'm not supposed to do anything of a jarring nature for eight weeks. I'm in the middle of the sixth week."

Kaminski offered a knowing smile that may have verged on a sneer. 'Okay. I'll handle it." Lewis had undergone recent eye surgery and Ace understood. Of course, he also understood he was going to absorb more recoil.

Kaminski settled into one of the plastic lawn chairs, picked up the slug launcher and loaded the two-round removable box magazine. He then stuffed another of the Winchester Premium slug rounds into the chamber before closing the bolt and pushing the magazine into its well. Using the wooden timbers as a forward rest, he leaned into the Model 695, pulled the trigger, and arose from the chair.

"I want to take a look," he announced, starting downrange,

The crosshairs in the scope are plainly visible in this photo. Shooting was done with the scope on the 2.5x setting.

Lewis in his wake. When the pair reached their wooden target, it was obvious the shot had been called correctly. Only a thin sliver of plywood separated the hole made by the slug from the bottom of the dead bolt lock.

"Let's try it again," Kaminski muttered and headed back to the table.

Settled in as before, he leveled the slug gun, the back of his left hand resting on the covered wooden blocks, the palm loosely holding the forend. Lewis watched as he took three deep breaths, exhaling each of them slowly.

Leaning into the stock, he again took aim, slowly drawing the trigger

back until it sent the firing pin into the primer. This time, Lewis noted that the forward end of the gun jerked upward from the covered rest. There was recoil for sure.

Ace Kaminski had been shooting with the scope set at its 2.5x setting, but now he cranked it all the way up to get a look at the door and, more specifically, the lock. Lewis was looking at the same thing with binoculars. The second slug had gone to the left of the lock, missing this time by roughly a quarter-inch.

"Well, they say third time's the charm," the shooter muttered as he readjusted his scope. Neither had thought to bring a sling that could be rigged for added stability, although there were studs for swivels fore and aft on the stock.

Settling into his shooting position once more, Kaminski took only one long breath, held it and fingered the trigger. Downrange, metal pieces flew in several directions. There should have been congratulations, perhaps a clap on the back, but all three participants already were on their way to the door!

The only evidence of the dead bolt lock was the ring that had surrounded it on the front and a metal plate that had covered the back. There was no evidence of the workings, although the Kaminskis and Lewis searched the pile of lava boulders behind the door for several minutes.

"Third time was the charm," Lewis belatedly agreed with the shooter.

"Want to try it again? Kaminski asked. "There's another door and another lock."

The differences in nose cavities on the two brands of slugs fired in the test are seen here. On the left is the Winchester one-ounce Premium load. The other is the imported Lightfield cartridge that has a slug weight of 1.25 ounces.

The gun features a heavy-duty rifle-type trigger and trigger guard. The trigger on the gun we checked out was not target rifle quality by any means; a bit of smoothing could be used to advantage. The magazine release is just forward of the guard.

The front sight is sturdy and features a white bead at the rear for better target acquisition. It is adjustable for windage. Note the ports for reducing felt recoil.

The shooter's third shot hit the lock dead center. These are the only parts found other than a few flakes of metal on the rocks behind the door.

The hull of the Winchester Premium round is a light gray in color. That of the Hungarian cartridge is a shade of royal blue. The latter round has been imported only recently.

"Might as well," Lewis agreed. "We're here."

While the Kaminskis removed the second wooden door from their truck and installed the new lock, Lewis continued to search for the missing parts of the destroyed mechanism. On the face of the rocks, he found several flakes of metal, all of them no larger than the head of a kitchen match; nothing more. Moving several tons of boulders to expand the search seemed a bit extreme. Besides, the second door was ready and Ace Kaminski was nailing it in place.

The means for standing the targets upright and keeping them that way was a steel stake on each side of the door. These stakes were the type used by concrete contractors to hold forms in place and have holes for nails. With the stakes snugged against the wood of the door frame, two nails were driven part way in, leaving enough of the head exposed so that they could be pulled with a claw hammer when time to clean up this temporary shooting range.

The lock on the first door had been positioned on the left side. For this one, it was on the right side. Lewis questioned the change and got a shrug with the answer: "Just seemed logical."

Ace Kaminski, a Hawaii State law enforcement officer, tested the Mossberg Model 625 in the abandoned arm of an old quarry. He seems intrigued with the trigger action.

Kaminski displays the damaged parts of the second lock, which rendered the mechanism non-functional.

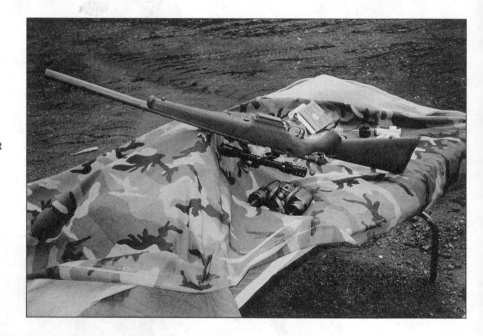

The slug gun, the ammo and the binoculars got a rest during the reworking of the tiny metallic target downrange.

The shooter prepares to reload the Model 625 magazine. At this time, he switched to the Hungarian-made Lightfield slugs which now are being imported into the U.S.

The camouflage cover on the table made an excellent shell catcher during the shooting test. In the beginning, tests were conducted with Winchester ammo.

The tent in the background has been erected in case of sudden rain. Kaminski checks out a Winchester Premium load before loading it into the two-round magazine.

The shooter contemplates the target downrange before assuming his shooting position. Firing from a benchrest, recoil is more pronounced than if the gun were fired offhand.

Kaminski walks the new door down to the 50-yard mark for installation.

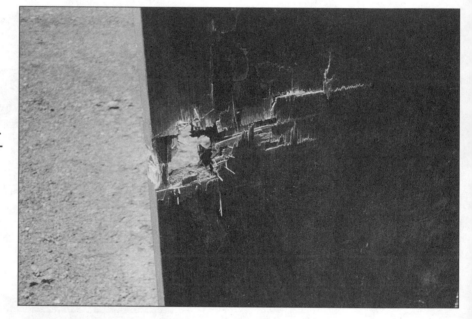

Damage to the back of the door is even more revealing. The lock was held precariously in place by a single small screw when the shooting ended.

The rounds fired by Kaminski on the second lock nearly surrounded the metal, with denting hits on top and bottom, but nothing to send the lock flying as before.

With the lock removed, one gets some idea of the damage done to it by the slugs, although there was not a direct hit.

Looking at the back of the door, one can see the amount of damage done. Making a forced entry in this instance would require no more than a shove of the door, as the lock no longer is functional.

This wreckage of the door shows the damage to the wood as the 12-gauge slug ripped the dead bolt away. It was not found.

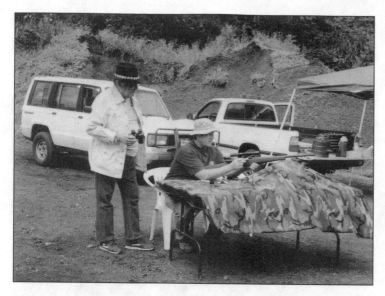

Jack Lewis, binoculars in hand, is ready to check the rounds that Kaminski fires on the door 50 yards downrange. Under the camouflage cover are lengths of timber being used as a rest for the shooting.

Loading the magazine into the well took a bit of experimentation before it became an automatic motion, Ace Kaminski found.

Again, Ace loaded the two-round magazine and stuffed a third Winchester Premium round into the chamber. Hunching over the table, he sighted on the dead bolt lock and fired. Since the lock failed to fly, he didn't check through the scope, but fired the other two rounds. Through the Bushnell binoculars, Lewis eyed the damage. All three rounds had cut holes in the wood in an arc around the bottom of the lock. In fact, one slug made a crease in the bottom of the circular metal frame that encased the lock's working elements.

"Close, but no cigar," Lewis commented.

Kaminski tried a couple more rounds of the Winchester ammo, only adding to the curve of his arc. By now, he was scowling. That was when Lewis handed him a box carrying five rounds of the 1.25-ounce Lightfield slugs.

"Here. Let's try these," he suggested.

Again, Kaminski loaded three rounds and settled into his shooting position. One at a time and with great concentration, he fired each round. The lock was still there. He loaded the other two rounds of the Hungarian-made ammo and fired off the two rounds. No change in target status.

Shaking his head, he massaged his shoulder for a moment, then settled the shotgun among the empty hulls and made for the target, Lewis in his footsteps.

When they drew close enough to see what actually had happened,

there was nothing but surprise. The lock was completely surrounded by holes in the wood, just a few strands of fibrous Philippine mahogany still holding it in place. Another slug had even creased the surrounding frame at the top of the lock.

Kaminski extended his trigger finger to punch at the lock and it fell away, still held to the wood by one stubborn screw.

"I don't think that would do much to slow down an entry," Lewis suggested. The holes now formed a nearly perfect half-circle around the lock.

With the lock removed, photos were taken to show the extent of the damage. Lewis packed the parts away in a box with the unfired ammo, while Ace Kaminski eyed the Model 695 thoughtfully.

"Let's find out what I can buy this for," the shooter suggested. "I think I ought to have it."

"I'll check with Bud Fini at Mossberg," Lewis promised. Then, on a tentative note, he added, "But if

it's going to be yours, maybe you ought to be certain it's cleaned properly."

Kaminski cast the other a glance with raised eyebrow to let it be known he realized he was being conned. Then his eyes went to the gun in his hands. "I'll clean it," he decided. "Then I'll know it's done right!"

Touche'!

Deciding to prove the shot on the bolt was not a fluke, Kaminski installs another new lock in the side of another reject door. This one is mounted on the opposite side from the lock on the first door shot.

Section VI

And In The 21st Century?

ASSAULT WEAPONS FOR THE MILLENNIUM

In The Coming New Century, Our Armed Forces Will Field Some All-New Weapons, As Well As Some That Just Look New.

IN SPITE OF all of the talk of Y2K and the fact that most of the computers of the world could crash, the search for new weaponry by our Department of Defense and the individual services continues without sign of a glitch.

During the coming century, there is no telling what will have been introduced. By the beginning of the 22nd century, we could well be battling in space. At this point, some of the weaponry under military consideration only looks as though it is something bought from the Star Wars prop department.

Military weapons are much like the U.S. freeway system. They are dreamed up, developed, prototyped, tested - perhaps adopted - then manufactured. By the time these weapons are in the hands of the troops who will train and perhaps fight with

them, they usually are obsolete in the eyes of weapons developers and their designers and scientists. This cadre already is off on another, usually more deadly tack.

At the other extreme, weapons that were considered to be obsolete suddenly are subjects of new interest. An example is the M14 rifle, which was designed to be the interim issue between the World War II-produced Garand M1 and the Vietnam era M-16. For the most part, these rifles have been stored away, coated in preservative cosmolene, for more than 30 years. Recently, however, the Armed Services called for a new sniper rifle. A number of models were considered, including the Stoner SR-25, but it finally was determined that the Department of Defense could save considerable amounts of

taxpayer money by using the M14.

Thus, more than 10,000 of these rifles were inspected by Marine Corps armorers and civilian military employees to select the best 1,000 of the cache. As decreed by the Government Accounting Office, the cost of the supposedly obsolete rifles to the Marines was one dollar each!

There were other costs, however. After study and testing by the Marksmanship Training Unit at the Marine Corps Base at Quantico, Virginia, the recommendation was to design a new barrel for the reclaimed war surplus, as well as a fiberglass stock. There were several other recommendations for improving the rifle's capabilities in various types of weather and physical environments.

The updated rifle is not referred to as a sniper weapon in official

The Heckler & Koch 9mm submachine gun has been a long-time standby of Marine Corps reconnaissance units and special Mission-trained units of other services. It is being replaced by the M-4A1 Carbine in its new guise.

This is not the M-14 rifle many of us remember from the 1960s. Reworked and furnished with a new synthetic stock, it is now listed as the Designated Marksman Rifle, the politically correct term for sniper!

correspondence, however. It now is called the DMR, which translates to Designated Marksman Rifle. Police departments began referring to their SWAT snipers as designated marksman some years ago to avoid using the less popular connotation in the civilian community that went with the word, sniper. Apparently, the Pentagon has taken similar steps to be politically correct in the current age.

In addition to the new barrel, the M14 has other improvements.

The synthetic stock incorporates a butt that is adjustable for length and there also is an adjustable cheek pad positioned to make shooting more comfortable and hopefully more accurate. A clutchable pistol grip is moulded into the stock and located directly behind the M14's trigger guard, while an integral bipod has been included as an aid to long range shooting. Another example of looking to the past for possible perfection is reflected in the fact that the nylon web sling is not part of this rig. Instead, the standard leather sling of decades past is being used.

Marines at the Corps' Marksmanship Training Unit where Designated Riflemen are trained report that the DMR, equipped with a 10-power Leupold scope and firing the 7.62 NATO round, can put down targets at 800 yards with no difficulty. This combination also is reported to allow the shooter to fire an aimed round every four seconds — or 15 rounds in a single minute.

The original M14 rifle, of course, had a selector switch that was instrumental in our infantry troops graduating from status of shooters to sprayers before the military brass realized what was happening and took the selector out of most of the rifles, leaving them to fire semi-automatic only. There is no selector switch on the converted M14s, either.

When the rifles came out of the preservative grease, which was washed off with steam hoses, each of them weighed about 10 pounds, depending upon the density of the wooden stocks. The new rifle, with the standard-weight synthetic stock, scales at an even 11 pounds.

Another oldie but goodie that has found a new life at a robust 88 years of age and a veteran of countless wars, revolutions and incidents is the familiar Model 1911 autoloading pistol, which fires the 45 ACP cartridge. The current model is designated as the M1911A1 and it is these pistols that were being pulled out of storage

during Desert Storm and rushed to the front, where they were found to operate better in sand and dust that did the M9 Beretta-made 9mm.

The Marines have gathered up a batch of M1911A1 pistols, which are being worked over by Corps gunsmiths and armorers. A new stainless steel trigger is being installed, one that can be adjusted by the individual Marine to his own tastes and standards. A new wrap-around grip made popular by competition shooters also has become a part of the handgun, as have ambidextrous safeties - one on each side of the gun. The 1911A1s being given the treatment also are receiving a new combat hammer with a combat sear and an easily maneuverable beavertail-type safety.

For this reconfiguration, Irv Stone III of Bar-Sto Precision Machine in Twenty-nine Palms, California, came up with a new drop-in barrel that makes the auto easier to assemble and disassemble. For years, Stone, his

The Objective Individual Combat Weapon (OICW) is the designation for this piece of armament that probably will be issued to troops in 2006. It combines the familiar gas-operated 5.56mm rifle with a 20mm gun that launches a round that explodes either on or above the intended target.

father before him and this shop have catered to some of the nation's top competitive pistol hawks.

These pistols, however, are being issued only to Marine Expeditionary Units. These are the special operations-qualified outfits — usually an infantry battalion with all of the logistical and supporting weapons units needed for an operation — about which we have been reading in the newspapers and seeing on television. These are the units that have sought to maintain the peace or rescue stranded American citizens in such unsettled areas a Haiti, Lebanon, Somolia, ad infinitum.

At this point in history, at least, the rest of the Marine Corps will have to struggle along the 9mm M9 pistol.

Of more recent vintage is the M4A1 Carbine, which is being issued to selected Army and Marine units at this writing. Originally, the intent was to furnish the carbine only to specialized elements such as recon and special response teams that have been armed with the MP5 submachine gun. The Heckler & Koch gun still is favored by most major police departments, according to recent information. In an effort to keep up with the times, the German manufacturers offered such accessories as a sound suppressors, a frame-mounted flashlight and a laser spotter.

More recently, the M4A1 Carbine

The OICW is being torture-tested currently by Army and Marine troops at various sites. The unit weighs 18 pounds without ammo, but efforts are being made to reduce its weight prior to production.

has been awarded a new designation: the CQBW, the acronym for Close Quarter Battle Weapon. A rework of the M-16 rifle, the 5.56mm-chambered carbine was developed by Colt Manufacturing Company as long ago as 1989. Apparently, it required almost a decade for the Pentagon to realize its potential.

Original purpose for the M4A1 was to provide a handier means for fighting in close confines such as ship's compartments and small rooms. To make the weapon live up to its new CQBW designation, a batch of accessories have been developed, the center of which is the M1913 rail adapter system. This system allows additions to be mounted on the gun that can include the M203 40mm grenade launcher, a sound suppressor, a detachable carrying handle and rear sight, a modified M203 leaf sight, a forward hand grip, the ACOG Reflex sight and the ACOG scope, as well as the AP/PEQ-4 laser dot pointer/illuminator.

The forward hand grip allows the shooter to fire the carbine in much the manner of a submachine gun, using 30-round magazines. The user will be packing 10 such magazines. Not previously mentioned is an optical unit known as the Advanced Optical Combat Gunsight. This device requires no batteries operating off of ambient light, while allowing the shooter to have both eyes open, as he looks down the barrel of his weapon.

The MP5 subgun served well during its period of tenure and be assured it is not being junked. It will end up in warehouse against the possibility of being needed again for special purposes. Any submachine gun firing the 9mm Parabellum cartridge has limited range, while the M4A1 Carbine can handle accurate fire missions to a minimum of 500

Designed to replace the Mark 19 40mm machine gun and the M2 50-caliber machine gun, the Objective Crew-Served Weapon (OCSW) fires 25mm exploding shells at the rate of 260 rounds per minute.

meters and, with the right ammo, to 1,000 meters, according to those who tested it. The CQBW weighs just under 6.5 pounds and is sealed and coated for protection against salt water. It has been submerged to a depth of 66 meters during Pentagon torture tests and, when brought to the surface, functioned perfectly.

A new cartridge also is under development for this firearm and may be in the supply system by the time this is read. Called Controlled Penetration Ammunition, this round has been proclaimed deadly, but when the bullet hits the target, its power drops rapidly, thus reducing the possibility of hitting a friendly trooper or even a civilian non-combatant farther downrange.

It is pretty well established that the carbine, even with its accessorized reidentification, is not likely to replace the M-16 rifle among regular infantry units, however

The weaponry discussed is being phased into the various armed services as this is written. However, the weaponry that already is being tested for introduction in the next century is considerably more exotic and expensive!

Probably closest to acceptance by the Pentagon for issue to Army and Marine Corps personnel is the OICW or Objective Individual Combat Weapon. Any number of "Space Age" designs were submitted for this new piece of individual armament, but in the end, there were only two contenders. Alliant Techsystems of Hopkins, Minnesota, won the competition and it is their entry that some say probably will replace the M-16 as the infantryman's weapon within the next decade!

The gas-operated OCSW weighs 37 pounds and requires two men to handle it, one acting as spotter and assistant gunner. Effective range of this weapon is 2000 meters.

Actually, the winning entry was a team effort, with Alliant Techsystems the prime contractor. Germany's Heckler & Koch actually built the prototype bullpup-style weapon, while the fire control system was produced by Contraves Brashear Systems of Pittsburgh, Pennsylvania. Another German firm, Dynamit Nobel AG, devised the high explosive propulsion system and has also worked at improving performance of the 5.56mm ammo.

The OICW carries two barrels, the top bore firing a 20mm high-explosive round, the lower barrel handling the familiar 5.56mm NATO round. Fully loaded, it weighs 18 pounds, but Matthew T. Zimmerman, manager of the Joint Service Small Arms Program at the Army's Picatinny Arsenal, says, "anticipated fielding weight for the fully loaded OICW is less than 14 pounds."

Zimmerman points out that "the OICW combines the lethality of 20mm airbursting munitions, 5.56mm NATO ammunition and a unique, full-solution fire control to affect decisively violent and suppressive target effects at extended ranges. The modular OICW can be fired as an integrated weapon system or separated for independent 5.56mm and 20mm firing."

One of the Alliant Techsystems' boasts is that the 20mm round makes possible an air burst over a defiladed target. "There's no place to hide," they declare. However, Virginia Hart Ezell, a Reserve major with the Ordnance Corps and president of the Institute for Research on Small Arms in International Security, has been quick to point out that while the airburst fuze and fragmenting warhead may offer lethality to the claimed 1,000 meters, "the problem for this small warhead in a round with a total weight of only 3.25 ounces is attaining lethality. Precision will be the key to its success."

To reduce weight, the barrel of the 20mm gun has been made from titanium. The two barrels share a single trigger mechanism, with a locking device that prevents the 5.56mm and 20mm from firing

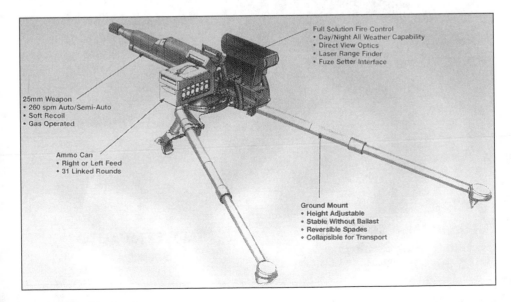

25mm Weapon
• 260 spm Auto/Semi-Auto
• Soft Recoil
• Gas Operated

Ammo Can
• Right or Left Feed
• 31 Linked Rounds

Full Solution Fire Control
• Day/Night All Weather Capability
• Direct View Optics
• Laser Range Finder
• Fuze Setter Interface

Ground Mount
• Height Adjustable
• Stable Without Ballast
• Reversible Spades
• Collapsible for Transport

The OCSW with tripod.

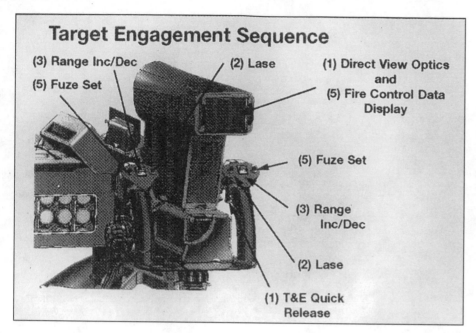

Target Engagement Sequence

(3) Range Inc/Dec

(5) Fuze Set

(2) Lase

(1) Direct View Optics and (5) Fire Control Data Display

(5) Fuze Set

(3) Range Inc/Dec

(2) Lase

(1) T&E Quick Release

Several steps are required for targeting and firing the OCSW effectively: (1) Squeeze the traverse and elevation levers for sight adjustments; (2) lase the target for range; (3) determine range for indirect fire if appropriate; (4) set the fire-control Aimpoint reticle on the target, using the T&E fine adjustments; (5) set the fuze mode for the proper type of explosion on target; (6) select the fire mode for semi- or full-auto; (7) depress the trigger.

T&E Controls

T&E Quick Release
- "Hands on" Release
- Rapid Target Acquisition
- Free Fire Mode

Elevation Fine Adjust:
- Mounted to Pintle
- Lock/Release on Right Handgrip
- 1 Mil Fine Adjust

Traverse Fine Adjust:
- Mounted to Pintle
- Lock/Release on Left Handgrip
- 1 Mil Fine Adjust

The T&E controls of the OCSW.

simultaneously. Recoil for the high-explosive system is reported to be less than that of the M14 rifle.

As for the 20mm high-explosive capability, David Broden, the technical director for Alliant Systems, states that performance consistency is controlled by "turns-count fuzing that is self-compensating regardless of the rate of speed of the round. It will always turn at the same rate, compensating for any variances caused by the manufacturing process."

Contraves Brashear Systems designed the fire control system to calculated the number of turns required for the round to reach its target. A laser incorporated as part of the fire control mechanism sends out pulses to the target, each pulse being analyzed to determine the exact range. According to Broden, "This fire control unit then communicates the information to the fuze even before the round leaves the barrel."

As of this writing, seven additional

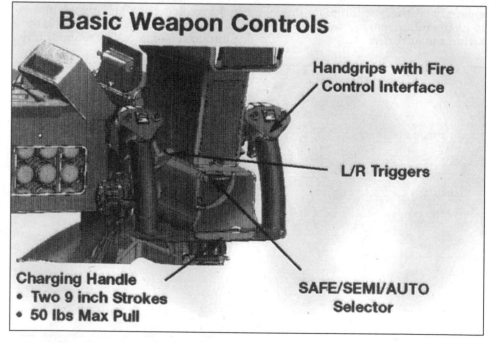

Basic Weapon Controls

Handgrips with Fire Control Interface

L/R Triggers

SAFE/SEMI/AUTO Selector

Charging Handle
- Two 9 inch Strokes
- 50 lbs Max Pull

Basic weapons controls of the OCSW.

Firing exercises such as this, with Marine Corps reconnaissance troops firing standard 9mm Parabellum cartridges, have led to concerns about pollution from lead and other materials. Work is now under way to substitute tungsten-tin bullets for lead in military small arms calibers.

guns have been built and delivered — at a cost of $8.5 million — to the Picatinny Arsenal in New Jersey for additional testing. When this testing is done, engineering and manufacturing development phases will begin in the year 2000. The government has requested a unit price estimate on 20,000 to 45,000 of these weapons. For what it may be worth, Matthew T. Zimmerman is on record as saying, "Cost is approximately $10,000 per system," but he adds that the OICW doubles the stand-off range, provides a 500-plus percent increase in probability of enemy incapacitation, reduces the soldier's load, and significantly increases combat versatility and survivability of the infantryman.

Assuming something better doesn't come along and the whole process starts over, it is estimated our troops will be armed with the OICW in 2006.

Those who have fired it during tests tend to feel another weapon of the near future opens up whole new vistas to the troops armed with it. This is the OCSW or Objective Crew-Served Weapon System. A product of General Dynamic's Armament Systems Division, the corporate developers are boasting that this may well be the weapon to replace both the 50-caliber M2 machine gun and the Mark 19 machine gun that fires 40mm grenades!

The OCSW is gas-operated to fire 25mm high-explosive shells at the cyclic rate of some 260 rounds per minute. It is tripod-mounted and offers the gunner a choice of semi-auto or full-automatic fire. Maximum effective range is 2,000 meters. The gun unloaded weighs 37 pounds. Like the Objective Individual Combat Weapon discussed earlier, it also is designed for overhead bursts that drive fragments into the unfortunates who may be under the burst.

Another innovation being pioneered at this writing by the U.S. Army is born of ecology efforts rather than combat needs. Contrary to some news reports, lead contamination at outdoor Military shooting ranges is not a current problem, although it is conceivable that lead could leach into surface water on some of the more heavily used firing installations.

"There is no problem now, but there could be," states Jim Arnold, chief of the pollution prevention and environmental technology division at the Aberdeen Proving Ground in Maryland. "We're looking ahead to anticipate problems and solve them before they start!"

In this connection, the Army now has begun producing environmentally friendly ammunition. The first million rounds, combining tungsten and tin in place of lead, are in production at Missouri's Lake City Army Ammunition Plant.

The 5.56mm bullets have a tungsten-tin core sheathed in copper. Developed by researchers at the the Army's Armament Research, Development and Engineering Center at Picatinny Arsenal in New Jersey, the new rounds proved to be slightly more accurate than the lead-cored versions during official tests. According the Jim Arnold, the new rounds are ballistically and visibly identical to the old and require no special handling.

At this writing, National Guard troops in Alaska have finished annual qualification firing with the new rounds. "There was no difference in the performance of these rounds in regard to bullet grouping or functioning of the weapons," according to Major Gary Curtiss, operations officer with the 1st Battalion (Scouts) of the 297th Infantry.

"We have been working on this

Marine recon personnel fire on silhouette targets, while others reload magazines with conventional ammo. The 9mm Heckler & Koch MP5 subgun is being phased out in favor of the M-4A1 Carbine. The latter will fire a non-toxic tungsten-tin bullet.

A Marine checks his hits on a silhouette target at Camp Pendleton, California. He used the MP5 9mm subgun, firing lead-core bullets. He probably wonders whether he would do as well with tungsten-tin 9mm bullets now under development.

project for about two years," Jim Arnold admits. "The concept is part of an Army initiative called Range 2 1. It involves the Army's efforts to be good stewards of their training and testing real estate."

The goal of the program, of course, is to reduce lead in the environment. The heavy metal and its chemical compounds are poisonous. Experience has shown that even small doses can cause irreversible brain damage, if ingested or breathed.

Arnold reports that the present concern is indoor ranges, such as those used regularly by the Reserve components of our Armed Services. He said that many indoor ranges of the military and some police departments have been closed due to the pollution hazard.

"While lead contamination is part of the total picture," he said,

"general health concerns about the vapors, residues and other pollutants created by firing lead rounds plays a larger part in closing indoor ranges.

"Still, lead is toxic, and if we can get rid of even the small chances of breathing lead, we should."

Arnold insists the tungsten-tin solution is comparatively inexpensive, the cost of the new rounds being comparable to that of the lead-loaded ammunition. Once in mass production, he declares, the tungsten-tin bullets may even be cheaper than those of lead. Incidentally, the Army buys all of the small arms ammunition for all

service branches. In fiscal 1998, our tax dollars paid for more than 200 million 5.56mm lead-copper rounds.

If the new 5.56 cartridge proves successful in actual field use, researchers at the New Jersey arsenal will move on to the 9mm Parabellum, the 7.62mm NATO cartridge and the 50- caliber Browning Machine Gun round.

According to Jim Arnold, "The 50-caliber will be next. There's a small amount of lead in this round we think we can get rid of simply by improving the industrial process used in its manufacture.

"The 9mm bullet is a somewhat tougher nut to crack," the military environmentalist adds. "The bullet is fairly large, so there has to be some cost reduction in tin and tungsten before this will work."

He points out, too, that the new bullets solve only the problem of reducing lead in the environment. Scientists also are working toward making bullet propellants and even primers more environmentally acceptable.

"All my young engineers have been been excited about working on this project," Jim Arnold says. "There really isn't any down-side to it."

Among the so-called Baby Boom generation and those even more ancient, the state-of-the-art computerization aspects of the OICW and OCSW are over the heads of many of us. Sciences — and particularly the sciences of warfare — are advancing far faster than many of us are able to grasp. However, for those in their teens and those with college credits, who now fill the ranks of our Armed Services, computers and electronics are anything but an impossible challenge. Youngsters today are introduced to computers in their first years of school. Growing up with these machines and the

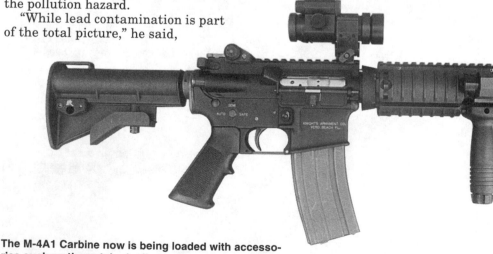

The M-4A1 Carbine now is being loaded with accessories such as the notched rail atop the unit that allows mounting of night sights and other optical devices. The forward hand grip gives the Carbine the characteristics of a submachine gun.

clones and variations, they have the ability and early training to handle such assignments as a matter of course.

The facet we find somewhat frightening is the likelihood that while we are perfecting such weapons and training our military to use them tactically, other nations — including the unfriendlies — are working on similar weapons that will be just as deadly against us in future battles! ●

COLT'S M-4 CARBINE ISSUE

This New, Shorter Version Of The M-16 Has Its Advantages.

COLT FIREARMS OFFICIALS should be bowing in thanks in the general direction of the Pentagon, headquarters for the Department of Defense. After some lean years and several reorganizations, the Connecticut company is back in the military arms business with DOD adoption of their M-4 Carbine.

As the first to manufacture the M-16 rifle, then a proprietary mechanism, Colt had a lock on that business for several years during the Vietnam hostilities. For recent replacement manufacture, the rifle contract has gone to others, including Belgium's FN. This company, incidentally, built a plant in South Carolina to soothe those congressmen who resented such contracts going out of the country.

As long ago as the 1980s, Colt designers began to reconfigure the M-16, seeking a design that would intrigue our nation's military arms buyers. The Colt Carbine was around for several years before the Pentagon became interested. Only now, as of this writing, has the Department of Defense begun issuing the M-4 Carbine to our troops.

According to Lieutenant Colonel Lester Knotts, plans and training officer for the 25th Light Infantry Division, the 5.56mm M-4, which fires semi-automatic or with a three-round burst, originally was destined to replace all the 45-caliber M-3 submachine guns, as well as selected M-9 pistols and M-16 series rifles. Other sources, however, state that the upgraded M-4A1, which also fires full-auto, probably will replace the current carbine by 2001.

"All division infantry units have received a partial issue of M-4 Carbines as a complement to the M-16. The weapon is being considered as a full replacement for the M-16A2," the officer told us.

The Carbines apparently are being phased into the various services a few at a time. For example, the 25th Light Infantry Division headquartered at Schofield Barracks in Hawaii has roughly 19,000 troops, but as of the date of this chapter being written—May, 1999—the division's infantry battalions have a ratio of one Carbine to every four M-16A2 rifles. Some of the new guns also have been issued to the division's artillery regiment and some other units.

As mentioned earlier in this book, the Marine Corps is in the process of phasing out the Heckler & Koch MP5 9mm submachine gun, which has been a mainstay of reconnaissance units in past years. Word had gone to the field that it would be replaced by the M-4A1 Carbine by March 31, 1999, but such did not happen by that date. An active-duty Marine friend feels it will be into the 21st century before the Corps has the necessary M-4A1s it requires to replace the 9mm subgun. It should be noted, however, that said friend is not necessarily noted for his positive attitude toward military supply functions, in general.

Field-stripped for cleaning, the M-4 is a relatively simple piece of armament. The soldier is Second Lieutenant Nick Hermes of the U.S. Army's 25th Light Infantry Division.

With the stock fully extended the M-4 Carbine measures only 33 inches in overall length. It is 6.63 inches shorter than the M-16 rifle from which it was derived.

With the stock extended, the Carbine is locked firmly in place for firing.

With the stock closed, the M-4 Carbine measures 29.75 inches in overall length, making it easy to handle in tight confines.

Through the Schofield Barracks public affairs officer, Lieutenant Colonel Debra Pressley, then First Lieutenant Joseph Michael Peters, media relations officer for the 25th Light Infantry Division, arrangements were made for Jack Lewis to spend time with division elements that were requalifying with their issued weapons that included both the M-16 and the newer M-4 Carbine.

Picked up at Honolulu International Airport by Lt. Peters, Lewis was impressed to find that the officer had shown the foresight to obtain an earlier edition of *The Gun Digest Book of Assault Weapons* and to look over the format and approach to the various military and law enforcement weapons covered in those pages. The 30-minute ride to the Army installation was filled with a discussion of modern military weaponry, each of them mentioning personal incidents leading to their likes and dislikes. Peters seems to favor the M-4 Carbine over the M-

16, declaring, "I find I shoot better scores with the M-4, and that's what it's all about."

The day Lewis spent on the range was devoted to requalification of personnel from one of the division's artillery units. He noted that most were armed with the M-16, a few with the M-4. He wanted to know where the line was drawn.

"In artillery—in fact, in most of the division—those who are going to be closest to the enemy are armed with the M-4," Lt. Peters explained. "For example, when I was in artillery, I was armed with the Carbine, because I was a forward observer. That meant I had to be up close, pooping and snooping, until I found a good position from which I could call in artillery on an enemy. It also meant I might be spotted and would have to move out in a hurry. The M-4 Carbine makes that easier to do."

While some 85 percent of the parts in the M-4 are interchangeable with the M-16, there are definite visible differences. For example, the Carbine

has an extendable three-position buttstock. Including the compensator, it measures 29.75 inches closed, 33.0 inches fully extended. The compensator-equipped, fixed-stock M-16 measures 39.63 inches. The barrel of the Carbine, including the compensator, is 15.5 inches in length, the M-16 is 21 inches with the compensating unit. With a sling and loaded magazine, the M-4's weight is seven pounds, five ounces. With the same outfitting, the M-16 weighs eight pounds, 13 ounces.

The rifling of both weapons is the same: six grooves in a right-hand twist, 1:7-inch twist. Other mechanical features are much the same, each boasting a trigger pull of 5.5 to 9.5 pounds. Cyclic rate of fire for the rifle is approximately 700 to 900 rounds per minute, while that of the Carbine is 700 to 970. Chamber pressure on both models is the same: 52,000 pounds per square inch. Muzzle velocity for the Carbine has been established at approximately 2970 feet per second, the rifle being clocked at 3100 fps.

The controls for the M-4 are essentially the same as those of the M-16. There is interchangability of 85 percent among the parts of the two models.

The stock slides on a steel tube and moves smoothly in and out. The chevron-shaped piece of metal at the bottom of the stock controls the length.

The compensator helps to reduce recoil and muzzle flash on the M-4. It is the same as that on the M-16.

Maximum range for both rifle and Carbine has been established as 3,938 yards. Maximum effffective range on area targets for both is being listed at 875 yards. For individual/point targets, the M-16 rifle is a trifle superior; its effectiveness is listed as 602 yards. For such targets, max range for the Carbine is tabbed at 547 yards.

There are numerous firing ranges at Schofield Barracks, but the one to which Lt. Peters took Jack Lewis was one of the requalification ranges. In the 25th Light Infantry Division, all personnel have to requalify twice annually, so the ranges are kept busy.

At one end of the spread is the zero range. This involves four small targets for each shooter, the distance established as 30 yards. Before each target is a permanent, manufactured "foxhole." This is a section of what appears, at first glance, to be concrete pipe sunk into the ground to a depth of about four feet. A closer look suggests that each of these positions has been individually cast. Each rifleman takes his position in one of these holes. In front of the hole are several sandbags, with a white stake at the right on which he rests his weapon.

Range personnel each oversee three shooters during the zeroing exercise, while other soldiers govern movement and firing from the three-story tower behind the firing line. A safe distance away, behind the tower and across a road, is the ammo supply. It is here that emptied magazines are refilled at specific intervals, the freshly loaded magazines being moved back across the road for issue to individual shooters in keeping with rules of the range. This is just one more facet of the safety precautions established and followed at this Army installation.

The initial challenge for each shooter is to zero his rifle. For this, each of the four targets on the board carries a miniature printed version of a standard silhouette target. The object is to zero the rifle to bring deadly fire on that small silhouette, which measures roughly five inches in height and three inches in width.

Several rounds are fired on the zeroing targets, then on command, weapons are cleared and the shooters move forward to inspect their targets and attempt to determine how the sights must be adjusted to bring them into zero. Assigned range personnel, of course, are looking at the same targets and advising the shooters as

As with the M-16, the adjustable rear sight is part of the Carbine's carrying handle. It can be removed for installation of a scope or night sighting device.

The handguard of the M-4 is shorter than that of the M-16, as is the barrel, but the front sights are identical.

The buttstock assembly carries the action spring and the buffer.

Troops of the 25th Light Infantry Division fire on the zeroing targets at a range of 30 yards in the beginning stage of requalification.

to what they must do to bring the sights into effective alignment.

The original firing order called for shooters to fire on the upper right of the four targets. On one stand, there were no bullet holes in the chosen target or in any of the other three. This led one of the range overseers to run a steel ramrod through the barrel of this M-4 Carbine to make certain no bullets were lodged in the bore, then the weapon was laid aside until time could be taken to check the sights out properly.

Two or three shots at a time, the shooters brought their weapons into

proper zero. As this was accomplished, the zeroed shooters came out of their emplacements and were replaced by a new contingent. Again, each retiring shooter had a ramrod shoved down the length of his weapon's bore before he was sent down the road in formation with the others who had passed this phase of requalification.

Under standing orders at Schofield Barracks, each unit that is requalifying soldiers must have its own range officer assigned to work with the contingent of regularly assigned range personnel. On the day Lewis donned one of the new Kevlar helmets and

served with the Army, First Lieutenant Michael K. Byard of a battery of the 11th Field Artillery was the unit range officer. He was among those checking bores and chambers as shooters came off the firing line.

Adjoining the zero range is another installation that features pop-up targets. These three-dimensional targets are light blue in color and are hidden behind dirt mounds scattered over the firing field. Again, there is a series of the manufactured foxholes and each hole has a number. Out beyond 300 yards are large numbered signs that indicate the area into which

REPAIR PARTS LIST

1	HANDLE ASSEMBLY, CHARGING
2	BOLT CARRIER ASSEMBLY
3	UPPER RECEIVER AND BARREL ASSEMBLY (M16A2)
3A	UPPER RECEIVER AND BARREL ASSEMBLY (M4)
4	MAGAZINE, CARTRIDGE (30 round)
5	SLING, SMALL ARMS (M16A2)
5A	SLING, SMALL ARMS (M4)
6	LOWER RECEIVER AND BUTTSTOCK ASSEMBLY (M16A2)
6A	LOWER RECEIVER AND BUTTSTOCK ASSEMBLY (M4)

This repair parts list explains the numbers on the right.

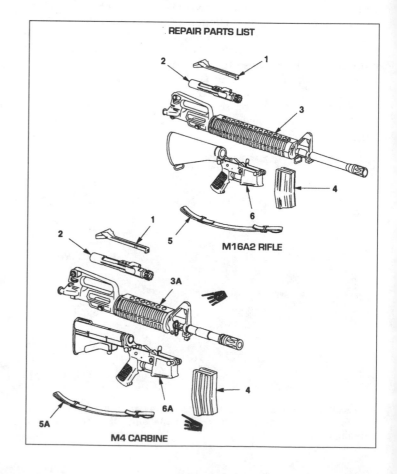

REPAIR PARTS LIST

M16A2 RIFLE

M4 CARBINE

The bolt carrier and bolt of the two firearms are identical and are treated the same in matters of maintenance and lubrication.

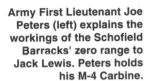

Army First Lieutenant Joe Peters (left) explains the workings of the Schofield Barracks' zero range to Jack Lewis. Peters holds his M-4 Carbine.

For zeroing M-16 rifles and M-4 Carbines, four small silhouette targets are stapled to a backing.

each rifleman should fire when he sees targets. In other words, if the number flanking the foxhole is six, at the far end of the range are two small billboards carrying the same number. The shooter fires only at the targets soon between his corresponding numbers. Also, about 25 yards in front of each foxhole is a white log that measures roughly five feet in length. It has a purpose, which will be described later.

"If someone happens to shoot on someone else's target, it plays hell with the scoring," Lt. Byard explained. "Everything from activating the targets and timing to the scoring are done electronically." During the sequence, each of the 20 targets scattered over the number-flanked areas are assigned to the individual marksman.

Each shooter is issued three magazines of ammo, each carrying 20 rounds. Ordered into the foxhole, he stacks the magazines on the edge of the concrete tube to keep them out of the red volcanic dirt. When the order comes from the rangemaster's public address system to lock and load, the clatter of bolts echoes along the firing line.

Each man hunches into position, using the sandbags for support of his rifle or Carbine and, as the targets suddenly begin to pop up over the range, firing begins. All of the targets are controlled by an electronic tape in the tower, each popping up for a period of five to eight seconds before it drops out of sight. That time span is peculiar to the Schofield Barracks range, incidentally. Other major

After firing three rounds, the soldiers check their targets with range personnel to determine what sight changes must be made to bring the sights into alignment.

Finished with the chore of zeroing, soldiers form up and are marched to the next phase of requalification, the unknown distance range.

While waiting for an earlier relay to finish firing, soldiers check their shooting logs to determine where sights should be set for this phase of training.

Specialist Timothy Mapes carries empty magazines from shooting positions to the ammunition point, where they will be reloaded.

Specialist Edwin S. Tracey is in charge of reloading magazines and issuing live ammo to those shooting on the requalification ranges. His station is removed from the shooting line.

Armed with M-4 Carbines, these two soldiers are waiting to be assigned to targets. The ammo point is visible on the other side of the road. The distance is a safety measure.

This left-handed shooter fires at targets at 100 yards. Behind each of the dirt berms is a pop-up target. In the distance are numbered signs that tell him the perimeters of his shooting range.

Wearing his own shooting jacket and a borrowed helmet, Jack Lewis gets the feel of the M-4 Carbine before moving to the range to fire a few rounds. At this point, the magazine is empty; a standard safety precaution.

This soldier demonstrates the protective mask meant to defeat chemical attacks by an enemy. Some of the qualification firing is done while wearing this mask. Night firing is another facet of the Army's program.

Army installations that have such courses may expose their pop-up targets for as few as three seconds and as many as 12.

Each rifleman hopes to acquire these targets and fire on them, but as widespread as some are, looking for them through the rifle's peep sight is a difficult chore. As soon as the sequence ends, the individual hits and misses are compiled by computers in the tower. In the second phase of qualification, the shooter comes out of his hole and lies prone on the packed ground beside the concrete tube.

One facet of training Lewis noted was that left-handers were allowed to shoot left-handed. No effort apparently had been made to make them right-handed shooters, as had

been his own experience many years ago at Parris Island, South Carolina.

As before, the standard orders and safety warnings were verbalized from the tower, and the downrange targets scattered at intervals of 50, 100, 150, 200, 250 and 300 yards began to pop up. Again, each soldier had 20 rounds for a like number of targets, but the firing seemed to be more sporadic. Lewis reasoned that in their prone positions, the shooters were having greater difficulty with proper target acquisition. Range personnel admitted that for some, the prone position is more difficult on the rapidly disappearing targets. To qualify for the right to wear

an expert rifleman's badge, the Army shooter must score with no less than 36 hits on the 40 targets presented in the two-stage training competition. For a sharpshooter's badge, a soldier must score 30 to 35 hits, and for marksman status, the score must be between 23 and 29 hits.

Then there were those white logs placed half way to the 50-yard targets. They are involved in a separate exercise that calls for donning the hooded gas mask that each soldier

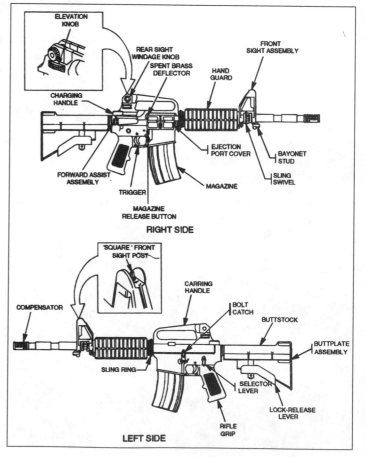

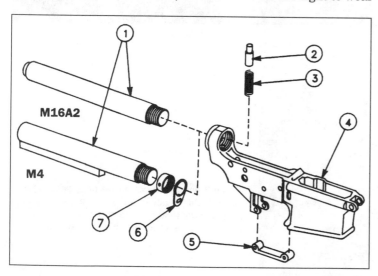

The M-4 Carbine has two extra parts in its design, the receiver end plate (6) and a locking nut (7). If either of these is damaged, it should be replaced. Other parts requiring periodic inspection are the buffer retainer (2), helical springs (3), lower receiver (4) and the trigger guards. All are easily replaced.

With magazine removed, this M-4 Carbine is equipped with a laser unit on the plugged barrel that allows for realistic war games. The yellow plug makes it easy to see that the Carbine is incapable of accepting live ammo.

The firing line and computer-operated targets on the unknown distance range at Schofield Barracks are operated from this tower. Shooters' scores also are recorded electronically.

carries in a rectangular pouch attached to his cartridge belt. Each of the shooters, carrying his last magazine of ammo, moved up beside one of the logs and again went into the prone position. That third magazine was loaded into the weapon upon order from the tower and each man settled into shooting position

Suddenly, the blue man-sized targets began to pop up in front of each shooter from behind the protective berm, then disappear. Each time this target appeared, a shot was fired at it. This exercise continued all along the line until ammunition and time were expended.

"They also have to do this same close-range exercise at night," Lt. Peters announced to his charge for the day. It seemed logical.

Lewis wanted to try the pop-up target range, but didn't want to interfere with training; another relay of shooters was waiting behind the tower. Instead, he and Lt. Peters

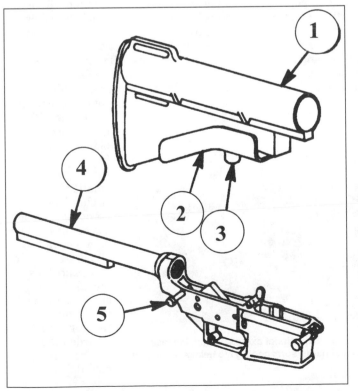

The M-4 buttstock assembly requires some special care not associated with the fixed-stock M-16. To remove the stock (1) from the lower receiver extension (4), one must grasp the lock release lever (2) in the area of the retaining pin then pull down and slide the stock to the rear to separate the two assemblies. The detent pin should be well lubricated.

Specifications

Name:	M-4 Carbine.
Caliber:	5.56mm NATO; fires ball, blank and tracer ammo.
Operation:	Gas-operated; semi-automatic or three-round burst; air-cooled, rotating bolt breech mechanism.
Cyclic Rate:	700-970 rounds per minute.
Weight:	7 pounds, 5 ounces (with loaded magazine, sling); 6 pounds (empty).
Length:	29.75 inches (buttstock closed); 33 inches (butt extended).
Barrel:	15.5 inches (with compensator); 1:7-inch right-hand twist; six-groove.
Magazine:	20-round, detachable.
Stock:	Three-position extendable tube.
Maker:	Colt's Manufacturing Co., Inc. P.O. Box 1868 Hartford, CT 06144-1868

moved back to the zero range, where they had started. There, Lewis had the opportunity to handle the M-4 Carbine and become familiar with its workings. With its similarities to the M-16, this was no great chore. He then fired a few rounds, choosing the offhand position. "This was done with the understanding that no one would check my target," he reports.

What this shooter was attempting to do was compare the feel of the M-4 to the M-16, and like Peters, he immediately came to favor the former. "The reduction in size and weight seems to have improved the balance and it's a lot easier to maneuver," he says. "It's a natural for urban house-to-house fighting. This one's going to be around for long while."

The Marine Corps has had pop-up targets of a sort; silhouettes were rigged to rise and fall on electronic impulse and the targets were set at alleged unknown distances. These ranges have been used primarily in field exercises, definitely not for rifle qualification

purposes. In fact, Lewis recalls firing the then-new M-60 machine gun on such a range in the early 1960s.

There is an ongoing question as to whether the Army's system is better or less instructive than that of the Corps in creating one-shot, one-kill shooters. Instead of the pop-up targets at unmarked distances used by the Army, Marines—in boot camp and each year thereafter—fire at stationary targets that are set at 200, 300 and 500 meters.

At 200 meters, each Marine fires five semi-auto rounds in each position: standing, kneeling and sitting. These positions are fired at five minute intervals. Then, from the kneeling position, each marksman must fire 10 rounds in the rapid-fire mode in 70 seconds.

At the 300-yard range, each Marine fires five rounds in five minutes from the kneeling position. This is followed by 10 rounds rapid-fire, again in 70 seconds.

At the 500-meter range, each shooter is allowed 10 minutes in which to fire 10 rounds on the distant target, using the prone position. In all, 50 rounds are fired.

On the 200-meter target, two points are allowed for each round in the target's smaller inner circle. Expert standing calls for a score of 40 to 65 points, while 35 to 39 points earns a sharpshooter's medal. Those shooters in the 25 to 34-point category are awarded the marksman's medal.

According to word out of the Marksmanship Training Unit at Quantico, Virginia's Marine Corps Base, the Corps is looking into constructing ranges with unmarked distances that will be operated electronically to score hits and misses. However, in an interview by Matthew Cox of *Army Times*, a weekly newspaper sold on bases and by subscription, Marine Chief Warrant Officer Steve Hesseltine, stated that even with the addition of such ranges, the Corps has no plan for abandoning the present system.

"The Marine Corps is not willing," he stated, "to sacrifice time on known distance targets to get the time for unknown distance training."

For the most part, the Marine Corps will continue to carry the M-16A2 rifle into combat, although the plan is to arm reconnaissance units, rapid response teams and similar specialties with the M-4A1. As for the comparison between the two, Schofield Barracks range personnel told Lewis there is virtually no difference in the scores registered between M-4 and M-16 shooters in requalification.

"Shooting is an individual talent," one staff noncommissioned officer said. "Some naturally shoot better than others. It looks as though some score better with the M-4. Others don't shoot quite as well as they do with the M-16. Growing familiarity may take care of that, of course, but again, some riflemen are just better than others."

Not to be forgotten, of course, is the fact that such companies as Knight's Industry have been thinking of the M-4 in modular terms. By the addition of specially designed accessories, the Carbine could fill any number of roles in a combat environment. The possibilities for modular weapon configurations are almost endless. ●

This soldier is involved in a realistic combat exercise using the laser unit. The band with the laser sensors surrounding his helmet will signal hits by an "enemy" laser.

CHAPTER 35

THE EYES OF BATTLE

In Wars Of The Future, Marksmen Still May Need To Identify Friend Or Foe Visually, But Modern Technology Will Be A Big Help!

WHEN WE THINK of the work of snipers—now referred to as Designated Marksmen—our first thoughts may well have to do with the type of individual chosen for such service. But the equipment with which he has to work in fulfilling the mission is deserving of consideration, too.

Snipers were in service as long ago as the French and Indian War, when Colonial frontiersmen fighting on the side of the British used "Native American" tactics to ambush the European armies who were intent on making the North American continent a French possession.

It wasn't until after the Civil War that any serious thought was given to using a telescope mounted atop a rifle. In fact, snipers of that day had to be satisfied with a piece of metal tubing that extended the full length of action and barrel to better their aim. Hence, the name "tube sight." There were no optical elements involved. Someone later decided that crosshairs mounted at the forward end of the tube would make centering the shot more simple.

Oddly, the Model 683 9mm submachine gun, introduced in 1984 by Saco Defense Systems, utilized the same approach. On top of the gun was a carrying handle that doubled as the sight. This handle was nothing more than a metal tube, with crosshairs situated at the forward open end. There were no optics.

During later wars, U.S. troops invariably used top-quality sporting scopes already in production that could be mounted on sniper rifles. But in the current Age of Electronics, all of that has changed. There are all sorts of sighting devices that make it easier to identify a target, night or day. Some of the nation's leading optical companies have entered the market, but so have major corporations that feel they can fill a need.

Aimpoint, Inc., for example, initially developed a major market among sportsmen with a sighting device that offered an illuminated red dot in the center of the optics, making it easy to follow a moving target. Some of these devices were tested extensively by the military and found to offer certain

As late as the 1980s, Saco Defense Industries mounted an open tube atop their Model 683 sub-machine gun. There were no lenses, but cross-hairs were situated in the forward end of the metal tube.

advantages, but they wanted more.

In 1996, the Herndon, Virginia, corporation introduced the Aimpoint Reflex Collimator Sight, more simply described, perhaps, as an electronic red dot sight. They also came up with mounts for the M-16 series of rifles as well as the M-4 Carbine. The result was a contract option to furnish up to 80,000 units of sights and mounts over four option years.

Designated as the Comp/M sight, it earlier had passed torture tests involving environments of extreme heat and cold, as well as torrential rains. Over a 12-month period of testing extremes, the sight was baked, frozen, dropped and drowned, but survived each test.

Aimpoint also came up with what they called the Rail Grabber mount featuring integral rings and a torque-limiting, quick-release knob. The mount was designed for use with the Aimpoint Comp and the same manufacturer's M-16 mount, or with any Military Standard-1913 rail.

The Comp/M sight can be mounted on any of the M-16 or AR-15 family of rifles using various approaches. It can be mounted on the carrying handle, still positioning the sight so that it lies low over the hand guard. This allows the iron sights to be used as backup. The sight also can be positioned on the rail forward of the carrying handle, but this blocks practical use of iron sights. A third method of mounting is to remove the carrying handle and install the sight on the rail directly over the gun's magazine well.

According to a corporate spokesperson, "Aimpoint sights offer a unique, parallax-free, double-lens shooting system that gives the shooter the advantage of getting on target quickly and shooting more accurately. With the patented double-lens system, the Aimpoint is the only red dot sight that does not require the shooter to center the red dot in the sight."

Another Virginia firm, operating out of Roanoke, is ITT Night Vision. This is a defense industry arm of the corporate giant better known in its younger years as International Telephone & Telegraph. Today, the parent organization is ITT Industries.

This particular offshoot of the parent corporation calls itself the "world leader in night vision technology." Whether that claim is

During the War Between The States, there were no optical sights, but snipers used long tubes attached to rifle barrels as a sighting aid to put them on target.

valid is something we can't answer, but the corporation is a prime supplier nationwide to law enforcement agencies.

One of the more recent ITT introductions is what is called the F7201A day/night weapon sight system. According to spokesperson Sandra Coan, this is "the first modular rifle scope for the law enforcement market that features interchangeable night vision and daytime eyepieces. Day or night, special operations personnel now can use one weapon with one scope for virtually any situation. Shooters merely interchange the eyepieces as circumstances require."

When the marksman is operating in darkness, the F7201A features

Generation 3 (G3) night vision, which ITT Night Vision calls "the highest level night vision technology available today." Incidentally, ITT has produced more than 70 percent of the G3 night vision goggles delivered to the Department of Defense.

The F7201A sight is a lightweight, precision-made, high-quality unit that offers police and SWAT shooters variable power of 2.5x to 10x. This is aided by means of a large 57mm focusable objective and detachable glare hood. This wide range of magnification is designed to provide shooters with optimal power at various ranges. From our point of view, it also should offer quick, reliable acquisition of

the target and positive identification, day or night.

In checking out one of the units mounted on a Remington Model 700 sniper rifle, Jack Lewis found that "zero of the weapon can be set with a pair of heavy-duty turret knobs that I found easy to manipulate for windage and elevation. The knobs are large enough that they'll be easy to use in any type of weather."

Not unlike many standard rifle scopes, the pair of turret knobs offer precise adjustment with distinct MOA (minute of angle) increments that can be heard and felt when turned.

We did not have an opportunity to check out the unit at either dusk or dawn, but Sandra Coan explained

In 1996, Aimpoint, a firm devoted previously to sporting sights, entered the military field with what they called their Reflex Collimator Sight or Comp/M. This was an electronic red dot unit that passed numerous torture tests.

There are various means of mounting the Aimpoint Comp/M on the M16 rifle series or the M4 Carbine. If mounted on the barrel ahead of the standard sights, it interferes with the latter. The carrying handle can be removed and the sight mounted on an added rail.

that the F7201A has specially coated optics that perform "exceptionally well with the daytime eyepiece during these times. There is no sacrifice of daytime performance compared to existing day scopes. The interchangeable daytime eyepiece provides plus-two to minus-two diopters of focus adjustment."

The F7201A's night vision module features a high-performance G3 image intensifier, with a manually adjustable gain of up to 50,000! Thus, the individual shooter is able to adjust the brightness level by means of a control knob mounted on the module. The unit also incorporates an integrated covert infrared illuminator. This is for additional illumination under conditions of extreme darkness.

The F7201A is powered by common AA alkaline batteries and it

can be mounted on the rifle by means of standard 30mm scope rings, which will handle the diameter of the 56mm objective.

Still another entry in the Antidarkness Sweepstakes is the AN/PAS-13 Thermal Weapon Sight, more commonly known as the TWS. This is an advanced infrared weapon sight developed jointly by the U.S. Army and Raytheon Systems, the latter headquartered in El Segundo, California.

This particular device is light enough that it can be used on rifles and other small arms. This versatile sight has shown that it can be utilized for surveillance and also for putting shoulder-launched missiles on target. The AN/PAS-13 currently is replacing earlier image-intensifying night sights that have been mounted on

small arms. Unlike the earlier models, the AN/PAS-13 not only can be used to see in total darkness, but it also is designed to function during adverse weather and under battlefield conditions that include smoke and heavy dust.

Engineers at Raytheon Systems describe their AN/PAS-13 as a second generation, forward-looking infrared sensor, acronymed to FLIR, as we might expect! This unit features both RS-170 and digital video output, making it compatible with the Army's current vision of the "digital battlefield." The sight was selected as the one to be used in the Army's current Land Warrior program, which is designed to lead our national defense system into the 21st century.

An improvement to the system called for by the Army adds a modular

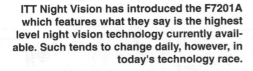
ITT Night Vision has introduced the F7201A which features what they say is the highest level night vision technology currently available. Such tends to change daily, however, in today's technology race.

The AN/PAS-13 thermal weapons sight developed by Hughes Aircraft, but now in the hands of Raytheon Systems, is an advance infrared weapon sight developed in cooperation with the U.S. Army. The Army has been using the sight in its Land Warrior evaluation program.

detachable laser rangefinder for disturbed reticle fire control, plus a high-magnification telescope for applications requiring performances at ranges greater than three kilometers.

The AN/PAS-13 package developed by Raytheon includes, we learned, interchangeable telescopes for quick adaptation to any mission. Their small size, coupled with high magnification, results in the shooter's hit probability being greater than that of image intensifiers or even other thermal images, according to the maker's claims.

Success of the AN/PAS-13 would appear to be based upon the fact that advanced technologies are employed to provide a rugged but portable infrared sensor that offers high performance at low cost. Involved in the design is high-sensitivity mercury cadmium telluride focal plane array technology. That mouthful means that the unit affords long-range target acquisition with a small telescope. The unit also employs binary optical elements with advance plastic housings for lower weight and higher transmission.

The AN/PAS-13 design also utilizes VLSI electronics for small size and low power, as well a thumbnail-size thermoelectric cooler for silent operation and high reliability. In field use, the brightness is adjustable and an eyecup-activated switching system puts the instrument in the standby mode for maximum battery life.

The reticles are electronically programmable for adaptation to a wide range of weapons, including the M-16 rifle family, the M-4A1 Carbine, the M-249 assault weapon,

the M-60 machine gun and the Mark 19 40mm machine gun. Perhaps most important of all is the fact that the device has completely modular architecture with only one moving part, which simplifies maintenance.

The AN/PAS-13 comes in three versions. The Basic System has no telescope and weighs 3.8 pounds with battery. The Medium System, which has a range of 1100 meters against personnel targets, weighs 4.5 pounds with battery. The Heavy System is designed for use against vehicular and storage unit targets at up to 2200 meters; this one weighs 5.0 pounds with battery. At the ranges listed, Raytheon claims 70 percent target recognition through clear air. Equipped with the standard BA-5847

Army battery, life exceeds 10 hours of typical mission use.

Every infantryman's dream is a rifle that shoots around corners. There are such weapons, including one used by the German army in World War II, but they have proved to be of only limited military value.

However, a gent named Matthew Hagerty of LandTec, Inc. (P.O. Box 5456, Sonora, California 95370), has come up with a device called the Sight Unseen SU-4 that performs a similar chore. The unit is available to military and law enforcement agencies only, as might be expected.

Hagerty, a shooter with more than 30 years experience, describes the SU-4 as "a remote infrared video sighting system" that is operable day or night;

This is the type of image that is produced for the W1000 user, when the unit is mounted on his weapon. One also is able to follow movement of the subjects with the Raytheon product.

the infrared beam undetectable to the naked eye. Over the past three years, Hagerty has fired more than 230,000 rounds in testing and demonstrating this device.

The entire unit, including its battery, weighs only 3.75 pounds. That may seem considerable weight to mount on a rifle barrel, but it doesn't work that way. The video camera, with included scope rings, is roughly the size of a 3-9x rifle scope and weighs only seven ounces. The lens offers 1x magnification, with a 30-degree aperture. The battery, weighing 32 ounces, is contained in a padded pouch that hangs on the furnished belt. This belt and the pouch weigh 7.5 ounces.

There is a headset that weighs a paltry 8.75 ounces and hangs the video screen in front of one eye, transmitting—with superimposed crosshairs—what is seen through the miniaturized camera mounted on the rifle. The uncovered eye allows normal vision.

Aiming is a bit different from the normal practice of drawing a fine bead on a target. One points the weapon at the target, but what is seen by the camera is viewed by the screen positioned in front of one eye. Admittedly, this technique takes a bit of time to be used effectively, but the big plus is that the only part of the shooter's body that need be exposed is the hand holding the weapon.

The crosshairs are adjustable so that the rig can be pre-zeroed for whatever mission is ahead. The unit also can be mounted on a handgun, which makes it even less conspicuous when edged around the corner of a building or out a closet door to determine target availability and the danger factor involved.

Matt Hagerty is the exclusive sales source for the unit, but the inventor is a gent named Larry Elliott, who was in the recording industry in New York City for a number of years.

As someone once said, "When you've listened to enough acid rock, almost anything is better." Elliott seemingly had this thought in mind when he transplanted to Southern California and looked into the possibilities of a self-defense system that would allow people to remain under virtually full cover while firing their weapon.

Elliott also is an avid shooter of some 25 years experience and a veteran of more than three decades' work with electronics. Realizing his own shortcomings in some fields, he hired several experts to help solve specific problems during early development. With the aid of one John

The Raytheon W1000 Nightsight can be mounted on a variety of today's weapons, including the M16 rifle series. The thermal imaging is reported to cut through smoke, dust, fog, haze and other battlefield obscurants. It has only one moving part.

With the rifle held around a corner, the rectangular television camera picks up the image of what - or who - lies in wait. The image appears on the tiny TV screen that covers one eye, offering warning of what to expect.

Davies, who financed some of the work, Elliott came up with a working system in 1995, and applied for patents. At this writing, the patents are still pending.

A number of veteran law enforcement officers and other experts have had an opportunity to try out the SU-4 and t a man express amazement at the advantage it offers over an armed foe. The possibility, incidentally, that haunts inventor Larry Elliott is the chance of the unit falling into the hands of the lawless. That is the chief reason he offers it

for sale only to law enforcement and the military.

Harry Lu is one of those who has had an opportunity to work with the SU-4. His declaration is that "this will change the entire technique of dynamic entry"—another of those politically correct terms that translates to: forced entry by armed officers.

A gunsmith and shooter for more than two decades, Harry Lu is a weapons specialist with the Stembridge Gun Room, a Hollywood area enterprise that has furnished the bulk of the armament used by actors

in action films such as the "Terminator" series, "Air Force One," and scores of others over the years.

Lu got his first hands-on look at the SU-4 early in 1997, when it was being demonstrated at the shooting range of the Los Angeles County Sheriff's Department. The video sight was mounted on an AR-15 rifle, and Lu had the opportunity to fire about 50 rounds. Using the television monitor that covered one eye, he zeroed in on a group of bowling pins that were set at about 25 yards downrange.

This manufacturer's photo offers some idea as to the size and complexity of the W1000 Nightsight. In foreground are the inner workings of the unit, while the protective, weather resistant black housing serves as a background.

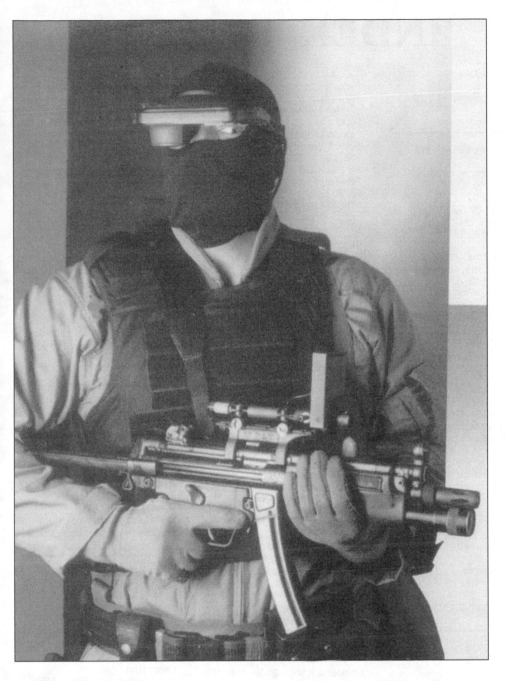

The Sight Unseen SU-4 is a remote video sighting system that allows the user to look around corners or over the top of a fighting hole while exposing nothing more than his hand. A tiny television screen covers one eye, showing what is out there. The camera is mounted on the weapon.

Malcolm Street, who writes an outdoor column for a Colorado newspaper, also has had an opportunity to test the SU-4. "When I first saw it, I thought it was a joke," he recalls. "With the camera mounted on a 9mm Beretta handgun and the headset's miniature TV covering one eye of the demonstrator, I thought it was some kind of a futuristic weapon that would be unveiled in some science fiction movie."

Once in his hands and with a bit of instruction from Matt Hagerty, Street soon found himself aiming the SU-4 with ease. Before he became an outdoor writer and started to write about shooting ducks, Street did a long stint as a police reporter, where he wrote about people being shot. That experience undoubtedly colored some of his thinking.

"I think some things still can be done to improve the SU-4," he opined. "All of the wires connecting the various parts tended to disturb me, but with the development of the digital sciences, there's no reason that approach could not be used and get rid of the wire." Like the inventor, he also worries about the possibility of the units finding their way into the hands of the lawless elements around the world.

As we understand it, the Department of Defense already has been taking a long look at the SU-4, although no large orders have been issued at this writing. It is known that a team of weapons experts in Crane, Indiana, have been testing and evaluating two of the SU-4 units. This is the site of the research and engineering facility of the Navy's Special Warfare Command. There the government folks are considering the SU-4 for use on the modified 5.56mm M-4A1 Carbine now being issued to selected personnel of Special Operations Forces.

One probably would not consider the Department of Energy as a federal entity that would need the SU-4, but like other agencies, they have a security division and the Sight Unseen is now in the hands of department tactical units.

The world of armament is on a fast track that seems to get faster with each passing year. Some of the items that have been discussed in this chapter probably will be considered obsolete by the time readers have this book in hand. In fact, we guarantee it! •

To make things difficult and add "some zest to the test," he assumed a crouch and laid the rifle across his knees, shooting from what he termed a "perpendicular position." It was nearly dark on the range, but Harry Lu hit a bowling pin with each pull of the trigger.

The movie gun expert then was led into a darkened room. He reported later that through the television monitor in front of his eye he saw some cardboard boxes stacked against the far wall. In total darkness, he was able to read the printing on them. This night sight capability is created by the 4.75-ounce infrared unit that is built into the Sight Unseen SU-4.

Other elements not mentioned previously are the lightweight housing fashioned from 7075 T6 aircraft alloy and an electronics module that scales at 8.75 ounces.

INDEX

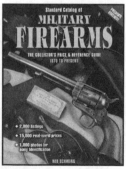
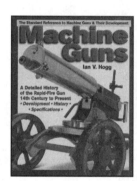

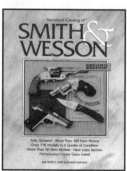
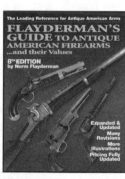

BARRON'S

AP*

ENVIRONMENTAL SCIENCE

5TH EDITION

Gary S. Thorpe, M.S.
AP Environmental Science Teacher (ret.)
Beverly Hills High School
Beverly Hills, CA

BARRON'S

Acknowledgments

I would like to thank my wife, Patti, and my two daughters, Kris and Erin, for their patience and understanding while I was writing this book. This book is dedicated in tribute to the late Dr. Jerry Bobrow of Bobrow Test Preparation Services, who was not only my publishing agent but a dear friend for many years. A special thanks also goes to the many professional and dedicated high school APES teachers across the United States who contributed their finest work in making this book possible.

All inquiries should be addressed to:
Barron's Educational Series, Inc.
250 Wireless Boulevard
Hauppauge, New York 11788
www.barronseduc.com

ISBN: 978-1-4380-0132-6 (book only)
ISBN: 978-1-4380-7260-9 (book and CD-ROM package)
ISSN: 2157-3824 (book only)
ISSN: 2157-3832 (book and CD-ROM package)

Printed in the United States of America

9 8 7 6 5

10%
POST-CONSUMER WASTE
Paper contains a minimum of 10% post-consumer waste (PCW). Paper used in this book was derived from certified, sustainable forestlands.

Contents

As you review the content in this book and work toward earning that **5** on your AP ENVIRONMENTAL SCIENCE exam, here are five things that you **MUST** do:

1 **Practice writing your own answers to the Free-Response Questions (FRQs).** After you review each FRQ, close this book and write your own response to the question. Then, compare your answer to the one in the book. The more you practice writing *your own* essays, the higher your score will be on the actual APES exam.

2 **Be sure to review the Case Studies presented in this book.** You will find several questions on the exam that focus on specific events that have occurred throughout history and involve environmental science principles and issues. When possible, reference these Case Studies in your responses to the FRQs.

3 **Thoroughly review Chapters 9 (Pollution) and 10 (Impacts on the Environment and Human Health).** About 25–30% of the multiple-choice questions on the APES exam will test your knowledge of the topics in these chapters. In particular,

- Be familiar with the differences between industrial and photochemical smog.
- Know the causes and effects of acid deposition.
- Know the causes and effects of global warming.
- Familiarize yourself with remediation and reduction strategies for environmental pollution.

4 **Become comfortable with doing the types of math problems found in this book, especially those involving energy calculations.** These problems are found in Chapter 8 and in both practice exams. Historically, question 1 of the FRQ section of the APES exam requires you to complete mathematical calculations.

5 **Review the relevant acts, laws, and treaties detailed in each chapter.** You will find several questions on the APES exam that test your knowledge on them; you can also reference them in your answers to the FRQs when appropriate.

What's New in the 5th Edition?

This 5th edition includes many new and important features: (1) a diagnostic test that consists of 100 brand new multiple-choice questions with all answers explained. At the end of the diagnostic test, a predictive rubric developed by the College Board will allow you to predict your final score on the APES exam; (2) all chapters have been fully updated to reflect recent changes in environmental laws; (3) case studies have been updated to reflect events that have recently occurred; e.g., 2011 earthquake and tsunami that hit Japan and the severe tornadoes that occurred in the United States in 2011–2012; (4) new charts have been re-formatted for students to make reviewing for the APES exam easier; (5) "Quick Review Checklists," which list the most important topics covered in each chapter, have been added. You can use the checklists to mark your progress in reviewing each topic; (6) a new "Vocabulary Review" for each chapter provides you with a handy list of the most important vocabulary words <u>and definitions</u> that you can review just before the exam, and finally (7) the 5th edition is available as a book/CD set that contains two *additional* APES exams with fully explained answers. Combine this 5th edition book and CD with Barron's AP Environmental Science Flash Cards, and you'll have everything you need to fully prepare yourself for the APES exam. No other APES review on the market today comes close to all that is included in this book.

Introductory Material

The introductory material contains information on the AP exam itself. It includes commonly asked questions, strategies for taking the exam, and techniques for writing outstanding essays.

Specific Topics

The majority of this book is divided into seven units. Each contains specific chapters on material covered on the APES exam. Each chapter provides a condensed review of key information, updated case studies, relevant and updated environmental laws, a topic-specific vocabulary list including definitions, multiple-choice questions, and free-response essay questions similar to the questions found on actual APES exams. Many of the free-response questions and explanations have been contributed by award-winning APES teachers from across the United States.

Practice Exams

The last part of this book contains two complete practice APES exams. All questions are thoroughly explained and the free-response questions provide a rubric for scoring your answers along with tips on how to score even higher.

If you have purchased a book that contains the CD-ROM, the software contains two additional practice tests and answers so you can practice taking the test under timed conditions and receive immediate scoring.

Format of the APES Exam

The APES exam is three hours long and is divided equally in time between a multiple-choice section and a free-response section. The multiple-choice section, which makes up 60% of the final score and lasts 90 minutes, consists of 100 multiple-choice questions and is designed to cover your knowledge and understanding of environmental science. Thought-provoking problems and questions based on fundamental ideas are included along with questions based on the recall of basic facts and major concepts. The number of multiple-choice questions taken from each major topic area is reflected in the percentages shown in "Topics Covered on the Exam" later in this section. For example, in Earth Systems and Resources, you will see "(10–15%)." Expect to find 10 to 15 multiple-choice questions from this area on the actual APES exam. Therefore, spend about 10–15% of your time reviewing this area.

The free-response section, which is also 90 minutes long, makes up 40% of your final score. It contains one data set question, one document-based question, and two synthesis and evaluation questions. The differences between these types of free-response questions will be explained later in this introductory section. You must organize your answers to demonstrate reasoning and analytical skills, as well as the ability to write clearly and concisely.

Test-Taking Strategies

The Educational Testing Service will send you your AP Environmental Science score in July. Depending upon your choice, the scores may also be sent to colleges and universities. The scores are reported on the following scale:

- 5—Extremely well qualified
- 4—Well qualified
- 3—Qualified
- 2—Possibly qualified
- 1—No recommendation

Most colleges and universities accept a score of 4 or 5 for credit and placement, while some may accept a score of 3. Scores of 1 or 2 are not accepted by colleges and universities for either credit or placement.

The rule of thumb in determining how well you will probably do on the AP Environmental Science Exam is to look at the number of multiple-choice questions you answer correctly on the practice exams in this book. If you consistently get between 50 and 60% correct, you should be able to score a minimum of a 3. If you score consistently between 65 and 75% of the multiple-choice questions correct, you should be able to achieve a 4, and if you score 80 to 100% correctly, you should be looking at a 5. This assumes, of course, that you adequately answer the questions in the free-response section.

The Multiple-Choice Questions

- Because there is no scoring penalty for guessing, it is to your advantage to answer as many multiple-choice questions as possible.
- When you reach a question that you are not quite sure of and need more time, place a "+" next to the number.
- When you reach a question that you cannot answer, place a "−" next to the number.
- After you have answered all of the questions you know for sure, go back to only your "+" questions. Remember, as there is no scoring penalty for guessing, eliminate any obvious incorrect answers and then guess.
- If time remains, scan through the "−" questions. Again, there is no scoring penalty for guessing, so eliminate any obvious incorrect answers and then guess.

TYPES OF MULTIPLE-CHOICE QUESTIONS

The AP Environmental Science Exam relies on a variety of multiple-choice questions including identification and analysis. Those kinds of questions can be further identified as generalizations, comparing and contrasting concepts and events, sequencing a series of related ideas or events, cause-and-effect relationships,

TIP

Always read the entire question. Underline key words in the question such as:

• *all of the following EXCEPT*
• *which of the following*
• *increases*
• *decreases*
• *are commonly used*
• *is responsible*
• *most accurately compares*
• *best describes*
• *is correct*
• *results*
• *reflects*
• *is most likely*
• *least likely*
• *which best DEFINES*

definitions, solutions to a problem, hypothetical situations, chronological problems, multiple correct answers, and negative questions. More than 75% of the multiple-choice questions fit into these categories.

In addition to identification and analysis questions, there are stimulus-based questions that rely on your interpretation and understanding of maps, graphs, charts, tables, pictures, flowcharts, photographs or sketches, cartoons, short narrative passages, surveys and poll data, quotations that come from primary source documents, and passages from environmental legislation and statutes, as well as questions that relate directly to laboratory and field investigations.

Identification and Analysis Questions

Question Type	Example
Definitional	Any factor that influences a natural process under study is a(n) (A) independent variable (B) dependent variable (C) control (D) placebo (E) experimental value
Cause-and-effect relationships	_____ contributes to the formation of _____ and thereby compounds the problem of _____ . (A) ozone, carbon dioxide, acid rain (B) carbon dioxide, carbon monoxide, ozone depletion (C) sulfur dioxide, acid deposition, global warming (D) nitrous oxide, ozone, industrial smog (E) nitric oxide, ozone, photochemical smog
Sequencing a series of related ideas or events	Which of the answers below correctly describes the order in which environmental legislation would pass through Congress? I. Reports the bill out of the appropriate committee II. Debates the bill on the floor of the respective houses III. Rejects or accepts amendments to the bill IV. Resolves any differences in a conference committee (A) I, II, III, IV (B) I, III, IV, II (C) II, IV, I, III (D) III, I, II, IV (E) IV, III, II, I

Question Type	Example

Generalization

What is generally considered to be the most significant factor in terms of being a causative agent for cancer?

(A) Smoking
(B) Diet
(C) Stress
(D) Heredity
(E) Pollution

Solution to a problem

A field biologist had been keeping density counts of the number of coastal side-blotched lizards (*Uta stansburiana hesperis* Richardson) that had recently been introduced into a large section of California desert. The yearly counts per acre were: 1998: 4; 1999: 8; 2000: 16. Assuming that the carrying capacity had not been reached, which of the following would be true?

(A) In 2001, there should be 20 lizards due to arithmetic growth.
(B) In 2001, there should be 20 lizards due to exponential growth.
(C) In 2001, there should be 32 lizards due to exponential growth.
(D) In 2001, there should be around 16 lizards due to population stability.
(E) It is impossible to predict how many lizards there would be in 2001.

Hypothetical situation

Converting to a solar-hydrogen energy source could theoretically be achieved by

(A) attracting private investors.
(B) passing legislation that would fund "seed money" for entrepreneurs.
(C) passing legislation that would discontinue government subsidies of fossil fuels.
(D) educating the public as to the environmental benefits of solar-hydrogen fuel sources.
(E) all of the above.

Question Type	Example
Chronological problem	The following events are related to major case studies of environmental pollution. Place the events in chronological order.

I. Bhopal, India
II. *Exxon Valdez*
III. Donora, Pennsylvania
IV. Three Mile Island
V. Chernobyl, Ukraine

(A) I, II, III, IV, V
(B) V, IV, III, II, I
(C) I, III, V, II, IV
(D) I, V, II, IV, III
(E) III, IV, V, I, II

| **Comparing and contrasting concepts and events** | Which of the following acts or treaties accurately compares the political, environmental, and economic goals of the participating nations to the goal of reducing global greenhouse gas emissions? |

(A) Clean Air Act of 1955
(B) National Environmental Policy Act (NEPA) 1969
(C) Comprehensive Environmental Response, Compensation, and Liability (Superfund) Act (CERCLA) 1980
(D) Pollution Prevention Act of 1990
(E) Kyoto Protocol of 1997

| **Multiple correct answers** | Nitrogen is assimilated in plants in what form? |

(A) NO_2^-
(B) NH_3
(C) NH_4^+
(D) NO_3^-
(E) Choices B, C, and D

| **Negative questions** | An effective method to decrease the amount of pesticide use would include all of the following EXCEPT |

(A) using monoculture techniques
(B) rotating crops
(C) using pheromones
(D) using polyculture techniques
(E) using insect-resistant crops

Stimulus-Based Multiple-Choice Questions

Question Type	Example

Short narrative passage

"Human beings are adaptable. They have survived and conquered when other species have become extinct. Granted, that we as humans have a long way to go in order to live in harmony with nature, nevertheless, the future looks bright for man to conquer all environmental problems. There is no limit to what problems humans can solve. If we all work together, we can solve any problem. The future is bright."

The quote above would be most closely associated with

(A) Malthusian principles.
(B) neo-Luddites.
(C) cornucopian fallacy.
(D) nihilists.
(E) utilitarianism.

Short quotation

As the troposphere warms, the stratosphere begins to cool and causes the formation of ice-clouds above the South Pole. The ice-clouds tend to accelerate the decrease of ozone above the South Pole by providing a surface for chemical reactions to occur. This is an example of

(A) serendipity.
(B) a positive feedback loop.
(C) a negative feedback loop.
(D) synergy.
(E) chaos.

Environmental case law

Which act established the first clear water purity standards?

(A) Water Resources Planning Act
(B) Water Resources Development Act
(C) Safe Drinking Water Act
(D) Surface Water Treatment Rule
(E) Water Quality Act

Sketch or diagram

The following diagram indicates

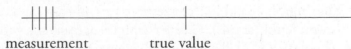

measurement   true value

(A) a measurement that is accurate and precise.
(B) a measurement that is accurate but not precise.
(C) a measurement that is precise but not accurate.
(D) a measurement that is neither accurate nor precise.
(E) a conclusion cannot be made regarding this distribution.

The Elimination Strategy

Take advantage of being able to mark in your test booklet. As you go through the "+" questions, eliminate choices from consideration by marking them out in your question booklet. Mark with question marks any choices you wish to consider as possible answers. See the following example:

A.
B. ?
C.
D.
E. ?

This technique will help you avoid reconsidering those choices that you have already eliminated and will thus save you time. It will also help you narrow down your possible answers. Remember, there is no penalty for guessing, so use this strategy to eliminate obvious incorrect choices!

Question Type	Example
Graph or table interpretation	Two varieties of the same species of voles (meadow mice), albino and red-backed, were used in an experiment. Both varieties were subjected to the predation of a hawk, under controlled laboratory conditions. During the experiment, the floor of the test room was covered on alternate days with white ground cover that matched the albino voles and red-brown cover that matched the red-backed voles. The results of fifty trials are shown in the following tabulation.

NUMBER OF VOLES CAPTURED

Variety	White Cover	Red-Brown Cover	Total
Albino	35	57	92
Red-backed	60	40	100
Total	95	97	192

Which result would have been most likely if only red-brown floor covering had been used?

(A) Ninety-seven red-backed voles would have survived.
(B) Ninety-five albino voles would have survived.
(C) The survival rate of the albino voles would have decreased markedly.
(D) A greater number of red-backed voles would not have survived.
(E) There would have been no change in the results.

A FINAL WORD ABOUT THE MULTIPLE-CHOICE QUESTIONS

Throughout the APES course, your teacher will be giving you a variety of sample multiple-choice questions with five possible answers. Other methods include:

- **Building:** Build up your own database of questions by using questions from this book and accompanying CD.
- **Using:** Use *Barron's AP Environmental Science Flash Cards*, available from your local bookstore.
- **Sharing:** Share and collect questions that other students come up with (the Internet is wonderful for this). Create reciprocal agreements with APES classes from other schools (e.g., "We'll give you 300 of our questions if you give us 300 of yours").
- **Creating:** Create a class database where everyone contributes ten questions per chapter in all question formats. Or make your own class APES web site—post questions, answers with explanations, class projects, photos, and so on.
- **Obtaining:** Obtain past questions from the Educational Testing Service—the people who create the APES exam. Yes, past questions are available!

- **Searching:** Search the Internet for web sites or social networking pages from other APES classes (I counted over sixty when I recently searched). Many of these web sites have practice questions posted.
- **Visiting:** Visit the web sites of publishers of environmental science textbooks. Often you will find many practice questions available for free on their sites.
- **Debriefing:** Right after you finish the AP exam, come immediately back to your APES teacher and let him or her know the type of questions that you found easy and the ones that you found more difficult. This will help your teacher to prepare for next year. After a few years of student feedback, your teacher will have a pretty good idea of what to expect.

The Free-Response Questions

There are three types of free-response questions: (1) data analysis, (2) document based, and (3) synthesis and evaluation.

The data analysis (or data set) question presents data in tabular or graphical form and measures your ability to interpret and analyze data. The document-based question (DBQ) presents material in the form of real-life documents (newspaper clippings, product advertisements, etc.). The synthesis and evaluation questions are in-depth essay questions, often with multiple parts.

In scoring the free-response essays, points are awarded only for arguments that are supported by scientific facts and principles. Each question is scored on a scale from 1 to 10, with 10 being the highest.

All four essay questions must be answered within 90 minutes. If you spend an equal amount of time on each essay, this averages to about 23 minutes per essay. Lists, outlines, and unlabeled drawings are not acceptable and will not be awarded credit.

THESIS STATEMENT

The thesis statement is a sentence or two toward the beginning of your response that tells the AP graders what your answer is going to be about. A thesis statement:

- tells the grader <u>how you will interpret</u> the significance of the subject matter under discussion;
- tells the grader <u>what to expect</u> from your response;
- and <u>presents your argument</u> to the grader. The rest of your response provides the evidence to support your thesis statement.

Examples of APES thesis statements:

1. Many of the problems faced by less-developed countries, such as poverty, hunger, and environmental destruction, are the consequences of excessive population growth.

2. Family structure and the status of women in society are the prime determinants of fertility and population growth.

3. Governmental run "food aid" programs often funnel tax dollars to large, worldwide corporate agribusinesses while increasing the influence of foreign food aid organizations; often at the expense of small, local food growers.

TIP

The best way to earn the highest score possible on the AP Exam is to look at other students' essays from past APES exams and see how their essays were graded by the College Board readers. Your teacher has access to these past exams at *www.apcentral. collegeboard.com.* This is the best kept secret there is for getting a 5.

The free-response questions often include phrases that should guide how you write your essays. The following table lists many of these key terms and what they actually mean.

Key Phrases

Key Term	Meaning	Example
Analyze the effect . . .	Evaluate the impact	<u>Analyze the effects</u> of major global wind patterns in determining the distribution of biomes.
Assess the accuracy . . .	Determine the truth	<u>Assess the accuracy</u> of the following statement, "A high birth rate corresponds to a high standard of living."
Compare the strengths and weaknesses . . .	Show differences	<u>Compare the strengths and weaknesses</u> of three government intervention programs to combat pollution.
Critically evaluate . . .	Give examples that agree and/or disagree	<u>Critically evaluate</u> evidence that both supports and refutes the claim that greenhouse gases are responsible for the hole in the ozone layer.
Define and evaluate . . .	Give a definition and analyze the point of view	<u>Define</u> ecofeminism <u>and evaluate</u> the contention that male-dominated societies are responsible for environmental imbalance and social oppression.
Discuss . . .	Give examples that illustrate	<u>Discuss</u> the rapid increase of African "killer bees" in the United States as an example of the process of natural selection.
Evaluate . . .	Determine the validity	<u>Evaluate</u> the claim that increasing the standard of living and improving the role of women will result in a lower birthrate.
Explain . . .	Offer the meaning, cause, effect, and influence	<u>Explain</u> three different theories of moral responsibility to the environment. Include in your discussion the major proponents of each theory and their specific ideas(s) or "school."
To what extent . . .	Explain the relationship and role	<u>To what extent</u> does moisture determine a soil profile? Provide specific soil types, overview of soil horizons, and geographic distribution.

Topics Covered on the Exam*

I. Earth Systems and Resources (10–15%)

A. **Earth Science Concepts**—Geologic time scale, plate tectonics, earthquakes, volcanism, seasons, solar intensity and latitude.

B. **The Atmosphere**—Composition, structure, weather, climate, atmospheric circulation and the Coriolis effect, atmosphere-ocean interactions, and ENSO.

C. **Global Water Resources and Use**—Freshwater, saltwater, ocean circulation, agriculture, industrial and domestic use, surface and groundwater issues, global problems, and conservation.

D. **Soil and Soil Dynamics**—Rock cycle, formation, composition, physical and chemical properties, main soil types, erosion and other soil problems, and soil conservation.

II. The Living World (10–15%)

A. **Ecosystem Structure**—Biological populations and communities, ecological niches, interactions among species, keystone species, species diversity, and edge effects, and major terrestrial and aquatic biomes.

B. **Energy Flow**—Photosynthesis and cellular respiration, food webs, and trophic levels, and ecological pyramids.

C. **Ecosystem Diversity**—Biodiversity, natural selection, evolution, and ecosystem services.

D. **Natural Ecosystem Change**—Climate shifts, species movement, and ecological succession.

E. **Natural Biogeochemical Cycles**—Carbon, nitrogen, phosphorus, sulfur, water, and conservation of matter.

III. Population (10–15%)

A. **Population Biology Concepts**—Population ecology, carrying capacity, reproductive strategies, and survivorship.

B. **Human Population**

1. Human population dynamics—Historical population sizes, distribution, fertility rates, growth rates and doubling times, demographic transition, and age-structure diagrams.

2. Population size—Strategies for sustainability, case studies, and national policies.

3. Impacts of population growth—Hunger, disease, economic effects, resource use, and habitat destruction.

---

*Advanced Placement Program Description—Environmental Science, 2010, AP College Board.

IV. Land and Water Use (10–15%)

A. Agriculture

1. Feeding a growing population—Human nutritional requirements, types of agriculture, green revolution, genetic engineering and crop production, deforestation, irrigation, and sustainable agriculture.
2. Controlling pests—Types of pesticides, costs and benefits of pesticide use, integrated pest management, and relevant laws.

B. Forestry—Tree plantations, old-growth forests, forest fires, forest management, and national forests.

C. Rangelands—Overgrazing, deforestation, desertification, rangeland management, and federal rangelands.

D. Other Land Use

1. Urban land development—Planned development, suburban sprawl, and urbanization.
2. Transportation infrastructure—Federal highway system, canals and channels, roadless areas, and ecosystem impacts.
3. Public and federal lands—Management, wilderness areas, national parks, wildlife refuges, forests, and wetlands.
4. Land conservation options—Preservation, remediation, mitigation, and restoration.
5. Sustainable land use strategies.

E. Mining—Mineral formation, extraction, global reserves, and relevant laws and treaties.

F. Fishing—Fishing techniques, overfishing, aquaculture, and relevant laws and treaties.

G. Global Economics—Globalization, World Bank, *Tragedy of the Commons*, and relevant laws and treaties.

V. Energy Resources and Consumption (10–15%)

A. Energy Concepts—Energy forms, power, units, conversions, and laws of thermodynamics.

B. Energy Consumption

1. History—Industrial Revolution, exponential growth, and energy crisis.
2. Present global energy use.
3. Future energy needs.

C. Fossil Fuel Resources and Use—Formation of coal, oil, and natural gas; extraction/purification methods; world reserves and global demand; synfuels; and environmental advantages/disadvantages of sources.

D. Nuclear Energy—Nuclear fission process, nuclear fuel, electricity production, nuclear reactor types, environmental advantages/disadvantages, safety issues, radiation and human health, radioactive wastes, and nuclear fusion.

E. Hydroelectric Power—Dams, flood control, salmon, silting, and other impacts.

F. **Energy Conservation**—Energy efficiency, CAFE standards, hybrid electric vehicles and mass transit.

G. **Renewable Energy**—Solar energy, solar electricity, hydrogen fuel cells, biomass, wind energy, small-scale hydroelectric, ocean waves and tidal energy, geothermal, and environmental advantages/disadvantages.

VI. Pollution (25–30%)

A. **Pollution Types**

1. Air pollution—Sources (primary and secondary) of major air pollutants, measurement units, smog, acid deposition—causes and effects, heat islands and temperature inversions, indoor air pollution, remediation and reduction strategies, Clean Air Act, and other relevant laws.

2. Noise pollution—Sources, effects, and control measures.

3. Water pollution—Types, sources, causes and effects, cultural eutrophication, groundwater pollution, maintaining water quality, water purification, sewage treatment/septic systems, Clean Water Act, and other relevant laws.

4. Solid waste—Types, disposal, and reduction.

B. **Impacts on the Environment and Human Health**

1. Hazards to human health—Environmental risk analysis, acute and chronic effects, dose-response relationships, air pollutants, smoking, and other risks.

2. Hazardous chemicals in the environment—Types of hazardous waste, treatment/disposal of hazardous waste, cleanup of contaminated sites, biomagnification, and relevant laws.

C. **Economic Impacts**—Cost-benefit analysis, externalities, marginal costs, and sustainability.

VII. Global Change (10–15%)

A. **Stratospheric ozone**—Formation of stratospheric ozone, ultraviolet radiation, causes of ozone depletion, effects of ozone depletion, strategies for reducing ozone depletion, and relevant laws and treaties.

B. **Global Warming**—Greenhouse gases and the greenhouse effect, impacts and consequences of global warming, reducing climate change, and relevant laws and treaties.

C. **Loss of Biodiversity**

1. Habitat loss—Overuse, pollution, introduced species, and endangered and extinct species.

2. Maintenance through conservation.

3. Relevant laws and treaties.

Questions Commonly Asked About the APES Exam

Q: What's the best way to prepare for the APES exam?

A: Don't wait until the last few weeks in April or May to start "cramming," as that seldom works. Instead, highly successful students use *Barron's AP Environmental Science* starting from the very first day of their high school AP Environmental Science class. They use this book *along with* their textbook and class lectures, covering each topic concurrently with their course schedule. This steady, slower-paced approach, which allows you to cover more information in greater depth, has proven highly successful.

Q: How are the multiple-choice questions graded?

A: Section I, worth 60% of the total score, is 90 minutes long and consists of 100 multiple-choice questions. The total score for Section I is the number of correct answers. If you leave a question unanswered, it does not count at all. You will need to answer around 50% of the multiple-choice questions correctly to obtain a 3 on the exam. The multiple-choice questions are based on recall of basic facts and major concepts of environmental science.

Q: How are the essay or free-response questions graded?

A: Your essays are read several times by both college and high school faculty who have taught environmental science for many years. These readers use a set of written guidelines or standards known as a rubric to come to a consensus on the overall score for each essay that you write.

Q: Will I find questions about labs?

A: Although the College Board does not specify the number or type of labs that must be completed in an APES course, there are several questions on the exam that will draw upon your lab experiences and your ability to analyze experimental data and make valid conclusions.

Q: What do the scores mean?

A: The APES exam is graded on a 5-point scale:

5: Passing. ~9% earn this score.
4: Passing. ~25% earn this score.
3: Passing. ~15% earn this score.
2: Not passing. ~25% earn this score.
1: Not passing. ~26% earn this score.

In summary, about half pass and half do not.

Q: What materials do I take with me to the exam?

A: Bring your admission ticket, an official photo including signature I.D., your social security number, several sharpened #2 pencils with non-smudging erasers, black or blue erasable pens for the free-response questions, and a watch. Do not bring food or drink, colored pencils, highlighters, rulers, or cell phones. Calculators are NOT allowed.

Q: Should I guess?

A: Yes. There is no penalty for wrong answers in the multiple-choice section, so you should answer all multiple-choice questions. Even if you have no idea of the correct answer, you should try to eliminate any obvious incorrect choices, and then guess!

Q: Can I cancel my scores?

A: Yes. Your request must be received in writing by June 15. You may also request that one or more of your AP grades NOT be sent to colleges.

Q: Can I write on the test booklet?

A: Yes. You will definitely want to make notes or brief outlines on the test booklet to help organize your free-response answers. Several examples of this technique are presented in this book.

Q: How do I get more information?

A: Log on to *http://apcentral.collegeboard.com* or *http://collegeboard.com/apstudents*

Answer Sheet
DIAGNOSTIC TEST

1 Ⓐ Ⓑ Ⓒ Ⓓ Ⓔ	26 Ⓐ Ⓑ Ⓒ Ⓓ Ⓔ	51 Ⓐ Ⓑ Ⓒ Ⓓ Ⓔ	76 Ⓐ Ⓑ Ⓒ Ⓓ Ⓔ
2 Ⓐ Ⓑ Ⓒ Ⓓ Ⓔ	27 Ⓐ Ⓑ Ⓒ Ⓓ Ⓔ	52 Ⓐ Ⓑ Ⓒ Ⓓ Ⓔ	77 Ⓐ Ⓑ Ⓒ Ⓓ Ⓔ
3 Ⓐ Ⓑ Ⓒ Ⓓ Ⓔ	28 Ⓐ Ⓑ Ⓒ Ⓓ Ⓔ	53 Ⓐ Ⓑ Ⓒ Ⓓ Ⓔ	78 Ⓐ Ⓑ Ⓒ Ⓓ Ⓔ
4 Ⓐ Ⓑ Ⓒ Ⓓ Ⓔ	29 Ⓐ Ⓑ Ⓒ Ⓓ Ⓔ	54 Ⓐ Ⓑ Ⓒ Ⓓ Ⓔ	79 Ⓐ Ⓑ Ⓒ Ⓓ Ⓔ
5 Ⓐ Ⓑ Ⓒ Ⓓ Ⓔ	30 Ⓐ Ⓑ Ⓒ Ⓓ Ⓔ	55 Ⓐ Ⓑ Ⓒ Ⓓ Ⓔ	80 Ⓐ Ⓑ Ⓒ Ⓓ Ⓔ
6 Ⓐ Ⓑ Ⓒ Ⓓ Ⓔ	31 Ⓐ Ⓑ Ⓒ Ⓓ Ⓔ	56 Ⓐ Ⓑ Ⓒ Ⓓ Ⓔ	81 Ⓐ Ⓑ Ⓒ Ⓓ Ⓔ
7 Ⓐ Ⓑ Ⓒ Ⓓ Ⓔ	32 Ⓐ Ⓑ Ⓒ Ⓓ Ⓔ	57 Ⓐ Ⓑ Ⓒ Ⓓ Ⓔ	82 Ⓐ Ⓑ Ⓒ Ⓓ Ⓔ
8 Ⓐ Ⓑ Ⓒ Ⓓ Ⓔ	33 Ⓐ Ⓑ Ⓒ Ⓓ Ⓔ	58 Ⓐ Ⓑ Ⓒ Ⓓ Ⓔ	83 Ⓐ Ⓑ Ⓒ Ⓓ Ⓔ
9 Ⓐ Ⓑ Ⓒ Ⓓ Ⓔ	34 Ⓐ Ⓑ Ⓒ Ⓓ Ⓔ	59 Ⓐ Ⓑ Ⓒ Ⓓ Ⓔ	84 Ⓐ Ⓑ Ⓒ Ⓓ Ⓔ
10 Ⓐ Ⓑ Ⓒ Ⓓ Ⓔ	35 Ⓐ Ⓑ Ⓒ Ⓓ Ⓔ	60 Ⓐ Ⓑ Ⓒ Ⓓ Ⓔ	85 Ⓐ Ⓑ Ⓒ Ⓓ Ⓔ
11 Ⓐ Ⓑ Ⓒ Ⓓ Ⓔ	36 Ⓐ Ⓑ Ⓒ Ⓓ Ⓔ	61 Ⓐ Ⓑ Ⓒ Ⓓ Ⓔ	86 Ⓐ Ⓑ Ⓒ Ⓓ Ⓔ
12 Ⓐ Ⓑ Ⓒ Ⓓ Ⓔ	37 Ⓐ Ⓑ Ⓒ Ⓓ Ⓔ	62 Ⓐ Ⓑ Ⓒ Ⓓ Ⓔ	87 Ⓐ Ⓑ Ⓒ Ⓓ Ⓔ
13 Ⓐ Ⓑ Ⓒ Ⓓ Ⓔ	38 Ⓐ Ⓑ Ⓒ Ⓓ Ⓔ	63 Ⓐ Ⓑ Ⓒ Ⓓ Ⓔ	88 Ⓐ Ⓑ Ⓒ Ⓓ Ⓔ
14 Ⓐ Ⓑ Ⓒ Ⓓ Ⓔ	39 Ⓐ Ⓑ Ⓒ Ⓓ Ⓔ	64 Ⓐ Ⓑ Ⓒ Ⓓ Ⓔ	89 Ⓐ Ⓑ Ⓒ Ⓓ Ⓔ
15 Ⓐ Ⓑ Ⓒ Ⓓ Ⓔ	40 Ⓐ Ⓑ Ⓒ Ⓓ Ⓔ	65 Ⓐ Ⓑ Ⓒ Ⓓ Ⓔ	90 Ⓐ Ⓑ Ⓒ Ⓓ Ⓔ
16 Ⓐ Ⓑ Ⓒ Ⓓ Ⓔ	41 Ⓐ Ⓑ Ⓒ Ⓓ Ⓔ	66 Ⓐ Ⓑ Ⓒ Ⓓ Ⓔ	91 Ⓐ Ⓑ Ⓒ Ⓓ Ⓔ
17 Ⓐ Ⓑ Ⓒ Ⓓ Ⓔ	42 Ⓐ Ⓑ Ⓒ Ⓓ Ⓔ	67 Ⓐ Ⓑ Ⓒ Ⓓ Ⓔ	92 Ⓐ Ⓑ Ⓒ Ⓓ Ⓔ
18 Ⓐ Ⓑ Ⓒ Ⓓ Ⓔ	43 Ⓐ Ⓑ Ⓒ Ⓓ Ⓔ	68 Ⓐ Ⓑ Ⓒ Ⓓ Ⓔ	93 Ⓐ Ⓑ Ⓒ Ⓓ Ⓔ
19 Ⓐ Ⓑ Ⓒ Ⓓ Ⓔ	44 Ⓐ Ⓑ Ⓒ Ⓓ Ⓔ	69 Ⓐ Ⓑ Ⓒ Ⓓ Ⓔ	94 Ⓐ Ⓑ Ⓒ Ⓓ Ⓔ
20 Ⓐ Ⓑ Ⓒ Ⓓ Ⓔ	45 Ⓐ Ⓑ Ⓒ Ⓓ Ⓔ	70 Ⓐ Ⓑ Ⓒ Ⓓ Ⓔ	95 Ⓐ Ⓑ Ⓒ Ⓓ Ⓔ
21 Ⓐ Ⓑ Ⓒ Ⓓ Ⓔ	46 Ⓐ Ⓑ Ⓒ Ⓓ Ⓔ	71 Ⓐ Ⓑ Ⓒ Ⓓ Ⓔ	96 Ⓐ Ⓑ Ⓒ Ⓓ Ⓔ
22 Ⓐ Ⓑ Ⓒ Ⓓ Ⓔ	47 Ⓐ Ⓑ Ⓒ Ⓓ Ⓔ	72 Ⓐ Ⓑ Ⓒ Ⓓ Ⓔ	97 Ⓐ Ⓑ Ⓒ Ⓓ Ⓔ
23 Ⓐ Ⓑ Ⓒ Ⓓ Ⓔ	48 Ⓐ Ⓑ Ⓒ Ⓓ Ⓔ	73 Ⓐ Ⓑ Ⓒ Ⓓ Ⓔ	98 Ⓐ Ⓑ Ⓒ Ⓓ Ⓔ
24 Ⓐ Ⓑ Ⓒ Ⓓ Ⓔ	49 Ⓐ Ⓑ Ⓒ Ⓓ Ⓔ	74 Ⓐ Ⓑ Ⓒ Ⓓ Ⓔ	99 Ⓐ Ⓑ Ⓒ Ⓓ Ⓔ
25 Ⓐ Ⓑ Ⓒ Ⓓ Ⓔ	50 Ⓐ Ⓑ Ⓒ Ⓓ Ⓔ	75 Ⓐ Ⓑ Ⓒ Ⓓ Ⓔ	100 Ⓐ Ⓑ Ⓒ Ⓓ Ⓔ

Diagnostic Test

The following diagnostic test will allow you to pinpoint your current strengths and weaknesses as you work toward the AP Environmental Science exam.

If you're just getting underway with your APES course, you may realize that you've already seen some of the topics found on the APES exam in other courses (AP Biology, AP Chemistry, etc.), but for many of you this will be your first exposure to this information.

Questions found on this diagnostic test reflect the actual percentage of questions that you will find for each topic; i.e., 10–15% of the questions on the actual APES exam cover earth science concepts (geology, tectonics, earthquakes, soil dynamics, etc.)—likewise, 10–15% of the questions on this diagnostic also cover these same topics). Furthermore, the questions on this diagnostic test are grouped into categories to make it easy for you and your teacher to identify areas in which you might need extra study. As on the actual APES exam, there is no penalty for guessing on this diagnostic test; however, for this practice diagnostic test *ONLY*, it is suggested that if you are not familiar with the question or answer choices, that you leave it blank. This will give you a clearer picture of where you currently are. Some students take this same diagnostic test again just before the actual APES exam, to see how far they have progressed—teachers refer to this as a "post" test.

An answer key with full explanations can be found following this diagnostic test. Also included in the scoring section is a predictive scale of what your actual APES score might be based on your performance on this diagnostic test. Free-Response Questions (FRQs) are not included in this diagnostic test as that would involve subjective grading.

For this Diagnostic Test *only*, if you do not know the answer for a particular question, do *not* guess; this will allow you to determine your strengths and weaknesses. If you know the answer or are pretty sure of the answer, then answer the question.

1. Approximately how old is the Earth?

   (A) 4,500,000 years
   (B) 45,000,000 years
   (C) 450,000,000 years
   (D) 4,500,000,000 years
   (E) 45,000,000,000 years

2. An earthquake of Richter magnitude 2 releases _____ times less energy than an earthquake of Richter magnitude 4?

   (A) 0.01
   (B) 0.5
   (C) two
   (D) 31.7 × 2 or 63.4
   (E) 100

3. The interface where tectonic plates slide or grind past each other is known as a

   (A) transform plate boundary
   (B) convergent plate boundary
   (C) divergent plate boundary
   (D) subduction zone
   (E) trench

4. Climate on Earth is primarily determined by

   (A) the distance between the Earth and the Sun during a particular season
   (B) the tilt of the Earth's axis as it rotates around the Sun
   (C) the amount of cloud cover over a particular region of the Earth
   (D) ocean temperatures
   (E) Earth's longitude

5. Which of the following gases found in the troposphere are greenhouse gases and are also gases produced by domestic livestock?

    I. CO
    II. CO_2
    III. CH_4
    IV. O_2
    V. H_2O

    (A) I and V
    (B) I and III
    (C) II and III
    (D) II, III, and V
    (E) II, III, IV, and V

6. Which area listed below would be found in the regions of the Earth influenced by Ferrel cells?

    (A) Ecuador—near the equator
    (B) Antarctica
    (C) Greenland
    (D) Mid-western states of the United States (e.g., Nebraska, Kansas, etc.)
    (E) Southern Africa

7. Which of the following events about El Niño are TRUE?

    I.   Just prior to an El Niño, the sea surface warms in the eastern equatorial Pacific Ocean
    II.   Just prior to an El Niño, trade winds weaken
    III. During an El Niño, the number of hurricanes in the Atlantic Ocean increases
    IV. During an El Niño, upwelling increases along the western coast of South America resulting in large schools of fish

    (A) I only
    (B) II only
    (C) I and II
    (D) III
    (E) I, III, and IV

8. Water in areas of upwelling are generally

   (A) warm and lacking in nutrients
   (B) warm and high in nutrients
   (C) cold and lacking in nutrients
   (D) cold and high in nutrients
   (E) very hot due to thermal vents and contain high amounts of sulfur

9. Which of the following choices below lists the amount of freshwater available on Earth in the correct descending order?
   (A) Groundwater > soil moisture > atmospheric moisture > lakes > rivers and streams > glaciers and ice caps
   (B) Glaciers and ice caps > atmospheric moisture > groundwater > rivers and streams > soil moisture > lakes
   (C) Glaciers and ice caps > groundwater > lakes > soil moisture > atmospheric moisture > rivers and streams
   (D) Lakes > groundwater > atmospheric moisture > glaciers and ice caps > soil moisture > rivers and streams
   (E) Atmospheric moisture > rivers and streams > ground water > soil moisture > lakes > glaciers and ice caps

10. Freshwater used in developing countries is primarily used for

    (A) agriculture
    (B) industrial purposes
    (C) drinking water
    (D) domestic needs
    (E) all of the above are used in approximate equal proportion

11. Currently, the use of freshwater by humans is increasing at about _____rate of worldwide population growth.

    (A) one-half the
    (B) the same
    (C) twice the
    (D) four times the
    (E) eight times the

For Questions 12–13 choose from the following

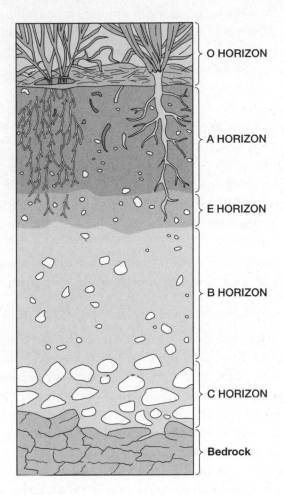

O HORIZON

A HORIZON

E HORIZON

B HORIZON

C HORIZON

Bedrock

(A) A
(B) B
(C) C
(D) O
(E) E

12. Which soil layer consists of clay, iron oxides, and other components that came from the zone of leaching?

13. Which soil layer consists of about equal amounts of organic material and minerals?

14. Tropical rain forests have a rich biodiversity primarily because

(A) warm, moist climates make it easier for living forms to survive
(B) they are generally very large allowing for many life-forms to coexist
(C) evolution occurs faster in warmer and more humid environments
(D) historically, there has been less human settlement and disturbance in tropical rain forests
(E) many diverse niche opportunities and habitats occur in tropical rain forests

15. Which of the following is NOT an example of commensalism?

   (A) Birds known as cattle egrets forage in fields among cattle or other livestock. As cattle, horses, and other livestock graze on the field, they cause movements that stir up various insects. As the insects are stirred up, the cattle egrets following the livestock catch and feed upon them.
   (B) In India, lone golden jackals expelled from their pack have been known to attach themselves to a particular tiger, trailing it at a safe distance in order to feed on the big cat's kills.
   (C) Bacteria living in the stomach of cows and other ruminant animals.
   (D) Birds will often follow army ant raids on a forest floor. As the army ant colony travels on the forest floor, it stirs up various flying insect species. As the insects flee from the army ants, the birds following the ants catch the fleeing insects.
   (E) Orchids and mosses grow on the trunks or branches of trees. They get the light they need as well as nutrients that run down along the tree.

16. "Sea otters are mammals who feed on a variety of marine invertebrates but who feed especially on sea urchins. Sea urchins are voracious herbivores that tend to feed on the base of the kelp until the whole plant detaches from the bottom and floats away. An overabundance of urchins can lead to overgrazing of the kelp and the depletion of sea urchins. Once abundant in California, sea otters were hunted down for their pelts to near extinction. After they were placed under federal protection to increase their numbers and save them from extinction, sea otters were able to begin naturally controlling the urchins so that the kelp forests had a chance to recover."

   In this example, sea otters are considered to be a(n)

   (A) indicator species
   (B) keystone species
   (C) ecotone species
   (D) niche specialist
   (E) niche generalist

17. Which of the following represents intraspecific interaction(s)?

   (A) mutualism
   (B) commensalism
   (C) parasitism
   (D) territoriality
   (E) predation

18. The marine zone that is essentially open ocean, and whose flora include surface seaweeds and whose fauna includes many species of fish and some mammals, such as whales and dolphins, is known as the

    (A) intertidal zone
    (B) pelagic zone
    (C) benthic zone
    (D) abyssal zone
    (E) hadal zone

19. Photosynthesis produces sugars from

    (A) carbon dioxide, water, and oxygen
    (B) oxygen, water, and energy
    (C) glucose, oxygen, and energy
    (D) carbon dioxide, water, and energy
    (E) oxygen, carbon dioxide, and energy

Use the following diagram for Questions 20 and 21.

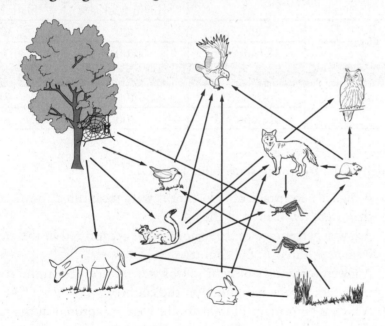

20. In the food web above, which of the following statements would be TRUE for the owl?

    I.   The owl is an omnivore
    II. The owl is a primary consumer
    III. The owl is a secondary consumer
    IV. The owl is a tertiary consumer
    V.   The owl is a primary producer

    (A) II only
    (B) III only
    (C) III and IV only
    (D) I, IV, and V only
    (E) II, III, and IV only

21. Energy enters this system as sunlight. If a leaf from the plant contains 10 calories of energy and the leaf is totally consumed by the grasshopper, which is then totally consumed by the songbird, which is then totally consumed by the owl, about how much of the energy from the leaf is eventually available as energy for the owl to use?

    (A) 0.0001 calories
    (B) 0.001 calories
    (C) 10 calories
    (D) 100 calories
    (E) 1,000 calories

22. An APES class performed an experiment of releasing and recapturing light and dark moths in the city and the country. The results are presented below:

Comparison of Light and Dark Moth Recaptures in the City and Country			
Location		Number of Light Moths	Number of Dark Moths
Country	Released	300	300
	Recaptured	200	100
City	Released	400	400
	Recaptured	200	300

Which of the following statements is TRUE?

    (A) A higher percentage of light moths were recaptured in the country than were recaptured in the city.
    (B) A lower percentage of dark moths were recaptured in the city than were recaptured in the country.
    (C) A lower percentage of light moths were recaptured in the country than dark moths recaptured in the country.
    (D) A higher percentage of light moths were recaptured in the city than dark moths recaptured in the city.
    (E) All statements are true.

23. In New York City, where the quality of drinking water had fallen below standards required by the U.S. Environmental Protection Agency (EPA), authorities opted to restore the polluted Catskill Watershed. Once the input of sewage and pesticides to the watershed area was reduced, natural abiotic processes such as soil adsorption and filtration of chemicals, together with biotic recycling via root systems and soil microorganisms, water quality improved to levels that met government standards. The cost of this investment in natural capital was estimated between $1–1.5 billion, which contrasted dramatically with the estimated $6–8 billion cost of constructing a water filtration plant plus the $300 million annual running costs.

    The Catskill Watershed provides _____ to New York City.

    (A) natural resource services
    (B) market services
    (C) social services
    (D) economic services
    (E) ecosystem services

24. In response to climate shifts due to global warming, terrestrial animals can adapt, migrate, or die. Which of the following factors below contribute to surviving the effects of global warming?

    I. Long generational times
    II. Being widely dispersed
    III. Having narrow climatic tolerances
    IV. Being an *r*-strategist rather than a *K*-strategist
    V. Being confined to one geographic location

    (A) I, II, and IV
    (B) II and IV
    (C) I, IV, and V
    (D) I, II, and V
    (E) All of the above

25. Which of the following would be subject to primary succession?

    (A) rock exposed by a retreating glacier
    (B) an abandoned farm
    (C) a forest that had been clear-cut
    (D) newly flooded agricultural land used to create a reservoir
    (E) a forest that has been burned

26. Which of the following would be TRUE regarding succession?

    I.   Growth of lichen on rocks after a fire destroyed a forest is an example of primary succession
    II.   Growth of grasses on a newly formed sand dune is an example of secondary succession
    III. Growth of algae on cooled lava rock is an example of secondary succession
    IV.   *K*-selected organisms are typical of primary succession
    V.   *r*-selected organisms are typical of secondary succession

    (A) III
    (B) I and III
    (C) II, IV, and V
    (D) I, III, IV, and V
    (E) None are true

27. The first compound that ammonia is converted into in the nitrogen cycle is

    (A) nitrate
    (B) urea
    (C) protein
    (D) nitrite
    (E) amino acid

28. Which of the following below are examples of density-independent factors that control population growth?

    I.   Droughts and floods
    II.   Fires
    III. Use of pesticides
    IV.   Release of a pollutant
    V.   Overhunting and fishing

    (A) I
    (B) I and II
    (C) III, IV, and V
    (D) IV
    (E) All choices are correct examples

29. The graph below is of a paramecium population growing in culture over a period of 30 hours. If food is a limiting factor for this population, then increasing the amount of food available in the water at the beginning of the experiment will . . .

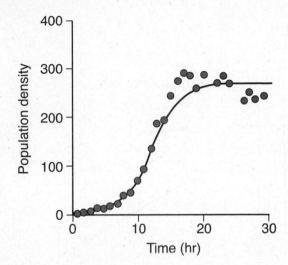

(A) increase the population density between 0–15 hours
(B) decrease the population density after the carrying capacity had been reached
(C) have no effect on the population density between 0 and 15 hours
(D) decrease the time it takes for the population to reach its carrying capacity
(E) All of the above are true

30. Consider the following organisms

I. Elephant
II. Weeds
III. Mice
IV. Acorn tree
V. Mosquitos

Which of the above would be considered *K*-strategists?

(A) I
(B) II, III, and V
(C) I and IV
(D) II and V
(E) V

31. In wild populations, individuals most often show a _____ pattern of dispersion.

    (A) clumped
    (B) uniform
    (C) random
    (D) scattered
    (E) chaotic

32. Examine the following diagram below.

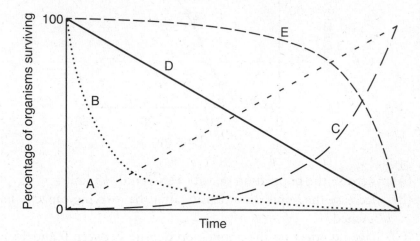

Which of the choices above would be a characteristic survivorship curve for a songbird?

    (A) A
    (B) B
    (C) C
    (D) D
    (E) E

33. Examine the diagram below.

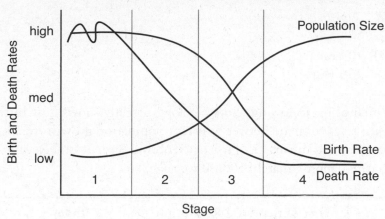

Model of Human Demographic Transition

Which of the following statements are TRUE of Stage 2?

I. This stage would be typical for countries today such as Afghanistan and much of sub-Saharan Africa.

II. Decline in death rates is primarily due to improvements in the food supply brought about by higher yields in agricultural practices and better transportation, which prevent death due to starvation and lack of water. Agricultural improvements included crop rotation, selective breeding, and seed drill technology.

III. Improvements in water supply, sewage treatment, food handling, and general personal hygiene following from growing scientific knowledge of the causes of disease and the improved education and social status of mothers are primarily responsible for decreasing the death rate.

IV. Growth in population is primarily due to an increase in death rates, not fertility rates.

V. The age structure of the population becomes increasingly older as more and more people live longer.

(A) I and IV
(B) I, II, and III
(C) I, II, IV, and V
(D) III, IV, and V
(E) All statements are true

34. A country with an annual population growth rate of 5% would double its population in approximately how many years?

    (A) 5 years
    (B) 7 years
    (C) 14 years
    (D) 70 years
    (E) 350 years

35. Which of the following choices below correctly shows how birthrates and death rates compare between current population growth trends and trends that occurred during the First or Neolithic Agricultural Revolution that occurred approximately 10,000 years ago?

	First Agricultural Revolution	Today
(A)	Birthrate: High	Birthrate: Low
	Death Rate: Low	Death Rate: High
(B)	Birthrate: Low	Birthrate: High
	Death Rate: High	Death Rate: Low
(C)	Birthrate: High	Birthrate: High
	Death Rate: Low	Death Rate: Low
(D)	Birthrate: High	Birthrate: Low
	Death Rate: High	Death Rate: Low
(E)	Birthrate: High	Birthrate: High
	Death Rate: Low	Death Rate: High

36. Examine the age distribution diagrams below.

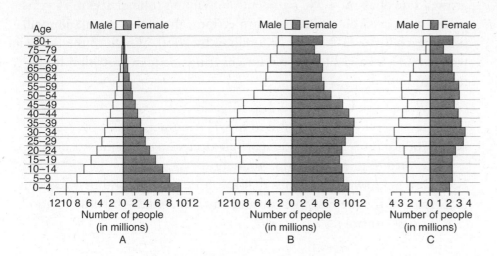

Which of the following statements would be TRUE?

I.   A is experiencing rapid growth, B is experiencing slow growth, and
     C is experiencing a decline in growth

II. A is experiencing slow growth, B is experiencing rapid growth, and
     C is experiencing a decline in growth

III. A is experiencing a decline in growth, B is experiencing a rapid
     growth, and C is experiencing a slow growth

IV. A would be typical for Nigeria, B would be typical for Germany, and
     C would be typical for the United States

V.   A would be typical for the United States, B would be typical for
     Nigeria, and C would be typical for Germany

(A) I
(B) I and III
(C) I and V
(D) II and IV
(E) III and IV

37. The most populous countries in the world are India, China, and

(A) Russia
(B) United States
(C) Mexico
(D) Indonesia
(E) Pakistan

38. The world's current population of approximately 7 billion people with a growth rate of about 1.3% represents a doubling time of about 54 years. At this rate, according to current projections, the global population will likely reach between 7.5 and 10.5 billion by 2050. Which of the following would NOT be a viable strategy for ensuring adequate nutrition for a population of that size?

    (A) Where feasible, switch to drip irrigation
    (B) Increase the efficiency of food distribution networks
    (C) Produce more meat products while decreasing the amount of land devoted to grain and crop production
    (D) Develop new hybrid crops that are more drought and pest resistant
    (E) Expand the use of non-toxic and environmentally-friendly methods of pest control

39. Worldwide human population growth within the last 100 years is primarily due to

    (A) increase in the birthrate
    (B) decrease in the death rate
    (C) a lower infant mortality rate
    (D) immigration
    (E) a desire to have more children

40. Which of the following was NOT a major component of the First Green Revolution?

    (A) Genetic engineering of food crops
    (B) Widespread use of synthetic nitrogen-based fertilizers
    (C) Widespread use of pesticides
    (D) Development of major modern irrigation projects
    (E) Development of new crop varieties through selective breeding technology

41. Which type of insecticide developed during the 19th century affects the nervous system of an insect by disrupting the enzyme that regulates acetylcholine, a neurotransmitter? They usually are not persistent in the environment. Common examples include parathion and malathion.

    (A) Carbamates
    (B) Pyrethroids
    (C) Organophosphates
    (D) DDT
    (E) Organochlorines

42. Which of the following is NOT a principle of integrated pest management (IPM)?

    (A) Establish acceptable pest thresholds
    (B) Selecting crop varieties best for local growing conditions
    (C) Visual inspection and using insect and spore traps to monitor pest levels while keeping accurate records
    (D) Using broad, non-specific insecticides to reduce or eliminate all pest populations before they have a chance to get out of control
    (E) Using mechanical methods to reduce pest populations, which include handpicking, erecting insect barriers, using traps, vacuuming, and tillage to disrupt breeding.

43. The type of timber-harvesting method shown below is known as

    (A) seed tree harvesting
    (B) group selection
    (C) clear-cutting
    (D) single tree selection
    (E) shelterwood cutting

44. Which of the choices below are effective method(s) of remediating the effects of desertification?

    I.   Reforestation
    II. Fixating the soil through the use of shelter belts, woodlots, and windbreaks or sand fences
    III. Planting legumes
    IV. Enabling native sprouting tree growth through selective pruning of shrub growth
    V.   Planting market gardens to keep soil from blowing away

    (A) I and II
    (B) I, III, IV
    (C) II, IV, V
    (D) I, III, IV, V
    (E) I, II, III, IV

45. Which of the following is a characteristic of urban sprawl?

    (A) Multi-use zoning
    (B) High-density zoning
    (C) Car-independent zoning
    (D) Job sprawl
    (E) High unemployment

46. During which U.S. presidency did the first federal highway system develop?

    (A) Abraham Lincoln (1860–1865)
    (B) Franklin Roosevelt (1933–1945)
    (C) Harry Truman (1945–1953)
    (D) Dwight Eisenhower (1953–1961)
    (E) Ronald Reagan (1981–1989)

47. Which of the following lists land use in order from the smallest collective area on Earth to the largest?

    (A) Agricultural < forests < cities
    (B) Forests < cities < agricultural
    (C) Cities < forests < agricultural
    (D) Forests < agricultural < cities
    (E) Agricultural < cities < forests

48. Which agency listed below is responsible for the management of public lands?

    (A) Bureau of Land Management
    (B) Environmental Protection Agency
    (C) National Park Service
    (D) Fish and Wildlife Service
    (E) Department of Agriculture

49. Rainwater runoff from US Route 7 in South Burlington, Vermont polluted local streams that fed into Lake Champlain, a source of drinking water. The city of South Burlington and the Vermont Agency of Natural Resources constructed a storm water treatment system along Bartlett Brook to control the pollution. The project also included the cleanup and widening of a stream channel and creation of a new wetland in the area from an area that had once been occupied by an industrial factory. This is an example of environmental

    (A) preservation
    (B) remediation
    (C) mitigation
    (D) restoration
    (E) all of the above

50.   The type of mining that produces 85% of minerals (excluding petroleum and natural gas) in the United States, including 98% of metallic ores, is known as

(A)   surface mining
(B)   subsurface mining
(C)   *in-situ* leaching
(D)   long wall mining
(E)   room and pillar mining

51.   The type of fishing illustrated below is

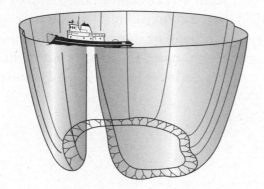

(A)   gill netting
(B)   long lining
(C)   reef netting
(D)   trolling
(E)   purse seining

52.   The "Tragedy of the Commons" illustrates how

(A)   individual rationality results in group irrationality
(B)   the pursuit of short-term individual gain often leads to long-term collective costs
(C)   the cost of a product also includes the cost of utilization of common property
(D)   "Commons" are real resources that are owned collectively by people occupying the area
(E)   common people who work for a living are often victims of environmental exploitation

53. A store uses one-hundred 200-watt lightbulbs for 10 hours per day. How many kilowatt-hours of electrical energy are used in one year if the store is open 50 weeks per year, 6 days per week?

    (A) 50,000
    (B) 60,000
    (C) 6,000,000
    (D) 30,000,000
    (E) 60,000,000

54. The gas mileage of one model of the 2003 Hummer 2 was determined to be 8 miles per gallon. The 2012 Mitsubishi i-MiEV is an all-electric vehicle and when using a conversion factor to convert the fuel economy into miles per gallon of gasoline equivalent (MPGe), it is rated at 112 miles per gallon of gasoline. How much more efficient in fuel consumption is the all-electric vehicle over the Hummer 2?

    (A) 13%
    (B) 14%
    (C) 130%
    (D) 140%
    (E) 1300%

55. In an internal combustion automobile engine, only about 20% of the high-quality chemical energy available in the gasoline is converted to mechanical energy used to propel the car; the remaining 80% is degraded to low-quality heat that is released into the environment. In addition, about 50% of the mechanical energy produced is also degraded to low-quality heat energy through friction, so that 90% of the energy in gasoline is wasted and not used to move the car. This best illustrates which principle below?

    (A) First Law of Thermodynamics
    (B) Second Law of Thermodynamics
    (C) Third Law of Thermodynamics
    (D) Enthalpy
    (E) None of the above

56. Per capita, the United States uses about _____ amount of oil per day than China.

    (A) half the
    (B) the same
    (C) twice the
    (D) ten times the
    (E) one hundred times the

57. In the United States, on average, _____ energy is used to heat homes than is used to cool them.
    (A) 25% less
    (B) 50% less
    (C) 50% more
    (D) 100% more
    (E) 250% more

58. Which sector listed below currently uses the largest amount of energy in the world?

    (A) Commercial (i.e., stores, restaurants, offices, etc.)
    (B) Industrial (i.e., manufacturing plants)
    (C) Residential (i.e., homes, apartments, etc.)
    (D) Transportation (i.e., cars, planes, etc.)
    (E) All of the above in roughly equal proportions

59. The estimated natural gas reserves in the United States are estimated at 2,170 trillion cubic feet (Tcf). The rate of consumption of natural gas in the United States is approximately 62 billion cubic feet per day. Approximately how long will the United States natural gas reserves last at the current rate of consumption?

    (A) 10 years
    (B) 25 years
    (C) 50 years
    (D) 100 years
    (E) 200 years

60. Which of the following has the largest potential negative environmental impact on global warming?

    (A) Coal
    (B) Oil
    (C) Natural gas
    (D) Solar
    (E) Nuclear

61. Which country listed below obtains the greatest percentage of its electricity from nuclear power?

    (A) United States
    (B) Russia
    (C) China
    (D) Japan
    (E) France

62. Examine the diagram of a nuclear power plant below

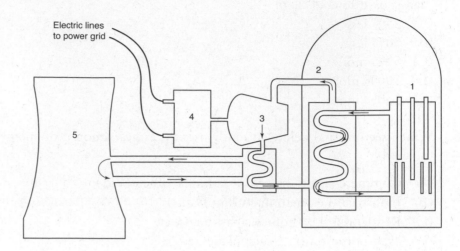

What is the name and function of the part labeled "5"?

(A) Heat exchanger—transfers heat from the fission reaction to water, which then turns to steam capable of powering steam turbines

(B) Generator—converts mechanical energy from the steam turbine into electrical energy

(C) Turbine—steam under very high pressure and temperature strikes blades or vanes mounted on a wheel enabling the large wheel to turn

(D) Moderator—the container holding a material, such as heavy water or graphite, used for slowing down neutrons in the cores of nuclear reactors so that they have a higher probability of inducing nuclear fission

(E) Cooling tower—cools or recycles water and releases unwanted heat to the environment

63. Which of the following current methods to produce 1 kWh of electricity is the MOST expensive?

(A) Nuclear
(B) Coal
(C) Natural gas
(D) Wind
(E) Hydroelectric

64. Which of the following is the LEAST likely environmental consequence of building hydroelectric dams?

(A) Dams change water temperatures downstream
(B) Dams increase the risk of predation
(C) Dams increase silting downstream
(D) Dams decrease the oxygen content of water downstream
(E) Dams decrease the flow of water downstream

65. Which government agency administers and regulates CAFE standards?

    (A) Environmental Protection Agency (EPA)
    (B) National Highway Traffic Safety Administration (NHTSA)
    (C) National Science Foundation (NSF)
    (D) National Transportation Safety Board (NTSB)
    (E) Office of Weights and Measures (OWM)

66. A 42 watt CFL (compact fluorescent light) bulb produces 2,600 lumens of light, lasts approximately 10,000 hours, and costs $13.00. A 150-watt incandescent lightbulb produces the same amount of light, lasts only 1,000 hours and costs $2.00. If electricity runs $0.10 per kWh, how much will the CFL save over the lifetime of the bulb compared to using the incandescent bulbs?

    (A) $7.00
    (B) $13.00
    (C) $42.00
    (D) $108.00
    (E) $115.00

67. Which of the following RENEWABLE energy sources listed below is used the LEAST in the United States?

    (A) Solar
    (B) Biomass
    (C) Wind
    (D) Hydroelectric
    (E) Geothermal

68. Which of the following would be classified as a secondary air pollutant?

    (A) Carbon monoxide
    (B) Acid rain
    (C) Carbon dioxide
    (D) Sulfur dioxide
    (E) Lead

69. Which of the following would NOT be classified as a criteria pollutant?

    (A) Carbon monoxide
    (B) Sulfur dioxide
    (C) Particulates
    (D) Ozone
    (E) Carbon dioxide

70. 1,500 parts per billion would be the same concentration as _____ parts per million.

    (A) 0.15
    (B) 1.5
    (C) 15
    (D) 150
    (E) 1,500

71. Which one of the following criteria pollutants listed below contributes to the formation of both acid deposition AND photochemical smog?

    (A) CO
    (B) NO_2
    (C) O_3
    (D) Particulates
    (E) SO_2

72. During summer months, Los Angeles, California often experiences a temperature inversion. During this event

    (A) Cold air that is heavier lies above a mass of warmer air that wants to rise, trapping particulates close to the ground.
    (B) Stable warm air lies above a mass of colder air, trapping air particulates close to the ground.
    (C) There is no colder air mass to provide a difference in temperature; therefore, the air stalls and traps particulates close to the ground.
    (D) Warmer air is trapped between two cold fronts, trapping the particulates within the warm air mass.
    (E) Warm air rises while colder air sinks. Particulates within the cold air are then brought closer to the ground and their concentration increases, producing smog.

73. Given the following pollutants

    I.   CFCs
    II. VOCs
    III. Radon
    IV. PANs
    V.   Asbestos

    Which are NOT naturally occurring indoor air pollutants?

    (A) I and II
    (B) I and IV
    (C) I, II, and IV
    (D) III, V
    (E) I, III, IV, V

74. Which of the following were the criteria used for acceptable exposure to specific air pollutants as addressed in the National Ambient Air Quality Standards set forth by the Clean Air Act?

   I. The amount of time exposed to the air pollutant
   II. The concentration of the air pollutant
   III. The toxicity of the air pollutant
   IV. The LD_{50} of the air pollutant
   V. The number of people that would be at risk if exposed to the air pollutant

   (A) I and II
   (B) II and III
   (C) I, II, and III
   (D) I, III, and IV
   (E) III, IV, and V

75. Which of the following statement(s) regarding noise pollution is/are TRUE?

   I. Noise pollution is a significant occupational hazard and is regulated and enforced by the Environmental Protection Agency.
   II. Sound measured at 40 decibels is twice as loud as sound measured at 20 decibels.
   III. Noise pollution is not a serious threat in the oceans as organisms that live underwater do not hear.
   IV. The Office of Noise Abatement and Control of the Environmental Protection Agency (EPA) is currently charged with regulating and overseeing noise-abatement activities.

   (A) I and II
   (B) I and III
   (C) II, III, and IV
   (D) I, III, and IV
   (E) All statements are false

76. Which of the following forms of water pollution affects the largest number of people worldwide?

   (A) Brackish water resulting from flooding
   (B) Water that is not properly processed through sewage treatment plants
   (C) Water containing pollutants from industrial factories
   (D) Waterborne pathogens and diseases
   (E) Groundwater contamination resulting from illegal dumping of toxic materials

77. An APES class was doing a field study of effluent water entering a river through a large drainage pipe from a large building. Which of the following would be a logical conclusion based upon their observations?

    (A) The students observed green algae covering a small area of the river a mile away from the factory and concluded that the factory was dumping hot water into the river as algae grow profusely in warm water.

    (B) The students detected measurable amounts of coliform bacteria in the river near the drainage pipe and concluded that the building could be a meatpacking plant.

    (C) The students detected high concentrations of metal ions in the river bottom upstream of the factory and found nothing but anaerobic bacteria, fungi, and sludge worms living in the mud. They concluded that the building was probably a factory producing inorganic fertilizer and releasing some of the fertilizer into the water.

    (D) The students observed a large number of insect larvae in the water 2 miles from the drainage pipe and concluded that the water was polluted by a factory that was releasing large amounts of food wastes into the water.

    (E) The students measured the turbidity of the water exiting the drainage pipe and found it to be extremely high and concluded that the building was probably a factory that produced pharmaceuticals.

78. Groundwater contamination is addressed in all of the following EXCEPT the

    (A) Clean Water Act
    (B) Safe Drinking Water Act
    (C) Resource Conservation and Recovery Act
    (D) Superfund
    (E) Groundwater contamination is addressed in all of the above

Questions 79 and 80 refer to the following graph.

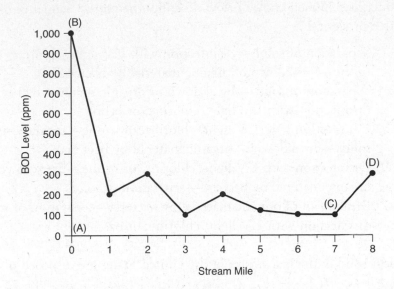

An APES class measured BOD along an 8-mile stretch of a stream. Their results are presented above.

79. BOD indicates

(A) the level of pollution in a sample of water

(B) the rate at which oxygen is being produced by aquatic plants

(C) the rate at which oxygen is being consumed by microorganisms living in the water

(D) the potential amount of oxygen that the water sample could contain given the pH, temperature, and volume of the sample

(E) the concentration of oxygen in a water sample that a living organism requires to survive

80. At which point on the graph would you expect to find the highest concentration of anaerobic bacteria?

(A) A

(B) B

(C) C

(D) D

(E) Anaerobic bacteria would not be found in a stream

81. Sewage treatment plants have three general processes that water undergoes. Which choice below describes the correct sequence of these three processes?

    (A) Separation of solids—disinfection with UV light, chlorine, or ozone—breakdown of organic material by bacteria
    (B) Separation of solids—breakdown of organic material by bacteria—disinfection with UV light, chlorine, or ozone
    (C) Disinfection with UV light, chlorine, or ozone—separation of solids—breakdown of organic material by bacteria
    (D) Disinfection with UV light, chlorine, or ozone—breakdown of organic material by bacteria—separation of solids
    (E) Breakdown of organic material by bacteria—separation of solids—disinfection with UV light, chlorine, or ozone

82. Most solid municipal wastes in the United States are disposed of by

    (A) taking the wastes far from land and dumping it into the sea
    (B) burning it at large municipal incinerators
    (C) burying it in giant pits
    (D) taking it to sanitary landfills
    (E) burning the wastes at the site (home, school, factory, etc.)

83. Three "environmentally friendly" methods of dealing with waste disposal are to reuse, reduce, and recycle. Which of the following choices below places these methods in order of increasing amounts of energy required for that particular process?

    (A) Reuse < reduce < recycle
    (B) Reuse < recycle < reduce
    (C) Recycle < reduce < reuse
    (D) Recycle < reuse < reduce
    (E) Reduce < reuse < recycle

84. A group of workers at a nuclear power plant received an acute exposure of radiation. This means

    (A) the workers received a high dosage of radiation over a long time period
    (B) the workers received a high dosage of radiation in a very short time period
    (C) the workers received a low dosage of radiation over a long time period
    (D) the workers received a low dosage of radiation over a short time period
    (E) the workers received a lethal dosage of radiation

85. A laboratory was testing the effectiveness of a new insecticide. The laboratory determined that the LD_{50} dosage level for rats was 150 milligrams per kilogram of body mass. Based on this information, which of the following statements would be most accurate?

   (A) Fifty out of 100 rats receiving 300 milligrams of the new insecticide per kilogram of body mass would die.

   (B) Fifty out of 100 rats receiving 150 milligrams of the new insecticide per kilogram of body mass would die.

   (C) Any amount more than 150 milligrams of the new insecticide per kilogram of body mass would be lethal to humans.

   (D) Out of the 100 rats tested, 50 of them would be perfectly normal with no ill-effects and 50 of them would eventually die from the new insecticide.

   (E) Fifty percent of any population of organism would die if given more than 150 milligrams of the new insecticide.

Questions 86–87 refer to the following dose-response curve.

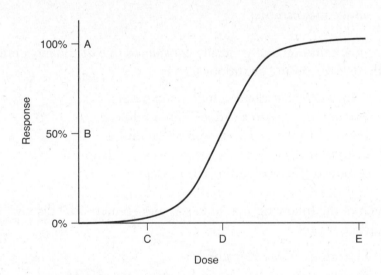

86. Which point represents the LD_{50}?

   (A) A
   (B) B
   (C) C
   (D) D
   (E) E

87. Which point represents the threshold?

   (A) A
   (B) B
   (C) C
   (D) D
   (E) E

88. Of the indoor pollutants that are listed below, which one has the highest total health care costs, affects the most people, and causes the most deaths?

(A) asbestos
(B) exposure to radon
(C) exposure to smog
(D) cigarette smoke
(E) ozone

89. DDT, a synthetic agricultural pesticide, was very effective in reducing incidents of malaria but caused shell thinning in certain species of birds particularly birds of prey such as the bald eagle, brown pelican, peregrine falcon, and osprey. DDT is classified as what type of hazardous waste?

(A) neurotoxin
(B) carcinogen
(C) teratogen
(D) mutagen
(E) endocrine disrupter

90. The most common and generally considered one of the most effective methods of disposing hazardous wastes is

(A) incinerate the waste at a high temperature
(B) entrap the waste in a surface impoundment
(C) dispose of the waste in a sanitary landfill
(D) dispose of the waste in a hazardous waste landfill
(E) dispose of the waste in injection wells

91. Which of the following acts addresses and regulates the disposal of hazardous wastes?

(A) Hazardous Waste Control Act
(B) Resource Conservation and Recovery Act (RCRA)
(C) Toxic Substance Control Act
(D) Comprehensive Response, Compensation, and Liability Act (CERCLA) – Superfund
(E) Pollution Prevention Act (PPA)

92. If the price of a barrel of oil from the Middle East were to suddenly double, it would

    (A) make it economically feasible to explore for new sources of oil within the United States; thereby increasing the supply, which would decrease the price for oil
    (B) make it economically unfeasible to explore for new sources of oil within the United States; thereby decreasing the supply, which would cause a decrease in demand for oil
    (C) make it economically feasible to use alternative sources of energy within the United States, thereby increasing the demand for oil and consequently increasing the supply of oil
    (D) make it economically unfeasible to use alternative sources of energy within the United States, thereby increasing the demand for oil, which would result in a decrease in the supply of gasoline
    (E) have no effect on exploring for new sources of oil within the United States, therefore the supply of oil in the United States would decrease and the price would then also decrease

93. Currently, the gas contributing most to stratospheric ozone breakdown is

    (A) Chlorofluorocarbons (CFCs) used in air conditioners
    (B) Carbon tetrachloride (CCl_4) used as an industrial solvent and in fire extinguishers
    (C) Methyl chloroform (CH_3CCl_3) used as a solvent for adhesives, for metal degreasing, and in textile processing
    (D) Methyl bromide (CH_3Br) used as a fumigant
    (E) Nitrous oxide (N_2O) released from livestock manure, sewage treatment, and industrial processes

94. An increase in greenhouse gases increases tropospheric temperatures. If ice melts due to global warming, it affects the Earth's albedo. Which of the following statements would be true regarding the effect of melting ice and its effect on the Earth's albedo?

(A) Melting ice would increase the Earth's albedo resulting in less heat absorbed, which in turn would result in more ice melting in what would be known as a positive feedback loop.

(B) Melting ice would decrease the Earth's albedo resulting in more heat being absorbed, resulting in more ice melting in what would be known as a positive feedback loop.

(C) Melting ice would increase the Earth's albedo resulting in less heat absorbed, which in turn would result in more ice melting in what would be known as a negative feedback loop.

(D) Melting ice would increase the Earth's albedo resulting in more heat absorbed, which in turn would result in less ice melting in what would be known as a negative feedback loop.

(E) Melting ice would decrease the Earth's albedo resulting in less heat being absorbed, resulting in less ice melting in what would be known as a negative feedback loop.

95. Which of the following was instrumental in significantly reducing the production of chlorofluorocarbons?

(A) Clean Air Act
(B) Montreal Protocol
(C) Kyoto Protocol
(D) National Environmental Policy Act
(E) Toxic Substances Control Act

96. The majority of the natural greenhouse effect is due to which gas listed below?

(A) Carbon dioxide (CO_2)
(B) Chlorofluorocarbons (CFCs)
(C) Water vapor (H_2O)
(D) Nitrous oxide (N_2O)
(E) Methane (CH_4)

97. Which of the following factors are primary reasons why sea level is rising?

I. Thermal expansion of the oceans
II. More frequent rain and flooding
III. Melting of sea ice
IV. Melting of land-based ice

(A) I and III
(B) II and IV
(C) III and IV
(D) I and IV
(E) I, II, III, and IV

98. Which countries listed below have recently either stated they would not enter a second round of carbon cuts under a new Kyoto Protocol due to go into effect in 2012 or never signed the original Kyoto Protocol of 1997?

    I.   Russia
    II. Canada
    III. United States
    IV. Japan
    V.   France

    (A) I, III
    (B) II, IV, and V
    (C) III, IV, and V
    (D) I, III, and IV
    (E) I, II, III, IV, and V

99. The greatest threat to a species survival is generally considered

    (A) lack of food
    (B) pollution
    (C) poaching
    (D) invasive species
    (E) loss of habitat

100. Which international agreement has been helpful in protecting endangered animals and plants by listing those species and products whose international trade is controlled?

    (A) Endangered Species Act
    (B) CITES
    (C) Fish and Wildlife Act
    (D) National Environmental Policy Act
    (E) International Treaty on Endangered and Threatened Species

DIAGNOSTIC TEST ANSWERS AND EXPLANATIONS

Directions: On the line to the left of each number, place a "C" if you got the question Correct, place an "X" if you answered the question incorrectly, and leave the line blank if you did not answer the question.

I. Earth Systems and Resources (10–15%)

_____ 1. **(D)** The age of the Earth is approximately 4.54 billion years. This age is based on evidence from radiometric age dating of meteorite material and is consistent with the ages of the oldest-known terrestrial and lunar samples. *Earth Science Concepts: Geologic Time Scale*

_____ 2. **(D)** The Richter scale is logarithmic, meaning that whole-number jumps indicate a tenfold increase (or decrease). In this case, the increase is in wave amplitude. That is, the wave amplitude in a level 6 earthquake is 10 times greater than in a level 5 earthquake, and the amplitude increases 100 times between a level 7 earthquake and a level 9 earthquake. However, the amount of energy released increases (or decreases) 31.7 times between whole number Richter values. *Earth Science Concepts: Earthquakes*

_____ 3. **(A)** Transform plate boundaries are locations where two plates slide past one another. The fracture zone that forms a transform plate boundary is known as a transform fault. Most transform faults are found in the ocean basin. Transform faults are locations of recurring earthquake activity and faulting. The earthquakes are usually shallow because they occur within and between plates that are not involved in subduction. Volcanic activity is normally not present because the typical magma sources of an upwelling convection current or a melting subducting plate are not present. *Earth Science Concepts: Plate Tectonics*

_____ 4. **(B)** The tilt of the Earth is responsible for the yearly cycle of seasonal-weather changes. Two factors change during the course of a year to give seasonal variations in temperatures: (1) the angle at which sunlight enters the atmosphere and strikes the ground and (2) the number of daylight hours. If sunlight enters the atmosphere at a direct angle, as it does in the Northern Hemisphere during the summer, it will go through less of the atmosphere. Sunlight entering the atmosphere at the Southern Hemisphere at this time has to pass through more of the atmosphere. Over time, the angle of Earth's tilt varies between 22.2 and 24.5 degrees. A larger tilt means that the summer hemisphere will receive more solar radiation, while the winter hemisphere will receive less. The Sun appears lower in the sky during winter, when the hemisphere affected is tilted away from it. This decreases the number of hours for the sun to heat the ground and lower temperatures result. *The Atmosphere: Climate*

_____ 5. **(D)** Products of cellular respiration are CO_2 and H_2O ($C_6H_{12}O_6 + 6O_2 \rightarrow 6H_2O + 6CO_2$). In addition to water and carbon dioxide being produced, livestock also produce methane (CH_4) through a process known as enteric fermentation. CO_2, H_2O, and CH_4 are all greenhouse gases. *The Atmosphere: Composition*

_____ 6. **(E)** The overall movement of surface air in the Ferrel cell occurs between the 30th to the 60th north and south latitudes. Ecuador and the majority of the United States including mid-western states occur in the Hadley cell, which lies between 30° north and 30° south latitudes while Antarctica and Greenland occurs in areas influenced by the polar cells. *The Atmosphere: Atmospheric Circulation*

_____ 7. **(C)** El Niño episodes are defined as sustained warming of the central and eastern tropical Pacific Ocean and results in a decrease in the strength of the Pacific trade winds. A deeper thermocline (often observed during El Niño years) limits the amount of nutrients brought to shallower depths by upwelling processes, greatly impacting the year's fish crop. *The Atmosphere: ENSO*

_____ 8. **(D)** Upwelling is a phenomenon that involves wind-driven motion of dense, cooler, and usually nutrient-rich water toward the surface, replacing the warmer, usually nutrient-depleted surface water. The increased availability in upwelling regions results in high levels of primary productivity and thus fishery production. Approximately 25% of the total global marine fish catches come from five upwellings that occupy only 5% of the total ocean area. Upwellings that are driven by coastal currents or diverging open ocean have the greatest impact on nutrient-enriched waters and global fishery yields. *The Atmosphere: ENSO*

_____ 9. **(C)** See diagram below. *Global Water Resources and Use: Freshwater/ Saltwater*

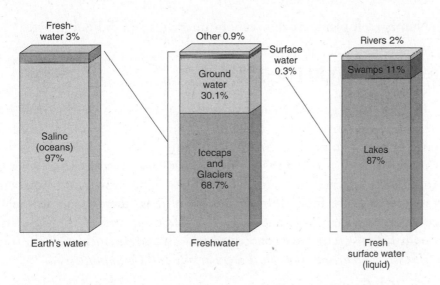

_____ 10. **(A)** The agricultural sector is the most dominant user of water, accounting for up to 70% of the world's freshwater usage. Agricultural water use is especially heavy in the developing world, with some countries in Asia, Africa, and South America using more than 79% of their total freshwater supply for agricultural purposes. In fact, 85–90% of all the freshwater that is used in Africa and Asia is for agriculture. Farmers in developing countries use up to twice as much water than their counterparts in industrialized countries, and often obtain crop yields that are three times less. *Global Water Resources and Use: Agricultural*

_____ 11. **(C)** Currently, 7 billion people use nearly 30% of the world's total accessible renewal supply of water. By 2025, with an estimated 8 billion people, that value is estimated to reach 70%. *Global Water Resources and Use: Global Problems*

_____ 12. **(B)** The B horizon is commonly referred to as "subsoil," and consists of mineral layers that may contain concentrations of clay or minerals such as iron or aluminum oxides or organic material that got there by leaching. Accordingly, this layer is also known as the "zone of accumulation." Plant roots penetrate through this layer, but it has very little humus. It is usually brownish or red because of the clay and iron oxides washed down from the A horizon. *Soil and Soil Dynamics: Main Soil Types*

_____ 13. **(A)** The A horizon is the top layer of the soil horizons and is often referred to as "topsoil." This layer has a layer of dark decomposed organic materials, which is called "humus." The A horizon is the zone in which most biological activity occurs. Soil organisms such as earthworms, arthropods, nematodes, fungi, and many species of bacteria are concentrated here, often in close association with plant roots. *Soil and Soil Dynamics: Main Soil Types*

RECAP FOR EARTH SYSTEMS AND RESOURCES

_____ Total number correct for this section

_____ Percent correct for this section
(number correct for this section / 13) × 100%

_____ Number wrong for this section (questions you thought you knew).
Do NOT count answers left blank.

_____ Number left blank for this section (questions you did not know)

II. The Living World (10–15%)

_____ 14. **(E)** As a general rule, diversity and ecosystem productivity increase with the amount of solar energy available to the system. The stable tropical rain forest environment promotes diversity by allowing plants and animals to interact all year round without needing to develop protection against severe weather conditions. In addition, because the sun shines all year long providing plants with the energy to manufacture food through photosynthesis, there is no seasonal food shortage in the ecosystem. Over the course of millions of years, with abundant food, tropical rain forest species have adapted to take full advantages of all the available niches. *Ecosystem Structure: Biological Populations and Communities*

_____ 15. **(C)** Commensalism is a class of relationship between two organisms where one organism benefits but the other is unaffected (there is no harm or benefit). Cows eat grass and hay almost exclusively. Cows, and other ruminant animals, have a special type of stomach called a rumen, which is home to billions of microbes that consume grass and hay. These bacteria, fungi, and protists provide nutrients that the cow can digest. Without these microbes, the cow would die. The ungulates benefit from the cellulase produced by the bacteria, which facilitates digestion; the bacteria benefit from having a stable supply of nutrients in the host environment. *Ecosystem Structure: Interactions Among Species*

_____ 16. **(B)** A keystone species is a species that has a disproportionately large effect on its environment relative to its abundance. Such species play a critical role in maintaining the structure of an ecological community, affecting many other organisms in an ecosystem, and helping to determine the types and numbers of various other species in the community. Similarly, an ecosystem may experience a dramatic shift if a keystone species is removed, even though that species was a small part of the ecosystem by measures of biomass or productivity. *Ecosystem Structure: Keystone Species*

_____ 17. (**D**) Territoriality is behavior by a single animal, mating pair, or group of animals of the same species of an area occupied and often vigorously defended against intruders, especially those of the same species. All of the other choices are interspecific interactions. *Ecosystem Structure: Interactions Among Species*

_____ 18. (**B**) See diagram below *Ecosystem Structure: Aquatic Biomes*

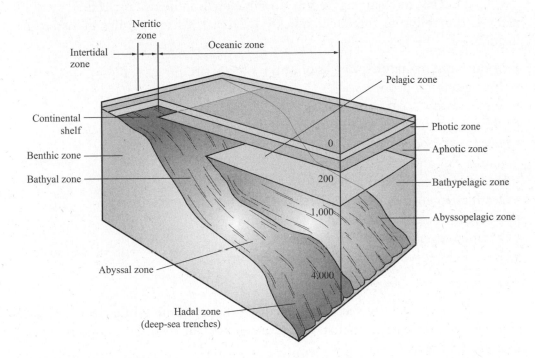

_____ 19. (**D**) Photosynthesis (plants): $6CO_2 + 6H_2O + $ energy (sunlight) $\rightarrow C_6H_{12}O_6 + 6O_2$

Cellular Respiration (animals): $C_6H_{12}O_6 + 6O_2 \rightarrow 6CO_2 + 6H_2O + $ energy *The Living World: Photosynthesis and Cellular Respiration*

_____ 20. (**C**) Producers are plants. Primary consumers eat plants. Secondary consumers eat primary consumers. Tertiary consumers eat secondary consumers. Two possible examples are provided below. *Energy Flow: Food Webs*

Secondary Consumer: plant (producer) > rabbit (primary consumer) > owl (secondary consumer)

Tertiary Consumer: plant (producer) > grasshopper (primary consumer) > songbird (secondary consumer) > owl (tertiary consumer)

_____ 21. (**B**) A general rule of thumb is that approximately 10% of the energy entering one level of a trophic level passes onto the next higher level. Leaf (10 calories) > grasshopper (1 calories) > songbird (0.1 calorie) > owl (0.001 calorie). This loss of energy is consistent with the Second Law of Thermodynamics, which states that no energy conversion is 100% efficient. The loss occurs as energy is trapped in indigestible parts and energy (heat) lost in metabolic processes. *Energy Flow: Trophic Levels*

_____ 22. **(A)** To find the percentage of moths recaptured, divide the number of moths recaptured by the number of moths released. *Ecosystem Diversity: Natural Selection*

_____ 23. **(E)** Humankind benefits from a multitude of resources and processes that are supplied by natural ecosystems. Collectively, these benefits are known as ecosystem services and include products like clean drinking water and processes such as the decomposition of wastes. *Ecosystem Diversity: Ecosystem Services*

_____ 24. **(B)** In changing and/or unstable environments, *r*-selection predominates as the ability to reproduce quickly is crucial. Characteristics of *r*-strategists include:

- Produce numerous offspring at once
- Short gestation period
- Less resources spent per offspring
- Offspring hatch or born capable of surviving on their own
- Have small bodies
- Mature fast and have short life span
- Able to disperse offspring widely
- Death rate generally not correlated with density of population
- Population size fluctuates and not stable
- Occupies a generalist role in ecology
- Use a high reproductive rate to high mortality rate

Natural Ecosystem Change: Climate Shifts

_____ 25. **(A)** Primary succession occurs in biotic communities in a previously uninhabited and barren habitat with little or no soil. *Natural Ecosystem Change: Ecological Succession*

_____ 26. **(E)** Primary succession occurs in biotic communities in a previously uninhabited and barren habitat with little or no soil. Secondary succession is a process started by an event (e.g., forest fire, harvesting, hurricane) that reduces an already established ecosystem (e.g., a forest or a wheat field) to a smaller population of species, and as such, secondary succession occurs on preexisting soil whereas primary succession usually occurs in a place lacking soil. Secondary succession is usually faster than primary succession as soil is already present, so there is no need for pioneer species and seeds, roots and underground vegetative organs of plants may still survive in the soil. In unstable or unpredictable environments, *r*-selection predominates as the ability to reproduce quickly is crucial. There is little advantage in adaptations that permit successful competition with other organisms because the environment is likely to change again. Traits that are thought to be characteristic of *r*-selection include: high fecundity, small body size, early maturity onset, short generation time, and the ability to disperse offspring widely. Examples include: bacteria and diatoms, insects, and weeds. In stable or predictable environments, *K*-selection predominates as the ability to compete successfully for limited resources is crucial. Traits that are thought to be characteristic of *K*-selection include: large body size, long life expectancy, and the production of fewer offspring, which require extensive parental care until they mature. Organisms with *K*-selected traits include large organisms such as elephants, trees, humans, and whales. *Natural Ecosystem Change: Ecological Succession*

_____27. **(D)** The conversion of ammonium (NH_4^+) to nitrate (NO_3^-) is performed primarily by soil-living bacteria and other nitrifying bacteria. In the primary stage of nitrification, the oxidation of ammonium (NH_4^+) is performed by bacteria such as the *Nitrosomonas* species, which converts ammonia (NH_3) to nitrites (NO_2^-). Other bacterial species, such as *Nitrobacter*, are responsible for the oxidation of the nitrites (NO_2^-) into nitrates (NO_3^-). It is important for the nitrites to be converted to nitrates because accumulated nitrites are toxic to plant life. *Natural Biogeochemical Cycles: Nitrogen Cycle*

RECAP FOR THE LIVING WORLD

_____ Total number correct for this section

_____ Percent correct for this section
(number correct for this section / 14) $\times$ 100%

_____ Number wrong for this section (questions you thought you knew).
Do NOT count answers left blank.

_____ Number left blank for this section (questions you did not know)

III. Population (10–15%)

_____ 28. **(E)** A density-independent factor is one where the effect of the factor on the size of the population is independent of and does NOT depend upon the original density or size of the population; e.g., a severe storm and flood coming through an area can just as easily wipe out a large population as a small one. *Population Biology Concepts: Population Ecology*

_____ 29. **(C)** Having extra food in the water between 0 and 15 hours will not affect the population density during this time period. Assuming ideal conditions with more than enough food available during this time period, the paramecium are already reproducing at their maximum capacity. However, if there is extra food available at all times during the 30 hours of the experiment, then the time period of exponential growth is extended, increasing the population density until a point is reached that another limiting factor such as oxygen content in the water begins to affect the density of paramecium that can survive; at which point a new carrying capacity is established. *Population Biology Concepts: Carrying Capacity*

_____ 30. **(C)** In stable or predictable environments, *K*-selection predominates as the ability to compete successfully for limited resources is crucial and populations of *K*-selected organisms typically are very constant and close to the maximum that the environment can bear (unlike *r*-selected populations, where population sizes can change much more rapidly). Traits that are thought to be characteristic of *K*-selection include: large body size, long life expectancy, and the production of fewer offspring, which require extensive parental care until they mature. Examples of organisms with *K*-selected traits include large organisms such as elephants, trees, humans, and whales. *Population Biology Concepts: Reproductive Strategies*

_____ 31. **(A)** In clumped distribution, the distance between neighboring individuals is minimized and is found in environments that are characterized by patchy resources. Clumped distribution is the most common type of dispersion found in nature because animals need certain resources to survive, and when these resources become scarce during certain parts of the year, animals tend to "clump" together around these crucial resources. Individuals might be clustered together in an area due to social factors such as herds or family groups. Organisms that usually serve as prey form clumped distributions in areas where they can hide and detect predators easily. Other causes of clumped distributions are the inability of offspring to independently move from their habitat. Clumped distribution in species also acts as a mechanism against predation as well as an efficient mechanism to trap or corner prey. *Population Biology Concepts: Survivorship*

_____ 32. (**D**) Choice D is known as a Type II survivorship curve and is typical of species in which a fairly constant mortality rate is experienced regardless of age. Type I survivorship curves (E) are characterized by high survival in early and middle life, followed by a rapid decline in survivorship in later life. Humans are one of the species that show this pattern of survivorship. In Type III curves (B), the greatest mortality is experienced early on in life, with relatively low rates of death for those surviving this bottleneck. This type of curve is characteristic of species that produce a large number of offspring. One example of a species that follows this type of survivorship curve is the frog. *Population Biology Concepts: Survivorship*

_____ _33. (**B**) Stage 2 sees a rise in population caused by a decline in the death rate while the birth rate remains high, or perhaps even rises slightly. The decline in the death rate is due initially to two factors: (1) improvements in food supply brought about by higher yields as agricultural practices were improved in the Agricultural Revolution of the 18th century and (2) significant improvements in public health that reduced mortality, particularly in childhood. As a consequence, there is an increasingly rapid rise in population growth (a "population explosion") as the gap between deaths and births grows wider; not due to an increase in fertility (or birthrates) but to a decline in deaths, which results in the increasing survival of children. Hence, the age structure of the population becomes increasingly youthful. This trend is intensified as these increasing numbers of children enter into reproduction while maintaining the high fertility rate of their parents. *Human Population: Demographic Transition*

_____ 34. (**C**) The Rule-of-70 provides a simple way to calculate the approximate number of years it takes for the level of a variable growing at a constant rate to double. This rule states that the approximate number of years n for a variable growing at the constant growth rate of R percent, to double is

$$n = \frac{70}{r} = \frac{70}{5} = 14$$

Human Population: Doubling Times

_____ 35. (**D**) Prior to the First or Neolithic Agricultural Revolution, humans were hunters-gatherers. During the First Agricultural Revolution, humans began to domesticate animals and raise crops, which allowed a steady food supply. With a steady food supply, the population increased. However, without the current advancements in medical care, sanitation, food preservation, etc., both birth and death rates were high. Today's birth and death rates in many areas of the world are significantly lower than 10,000 years ago due to these advancements along with women joining the workforce, family planning, etc. *Human Population: Historical Population Sizes*

_____ 36. (**A**) Four general types of age-structure diagrams have been identified by the fertility and mortality rates of a country.

(1) Stable pyramid—A population pyramid showing an unchanging pattern of fertility and mortality.

(2) Stationary pyramid—A population pyramid typical of countries with low fertility and low mortality, very similar to a constrictive pyramid.

(3) Expansive pyramid—A population pyramid showing a broad base, indicating a high proportion of children, a rapid rate of population growth, and a low proportion of older people. This wide base indicates a large number of children. A steady upward narrowing shows that more people die at each higher age band. This type of pyramid indicates a population in which there is a high birthrate, a high death rate, and a short life expectancy. This is the typical pattern for less economically developed countries, due to little access to and incentive to use birth control, negative environmental factors (for example, lack of clean water), and poor access to health care. This age structure diagram would be typical for a country such as Nigeria.

(4) Constrictive pyramid—A population pyramid showing lower numbers or percentages of younger people. The country will have a greying population, which means that people are generally older, as the country has long life expectancy, a low death rate, but also a low birthrate. This pyramid is often a typical pattern for a very developed country, a high over-all education, and easy access and incentive to use birth control, good health care, and few or no negative environmental factors. This age structure diagram would be typical for a country such as Germany and to a lesser extent the United States. *Human Population: Age-Structure Diagram*

_____37. (**B**) *Human Population: Population Size*

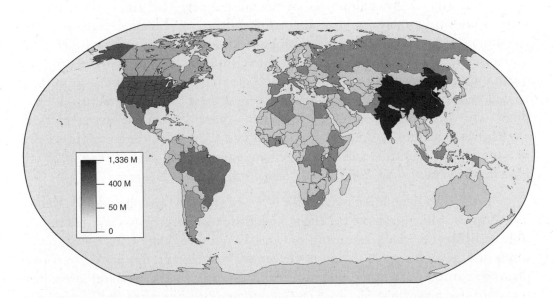

_____ 38. (**C**) It takes up to 16 pounds of grain to produce just 1 pound of meat and raising animals for food (including land used for grazing and land used to grow feed crops) uses 30% of the Earth's landmass. Raising animals for food is grossly inefficient, because while animals eat large quantities of grain, soybeans, oats, and corn, they only produce comparatively small amounts of meat, dairy products, or eggs in return. That is why more than 70% of the grain and cereals that are grown in the United States are fed to farmed animals. In addition, it takes more than 11 times as much fossil fuel to produce 1 calorie from animal protein as it does to produce 1 calorie from plant protein. *Human Population: Impacts of Population Growth*

_____ 39. (**B**) The combination of decreasing death rate due to the march of progress in sanitation and medicine, coupled later with the decrease in birthrate due to changes in the economies, has led to a significant change in the population growth in the developed world. *Human Population: Human Population Dynamics*

RECAP FOR POPULATION

_____ Total number correct for this section

_____ Percent correct for this section
(number correct for this section / 12) × 100%

_____ Number wrong for this section (questions you thought you knew).
Do NOT count answers left blank.

_____ Number left blank for this section (questions you did not know)

IV. Land and Water Use (10–15%)

_____ 40. (**A**) Genetically modified crops are crops that have been genetically modified in a lab setting. The majority of processed foods in the United States contain food products that have been genetically modified. The DNA of the organism is spliced and swapped out for "better" genes, which are theoretically designed to create stronger, more resistant, and more productive plants. *Agriculture: Feeding a Growing Population: Green Revolution*

_____ 41. (**C**) Organophosphates are the most widely used group of insecticides used in the world today (approximately 40% of the world market) and are generally among the most acutely toxic of all pesticides to vertebrate animals. They are also unstable and therefore break down relatively quickly in the environment. Most organophosphate pesticides are insecticides, although there are also a number of related herbicide and fungicide compounds. In developing countries, organophosphates are widely used because they are less expensive than the newer pesticide alternatives. Their use is banned or restricted in 23 countries, their import is illegal in a total of 50 countries, and they were banned in the United States in 2000 and have not been used since 2003. *Controlling Pests: Types of Pesticides*

_____ 42. (**D**) In addition to (A), (B), (C), and (E), IPM also includes (1) biological controls, which promote beneficial insects that eat target pests and (2) responsible pesticide use, which is generally only used as required and often only at specific times in a pest's life cycle. Many of the newer pesticide groups are derived from plants or naturally occurring substances (e.g., nicotine, pyrethrum, and insect juvenile hormone analogues). *Agriculture: Controlling Pests: Integrated Pest Management*

_____ 43. (**E**) In a shelterwood cut, mature trees are removed in two or three harvests over a period of 10 to 15 years. This method allows regeneration of medium to low shade-tolerant species because a "shelter" is left to protect them. *Forestry: Forest Management*

_____ 44. (**E**) Market gardening is growing of vegetables and flowers on suburban land of high value for the supply of nearby cities. Heavy fertilizing, regular watering, and the planting of successive crops are employed to obtain continuous returns from the acreage. *Rangelands: Desertification*

_____ 45. (**D**) Job sprawl is defined as low-density, geographically spread-out patterns of employment, where the majority of jobs in a given metropolitan area are located outside of the main city's central business district, and increasingly in the suburban periphery. It is often the result of urban disinvestment, the geographic freedom of employment location allowed by predominantly car-dependent commuting patterns of many American suburbs, and many companies' desire to locate in low-density areas that are often more affordable and offer potential for expansion. *Other Land Use: Urban Land Development: Suburban Sprawl*

_____ 46. (**D**) In 1919 when Dwight Eisenhower was a young officer in the U.S. Army, it took two months for a military convoy to go from Washington, D.C. to San Francisco. Later, when Eisenhower was a general during WWII, he had first-hand knowledge of the German autobahn. Through his first-hand knowledge and urging, the expanded Federal-Aid Highway Act of 1956 authorized a budget of $25 billion to build an extended federal highway system network of 41,000 miles (66,000 km) that included: a minimum of two lanes in each direction; lanes that were 12 feet (3.7 m) in width; a 10-foot (3-m) right paved shoulder and design speeds of 50–70 mph (80–113 km per hour). Today the network stretches 47,000 miles (75,000 km). *Other Land Use: Transportation Infrastructure: Federal Highway System*

_____ 47. (**C**) Cities occupy approximately 5% of the Earth's land surface; forests occupy approximately one-third of the Earth's surface, and land used for agricultural purposes occupies approximately half of all the Earth's land surface. *Other Land Use: Public and Federal Lands: Management*

_____ 48. (**A**) The Bureau of Land Management (BLM) is an agency within the U.S. Department of the Interior, which administers America's public lands, totaling approximately 253 million acres (1,020,000 sq. km), or one-eighth of the landmass of the United States. The BLM also manages 700 million acres (2,800,000 sq. km) of subsurface mineral rights underlying federal, state, and private lands. Most public lands are located in western states, including Alaska. The BLM's stated mission is to sustain the health, diversity, and productivity of the public lands for the use and enjoyment of present and future generations. *Other Land Use: Public and Federal Lands: Management*

_____ 49. (**C**) Environmental mitigation involves steps taken to avoid or minimize negative environmental impacts. Mitigation can include: avoiding the impact by not taking a certain action; minimizing impacts by limiting the degree or magnitude of the action; rectifying the impact by repairing or restoring the affected environment; reducing the impact by protective steps required with the action; and/or compensating for the impact by replacing or providing substitute resources. The example is not preservation as nothing was preserved. Environmental remediation deals with the removal of pollution or contaminants from environmental media such as soil, groundwater, sediment, or surface water. Restoration involves bringing back to a former or original state. *Other Land Use: Land Conservation Options: Preservation, Remediation, Mitigation, Restoration*

_____ 50. (**A**) Surface mining is done by removing (stripping) surface vegetation, dirt, and if necessary, layers of bedrock in order to reach buried ore deposits. Techniques of surface mining include open-pit mining, which consists of recovery of materials from an open pit in the ground, quarrying or gathering building materials from an open pit mine; strip mining, which consists of stripping surface layers off to reveal ore/seams underneath; and mountaintop removal, commonly associated with coal mining, which involves taking the top of a mountain off to reach ore deposits at depth. *Other Land Use: Mining: Extraction*

_____ 51. (**E**) Purse seining establishes a large wall of netting to encircle schools of fish. Fishermen pull the bottom of the netting closed—like a drawstring purse—to herd fish into the center. This method is used to catch schooling fish, such as sardines, or species that gather to spawn, such as squid. *Other Land Use: Fishing: Fishing Techniques*

_____ 52. (**B**) "The Tragedy of the Commons," written by ecologist Garrett Hardin in 1968, illustrates the argument that free access and unrestricted demand for a finite resource ultimately reduces the resource through overexploitation. This occurs because the benefits of exploitation accrue to individuals or groups, each of whom is motivated to maximize use of the resource to the point in which they become reliant on it, while the costs of the exploitation are borne by all those to whom the resource is available (which may be a wider class of individuals than those who are exploiting it). This, in turn, causes demand for the resource to increase, which causes the problem to increase to the point that the resource is depleted. *Global Economics: Tragedy of the Commons*

RECAP FOR LAND AND WATER USE

_____ Total number correct for this section

_____ Percent correct for this section
(number correct for this section / 13) × 100%

_____ Number wrong for this section (questions you thought you knew).
Do NOT count answers left blank.

_____ Number left blank for this section (questions you did not know)

V. Energy/Resources and Consumption (10–15%)

_____ 53. (**B**) *Energy Concepts: Conversions*

$$\frac{100 \text{ lightbulbs}}{1} \times \frac{200 \text{ watts}}{1 \text{ lightbulb}} \times \frac{10 \text{ hours}}{1 \text{ day}} \times \frac{6 \text{ days}}{1 \text{ week}} \times \frac{50 \text{ weeks}}{1 \text{ year}} \times \frac{1 \text{ kilowatt}}{1,000 \text{ watts}} = \frac{60,000 \text{ kilowatt} \cdot \text{hrs}}{\text{year}}$$

_____ 54. (**E**) The percent change is calculated as $\% = \frac{V_f - V_i}{V_i} \times 100\%$ where V_f is the final value and V_i is the initial V_i value. Therefore, $\% = \frac{112 - 8}{8} \times 100\% = 1300\%$. *Energy Concepts: Conversions*

_____ 55. (**B**) The Second Law of Thermodynamics states that energy varies in its quality or ability to do useful work. For useful work to occur energy must move or flow from a level of high-quality (more concentrated) energy to a level of lower-quality (less concentrated) energy. The chemical potential energy concentrated in a tank of gasoline and the concentrated heat energy at a high temperature are forms of high-quality energy. Because the energy in gasoline is concentrated, it has the ability to perform useful work in moving or changing matter. In contrast, less concentrated heat energy at a low temperature has little remaining ability to perform useful work. *Energy Concepts: Laws of Thermodynamics*

_____ 56. (**D**) According to the United States Energy Information Administration, the United States consumes about 19 million barrels of oil per day; oil that is used to produce gasoline, manufacturing products, heating and power, etc. Since each barrel of oil equates to 42 gallons (160 L), this represents about 800 million gallons (3 billion L) of oil per day. With the United States population at approximately 313 million, this works out to be about 2.5 gallons (10 L) of oil per person per day. In contrast, China with a population of 1.4 billion people (almost three times that of the United States) currently consumes 8.2 million barrels of oil (345 million gallons (1.3 billion L)) per day, which represents about 0.25 gallons per person per day. However, with a rising standard of living, this figure is expected to rise, and compounded with the larger population, China is expected to become the world's primary oil consumer. Because oil is a finite resource, according to the Law of Supply and Demand, prices are expected to rise. *Energy Consumption: Present Global Energy Use*

_____ 57. (**E**) In the United States on average the amount of energy required for heating a home far outpaces that used to cool it. In fact, over the course of a year nearly one-third of a typical utility bill goes to heating. For most of the United States on average the temperature difference in the winter is about twice that of the summer to maintain an indoor temperature of 75°F (24°C). For example, during the winter, if the temperature outside is 35°F (2°C), that represents a 40°F difference. In summer, if the outdoor temperature reaches 95°F (35°C), that represents a 20°F difference in order to keep the indoor temperature at 75°F (24°C). *Energy Consumption: Present Global Energy Use*

_____ 58. (**B**) *Energy Consumption: Present Global Energy Use*

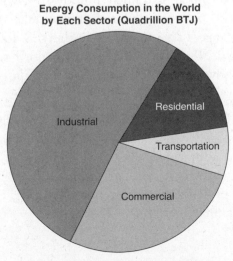

Energy Consumption in the World by Each Sector (Quadrillion BTJ)

Source: U.S. Energy Information Administration

_____59. (**D**) *Fossil Fuel Resources and Use: World Reserves and Global Demand*

$$\frac{2{,}170 \times 10^{12} \text{ ft}^3}{62 \times 10^9 \text{ ft}^3/\text{day}} \times \frac{1 \text{ year}}{365 \text{ day}} = 35 \times 10^3 \div 365 \approx 100 \text{ years}$$

_____60. (**C**) Natural gas (mostly methane) when burned produces 45% less carbon dioxide than coal and 30% less carbon dioxide than oil. However, methane is 21 times more dangerous for greenhouse warming than carbon dioxide so incomplete combustion or any leakage of natural gas (from animals, pipelines, landfills, melting tundra, sea floor hydrates, etc.) contributes strongly to greenhouse emissions and global warming. *Fossil Fuel Resources and Use: Environmental Advantages/ Disadvantages of Sources*

_____ 61. (**E**) Nuclear power provides 79% of the electricity produced in France and France's electricity price is among the lowest in Europe. Following the 2011 Fukushima nuclear accident, there have been active debates in France as to whether to upgrade the existing nuclear reactors or whether to begin phasing them out. The following represent the amount of electricity generated from nuclear power: United States (20%), Russia (18%), China (2%), and Japan (29%). *Nuclear Energy: Electricity Production*

_____ 62. (**E**) For every three units of energy produced by the reactor core of a U.S. nuclear power plant, two units are discharged to the environment as waste heat. Nuclear plants are often built on the shores of lakes, rivers, and oceans because these bodies provide the large quantities of cooling water needed to handle the waste heat discharge that results in thermal pollution. *Nuclear Energy: Electricity Production*

_____ 63. (**C**) In order (most expensive to least expensive): Natural Gas: $0.081 > Wind: $0.030 > Coal: $0.027 > Nuclear: $0.019 (*includes eventual decommissioning costs*) > Hydroelectric: $0.009. *Nuclear Energy: Electricity Production*

_____ 64. (**C**) Dams built across rivers slow down the river's flow and cause sediments in the water to deposit to the bottom of the reservoir behind the dam. As the sediments accumulate in the reservoir, the dam gradually loses its ability to store water for the purpose(s) for which it was built. The rate of reservoir sedimentation depends mainly on the size of a reservoir relative to the amount of sediment flowing into it: a small reservoir on an extremely muddy river will rapidly lose capacity whereas a large reservoir on a very clear river may take some time to lose an appreciable amount of storage. Large reservoirs in the U.S. lose storage capacity at an average rate of around 0.2% per year while most major reservoirs in China lose capacity at an annual rate over 2%. *Hydroelectric Power: Silting*

_____ 65. (**B**) First enacted by Congress in 1975, the purpose of CAFE (Corporate Average Fuel Economy) is to reduce energy consumption by increasing the fuel economy of cars and light trucks. The National Highway Traffic Safety Administration (NHTSA) administers the CAFE program and sets fuel economy standards for cars and light trucks sold in the U.S., while the Environmental Protection Agency (EPA) provides the fuel economy data and calculates the average fuel economy for each manufacturer.

_____ 66. (**E**) To begin with, you will need to buy 10 incandescent lightbulbs to last the same amount of time as the CFL: 10 × $2.00 = $20. By buying the CFL, you therefore save $20 − $13 = $7.

The total cost of energy for the incandescent bulbs would be:

$$\frac{10 \text{ incandescent lightbulbs}}{1} \times \frac{150 \text{ watts}}{1 \text{ incandescent lightbulb}} \times \frac{1 \text{ kilowatt}}{1,000 \text{ watts}} \times \frac{1,000 \text{ hours}}{1} \times \frac{\$0.10}{1 \text{ kWh}} = \$150.$$

The total cost of energy for the single CFL bulb would be:

$$\frac{10 \text{ CFL bulbs}}{1} \times \frac{42 \text{ watts}}{1 \text{ CFL bulb}} \times \frac{1 \text{ kilowatt}}{1,000 \text{ watts}} \times \frac{10,000 \text{ hours}}{1} \times \frac{\$0.10}{1 \text{ kWh}} = \$42.00$$

Therefore, you save $150.00 − $42.00 = $108.00 in energy for a total savings of $108.00 in energy + $7.00 saving in cost of bulb = $115.00 *Energy Conservation: Energy Efficiency*

_____ 67. (**A**) *Solar Energy is currently used the least in the U.S.*

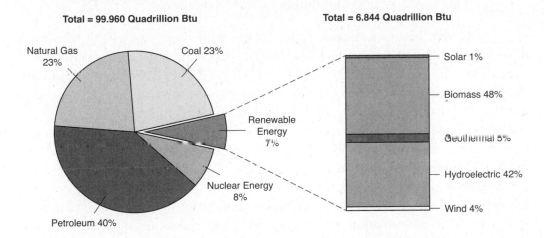

Total = 99.960 Quadrillion Btu

Total = 6.844 Quadrillion Btu

RECAP FOR ENERGY RESOURCES AND CONSUMPTION

_____ Total number correct for this section

_____ Percent correct for this section
(number correct for this section / 15) × 100%

_____ Number wrong for this section (questions you thought you knew).
Do NOT count answers left blank.

_____ Number left blank for this section (questions you did not know)

VI. Pollution (15–30%)

_____ 68. (**B**) Primary air pollutants are pollutants that are released directly into the lower atmosphere (troposphere) and are toxic. Secondary air pollutants are those pollutants that are formed by the combination or chemical reaction of primary pollutants in the atmosphere. Acid rain forms from the chemical reaction in the atmosphere. Acid rain is formed by the reaction of sulfur dioxide (SO_2) and water vapor. Another example of a secondary air pollutant would be PANs (peroxacyl nitrates), which are formed by the reaction of hydrocarbons, oxygen, and nitrogen dioxide. *Air Pollution: Sources—Primary and Secondary.*

_____ 69. (**E**) Criteria pollutants are pollutants that do the most harm to humans. In addition to those listed by the Environmental Protection Agency (EPA), nitrogen dioxide (NO_2), and lead (Pb) are also included. *Air Pollution: Major Air Pollutants*

_____ 70. (**B**) This type of problem can easily be solved by factor analysis. *Air Pollution: Measurement Units*

$$\frac{1{,}500 \text{ parts}}{1 \text{ billion}} \times \frac{1 \text{ billion}}{1{,}000{,}000{,}000 \text{ parts}} \times \frac{1{,}000{,}000 \text{ parts}}{1 \text{ million}} = 1.5 \text{ ppm}$$

_____ 71. (**B**) Nitrogen dioxide (NO_2) reacts with water vapor (H_2O) to form nitrous acid (HNO_2) and nitric acid (HNO_3), which are both components found in acid deposition (rain): $2NO_2 + H_2O \rightarrow HNO_2 + HNO_3$. Nitrogen dioxide also absorbs light energy and breaks down to form nitric oxide (NO) and atomic oxygen (O). Nitric oxide can then combine with ozone (O_3) to form nitrogen dioxide (NO_2) and oxygen (O_2): $NO + O_3 \rightarrow NO_2 + O_2$. If the concentration of nitrogen dioxide is greater than the concentration of nitric oxide, then ozone is formed and can reach dangerous levels. If the concentration of nitrogen dioxide is less than the concentration of nitric acid, then the ozone is destroyed almost instantly, keeping the concentration of ozone stable and below a harmful threshold. Sulfur dioxide is only involved in formation of acid rain, not photochemical smog. *Air Pollution: Acid Deposition and Smog.*

_____ 72. (**B**) Temperature inversions usually occur in urban areas when air pollutants are trapped close to the ground and not able to rise into the atmosphere. Under normal conditions, warmer air, which is less dense than cooler air, will rise into the cooler atmosphere above. However, during a temperature inversion, the air above a city is warm, and prevents the polluted warmer air from rising, causing smog levels to increase, which results in increased respiratory distress. *Air Pollution: Temperature Inversions*

_____ 73. (**C**) "Naturally occurring" means occurring in nature in a free state. Both radon and asbestos are found in nature and are sometimes found in indoor air samples. If radioactive radon occurs in the bedrock near a building, it can seep into a basement or crawlspace and eventually result in lung cancer. Asbestos was often used as insulation material. When asbestos fibers are inhaled, they are trapped in the lungs, which causes the lungs to produce acids. In time, this can lead to diseases such as asbestosis, lung cancer, or mesothelioma. Chlorofluorocarbons and peroxyacylnitrates (PANs) are not naturally occurring in their free state and generally not considered indoor air pollutants. VOCs (volatile organic compounds) such as formaldehyde, are indoor air pollutants and are commonly found in carpet, paneling, furniture, paint, plastics, cleaning fluids, etc., but like CFCs and PANs, they are not naturally occurring. *Air Pollution: Indoor Air Pollution*

_____ 74. (**A**) National Ambient Air Quality Standards (NAAQS) are standards established by the U.S. Environmental Protection Agency (EPA) under authority of the Clean Air Act that apply for outdoor air throughout the country. Primary standards are designed to protect human health, with an adequate margin of safety, including sensitive populations such as children, the elderly, and individuals suffering from respiratory diseases. Secondary standards are designed to protect public welfare from any known or anticipated adverse effects of a pollutant. *Air Pollution: Clean Air Act and Other Relevant Laws*

_____ 75. (**E**) Noise pollution in the workplace is regulated and enforced by OSHA (Occupational Safety and Health Administration) a branch of the U.S. Department of Labor. A difference of 20 decibels corresponds to an increase of 10 × 10 or 100 times in intensity. Reef fish, whales, dolphins, and other marine species rely on sounds to communicate. Under the Clean Air Act, the EPA established the Office of Noise Abatement and Control (ONAC) to carry out investigations and studies on noise and its effect on the public health and welfare. Through ONAC, the EPA coordinated all federal noise control activities, but in 1981 the administration concluded that noise issues were best handled at the state and local level. As a result, ONAC was closed and primary responsibility of addressing noise issues was transferred to state and local governments. However, EPA retains authority to investigate and study noise and its effect, disseminate information to the public regarding noise pollution and its adverse health effects, respond to inquiries on matters related to noise, and evaluate the effectiveness of existing regulations for protecting the public health and welfare. *Noise Pollution: Effects*

_____ 76. (**D**) The World Health Organization (WHO) has estimated that 1.1 billion people globally lack basic access to drinking water resources, while 2.4 billion people have inadequate sanitation facilities, which accounts for many water related acute and chronic diseases. Some 3.4 million people, many of them young children, die each year from water-borne diseases, such as intestinal diarrhea (cholera, typhoid fever, and dysentery), caused by microbially-contaminated water supplies that are linked to deficient or non-existent sanitation and sewage disposal facilities. Globally, water-borne diseases are the second leading cause of death in children below the age of five years, while childhood mortality rates from acute respiratory infections ranks first. *Water Pollution: Causes and Effects*

_____ 77. (**B**) In choice (A), hot water does not promote the growth of algae— phosphates and/or nitrates do. With an algal bloom being a mile away from the factory, it would be more likely that phosphates and/or nitrates were coming from another source. In choice (C), finding high concentrations of metal ions upstream of the drainage pipe would generally rule out the factory. Furthermore, metal ions would generally not be a waste product from a fertilizer plant. In choice (D), large numbers of insect larvae, also known as indicator species, probably indicates that the water this far from the factory may be very clean. Large amounts of food wastes dumped into the water at the site of the drainage pipe would supply vital nutrients to bacteria that would thrive and use up large amounts of oxygen for their metabolic requirements and deprive other organisms of oxygen that they would need (cultural eutrophication). Turbidity measures the amount of suspended material in the water and would probably not have much to do with the release of waste water from the production of pharmaceuticals. *Water Pollution: Sources*

_____ 78. **(A)** The Clean Water Act passed in 1972 was enacted to reduce point source pollution and addressed protecting surface water. It did not directly address groundwater contamination. The Safe Drinking Water Act, Resource Conservation and Recovery Act, and the Superfund Act did address groundwater contamination. *Water Pollution: Clean Water Act and Other Relevant Laws*

_____ 79. **(C)** Biochemical oxygen demand or BOD is the amount of dissolved oxygen needed by aerobic biological organisms in a body of water to break down organic material present in a given water sample at certain temperature over a specific time period. The term also refers to a chemical procedure for determining this amount. *Water Pollution: Causes and Effects*

_____ 80. **(B)** Anaerobic decomposition is a biological process in which decomposition of organic matter occurs without oxygen. The area of the graph where oxygen in the water is lowest is the area where BOD is the highest. Two processes occur during anaerobic decomposition. First, facultative acid forming bacteria use organic matter as a food source and produce volatile (organic) acids, gases such as carbon dioxide and hydrogen sulfide, stable solids, and more facultative organisms. Second, anaerobic methane formers use the volatile acids as a food source and produce methane gas, stable solids, and more anaerobic methane formers. *Water Pollution: Cultural Eutrophication*

_____ 81. **(B)** Suspended solid matter is usually removed first by screens and/or sedimentation tanks. Next, the biological material from human wastes, food wastes, soaps, etc., is removed by allowing bacteria to break down the material. Finally, the last stage uses a form of disinfection. *Water Pollution: Sewage Treatment*

_____ 82. **(D)** Sanitary landfills are one of the most popular forms of waste disposal in the United States, primarily because they are the least expensive way to dispose of waste. In a sanitary landfill, waste is spread in layers on a piece of property, usually on marginal or submarginal land. The waste is spread into layers and then compacted tightly, greatly reducing the volume of the waste. The waste is then covered by soil. Problems that are encountered in open dumping, including insects, rodents, safety hazards, and fire hazards, are usually avoided with landfilling. A landfill should not be located in areas with high groundwater tables. Leachate migration control standards must be followed in the design, construction, and operation of landfills during the use of the facility and during the post closure period. Much of the waste in a sanitary landfill will decompose through biological and chemical processes that produce solid, liquid, and gaseous products. Food wastes degrade rapidly, whereas plastics, glass, and construction wastes do not. The most common types of gas produced by the decomposition of the wastes are methane and carbon dioxide. After a landfill has reached capacity, it is closed for waste deposition and covered. In some cases it can be used as pasture, cropland, or for recreational purposes. Maintenance of the closed landfill is important to avoid soil erosion and excess runoff into desirable areas. *Solid Waste: Types*

_____ 83. **(E)** Wherever possible, waste reduction is the least expensive option. If waste is produced, every effort should be made to reuse it if practicable. Recycling is the third option in the waste management hierarchy. Although recycling does help to conserve resources and reduce wastes, there are economic and environmental costs associated with waste collection and recycling. For this reason, recycling should only be considered for waste that cannot be reduced or reused. Finally, it may be possible to recover materials or energy from waste that cannot be reduced, reused, or recycled. *Solid Waste: Reduction*

_____ 84. (**B**) An acute exposure refers to a single exposure to a harmful substance that results in severe biological harm or death. *Hazards to Human Health: Acute and Chronic Effects*

_____ 85. (**B**) The median lethal dose, LD_{50} of a toxin, radiation, or pathogen is the dose required to kill half the members of a tested population after a specified test duration. LD_{50} figures are frequently used as a general indicator of a substance's acute toxicity. *Hazards to Human Health: Dose-Response Relationships*

_____ 86. (**D**) Follow the Y axis up to 50%, then move right until you reach the curve, then read straight down. *Hazards to Human Health: Dose-Response Relationships*

_____ 87. (**C**) The first point along the graph where a response above zero is reached is referred to as a threshold dose. For most drugs, the desired effects are found at doses slightly greater than the threshold dose. At higher doses, undesired side effects appear and grow stronger as the dose increases. The more potent a particular substance is, the steeper this curve will be. *Hazards to Human Health: Dose-Response Relationships*

_____88. (**D**) Cigarette smoke causes about half a million deaths a year in the United States; this represents 1 of every 5 deaths. On average, adults who smoke cigarettes die 14 years earlier than nonsmokers. Based on current cigarette smoking patterns, an estimated 25 million Americans who are alive today will die prematurely from smoking-related illnesses, including 5 million people younger than 18 years of age. Smokers increase their risk of dying from bronchitis by nearly 10 times, from emphysema by nearly 10 times, and from lung cancer by up to 22 times. The total cost of caring for people with health problems caused by cigarette smoking—counting all sources of medical payments—is about $73 billion per year. *Hazards to Human Health: Smoking and Other Risks*

_____ 89. (**E**) Endocrine disruptors are substances that interfere with the synthesis, secretion, transport, binding, action, or elimination of natural hormones in the body that are responsible for development, behavior, fertility, and maintenance of homeostasis.

Studies have shown that endocrine disruptors can cause adverse biological effects in animals, and low-level exposures also cause similar effects in human beings. In the late 1950s, Rachel Carson, a marine biologist, turned her attention to conservation and the environmental problems caused by synthetic pesticides. Her book, *Silent Spring* (1962), brought environmental concerns to an unprecedented portion of the American public. *Silent Spring*, while met with fierce denial from chemical companies, spurred a reversal in national pesticide policy—leading to a nationwide ban on DDT and other pesticides—and led to the creation of the Environmental Protection Agency (EPA). *Hazardous Chemicals in the Environment: Types of Hazardous Waste*

_____ 90. (**D**) Following is a diagram of a hazardous waste landfill. *Hazards to Human Health: Waste Treatment/Disposal of Hazardous Waste*

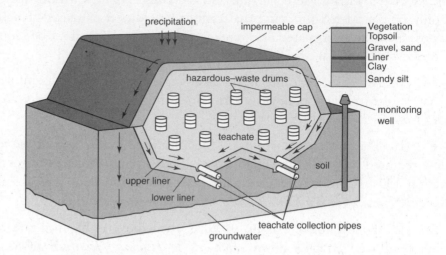

_____ 91. (**B**) Congress enacted the Resource Conservation and Recovery Act (RCRA) in 1976 to address the increasing problems the nation faced from its growing volume of municipal and industrial waste. RCRA amended the Solid Waste Disposal Act of 1965. It set national goals for:

- Protecting human health and the natural environment from the potential hazards of waste disposal.
- Energy conservation and natural resources.
- Reducing the amount of waste generated, through source reduction and recycling.
- Ensuring the management of waste in an environmentally sound manner. It is now most widely known for the regulations promulgated under RCRA that set standards for the treatment, storage, and disposal of hazardous waste in the United States. *Hazards to Human Health: Relevant Laws*

RECAP FOR POLLUTION

_____ Total number correct for this section

_____ Percent correct for this section
(number correct for this section / 24) × 100%

_____ Number wrong for this section (questions you thought you knew).
Do NOT count answers left blank.

_____ Number left blank for this section (questions you did not know)

VII. Global Change (10–15%)

_____ 92. (**A**) The marketplace forces of supply and demand determine the price of fuel. If demand grows or if a disruption in supply occurs, there will be upward pressure on prices. By the same token, if demand falls or there is an oversupply of product in the market, there will be downward pressure on prices. Recently, crude oil prices have risen dramatically, driven by rising global demand, speculation on prices, and political instability in several oil producing countries. *Economic Impacts*

_____ 93. (**E**) Currently, nitrous oxide emissions from human activities are more than twice as high as the next leading ozone-depleting gas. Nitrous oxide is emitted from natural sources and as a by-product of agricultural fertilization, livestock manure, sewage treatment, and other industrial processes. With CFCs and certain other ozone-depleting gases coming in check as a result of the 1987 Montreal Protocol, the international treaty that phased out ozone-destroying compounds, anthropogenic nitrous oxide is becoming an increasingly larger fraction of the emissions of ozone-depleting substances. Nitrous oxide is not regulated by the Montreal Protocol. Nitrous oxide is also a greenhouse gas. *Stratospheric Ozone: Causes of Ozone Depletion*

_____ 94. (**B**) Ice-albedo feedback (or snow-albedo feedback) is a positive feedback climate process whereby a change in the area of snow-covered land, ice caps, glaciers, or sea ice alters the albedo (Earth's reflectivity). Global warming tends to decrease ice cover allowing for greater exposure of darker land to increase absorption of solar energy, leading to more warming and more ice melting. *Global Warming: Impacts and Consequences of Global Warming*

_____ 95. (**B**) The Montreal Protocol on Substances That Deplete the Ozone Layer is an international treaty designed to protect the ozone layer by phasing out the production of numerous substances believed to be responsible for ozone depletion. The treaty went into effect on January 1, 1989. It is widely believed that if the international agreement is adhered to, the ozone layer may be expected to recover by 2050; however, increasing anthropogenic nitrous oxide emissions may delay that goal. *Stratospheric Ozone: Relevant Laws and Treaties*

_____ 96. (**C**) Water vapor is one of the most important elements of the climate system. As a greenhouse gas, it represents around 80% of total greenhouse gas mass in the atmosphere and 90% of greenhouse gas volume. The primary reasons why water vapor cannot be a cause of climate change are its short atmospheric residence time and a basic physical limitation on the quantity of water vapor in the atmosphere for any given temperature (its saturation vapor pressure). The addition of a large amount of water vapor to the troposphere would have little effect on global temperatures in the short term due to the thermal inertia of the climate system. *Global Warming: Greenhouse Gases and the Greenhouse Effect*

_____ 97. (**D**) Global sea level rose at an average rate of about 3.3 ± 0.4 mm per year from 1993 to 2009. Two main factors contribute to sea level rise. The first is thermal expansion: as ocean water warms, it expands. The second is from the contribution of land-based ice due to increased melting. The major store of water on land is found in glaciers and ice sheets. Melting of sea ice does not result in a rise in sea level. *Global Warming: Impacts and Consequences of Global Warming*

_____ 98. (**E**) In 1997, delegates from 194 nations met in Kyoto, Japan, and collectively promised to reduce greenhouse gas emissions by about 5% below 1990 levels by 2012, as a first step toward global cooperation on limiting carbon-driven climate change. The treaty they produced, known as the Kyoto Protocol, expires at the end of 2012. The treaty required the major industrialized nations to meet targets on emissions reduction but imposed no mandates on developing countries, including emerging economic powers and sources of global greenhouse gas emissions like China, India, Brazil, and South Africa. Major countries, including

Canada, France, Japan, and Russia, have said they will not agree to an extension of the protocol unless the unbalanced requirements of developing and developed countries are changed. That is similar to the United States' position, which is that any successor treaty must apply equally to all major economies. The United States has never been a party to the protocol. *Global Warming: Relevant Laws and Treaties*

_____ 99. (**E**) Habitat loss due to destruction, fragmentation, or degradation of habitat is the primary threat to the survival of wildlife. When an ecosystem has been dramatically changed by human activities—such as agriculture, oil and gas exploration, commercial development, or water diversion—it may no longer be able to provide the food, water, cover, and/or places for endangered species to live and raise young. *Loss of Biodiversity: Habitat Loss*

_____ 100. (**B**) CITES (the Convention on International Trade in Endangered Species of Wild Fauna and Flora) is an international agreement between governments. Its aim is to ensure that international trade in specimens of wild animals and plants does not threaten their survival. *Loss of Biodiversity: Relevant Laws and Treaties*

RECAP FOR GLOBAL CHANGE

_____ Total number correct for this section

_____ Percent correct for this section
(number correct for this section / 9) × 100%

_____ Number wrong for this section (questions you thought you knew).
Do NOT count answers left blank.

_____ Number left blank for this section (questions you did not know)

Assess Your Strengths and Weaknesses

    I. Earth Systems and Resources: _____ correct

   II. The Living World: _____ correct

  III. Population: _____ correct

  IV. Land and Water Use: _____ correct

   V. Energy Resources and Consumption: _____ correct

  VI. Pollution: _____ correct

 VII. Global Change: _____ correct

TOTAL: _____

PREDICTED AP SCORE

Less than 50 correct:	1 or 2 (not passing)
50–60 correct:	3 on the APES exam
61–75 correct:	4 on the APES exam
76+ correct:	5 on the APES exam

UNIT I: EARTH SYSTEMS AND RESOURCES (10–15%)

Areas on Which You Will Be Tested

A. Earth Science Concepts—geologic time scale, plate tectonics, earthquakes, volcanism, seasons, solar intensity, and latitude.

B. The Atmosphere—composition, structure, weather, climate, atmospheric circulation and the Coriolis effect, atmosphere-ocean interactions, and ENSO.

C. Global Water Resources and Use—freshwater, saltwater, ocean circulation, agriculture, industrial and domestic use, surface and groundwater issues, global problems, and conservation.

D. Soil and Soil Dynamics—rock cycle, formation, composition, physical and chemical properties, main soil types, erosion and other soil problems, and soil conservation.

The Earth

CHAPTER 1

GEOLOGIC TIME SCALE

Two time scales are used to measure the age of Earth. One is based on the sequence of layering of the rocks and the evolution of life. The other is the radiometric time scale, based on the natural radioactivity of chemical elements in rocks. Earth's past has been organized into various units according to events that took place in each period. Different spans of time on the time scale are usually separated by major geologic or paleontological events, such as mass extinctions. For example, the boundary between the Cretaceous period and the Paleogene period is defined by the extinction of the dinosaurs and many marine species. The largest defined unit of time is the eon. Eons are dived into eras, which are in turn divided into periods, epochs, and stages (Eon → Eras → Periods → Epochs → Stages). Key principles of the geological time scale:

1. Rock layers (strata) are laid down in succession with each strata representing a "slice" of time.

2. The principle of superposition—any given layer is probably older than those above it and younger than those below it.

Several factors complicate the geologic time scale:

1. Layers are often eroded, distorted, tilted, or even inverted after deposition.

2. Layers laid down at the same time in different areas can have entirely different appearances.

3. A layer from any given area represents only part of Earth's history.

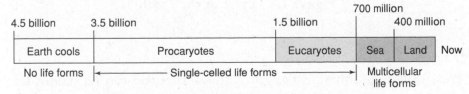

Figure 1.1 Timeline of life development

THE GEOLOGIC TIME SCALE

Era	When period began (millions of years ago)	Period	Animal life	Plant life	Major geologic events
Cenozoic	2	Neogene	Rise of civilizations	Increase in number of herbs and grasses	Ice Age
		Paleogene	Appearance of first men; dominance on land of mammals, birds, and insects	Dominance of land by flowering plants	
	65				
Mesozoic	135	Cretaceous		Dominance of land by conifers; first flowering plants appear	Building of the Rocky Mountains
		Jurassic	Age of dinosaurs		
	180	Triassic	First birds		
	225				
Paleozoic	275	Permian	Expansion of reptiles		Building of the Appalachian Mountains
		Carboniferous	Age of amphibians	Formation of great coal swamps	
	350	Devonian	Age of fishes		
	413	Silurian	Invasion of land by invertebrates	Invasion of land by primitive plants	
	430	Ordovician	Appearance of first vertebrates (fish)	Abundant marine algae	
	500	Cambrian	Abundant marine invertebrates	Appearance of primitive marine algae	
	570				
Precambrian		—	Primitive marine life		

Figure 1.2 Geologic time scale

EARTH STRUCTURE

Earth, which formed about 4.6 billion years ago, is the third planet away from the sun in the solar system and is the only planet known to support life. Earth can be divided into three sections: the biosphere, the hydrosphere, and the internal structure. The biosphere includes all forms of life (plants and animals) both on land and in the sea. The hydrosphere includes all forms of water (fresh and saltwater, snow, and ice). The internal structure of Earth is divided into the crust, mantle, and core.

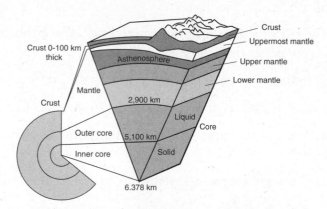

Figure 1.3 Layers of the Earth

Crust

The crust makes up only 0.5% of Earth's total mass and can be subdivided into two main parts: basalt-rich oceanic crust and granite-rich continental crust. The crust floats on top of the mantle. Oceanic crust covers about two-thirds of Earth's surface but comprises about only one-third of the crustal mass, as the continental crust is much thicker. Being relatively cold, the crust is rocky and brittle, so it can fracture in earthquakes.

CONTINENTAL CRUST

The continental crust extends from the surface of Earth down to 20–30 miles (30–50 km). The exposed parts of the continental crust are less dense than oceanic crust because oceanic crust contains minerals rich in heavier elements such as iron and magnesium. However, continental crust appears to be stratified (layered) and becomes denser with depth. It is largely composed of volcanic, sedimentary, and granite-type rocks, although the older areas are dominated by metamorphic rocks.

OCEANIC CRUST

From the surface of Earth down to about 7 miles (11 km) is the oceanic crust. The oceanic crust can be divided into ocean basins where water depth exceeds 2 miles (3 km), and the crust is layered and very uniform.

MOHO

The Mohorovicic discontinuity, usually referred to as the Moho, is the boundary between the Earth's crust and the mantle. The Moho serves to separate both oceanic crust and continental crust from underlying mantle. It lies 3 miles (5 km) below the ocean floor and 19–31 miles (30 to 50 km) beneath the continents. It was first identified in 1909, when abrupt increases in the velocity of earthquake waves (specifically P-waves) occurred in this area. During the late 1950s, Project Mohole was proposed to drill a hole through the ocean floor to reach this boundary, but the project was cancelled in 1967.

MANTLE

Most of Earth's mass is in the mantle, which is composed of iron, magnesium, aluminum, and silicon-oxygen compounds. At over 1800°F (1000°C), most of the mantle is solid. However, the upper third (known as the asthenosphere) is more plastic-like in nature.

CORE

The core is composed mostly of iron and is so hot that the outer core is molten. The inner core is under such extreme pressure that it remains solid.

PLATE TECTONICS

Plate tectonic theory arose out of two separate geological observations: continental drift and sea-floor spreading.

Latitude and Longitude

Longitude specifies east-west positions on the Earth. 0° longitude begins at the Prime Meridian in Greenwich, England. The degrees continue 180° east and 180° west until they meet and form the International Date Line in the Pacific Ocean. Latitude specifies north-south positions. 0° lati-

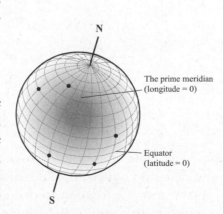

The prime meridian (longitude = 0)

Equator (latitude = 0)

tude is the equator. 90° north latitude is the north pole while 90° south latitude is the south pole. Each degree of latitude is approximately 69 miles (111 km) apart.

The Continental Drift Theory

In 1915, Alfred Wegener proposed that all present-day continents originally formed one landmass (Pangaea). Wegener believed that this supercontinent began to break up into smaller continents around 200 million years ago. He based his theory on five factors:

1. Fossilized tropical plants were discovered beneath Greenland's icecaps.

2. Glaciated landscapes occurred in the tropics of Africa and South America.

3. Tropical regions on some continents had polar climates in the past, based on paleoclimatic data.

4. The continents fit together like pieces of a puzzle.

5. Similarities existed in rocks between the east coasts of North and South America and the west coasts of Africa and Europe.

Continental drift gained acceptance in the 1960s when the theory of plate tectonics provided a mechanism that would account for the movement of the continents.

The Seafloor Spreading Theory

During the 1960s, alternating patterns of magnetic properties were discovered in rocks found on the seafloor. Similar patterns were discovered on either side of mid-oceanic ridges found near the center of the oceanic basins. Dating of the rocks indicated that as one moved away from the ridge, the rocks became older. This suggested that new crust was being created at volcanic rift zones.

The lithosphere (crust and upper mantle, approximately 62 miles (100 km) thick) is divided into massive sections known as plates, which float and move on the viscous asthenosphere. Subduction zones are areas on the Earth where two tectonic plates meet and move toward each other, with one sliding underneath the other and moving down into the mantle.

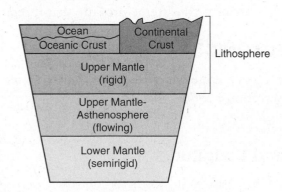

Figure 1.4 The outer layers of Earth

The plates move slowly over time and sink in areas of volcanic island chains, folded mountain belts, and trenches, and rise up from ridges and rift valleys. These plates move in relation to one another at one of three types of plate boundaries: transform, divergent, and convergent.

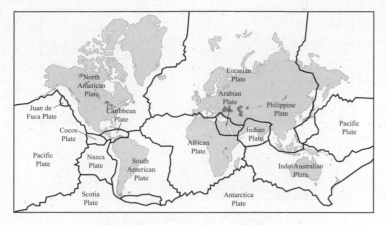

Figure 1.5 Earth's major plates

TRANSFORM BOUNDARIES

Transform boundaries occur where plates slide *past* each other. The friction and the stress buildup from the sliding plates frequently cause earthquakes—a common feature along transform boundaries. The San Andreas Fault, which is found near the western coast of North America, is where the Pacific and North American plates move relative to each other such that the Pacific plate is moving northwest with respect to North America. In about 50 million years, the part of California that is west of the San Andreas Fault will be a separate island near Alaska.

DIVERGENT BOUNDARIES

Divergent boundaries occur where two plates slide *apart* from each other with the space that was created being filled with molten magma from below. Examples of areas of oceanic divergent boundaries include the Mid-Atlantic Ridge and the East Pacific Rise. Examples of areas of continental divergent boundaries include the East African Great Rift Valley. Divergent boundaries can create massive fault zones in the oceanic ridge system and are areas of frequent oceanic earthquakes.

CONVERGENT BOUNDARIES

Convergent boundaries occur where two plates slide *toward* each other, commonly forming either a subduction zone (if one plate moves underneath the other) or an orogonic belt (if the two plates collide and compress). When a denser oceanic plate moves underneath (subducts) a less-dense continental plate, an oceanic trench is produced on the ocean side and a mountain range on the continental side. One example is the Cascade Mountain range, which extends north from California's Sierra Nevada Mountains and includes Mount Saint Helens.

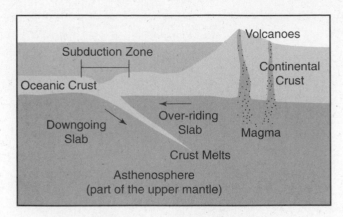

Figure 1.6 Subduction

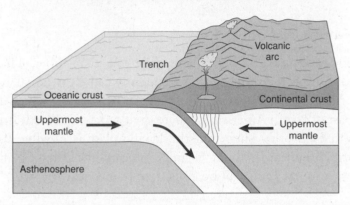

Figure 1.7 Oceanic-continental convergence

When *two oceanic plates converge*, they create an island arc—a curved chain of volcanic islands rising from the deep seafloor and near a continent. They are created by subduction processes and occur on the continent side of the subduction zone. Their curve is generally convex toward the open ocean. A deep undersea trench is located in front of such arcs where the descending plate dips downward. Examples include Japan and the Aleutian Islands in Alaska.

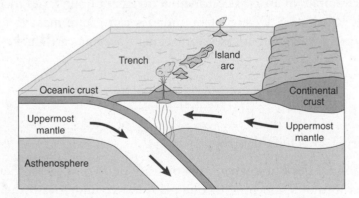

Figure 1.8 Oceanic-oceanic convergence

When *two continental plates collide*, mountain ranges are created as the colliding crust is compressed and pushed upward. An example is the northern margins of the Indian subcontinental plate being thrust under a portion of the Eurasian plate, lifting it and creating the Himalayas.

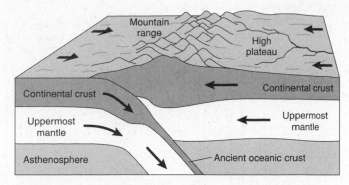

Figure 1.9 Continental-continental convergence

EARTHQUAKES

Earthquakes occur during abrupt movement on an existing fault, along tectonic plate boundary zones or along mid-oceanic ridges. A massive amount of stored energy, held in place by friction, is released in a very short period of time. The area where the energy is released is called the focus. From the focus, seismic waves travel outward in all directions. Directly above the focus, on Earth's surface, is the epicenter.

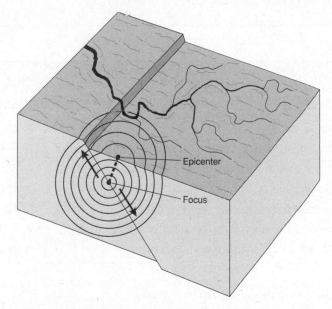

Figure 1.10 Relationship of an epicenter to a focus

The strength or magnitude of an earthquake is commonly measured by the logarithmic Richter scale and is recorded by a seismograph onto a seismogram.

However, the Richter magnitude scale is really comparing amplitudes of waves on a seismogram, not the strength (energy) of the quakes. Because of the logarithmic basis of the scale, each whole number increase in magnitude on the Richter scale represents a tenfold increase in measured amplitude. In terms of energy, each whole number increase corresponds to an increase of about 32 times the amount of energy released. It is the energy or strength of the earthquake that knocks down buildings and causes damage.

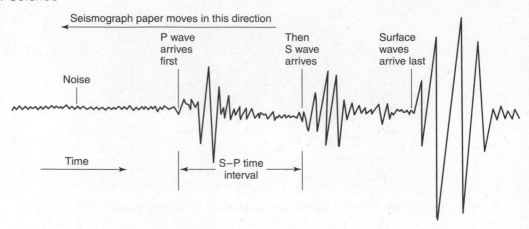

Figure 1.11 Seismogram

There are two classes of seismic waves: body waves and surface waves. Body waves travel through the interior of Earth. There are two types of body waves: P waves and S waves. P waves travel through Earth and are caused by expansion and contraction of bedrock. S waves are produced when material moves either vertically or horizontally and travel only within the uppermost layers of Earth (along its surface). Surface waves produce rolling and/or swaying motion and are slower than P or S waves. Surface waves cause ground motion and damage.

The Richter Scale

Severity	Richter scale	Description	Occurrence (per year)
Minor	3.0–3.9	Rarely causes damage.	~ 50,000
Light	4.0–4.9	Shaking of indoor items. No significant damage.	~ 6,000
Moderate	5.0–5.9	Major damage to poorly constructed buildings.	~ 800
Strong	6.0–6.9	Destructive up to 100 miles (160 km).	~ 120
Major	7.0–7.9	Serious damage over large areas.	~ 18
Great	8.0–8.9	Serious damage over several thousand miles.	~ 1
Extreme	9.0+	Devastating for thousands of miles.	1 in 20 years

The severity of an earthquake depends upon:

1. The amount of potential energy that had been stored

2. The distance the rock mass moved when the energy was released

3. How far below the surface the movement occurred

4. The makeup of the rock material

Primary effects are due to the shaking and resulting damage to buildings and infrastructure and due to the loss of life or injury. Secondary effects include rock slides, flooding due to subsidence (sinking) of land, liquefaction of recent sediments, fires, and tsunamis. Damage due to earthquakes can be reduced through mapping of faults, preparing computer models and simulations, strengthening building codes, preparing emergency teams with adequate training, upgrading communication technology and availability, storing emergency supplies, and educating the public.

> **CASE STUDIES**
>
> - **Haiti, 2010:** The January 2010 earthquake in Haiti was a catastrophic, magnitude 7.0 quake that occurred at a depth of 8 miles (13 km) below the surface. About 3 million people were affected by the quake, with close to 200,000 people killed directly and more than 250,000 severely injured. The capital of Port-au-Prince and surrounding cities were entirely destroyed primarily due to inadequate building codes, making rescue attempts extremely difficult. The quake occurred in the vicinity of the northern boundary of the Caribbean tectonic plate, where it shifts eastward by about 0.79 inches (20 mm) per year in relation to the North American plate.
> - **San Andreas Fault:** The San Andreas Fault, first discovered in 1895, is a continental transform fault that extends 800 miles (1,300 km) through California to Baja California in Mexico, forming the tectonic boundary between the Pacific plate and the North American plate. All land west of the fault on the Pacific plate is moving slowly to the northwest, while all land east of the fault is moving southwest. The rate of slippage averages about 1.5 inches (38 mm) per year. In 1906 a portion of the fault ruptured near San Francisco; the earthquake (estimated at 7.8) caused 3,000 deaths, many due to the resulting fires.

TSUNAMIS

Tsunamis are a series of waves created when a body of water is rapidly displaced usually by an earthquake. The effects of a tsunami can be devastating due to the immense volumes of water and energy involved. A tsunami can be generated when plate boundaries abruptly move and vertically displace the overlying water. Subduction-zone-related earthquakes generate the majority of all tsunamis. Tsunamis formed at divergent plate boundaries are rare since they do not generally disturb the vertical displacement of the water column. Tsunamis have a small wave height offshore, very long wavelength, and generally pass unnoticed at sea. Most tsunamis are generated in the Pacific and Indian Ocean basins. In 2004, the Indian Ocean 9.3 earthquake created tsunamis that killed ~300,000 people—one of the deadliest natural disasters in recorded history.

> **CASE STUDY**
>
> - **Tōhoku Earthquake and Tsunami:** In 2011, northern Japan was hit by a 9.0 magnitude earthquake that triggered a deadly 23-foot tsunami. The giant waves deluged cities and rural areas alike leaving a path of death and devastation in its wake. According to the official toll, the earthquake and resulting tsunami left 15,839 dead and 3,647 missing. In addition, cooling systems at a nearby nuclear power station failed shortly after the earthquake, causing a nuclear crisis. The initial nuclear reactor failure was followed by an explosion and eventual partial meltdowns and fires in other reactors, which resulted in the release of radioactivity directly into the atmosphere. More than 200,000 residents were evacuated from affected areas putting the disaster on par with the 1986 Chernobyl nuclear reactor explosion.

VOLCANOES

Active volcanoes produce magma (melted rock) at the surface. Other types of volcanoes are classified as intermittent, dormant, or extinct. The majority of volcanoes—95%—occur at subduction zones and mid-oceanic ridges. The remaining 5% occur at hot spots, areas where plumes of magma come close to the surface. Volcanoes may produce ejecta (lava rock and/or ash), molten lava, and/or toxic gases. The most common gases released by volcanoes are steam, carbon dioxide, sulfur dioxide, and hydrogen chloride. Volcanoes affect the climate by introducing large quantities of sulfur dioxide (SO_2) into the atmosphere that is later converted to sulfate ions (SO_4^{2-}) in the stratosphere. The sulfate particles reflect shorter wavelengths of solar radiation and serve as condensation nuclei for high clouds. In 1992, the year after the Mt. Pinatubo eruption, the effect of stratospheric sulfate particles decreased the average global temperature by as much as 1°F (0.5°C) by decreasing the amount of sunlight reaching Earth. The particles settle out of the atmosphere usually within two years and contribute to acid rain.

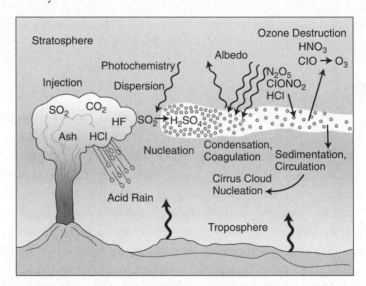

Figure 1.13 Atmospheric effects of volcanoes

Eruptions occur when pressure within a magma chamber forces molten magma up through a conduit (pipe) and out a vent at the top of the volcano. The type of eruption depends on the gases, the amount of silica in the magma (which determines viscosity), and how free the conduit is (whether the volcano flows or explodes). Correlation exists between seismic and volcanic activity. Benefits of volcanic eruptions include producing new landforms as seen in the Hawaiian Islands and increased soil nutrient levels produced from erosion of lava rock. Methods of dealing with threats from volcanoes include:

1. Modeling and data analysis for better volcanic activity prediction

2. Better evacuation plans

3. Study of precursors such as changes in the cone

4. Measuring changes in temperature and gas composition

5. Magnetic changes

6. Changes in seismic activity

Volcano Structure

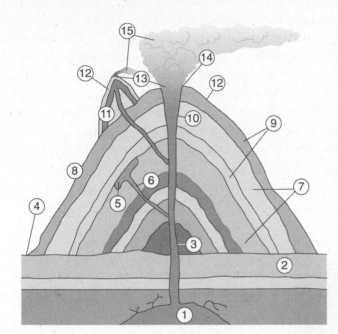

1. Magma chamber
2. Bedrock
3. Conduit (pipe)
4. Base
5. Sill
6. Branch pipe
7. Layers of ash emitted by the volcano
8. Flank
9. Layers of lava emitted by the volcano
10. Throat
11. Parasitic cone
12. Lava flow
13. Vent
14. Crater
15. Ash cloud

Figure 1.14 General volcano structure

CASE STUDIES

- **Mount Saint Helens:** Located in Washington State, Mount Saint Helens erupted in 1980. The earthquake removed trees, increased soil erosion, destroyed wildlife, and polluted the air with gases and ash. Other effects included mudflows, melting of glacial ice and snow, and clogged rivers that caused flooding. Fifty-seven people were killed.

- **Mount Pinatubo:** Mount Pinatubo is part of a chain of composite volcanoes on the west coast of the island of Luzon in the Philippines. In June 1991, Mount Pinatubo erupted for 9 hours, disgorged a cubic mile of volcanic debris, and vented 18 million metric tons of sulfur dioxide into the atmosphere which encircled Earth in three weeks after reaching the stratosphere. This was the largest sulfur dioxide cloud ever detected to date. The sulfate aerosols formed in the stratosphere increased reflection of solar radiation and within 3 years caused over a 2°F (1°C) overall cooling of Earth.

SEASONS, SOLAR INTENSITY, AND LATITUDE

Factors that affect the amount of solar energy at the surface of Earth (which directly affects plant productivity) include Earth's rotation (once every 24 hours), Earth's revolution around the sun (once per year), tilt of Earth's axis (23.5°), and atmospheric conditions. Summer (the period of greatest solar radiation) occurs in the Northern Hemisphere when the Northern Hemisphere is tilted toward the sun. The sun rises higher in the sky and stays above the horizon longer, with the rays of the sun striking the ground more directly (at less of an angle). Likewise, in the Northern Hemisphere winter, the hemisphere is tilted away from the sun. The Sun rises lower in the sky and stays above the horizon for a shorter period, with the rays of the sun striking the ground at a greater angle.

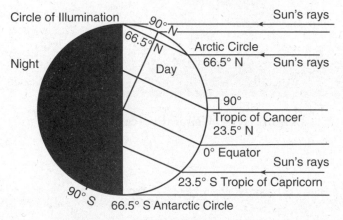

Figure 1.15 Summer solstice

Earth is closest to the sun during the Northern Hemisphere winter (December, January, and February) and farthest away during the Northern Hemisphere summer (June, July, and August). Seasons are NOT caused by Earth's distance from the sun, but rather by the angle of sunlight hitting the Earth.

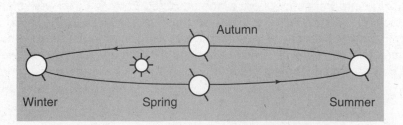

Figure 1.16 Seasons in the Northern Hemisphere

SOIL

Soils are a thin layer on top of most of Earth's land surface. This thin layer is a basic natural resource and deeply affects every other part of the ecosystem. For example, soils hold nutrients and water for plants and animals; water is filtered and cleansed as it flows through soils; and soils affect the chemistry of water and the amount of water that returns to the atmosphere to form rain. Soils are composed of three main ingredients: minerals of different sizes, organic materials from the remains of dead plants and animals, and open space that can be filled with water or air. A good soil for growing most plants should have about 45% minerals (with a mixture of sand, silt, and clay), 5% organic matter, 25% air, and 25% water.

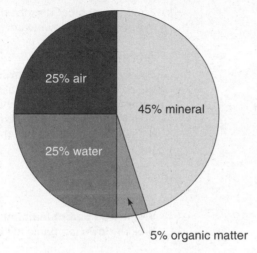

Figure 1.17 Soil components

Soils develop in response to several factors:

1. **Parent material.** This refers to the rock and minerals from which the soil derives. The nature of the parent rock, which can be either native to the area or transported to the area by wind, water, or glacier, has a direct effect on the ultimate soil profile.

2. **Climate.** This is measured by precipitation and temperature. It results in partial weathering of the parent material, which forms the substrate for soil.

3. **Living organisms.** These include the nitrogen-fixing bacteria *Rhizobium*, fungi, insects, worms, snails, etc., that help to decompose litter and recycle nutrients.

4. **Topography.** This refers to the physical characteristics of the location where the soil is formed. Topographic factors that affect a soil's profile include drainage, slope direction, elevation, and wind exposure.

With sufficient time, a mature soil profile reaches a state of equilibrium. Feedback mechanisms involving both abiotic and biotic factors work to preserve the mature soil profile. The relative abundance of sand, silt, and clay is called the soil texture.

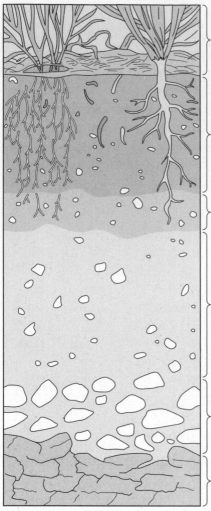

O HORIZON
Surface litter: leaves and partially decomposed organic debris. May be very thick in deciduous forests and very thin in tundra and desert.

A HORIZON
Topsoil: organic matter (humus), living organisms, inorganic minerals. The topsoil is typically very thick in grasslands.

E HORIZON
Zone of leaching: dissolved and suspended materials move downward.

B HORIZON
Subsoil: tends to be yellowish in color due to the accumulation of iron, aluminum, humic compounds, and clay leached down from the A and E horizons. It can be rich in nutrients in areas where rainwater leeched nutrients from the topsoil.

C HORIZON
Weathered parent material: partially broken-down inorganic minerals.

Bedrock

Figure 1.18 Soil profile

Soil Components

Component	Description
Clay	Very fine particles. Compacts easily. Forms large, dense clumps when wet. Low permeability to water; therefore, upper layers become waterlogged.
Gravel	Coarse particles. Consists of rock fragments.
Loam	About equal mixtures of clay, sand, silt, and humus. Rich in nutrients. Holds water but does not become waterlogged.
Sand	Sedimentary material coarser than silt. Water flows through too quickly for most crops. Good for crops and plants requiring low amounts of water.
Silt	Sedimentary material consisting of very fine particles between the size of sand and clay. Easily transported by water.

Organic vs. Inorganic Fertilizers

Organic Fertilizer	Inorganic Fertilizer
Three common forms: animal manure, green manure, and compost.	Does not add humus to the soil, resulting in less ability to hold water and support living organisms (earthworms, beneficial bacteria, and fungi, etc.).
Improves soil texture, adds organic nitrogen, and stimulates beneficial bacteria and fungi.	Lowers oxygen content of the soil thereby keeping fertilizer from being taken up efficiently.
Improves water-holding capacity of soil.	Supplies only a limited number of nutrients (usually nitrogen and phosphorus).
Helps to prevent erosion.	Requires large amounts of energy to produce, transport, and apply.
	Releases nitrous oxide (N_2O)—a greenhouse gas.

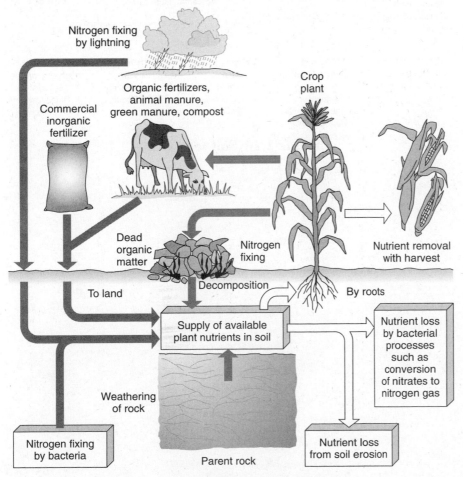

Figure 1.19 Plant nutrient pathways

SOIL FOOD WEB

The soil food web is the community of organisms living all or part of their lives in the soil. It describes a complex living system in the soil and how it interacts with the environments, plants, and animals.

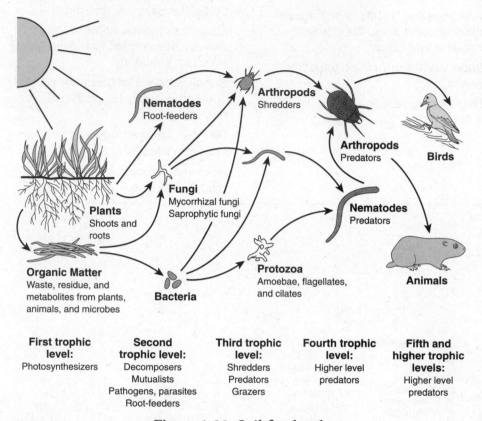

Figure 1.20 Soil food web

EROSION

Soil erosion is the movement of weathered rock or soil components from one place to another. It is caused by flowing water, wind, and human activity such as cultivating inappropriate land, burning of native vegetation, deforestation, and construction. Soil erosion destroys the soil profile, decreases the water-holding capacity of the soil, and increases soil compaction. Because water cannot percolate through the soil, it runs off the land, taking more soil with it (positive feedback loop). Because the soil cannot hold water, crops grown in areas of soil erosion frequently suffer from water shortage. In areas of low precipitation, erosion leads to significant droughts. Poor agricultural techniques that lead to soil erosion include monoculture, row cropping, overgrazing, improper plowing of the soil, and removing crop wastes instead of plowing the organic material back into the soil. There are three common types of soil erosion:

1. **Sheet erosion**—soil moves off as a horizontal layer

2. **Rill erosion**—fast-flowing water cuts small channels in the soil

3. **Gully erosion**—extreme case of rill erosion, where over time, channels increase in size and depth.

Soil erosion causes damage to agriculture, waterways (canals), and infrastructures (dams). It interferes with wetland ecosystems, reproductive cycles (as in salmon), oxygen capacity, and the pH of the water.

Soil Erosion

Desertification	Salinization	Waterlogging
Definition: Productive potential of arid or semiarid land falls by at least 10% due to human activity and/or climate change.	**Definition:** Water that is not absorbed into the soil and evaporates leaves behind dissolved salts in topsoil.	**Definition:** Saturation of soil with water resulting in a rise in the water table.
Symptoms: Loss of native vegetation; increased wind erosion; salinization; drop in water table; reduced surface water supply.	**Symptoms:** Stunted crop growth; lower yield; eventual destruction of plant life.	**Symptoms:** Saline water envelops deep roots killing plants; lowers productivity; eventual destruction of plant life.
Remediation: Reduce overgrazing; reduce deforestation; reduce destructive forms of planting, irrigation, and mining. Plant trees and grasses to hold soil.	**Remediation:** Take land out of production for a while; and/or install underground perforated drainage pipes; flush soil with freshwater into separate lined evaporation ponds; plant halophytes (salt-loving plants) such as barley, cotton, sugar beet and/or semi-dwarf wheat.	**Remediation:** Switch to less water-demanding plants in areas susceptible to waterlogging; utilize conservation-tillage farming; plant waterlogging-resistant trees with deep roots; take land out of production for a while; and/or install pumping stations with drainage pipes that lead to catchment-evaporation basins.

LANDSLIDES AND MUDSLIDES

Landslides occur when masses of rock, earth, or debris move down a slope. Mudslides, also known as debris flows or mudflows, are a common type of fast-moving landslide that tends to flow in channels. Landslides are caused by disturbances in the natural stability of a slope. They can happen after heavy rains, droughts, earthquakes, or volcanic eruptions. Mudslides develop when water rapidly collects in the ground and results in a surge of water-soaked rock, earth, and debris. Mudslides usually begin on steep slopes and can be triggered by natural disasters. Areas where wildfires or construction have destroyed vegetation on slopes are at high risk for landslides during and after heavy rains. Some areas are more likely to experience landslides or mudslides, including:

* Areas where wildfires or construction have destroyed vegetation
* Areas where landslides have occurred before
* Steep slopes and areas at the bottom of slopes or canyons
* Slopes that have been altered for construction of buildings and roads
* Channels along a stream or river
* Areas where surface runoff is directed

THE ROCK CYCLE

There are three main categories of rocks: metamorphic, igneous, and sedimentary.

1. **Igneous**—formed by cooling and classified by their silica content. Intrusive igneous rocks solidify deep underground, cool slowly and have a large-grained texture (e.g., granite). Extrusive igneous rocks solidify on or near the surface, cool quickly, and have a fine-grained smooth texture (e.g., basalt). Igneous rocks are broken down by weathering and water transport. Most soils come from igneous rocks.

2. **Metamorphic**—formed by intense heat and pressure. Those with high quartz content form sandy soil (e.g., gneiss). Slate forms silty soil. Marble forms limestone clay. Common examples: diamond, marble, asbestos, slate, anthracite coal.

3. **Sedimentary**—formed by piling and cementing of various materials (diatoms, weathered chemical precipitates, fragments of older rocks) over time in low-lying areas. Fossils form only in sedimentary rock.

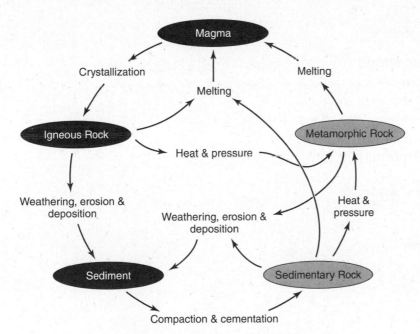

Figure 1.22 The rock cycle

QUICK REVIEW CHECKLIST

- **Geologic Time Scale**
  - eon, era, periods, epochs, stages
  - timeline of development

- **Earth Structure**
  - layers of the Earth (crust-oceanic-continental, mantle, and core)
  - Continental Drift Theory
  - seafloor spreading
  - plate tectonics
  - boundaries (differences between transform, divergent, and convergent)

- **Earthquakes**
  - epicenter, focus
  - Richter scale vs. magnitude
  - P wave vs. S wave
  - primary vs. secondary effects
  - mitigation
  - tsunamis

- **Volcanoes**
  - where they occur
  - how they are formed
  - atmospheric effects of volcanic eruptions
  - basic structure
  - mitigation

- **Seasons**
  - angle of sun and how it affects season

- **Soil**
  - components
  - factors that affect soil development
  - horizons (O, A, E, B, C)
  - types (clay, gravel, loam, sand, silt)
  - organic vs. inorganic fertilizers
  - disadvantages of inorganic fertilizers
  - soil cycle

- **Erosion**
  - types (sheet, rill, and gully)

- **Rock Cycle**
  - metamorphic—how it is formed and examples
  - igneous—how it is formed and examples
  - sedimentary—how it is formed and examples

MULTIPLE-CHOICE QUESTIONS

1. The majority of the rocks in the Earth's crust are:

   (A) igneous
   (B) metamorphic
   (C) sedimentary
   (D) basalt
   (E) volcanic

2. Which of the following is an example of an igneous rock?

   (A) Marble
   (B) Slate
   (C) Limestone
   (D) Granite
   (E) Sandstone

3. The smallest particle of soil is known as

   (A) clay
   (B) sand
   (C) silt
   (D) gravel
   (E) humus

4. Acid rain affects soil by

   (A) decreasing soil porosity
   (B) decreasing the pH
   (C) decreasing soil aeration
   (D) lowering nutrient capacity
   (E) All of the above

5. Which of the types of soil listed below contains the highest amount of nutrients?

   (A) clay
   (B) silt
   (C) sand
   (D) gravel
   (E) loam

6. An example of a volcano with broad, gentle slopes and built by the eruption of runny, fluid-type basalt lava would be

   (A) Mount Saint Helens
   (B) Krakatau
   (C) Kilauea
   (D) Vesuvius
   (E) Mount Rainier

7. Which of the following is at a convergent boundary where two continental plates are presently colliding?

   (A) The Appalachian Mountains
   (B) The Himalayas
   (C) The Andes Mountains
   (D) The Rocky Mountains
   (E) None of the above

8. The Dust Bowl of the 1930s resulted in the passage of what legislation?

   (A) Endangered American Wilderness Act
   (B) Soil and Water Conservation Act
   (C) Federal Land Management Act
   (D) Public Rangelands and Improvement Act
   (E) Soil Erosion and Conservation Act

9. Poor nutrient-holding capacity, good water infiltration capacity, and good aeration properties are examples of what type of particle found in soil?

   (A) Clay
   (B) Silt
   (C) Sand
   (D) Loam
   (E) Humus

10. An alkaline, dark soil, rich in humus, found in a semiarid climate would be most characteristic of

    (A) deserts
    (B) grasslands
    (C) tropical rain forests
    (D) deciduous forests
    (E) coniferous forests

11. Which period in geological time describes the following: "Development of flowering plants. Large diversity in dinosaurs but ending with their sudden extinction approximately 65 million years ago. Formation of the Andes Mountains. African and South American plates begin to separate. Climate is cooling. Shallow seas are prominent."?

    (A) Paleogene
    (B) Neogene
    (C) Jurassic
    (D) Cretaceous
    (E) Permian

12. The process of weathering produces what type of rock?

    (A) Igneous
    (B) Metamorphic
    (C) Sedimentary
    (D) Volcanic
    (E) None of the above

13. A rock that would most likely contain a fossil would be

    (A) igneous
    (B) metamorphic
    (C) sedimentary
    (D) volcanic
    (E) All of the above

14. The most common element found in Earth's crust is

    (A) oxygen
    (B) hydrogen
    (C) iron
    (D) silicon
    (E) aluminum

15. The horizon of soil also known as the topsoil layer, that contains humus, minerals, and roots, and that is rich in living organisms is known as the

    (A) A layer
    (B) B layer
    (C) C layer
    (D) D layer
    (E) O layer

16. Earth is closest to the sun in the Northern Hemisphere during

    (A) winter
    (B) summer
    (C) spring
    (D) fall
    (E) all seasons

17. An earthquake of Richter magnitude 5 is how many times larger on the Richter scale than an earthquake of Richter magnitude 3?

    (A) One-fourth
    (B) One-half
    (C) Twice
    (D) Four times
    (E) One hundred times

Refer to the following table to answer Question 18.

	Most Stable	Least Stable
A	Bedrock	Sand
B	Unconsolidated sand	Bedrock
C	Clay	Bedrock
D	Sand and mud	Clay
E	Water-saturated sand	Sand

18. Which of the choices above represents the most stable and the least stable foundation material to build upon in areas that are frequented by earthquakes?

    (A) A
    (B) B
    (C) C
    (D) D
    (E) E

19. The San Andreas Fault in California occurs at

    (A) a convergent boundary
    (B) a divergent boundary
    (C) a transform boundary
    (D) a subduction zone
    (E) an oceanic ridge

20. Earth's surface is part of the

    (A) asthenosphere
    (B) lithosphere
    (C) benthosphere
    (D) troposphere
    (E) stratosphere

FREE-RESPONSE QUESTION

By: Dr. Ian Kelleher, Brooks School, North Andover, MA
B.S. University of Manchester, England;
Ph.D. Cambridge University

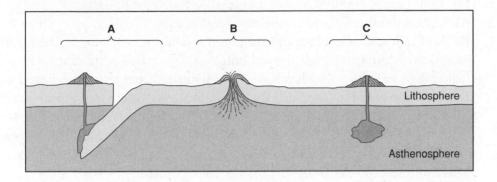

(a) Geological features A–C above are formed as a consequence of plate tectonics. For EACH feature above

    (i) Identify AND describe the geological action that is occurring there

    (ii) For each of the phenomena described in (i), give an actual example occurring on Earth

(b) Charles Darwin was the geologist, botanist, and zoologist on the research vessel *Beagle* when he made observations that lead to his book, *The Origin of Species*, in which the theory of evolution and natural selection was first introduced. A century later, scientists developed the theory of plate tectonics, describing how the solid Earth formed. Describe two ways in which evolution and/or speciation may occur as a consequence of plate tectonics.

(c) Mount Pinatubo in the Philippines erupted in 1991. Examine the temperature graph below and answer the following questions.

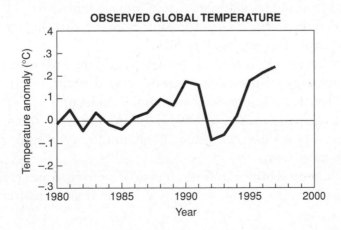

    (i) Compare Earth's climate before and after the eruption of Mount Pinatubo.

    (ii) Explain how the eruption of Mount Pinatubo might affect short-term and long-term climate change.

MULTIPLE-CHOICE ANSWERS AND EXPLANATIONS

1. **(A)** Igneous rocks are solidified from magma. If the magma cools slowly, the rocks are coarser in nature. Had the question been worded "the majority of the rocks on the surface of Earth," the answer would have been sedimentary.
2. **(D)** Other examples of igneous rocks include basalt and quartz.
3. **(A)** Clay is the smallest-sized particle found in soil.
4. **(E)** Acid rain causes calcium and magnesium compounds to be leached from the soil, which decreases the natural buffering effect and reduces the soil pH (makes it more acidic). Acids release toxic materials from compounds and are absorbed by vegetation (mercury, lead, cadmium, etc.). Acid rain promotes the growth of mosses that tend to retain water in the soil, thereby decreasing soil aeration (waterlogged). Mosses decrease the abundance of mycorrhizal fungi that help plants absorb nutrients. Acid rain decreases plants' resistance, making them more susceptible to disease, insects, drought, etc.
5. **(E)** Loam is soil composed of sand, silt, and clay in relatively even concentrations. Loam soils generally contain more nutrients and humus than sandy soils, have better infiltration and drainage than silty soils, and are easier to till than clay soils.
6. **(C)** Kilauea is a shield volcano that is characterized by basalt lava building enormous, low-angle, gently sloping cones. The fluid nature of the lava prevents it from piling in steep mounds. Shield volcanoes occur along the mid-oceanic ridge, where seafloor spreading is in progress and along subduction zones related to volcanic arcs. The largest volcanoes on Earth are shield volcanoes.
7. **(B)** Notice the word "presently." The Appalachian and Rocky mountains were formed at *ancient* convergent plate boundaries. The Andes lie at a convergent boundary where oceanic lithosphere is being subducted under the South American continent.
8. **(B)** Refer to the case study presented in this chapter.
9. **(C)** Water flows through sandy soils too fast for many crops and requires frequent irrigation.
10. **(B)** Soils found in grasslands are rich in organic nutrients.
11. **(D)** Refer to the section "Geologic Time Scale" in this chapter.
12. **(E)** Weathering does not produce rock.
13. **(C)** Sedimentary rock is formed by the piling of material over time. If conditions are right, organisms that die may be covered by this material and become fossilized. Fossils are impressions made up of minerals.
14. **(A)** Eight elements make up 99% of Earth's crust. In order of decreasing abundance, they are oxygen, silicon, aluminum, iron, calcium, sodium, potassium, and magnesium.
15. **(A)** If the topsoil is brown or black, it is rich in nitrogen and is good for crops. If the topsoil is gray, yellow, or red, it is low in organic matter and poor for crops.
16. **(A)** The angle of sunlight determines the season, not how close Earth is to the sun.

17. **(E)** The Richter scale is a $\log_{10}$ scale and measures the magnitude of an earthquake. $5 - 3 = \underline{2}$ and $10^2 = 100$. However, the Richter scale does NOT measure the energy of an earthquake. The energy of a Richter magnitude 5 has 32 times more energy than a Richter magnitude of 4.

18. **(A)** Soil type can substantially increase earthquake risk. The worst soils to build upon include deep, loose sand; silty clays; sand and gravel; and soft, saturated granular soils. Earthquake forces are amplified on water-saturated soils, changing the soil from a solid to a liquid, a process known as liquefaction. Liquefaction makes the ground incapable of supporting a foundation. During liquefaction, the ground can crack or heave, causing uneven settling or building collapse. The best soils to build upon to reduce damage from earthquakes are bedrock (deep and unbroken rock formations) and stiff soils. These soil types are best, since much less vibration is transferred through the foundation to the structure above.

19. **(C)** Places where plates slide past each other are called transform boundaries. The most famous transform boundary in the world is the San Andreas fault.

20. **(B)** The asthenosphere is the region below the lithosphere, estimated as being from 50 to several hundred miles (85 to several hundred km) thick.

IMPORTANT NOTE TO STUDENT

Your answers to the Free Response Questions (FRQs) will most likely be <u>much</u> shorter than what you see in this book and that is perfectly fine and expected. The answers presented in this book are very comprehensive and try to cover a wide range of possible student responses. When comparing your essays with the essays presented in this book, try to see if there are any major topics that you may have left out or if you have made any factual errors in what you did write about. Remember, you only have on average 23 minutes to write each essay.

FREE-RESPONSE ANSWER

(a) Feature *A* is a subduction zone. One lithospheric plate is subducting (sinking) below another, largely due to differences in density (the denser plate sinks). This is an example of a convergent plate boundary. As the subducted plate sinks to greater depths, the temperature increases to the point where it begins to melt. This molten magma is less dense than the solid rock around it, so it rises up and forms a chain of volcanic mountains parallel to the plate boundary. The Cascade Mountains in Washington State are examples of a volcanic arc. When two oceanic plates converge, they create an island arc—a curved chain of volcanic islands rising from the deep seafloor and near a continent. They are created by subduction processes and occur on the continent side of the subduction zone. Japan is an example of an island arc.

Feature *B* is a divergent plate boundary. Lithospheric plates are moving apart. The space created between them is filled by hot molten magma coming up from the asthenosphere that then cools and adds to the crust. In oceanic crust, they are known as a mid-oceanic ridge. The Mid-Atlantic Ridge is an example. When they form on continental crust, they are known as rift valleys, such as the African Rift Valley.

Feature *C* is a hot spot. This is a place in the asthenosphere where the temperature is higher than average such that localized melting occurs. This molten rock, being less dense due to its temperature and state of matter, rises up. It forms a volcano on Earth's surface. Over geologic time, the location of the hot spot remains constant, whereas the lithospheric plate moves over it. This causes a chain of volcanoes to form over time from a single hot spot. The Hawaiian Islands are an example of the consequences of hot spots.

(b) Evolution may occur as a consequence of geographic separation of one population of a species into two or more populations. Plate tectonics may cause this separation by either of two methods.

First, a divergent (constructive) plate boundary could cause one landmass to be divided into two or more distinct parts, perhaps even separated by an ocean. For example, identical fossils can be found on the east cost of South America and the west coast of Africa, indicating that these were once the same connected landmass. After these two continents diverged, different species would evolve from this common ancestor as a reaction to the different environments and consequent environmental pressures on the different landmasses.

Second, faulting occurring as a consequence of plate tectonics may cause a river to be diverted. The new path of the river could divide a population into two and serve as a geographic barrier preventing gene flow. Different conditions in geographically separated regions would eventually lead to the evolution of different species as each population adapted to its environment in different ways.

Plate tectonics may result in climatic change in one of the following ways: First, Earth's atmosphere has changed considerably throughout geological history, largely as a consequence of gases emitted through volcanic activity caused by plate tectonics. These changes in the atmosphere have caused climate change. For example, there is evidence that the Earth was much warmer hundreds of millions of years ago.

Second, lithospheric plates move over the surface of Earth at speeds of a few centimeters a year. Individual plates have moved thousands of miles over geologic history. As the latitude of the plate changes, so will its climate. For example, some rocks in Alaska indicate that they were originally deposited at a time when the plate had a tropical climate and so must have been closer to the equator.

Species evolve in reaction to these climate changes. For example, animals will adapt to shifting food sources as different plants grow in different climates. A species of animal may develop fur over time (through natural selection) as temperatures decrease over time.

As lithospheric plates move to latitudes further from the equator, climates will have greater seasonal variations. This could lead to evolutionary adaptations such as plants shedding their leaves to conserve resources or animals hibernating during winter months to conserve energy.

Evidence suggests that some mass extinctions in Earth's history may have been caused by large-scale volcanic activity, such as flood basalts, which occur as a consequence of plate tectonics. These mass extinctions tend to be followed by periods with high rates of evolution (punctuated) and increase in species diversity (adaptive radiation) as ecological niches are filled.

(c)

(i)   After the eruption of Mount Pinatubo, Earth's temperature was approximately 0.3°C lower for the next two years. Earth's temperature rose by approximately 0.1°C during the third year. By the fourth year after the eruption, Earth's temperature had returned to the pre-eruption level.

(ii)   In the short term, dust and other particulates released into the atmosphere from the eruption would block the Sun's rays and tend to decrease temperatures. For example, sulfur dioxide gas that is injected into the stratosphere from volcanic activity chemically reacts with oxygen to form sulfate aerosols (solid particles), which tend to reflect solar radiation back into space. The aerosol remains in suspension long after solid ash particles have fallen to Earth. Without replenishment, the sulfuric acid aerosol layer is gradually depleted. This decrease in energy reaching the Earth would result in lower global temperatures. Fine ash particles from an eruption column fall out too quickly to significantly cool the atmosphere over an extended period of time.

In the long term, gases such as carbon dioxide released during the eruption would accumulate in the stratosphere. There they would contribute to the greenhouse effect. They would absorb energy radiated back from the Earth, leading to an increase in global temperature. The degree of temperature change from the Mount Pinatubo eruption via this mechanism would be much less than that by dust blocking the sun, but the effect would last much longer.

The Atmosphere

CHAPTER 2

COMPOSITION

Earth's atmosphere is composed of seven primary compounds:

Component

NITROGEN (N$_2$)   78%

Fundamental nutrient for living organisms. Deposits on Earth through nitrogen fixation and reactions involving lightning and subsequent precipitation. Returns to the atmosphere through combustion of biomass and denitrification.

OXYGEN (O$_2$)   21%

Oxygen molecules are produced through photosynthesis and are utilized in cellular respiration.

WATER VAPOR (H$_2$O)   0–4%

Largest amounts occur near equator, over oceans, and in tropical regions. Areas where atmospheric water vapor can be low are polar areas and deserts.

CARBON DIOXIDE (CO$_2$)   <<1%

Volume of CO$_2$ has increased about 25% in the last 300 years due to the burning of fossil fuels and deforestation. CO$_2$ is produced during cellular respiration and the decay of organic matter. It is a reactant in photosynthesis. CO$_2$ is also a major greenhouse gas. Humans are responsible for about 5,500 million tons of CO$_2$ per year. The average time of a CO$_2$ molecule in the atmosphere is approximately 100 years.

METHANE (CH$_4$)   <<<1%

Methane contributes to the greenhouse effect. Since 1750, methane has increased about 150% due to the use of fossil fuels, coal mining, landfills, grazers, and flooding of rice fields. Human activity is responsible for about 400 million tons per year as compared with approximately 200 million tons per year produced naturally. Average cycle of a methane molecule in the atmosphere is approximately 10 years.

NITROUS OXIDE (N$_2$O)   <<<1%

Concentration increasing about 0.3% per year. Sources include burning of fossil fuels, use of fertilizers, burning biomass, deforestation, and conversion to agricultural land. Humans are responsible for about 6 million tons per year. N₂O is a contributor to the greenhouse effect. Average time of a N₂O molecule in the atmosphere is approximately 170 years.

OZONE (O₃)   <<<1%

97% of ozone is found in the stratosphere (ozone layer) 9–35 miles (15–55 km) above Earth's surface. Ozone absorbs UV radiation. Ozone is produced in the production of photochemical smog. A "hole" in the ozone layer occurs over Antarctica. Chlorofluorocarbons (CFCs) are the primary cause of the breakdown of ozone.

STRUCTURE

The atmosphere consists of several different layers:

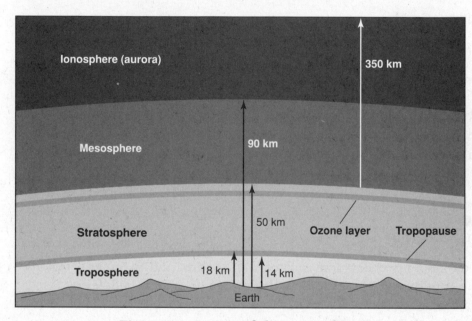

Figure 2.1 Layers of the atmosphere

Layers

TROPOSPHERE

0–7 miles (0–11 km) above surface. 75% of atmosphere's mass is in the troposphere. Temperature decreases with altitude, reaching –76°F (–60°C) near the top. Weather occurs in this zone.

STRATOSPHERE

Temperature increases with altitude due to absorption of heat by ozone. Ozone is produced by UV radiation and lightning. Contains the ozone layer.

MESOSPHERE

Temperature decreases with altitude. Coldest layer. Ice clouds occur here. Meteors (shooting stars) burn up in this layer.

TIP

Don't confuse weather and climate. Weather describes whatever is happening outdoors in a given place at a given time. Weather is what happens from minute to minute. Climate describes the total of all weather occurring over a period of years in a given place. This includes average weather conditions, regular weather sequences (like winter, spring, summer, and fall), and special weather events (like tornadoes and floods.)

THERMOSPHERE (IONOSPHERE)

Temperature increases with height due to gamma rays, X-rays, and UV radiation. Molecules are converted into ions which results in the aurora borealis (northern lights) in the northern hemisphere and the aurora australis (southern lights) in the southern hemisphere. The aurora borealis most often occurs from September to October and from March to April.

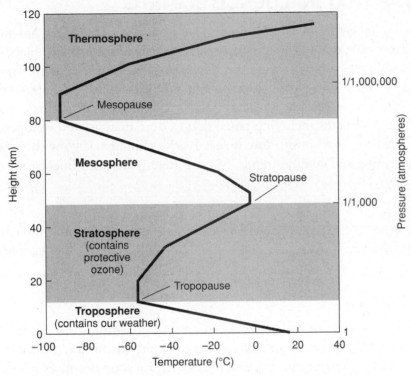

Figure 2.2 Changes in temperature in the atmosphere

WEATHER AND CLIMATE

Weather is caused by the movement or transfer of heat energy, which influences the following physical properties: temperature, air pressure, humidity, precipitation, available sunshine determined by cloud cover, wind speed, and wind direction. Climate describes the total of all weather occurring over a period of years in a given place. Energy can be transferred wherever there is a temperature difference between two objects. Energy can be transferred through radiation, conduction, and convection.

Radiation is the flow of electromagnetic radiation. It is the method by which Earth receives solar energy.

Conduction involves the transfer of heat through a substance that results from a difference in temperature between different parts of the substance.

Convection is the primary way energy is transferred from hotter to colder regions in Earth's atmosphere and is the primary determinant of weather patterns. Convection involves the movement of the warmer and therefore more energetic molecules in air. Convection takes place both vertically and horizontally. When air near the ground becomes warmer and therefore less dense than the air above it, the air rises. Pressure differences that develop because of temperature differences result in wind or horizontal convection.

TIP

Several different factors influence climate:

- Air mass
- Air pressure
- Albedo
- Altitude
- Angle of sunlight
- Clouds
- Distance to oceans
- Fronts
- Heat
- Land changes
- Latitude
- Location
- Humidity or moisture content of air
- Mountain ranges
- Pollution
- Rotation
- Wind patterns
- Human activity

Regions nearer the equator receive much more solar energy than regions nearer the poles and are consequently much warmer. These latitudinal differences in surface temperature create global-scale flows of energy within the atmosphere, giving rise to the major weather patterns of the world. Without convection and the transfer of energy, the equator would be about 27°F (15°C) warmer and the Arctic would be about 45°F (25°C) colder than they actually are.

FACTORS THAT INFLUENCE CLIMATE

Evidence for changes in the climate come from data used to measure climate (which is available for only the last few hundred years), written accounts (subjective), and data from material present at the time. These materials consists of tree rings, fossilized plants, insect and pollen samples, gas bubbles trapped in glaciers, deep ice core samples, lake sediments, stalactites and stalagmites, marine fossils including coral analysis, sediments including rafted debris, dust analysis, and isotope ratios in fossilized remains. The bottom line is that Earth's climate has gone through many cycles of warming and cooling trends. Many different factors influence the climate.

AIR MASS

An air mass is a large body of air that has similar temperatures and moisture content. Air masses can be categorized as equatorial, tropical, polar, arctic, continental, or maritime.

AIR PRESSURE

Most of the total mass of the atmosphere—99%—is within 20 miles (32 km) of Earth's surface. Gravity on an air mass results in air pressure and is measured in millibars, inches of mercury, or hectopascals (hPa). Air pressure decreases with altitude. Low pressure usually produces cloudy and stormy weather. High pressure masses contain cool, dense air that descend toward Earth's surface and becomes warmer. High pressure is usually associated with fair weather.

ALBEDO

Albedo is reflectivity. Materials like ocean water have low albedo, whereas land masses have moderate albedo. The highest albedo is snow and ice. Hence, periods when polar ice is highly extended will promote further cooling. This is a positive-feedback mechanism. Dust in the atmosphere has the same effect. It forms a high albedo veil around Earth so that a significant amount of solar radiation is reflected before it reaches the surface. The dust may come from dry climate periods, volcanic eruptions, meteor impacts, and so on.

ALTITUDE

For every 1,000 feet (300 m) rise in elevation, there is a 3°F (1.5°C) drop in temperature. Every 300 feet (90 m) rise in elevation is equivalent to a shift of 62 miles (100 km) north in latitude and biome similarity.

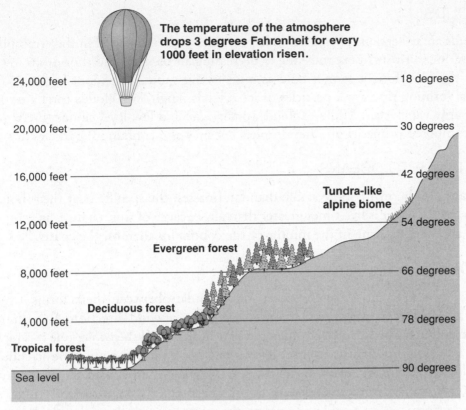

The temperature of the atmosphere drops 3 degrees Fahrenheit for every 1000 feet in elevation risen.

24,000 feet	18 degrees
20,000 feet	30 degrees
16,000 feet	42 degrees
12,000 feet	54 degrees
8,000 feet	66 degrees
4,000 feet	78 degrees
	90 degrees
Sea level	

Tundra-like alpine biome

Evergreen forest

Deciduous forest

Tropical forest

Figure 2.3 Change in temperature in response to change in altitude

ANGLE OF SUNLIGHT

In the Northern Hemisphere winter, Earth is closest to the sun. The angle of sunlight reaching Earth affects the climate. Areas closest to the equator receive the most sunlight and therefore higher temperatures.

CARBON CYCLE

The consumption of carbon in the form of carbon dioxide (CO_2) results in cooling. Two different processes consume carbon dioxide: carbonate rock weathering and silicate rock weathering.

Carbonate rock weathering: $\mathbf{CO_2} + H_2O + CaCO_3 \rightarrow Ca^{2+} + 2HCO_3^-$

Silicate rock weathering: $2\mathbf{CO_2} + H_2O + CaSiO_3 \rightarrow Ca^{2+} + 2HCO_3^- + SiO_2$

The production of carbon in the form of carbon dioxide results in warming. Both carbonate formation in the oceans and metamorphic breakdown of carbonate yield carbon dioxide.

Carbonate formation in the oceans: $Ca^{2+} + 2HCO_3^- \rightarrow \mathbf{CO_2} + H_2O + CaCO_3$

Metamorphic breakdown of carbonate: $SiO_2 + CaCO_3 \rightarrow \mathbf{CO_2} + CaSiO_3$

CLOUDS

Clouds are collections of water droplets or ice crystals suspended in the atmosphere. As warmer air rises, it expands due to decreasing air pressure and thus drops in temperature; therefore, it cannot hold as much water vapor. The vapor begins to condense forming tiny water particles or ice crystals. High-level clouds (prefix *cirr*) are primarily ice crystals. Midlevel clouds (prefix *alto*) and low-level clouds (prefix *strat*) are composed primarily of water droplets but may also contain ice particles or snow.

DISTANCE TO OCEANS

Oceans are thermally more stable than landmasses; the specific heat (heat-holding capacity) of water is five times greater than air. Because of this, changes in temperature are more extreme in the middle of the continents than on the coasts.

FRONTS

When two different air masses meet, the boundary between them forms a front. The air masses can vary in temperature, dew point, or wind direction. A warm front is the boundary between an advancing warm air mass and the cooler one it is replacing. Since warm air is less dense, it rises and cools, and the moisture it contains is released as rain. A cold front is the leading edge of an advancing mass of cold air. Cold fronts are associated with thunderhead clouds, high surface winds, and thunderstorms. After a cold front passes, the weather is usually cool with clear skies.

GREENHOUSE EFFECT

The most important greenhouse gases are water (H_2O), carbon dioxide (CO_2), and methanae (CH_4). Without this effect, Earth would be cold and inhospitable. If taken too far, Earth could evolve into a hothouse.

HEAT (CONVECTION)

Climate is influenced by how heat energy is exchanged between air over the oceans and the air over land.

LAND CHANGES

Climate is influenced by urbanization and deforestation.

LANDMASS DISTRIBUTION

Materials absorb and reflect solar radiation to different extents. Ocean water is much more absorbent than landmasses so that continents reflect a lot more solar energy back into space than the oceans. Earth receives more solar radiation at low latitudes (near the equator) than near the poles. An Earth with landmasses clustered at low latitudes would reflect more solar energy into space, resulting in a cooler planet than one with more equatorial ocean area. Approximately 600–800 million years ago, there were significant glacial deposits in North America, Australia, and Africa. At this time, paleomagnetism of rocks suggests that these continents were near the south pole and that the equatorial Earth was largely ocean.

LATITUDE

The higher the latitudes, the less solar radiation. This affects the climate.

LOCATION

Climate is influenced by the location of high and low air pressure zones and where landmasses are distributed.

MOISTURE CONTENT OF AIR (HUMIDITY)

The moisture content of air is a primary determinant of plant growth and distribution and is a major determinant of biome type (desert vs. tropical forest). Atmospheric water vapor supplies moisture for clouds and rainfall, and it plays a role in energy exchanges within the atmosphere. Water vapor is also a greenhouse gas as it traps heat energy leaving Earth's surface. The dew point is the temperature at which condensation takes place.

MOUNTAIN RANGES

The presence or absence of mountain ranges affects the climate. Mountains influence whether one side of the mountain will receive rain or not (rain shadow effect). The side facing the ocean is the windward side and receives the most rain; the side of the mountain opposite the ocean is the leeward side and receives little rain. Temperatures decrease as the altitude increases. Orographic lifting occurs when an air mass is forced from a low elevation to a higher elevation as it moves over rising terrain. As the air mass gains altitude, it expands and cools, which can raise the relative humidity and create clouds and, under the right conditions, precipitation.

PLATE TECTONICS AND VOLCANOES

Plate tectonics affect atmospheric carbon dioxide, which factors into climate changes through the greenhouse effect. Volcanoes produce carbon dioxide. If global volcanism slows, as would be the case when supercontinents stabilize, less atmospheric carbon dioxide released into the atmosphere would trigger global cooling. Increased volcanism puts more carbon dioxide in the atmosphere and results in more greenhouse warming.

POLLUTION

Greenhouse gases are emitted from both natural sources (e.g., volcanoes) and anthropogenic (human) sources (e.g., industry, transportation, etc.).

PRECESSION

The wobble of Earth on its axis changes the amount of energy received by the sun. Changes in the orientation of Earth in space (tilt and obliquity) also have an effect on climate.

ROTATION

Daily temperature cycles are primarily influenced by Earth's rotation on its axis (once every 24 hours). At night, heat escapes from the surface. Daily minimum temperatures occur just before sunrise.

SOLAR OUTPUT

Changes in solar output of only 1% per 100 years would change Earth's temperature by up to 1°F (0.5°C). Times of sunspot activity (every 11, 90, and 180 years) correspond to decreases in solar radiation reaching Earth. The sun's magnetic field reverses every 22 years.

VOLCANOES

Sulfur-rich volcanic eruptions can eject material into the stratosphere, potentially causing tropospheric cooling and stratospheric warming. Volcanic aerosols exist in the atmosphere for an average of one to three years, and may result in tropospheric cooling. Volcanic aerosols injected into the stratosphere can also provide surfaces for ozone-destroying reactions. Over the course of millions of years, large volumes of volcanic ash deposited in the oceans can increase the iron content in seawater. This additional iron can promote biotic activity, which can lower the CO_2 concentration of seawater, and hence atmospheric CO_2 levels, resulting in global cooling. Over the course of weeks to years, ongoing production of ash from volcanoes may locally change climate by modifying the local atmosphere. Recent research also suggests that large eruptions may trigger El Niño climatic events.

WIND PATTERNS

Wind patterns are influenced by temperature, pressure differences (gradients), and the Coriolis effect.

- The Sun heats the atmosphere unevenly.
- The air closest to the surface is warmer and rises.
- Air at high elevations is cooler and sinks.
- This rising and falling sets up convection processes and is the primary cause of winds.
- Global air circulation is caused and affected by:
  - uneven heating of the Earth's surface.
  - seasons.
  - the Coriolis effect.
  - the amount of solar radiation reaching the Earth's surface over a period of time.
  - convection cells created by areas of warm ocean water which in turn are caused by differences in water density, winds, and the Earth's rotation.

During relatively calm, sunny days, the land warms up faster than the sea. This causes the air above it to become less dense than the air over the sea, which results in a sea breeze. A land breeze occurs during relatively calm, clear nights when the land cools down faster than the sea. This results in the air above the land becoming denser than the air over the sea. As a result, air moves from the land towards the coast.

Once air has been set in motion by the pressure gradient force, it undergoes an apparent deflection from its path. This apparent deflection is called the "Coriolis force" and is a result of the Earth's rotation. As air moves from high to low pressure in the Northern Hemisphere, it is deflected to the right by the Coriolis force. In the Southern Hemisphere, air moving from high to low pressure is deflected to the left by the Coriolis force. The amount of deflection the air makes is directly related to both the speed at which the air is moving and its latitude. Therefore, slowly blowing winds will be deflected only a small amount, while stronger winds will be deflected more. Likewise, winds blowing closer to the poles will be deflected more than winds at the same speed closer to the equator. The Coriolis force is zero at the equator.

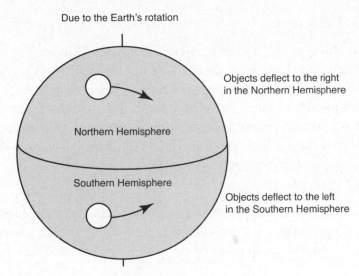

Figure 2.4 Coriolis effect

HUMAN ACTIVITY

Climate can also be influenced by human activity. Deforestation, urbanization, heat island effects, release of pollutants including greenhouse gases and the burning of fossil fuels, and the production of acid rain are examples of how humans have altered climatic patterns. Increased pollution alone, combined with an increase in convectional uplift in urban areas, tends to increase the amount of rainfall in urban areas as much as 10% when compared with undeveloped areas.

Major Climatic Periods

Several major climatic periods have occurred. They are described below.

2,000,000 B.C.E. TO 12,000 B.C.E. (PLEISTOCENE ICE AGE)

Large glacial ice sheets covered much of North America, Europe, and Asia. The Pleistocene had periods when the glaciers retreated (interglacial) because of warmer temperatures and advanced because of colder temperatures (glacial). During the coldest periods of the Pleistocene Ice Age, average global temperatures were probably 7°F–9°F (4–5°C) colder than they are today.

12,000 B.C.E. TO 3000 B.C.E.

This warming of Earth and subsequent glacial retreat began about 14,000 years ago. The warming was shortly interrupted by a sudden cooling period between 10,000–8500 B.C.E. Scientists speculate that this cooling may have been caused by the release of fresh water trapped behind ice on North America draining into the North Atlantic Ocean. The release altered vertical currents in the ocean, which exchange heat energy with the atmosphere. The warming resumed by 8500 B.C.E. By 5000 to 3000 B.C.E., average global temperatures reached their maximum level and were 2°F–4°F (1–2°C) warmer than they are today, a period known as the Climatic Optimum. During the Climatic Optimum, many of Earth's great ancient civilizations began and flourished. In Africa, the Nile River had three times its present volume, indicating a much larger tropical region.

3000 B.C.E. TO 750 B.C.E.

From 3000 to 2000 B.C.E., a cooling trend occurred. This cooling caused large drops in sea levels and the emergence of many islands (Bahamas) and coastal areas that are still above sea level today. A short warming trend took place from 2000 to 1500 B.C.E., followed once again by colder conditions. Colder temperatures from 1500 to 750 B.C.E. caused renewed ice growth in continental glaciers and alpine glaciers and a sea level drop of between 6 to 10 feet (2–3 m) below present-day levels.

750 B.C.E. TO 900 C.E.

The period from 750 B.C.E. to 900 C.E. saw warming up to 150 B.C.E. During the time of the Roman Empire (150 B.C.E. to 300 C.E.) a cooling began that lasted until about 900 C.E. At its height, the cooling caused the Nile River and the Black Sea to freeze.

900 C.E. TO 1200 C.E. (LITTLE CLIMATIC OPTIMUM)

During this warm period, the Vikings established settlements on Greenland and Iceland. The snow line in the Rocky Mountains was about 1,200 feet (370 m) above current levels. A period of cool and more extreme weather followed the Little Climatic Optimum. There are records of floods, great droughts, and extreme seasonal climate fluctuations up to the 1400s.

1550 C.E. TO 1850 C.E. (LITTLE ICE AGE)

From 1550 to 1850 C.E., global temperatures were at their coldest since the beginning of the Holocene. During the Little Ice Age, the average annual temperature of the Northern Hemisphere was about 2°F (1.0°C) lower than today.

1850 C.E. TO PRESENT

The period from 1850 to the present is one of general warming.

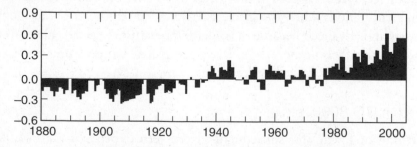

Figure 2.5 Average changes in ocean and land temperatures (°C) from 1880 to 2000

ATMOSPHERIC CIRCULATION AND THE CORIOLIS EFFECT

Due to the rotation of Earth on its axis, rotation around the sun, and the tilt of Earth's axis, the sun heats the atmosphere unevenly. Air closer to Earth's surface is the warmest and rises. Air at higher elevations is cooler and, as such, more dense and sinks. This sets up convection processes and is the primary cause for winds. Global air circulation is also affected by uneven heating of Earth's surface, seasons, the Coriolis effect, the amount of solar radiation reaching the Earth over long periods of time, convection cells created by warm ocean waters that commonly leads to hurricanes, and ocean currents, which are caused by differences in water density, winds, and Earth's rotation.

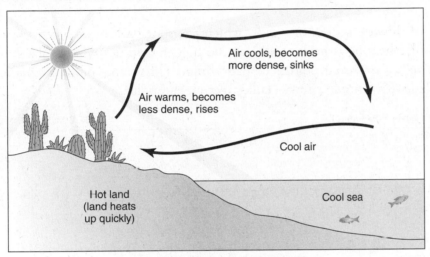

Figure 2.6 Convection cell

The trade winds are the prevailing pattern of easterly surface winds found in the tropics, within the lower portion of the Earth's atmosphere, in the lower section of the troposphere near the Earth's equator. The trade winds blow predominantly from the northeast in the Northern Hemisphere (northeast trade winds) and from the southeast in the Southern Hemisphere (southeast trade winds), strengthening during the winter. Historically, the trade winds have been used by captains of sailing ships to cross the world's oceans for centuries; they also enabled European empire expansion into the Americas and helped trade routes to become established across the Atlantic and Pacific oceans. The trade winds act as the steering flow for tropical storms that form over the Atlantic, Pacific, and south Indian oceans and make landfall in North America, Southeast Asia, and India, respectively. Trade winds also steer African dust westward across the Atlantic Ocean into the Caribbean Sea, as well as portions of southeast North America.

Horizontal winds move from areas of high pressures to areas of low pressures. Wind speed is determined by pressure differences between air masses. The greater the pressure difference is, the greater the wind speed. Wind direction is based upon from where the wind is coming. A wind coming from the east is called an easterly. Wind speed is measured with an anemometer, and wind direction is measured with a wind vane.

Earth's rotation on its axis causes winds not to travel straight. This is called the Coriolis effect. It causes prevailing winds in the Northern Hemisphere to spiral clockwise out from high-pressure areas and spiral counterclockwise in toward low-pressure areas.

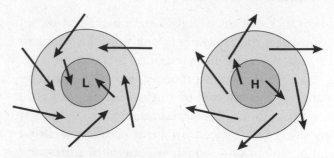

Figure 2.7 Circulation wind patterns of high- and low-pressure systems in the Northern Hemisphere. The pattern reverses in the Southern Hemisphere

The worldwide system of winds, which transports warm air from the equator where solar heating is greatest toward the higher latitudes where solar heating is diminished, gives rise to Earth's climatic zones. Three types of air circulation cells associated with latitude exist—Hadley, Ferrel, and polar.

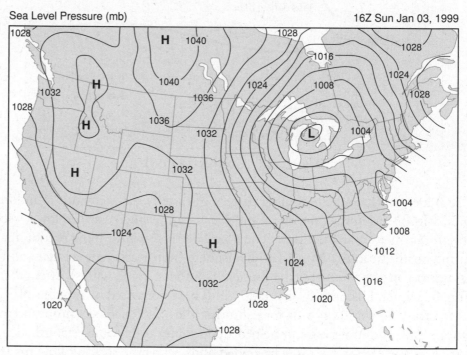

Figure 2.8 Wind speed is directly related to the distance between the isobars. The closer together they are, the stronger the wind

Hadley Air Circulation Cells

Air heated near the equator rises and spreads out north and south. After cooling in the upper atmosphere, the air sinks back to Earth's surface within the subtropical climate zone (between 25° and 49° north and south latitudes). Surface air from subtropical regions returns toward the equator to replace the rising air. The equatorial regions of the Hadley cells are characterized by high humidity, high clouds, and heavy rains. The monthly average temperatures are around 90°F (32°C) at sea level, and there is no winter. The vegetation is tropical rain forest. Temperature variation from day to night (diurnal) is greater than from season to season.

Subtropical regions of the Hadley cell are characterized by low relative humidity, little cloud formation, high ocean evaporation due to low humidity, and many of the world's deserts. The climate is characterized by warm to hot summers and mild winters.

The tropical wet and dry (or savanna) climate has a dry season more than two months long. Annual losses of water through evaporation in this region exceed annual water gains from precipitation.

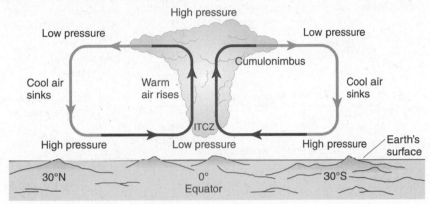

Figure 2.9 Hadley Cell

Ferrel Air Circulation Cells

Ferrel cells develop between 30° and 60° north and south latitudes. The descending winds of the Hadley cells diverge as moist tropical air moves toward the poles in winds known as the westerlies. Midlatitude climates can have severe winters and cool summers due to midlatitude cyclone patterns. The western United States is drier in summer than the eastern United States due to oceanic high pressures that brings cool, dry air down from the north. The climate of this area is governed by both tropical and polar air masses. Defined seasons are the rule, with strong annual cycles of temperature and precipitation. The seasonal fluctuation of temperature is greater than the change in temperature occurring in a 24-hour cycle. Climates of the middle latitudes have a distinct winter season. The area of Earth controlled by Ferrel cells contains broadleaf deciduous and coniferous evergreen forests.

Polar Air Circulation Cells

The polar cells originate as icy-cold, dry, dense air that descends from the troposphere to the ground. This air meets with the warm tropical air from the midlatitudes. The air then returns to the poles, cooling and then sinking. Sinking air suppresses precipitation; thus, the polar regions are deserts (deserts are defined by moisture, not temperature). Very little water exists in this area because it is tied up in the frozen state as ice. Furthermore, the amount of snowfall per year is relatively small.

In general, climates in the polar domain are characterized by low temperatures, severe winters, and small amounts of precipitation, most of which falls in summer. The annual fluctuation of temperature is greater than the change in temperature occurring in a 24-hour cycle. In this area where summers are short and temperatures are generally low throughout the year, temperature rather than precipitation is the critical factor in plant distribution and soil development. Two major biomes exist—the tundra and the taiga.

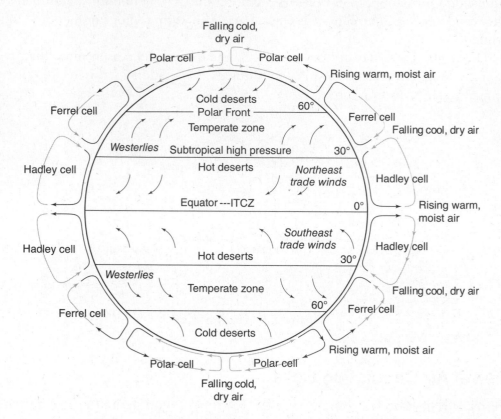

Figure 2.10 The Hadley, Ferrel, and polar cells

Hurricanes, Cyclones, and Tornadoes

Hurricanes are the most severe weather phenomenon on the planet. Hurricane Katrina that hit New Orleans, Louisiana, in 2005 was responsible for about $81 billion in damage and approximately 1,830 deaths. Hurricanes begin over warm oceans in areas where the trade winds converge. A subtropical high-pressure zone creates hot daytime temperatures with low humidity that allows for large amounts of evaporation. The Coriolis effect initiates the cyclonic flow.

The stages of hurricane development include the presence of separate thunderstorms that have developed over tropical oceans, and cyclonic circulation that begins to cause these thunderstorms to move in a circular motion. This cyclonic circulation allows them to pick up moisture and latent heat energy from the ocean. In the center of the hurricane is the eye, an area of descending air and low pressure. The energy of a hurricane dissipates as it travels over land or moves over cooler bodies of water. Rainfall can be as much as 24 inches (0.6 m) in 24 hours. A storm surge, which results from the increase in the height of the ocean near the eye of a hurricane, can cause extensive flooding.

Tornadoes are swirling masses of air with wind speeds close to 300 miles per hour (485 kph). Like hurricanes, the center of the tornado is an area of low pressure. In the United States, tornadoes are frequent from April through July and occur in the center of the United States in an area known as "Tornado Alley." Due to advances in weather forecasting, modeling, and warning systems, the death rate due to tornadoes has decreased significantly.

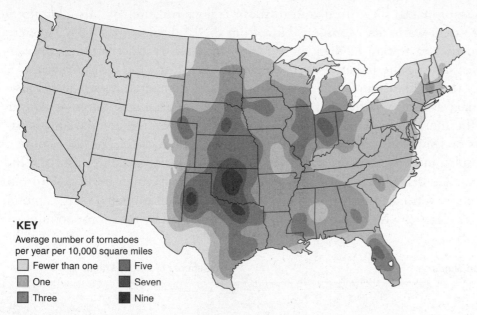

KEY

Average number of tornadoes
per year per 10,000 square miles

Fewer than one   Five

One   Seven

Three   Nine

Figure 2.11 Average number of tornadoes per year

While both tornadoes and tropical cyclones are spinning, turbulent vortices of wind, they have little in common. Tornadoes have diameters on the scale of hundreds of meters and are produced from a single convective storm, such as a thunderstorm. Tropical cyclones, on the other hand, have diameters of hundreds of kilometers and are comprised of many convective storms. Tornadoes occur primarily over land, as solar heating of the land surface usually contributes the development of the thunderstorm that spawns the vortex. In contrast, tropical cyclones are an oceanic phenomenon and die out over land due to the loss of a moisture source. Additionally, while tornadoes require substantial vertical shear of the horizontal winds (i.e., change of wind speed and/or direction with height) to form, tropical cyclones require very low values of vertical shear in order to form and grow. Finally, tropical cyclones have lifetimes that are measured in days, while tornadoes typically last for less than an hour.

CASE STUDY

Hurricane Katrina in 2005 was one of the deadliest and most destructive hurricanes in the history of the United States. Nearly 2,000 people died in the actual hurricane and in the subsequent floods. Total property damage was estimated at $81 billion. Katrina caused severe destruction along the Gulf coast from central Florida to Texas, much of it due to the storm surge. The largest number of deaths occurred in New Orleans, Louisiana, which flooded as the levee system failed and 80% of the city and the surrounding areas became flooded. The worst property damage occurred in coastal areas, such as Mississippi beachfront towns with storm surge waters reaching 6–12 miles (10–19 km) inland.

Monsoons

Monsoons are strong, often violent winds that change direction with the season. Monsoon winds blow from cold to warm regions because cold air takes up more space than warm air. Monsoons blow from the land toward the sea in winter and from the sea toward land in the summer. India's climate is dominated by monsoons. During the Indian winter, which is hot and dry, the monsoon winds blow from the northeast and carry little moisture. The temperature is high because the Himalayas form a barrier that prevents cold air from passing onto the subcontinent. Furthermore, most of India lies between the Tropic of Cancer and the equator, so the sun's rays shine directly on the land. During the summer the monsoons move onto the subcontinent from the southwest. The winds carry moisture from the Indian Ocean and bring heavy rains from June to September. Farmers in India rely on these torrential summer rainstorms to irrigate their land. Additionally, a large amount of India's electricity is generated by water power provided by the monsoon rains.

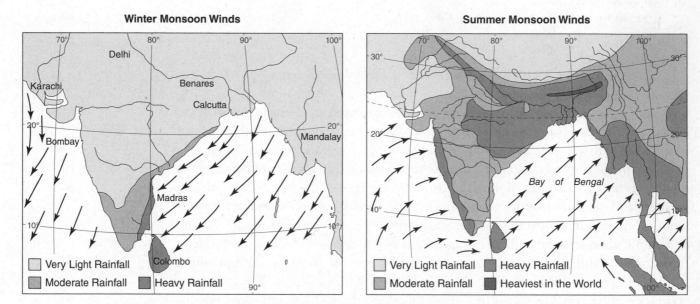

Figure 2.12 Winter and summer monsoon wind patterns

Rain Shadow Effect

A rain shadow is a dry area on the mountainside facing away from the direction of the wind. The mountains block the passage of rain-producing weather systems, casting a "shadow" of dryness behind them. Warm, moist air rises through orographic lifting to the top of a mountain range or large mountain, where, due to decreasing atmospheric pressure with increasing altitude, it expands and cools to reach its dew point. At the dew point, moisture condenses onto the mountain, and it precipitates on the top and windward sides of the mountain. The air descends on the leeward side, but due to the process of precipitation, it has lost much of its initial moisture. Typically, descending air also gets warmer down the leeward side of the mountain, creating an arid region.

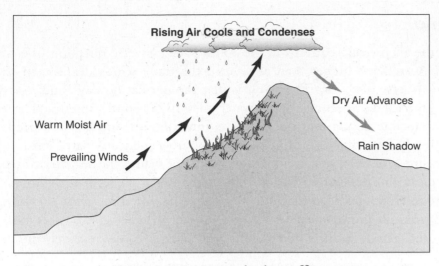

Figure 2.13 Rain shadow effect

EL NIÑO AND LA NIÑA

Normal State

During normal (non-El Niño or "La Nada") conditions, easterly trade winds move water and air warmed by the sun toward the west (Walker circulation). The ocean is generally around 24 inches (60 cm) higher in the western Pacific and the water about 14°F warmer. The trade winds, in piling up water in the western Pacific, make a deep—450 feet (150 m)—warm layer in the west that pushes the thermocline down while it rises in the east. The shallow—90 feet (30 m)—eastern thermocline allows the winds to pull up nutrient-rich water from below, which increases fishing stocks. The western side of the equatorial Pacific is characterized by warm, wet low-pressure weather, as the collected moisture is released in the form of typhoons and thunderstorms.

TIP

Questions about El Niño and La Niña are very common on the APES exam. Be sure you know these two processes!

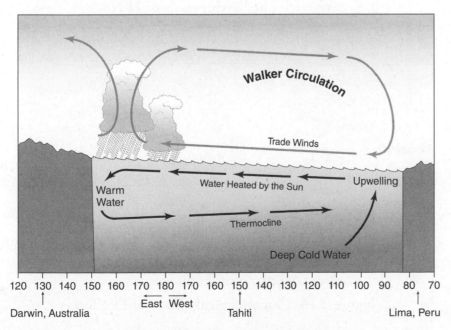

Figure 2.14 Normal conditions

El Niño

When the air pressure patterns in the South Pacific reverse direction (the air pressure at Australia is higher than at Tahiti), the trade winds decrease in strength and can reverse direction. The result is that the normal flow of water away from South America decreases and ocean water piles up off South America. This pushes the thermocline deeper and decreases the upwelling of nutrient-rich deep water, which results in extensive fish kills off the South American coast. With a deeper thermocline and decreased westward transport of water, the sea surface temperature increases in the eastern Pacific. This is the warm phase of El Niño-Southern Oscillation (ENSO) called El Niño. The net result is a shift of the prevailing rain pattern from the normal western Pacific to the central Pacific; rainfall is more common in the central Pacific while the western Pacific becomes relatively dry.

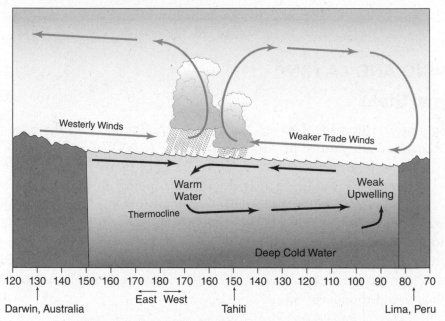

Figure 2.15 The development of El Niño

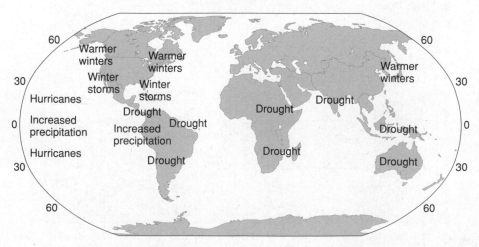

Figure 2.16 Climatological effects of El Niño

La Niña

There are occasions when the trade winds that blow west across the tropical Pacific are stronger than normal, leading to increased upwelling off South America and hence *cooler-than-normal* sea surface temperatures. The prevailing rain pattern also shifts farther west than normal. These winds pile up warm surface water in the western Pacific. This is the cool phase of ENSO called La Niña. La Niña is characterized by unusually cold ocean temperatures in the eastern equatorial Pacific. La Niña tends to bring nearly the opposite effects of El Niño to the United States, with wetter-than-normal conditions across the Pacific Northwest and both dryer and warmer-than-normal conditions in the southern states. Winter temperatures are warmer than normal in the southeastern United States and cooler than normal in the northwest. The increased temperatures in the southeast during La Niña years correlate with the substantial increase in hurricanes that occurs during the same time period. La Niña is also responsible for heavier-than-normal monsoons in India and Southeast Asia.

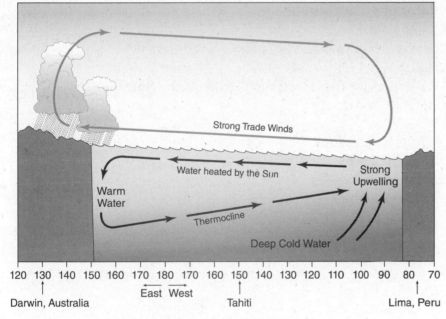

Figure 2.17 La Niña

QUICK REVIEW CHECKLIST

☐ **Atmosphere Composition**
  ☐ Nitrogen, oxygen, water vapor, carbon dioxide, methane, nitrous oxide, ozone

☐ **Structure of the Atmosphere**
  ☐ Ionosphere, mesosphere, stratosphere, troposphere

☐ **Weather and Climate**
  ☐ Differences between weather and climate
  ☐ Factors that affect climate: air mass, air pressure, albedo, altitude, angle of sunlight, clouds, distance to oceans, fronts, heat, land changes, latitude, location, humidity, mountain ranges, pollution, rotation, wind patterns
  ☐ Human activity and influence on climate

☐ **Atmospheric Circulation**
  ☐ Coriolis effect
  ☐ Types of winds (breezes): sea breeze, land breeze
  ☐ Hadley, Ferrel, and polar cells
  ☐ Hurricanes and Tornadoes: what causes them, mitigation, case studies (Katrina)

☐ **El Niño and La Niña**
  ☐ How they develop
  ☐ Environmental effects

MULTIPLE-CHOICE QUESTIONS

1. The zone of the atmosphere in which weather occurs is known as the

   (A) ionosphere
   (B) mesosphere
   (C) troposphere
   (D) thermosphere
   (E) stratosphere

2. 99% of the volume of gases in the lower atmosphere, listed in descending order of volume, are

   (A) O_2, N_2, CO_2, H_2O
   (B) H_2O, N_2, O_2, CO_2
   (C) O_2, CO_2, N_2, H_2O
   (D) CO_2, H_2O, O_2, N_2
   (E) N_2, O_2, H_2O, CO_2

3. Regional climates are most influenced by

   (A) latitude and altitude
   (B) prevailing winds and latitude
   (C) altitude and longitude
   (D) latitude and longitude
   (E) Coriolis effect and trade winds

4. A low-pressure air mass is generally associated with

   (A) hot, humid weather
   (B) fair weather
   (C) tornadoes
   (D) cloudy or stormy weather
   (E) hurricanes

5. La Niña would produce all the following effects EXCEPT

   (A) more rain in southeast Asia
   (B) wetter winters in the Pacific Northwest region of the United States
   (C) warmer winters in Canada and northeast United States
   (D) warmer and drier winters in the southwest and southeast United States
   (E) more Atlantic hurricanes

6. On the leeward side of a mountain range, one would expect

   (A) more clouds and rain than on the windward side
   (B) more clouds but less rain than on the windward side
   (C) colder temperatures
   (D) less clouds and less rain than on the windward side
   (E) no significant difference in climate compared with the windward side

7. The ozone layer exists primarily in what section of the atmosphere?

   (A) Troposphere
   (B) Stratosphere
   (C) Mesosphere
   (D) Thermosphere
   (E) Ionosphere

8. Along the equator,

   (A) warm, moist air rises
   (B) warm, moist air descends
   (C) warm, dry air descends
   (D) cool, dry air descends
   (E) cool, moist air descends

9. The gas that is responsible for trapping most of the heat in the lower atmosphere is

   (A) water vapor
   (B) ozone
   (C) carbon dioxide
   (D) oxygen
   (E) nitrogen

10. Characteristics or requirements of a monsoon include all of the following EXCEPT

    (A) a seasonal reversal of wind patterns
    (B) large land areas cut off from continental air masses by mountain ranges and surrounded by large bodies of water
    (C) different heating and cooling rates between the ocean and the continent
    (D) extremely heavy rainfall
    (E) heating and cooling rates between the oceans and the continents that are equal

11. An atmospheric condition in which the air temperature rises with increasing altitude, holding surface air down and preventing dispersion of pollutants, is known as (a)

    (A) temperature inversion
    (B) cold front
    (C) warm front
    (D) global warming
    (E) upwelling

12. The surface with the lowest albedo is

    (A) snow
    (B) ocean water
    (C) forest
    (D) desert
    (E) black topsoil

13. Jet streams over the U.S. travel primarily

    (A) north to south
    (B) south to north
    (C) east to west
    (D) west to east
    (E) in many directions

14. The correct arrangement of atmospheric layers, arranged in order from the most distant from Earth's surface to the one closest to Earth's surface, is

    (A) troposphere, stratosphere, mesosphere, thermosphere
    (B) thermosphere, mesosphere, stratosphere, troposphere
    (C) stratosphere, troposphere, mesosphere, thermosphere
    (D) thermosphere, mesosphere, troposphere, stratosphere
    (E) None of the above

TIP

Be careful when answering questions that involve placing items in order that you have the order going in the proper direction. A common trick is to have the correct choices in the opposite direction.

15. Areas of low pressure are typically characterized by _____ air and move toward regions where the pressure is _____ with time.

    (A) sinking, falling
    (B) rising, falling
    (C) sinking, rising
    (D) rising, rising
    (E) None of the above

16. The global circulation pattern that dominates the tropics is called the

    (A) Ferrel cell
    (B) Polar cell
    (C) Bradley cell
    (D) Hadley cell
    (E) Tropical cell

17. The date with the shortest amount of daylight in the Southern Hemisphere is

    (A) June 22
    (B) January 1
    (C) December 21
    (D) September 1
    (E) March 18

18. Jet streams follow the sun in that as the sun's elevation _____ (increases, decreases) each day in the spring, the jet stream shifts by moving _____ (north, south) during the Northern Hemisphere spring.

    (A) increases, north
    (B) increases, south
    (C) decreases, north
    (D) decreases, south
    (E) None of the above

19. Usually, fair and dry/hot weather is associated with high pressure around _____ latitude with rainy and stormy weather associated with low pressure around _____ latitude.

    (A) 0 degrees N/S, 90 degrees E/W
    (B) 90 degrees E/W, 90 degrees N/S
    (C) 30 degrees N/S, 50–60 degrees N/S
    (D) 50–60 degrees N/S, 30 degrees N/S
    (E) 45 degrees N/S, 45 degrees E/W

20. The three necessary ingredients for thunderstorm formation are

    (A) moisture, lifting mechanism, instability
    (B) lifting mechanism, mountains, oceans
    (C) stability, moisture, heat
    (D) lifting mechanism, fronts, moisture ·
    (E) deserts, mountains, clouds

TIP

Before writing your essays, be sure to map out or brainstorm what you are going to write about. A few minutes planning and organizing your essays will get you a much higher score.

FREE-RESPONSE QUESTION

(a) Choose ONE of the following: Hadley cell, Ferrel cell, or polar cell. In your description, include the following:

   (i)   A description of the type of cell
   (ii) An explanation of how that cell develops
   (iii) The cell's location with respect to the equator

(b) Describe the characteristics of that cell in terms of climatic conditions. In your description, include temperature, relative humidity, and prevailing winds.

   (i)   Identify and describe ONE biome that would exist at sea level within the specific latitudes of that cell. In your description, give examples of both plants and animals that would be found within that biome.

MULTIPLE-CHOICE ANSWERS AND EXPLANATIONS

1. **(C)** The troposphere is the atmospheric layer closest to Earth and extends for about 11 miles (18 km) above Earth at the equator and about 5 miles (8 km) above Earth at the poles. Temperature declines as altitude increases.

2. **(E)** Nitrogen (78%), oxygen (21%), water vapor (about 0–4%), and the rest below 1%.

3. **(A)** Latitude expresses how far north or south of the equator a location is. The equator is 0° latitude, and the poles are at 90°. For every 1,000 feet (300 m) in altitude, there is a 3°F (1.5°C) drop in temperature.

4. **(D)** A low-pressure air mass (low) occurs when warm air, which is less dense than cooler air, spirals inward toward the center of a low-pressure area. Since the center of the low-pressure area is of even less density and pressure, the air in this section rises and the warm air cools as it expands. The temperature begins to fall and may go below the dew point—the point at which air condenses into water droplets. These water droplets make up clouds. If the droplets begin to coalesce on condensation nuclei, rain follows.

5. **(C)** During La Niña, large portions of central North America experience increased storminess, increased precipitation, and an increased frequency of significant cold-air outbreaks, while the southern states experience less storminess and precipitation. Also, there tends to be considerable month-to-month variations in temperature, rainfall, and storminess across central North America during the winter and spring seasons.

6. **(D)** The rain shadow effect occurs on the leeward side of a mountain, the side away from the ocean. Moist air from the ocean rises when it hits mountains, cools, and loses its moisture on the windward side. On the leeward side, air is much drier. For example, the western side of the Sierra Nevada Mountain Range in California is much wetter than the eastern side.

7. **(B)** 97% of ozone (O_3) is found in the lower stratosphere, which is 9 to 35 miles (15–55 km) above Earth's surface. Temperature increases with altitude in the stratosphere due to absorption of heat energy by ozone molecules.

8. **(A)** Hadley cells occur between 0° and 25° north and south latitudes (equatorial region). In this area, there is upward air motion, cooling of the air due to uplift, high humidity, high clouds, and heavy rains.

9. **(A)** Water vapor is present in such abundance throughout the atmosphere that it acts like a blanket of insulation, trapping heat and forcing surface temperatures higher than they would be otherwise. Water vapor is roughly eight times more effective than carbon dioxide as a greenhouse gas.

10. **(E)** During monsoon season, winds blow from cooler ocean areas (higher pressure) to warmer landmasses (lower pressure). As the air rises over the land masses, it cools and is unable to retain water, producing great amounts of precipitation. In winter, the ocean is now warmer and the cycle reverses. Drier air travels from the land out to the ocean. Monsoons exist in Australia, Africa, and North and South America.

11. **(A)** Temperature inversions are atmospheric conditions in which the air temperature rises with increasing altitude, holding surface air down and preventing dispersion of pollutants.

12. **(E)** Albedo is a measure of reflection of sunlight from a surface. Of the choices, dark topsoil absorbs the most energy and therefore reflects the least amount of energy, resulting in the lowest albedo.

13. **(D)** Jet streams are large-scale upper air flows that travel from west to east and are produced by differences in temperature. They can travel as fast as 250 miles per hour (400 kph) and travel between 3 and 8 miles (5–13 km) above Earth's surface.

14. **(B)** Remember, the question required you to place the layers in order from the most distant to the closest.

15. **(B)** In a high-pressure system, air pressure is greater than the surrounding areas. This difference in air pressure results in wind. In a high-pressure area, air is denser than in areas of lower pressure. The result is that air will move from the high-pressure area to an area of lower pressure. Clear skies and fair weather usually occur in these regions. On the other hand, winds tend to blow into a low-pressure system because air moves from areas of higher pressure into areas of lower pressure. As winds blow into a low-pressure system, the air moves up. This upward flow of air can cause clouds, strong winds, and precipitation to form.

16. **(D)** Hadley cells dominate the tropics.

17. **(A)** The seasons in the Southern Hemisphere are opposite that of the Northern Hemisphere. For example, spring in the Northern Hemisphere is fall in the Southern Hemisphere.

18. **(A)** The position of the jet stream also determines where the storm track is. As the jet stream moves north during spring, the storm track moves north, leaving the southern plains of Texas and Oklahoma and moving into the northern plains near the Dakotas.

19. **(C)** Except for a few locations, most of the world's deserts are located along 30 degrees N/S latitude with lush forests from abundant rains located around 50–60 degrees N/S latitude.

20. **(A)** Moisture, a lifting mechanism, and instability are all needed for thunderstorms to form. The moisture is needed for rain. The lifting mechanism is needed to get the air moving initially in an upward direction, and the unstable atmosphere insures the upward-moving air continues to do so.

FREE-RESPONSE ANSWER

Let's do this essay together, using it as a teaching tool rather than just providing an answer and rubric. Let's choose the Hadley cell for this example.

The first step is to brainstorm. Write a list of key words that would apply to the question. Remember that the order of the keywords is not important, we will put them into the correct order later. Here is a sample of key words: Hadley, Ferrel, polar, temperature, solar insolation, humidity, biomes, plants, and animals.

Now that we have around 10 key words, let's expand the list by adding details—items that we will discuss in our essay. We can also begin to map out the order in which we will discuss the items.

- Hadley: 0° to 30°, deserts, equatorial regions, tropical rain forests, subtropical areas, savannas
- Location
- Temperature (heat moves from equator to colder areas)
- Relative humidity

- Prevailing winds
- Solar insolation
- Biomes
- Animals
- Plants

Remember, you have 23 minutes to spend on this essay, so do not spend more than 5 minutes in organization. Now look over the list and add anything that you have missed. Now it is time to begin writing.

The first step is to write a thesis statement: **"The world's biomes are primarily determined by climatic conditions. Deserts are characterized as areas of low precipitation, while tropical rain forests are characterized by areas of high precipitation."**

The next step is to begin describing what determines climatic conditions that, in turn, affect the type of life present within that zone. **"Solar insolation, that is the amount of sunlight received on Earth, is greatest at the equator and diminishes toward the poles. Since heat flows from warmer regions to cooler regions, the warmer air produced at the equator moves through major worldwide wind patterns that distribute this energy worldwide. As one moves from the equator to the poles, there are three major air circulation cells—Hadley, Ferrel, and polar."** At this point, a labeled sketch would be helpful.

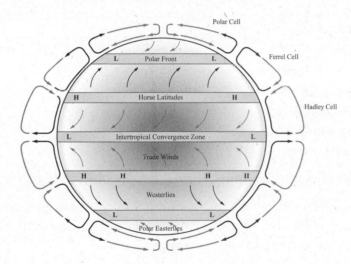

TIP

When writing your FRQ essays, a picture is worth a thousand words! If you can sketch out a labeled diagram of what you are describing it will go a long way in improving your score.

Now, for the remaining time, we can refer to the detailed essay outline and complete the essay, adding details and examples where necessary.

From the equator to 30° north and south latitudes, Hadley cells exist. Since this area of Earth receives the greatest solar radiation due to Earth's axis tilt, this area of Earth is the warmest. Near the equator, this warm, moist air rises. As the warm air rises, it begins to cool and become denser. Since cooler air cannot hold as much water vapor as warmer air, the humidity of the air increases to the point where clouds are produced. This, in turn, causes great amounts of rainfall. Monthly average temperatures are quite high at sea level, and there is no winter. Vegetation near sea level is tropical rain forest. In these tropical systems, temperature variations from day to night are greater than

from season to season. Tropical rain forests, which extend about 1,500 miles (2,400 km) north and south of the equator, are found in South and Central America, Africa, and southeast Asia. Climatic conditions can include rain throughout the year, monsoons—a short, dry season followed by a heavy, rainy period, and tropical savanna with characteristic wet and dry seasons.

Tropical rain forests have characteristically high-species plant and animal diversity. Vegetation is dense. Bromeliads, orchids, ferns, and palms are present. Leaves are large in an effort to absorb sunlight, and there is little need to conserve water lost through transpiration. Soils are characteristically low in nutrients with the nutrients being stored in vegetation. Soil is characteristically acidic. Decomposition of organic material is high due to temperature and moisture. Leaching of soil nutrients is high; therefore, soil quality is very low. Abundant insects and animal biodiversity are characteristic. Examples of animals that one might find in a tropical rain forest biome might include numerous species of butterflies, ants, mosquitoes, millipedes, bats, monkeys, sloths, tarsiers, hippopotamuses, macaws, toucans, parrots, anacondas, alligators, and numerous species of frogs.

At this point, we think we are done. Our last job is to be sure that we have answered all questions. Let's put a check beside each topic that we answered and that we were required to address:

- Describe the cell ✔
- How it develops ✔
- Location of the cell ✔
- Characteristics of the cell

  1. Temperature ✔
  2. Relative humidity ✔
  3. Prevailing winds ✔
  4. Solar insolation ✔

- List examples of plants and animals living within a biome in that cell ✔

Now it is your turn. Take the same question, but this time answer it in terms of either a Ferrel or polar cell. Your teacher may wish to collect your essay and give you pointers on your strengths and weaknesses.

CHAPTER 3

Global Water Resources and Use

FRESHWATER AND SALTWATER

Over 70% of Earth's surface is covered by water. Oceans hold about 97% of all water on Earth, while freshwater constitutes about 3%. Of the freshwater that is available, most of it is trapped in glaciers and ice caps. The rest is found (in descending order) in groundwater, lakes, soil moisture, atmospheric moisture, rivers, and streams.

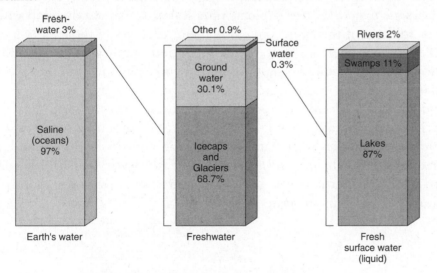

Figure 3.1 Distribution of Earth's water

Water has many unique properties:

1. Strong hydrogen bonds hold water molecules to each other.

2. The temperature of water changes slowly due to its high specific heat capacity.

3. Water has a high boiling point.

4. A lot of energy is needed to evaporate water.

5. Water dissolves many compounds.

6. Water filters out harmful UV radiation in aquatic ecosystems.

7. Water adheres to many solid surfaces.

8. Water expands when it freezes.

Most human settlements are determined by the availability of freshwater. The highest per capita supplies of freshwater are in countries with high precipitation and small populations (Iceland, Norway, and so on). Lowest per capita freshwater supplies are in areas with low rainfall and high populations (Egypt, Israel, and so on).

The use of freshwater, a limited resource, is growing at twice the rate of population growth. In the United States, the average amount of freshwater allocated per person for all purposes is approximately 500,000 gallons (1,900,000 l) per year.

LAKES

Most lakes on Earth are located in the Northern Hemisphere at higher latitudes and are generally found in mountainous areas, rift zones, areas with ongoing or recent glaciations, or along the courses of mature rivers. Processes that form lakes include: (1) tectonic uplift of a mountain range that creates a depression that accumulates water; (2) advance and retreat of glaciers that scrape depressions in the Earth's surface where water accumulates (e.g., the Great Lakes of North America); (3) salt or saline lakes that form where there is no natural outlet or where the water evaporates rapidly and the drainage surface of the water table has a higher-than-normal salt content (e.g., the Great Salt Lake, the Aral Sea, and the Dead Sea); (4) oxbow lakes formed by erosion in river valleys; and (5) crater lakes formed in volcanic craters and calderas that fill up with water more rapidly than they empty (e.g., Crater Lake in Oregon).

All lakes are temporary over geologic time scales, as they slowly fill in with sediments or spill out of the basin containing them. Changes in the level of a lake are controlled by the difference between the input and output compared to the total volume of the lake. Significant input sources are precipitation onto the lake, runoff carried by streams and channels from the lake's catchment area, groundwater channels and aquifers, and artificial sources from outside the catchment area. Output sources include evaporation from the lake, surface and groundwater flows, and any extraction of lake water by humans. Variations in climate conditions and human water requirements will create fluctuations in the lake level. Artificial lakes are constructed for hydroelectric power generation, recreational purposes, industrial use, agricultural use, or domestic water supply.

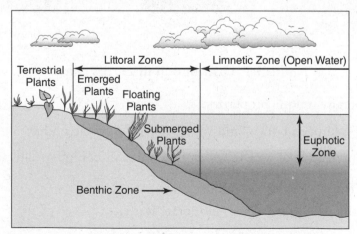

Figure 3.2 Lake zonation

Lakes have three zones: the littoral zone, which is a sloped area close to land; the photic or open-water zone, where sunlight is abundant; and the deep-water benthic zone. The depth to which light can reach in lakes depends on turbidity, or the amount and type of suspended particles in the water. These particles can be either sedimentary (i.e., silt) or biological (e.g., algae or detritus) in origin.

The material at the bottom of a lake can be composed of a wide variety of inorganic material, such as silt or sand, and organic material, such as decaying plant or animal matter. The composition of the lake bed has a significant impact on the flora and fauna found near the lake, as it contributes to the amount and the types of nutrients available. A lake may be in-filled with deposited sediment and gradually become wetland.

Oligotrophic lakes are generally clear due to low nutrient levels and have little plant life. Mesotrophic lakes have good clarity and an average level of nutrients. Eutrophic lakes are enriched with nutrients, resulting in large amounts of plant growth with possible algal blooms. Hypertrophic lakes have been excessively enriched with nutrients, have poor water clarity, and are subject to devastating algal blooms. These lakes usually result from human activities, such as heavy use of fertilizers or sewage outlets in the lake catchment area. Such lakes are of little use to humans and have a poor ecosystem due to decreased amounts of dissolved oxygen. Oligotrophic lakes are lakes with low primary productivity, the result of low nutrient content. These lakes have low algal production, and consequently, often have very clear waters, with high drinking water quality.

Because of the high specific heat capacity of water, lakes moderate the surrounding region's temperature and climate. In the daytime, a lake can cool the land beside it with local winds, resulting in a sea breeze; at night, it can warm it with a land breeze.

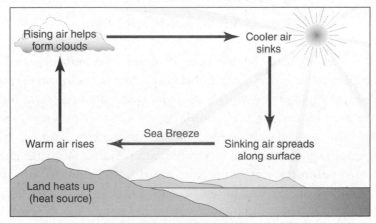

Figure 3.3 Sea breeze

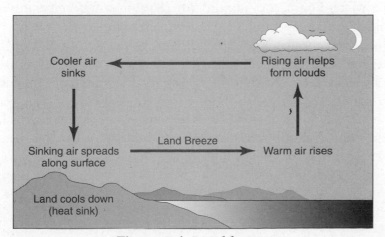

Figure 3.4 Land breeze

The stratification or layering of water in lakes is due to density changes caused by changes in temperature. The density of water increases as temperature decreases until it reaches its maximum density at about 39°F (4°C), causing thermal stratification—the tendency of deep lakes to form distinct layers in the summer months. Deep water is insulated from the sun and stays cool and denser, forming a lower layer called the hypolimnion. The surface and water near the shore are warmed by the sun, making them less dense, so that they form a surface layer called the epilimnion.

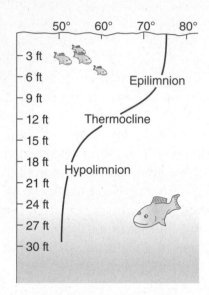

Figure 3.5 Thermal stratification

Seasonal turnover refers to the exchange of surface and bottom water in a lake or pond that happens twice a year (spring and fall). During the summer, the sun heats water near the surface of lakes, which results in a well-defined warm layer of water occurring over a cooler one (stratification). As the summer progresses, temperature differences increase between the layers, and a thin middle layer, or thermocline, develops, where a rapid transition in temperature occurs. With the arrival of fall and cooler air temperatures, water at the surface of lakes begins to cool and becomes heavier. During this time, strong fall winds move the surface water around, which promotes mixing with deeper water—a condition known as *fall turnover*. As the mixing continues, lake water becomes more uniform in temperature and oxygen level. As the winter approaches in areas where subfreezing temperatures are common, the lake surface temperatures approach the freezing mark (water is most dense at 4°C). Thus, as lake waters move toward freezing, the water sinks to the lake bottom when it reaches 4°C. Colder water remains above, perhaps eventually becoming capped by an ice layer, which further prevents the winds from stirring the water mass. With spring, the surface ice begins to melt, and cold surface waters warm until they reach the temperatures of the bottom waters, again producing a fairly uniform temperature distribution throughout the lake. When this occurs, winds blowing over the lake again set up a full circulation system known as *spring turnover*.

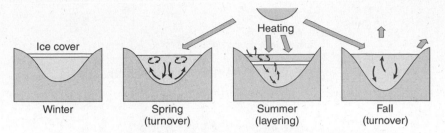

Figure 3.6 Seasonal lake turnover

WETLANDS

Wetlands include swamps, estuaries, marshes, and bogs. Wetlands are characterized by a water table that stands at or near the land surface for a long enough season each year to support aquatic plants. They are considered the most biologically diverse of all ecosystems and occur where the soil is either permanently or seasonally saturated with moisture, often covered partially or completely by shallow pools of water. The water found in wetlands can be saltwater, freshwater, or brackish (water that has more salinity than freshwater, but not as much as seawater). Plant life found in wetlands includes mangrove, water lilies, cattails, sedges, tamarack, black spruce, and cypress. Animal life includes many different amphibians, reptiles, birds, and mammals.

Wetlands have historically been drained for real estate development or flooded for use as recreational lakes. By 1993, half of the world's wetlands had been drained. Wetlands provide a valuable flood control function and are very effective at filtering and cleaning water.

AQUIFERS

An aquifer is a geologic formation that contains water in quantities sufficient to support a well or spring. Unconfined aquifers have as their upper boundary the water table. Typically (but not always), the shallowest aquifer at a given location is unconfined, meaning it does not have a confining layer between it and the surface. Unconfined aquifers usually receive recharge water directly from the surface, from precipitation or from a body of surface water (e.g., a river, stream, or lake). Confined aquifers have the water table above their upper boundary and are typically found below unconfined aquifers. The term "perched" refers to groundwater accumulating above an area of low permeability such as clay. The unsaturated zone is directly below the surface and contains some water. In the unsaturated zone, water and air fill the voids between soil or rock particles. Deeper in the ground is the zone of saturation. In the zone of saturation, the subsurface is completely saturated with water. The point where the zone of aeration meets the zone of saturation is known as the water table. Water table levels fluctuate naturally throughout the year based on seasonal variations. In addition, the depth of the water table varies.

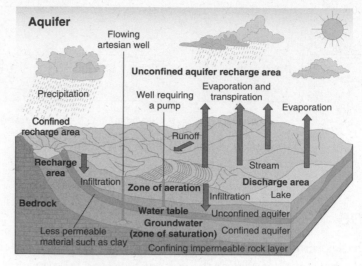

Figure 3.7 A typical aquifer

OCEANS

Approximately 71% of the Earth's surface is covered by the oceans. More than half of this area is below 10,000 feet (3,000 m) deep, with the average salt content of seawater being around 3.5%. The oceanic crust is composed of a dense, thin layer of solidified volcanic basalt as compared to the thicker but less dense continental crust, which is composed primarily of granite. The ocean floor spreads from mid-ocean ridges, where two tectonic plates adjoin. Where two plates move toward each other, one plate subducts or moves under another plate (oceanic or continental), leading to an oceanic trench.

Oceans have a significant effect on the biosphere, as oceanic evaporation is the primary source for precipitation and ocean temperatures affect climate and wind patterns. Approximately 250,000 marine life-forms are currently known, with many times that number yet to be discovered. Oceans are divided into specific zones:

Oceanic Zones

Aphotic	The depths beyond which less than 1% of sunlight penetrates.
Benthic	The ecological region at the lowest level of a body of water.
Disphotic	The zone that is dimly lit and does not have enough light penetrating from the surface to carry out photosynthesis.
Neritic	Extends from the low tide mark to the edge of the continental shelf, with a relatively shallow depth extending to about 650 feet (200 m). Generally well-oxygenated water, low water pressure, available light for photosynthesis, and relatively stable temperature and salinity levels. High biodiversity. Also known as sublittoral or photic zone.
Oceanic	The region of open sea beyond the edge of the continental shelf; includes 65% of the ocean's open water.
Pelagic	Includes all open ocean regions.
Photic (Euphotic)	The depth of the water that is exposed to sufficient sunlight for photosynthesis to occur. Biologically diverse.

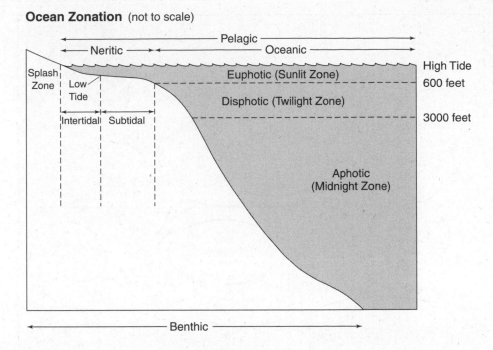

Figure 3.8 Ocean zonation

OCEAN CIRCULATION

The Northern Hemisphere is dominated by land and the Southern Hemisphere by oceans. Temperature differences between summer and winter are more extreme in the Northern Hemisphere because the land warms and cools more quickly than water. Heat is transported from the equator to the poles mostly by atmospheric air currents but also by oceanic water currents. The warm waters near the surface and colder waters at deeper levels move by convection. Changes in ocean temperatures have a direct bearing on ocean currents. During summers, a thermocline develops in ocean waters between the warm surface water and the cooler bottom water.

Surface ocean currents are driven by wind patterns that result from the flow of high thermal energy sources generated at the tropics (higher pressure) to low-energy sources in polar areas (lower pressure). They serve to distribute the heat generated near the tropics. Deep-water, density-driven currents are controlled primarily by differences in temperature and salt content. Denser, saltier water sinks, and less-dense water rises. About 90% of the ocean volume circulates due to density differences in temperature and salinities, while the remaining 10% is involved in wind-driven surface currents. In the Northern Hemisphere, north-flowing currents are warm (originating near the equator), and south-flowing currents are colder (originating from the Arctic area).

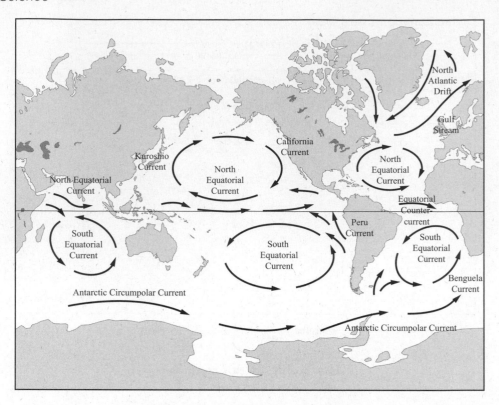

Figure 3.9 Ocean surface currents

Ocean water has warmed significantly during the past 50 years. The greatest amount of warming has occurred in the top surface layers of the ocean. The temperature of the Antarctic Southern Ocean rose by 0.31°F (0.17°C) between the 1950s and the 1980s—twice the rate for the world's oceans as a whole. Since the 1950s, the California Current that runs southward along the west coast of the United States has risen about 2.7°F (1.5°C) and has resulted in a significant decrease in plankton with resulting rippling effects within the food web. Possible reasons for dramatic increases in ocean temperatures include:

1. Significant slowing of the ocean circulation that transports warm water to the North Atlantic

2. Large reductions in the Greenland and West Antarctic ice sheets

3. Accelerated global warming due to carbon cycle feedbacks in the terrestrial biosphere

4. Decreases in upwelling

5. Releases of terrestrial carbon from permafrost regions and methane from hydrates in coastal sediments.

The Gulf Stream transports warm water from the Caribbean northward. A branch of the Gulf Stream known as the North Atlantic Drift is responsible for bringing warmer temperatures to Europe. Evaporation of ocean water in the North Atlantic results in a cooling effect and a higher salt concentration, both of which increase the density of the water. As the denser water sinks, it creates a southern circulation pattern. As glaciers in Greenland melt due to the effects of global warming, the density of this ocean water decreases due to more freshwater. This, in effect, could stall the North Atlantic Drift and bring colder temperatures and flooding to Europe.

The Great Ocean Conveyor Belt

There is constant motion in the ocean in the form of a global ocean "conveyor belt" driven by thermohaline currents. These currents are density driven and are affected by both temperature and salinity. Cold, salty water is dense and sinks to the bottom of the ocean, while warm water is less dense and rises to the surface. Warm water from the Gulf Stream enters the Norwegian Sea and provides heat to the atmosphere in the northern latitudes. The loss of heat by the water in this area makes the water cooler and denser, causing it to sink. As more warm water is transported north, the cooler water sinks and moves south, making room for the incoming warm water. This cold bottom water flows south to Antarctica. Eventually, the cold bottom waters warm and rise to the surface in the Pacific and Indian oceans. It takes water about 1,600 years to move through the entire conveyor belt. The ocean conveyor belt plays an important role in supplying heat to the polar regions, and thus in regulating the amount of sea ice in these regions. Insofar as thermohaline circulation governs the rate at which deep waters are exposed to the surface, it may also play an important role in determining the concentration of carbon dioxide in the atmosphere. For more information on global warming and its effect on thermohaline circulation, refer to Chapter 11.

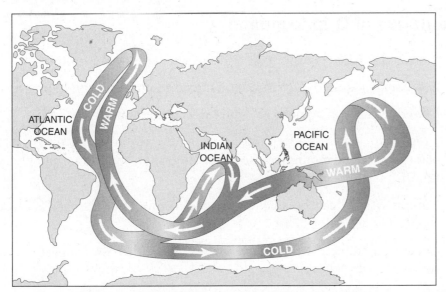

Figure 3.10 The Great Ocean Conveyor Belt

Upwellings

Upwellings occur when prevailing winds produced through the Coriolis effect, and moving clockwise in the Northern Hemisphere, push warmer, nutrient-poor surface waters away from the coastline. This surface water is then replaced by cooler, nutrient-rich deeper waters. The deeper waters contain high levels of nitrates and phosphates, which result from the decomposition and sinking of surface water plankton. When these nutrients are brought to the surface through upwelling, they supply necessary nutrients for phytoplankton, which form the base of the oceanic food chain.

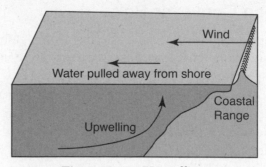

Figure 3.11 Upwelling

AGRICULTURAL, INDUSTRIAL, AND DOMESTIC USE

About 70% of freshwater is used for agriculture. Use of water for agriculture depends upon national wealth, climate, and degree of industrialization. Canada uses about 10% of its freshwater resources for agriculture, whereas India uses about 90%. Up to 70% of water intended for agriculture in developing countries may not reach crops due to seepage, evaporation, and leakage. Drip irrigation, the most efficient type of irrigation, is used on less than 1% of crops worldwide.

Advantages of Drip Irrigation

1. Increased efficiency. Almost all water reaches crops—no runoff.

2. Less energy required. Lower water demand results in less pumping costs.

3. Lower demand on aquifers or depleted water resources.

4. Crop yield increases—fertilizer is accurately applied directly to roots of plants and can be monitored. Reduces salinization and nitrate and phosphate runoff.

5. Tubing systems can be adapted to meet contours of the land and can be changed as needed.

6. Correct amounts of water means plants are neither waterlogged nor water stressed.

Industry uses about 25% of all freshwater, ranging from a high of about 75% in Europe to less than 5% in developing countries. Water used for cooling power plants is the largest sector. Water returns 60 times its economic value when used for industrial purposes rather than for agriculture.

Domestic uses of freshwater include water being used for flushing toilets, bathing, drinking, and so on. People living in developed countries use about 10 times more water for personal use than people living in less-developed countries.

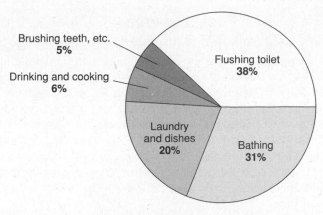

Figure 3.12 Water use

SURFACE AND GROUNDWATER ISSUES

Surface water infiltrates and percolates through the soil into aquifers—layers of porous rock, sand, and gravel where water is trapped above a nonporous layer or bedrock. The surface area in which water infiltrates into the aquifer is called the recharge zone. If pollution enters an aquifer, the aquifer is no longer a source of safe drinking water. Movement of water through aquifers is very slow. Artesian wells occur where the water breaks through to the surface. Aquifers in the United States hold 30 times more water than all U.S. lakes and rivers combined, with groundwater supplying almost 40% of all freshwater in the United States. When removal of water exceeds the recharge rate, the land sinks (subsidence). Depletion of water in aquifers also leads to sinkholes and saltwater intrusion—a condition in which seawater replaces the freshwater in the aquifer, making it unusable for human use. The region where water-saturated soil meets water-unsaturated soil is called the water table. The water table is unique to a region and can rise and fall with rainfall variations, depletion rates, etc.

Groundwater is considered to be one of the last "free resources," as anyone who can afford to drill can draw up water. Thus, the extraction of groundwater becomes a "Tragedy of the Commons," with high economic externalities.

Water-Renewal Rates

Source of Water	Average Renewal Rate
Groundwater (deep)	~ 10,000 years
Groundwater (near surface)	~ 200 years
Lakes	~ 100 years
Glaciers	~ 40 years
Water in the soil	~ 70 days
Rivers	16 days
Atmosphere	8 days

CASE STUDIES

San Joaquin Valley, California: Groundwater-related subsidence is the sinking of land resulting from groundwater extraction. Land subsidence occurs when large amounts of ground water have been withdrawn from certain types of rocks, such as fine-grained sediments. The rock compacts because the water is partly responsible for holding the ground up. When the water is withdrawn, the rocks fall in on themselves. The desert areas of the world are requiring more and more water for growing populations and agriculture. In the San Joaquin Valley of the United States, groundwater pumping for crops has gone on for generations and has resulted in the entire valley sinking up to thirty feet.

Mexico City: A city of 22 million people, Mexico City is almost entirely dependent on exploiting groundwater for its needs. The water table in Mexico City is dropping almost six feet (2 meters) per year. Such a dramatic change in land elevation causes massive impacts on buildings and infrastructure, such as cracking and tilting.

GLOBAL PROBLEMS

Both water shortages and rising sea levels are global problems.

Water Shortages

The rate of water consumption is growing twice as fast as the population growth rate. Freshwater shortages that result from this demand can be due to natural weather patterns that reduce rainfall, rivers changing course, flooding that contaminates existing supplies, competition for available water, overgrazing and the resulting erosion, pollution of existing supplies, and competing interests that reduce water conservation programs. Water is a limiting factor as it limits the amount of food that can be produced in a region. If food cannot be grown locally due to water shortages, then food must be imported at additional costs.

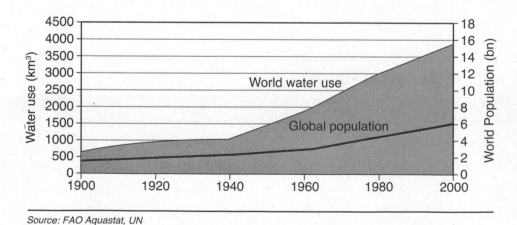

Source: FAO Aquastat, UN

Figure 3.13 Global Water Use vs. Population Growth

Rising Sea Levels

Rising sea level is primarily due to two factors: thermal expansion of water and the melting of ice caps and glaciers. Thermal expansion of seawater involves increasing the distance between neighboring water molecules, and this distance increases with increasing temperature. Translated over the mean depth of the ocean 2.4 miles (3.8 km), a 1-degree increase in temperature will cause a sea level rise of about 28 inches (70 cm).

During the end of the last ice age about 18,000 years ago, when global temperatures were about 10°F (5°C) warmer than they are today, sea level was about 430 feet (130 m) higher than it is today. Much of the rise was due to ice that was on land melting and filling the oceans. When ice that is floating on the water melts, it does not contribute to a rise in sea level. However, it does affect climate by changing the albedo. With higher sea levels and more water covering Earth's surface, more heat energy is absorbed by the water and less is reflected back into space, resulting in higher temperatures.

During the 20th century, sea levels rose 6–8 inches (15–25 cm). Approximately 1–2 inches (2–5 cm) of the rise resulted from the melting of mountain glaciers. Another 1–2 inches (2–5 cm) resulted from the expansion of ocean water that resulted from warmer ocean temperatures. Best scientific estimates indicate that sea levels will rise 7 inches (18 cm) by the year 2030 and 23 inches (58 cm) by the year 2090. Climate models have suggested that temperatures in polar regions will increase more and at a faster pace than in other areas of the world. Since 1995, more than 5,400 square miles, an area equal to Connecticut and Rhode Island combined, have broken off the Antarctic ice shelves and melted.

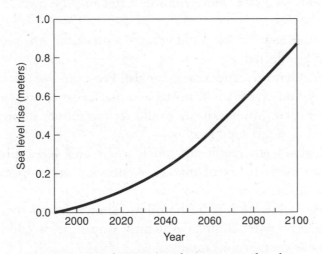

Figure 3.14 Projected rise in sea level

Wetlands are the most-impacted areas affected by rising sea levels. A 1-foot (30 cm) increase in sea level would result in up to 40% of the U.S. wetlands being destroyed. Other impacts would include: erosion of beaches and bluffs, salt intrusion into aquifers and surface waters, inundation of seawater into low-lying areas, and increased flooding and storm damage.

Much of the world's population—20%—lives in coastal regions, and half of the world's population lives within 120 miles (200 km) of the coast. Asia, Latin America, and the Caribbean have the highest percentages of people living near the coast.

FRESHWATER CONSERVATION

Several conservation methods can be used to increase the quantity of available freshwater:

Methods to Increase Supplies of Freshwater: Description and Drawbacks

- **Changes in personal habits:** Turn off shower while washing. Wash only full loads of clothes and dishes; turn off water when brushing teeth. Check for and repair leaks around the home. Use a broom when cleaning driveways and patios. Adjust sprinklers to prevent runoff. Water at night or early morning.
- **Construct dams and reservoirs:** Interferes with fish migration and destroys natural rivers. Leakages, earthquakes, evaporation, sediment buildup, and displacement of people are also consequences. Up to 60 million people worldwide (many being indigenous minorities) have been relocated due to dam and reservoir construction.
- **Desalinate water:** Rate of production is low and is expensive (three to four times more expensive than any other process). Issues of brine disposal.
- **Drip irrigation:** Drip irrigation conserves water by reducing evaporation, but it is expensive. Most large agricultural corporations can afford it, but small, independent farmers cannot. Not suitable for annual crops.
- **Education:** Informing and educating the public on water conservation.
- **Encourage the use of recycled products that require less water to produce:** Costs of collecting products may be outweighed by savings.
- **Engineer systems to collect more runoff:** Water may be high in pollutants and expensive to reprocess.
- **Levy taxes or user fees:** Prices would go up on products. International competitiveness would be affected.
- **Line irrigation channels and cover canals:** Prevents loss of irrigation water through seepage and evaporation. Initial and maintenance costs are expensive.
- **Meter all water used:** Municipalities would recoup money on meter installation with paying less to water suppliers.
- **Plant crops that do not require as much water and xeriscaping:** Xeriscaping reduces urban runoff. Issues of market economies, crop prices and demand, weather patterns, and so on.
- **Rebates or legislation of low-flush toilets, shower restrictors, etc.:** Rebates would be offered by water companies, which, over time, would recoup costs by having to buy less water from suppliers.
- **Reduce government subsidies:** Increased water costs would be passed on to consumers and result in greater personal conservation.
- **Reprocess (recycle) water:** The public is not supportive of using reprocessed toilet water. Reprocessed water could be used for irrigation but would require separate pipeline systems. Reuse of gray water is becoming popular in new developments.
- **Seed clouds:** Water availability to other areas would be affected.
- **Tiered price scale:** Would reduce effective family income for larger families. Could be remedied through exemptions or allocated share of water per family member.

- **Use of icebergs:** Expensive and most of it would be lost before it reached final destination.
- **Use more groundwater:** If rate of use exceeds rate of recharge, then subsidence, sinkholes, and saltwater intrusion could occur.

CASE STUDIES

- **Aswan High Dam, Egypt:** Completed in the 1970s, the Aswan High Dam in Egypt was built to supply irrigation water. The water that is available is only half of what was expected due to evaporation and seepage losses in unlined canals. Several other problems were encountered. First, the elimination of nutrients onto farmlands now requires the use of expensive fertilizers. Second, the depletion of nutrients into the Mediterranean caused a decline in certain fish catches. Third, large amounts of standing water caused the proliferation of snails and ultimately resulted in a debilitating disease known as schistosomiasis, with some areas having infection rates of 80%.

- **Bangladesh:** In the 1960s, thousands of wells were dug in Bangladesh by foreign governments and humanitarian organizations in an effort to supply freshwater to the population. Shortly thereafter, arsenic compounds from the soil began to leach into the groundwater. Arsenic poisoning began to appear among the population, with millions of people showing symptoms.

- **Colorado River Basin:** Diversion of water from the Colorado River has led to water right disputes between California, Arizona, and Mexico. Dams on the Colorado River trap large quantities of silt (over 10 million metric tons per year) and reduce nutrient levels in farmlands below the dam. As a result, more fertilizer is required. Farm irrigation has resulted in high levels of salts in the alkaline soils to become incorporated in agricultural runoff. Millions of acres of once-valuable farmland are now useless due to the salt buildup in soil, a process known as salinization.

- **James Bay, Canada:** Diversion of rivers into Hudson Bay to generate electrical power has resulted in massive flooding. During one flood, up to 10,000 caribou drowned. In addition, mercury has leached out of rocks and into water, with nearby residents showing signs of mercury poisoning. The project also created expensive legal battles and created many issues with indigenous people whose land was flooded.

- **Ogallala Aquifer:** The Ogallala Aquifer underlies eight states from Texas to North Dakota. The Ogallala Aquifer used to hold more freshwater than all freshwater lakes, streams, and rivers on Earth. Due to pumping of this groundwater for agricultural, domestic, and industrial uses, many locations are experiencing water shortages.

- **Three Gorges Dam, China:** In 1949, China had no large reservoirs and only 40 small hydroelectric stations. By 1985, there were 80,000 reservoirs and 70,000 hydroelectric stations. The Three Gorges Dam required relocation of 1.2 million people.

TIP

Case studies can be brought into your essay answers to bring a historical connection to the question. Try to bring at least one case study into your essays—your score will go higher. You will also find several multiple-choice questions on the test that focus on case studies. Only the most relevant case studies are included in this book.

QUICK REVIEW CHECKLIST

☐ **Properties of Water**
- ☐ name five physical properties of water
- ☐ various forms and amounts of freshwater available (lakes, glaciers, ice caps, etc.)

☐ **Ocean Circulation**
- ☐ causes of currents (winds, densities, temperature, thermoclines, etc.)
- ☐ differences between Northern Hemisphere and Southern Hemisphere currents
- ☐ causes and consequences of increases in ocean temperatures

☐ **Water Usage**
- ☐ agricultural usage (various forms, advantages and disadvantages of irrigation)
- ☐ industrial usage (relative amount compared to other uses, recycling methods)
- ☐ domestic usage (relative amount compared to other uses)

☐ **Surface Water vs. Groundwater**
- ☐ relative amount of freshwater available
- ☐ relative renewal rates
- ☐ pollution (current status, mitigation)

☐ **Rising Sea Level**
- ☐ historical perspective
- ☐ contributing factors
- ☐ impact (financial and cultural)

☐ **Conservation**
- ☐ name five conservation methods for industrial, agricultural, and domestic water usage

☐ **Case Studies**
- ☐ Aswan High Dam
- ☐ Bangladesh
- ☐ Colorado River Basin
- ☐ James Bay
- ☐ Ogallala Aquifer
- ☐ Three Gorges

MULTIPLE-CHOICE QUESTIONS

1. Water vapor returning to the liquid state is called

    (A) evaporation
    (B) transpiration
    (C) boiling
    (D) condensation
    (E) vaporization

2. The temperature at which air becomes saturated and produces liquid is called

    (A) the saturation point
    (B) the dew point
    (C) the condensation point
    (D) relative humidity
    (E) absolute humidity

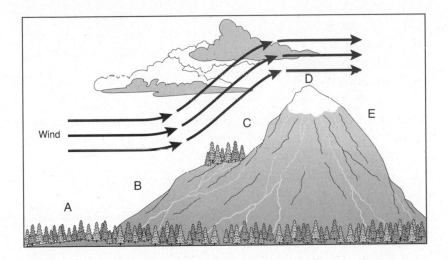

3. The area that would receive the most precipitation would be

    (A) *A*
    (B) *B*
    (C) *C*
    (D) *D*
    (E) *E*

4. The rain shadow effect would be located at point

    (A) *A*
    (B) *B*
    (C) *C*
    (D) *D*
    (E) *E*

5. Of the freshwater on Earth that is not trapped in snow packs or glaciers, most of it (95%) is trapped in

  (A) lakes
  (B) rivers
  (C) aquifers
  (D) dams
  (E) estuaries, marshes, and bogs

6. The primary use of freshwater is for

  (A) industry
  (B) domestic use
  (C) fishing
  (D) agriculture
  (E) landscaping

7. A mixture of freshwater and saltwater is known as
  (A) brackish water
  (B) gray water
  (C) black water
  (D) connate water
  (E) lentic water

8. A temperate lake is most likely to show thermal stratification and limited mixing of surface and deeper waters during the _____ season.

  (A) winter
  (B) spring
  (C) summer
  (D) fall
  (E) None of the above

9. Of the following methods of irrigation, the one that currently conserves the most water is

  (A) flooding fields
  (B) irrigation channels
  (C) sprinklers
  (D) drip irrigation
  (E) misters

10. The largest use for industrial water is for

  (A) cooling electrical power plants
  (B) automobile manufacturing
  (C) mining
  (D) the food and beverage industry
  (E) aquaculture

11. A country that would represent large per capita water use would be

    (A) China
    (B) India
    (C) Israel
    (D) United States
    (E) Iceland

12. When compared with the rate of population growth, the worldwide demand rate for water is

    (A) about half
    (B) about the same
    (C) about two times
    (D) about three times
    (E) about ten times

13. The U.S. per capita use of water on a daily basis is closest to

    (A) 50 gallons
    (B) 100 gallons
    (C) 1,500 gallons
    (D) 5,000 gallons
    (E) 10,000 gallons

14. Countries that are more likely to suffer from water stress would be located in

    (A) North America
    (B) South America
    (C) western Europe
    (D) the Middle East
    (E) Asia

15. What fraction of the world's population does not have access to adequate amounts of safe drinking water?

    (A) 1/2
    (B) 1/3
    (C) 1/4
    (D) 1/6
    (E) 1/10

16. The oceanic zone that extends from the low tide mark to the edge of the continental shelf is known as the

    (A) aphotic zone
    (B) benthic zone
    (C) neritic zone
    (D) pelagic zone
    (E) photic zone

17. Rising sea levels due to global warming would be responsible for all of the following EXCEPT

    (A) destruction of coastal wetlands
    (B) beach erosion
    (C) increased damage due to storms and floods
    (D) increased salinity of estuaries and aquifers
    (E) all would be the result of rising sea levels

18. What does La Niña bring to the southeastern United States?

    (A) Warm winters
    (B) Extremely cold winters
    (C) Hot summers
    (D) Cooler than normal summers
    (E) None of the above

19. Which of the following ocean currents flows without obstruction or barriers around Earth?
    (A) Gulf Stream
    (B) California Current
    (C) Antarctic Circumpolar Current
    (D) Aghulas Current
    (E) They all flow unimpeded

20. Saltwater intrusion into groundwater occurs most often when

    (A) the water table near the coast drops
    (B) surface salts from irrigation water seep into the ground
    (C) storms at sea create unusually low tides
    (D) less surface water reaches the water table
    (E) salt water is pumped into aquifers to replenish water tables

FREE-RESPONSE QUESTION

An APES class visited a local freshwater stream near their high school and performed several tests to determine the water quality of the stream.

(a) Choose ONE test of water quality. For that test, provide

    (i)   A description of exactly what that water quality test measures
    (ii)   A brief explanation of how that test is performed
    (iii) How the results of that test are interpreted and they relate to overall water quality

(b) Assume that the results of the water quality test that you chose in (a) are such that they are negatively impacting stream water quality. Describe ONE remediation technique that could be used to reduce the environmental impact.

(c) Sketch a food web of a freshwater or riparian ecosystem. In your diagram

    (i)   Include at least one producer, one primary consumer, one secondary consumer, and one tertiary consumer and label one of each type as to their role in the pyramid
    (ii)   Use arrows to show the relationships that exist in your diagram between the producers and the consumers

MULTIPLE-CHOICE ANSWERS AND EXPLANATIONS

1. **(D)** Evaporation is water changing from a liquid state to a gaseous state below the boiling point. Transpiration is water moving through a plant. Vaporization is moving from a liquid state to a gaseous state.

2. **(B)** The saturation point is the maximum amount of water vapor that a particular volume of air at a given temperature can hold. The condensation point is the temperature and pressure at which water vapor turns into liquid water. Absolute humidity is the mass of water vapor in a given volume of air. Relative humidity is the ratio of the actual amount of water vapor held in the atmosphere compared with the maximum amount that the air could hold and is influenced by temperature and atmospheric pressure.

3. **(C)** As the air lifts (orographic lifting), it becomes cooler. Cooler air holds less water vapor. At location *C*, the air is holding the maximum amount of water vapor. Given the fact that the temperature has decreased, it would receive the maximum amount of rain. At the top of the mountain at location *D*, much of the water vapor has been depleted from the air.

4. **(E)** Point *E* is on the leeward side of the mountain. This side receives little precipitation because most of the rain has been deposited on the windward side. The leeward side is experiencing the rain shadow effect.

5. **(C)** The oceans hold 97% of all water on Earth. Freshwater only makes up 3%. Of that 3%, 90% of it is trapped in ice and snow, which is rapidly melting due to global warming. Of the freshwater left, the majority is found in groundwater, with the remaining 3% of freshwater found in lakes, rivers, and

streams. Of the total amount of water on Earth, only 0.01% is located in lakes, rivers, and streams.

6. **(D)** Agriculture uses about 70% of all freshwater. Use for agriculture depends upon national wealth, climate, and degree of industrialization. Industry uses about 25% of all freshwater, with Europe using the most and developing countries using the least. Water used for cooling of power plants is the largest sector.

7. **(A)** Gray water is sewage water that does not contain toilet wastes. Black water is sewage that does contain toilet wastes. Connate water is also known as fossil water and is water that has been trapped within sediment or rock structures at the time the rock was formed. Lentic water is the standing water of lakes, marshes, ponds, and swamps.

8. **(C)** During the summer, the surface water warms up much faster than the deep water. The warmer surface water is less dense than the cooler, deep water, so it stays on the surface. The wind mixes the surface water but only near the surface. The lake tends to become stratified, with a warmer upper layer or epilimnion and a cooler lower layer or hypolimnion. The boundary between these layers is called the thermocline.

9. **(D)** Drip irrigation can increase yields and decrease water requirements and labor. It provides the plant with continuous, near-optimal soil moisture by conducting water directly to the plant. It saves water because only the plant's root zone receives moisture.

10. **(A)** Industry used about 25% of all freshwater, ranging from 75% in Europe to less than 5% in developing countries.

11. **(D)** Highest per capita supplies of freshwater are in countries with high rainfall and low populations (Iceland, Norway, and so on). These water-rich countries have low water withdrawals. Remember, *per capita* means "per person."

12. **(C)** Since populations are increasing and increased populations result in higher levels of pollution and since freshwater sources are finite, the amount of freshwater per person is decreasing each year.

13. **(C)** In the United States, renewable or replacement water averages 2.4 million gallons (9 million L) per person per year. The average amount withdrawn from water supplies in the United States is about 500,000 gallons (1.9 million L) per person per year (1,500 gallons [5,700 L] per day).

14. **(D)** Areas that do not receive as much precipitation include polar regions (cold air cannot hold as much water as warmer air), midcontinental areas (they are too far from oceans and the clouds have released much of their moisture before they reach inland), subtropical deserts (air masses are subsiding), and the leeward sides of mountains near coastal regions (rain shadow effect).

15. **(D)** It is estimated that over 1 billion people lack access to safe drinking water. A child dies every 8 seconds worldwide from contaminated water sources (over 5 million children each year).

16. **(C)** The neritic zone, also called coastal waters or the sublittoral zone, is the part of the ocean extending from the low tide mark to the edge of the continental shelf, with a relatively shallow depth extending to about 650 feet (200 m). The neritic zone has generally well-oxygenated water, low water pressure, and relatively stable temperature and salinity levels. These, combined with presence of light and the resulting photosynthetic life, such as phytoplankton and floating seaweed, make the neritic zone the location of the majority of sea life.

17. **(E)** Sea levels are rising and are caused by both natural and human factors. A 0.5-inch (1 cm) rise in sea level erodes beaches about 3 feet (1 m) horizontally. It is predicted that within 100 years, there will be a net loss of up to 43% in coastal wetlands due to rising sea levels.

18. **(A)** La Niña can bring warm winters to the southeast and cooler-than-normal winter temperatures to the northwest United States. It is the cold counterpart of El Niño. La Niña's strong easterly winds bring cold ocean water to the surface in the eastern Pacific and causes increased rainfall in the western Pacific. The jet stream rather than coming through the Pacific Northwest is diverted over Alaska and into the Great Lakes region.

19. **(C)** The Antarctic Circumpolar Current is the most powerful ocean current system on Earth and exerts a strong influence on climate. It circles Earth in the southern hemisphere and connects the three great ocean basins—Atlantic, Indian, and Pacific. Unlike in the Northern Hemisphere, there are no landmasses to break up this large, continuous stretch of water.

20. **(A)** Normally, the groundwater underlying coastal regions has an upper layer of freshwater with salt water beneath it. The layering occurs because rain, falling as freshwater, is less dense than salt water. When freshwater is withdrawn at a faster rate than it can be replenished, a drawdown of the water table occurs, with a resulting decrease in the overall hydrostatic pressure. When this happens near an ocean coastal area, saltwater from the ocean intrudes into the freshwater aquifer.

FREE-RESPONSE ANSWER

(a) Choose ONE test of water quality. For that test, provide

   (i)   A description of exactly what that water quality test measures

   Biological oxygen demand (BOD) is a measure of the oxygen used by microorganisms to decompose organic wastes. If there is a large quantity of organic waste in the water supply, bacterial counts will be high. Therefore, the demand for oxygen will be high, resulting in a high BOD level. As the waste is consumed or dispersed through the water, BOD levels will begin to decline. Nitrates and phosphates in a body of water can also contribute to high BOD levels. Nitrates and phosphates are plant nutrients and can cause plant life and algae to grow quickly. When plants grow quickly, they also die quickly. This contributes to the organic waste in the water, which is then decomposed by bacteria—resulting in a high BOD level. When BOD levels are high, dissolved oxygen (DO) levels decrease because the oxygen that is available in the water is being consumed by the bacteria. Because less dissolved oxygen is available in the water, fish and other aquatic organisms may not survive.

   (ii) A brief explanation of how that test is performed

   The BOD test takes five days to complete and is performed using a dissolved oxygen test kit. The BOD level is determined by comparing the DO level of a water sample taken immediately with the DO level of a water sample that has been incubated in the dark for five days. The difference between the two DO levels represents the amount of oxygen required for the decomposition of any organic material in the sample and is a good approximation of the BOD level.

(iii) How the results of that test are interpreted and how they relate to overall water quality

BOD levels of 1–2 ppm are indicative of good water quality without much organic waste present in the water supply. A water supply with a BOD level of 3–5 ppm is considered moderately clean. In water with a BOD level of 6–9 ppm, the water is considered somewhat polluted because there is usually organic matter present, and bacteria are decomposing this waste. At BOD levels of 10 ppm or greater, the water supply is considered very polluted with organic wastes. At these BOD levels, organisms that are more tolerant of lower dissolved oxygen may appear and become numerous (such as leeches and sludge worms). Organisms that need higher oxygen levels (like caddis fly larvae and mayfly nymphs) will not survive.

(b) Assume that the results of the water quality test that you chose in (a) are such that they are negatively impacting stream water quality. Describe ONE remediation technique that could be used to reduce the environmental impact.

High BOD usually indicates the presence of organic waste(s) in the water. The first step in reducing the environmental impact of low dissolved oxygen content in the water is to identify the source of the waste. By carefully testing various sites along the stream, it may be possible to identify exactly the source of the organic pollution; i.e., leaking sewer line, leaking septic tank, discharge from a factory, runoff from a cattle feedlot, etc. Once the source has been identified, several options are available: (1) contact the polluter and let them know your results and/or (2) contact local, state, or national authorities. If the source of pollution is a point-source such as a leak in a sewer line, this can generally be easily corrected. However, non-point pollution sources such as agricultural runoff may be more difficult to locate and identify. However, remediation techniques could involve changes in: the type of fertilizer being used and its application; erosion and sediment control techniques; changes in animal feeding operations; changes in cattle grazing management; and/or changes in irrigation water management.

A sample food web is included here ONLY for reference. The student does NOT need to include any of the organisms listed here to receive full credit. However, the food web that is drawn must be correct.

(c) Sketch a food web of a freshwater or riparian ecosystem. In your diagram

(i) include at least one producer, one primary consumer, one secondary consumer, and one tertiary consumer and label each as to its role in the pyramid

(ii) use arrows to show the relationships that exist in your diagram between the producers and the consumers

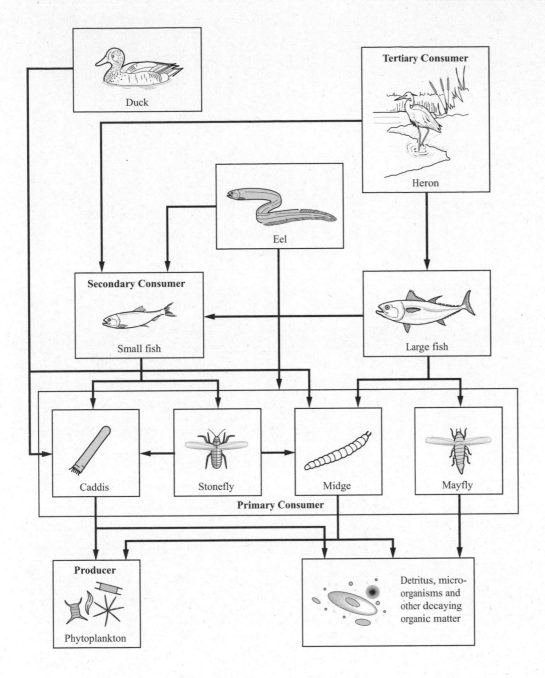

UNIT II: THE LIVING WORLD (10–15%)

Areas on Which You Will Be Tested

A. **Ecosystem Structure**—biological populations and communities, ecological niches, interactions among species, keystone species, species diversity and edge effects, major terrestrial and aquatic biomes.

B. **Energy Flow**—photosynthesis and cellular respiration, food webs and trophic levels, and ecological pyramids.

C. **Ecosystem Diversity**—biodiversity, natural selection, evolution, and ecosystem services.

D. **Natural Ecosystem Change**—climate shifts, species movement, and ecological succession.

E. **Natural Biogeochemical Cycles**—carbon, nitrogen, phosphorus, sulfur, water, and conservation of matter.

Ecosystems

CHAPTER 4

ECOLOGY

Ecology is the branch of biology that deals with the relations of organisms to one another and to their physical surroundings. Understanding ecosystems requires having an understanding of ecology.

Biological Populations and Communities

Organisms that resemble each other, that are similar in genetic makeup, chemistry, and behavior, and that are able to interbreed and produce fertile offspring belong to the same species. Organisms of the same species (intraspecific) that interact with each other and occupy a specific area form a population. Populations of different species (interspecific) living and interacting within an area create communities. A community is made up of all the populations of different species that live together within a particular area. An ecosystem is a system formed by the interaction of a community of organisms with their physical environment. Organisms make up populations that make up communities that make up ecosystems that make up the biosphere: biosphere → ecosystems → communities → populations → species → organisms.

Members of a population can be dispersed in an area in three ways:

> **Remember**
>
> "Intra" means within. "Inter" means between.

1. **Clumped.** Some areas within the habitat are dense with organisms, while other areas contain few members. This type of distribution is found in environments that are characterized by patchy resources. Clumped distribution is the most common type of dispersion found in nature because animals need certain resources to survive, and when these resources become scarce during certain parts of the year, animals tend to "clump" together around these crucial resources; e.g., elephants in Africa clumped together near water holes during the dry season. Individuals might also be clustered together in an area due to social factors such as family groups; e.g., wildebeests. Organisms that usually serve as prey also form clumped distributions in areas where they can hide and detect predators easily; e.g., ducks. Other causes of clumped distributions are the inability of offspring to independently move from their habitat. This is seen in juvenile animals that are immobile and strongly dependent upon parental care; e.g., chimpanzees. Clumped distribution in species also acts as a mechanism against predation as well as an efficient mechanism to trap or corner prey; e.g., lions. Threatened or endangered species are also more likely to be clumped in their distribution.

2. **Random.** Little interaction between members of the population leading to random spacing patterns. Random distribution usually occurs in habitats where environmental conditions and resources are consistent. This pattern of dispersion is characterized by the lack of any strong social interactions between species; e.g., dandelion seeds being dispersed by wind.

3. **Uniform.** Fairly uniform spacing between individuals. Uniform distributions are found in populations in which the distance between neighboring individuals is maximized. The need to maximize the space between individuals generally arises from competition for a resource such as moisture or nutrients, or as a result of direct social interactions between individuals within the population, such as territoriality; e.g., penguins often exhibit uniform spacing by aggressively defending their territory among their neighbors or creosote bushes releasing chemicals that inhibit the growth of other plants around them (allelopathy).

Ecosystem (Community) Characteristics

(1) Physical appearance	Relative size; stratification; distribution of populations and species
(2) Species diversity	Number of different species
(3) Species abundance	Number of individuals of each species
(4) Niche structure	Number of ecological niches; how they resemble or differ from each other; species interactions

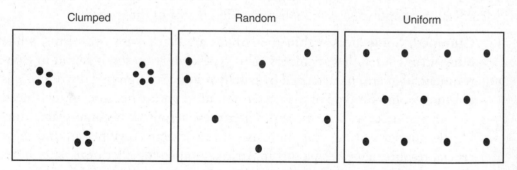

Figure 4.1 Clumped, random, uniform distribution

Ecological Niches

An ecological niche is the particular area within a habitat occupied by an organism and includes the function of that organism within an ecological community. The physical environment influences how organisms affect and are affected by resources and competitors. The niche reflects the specific adaptations that a species has acquired through evolution. To describe an organism's niche involves a description of the organism's adaptive traits, habitat, and place in the food web. A niche also takes into account the types and amounts of resources the species uses and its interactions with both living (biotic) and nonliving (abiotic) factors in its habitat.

Generalist species (*K*) live in broad niches. They are able to withstand a wide range of environmental conditions. Examples of generalist species include cockroaches, mice, and humans. Specialist species (*r*) live in narrow niches and are sensitive to environmental changes. Since they cannot tolerate change, they are more prone to extinction. An example of a specialist species is the giant panda, which only eats a certain type of bamboo. When environmental conditions are stable, specialist species have an advantage since there are few competitors as each species occupies its own unique niche (competitive exclusion principle). However, when habitats are subjected to rapid changes, the generalist species usually fare better since they are more adaptable.

Law of Tolerance and Limiting Factors

Earth's ecosystems are affected by both biotic (living) and abiotic (nonliving) factors, and are regulated by the Law of Tolerance, which states that the existence, abundance, and distribution of species depends on the tolerance level of each species to both physical and chemical factors. The abundance or distribution of an organism can be controlled by certain factors (e.g., the climatic, topographic, and biological requirements of plants and animals) where levels of these exceed the maximum or minimum limits of tolerance of that organism. A limiting factor is any abiotic factor that limits or prevents the growth of a population. Limiting factors in terrestrial ecosystems may include the level of soil nutrients, amount of water, light, and temperature. In aquatic ecosystems, major limiting factors include pH, the amount of dissolved oxygen in the water, and salinity.

Resource Partitioning

Resources in an environment are limited. Some species have evolved to "share" a specific resource. This sharing may take the form of two species eliminating direct competition by utilizing the same resource at different times (temporal partitioning)—e.g., one species of spiny mouse feeds on insects during the day while a second species of spiny mouse feeds on the same insects at night or when competing species use the same resource by occupying different areas or habitats within the range of occurrence of the resource (spatial partitioning)—e.g., different species of fish feeding at different depths in a lake or different species of monkey feeding at different heights in a tree. A third form of resource partitioning occurs when two species share the same resource but have evolved slightly different structures to utilize the same resource (morphological partitioning)—e.g., two different species of bees have evolved different proboscis lengths to utilize various sized flowers of the same species.

Interactions Among Species

Various types of interactions occur among species. They can benefit one or both species, harm one or both species, or not affect one of the species involved.

Interactions Among Species

Interaction	Description
Amensalism	The interaction between two species whereby one species suffers and the other species is not affected. Usually this occurs when one organism releases a chemical compound that is detrimental to another organism. Examples: The bread mold *Penicillium* secretes penicillin, which is a chemical that kills bacteria. The black walnut tree releases a chemical that kills neighboring plants. Amensalism is common in chaparral and desert communities as it stabilizes the community by reducing competition for scarce nutrients in the water. This chemical interaction is known as allelopathy.
Commensalism	The interaction between two species whereby one organism benefits and the other species is not affected. Forms of commensalism include: (1) using another organism for transportation such as the remora on a shark or mites on dung beetles; (2) using another organism for housing such as epiphytic plants like orchids growing on trees or birds living in the holes of trees; and (3) using something that another organism created such as hermit crabs using the shells of marine snails for protection.
Competition	Competition can be either intraspecific (competition between members of the same species) or interspecific (competition between members of different species). Competition is the driving force of evolution whether it is for food, mating partners, or territory. Intraspecific competition results in organisms best suited for surviving in a changing environment. Competition is prominent in predator-prey relationships with the predator (seeking food) and the prey (seeking survival). Examples of types of competition include: (1) interference—occurs directly between individuals by interfering with foraging, survival, or reproduction or by preventing a species to establish itself within a habitat; (2) exploitation—occurs indirectly through a common limiting resource that acts as an intermediate; by using the resource it depletes the amount available to others; and (3) apparent—occurs indirectly between two species, which are both sought after by the same predator.
Mutualism	The interaction between two species whereby both species benefit. Symbiosis is a lifelong positive interaction that involves close physical and/or biochemical contact such as the relationship between trees and mycorrhizal fungi, or the relationships can be shorter as in the case of bees pollinating flowers. Mutualism can be obligatory such as mycorrhizal fungi being totally dependent on their plant hosts, or it can be nonobligatory as seen in *Rhizobia* bacteria reproducing either in the soil or in a symbiotic relationship with legumes.
Parasitism	The interaction between two species whereby one species is benefited at the expense of the other. If the parasite lives on the host, it is known as an ectoparasite (mosquito) and often has elaborate mechanisms and strategies for acquiring a host (leeches that locate their host by sensing movement and confirming the identity through skin temperature and chemical cues before attaching). If the parasite lives within the host, it is known as an endoparasite (tapeworm) and acquires its hosts by passive mechanisms such as the ingestion of egg cells. Epiparasites feed on other parasites. Biotrophic parasites must keep their hosts alive and represent a successful mode of life; many viruses are examples of biotrophic parasites because they use the host's genetic and cellular processes to multiply. Necrotrophs are parasites that eventually kill their hosts. Social parasites involve behaviors that benefit the parasite and harm the host (e.g., cuckoo birds that use other birds to raise their young or the nectar-robbing behavior of insects and birds). Hosts have evolved defense mechanisms (immune systems, plant toxins) to diminish parasitism.

Interactions Among Species (continued)

Interaction	Description
Predation	Predators hunt and kill prey through the act of predation. Whereas predators kill their prey, parasites have evolved mechanisms to keep their host alive, since their survival depends on a viable host. Predators can be opportunistic and kill and eat almost anything, or they may be specialists and only prey upon certain organisms. Predators that eat only meat are called carnivores; those that eat both meat and vegetation are known as omnivores.
Saprotrophism	Saprotrophs obtain their nutrients from dead or decaying plants or animals through absorption of soluble organic compounds. Saprotrophs include many fungi, bacteria, and protozoa. Vultures and dung beetles are also saprotrophs.

Keystone Species

A keystone species is a species whose very presence contributes to a diversity of life and whose extinction would lead to the extinction of other forms of life. Through various interactions, a small number of individuals from a keystone species have a very large and disproportionate impact on how ecosystems function. An ecosystem may experience a dramatic shift if a keystone species is removed even though that keystone species was a small part of the ecosystem as measured by biomass or productivity. A classic keystone species is a small predator that prevents a particular herbivorous species from decimating a dominant plant species. Since the prey numbers are low, the keystone predator numbers could be even lower and still be effective. Yet without the predators, the herbivorous prey would explode in numbers, wipe out the dominant plants, and dramatically alter the character of the ecosystem. Two examples of keystone species are listed below:

STARFISH (SEA STARS)

Starfish prey on sea urchins, mussels, and other shellfish that have no other natural predators. If starfish are removed from the ecosystem, mussel populations explode and drive out other species, and sea urchin populations rise to the point where they begin to decimate coral reefs

SEA OTTERS IN KELP FORESTS

Sea otters prey on sea urchins. Kelp roots serve as anchors and not as nutrient-absorbing systems as found in land plants. If left unchecked, the sea urchins destroy the kelp forests by foraging on kelp roots.

Species Diversity

Organisms that live in different environments are specifically adapted to their particular biome.

AQUATIC ORGANISMS

Water provides buoyancy and reduces the need for support structures such as legs and trunks. Water has high thermal capacity, so most aquatic organisms do not spend energy on temperature regulation. Many organisms obtain nutrients directly from the water, thereby reducing energy spent on searching for food. These include filter feeders such as barnacles, clams, and oysters. Water allows dispersal of gametes and larvae to new areas. Water screens out UV radiation. Intertidal organisms have evolved methods of not being swept away by waves and prevent water loss during low tide through shells and exoskeletons, salt-removing mechanisms, and lower metabolic rates due to cooler ambient temperatures.

DESERT ORGANISMS

Desert plants are spaced apart due to limiting factors and consist primarily of succulents (cactus) and short-lived annuals (wildflowers). Succulents store water, have small surface areas exposed to sunlight, have vertical orientation to minimize exposure to the sun, open their stomata at night, have waxy leaves to minimize transpiration, have deep roots to tap groundwater (mesquite and creosote), and have shallow roots to collect water after short rainfalls (prickly pear and saguaro cactus). Sharp spines on cacti reflect sunlight, create shade, and discourage herbivores. Cacti secrete toxins into the soil to prevent interspecific competition (allelopathy). Desert plants store biomass in seeds. Wildflowers have short life spans and are dependent on water for germination.

Desert animals are small and have small surface areas. They spend time in underground burrows where it is cooler, and they are often nocturnal. Aestivation is common. Some animals are able to metabolize dry seeds. Kangaroo rats produce their own water and secrete concentrated urine. Insects and reptiles have thick outer coverings to minimize water loss.

GRASSLAND ORGANISMS

Grasses grow out from the bottom (basal meristem) so they can grow again after being nibbled by grazing animals. Grass species are drought resistant. Deciduous trees and shrubs shed leaves during the dry season to conserve water. Grazers and browsing animals eat vegetation at different heights so as to not compete. Giraffes eat near the top of trees, elephants eat lower down, zebras eat taller grasses, and gazelles eat shorter grasses. Some animals migrate to find water. Others become dormant. Still others survive on seeds during the dry season. Some animals live in burrows to hide and escape predators. In addition, their fur color sometimes matches the color of the surroundings to act as camouflage.

FOREST ORGANISMS

In the tropics, some animals live in tree canopies where shelter and available food supplies (leaves, flowers, and fruits) are abundant and where they can escape from predators that live closer to the ground. Epiphytes (orchids and bromeliads) live on trunks and branches of trees, and they catch organic matter falling from the canopy. Epiphytes do not root in the soil. Instead, they obtain their moisture from the air or from dampness on the surface of their host. Some plants have very large leaves to capture scarce light. Roots of trees are shallow and spread out to capture nutrients in poor soil. To compensate for little support by shallow roots, trees may have buttresses. Flowers have elaborate devices to attract pollinators since wind is minimal in dense growth.

In temperate deciduous forests, broadleaf deciduous trees lose their leaves in winter and become dormant to conserve water and energy. Deciduous trees shift their metabolism from a photosynthesis-based system when light and temperature are favorable to one utilizing glucose and amino acids during the winter. This also helps keep the tree from freezing and acts as a kind of antifreeze.

In evergreen coniferous forests, small, waxy-coated needles are able to withstand the cold and drought of winter and have low surface area to reduce transpiration. Furthermore, conifers are always replacing their needles, unlike deciduous trees that replace their leaves only once a year. Decomposed needles make soil acidic, preventing many competing species from surviving in the soil environment. Some animals hibernate to conserve energy during winter when resources are scarce.

TEMPERATE SCRUB FOREST LAND ORGANISMS

Chaparral plants have small, waxy-coated leaves to reduce transpiration. Many plants produce toxins that leach into the soil to prevent competition (allelopathy). Vegetation becomes dormant during the dry season. Leaves do not fall during the dry season due to the stress of replacing leaves without an adequate water supply. Plant thorns are common for protection. Vegetation is adapted to fires and is common due to the high oil content in the brush. Fires reduce competition and allow seeds to germinate. Rodents are common and store seeds in underground burrows.

TUNDRA ORGANISMS

Polar grassland plants are adapted to low sunlight, low amounts of free water, high winds, and low temperatures. Tundra plants primarily grow during summer months. Leaves on plants have waxy outer coatings. Many plants survive winter as roots, stems, bulbs or tubers. Lichens dehydrate during winter to avoid frost damage.

Animals have adapted in several ways. They have extra layers of fat, chemicals in the blood to keep it from freezing, and compact bodies to conserve heat. They also have thick skin, thick fur, and waterproof feathers above downy insulating feathers. Additionally, animals either migrate during the coldest months or live underground (lemmings).

Edge Effects

An edge effect refers to how the local environment changes along some type of boundary or edge. Forest edges are created when trees are harvested, particularly when they are clear-cut. Tree canopies provide the ground below with shade and maintain a cooler, moister environment below. In contrast, a clear-cut allows sunlight to reach the ground, making the ground warmer and drier—environments not suitable for many forest plants. As time passes and a stand of young trees emerges on a clear-cut, the environment in the young stand changes and the edge begins to fade. As the mature forest develops, the edge fades away.

The edge effect is the result of two different conditions influencing the plants and animals that live on the edge. Some animal species (deer, elk, white-tailed deer, and pheasants) survive well in a forest edge since they are able to find food in the clearing, are able to benefit due to various habitats near one another, are able to hide in the nearby trees, or are well-adapted to human disturbances. These animals are called "edge species." Other animals, such as the spotted owl, do not do well in edges. Negative edge effects become most extreme when forest lands share the edge with agriculture or suburbs. Species composition and diversity can change dramatically if organisms adapted to one set of conditions cannot adapt to the change. If the edge effect is gradual or has indistinct boundaries and over which many species cross, it is called an open community. A community that is sharply divided from its neighbors is called a closed community. Preservation of large blocks of habitat and linking smaller habitat blocks together with migration corridors are techniques to protect rare and endangered species.

Major Terrestrial and Aquatic Biomes

Biomes are a major regional or global biotic community characterized by the dominant forms of plant life and the prevailing climate. Temperature and precipitation are the most important determinants of biomes. Biomes are classified by the type of dominant plant and animal life. Species diversity within a biome is directly related to net productivity, availability of moisture, and temperature.

Biomes

ANTARCTIC

Area surrounding south pole. Rainfall <2 inches (5 cm) per year.

BENTHOS (HADAL)

Bottom of oceans. No sunlight, therefore no plant life. Primary input of energy comes from dead organic matter settling and chemosynthesis.

COASTAL ZONES

Includes estuaries, wetlands, and coral reefs. High diversity and counts of animal and plant species due to runoff from land.

CORAL REEFS

Warm, clear, shallow ocean habitats near land and generally in the tropics. There are three types of coral reefs. Fringing reefs grow on continental shelves near the coastline. Barrier reefs are parallel to shoreline but farther from shore. Coral atolls are rings of coral that grow on top of sunken oceanic volcanoes. Coral reefs are disappearing at an alarming rate due to increase in sea temperature, pollution, dredging, and sedimentation.

DESERTS

Occur between 15° and 25° north and south latitude and generally occur in the interior of continents. Occupy about 20% of all landmass. Rainfall less than 20 inches (50 cm) per year. Air currents are descending, which generally diminishes the formation of rain (rain requires ascending air—orographic lifting). Soils often have abundant nutrients but lack organic matter and consist of sand and closely packed boulders. Little humus in the soil profile.

FRESHWATER WETLANDS

Freshwater wetlands include freshwater swamps, marshes, bogs, prairie potholes (important stopping grounds for migrating birds), ponds, peat bogs, and riparian areas (areas near rivers and streams). Ground is saturated with freestanding water, although standing water can be seasonal. Soil is low in oxygen. Important breeding areas rich in insects, amphibians, and reptiles. Prime areas for human development and recreation resulting in large amounts of habitat destruction. Critical for freshwater supplies. Easily polluted. Dominant plants are floating plants (phytoplankton). Animal life is abundant. Estuaries are rich in nutrients and are breeding grounds for fish. Water input includes runoff, groundwater flow, and streams. A lake is a body of water of considerable size surrounded by land. The vast majority of lakes on Earth are freshwater and most, like in the Northern Hemisphere, are at higher altitudes. Lakes can be classified on the basis of their richness of nutrients, which affects plant growth and animal diversity. Oligotrophic lakes are clear and low in nutrients, which results in a small amount of plant life and other forms of biomass. Eutrophic lakes are rich in nitrogen and phosphorus with large and diverse populations of phyto- and zooplankton, which supports a large diversity of fish. During warm weather, the oxygen content of the water may decrease resulting in die-offs. Hypertrophic lakes are excessively enriched with nutrients and subject to algal blooms. These lakes result from human activity such as the heavy use of fertilizers in the lake catchment area.

GRASSLANDS

Found in areas too dry for forests and too wet for deserts. Rainfall is seasonal. Temperatures are moderate. Grasslands occupy approximately 25% of all land area on Earth. Few trees and shrubs due to frequent seasonal fires and water availability. Dominant plants are grasses and perennials with extensively developed roots. Soils are rich in organic matter. Upper soil horizons are alkaline, dark, and rich in humus. Extensively used by humans for agriculture.

HYDROTHERMAL VENTS

Occur in the deep ocean where hot-water vents rich in sulfur compounds are found, which provide energy for chemosynthetic bacteria.

INTERTIDAL

The area of the shoreline exposed to water during high tide and air during low tide. Water movement brings in nutrients and removes waste products. Extremely rich in biodiversity. Susceptible and sensitive to pollution from land runoff and ocean pollution.

OCEAN

Oceans occupy 75% of Earth's surface. Areas of low diversity and low productivity except near the shoreline. Low in nitrogen and phosphorus, which limits plant growth and the smaller organisms that feed on them. Large animals occur but in low density.

SAVANNAS

Warm year-round. Scattered trees. Environment is intermediate between grassland and forest. Extended dry season followed by a rainy season. Consists of grasslands with stands of deciduous shrubs and trees. Trees and shrubs generally shed leaves during the dry season, which reduces the need for water. Food is limited during the dry season, requiring many animals to migrate. Soils are rich in nutrients. Contain large herds of grazing animals and browsing animals that provide resources for predators.

TAIGA (CONIFEROUS OR BOREAL FORESTS)

Generally found between 45° and 60° north latitude. Occupies approximately 17% of land surface. Forests of cold climates of high latitudes and altitudes. Two types of taiga: open woodland and dense forest. More precipitation than the tundra. Generally precipitation occurs during the summer months due to midlatitude cyclones. Soils are generally poor in nutrients because of large amounts of leaching caused by rainfall. The soils are acidic due to the decomposition of needles (an adaptation to conserve water). Deep layer of litter on the surface, and decomposition is slow because of low temperatures. Dense stands of small trees cause understory to be low in light. Low biodiversity due to harshness of environment. Disturbances include fires, storms, and insect infestations.

TEMPERATE DECIDUOUS FORESTS

Forests found in milder temperatures than boreal forests of the taiga. Rapid decomposition due to mild temperatures and precipitation, which results in a small amount of litter on surface. Because of the mild climate, this biome has been greatly exploited by humans for agriculture, lumber, and urban development. Soil is generally poor in nutrients. Tall deciduous trees. Rich and diverse understory. Low density of large mammals due to shade that prevents much ground vegetation.

TEMPERATE RAIN FORESTS

Moderate temperatures and rainfall exceeding 100 inches (250 cm) per year. Low biodiversity because of limited light, which limits food for herbivores. Major resource for timber.

TEMPERATE SHRUBLAND (CHAPARRAL)

Hot, dry summers with mild, cool, and rainy winters. During summer and spring, a subtropical high-pressure zone exists over the area. Rain falls during the winter due to midlatitude cyclones. Average rainfall is between 15–40 inches (30–75 cm) per year. Characterized by dense shrub growth. Decomposition is slow during dry months. Few large mammals. Erosion is common after fires. Because of climate, this area is being utilized for urbanization. Found in select coastal regions.

TEMPERATE WOODLANDS

Drier climate than deciduous forests. Dominated by small trees. Stands of trees are open, allowing light to reach ground. Fires are common.

TROPICAL RAIN FORESTS

High and constant temperature (average approximately 80°F [27°C]). Rainfall ranges between 75–100 inches (200–250 cm) per year. Found within Hadley cells. High species diversity for both plants and animals (up to 100 different tree species per square kilometer as opposed to three to five in temperate zones). Vegetation is dense. Soils are low in nutrients, and most nutrients are stored in vegetation. Soil is acidic. Decomposition of organic material is very fast due to temperature and moisture. Leaching is high. Abundant insect and animal biodiversity. Humans are clearing tropical rain forests for agriculture and cattle raising through a technique called slash and burn. Due to poor soil nutrient levels, agricultural activity lasts for only a limited time and can be sustained only by applying expensive fertilizer, which causes farmers to destroy even more forest.

TROPICAL SEASONAL FOREST

Occurs in areas of seasonal rainfall (monsoon) that is followed by long, dry season. Warm temperatures year-round. Contains mixture of deciduous and drought-tolerant evergreen trees.

TUNDRA

60° north latitude and above. Influenced by polar cells. Alpine tundra is located in mountainous areas, above the tree line with well-drained soil. Dominant animals include small rodents and insects. Arctic tundra is frozen, treeless plains, low rainfall, and low average temperatures with poor drainage due to the frozen ground. Growing season lasts about 2 months. Soil has few nutrients because of low vegetation and little decomposition. Permafrost is permanently frozen ground and a barrier for roots.

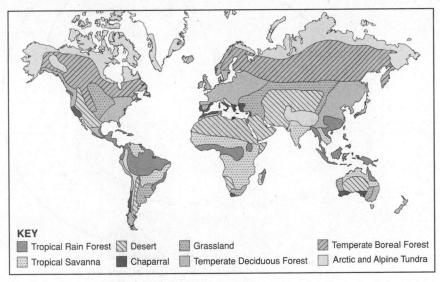

KEY

▓ Tropical Rain Forest	▨ Desert	▦ Grassland	▨ Temperate Boreal Forest
▦ Tropical Savanna	■ Chaparral	▥ Temperate Deciduous Forest	▦ Arctic and Alpine Tundra

Figure 4.2 Major biomes of the world

ENERGY FLOW

The ultimate source of energy is the sun. Plants are able to use this light energy to create food. The energy in food molecules flows to animals through food webs.

Photosynthesis and Cellular Respiration

$$6CO_2 + 6H_2O + sunlight \rightarrow C_6H_{12}O_6 + 6O_2$$

Plants remove carbon dioxide from the atmosphere by a chemical process called photosynthesis, which uses light energy to produce carbohydrates and other organic compounds. Plants capture light primarily through the green pigment chlorophyll.

Chlorophyll is contained in organelles called chloroplasts. The glucose or the energy derived from its oxidation during cellular respiration is then used to form other organic compounds such as cellulose (for support), lipids (waxes and oils), and amino acids and then proteins. Oxygen gas is released into the atmosphere during photosynthesis. Plants also emit carbon dioxide during respiration. They produce less carbon dioxide than they absorb and therefore become net sinks of carbon.

Organisms that undergo photosynthesis are called photoautotrophs. Factors that affect the rate of photosynthesis are the amount of light and its wavelength, carbon dioxide concentration, the availability of water, and temperature.

Organisms dependent on photosynthetic organisms (autotrophs) are called heterotrophs. In general, cellular respiration is the opposite of photosynthesis. In respiration, glucose is oxidized by the cells to produce carbon dioxide, water and chemical energy. This energy is then stored in the molecule adenosine triphosphate (ATP).

$$C_6H_{12}O_6 + 6O_2 \rightarrow 6CO_2 + 6H_2O + \text{energy}$$

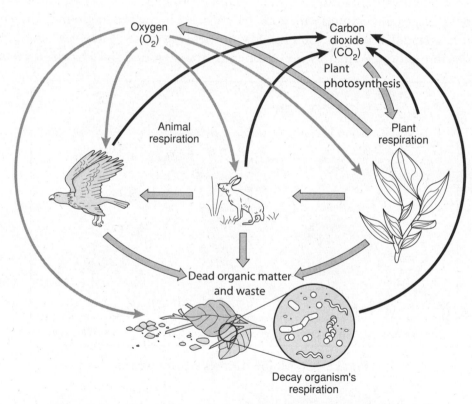

Figure 4.3 The carbon cycle viewed as an ecosystem cycle

Food Webs and Trophic Levels

Primary producers (autotrophs) are plants. They convert solar energy into chemical energy through photosynthesis. Primary consumers are heterotrophs (herbivores—plant eaters) and get their energy by consuming primary producers. Primary consumers have developed defense mechanisms against predation, some of which include speed, flight, quills, tough hides, camouflage, and horns and antlers.

Secondary (and higher) consumers are also heterotrophs and may be either strictly carnivores (meat eaters) or omnivores (eat both plants and animals).

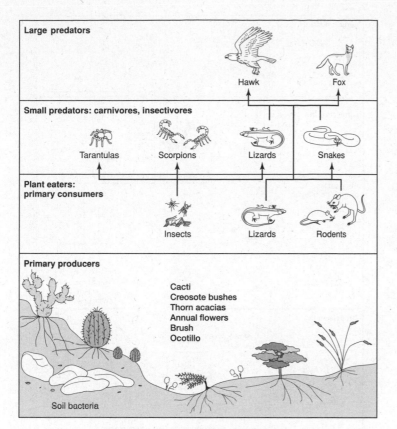

Figure 4.4 Desert food web

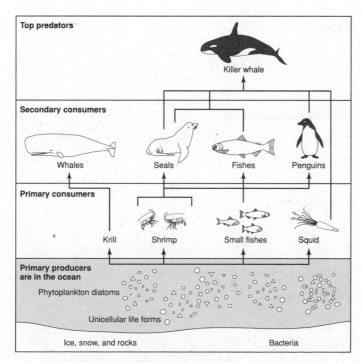

Figure 4.5 Oceanic food web

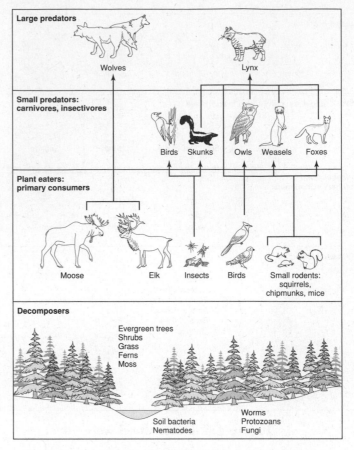

Figure 4.6 Coniferous forest food web

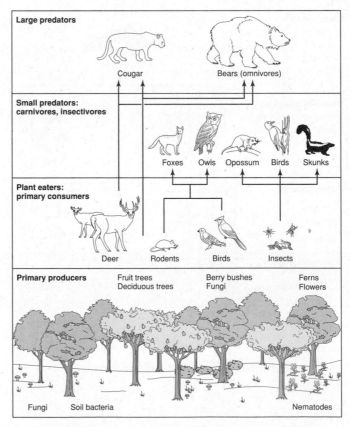

Figure 4.7 Deciduous forest food web

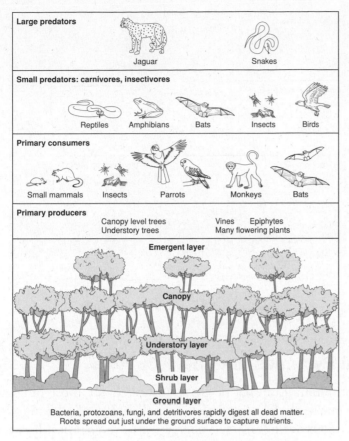

Large predators
Jaguar   Snakes

Small predators: carnivores, insectivores
Reptiles   Amphibians   Bats   Insects   Birds

Primary consumers
Small mammals   Insects   Parrots   Monkeys   Bats

Primary producers
Canopy level trees   Vines   Epiphytes
Understory trees   Many flowering plants

Emergent layer
Canopy
Understory layer
Shrub layer
Ground layer
Bacteria, protozoans, fungi, and detritivores rapidly digest all dead matter.
Roots spread out just under the ground surface to capture nutrients.

Figure 4.8 Tropical rain forest food web

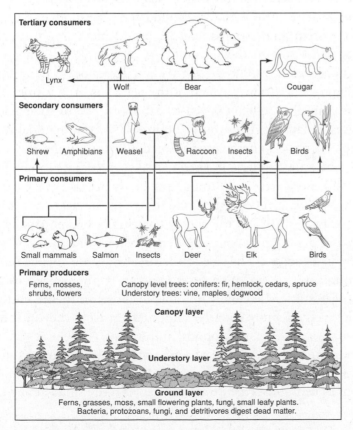

Tertiary consumers
Lynx   Wolf   Bear   Cougar

Secondary consumers
Shrew   Amphibians   Weasel   Raccoon   Insects   Birds

Primary consumers
Small mammals   Salmon   Insects   Deer   Elk   Birds

Primary producers
Ferns, mosses,   Canopy level trees: conifers: fir, hemlock, cedars, spruce
shrubs, flowers   Understory trees: vine, maples, dogwood

Canopy layer
Understory layer
Ground layer
Ferns, grasses, moss, small flowering plants, fungi, small leafy plants.
Bacteria, protozoans, fungi, and detritivores digest dead matter.

Figure 4.9 Temperate rain forest food web

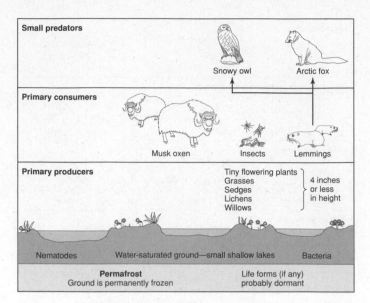

Figure 4.10 Tundra food web

Ecological Pyramids and the 10% Rule

Sunlight is the ultimate source of energy required for most biological processes (except for chemosynthetic organisms). Less than 3% of all sunlight that reaches Earth is used in photosynthesis. The energy stored in chemical bonds is released to animals and plants through cellular respiration.

Losses of potential energy (in the form of heat energy) occur as one moves up an energy pyramid and conforms with the second law of thermodynamics, which states that any closed system tends spontaneously toward increasing disorder (entropy); some energy is transferred to the surroundings as heat in any energy conversion; and no real process can be 100% efficient. These losses occur in various ways. For example, in digestive inefficiency, much of the plant material is not able to be broken down. For example, elephants need to eat about 5% of their body weight in plant material each day but digest only about 40% of the material that they consume. Other losses occur in energy used by predators for cellular respiration, energy required for temperature regulation, energy used by predators to obtain food or for reproduction, and energy released through the decay of waste products. There is an average 90% loss in available energy as one moves to the next-higher trophic level. Likewise, approximately 10% of the energy entering one level passes to the next.

Detritus energy pyramids (organisms that consume organic wastes) are significantly different in structure. The size of the organisms are smaller, and organisms exist in environments rich in nutrients so energy is not needed to obtain food. Additionally, organisms are generally not able to move on their own to any degree. Finally, trophic levels are more complex and interrelated as they include algae, bacteria, fungi, protozoa, insects, arthropods, and worms.

A notable exception in the scheme of a pyramid of biomass occurs in aquatic ecosystems. In this ecosystem, the producers are mainly microscopic algae. Although the total number of algae is great, their total biomass is quite small at any given time.

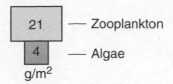

21 — Zooplankton

4 — Algae

g/m²

Figure 4.11 Inverted pyramid of biomass—aquatic ecosystem

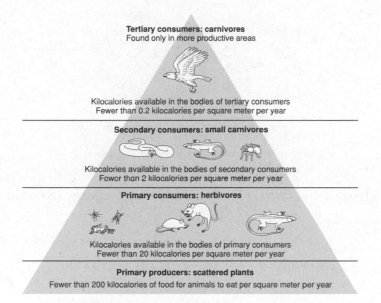

Tertiary consumers: carnivores
Found only in more productive areas

Kilocalories available in the bodies of tertiary consumers
Fewer than 0.2 kilocalories per square meter per year

Secondary consumers: small carnivores

Kilocalories available in the bodies of secondary consumers
Fewer than 2 kilocalories per square meter per year

Primary consumers: herbivores

Kilocalories available in the bodies of primary consumers
Fewer than 20 kilocalories per square meter per year

Primary producers: scattered plants
Fewer than 200 kilocalories of food for animals to eat per square meter per year

Figure 4.12 Desert biomass—energy pyramid

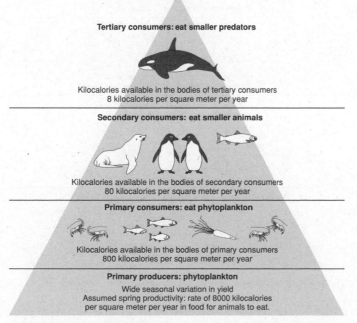

Tertiary consumers: eat smaller predators

Kilocalories available in the bodies of tertiary consumers
8 kilocalories per square meter per year

Secondary consumers: eat smaller animals

Kilocalories available in the bodies of secondary consumers
80 kilocalories per square meter per year

Primary consumers: eat phytoplankton

Kilocalories available in the bodies of primary consumers
800 kilocalories per square meter per year

Primary producers: phytoplankton
Wide seasonal variation in yield
Assumed spring productivity: rate of 8000 kilocalories
per square meter per year in food for animals to eat.

Figure 4.13 Marine biomass—energy pyramid

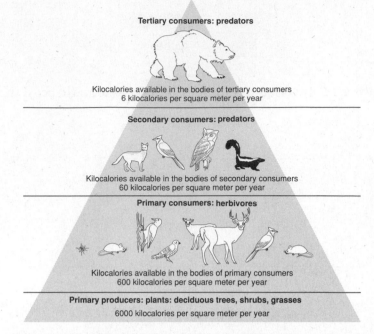

Figure 4.14 Deciduous forest biomass—energy pyramid

TIP

As energy flows through systems, more of it becomes unusable at each step.

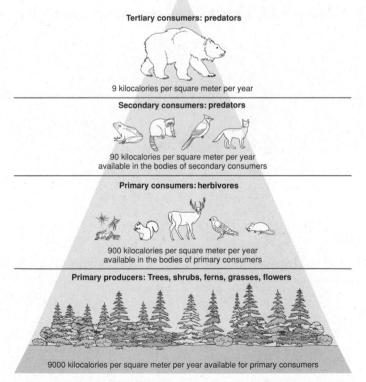

Figure 4.15 Temperate rain forest biomass—energy pyramid

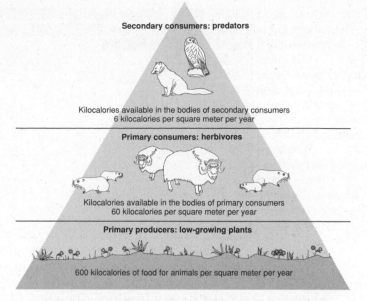

Figure 4.16 Tundra biomass—energy pyramid

ECOSYSTEM PRODUCTIVITY: GPP AND NPP

Of all available sunlight that reaches the Earth, less than 3% for land plants and less than 1% for aquatic plants is used for photosynthesis. This relatively low efficiency of the conversion of solar energy into energy stored in carbon compounds sets the overall amount of energy available to heterotrophs at all other trophic levels. Gross primary production (GPP) is the rate at which plants capture and fix (store) a given amount of chemical energy as biomass in a given length of time. Some fraction of this fixed energy is used by primary producers for cellular respiration and the maintenance of existing tissues. The remaining fixed energy is referred to as net primary production (NPP) and is the rate at which all the plants in an ecosystem produce net useful chemical energy and is equal to the difference between the rate at which the plants produce useful chemical energy (GPP) and the rate at which they use some of that energy during respiration.

$$NPP = GPP - \text{plant respiration}$$

Some net primary production goes toward growth and reproduction of primary producers, while some is consumed by herbivores. Open oceans, due to their large proportion of the Earth's surface, collectively have the highest new productivity. However, when compared on a one-to-one per square meter basis, estuaries have the highest net primary productivity.

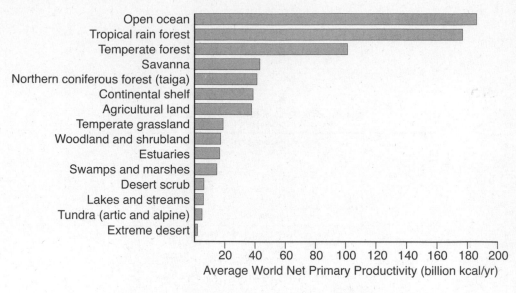

Figure 4.17 Net Primary Productivity—compared by total surface area on Earth

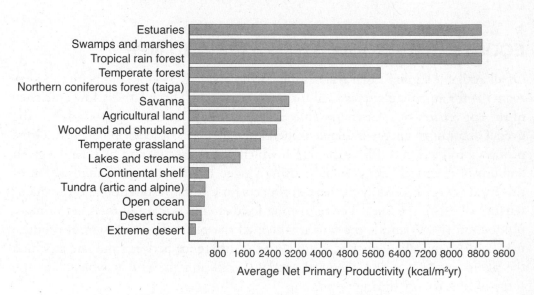

Figure 4.18 Net Primary Productivity—compared per square meter

ECOSYSTEM DIVERSITY

The topic of ecosystem diversity involves biodiversity, natural selection, evolution, and ecosystem services.

Biodiversity

Biodiversity attempts to describe diversity at three levels: genetic, species, and ecosystem. Genetic diversity involves the range of all genetic traits, both expressed and recessive, that makes up the gene pool for a particular species. Species diversity is the number of different species that inhabit a specific area. For example, tropical rain forests have a higher species diversity than extreme deserts. Ecosystem diversity concerns the range of habitats that can be found in a defined area. Ecosystems are composed of both biotic and abiotic components.

Biodiversity

Diversity Increasers	Diversity Decreasers
Diverse habitats	Environmental stress
Disturbance in the habitat (fires, storms, etc.)	Extreme environments
Environmental conditions with low variation	Extreme limitations in the supply of a fundamental resource
Trophic levels with high diversity	Extreme amounts of disturbance
Middle states of succession	Introduction of species from other areas
Evolution	Geographic isolation

Most scientists believe the total number of species on Earth to be between 10 and 30 million. Tropical rain forests cover approximately 7% of the total dry surface of Earth but hold over half of all of the species. Scientists have given names to only about 1.5 million species.

Natural Selection

Natural selection is the mechanism of how organisms evolve. Natural selection works on the individual level by determining which organisms have adaptations that allow them to survive, reproduce, and be able to pass on those adaptive traits to their offspring. Natural selection occurs over successive generations. Evolution works on the species level by describing how the species attains the genetic adaptations that allow them to survive in a changing environment. Without a changing environment, neither evolution nor natural selection would exist.

The range of genetic variation within a species's gene pool determines whether or not the species, not the individual, has the capacity to adapt and survive to changes in the environment. The expression of that variation in phenotypic and behavioral expressions determines whether the individual survives and is commonly referred to as survival of the fittest. "Fittest" means the ability to reproduce and pass on genes to offspring. New genes enter the gene pool through mutation and when combined with a change in gene frequency, results in evolution at the species level. Natural selection operates in three ways: stabilizing, directional, and disruptive.

STABILIZING SELECTION

Stabilizing selection affects the extremes of a population and is the most common form of natural selection. The individuals that deviate too far from the average conditions are removed. The results are a decrease in diversity, maintenance of a stable gene pool, and no evolution. For example, human babies that are too low in weight or too high in weight have survival problems.

Natural Selection

Process of Natural Selection	Description
Competition	There is a struggle to survive, and competition exists for limited resources.
Disproportionate increase and persistence in phenotypic adaptation in successive populations	Variations that are advantageous to the individual in terms of survival allow more organisms possessing the trait(s) to survive, reproduce, and pass on the characteristic(s) to future generations.
Geometric (or exponential) increase in population	If all offspring survived, there would be astronomical numbers of individuals.
Individual variations	There is variation in offspring. For natural selection, the variations must be gene expressed and be capable of being inherited.
Limited resources	Earth has finite resources.

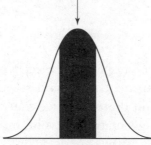

Figure 4.19
Stabilizing selection

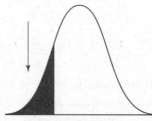

Figure 4.20
Directional selection

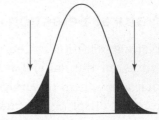

Figure 4.21
Disruptive selection

DIRECTIONAL SELECTION

Directional selection affects the extremes of a population. Individuals toward one end of the distribution may do especially well, resulting in a frequency distribution toward this advantage in future generations. An example is the industrial melanism of the peppered moth and the evolution of the horse. The early horse present during the early Eocene was a small-bodied creature that moved well through heavy brush and woodlands. Today's horse, with its long legs designed for speed in the open grassland and changes in its dental and toe structure, looks nothing like its ancestor.

DISRUPTIVE SELECTION

Disruptive selection acts against individuals that have the average condition and favors individuals at the extreme ends (bimodal). The population is essentially split into two. Both directional and disruptive selection affects the gene pool. In both cases, the population changes and evolution occurs.

More often than not, natural selection is based upon the cumulative effects of numerous genes, each responsible for slight changes. When genes at more than one locus contribute to the same trait, the result is called a polygenic effect.

Polyploidy occurs in plants when the entire set of chromosomes is multiplied. It is an example of sympatric speciation in which species arise within the same, overlapping geographic range. This can occur through the process of hybridization. In hybridization, chromosomes from two different species are artificially combined to form a new species (hybrid). In another type of hybridization, chromosomes naturally fail to segregate during meiosis, producing diploid gametes. If the hybrid has adaptive traits to survive in the new environment, a new species of plant has been produced. Although the plant may not be able to reproduce sexually, it may be able to reproduce through vegetative means. Examples of polyploidy include cotton, tobacco, sugarcane, bananas, potatoes, and wheat. More than half of all known species of plants today (260,000 species) may have originated through polyploidy.

Evolution

Change generally takes a very long time and is supported by the fossil record. Evolution is the change in the genetic composition of a population during successive generations as a result of natural selection acting on the genetic variation among individuals and results in the development of new species. The concept of a "common ancestor" states that similarities among species can be traced back through a phylogenetic tree.

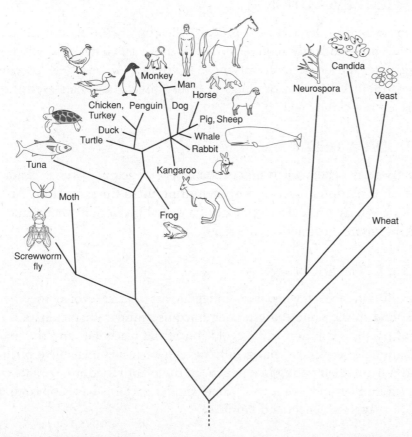

Figure 4.22 Phylogenetic tree traced through analysis of cytochrome C.

SPECIATION

Speciation results when segments of a population of one species become so isolated that gene flow stops. Adaptive radiation describes rapid speciation to fill ecological niches and is driven by either mutation and/or natural selection. Three basic types of adaptive radiation are: general adaptation, environmental change, and geographic isolation.

Adaptive Radiation

Type	Definition	Example
General	Species develop a radical new ability to reach new parts of its environment.	Bird flight
Environmental Change	Due to large changes in the environment, species branch into new species and occupy new niches.	Rapid spread and development of mammalian species after extinction of dinosaurs.
Geographic Isolation	Isolated ecosystems are colonized by species that undergo rapid divergent evolution.	Darwin finches in the Galapagos Islands.

CONVERGENT EVOLUTION

Convergent evolution describes the process whereby organisms not closely related to each other independently acquire similar (analogous) characteristics while evolving in separate and sometimes varying ecosystems. An example of convergent evolution is the development of wings in birds, insects, and bats even though the organisms are not closely related.

EVOLUTIONARY RELAY

Evolutionary relay occurs when independent species acquire similar characteristics through their evolution in similar ecosystems but not at the same time. An example of evolutionary relay is the development of a dorsal fin in both sharks and the prehistoric ichthyosaurs (extinct marine reptiles).

PARALLEL EVOLUTION

Parallel evolution occurs when two independent species evolve together at the same time and in the same ecosystem and acquire similar characteristics. A classic example of parallel evolution is the evolution of the placentals and the marsupials. Placental animals bear their young fully developed. Marsupials give birth prematurely and nurture their young in a pouch. In the plant kingdom, parallel evolution is seen in the similar forms of leaves, where similar patterns have appeared over and over again in separate genera and families.

GRADUALISM AND PUNCTUATED EQUILIBRIUM

Gradualism views evolution as a slow, stepwise development of a species over long periods of time (millions of years). Punctuated equilibrium proposes that some species arose suddenly in a short period of time (thousands of years) after long periods of stability. These bursts of rapid evolution are thought to have been triggered by changes in the physical or biological environment—perhaps a period of drought or the appearance of a new, more challenging predator. A classic example of punctuated equilibrium is the abrupt appearance of flowering plants without a fossil record.

Ecosystem Services

Ecosystem services are the processes by which the environment produces resources. Examples include clean water, timber, habitat for fisheries, and pollination of native and agricultural plants. Ecosystems provide the following services:

- Moderate weather extremes and their impacts
- Disperse seeds
- Mitigate droughts and floods
- Protect people from the sun's harmful ultraviolet rays
- Cycle and move nutrients
- Protect stream and river channels and coastal shores from erosion
- Detoxify and decompose wastes
- Control agricultural pests
- Maintain biodiversity
- Generate and preserve soils and renew their fertility
- Contribute to climate stability
- Purify the air and water
- Regulate disease-carrying organisms
- Pollinate crops and natural vegetation

Species Movements

Many of the different types of organisms that inhabit Earth have the ability to move. This movement can be accomplished either passively or actively. Examples of active movement include walking, running, flying, or swimming. In passive movement, the organism uses some external force to cause transit. For example, plants can use wind for seed dispersal while oyster larvae can passively travel great distances by sea currents.

One common factor of why organisms move is to disperse to new habitats to reduce intraspecific competition. By finding new suitable habitats, individuals can increase the range of their species. A larger range makes the species better off in terms of evolution.

The geographic distributions of plant and animal species are never fixed over time. Geographic ranges of organisms shift, expand, and contract. These changes are the result of two contrasting processes: (1) colonization and establishment, and (2) localized extinction. Colonization and establishment takes place when populations expand into new areas. A number of processes can initiate this process, including disturbance and abiotic environmental change. Localized extinction results in the elimination of populations from all or part of their former range. It can be caused by biotic interactions or abiotic environmental change.

Plants have developed a number of different mechanisms for dispersing their offspring:

1. The use of specialized structures to aid the transport of an individual by wind

2. The employment of particular structures to transport the individual by moving water

3. The production of fruit-encased seeds that other organisms consume and disperse

4. Adhesion mechanisms

5. The physical ejection of seeds

Once dispersed, an individual can colonize a new site only if it is devoid of other organisms and if the necessary abiotic requirements and conditions exist for its survival. Sites within ecosystems become devoid of organisms through disturbance. A disturbance can be caused by predation, climate variations, earthquakes, volcanoes, fire, animal burrowing, and even the impact of a raindrop. Often the struggle for survival does not end with colonization of an individual on a vacant site. Once colonized, an individual may not be able to establish itself over the long term because of abiotic and biotic influences. The death of the individual may occur through competitive interaction, predation, or an abiotic factor like fire.

Ecological Succession

Succession is the gradual and orderly process of ecosystem development brought about by changes in community composition and the production of a climax community characteristic of a particular geographic region. It describes the changes in an ecosystem through time and disturbance. Rates of succession are affected by several factors.

- Facilitation is when one species modifies an environment to the extent it meets the needs of another species.
- Inhibition is when one species modifies the environment to an extent that it is not suitable for another species.
- Tolerance is when species are not affected by the presence of other species.

Earlier successional species frequently called pioneer species are generalists. Pioneer plants have short reproductive times (annuals), and pioneer animals have low biomass and fast reproductive rates. Later successional species include larger perennial plants and animals with greater biomass, longer generational times, and higher parental care.

Types of Succession

Type	Description
Allogenic	Changes in the environmental conditions create conditions beneficial to new plant communities.
Primary	The colonization and establishment of pioneer plant species on bare ground. (Example: lichens on bare rocks)
Progressive	Communities become more complex over time by having a higher species diversity and greater biomass.
Retrogressive	The environment deteriorates and results in less biodiversity and less biomass.
Secondary	Begins in an area where the natural community has been disturbed but topsoil remains. (Example: forest fire)

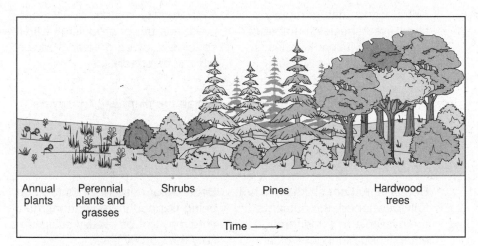

Annual plants   Perennial plants and grasses   Shrubs   Pines   Hardwood trees

Time ⟶

Figure 4.23 Stages of succession in a temperate deciduous forest. The time span from annual plants to hardwood trees is over 100 years

The following table lists the characteristics of succession within plant communities:

Characteristics of Succession-Plant Communities

Characteristic	Early Successional Stage	Late Successional Stage
Biomass	Limited.	High in tropics and wetlands; limited in deserts.
Consumption of soil nutrients	Nutrients are quickly absorbed by simpler plants.	Since biomass is greater and more nutrients are contained within plant structures, nutrient cycling between the plant and soil tends to be slower.
Impact of macroenvironment	Early plants depend primarily on conditions created by macro-environmental changes (fires, floods, etc.).	These plant species appear only after pioneer plant communities have adequately prepared the soil.
Life span of seed	Long. Seeds may become dormant and able to withstand wide environmental fluctuations.	Short. Not able to withstand wide environmental fluctuations.
Life strategy	*r*-strategists: mature rapidly; short-lived species; number of organisms within a species is high; low biodiversity; niche generalists.	*K*-strategists: mature slowly; long-lived; number of organisms within a species is lower; greater biodiversity; niche specialists.
Location of nutrients	In the soil and in leaf litter.	Within the plant and top layers of soil.
Net primary productivity	High.	Low.
Nutrient cycling by decomposers	Limited.	Complex.
Nutrient cycling through biogeochemical cycles	Because nutrient sinks have not fully developed, the nutrients are available to cycle through established biogeochemical cycles fairly rapidly.	Because of nutrient sinks (carbon being trapped in vegetation), nutrients may not be readily available to flow through cycles.
Photosynthesis efficiency	Low.	High.
Plant structure complexity	Simple.	More complex.
Recovery rate of plants from environmental stress	Plants quickly and easily come back.	Recovery is slow.
Seed dispersal	Widespread	Limited in range.
Species diversity	Limited	High.
Stability of ecosystem	Since diversity is limited, ecosystem is subject to instability.	Due to high diversity, ecosystem can withstand stress.

QUICK REVIEW CHECKLIST

- [ ] **Biological Populations and Communities**
  - [ ] ecosystem characteristics
  - [ ] population dispersal patterns
  - [ ] ecological niches—generalists vs. specialists
  - [ ] biological interactions
    - [ ] amensalism
    - [ ] commensalism
    - [ ] competition
    - [ ] mutualism
    - [ ] parasitism
    - [ ] predation
    - [ ] saprotrophism
    - [ ] keystone species (examples)

- [ ] **Species Diversity (Adaptations)**
  - [ ] aquatic organisms
  - [ ] desert organisms
  - [ ] grassland organisms
  - [ ] forest organisms
  - [ ] temperate scrub forest land organisms
  - [ ] tundra organisms

- [ ] **Edge Effects**

- [ ] **Biomes**
  - [ ] Antarctic
  - [ ] benthos
  - [ ] coastal zones
  - [ ] coral reefs
  - [ ] deserts
  - [ ] freshwater wetlands
  - [ ] grasslands
  - [ ] hydrothermal vents
  - [ ] intertidal zones
  - [ ] ocean
  - [ ] savannas
  - [ ] taiga
  - [ ] temperate deciduous forests
  - [ ] temperate rain forests
  - [ ] temperate scrubland (chaparral)
  - [ ] temperate woodlands
  - [ ] tropical rain forests
  - [ ] tropical seasonal forests
  - [ ] tundra

- [ ] **Energy flow**
  - [ ] photosynthesis
  - [ ] cellular respiration

QUICK REVIEW CHECKLIST (continued)

- ☐ **Food Webs and Trophic Levels**
  - ☐ desert food web
  - ☐ oceanic food web
  - ☐ coniferous forest food web
  - ☐ deciduous forest food web
  - ☐ tropical rain forest food web
  - ☐ temperate rain forest food web
  - ☐ tundra food web

- ☐ **Ecological Pyramid**
  - ☐ aquatic ecosystem (inverted)
  - ☐ desert biomass
  - ☐ marine biomass
  - ☐ deciduous forest biomass
  - ☐ temperate rain forest biomass
  - ☐ tundra biomass
  - ☐ net primary productivity

- ☐ **Ecosystem Diversity**
  - ☐ diversity increasers
  - ☐ diversity decreasers

- ☐ **Natural Selection**
  - ☐ stabilizing selection
  - ☐ directional selection
  - ☐ disruptive selection

- ☐ **Evolution**
  - ☐ speciation
  - ☐ convergent evolution
  - ☐ evolutionary relay
  - ☐ parallel evolution
  - ☐ gradualism
  - ☐ punctuated equilibrium

- ☐ **Ecosystem Services**

- ☐ **Species Movements**

- ☐ **Ecological Succession**
  - ☐ types of succession
    - ☐ allogenic
    - ☐ primary
    - ☐ progressive
    - ☐ retrogressive
    - ☐ secondary
  - ☐ stages of succession

- ☐ **Ecological Succession**
  - ☐ characteristics of succession (plant communities)

MULTIPLE-CHOICE QUESTIONS

For questions 1–3, choose from the following items:

  (A) Tropical rain forest
  (B) Temperate deciduous forest
  (C) Savanna
  (D) Taiga
  (E) Tundra

1. Forests of cold climates of high latitudes and high altitudes.

2. Warm year-round; prolonged dry seasons; scattered trees.

3. Low biodiversity due to lots of shade, which limits food for herbivores. Major resource for timber.

4. The annual productivity of any ecosystem is greater than the annual increase in biomass of the herbivores in the ecosystem because

  (A) plants convert energy input into biomass more efficiently than animals
  (B) there are always more animals than plants in any ecosystem
  (C) plants have a greater longevity than animals
  (D) during each energy transformation, some energy is lost
  (E) animals convert energy input into biomass more efficiently than plants do

5. Net primary productivity per square meter is highest in which biome listed below?

  (A) Deserts
  (B) Grasslands
  (C) Boreal forests
  (D) Open oceans
  (E) Estuaries

6. All of the following are factors that increase population size EXCEPT

  (A) ability to adapt
  (B) specialized niche
  (C) few competitors
  (D) generalized niche
  (E) high birthrate

7. A specialist faces _____ competition for resources and has _____ ability to adapt to environmental changes. A generalist faces _____ competition for resources and has _____ ability to adapt to environmental changes.

    (A) less, greater, greater, less
    (B) greater, less, less, greater
    (C) less, less, greater, greater
    (D) greater, greater, less, less
    (E) None of the above

8. Whether a land area supports a deciduous forest or grassland depends primarily on

    (A) changes in temperature
    (B) latitude north or south of the equator
    (C) consistency of rainfall from year to year and the effect that it has on fires
    (D) changes in length of the growing season
    (E) None of the above

9. The main difference between primary and secondary succession is that

    (A) primary succession occurs in the year before secondary succession
    (B) primary succession occurs on barren, rocky areas and secondary succession does not
    (C) secondary succession ends in a climax species and primary succession ends in a pioneer species
    (D) secondary succession occurs on barren, rocky areas and primary succession does not
    (E) All of the above statements are true

10. The biggest threat to species is

    (A) low reproductive rates
    (B) disease
    (C) alien, invasive species
    (D) collecting, hunting, and poaching
    (E) loss of habitat

11. Darwin noted that the Patagonian hare was similar in appearance and had a niche similar to the European hare. However, the Patagonian hare is not a rabbit. It is a rodent related to the guinea pig. This example illustrates the principle known as

    (A) allopatric speciation
    (B) adaptive radiation
    (C) divergent evolution
    (D) coevolution
    (E) convergent evolution

For questions 12–14, choose from the following items:

    (A) Adaptive radiation
    (B) Isolation
    (C) Natural selection
    (D) Stable gene pool
    (E) Convergent evolution

12. Members of the same species of moths are prevented from interbreeding because they live on opposites sides of a mountain range.

13. Darwin's finches are a good example of this biological principle.

14. In the evolutionary history of the horse, the early horse (*Eohippus*) was replaced by the modern one-toed horse.

15. As one travels from the tropical rain forests near the equator to the frozen tundra, one passes through a variety of biomes including deserts, temperate and deciduous forests, etc. The primary reason for the change in vegetation is due to

    (A) evolution
    (B) succession
    (C) the hours of sunlight reaching a particular region
    (D) changes in temperature and amount of rainfall
    (E) the amount of relative cloud cover and ocean currents

16. Species that serve as early warnings of environmental damage are called

    (A) keystone species
    (B) native species
    (C) specialist species
    (D) indicator species
    (E) generalist species

17. Which one of the following statements is false?

    (A) When environmental conditions are changing rapidly, a generalist is usually better off than a specialist.
    (B) The fundamental niche of a species is the full range of physical, chemical, and biological factors it could use if there were no competition.
    (C) The competitive exclusion principle states that no two species with the same fundamental niche can indefinitely occupy the same habitat.
    (D) Interspecific competition is competition between two members of the same species.
    (E) Resource partitioning limits competition by two species using the same scarce resource at different times, in different ways, or in different places.

18. Which of the following best describes a nonanthropogenic secondary succession?

    (A) Plants and other vegetation die gradually due to drought
    (B) Wildflowers grow in an area that was previously destroyed by fire
    (C) A farmer removes weeds using a herbicide
    (D) Lichens and mosses secrete acids that allow other plants to grow
    (E) None of the above

19. The location of where an organism lives would be best described as its

    (A) niche
    (B) habitat
    (C) range
    (D) biome
    (E) ecosystem

For Question 20, refer to the locations marked by letters in the world map below

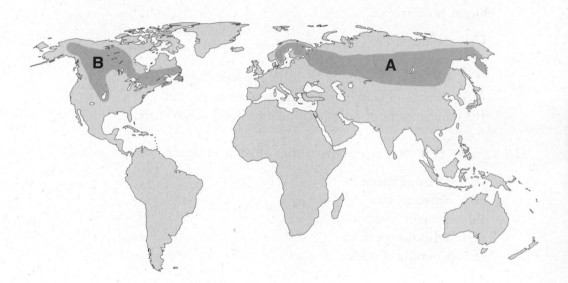

20. The locations shaded in the map above are known as

    (A) tropical rain forests
    (B) grasslands
    (C) taiga (boreal forest)
    (D) chaparral
    (E) tundra

FREE-RESPONSE QUESTION

There are over 25,000 species of bees in the world today. Africanized honey bees (AHB), *Apis mellifera L. scutellata* (Lepetelier), sometimes referred to as killer bees, are the same species as European honeybees (EHB) but a different subspecies. Only through careful examination under a microscope, or through DNA tests, can AHBs be distinguished from EHBs. AHBs are called "Africanized" honeybees as a result of interbreeding experiments. The thought was that AHBs might be better suited for the tropical climates of South America than EHBs. In the 1950s, AHBs were inadvertently released in Brazil. AHBs began migrating (about 300 miles per year), arriving in southern Texas in 1990, Arizona and New Mexico in 1993, and southern California in 1994. Since 1994, migration has appeared to slow down significantly. Although the two subspecies are virtually indistinguishable, it is the behavior of the two subspecies that sets them apart. AHBs defend their colonies much more vigorously than do EHBs. When AHBs sting, more of them participate in extremely aggressive behavior. AHBs nest where EHBs do not, such as small, confined spaces near the ground such as flowerpots, abandoned tires, and cracks in building foundations.

(a) Discuss the influx of AHBs in the southwest United States in terms of the processes of natural selection.

    (i)   In what areas do the processes of natural selection apply to the colonization of AHBs?

    (ii)   In what areas do the processes of natural selection NOT apply to the colonization of AHBs?

    (iii) What issues regarding the influx of AHBs warrant further study?

(b) Provide possible explanations of why the expansion of AHBs may have stopped.

(c) What adaptations have honeybees in general developed to be able to survive?

(d) Provide some possible methods to control AHBs.

(e) What are possible economic implications of AHBs to agriculture?

TIP

Be sure to explain technical terms when you use them in an answer. Dropping in terms like "bioaccumulation" without demonstrating an understanding of the term will not earn you any credit.

MULTIPLE-CHOICE ANSWERS AND EXPLANATIONS

1. **(D)** Refer to the biome descriptions (pages 170–173).
2. **(C)** Refer to the biome descriptions (pages 170–173).
3. **(B)** Refer to the biome descriptions (pages 170–173).
4. **(D)** Less energy is available at each trophic level because energy is lost by organisms through cellular respiration and incomplete digestion of food sources.
5. **(E)** Estuaries form a transition zone between river environments and ocean environments and are subject to both marine influences, such as tides, waves, and the influx of saline water; and riverine influences, such as flows of freshwater and sediment. The inflow of both seawater and freshwater provide high levels of nutrients in both the water column and sediment, making estuaries the most productive natural habitats in the world and also the most threatened.
6. **(B)** Specialized niches are more susceptible to environmental changes and have a direct effect on the stability of populations (population size).
7. **(C)** Specialist species are adapted to a narrow range of habitats and conditions, while generalist species are able to live in a variety of habitats.
8. **(C)** The question of determining whether it is a deciduous forest or grassland is dependent on yearly patterns of rainfall since both biomes can exist over similar temperature ranges. Frequent fires are an important factor in determining grasslands.
9. **(B)** Primary succession occurs on bare rocks and starts with lichens. Secondary succession occurs in areas where there is intact topsoil.
10. **(E)** Scientists warn that human activities may be bringing about the sixth mass extinction of species in the world's history.
11. **(E)** Convergent evolution describes the process whereby organisms not closely related independently acquire similar characteristics while evolving in separate and sometimes varying environments.
12. **(B)** "Species" is defined as a group of organisms that look similar, have the ability to interbreed, and produce fertile offspring. Two forms of isolation that prevent interbreeding are geographic isolation and reproductive isolation.
13. **(A)** Adaptive radiation is the development of many species that are derived from a single, ancestral population.
14. **(C)** Natural selection is the process by which only the organisms that are best adapted to their environment tend to survive and transmit their genes to successive generations.
15. **(D)** The distribution of biomes is primarily determined by global climatic zones as measured by average annual temperature and rainfall. An area's climate will determine what sort of biome can be sustained in that area. Other determining factors include sun angle, heat import, and the angle of the Earth's rotation. Regional climates, which also determine the distribution of biomes, are affected by rain shadows and cold or warm ocean currents.
16. **(D)** An indicator species is a species whose presence, absence, or relative well-being in a given environment is indicative of the health of the ecosystem as a whole.
17. **(D)** Interspecific competition is competition among members of different species.

18. **(B)** Ecosystems undergo secondary succession following some artificial or natural disturbance such as a forest fire or farming. The question included the word "nonanthropogenic" which would rule out choice (C) since anthropogenic refers to something caused by humans.

19. **(B)** A habitat is the location where a particular species lives and grows. A microhabitat is the immediate surroundings and other physical factors of an individual plant or animal within its habitat. Habitat destruction is a major factor in causing a species population to decrease, eventually leading to it being endangered or becoming extinct. A biome is the set of flora and fauna that lives in a habitat and occupy certain geography.

20. **(C)** Taiga, also known as boreal forest, is the world's largest land biome, and makes up almost a third of the world's forest cover with the largest areas located in Russia and Canada. The taiga has a subarctic climate with very large temperature range between seasons, but the long and cold winter is the dominant feature.

    Lakes and other water bodies are very common. The taiga experiences relatively low precipitation, 8"–30" (200–750 mm), throughout the year, primarily as rain during the summer months, but also as fog and snow. As evaporation is consequently low for most of the year, precipitation exceeds evaporation, and is sufficient to sustain the dense vegetation growth. Snow may remain on the ground for as long as nine months in the northernmost extensions of the taiga.

    Taiga soil tends to be young and poor in nutrients and lacks the deep, organically enriched profile present in temperate deciduous forests. The thinness of the soil is due largely to the cold, which hinders the development of soil and the ease with which plants can use its nutrients. Since the soil is acidic due to the falling pine needles, the forest floor has only lichens and some mosses growing on it. Diversity of soil organisms in the boreal forest is high, comparable to the tropical rain forest.

    Because the sun is low in the horizon for most of the year, it is difficult for plants to generate energy from photosynthesis. Pine, spruce, and fir do not lose their leaves seasonally and are able to photosynthesize with their older leaves in late winter and spring when light is good but temperatures are still too low for new growth to commence. The adaptation of evergreen needles limits the water lost due to transpiration and their dark green color increases their absorption of sunlight. Although precipitation is not a limiting factor, the ground freezes during the winter months and plant roots are unable to absorb water, so desiccation can be a severe problem in late winter.

    The taiga stores enormous quantities of carbon, more than the world's temperate and tropical forests combined, much of it in wetlands and peatland. Current estimates place boreal forests as storing twice as much carbon per unit area as tropical forests.

FREE-RESPONSE ANSWER

Ten points possible for full credit. Parts A, B, C, D, and E are worth 2 points maximum each.

(a) The range of genetic variation within a species's gene pool determines whether or not the species, not the individual, has the capacity to adapt and survive to changes in the environment. The colonization of the American southwest by AHBs differs from classical theories of natural selection in that AHBs and EHBs belong to the same species and therefore are presumably able to interbreed and produce fertile offspring. The two subspecies seem to differ only in behavioral patterns. As to whether the behavioral patterns of the two subspecies are so radically different as to cause a prezygotic reproductive barrier or not is worth investigation.

Another issue that differs from classical natural selection theory is that, in this case, the environment, over such a short time span, is not changing. In effect, it is not a variable involved in survival rates. Both subspecies can and do survive in the environment. Additionally, the environment is not affecting disproportionate natality rates between the two subspecies based upon one subspecies having a survival advantage over the other.

In terms of following classic natural selection theory, what exists in this scenario is competition between the two subspecies for limited resources. Both subspecies are competing for space and food supplies. As to whether or not the more aggressive behavior of protecting the nest allows more AHBs to survive disproportionately, thereby increasing the ratio of AHBs to EHBs is another factor that warrants further study.

(b) It appears that since 1994, the expansion of AHBs into the southwestern United States has slowed down. Possible reasons might include the following.

(1) AHBs are adapted to tropical climates (Africa and Brazil). Their ability to survive may be restricted to climatic zones that have warm temperatures most of the year (similar to the American Southwest). Cold temperatures (common in the Midwest and northeast U.S.) may influence the viability of offspring and, consequently, their expansion into these areas.

(2) Geographic barriers may be another reason for a decline in the expansion of AHBs. Mountain ranges, dry deserts with low humidity, and the lack of adequate food resources may also be slowing expansion. Finally, variation in seasonal photoperiod, timing of forage availability, and/or the existence of parasites such as mites, pathogenic bacteria, or viruses may be having an effect on the newly introduced subspecies.

(c) Three adaptations of honeybees have been essential to their evolution and biology. First is clustering behavior, which is working as a social unit with specific predetermined behavioral patterns and duties of each class in the hierarchy. The second is the ability to cool the hive through the process of evaporation of water collected outside the hive, ensuring a stable internal temperature. The ability to ensure temperature stability within the nest allows honeybees to colonize a wide variety of environments, as opposed to bees that lack this trait and are therefore restricted to thermally stable environments (tropics). The third is the ability to communicate information about food sources, direction, and distance through dance behavior. The ability to communicate such a wide

Notable points:

(a) Recognition of genetic variation as a determinant in the process of natural selection.

Recognition that subspecies are able to interbreed.

Recognition that behavior may be a reproductive barrier.

Recognition that the environment is remaining constant and not acting to select one subspecies over another.

Recognition that the two subspecies are competing for the same limited natural resources—a basic tenet of natural selection.

Recognition that more study is needed in the advantage of aggressive behavior and its effect on survivability of the colony.

(b) Specific adaptations of AHBs to tropical climates.

Temperature tolerances may be narrower in AHBs.

Geographic barriers.

Mountain ranges.

Low humidity in deserts.

Lack of sufficient food resources in deserts.

Variation in seasonal photoperiod.

Timing of forage availability (seasons) as opposed to no season in the tropics.

Parasites.

Pathogenic organisms.

(c) Clustering behavior.

variety of complex information is unparalleled in the animal kingdom (except for humans).

(d) Since AHBs and EHBs are coexisting within the same areas, any attempt to control the AHBs through pesticides or other extermination techniques would probably have an effect on the EHBs as well. For the most part, EHBs and their less-aggressive behavior are more suited to coexist with humans for agricultural pollination purposes than are AHBs. Introduction of any bacterial agent, parasite, or other biological controlling mechanism would also probably affect the EHBs. One method that might work to control the domination of an area by AHBs would be to ensure that there are sufficient EHBs in the area. First, this would provide competition for resources between the two subspecies, thereby reducing the carrying capacity of the area. In turn, this would limit expansion of the AHB population. Second, ensuring sufficient EHBs in the area might allow interbreeding of an AHB queen with EHB males. The goal of interbreeding would be to possibly dampen the highly aggressive behavioral characteristics of the AHBs. Third, introducing large numbers of sterile, male AHBs into hives might result in smaller populations. Physically disrupting hives would only enhance recolonization.

(e) Agriculture as practiced today requires the use of honeybees for pollination. Honeybees are rented and placed into fields for this purpose by beekeepers. Urban expansion, human population increases, and sophisticated transportation systems have all made rural areas more accessible. AHBs strike terror in many people, and yet documented cases of deaths due to AHBs are rather low and exaggerated. Public pressure to eradicate "killer bees" will certainly involve economics. The cost of renting EHBs would certainly increase due to issues of suitability and availability of sites, public concerns, legislative mandates, and destroying EHBs in an attempt to control AHBs. As costs of renting EHBs increase, profit margins could decrease, forcing many beekeepers out of business. The result would be fewer bees for the needs of agriculture. This, in turn, could result in less agricultural production and, consequently, higher prices to the consumer.

(margin notes:)

Predetermined roles.

Temperature regulation of hive to create stable environment for young.

Internal stability of nest temperature allows colonization into more diverse areas.

Ability to communicate.

(d) Recognition that wide use of pesticides would not be effective.

EHBs are more suitable for agriculture.

Bacterial agents or viruses would affect both subspecies.

Only way to control AHBs would be to ensure competitive population numbers of EHBs.

Reduce carrying capacity of environment.

Interbreeding and its role to diminish aggressive behavior.

Introduction of sterile males.

(e) Bees are necessary for agriculture.

People are closer today to agricultural areas and are thereby more impacted.

Public fear and hysteria of AHBs.

Availability of suitable sites for EHBs.

Public pressure.

Liability issues (insurance).

Legislative mandates.

Fewer beekeepers.

Cost of maintaining EHBs would increase.

As cost of bees goes up, so would cost of agricultural products.

YOUR TURN

- Let's practice the skills required for answering Free Response Questions. Read and review the essay above several times. Take very brief notes of important points and use them for now if you wish. When you are ready, set a timer for 23 minutes—the average amount of time you will have for each FRQ. Begin answering each question as best you can in your best writing style. STOP after 23 minutes. Take a breath! Then later, go back over the essay you wrote. REMEMBER: I had days to write my answer and you had 23 minutes. Your essay will be **much** shorter than mine but the thing you are looking for now is: (1) Did you answer the questions? (2) Do you feel comfortable with what you wrote? (3) Were you able to incorporate some of the material in my answers into your answers? (4) Do your answers flow and seem organized? (5) Were you able to back up or support your statements with facts, examples, etc.? (6) Does your essay look neat and legible? If any of the answers above were "no"—then try this same exercise again until you are finally satisfied. As you continue this method for each chapter, you are getting closer and closer to that 5!

CHAPTER 5

Natural Biogeochemical Cycles

CARBON CYCLE

Carbon is the basic building block of life and the fundamental element found in carbohydrates, fats, proteins, and nucleic acids (DNA and RNA). Carbon is exchanged among the biosphere, geosphere, hydrosphere, and atmosphere. Although carbon is found in rocks, it is a minor component when compared with the mass of either oxygen or silicon atoms in rocks. Carbon is found in carbon dioxide (CO_2), which makes up less than 1% of the atmosphere.

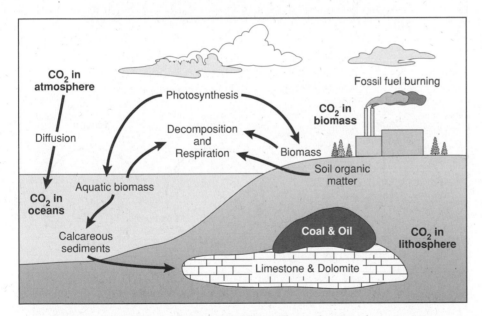

Figure 5.1 The carbon cycle viewed as chemical processes

The major reservoirs or "sinks" of carbon include:

- **Plant matter:** A portion of atmospheric carbon (15%) is removed through photosynthesis by which carbon is incorporated into plant structures and compounds:

$$6CO_2 + 6H_2O + \text{energy (sunlight)} \rightarrow C_6H_{12}O_6 + 6O_2$$

- **Terrestrial biosphere:** Forests store 86% of the planet's above-ground carbon and 73% of the planet's soil carbon. Carbon can be stored up to several hundreds of years in trees and up to thousands of years in soils.

- **Oceans:** Dissolved inorganic carbon in the form of CO_2 and living and nonliving marine biota (i.e., shells and skeletons) are included. The oceans are gaining approximately 2 gigatons (4×10^{12} kg) of carbon each year; however, most of it is not involved with rapid exchanges with the atmosphere. Removing carbon dioxide from water raises the pH, making the water more basic.
- **Sedimentary deposits:** Limestone Ca$\underline{C}O_3$) and carbon trapped in fossil fuels and coal. Limestone is the largest reservoir of carbon in the carbon cycle. The calcium comes from the weathering of calcium-silicate rocks, which causes the silicon in the rocks to combine with oxygen to form sand or quartz (silicon dioxide), leaving calcium ions available to form limestone.

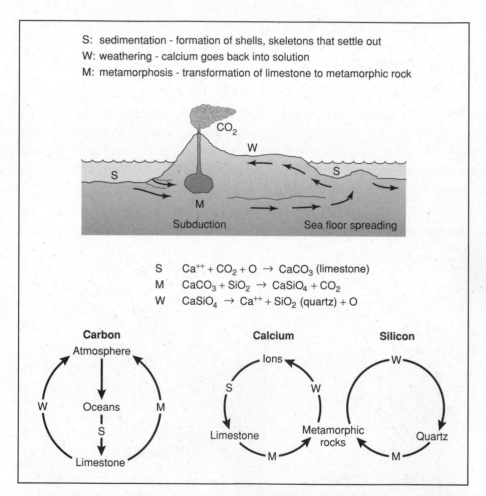

Figure 5.2 Inorganic carbon cycle

Carbon is released back into the atmosphere through:

1. Cellular respiration of plants and animals that break down glucose into carbon dioxide and water: $C_6H_{12}O_6 + 6O_2 \rightarrow 6CO_2 + 6H_2O +$ energy. When oxygen is not present, anaerobic respiration occurs and releases carbon into the atmosphere in the form of methane (CH_4) (e.g., as marsh gas or flatulence).

2. Decay of organic material by the action of decomposers; if oxygen is present, the carbon is released in the form of carbon dioxide; if oxygen is absent, it is released in the form of methane (CH_4).

3. Burning fossil fuels, wood, coal, etc.

4. Weatherization of rocks and especially the erosion of limestone, marble, and chalk, which break down to carbon dioxide and carbonic acid (H_2CO_3).

5. Volcanic eruptions.

6. Release of carbon dioxide by warmer ocean waters.

Prior to the Industrial Revolution, transfer rates of carbon dioxide due to photosynthesis and respiration (including decay) were fairly balanced. However, since the Industrial Revolution, more carbon dioxide is being deposited in the Earth's atmosphere than is being removed. This increase is believed to be due to the burning of wood and fossil fuels and deforestation.

Carbon Sinks

Carbon Sink	Amount (Billions of Metric Tons)
Marine sediments and sedimentary rocks	~ 75,000,000
Ocean	~ 40,000
Fossil fuel deposits	~ 4000
Soil organic matter	~ 1500
Atmosphere	578 (in 1700 c.e.) to 766 (in 2000 c.e.)
Terrestrial plants	~ 580

NITROGEN CYCLE

Nitrogen makes up 78% of the atmosphere. Nitrogen is also an essential element needed to make amino acids, proteins, and nucleic acids. Other nitrogen stores include organic matter in the soil and the oceans (1 million times more nitrogen is found in the atmosphere than is contained in either land or ocean waters).

The natural cycling of nitrogen, in which atmospheric nitrogen is converted to nitrogen oxides by lightning and deposited in the soil by rain where it is assimilated by plants and either eaten by animals (and returned as feces) or decomposed back to elemental nitrogen by bacteria, includes the following processes:

- Nitrogen fixation
- Nitrification
- Assimilation
- Ammonification
- Denitrification

Nitrogen Fixation

Nitrogen fixation is the conversion of atmospheric nitrogen (N_2) to ammonia (NH_3) or nitrate (NO_3^-) ions. Nitrate is the product of high-energy fixation by lightning, cosmic radiation, or meteorite trails. In high-energy fixation, atmospheric nitrogen and oxygen combine to form nitrates, which are carried to Earth's surface in rainfall

TIP

Know *all* steps involved in the nitrogen cycle. You will find more questions about the nitrogen cycle than any other cycle on the APES exam.

as nitric acid (HNO_3). High-energy fixation accounts for **about 10%** of the nitrate entering the nitrogen cycle.

In contrast, biological fixation accounts for 90% of the fixed nitrogen in the cycle. In biological fixation, molecular nitrogen (N_2) is split into two free nitrogen atoms ($N_2 \rightarrow N + N$). The nitrogen atoms combine with hydrogen to yield ammonia (NH_3).

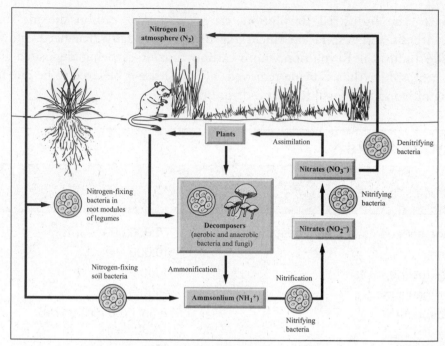

Figure 5.3 The nitrogen cycle

The fixation process is accomplished by a series of different microorganisms. The symbiotic bacteria *Rhizobium* is associated with the roots of legumes such as beans or clover. To a lesser extent, some non-leguminous plants also exhibit symbiotic relationships with bacteria.

Nitrification

Nitrification is the process in which ammonia is oxidized to nitrite (NO_2^-) and nitrate (NO_3^-), the forms most usable by plants. Two groups of microorganisms are involved in nitrification. *Nitrosomonas* oxidize ammonia to nitrite and water. *Nitrobacter* oxidize the nitrite to nitrate.

Assimilation

Nitrates are the form of nitrogen most commonly assimilated by plants through their root hairs. Nitrogen is used by plants to synthesize amino acids, oils, and nucleic acids. Rains and extensive irrigation can leach soluble nitrates and nitrites into groundwater, which, in high amounts, can interfere with blood-oxygen levels in human infants. Soluble nitrates that run off the land and enter aquatic and wetland habitats result in cultural eutrophication and the destruction of these habitats. Animals assimilate nitrogen-based compounds by consuming plants and other organisms that consume plants.

Ammonification

When a plant or animal dies, or an animal excretes, the initial form of nitrogen is found in amino acids and nucleic acids. Bacteria, or in some cases, fungi, convert this organic nitrogen within the remains back into ammonia (NH_3).

Denitrification

Denitrification is the process in which nitrates are reduced to gaseous nitrogen. This process is used by facultative anaerobes. These organisms flourish in an aerobic environment but are also capable of breaking down oxygen-containing compounds (NO_3^-) to obtain oxygen in anaerobic environments. Examples include fungi and the bacteria *Pseudomonas*.

Effects of Excess Nitrogen

Fossil fuel combustion has contributed to a sevenfold increase in nitrogen oxides (NO_x) to the atmosphere, particularly nitrogen dioxide (NO_2). NO_x is a precursor of tropospheric (lower atmosphere) ozone production and contributes to smog and acid rain and increases nitrogen inputs to ecosystems.

Ammonia (NH_3) in the atmosphere has tripled as the result of human activities since the Industrial Revolution. Ammonia acts as an aerosol and decreases air quality.

Nitrous oxide (N_2O) is a significant greenhouse gas and has deleterious effects in the stratosphere, where it breaks down and acts as a catalyst in the destruction of atmospheric ozone. N_2O is in a large part emitted during nitrification (conversion of ammonium to nitrate and nitrite) and denitrification (converting oxides back to nitrogen gas or nitrous oxides for energy generation) processes that take place in the soil. The largest N_2O emissions are observed where nitrogen-containing fertilizer is applied in agriculture.

Human activity has more than doubled the annual transfer of nitrogen into biological available forms through:

- Extensive cultivation of legumes (particularly soy, alfalfa, and clover)
- The extensive use of chemical fertilizers and pollution emitted by vehicles and industrial plants (NO_x)
- Biomass burning
- Cattle and feedlots
- Industrial processes

PHOSPHORUS CYCLE

Phosphorus is essential for the production of nucleotides, production of ATP, fats in cell membranes, bones, teeth, and shells. Phosphorus is not found in the atmosphere but, rather, the primary sink for phosphorus is in sedimentary rocks. Generally, phosphorus is found in the form of the phosphate ion (PO_4^{3-}) or the hydrogen phosphate ion (HPO_4^{2-}). Phosphorus is slowly released from terrestrial rocks by weathering and the action of acid rain. It then dissolves into the soil and is taken up by plants. It is often a limiting factor for soils due to its low concentration and solubility. Phosphorus is a key element in fertilizer. A fertilizer labeled 6-24-26 contains 6% nitrogen, 24% phosphorus, and 26% potassium.

Humans have impacted the phosphorus cycle in several ways: First, humans have mined large quantities of rocks containing phosphorus for inorganic fertilizers and detergents. Second, clear-cutting tropical habitats for agriculture decreases the amount of available phosphorus as it is contained in the vegetation. Third, humans allow runoff from feedlots, from fertilizers, and from the discharge of municipal sewage plants. The runoff collects in lakes, streams, and ponds. It causes an increase in the growth of cyanobacteria (blue-green bacteria), green algae, and aquatic plants. In turn, this growth results in decreased oxygen content in the water, which then kills other aquatic organism in the food web. Fourth, humans apply phosphorus-rich guano and other phosphate-containing fertilizers to fields.

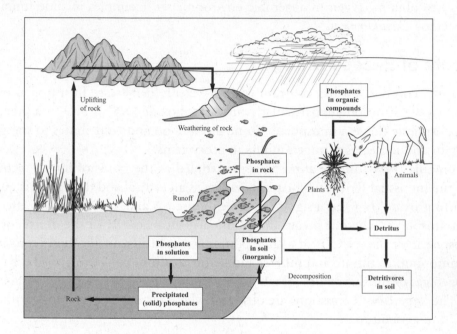

Figure 5.4 The phosphorus cycle

SULFUR CYCLE

Elemental or pure sulfur is commonly found in underground deposits or near natural hot springs or volcanoes. It's also found in the combined form in many minerals.

Sulfur in Lithosphere

Sulfur is the thirteenth most abundant element in Earth's crust and the ninth most abundant in sediments. Sulfur content of rocks varies considerably (e.g., sedimentary rocks have the most while igneous rocks have the least). Sulfur in lithosphere is mobilized by slow weathering of rock material. Dissolved in runoff, it moves with river water and is deposited in continental shield sediments in oceans. Eventually on geological timescale, this uplifts to surface again thus completing the geological part of the sulfur cycle.

Sulfur in Hydrosphere

Main storage of sulfur in the oceans is through dissolved sulfate. The most volatile sulfur compound in seawater is dimethyl sulfide (DMS; $(CH_3)_2S$), which is produced by algal and bacterial decay. Its highest concentrations are in coastal marshes and wetlands. Sulfur is the second most abundant compound in rivers with concentrations fluctuating highly with seasons and frequency of drought, flood, and normal flow. Rivers transport about 110 million tons (100 Tg) of sulfur per year to the oceans.

Sulfur in Soil and Biosphere

Sulfur is a major essential nutrient in the biosphere and is concentrated mainly in soil from where it enters the biosphere through plant uptake. Its main sources are deposition from the atmosphere, weathering of rocks, release from decay of organic matter and anthropogenic fertilizer, pesticides, and irrigation water. In soil, it is present mainly in the oxidized state (e.g., SO_4^{2-}). Rich organic soils may have up to 0.5% sulfur by dry weight. Sulfur in soil may be in bound or unbound form, as organic or inorganic compounds, organic sulfur being most prevalent. Plants take up sulfur from the soil mainly as sulfate and it is passed on with the food chain in the biosphere. It leaves the biosphere on death of living organisms when aerobic decay and decomposition brings back sulfate into the soil. Finally, anaerobic decomposition in soil releases part of organic sulfur as hydrogen sulfide (H_2S), dimethyl sulfide ($(CH_3)_2S$, and other organic compounds into the atmosphere. The release of sulfur is dependent upon warmer temperatures.

Sulfur in the Atmosphere

Six important sulfur compounds are released into the atmosphere due to interaction of processes between Earth's surface and the atmosphere.

1. **Carbonyl sulfide (COS):** The most abundant sulfur species in atmosphere and in nature is mainly produced by decomposition processes in soil, marshes and wetlands along ocean coasts, and areas of ocean upwelling that are rich in nutrients. Anthropogenic combustion processes produce less than 25% of COS. It has a lifetime of 44 years with the only sink being stratospheric photolysis and slow photochemical reactions in troposphere. Oceans may act both as source and sink. About 80% of total atmospheric sulfur is COS, but it is relatively inert and does not add much to the atmospheric sulfur pollution problem.

2. **Carbon disulfide (CS_2):** It is far more reactive than COS and has similar sources. It has a lifetime of 12 days and its major sink is photochemical reactions. Its concentration decreases rapidly with altitude. The most important source of the compound is microbial processes in warm tropical soils. Major secondary sources are marshes and wetlands along sea coasts. Small anthropogenic inputs are from fossil fuel combustion.

3. **Dimethyl sulfide ($(CH_3)_2S$:** DMS is released from oceans in much greater amounts than COS or CS_2 and is rapidly oxidized to sulfur dioxide or is redeposited to the oceans. In the sulfur cycle, most of the natural gas released from oceans is DMS. Its concentrations are highest during the night.

4. **Hydrogen sulfide (H_2S):** Mainly produced in nature during anaerobic decay in soils, wetlands, salt marshes, and other areas of stagnant water with maximum concentrations occurring over tropical forests. This highly

reactive compound is removed by reaction with hydroxyl radical (OH^-) and COS. Its highest concentrations occur at night and in the early morning when photochemical activity is at a minimum.

5. **Sulfur dioxide (SO_2):** Its natural source is oxidation of H_2S and its major anthropogenic source is combustion of fossil fuels. Its atmospheric concentrations are most influenced by anthropogenic emissions. In some industrialized areas such as eastern North America, over 90% of SO_2 is from anthropogenic sources while half of global SO_2 originates from natural sources. The lifetime of SO_2 is 2–4 days indicating losses due to photochemical conversion. The rest of the gas is removed from the atmosphere by wet and dry deposition.

6. **Sulfate aerosol (SO_4^{2-}):** The largest natural source of sulfate aerosol particles originate from sea spray. About 3.3 million tons (3 Tg) per year of sulfate is added to the atmosphere from anthropogenic sources directly but much greater amounts are formed through secondary reactions from various sulfur species in the atmosphere. Most of the salt spray sulfate falls back to oceans but some is carried over the continents to be included in deposition processes there.

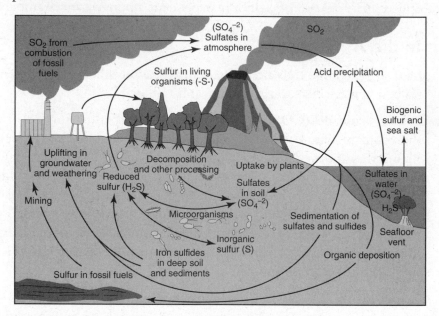

Figure 5.5 The sulfur cycle

WATER CYCLE

The water cycle is powered by energy from the sun. Solar energy evaporates water from oceans, lakes, rivers, streams, soil, and vegetation. The oceans hold 97% of all water on the planet and are the source of 78% of all global precipitation. Oceans are also the source of 86% of all global evaporation, with evaporation from the sea surface keeping Earth from overheating. If there were no oceans, surface temperatures on land would rise to an average of 153°F (67°C).

The water cycle is in a state of dynamic equilibrium by which the rate of evaporation equals the rate of precipitation. Warm air holds more water vapor than cold air. Processes involved in the water cycle include evaporation, evapotranspiration, condensation, infiltration, runoff, and precipitation.

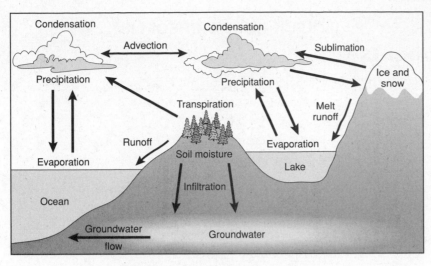

Figure 5.6 The water cycle

Human Impact on Water Cycle

Human Activity	Impact on Water Cycle
Withdrawing water from lakes, aquifers, and rivers	Groundwater depletion and saltwater intrusion
Clearing of land for agriculture and urbanization	Increased runoff Decreased infiltration Increased flood risks Accelerated soil erosion
Agriculture	Runoff contains nitrates, phosphates, ammonia, etc.
Destruction of wetlands	Disturbing natural processes that purify water
Pollution of water sources	Increased occurrences of infectious agents such as cholera, dysentery, etc.
Sewage runoff, feedlot runoff	Cultural eutrophication
Building power plants	Increased thermal pollution

CONSERVATION OF MATTER AND ENERGY

The law of conservation of matter states that during an ordinary chemical change, there is no detectable increase or decrease in the quantity of matter. The total quantity of matter and energy available in the universe is a fixed amount and is never any more or less. The law of conservation of energy states that energy cannot be created or destroyed but can change its form. Conversion of one type of matter into another is always accompanied by the conversion of one form of energy into another. Usually heat is either given off or absorbed, but sometimes the conversion involves light or electrical energy in addition to heat.

QUICK REVIEW CHECKLIST

☐ **Carbon Cycle**
   ☐ carbon sink

☐ **Nitrogen Cycle**
   ☐ nitrogen fixation
   ☐ nitrification
   ☐ assimilation
   ☐ ammonification
   ☐ denitrification

☐ **Phosphorus Cycle**

☐ **Sulfur Cycle**

☐ **Energy Flow**
   ☐ photosynthesis
   ☐ cellular respiration

☐ **Water Cycle**
   ☐ human impact on water cycle

☐ **Conservation of Matter and Energy**

MULTIPLE-CHOICE QUESTIONS

1. Which of the following is NOT a primary depository for the element listed?

   (A) Carbon—coal
   (B) Nitrogen—nitrogen gas in the atmosphere
   (C) Phosphorus—marble and limestone
   (D) Sulfur—deep ocean deposits
   (E) All are correct

2. Burning fossil fuels coupled with deforestation increases the amount of _____ in the atmosphere.

   (A) NO_2
   (B) CO_2
   (C) SO_2
   (D) O_3
   (E) All of the above are correct

3. In the nitrogen fixation cycle, cyanobacteria in the soil and water and *Rhizobium* bacteria in root systems are responsible for converting

   (A) organic material to ammonia and ammonium ions
   (B) ammonia, ammonium ions, and nitrate ions to DNA, amino acids, and proteins
   (C) ammonia and nitrite ions to nitrate ions
   (D) nitrogen and hydrogen gas to ammonia
   (E) ammonia to nitrite and nitrate ions

4. The cycle listed that has the most immediate effect on acid precipitation would be the

   (A) carbon cycle
   (B) sulfur cycle
   (C) water cycle
   (D) phosphorous cycle
   (E) rock cycle

5. Nitrogen is assimilated in plants in what form?

   (A) Nitrite, NO_2^-
   (B) Ammonia, NH_3
   (C) Ammonium, NH_4^+
   (D) Nitrate, NO_3^-
   (E) Choices B, C, and D

6. Plants assimilate sulfur primarily in what form?

   (A) Sulfates, SO_4^{2-}
   (B) Sulfites, SO_3^{2-}
   (C) Hydrogen sulfide, H_2S
   (D) Sulfur dioxide, SO_2
   (E) Elemental sulfur, S

7. Humans increase sulfur in the atmosphere and thereby increase acid deposition by all of the following activities EXCEPT

   (A) industrial processing
   (B) processing (smelting) ores to produce metals
   (C) burning coal
   (D) refining petroleum
   (E) clear-cutting

8. Phosphorus is being added to the environment by all of the following activities EXCEPT

   (A) runoff from feedlots
   (B) slashing and burning in tropical areas
   (C) stream runoff
   (D) burning coal and fossil fuels
   (E) mining to produce inorganic fertilizer

9. Carbon dioxide is a reactant in

   (A) photosynthesis
   (B) cellular respiration
   (C) the Haber-Bosch process
   (D) nitrogen fixation
   (E) None of the above

10. Human activity adds significant amounts of carbon dioxide to the atmosphere by all of the following EXCEPT

    (A) brush clearing
    (B) burning wood
    (C) burning fossil fuels
    (D) clear-cutting
    (E) agricultural runoff

11. Clearing of land for either habitation or agriculture does all of the following EXCEPT

    (A) increases runoff
    (B) increases flood risks
    (C) increases potential for landslides
    (D) increases infiltration
    (E) accelerates soil erosion

12. All of the following have an impact on the nitrogen cycle EXCEPT

    (A) the application of inorganic fertilizers applied to the soil
    (B) the action of aerobic bacteria acting on livestock wastes
    (C) the overplanting of nitrogen-rich crops
    (D) the discharge of municipal sewage
    (E) the burning of fossil fuels

13. Which of the following is a macronutrient essential for the formation of proteins?

    (A) Sulfur
    (B) Nitrogen
    (C) Iron
    (D) Cobalt
    (E) Molybdenum

14. Which of the following bacteria are able to convert soil nitrites to nitrates?
    (A) *Nitrosomonas*
    (B) *Nitrobacter*
    (C) *Rhizobium*
    (D) *Penicillium*
    (E) *Clostridium*

15. Which of the following cycles would be considered sedimentary?

    (A) Carbon cycle
    (B) Water cycle
    (C) Phosphorus cycle
    (D) Nitrogen cycle
    (E) Sulfur cycle

16. The cycle that is most common to all other cycles is the

    (A) nitrogen cycle
    (B) carbon cycle
    (C) hydrologic cycle
    (D) life cycle
    (E) the rock cycle

17. The energy that drives the hydrologic cycle comes primarily from

    (A) trade winds
    (B) solar energy and gravity
    (C) Earth's rotation on its axis
    (D) ocean currents and wind patterns
    (E) solar radiation

18. Which one of the following processes is working against gravity?

    (A) Precipitation
    (B) Percolation
    (C) Runoff
    (D) Transpiration
    (E) Infiltration

19. Ammonium ions (NH_4^+) are converted to nitrate (NO_3^-) and nitrite ions (NO_2^-) through which process?

    (A) Assimilation
    (B) Denitrification
    (C) Nitrogen fixation
    (D) Nitrification
    (E) Ammonification

20. Which form of nitrogen is most usable by plants?

    (A) Nitrate
    (B) Nitrite
    (C) Nitrogen gas
    (D) Ammonia
    (E) Atomic nitrogen

FREE-RESPONSE QUESTION

By: Sarah E. Utley
College Board APES Reader; Princeton, New Jersey
Environmental Content Specialist
Center for Digital Innovation
AP Environmental Science Division
University of California at Los Angeles

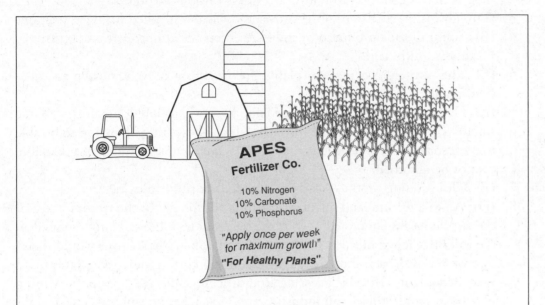

The APES Fertilizer Company manufactures a soil additive that contains 10% (w/v) of nitrogen, carbonate, and phosphorus. Use this information to answer the following questions.

(a) Choose either carbon or nitrogen and clearly explain the biogeochemical cycle of that nutrient. Include all of the important steps in the cycle and indicate movement from the atmosphere, water, and soil where necessary.

(b) Agricultural runoff from overapplication of fertilizers is a major source of water pollution. Choose either nitrogen or phosphorus and fully explain the cause and effect of this excess on the aquatic ecosystem.

(c) Rather than rely on the application of fertilizers, current agricultural research is encouraging the practice of more conservation-minded farming. Name and explain one such environmental practice that can decrease dependence on human-applied nutrients without causing a significant decrease in crop yield.

MULTIPLE-CHOICE ANSWERS AND EXPLANATIONS

1. **(C)** The primary sinks for phosphorus are ocean sediments and certain islands rich in guano.

2. **(B)** Burning fossil fuels releases sulfur oxides (SO_x), carbon oxides (carbon dioxide on complete combustion, or carbon monoxide on incomplete combustion) and nitrogen oxides (NO_x). Ozone is not produced by burning fossil fuels. Deforestation releases carbon dioxide. Since the question said "coupled," the gas that is common to both processes is carbon dioxide.

3. **(D)** This is the first step in the nitrogen cycle and is called nitrogen fixation.

4. **(B)** Sulfur dioxide produced by industry enters the atmosphere and returns to Earth as sulfuric acid.

5. **(E)** The nitrite ion is toxic to plants. In the nitrogen cycle, during assimilation, plant roots absorb nitrate.

6. **(A)** Hydrogen sulfide and sulfur dioxide are toxic to living organisms. Some sulfate compounds are soluble in water, which allows the sulfate ion to be able to be absorbed by plants. Elemental sulfur is not soluble in water and therefore cannot be absorbed.

7. **(E)** Clear-cutting produces carbon dioxide, not sulfur dioxide.

8. **(D)** Animal manure and guano are rich in phosphate. In the tropics, most of the nutrients are contained within the vegetation. Little is being retained in the soil since much of it leaches due to high rainfall. Phosphorus would therefore be released back into the environment by cutting down vegetation and then burning it—thereby releasing it and being subjected to runoff. Mining phosphates for fertilizer and industrial products takes phosphorus out of sinks and puts it into the environment. Burning coal and petroleum does not add appreciable amounts of phosphorus to the environment.

9. **(A)** The reaction for photosynthesis is $6CO_2 + 6H_2O + \text{sunlight} \rightarrow C_6H_{12}O_6 + 6O_2$. Cellular respiration is the reverse of photosynthesis.

10. **(E)** Agricultural runoff, primarily from fertilizers and feedlots, adds nitrates and phosphates to streams and results in cultural eutrophication. All other choices involve combustion, which produces carbon dioxide.

11. **(D)** Infiltration is the movement of water into the soil. Removing vegetation decreases infiltration by not allowing water to percolate through the soil slowly. Since runoff is increased, the potential for flooding increases. As the soil structure loses its integrity, the chances of landslides increase. Runoff also carries with it topsoil and nutrients, thus accelerating soil erosion.

12. **(B)** The bacteria that normally work to decompose livestock wastes are anaerobic, operate only in environments with little or no oxygen, and produce nitrous oxide (N_2O). Digesters can be constructed to reduce livestock wastes to methane gas (CH_4), which can then be burned as a fuel.

13. **(B)** The growth of all organisms depends on the availability of macro- and micronutrients, and none is more important than nitrogen, which is required in large amounts as an essential component of proteins, nucleic acids, and other cellular constituents.

14. **(B)** *Nitrosomonas* bacteria oxidize ammonia to nitrite: $NH_3 \rightarrow NO_2^-$. *Nitrobacter* then oxidize nitrite to nitrate: $NO_2^- \rightarrow NO_3^-$. Denitrifying bacteria anaerobically reduce nitrate to nitrogen gas: $NO_3^- \rightarrow N_2$.

15. **(C)** The largest reservoir of phosphorus is sedimentary rock. The phosphorus cycle originates with the introduction of phosphate (PO_4^{3-}) into soils from the weathering of rocks. Phosphate enters living ecosystems when plants take up phosphate ions from the soil.

16. **(C)** Water plays a part somewhere in every cycle.

17. **(B)** Solar energy allows water to change phase (water to gas, liquid to ice, etc.) and gravity causes rain to fall and rivers to flow.

18. **(D)** Transpiration is the process by which water moves upward (against gravity) from the soil through the roots and out through the leaves of plants.

19. **(D)** Nitrification is the biological oxidation of ammonia into nitrite ions followed by the oxidation of nitrites into nitrates. The oxidation of ammonia into nitrites is done by bacteria belonging to the genera *Nitrosomonas* and *Nitrosococcus*. The oxidation of nitrite ions into nitrate ions is done by bacteria belonging to the genus *Nitrobacter*.

20. **(A)** Nitrite and ammonia are more toxic to plants than nitrate. Plants cannot use nitrogen from the atmosphere directly.

FREE-RESPONSE ANSWER

Part (a): Maximum 5 points
Part (b): Maximum 3 points
Part (c): Maximum 2 points

Total: maximum 10 points

(a) Earth is a closed system. A finite amount of matter (such as life-supporting nutrients) is found in the biosphere. These nutrients cycle through Earth's varied support systems in different forms. Nitrogen, an essential nutrient for life, is found primarily in the atmosphere (making up 78% by volume). However, it also cycles through the lithosphere and the biomass of organisms. Unfortunately, the producers cannot absorb nitrogen in its most commonly found form, N_2. In order for this gaseous element to be used by living organisms, it has to be converted in a series of steps called the nitrogen cycle.

    The first step in the cycle is called nitrogen fixation. This is the process by which atmospheric nitrogen is converted to ammonia (NH_3). There are some natural sources of nitrogen fixing such as lightning and volcanoes. However, most of the biological fixing is done by nitrogen-fixing bacteria that live in the root nodules of certain plants called legumes, such as peas and clover. The nitrogen (N_2) is converted to ammonia (NH_3) using the enzyme nitrogenase.

    After the nitrogen is fixed into ammonia, it goes through a process called nitrification. This is a two-step process where special soil bacteria first convert the ammonia to nitrite (NO_2^-) and then to nitrate (NO_3^-), the form that plants can most easily absorb through their roots. Plants can also take up a limited amount of ammonia. The process by which the roots absorb the nitrate and ammonia is called assimilation. During this step, the plants incorporate nitrogen into their tissues. This absorbed nitrogen is used by plants to form nitrogen-containing molecules such as proteins and nucleic acids.

Notable points:

Movement through Earth's life support systems (atmosphere, lithosphere, biomass).

Introduction to nitrogen cycle.

Definition of nitrogen fixation.

Sources of fixation.

Next step— nitrification.

Definition of nitrification (step 1).

Definition of nitrification (step 2).

Next step in cycle— assimilation.

Next step in cycle— ammonification.

Next step in cycle— denitrification.

Final step in cycle—conversion into gaseous N₂.

Since animals cannot directly absorb nitrogen, they assimilate it into their body tissues when they eat plants or other animals. After animals absorb the nitrogen into their tissues, it is excreted as urea or uric acid. Uric acid is the end product of nitrogen metabolism in birds and reptiles. In humans and most other higher animals, the main product of nitrogen detoxification is urea. In fish, bacteria, and protozoa, it is ammonia. In those animals that do produce uric acid in high quantities, it is excreted in the feces as a dry mass. Although this compound is produced through a complex and energetically costly metabolic pathway (in comparison with the production of other nitrogenous wastes), its elimination minimizes water loss and is therefore commonly found in the excretions of animals that live in desert habitats.

In addition, when the organism dies, the nitrogen in the tissues is released back into the cycle. There nitrogen-containing substances are decomposed into ammonia in a process called ammonification. Then during denitrification, other bacteria convert the ammonia found in the soil into nitrate and nitrite. The nitrite and nitrate are further converted into gaseous nitrogen, which is then available to be refixed and used by other organisms.

Cause of the aquatic pollution.

Initial effect of excessive fertilizer.

Effect after initial algal bloom.

Result of overapplication of fertilizer.

Final result of excessive application.

(b) When fertilizers such as phosphorus are overapplied, rain or irrigation causes the excess fertilizer to run off into local waterways. Since phosphorus is often a limiting factor in aquatic ecosystems, this excess amount results in proliferation of algae and is known as an algal bloom. When these algal populations die, they are decomposed by large amounts of bacteria that consume much of the dissolved oxygen in the water. This, in turn, causes aquatic organisms to die from lack of oxygen. The result is a sterile lake or stream that lacks the nutrients necessary to support life.

Name of the conservation method.

Initial description of the method.

Further explanation of the conservation-minded agricultural method.

Reason why the crop yield will not decrease.

Further explanation of the yield maintenance.

(c) Conservation-minded agriculture can lead to a decreased dependence on human-applied nutrients. One of the most common, environmentally conscious agricultural practices is conservation or no-till farming. In this practice, the fields are not plowed under at the end of the growing season. The old stalks and vegetation are left on the fields over the winter. Then, in the spring, special machinery is used to plant the new crop on the untilled field. By leaving the previous season's biomass on the untilled land, the natural decomposition process can occur. The nutrients that would normally have been removed and lost are allowed to decompose back into the soil. This leads to a decreased need for artificial fertilizers without a loss of crop yield.

UNIT III: POPULATION
(10–15%)

Areas on Which You Will Be Tested

A. Population Biology Concepts—population ecology, carrying capacity, reproductive strategies, and survivorship.

B. Human Population—
1. Human population dynamics—historical population sizes, distribution, fertility rates, growth rates and doubling times, demographic transition, and age-structure diagrams.
2. Population size—strategies for sustainability, case studies, and national policies.
3. Impacts of population growth—hunger, disease, economic effects, resource use, habitat destruction.

Populations

CHAPTER 6

POPULATION BIOLOGY CONCEPTS

Several topics must be considered when discussing population biology:

- Population ecology
- Carrying capacity (K)
- Reproductive strategies
- Survivorship

Population Ecology

Population ecology studies the dynamics of species' populations and how these populations interact with the environment. Most organisms live in groups (flocks, schools, nests, etc.) and living in groups provides several advantages: increased protection from predators, increased chances for mating, and division of labor.

Population ecology plays an important role in the development of the field of conservation biology, especially in predicting the long-term probability of a species persisting in a given habitat. The following table lists those factors that affect population viability.

Carrying Capacity (*K*)

Carrying capacity refers to the number of organisms that can be supported in a given area sustainably. It varies from species to species and is subject to changes over time. As an environment degrades, the carrying capacity decreases. Factors that keep population sizes in balance with the carrying capacity are called regulating factors. They include food availability, space, oxygen content in aquatic ecosystems, nutrient levels in soil profiles, and the amount of sunlight. Below the carrying capacity, populations tend to increase in size. Population size cannot be sustained above the carrying capacity; eventually the population will crash.

A population's biotic potential is the maximum rate at which a population can grow. Its biotic potential, given optimal conditions (food, water, and space), occurs when resources are unlimited. Factors that influence biotic potential include age at reproduction, frequency of reproduction, number of offspring produced, reproductive life span, and average death rate under ideal conditions. If a population in a community is left unchecked, the maximum population growth rate can increase exponentially and takes on a J-shaped curve.

Factors That Affect Population Viability

Increase (+) Viability	Decrease (–) Viability
Favorable environmental conditions (light, temperature, and nutrients)	Unfavorable environmental conditions (insufficient light, temperature extremes, and/or poor supply of nutrients)
High birthrate	Low birthrate
Generalized niche	Specialized niche
Satisfactory habitat	Habitat not satisfactory or has been seriously impacted
Few competitors	Too many competitors
Suitable predatory defense mechanism(s)	Unsuitable predatory defense mechanism(s)
Adequate resistance to diseases and parasites	Little or no suitable defense mechanisms against diseases or parasites
Able to migrate	Unable to migrate
Flexible—able to adapt	Inflexible—unable to adapt
Sufficient food supply	Deficient food supply

Predation not only removes the very old, the very young, and the weaker members from the population, it may also reduce the population of the prey. If the predators do not keep the prey population in balance, the carrying capacity is exceeded and the prey may starve. Predator and prey populations are closely interdependent. Populations of algae, annual plants, and insects with short life spans are controlled by seasonal and nutritional environmental changes. A J-shaped growth curve may show a plunge in population as the reproductive potential declines because of environmental changes. The following year, there may be an exponential increase in the population.

Figure 6.1 J-shaped curve

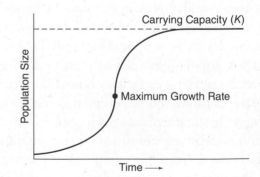

Figure 6.2 S-shaped curve (logistics model)

An S-shaped curve is used to describe the pattern of growth over extended periods of time when organisms move into an empty niche. Growth rates are density-dependent. They are characterized by maximum population growth rate and the carrying capacity. In an S-shaped curve, population size initially increases due to unlimited resources for a small population. However, as resources become limited, the population growth rate slows down and stabilizes around the limits of the carrying capacity at the point where the birthrate equals the death rate. The average American's ecological footprint (the demand of an individual with an average amount of resources) is about 12 acres.

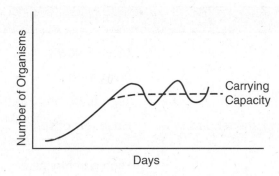

Figure 6.3 Fluctuations around the carrying capacity

Thomas Malthus

Thomas Malthus was a political economist who was concerned about what he saw as the decline of living conditions in 19th-century England. He blamed this decline on three elements: (1) the overproduction of young; (2) the inability of resources to keep up with the rising human population; and (3) the irresponsibility of the lower classes. To combat this, Malthus suggested the family size of the lower class ought to be regulated such that poor families do not produce more children than they can support. In his 1798 work, *Essay on Population*, Malthus hypothesized that unchecked population growth always exceeds the means of supporting a larger population. He argued that actual population growth is kept in line with food supply by "positive checks" such as starvation and disease, which elevate the death rate, and by "preventive checks" (e.g., postponement of marriage), which keep down the birthrate. Malthus's hypothesis implied that actual population growth always has the tendency to push above the available food supply. Because of this tendency, any attempt to correct the condition of the lower classes by increasing their living standards or improving agricultural productivity would not be possible, as any extra means of subsistence would be completely absorbed by an increase in the population. Charles Darwin incorporated some of Malthus's ideas into his 1859 book, *On the Origin of Species*, by stating that limited resources result in competition, with those organisms that survive being able to pass on those adaptations through their genes to their offspring.

Reproductive Strategies

Organisms have adapted either to maximize growth rates in environments that lack limits or to maintain population size at close to the carrying capacity in stable environments. Species that have high reproductive rates are known as *r*-strategists. Species that reproduce later in life and with fewer offspring are known as *K*-strategists.

Reproductive Strategies

r-Strategists	*K*-Strategists
Mature rapidly	Mature slowly
Short lived	Long lived
Tend to be prey	Tend to be both predator and prey
Have many offspring and tend to overproduce	Have few offspring
Low parental care	High parental care
Are generally not endangered	Most endangered species are *K*-strategists
Wide fluctuations in population density (booms and busts)	Population size stabilizes near the carrying capacity
Population size limited by density-independent limiting factors, including climate, weather, natural disasters, and requirements for growth	Density-dependent limiting factors to population growth stem from intra-specific competition and include competition, predation, parasitism, and migration
Tend to be small	Tend to be larger
Type III survivorship curve	Type I or II survivorship curve
Examples: most insects, algae, bacteria, rodents, and annual plants	Examples: humans, elephants, cacti, and sharks

Survivorship

Survivorship curves show age distribution characteristics of species, reproductive strategies, and life history. Reproductive success is measured by how many organisms are able to mature and reproduce. Each survivorship curve represents a balance between natural resource limitations and interspecific and intraspecific competition. For example, humans could not survive in a Type III survivorship mode, where human females would produce thousands of offspring. Likewise, ants could not survive in a Type I mode, where each queen ant would produce only a few eggs during her lifetime and where she would spent most of her time and energy raising offspring.

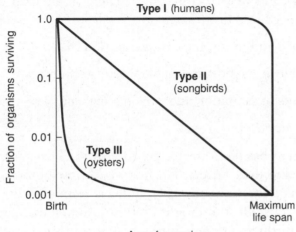

Figure 6.4 Survivorship curve

Survivorship Curves

Type	Description
I Late Loss	Reproduction occurs fairly early in life. Most deaths occur at the limit of biological life span. Low mortality at birth; high probability of surviving to advanced age. Death rates increase during old age. Advances in prenatal care, nutrition, disease prevention, and cures including immunization have meant longer life spans for humans. Examples: humans, annual plants, sheep, and elephants.
II Constant Loss	Individuals in all age categories have fairly uniform death rates. Predation affecting all age categories is primary means of death. Typical of organisms that reach adult stages quickly. Examples: rodents, perennial plants, and songbirds.
III Early Loss	Typical of species that have great numbers of offspring and reproduce for most of their lifetime. Death is prevalent for younger members of the species (environmental loss and predation) and declines with age. Examples: sea turtles, trees, internal parasites, fish, and oysters.

HUMAN POPULATION DYNAMICS

Many different factors affect the human population: historical population sizes, population distribution, fertility rates, growth rates, doubling times, and demographic transition. Age-structure diagrams act as indicators of future population trends.

Historical Population Sizes

The rapid growth of the world's human population over the past 100 years has been due primarily to a decrease in death rates. In 1900, the overall death rate in the United States was 1.7%. In 2000, the death rate had dropped to 0.9% (almost half). Children in 1900 were 10 times more likely to die than children in 2000. Several factors have reduced death rates:

1. Increased food and more efficient distribution that result in better nutrition

2. Improvements in medical and public health technology

3. Improvements in sanitation and personal hygiene

4. Safer water supplies

Human population has had three surges in growth. These surges in population have been attributed to three factors: The first was the use of tools and fire. The second was the agricultural revolution, when humans stopped being hunter-gatherers and began to raise crops. The third was the industrial and medical revolutions within the last 200 years. Birthrate or crude birthrate is equal to the number of live births per 1,000 members of the population in one year. Death rate or crude death rate is equal to the number of deaths per 1,000 members of the population in one year. Immigration refers to the number of individuals that enter the population, while emigration refers to the number of individuals that leave the population. Population change can be calculated from the following formula:

Population change = (crude birthrate + immigration) – (crude death rate + emigration)

EXAMPLE

In 1950, the population of a small suburb in Los Angeles, California, was 20,000. The birthrate was measured at 25 per 1,000 population per year, while the death rate was measured at 7 per 1,000 population per year. Immigration was measured at 600 per year, while emigration was measured at 200 per year. By how much did the population increase (or decrease) in that year?

Answer:

Population change = (crude birthrate + immigration) – (crude death rate + emigration)

$$= (25(20) + 600) \quad - \quad (7(20) + 200)$$

$$= +760$$

The population grew from 20,000 to 20,760 in one year.

The actual rate of population change can be determined by using the following formula:

$$\text{Actual growth rate (\%)} = \frac{\text{birthrate} - \text{death rate}}{10}$$

EXAMPLE

The United States had a birthrate of 14.6 live births per 1,000 population in one year, compared to India's birthrate of 22.2 in that same year. The death rate in that year for the United States was 8.3 deaths per 1,000 population, compared to India's rate of 6.4. Calculate the population growth rates (%) for both the United States and India for that year.

Answer:

$$\text{United States: } \frac{\text{birthrate} - \text{death rate}}{10} = \frac{14.6 - 8.3}{10} = 0.6$$

$$\text{India: } \frac{\text{birthrate} - \text{death rate}}{10} = \frac{22.2 - 6.4}{10} = 1.6$$

A current world growth rate of approximately 1.3% when applied to the about 7 billion people on Earth yields an annual increase of about 85 million people. Because of the large and increasing population size, the number of people added to the global population will remain high for several decades, even if growth rates decline.

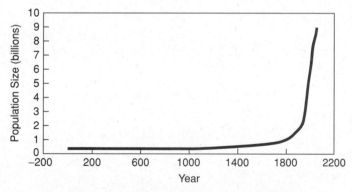

Figure 6.5 Estimated human population growth from 200 B.C.E. to 2200 C.E.

Distribution

In 1800, the vast majority of the world's population (65%) resided in Asia and Europe. By 1900, 25% of the human population lived in Europe largely due to the Industrial Revolution. Between 2000 and 2030, most of the growth will occur in the less-developed countries in Africa, Asia, and Latin America whose growth rates are much higher than those in more-developed countries. The more-developed countries in Europe and North America will have growth rates less than 1%. Some countries such as Russia, Germany, Italy, and Japan will even experience negative growth rates.

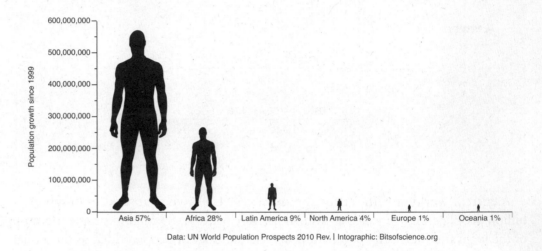

Data: UN World Population Prospects 2010 Rev. | Intographic: Bitsofscience.org

Figure 6.6 Distribution of the last billion people on Earth

Human Population Growth

Time Period	Description	Practicing Worldview
Before Agricultural Revolution	~ 1 million to 3 million humans. Hunter-gatherer lifestyle.	**Earth Wisdom**—Natural cycles that can serve as a model for human behavior.
8000 B.C.E. to 5000 B.C.E.	~ 50 million humans. Increases due to advances in agriculture, domestication of animals, and the end of a nomadic lifestyle.	
5000 B.C.E. to 1 B.C.E.	~ 200 million humans. Rate of population growth during this period was about 0.03 to 0.05%, compared with today's growth rate of 1.3%.	**Frontier Worldview**—Viewed undeveloped land as a hostile wilderness to be cleared and planted, then exploited for its resources as quickly as possible.
0 C.E. to 1300 C.E.	~ 500 million humans. Population rate increased during the Middle Ages because new habitats were discovered. Factors that reduced population growth rate during this time were famines, wars, and disease (density-dependent factors).	
1300 C.E. to 1650 C.E.	~ 600 million humans. Plagues reduced population growth rate. Up to 25% mortality rates are attributed to the plagues that reached their peak in the mid-1600s.	
1650 C.E. to present	Currently ~ 6 billion humans. In 1650 C.E. growth rate was ~ 0.1%. Today it is ~ 1.3%. Health care, health insurance, vaccines, medical cures, preventative care, advanced drugs and antibiotics, improvements in hygiene and sanitation, advances in agriculture and distribution, and education are factors that have increased the growth rate.	**Planetary Management**—Beliefs that as the planet's most important species, we are in charge of Earth; we will not run out of resources because of our ability to develop and find new ones; the potential for economic growth is essentially unlimited; and our success depends on how well we manage Earth's life-support systems mostly for our own benefit.
Present to 2050 C.E.	Estimates are as high as ~ 15 billion.	**Earth Wisdom**—Beliefs that nature exists for all Earth's species and we are not in charge of the Earth; resources are limited and should not be wasted. We should encourage Earth-sustaining forms of economic growth and discourage Earth-degrading forms of economic growth; and our success depends on learning how Earth sustains itself and integrating such lessons from nature into the ways we think and act.

Fertility Rates

Replacement level fertility (RLF) is the level of fertility at which a couple has only enough children to replace themselves, or about 2 children per couple. It takes a RLF of 2.1 to replace each generation since some children will die before they grow up to have their own two children. RLF rates are lower in moderately developed countries (MDC) and higher in less-developed countries (LDC) due to higher infant mortality rates in LDCs. Infant mortality rates are good indicators of comparative standards of living. The total fertility rate (TFR) is the average number of children that each woman will have during her lifetime. The country of Niger in Africa leads the world's TFR at 7.68.

Worldwide Total Fertility Rate	
Country	**TFR**
Niger	7.68
India	2.65
Israel	2.72
Mexico	2.31
United States	2.06
China	1.54
Russia	1.54
Japan	1.21
World average	**2.59**

Despite half of the world's population having subreplacement fertility rates, the world's population is still growing quickly. This growth is due to nations with above-replacement TFRs and a population momentum caused by large numbers of younger females who have as yet not had children.

Declines in fertility rates can be attributed to several factors. Urbanization results in a higher cost of living. Urbanization reduces the need for extra children to work on farms. There is a greater personal acceptance and government encouragement of contraception and abortion. The numbers of females in the workforce and female educational opportunities are increasing. More individuals desire to increase their standard of living by having less children. Many people are postponing marriage until their careers are established.

The two main effects of TFRs less than 2.1 without additions through immigration are population decline and population aging. In the United States the TFR has been inconsistent. The greatest TFR occurred during the post-World War II years (baby boomers). New immigrants and their descendants are projected to contribute 66% of the expected growth by 2050.

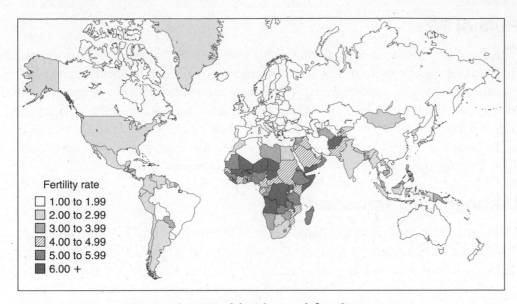

Figure 6.7 Worldwide total fertility rates

Growth Rates and Doubling Times

The 20th century saw the largest increase in the world's population in human history. The following chart shows the doubling times of the world's population:

950 C.E. to 1600	650 years
1600 to 1800	200 years
1800 to 1925	125 years
1925 to 1975	50 years
1975 to 2025	50 years

Note that the doubling times from 1925 to 1975 and projected from 1975 to 2025 remain constant. This does NOT mean that the world is not increasing in population—it means that the growth *rate* has decreased as shown in the following figure.

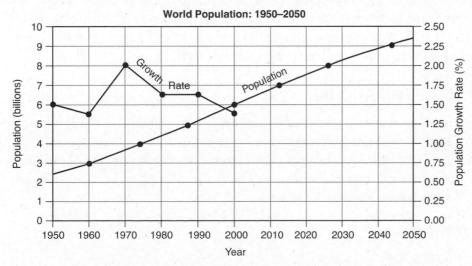

Source: U.S. Census Bureau. International Data Base, December 2010 Update

Figure 6.8 Yearly growth rate of human population (1950–2050)

Rule of 70

The Rule of 70 is a useful rule of thumb that roughly explains the time periods involved in exponential growth at a constant rate. To find the doubling time of a quantity growing at a given annual percentage rate, divide the percentage number into 70 to obtain the approximate number of years required to double. For example, at a 2% annual growth rate, doubling time is 70 / 2 = 35 years.

To find the annual growth rate, divide 70 by the doubling time. For example, 70 / 35 years doubling time = 2, or a 2% annual growth rate.

Demographic Transition

Demographic transition is the name given to the process that has occurred during the past century. It leads to a stabilization of population growth in the more highly developed countries and is generally characterized as having four separate stages: preindustrial, transitional, industrial, and postindustrial.

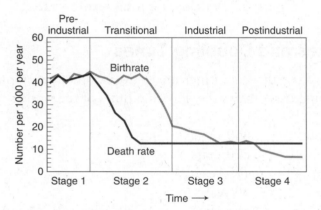

Figure 6.9 Demographic transitions occurring in human populations.

STAGE 1: PRE-INDUSTRIAL

Living conditions are severe, medical care is poor or nonexistent, and the food supply is limited due to poor agricultural techniques, preservation, and pestilence. Birthrates are high to replace individuals lost through high mortality rates. The net result is little population growth. Many countries in sub-Saharan Africa have reverted back to this stage due to the increase of AIDS.

STAGE 2: TRANSITIONAL

This stage occurs after the start of industrialization. Standards of hygiene, advances in medical care, improved sanitation, cleaner water supplies, vaccination, and higher levels of education begin to drive down the death rate, leading to a significant upward trend in population size. The net result is a rapid increase in population. Examples include India, Pakistan, and Mexico.

STAGE 3: INDUSTRIAL

Urbanization decreases the economic incentives for large families. The cost of supporting an urban family grows, and parents are more actively discouraged from having large families. Educational and work opportunities for women decrease birthrates. Obtaining food is not a major focus of the day. Leisure time is available. Retirement safety nets are in place, reducing the need for extra children to support parents. In response to these economic pressures, the birthrate starts to drop, ultimately coming close to the death rate. An example is China.

STAGE 4: POST-INDUSTRIAL

Birthrates equal mortality rates, and zero population growth is achieved. Birth and death rates are both relatively low, and the standard of living is much higher than during the earlier periods. In some countries, birthrates may actually fall below mortality rates and result in net losses in population. Examples of declining populations include Russia, Japan, and many European countries. The developed world currently remains in this fourth stage of demographic transition.

STAGE 5: SUB-REPLACEMENT FERTILITY

The original demographic transition model has just four stages; however, some theorists consider that a fifth stage is needed to represent countries that have sub-replacement fertility (that is, below 2.1 children per woman). Most European and many East Asian countries now have higher death rates than birthrates. In this stage, population aging and population decline will eventually occur to some extent, presuming that sustained mass immigration does not occur.

Age-Structure Diagrams

A good indicator of future trends in population growth is furnished by age-structure diagrams. Age-structure diagrams are determined by birthrate, generation time, death rate, and sex ratios. There are three major age groups in a population: pre-reproductive, reproductive, and post-reproductive. A pyramid-shaped age structure diagram (i.e., Nigeria) indicates the population has high birthrates and the majority of the population is in the reproductive age group (generally late teens to mid-40s). A bell-shape indicates that pre-reproductive and reproductive age groups are more nearly equal, with the post-reproductive group being smallest due to mortality; this is characteristic of stable populations (i.e., United States). An urn-shaped diagram indicates the post-reproductive group is largest and the pre-reproductive group is smallest, a result of the birthrate falling below the death rate and is characteristic of declining populations (i.e., Germany).

The age-structure diagrams in the figure below show age distributions of less-developed countries compared with more developed countries. When the base is large (greater number of younger individuals in the population), there is a potential for an increase in the population as these younger individuals mature and have children of their own (population momentum). When the top of the pyramid is larger, it indicates a large segment of the population is past their reproductive years (post-reproductive) and indicates a future slowdown in population growth. Age-structure diagrams reflect demographic transitions.

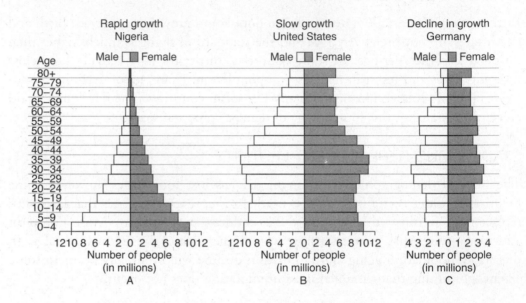

Figure 6.10 Age structure diagrams for countries with rapid, slow, and declining birthrates

In Mexico, large family size is due to the necessity for farm labor, the need to support parents when they no longer work, a need to increase family income, and cultural and religious beliefs. The death rate has declined due to social and medical programs. However, the birthrate continues to remain high.

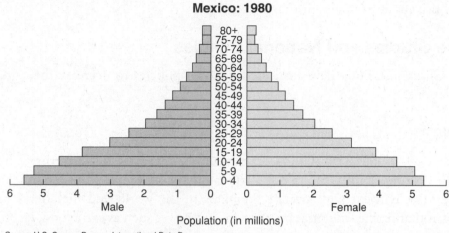

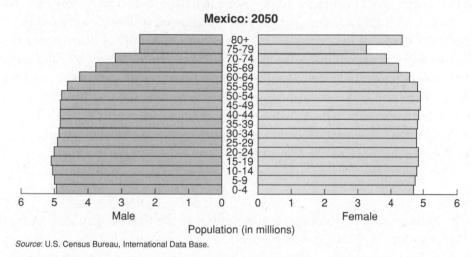

Figure 6.11 Age structure in Mexico, 1980 and 2050 (estimated)

POPULATION SIZE

This section discusses several strategies to sustain population size. It then provides a few case studies.

Strategies for Sustainability

- Provide economic incentives for having fewer children.
- Empower and educate women. The low status of women is the number one problem.
- Education usually leads to higher incomes. Higher incomes decrease the need for having extra children to take care of older parents.
- Higher education usually results in having children later in life.

- Provide government family planning services. These practices have ranged from education and birth control to sterilization and abortion.
- Improve prenatal and infant health care. Women would not need more children if the ones they had survived.
- Increase economic development in less-developed countries through free trade and private investment with tax incentives.

Case Studies and National Policies

Both China and India have instituted national policies to decrease their growing populations.

CHINA

Between 1972 and 2000, China dramatically reduced its crude birthrate by half (the TFR dropped from 5.7 to 1.8). The family planning program in China is one of the most efficient and strictest programs in the world and includes a mobile program that reaches the rural population. Incentives such as extra food, larger pensions, better housing, free medical care, free school tuition, and salary bonuses for parents who limit their number of children are responsible for the success of this program. Couples are encouraged to postpone marriage and to have only one child. (If the first child is female, then the parents are allowed to have another child and still retain the financial incentives.) After a mother's first child is born, a woman is required to wear an intrauterine device. Removal of the device is a crime subject to sterilization. Physicians receive bonuses for sterilization procedures. Couples are punished for refusing to terminate unapproved pregnancies and for giving birth under the legal marriage age. Penalties include fines (up to 50% of their yearly salary), loss of land, less food, a decrease in farm supplies, loss of government benefits, and/or discharge from the Communist Party.

INDIA

In 1952, India (with a population of 400 million at the time) began its first family planning program. In 2000, India's population was 1 billion, or 16% of the world's population. Each day there are 50,000 live births in India. One-third of the population of India earns less than 40 cents per day, and cropland has decreased 50% per capita since 1960. In the 1970s, India instituted a mandatory sterilization program involving vasectomies. Some of the reasons for India's failures were poor planning, low status of women, favoring male children, and insensitivity to cultures and religion. Tubal ligation is the preferred method of family planning in India today. Condoms are free from the Indian government but have less than 10% use. Other birth control methods are usually accepted by only the upper/educated class.

IMPACTS OF POPULATION GROWTH

When left unchecked, population growth often results in hunger. Diseases and economics also affect population growth.

Hunger

A large portion of the world's population—25%—is malnourished. Areas of greatest malnutrition are Africa, Asia, and parts of Latin America. Consequently, these are areas with the highest TFRs. Several factors contribute to malnutrition.

1. Poverty

2. Droughts, which will only increase as the impact of global warming becomes more severe

3. Populations that have surpassed their carrying capacity

4. Political instability and wars, which cause mass migrations

5. Pestilence

6. Foreign investors who own large landholdings and whose sole motivation is profit (selling the food to the highest bidder, which often means exporting it)

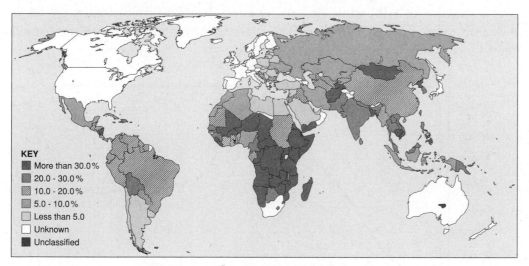

KEY
- More than 30.0%
- 20.0 - 30.0%
- 10.0 - 20.0%
- 5.0 - 10.0%
- Less than 5.0
- Unknown
- Unclassified

Figure 6.12 Worldwide malnutrition

Advances made during the first and second green revolutions (which focused on food production) are not ending world famine. In India, Mexico, and the Philippines, where large advances were made in crop production, famine is still common. Exports from these and other poor countries caused by distributors receiving higher profits from richer countries is actually making famine worse. Profit motives result in removing food from countries that grow it and sending the food to other countries that are able to pay higher prices.

Large-scale agribusiness or corporate ownership of farmland will not solve world hunger. Land reform in Japan, Zimbabwe, Taiwan, and Brazil has redistributed land into smaller holdings. It has also raised agricultural output an average of 80%.

The issue of malnutrition is not that the world does not produce enough food. The issue is that too many people cannot afford it or that it is not distributed efficiently. Enough wheat, rice, and grain are produced on Earth each day to provide each human with 3,500 calories per day (2,500 calories is the minimum daily requirement for men, and 2,000 calories is the minimum daily requirement for women). This does not even include vegetables, beans, nuts, meats, and fish processed each day. If all food grown and raised on Earth was distributed equally, it would result in 4.3 pounds (2 kg) per person per day.

Disease and Economic Impact

This section discusses how disease and economic realities affect population growth.

AIDS

In the United States, more than half a million people have died from complications arising from AIDS since 1981. An estimated 15,000 currently die annually according to the Federal Centers for Disease Control and Prevention. More than 1 million people in the United States are living with the virus, and 40,000 become infected each year. African-Americans, who make up approximately 13% of the U.S. population, account for half of new U.S. infections and a third of all AIDS-related deaths. African-American males are 7 times more likely as Caucasian males to be infected with HIV, while African-American females are 20 times more likely to be infected as Caucasian females. The fastest growing population in the United States for new infections are 15 to 24 years old.

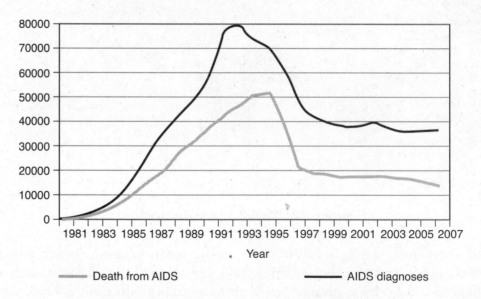

Figure 6.13 AIDS diagnoses and death rates in the United States between 1981–2007

AIDS—WORLDWIDE

In 2009, 33 million people around the world were living with HIV/AIDS. More than 60 million people have been infected with HIV and 25 million people have died of AIDS since the pandemic began in the early 1980s with currently over

7,000 new HIV infections occurring each day. AIDS is the leading cause of death in sub-Saharan Africa and the fourth leading cause of death globally with 5,000 people worldwide dying each day due to AIDS. About half of all new adult HIV infections occur among 15–24-year-olds. Approximately 97% of people living with HIV/AIDS live in low- and middle-income countries. Sub-Saharan Africa is the hardest-hit region and is home to two-thirds of all people living with HIV worldwide. Parts of Asia and Latin America are experiencing severe epidemics at the national or local level. Eastern Europe and central Asia is the region with the fastest growing HIV/AIDS epidemic in the world.

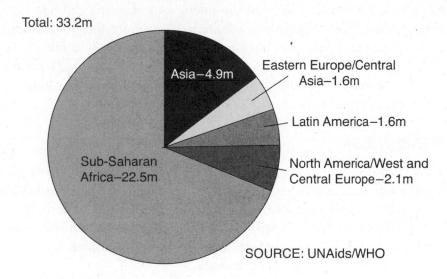

Figure 6.14 People living with HIV (by region)

AIDS—ECONOMIC IMPACT

For many less-developed countries with higher incidences of HIV-AIDS, the disease affects economic growth by reducing human capital. Those infected require significant medical care straining emerging economies. Higher mortality rates also creates a smaller skilled labor force, which results in a smaller tax base, which in turn reduces the resources available for public expenditures such as education, other health care services, etc. On the level of the household, AIDS results in both the loss of income and increased costs for medical care.

Worldwide, at least 25 million people have died from AIDS, and 2.8 million died in 2006, according to the World Health Organization. AIDS could kill 31 million people in India and 18 million in China by 2025, according to projections by U.N. population researchers. The toll from AIDS over the next 25 years will go far beyond the 34 million people thought to have died from the bubonic plague in the 14th century or the 20 to 40 million people who perished in the 1918 Spanish flu pandemic. AIDS is the leading cause of death in Africa, which has accounted for nearly half of all global AIDS deaths.

The epidemic is still growing. Its peak could be a decade or more away. In at least seven countries, the U.N. estimates that AIDS has reduced life expectancy to 40 years or less. Botswana has the highest HIV prevalence in the world; 36% of the country's 1.6 million people are HIV positive. AIDS experts predict that in the next few years, more than 50% of Botswana's children will be AIDS orphans and the average life expectancy will have fallen from 47 years to 27 years.

PANDEMICS

The Spanish influenza pandemic of 1918 to 1919 killed somewhere between 20 and 40 million people worldwide, with 28% of all Americans infected. It has been cited as the most devastating pandemic in recorded world history. More people died of Spanish influenza in a single year than in the four years of the plague from 1347 to 1351. The flu was most deadly for people ages 20 to 40. This was unusual for influenza, which is normally a killer of the elderly and of young children.

According to the World Health Organization, if a mutant form of bird flu virus (H5N1) develops that could pass from person to person, it could kill as many as 7 million people worldwide and infect nearly one-third of the world's population. Infectious disease experts fear the virus may mutate within a pig that harbors both human and avian forms of the flu virus.

OTHER DISEASES

The World Health Organization estimates that by 2020, tobacco-related illnesses, including heart disease, cancer, and respiratory disorders, will be the world's leading killer. They will be responsible for more deaths than AIDS, tuberculosis, road accidents, murder, and suicide combined. In 2005, estimated losses in national income from heart disease, strokes, and diabetes was $18 billion in China, $11 billion in the Russian Federation, and $9 billion in India.

Tuberculosis is the leading cause of death in many poorer countries. Its economic impact on global economies is estimated to be $12 billion.

Each year, approximately 500 million malaria infections lead to over 1 million deaths, 75% of which occur among children living in Africa. Mortality rates due to malaria are rising among young children, and drug therapies that were once fairly effective in treating malaria are becoming less effective as newer strains become more drug-resistant.

Resource Use and Habitat Destruction

Three methods are used to estimate the effects of humans on patterns of resource utilization: measure net primary productivity, estimate how much impact humans have had on Earth, and examine finite resources and from that draw conclusions on increasing productivity. Net primary productivity (NPP) is the total amount of solar energy converted into biochemical energy through photosynthesis minus the energy needed by those plants for their own metabolic requirements. It is a quantifiable measure of resources available on Earth. The NPP without human activity has been estimated to be 150 billion tons of organic matter per year. Human activity has caused a 12% decline in the NPP due to deforestation. Humans utilize about 27% of the NPP for their own purposes (food, building material, energy, and so on) or by converting productive land to nonproductive purposes. When added up, humans utilize about 40% of the NPP and leave all other life on Earth with 60%. The difference grows with the ever-increasing human population growth.

Of the NPP of the oceans, about 8% is utilized for human purposes. In nutrient-rich upwelling areas, humans utilize about 25%. In temperate continental shelf waters, humans utilize approximately 35% of the NPP.

If humans utilized 100% of the NPP (leaving nothing for all other life-forms on Earth), the theoretical maximum sustainable human population at 100% of the carrying capacity would be 15 billion people—which could be achieved during the 21st century. In this scenario, every square centimeter of Earth would be utilized for human needs. The following table lists factors that affect resource utilization.

Factors That Affect Resource Utilization

Factor	Description
Carrying capacity	See the section "Carrying Capacity (K)" in this chapter.
Energy resources	One average American consumes as much energy as 500 Ethiopians or 35 people from India.
Environmental degradation	Due to increased population size, erosion, desertification, pollution, impact on the ozone layer, and gases that contribute to global warming all increase.
Exploitation of natural resources as a function of gross domestic product	The richest 20% of the world's population contribute to resource depletion of energy and raw materials through overconsumption. This, in turn, leads to disproportionate amounts of pollution. The poorest 20% of the world's population are forced to deplete resources by being forced to cut down forests, clear land, and farm marginal land.
Extinction of animal and plant species	Close to 50% of all species of animals and plants on Earth could be on a path toward extinction within 100 years. 11% of all bird species and 13% of all plant species are at risk for extinction.
Famine	See the section "Hunger" in this chapter.
Political unrest	Affects employment, food distribution and standard of living that, in turn, affect utilization of resources.
Population density	Density, more than population size, has a greater effect on the amount of pollution and use of energy.
Population size	Large numbers of people lead to high rates of habitat loss and natural resource depletion.
Poverty	20% of the world's richest countries control 80% of the world's wealth. The poorest 20% of the world's population controls just 1.5% of the world's economic resources.
Technological development	More-developed countries consume more resources than less-developed countries. The United States represents about 5% of the world's population but consumes 25% of the world's resources and generates 25% of the world's waste.

TIP

Do NOT start preparing for the APES exam a few weeks ahead of time. The APES exam is actually one of the toughest AP Exams given. In 2011, half of all students taking the exam received a 1 or 2. Pace yourself and be sure to get lots of rest before the exam day. Don't just read the practice essays in this book— write them out.

QUICK REVIEW CHECKLIST

- [ ] **Population Biology Concepts**
  - [ ] population ecology
  - [ ] factors that affect population viability
  - [ ] carrying capacity
  - [ ] J-curves
  - [ ] S-curves
  - [ ] reproductive strategies
    - [ ] *r*-strategists
    - [ ] *K*-strategists
  - [ ] survivorship
    - [ ] survivorship curves
      - [ ] Type I
      - [ ] Type II
      - [ ] Type III

- [ ] **Human Population Dynamics**
  - [ ] historical population sizes
  - [ ] calculating population change
    - [ ] crude birthrate
    - [ ] crude death rate
    - [ ] immigration
    - [ ] emigration
  - [ ] distribution

- [ ] **Fertility Rates**
  - [ ] replacement fertility rate (RLF)
  - [ ] total fertility rate
  - [ ] growth rates
  - [ ] doubling time

- [ ] **Demographic Transition**
  - [ ] stage 1
  - [ ] stage 2
  - [ ] stage 3
  - [ ] stage 4

- [ ] **Age Structure Diagrams**

- [ ] **Population Size**
  - [ ] strategies for sustainability

- [ ] **Case Studies**
  - [ ] China
  - [ ] India

QUICK REVIEW CHECKLIST (continued)

☐ **Impacts of Population Growth**
    ☐ hunger
    ☐ disease and economic impact
        ☐ AIDS
        ☐ pandemics
        ☐ other diseases

☐ **Resource Use and Habitat Destruction**
    ☐ factors that affect resource utilization

MULTIPLE-CHOICE QUESTIONS

1. Which would be least likely to be affected by a density-dependent limiting factor?

    (A) A small, scattered population
    (B) A population with a high birthrate
    (C) A large, dense population
    (D) A population with a high immigration rate
    (E) None of the above

2. A population showing a growth rate of 20, 40, 60, 80 . . . would be characteristic of
    (A) logarithmic growth
    (B) exponential growth
    (C) static growth
    (D) arithmetic (linear) growth
    (E) power curve growth

3. If a population doubles in about 70 years, it is showing a ____ % growth rate.

    (A) 1
    (B) 5
    (C) 35
    (D) 140
    (E) 200

4. An island off Costa Rica includes 500 birds of a particular species. Population biologists determined that this bird population was isolated with no immigration or emigration. After one year, the scientists were able to count 60 births and 10 deaths. The net growth for this population was

   (A) 0.5
   (B) 0.9
   (C) 1.0
   (D) 1.1
   (E) 1.5

5. Afghanistan has a current growth rate of 4.8%, representing a doubling time of approximately

   (A) 4.8 years
   (B) 9.6 years
   (C) 14.5 years
   (D) 35 years
   (E) 70 years

6. Biotic potential refers to

   (A) an estimate of the maximum capacity of living things to survive and reproduce under optimal environmental conditions
   (B) the proportion of the population of each sex at each age category
   (C) the ratio of total live births to total population
   (D) a factor that influences population growth and that increases in magnitude with an increase in the size or density of the population
   (E) events and phenomena of nature that act to keep population sizes stable

7. The number of children an average woman would have, assuming that she livers her full reproductive lifetime, is known as the
   (A) birthrate
   (B) crude birthrate
   (C) TFR
   (D) RLF
   (E) zero population growth rate

8. The average American's ecological footprint is approximately

   (A) the size of a shoe
   (B) 0.5 acres
   (C) 3 acres
   (D) 6 acres
   (E) 12 acres

9. Which of the following statements is FALSE?

   (A) The United States, while having only 5% of the world's population, consumes 25% of the world's resources.
   (B) Up to 50% of all plants and animals could become extinct within the next 100 years.
   (C) In 1990, 20% of the world's population controlled 80% of the world's wealth.
   (D) Every second, five people are born and two people die, a net gain of three people.
   (E) They are all true statements.

10. Pronatalists (people in favor of having many children) would include all of the following EXCEPT

   (A) many children die early due to health and environmental conditions
   (B) children are expensive and time intensive
   (C) children provide extra income for families
   (D) children provide security for parents when the parents reach old age
   (E) status of the family is often determined by the number of children

11. The most successful method of controlling a country's population has been

   (A) required sterilization
   (B) government quotas on children produced
   (C) birth control
   (D) financial incentives
   (E) All of the above

12. The following age-structure diagram would be typical of

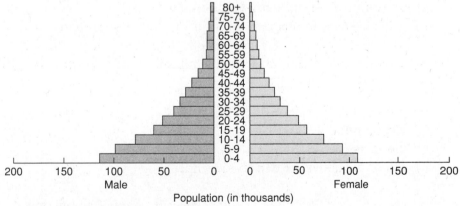

Source: U.S. Census Bureau, International Data Base.

   (A) Russia
   (B) China
   (C) the United States
   (D) Niger or Peru
   (E) Canada

13. Examine the following age-structure diagram.

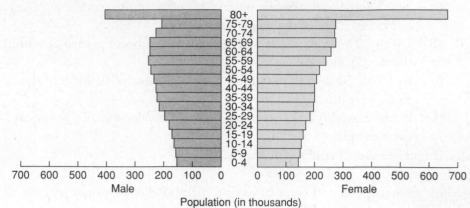

Source: U.S. Census Bureau, International Data Base.

This population will be

(A) declining rapidly in the future
(B) growing slowly in the future
(C) remaining stable
(D) growing rapidly in the future
(E) declining slowly in the future

14. Which of the following examples does NOT demonstrate a density-dependent factor affecting the population size?

(A) The "black plagues" that occurred in Europe during the mid 14th century and which are estimated to have killed up to ⅓ of the European population
(B) The number of lions inhabiting a grassland in Africa
(C) Tropical plants located near the ground in a tropical rain forest
(D) An outbreak of influenza in a hospital
(E) The destruction of a rain forest in Brazil due to drought

15. Density-independent factors would include all of the following EXCEPT

(A) drought
(B) fires
(C) predation
(D) flooding
(E) All of the above are density-dependent

16. Between 1963 and 2000, the rate of the world's annual population change _____ but the human population size _____ .

(A) dropped 40%; rose 90%
(B) rose 90%; dropped 40%
(C) dropped 90%; rose 40%
(D) remained stable; tripled
(E) rose 40%; dropped 2.9%

17. RLF for a couple is

   (A) 1.0
   (B) 2.0
   (C) 2.1
   (D) 3.0
   (E) varies depending on country

18. Which of the following factors is associated with the highest potential for population growth?

   (A) High percentage of people under age 18
   (B) High percentage of people in their 30s
   (C) High percentage of people in their 50s
   (D) High percentage of people in high-income groups
   (E) High percentage of people in low-income groups

19. Using the demographic transition model, what stage would be characteristic of death rates falling while birthrates remain high?

   (A) Preindustrial
   (B) Industrial
   (C) Postindustrial
   (D) Transitional
   (E) None of the above

20. All of the following factors tend to cause women to have fewer children EXCEPT

   (A) higher education
   (B) high infant mortality
   (C) better prenatal care
   (D) birth control education
   (E) human rights are protected

FREE-RESPONSE QUESTION

By: William Aghassi
Brooklyn Technical High School, Brooklyn, NY
B.S. (Mechanical Engineering- Polytechnic University)
M.S. (Environmental Engineering- New Jersey Inst. of Technology)

The 1990 U.S. census revealed that, for the first time, a majority of Americans live in suburbs of major cities or in suburban-like communities.

(a) List three factors why this trend may not be sustainable from a resource point of view.

(b) Explain why each of the three reasons you have listed is not sustainable and the possible consequence of each.

(c) What national public policy decision(s) made the United States into a suburban country as opposed to Europe, which is largely urbanized?

(d) Many environmentalists think of the 21st century as the "Century of the City." State whether or not you agree or disagree with this statement and include your reasons.

MULTIPLE-CHOICE ANSWERS AND EXPLANATIONS

1. **(A)** Increasing population size reduces available resources, thus limiting population growth. In restricting population growth, a density-dependent factor intensifies as the population size increases, affecting each individual more strongly. Population growth declines because of death rate increase, birthrate decrease, or both. There is a reduction in the food supply, which restricts reproduction resulting in less offspring. The competition for space to establish territories is a behavioral mechanism that may restrict population growth. Predators concentrate in areas where there is a high concentration of prey. As long as the natural resources are available in sufficient quantity, the population will remain constant. As the population decreases, so do predators. The accumulation of toxic wastes may also limit the size of a population. Intrinsic factors may play a role in limiting a population size. High densities may cause stress syndromes, resulting in hormonal changes that may delay the onset of reproduction. It has also been reported that immune disorders are related to stress in high densely populated areas. Density-independent factors include weather, climate, and natural disasters such as freezes, seasonal changes, hurricanes, and fires. These factors affect all individuals in the population, regardless of population size.

2. **(D)** Arithmetic or linear growth is characterized by a constant increase per unit of time. In this case, the constant is an increase of 20.

3. **(A)** A 1% growth rate would cause a population to double in 70 years. Hint: divide 70 by the annual percentage growth rate to get the doubling time in years.

4. **(D)** Population size = original size (500) + births (60) − deaths (10) + immigration (0) − emigration (0) = 550. Net growth *rate* = 550/500 = 1.1.

5. **(C)** Using the Rule of 70, 70/4.8 = 14.5 years.

6. **(A)** The maximum reproductive rate is called the biotic potential.

7. **(C)** Global TFR is approximately 2.6.

8. **(E)** An ecological footprint is a metaphor used to depict the amount of land a person would hypothetically need to provide the resources required to support himself.

9. **(E)** No explanation needed.

10. **(B)** Pronatalists urge people to have many children. Choice (B) is the only argument provided that does not promote having children.

11. **(E)** All of the choices listed have had some measure of success.

12. **(D)** Age-structure diagrams with a wide base are populations that have a high proportion of young, which results in a powerful, built-in momentum to increase population size, assuming death rates do not unexpectedly increase.

13. **(A)** This graph is the reverse of the diagram in Question 12. In this case, the majority of the population is beyond reproductive years and the death rate exceeds the birthrate. This projected age structure diagram is for Hong Kong in 2050.

14. **(E)** Choices A–D are examples of density-dependent factors, wherein large, dense populations are more strongly affected than small, less crowded ones. Drought is a naturally occurring event and does not depend on the density of any organism(s) occurring in the area. However, had the destruction of the rain forest been due to ranching, timber harvesting, and/or agriculture (as is the most common cause), then an increase in the number of humans in the rain forest would increase the amount of rain forest destruction in which case the destruction would be due to density-dependent elements.

15. **(C)** Density-independent factors influence population growth and do not depend on the size or density of the population. Predation rates are affected by population size.

16. **(A)** Population change is an increase or decrease in the size of a population. It is equal to (births + immigration) − (deaths + emigration). Population size is the number of individuals in the population.

17. **(C)** A TFR of 2.1 is considered the replacement rate. Once the TFR of a population reaches 2.1, the population will remain stable, assuming no immigration or emigration takes place.

18. **(A)** Population momentum is the tendency for changes in population growth rates to lag behind changes in childbearing behavior and mortality conditions. Momentum operates through the population age distribution. A population that has been growing rapidly for a long time acquires a "young" age distribution that will result in positive population growth rates for many decades into the future.

19. **(D)** In the preindustrial stage, living conditions are harsh, birth and death rates are high, and there is little increase in population size. In the transitional stage, living conditions improve, the death rate drops, and birthrates remain high. In the industrial stage, growth slows. In the postindustrial stage, zero population growth is reached and the birthrate falls below the death rate.

20. **(B)** Countries with high infant mortality rates generally have high TFRs.

FREE-RESPONSE ANSWER

(a) Three factors may limit the trend to American suburbanization:
1. Limit to the amount of open space available near cities
2. Non-point-source pollution (runoff) that could jeopardize the integrity of the region's watershed
3. Traffic congestion
4. Diversity of plant and animal ecosystems could be jeopardized
5. Degradation of air quality
6. Loss of agricultural lands
7. Scarcity of available and inexpensive energy sources

(b) 1. The two features that distinguish land use in suburban areas are low-density housing and that over 60% of available land is devoted to the needs of the automobile. As suburbanization increases, these two factors tend to diminish the availability of open space.
2. Suburbanization near cities tends to encroach upon the watersheds of these regions. Suburban lawns, parking lots, and roads are responsible for a much greater nutrient and chemical loading than undeveloped land and greatly affect the water quality of the region's drinking water.
3. Suburban communities are low density and widely dispersed. Since suburban residents do not commute from or to a central location, they are usually ill served by mass transit and carpooling is sometimes not practical. Commuting times therefore lengthen to intolerable levels, resulting in high air pollution levels.
4. Suburban sprawl can destroy many unique and/or productive ecosystems such as wetlands and forests, thus limiting regional diversity.
5. Since suburbs are decentralized, residents must rely on the automobile for every errand, and all of their goods must be transported by truck. This often results in traffic congestion and air quality degradation that leads to respiratory distress in humans, damage to plants, and damage to buildings.
6. Land goes toward the highest value use. As suburbs encroach on agricultural areas, farmers may be forced to sell to developers due to rezoning and a resulting increase in real estate taxes or simply a higher rate of return than that of farming.
7. Low-density single-family housing and exclusive reliance on the automobile to get around are energy inefficient. As imported oil supplies become expensive or hard to obtain, this could limit suburban growth.

(c) After World War II, the decision to invest infrastructure dollars on roads and disinvest in mass transit made suburbanization possible.

The public policy decision to keep energy prices low through relatively low taxation compared with Europe, which has high energy taxation and high energy prices, made suburban sprawl possible.

(d) Agree: Cities are more energy efficient and, if well planned, are more convenient and offer a better sense of community than many suburbs. This will attract more Americans to move back to cities.

Disagree: Americans are reluctant to forgo the American dream of the single-family home and the automobile to ever return to cities in large numbers.

UNIT IV: LAND AND WATER USE (10–15%)

Areas on Which You Will Be Tested

A. Agriculture

1. Feeding a growing population—human nutritional requirements, types of agriculture, green revolution, genetic engineering, crop production, deforestation, irrigation, and sustainable agriculture.
2. Controlling pests—types of pesticides, costs and benefits of pesticide use, integrated pest management, and relevant laws.

B. Forestry—tree plantations, old-growth forests, forest fires, forest management, and national forests.

C. Rangelands—overgrazing, deforestation, desertification, rangeland management, and federal rangelands.

D. Other Land Use

1. Urban land development—planned development, suburban sprawl, and urbanization.
2. Transportation infrastructure—federal highway system, canals and channels, roadless areas, and ecosystem impacts.
3. Public and federal lands—management, wilderness areas, national parks, wildlife refuges, forests, and wetlands.
4. Land conservation options—preservation, remediation, mitigation, and restoration.
5. Sustainable land use strategies.

E. Mining—mineral formation, extraction, global reserves, and relevant laws and treaties.

F. Fishing—fishing techniques, overfishing, aquaculture, and relevant laws and treaties.

G. Global Economics—globalization, World Bank, "Tragedy of the Commons," and relevant laws and treaties.

Land and Water Use

CHAPTER 7

FEEDING A GROWING POPULATION

In order to feed a population adequately, several factors must be taken into account. The following sections discuss these in detail.

Human Nutritional Requirements

A healthy diet generally requires 2,500 calories per day for the average male and 2,000 calories per day for the average female. Proper nutrition also requires a balanced intake of protein, carbohydrates, and fat. Protein produces 4 calories of energy per gram and should make up about 30% of all calories. Carbohydrates also produce 4 calories of energy per gram and should make up approximately 60% of the daily diet. Fats produce 9 calories of energy per gram and should not make up more than 10% of the total daily caloric intake.

Only about 100 species of plants of the 350,000 known are commercially grown to meet human nutritional needs. Of these, wheat and rice supply over half the human caloric intake. Just 8 species of animal protein supply over 90% of the world's needs. It takes about 16 pounds (7 kg) of grain to produce 1 pound (0.5 kg) of edible meat, and 20% of the world's richest countries consume 80% of the world's meat production. About 90% of the grain grown in the United States is grown for animal feed. By consuming the grain directly instead of consuming the animals that feed upon it, there would be a 20-fold increase in the amount of calories available and an 8-fold increase in the amount of protein available. The benefit of consuming meat products is that they are concentrated sources of protein that are broken down through digestion into amino acids.

Malnutrition

In terms of famine and malnutrition, about 11 million children die each year from starvation, with 850 million people (13% of the world population) considered malnourished. Chronic undernourishment and vitamin or mineral deficiencies result in stunted growth, weakness, and increased susceptibility to illness.

Most of the undernourished are in developing countries. Marasmus and kwashiorkor are protein deficiency diseases in which victims may become so emaciated that they may be less than 80% of their normal weight for their height.

Types of Agriculture

AGROFORESTRY

A system of land use in which harvestable trees or shrubs are grown among or around crops or on pastureland as a means of preserving or enhancing the productivity of the land.

ALLEY CROPPING

A method of planting crops in strips with rows of trees or shrubs on each side. Alley cropping increases biodiversity, reduces surface water runoff and erosion, improves the utilization of nutrients, reduces wind erosion, modifies the microclimate for improved crop production, and improves wildlife habitat.

Figure 7.1 Alley cropping

CROP ROTATION

Planting a field with different crops from year to year to reduce soil nutrient depletion. Example: Rotating corn or cotton, which removes large amounts of nitrogen from the soil, with soybeans that then add nitrogen to the soil.

Crop Rotation Schedule			
	Field 1	**Field 2**	**Field 3**
1st Year	Wheat and rye	Oats and barley	Fallow
2nd Year	Fallow	Wheat and rye	Peas and beans
3rd Year	Peas and beans	Fallow	Wheat and rye

HIGH-INPUT AGRICULTURE

Includes the use of mechanized equipment, chemical fertilizers, and pesticides.

INDUSTRIAL AGRICULTURE OR CORPORATE FARMING

A system characterized by mechanization, monocultures, and the use of synthetic inputs such as chemical fertilizers and pesticides, with an emphasis on maximizing productivity and profitability.

INTERCROPPING

To grow more than one crop in the same field, especially in alternating rows or sections.

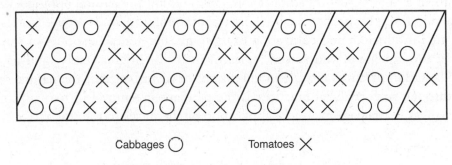

Cabbages ◯   Tomatoes ✕

Figure 7.2 Example of intercropping

INTERPLANTING

Growing two different crops in an area at the same time. To interplant successfully, plants should have similar nutrient and moisture requirements.

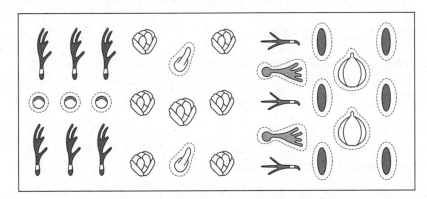

Figure 7.3 Example of interplanting

LOW INPUT

Depends on hand tools and natural fertilizers; lacks large-scale irrigation.

LOW-TILL, NO-TILL, OR CONSERVATION-TILL AGRICULTURE

Soil is disturbed little or not at all to reduce soil erosion. Has lower labor costs, reduces the need for fertilizer, and saves energy.

MONOCULTURE

The cultivation of a single crop.

ORGANIC FARMING

A form of agriculture that relies on crop rotation, green manure, compost, biological pest control, and mechanical cultivation to maintain soil productivity and control pests. This practice excludes or strictly limits the use of synthetic fertilizers, synthetic pesticides, plant growth regulators, livestock feed additives, and genetically modified organisms.

PLANTATION

A commercial tropical agriculture system that is essentially export oriented. The local government and foreign/international companies exploit the natural resources of the tropical rain forest for profit, usually short-term economic gain. It often involves the deliberate introduction and cultivation of economically desirable species of tropical plants at the expense of widespread replacement of the original native and natural flora. Plantation practices include modifications or disturbance of the natural landscape through such artificial practices as the permanent removal of natural vegetation, changes in drainage channels, application of chemicals to the soil, etc.

POLYCULTURE

Polyculture uses *different* crops in the same space, in imitation of the diversity of natural ecosystems, and avoids large stands of a single crop (monoculture). It includes crop rotation, multicropping, intercropping, and alley cropping. Polyculture, though it often requires more labor, has several advantages over monoculture. The diversity of crops avoids the susceptibility of monocultures to disease. The greater variety of crops provides habitat for more species, increasing local biodiversity.

POLYVARIETAL CULTIVATION

Planting a plot of land with several varieties of the *same* crop.

SUBSISTENCE

Agriculture carried out for survival—with few or no crops available for sale. It is usually organic, due to lack of money to buy industrial inputs such as fertilizer, pesticides, or genetically modified seeds.

TILLAGE

Conventional method in which the surface is plowed which then breaks up and exposes the soil. This is then followed by smoothing the surface and planting. This method exposes the land to water and wind erosion.

Green Revolution

The first green revolution occurred between 1950 and 1970. It involved planting monocultures, using high applications of inorganic fertilizers and pesticides, and the widespread use of artificial irrigation systems. Before the first green revolution, crop production was correlated with increases in acreage under cultivation. After the first green revolution, crop acreage increased about 25%, but crop yield increased 200%. Crop yield then reached a plateau since it was easier and more economical to increase crop production through various agricultural techniques than to buy and clear new land.

The second green revolution began during the 1970s and is continuing today. It involves growing genetically engineered crops that produce the most yields per acre. It is in contrast with past agricultural practices in which farmers planted a variety of locally adapted strains. For example, of all wheat grown in the United States today, 50% comes from 9 different genotypes.

CRITICISMS OF THE GREEN REVOLUTION

Critics cite the following as problems and/or failures of the Green Revolution:

- The Green Revolution is unsustainable.
- Increasing food production is not synonymous with increasing food security, i.e., famines are not caused by decreases in food supply but by socioeconomic dynamics and a failure of public action.
- Green Revolution agriculture produces monocultures of cereal grains, while traditional agriculture usually incorporates polycultures.
- There has been a drop in the productivity of land that has been intensively farmed for the past 30 years due to desertification and other forms of land degradation.
- The necessary purchase of inputs led to the widespread establishment of rural credit institutions, which then caused many smaller farmers to go into debt and in many cases resulted in a loss of their farmland.
- Green Revolution agriculture increases the use of pesticides, which are necessary to limit the high levels of pest damage that inevitably occur in monoculture.
- Salinization, water logging, and lowering of water levels in certain areas increased as consequences of increased irrigation.
- The Green Revolution reduced agricultural biodiversity, as it relied upon only a few high-yield varieties of each crop. This led to the susceptibility of the food supply to pathogens that cannot be controlled by agrochemicals, as well as the permanent loss of many valuable genetic traits bred into traditional varieties over thousands of years.

Genetic Engineering and Crop Production

Genetic engineering involves moving genes from one species to another or designing gene sequences with desirable characteristics. These include pest, drought, mold, and saline resistance, higher protein yields, and higher vitamin content. About 75% of all crops grown derive from genetically engineered or transgenic crop species.

In 2006, 10 million farmers in 22 countries planted 252 million acres of transgenic crops. The majority of these crops were herbicide- and insect-resistant soybeans, corn, cotton, canola, and alfalfa. Other examples included sweet potatoes resistant to a virus that could seriously reduce most of the African harvest, rice with increased iron and vitamins that may alleviate chronic malnutrition (golden rice), and a variety of plants able to survive weather extremes. In the near future, genetically modified bananas may produce human vaccines to prevent infectious diseases such as hepatitis B. Genetic modification may produce fish that mature more quickly,; allow cows to become resistant to bovine spongiform encephalopathy (mad cow disease); produce fruit and nut trees that yield years earlier; and plants that can make new plastics with unique properties. The future will see exponential growth in developing genetically modified products.

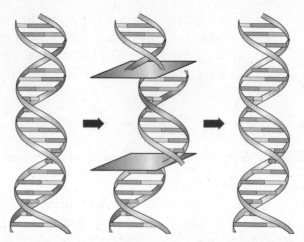

Figure 7.4 Example of gene splicing, a process by which a segment of DNA from one source is attached to or inserted into a strand of DNA from another source.

CASE STUDY

Golden rice is produced by splicing three foreign genes, two from the daffodil and one from a bacterium, into a variety of rice that supplies vitamin A to populations that frequently suffer from vitamin A deficiency.

Genetically Engineered Crops

Pros	Cons
May require less water and fertilizer	Unknown ecological effects
Higher crop yields	Less biodiversity
Less spoilage	May harm beneficial insects
Faster growth which may mean greater productivity, resulting in lower operating costs	May pose allergen risk
More resistant to disease, drought, frost, and insects	May result in mutations with unknown consequences
May be able to grow in saltier soils	May cause pesticide-resistant strains

Irrigation

Three-quarters of all freshwater used on Earth is used for agriculture. Worldwide, approximately 40% of all crop yields come from 16% of all cropland that is irrigated. The use of irrigation depends on the climate and the degree of industrialization. For example, Canada irrigates about 10% of its crops, whereas India requires 90% of its crops to be irrigated. With inefficiencies such as seepage, leakage, and evaporation, up to 70% of all irrigation water can be lost. A drip irrigation system, which solves many of these problems but is more expensive to install, is used on approximately 1% of crops worldwide.

Increases in human population growth are outpacing the rate of land that is being irrigated. Sustainable irrigation is limited as a result of increases in costs, depletion of current sources of water, competition for water by urban areas, restoration of wetlands and fisheries, waterlogging, and salinization. Future water capacity will increase through increases in efficiency.

Sustainable Agriculture

Sustainable agriculture involves a variety of approaches. It integrates three main goals: environmental health, economic profitability, and social and economic equity. Specific strategies must take into account topography, soil characteristics, climate, pests, local availability of inputs, and the individual grower's goals. Despite the site-specific and individual nature of sustainable agriculture, several general principles can be applied to help growers select appropriate management practices and are described below.

Changes in agriculture have had many positive effects and reduced many risks in farming. However, there have also been significant costs. Prominent among these are topsoil depletion, groundwater contamination, the decline of family farms, continued neglect of the living and working conditions for farm laborers, increasing costs of production, and the disintegration of economic and social conditions in rural communities.

EFFICIENT USE OF INPUTS

Sustainable farmers maximize reliance on natural, renewable farm inputs with the goal to develop efficient, biological systems that do not need high levels of material inputs. Sustainable approaches are those that are the least toxic and least energy intensive and yet maintain productivity and profitability. Preventive strategies and other alternatives (such as integrated pest management) should be employed before using chemical inputs from any source.

SELECTION OF SITE, SPECIES, AND VARIETY

Preventive strategies, when adopted early, can reduce inputs and help establish a sustainable production system. When possible, pest-resistant crops should be selected that are tolerant of existing soil or site conditions. When site selection is an option, factors such as soil type and depth, previous crop history, and location (climate and topography) should be taken into account before planting.

SOIL MANAGEMENT

Proper soil, water, and nutrient management can help prevent some pest problems brought on by crop stress or nutrient imbalance. Furthermore, crop management systems that impair soil quality often result in greater inputs of water, nutrients, pesticides, and/or energy for tillage to maintain yields. In sustainable systems, the soil is viewed as a fragile and living medium that must be protected and nurtured to ensure its long-term productivity and stability. Methods to protect and enhance the productivity of the soil include using cover crops, compost, and/or manures, reducing tillage, and maintaining soil cover with plants and/or mulches. Regular additions of organic matter or the use of cover crops can increase soil aggregate stability, soil tilth, and the diversity of soil microbial life.

SPECIES DIVERSITY

By growing a variety of crops, farmers spread out the economic risk and are less susceptible to the radical price fluctuations associated with changes in supply and demand. For example, in annual cropping systems, crop rotation can be used to suppress weeds, pathogens, and insect pests. Also, cover crops can have stabilizing effects on the agroecosystem by holding soil and nutrients in place, conserving soil moisture with dead mulches, and increasing the water infiltration rate and soil water-holding capacity. Optimum diversity may be obtained by integrating both crops and livestock in the same farming operation. Growing row crops on more level land and pasture or forages on steeper slopes will reduce soil erosion. Planting pasture and forage crops in rotation enhances soil quality and reduces erosion. Livestock manure, in turn, contributes to soil fertility. Livestock can buffer the negative impacts of low rainfall periods by consuming crop residue that in plant-only systems would have been considered crop failures. Feeding and marketing are flexible in animal production systems. This can help cushion farmers against trade and price fluctuations and, in conjunction with cropping operations, make more efficient use of farm labor and resources.

CONTROLLING PESTS

Pesticides can be used to control pests, but their use has drawbacks. Integrated pest management is another strategy to control pests.

Types of Pesticides

Pesticides differ in several ways. Their chemistry, how long they remain effective in the environment (environmental persistence), and their effect on the food web (bioaccumulation and biomagnification) are just a few concerns. Others include what type of organisms are affected, how the pesticides work (nervous system, reproductive cycles, blood chemistry), how fast they work, and their application.

BIOLOGICAL

Living organisms are used to control pests. Examples include bacteria, Bt (*Bacillus thuringiensis*), ladybugs, milky spore disease, parasitic wasps, and certain viruses.

CASE STUDY

Bacillus thuringiensis (Bt) is a soil-dwelling bacterium that also occurs naturally in the gut of caterpillars of various types of moths and butterflies, as well as on the dark surface of plants. Proteins produced by Bt are used as specific insecticides. It works by secreting one or more toxins after being ingested by an insect. The toxins are often specific to a family of insects, and because of their specificity, these pesticides are regarded as environmentally friendly. Advantages of using Bt include:

  (i) The level of toxin can be very high, thus delivering sufficient dosage to the pest.
  (ii) It is contained within the plant system; therefore only those insects that feed on the crop perish.
  (iii) It replaces the use of synthetic pesticides in the environment.

A possible drawback to Bt may be that constant exposure to a toxin creates evolutionary pressure for pests resistant to that toxin.

CARBAMATES

Carbamates, also known as urethanes, affect the nervous system of pests. 100 grams of a carbamate has the same effect as 2,000 grams of a chlorinated hydrocarbon such as DDT. Carbamates are more water soluble than chlorinated hydrocarbons, which brings a greater risk of them being dissolved in surface water and percolating into groundwater.

CASE STUDY

On December 2, 1984 at the Union Carbide pesticide plant in Bhopal, India, a leak of chemicals from a plant manufacturing a carbamate pesticide leaked, which resulted in the exposure of hundreds of thousands of people. Roughly 8,000 people have since died from gas-related diseases with 200,000 people having permanent injuries.

CHLORINATED HYDROCARBONS AND OTHER PERSISTENT ORGANIC COMPOUNDS (POPS)

Chlorinated hydrocarbons, such as the pesticide DDT, are synthetic organic compounds belonging to a group of chemicals known as persistent organic pollutants or POPs. Persistent organic pollutants (POPs) are organic compounds that are resistant to environmental degradation through chemical, biological, and photolytic processes. Because of this, they have been observed to persist in the environment, to be capable of long-range transport, bioaccumulate in human and animal tissue, biomagnify in food chains, and to have potential significant impacts on human health and the environment. Many POPs are currently or were in the past used as pesticides. Others are used in industrial processes and in the production of a range of goods such as solvents, polyvinyl chloride, and pharmaceuticals. Some of the chemical characteristics of POPs include low water solubility, high lipid solubility, semi-volatility, and high molecular masses. POPs are frequently halogenated, usually with chlorine. The more chlorine or other halogen groups a POP has, the more resistant it is to being broken down over time. One important factor of their chemical properties, such as lipid solubility, results in the ability to pass through biological phospholipid membranes and bioaccumulate in the fatty tissues of living organisms. The chemicals' semi-volatility allows them to travel long distances through the atmosphere before being deposited. Thus POPs can be found all over the world, including in areas where they have never been used and remote regions such as the middle of oceans and Antarctica. The chemicals' semi-volatility also means that they tend to volatilize in hot regions and accumulate in cold regions, where they tend to condense and persist. As pesticides, they affect the nervous system of pests. In the 1950s, DDT was linked with the thinning of eggshells in certain species of birds (e.g., bald eagle).

FUMIGANTS

Used to sterilize soil and prevent pest infestation of stored grain.

INORGANIC

Broad-based pesticides. Includes arsenic, copper, lead, and mercury. Highly toxic and accumulate in the environment.

ORGANIC OR NATURAL

Natural poisons derived from plants such as tobacco or chrysanthemum.

ORGANOPHOSPHATES

Extremely toxic but remain in the environment for only a brief time. Examples include malathion to control mosquitoes and West Nile Virus, and parathion.

Costs and Benefits of Pesticide Use

Despite the use of pesticides, many pests worldwide have increased in numbers. This is due to genetic resistance, reduced crop rotation, increased mobility of pests due to increased world trade, and reduction in crop diversity. The following table shows the pros and cons of pesticide use.

The Pros and Cons of Pesticides

Pros	Cons
Kill unwanted pests that carry disease	Accumulate in food chains
Increase food supplies	Pests develop resistance and create a pesticide treadmill
More food means food is less expensive	Estimates range from $5 to $10 in damage done to the environment for every $1 spent on pesticides; pesticides are expensive to purchase and apply
Newer pesticides are safer and more specific	Pesticide runoff and its effect on aquatic environments through biomagnification
Reduces labor costs	Inefficiency—only 5% of a pesticide reaches a pest
Agriculture is more profitable	Threatens endangered species and pollinators; also affects human health

Integrated Pest Management

Integrated pest management (IPM) is an ecological pest control strategy that uses a variety of methods. When used in combination, these methods working together can reduce or eliminate the use of traditional pesticides. The aim of IPM is not to eradicate pests but to control their numbers to acceptable levels. In integrated pest management, chemical pesticides are the last resort. Methods employed in IPM include:

- Polyculture
- Intercropping
- Planting pest-repellent crops
- Using mulch to control weeds
- Using pyrethroids or naturally occurring microorganisms (such as Bt) instead of toxic pesticides
- Natural insect predators
- Rotating crops often to disrupt insect cycles
- Using pheromones or hormone interrupters
- Releasing sterilized insects
- Developing genetically modified crops that are more insect resistant
- Regular monitoring through visual inspection and traps followed by record keeping
- Construction of mechanical controls such as traps, tillage, insect barriers, or agricultural vacuums equipped with lights

> **RELEVANT LAWS**
>
> **Federal Insecticide, Fungicide and Rodenticide Control Act (FIFRA) (1947):** Regulates the manufacture and use of pesticides. Pesticides must be registered and approved. Labels require directions for use and disposal.
>
> **Federal Environmental Pesticides Control Act (1972):** Requires registration of all pesticides in U.S. commerce.
>
> **Food Quality Protection Act (FQPA) (1996):** Emphasizes the protection of infants and children in reference to pesticide residue in food.

FORESTRY

Forestry involves the management of forests. Sometimes this involves planting new trees, and sometimes it involves fires.

Ecological Services

Forests are an important global reserve. The ecological services of forests include:

1. Providing wildlife habitats
2. Carbon sinks
3. Affecting local climate patterns
4. Purifying air and water
5. Reducing soil erosion as they serve as a watershed, absorbing and releasing controlled amounts water
6. Providing energy and nutrient cycling

Tree Plantations

Tree plantations are large, managed commercial or government-owned farms with uniformly aged trees of one species (monoculture). Trees may not be native to the area and may be hybrids (genetically modified). The primary use of plantation trees is for pulp and lumber. Pine, spruce, and eucalyptus are widely used due to their fast growth rates and can be used for paper and timber. Trees are harvested by clear-cutting. Short rotation cycles of 25–30 years or 6–10 years in the tropics are economically important factors. Just 5% of the world's forests are tree plantations, but they account for 20% of the current world wood production. In comparison, 63% of the world's forests are secondary-growth forests, and 22% are old-growth forests.

Annually, tropical tree plantations yield much more wood (25 m³/hectare) than traditional forests (1–3 m³/hectare). Some of the natural closed forests—7%—are being lost in the tropics due to land conversion to tree plantations. Tree plantations do not support food webs found in old-growth forests, and they contain little biodiversity. Decaying wood is absent, which provides a vital link in an old-growth forest. Conversion to tree plantations may result in draining wetlands and replacing traditional hardwoods. Newer techniques allow leaving blocks of native species within the plantation or retaining corridors of natural forest. The Kyoto Protocol encourages use of tree plantations to reduce carbon dioxide levels although carbon dioxide may eventually re-enter the atmosphere after harvesting.

Old-Growth Forests

Old-growth forests are forests that have not been seriously impacted by human activities for hundreds of years. Old-growth forests are rich in biodiversity. Old-growth forests are characterized by:

TIP

"in situ" means "in its original place."

- Older and mixed-aged trees
- Minimal signs of human activity
- Multilayered canopy openings due to tree falls
- Pit-and-mound topography due to trees falling and creating new microenvironments by recycling carbon-rich organic material directly to the soil and providing a substrate for mosses, fungi (necessary for *in situ* recycling), and seedlings
- Decaying wood and ground layer that provides a rich carbon sink
- Dead trees (snags) that are necessary nesting sites for woodpeckers and spotted owls
- Healthy soil profiles
- Indicator species
- Little vegetation on the forest floor due to light being a limiting factor.

Depletion of old-growth forests increases the risk of climatic change. Many old-growth forests contain species of trees that have high economic value but that require a long time to mature (mahogany, oak, etc.).

Forest Fires

Forests are unique in terms of their ecological significance and the number and frequency of forest fires. Current wildfire frequency in the United States is about 4 times the average of 1970–1986. The total area burned by current fires is about 7 times its previous level. The U.S. Forest Service has lengthened the wildfire season by 78 days. The change in wildfire frequency appears to be linked to annual spring and summer temperatures. Longer, warmer summers are documented with an increase in the number of forest fires. A correlation exists between early arrivals of the spring snowmelt in the mountainous regions and the incidence of large forest fires. An earlier snowmelt can lead to an earlier and longer dry season, which provides greater opportunities for larger fires. As forests burn, they release their stored carbon as carbon dioxide into the atmosphere, further compounding the problems of global warming. Another reason for the increase in forest fires is a change in fire management philosophy. Any naturally started fire on federal land that is not threatening resources (homes or commercial structures) is allowed to burn.

CROWN FIRES

Occur in forests that have not had surface fires for a long time. Extremely hot. Burn entire trees and leap from treetop to treetop. Kills wildlife, increases soil erosion, and destroys structures.

GROUND FIRES

Fires that occur underground and burn partially decayed leaves. Common in peat bogs. Difficult to detect and extinguish.

SURFACE FIRES

Burns undergrowth and leaf litter. Kills seedlings and small trees. Spares older trees, and allows many wild animals to escape. Advantages: burns away flammable ground litter, reducing larger fires later; releases minerals back into soil profile; stimulates germination for some species with cones that require heat to open up and release the seeds, such as giant sequoia and jack pine; helps to keep pathogens and insects in check; and allows vegetation to grow in clearings that provides food for deer, moose, elk, muskrat, and quail.

METHODS TO CONTROL FIRES

Two methods are used to control forest fires: prevention and prescribed burning. Prevention involves burning permits, closing parts of the forest during times of the year when the number of visitors is high and during periods of drought, and educating the public. Prescribed burning involves purposely setting controlled surface fires and setting small, prescribed fires to thin out underbrush in high-risk areas. It requires careful planning and monitoring. Other strategies include allowing fires to burn themselves out and creating large, clear areas around structures.

Deforestation

Deforestation is the conversion of forested areas to nonforested areas. They are then used as grasslands for livestock grazing, grain fields, mining, petroleum extraction, fuel wood cutting, commercial logging, tree plantations, and urban sprawl. Natural deforestation can be caused by tsunamis, forest fires, volcanic eruptions, glaciation, and desertification. Deforestation results in a degraded environment with reduced biodiversity and reduced ecological services. Deforestation threatens the extinction of species with specialized niches, reduces the available habits for migratory species of birds and butterflies, decreases soil fertility brought about by erosion, and allows runoff into aquatic ecosystems. It also causes changes in local climate patterns and increases the amount of carbon dioxide released into the air from burning and tree decay. In addition to the direct effects brought about by deforestation, indirect effects caused by edge effects and habitat fragmentation can also occur.

Methods that are currently employed to manage and harvest trees include:

- **Even-age management**—Essentially the practice of tree plantations.
- **Uneven-age management**—Maintain a stand with trees of all ages from seedling to mature.
- **Selective cutting**—Specific trees in an area are chosen and cut.
- **High grading**—Cutting and removing only the largest and best trees.
- **Shelterwood cutting**—Removes all mature trees in an area within a limited time.
- **Seed tree cutting**—Majority of trees are removed except for scattered, seed-producing trees used to regenerate a new stand.
- **Clear-cutting**—All of the trees in an area are cut at the same time. This technique is sometimes used to cultivate shade-intolerant tree species.
- **Strip cutting**—Clear-cutting a strip of trees that follows the land contour. The corridor is allowed to regenerate.

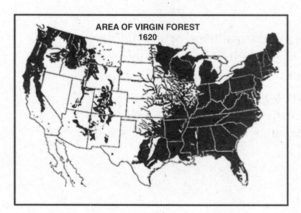 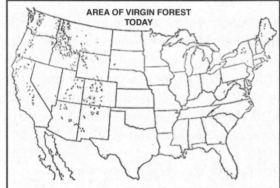

Figure 7.5 Deforestation in the United States (1620–present)

Deforestation alters the hydrologic cycle, potentially increasing or decreasing the amount of water in the soil and groundwater. This then affects the recharge of aquifers and the moisture in the atmosphere. Shrinking forest cover lessens the landscape's capacity to intercept, retain, and transport precipitation. Instead of trapping precipitation, which then percolates to groundwater systems, deforested areas become sources of surface water runoff, which moves much faster than subsurface flows. The faster transport of surface water can translate into flash flooding and more extreme floods than would occur with the forest cover.

Tree Plantations

Pros	Cons
Practical method for trees that require full or moderate sunlight in order to grow.	Reduces recreational value of land.
Efficient and economical method.	If done on steeply sloped areas, will often cause soil erosion, water pollution, and flooding.
Genetically improved species of trees that resist disease and grow faster can be grown.	Causes habitat fragmentation.
Increases economic returns on investments.	Reduces biodiversity.
Produces a high yield of timber at the lowest cost, and provides jobs.	Promotes monoculture and tree plantations that are prone to disease or infestation through the lack of diversity.

Deforestation also contributes to decreased evapotranspiration. This lessens atmospheric moisture and precipitation levels. It also affects precipitation levels downwind from the deforested area as water is not recycled to downwind forests but, instead, is lost in runoff and returns directly to the oceans. Forests are also important carbon sinks. Forests can extract carbon dioxide and pollutants from the air, thus contributing to biosphere stability and reducing the greenhouse effect. Forests are also valued for their aesthetic beauty and as a cultural resource and tourist attraction.

Three schools of thought exist with regard to the causes of deforestation—the impoverished school, the neoclassical school, and the political-ecology school. The impoverished school believes that the major cause of deforestation is the growing number of poor. The neoclassical school believes that the major cause is "open-access property rights." The political-ecology school believes that the major cause of deforestation is due to entrepreneurs.

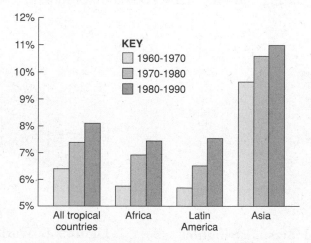

Figure 7.6 Rate of deforestation in tropical rain forests

Forest Management

Forests cover about one-third of all land surface worldwide. Most—80%—of these forests are closed canopies (tree crowns covering more than 20% of the ground), and 20% are classified as open canopy (tree crowns covering less than 20% of the ground surface). Most forests (70%) are located in North America, the Russian Federation, and South America. In the United States, the largest area of timbering is in the Pacific Northwest, employing 150,000 people and representing a $7 billion per year industry.

Forests account for about a third of the land in the United States, the largest of any land use category. Out of the 747 million acres of U.S. forest land, two-thirds (500 million acres) are nonfederal.

The Forest Service was established in 1905 as an agency of the U.S. Department of Agriculture and consists of 155 national forests and 22 grasslands. The Forest Service manages public lands in national forests and grasslands and encompasses 193 million acres (approximately the size of Texas). These resources are used for logging, farming, recreation, hunting, fishing, oil and gas extraction, watersheds, mining, livestock grazing, farming, and conservation purposes.

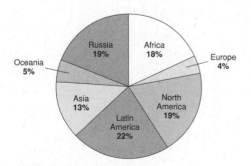

Figure 7.7 World forest distribution

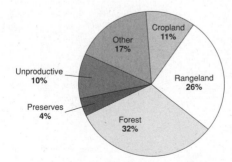

Figure 7.8 World land use

The Forest Service protects and manages natural resources on National Forest System lands. It sponsors research on all aspects of forestry, rangeland management, and forest resource utilization. It provides community assistance and cooperation with state and local governments, forest industries and private landowners to help protect and manage nonfederal forests, associated ranges, and watersheds to improve conditions in rural areas. The Forest Service also provides international assistance in formulating policy and coordinating U.S. support for the protection and sound management of the world's forest resources.

RELEVANT LAWS

Wilderness Act (1964): Created the legal definition of wilderness in the United States. Currently four agencies (National Park Service, U.S. Forest Service, U.S. Fish and Wildlife Service, and the Bureau of Land Management) are in charge of more than 106 million acres (429,000 km²) of federal wilderness.

Wild and Scenic Rivers Act (1968): Preserves and protects certain rivers with outstanding natural, cultural, and recreational values in a free-flowing condition for the enjoyment of present and future generations. Classified rivers as wild, scenic, or recreational.

RANGELANDS

Rangelands are being compromised by overgrazing and desertification. The federal government is trying to manage and sustain the rangelanads.

Overgrazing

The consequences of overgrazing and its effect on sustainability, which was the theme of the essay "The Tragedy of the Commons," occurs when plants are exposed to grazing for too long without sufficient recovery periods. When a plant is grazed severely, it uses energy stored in its roots to support regrowth. As this energy is used, the roots die back. The degree to which the roots die back depends on the severity of the grazing. Root dieback does add organic matter to the soil, which increases soil porosity, the infiltration rate of water, and the soil's moisture-holding capacity. If sufficient time has passed, enough leaves will regrow and the roots will regrow as well. A plant is considered overgrazed when it is regrazed before the roots recover. Overgrazing can reduce root growth by up to 90%.

Consequences to overgrazing include pastures becoming less productive, soils having less organic matter and becoming less fertile, and a decrease in soil porosity. The infiltration rate and moisture-holding capacity of the soil drops and susceptibility to soil compaction increases. Additionally, desirable plants become stressed, while weedier species thrive in these harsher conditions. Overgrazing causes biodiversity to decrease by reducing native vegetation, which leads to erosion. Riparian areas are affected by cattle destroying banks and streambeds, thereby increasing silting. Eutrophication increases due to cattle wastes. Therefore, aquatic environments are negatively impacted. Predator-prey relationships and the balance achieved through predator control programs are affected. Overgrazing increases the incidence of disease in native plant species. Finally, land is affected to the point where sustainability is threatened.

Desertification

Desertification is the conversion of marginal rangeland or cropland to a more desert-like land type. It is often caused by overgrazing, soil erosion, prolonged drought, or climate changes as well as the overuse of available resources such as nutrients and water. Desertification proceeds with the following steps: First, overgrazing results in animals eating all available plant life. Next, rain washes away the trampled soil, since nothing holds water anymore. Wells, springs, and other sources of water dry up. What vegetation is left dies from drought or is taken for firewood. Then weeds that are unsuitable for grazing may begin to take over. The ground becomes unsuitable for seed germination. Finally, wind and dry heat blow away the topsoil.

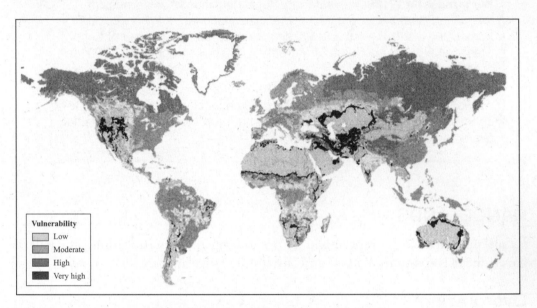

Figure 7.9 Desertification vulnerability

Federal Rangeland Management

Rangelands comprise about 40% of the landmass of the United States and are the dominant type of land in arid and semiarid regions. Nearly 80% of the lands of the western United States are classified as rangelands, whereas only 7% of some areas near the East Coast are classified as rangelands. Rangelands provide valuable grazing lands for livestock and wildlife. Rangelands serve as a source of high-quality water, clean air, and open spaces. They benefit people as a setting for recreation and as an economic means for agriculture, mining, and living communities. Rangelands serve multiple purposes:

- A habitat for a wide array of game and nongame animal species
- A habitat for a diverse and wide array of native plant species
- A source of high-quality water, clean air, and open spaces
- A setting for recreational hiking, camping, fishing, hunting, and nature experiences
- The foundation for low-input, fully renewable food production systems for the cattle industry

Jurisdiction of public grazing rangelands is coordinated through the Forest Service and the Bureau of Land Management (BLM). Before 1995, grazing policies were determined by rancher advisory boards composed of permit holders. After 1995, resource advisory councils were formed made up of diverse groups representing different viewpoints and interests. Forty percent of all federal grazing permits are owned by 3% (or approximately 2000) of all livestock operators. Federal grazing permits average about 5 cents per day per animal through federal subsidies. The true cost of doing business would make this fee closer to $10 to $20 per animal per day.

Methods of rangeland management include:

1. Controlling the number and distribution of livestock so that the carrying capacity is not exceeded

2. Restoring degraded rangeland

3. Moving livestock from one area to another to allow the rangeland to recover

4. Fencing off riparian (stream) areas to reduce damage to these sensitive areas

5. Suppressing the growth of invasive plant species

6. Replanting barren rangeland with native grass seed to reduce soil erosion

7. Providing supplemental feed at selected sites

8. Locating water holes, water tanks and salt blocks at strategic points that do not degrade the environment

Land administered by the BLM is inhabited by 219 endangered species of wildlife. Livestock grazing is the fifth-rated threat to endangered plant species, the fourth leading threat for all endangered wildlife, and the number one threat to all endangered species in arid regions of the United States.

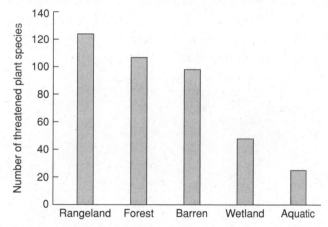

Figure 7.10 Endangered plant species as a function of biome

URBAN LAND DEVELOPMENT

The following sections discuss another form of land use—urban land development.

Planned Development

There are more than 76 million residential buildings and approximately 5 million commercial buildings in the United States alone. Together, these buildings use one-third of all the energy and two-thirds of all the electricity consumed in the United States. Energy needs of buildings account for almost half of the sulfur dioxide emissions, one-fourth of the nitrous oxide emissions, and one-third of the carbon dioxide emissions.

Green building and city characteristics focus on whole-system approaches. They include:

- Energy conservation through government and private industry rebates and tax incentives for solar and other less-polluting forms of energy
- Resource-efficient building techniques and materials
- Indoor air quality
- Water conservation through the use of xeriscaping
- Designs that minimize waste while utilizing recycled materials
- Placing buildings whenever possible near public transportation hubs that use a multitude of venues such as light rail, subways, and park and rides
- Creating environments that are pedestrian friendly by incorporating parks, green-belts, and shopping areas in accessible areas
- Preserving historical and cultural aspects of the community while at the same time blending into the natural feeling and aesthetics of a community

Suburban Sprawl and Urbanization

Urbanization refers to the movement of people from rural areas to cities and the changes that accompany it. Areas that are experiencing the greatest growth in urbanization are countries in Asia and Africa. Asia alone has close to half of the world's urban inhabitants even though 60% of its population still lives in rural areas. Africa, which is generally considered overwhelmingly rural, now has a larger urban population than North America. Reasons for this include access to jobs, higher standards of living, easier access to health care, mechanization of agriculture, and access to education. Nations with the most rapid increases in their urbanization rates are generally those with the most rapid economic growth. From 1950 to 1990, the world's economy increased fivefold.

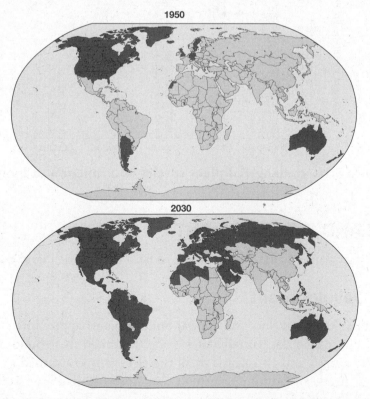

Figure 7.11 Projected worldwide urban growth from 1950–2030

Urbanization

Pros	Cons
Uses less land—less impact on the environment.	Impact on land is more concentrated and more pronounced. Examples include water runoff and flooding.
Better educational delivery system.	Overcrowded schools.
Mass transit systems decrease reliance on fossil fuels—commuting distances are shorter.	Commuting times are longer because the infrastructure cannot keep up with growth.
Better sanitation systems.	Sanitation systems have greater volumes of wastes to deal with.
Recycling systems are more efficient.	Solid-waste buildup is more pronounced. Landfill space becomes scarce and costly.
Large numbers of people generate high tax revenues.	Large numbers of poor people place strains on social services. This results in wealthier people moving away from urban areas into suburbs and decreasing the tax base.
Urban areas attract industry due to availability of raw materials, distribution networks, customers, and labor pool.	Higher population densities increase crime rates. Population increase may be higher than job growth.
Much of the pollution comes from point sources, enabling focused remediation techniques.	Since population densities are high, pollution levels are also high (urban heat islands, ozone levels, and water and soil pollution).

TRANSPORTATION INFRASTRUCTURE

Transportation can be via roadways or water channels. Areas without transportation infrastructure suffer an ecosystem impact.

Federal Highway System

The federal highway system contains approximately 160,000 miles (256,000 km) of roadway important to the nation's economy, defense, and mobility. Although interstate highways usually receive substantial federal funding and comply with federal standards, they are owned, built, and operated by the states in which they are located. Current federal highway taxes include an 18-cents per gallon tax on gasoline, a 25-cent per gallon tax on diesel, and a tax on heavy vehicles.

The system serves all major U.S. cities. Unlike counterparts in most industrialized countries, interstates go through downtown areas and facilitate urban sprawl. The distribution of virtually all goods and services involve interstate highways at some point. Residents of American cities commonly use urban interstates to travel to their employment.

An efficient and well-maintained federal highway system can have the following impacts on the environment:

LESS POLLUTANTS

Vehicles caught in stop-and-go traffic emit far more pollutants, particularly carbon monoxide, nitrogen oxides, and smog-forming volatile organic compounds, than they do without frequent braking and acceleration.

REDUCE GREENHOUSE GASES

Improving traffic flow and reducing congestion will decrease atmospheric carbon dioxide.

IMPROVE FUEL ECONOMY AND REDUCE FOREIGN OIL DEPENDENCE

For vehicles stuck in traffic, not only do tailpipe emissions go up but fuel economy goes down. Modest improvements to the nation's worst traffic bottlenecks would save 1 billion gallons of fuel each year.

IMPROVE THE ECONOMY

Interstates return $6 in economic productivity for every $1 invested.

IMPROVE THE QUALITY OF LIFE

An interstate highway system allows products (both perishable and nonperishable) to be distributed throughout the country in a short period of time.

Canals and Channels

The term channel is another word for strait, which is defined as a relatively narrow body of water that connects two larger bodies of water. Channels can occur naturally or be constructed. Repeated dredging of canals and channels is often necessary because of silting.

In the United States, channels frequented by ships are generally maintained by the United States Department of the Interior and monitored and policed by the United States Coast Guard. Smaller channels are maintained by the various states or local governments.

The two largest canals in the world of major economic value are the Panama Canal and the Suez Canal. The 48-mile (77 km) Panama Canal connects the Pacific Ocean with the Atlantic. It allows water transport without having to circumnavigate South America. The 163-mile (190 km) Suez Canal connects the Red Sea with the Mediterranean. It allows water transport between Europe and Asia without traveling around Africa, and 8% of the world's shipping runs through the Suez Canal.

> ### CASE STUDY
>
> Gatún Lake is an artificial lake created for the operation of the locks in the Panama Canal. A significant environmental problem that occurs with Gatún Lake is the drainage of water (up to 52 million gallons [197 million L] of freshwater leaves the lake every time a ship passes through the canal). Although there is sufficient annual rainfall to replenish the water used by the canal, the seasonal nature of the rainfall requires storage of water from one season to the next. The rainforest surrounding the lake traditionally played a major role by absorbing rainwater and releasing it slowly. However, due to recent deforestation of the land around the lake, rain flows rapidly down through the deforested slopes, carrying silt into the lake. The excess water is spilled out into the ocean. This results in a shortfall during the dry season and silt buildup in the lake, which must be periodically dredged.

Roadless Areas and Ecosystem Impacts

Roadless areas are places where no roads have been built and where, as a result, no logging or other development can occur. Roadless areas are havens for fish and wildlife whose habitats in many other forest areas has been fragmented or entirely destroyed. They provide habitats for more than 1,600 threatened, endangered, or sensitive plant and animal species and include watersheds that supply clean drinking water. The roadless rule protects 60 million acres, or 31%, of National Forest System lands—about 2% of the total land base of the United States.

PUBLIC AND FEDERAL LANDS

The federal government manages public lands. It sets aside areas as national parks, wildlife refuges, and wetlands.

Management

The Bureau of Land Management (BLM) is responsible for managing 262 million acres (105 million ha) of land, about one-eighth of the land in the United States. The BLM also manages about 300 million additional acres (120 million ha) of subsurface mineral resources. The bureau is also responsible for wildfire management and preservation on 400 million acres (162 million ha). Most of the lands the BLM manages are located in the western United States, including Alaska. They are dominated by extensive grasslands, forests, high mountains, arctic tundra, and deserts. The BLM manages a wide variety of resources and uses including energy and minerals, timber, forage, wild horse and burro populations, fish and wildlife habitats, wilderness areas, and archaeological, paleontological, and historical sites.

National Parks

There are over 1,100 national parks in the world today. However, many of them do not receive proper protection from poachers, loggers, miners, or farmers due to the costs involved.

The United States National Park System encompasses approximately 84 million acres (34 million ha), of which more than 4 million acres (1.6 million ha) remain in private ownership. The largest area is in Alaska and is more than 16% of the entire system. U.S. National parks are threatened by high demand by large numbers of visitors, which leads to congestion, eroded trails, noise that disrupts wildlife, and pollution from autos and visitors. Other threats include off-road vehicles, introduction of nonnative species that impact biodiversity, and commercial activities such as mining, logging, livestock grazing, and urban development.

There are several solutions to these problems:

- Reducing the amount of private land within national parks through incentives to current owners
- Providing education programs to the public
- Setting quotas on attendance through advanced reservation systems
- Adopting a fee system that covers external costs
- Banning off-road vehicles
- Banning autos and instead provide shuttle buses to control traffic
- Providing tax incentives for property owners near national parks to use land grants
- Conducting periodic and detailed wildlife and plant inventories

---

RELEVANT LAWS

Wilderness Act (1964): Wilderness was defined by its lack of noticeable human modification or presence. Federal officials are required to manage wilderness areas in a manner conducive to retention of their wilderness character.

Wild and Scenic Rivers Act (1968): Established a system of areas distinct from the traditional park concept to ensure the protection of each river's unique environment. It also preserves certain selected rivers that possess outstanding scenic, recreational, geological, cultural, or historic values and maintains their free-flowing condition.

Food Security Act (1985): Also known as "Swampbuster," this act contains provisions designed to discourage the conversion of wetlands into non-wetland areas. The act also created a system for farmers to regain lost federal benefits if they restored converted wetlands.

Wildlife Refuges

President Theodore Roosevelt designated 4-acre (1.6 ha) Pelican Island, off Florida, in 1903 as the first national wildlife refuge, designed to protect breeding birds. Roosevelt designated another 52 wildlife refuges before he left office in 1909. The early refuges were established primarily to protect wildlife such as the overhunted bison and birds killed by market hunters, such as egrets and waterfowl. During the drought years of the Great Depression, refuges were created to protect waterfowl. The system developed piecemeal largely in response to such wildlife crises. The National Wildlife Refuge System, consisting today of 547 refuges encompassing more than 93 million acres (37 million ha), is managed by the U.S. Fish and Wildlife Service.

Wetlands

Wetlands are areas that are covered by water and support plants that can grow in water-saturated soil. High plant productivity supports a rich diversity of animal life. Countries with the most wetlands are Canada (14% of land area), the Russian Federation (including Siberia), and Brazil. Wetlands were once about 10% of the land area in the United States but have been reduced to about 5%, with most of them in Louisiana and Florida. Most wetland habitat loss—90%—is due to conversion of the land to agriculture with the rest of the loss due to urbanization. Wetlands are home to a wide variety of species. One-third of all endangered species in the United States spend part of their life span in wetlands. Wetlands serve as natural water purification systems removing sediments, nutrients, and toxins from flowing water. Wetlands along lakes and oceans stabilize shorelines and reduce damage caused by storm surges, reduce the risks of flooding, and reduce saltwater intrusion.

Fens are wetlands characterized by continuous sources of groundwater rich in magnesium and calcium, which makes a fen very alkaline. This groundwater comes from glaciers that have melted, depositing their water in layers of gravel and sand. The water sits upon layers of soil (glacial drift) that are not permeable, thus keeping the water from sinking beneath the surface. The water is then forced to flow sideways along the surface, where it picks up minerals in its path.

A bog is a type of wetland that accumulates acidic peat, a deposit of dead plant material that can be dried and burned for fuel. Bogs are located in cold, temperate climates. They are usually in boreal biomes such as western Siberia, parts of Russia, Ireland, Canada, and the states of Minnesota and Michigan. Bogs are generally low in nutrients and highly acidic. Carnivorous plants have adapted to these conditions by using insects as their nutrient source.

Wilderness Areas

Wilderness areas are wild or primitive portions of national forests, parks, and wildlife refuges where timbering, most commercial activity, motor vehicles, and human-made structures are prohibited. The Wilderness Act (1964) created the National Wilderness Preservation System, the system that collectively unites all individual wilderness areas. This system encompasses a wide variety of ecosystems throughout the country including swamps in the Southeast, tundra in Alaska, snowcapped peaks in the Rocky Mountains, hardwoods forests in the Northeast, and deserts in the Southwest.

LAND CONSERVATION OPTIONS

Preservation, remediation, mitigation, restoration and sustainable land use strategies are land conservation options. Several principles can be employed in land conservation using a land-use ethic model:

1. Protect biodiversity, wildlife habitats, and the ecological functioning of public land ecosystems through careful monitoring and enforcement.

2. Adopt a user pay approach for extracting resources from public lands. Eliminate government subsidies and tax breaks to corporations that extract publicly owned resources.

3. Institute fair compensation for resources extracted from public land. Instead of the government subsidizing the extraction of resources, the corporations should be paying the government fair market value for natural resources.

4. Require responsibility for any user who damages or alters public land.

5. Adopt uneven-aged management forestry practices that foster maintaining a variety of tree species at various ages and sizes. Uneven-aged management fosters biological diversity, long-term sustainable production of high-quality timber, selective cutting, and the principle of multiple use of the forests for recreation, watershed protection, wildlife, and timber.

6. Include ecological services of trees in estimating valuation.

7. Reduce road building into uncut forest areas. Require restoration plans for those roads that are currently in place, and require such plans for any future roads.

8. Coordinate with the Forest Service on leaving fallen timber and standing dead trees in place to promote nutrient cycling and providing wildlife habitats.

9. Grow timber on longer rotations.

10. Reduce or eliminate clear-cutting, shelter wood cutting, or seed tree cutting on sloped land.

11. Rely on more sustainable tree-cutting methods such as selective and strip cutting.

12. Reduce fragmentation of remaining large forests.

13. Require certification of lumber that is cut according to sustainable forest practices.

14. Use sustainable techniques for tropical forests. These include: educating settlers about sustainable forest practices and their advantages, monitoring and enforcing cutting based on sound ecological principles, and reducing subsidies that encourage tropical deforestation. Other techniques include instituting debt-for-nature and conservation easements, creating subsidies for sustainable practices, and rehabilitating areas that have already been degraded.

15. Solutions to urban land use problems include zoning. Various parcels of land are designated for certain uses but can be influenced by developers. Local governments can limit permits, require environmental impact analyses, require developer fees for services, tax farmland on the basis of its actual (not potential) use, promote compact development and preservation of open space, and establish green spaces, urban boundaries, and land trusts.

The following items describe some land conservation options:

PRESERVATION OR SUSTAINABLE

To keep or maintain intact. Example: Land trusts are private, nonprofit organizations that actively work to conserve land by undertaking or assisting in land or conservation acquisition, or by stewardship of such land.

REMEDIATION

The act or process of correcting a fault or deficiency. Example: Cleanup from the 1989 *Exxon Valdez* Alaskan oil spill or from the 2010 BP Deepwater Horizon oil spill affecting the Gulf of Mexico and the gulf coast of the United States.

MITIGATION

To moderate or alleviate in force or intensity. Example: Numerous vehicle-deer collisions in Georgia led officials to implement a system of wildlife warning reflectors along local roads. The county installed several thousand reflectors designed to make deer freeze in place before approaching the roadway. The reflectors reduced wildlife mortality and saved motorists thousands of dollars in collision costs.

RESTORATION

To restore to its former good condition. Ecosystem restoration involves management actions designed to facilitate the recovery or reestablishment of native ecosystems. A central premise of ecological restoration is that restoration of natural systems to conditions consistent with their evolutionary environments will prevent their further degradation while simultaneously conserving their native plants and animals. Example: Removing a dam, which will allow the return of native fish to a river or the removal of harmful, invasive exotic species from a riparian environment.

MINING

The following table provides an overview of mining.

Overview of Mining		
Steps	**Descriptions**	**Environmental Effects and Issues**
Mining	Removing mineral resource from the ground. Can involve underground mines, drilling, room-and-pillar mining, long-wall mining, open pit, dredging, contour strip mining, and mountaintop removal.	Mine wastes—acids and toxins. Displacement of native species. Reclamation of land and recycling.
Processing	Removing ore from gangue. Involves transportation, processing, purification, smelting, and manufacturing.	Pollution (air, water, soil, and noise). Human health concerns, risks, and hazards.
Use	Involves distribution to end user.	

Extraction

Before mining begins, economic decisions are made to determine whether a site will be profitable. Factors that enter into the decision include current and projected price, amount of ore at the site, concentration, type of mining required, cost of transporting the ore to a processing facility, and cost of reclamation. After all factors are analyzed, several steps are employed.

SITE DEVELOPMENT

Samples are taken from an area to determine the quality and quantity of minerals in a location. Roads and equipment are brought in.

EXTRACTION

Three main methods of extraction exist: surface mining, underground mining, and *in situ* leaching. Surface mining is a type of mining in which the soil and rock overlying the mineral deposit (known as overburden) is removed and stored (spoilbank). Surface mining is used where deposits of commercially useful minerals are found near the surface, and where the overburden is relatively thin or the area is unsuitable for tunneling. Surface mines are typically enlarged until either the mineral deposit is exhausted, or the cost of removing larger volumes of overburden makes further mining impractical.

There are five main forms of surface mining: (1) Strip mining, the most commonly used method to mine coal or tar sand, is the practice of mining a seam of mineral by first removing a long strip of overburden. Area stripping is used on fairly flat terrain to extract deposits over a large area. As each long strip is excavated, the overburden is placed in the excavation produced by the previous strip. Contour stripping involves removing the overburden above the mineral seam near the outcrop in hilly terrain, where the mineral outcrop usually follows the contour of the land. This method commonly leaves behind terraces in mountainsides. (2) Open-pit mining refers to a method of extracting rock or minerals from the earth by their removal from an open pit. (3) Mountaintop removal mining is used where a coal seam outcrops all the way around a mountaintop. All the rock and soil above the coal seam are removed, and the soil is placed in adjacent lows such as hollows or ravines. Mountaintop removal replaces previously steep topography with a relatively level surface. (4) Dredging is a method often used to bring up underwater mineral deposits. Although dredging is usually employed to clear or enlarge waterways for boats, it can also recover significant amounts of underwater minerals relatively efficiently and cheaply. (5) Highwall mining uses a continuous mining machine driven under remote control into the seam exposed by previous open-cut operations. A continuous haulage system carries the coal from the mine to an open-air installation for stockpiling and transport.

In underground mining, large shafts are dug into the earth. There is less surface destruction and waste rock produced than in surface mining, but it is unsafe. Sub-surface mining often occurs below the water table, so water must be constantly pumped out of the mine in order to prevent flooding. When a mine is abandoned, the pumping ceases and water floods the mine. This introduction of water often results in acid rock drainage, which is caused by certain bacteria accelerating the decomposition of metal sulfide ions that have been exposed to air and water.

Finally, with *in situ* leaching, small holes are drilled into the site. Water-based chemical solvents are used by miners to extract the resources. Advantages of *in situ* mining include: it is a less-expensive method since rocks do not have to be broken up or removed; there are shorter lead times to production; and it requires less surface ground disturbance and less mediation. On the negative side, fluids injected into the earth are toxic and enter the groundwater supply.

PROCESSING

Processing involves intensive chemical processing during smelting. This is the method by which a metal is obtained from its ore, either as an element or as a simple compound. It is usually accomplished by heating beyond the melting point, ordinarily in the presence of reducing agents such as coke or oxidizing agents such as air. A metal whose ore is an oxygen compound (iron, zinc, or lead oxides) is heated (reduction smelting) in a blast furnace to a high temperature. The oxide combines with the carbon in the coke, escaping as carbon monoxide or carbon dioxide. Other impurities are removed by adding flux, with which they combine to form slag. If the ore is a sulfide mineral (copper, nickel, lead, or cobalt sulfides) air or oxygen is introduced to oxidize the sulfide to sulfur dioxide and any iron to slag, leaving the metal.

In cyanide heap leaching, gold ore is heaped into a large pile. Cyanide solution is then sprayed on top of the pile. As the cyanide percolates downward, the gold leaches out of the ore and collects in pools at the bottom. The gold extracted may be only 0.01% of the total ore processed. Liquid wastes containing cyanide and other toxins are kept in tailing ponds, which eventually leak and enter groundwater supplies.

Tailings are the materials left over after the process of separating the valuable fraction from the ore. Tailings represent an external cost of mining. In coal and oil sands mining, the word "tailings" refers specifically to fine waste suspended in water.

TIP

coke—a solid fuel made by heating coal in the absence of air so that the volatile components are driven off.

flux—a mineral added to the metals in a furnace to promote fusing or to prevent the formation of oxides.

slag—waste matter separated from metals during the smelting or refining of ore.

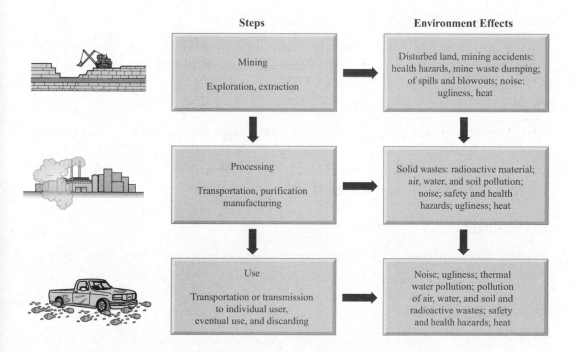

Figure 7.12 Steps required for manufacturing products and their environmental consequences

Global Reserves

Two billion tons (1.8 billion m.t.) of minerals are extracted and used each year in the United States (about 10 tons [9.1 m.t.] for every American). At the same time, the United States imports more than 50% of its most needed minerals. As mineral reserves become depleted, lower grades of ore are mined, which causes more processing and consequently more pollution.

The United States, Germany, and Russia represent 8% of the world's population, yet they consume 75% of the most widely used metals, with the United States consuming 20%.

RELEVANT LAWS

General Mining Law (1872): Grants free access to individuals and corporations to prospect for minerals in public domain lands and allows them, upon making a discovery, to stake a claim on that deposit.

Mineral Leasing Act (1920): Authorizes and governs leasing of public lands for developing deposits of coal, petroleum, natural gas and other hydrocarbons, phosphates, and sodium in the United States. Prior to the act, these materials were subject to mining claims under the General Mining Act of 1872.

Surface Mining Control and Reclamation Act (1977): Established a program for regulating surface coal mining and reclamation activities.

FISHING

Different techniques are used to fish the planet's waters:

BOTTOM TRAWLING

Uses a funnel-shaped net to drag the ocean bottom. Shrimp, cod, flounder, and scallops. Analogous to clear-cutting forests. Species not wanted is called bycatch.

DRIFT NET

Long expanses of nets that hang down in water. Traps turtles, seabirds, and marine mammals. During the 1980s, 10,000 dolphins and whales and millions of sharks were killed each year by drift nets. The 1992 U.N. voluntary ban on drift nets longer than 1.5 miles (2.4 km) has made some progress.

LONGLINE

Placing very long lines with thousands of baited hooks. Swordfish, tuna, sharks, halibut, and cod. Endangers sea turtles, pilot whales, and dolphins.

PURSE SEINE

Surrounds large schools of fish spotted by aircraft with a large net. Net is then drawn tight. Tuna, mackerel, anchovies, and herring.

Overfishing

The oceans have been looked on as unlimited resources. Ocean productivity is generally low and results from spatial separation of required plant nutrients. Light is restricted to surface waters.

The oceans supply 1% of all human food and represent 10% of the world's protein source. China is responsible for about one-third of all fish harvesting from the oceans. About one-third of the total catch of fish is used for purposes other than human consumption, such as fish oil, fish meal, and animal feed. Another one-third of global catches consists of bycatch. These are marine mammals, sea turtles, birds, noncommercial fish, and shellfish that are ensnared in fishing nets or dredged up by trawling and discarded.

Maximum sustained yield is the largest amount of marine organisms that can be continually harvested without causing the population to crash. This yield generally occurs when a population is maintained at half the carrying capacity.

Methods to manage fisheries in a sustainable manner include:

1. Regulate locations and numbers of fish farms and monitor their pollution output

2. Encourage the production of herbivorous fish species

3. Require and enforce labeling of fish products that were raised or caught according to sustainable methods

4. Set catch limits far below maximum sustainable yields

5. Eliminate government subsidies for commercial fishing

6. Prevent importation of fish from foreign countries that do not adhere to sustainable-harvesting methods

7. Place trading sanctions on foreign countries that do not respect the marine habitat, including countries that hunt whales

8. Assess fees for harvesting fish and shellfish from public waters

9. Increase the number of marine sanctuaries and no-fishing areas

10. Increase penalties for fishing techniques that do not allow escape of bycatch, including unwanted fish species, marine mammals, sea birds, and sea turtles

11. Ban the throwing back of bycatch

12. Monitor and destroy invasive species transported through ship ballast

Several methods can restore habitats suitable for freshwater fish. These include: planting native vegetation on stream banks, rehabilitating in-stream habitats, controlling erosion, and controlling invasive species. Other restsorative methods include restoring fish passages around human-made impediments, monitoring, regulating, and enforcing recreational and commercial fishing; and protecting coastal estuaries and wetlands.

Aquaculture

Aquaculture, commonly known as mariculture or fish farming, includes the commercial growing of aquatic organisms for food. It involves stocking, feeding, protection from predators, and harvesting. Aquaculture is growing about 6% annually and provides 5% of the total food production worldwide, most of it coming from less-developed countries. Currently, the most popular products being produced through aquaculture include seaweeds, mussels, oysters, shrimp, and certain species of fish (primarily salmon, trout, and catfish). Kelp makes up about 17% of aquaculture output and is used as a food product and as a source of various products used in the food industry. Aquaculture is used to raise 80% of all mollusks, 40% of all shrimp, and 75% of all kelp.

Aquaculture offers several advantages over raising livestock in that cold-blooded organisms convert more feed to usable protein. For example, for every 1 million calories of feed required, a trout raised on a farm produces about 35 grams of protein whereas a chicken produces 15 grams of protein and cattle produce 2 grams of protein. For every hectare of ocean, intense oyster farming can produce 58,000 kg of protein while natural harvesting of oysters produces 10 kg of protein.

For aquaculture to be profitable, the species must be marketable, inexpensive to raise, trophically efficient, at marketable size within 1 to 2 years, and disease resistant. Aquaculture creates dense monocultures that reduce biodiversity within habitats and requires large levels of nutrients in the water.

Aquaculture offers possibilities for sustainable protein-rich food production and for economic development to local communities. However, aquaculture on an industrial scale may pose several threats to marine and coastal biological diversity. It creates wide-scale destruction and degradation of natural habitats and leaves nutrients and antibiotics in aquaculture wastes. Accidental releases of alien or modified organisms into native waters, transmission of diseases to wild stocks, and displacement of local and indigenous human communities are also side effects.

CASE STUDY

Polychlorinated biphenyls (PCBs) were banned in the U.S. in the late 1970s and are slated for global phase-out under the United Nations treaty on persistent organic pollutants. PCBs are highly persistent and have been linked to cancer and impaired fetal brain development. Salmon farming has made salmon the third most popular fish in America and comprises 22 percent of all retail seafood counter sales. Many consumers eat more salmon today to avoid over-consumption of beef and poultry, and to benefit from anti-cancer and anti-heart disease properties of oily fish. However, analysis of U.S. government data found that farmed salmon are likely the most PCB-contaminated protein source in the current U.S. food supply. Approximately 800,000 U.S. adults have an increased cancer risk by eating PCB-contaminated salmon. Farmed salmon are fattened with ground fishmeal and fish oils that are high in PCBs. As a result, salmon farming operations that produce inexpensive fish unnaturally concentrate PCBs. Furthermore, farmed salmon contains 52 percent more fat than wild salmon, according to the U.S. Department of Agriculture.

RELEVANT LAWS

Anadromous Fish Conservation Act (1965): Authorizes the Secretary of the Interior to enter into agreements with states and other non-federal interests to conserve, develop, and enhance the anadromous fish (fish that migrate from the sea to fresh water to spawn) resources of the United States.

Magnuson Fishery Conservation and Management Act (1976): Governs marine fisheries management in United States federal waters. Aids in the development of the domestic fishing industry by phasing out foreign fishing. To manage the fisheries and promote conservation, the Act created eight regional fishery management councils. The 1996 amendments focused on rebuilding overfished fisheries, protecting essential fish habitat, and reducing bycatch.

United Nations Treaty on the Law of the Sea (1982): Defines the rights and responsibilities of nations in their use of the world's oceans, establishing guidelines for businesses, the environment, and the management of marine natural resources.

GLOBAL ECONOMICS

The economy and the environment are intrinsically linked such that both are simultaneously causes and effects and are inputs and outputs of each other. The environment contains all the resources that can be used in the economy. The use of resources for economic purposes continuously creates new environmental situations. For example, while some resources are depleted and transformed from usable to unusable states, economic resources are used to expand additional resources. This occurs through increasing the available supply of materials, opening land to agricultural production, transporting resources from locations where they are in surplus to areas of shortage, and so on.

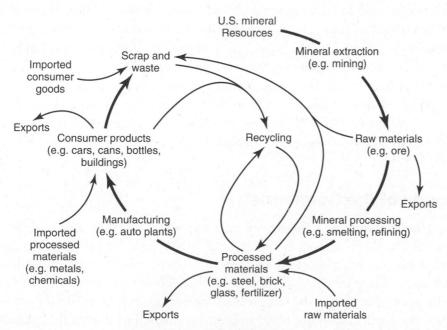

Figure 7.13 Resources cycle

Increased levels of economic activity and improvements in living standards have occurred since the end of World War II. People in the wealthiest countries constitute 15% of the global population and enjoy average levels of income that are about 20 times greater than the 85% of the global population that live in poorer countries.

If the income of the poorest 85% were raised to only one-third that of the richest countries, the level of total world production and consumption would have to double, with a similar increase in the use of Earth's resources. The conclusion is that continued increases in living standards in poorer countries will increase pressure on the carrying capacity of the planet.

Until recently, developments in local economies and local environments were dispersed and, to a great extent, isolated. They did not typically result in cumulative processes that had widespread or global impact. However, as with the economy, over the past century or so, the growth of human populations throughout the world (and the greater vigor with which these populations have assaulted the environment in their pursuit of higher production and consumption levels) has led to a significant increase in global environmental disruption. The effects of these disruptions have become increasingly interlinked. A global environment—a set of interrelated processes, causes and effects, not simply a group of unrelated ecological events—has come into being.

World Bank

The World Bank is a source of financial and technical assistance to developing countries around the world. The World Bank (owned by 184 member countries) provides low-interest loans, interest-free credit, and grants to developing countries for education, health, infrastructure, communications, and environmental issues. In 2001, the World Bank Board of Directors endorsed an environment strategy to guide the bank's actions in environmental areas. The strategy emphasizes three objectives: improving the quality of life, improving the quality of growth, and protecting the quality of the regional and global commons through the "greening" of investments in agriculture, water sanitation, and other environmental projects. The World Bank in 2005 has distributed $13.8 billion in public and private funds in the areas of biodiversity, conservation, climate change, and international waters; funded $740 million in projects to phase out ozone-depleting substances; and funded $1.6 billion into projects that reduce greenhouse gas emissions.

The World Bank is also the greatest single source of funds for large dam projects, having provided more than $50 billion for construction of more than 500 large dams in 92 countries. Since 1948, theses large dam projects have forcibly displaced approximately 10 million people from their land.

"Tragedy of the Commons"

Garrett Hardin wrote the "Tragedy of the Commons" in 1968, and it appeared in the journal *Science*. The story parallels what is happening worldwide in regard to resource depletion and pollution. The seas, air, water, animals, and minerals are all the commons. They are there for humans to use. Those who exploit them become rich. The price of depleting the resources of the commons is an external cost paid by all people on Earth. Examples of current environmental problems that parallel the issues of sustainability brought up in the "Tragedy of the Commons" include:

- Uncontrolled human population growth leading to overpopulation
- Air pollution
- Overextraction of groundwater and wasting water due to excessive irrigation
- Frontier logging of old growth forest and slash and burn
- Burning of fossil fuels and consequential global warming
- Habitat destruction and poaching
- Overfishing

Limits to the "Tragedy of the Commons" include the following:

- Economic decisions are generally short term, based on reactions in the world market. Environmental decisions are long term.
- Land that is privately owned is subject to market pressure. For example, if privately owned timberland is increasing in value at an annual rate of 3% but interest rates on loans to purchase the land are 7%, this could result in the land being sold or the timber being harvested for short-term profits.
- Some commons are easier to control than others. Land, lakes, rangeland, deserts, and forests are geographically defined and easier to control than air or the open oceans that do not belong to any one group.
- Incorporating discount rates into the valuation of resources would be an incentive for investors to bear a short-term cost for a long-term gain.
- Breaking a commons into smaller, privately owned parcels fragments the policies of governing the entire commons. Different standards and practices used on one parcel may or may not affect all other parcels.

NAMES TO KNOW

Rachel Carson: Wrote *Silent Spring*, which spurred a reversal in national pesticide policy and led to a nationwide ban on DDT and other pesticides, and which inspired a grassroots environmental movement that led to the creation of the Environmental Protection Agency.

Aldo Leopold: Best known for his book *A Sand County Almanac*. Influential in the development of modern environmental ethics and in wilderness conservation emphasizing biodiversity and ecology. Developed the science of wildlife management.

John Muir: Helped to save the Yosemite Valley, Sequoia National Park, and other wilderness areas. The Sierra Club, which he founded, is now one of the most important environmental conservation organizations in the United States.

Theodore Roosevelt: As the twenty-sixth president of the United States, he used his position to pave the way for environmentalists of the future. He is known for setting aside land for national forests, establishing wildlife refuges, developing the farmlands of the American West, and advocating protection of natural resources. Roosevelt set aside 150 million acres for forest reserves, created 50 wildlife refuges, turned much of the arid land of the southwestern United States into farmland, and initiated sixteen major reclamation projects in the southwest.

Henry David Thoreau: Author of *Walden*, which viewed unity and community as important aspects of nature, and wrote that all disturbances in these links are caused by human beings and that modern materialism would lead to the destruction of the environment needed for humans and other living things to survive. Wrote about the need for national forest preserves and about the destruction caused by dams. His work raised the environmental consciousness of many generations of readers.

QUICK REVIEW CHECKLIST

☐ **Feeding a Growing Population**
- ☐ human nutritional requirements
- ☐ types of agriculture
  - ☐ agroforestry
  - ☐ alley cropping
  - ☐ crop rotation
  - ☐ high-input agriculture
  - ☐ industrial agriculture (corporate farming)
  - ☐ intercropping
  - ☐ interplanting
  - ☐ low input agriculture
  - ☐ low-till agriculture
  - ☐ no-till agriculture
  - ☐ conservation-till agriculture
  - ☐ monoculture
  - ☐ plantation
  - ☐ polyculture
  - ☐ polyvarietal cultivation
  - ☐ subsistence agriculture
  - ☐ tillage

☐ **Green Revolution**
- ☐ first green revolution
- ☐ second green revolution

☐ **Genetic Engineering and Crop Production**
- ☐ genetically engineered crops

☐ **Irrigation**

☐ **Sustainable Agriculture**
- ☐ efficient use of inputs
- ☐ selection of site, species, and variety
- ☐ soil management
- ☐ species diversity

☐ **Controlling Pests**
- ☐ types of pesticides
  - ☐ biological
  - ☐ carbamates
  - ☐ chlorinated hydrocarbons
  - ☐ fumigants
  - ☐ inorganic
  - ☐ organic or natural
  - ☐ organophosphates
- ☐ pros and cons of using pesticides

QUICK REVIEW CHECKLIST (continued)

☐ **Integrated Pest Management**

☐ **Forestry**
  ☐ ecological services
  ☐ tree plantations (pros and cons)
  ☐ old-growth forests

☐ **Forest Fires**
  ☐ crown fires
  ☐ ground fires
  ☐ surface fires
  ☐ methods to control fires

☐ **Deforestation**
  ☐ even-age management
  ☐ uneven-age management
  ☐ selective cutting
  ☐ high grading
  ☐ shelterwood cutting
  ☐ seed tree cutting
  ☐ clear-cutting
  ☐ strip cutting

☐ **Case Study**
  ☐ Hubbard Brook Experimental Forest

☐ **Forest Management**
  ☐ Responsibilities of the U.S. Forest Service

☐ **Rangelands**
  ☐ overgrazing
  ☐ desertification
  ☐ remediation

☐ **Federal Rangeland Management**
  ☐ factors that affect resource utilization

☐ **Urban Land Development**
  ☐ planned development
  ☐ suburban sprawl and urbanization

☐ **Transportation Infrastructure**
  ☐ Federal Highway System

☐ **Canals and Channels**
  ☐ Case Study (Gatún Lake)

QUICK REVIEW CHECKLIST (continued)

- ☐ **Roadless Areas and Ecosystem Impacts**
  - ☐ Roadless Area Conservation Rule (2001)

- ☐ **Public and Federal Lands**
  - ☐ management
  - ☐ Federal Land Policy and Management Act (1976)
  - ☐ National Parks
    - ☐ Wilderness Act (1964)
    - ☐ Wild and Scenic Rivers Act (1968)

- ☐ **Wildlife Refuges**

- ☐ **Wetlands**

- ☐ **Land Conservation Options**

- ☐ **Mining**
  - ☐ extraction
  - ☐ site development
  - ☐ extraction
  - ☐ processing

- ☐ **Fishing**
  - ☐ bottom trawling
  - ☐ drift net
  - ☐ long line
  - ☐ purse seine
  - ☐ overfishing

- ☐ **Aquaculture**
  - ☐ Anadromous Fish Conservation Act (1965)
  - ☐ Marine Mammal Protection Act (1972)
  - ☐ Magnuson Fishery Conservation and Management Act (1976)
  - ☐ United Nations Treaty on the Law of the Sea (1982)

- ☐ **Global Economics**
  - ☐ World Bank

- ☐ **Tragedy of the Commons**

MULTIPLE-CHOICE QUESTIONS

1. Chronically undernourished people are those who receive approximately _____ calories or less per day.

   (A) 500
   (B) 1,000
   (C) 1,500
   (D) 2,000
   (E) 3,000

2. The greatest threat to the success of a species is

   (A) environmental pollution
   (B) loss of habitat
   (C) poaching
   (D) hunting
   (E) introduction of new predators into the natural habitat

3. The second law of thermodynamics would tend to support

   (A) people eating more meat than grain
   (B) people eating more grain than meat
   (C) people eating about the same amount of grain as meat
   (D) people being undernourished
   (E) people eating a balanced diet from all food groups

4. The majority of nutrients and calories in the average human diet come from

   (A) potatoes, corn, and rice
   (B) wheat, rice, and soybeans
   (C) wheat, corn, and rice
   (D) wheat, corn, and oats
   (E) wheat, corn, and soybeans

5. Planting trees and/or shrubs between rows of crops is known as

   (A) contour farming
   (B) planting windbreaks
   (C) strip cropping
   (D) alley cropping
   (E) tillage farming

6. The one area of the world that is NOT expected to increase food production soon is

   (A) Asia
   (B) Latin America
   (C) sub-Saharan Africa
   (D) China
   (E) India

7. Most foods derived from genetically modified crops contain
   (A) the same number of genes as food produced from conventional crops
   (B) the same number of genes as foods produced from hybrid crops
   (C) one or two additional genes
   (D) hundreds of additional genes
   (E) no genes at all

8. Which region of the developing world is currently as urbanized as the developed world?

   (A) Africa
   (B) Asia
   (C) Latin America
   (D) Europe
   (E) North America

9. Malnutrition primarily refers to

   (A) lack of carbohydrates in the diet
   (B) lack of protein in the diet
   (C) lack of fat in the diet
   (D) a deficiency of micronutrients in the diet
   (E) a deficiency of vitamins in the diet

10. Adding more fertilizer does NOT necessarily increase crop production is an example of

    (A) law of supply and demand
    (B) Leibig's law of minimum
    (C) limiting factors
    (D) second law of thermodynamics
    (E) Gaia hypothesis

11. Soil that is transported by the wind is

    (A) alluvial
    (B) feral
    (C) gangue
    (D) rill
    (E) aeolian

12. Most of Earth's land area is

    (A) urban
    (B) forest
    (C) desert
    (D) rangeland
    (E) agricultural

13. Cities experiencing the greatest urban growth are found in
    (A) Asia
    (B) Africa
    (C) Europe
    (D) North America
    (E) both choices (A) and (B)

14. Which of the following is NOT a concept designed to create a sustainable city?

    (A) Conserve natural habitats
    (B) Focus on energy and resource conservation
    (C) Design affordable and fuel-efficient automobiles
    (D) Provide ample green space
    (E) All are correct

15. Approximately what percentages of the world depends upon wood or charcoal for heating and/or cooking?

    (A) Less than 10%
    (B) Between 20% and 30%
    (C) Between 50% and 60%
    (D) More than 75%
    (E) Has not been determined

16. Of all the jobs in the U.S. Forest Service, the majority are concerned with

    (A) lumber management
    (B) fire management
    (C) mining management
    (D) recreation
    (E) administrative functions

17. In which of the following states or areas would you NOT find significant amounts of old-growth forests?

    (A) New England
    (B) Appalachia
    (C) British Columbia
    (D) Washington State
    (E) California

18. Most grain that is grown in the United States is used

    (A) for export to countries that need grain
    (B) for cereals and baked goods
    (C) to feed cattle
    (D) for trade with other countries
    (E) to create fuel and liquor

19. What is the number one source of soil erosion?

    (A) Physical degradation
    (B) Chemical degradation
    (C) Water erosion
    (D) Wind erosion
    (E) All forms contribute equally

20. A process in which small holes are drilled into Earth and water-based chemical solvents are used to flush out desired minerals is known as

    (A) chemical leaching
    (B) *ex-situ* leaching
    (C) beneficiation
    (D) heap leaching
    (E) *in situ* leaching

FREE-RESPONSE QUESTION

by: Sarah E. Utley
    College Board APES Reader; Princeton, NJ
    Environmental Content Specialist, Center for Digital Innovation
    AP Environmental Science Division, UCLA

TIP

The Free-Response section of the APES exam consists of four required questions: one data-set question, one document-based question, and two synthesis and evaluation questions. Be sure you are comfortable with and know what is required for each type of question.

Deposits of coal were recently discovered in a small valley in the eastern foothills of the Rocky Mountains. These deposits were found both near the surface and underneath the ground.

(a) Describe a method that could be used to mine the coal.

(b) Using coal as an energy source can have serious environmental consequences. Discuss current technological methods employed to reduce the impact of using coal as an energy source.

(c) The residents of this small town have mixed opinions about the impact of the mine on their community. Some residents support the mine because of the increased employment opportunities and increased tax base that supports projects such as schools and roads. Others are concerned about current or possible future environmental impacts on this region of the state. Discuss two of these possible environmental impacts.

MULTIPLE-CHOICE ANSWERS AND EXPLANATIONS

1. **(D)** Chronic malnutrition is defined as receiving fewer than 2,000 calories per day. People who live in developed nations receive an average of 3,340 calories per day.

2. **(B)** There are many reasons why certain species decline and become endangered; however, most environmentalists agree that the most significant factor is habitat loss and degradation.

3. **(B)** The second law of thermodynamics states that there is about a 10% loss in each successive higher trophic level in the energy pyramid.

4. **(C)** Wheat and rice supply approximately 60% of worldwide human calories.

5. **(D)** See the table in the section "Types of Agriculture" for a more detailed explanation about alley cropping.

6. **(C)** Droughts, pestilence, AIDS, and civil strife in this area have had serious impacts on food production in this part of the world.

7. **(C)** Combining genes from different organisms is known as recombinant DNA technology, and the resulting organism is said to be "genetically modified," "genetically engineered," or "transgenic." Genetically modified products include medicines and vaccines, foods and food ingredients, feeds, and fibers.

8. **(C)** Despite the rapid growth in urbanization in Asian and African countries, their current percentage of people living in urban areas is still half of that of Latin America. About 75% of Latin America's population currently lives in urban areas.

9. **(B)** Protein malnutrition, more commonly referred to as protein-energy malnutrition, is the most lethal form of malnutrition. Protein is necessary for key body functions, including provision of essential amino acids and development and maintenance of muscles.

10. **(C)** There is a limit to crop yield versus fertilizer application. Additional fertilizer past a certain point can actually harm plants.

11. **(E)** Aeolian soils are sand-sized particles transported by wind action.

12. **(B)** About one-third of Earth's surface is covered by forests.

13. **(E)** In 2015, the largest cities in the world are projected to be Tokyo (Japan), Bombay (India), Lagos (Nigeria), and Dhaka (Bangladesh).

14. **(C)** Designing affordable and fuel-efficient cars would increase the number of automobiles already in cities since more people could afford them. More private vehicles results in congestion, pollution, and so on.

15. **(C)** As late as the 1850s, wood supplied over 90% of the energy requirements in the United States. Half of the energy currently used in Africa is fuel wood.

16. **(D)** The number of recreational visitors in all National Forests in 1993 was 730 million. By the year 2045, the number is projected to rise by approximately 63 percent.

17. **(A)** Only 20% of the worlds' original forests remain intact. In New England, the first area to be colonized by Europeans, 99% of the frontier forests have been destroyed.

18. **(C)** There are about 1.5 billion cattle on Earth. They graze on 25% of the landmass and consume enough grain to feed hundreds of millions of people. In the United States, cattle consume 70% of all grain produced.

19. **(C)** Water erosion is about half of the problem.

20. **(E)** See the section "Extraction" for a more detailed explanation.

FREE-RESPONSE ANSWER

Ten points necessary for full-credit.
Section (a): worth 2 points. Describe either surface or subsurface mining.
Section (b): worth 4 points. Explain at least two remediation techniques.
Section (c): worth 4 points. Two points awarded for each completely described
environmental impact.

(a) 1. Coal that is located close to the surface is frequently extracted by strip-mining. In surface mining, the rock, soil, and vegetation layers that are on top of the coal are scraped away and removed. The removed rock and soil are called overburden. Specifically, in strip mining, a long trench is dug, removing the overburden and the coal. Then a second trench is dug parallel to the first, and the overburden from the second is used to fill the first trench. The hill of loose overburden that fills the previous trench is called a spoil bank. The process continues until the coal is depleted or the cost of future extraction is prohibitive.

Notable points:

Description of mining type.

Specific description of coal removal.

or

2. Coal that is located deep underneath the surface of Earth is removed through underground or subsurface mining techniques. A deep shaft must be dug or blasted into the area. An extensive network of tunnels (which are supported with wooden or metal beams) is then dug, and these extend out from the main shaft. Sometimes part of the coal vein is left intact to support the shafts and tunnels. If the mine is large enough, electricity is wired, an elevator is installed to take workers to the active part of the mine, and tracks are laid on which the loaded bins of coal travel. The coal itself can be removed with special mining machines equipped with large drills. The mined coal is then loaded into the mining bins and taken to the surface.

Description of mining type.

Description of coal removal.

(b) Coal can contain contaminants such as rocks, ash, mineral dust, and sulfur. These contaminants decrease the efficiency of the coal and can increase the environmental impact of burning the fossil fuel. When coal with high sulfur content is burned, the sulfur can enter the atmosphere as sulfur dioxide—a component of acid rain. Several techniques can decrease the environmental impact of coal use. When coal is initially mined, it is usually washed. Washing involves separating the impurities from the coal based on density. The contaminants are generally denser than the coal and sink in the separation fluid. The process involves first grinding the coal into small pieces. Then the pieces are placed onto a separation table with a fluid. The coal is skimmed off the top. The contaminants, such as pyrite (a sulfur derivative), sink to the bottom. In addition to the initial washing of coal, remediation techniques can decrease the amount of pollutants that result from the burning or use of coal.

The Clean Air Act (revised in 1990) requires that all new coal-burning plants built after 1978 must be equipped with air quality structures that remove the sulfur from the combustion gases before they are released through the smokestack. These structures are called scrubbers. In a scrubber, a mixture of water and crushed limestone is sprayed into the gases. The sulfur from the emissions and the limestone chemically combine to form a solid (calcium sulfate). This solid is then disposed in a solid waste disposal facility or can be used in the production of some building products.

Though an answer may contain more than two remediation techniques, at a minimum, a full-credit answer should contain two techniques.

Introduction of techniques.

Purpose of washing.

Description of washing (performed after excavation and prior to combustion).

Purpose of scrubbers.

Description of scrubbers.

Description of fluidized bed combustion.

Purpose of fluidized bed combustion.

The question specifically asks for two environmental implications.

Name of each concern.

Cause of each impact.

Environmental result of each.

In addition to scrubbers, there is additional technology that can decrease the environmental impact of coal burning. In a fluidized bed combustion plant, the coal particles are suspended within the boiler on jets of air. This tumbling of the burning coal allows limestone to be introduced into the plant prior to the smokestack. The limestone combines with the sulfur and chemically bonds with it to capture a greater amount of sulfur pollutants. In addition to removing the sulfur prior to entering the smokestack, a fluidized bed boiler burns at a cooler temperature than a conventional boiler. This cooler temperature prevents the smog-forming NO_x pollutants from becoming volatile and being released into the air.

(c) (Give two implications.)

(1) Water pollution is frequently a concern with the mining of coal. Water is used throughout the mining process, from cooling machinery and smelters to washing coal. If this contaminated water is not contained and purified, it can seep into the local waterways or water table. In addition, precipitation that percolates through the area can leach soil contaminants from the mining process into the local water table or waterways. The water table of the areas located close to the mines must be carefully monitored for quality.

(2) Air pollution is also a concern in the mining industry. The mining machinery, which is frequently powered by diesel engines, contributes to air pollution in the mine vicinity. In addition, the burning of coal often releases air toxins such as sulfur dioxide, nitrogen oxides, and particulate matter into the atmosphere. New combustion units are now mandated by the Clean Air Act to be fitted with scrubbers and other clean air apparatuses. Many states are now requiring that even older equipment must meet new clean air requirements.

(3) There is also the concern of habitat destruction and wildlife–native plant displacement. The process of surface mining, which requires the removal of many tons of soil, disturbs the natural ecosystem and displaces native animals. Subsurface mining is often less disruptive to soil and the soil surface but has its own concerns, such as subsidence and land instability. Though mining corporations are required by law to return the land to the original topography, since the soil structure has been altered, native plant revegetation techniques often fail. When the native plants fail to thrive, reintroducing native wildlife is difficult.

(4) Mining can also be harmful to human health. With subsurface mining, workers must be protected against unstable mine shafts, generally dangerous working conditions, and health concerns such as poor air quality. Safely ventilating the mines below the ground can be difficult, and care must be taken to protect the workers from the respiratory diseases such as emphysema and lung cancer. With the large amount of mining equipment (large cranes, bulldozers, and so on) required in surface mining, human safety is always a concern.

UNIT V: ENERGY RESOURCES AND CONSUMPTION (10–15%)

Areas on Which You Will Be Tested

A. Energy Concepts—energy forms, power units, conversions, and laws of thermodynamics.

B. Energy Consumption
1. History—Industrial Revolution, exponential growth, and energy crisis.
2. Present global energy use.
3. Future energy needs.

C. Fossil Fuel Resources and Use—formation of coal, oil, and natural gas, extraction/purification methods, world reserves and global demand, synfuels, and environmental advantages/disadvantages of sources.

D. Nuclear Energy—nuclear fission process, nuclear fuel, electricity production, nuclear reactor types, environmental advantages/disadvantages, safety issues, radiation and human health, radioactive wastes, and nuclear fusion.

E. Hydroelectric Power—dams, flood control, salmon, silting, and other impacts.

F. Energy Conservation—energy efficiency, CAFE standards, hybrid electric vehicles, and mass transit.

G. Renewable Energy—solar energy, solar electricity, hydrogen fuel cells, biomass, wind energy, small-scale hydroelectric, ocean waves and tidal energy, geothermal, and environmental advantages/disadvantages.

Energy

CHAPTER 8

ENERGY CONCEPTS

Energy is the ability to do work. In the SI system, the unit of energy is the joule. Power is work divided by time. The unit of power is the joule/s, which is also called a watt. The following table describes the different energy forms.

Forms of Energy

Form	Description
Mechanical	There are two types of mechanical energy: potential energy (a book sitting on a table) and kinetic energy (a baseball flying through the air).
Thermal	Heat is the internal energy in substances—the vibration and movement of the atoms and molecules within substances.
Chemical	Chemical energy is stored in bonds between atoms in a molecule.
Electrical	Electrical energy results from the motion of electrons.
Nuclear	Nuclear energy is stored in the nuclei of atoms. It is released by either splitting or joining of atoms.
Electromagnetic	Electromagnetic energy travels by waves.

Power and Units

Power is the amount of work done per time. The most common unit of power is the kilowatt-hour (kWh).

Units of Energy/Power

Unit or Prefix	Description
Btu (British Thermal Unit)	Btu is a unit of energy used in the United States. In most countries it has been replaced with the joule. A Btu is the amount of heat required to raise the temperature of 1 pound of water by 1°F. 1 watt is approximately 3.4 Btu/hr. 1 horsepower is approximately 2,540 Btu/hr. 12,000 Btu/hr. is referred to as a "ton" in many air-conditioning applications.
Horsepower	Primarily used in the automobile industry. 1 horsepower (HP) is equivalent to 746 watts.
Kilo-	1,000 or 10^3. 1 kW = 10^3 watts.
Mega- (M)	1,000,000 or 10^6. 1 MW = 10^6 watts.
Kilowatt hour (kWh)	Unit of energy equal to 1,000 watt hours or 3.6 megajoules. The kilowatt hour is most commonly known as a billing unit for energy delivered to consumers by electric utilities. Examples: A heater rated at 1,000 watts (1 kilowatt), operating for one hour uses one kilowatt hour (equivalent to 3.6 megajoules) of energy. Using a 60 watt lightbulb for one hour consumes 0.06 kilowatt hours of electricity. Using a 60 watt lightbulb for 1,000 hours consumes 60 kilowatt hours of electricity.

Conversions

Let's do a sample conversion problem that you might experience on the APES exam. We will break it down into steps and show you how it might be graded.

TIP

Be sure to practice these types of conversion problems. They appear very frequently in the Free-Response Question on the APES test. Also, be sure you are comfortable with scientific notation and the factor-label method.

EXAMPLE PROBLEM #1

Thorpeville is a rural community with a population of 8,000 homes. It gets its electricity from a small, municipal coal-burning power plant just outside of town. The power plant's capacity is rated at 20 megawatts with the average home consuming 10,000 kilowatt hours (kWh) of electricity per year. Residents of Thorpeville pay the utility $0.12 per kWh. A group of entrepreneurs is suggesting that the residents support a measure to install 10 wind turbines on existing farmland. Each wind turbine is capable of producing 1.5 MW of electricity. The cost per wind turbine is $2.5 million dollars to purchase and operate for 20 years.

(a) The existing power plant runs 8,000 hours per year. How many kWh of electricity is the current plan capable of producing?

2 points. 1 point for correct setup. 1 point for correctly calculating the amount of electricity generated. You must correctly convert MW to kW. No points will be awarded without showing your work. Alternative setups are acceptable.

$$\frac{20\,\text{MW}}{1} \times \frac{(1 \times 10^6\,\text{watts})}{1\,\text{MW}} \times \frac{1\,\text{kW}}{10^3\,\text{watts}} = 2 \times 10^4\,\text{kW}$$

$$\frac{(2 \times 10^4\,\text{kW})}{1} \times \frac{8{,}000\,\text{hours}}{1\,\text{yr.}} = 16{,}000 \times 10^4\,\text{kWh/yr}$$

$$= 1.6 \times 10^8\,\text{kWh/yr.}$$

(b) How many kWh of electricity do the residents of Thorpeville consume in one year?

2 points. 1 point for correct setup. 1 point for correctly calculating the amount of electricity generated. You must correctly convert MW to kW. No points will be awarded without showing your work. Alternative setups are acceptable.

$$\frac{8 \times 10^3\,\text{homes}}{1} \times \frac{1 \times 10^4\,\text{kWh/home}}{1\,\text{yr.}} = 8 \times 10^7\,\text{kWh/yr.}$$

(c) Compare answers (a) and (b). What conclusions can you make?

2 points, plus 1 possible elaboration point. 1 point for comparing answers (a) with (b) with an explanation of why the numbers in parts (a) and (b) would be the same or different (must be a viable reason).

OR

1 point for a solid or accurate explanation of why (a) and (b) are different even if the calculations were not attempted.

1 possible elaboration point for explanations that go into great detail about why the numbers differ.

Note: If you say that (a) and (b) are the same, you must state that this can only occur if the households have backup systems that will produce energy for them if they exceed the power generated by the plant.

The power plant produces 1.6×10^8 kWh per year. The residents, however, only use 8×10^7 kWh per year. This leaves a surplus of $1.6 \times 10^8 - 8 \times 10^7 = 8 \times 10^7$ kWh in one year that can be sold to other towns. At a rate of $0.12 per kWh, this provides a surplus of 8×10^7 kWh × \$0.12/kWh = $0.96 \times 10^7 = \$9,600,000$.

Additional revenues could be generated by running the power plant 24 hours a day, 365 days a week.

Differences between Thorpeville's consumption and the power plant's output could be attributed to the following:

- The power plant needs to produce higher amounts of power to compensate for line loss.
- The power plant needs to produce higher amounts of power to supply energy to the town during peak hours, not just the average usage.
- The power plant needs to plan for possible future growth of the town.
- The power plant was built over capacity to provide a source of income to the town.

(d) Assuming that the population of Thorpeville remains the same for the next 20 years, and that electricity consumption remains stable per household, what would be the cost (expressed in $ per kWh) of electricity to the residents over the next 20 years if they decided to go with wind turbines?

2 points. 1 point for correct setup. 1 point for correct answer with calculations. Alternative setups are acceptable. If your answer in part (b) is incorrect but you appropriately use it as the basis for the calculations for answering the question in part (d), you will receive full credit for answering part (d) if the setup and calculations are correct, even if the answer is not correct.

Based on current community consumption of 8×10^7 kWh/yr from part (b).

$$\text{kWh for 20 years} = \frac{8 \times 10^7 \text{ kWh}}{\text{year}} \times 20 \text{ years} = 1.6 \times 10^9 \text{ kWh}$$

$$\text{Direct cost for 20 years} = 10 \text{ turbines} \times \frac{\$2.5 \times 10^6}{\text{turbine}} = \$2.5 \times 10^7$$

$$\text{cost/kWh} = \frac{\$2.5 \times 10^7}{1.6 \times 10^9 \text{ kWh}} = \$1.6 \times 10^{-2}/\text{kWh} = \$0.016/\text{kWh}$$

(e) What are the pros and cons of the existing coal-burning plant compared with the proposed wind farm?

Pros	Cons
WIND: The electricity produced from the wind turbines costs $0.016 per kWh, but each homeowner would also have to pay $25,000,000/8,000 homes = $3,125.00 over 20 years ($156.25/yr.) to pay for the wind turbines. 10,000 kWh at $0.016 per kWh for electricity produced from wind turbines = $160 plus $156.25 per year to pay for the wind turbines = $316.25 per year.	COAL: Electricity costs $0.12 per kWh produced from the coal-burning plant. 10,000 kWh of electricity per year from the coal-burning plant at $0.12 per kWh = $1,200 per year. Clearly, electricity produced from wind turbines is much cheaper.
WIND: Zero emissions. Acid rain would be reduced as well as photochemical smog.	COAL: Produces air pollution, specifically SO_2 and NO_x.
WIND: The wind is free.	COAL: As labor prices increase, the price of coal would be expected to increase over the next 20 years.
WIND: No heavy-metal or radioactive emissions.	COAL: Coal-burning plants produce heavy metals such as mercury, lead, and cadmium pollution along with radio-active contaminants.
WIND: No thermal pollution.	COAL: Can produce thermal pollution to local streams. However, cooling towers can be installed to reduce this form of pollution.
WIND: Multiple use of the land.	COAL: Cannot utilize the concept of multiple use of land.

EXAMPLE PROBLEM #2

(a) An electric water heater requires 0.30 kWh to heat a gallon of water. The thermostat is set to 150°F. The cost of electricity is $0.20 per kWh. A washing machine with a flow rate of 6.0 gallons per minute runs four times each Saturday. Each time it runs it takes in water for a total of 15 minutes. How much total water does the washing machine use in one year?

$$\frac{4 \text{ cycles}}{\text{Saturday}} \times \frac{15 \text{ minutes}}{1 \text{ cycle}} \times \frac{6.0 \text{ gallons}}{1 \text{ minute}} \times \frac{52 \text{ Saturdays}}{1 \text{ year}} = 18{,}720 \text{ gallons / year}$$

2 points. 1 point for correct setup. 1 point for correct answer with calculations. Alternative setups are acceptable.

(b) Calculate the annual cost of the electricity for the washing machine, assuming that 3.0 gallons per minute of the water used by the machine comes from the hot-water heater.

18,720 gallons / 2 = 9,360 gallons of hot water per year

$$\frac{9{,}360 \text{ gallons}}{1 \text{ year}} \times \frac{0.30 \text{ kWh}}{1 \text{ gallon}} \times \frac{\$0.20}{\text{kWh}} = \$561.60 \text{ / year}$$

2 points. 1 point for correct setup. 1 point for correct answer with calculations. Alternative setups are acceptable. If your answer in part (b) is incorrect but you appropriately used information from part (a) as the basis for answering the question, you will receive full credit, even if the numerical answer is wrong.

Laws of Thermodynamics

FIRST LAW

Energy cannot be created or destroyed.

SECOND LAW

When energy is converted from one form to another, a less useful form results (energy quality). Energy cannot be recycled to a higher quality. Only 20% of the energy in gasoline is converted to mechanical energy. The rest is lost as heat and is known as low-quality energy.

ENERGY CONSUMPTION

Wood (a renewable energy source) served as the predominant form of energy up until the Industrial Revolution. During the Industrial Revolution, coal (a nonrenewable energy source) surpassed wood's usage. Coal was overtaken by petroleum during the middle of the 20th century, with petroleum continuing to be the primary source of energy worldwide. Natural gas and coal experienced rapid development in the second half of the 20th century.

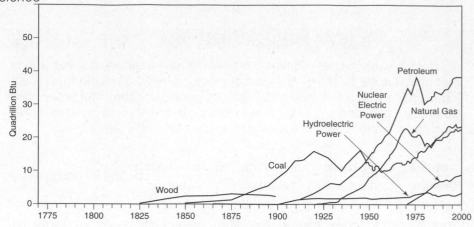

Figure 8.1 Energy consumption by source

Source: Energy Information Administration

The United States was self-sufficient in energy until the late 1950s. At that time, energy consumption began to outpace domestic production, which then led to oil imports.

The industrial sector in the United States has traditionally used the largest share of energy, followed by transportation and then residential and commercial uses. While coal was once the predominant form of energy in the industrial sector, it gave way to natural gas and petroleum in the late 1950s, with rapid increases occurring through the 1970s.

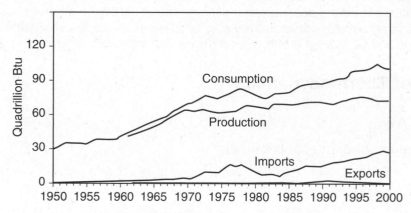

Figure 8.2 U.S. energy overview

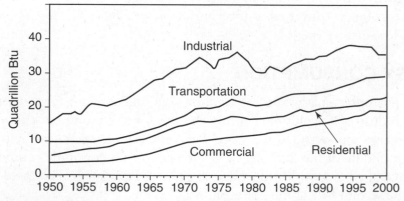

Figure 8.3 Energy consumption in the United States by end use

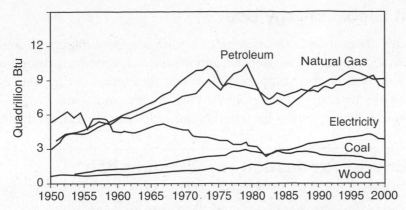

Figure 8.4 Industrial energy consumption

Beginning in 1998, net imports of oil surpassed the domestic oil supply in the United States. The United States accounts for 25% of the world consumption of petroleum.

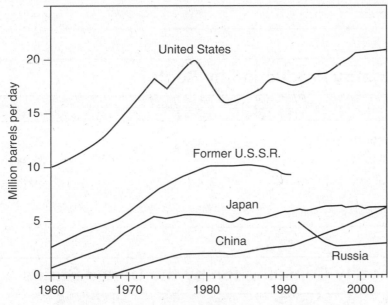

Figure 8.5 Leading petroleum consumers

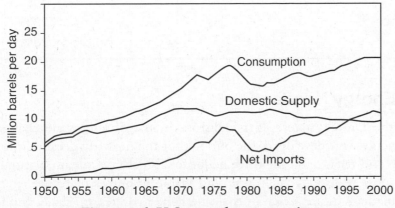

Figure 8.6 U.S. petroleum overview

Present Global Energy Use

In the United States, most of the energy comes from nonrenewable energy sources such as coal, petroleum, natural gas, propane, and uranium. These energy sources are called nonrenewable because their supplies are limited. Renewable energy sources include biomass, geothermal energy, hydropower, solar energy, and wind energy. They are called renewable energy sources because they are replenished in a relatively short time.

U.S. Energy Production vs. Consumption

Commodity	U.S. Production	U.S. Consumption
Oil	18%	39%
Natural gas	27%	23%
Coal	33%	23%
Nuclear	10%	7%
Renewable (geothermal, biomass, solar, wind)	9%	3.6%
Hydroelectric	5%	4%

U.S. Energy Production by Sector

Sector	%
Transportation	27%
Industrial	38%
Residential and commercial	36%

*Source: U.S. Geological Survey

Commodity Consumption by the United States

Commodity	%
(% of Total World Usage)	
Oil	40%
Natural gas	23%
Coal	23%

Future Energy Needs

Although the United States's energy history is one of large-scale change as new forms of energy were developed, the outlook for the next few decades is for continued growth and reliance on the three major fossil fuels: petroleum, natural gas, and coal. The most realistic, economical, and viable resources of future energy needs for the immediate future are clean coal, methane hydrates, oil shale, and tar sands.

CLEAN COAL

The world's supply of coal is substantial and can be expected to meet the world's energy needs for many years to come. Clean-coal technology refers to processes that reduce the negative environmental effects of burning coal. The processes include washing the coal to remove minerals and impurities and capturing the sulfur dioxide and carbon dioxide from the flue gases. Other clean-coal technology is focusing on natural gas or microbial fuel cells charged from biomass or sewage.

In the following diagram, oxygen is introduced to burn coal completely at Step 1. At Step 2, coal is pulverized in order to burn more completely. Coal is also washed at this point to remove contaminants. At Step 3, ash is removed using electrostatic precipitators. At Step 4, steam is condensed and returned to the boiler. And at Step 5, CO_2 is recovered using lime and then sequestered.

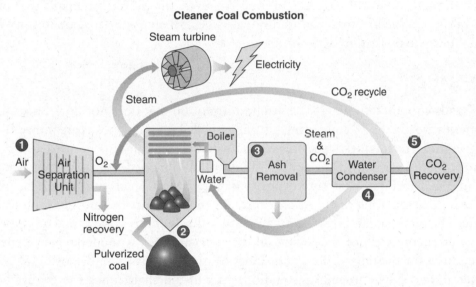

Figure 8.7 Steps used in producing clean coal

METHANE HYDRATES

Methane hydrates (methane locked in ice) are a recently discovered source of methane that form at low temperature and high pressure. They are found in two types of geologic settings: on land in permafrost regions where cold temperatures persist in shallow sediments and beneath the ocean floor at water depths greater than 1,640 feet (500 m) where high pressures dominate and where the hydrate deposits themselves may be several hundred meters thick. Some believe there is enough methane in the form of hydrates to supply energy for hundreds or thousands of years.

Natural gas is expected to take on a greater role in power generation. This is largely because of increasing pressure for clean fuels and the relatively low capital costs of building new natural gas–fired power equipment. The United States will consume increasing volumes of natural gas well into the 21st century. U.S. natural gas consumption is expected to increase 40%. Also, natural gas demand is expected to grow because of its expanded use as a transportation fuel and potentially, in the long-term, as a source of alternative liquid fuels and a source of hydrogen for fuel cells. The primary waste product of burning natural gas is carbon dioxide—a greenhouse gas that contributes to global warming.

OIL SHALE

Oil shales contain an organic material called kerogen. If the oil shale is heated in the absence of air, the kerogen converts to oil. There are approximately 3 trillion barrels of recoverable oil from oil shale in the world, with 750 billion of it being located in the United States. Oil shale can be extracted through either surface mining or *in situ* methods that consist of heating the oil shale underneath the ground and extracting the oil and gases through pumping. Most of the oil shale in the United States is found in Wyoming, Utah, and Colorado. The largest world reserves are found in Estonia, Australia, Germany, Israel, and Jordan.

Surface mining of oil shale negatively impacts the environment. The net energy yield of producing oil through oil shale is moderate since energy is required for blasting, drilling, crushing, heating the material, disposing of waste material, and environmental restoration. *In situ* methods have the potential of affecting aquifers. Even though the world has large oil shale reserves, the problem remains that once the oil is obtained from shale, traditional issues of environmental pollution, acid rain, and global warming will continue.

TAR SANDS

Tar sands contain bitumen—a semisolid form of oil that does not flow. Specialized refineries are capable of converting bitumen to oil. Tar sand deposits are mined using strip-mining techniques. *In situ* methods using steam can also be used to extract bitumen from tar sands. The sulfur content of oil obtained from tar sands is high, about 5%. Most of the tar sand deposits are located in Canada and Venezuela, with those in Canada being the most concentrated and therefore the most economical to mine. The oil in tar sands represents about two-thirds of the world's total oil reserves. The net-energy yield of producing oil through tar sands is moderate since energy is required for blasting, drilling, crushing, heating the material, disposing of waste material, and environmental restoration. As with oil shale, once the oil has been extracted from tar sands, the problems of environmental pollution, acid rain, and global warming continue.

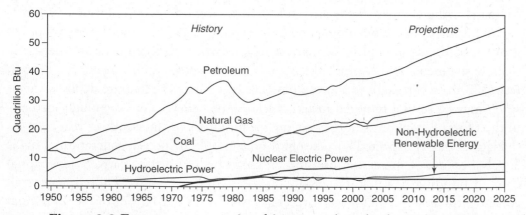

Figure 8.8 Energy consumption history and outlook, 1949–2025

Energy Crisis

In a free-market economy, the price of energy is driven by the principle of supply and demand. Sudden changes in the price of energy can occur if either supply or demand changes. In some cases, an energy crisis is brought on by a failure of world markets to adjust prices in response to shortages. Oil supply is largely controlled by nations with significant reserves of easily extractable oil, such as Saudi Arabia and Venezuela, who belong to an association of oil-producing countries known as OPEC (Organization of Petroleum Exporting Countries). When OPEC reduces the output quotas of its member countries, the price of oil increases as the supply diminishes. Similarly, OPEC can boost oil production in order to increase supplies, which drives down the price. When OPEC raises the price of oil too high, demand decreases and the production of oil from alternative sources becomes profitable. Historically, there have been several energy crises.

Most of the world's energy is supplied by burning oil. At current rates of consumption, world oil reserves are predicted to last 50 years, with oil reserves in the United States predicted to last 25 years. The industrialization of China will significantly decrease this predicted number of years. As supply decreases, prices will increase. Higher prices for oil may make other sources (shale oil and tar sands) more economical.

FOSSIL FUEL RESOURCES AND USE

Coal is produced by decomposition of ancient (286 million-year-old) organic matter under high temperature and pressure. Sulfur from the decomposition of hydrogen sulfide (H_2S) by anaerobic bacteria became trapped in coal. There are three types of coal: lignite, bituminous, and anthracite. Lignite or brown is the softest and has the lowest heat content. Bituminous is soft, has a high sulfur content, and constitutes 50% of the U.S. reserve. Anthracite is hard, has a high heat content and low sulfur content, and makes up 2% of the U.S. reserve. Peat is precoal and is used in some countries for heat but it has low heat content. Coal supplies 25% of the world's energy, with China and the United States consuming the most. In the United States, 87% of the coal is used for power plants to produce electricity. The Clean Air Act requires up to a 90% reduction in the release of sulfur-containing gases.

Oil is a fossil fuel produced by the decomposition of deeply buried organic material (plants) under high temperatures and pressures for millions of years. Compounds derived from oil are known as petrochemicals. They are used in the manufacture of paints, drugs, plastics, etc.

Natural gas (known as methane or CH_4) is produced by the decomposition of ancient organic matter under high temperatures and pressure. Conventional sources of methane are found associated with oil deposits. Unconventional sources include coal beds, shale, gas hydrates, and tight sands. Methane can be liquefied (LNG), which allows for worldwide distribution.

Extraction-Purification Methods

COAL

There are two primary methods of mining coal: surface mining and underground mining. Coal that is going to be burned in solid form may go through a variety of preparation processes. These include removing foreign material, screening for size, crushing, and washing to remove contaminants. It is also possible to turn solid coal into a gas or liquid fuel through clean-coal technologies.

OIL

Oil occurs in certain geologic formations at varying depths in Earth's crust. In many cases, elaborate, expensive equipment is required to extract it. Oil is usually found trapped in a layer of porous sandstone, which lies just beneath a dome-shaped or folded layer of some nonporous rock such as limestone. In other formations, the oil is trapped at a fault, or break in the layers of the crust. Natural gas is usually present just below the nonporous layer and immediately above the oil. Below the oil layer, the sandstone is usually saturated with salt water. The oil is released from this formation by drilling a well and puncturing the limestone layer. The oil is usually under such great pressure that it flows naturally, and sometimes with great force, from the well. However, in some cases, this pressure later diminishes so that the oil must be pumped. Once the oil has been collected, it is sent to a refinery, where it is cracked. Cracking involves separating the components of oil by their boiling points. Refining crude oil produces gasoline, heating oil, diesel oil, asphalt, etc.

CASE STUDY

Arctic National Wildlife Refuge (ANWR): The largest national wildlife refuge in the United States, the ANWR is located in northeastern Alaska and consists of 19 million acres (78,000 km^2). The question of whether to drill for oil in the ANWR has been an ongoing political controversy in the United States since 1977. Much of the debate over whether to drill in ANWR rests on the amount of economically recoverable oil, as it relates to world oil markets, weighed against the potential harm oil exploration might have on the wildlife.

The Keystone Pipeline System is a pipeline concept to transport synthetic crude oil and diluted bitumen from oil sands in Canada to multiple destinations in the United States, which include refineries in Illinois, a distribution hub in Oklahoma, and proposed connections to refineries along the Gulf Coast of Texas. As of October 2012, the plan has not been approved by Congress.

NATURAL GAS

Natural gas typically flows from wells under its own pressure. It is collected by small pipelines that feed into the large gas transmission pipelines. In the United States, about 20 trillion cubic feet (560 billion m^3) of gas is produced each year.

Hydrofracking

Natural gas from dense shale rock formations that have previously been uneconomical to extract has become the fastest-growing source of natural gas in the United States and could become a significant new global energy source. In hydraulic fracturing, or hydrofracking, chemicals are mixed with large quantities of water and sand and injected into wells at extremely high pressure to create fractures in rock that allow oil and natural gas to escape and flow out of the well. Studies estimate that up to 80% of natural gas wells drilled in the next decade will require hydraulic fracturing.

Hydrofracking

Pros	Cons
Process of bringing a well to completion is short, after which the well can be in production for 20 to 40 years.	Dangerous chemicals are used in the process and can enter the water table.
Makes it possible to produce oil and natural gas in places where conventional technologies were ineffective or cost-prohibitive.	Toxic, radioactive, and caustic liquid waste by-products pose storage, treatment, and disposal problems. There are no adequate safeguards or regulations currently in place for this process.
Allows greater independence from foreign sources of energy and helps create new jobs, which in turn stimulates the economy.	Hydrofracking results in contaminated water supplies, air pollution, destroyed streams, and negative environmental impacts on local flora and fauna.

World Reserves and Global Demand

Coal, oil, and natural gas are nonrenewable energy resources. Following is a brief description of the known world reserves of these energy sources and their expected demands in the future.

COAL

Coal is currently the world's single largest source of fuel used to produce electricity. The United States has the largest proven recoverable coal reserves in the world, whereas China is the world's largest producer of coal. Global coal reserves are estimated to last about 300 years at current levels of extraction with continuing issues of CO_2 emissions and global warming.

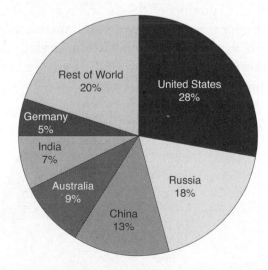

Figure 8.9 World recoverable coal reserves by region

OIL

A large portion of the Earth's global crude oil reserve—45% to 70%—has already been depleted. It is estimated that there is a 50-year supply left on Earth, with countries in the Middle East owning about half of what's left. The United States owns

3% of the world's oil reserves but uses 30% of the oil extracted in the world each year. Increased competition for foreign oil by China and India increases the world's cost of oil. Two-thirds of the oil used in the United States is used for transportation (gasoline, diesel, jet fuel, etc.). About one-fourth of it is used in industries such as plastics, medicines, etc. Oil imports in the United States have decreased slightly in the last few years due to improvements in energy efficiency and higher fuel economy standards. Of all known oil reserves, 65% is found in 1% of all fields—primarily in the Middle East.

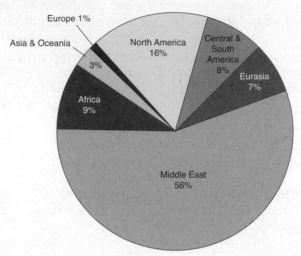

Figure 8.10 World oil reserves by region

NATURAL GAS

Most of the world's natural gas reserves are located in the Middle East (34% of the world total). Russia and Kazakhstan combined have approximately 40% of the world's natural gas reserves, the Middle East has about 25%, and the United States has about 3%. Given U.S. production levels, there is enough natural gas in the United States to meet approximately 75 years of domestic production. This estimate does not take into account expected increasing levels of domestic production or the potential opening up of access to currently restricted land such as the Arctic National Wildlife Refuge.

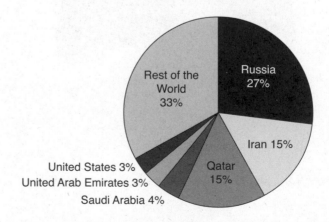

Data from CIA *World Factbook 2008*

Figure 8.11 World natural gas reserves by region

Synfuels

A synthetic fuel (synfuel) is any fuel produced from coal, natural gas, or biomass through chemical conversion. The conversion process creates substances that are chemically the same as crude oil or processed fuels, but were synthesized through artificial means. The raw materials used to make synfuels have to be subjected to intense chemical and physical changes to be usable as crude oil or processed fuel. An example is synthetic natural gas (SNG), which is chemically produced from coal liquefaction.

SOLID COAL TO SYNTHETIC NATURAL GAS (SNG), METHANOL, OR SYNTHETIC GASOLINE

Pros

- Easily transported through pipelines.
- Produces less air pollution.
- Large supply of raw materials available worldwide to meet current demands for hundreds of years.
- Can produce gasoline, diesel, or kerosene directly without reforming or cracking.

Cons

- Low net energy yield and requires energy to produce SNG.
- Plants are expensive to build.
- Would increase depletion of coal due to inherent inefficiencies.
- Product is more expensive than petroleum products.

Environmental Advantages/Disadvantages of Sources

COAL

Pros

- Abundant, known world reserves will last approximately 300 years at current rate of consumption.
- Unidentified world reserves are estimated to last 1,000 years at current rate of consumption.
- United States reserves are estimated to last about 300 years at current rate of consumption.
- Relatively high net-energy yield.
- U.S. government subsidies keep prices low.
- Stable; nonexplosive; not harmful if spilled.

Cons

- Most extraction in the United States is done through either strip mining or underground mining. These methods cause disruption to the land through erosion, runoff, and decrease in biodiversity.
- Up to 20% of coal ends up as fly ash, boiler slag, or sludge. Burning coal releases mercury, sulfur, and radioactive particles into the air. Thirty-five percent of all CO_2 releases are due to the burning of coal, with 30% of all pollution due to NO_x.

- Underground mining is dangerous and unhealthy.
- Expensive to process and transport. Cannot be used effectively for transportation needs.
- Pollution causes global warming. Scrubbers and other antipollution control devices are expensive.

OIL

Pros

- Inexpensive; however, prices are increasing, making alternatives more attractive.
- Easily transported through established pipelines and distribution networks.
- High net-energy yield.
- Ample supply for immediate future.
- Large U.S. government subsidies in place.
- Versatile—used to manufacture many products (paints, medicines, plastics, etc.).

Cons

- World oil reserves are limited and declining.
- Produces pollution (SO_2, NO_x, and CO_2). Production releases contaminated wastewater and brine.
- Causes land disturbances in the drilling process, which accelerates erosion.
- Oil spills both on land and in the ocean from platforms and tankers.
- Disruption to wildlife habitats (e.g., Arctic Wildlife Refuge).
- Supplies are politically volatile.

NATURAL GAS

Pros

- Pipelines and distribution networks are in place. Easily processed and transported as LNG over rail or ship.
- Relatively inexpensive, but prices are increasing. Viewed by many as a transitionary fossil fuel as the world switches to alternative sources.
- World reserves are estimated to be 125 years at current rate of consumption.
- High net energy yield.
- Produces less pollution than any other fossil fuel.
- Extraction is not as damaging to the environment as either coal or oil.

Cons

- H_2S and SO_2 are released during processing.
- LNG processing is expensive and dangerous, and results in lower net energy.
- Leakage of CH_4 has a greater impact on global warming than does CO_2.
- Disruption to areas where it is collected.
- Extraction releases contaminated wastewater and brine.
- Land subsidence.

Fuel Type	Btu Value per Unit	Units Req'd to Produce 1,000,000 Btus	Fuel Price per Unit	Cost to Produce 1,000,000 Btus	Appliance Efficiency[3]	Effective Cost per 1,000,000 Btus
Electricity	3,413 per kWh	293 kWh	$0.14	$41.84	100%	$41.84[1]
Natural Gas	1,000 per ft³ 1 therm = 100 ft³	10 therms	$1.35 per therm	$13.50	80%	$16.88[1]
Fuel Oil	139,000 per gallon	7.1 gallons	$2.86 per gallon	$20.30	80%	$25.38
LP Gas	91,690 per gallon	11 gallons	$2.95 per gallon	$32.45	80%	$40.56
Wood	22,000,000 per cord	0.0607 cords	$225 per cord	$13.66	60%	$22.77[2]
Wood Pellets	8,000 per pound	125 pounds	$0.12 per pound	$14.69	80%	$18.36
Kerosene	135,000 per gallon	7.41 gallons	$3.30 per gallon	$24.45	95%	$25.68

[1] Does not include a fixed monthly charge.

[2] Includes delivery.

[3] Electricity is set at 100% for comparative purposes.

Figure 8.12 Comparisons of U.S. Fuel Prices (as of March 2010)

NUCLEAR ENERGY

During nuclear fission, an atom splits into two or more smaller nuclei along with by-product particles (neutrons, photons, gamma rays, and beta and alpha particles). The reaction gives off heat (exothermic). If controlled, the heat that is produced is used to produce steam that turns generators that then produces electricity. If the reaction is not controlled, a nuclear explosion can result.

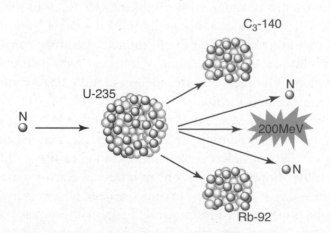

Figure 8.13 Nuclear fission

The amount of potential energy contained in nuclear fuel is 10 million times more than that of more traditional fuel sources such as coal and petroleum. The downside is that nuclear wastes remain highly radioactive for thousands of years and are difficult to dispose. The most common nuclear fuels are U-235, U-238, and Pu-239.

Nuclear Fuel

U-235

U-235 differs from U-238 in its ability to produce a fission chain reaction. The minimum amount of U-235 required for a chain reaction is called the critical mass. Low concentrations of U-235 can be used if the speed of the neutrons is slowed down through the use of a moderator. Less than 1% of all natural uranium on Earth is U-235. Uranium that has been processed to separate out U-235 is known as enriched uranium and is a subject of current controversy with Iran and North Korea. Nuclear weapons contain 85% or more U-235; nuclear power plants contain about 3% U-235. The half-life of U-235 is 700 million years.

U-238

U-238 is the most common (99.3%) isotope of uranium and has a half-life of 4.5 billion years. When hit by a neutron, it eventually decays into Pu-239, which is used as a fuel in fission reactors. Most depleted uranium is U-238.

Pu-239

Pu-239 has a half-life of 24,000 years. It is produced in breeder reactors from U-238. Plutonium fission provides about one-third of the total energy produced in a typical commercial nuclear power plant. Control rods in nuclear power plants need to be changed frequently due to the buildup of Pu-239 that can be used for nuclear weapons and due to the buildup of Pu-240, a contaminant. International inspections of nuclear power plants regulate the amount of Pu-239 produced by power plants.

Electricity Production

The use of nuclear energy as a source for producing electricity in the United States started during the 1960s and increased rapidly until the late 1980s. Reasons for its decline included cost overruns, higher-than-expected operating costs, safety issues, disposal of nuclear wastes, and the perception of it being a risky investment. However, due to electricity shortages, fossil fuel price increases, and global warming, there is a renewed interest and demand for nuclear power plants. As of 2005, nuclear power provided 6% of the world's energy and 15% of the world's electricity, with the U.S., France, and Japan together accounting for 57% of nuclear generated electricity. As of 2007, there were 439 nuclear power reactors in operation in the world, operating in 31 countries. Globally, during the 1980s, one new nuclear reactor started up every 17 days on average; by the year 2015 this rate could increase to one every 5 days.

The United States produces the most nuclear energy, with nuclear power providing 19% of the electricity it consumes, while France produces the highest percentage of its electrical energy from nuclear reactors—78% as of 2006. In the European Union as a whole, nuclear energy provides 30% of the electricity.

Proponents of nuclear energy assert that nuclear power is a sustainable energy source that reduces carbon emissions and increases energy security by decreasing dependence on foreign oil. Proponents also claim that the risks of storing waste are small and can be further reduced by the technology in the new reactors. Furthermore, the operational safety record is already good when compared to the other major kinds of power plants. Critics believe that nuclear power is a potentially dangerous and declining energy source, with decreasing proportions of nuclear energy in power production, and dispute whether the risks can be reduced through new technology. Critics also point out the problem of storing radioactive waste, the potential for possibly severe radioactive contamination by accident or sabotage, the possibility of nuclear proliferation, and the disadvantages of centralized electrical production.

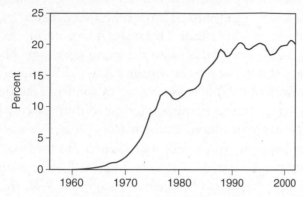

Figure 8.14 Nuclear share of electricity in the United States

Nuclear Reactor Types

Several different nuclear reactor types are in use: light-water reactors, heavy-water reactors, graphite-moderated reactors, and exotic reactors. However, they all have several features in common (see Figure below).

A. The *core* contains up to 50,000 fuel rods. Each fuel rod is stacked with many fuel pellets, each pellet having the energy equivalent of 1 ton (0.9 m.t.) of coal, 17,000 cubic feet (481 m³) of natural gas, or 149 gallons (564 L) of oil.

B. Enriched or concentrated U-235 is usually the *fuel*. The fission of an atom of uranium produces 10 million times the energy produced by the combustion of an atom of carbon from coal.

C. *Control rods* (usually made of boron) move in and out of the core to absorb neutrons and slow down the reaction.

D. A neutron *moderator* is a medium that reduces the velocity of fast neutrons, thereby turning them into thermal neutrons capable of sustaining a nuclear chain reaction. Moderators can be water, graphite (can produce plutonium for weapons), or deuterium oxide (heavy water).

E. *Coolant* removes heat and produces steam to generate electricity.

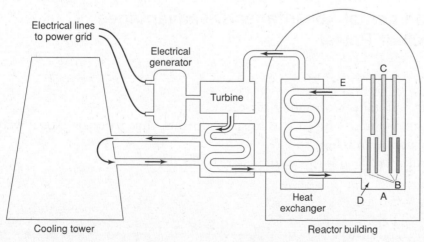

Figure 8.15 Diagram of nuclear power plant

LIGHT-WATER REACTORS

Both the moderator and coolant are light or normal water (H_2O). To this category belong the pressurized-water reactors (PWR) and boiling-water reactors (BWR).

In PWR, the water coolant operates at a high pressure and is then pumped through the reactor core, where it is heated to about 620°F (325°C). The superheated water is pumped through a steam generator. Through heat exchangers, a secondary loop of water is heated and converted to steam. This steam drives one or more turbine generators, is condensed, and is pumped back to the steam generator. The secondary loop is isolated from the water in the reactor core and is not radioactive. A third stream of water from a lake, river, or cooling tower is used to condense the steam.

In BWR, the water coolant is permitted to boil within the core by operating at a lower pressure. The steam produced in the reactor pressure vessel is piped directly to the turbine generator, is condensed, and is then pumped back to the reactor. Although the steam is radioactive, there is no intermediate heat exchanger between the reactor and turbine to decrease efficiency. As in the PWR, the condenser cooling water has a separate source such as a lake or river.

HEAVY-WATER REACTORS

Heavy water, also known as deuterium oxide (D_2O), is a form of water in which each hydrogen in the water molecule contains one proton, one electron, and one neutron. Heavy water is used in certain types of nuclear reactors where it acts as a neutron moderator to slow down neutrons so that they can react with the uranium in the reactor. The use of heavy water essentially increases the efficiency of the nuclear reaction.

GRAPHITE-MODERATED REACTORS

This category uses light water for cooling, graphite for moderation, and uranium for fuel. These reactors require no separated isotopes such as enriched uranium or heavy water. This type of reactor, built by the Russians, was very unstable and is no longer being produced (see the Chernobyl case study).

EXOTIC REACTORS

Fast-breeder reactors and other experimental installations are in this group. Breeder reactors produce more fissionable material than they consume.

Environmental Advantages/Disadvantages of Nuclear Power

PROS

- No air pollutants if operating correctly.
- Releases about 1/6 the CO_2 as fossil fuel plants, thus reducing global warming.
- Water pollution is low.
- Disruption of land is low to moderate.

CONS

- Nuclear wastes take millions of years to degrade. Problem of where to store them and keeping them out of hands of terrorists.
- Nuclear power plants are licensed in the United States by the Nuclear Regulatory Commission (NRC) for 40 years. After that, they can ask to renew their license, or they can shut down the plant and decommission it. Decommissioning means shutting down the plant and taking steps to reduce the level of radiation so that the land can be used for other things. Since it may cost $300 million or more to shut down and decommission a plant, the NRC requires plant owners to set aside money when the plant is still operating to pay for future shutdown costs.
- Low net-energy yield—energy required for mining uranium, processing ore, building and operating plant, dismantling plant, and storing wastes.
- Safety and malfunction issues.

Safety Issues (Radiation and Human Health)

The U.S. Department of Energy (DOE) estimates that up to 50,000 radioactive contaminated sites within the United States require cleanup with a projected cost of $1 trillion dollars. The situation is many times worse in the former Soviet Union.

Estimated Health Risks per Year in the United States

	Nuclear	Coal
Premature death	6,000	65,000
Genetic defects/damage	4,000	200,000

CASE STUDY

Chernobyl, Ukraine (1986): Explosion in a nuclear power plant sent highly radioactive debris throughout northern Europe. Estimates run as high as 32,000 deaths, and 62,000 square miles (161,000 sq km) remain contaminated. About 500,000 people were exposed to dangerous levels of radiation. According to the World Health Organization, the Chernobyl nuclear disaster will cause 50,000 new cases of thyroid cancer among young people living in the areas most affected by the nuclear disaster, and the incidence of thyroid cancer in children rose tenfold in the Ukraine region. In certain parts of Belarus, 36% percent of children who were under four when the accident occurred can expect to develop thyroid cancer. Cost estimates run as high as $400 billion. The cause was determined to be both design and human error.

Nuclear Fusion

Nuclear fusion can occur when extremely high temperatures are used to force nuclei of isotopes of lightweight atoms to fuse together, which causes large amounts of energy to be released. A coal-fed electrical generating plant producing 1,000 megawatts of electricity in one day produces 30,000 tons of CO_2 gases, 600 tons of SO_2 gas, and 80 tons of NO_2 gas. In contrast, a fusion plant producing the same amount of electricity would produce 4 pounds of harmless helium as a waste product.

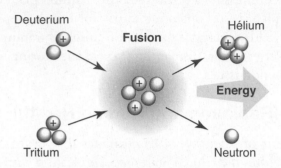

Figure 8.16 Nuclear fusion

HYDROELECTRIC POWER

Dams are built to trap water, which in turn is then released and channeled through turbines that generate electricity. Hydroelectric power supplies about 10% of the electricity in the United States and approximately 3% worldwide.

Pros

- Dams control flooding.
- Low operating and maintenance costs.
- No polluting waste products.
- Long life spans.
- Moderate to high net-useful energy.
- Areas of water recreation.

Cons

- Dams create large flooded areas behind the dam from which people are displaced. Water is slow moving and can breed pathogens.
- Dams destroy wildlife habits and keep fish from migrating.
- Sedimentation requires dredging. Prevents sedimentation from reaching downstream and enriching farmland.
- Expensive to build.
- Destroys wild rivers.
- Large-scale projects are subject to earthquakes.
- Water loss due to increased water surface areas.

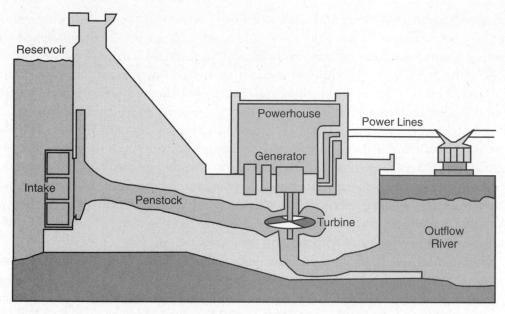

Figure 8.17 Typical hydroelectric dam

Flood Control

Methods to control floods include:

CHANNELIZATION

Straighten and deepen streams. Cons: removes bank vegetation and increases stream velocity, which causes erosion; may increase downstream flooding and sedimentation, which negatively impacts aquatic habitats.

DAMS

Dams store water in reservoirs. During periods of excessive rainfall, dams can be overwhelmed and excess water needs to be released.

IDENTIFY AND MANAGE FLOOD-PRONE AREAS

By identifying flood-prone areas, precautionary building practices such as floodways, building elevation, and pumping stations can be adopted.

LEVEES OR FLOODWALLS

Levees are raised embankments to prevent a river from overflowing. Levees contain river and stream flows but increase water velocity. Levees can break as they did in New Orleans during Hurricane Katrina in 2005.

PRESERVE WETLANDS

This technique preserves natural flood plains and maintains biodiversity.

Salmon

There are an estimated 74,993 dams in America, blocking 600,000 miles (965,000 km) of what had once been free-flowing rivers. Salmon are migratory fish that hatch in streams and rivers and then swim downstream to the ocean to live most of their lives. They return to the rivers and streams from which they hatched to spawn. Dams now block almost every major river system in the West. Many of those dams have destroyed important spawning and rearing habitats for salmon. In the Sacramento Valley in California, less than 5% of the salmon's original habitat is still available. In the Columbia River Basin, once the most productive salmon river system in the world, less than 70 miles (110 km) still remains free-flowing. As a result of habitat destruction, at least 106 major U.S. west coast salmon runs are extinct, and 25 more are now endangered. Dams also change the character of rivers, creating slow-moving, warm-water pools that are ideal for predators of salmon. Low water velocities in large reservoirs can also delay salmon migration and expose fish to higher water temperatures and disease. Cutting trees in forests near the streams and rivers clouds the water with silt and reduces water quality.

Things that have been done to reduce the impacts of dams on fish include fish passage facilities and fish ladders that help juvenile and adult fish migrate over or around many dams. Spilling water at dams over the spillway can help pass juvenile fish downstream because it avoids sending the fish through turbines. Water releases from upstream storage reservoirs have been used to increase water velocities and to reduce water temperatures in order to improve migration conditions through reservoirs. Juvenile fish also are collected and transported downstream in barges and trucks.

Silting and Other Impacts

DISEASE

Dam reservoirs in tropical areas, due to their slow movement, are literally breeding grounds for mosquitoes, snails, and flies—the vectors that carry malaria, schistosomiasis, and river blindness.

DISPLACEMENT

Flooded areas behind dams destroy rich croplands and displace people.

EFFECTS ON WATERSHED

Downstream areas are deprived of the nutrient-rich silt that would revitalize depleted soil profiles.

IMPACT ON WILDLIFE

Migration and spawning cycles are disrupted.

SILTING

Silting occurs when silt (very fine particles intermediate in size between sand and clay) that is dissolved in river water settles out behind dams. Over time, the silt builds up and must be removed (dredged).

WATER LOSS

Large losses of freshwater occur through evaporation and seepage through porous rock beds.

ENERGY CONSERVATION

Energy Star is a joint program of the U.S. Environmental Protection Agency and the U.S. Department of Energy. It is designed to protect the environment through energy-efficient products and practices. Programs coordinated through Energy Star saved enough energy in 2005 to avoid greenhouse gas emissions equivalent to 23 million cars and $12 billion in utility bills. The symbol shown below appears on products that meet Energy Star standards.

CAFE Standards

Transportation needs consume two-thirds of the petroleum consumption in the United States. This sector of energy consumption is increasing faster than any other sector (1.8% growth per year). Imports of crude oil and other petroleum products are expected to increase 66% by 2020. CAFE (Corporate Average Fuel Economy) standards are the average fuel economies of a manufacturer's fleet of passenger cars or light trucks. The testing follows the guidelines established by the Environmental Protection Agency. It is estimated that CAFE standards result in savings of over 55 billion gallons (210 billion L) of fuel annually with a substantial reduction in carbon dioxide emissions of approximately 10%. CAFE standards are achieved through better engine design, efficiency, and weight reduction. The average CAFE standard of 27.5 miles per gallon (11.7 km/L) for automobiles has not increased in the United States since 1996 with SUV standards less than those for light trucks. Significant improvements in fuel mileage could be achieved by expanding CAFE standards to include:

1. Streamlining

2. Reduced tire-rolling resistance

3. Engine improvements, especially transitioning to a hybrid technology

4. Optimized transmission improvements

5. Transition to higher voltage automotive electrical systems

6. Performance-based tax credits

Hybrid Electric Vehicles

Cars should be able to drive at least 300 miles (482 km) between refuelings, be refueled quickly and easily, and keep up with the other traffic on the road. A gasoline-powered car meets these requirements but produces a relatively large amount of pollution and generally gets poor gas mileage. For example, 1 gallon (4 L) of gasoline weighs 6 pounds (2.7 kg). When burned, the carbon in it combines with oxygen from the air to produce nearly 20 pounds (9 kg) of carbon dioxide. An electric car, however, produces almost no pollution but has limited range between charges. A hybrid vehicle attempts to increase the mileage and reduce the emissions of a gas-powered car significantly while overcoming the shortcomings of an electric car.

Gasoline-electric hybrid cars contain five important parts. First, it has an engine. The gasoline engine on a hybrid is smaller than on a gas-only car and uses advanced technologies to reduce emissions and increase efficiency. Second, the fuel tank in a hybrid is the energy storage device for the gasoline engine. Gasoline has a much higher energy density than batteries do. For example, about 1,000 pounds (455 kg) of batteries are needed to store as much energy as 1 gallon (3.7 L) or 6 pounds (2.7 kg) of gasoline. Third, advanced electronics allow the electric motor to act as a generator. For example, when it needs to, the motor can draw energy from the batteries to accelerate the car. When acting as a generator, it can slow down the car and return energy to the batteries. Fourth, the generator is similar to an electric motor, but it acts only to produce electrical power. It is used mostly on series hybrids. Fifth, the batteries in a hybrid car are the energy storage device for the electric motor. Unlike the gasoline in the fuel tank, which can power only the gasoline engine, the electric motor on a hybrid car can put energy into the batteries as well as draw energy from them.

A parallel hybrid has a fuel tank that supplies gasoline to the engine and a set of batteries that supplies power to the electric motor. Both the engine and the electric motor power the car at the same time. In a series hybrid, the gasoline engine turns a generator, which charges the batteries and/or powers an electric motor. The gasoline engine never directly powers the vehicle.

Plug-in hybrid electric vehicles are hybrid cars with an added battery. Plug-in hybrids can be plugged in to a 120-volt outlet and charged. Plug-ins run on the stored energy for much of a typical day's driving—up to 60 miles per charge. When the charge is used up, plug-in hybrids automatically keep running on the fuel in the fuel tank. A plug-in does not entail any sacrifice of vehicle performance or driver amenities. A midsize plug-in can accelerate from 0 to 60 miles per hour (0–96 kph) in less than 9 seconds and sustain a top speed of 97 miles per hour (156 kph). Higher initial costs are partly offset by lower operating costs.

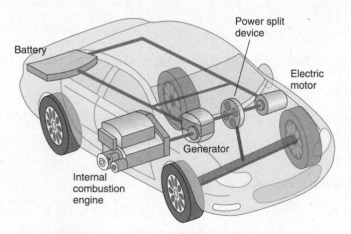

Figure 8.18 Hybrid electric vehicle

Alternative Fuels (LNG and CNG)

A natural gas vehicle or NGV is an alternative fuel vehicle that uses compressed natural gas (CNG). In 2010, there were 12.7 million natural gas vehicles throughout the world, led by Pakistan with 2.7 million vehicles. The Asia-Pacific region leads the world with 6.8 million NGVs, followed by Latin America with 4.2 million vehicles. In the Latin American region, almost 90% of NGVs have bi-fuel engines, allowing these vehicles to run on either gasoline or CNG.

Vehicles running on CNG require high compression and thus thick walled tanks, adding to the material cost and weight. CNG is also lighter than air, dispersing upwards in case of a leak. The cost of CNG is much cheaper than oil based products; some areas of the United States in April 2012 were selling a gallon's equivalent of CNG for $1.09. NGVs and especially CNG tends to corrode and wear the parts of an engine less rapidly than gasoline. Driving 500,000 miles (800,000 km) on an engine designed to run on CNG is not uncommon.

Finally, emissions are cleaner with NGVs, there is generally less wasted fuel, and lower emissions of carbon and lower particulate emissions per equivalent distance traveled.

Electric Cars

An electric car is an automobile that is propelled only by an electric motor and using electrical energy stored in batteries. Electric cars were popular in the late-19th century and early 20th century until advances in internal combustion engine technology and mass production of cheaper gasoline vehicles led to a decline in the use of the electric drive vehicle. A renewed interest in the production of electric cars occurred during the mid 2000s due mainly to concerns about rapidly increasing oil prices and the need to curb greenhouse gas emissions.

Electric cars have several potential benefits compared to conventional internal combustion automobiles, including: a significant reduction of urban air pollution as they do not emit harmful tailpipe pollutants from the onboard source of power at the point of operation, reduced greenhouse gas emissions from the onboard source of power, and less dependence on foreign oil.

Electric cars, however, are significantly more expensive than conventional internal combustion engine vehicles and hybrid electric vehicles due to the additional cost of their lithium-ion battery pack. Other factors discouraging the adoption of electric cars are the lack of public and private recharging infrastructure and the driver's fear of the batteries running out of energy before reaching their destination due to the limited range of existing electric cars.

Mass Transit

Mass transit includes rail, bus services, subways, airlines, ferries, and so on. Mass transit often determines where people live, where they work, and how much air pollution they are subjected to. In the United States, private cars are the primary mode of transportation. In the rest of the world, mass transport is the primary form. For example, in the United States, only 3% of the population utilizes mass transit on a regular basis. In Japan, that figure expands to 47%. Land availability and whether cities expand vertically (land is not available) or expand horizontally (land is available) often determines the preferred mode of transportation. Use of mass transit rises sharply with population density. Mass transit can be faster than private cars when either a separate infrastructure is reserved for mass transit or special lanes on shared highways are designated for mass transit vehicles, which results in higher speeds and less delay. In some areas, public transport systems are poorly developed and take significantly longer than an equivalent trip in a private vehicle. Perhaps the most efficient method to promote mass transit is to adopt a user-pay approach, where all external costs of operating a private vehicle are factored into license fees and/or vehicle taxes. However, this approach would be met with fierce private and political opposition.

LIGHT RAIL

Consists of trains that share space with road traffic and trains that have their own right-of-way and are separated from road traffic.

BUS RAPID TRANSIT

Includes bus-dedicated and grade-separated right-of-ways, bus lanes, bus signal preference and preemption, bus turnouts, bus-boarding islands, curb realignment, off-bus fare collection, and level boarding.

CAR SHARING

Car sharing is a model of car rental where people rent cars for short periods of time, often by the hour. It is often promoted as an alternative to owning a car where public transit, walking, and bicycling can be used most of the time and a car is only necessary for out-of-town trips, moving large items, or special occasions. It can also be an alternative to owning multiple cars for households with more than one driver. Car sharing differs from traditional car rentals in the following ways: Car sharing is not limited by office hours; reservation, pickup, and return is all self-service; vehicles can be rented by the hour, as well as by the day; vehicle locations are distributed throughout the service area, and often located for access by public transport; and insurance and fuel costs are included in the rates.

Recent studies have found that 30% of households that participated in car sharing sold a car; others delayed purchasing one while transit use, bicycling, and walking also increased among members. Car sharing is generally not cost-effective for commuting to a full-time job on a regular basis. Car sharing can also help reduce congestion and pollution. Replacing private automobiles with shared ones directly also reduces demand for parking spaces.

Successful car sharing development has tended to be associated mainly with densely populated areas. Low-density areas are considered more difficult to serve with car sharing because of the lack of alternative modes of transportation and the potentially larger distance that users must travel to reach the cars.

RENEWABLE ENERGY

Several different forms of renewable energy can be used.

Solar Energy

Solar energy consists of collecting and harnessing radiant energy from the sun to provide heat and/or electricity. Electrical power and/or heat can be generated at home and industrial sites through photovoltaic cells, solar collectors or at a central solar-thermal plant.

Active solar collectors use the sun's energy to heat water or air inside a home or business. It requires an electrical input for pumps and fans. Passive solar requires no moving parts. The structure is built to maximize solar capture, such as large, south-facing windows. Photovoltaic cells are used to generate electricity.

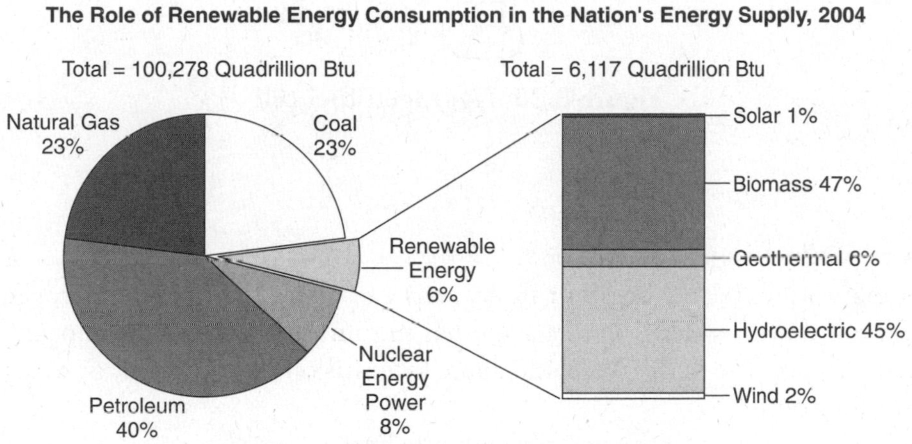

The Role of Renewable Energy Consumption in the Nation's Energy Supply, 2004

Total = 100,278 Quadrillion Btu   Total = 6,117 Quadrillion Btu

Natural Gas 23%
Coal 23%
Solar 1%
Biomass 47%
Renewable Energy 6%
Geothermal 6%
Hydroelectric 45%
Nuclear Energy Power 8%
Wind 2%
Petroleum 40%

Figure 8.19 Renewable energy sources

Pros

- Supply of solar energy is limitless.
- Reduces reliance on foreign imports.
- Only pollution is in manufacture of collectors. Little environmental impact.
- Can store energy during the day and release it at night—good for remote locations.

Cons

- Inefficient where sunlight is limited or seasonal.
- Maintenance costs are high.
- Systems deteriorate and must be periodically replaced.
- Current efficiency is between 10%–25% and not expected to increase soon.

Hydrogen Fuel Cells

Nine million tons of hydrogen is produced in the United States each day—enough to power 20 to 30 million cars or 5 to 8 million homes. Most of this hydrogen is used by industry in refining, treating metals, and processing foods.

The hydrogen fuel cell operates similar to a battery. It has two electrodes, an anode and a cathode, that are separated by a membrane. Oxygen passes over one electrode and hydrogen over the other. The hydrogen reacts with a catalyst on the anode that converts the hydrogen gas into negatively charged electrons and positively charged hydrogen ions. The electrons flow out of the cell to be used as electrical energy. The hydrogen ions move through the electrolyte membrane to the cathode, where they combine with oxygen and the electrons to produce water. Unlike batteries, fuel cells never run out.

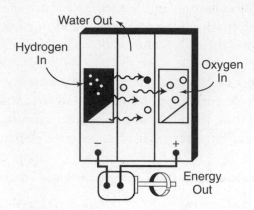

Figure 8.20 Hydrogen fuel cell

Pros

- Waste product is pure water.
- Ordinary water (either ocean or freshwater) can be used to obtain hydrogen.
- Does not destroy wildlife habitats and has minimal environmental impact.
- Energy to produce hydrogen could come from fusion reactor, solar, or other less-polluting source.
- Hydrogen is easily transported through pipelines.
- Hydrogen can be stored in compounds to make it safe to handle. Hydrogen is explosive, but so are methane, propane, butane, and gasoline.

Cons

- Takes energy to produce the hydrogen from either water or methane.
- Changing from a current fossil fuel system to a hydrogen-based system would be very expensive.
- Hydrogen gas is explosive.
- At the current time, it is difficult to store hydrogen gas for personal cars.

Biomass

Biomass is any carbon-based, biologically derived fuel source such as wood, manure, charcoal, or bagasse grown for use as a biofuel. Examples include biodiesel, methanol, and ethanol. Plants that are suitable for biofuel include switch grass, hemp, corn, and sugarcane. Biomass can also be used for building materials and biodegradable plastics and paper. Approximately 15% of the world's energy supply is derived from biomass and is most commonly used in developing nations.

Pros

- Renewable energy source as long as used sustainably.
- Can be sustainable if issue of deforestation and soil erosion are controlled.

- Could supply half of the world's demand for electricity.
- Biomass plantations (cottonwoods, poplars, sycamores, switch grass, and corn) can be located in less desirable locations and can reduce soil erosion and restore degraded land. In the U.S. alone, 200 million acres (80 million ha) are suitable for biomass plantations.

Cons

- Requires adequate water and fertilizer, of which sources are declining.
- Use of inorganic fertilizers, herbicides, and pesticides would harm environment.
- Corn being diverted to produce ethanol raises food prices.
- Would cause massive deforestation and loss of habitat, resulting in a decrease in biodiversity.
- Inefficient methods of burning biomass would lead to large levels of air pollution, especially particulate matter.
- Expensive to transport because it is heavy.
- Not efficient. About 70% of the energy derived from burning biomass is lost as heat.

Biomass can also be burned in large incinerators as an energy source.

Pros

- Crop residues are available (e.g., sugarcane in Hawaii).
- Ash can be collected and recycled.
- Reduces impact on landfills.

Cons

- Net-energy yield is low to moderate. Energy required for drying and transporting material to a centralized facility is prohibitive.
- Severe air pollution if not burned in a centralized facility.
- CO_2 production would have a major impact on global warming.

CASE STUDY

Bagasse is the fibrous matter that remains after sugarcane or sorghum stalks are crushed to extract their juice. It is currently used as a biofuel and in the manufacture of paper and building materials. For each 10 tons of sugarcane crushed, a sugar factory produces nearly 3 tons of bagasse. The high moisture content of bagasse, typically 40 to 50%, is a drawback to its use as a fuel. Approximately 90% of the cars in Brazil run on either alcohol or gasohol (a mixture of gasoline and ethanol) produced from sugarcane grown in Brazil.

Using the by-products of agricultural crops such as bagasse for paper production, rather than wood, does offset commercial forestry practices and reduces the rate of conversion of the rain forest to commercial tree stock; however, this is offset by the clearing of tropical rain forests to areas suitable for growing sugarcane.

Bagasse has been used as a sorbent material to clean up oil spills and to make disposable food containers, replacing materials such as Styrofoam.

Wind Energy

Wind turns giant turbine blades that then power generators. Turbines can be grouped in clusters called wind farms.

Pros

- All electrical needs of the United States could be met by wind in North Dakota, South Dakota, and Texas.
- Wind farms can be quickly built and can also be built out on sea platforms.
- Maintenance is low and the farms are automated.
- Moderate-to-high net-energy yield.
- No pollution. Wind farms are in remote areas so noise pollution is minimal to humans.
- Land underneath wind turbines can be used for agriculture (multiple-use).

Cons

- Steady wind is required to make investment in wind farms economical. Few places are suitable.
- Backup systems need to be in place when the wind is not blowing.
- Visual pollution.
- May interfere with flight patterns of birds.
- May interfere with communication, such as microwaves, TV, and cell phones.
- Noise pollution.

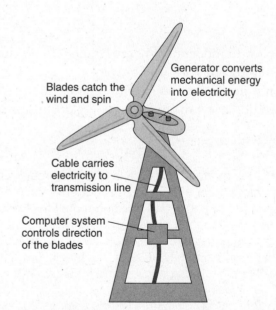

Figure 8.21 Wind turbine

Small-Scale Hydroelectric

Small-scale hydropower utilizes small turbines connected to generators submerged in streams to generate power. Generally, the capacity of small-scale hydropower is 100 kW or less. This technology does not impede stream navigation or fish movement. This technology is especially attractive in remote areas where power lines are not available. Several factors should be considered when installing small-scale hydropower:

- The amount of water flow available on a consistent basis
- The amount of drop (head) the water has between the intake and output of the system
- Regulatory issues such as water rights and easements.

In many cases, there are economic incentives for installing small-scale hydropower systems through grants, loans, and tax incentives.

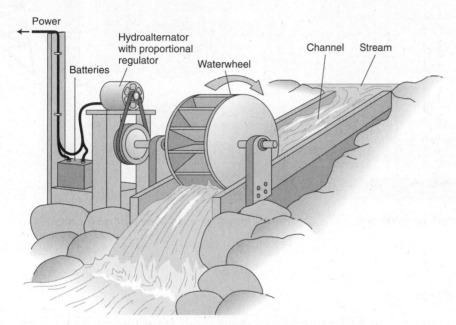

Figure 8.22 Small-scale hydroelectric generator

Ocean Waves and Tidal Energy

The natural movement of tides and waves spin turbines that generate electricity. Only a few plants are currently operating worldwide. They are on the north coast of France and in the Bay of Fundy between the United States and Canada.

Pros
- No pollution.
- Minimal environmental impact.
- Net-energy yield is moderate.

Cons
- Construction is expensive.
- Few suitable sites.
- Equipment can be damaged by storms and corrosion.

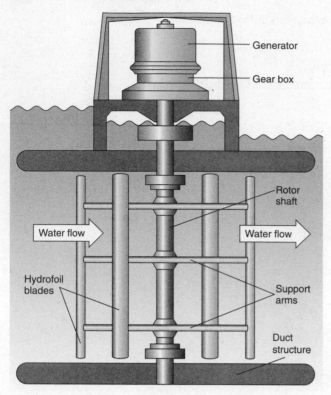

Figure 8.23 Tide turbine used to generate electricity

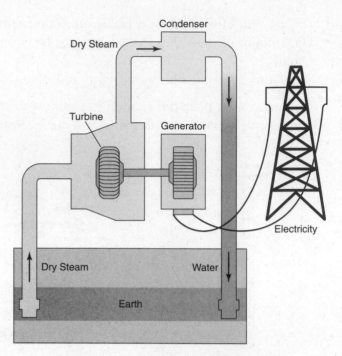

Figure 8.24 Geothermal generator

Geothermal

Heat contained in underground rocks and fluids from molten rock (magma), hot dry-rock zones, and warm-rock reservoirs produce pockets of underground dry steam, wet steam, and hot water. This steam can be used to drive turbines, which can then generate electricity. Geothermal energy supplies less than 1% of the energy needs in the United States. Geothermal energy is currently being used in Hawaii, Iceland, Japan, Mexico, New Zealand, Russia, and California. Areas of known geothermal resources tend to follow tectonic plate boundaries.

Pros

• Moderate net-energy yield.
• Limitless and reliable source if managed properly.
• Little air pollution.
• Competitive cost.

Cons

• Reservoir sites are scarce.
• Source can be depleted if not managed properly.
• Noise, odor, and land subsidence.
• Can degrade ecosystem due to corrosive, thermal, or saline wastes.

RELEVANT LAW

Renewable Energy Law, China (2007): Rapid economic development throughout China has resulted in a significant increase in energy consumption, leading to a rise in harmful emissions and power shortages. China's 2007 Renewable Energy Law requires power grid operators to purchase resources from registered renewable energy producers. The law also offers financial incentives, such as a national fund to foster renewable energy development, and discounted lending and tax preferences for renewable energy projects. The Renewable Energy Law is designed to help protect the environment, prevent energy shortages, and reduce dependence on imported energy. The law includes the use of solar photovoltaics and active solar water heating. Finally, the law includes specific penalties for noncompliance. In 2003, China's renewable energy consumption accounted for only 3% of the country's total energy consumption. The government plans to increase this figure to 10% by 2020. The United States now stands at about 2% usage of renewable energy sources.

CASE STUDY

Bloom Boxes: A Bloom Box is a collection of solid oxide fuel cells that use liquid or gaseous hydrocarbons (such as gasoline, diesel, or propane produced from fossil or bio sources) to generate electricity on the site where it will be used. 20 percent of Bloom Box cost savings result from avoiding transfer losses associated with transmitting energy over an electrical grid. 15 percent of the power at eBay is currently created with Bloom Boxes. Other large companies that are using Bloom Boxes include Google, Staples, Walmart, FedEx, Coca-Cola, and Bank of America.

QUICK REVIEW CHECKLIST

- [ ] **Energy Concepts**
  - [ ] forms of energy
  - [ ] power and units
  - [ ] conversion problems
  - [ ] laws of thermodynamics
- [ ] **Energy Consumption**
  - [ ] present global energy use
  - [ ] energy production vs. consumption
  - [ ] energy production by sector
  - [ ] commodity consumption
- [ ] **Future Energy Needs**
  - [ ] clean coal
  - [ ] methane hydrates
  - [ ] oil shale
  - [ ] tar sands
  - [ ] energy crisis

QUICK REVIEW CHECKLIST (continued)

- ☐ **Fossil Fuel Resources and Use**
  - ☐ extraction-purification methods
    - ☐ coal
    - ☐ oil
    - ☐ natural gas
  - ☐ world reserves and global demand
    - ☐ coal
    - ☐ oil
    - ☐ natural gas
    - ☐ synfuels
- ☐ **Environmental Advantages/Disadvantages of Sources**
  - ☐ coal
  - ☐ oil
  - ☐ natural gas
- ☐ **Nuclear Energy**
  - ☐ nuclear fuel
  - ☐ electricity production
  - ☐ nuclear reactor types
    - ☐ light-water reactors
    - ☐ heavy-water reactors
    - ☐ exotic reactors
  - ☐ environmental advantages/disadvantages of nuclear power
  - ☐ safety issues
  - ☐ Chernobyl
  - ☐ nuclear fusion
- ☐ **Hydroelectric Power**
  - ☐ diagram
  - ☐ pros/cons
  - ☐ flood control
  - ☐ channelization
  - ☐ levees-floodwalls
  - ☐ salmon
  - ☐ silting and other impacts
- ☐ **Energy Conservation**
  - ☐ CAFE standards
  - ☐ hybrid electric vehicles
    - ☐ regenerative braking
    - ☐ electric motor/drive assist
    - ☐ automatic start/shutoff
    - ☐ plug-ins

QUICK REVIEW CHECKLIST (continued)

☐ **Mass Transit**
- ☐ light rail
- ☐ group or personal rapid transit
- ☐ automated highway systems
- ☐ bus rapid transit
- ☐ maglev
- ☐ tubular rail

☐ **Renewable Energy**
- ☐ solar energy (pros/cons)
- ☐ hydrogen fuel cells
  - ☐ diagram
  - ☐ pros/cons
- ☐ biomass
  - ☐ relation to carbon sink
  - ☐ pros/cons
  - ☐ Brazil and biomass

☐ **Wind Energy**
- ☐ diagram
- ☐ pros/cons

☐ **Small-Scale Hydroelectric**
- ☐ diagram
- ☐ pros/cons

☐ **Ocean Waves and Tidal Energy**
- ☐ diagram
- ☐ pros/cons

☐ **Geothermal**
- ☐ dry steam
- ☐ hot water
- ☐ hot dry rock
- ☐ geopressurized systems
- ☐ diagram
- ☐ pros/cons

☐ **Renewable Energy Law (China, 2007)**

MULTIPLE-CHOICE QUESTIONS

1. Which of the following forms of energy is a renewable resource?

   (A) Synthetic oil
   (B) Breeder fission
   (C) Biomass
   (D) Oil shale
   (E) Synthetic natural gas

2. Which of the following forms of energy has low, short-term availability?

(A) Solar energy
(B) Synthetic oil derived from coal
(C) Nuclear energy
(D) Coal
(E) Petroleum

3. Which of the following is a source of high net energy?

(A) Tar sands
(B) Wind
(C) Fission
(D) Synthetic natural gas
(E) Geothermal

4. Which of the following alternatives would NOT lead to a sustainable energy future?

(A) Phase out nuclear power subsidies.
(B) Create policies to encourage governments to purchase renewable energy devices.
(C) Assess penalties or taxes on continuous use of coal and oil.
(D) Decrease fuel-efficiency standards for cars, appliances, and HVAC (Heating, Ventilation, and Air Conditioning) systems.
(E) Create tax incentives for independent power producers.

5. At today's rate of consumption, known U.S. oil reserves will be depleted in about

(A) 100 years
(B) 50 years
(C) 25 years
(D) 10 years
(E) 3 years

6. Which country currently ranks number one in both coal reserves and use of coal as an energy source?

(A) Russian Federation
(B) United States
(C) China
(D) India
(E) Brazil

7. The lowest average generating cost (cents per kWh) comes from what energy source?

(A) Large hydroelectric facilities
(B) Geothermal
(C) Nuclear
(D) Solar photovoltaic
(E) Coal

8. The fastest-growing renewable energy resource today is

   (A) nuclear
   (B) coal
   (C) wind
   (D) large-scale hydroelectric
   (E) geothermal

9. The least-efficient energy conversion device listed is

   (A) steam turbine
   (B) fuel cell
   (C) fluorescent light
   (D) incandescent light
   (E) internal combustion engine

10. Which is NOT an advantage of using nuclear fusion?

    (A) Abundant fuel supply
    (B) No generation of weapons-grade material
    (C) No air pollution
    (D) No high-level nuclear waste
    (E) All are advantages

11. Only about 10% of the potential energy of gasoline is used in powering an automobile. The remaining energy is lost as low-quality heat. This is an example of the

    (A) first law of thermodynamics
    (B) second law of thermodynamics
    (C) law of conservation of energy
    (D) first law of efficiency
    (E) law of supply and demand

12. The law of conservation of mass and energy states that matter can neither be created nor destroyed and that the total energy of an isolated system is constant despite internal changes. Which society offers the best long-term solution to the constraints of this law?

    (A) Low-throughput society
    (B) High-throughput society
    (C) Matter-recycling society
    (D) Free-market economy
    (E) Global market economy

13. Which of the following methods CANNOT be used to produce hydrogen gas?

    (A) Reforming
    (B) Thermolysis
    (C) Producing it from plants
    (D) Coal gasification
    (E) All are methods of producing hydrogen gas

14. Energy derived from fossil fuels supplies approximately what percentage of the world's energy needs?

    (A) 10%
    (B) 33%
    (C) 50%
    (D) 85%
    (E) 99%

15. Which of the following terms is NOT a unit of power?

    (A) Watt
    (B) Kilowatt
    (C) Horsepower
    (D) Joule
    (E) All are units of power

16. Automobile manufacturers make money by selling cars. Cars pollute and use fossil fuels. Traditionally, American auto manufacturers have encouraged customers to buy bigger and more powerful cars. This lack of incentive to improve energy efficiency is known as a

    (A) harmful, positive-feedback loop
    (B) beneficial, positive-feedback loop
    (C) harmful, negative-feedback loop
    (D) beneficial, negative-feedback loop
    (E) mutualistic, positive-feedback loop

17. If you were designing a house in the United States, you lived in a cold climate, and you wanted it to be as energy efficient as possible, you would place large windows to capture solar energy on which side of the house?

    (A) North
    (B) South
    (C) East
    (D) West
    (E) It makes no difference which side

18. Which of the following is NOT an advantage of building a hydroelectric power plant?

    (A) Low pollution
    (B) High construction cost
    (C) Relatively low operating cost
    (D) Control flooding
    (E) Moderate-to-high net-useful energy

19. The country that has made the largest commitment to increasing its share of renewable energy resources is

    (A) the United States
    (B) the Russian Federation
    (C) China
    (D) Saudi Arabia
    (E) Iran

20. Which of the following nonrenewable energy sources has the least environmental impact?

    (A) Gasoline
    (B) Coal
    (C) Oil shale
    (D) Tar sands
    (E) Natural gas

FREE-RESPONSE QUESTION

A large, natural gas–fired electrical power facility produces 15 million kilowatt-hours of electricity each day it operates. The power plant requires an input of 13,000 Btus of heat to produce 1 kilowatt-hour of electricity. One cubic foot of natural gas supplies 1,000 Btus of heat energy.

(a) Showing all steps in your calculations, determine the:
   (i) Btus of heat needed to generate the electricity produced by the power plant in 2 hours.
   (ii) Cubic feet of natural gas consumed by the power plant each year.
   (iii) Cubic feet of carbon dioxide gas released by the power plant each day. Assume that methane combusts with oxygen to produce only carbon dioxide and water vapor and that the pressures and temperatures are kept constant.
   (iv) Gross profit per year for the power company. The power company is able to sell electricity at $50 per 500 kWh. They pay a wholesale price of $5.00 per 1,000 cubic feet of natural gas.
(b) What environmental effect might the production of electricity through the burning of natural gas pose?
(c) Describe two other methods of producing electricity, and provide technological, economic, and environmental pros and cons for each method discussed.

MULTIPLE-CHOICE ANSWERS AND EXPLANATIONS

1. **(C)** Renewable resources are those resources that theoretically will last indefinitely either because they are replaced naturally at a higher rate than they are consumed or because their source is essentially inexhaustible.

2. **(E)** At the current rate of consumption, global oil reserves are expected to last another 45–50 years. With projections of increased consumption in the near future, this figure will be even lower.

3. **(B)** Net-useful energy is defined as the total amount of useful energy available from an energy resource over its lifetime minus the amount of energy used in extracting it and delivering it to the end user.

4. **(D)** The key word in this question is "NOT." To foster a sustainable energy future, fuel efficiency standards would have to increase.

5. **(C)** World oil demand is increasing at a rate of about 2% per year. Known U.S. oil reserves are projected to last another 25 years.

6. **(C)** China gets approximately 75% of its energy from coal.

7. **(A)** Nonrenewable resources of energy, such as natural gas or oil, have had recent and dramatic price increases that have resulted in major increases in the cost of electricity. Renewable resources of energy, especially hydroelectric and wind, provide the least-expensive method of producing electricity.

8. **(C)** During the 1990s, wind power experienced an annual growth of 22%. Wind power supplies less than 2% of the energy used in the United States. The country with the largest sector of its energy needs met through wind power is Denmark at 8%.

9. **(D)** An incandescent lightbulb is only 5% efficient as compared with a fluorescent light at 22%. The typical internal combustion engine is 10% efficient, and a hydrogen fuel cell is 60% efficient. The United States wastes as much energy each day as two-thirds of the world consumes.

10. **(E)** The major fuel used in fusion reactors, deuterium, could be readily extracted from ordinary water. The tritium required would be produced from lithium, which can be extracted from seawater and land deposits.

11. **(B)** The second law of thermodynamics states that when energy changes from one form to another, some of the useful energy is always degraded into a lower-quality, more dispersed (higher entropy), and less-useful form.

12. **(A)** A low-throughput society, also known as a low-waste society, focuses on matter and energy efficiency through reusing and recycling, using renewable resources at a rate no faster than can be replenished, reducing unnecessary consumption, emphasizing pollution prevention rather than waste reduction, and controlling population growth.

13. **(E)** Reforming is a chemical process of splitting water molecules. Thermolysis is breaking water molecules apart at high temperatures. Hydrogen gas can be produced from algae by depriving the algae of oxygen and sulfur. Coal gasification is the conversion of coal into synthetic natural gas (SNG), which can then be converted into hydrogen.

14. **(D)** Oil supplies about 36%, coal about 26%, and natural gas about 23%.

15. **(D)** A joule is a unit of energy.

16. **(A)** Pollution is harmful, which is the first part of the answer. A negative-feedback loop tends to slow down a process, while a positive-feedback loop tends to speed it up. Speeding up or increasing sales would be a positive feedback, which is the second half of the answer.

17. **(B)** In cold climates, large south-facing windows allow significant solar energy into the house and also provide daylighting. Properly sized overhangs can prevent overheating in the summer. In hot climates, north-facing windows can provide daylighting without heating the house. East- and west-facing windows generally cause excessive heat gains in the summer and heat losses in the winter, so they are usually small. Although overhangs are impractical for east- and west-facing windows, vertical shading can be used or trees and shrubs can be strategically located to shade the windows.

18. **(B)** The construction of hydroelectric plants is initially expensive but the operating costs are low since there are no fuel costs.

19. **(C)** China has passed legislation to increase its percentage of renewable energy to 10%. The United States' percentage is about 2%.

20. **(E)** The combustion of natural gas releases very small amounts of sulfur dioxide and nitrogen oxides, virtually no ash or particulate matter, and lower levels of carbon dioxide, carbon monoxide, and other reactive hydrocarbons when compared with coal or oil. The following chart compares emission levels of various pollutants for three forms of energy: natural gas, oil, and coal.

Fossil Fuel Emission Levels

Pollutant	Natural Gas	Oil	Coal
(pounds of pollutant per billion Btu of energy input)			
Carbon dioxide	117,000	164,000	208,000
Carbon monoxide	40	33	208
Nitrogen oxides	92	448	457
Sulfur dioxide	1	1,122	2,591
Particulates	7	84	2,744
Mercury	0.000	0.007	0.016

FREE-RESPONSE ANSWER

(a)

(i)

$$\frac{24 \text{ hours}}{1 \text{ days}} \times \frac{1.5 \times 10^7 \text{ kWh}}{24 \text{ hours}} \times \frac{13,000 \text{ Btu}}{1 \text{ kWh}} = 2.0 \times 10^{11} \text{ Btu per day}$$

(ii)

$$\frac{2 \times 10^{11} \text{ Btu}}{\text{day}} \times \frac{1 \text{ ft}^3}{1,000 \text{ Btu}} \times \frac{1 \text{ day}}{24 \text{ hours}} = 8.3 \times 10^6 \text{ ft}^3 \text{ natural gas/hr}$$

(iii) $CH_{4(g)} + 2O_{2(g)} \rightarrow CO_{2(g)} + 2H_2O_{(g)}$. If everything is a gas, and if temperature and pressure are kept constant, then the coefficients can represent volume. Therefore, we could say that 1 ft³ of methane gas combines with 2 ft³ of oxygen gas to produce 1 ft³ of carbon dioxide gas and 2 ft³ of water vapor.

$$\frac{9.3 \times 10^6 \; \text{ft}^3 \; \text{CH}_4}{\text{hr}} \times \frac{1 \; \text{ft}^3 \; \text{CO}_2}{1 \; \text{ft}^3 \; \text{CH}_4} \times \frac{24 \; \text{hours}}{1 \; \text{day}} = 2.2 \times 10^8 \; \text{ft}^3 \; \text{CO}_2 \; \text{per day}$$

Income:

$$\frac{1.57 \; \text{kWh}}{\text{day}} \times \frac{365 \; \text{days}}{\text{year}} \times \frac{\$50}{500 \; \text{kWh}} = \$5.48 \times 10^8 \; (\$548 \; \text{million}) \; \text{per year}$$

Costs that the power company spends on natural gas:

$$\frac{8.36 \times 10^6 \; \text{ft}^3 \; \text{natural gas}}{\text{hour}} \times \frac{24 \; \text{hours}}{1 \; \text{day}} \times \frac{365 \; \text{days}}{\text{year}} \times \frac{\$5.00}{1{,}000 \; \text{ft}^3 \; \text{natural gas}} =$$

$$\$3.66 \times 10^8 \; (\$366 \; \text{million}) \; \text{per year}$$

Gross profit: $(\$5.48 \times 10^8) - (\$3.66 \times 10^8) = \$1.82 \times 10^8 \; (\$182 \; \text{million})$

(b) An environmental effect that results from the burning of natural gas to produce electricity is the production of carbon dioxide gas—a greenhouse gas. As a greenhouse gas, the carbon dioxide gas molecules absorb radiant energy reflected from Earth's surface and re-radiate this energy as long-wave infrared radiation back to Earth. This trapping of Earth's heat has serious environmental consequences in terms of its effect on global weather patterns, local climate conditions, and the glaciers and polar ice caps.

Other environmental effects produced by burning natural gas include the production of hydrogen sulfide gas (H_2S) and sulfur dioxide gas (SO_2) as production by-products. Sulfur dioxide gas when combined with atmospheric water vapor produces what is known as acid rain. Acid rain has serious environmental effects primarily on aquatic organisms in lower trophic levels and on the reproduction of developing aquatic organisms. Hydrogen sulfide has serious environmental effects as a toxic pollutant and respiratory irritant. Leakage of CH_4 during processing adds methane to the atmosphere, which has a more deleterious effect as a greenhouse gas than does carbon dioxide.

Drilling platforms to extract natural gas, the production of contaminated wastewater and brine, the possibility of land subsidence, and the disruption of wildlife and habitat refuges are other deleterious side effects of using natural gas. However, these negative side effects have less environmental impacts than does using other forms of fossil fuels.

(c) Other methods of producing electricity include burning coal and using dams. The advantages of using coal are that it is plentiful and relatively inexpensive. Currently, the world used 4 billion metric tons of coal per year. At this rate, the world has enough coal to last for the next 200 years. Drawbacks to using coal are that current extraction methods are environmentally damaging to the land and natural habitat and are potentially dangerous to miners. Burning coal also releases radioactive particles and mercury into the air. Carbon dioxide produced from burning coal adds to the problem of global warming. The nitrogen oxides released add to the problems of acid precipitation.

Dams create large flooded areas that destroy natural habitats and disrupt the lives of the people who inhabit the area. The collection of sediment by the dam, the loss of this valuable sediment downstream and thereby making the land less productive, the obstructions that dams cause to migrating fish populations, and the aesthetic loss of a wild river are detractors of hydroelectric power. On the positive side, hydroelectric power does not significantly add to global pollution.

TIP

When answering essay and short answer questions, use the analyze, organize, and respond model.

Analyze—Write down key phrases. Even if a key phrase pops into your mind for another question, write it down immediately or you risk forgetting it.

Organize—Sequence your ideas. This ensures that your answer is logically developed and will be clear to the grader.

Respond—Try to provide support for claims that you make in your answer using Case Studies when possible. Star or underline important points. Write legibly. If your handwriting is poor, then print. Use proper grammar and be neat.

UNIT VI: POLLUTION
(25–30%)

Areas on Which You Will Be Tested

A. Pollution Types
1. **Air pollution**—primary and secondary sources, major air pollutants, measurement units, smog, acid deposition—causes and effects, heat islands and temperature inversions, indoor air pollution, remediation and reduction strategies, Clean Air Act, and other relevant laws.
2. **Noise pollution**—sources, effects, and control measures.
3. **Water pollution**—types, sources, causes and effects, cultural eutrophication, groundwater pollution, maintaining water quality, water purification, sewage treatment/septic systems, Clean Water Act, and other relevant laws.
4. **Solid waste**—types, disposal, and reduction.

B. Impacts on the Environment and Human Health
1. **Hazards to human health**—environmental risk analysis, acute and chronic effects, dose-response relationships, air pollutants, smoking, and other risks.
2. **Hazardous chemicals in the environment**—types of hazardous waste, treatment/disposal of hazardous waste, cleanup of contaminated sites, biomagnification, and relevant laws.

C. Economic Impacts—cost-benefit analysis, externalities, marginal costs, and sustainability.

Pollution

CHAPTER 9

AIR POLLUTION

Primary pollutants are emitted directly into the air from natural sources such as volcanoes, mobile sources such as cars, or stationary sources such as industrial smokestacks. Examples include: particulate matter or soot (PM_{10}), nitric oxide (NO), nitrogen dioxide (NO_2), sulfur dioxide (SO_2), carbon dioxide (CO_2), and carbon monoxide (CO).

Secondary pollutants result from the reaction of primary pollutants in the atmosphere to form a new pollutant. Examples include sulfur trioxide (SO_3), sulfuric acid (H_2SO_4), ozone (O_3), and chemicals found in photochemical smog such as PANS and peroxyacyl nitrates.

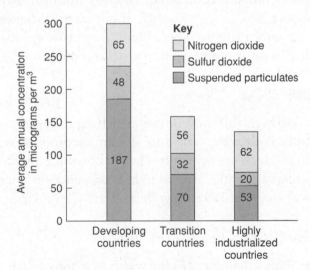

Figure 9.1 Particulate matter pollution in developing countries

Source: World Resources Institute.

Major Air Pollutants

NITROGEN DIOXIDE (NO_2)

Forms when fuels are burned at high temperatures. Also results from forest fires, volcanoes, lightning, and bacterial action in soil. Forms nitric acid (HNO_3) in the air and contributes to acid deposition and cultural eutrophication. Results in lung irritation and damage, suppresses plant growth, and may be a carcinogen.

CRITERIA AIR POLLUTANTS

Criteria air pollutants are a set of air pollutants that cause smog, acid rain, and other health hazards and are typically emitted from many sources in industry, mining, transportation, power generation, and agriculture. They were the first set of pollutants recognized by the U.S. Environmental Protection Agency as needing standards on a national level. In most cases they are the products of the combustion of fossil fuels or industrial processes. They include: ozone; particulate matter; carbon monoxide; sulfur dioxide; nitrogen oxides; and lead.

OZONE (O_3)

Major component of photochemical smog. Formed by sunlight reacting with NO_x and VOCs in the air. Causes lung irritation and damage, bronchial constriction, coughing, wheezing, and eye irritation. Damages plants, rubber, and plastics.

PEROXYACYL NITRATES (PANs)

PANs are secondary air pollutants formed from the reaction of various hydrocarbons combining with oxygen and nitrogen dioxide and being catalyzed by ultraviolet radiation from the sun: hydrocarbons + O_2 + NO_2 + light $\rightarrow$ $CH_3COOONO_2$ (PAN). Since they dissociate quite slowly in the atmosphere into radicals and NO_2, PANs are able to transport these unstable compounds far away from the urban and industrial origin. PANs transport NO_x to regions where it can more efficiently produce ozone. At concentrations of only a few parts per billion, they cause eye irritation. At higher concentrations, they cause extensive damage to vegetation.

SULFUR DIOXIDE (SO_2)

Produced by burning high-sulfur oil or coal, smelting of metals, and paper manufacturing. Combines with water vapor in the air to produce acid precipitation, which reduces the productivity of plants. Causes breathing difficulties. Significant decreases in concentrations and emissions in SO_2 concentration in the United States reflect the success of the Acid Rain Program and the Clean Air Act.

SUSPENDED PARTICULATE MATTER (PM_{10})

PM_{10}s are particles with a diameter 1/7 the width of a human hair or less (< 10 μm) and include smoke, dust, diesel soot, lead, and asbestos. PM_{10}s cause lung irritation and damage. Many are known mutagens, teratogens, and carcinogens. Reduction in PM_{10}s would produce health benefits 10 times greater than similar reductions in all other air pollutants combined.

VOLATILE ORGANIC COMPOUNDS (VOCs)

Include organic compounds that have a high vapor pressure. Over 600 compounds have been identified. Examples of VOCs include toluene, xylene, formaldehyde, benzene, and acetone. These are found in paints, aerosol sprays, dry-cleaning fluids, and industrial solvents. Causes respiratory irritation and damage. Most are carcinogenic and cause liver, kidney, and central nervous system damage. Concentration of VOCs may be 1,000 times higher indoors than outdoors.

Measurement Units

The most common form of expressing air pollutants is parts per million (ppm); 1 ppm represents one particle of a pollutant for every 999,999 particles of air. The symbol μ is often used to represent a millionth. This concentration is equivalent to one drop of ink in 40 gallons (150 L) of water or one second in 280 hours. To change ppm to a percentage, move the decimal place four places to the left and add a % sign. For example, a concentration of 400 ppm (0.04%) of carbon monoxide may be fatal. Two other common measurements are parts per billion (ppb or nano) and parts per trillion (ppt or pico).

Smog

There are two forms of smog: industrial smog and photochemical smog. Industrial smog tends to be sulfur-based and is also called grey-air smog. Photochemical smog is catalyzed by UV radiation and tends to be nitrogen-based. Photochemical smog is also called brown-air smog.

Formation of Industrial Smog

Step	Chemical Reaction
1. Carbon in coal or oil is burned in oxygen gas to produce carbon dioxide and carbon monoxide gas.	$C + O_2 \rightarrow CO_2$ $C + O_2 \rightarrow CO$
2. Unburned carbon ends up as soot or particulate matter (PM).	C
3. Sulfur in oil and coal reacts with oxygen gas to produce sulfur dioxide.	$S + O_2 \rightarrow SO_2$
4. Sulfur dioxide reacts with oxygen gas to produce sulfur trioxide.	$SO_2 + O_2 \rightarrow SO_3$
5. Sulfur trioxide reacts with water vapor in the air to form sulfuric acid.	$SO_3 + H_2O \rightarrow H_2SO_4$
6. Sulfuric acid reacts with atmospheric ammonia to form brown, solid ammonium sulfate.	$H_2SO_4 + NH_3 \rightarrow (NH_4)_2SO_4$

FORMATION OF PHOTOCHEMICAL SMOG

Net result: $NO + VOCs + O_2 + uv \rightarrow O_3 + PANs$

- **6 A.M.–9 A.M.**
  As people drive to work, concentrations of nitrogen oxides and VOCs increase:

$$N_2 + O_2 \rightarrow 2NO$$

$$NO + VOCs \rightarrow NO_2$$

$$NO_2 \xrightarrow{uv} NO + O$$

- **9 A.M.–11 A.M.**

  As traffic begins to decrease, nitrogen oxides and VOCs begin to react, forming nitrogen dioxide:

$$2NO + O_2 \rightarrow 2NO_2$$

- **11 A.M.–4 P.M.**

  As the sunlight becomes more intense, nitrogen dioxide is broken down and the concentration of ozone increases:

$$NO_2 \overset{uv}{\rightarrow} NO + O$$

$$O_2 + O \rightarrow O_3$$

Nitrogen dioxide also reacts with water vapor to produce nitric acid and nitric oxide:

$$3NO_2 + H_2O \rightarrow 2HNO_3 + NO$$

Nitrogen dioxide can also react with VOCs released by vehicles, refineries, gas stations, and so on to produce toxic PANs (peroxacyl nitrates):

$$NO_2 + VOCs \rightarrow PANs$$

- **4 P.M.–Sunset**

  As the sun goes down, the production of ozone is halted.

> ## CASE STUDY
>
> **Great Smog of '52:** A period of cold weather, combined with windless conditions, collected airborne pollutants mostly from the use of coal to form a thick layer of (gray) smog over London in 1952. It lasted from December 5–9, 1952, and then dispersed quickly after a change of weather. Estimates run as high as 100,000 people becoming ill and over 12,000 deaths.

Catalytic Converters

A catalytic converter is an exhaust emission control device that converts toxic chemicals in the exhaust of an internal combustion engine into less noxious substances. Inside a catalytic converter, a catalyst stimulates a chemical reaction in which noxious by-products of combustion are converted to less toxic substances by way of catalysed chemical reactions. Most present-day vehicles that run on gasoline are fitted with a "three way" converter, since it converts the three main pollutants:

(a) Reduction of nitrogen oxides to nitrogen and oxygen: $NO_x \rightarrow O_2 + N_2$
(b) Oxidation of carbon monoxide to carbon dioxide: $CO + O_2 \rightarrow CO_2$
(c) Oxidation of unburned hydrocarbons to carbon dioxide and water:
$C_xH_{2x} + O_2 \rightarrow CO_2 + H_2O$

Although catalytic converters are effective at removing hydrocarbons and other harmful emissions, they do not reduce the emission of carbon dioxide produced when fossil fuels are used for fuel. Additionally, the Environmental Protection Agency (EPA) has stated catalytic converters are a significant and growing cause of global warming, because of their release of nitrous oxide (N_2O), a greenhouse gas over 300 times more potent than carbon dioxide. The EPA states that motor vehicles contribute approximately 50% of nitrous oxide emissions and nitrous oxide makes up 7% of greenhouse gases.

Acid Deposition—Causes and Effects

Acid rain is a broad term used to describe several ways that acids fall out of the atmosphere. A more precise term is acid deposition, which has two parts: wet and dry. Wet deposition refers to acidic rain, fog, and snow. As this acidic water flows over and through the ground, it affects a variety of plants and animals. The strength of the effects depends on many factors, including how acidic the water is, the chemistry and buffering capacity of the soils involved, and the types of organisms, such as fish, macroinvertebrates, trees, and other living things that rely on water and soil.

Dry deposition refers to acidic gases and particles. About half of the acidity in the atmosphere falls back to Earth through dry deposition. Wind blows these acidic particles and gases onto buildings, cars, homes, and trees. Dry-deposited gases and particles can also be washed from trees and other surfaces by rainstorms. When that happens, the runoff water adds those acids to the acid rain, making the combination more acidic than the falling rain alone.

Acid deposition due to sulfur dioxide (SO_2) begins with sulfur dioxide being introduced into the atmosphere by burning coal and oil, smelting metals, organic decay, and ocean spray. It then combines with water vapor to form sulfurous acid ($SO_2 + H_2O \rightarrow H_2SO_3$). Finally, the sulfurous acid reacts with oxygen to form sulfuric acid ($H_2SO_3 + \frac{1}{2}O_2 \rightarrow H_2SO_4$).

Acid deposition due to nitrogen oxides (NO_x) begins with nitrogen oxides formed by burning oil, coal, or natural gas. They also are found in volcanic vent gases and formed by forest fires, bacterial action in soil, and lightning-induced atmospheric reactions. Nitrogen monoxide, also known as nitric oxide (NO), reacts with oxygen gas to produce nitrogen dioxide gas ($NO + \frac{1}{2}O_2 \rightarrow NO_2$). Finally, nitrogen dioxide reacts with water vapor in the atmosphere to produce nitrous and nitric acids ($2NO_2 + H_2O \rightarrow HNO_2 + HNO_3$).

Acid rain causes acidification of lakes and streams. It contributes to the damage of trees at high elevations and many sensitive forest soils through nitrogen saturation and creating acidic conditions that are unhealthy for decomposers and mycorrhizal fungi. Acid shock, which is caused by the rapid melting of snow pack that contains dry acidic particles, results in acid concentrations in lakes and streams 5 to 10 times higher than acidic rainfall. In addition, acid rain accelerates the decay of building materials and paints, including irreplaceable statues and sculptures. Acid rain also leaches essential plant nutrients from the soil such as Ca^{2+}, K^+ and Mg^{2+}. Heavy metal ions such as Pb^{2+}, Cd^{2+}, and Hg^{2+} that are contained within rock structures may be leached out of the rocks and into the soil structure. Prior to falling to Earth, SO_2 and NO_x gases and their particulate matter derivatives (sulfates and nitrates) contribute to breathing difficulties and other health matters.

Heat Islands and Temperature Inversions

Urban heat islands occur in metropolitan areas that are significantly warmer than their surroundings. Urban air can be 10°F (6°C) warmer than the surrounding area. Since warmer air can hold more water vapor, rainfall can be as much as 30% greater downwind of cities when compared with areas upwind. One of the main reasons for higher-than-normal nighttime air temperatures in urban areas are buildings that reduce the radiation of urban heat to the night sky. Thermal properties of surface materials (bricks, concrete, and asphalt) store heat longer. The lack of vegetation and standing water in many urban areas also increase urban temperatures. The canyon effect results from buildings reflecting and absorbing heat and blocking winds that reduce heat through convection. Human activities that increase the heat island effect include the operation of automobiles, air conditioners, and industry. Since demand for air-conditioning rises during summer months, problems associated with energy availability and pricing become compounded.

High levels of pollution in urban areas can also create a localized greenhouse effect. Urban heat islands can directly influence the health and welfare of urban residents who cannot afford air-conditioning. As many as 1,000 people per year die in the United States due to excessive temperatures. Urban heat islands can produce secondary effects on local meteorology, including the altering of local wind patterns, the development of clouds and fog, the number of lightning strikes, and the rate of precipitation. The heat island effect can be slightly reduced by using white or reflective building materials and increasing the amount of landscaping and parks.

Temperature inversions occur when air temperature increases with height above the ground, as opposed to the normal decrease in temperature with height. This effect can lead to pollution such as smog being trapped close to the ground, with possible adverse effects on human health (asthma, emphysema, and increases in lung cancer). Temperature inversions commonly occur at night when solar heating ceases and the surface cools, which then cools the atmosphere immediately above it. A warm air mass then moving over a colder one keeps the cooler air mass trapped below, and the air becomes still. This results in dust and pollutants being trapped and their concentrations increasing. A nearly permanent temperature inversion occurs over Antarctica.

CASE STUDY

In 1948, 20 people were asphyxiated and over 7,000 were hospitalized or became ill as the result of severe air pollution over Donora, PA, a town of 14,000. Smog from the local zinc and steel smelting plants settled in the valley where the town was located. Four days later, winds finally cleared the toxins from the town. The investigation of this incident by state and federal health officials resulted in the first meaningful federal and state laws to control air pollution and marked the beginning of modern efforts to assess and deal with the health threats from air pollution.

Indoor Air Pollution (Sick Building Syndrome)

Many people spend the majority of their lives indoors sleeping, working, eating, and relaxing, where air circulation may be restricted and where indoor air pollutant levels may be 25% to 60% greater than outdoor levels. Sick building syndrome (SBS) is a term used to describe a combination of ailments (a syndrome) associated with an individual's place of work or residence. Up to a third of new and remodeled buildings worldwide may be linked to symptoms of SBS. The most common pollutants found indoors include molds, bacteria, carbon monoxide, radon, allergens, asbestos, tobacco smoke, and formaldehyde and other volatile organic compounds (VOCs) released from carpeting, adhesives, and particleboard. SBS is frequently pinned down to flaws in heating, ventilation, and air conditioning (HVAC) systems. Symptoms of indoor air pollution can range from headaches, breathing difficulties, and allergies to asthma, cancer, emphysema, and various nerve disorders.

Remediation and Reduction Strategies

Strategies designed to improve air quality in general include:

1. Emphasizing tax incentives for pollution control rather than fines and penalties

2. Setting legislative standards for energy efficiency

3. Increasing funding for research into renewable energy sources

4. Incorporating incentives for reducing air pollution into trade policies

5. Distributing solar cookstoves to developing countries to replace coal and firewood

6. Phasing out two-cycle gasoline engines

7. For issues involving sick building syndrome: (a) modify building codes to control materials used in construction; (b) replace and repair areas that have received water damage in order to control mold (carpeting, ceiling tiles, inside walls, etc.); (c) use paints, adhesives, solvents, cleaning products, and pesticides in well-ventilated areas and during periods of non-occupancy; (d) increase the number of complete air exchanges in the building; and (e) ensure proper maintenance of HVAC systems.

8. Providing incentives to use mass transit

Several strategies have been designed to reduce the effects of acid rain. They include designing more efficient engines to reduce NO_x emissions and increasing the efficiency of coal-burning plants to reduce SO_2, NO_x, and particulates through washing coal and using scrubbers, advanced filtration on smokestacks, electrostatic precipitators, and staged catalytic burners with afterburners. Other strategies include increasing penalties on stationary sources that do not reduce emissions, providing tax incentives to companies that do reduce pollutants, providing incentives to consumers to purchase Energy Star appliances and products that conserve energy, and increasing CAFE standards.

The EPA's Acid Rain Program is designed to achieve significant environmental and public health benefits through reductions in emissions of sulfur dioxide (SO_2) and nitrogen oxides (NO_x), the primary causes of acid rain. To achieve this goal at the lowest cost to society, the program employs both traditional and innovative market-based approaches for controlling air pollution. In addition, the program encourages energy efficiency and pollution prevention. Specific strategies employed include an allowance trading system, an opt-in program that allows nonaffected industrial and small utility units to participate in allowance trading, setting new NO_x emissions standards for existing coal-fired utility boilers, and allowing emissions averaging to reduce costs. Another method is a permit process that affords sources maximum flexibility in selecting the most cost-effective approach to reducing emissions. Continuous emission monitoring (CEM) requirements provide credible accounting of emissions to ensure the integrity of the market-based allowance system and to verify the achievement of the reduction goals. The excess emissions provision provides incentives to ensure self-enforcement. Another strategy is an appeals procedure that allows the regulated community to appeal decisions with which it may disagree.

The Clean Air Act was originally signed into law in 1963. Its goal was to protect public health from air pollution and limit the effects of air pollution on the environment. Early versions allowed individual states to set their own standards. Later versions of the act switched responsibility of setting uniform standards to the federal government. Primary standards protect human health. Secondary standards protect materials, crops, climate, visibility, and personal comfort. The 1990 version addressed acid rain, urban smog, air pollutants, ozone protection, marketing pollution rights, and VOCs. Estimates are that the Clean Air Act is responsible each year for saving 15,000 lives, reducing bronchitis cases by 60,000, and reducing 9,000 hospital admissions due to respiratory illnesses. The following chart shows some of the progress that the Clean Air Act has been responsible for since it was passed into law. Notice however, the increase in PM_{10} and NO_x levels.

Pollutant	% Change
Pb	−98%
VOC	−42%
SO_2	−37%
CO	−31%
NO_x	+17%
PM_{10}	+266 %

The 1997 Kyoto Protocol would have required the United States to reduce greenhouse emissions by 7% when compared with 1990 levels over a five-year period. Under this agreement, the United States would have faced penalties if it did not meet its emission cuts. The United States saw this as an unattainable target since carbon dioxide and greenhouse gases continue to increase and are projected to increase for the next 20 years. The United States felt that the protocol held developed nations responsible for meeting the cuts but did not apply the same standards to developing nations. Reasons given for not agreeing with the rest of the signing members of the Kyoto Protocol were the cost of meeting the emission targets would be too high, the time frame was too short for implementation, and there was no evidence of a correlation between greenhouse gases and global warming.

In 2012, the year the 1997 Kyoto Protocol expired, Canada, Japan, and Russia joined the United States stating that they will not agree to an extension of the Kyoto Protocol unless the unbalanced requirements of developing and developed countries are changed.

RELEVANT LAWS AND PROTOCOLS

Air Pollution Control Act (1955): The nation's first piece of federal legislation regarding air pollution. Identified air pollution as a national problem and announced that research and additional steps to improve the situation needed to be taken. It was an act to make the nation more aware of this environmental hazard.

Clean Air Act (1963): The Clean Air Act is designed to control air pollution on a national level. It requires the Environmental Protection Agency (EPA) to develop and enforce regulations to protect the general public from exposure to airborne contaminants that are known to be hazardous to human health. The act (amended in 1967, 1977, and 1990):

- required comprehensive federal and state regulations for both stationary (industrial) and mobile sources of air pollution.
- expanded federal enforcement authority.
- addressed acid rain, ozone depletion, and toxic air pollution.
- established new auto gasoline reformulation requirements.
- was the first major environmental law in the United States to include a provision for citizen suits.

National Environmental Policy Act (1970): Created the Environmental Protection Agency (EPA). Also mandated creation of Environmental Impact Statements.

Montreal Protocol (1989): An agreement among nations requiring the phaseout of chemicals that damage the ozone layer.

Pollution Prevention Act (1990): Requires industries to reduce pollution at its source. Reduction can be in terms of volume and/or toxicity.

Kyoto Protocol (1997 and 2001): An agreement among 150 nations requiring greenhouse gas reductions.

NOISE POLLUTION

Noise pollution is unwanted human-created sound that disrupts the environment. The dominant form of noise pollution is from transportation sources, primarily motor vehicles, aircraft noise, and rail transport noise. Besides transportation noise, other prominent sources are office equipment, factory machinery, appliances, power tools, and audio entertainment systems. Noise regulation by governmental agencies effectively began in the United States with the 1972 Federal Noise Control Act.

Effects

Normal hearing depends on the health of the inner, middle, and outer ear. Three kinds of hearing loss occur: conductive, sensory, and neural. Sensory hearing loss is caused by damage to the inner ear and is the most common form associated with noise.

In addition to contributing to hearing loss, too much noise can affect health in other ways too. Immediate effects may be temporary or may become permanent. They may include cardiovascular problems with an accelerated heartbeat and high blood pressure, gastric-intestinal problems, a decrease in alertness and ability to memorize, nervousness, pupil dilation, and a decrease in the visual field. Effects that may be longer lasting include insomnia, nervousness, bulimia, chronically high blood pressure, anxiety, depression, and sexual dysfunction.

Control Measures

Roadway noise can be reduced through the use of noise barriers, limitations on vehicle speed, newer roadway surface technologies, limiting times for heavy-duty vehicles, computer-controlled traffic flow devices that reduce braking and acceleration, and changes in tire design. Aircraft noise can be reduced through developing quieter jet engines and rescheduling takeoff and landing times. Industrial noise can be reduced through new technologies in industrial equipment and installation of noise barriers in the workplace. Residential noise such as power tools, garden equipment, and loud radios can be controlled through local laws and enforcement.

RELEVANT LAW

Noise Control Act (1972): Establishes a national policy to promote an environment for all Americans free from noise that jeopardizes their health and welfare. To accomplish this, the act establishes a means for the coordination of federal research and activities in noise control, authorizes the establishment of federal noise emissions standards for products distributed in commerce, and provides information to the public respecting the noise emission and noise reduction characteristics of such products.

WATER POLLUTION

Water pollution can originate from either a point or a nonpoint source. A point source occurs when harmful substances are emitted directly into a body of water. An example of a point source of water pollution is a pipe from an industrial facility discharging effluent directly into a river. Point source pollution is usually monitored and regulated in developed countries.

Nonpoint sources deliver pollutants indirectly through transport or environmental change. An example of a nonpoint source of water pollution is when fertilizer from a farm field is carried into a stream by rain (run off). Nonpoint sources are much more difficult to monitor and control, and they account for the majority of contaminants in streams and lakes.

Sources of Water Pollution

The following sections describe the varied sources of water pollution. They include air pollution, chemicals, microbiological sources, mining, noise, nutrients, oxygen-depleting substances, suspended matter, and thermal sources.

AIR POLLUTION

Pollutants like mercury, sulfur dioxide, nitric oxides, and ammonia fall out of the air and into the water. They can then cause mercury contamination in fish and acidification and eutrophication of lakes. The oceans have absorbed enough carbon dioxide to have already caused a slight increase in ocean acidification and which may be causing the carbonate structures of corals, algae, and marine plankton to dissolve. These organisms form the base of the food pyramid in the ocean.

METHYL MERCURY

Mercury has been well known as an environmental pollutant for several decades. There are many sources of mercury in the environment, both natural and human made. Natural sources include volcanoes, natural mercury deposits, and volatilization from the ocean. The primary human-related sources include: coal combustion, waste incineration, and metal processing. Best estimates to date suggest that human activities have about doubled or tripled the amount of mercury in the atmosphere, and the atmospheric burden is increasing by about 1.5% per year. Like many environmental contaminants, mercury undergoes bioaccumulation. The bioaccumulation effect is generally compounded the longer an organism lives, so that larger predatory game fish will likely have the highest mercury levels. Adding to this problem is the fact that mercury concentrates in the muscle tissue of fish. Humans generally uptake mercury in two ways: (1) as methylmercury (CH_3Hg^+) from fish consumption, or (2) by breathing vaporous mercury in the ambient air. The ultimate source of mercury to most aquatic ecosystems is deposition from the atmosphere, primarily associated with rainfall. Once in surface water, mercury enters a complex cycle in which one form can be converted to another. Studies have shown that bacteria that process sulfate (SO_4^{2-}) in the environment take up mercury in its inorganic form, and through metabolic processes convert it to methylmercury. The conversion of inorganic mercury to methylmercury is important for two reasons: (1) methylmercury is much more toxic than inorganic mercury, and (2) organisms require considerably longer to eliminate methylmercury than elemental mercury. At this point, the methylmercury-containing bacteria may be consumed by the next higher level in the food chain, or the bacteria may release the methylmercury to the water where it can quickly adsorb to plankton, which are also consumed by the next level in the food chain.

OTHER CHEMICALS

A variety of chemicals from industrial and agricultural sources can cause water pollution. Examples include metals, solvents and oils, detergents, and pesticides. These can accumulate in fish and shellfish, poisoning the people, animals, and birds that consume them. On a square-foot basis, homeowners apply more chemicals to their lawns than farmers do to their fields. Each year, road runoff and other nonspill sources impart an amount of oil to the oceans that is more than 5 times greater than the *Exxon Valdez* spill—about 21 million barrels. Discharge of oily wastes and oil-contaminated ballast water and wash water are all significant sources of marine pollution. Drilling and extraction operations for oil and gas can also contaminate coastal waters and groundwater. The EPA estimates that about 100,000 gasoline storage tanks are leaking chemicals into groundwater. In Santa Monica, California, wells supplying half the city's water have been closed because of dangerously high levels of the gasoline additive MTBE. New evidence strongly suggests that components of crude oil, called polycyclic aromatic hydrocarbons (PAHs), persist in the marine environment for years and are toxic to marine life at concentrations in the low parts per billion (ppb) range. Chronic exposure to PAHs can affect the development of marine organisms, increase susceptibility to disease, and jeopardize normal reproductive cycles in many marine species.

Studies have shown that up to 90% of drug prescriptions pass through the human body unaltered. Animal farming operations that use growth hormones and antibiotics also send large quantities of these chemicals into the water. Most wastewater treatment facilities are not equipped to filter out personal care products, household products, or pharmaceuticals. As a result, a large portion of these chemicals pass directly into local waterways. Studies on the effects of these chemicals have discovered fragrance molecules inside fish tissues, ingredients from birth control pills causing gender-bending hormonal effects in frogs and fish, and the chemical nonylphenol, a remnant of detergent, disrupting fish reproduction and growth.

MICROBIOLOGICAL SOURCES

Disease-causing (pathogenic) microorganisms such as bacteria, viruses, and protozoa can result in swimmers getting sick and fish and shellfish becoming contaminated. Examples of waterborne diseases include cholera, typhoid, shigella, polio, meningitis, and hepatitis. In developing countries, an estimated 90% of the wastewater is discharged directly into rivers and streams without treatment. In the United States, 850 billion gallons (3 trillion L) of raw sewage are dumped into rivers, lakes, and bays each year by leaking sewer systems and inadequate combined sewer/storm systems that overflow during heavy rains. Leaking septic tanks and other sources of sewage can also cause groundwater and stream contamination. Beaches suffer the effects of water pollution from sewage. About 25% of all beaches in the United States annually have water pollution advisories or are closed each year due to bacterial buildup caused by sewage.

MINING

Mining causes water pollution in a number of ways. The mining process exposes heavy metals and sulfur compounds that were previously locked away in Earth. Rainwater leaches these compounds out of the exposed Earth, resulting in acid mine drainage and heavy-metal pollution that can continue long after the mining operations have ceased. Second, the action of rainwater on piles of mining waste (tailings) transfers pollution to freshwater supplies. In the case of gold mining, cyanide is intentionally poured on piles of mined rock (a leach heap) to extract the gold from the ore chemically. Some of the cyanide ultimately finds its way into nearby water. Additionally, huge pools of mining waste slurry are often stored behind containment dams that often leak or infiltrate ground water supplies. Fourth, mining companies in developing countries often dump mining waste directly into rivers or other bodies of water as a method of disposal.

The U.S. government in 2003 reclassified mining waste from mountaintop removal (a type of coal mining) so it could be dumped directly into valleys and burying streams altogether. The Iron Mountain mine in California has been closed since 1963 but continues to drain sulfuric acid and heavy metals into the Sacramento River. Experts say the pollution from this particular mine may continue for another 3,000 years.

NOISE

Many marine organisms, including marine mammals, sea turtles, and fish, use sound to communicate, navigate, and hunt. Because of oceanic water noise pollution caused by commercial shipping, military sonar, and recreational boating, some species may have a harder time hunting or detecting predators. They may also not being able to navigate properly.

NUTRIENTS

Phosphorus and nitrogen are necessary for plant growth and are plentiful in untreated wastewater. When added to lakes and streams, they can cause the growth of aquatic weeds that block waterways as well as algal blooms. If the source is from humans, it is called cultural eutrophication. Deposition of atmospheric nitrogen (from nitrogen oxides) also causes nutrient-type water pollution. Nutrient pollution is also a problem in estuaries and deltas, where the runoff that was aggregated by watersheds is finally dumped at the mouths of major rivers.

OIL SPILLS

Oil is one of the world's main sources of energy, but because it is unevenly distributed worldwide, it must be transported by ship across oceans and by pipelines across land. This can result in accidents when transferring oil to vessels, when transporting oil, and when pipelines break, as well as when drilling for oil. Oil accidentally released into a marine environment drastically affects wildlife. The oil penetrates the feathers of seabirds, reducing the feathers' insulating ability and making the birds more vulnerable to temperature fluctuations and much less buoyant in the water. It also impairs seabirds' flight, and thus their abilities to forage and escape from predators. As they attempt to preen, birds typically ingest oil that covers their feathers, causing kidney and liver damage. This, along with the limited foraging ability, quickly results in dehydration. Marine mammals exposed to oil spills are affected in similar ways as seabirds. Because oil floats on top of water, less sunlight penetrates into the water, limiting the photosynthesis of marine plants and phytoplankton and affecting the food web in the ecosystem.

Recovering the oil is difficult and depends on many factors, including the type of oil spilled, the temperature of the water, and the types of shorelines and beaches involved. Methods for cleaning up include the use of microorganisms to break down oil; chemical agents, dispersants, sorbents, and detergents that act to disperse the oil, absorb it, or cause it to clump into gel-like agglomerations that sink; controlled burning; and booming, skimming, and/or vacuuming the oil from the surface or shoreline.

OXYGEN-DEPLETING SUBSTANCES

Biodegradable wastes are used as nutrients by bacteria and other microorganisms. Excessive biodegradable wastes can cause oxygen depletion in receiving waters. This can result in increases in anaerobic bacteria that produce ammonia, amines, sulfides, and methane (swamp gas) and decreases of aerobic organisms such as fish.

PLASTIC

The Great Pacific Garbage Patch, or Pacific Trash Vortex, is a large system of rotating ocean currents (gyre) of marine litter in the central North Pacific Ocean and is characterized by high concentrations of floating plastics, chemical sludge, and other debris that have been trapped by the currents of the North Pacific Gyre. It was formed gradually as a result of marine pollution gathered by oceanic currents. The gyre's rotational pattern draws in waste material from across the North Pacific Ocean, including coastal waters off North America and Japan. As material is captured in the currents, wind-driven surface currents gradually move floating debris toward the center, trapping it in the region. Estimates of its size range from 0.5% to 8.1% of the size of the Pacific Ocean. As the plastic photodegrades into smaller and smaller pieces, it remains as plastic polymers with some leaching toxic chemicals such as bisphenol A and PCBs, which then concentrate in the upper water column. As it disintegrates, the plastic ultimately becomes small enough to be ingested by aquatic organisms that reside near the ocean's surface and enters the marine food chain. Some of these long-lasting plastics end up in the stomachs of marine birds and animals, and their young. The floating debris can also absorb organic pollutants from sea water, which ultimately results in bioaccumulation of these toxins throughout the food chain. Marine plastics also facilitate the spread of invasive species that attach to floating plastic in one region and drift long distances to colonize other ecosystems. On the macroscopic level, the physical size of the plastic kills birds and turtles as the animals' digestion cannot break down the plastic inside their stomachs. Another effect of the macroscopic plastic is that it makes it much more difficult for animals to see and detect their normal sources of food through the water column. Research has shown that this plastic marine debris affects over 250 species worldwide.

SUSPENDED MATTER

Suspended wastes eventually settle out of water and form silt or mud at the bottom. Toxic materials can also accumulate in the sediment and affect organisms throughout the food web. When forests are clear-cut, the root systems that previously held soil in place die and the sediment is free to run off into nearby streams, rivers, and lakes.

Plastics and other plastic-like substances (such as nylon from fishing nets and lines) can entangle fish, sea turtles, and marine mammals, causing injury and death. Certain types of plastic can break down into microparticles and become ingested by tiny marine organisms and move up the marine food chain. Plastic remains in the ecosystem and will continue to harm marine organisms far into the future.

THERMAL SOURCES

Produced by industry and power plants. Heat reduces the ability of water to hold oxygen and causes death to organisms that cannot tolerate heat and/or low oxygen levels. Global warming is also imparting additional heat to the oceans, rivers, and streams with unknown consequences.

CASE STUDIES

Minamata disease: Twenty-seven tons of mercury-containing compounds from industrial processes were dumped into Minamata Bay in Japan between 1932 and 1968. The mercury collected in fish and shellfish caught from the bay. Symptoms included blurred vision, hearing loss, loss of muscular coordination, and reproductive disorders.

Exxon Valdez **(1989):** In 1989, the oil tanker *Exxon Valdez* spilled 11 to 30 million gallons (42 to 110 million L) of crude oil into Prince William Sound, Alaska. As a result, 250,000 sea birds, 3,000 otters, 300 seals, 300 bald eagles, and 22 whales died along with billions of salmon and herring eggs. The oil also destroyed the majority of the plankton in the sound.

Gulf of Mexico Oil Spill (2010): In April 2010, a massive oil spill followed an explosion on the *Deepwater Horizon* offshore drilling rig operated by British Petroleum, becoming the most significant environmental disaster to occur in the United States. As the oil from the well site reached the Gulf coast, billions of dollars in damage was done to the Gulf of Mexico fishing industry, the tourism industry, and the habitat of hundreds of bird, fish, and other wildlife species.

Cultural Eutrophication

Cultural eutrophication is defined as the process whereby human activity increases the amount of nutrients entering surface waters. The two most important nutrients that cause cultural eutrophication are nitrates (NO_3^-) and phosphates (PO_4^{3-}) that come from fertilizer, sewage discharge, and animal wastes.

Nitrates are water soluble. Nitrates found in fertilizers can remain on fields and accumulate, leach into groundwater, end up in surface runoff, and/or volatize and enter the atmosphere where they contribute to acid precipitation. Nitrates cause nitrate poisoning in water supplies, reduce the effectiveness of hemoglobin, and may be responsible for worldwide declines in amphibians.

Phosphates are also a component of inorganic fertilizers. However, they are not water soluble and adhere to soil particles. Soil erosion contributes to the buildup of phosphates in water supplies. Phosphate levels in water supplies are 75% higher than they were during preindustrial times. Phosphate buildup is more damaging in freshwater systems. In contrast, nitrate pollution is more damaging in wetlands where nitrogen is the limiting factor.

Nitrates and phosphates are algal nutrients. Increased concentrations of these nutrients increase the carrying capacity of lakes and streams. Explosions in the amount of algae as a result of cultural eutrophication are called algal blooms. The steps involved in algal bloom include the following:

- Increased algae due to increased nitrate and/or phosphate concentrations result in decreased light penetration and killing off of deeper plants and their supply of oxygen to water.
- Oxygen concentration decreases in the water due to the consequences of increased material for decomposers.
- Lower oxygen concentrations cause fish and other aquatic organisms to die and contaminate the water at a high rate.
- Decaying fish and algae produce toxins in the water.

Several methods can control cultural eutrophication. Planting vegetation (buffer zones) along streambeds slows erosion and absorbs some of the nutrients. Controlling the application and timing of applying fertilizer, controlling runoff from feedlots, and using biological controls such as denitrifying bacteria that convert nitrates into atmospheric nitrogen are other methods.

Groundwater Pollution

About 50% of the people in the United States depend on groundwater for their water supplies. In some countries, it may reach as high as 95%. Almost half of the water used for agriculture in the United States comes from groundwater. The Environmental Protection Agency (EPA) estimates that each day, 4.5 trillion liters of contaminated water seep into groundwater supplies in the United States. In the United States, 34 billion liters per year (60%) of the most hazardous liquid waste solvents, heavy metals, and radioactive materials are injected directly into deep groundwater via thousands of injection wells. Although the EPA requires that these effluents be injected below the deepest source of drinking water, some pollutants have already entered underground water supplies in Florida, Texas, Ohio, and Oklahoma.

Water entering an aquifer remains there for approximately 1,400 years compared with 16 days for water entering a river system. Once an aquifer is contaminated, it is practically impossible to remove the pollutants. For example, in Denver, Colorado, just 80 liters of organic solvents contaminated 4.5 trillion liters of groundwater. Initial cleanup of contaminated groundwater locations in the United States could cost up to $1 trillion over the next 30 years.

Maintaining Water Quality and Water Purification

DRINKING WATER TREATMENT METHODS

- **Adsorption**—Contaminants stick to the surface of granular or powdered activated charcoal.
- **Disinfection**—Chlorine, chloramines, chlorine dioxide, ozone, and UV radiation.
- **Filtration**—Removes clays, silts, natural organic matter, and precipitants from the treatment process. Filtration clarifies water and enhances the effectiveness of disinfection.
- **Flocculation-Sedimentation**—Process that combines small particles into larger particles that then settle out of the water as sediment. Alum, iron salts, or synthetic organic polymers are generally used to promote coagulation.
- **Ion Exchange**—Removes inorganic constituents. It can be used to remove arsenic, chromium, excess fluoride, nitrates, radium, and uranium.

WATER TREATMENT REMEDIATION TECHNOLOGIES

- **Adsorption/absorption**—Solutes concentrate at the surface of a sorbent (an absorbing surface), thereby reducing their concentration.
- **Aeration**—Bubbling air through water increases rates of oxidation.
- **Air stripping**—VOCs are separated from groundwater by exposing water to air (the VOCs evaporate due to their high vapor pressure).
- **Bioreactors**—Groundwater is acted upon by microorganisms.
- **Constructed wetlands**—Uses natural geochemical and biological processes that parallel natural wetlands. Also known as living machines.

- **Deep-well injection**—Uses injection wells to place treated or untreated liquid waste into geologic formations that do not pose a potential risk to groundwater.
- **Enhanced bioremediation**—The natural rate of bioremediation is enhanced by adding oxygen and nutrients into groundwater.
- **Fluid-vapor extraction**—A vacuum system is applied to low-permeable soil to remove liquids and gases.
- **Granulated activated carbon (GAC)**—Groundwater is pumped through a series of columns containing activated carbon.
- **Hot water or steam flushing**—Steam or hot water is forced into an aquifer to vaporize volatile contaminants and is then treated through fluid-vapor extraction.
- **In-well air stripping**—Air is injected into wells—the air picks up various contaminants, particularly VOCs. Vapors are drawn off by vapor extraction.
- **Ion exchange**—Involves exchange of one ion for another.
- **Phytoremediation**—Uses plants to remove contamination.
- **UV oxidation**—Uses ultraviolet light, ozone, or hydrogen peroxide to destroy microbiological contaminants.

Sewage Treatment/Septic Systems

Sewage treatment incorporates physical, chemical, and biological processes to remove contaminants from wastewater. There are three stages of wastewater treatment.

A septic system consists of a tank and a drain field. Wastewater enters the tank, where solids settle. Anaerobic digestion using bacteria treats the settled solids and reduces their volume. Excess liquid leaves the tank and moves through a pipe with holes in it to a leach field where the water then percolates into the soil.

Some pollutants, especially nitrogen, do not decompose in a septic system and may contaminate the groundwater. Approximately 25% of Americans rely on septic systems.

PRIMARY TREATMENT—SEPARATION OF SOLIDS

Primary treatment is to reduce oils, grease, fats, sand, grit, and coarse solids. Specific steps include sand catchers, screens, and sedimentation. This is a physical method of cleaning.

SECONDARY TREATMENT—BREAKDOWN BY BACTERIA

Secondary treatment is designed to degrade substantially the biological content of the sewage derived from human waste, food waste, soaps, and detergent. Specific steps include filters, activated sludge, filter (oxidizing) beds, trickling filter beds using plastic media, and secondary sedimentation. This is a biological method of cleaning.

TERTIARY TREATMENT—DISINFECTION

Tertiary treatment provides a final stage to raise the effluent quality to the standard required before it is discharged to the receiving environment (sea, river, lake, or ground). Specific steps may include sand filtration, lagooning, constructed wetlands, nutrient removal through biological or chemical precipitation, denitrification using bacteria, phosphorous removal using bacteria, microfiltration, and disinfection using UV light, chlorine, or ozone.

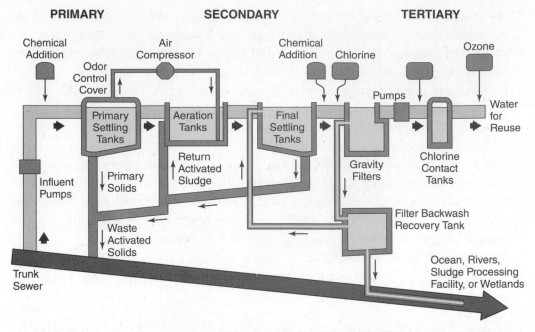

Figure 9.2 Sewage treatment plant

TIP

Reference relevant laws in your essay answers whenever possible. They will substantiate your thoughts and provide a historical framework for the issue.

RELEVANT LAWS

Clean Water Act (1972): Established the basic structure for regulating discharges of pollutants into the waters of the United States. It gave the EPA the authority to implement pollution control programs such as setting wastewater standards for industry. The Clean Water Act also continued requirements to set water quality standards for all contaminants in surface waters. The act made it unlawful for any person to discharge any pollutant from a point source into navigable waters unless a permit was obtained under its provisions. It also funded the construction of sewage treatment plants under the construction grants program and recognized the need for planning to address the critical problems posed by nonpoint source pollution.

Safe Drinking Water Act (1974): Established standards for safe drinking water in the United States.

Ocean Dumping Ban Act (1988): Made it unlawful for any person to dump or transport for the purpose of dumping sewage, sludge, or industrial wastes into the ocean.

Oil Spill Prevention and Liability Act (1990): Strengthened the EPA's ability to prevent and respond to catastrophic oil spills.

SOLID WASTE

Types of solid waste include:

- **Organic**—Kitchen wastes, vegetables, flowers, leaves, or fruits. Usually decomposes within 2 weeks. Wood can take 10 to 15 years to decompose.
- **Radioactive**—Spent fuel rods and smoke detectors. Radioactive wastes can take hundreds of thousands of years to decompose.
- **Recyclable**—Paper, glass, metals, and some plastics. Paper decomposes in 10 to 30 days. Glass does not decompose. Metals decompose in 100 to 500 years. Some plastics can take up to 1 million years to decompose.

- **Soiled**—Hospital wastes. Cotton and cloth can take 2 to 5 months to decompose.
- **Toxic**—Paints, chemicals, pesticides, and so on. Toxic wastes can take hundreds of years to decompose.

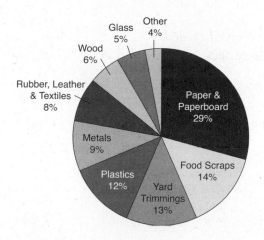

Figure 9.3 Amounts and types of municipal solid wastes (MSW) in the U.S.

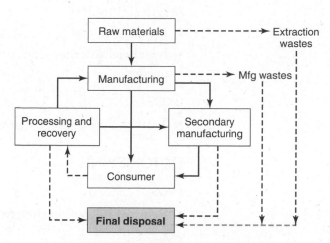

Figure 9.4 Solid waste flow diagram

Disposal and Reduction

BURNING, INCINERATION, OR ENERGY RECOVERY

Pros

- Heat can be used to supplement energy requirements.
- Reduces impact on landfills.
- Mass burning is inexpensive.
- What is left is 10% to 20% of original volume.
- U.S. incinerates 15% of its wastes.
- France, Japan, Sweden, and Switzerland incinerate > 40% of their wastes and use the heat to generate electricity.

Cons

- Air pollution including lead, mercury, NO_x, cadmium, SO_2, HCl, and dioxins.
- Sorting out batteries, plastics, etc., is expensive.
- No way of knowing toxic consequences.
- Ash is more concentrated with toxic materials.
- Initial costs of incinerators are high.
- Adds to acid precipitation and global warming.

COMPOSTING

Pros

- Creates nutrient-rich soil additive.
- Aids in water retention.
- Slows down soil erosion.
- No major toxic issues.

Cons

- Public reaction to odor, vermin, and insects.
- Not in my backyard (NIMBY).

REMANUFACTURING

Pros

- Recovers materials that would have been discarded.
- Beneficial to inner cities as an industry because material is available and jobs are needed.

Cons

- Toxic materials may be present (CFCs, heavy metals, toxic chemicals, etc.).

DETOXIFYING

Pros

- Reduces impact on the environment.

Cons

- Expensive.

EXPORTING

Pros

- Gets rid of problem immediately.
- Source of income for poor countries.

Cons

- Garbage imperialism or environmental racism.
- Long-term effects not known.
- Expensive to transport.

LAND DISPOSAL—SANITARY LANDFILLS

Pros

- Waste is covered each day with dirt to help prevent insects and rodents.
- Plastic liners, drainage systems, and other methods help control leaching material into groundwater.
- Geologic studies and environmental impact studies are performed prior to building.
- Collection of methane and use of fuel cells to supplement energy demand.
- Use of anaerobic methane generators reduces dependence on other energy sources.

Cons

- Rising land prices. Current costs are $1 million per hectare.
- Transportation costs to the landfill.
- High cost of running and monitoring landfill.
- Legal liability.

- Suitable areas are limited.
- NIMBY.
- Degradable plastics do not decompose completely.

LAND DISPOSAL—OPEN DUMPING

Pros

- Inexpensive.
- Provides a source of income to the poor by providing recyclable products to sell.

Cons

- Trash blows away in the wind.
- Vermin and disease.
- Leaching of toxic materials into the soil.
- Aesthetics.

OCEAN DUMPING

Pros

- Inexpensive.

Cons

- Debris floats to unintended areas.
- Marine organisms and food webs are impacted.
- Illegal in the United States.

RECYCLING

Pros

- Turns waste into an inexpensive resource.
- Reduces impact on landfills.
- Reduces need for raw materials and the costs associated with it.
- Reduces energy requirements to produce product. For example: recycling aluminum cuts energy use 95% and producing steel from scrap reduces energy requirements 75%.
- Reduces dependence on foreign oil.
- Reduces air and water pollution.
- Bottle bills provide economic incentive to recycle.

Cons

- Poor regulation.
- Fluctuations in market price.
- Throwaway packaging is more popular.
- Current policies and regulations favor extraction of raw materials. Energy, water, and raw materials are sold below real costs to stimulate new jobs and the economy.

REUSE

Pros

- Most efficient method of reclaiming materials.
- Industry models already in place—auto salvage yards, building materials, and so on.
- Refillable glass bottles can be reused approximately 15 times.
- Cloth diapers do not impact landfills.

Cons

- Cost of collecting materials on a large scale is expensive.
- Cost of washing and decontaminating containers is expensive.
- Only when items are expensive and labor is cheap is reuse economical.

RELEVANT LAWS

Resource Conservation and Recovery Act (RCRA) (1976): Encouraged states to develop comprehensive plans to manage nonhazardous industrial solid and municipal wastes. Set criteria for municipal landfills and disposal facilities, and prohibited open dumping of solid wastes.

Toxic Substances Control Act (TOSCA) (1976): Gave the EPA the authority to track industrial chemicals produced within or imported into the United States. Allows the EPA to ban the manufacture or importation of chemicals that pose risks.

Comprehensive Environmental Response, Compensation, and Liability Act (CERCLA—Superfund) (1980): Provided authority for the federal government to respond to releases or possible releases of hazardous substances that could threaten public health and/or the environment. Established rules for closed and abandoned hazardous waste sites. Established liability for corporations responsible for hazardous waste sites. Created a trust fund for cleanup if responsible parties for contaminated sites could not be found.

Nuclear Waste Policy Act (1982): Established federal authority to provide locations for permanent disposal of high-level radioactive wastes and required the operators of nuclear power plants to pay the costs of permanent disposal.

QUICK REVIEW CHECKLIST

- ☐ **Air Pollution**
  - ☐ major air pollutants
    - ☐ nitrogen dioxide
    - ☐ ozone
    - ☐ sulfur dioxide
    - ☐ suspended particulate matter (PM_{10})
    - ☐ volatile organic compounds (VOCs)
  - ☐ measurement units
  - ☐ smog
    - ☐ formation of industrial smog
    - ☐ formation of photochemical smog
  - ☐ acid deposition
    - ☐ causes and effects
  - ☐ heat islands
  - ☐ temperature inversions
  - ☐ indoor air pollution
  - ☐ remediation and reduction strategies
  - ☐ relevant laws and protocols
    - ☐ Air Pollution Control Act (1955)
    - ☐ Clean Air Act (1963)
    - ☐ National Environmental Policy Act (1969)
    - ☐ Montreal Protocol (1989)
    - ☐ Pollution Prevention Act (1990)
    - ☐ Kyoto Protocol (1997)

- ☐ **Noise Pollution**
  - ☐ causes
  - ☐ effects
  - ☐ control measures
  - ☐ Noise Control Act (1972)

- ☐ **Water Pollution**
  - ☐ sources
    - ☐ air pollution
    - ☐ chemicals
    - ☐ microbiological
    - ☐ mining
    - ☐ noise
    - ☐ nutrients
    - ☐ oxygen-depleting substances
    - ☐ suspended matter
    - ☐ thermal sources
  - ☐ Minamata disease
  - ☐ *Exxon Valdez* (1989)

- ☐ **Cultural Eutrophication**

QUICK REVIEW CHECKLIST (continued)

☐ **Groundwater Pollution**

☐ **Maintaining Water Quality and Water Purification**
   ☐ drinking water treatment methods
   ☐ water treatment remediation technologies

☐ **Sewage Treatment/Septic Systems**
   ☐ primary treatment
   ☐ secondary treatment
   ☐ tertiary treatment

☐ **Relevant Laws**
   ☐ Clean Water Act (1972)
   ☐ Safe Drinking Water Act (1974)
   ☐ Ocean Dumping Ban Act (1988)
   ☐ Oil Spill Prevention and Liability Act (1990)

☐ **Solid Wastes**
   ☐ different types
      ☐ organic
      ☐ radioactive
      ☐ recyclable
      ☐ soiled
      ☐ toxic
   ☐ amounts and type of MSW
   ☐ disposal and reduction methods
      ☐ incineration
      ☐ composting
      ☐ remanufacturing
      ☐ detoxifying
      ☐ exporting
      ☐ land disposal—sanitary landfills
      ☐ land disposal—open dumping
      ☐ ocean dumping
      ☐ recycling
      ☐ reuse
      ☐ solid waste flow diagram

☐ **Relevant Laws**
   ☐ Resource Conservation and Recovery Act (1976)
   ☐ Toxic Substances Control Act (TOSCA) (1976)
   ☐ Comprehensive Environmental Response, Compensation, and Liability Act (CERCLA-Superfund) (1980)
   ☐ Nuclear Waste Policy Act (1982)

MULTIPLE-CHOICE QUESTIONS

1. _____contributes to the formation of _____ and thereby compounds the problem of _____.

   (A) ozone, carbon dioxide, acid rain
   (B) carbon dioxide, carbon monoxide, ozone depletion
   (C) sulfur dioxide, acid deposition, global warming
   (D) nitrous oxide, ozone, industrial smog
   (E) nitric oxide, ozone, photochemical smog

2. Photochemical smog does NOT require the presence of

   (A) nitrogen oxides
   (B) ultraviolet radiation
   (C) peroxyacyl nitrates
   (D) volatile organic compounds
   (E) ozone

3. Which of the following is generally NOT considered to be a teratogen?

   (A) Ethanol or drinking alcohol
   (B) Benzene
   (C) Radiation
   (D) PCBs or polychlorinated biphenyls
   (E) All are considered teratogens

4. Which of the following steps is NOT involved in the production of industrial smog?

   (A) $C + O_2 \rightarrow CO_2$
   (B) $C + O_2 \rightarrow CO$
   (C) $S + O_2 \rightarrow SO_2$
   (D) $NO_2 \rightarrow NO + O$
   (E) $SO_2 + O_2 \rightarrow SO_3$

5. Household water is most likely to be contaminated with radon in homes that

   (A) are served by public water systems that use a groundwater source
   (B) are served by public water systems that use a surface water source
   (C) have private wells
   (D) use bottled water
   (E) are served by water agencies that use ozone to disinfect the water

6. Which reaction is NOT involved in the formation of acid deposition?

   (A) $O_3 + C_xH_y \rightarrow$ PANs
   (B) $SO_2 + H_2O \rightarrow H_2SO_3$
   (C) $H_2SO_3 + \frac{1}{2}O_2 \rightarrow H_2SO_4$
   (D) $NO + \rightarrow \frac{1}{2}O_2 \rightarrow NO_2$
   (E) $2NO_2 + H_2O \rightarrow HNO_2 + HNO_3$

7. Normal rainfall has a pH of about

   (A) 2.3
   (B) 5.6
   (C) 7.0
   (D) 7.6
   (E) 8.3

8. According to the Environmental Protection Agency, about _____ of all commercial buildings in the United States are classified as sick.

   (A) 5%
   (B) 15%
   (C) 50%
   (D) 75%
   (E) 100%

9. In developing countries, the most likely cause of respiratory disease would be

   (A) photochemical smog
   (B) industrial smog
   (C) smoking
   (D) PM_{10}
   (E) asbestos

10. Humans LEAST susceptible to the effects of air pollution are

    (A) newborns
    (B) children between the age of 2 and 10
    (C) teenagers
    (D) adult males
    (E) the elderly

11. Acid precipitation, leaching out the metal _____ , causes fish and other aquatic organisms to die from acid shock.

    (A) Al
    (B) Pb
    (C) Hg
    (D) Cd
    (E) Fe

12. Which pollutant best illustrates the effectiveness of legislation?

    (A) NO_2
    (B) SO_2
    (C) CO_2
    (D) O_3
    (E) Pb

13. The diagram below shows the range of organisms found within certain sections of a river in an industrial area. Which section of the river most likely has the LOWEST level of dissolved oxygen?

Effects of Sewage Discharge in a River
Organisms commonly found in discharge zone

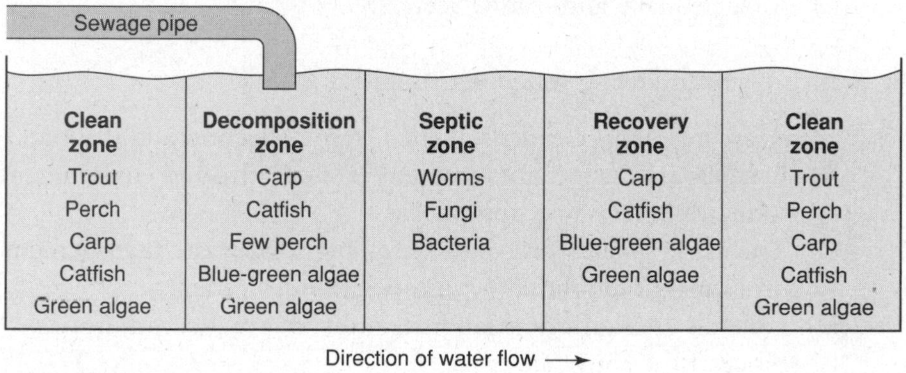

Clean zone	Decomposition zone	Septic zone	Recovery zone	Clean zone
Trout	Carp	Worms	Carp	Trout
Perch	Catfish	Fungi	Catfish	Perch
Carp	Few perch	Bacteria	Blue-green algae	Carp
Catfish	Blue-green algae		Green algae	Catfish
Green algae	Green algae			Green algae

Direction of water flow ⟶

    (A) Clean zone
    (B) Decomposition zone
    (C) Septic zone
    (D) Recovery zone
    (E) None of the above

14. Which country listed below did NOT agree to the Kyoto Protocol to reduce its greenhouse gas emissions in 1997 and the extension in 2012?

    (A) Canada
    (B) United States
    (C) Russia
    (D) Australia
    (E) Brazil

15. The major source of solid waste in the United States comes from what source?

    (A) Homes
    (B) Factories
    (C) Agriculture
    (D) Petroleum refining
    (E) Mining wastes

16. What is the largest type of domestic solid waste in the United States?

   (A) Yard wastes
   (B) Paper
   (C) Plastic
   (D) Glass
   (E) Metal

17. Which of the following is most readily recyclable?

   (A) Plastic
   (B) Paper
   (C) Metal
   (D) Glass
   (E) All are equally and readily recyclable

18. Which of the following statements is TRUE?

   (A) Recycling is more expensive than trash collection and disposal.
   (B) Landfills and incinerators are more cost effective and environmentally sound than recycling options.
   (C) The marketplace works best in solving solid waste management problems; no public sector intervention is needed.
   (D) Landfills are significant job generators for rural communities.
   (E) None of the above are true.

19. In the 1970s, houses were built over a toxic chemical waste disposal site. This case study is known as

   (A) Love Canal
   (B) Bet Trang
   (C) Bhopal
   (D) Brownfield
   (E) Chernobyl

20. Which of the following methods of handling solid wastes is against the law in the United States?

   (A) Incineration
   (B) Dumping it in open landfills
   (C) Burying it underground
   (D) Exporting the material to foreign countries
   (E) Dumping the material in the open ocean

FREE-RESPONSE QUESTION

By Dr. Ian Kelleher
Brooks School
North Andover, MA

(a) Study the following graph, which shows projected trends in annual carbon dioxide emissions, and then answer the following questions.

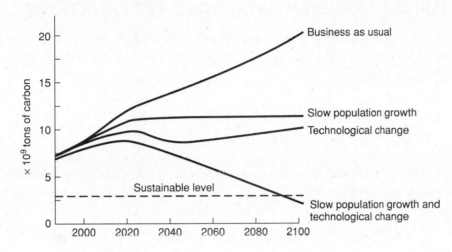

  (i) In the "business as usual" model, what factors do you think might contribute to the increase in carbon dioxide emissions?
 (ii) Given the shape of the graph, what do you think is meant in this case by "technological change"?
(iii) What is meant by a "sustainable level" of carbon dioxide emissions? According to these predictions, what needs to happen for this level to be brought about?

(b) Use the example of acid deposition to illustrate the difference between remediation and alleviation of an environmental problem.

(c) Look at the graph of CFC production and account for the trends you observe.

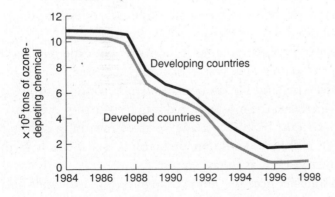

(d) In 1992, the World Bank designated indoor air pollution in developing countries as one of the four most critical global environmental problems. Use examples of major sources of indoor pollutants to illustrate how the issue of indoor air quality in developing countries differs from that in developed countries.

MULTIPLE-CHOICE ANSWERS AND EXPLANATIONS

1. **(E)** As the sunlight becomes more intense, nitrogen dioxide (NO_2) is broken down into nitric oxide (NO) and oxygen atoms, and the concentration of ozone increases:

$$NO_2 \xrightarrow{uv} NO + O$$

$$O_2 + O \rightarrow O_3$$

2. **(C)** Nitrogen dioxide can also react with volatile organic compounds (VOCs) released by vehicles, refineries, gas stations, and the like to produce toxic chemicals such as peroxyacyl nitrates (PANs):

$$NO_2 + VOCs \rightarrow PANs$$

3. **(E)** Teratogens are substances or environmental agents that cause abnormalities in a fetus during pregnancy. Choices (A)–(D) are all known teratogens.

4. **(D)** This step is present in the formation of photochemical smog.

5. **(C)** Radon is a naturally occurring radioactive gas that causes cancer and may be found in drinking water and indoor air. The Safe Drinking Water Act requires the EPA to develop regulations to reduce radon in drinking water.

6. **(A)** Review the reactions required to form acid deposition.

7. **(B)** Rain is naturally acidic due to the presence of carbon dioxide in the air, which forms carbonic acid with rainwater.

8. **(B)** The World Health Organization (WHO) estimates that up to 30% of commercial buildings worldwide may be unhealthy with up to one-third of the people who work in these buildings experiencing health effects. In the United States, with more stringent building codes, approximately 15% of commercial buildings are classified as unhealthy.

9. **(D)** Developing countries around the world are experiencing increased levels of particulate matter as a result of rapid increases in energy consumption, motor vehicle use, and rapid population and economic growth.

10. **(D)** The elderly are the most affected group since they may have compromised respiratory systems based on many years of breathing pollutants. Newborns are a very close second. Children are highly affected due to high activity levels and increased cases of asthma.

11. **(A)** Aluminum reduces the ion exchange through the gills and causes fish to excrete excess mucus, which reduces oxygen uptake.

12. **(E)** From 1976 to 1980, the average amount of lead in children was 15 µg/dL. From 1991 to 1994, the average level had been reduced to 2.7 µg/dL.

13. **(C)** The level of dissolved oxygen in the septic zone is too low to support organisms that live by aerobic respiration. In this region, anaerobic bacteria flourish and produce waste products such as hydrogen sulfide (H_2S) and methane (CH_4).

14. **(B)** The United States is the only country listed to have failed to agree to the Kyoto Protocol in 1997 to reduce its greenhouse gases and its extension in 2012. In 2011, Canada withdrew from the Protocol.

15. **(E)** Mining wastes, along with oil and gas production, constitute about 75% of all solid wastes generated in the United States.

16. **(B)** Paper accounts for approximately 35% of domestic solid waste in the United States.

17. **(B)** Paper can be broken down into fibers and reused generally without requiring a sorting process. For some refined paper products, recycled paper must be sorted based on ink types.

18. **(E)** In choice (A), when designed properly, recycling programs are cost-competitive with trash collection and disposal. In choice (B), properly designed recycling programs are cost competitive with landfills and incinerators. In choice (C), solid waste systems generally operate under public sector guidelines. In choice (D), recycling creates many more jobs in rural and urban communities than landfill employment.

19. **(A)** Love Canal is an abandoned canal in New York where a huge amount of toxic waste was buried. The waste was composed of at least 300 different chemicals, totaling an estimated 20,000 metric tons.

20. **(E)** The Ocean Dumping Act prohibits dumping of wastes into territorial ocean waters.

FREE-RESPONSE ANSWER

(a) (i) Increased carbon dioxide emissions primarily come from increased burning of fossil fuels worldwide. The "business as usual" model would include an increasing global population, which would mean an increase in the demand for energy. In the "business as usual" model, this need would be met primarily by increased use of fossil fuels, by far the most common source of energy in the world today. Increasing rates of development, particularly of developing countries in this model, would also lead to an increase in fossil fuel use.

(a) (ii) "Technological change" reduces carbon dioxide emissions on the graph. Increased use of alternative sources of energy such as nuclear power, hydro-electric, solar, and tidal energy would all decrease fossil fuel emissions. Technologies that increase energy efficiency and save power, such as more efficient car engines, would also decrease the use of fossil fuels and thus carbon dioxide emissions.

(a) (iii) A "sustainable level" of carbon dioxide emissions is one in which the amount absorbed by Earth's natural systems, such as oceans and plants, equals the amount released into the atmosphere. A combination of both technologi-

Notable points:

Cover all of the relevant aspects of "business as usual," such as increasing size and development of populations.

"Technological change" is a vague phrase that could mean many things. In this case, the curve thus labeled shows a dramatic reduction in carbon dioxide emissions, so the question is asking about technologies that reduce fossil fuel use.

cal change and slowed population growth is needed to bring carbon dioxide emissions to sustainable levels. As the graph shows, neither factor can produce sustainable levels on its own.

Explaining the difference between these two similar terms would be a good way to start. These are basic terms that you should know. Starting like this should lessen the chance of mixing them up.

Thus, cause and effect must both be covered in the answer, and you must take care to distinguish the two. Acid deposition is a secondary pollutant. Explaining the sequence of events that leads to its formation might be helpful in distinguishing cause from effect.

Anything that reduces the use of fossil fuels or limits the emissions of sulfur and nitrogen oxides would be an example of alleviation. Anything that neutralizes the effects of acid in the environment would be an example of remediation. Be careful in giving just an appropriate level of detail.

When asked to explain the trends shown in a graph, a good starting point is to describe what they are. Writing this down first should also help you compose your explanation.

This sample essay may provide more detail than necessary. The important point is that the amounts for both developed and developing countries fell dramatically at the same time and basically at the same rate. This suggests that the drops come as a result of the implementation of new laws. Since we are dealing with a global situation, it is likely to be in the form of an international agreement.

(b) Alleviation of an environmental problem means stopping or lessening its cause. Remediation means cleaning up the effects of the problem.

Acid deposition forms in the atmosphere mainly from sulfur oxides (SO_x) and nitrogen oxides (NO_x). Both are present primarily as a consequence of the combustion of fossil fuels.

Methods of alleviation may concentrate on decreasing the amount of sulfur and nitrogen oxides released into the atmosphere. Any method of reducing the rate of consumption of fossil fuels, such as increased use of nuclear power and alternative energy sources, or laws and education to help conserve energy would decrease the amount of sulfur and nitrogen oxides released. Clean-fuel technologies, such as fluidized-bed combustion of coal, would result in less of these gases being produced on combustion. Scrubbers in smokestacks can remove much of what is produced. Perhaps the most important step in reducing emissions in the United States, however, was the passing of the Clean Air Act in 1963 and its subsequent amendments.

Methods of remediation may concentrate on neutralizing the acid deposited in an environment. Acids can be neutralized by adding a base. Since an abundant, low-cost, and nontoxic material is often needed, limestone, $CaCO_3$, is commonly used. For example, limestone might be added to a lake to increase its pH. Powdered limestone could also be spread over agricultural lands to increase the pH of the soil. Many nutrients are more soluble in acidic soils and therefore might be washed away by rain. As a result, the addition of fertilizer is also required. Deforestation caused by acid deposition may be addressed by treating the soil and then replanting.

(c) Between 1984 and 1988, both developed and developing countries used ozone-depleting chemicals at a fairly consistent rate of approximately 1 million tons per year. After 1988, the amount used by both developed and developing countries decreased sharply and at a fairly constant rate for the next seven years. By 1996, developed countries used 50,000 tons per year and developing countries used 150,000 tons. Use remained at approximately these levels for the next two years.

The reduction is likely to be due to countries implementing technologies to comply with the Montreal Protocol (1989), which set limits for the emission of chemicals that cause depletion of the ozone layer. The biggest reduction has come from using alternatives to chlorofluorocarbons (CFCs)—the principal ozone-depleting agents. Alternatives include HFCs and HCFCs.

(d) Homes are perhaps the most important factor when considering indoor air quality since people tend to spend more time there than anywhere else. The majority of people in developing countries live in homes with much simpler technologies. Many of the pollutants found in houses in developed countries are not present. The major source of indoor air pollutants in developing countries, therefore, is the combustion of poor-quality fuels for heating, lighting, and cooking. Such dirty fuels include animal wastes, kerosene, and low-grade coal that may release large amounts of particulates, carbon monoxide, sulfur oxides, and other toxins on combustion. As fires are often burned indoors in places with inadequate ventilation, the levels of these pollutants and carbon monoxide can be greatly concentrated.

Energy sources are much more technologically advanced in developed countries, so this is not such an important source of indoor air pollution. For example, poorly maintained furnaces may produce some carbon monoxide. However, this problem is not nearly as widespread or generally as serious as the energy issue in developing countries. Instead, major sources of air pollution include lead (from lead paints), asbestos, and fumes from volatile organic compounds (VOCs) in paints, glues, plastics, and furniture. These things will be less common in houses in developing countries. Houses in developed countries are often tightly sealed, more so than in developing countries. This leads to increased levels of concentration. For example, radon gas, which occurs naturally from radioactive decay in certain rocks, might accumulate to dangerous levels in a modern air-conditioned house but not in a simpler hut with no glass in the windows.

The wording of the World Bank designation suggests that the question is referring to the general masses of the population in developing countries rather than the small, technologically developed percentage. The answer is thus strongly focused on this difference in lifestyle.

Impacts on the Environment and Human Health

HAZARDS TO HUMAN HEALTH

Environmental risk analysis is the comparing of the risk of a situation to its related benefits. It is the overall process that allows one to evaluate and deal with the consequences of events, based on their probability. There are four classes of risk:

1. High risk—such as smoking or driving while intoxicated.

2. Low risk—infrequent events that may have a large consequence, such as an earthquake on the East Coast of the United States.

3. Very low risk—events that have never occurred in recorded history, such as a major meteor striking the North American continent.

4. Mixed risk—outcomes that increase in frequency against a background of occurrences, such as additional cases of cancer beyond that normally expected.

Understanding how people accept risk requires an understanding of how preferences are accepted and measured. The three types of preferences are revealed, expressed, and natural standards. Revealed preferences are observations on the risks people actually take. Expressed preferences are often measured through public opinion polls. Natural standards are levels of risk humans have lived with in the past.

Risk estimation is a scientific question, while acceptability of a given level of risk is a political question. We can see this distinction by comparing the risk of smoking with working in a coal mine. If the United States spent as much money on premature deaths and illnesses caused by smoking tobacco as we do on coal mine safety, there would be little money left in the United States for any other purpose. This is the political reality of risk acceptance that goes beyond risk estimation.

External influences are factored into decisions regarding environmental risk. These influences include public concern, economic interest, and legislative actions that affect the possible choices available.

Risk analysis is divided into risk assessment and risk management. Risk assessment is an objective estimation of risk. It includes the identification of hazards, dose-response assessment, exposure assessment, and risk characterization.

Risk management is the process of determining what to do about risk. This includes risk identification and use of mitigating measures to reduce risk.

Acute and Chronic Effects

Acute health effects are characterized by sudden and severe exposure and rapid absorption of the substance. Normally, a single large exposure is involved. Acute health effects are often reversible, such as carbon monoxide poisoning.

Chronic health effects are characterized by prolonged or repeated exposures over many days, months, or years. Symptoms may not be immediately apparent. Chronic health effects are often irreversible. Examples include lead or mercury poisoning, asbestosis, or cancer.

Dose-Response Relationships

Dose-response relationships describe the change in effect on an organism or a population caused by differing levels of exposures to a substance. These relationships are used to determine whether various environmental risks are safe or hazardous.

A dose-response curve is a graph that relates the amount of drug or toxin given (plotted on the x-axis and usually the logarithm of the dose) compared with the response (plotted on the y-axis and usually provided in percentages). The point on the graph where the response is first observed is known as the threshold dose. For most drugs, the desired effect is found slightly above the threshold dose. When past this point, negative side effects begin to appear.

LD_{50} (lethal dose, 50%) is the median lethal dose of a pollutant or drug that kills half the members of a tested population within 14 days and is the most common indicator of toxicity. EC_{50} is the concentration of a compound where 50% of its effect is observed.

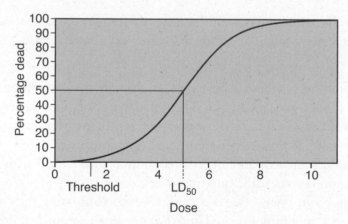

Figure 10.1 A dose-response curve

Air Pollutants and Their Effect on Human Health

AIR TOXICS

Air toxics are a group of air pollutants that are known or suspected to cause serious health problems. Examples of air toxics include asbestos, benzene, chloroform, formaldehyde, lead, mercury and nickel compounds, and perchloroethylene. People exposed to air toxics at sufficient concentrations and durations may have an increased chance of developing cancer or other serious health problems. These include damage to the immune system as well as neurological, reproductive (reduced fertility), developmental, and respiratory problems.

ASBESTOS

Studies of people who were exposed to asbestos in factories and shipyards have shown that breathing high levels of asbestos fibers can lead to an increased risk of lung cancer, mesothelioma (a cancer of the lining of the chest and the abdominal cavity), and asbestosis (the lungs become scarred with fibrous tissue). Researchers have not yet determined a safe level of exposure. However, they know that the greater and longer the exposure, the greater the risk of contracting an asbestos-related disease. Risks of lung cancer and mesothelioma increase with the number of fibers inhaled. The risk of lung cancer from inhaling asbestos fibers is also greater for smokers. People who develop asbestosis have usually been exposed to high levels of asbestos for a long time. The symptoms of these diseases do not usually appear until about 20 to 30 years after the first exposure.

CARBON MONOXIDE (CO)

Carbon monoxide enters the bloodstream through the lungs and binds chemically to hemoglobin, the substance in blood that carries oxygen to cells. In this way, CO interferes with the ability of the blood to transport oxygen to organs and tissue throughout the body. This can cause slower reflexes, confusion, and drowsiness. It can also reduce visual perception and coordination and can decrease the ability to learn. People with cardiovascular disease, such as angina, are most at risk from exposure to CO. These individuals may experience chest pain and other cardiovascular symptoms if they are exposed to CO, particularly while exercising.

INDOOR AIR POLLUTANTS

Health effects from indoor air pollutants may be acute and experienced soon after exposure or may be chronic. Immediate effects may show up after a single exposure or repeated exposures. These include headaches, dizziness, fatigue, and irritation of the eyes, nose, and throat. Such immediate effects are usually short term and treatable. The likelihood of immediate reactions to indoor air pollutants depends on several factors: age, preexisting medical conditions, and individual sensitivity. Certain immediate effects are similar to those from colds or other viral diseases. Other health effects from exposure to indoor air pollutants may show up either years after exposure has occurred or only after long or repeated periods of exposure. These effects, which include some respiratory diseases, heart disease, and cancer, can be severely debilitating or fatal.

Remember

Environmental problems have a cultural and social context. Understanding the role of cultural, social, and economic factors is vital to the development of solutions.

LEAD (Pb)

Exposure to lead can occur through inhalation of air and ingestion of lead in food, water, soil, or dust. Excessive lead exposure can cause seizures, brain and kidney damage, mental retardation, and/or behavioral disorders. Children six and under are most at risk because their bodies are growing quickly.

NITROGEN DIOXIDE (NO₂)

Health effects of exposure to nitrogen dioxide include coughing, wheezing, and shortness of breath in children and adults with respiratory disease such as asthma. Even short exposures to nitrogen dioxide can affect lung function and may cause permanent structural changes in the lungs.

OZONE (O₃)

The reactivity of ozone causes health problems because it damages lung tissue, reduces lung function, and sensitizes the lungs to other irritants. Exposure to ozone for several hours at relatively low concentrations has been found to reduce lung function significantly and to induce respiratory inflammation in normal, healthy people during exercise. This decrease in lung function is generally accompanied by symptoms including chest pain and pulmonary congestion.

PM₁₀

Coarse particles can aggravate respiratory conditions such as asthma. Exposure to fine particles is associated with several serious health effects, including premature death. When exposed to PM_{10}, people with existing heart or lung diseases such as asthma, chronic obstructive pulmonary disease, and congestive or ischemic heart disease are at increased risk of premature death. Older persons are especially sensitive to PM_{10} exposure. When exposed to PM_{10}, children and people with existing lung disease may not be able to breathe as deeply or as vigorously as they normally would. They may also experience symptoms such as coughing and shortness of breath. PM_{10} can increase susceptibility to respiratory infections and can aggravate existing respiratory diseases, such as asthma and chronic bronchitis.

RADON

Radon is an invisible, radioactive gas that results from the radioactive decay of radium, which may be found in rock formations beneath buildings or in certain building materials. Radon is probably the most pervasive serious hazard for indoor air in the United States and Europe, probably responsible for tens of thousands of deaths from lung cancer each year. Radon is a heavy gas and thus will tend to accumulate at the floor level, and radon accumulation is greatest for well-insulated homes. Radon mitigation methods include sealing concrete slab floors, basement foundations, water drainage systems, or by increasing ventilation.

SULFUR DIOXIDE (SO₂)

High concentrations of sulfur dioxide affect breathing and may aggravate existing respiratory and cardiovascular disease. Sensitive populations include asthmatics, individuals with bronchitis or emphysema, children, and the elderly.

Smoking and Other Preventable Risks

Cigarette smoke contains over 4,700 chemical compounds including 60 known carcinogens. No threshold level of exposure to cigarette smoke has been defined. However, conclusive evidence indicates that long-term smoking greatly increases the likelihood of developing numerous fatal conditions.

Cigarette smoking is responsible for more than 85% of lung cancers and is also associated with cancers of the mouth, pharynx, larynx, esophagus, stomach, pancreas, kidney, bladder, and colon. Cigarette smoking has also been linked to leukemia. Apart from the carcinogenic aspects of cigarette smoking, links to increased risks of cardiovascular diseases (including stroke), sudden death, cardiac arrest, peripheral vascular disease, and aortic aneurysm have also been established. Many components of cigarette smoke have also been characterized as ciliotoxic materials. These irritate the lining of the respiratory system, resulting in increased bronchial mucus secretion and chronic decreases in pulmonary and mucociliary function.

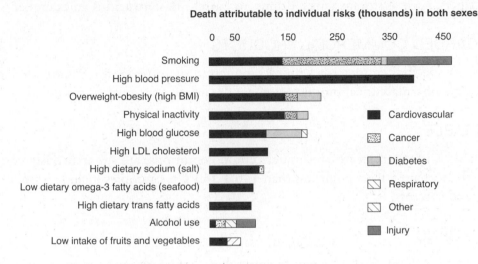

Source: U.S. National Library of Medicine; National Institutes of Health

Figure 10.2 Preventable risks and death rates in the United States

RELEVANT LAWS

Federal Hazardous Substances Act (1960): Required that certain hazardous household products bear cautionary labels to alert consumers to the potential hazards of these products.

Federal Environmental Pesticides Control Act (1972): Required registration of all pesticides in the United States.

Hazardous Materials Transportation Act (HAZMAT) (1975): Governs the transportation of hazardous materials and wastes. Covers containers, labeling, and marking standards.

Toxic Substances Control Act (1976): Gives the Environmental Protection Agency (EPA) the ability to track the 75,000 industrial chemicals currently produced in or imported into the United States.

Comprehensive Environmental Response, Compensation and Liability (CERCLA or SUPERFUND) (1980): Established federal authority for emergency response and cleanup of hazardous substances that have been spilled, improperly disposed of, or released into the environment.

Nuclear Waste Policy Act (1982): Established a study to find a suitable site for disposal of spent fuel from nuclear reactors. Yucca Mountain, Nevada, seems most feasible at this time.

HAZARDOUS CHEMICALS IN THE ENVIRONMENT

A hazardous waste is a waste with properties that make it dangerous or potentially harmful to human health or the environment. Hazardous wastes can be liquids, solids, contained gases, or sludges. The Environmental Protection Agency has separated hazardous wastes into the following categories:

CORROSIVE

Corrosive wastes are strong acids or strong bases that are capable of corroding metal containers, such as storage tanks, drums, or barrels. Battery acid is an example.

DISCARDED COMMERCIAL PRODUCTS

These are specific commercial chemical products in an unused form. Some pesticides and some pharmaceutical products become hazardous wastes when discarded.

IGNITABLE

Ignitable wastes can create fires under certain conditions, are spontaneously combustible, or have a flash point less than 140°F (60°C). Examples include waste oils and used solvents.

MUTAGENS

A mutagen is a physical or chemical agent that changes the genetic material, usually DNA, of an organism and thus increases the frequency of mutations above the natural background level. Many mutations cause cancer, as mutagens are typically also carcinogens. Examples of common mutagens include nitrous acid, bromine and bromine-containing compounds, sodium azide (as found in car safety air bag systems), and benzene.

NONSPECIFIC SOURCE

These include wastes from common manufacturing and industrial processes, such as solvents that have been used in cleaning or degreasing operations.

REACTIVE

Reactive wastes are unstable under normal conditions. They can cause explosions, toxic fumes, gases, or vapors when heated, compressed, or mixed with water. Examples include lithium batteries and explosives.

SOURCE SPECIFIC

These are wastes from specific industries, such as petroleum refining or pesticide manufacturing. Examples include certain sludges and wastewaters from treatment and production processes.

TERATOGENS

Teratogens are substances found in the environment that can cause a birth defect. Examples of teratogens include drinking alcohol (ethanol), radioactive compounds, dioxin, certain pharmaceuticals (e.g., Dilantin, which is used to treat seizures and certain heart arrhythmias), lithium, mercury, tetracyclines, ethers, tobacco, and excessive caffeine.

TOXIC

Toxic wastes are harmful or fatal when ingested or absorbed. They may contain mercury or lead for example. When toxic wastes are disposed of on land, contaminated liquid may leach from the waste and pollute groundwater.

Treatment, Disposal, and Cleanup of Contaminated Sites

Reduction and cleanup of hazardous wastes can occur by producing less waste, converting the hazardous material to less hazardous or nonhazardous substances, and placing the toxic material into perpetual storage.

PRODUCE LESS WASTE

- **Recycle**—Improved technology seeks ways of collecting hazardous wastes and using them as raw materials for new products.
- **Reduce or eliminate toxicity**—Improved technology seeks substitutes for hazardous chemicals. For example, Puron replaced Freon.

CONVERSION TO LESS HAZARDOUS OR NONHAZARDOUS SUBSTANCES

Chemical, physical, and biological treatment

Bioremediation is the use of bacteria and enzymes to break down hazardous materials. Phytoremediation involves rhizofiltration (using sunflowers to absorb radioactive wastes), phytostabilization (e.g., using willow and poplar trees to absorb organic contaminants), phytodegradation (e.g., using poplars to absorb and break down contaminants), and phytoextraction (e.g., using Indian mustard and brake ferns to absorb inorganic metal contaminants). Pros: inexpensive, low energy use, little to no air pollution, easy to build. Cons: slow, effective only as far down as roots will reach, some toxic materials can evaporate through plants. Plants would be toxic and need to be properly disposed. Chemical methods involve use of cyclodextrin.

Incineration

Can release air pollutants and toxic ash (such as lead, mercury, and dioxins).

Thermal Treatment

Plasma arcs. Pros: small, mobile, no toxic ash. Cons: expensive and can release particulates, chlorine gas, toxic metals, and radioactive wastes.

PERPETUAL STORAGE

Arid Region Unsaturated Zone

The unsaturated zone is the subsurface between the land surface and underlying aquifers. It includes sites in the arid western United States that are being relied upon to isolate a significant portion of the nation's radioactive and other hazardous wastes for thousands of years.

Capping

Capping, often used in combination with other cleanup methods, covers buried wastes to prevent contaminants from spreading. Spreading or migration of buried wastes can be caused by rainwater or surface water moving through the site or by wind blowing dust off the site. The primary purpose of a cap is to minimize contact between rain or surface water and the buried waste. Caps: (a) minimize water movement through the wastes by using efficient drainage; (b) resist damage caused by settling; and (c) prevent standing water by funneling away as much water as the underlying filter or soils can handle. Capping is used when the underground contamination is so extensive that excavating and removing it isn't practical, or when removing wastes would be more dangerous to human health and the environment than leaving them in place. Wells are often used to monitor groundwater where a cap has been installed to detect any movement of the wastes.

Landfill

Pros: inexpensive. Cons: groundwater seepage and contamination.

Salt Formations

Toxic wastes are deposited in deep salt formations. The absence of flowing water within natural salt formations prevents dissolution and subsequent spreading of the waste products. Rooms and caverns in the salt can be sealed, thus isolating the waste from the biosphere.

Surface Impoundments

Excavated ponds, pits, or lagoons. Pros: low cost, low operating cost, built quickly, wastes can be retrieved and, if lined, can store wastes for long periods. Cons: groundwater contamination, VOC pollution, overflow if flooding occurs, earthquake issues, promotes waste production.

Underground Injection

Pros: low cost, wastes can be retrieved, simple technology. Cons: leaks, earthquake issues, groundwater contamination.

Waste Piles

Storage of toxic materials in drums, underground vaults, or above-ground buildings. Pros: easy to identify leaks. Cons: shipping of materials to facilities results in accidents.

Bioaccumulation

Bioaccumulation is the increase in concentration of a pollutant from the environment in an organism or part of an organism. It involves the biological sequestering of substances that enter the organism through respiration, food intake, or epidermal (skin) contact with the substance. The level at which a given substance is bioaccumulated depends on:

- Rate of uptake
- Mode of uptake (gills, ingested along with food, contact with skin, etc.)
- Rate the substance is eliminated from the organism
- Transformation of the substance by metabolic processes
- Lipid (fat) content of the organism
- Environmental factors

Biomagnification

Biomagnification is the increase in concentration of a pollutant from one link in a food chain to another. In order for biomagnification to occur, the pollutant must be long-lived, mobile, soluble in fats, and biologically active. If a pollutant is short-lived, it will be broken down before it can become dangerous. If it is not mobile, it will stay in one place and be less likely to be taken up by many organisms. If the pollutant is soluble in water, it will be excreted by the organism. Pollutants that dissolve in fats, however, may be retained for a long time. It is traditional to measure the amount of pollutants in fatty tissues of organisms such as fish. In mammals, milk produced by females is often tested since the milk is high in fat and because the young are often more susceptible to damage from toxins.

Bioaccumulation vs. Biomagnification

For example, methylmercury is taken up by bacteria and phytoplankton. Small fish eat the bacteria and phytoplankton and *accumulate* the mercury. The small fish are in turn eaten by larger fish, which can become food for humans and animals resulting in the buildup (*biomagnification*) of large concentrations of mercury in human and animal tissue. As a general rule, the more fat-like a substance is, the more likely it is to bioaccumulate in organisms, such as fish.

ECONOMIC IMPACTS

A cost-benefit analysis is a technique for deciding whether to make a change. To use the technique, one adds up the value of the benefits of a course of action and subtracts the costs associated with it.

Costs are either one time or ongoing. Benefits are most often received over time. Time is factored into a cost-benefit analysis by calculating a payback period—the time for the benefits of a change to repay its costs.

In its simple form, a cost-benefit analysis is carried out using only financial costs and benefits. For example, a simple cost-benefit analysis of a new road would measure the cost of building the road and subtract this from the economic benefit of improving transport links. It would not measure either the cost of environmental damage or the benefit of quicker and easier travel to work. A more sophisticated approach is to attempt to put a financial value on intangible costs and benefits, which is highly subjective.

A cost-benefit analysis applies to three economic situations: First, it can help judge whether public services provided by the private sector are adequate. Second, it can be used when judging and assessing inefficiencies (market failures) in the private sector and their impact on the health, safety, and environmental needs of the country. Third, it helps in determining how to meet societal needs in a cost-effective manner in areas that only government can address. These include defense, preservation of scenic areas, environmental protection, and so on.

A cost-benefit analysis can be used for evaluating policy alternatives, shaping regulatory strategies, and evaluating specific regulations. A cost-benefit analysis requires:

1. Gathering all information and data about a public issue, including history and background

2. Defining the possible solutions to solving the issue

3. Brainstorming the possible environmental and societal consequences of the alternatives

4. Quantifying the benefits and the costs

5. Making decisions and balancing concerns

Framework of Cost-Benefit Analysis

Step	Description
Cost-benefit	Determine an action and levels of action that achieve the greatest net economic benefit. Exploring options and determining incremental levels of remediation provide the most benefit for the least cost.
Cost-effectiveness	Implementing a specific environmental, health, or safety objective at the least cost. Emphasis is on achieving the objective. Flexible regulatory guidelines are adapted to find the lowest cost to solve a problem.
Health or environmental protection standards	Reducing risk to the public whatever the cost.
Risk-benefit	Balancing health or environmental protection with the costs of providing the protection.
Technology	To achieve results that are predictable and certain.

External Costs

An external cost occurs when the product(s) or activities of one group has a negative impact on another group and when that impact is not fully accounted, or compensated for, in the price of the product. Example: A power station generates emissions of SO_2 causing damage to buildings and human health. In this case, the cost to the owners of the buildings and to those who suffer from respiratory issues is not taken into account in the cost of the electricity produced. In this example, the environmental costs are "external" because, although they are real costs to society, the owner of the power station is not taking them into account when setting the price of electricity.

The total cost of a good to society (called the social cost) includes the costs or production incurred by the industry as well as the external costs. One possibility for accounting for external costs in setting the true social cost would be via eco-taxes; i.e., taxing damaging fuels and technologies in proportion to their external costs. Another possible solution would be to subsidize cleaner technologies thus avoiding the social and environmental costs altogether. And finally, accounting for external cost estimates in the cost-benefit-analysis. In such an analysis, the costs to establish measures to reduce a certain environmental burden are compared with the benefits.

Ecotaxes (Green Taxes)

Ecotaxes are intended to promote ecologically sustainable activities by providing economic incentives and can complement or reduce the need for regulatory (command and control) approaches. Often, an ecotax may attempt to maintain overall tax revenue by proportionately reducing other taxes (green tax shift). Examples of ecotaxes would be:

- taxes on the use of fossil fuels by greenhouse gases produced.
- duties on imported goods produced by ecologically unsound methods.
- taxes on mineral, energy, and forestry products that were produced by ecologically unsound methods.
- fees for camping, hiking, fishing, and hunting.
- taxes on technologies and products, which are associated with substantial negative externalities.
- waste disposal taxes.
- taxes on effluents, pollution, and other hazardous wastes.

Cap and Trade

Cap and trade, also known as emissions trading, is a market approach used to control pollution by providing economic incentives for achieving reductions in the emissions of pollutants. With cap-and-trade policies, the government sets a limit or "cap" on the amount of a pollutant that can be emitted. Companies or other groups are then issued emission permits and are required to hold an equivalent number of allowances or credits, which represent the right to emit a specific amount of pollutants. The total amount of allowances and credits cannot exceed the cap, limiting total emissions to that level. Companies that need to increase their emission allowance must then buy credits from those who pollute less. The transfer of allowances is referred to as a "trade." In effect, the buyer is paying a charge for polluting, while the seller is being rewarded for having reduced emissions by more than was needed. Therefore, those who can reduce emissions more cheaply will do so, achieving pollution reduction at the lowest cost to society.

Sustainability

Sustainability deals with the continuity of the economic, social, and institutional aspects of human society while at the same time preserving biodiversity and the environment. Sustainable activities seek to provide the best outcomes for both human societies and natural ecosystems. Several issues are common to both interests:

- Consideration of risk, uncertainty, and irreversibility
- Ensuring appropriate valuation, appreciation, and restoration of nature
- Integration of environmental, social, and economic goals in policies and activities
- Equal opportunity and community participation
- Conservation of biodiversity and ecological integrity
- A commitment to best practice
- No net loss to either human or natural capital
- Continuous improvement
- The need for good governance

Unlimited economic and population growth puts many demands on natural resources. Its effects on pollution and the carrying capacity of Earth are factors that impact sustainability. These are all analyzed using life cycle assessments and ecological footprint analyses.

Ecological Footprint

The "ecological footprint" is a measure of human demand on the Earth's ecosystems. It is a standardized measure of demand for natural capital that may be contrasted with the planet's ecological capacity to regenerate and represents the amount of biologically productive land and sea area necessary to supply the resources a human population consumes, and to assimilate associated waste. Currently, humanity's total ecological footprint is estimated at 1.5 planet Earths—in other words, humanity uses ecological services 1.5 times as fast as Earth can renew them.

The "carbon footprint" is the amount of carbon being emitted by an activity or organization. The carbon component of the ecological footprint converts the amount of carbon dioxide being released into the amount of productive land and sea area required to sequester it and tells the demand on the Earth that results from burning fossil fuels. The carbon footprint is 54% of the ecological footprint and its most rapidly-growing component having increased 11-fold since 1961.

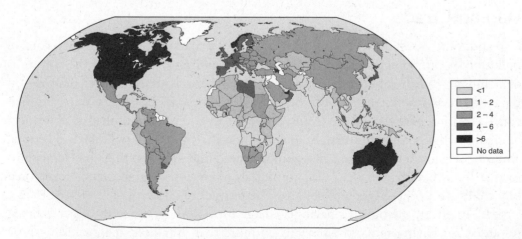

Figure 10.3 Ecological footprints of various countries measured in global hectares per person (gha)

QUICK REVIEW CHECKLIST

☐ **Hazards to Human Health**
  ☐ types of risks
  ☐ risk management strategies
  ☐ acute and chronic effects
  ☐ dose-response relationships
    ☐ LD_{50}
    ☐ EC_{50}
    ☐ dose-response curves

☐ **Air Pollutants and Effect on Human Health**
  ☐ air toxics
  ☐ asbestos
  ☐ carbon monoxide
  ☐ indoor air pollutants
  ☐ lead
  ☐ nitrogen dioxide
  ☐ ozone
  ☐ PM_{10}
  ☐ sulfur dioxide
  ☐ smoking

☐ **Hazardous Chemicals in the Environment**
  ☐ corrosive
  ☐ discarded commercial products
  ☐ ignitable
  ☐ nonspecific sources
  ☐ reactive
  ☐ source specific
  ☐ toxic

☐ **Treatment, Disposal, and Cleanup of Contaminated Sites**
  ☐ conversion techniques
    ☐ chemical, physical, or biological treatment
    ☐ incineration
    ☐ thermal treatment
    ☐ perpetual storage
    ☐ arid region unsaturated zone
    ☐ landfill
    ☐ salt formations
    ☐ surface impoundments
    ☐ underground injection
    ☐ waste piles

☐ **Case Study—DDT**

QUICK REVIEW CHECKLIST (continued)

☐ **Relevant Laws**
- ☐ Federal Hazardous Substances Act (1960)
- ☐ Federal Environmental Pesticides Control Act (1972)
- ☐ Hazardous Materials Transportation Act (HAZMAT) (1975)
- ☐ Toxic Substances Control Act (1976)
- ☐ Comprehensive Environmental Response, Compensation, and Liability Act (CERCLA or Superfund) (1980)
- ☐ Nuclear Waste Policy Act (1982)

☐ **Biomagnification**

☐ **Cost-Benefit Analysis**

☐ **Externalities**

☐ **Marginal Costs**

☐ **Sustainability**

MULTIPLE-CHOICE QUESTIONS

1. About 70% of U.S. hazardous wastes come from

   (A) agricultural pesticides
   (B) smelting, mining, and metal manufacturing
   (C) nuclear power plants
   (D) chemical and petroleum industries
   (E) households

2. Which act established federal authority for emergency response and cleanup of hazardous substances that have been spilled, improperly disposed of, or released into the environment?

   (A) Resource Recovery Act
   (B) Resource Conservation and Recovery Act
   (C) Solid Waste Disposal Act
   (D) Superfund
   (E) Hazardous Materials Transportation Act

3. Effects produced from a long-term, low-level exposure are called

   (A) acute
   (B) chronic
   (C) pathological
   (D) symptomatic
   (E) synergistic

4. Which of the following techniques is NOT an example of bioremediation?

   (A) land farming
   (B) composting
   (C) rhizofiltration
   (D) phytoremediation
   (E) All are examples of bioremediation

5. The following dose-response curve shows that

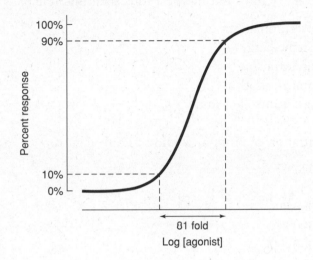

   (A) larger amounts of agonist produce a corresponding increase in response
   (B) 80% more agonist is required to achieve 80% more response
   (C) 81 times more agonist is needed to achieve a 90% response than a 10% response
   (D) an 80% high response is achieved with a tenfold increase in agonist
   (E) None of the above are true

6. A dose that is represented as LD_{50}

   (A) shows a response in 50% of the population
   (B) kills half of the study group
   (C) is a dose that has an acceptable risk level of 50%
   (D) is a dose that has a threshold response of 50%
   (E) is a dose that is administered to 50% of the population

7. Problem(s) associated with risk management include

   (A) people making a risk assessment vary in their conclusions of long-term versus short-term risks and benefits
   (B) some technologies benefit some groups and harm others
   (C) there is consideration of the cumulative impacts of various risks rather than consideration of each impact separately
   (D) there may be conflict of interest in those carrying out the risk assessment and review of the results
   (E) All of the above are true

8. Currently, the single-most significant threat to human health is

   (A) toxic chemicals
   (B) accidents
   (C) pathogenic organisms
   (D) pollution
   (E) nontransmissible diseases such as cancer and cardiovascular disease

9. The accumulation of DDT by peregrine falcons, brown pelicans, and other predatory birds during the 1960s is an example of

   (A) bioaccumulation
   (B) bioremediation
   (C) acute exposure
   (D) biomagnification
   (E) a case-controlled study

10. A concentration of 30 ppm would be equivalent to

    (A) 0.3%
    (B) 0.03%
    (C) 0.003%
    (D) 0.0003%
    (E) 0.00003%

11. Preserving the value of a resource for the future is a(n)

    (A) aesthetic value
    (B) cultural value
    (C) existence value
    (D) use value
    (E) option value

12. It costs a copper smelter $200 to reduce emissions by 1 ton and $250 for each additional ton. It costs an electric company $100 to reduce its emissions by 1 ton and $150 for each additional ton. What is the least expensive way of reducing total emissions by 2 tons?

    (A) Legislate that both firms must reduce emissions by 1 ton
    (B) Charge both firms $251 for every ton they emit
    (C) Allow each firm to buy a $151 permit to pollute
    (D) File an injunction to halt production until the firms reduce emissions by 2 tons
    (E) None of the above

13. In economic analysis, the optimum level of pollution

    (A) is always zero
    (B) is where the marginal benefits from further reduction equals the marginal cost of further reduction
    (C) occurs when demand crosses the private cost supply curve
    (D) should be determined by the private market without any government intervention
    (E) None of the above

14. Externalized costs of nuclear power include all of the following EXCEPT

    (A) disposing of nuclear wastes
    (B) government subsidies
    (C) costs associated with Three Mile Island
    (D) Price-Anderson Indemnity Act
    (E) All are external costs

15. Which of the following is NOT part of a cost-benefit analysis?

    (A) Judging whether public services provided by the private sector are adequate
    (B) Judging and assessing inefficiencies in the private sector and their impact on health, safety, and environmental need
    (C) Determining external costs to society
    (D) Meeting societal needs in a cost-effective manner
    (E) All are part of a cost-benefit analysis

16. A federal tax on a pack of cigarettes is an example of

    (A) full-cost pricing
    (B) an internal cost
    (C) an external cost
    (D) a marginal cost
    (E) a life cycle cost

17. The threshold dose-response model

    (A) cannot be used to determine how toxic a substance is
    (B) implies a risk associated with all doses
    (C) implies that no detectable harmful effects can occur below a certain dose
    (D) is similar to a linear dose-response model
    (E) All of the above are true

18. Approximately how many people aged 15–24 are newly infected world-wide with the AIDS virus each day?

    (A) 60
    (B) 600
    (C) 6,000
    (D) 60,000
    (E) 600,000

19. Which of the following is NOT part of risk assessment?

    (A) Determining the probability of a particular hazard
    (B) Determining types of hazards
    (C) Coming up with an estimate on the chances of how many people could be exposed to a particular risk
    (D) Informing the public about the chances of risks
    (E) All are part of risk assessment

20. Which factor listed below is generally considered to be the primary cause of reduced human life span?

    (A) AIDS
    (B) Infectious disease
    (C) Cancer
    (D) Poverty
    (E) Heart disease

FREE-RESPONSE QUESTION

By: Annaliese Berry, B.A.
California Institute of Technology
Williams College
A.P. Environmental Science Teacher
Marin Academy, San Rafael, California

Part (a): 2 points
Part (b): 2 points
Part (c): 4 points
Part (d): 2 points

Total: 10 points

In 1989, the oil tanker *Exxon Valdez* struck an offshore reef in Alaska and spilled more than 11 million gallons of crude oil into Prince William Sound. It was the largest spill in U.S. history. Although Exxon spent $2.2 billion in partially dispersing and removing the oil, many seabirds and mammals died as a result of this catastrophe.

Ironically, environmental accidents such as the *Exxon Valdez* oil spill actually stimulate our nation's economy by causing an increase in gross domestic product and gross national product. Using this information, answer the following questions.

(a)   Explain what gross domestic product (GDP) or gross national product (GNP) is a measure of and give examples of a possible cause for an increase in the GDP or GNP following the *Exxon Valdez* oil spill.

(b)   Give at least one criticism of GDP and GNP as progress indicators, and mention an alternative progress indicator. What does that alternative attempt to measure?

(c)   Name and explain one internal cost and one external cost that might be associated with the oil industry. Include in your answer an explanation of what internal and external costs are.

(d)   How would internalizing external costs (sometimes called full-cost analysis or true-cost analysis) affect the pricing and economic competitiveness of petroleum products?

TIP

For Free Response essays, be sure to practice making good arguments in favor of, or against, a particular position on an environmental issue. Make sure you understand that restating the question is a waste of time in a timed test, and doing so will never earn you any points.

MULTIPLE-CHOICE ANSWERS AND EXPLANATIONS

1. **(D)** In 1999, over 20,000 hazardous waste generators produced over 40 million tons of hazardous wastes.
2. **(D)** The Superfund program began in 1980 to locate, investigate, and clean up the most polluted sites nationwide.
3. **(B)** Chronic diseases are of long duration with slow progress. Examples would include congestive heart failure, Parkinson's disease, and cerebral palsy.
4. **(E)** Land farming, composting, rhizofiltration, and phytoremediation all involve the use of bacteria and enzymes to break down hazardous materials.
5. **(C)** "81 fold" means 81 more times. An agonist is a drug or other chemical that produces a reaction typical of a naturally occurring substance.

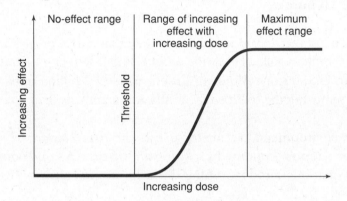

6. **(B)** The LD_{50} value is typically expressed in milligrams of material per kilogram of body weight. It indicates the quantity of material that will cause 50% of the subjects to perish.
7. **(E)** Risk assessment is the process of evaluating the likelihood of an adverse health effect. Risk assessment does NOT determine the level of allowable or acceptable risk—that is risk management.
8. **(E)** For most of human history, pathogenic (disease-causing) organisms were the greatest threat to health. Today cardiovascular, cancer, and other non-infectious diseases have become the major killers.
9. **(D)** Biomagnification is the increase in the concentration of toxic substances as one moves up the food chain. Animals at the top of the food chain receive the highest concentration of toxins and experience the worst effects.
10. **(C)** To change ppm to a percentage, move the decimal place four places to the left and add a % sign.
11. **(E)** An option value is the value that people place on having the option to enjoy something in the future.
12. **(C)** The copper smelter would pay $450 to emit 2 tons of pollutants. The electric company would pay $250 to emit 2 tons of pollutants. Clearly, $151 would be the least expensive option available.

13. **(B)** The marginal benefit of pollution control declines as the level of environmental quality goes up. At the same time, the marginal cost of pollution tends to increase. The optimal level of pollution from an economic standpoint is where the marginal benefit equals the marginal cost. As long as the marginal benefit exceeds the marginal cost, there is economic incentive for cleaning up.

14. **(E)** External costs are the costs that are borne by people other than the producer of a good.

15. **(C)** Cost-benefit analysis is a technique for deciding whether to make a change and requires adding up the value of the benefits of a course of action and subtracting the costs associated with it.

16. **(A)** Full-cost pricing accounts for the cost of a good when its internal costs and its estimated short- and long-term external costs are included in its market price. Washington State increased its cigarette tax to $1.425 a pack on Jan. 1, 2002, making it the nation's highest. Virginia has the lowest state sales tax of 2.5 cents per pack. There is a 39-cent per pack federal excise tax.

17. **(C)** The threshold dose-response model has long been recognized as the most important tool in understanding the risk assessment processes used by regulatory and public health agencies worldwide.

18. **(C)** An estimated 10 million people aged 15–24 are living with HIV/AIDS. Half of all new infections, more than 6,000 each day, occur among the young. However, in countries where HIV transmissions have been reduced, the greatest reductions have been among young people.

19. **(D)** Risk assessment is the process of quantifying the probability of a harmful effect. In most countries, the approval of certain pesticides, industrial chemicals, power plants, and so on is not allowed unless it can be demonstrated through risk assessment that they do not increase the risk, death, or illness above a certain level. Educating the public is not part of risk assessment. That is left up to the media, public interest groups, and special interest groups.

20. **(D)** Poverty is the fundamental issue that affects human life span. People who are without financial resources suffer from malnutrition, exposure, and disease. Those with financial resources are able to obtain proper nutrition, have shelter, and are able to seek medical treatment.

FREE-RESPONSE ANSWER

(a) Gross domestic product (GDP) is a measure of the market value of goods and services transacted within a country during a year, so it increases any time products or services are paid for. This means that the additional expense that Exxon (now Exxon-Mobil) incurred by controlling the spill ($2.2 billion) increased the GDP. For example, money was spent to hire boats with skimmers in an attempt to capture and contain floating oil.

Notable points:

Explanation of GDP or GNP.

Example of how cleaning up the spill or replacing lost equipment/oil causes goods or services to be transacted.

GDP and GNP are economic measures, not direct quality of life measures.

Example of alternative indicator. Examples include the NNP, ISEW, GPI, or NEW. A general alternative is to take into account any standard of living data (literacy rate, percent of population below poverty line, and so on).

Explanation of what example indicator measures.

Naming of an internal cost. Costs may be expenses related to cleanup, ship or oil replacement, cost of labor, and so on.

Explanation that internal costs are costs paid for by the organization producing the product.

Naming of an external cost such as water pollution left behind after a spill, air or water pollution from operating tankers, or an increase of CO₂ in the atmosphere when the petroleum products are consumed.

Explanation that external costs are harmful effects of the product that are not paid for by the organization.

Price of product would increase as external costs are paid for by the producer and passed along to the consumer.

Petroleum products would become less economically competitive.

(b) GDP and GNP have been criticized as progress indicators because economic growth is only indirectly related to quality of life. The GDP and GNP are often stimulated by events that directly lower quality of life, such as the *Exxon Valdez* oil spill, the Oklahoma City bombing, Hurricane Katrina in New Orleans, or the events of 9/11 in New York City. Alternative progress indicators attempt to capture quality of life or standard of living, although these are often harder to define and measure than the flow of dollars. One such indicator is the net national product (NNP), which accounts for depletion and destruction of natural resources along with changes in GNP.

(c) An internal cost is a cost that is paid for by the organization producing a product. This cost is typically passed along to the consumers when they purchase the product. One internal cost of the petroleum industry could be the cost of extracting petroleum using oil drills and platforms.

(d) Internalizing external costs would mean that organizations producing a product would pay for any harmful effects (the external costs) of their products. This would allow the market price of a product to reflect the full cost of producing and cleaning up the product. It would also increase the price of any product that has external costs. A product with high external costs would become substantially more expensive and less economically competitive when this happened. In the energy industry, sources of power such as oil and gas have relative high external costs and could become more expensive than lower-impact sources of energy such as wind power.

UNIT VII: GLOBAL CHANGE (10–15%)

Areas on Which You Will Be Tested

A. Stratospheric Ozone—formation of stratospheric ozone, ultraviolet radiation, causes of ozone depletion, effects of ozone depletion, strategies for reducing ozone depletion, and relevant laws and treaties.

B. Global Warming—greenhouse gases and the greenhouse effect, impacts and consequences of global warming, reducing climate change, and relevant laws and treaties.

C. Loss of Biodiversity
1. Habitat loss—overuse, pollution, introduced species, and endangered and extinct species.
2. Maintenance through conservation.
3. Relevant laws and treaties.

Stratospheric Ozone and Global Warming

CHAPTER 11

STRATOSPHERIC OZONE

The stratosphere contains approximately 97% of the ozone in the atmosphere, and most of it lies between 9 and 25 miles (15 to 40 km) above Earth's surface. Most ozone is formed over the tropics. However, slow circulation currents carry the majority of it to the poles, resulting in the thickest layers over the poles and the thinnest layer above the tropics. It also varies somewhat due to season, being somewhat thicker in the spring and thinner during the autumn. The increase in temperature with height in the stratosphere occurs because of absorption of ultraviolet radiation by ozone.

Ozone is formed in the stratosphere by the reaction of ultraviolet radiation striking an oxygen molecule. This results in the oxygen molecule splitting apart and forming atomic oxygen: $O_2 + hv \rightarrow O + O$. Atomic oxygen can now react with molecular oxygen to form ozone: $O + O_2 \rightarrow O_3$. The reverse reaction also occurs when ultraviolet radiation strikes an ozone molecule, causing it to form atomic oxygen and molecular oxygen: $O_3 + hv \rightarrow O + O_2$. Atomic oxygen can also react with ozone to produce oxygen gas: $O + O_3 \rightarrow O_2 + O_2$. Generally, these reactions balance each other so that the concentration of ozone in the stratosphere remains fairly constant, which keeps the amount of UV radiation reaching Earth also constant. Various forms of life on Earth have evolved over millions of years with fairly constant amounts of UV radiation.

Ultraviolet Radiation

The sun emits a wide variety of electromagnetic radiation, including infrared, visible, and ultraviolet. Ultraviolet radiation can be subdivided into three forms: UVA, UVB, and UVC.

UVA

320 to 400 nm wavelength. Closest to blue light in the visible spectrum. The form that usually causes skin tanning. UVA radiation is 1,000 times less effective than UVB in producing skin redness, but more of it reaches Earth's surface than UVB. Birds, reptiles, and bees can see UVA. Many fruits, flowers, and seeds also stand out more strongly from the background in ultraviolet wavelengths. Many birds have patterns in their plumage that are not visible in the normal spectrum (white light) but become visible in ultraviolet. Urine of some animals is also visible only in the UVA spectrum.

UVB

290 to 320 nm wavelength. Causes blistering sunburns and is associated with skin cancer.

UVC

10 to 290 nm. Found only in the stratosphere and largely responsible for the formation of ozone.

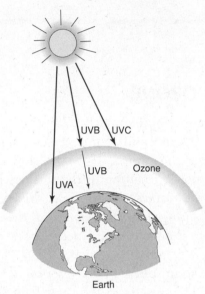

Figure 11.1 Ultraviolet radiation reaching Earth

Causes of Ozone Depletion

Thinning of the ozone layer was first discovered in 1985. It occurs seasonally and is due to the presence of human-made compounds containing halogens (chlorine, bromine, fluorine, or iodine). Measurements indicate that the ozone over the Antarctic has decreased as much as 60% since the late 1970s with an average net loss of about 3% per year worldwide.

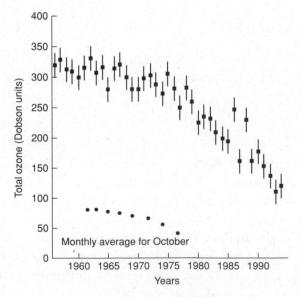

Figure 11.2 Ozone concentration over Antarctica (1955–1995)

The main culprits in the depletion of the ozone layer are compounds known as CFCs (chlorofluorocarbons). First manufactured during the 1920s, they are used as refrigerants (for example, Freon), aerosol propellants, electrical part cleaning solvents, and in the manufacture of foam products and insulation. By 1974, nearly 1 million tons of CFC gases were produced each year, and the chemicals were generating $8 billion worth of business. The largest single source of CFCs to the atmosphere is leakage from air conditioners. The average residence time of CFCs in the environment is 200 years.

When a CFC molecule enters the stratosphere, ultraviolet radiation causes it to decompose and produce atomic chlorine:

$$
\underset{\displaystyle F}{\overset{\displaystyle Cl}{F-C-Cl}} \quad \xrightarrow{\text{photon of UV radiation}} \quad \underset{\displaystyle F}{\overset{\displaystyle Cl}{F-C\cdot}} \; + \; \cdot Cl
$$

This atomic chlorine then reacts with the ozone in the stratosphere to produce chlorine monoxide (ClO):

$$Cl + O_3 \rightarrow ClO + O_2$$

The chlorine monoxide then reacts with more ozone to produce even more atomic chlorine in what becomes essentially a chain reaction:

$$ClO + O_3 \rightarrow Cl + 2O_2$$

Thus, one chlorine atom released from a CFC can ultimately destroy over 100,000 ozone molecules. Much of the destruction of the ozone layer that is occurring now is the result of CFCs that were produced many years ago since a CFC molecule takes 8 years to reach the stratosphere and the residence time in the stratosphere for a CFC molecule is over 100 years.

Bromine, found in much smaller quantities than chlorine, is about 50 times more effective than chlorine in its effect on stratospheric ozone depletion and is responsible for about 20% of the problem. Bromine is found in halons, which are used in fire extinguishers. Methyl bromide is used in fumigation and agriculture. It is naturally released from phytoplankton and biomass burning.

Effects of Ozone Depletion

During the onset of the 1998 Antarctic spring, a hole three times the size of Australia (over 3,500 miles [5,600 km] in diameter) developed in the ozone layer over the South Pole. Stratospheric ozone protects life from harmful ultraviolet radiation. Harmful effects of increased UV radiation include:

- Increases in skin cancer
- Increases in sunburns and damage to the skin
- Increases in cataracts of the eye
- Reduction in crop production
- Deleterious effects to animals (they don't wear sunglasses or sunscreen)
- Reduction in the growth of phytoplankton and the cumulative effect on food webs
- Increases in mutations since UV radiation causes changes in DNA structure

- Cooling of the stratosphere
- Reduction in the body's immune system
- Climatic change

Strategies for Reducing Ozone Depletion

Although most developed countries have phased out ozone-destroying chemicals, they are still legal in developing nations. There are several alternatives to CFC use. First, HCFC replaces chlorine with hydrogen. Unfortunately, it is still capable of destroying ozone albeit less effectively because it breaks down more readily in the troposphere. Second, alternatives to halons can be used in fire extinguishers. Third, helium, ammonia, propane, or butane can be used as a coolant. Helium-cooled refrigerators use 50% less electricity than those using CFCs or HCFCs. Individuals can use pump sprays instead of aerosol spray cans when possible, comply with disposal requirements of the Clean Air Act for old refrigerators and air conditioners, read labels and, when choices are available, use ozone friendly products, and support legislation that reduces ozone-destroying products.

> ### RELEVANT TREATY
>
> **Montreal Protocol (1987):** Designed to protect the stratospheric ozone layer. The treaty was originally signed in 1987 and substantially amended in 1990 and 1992. The Montreal Protocol stipulated that the production and consumption of compounds that deplete ozone in the stratosphere—chlorofluorocarbons (CFCs), halons, carbon tetrachloride, and methyl chloroform—were to be phased out by 2000 (2005 for methyl chloroform).

GLOBAL WARMING

When sunlight strikes Earth's surface, some of it is reflected back toward space as infrared radiation (heat). Greenhouse gases absorb this infrared radiation and trap the heat in the atmosphere.

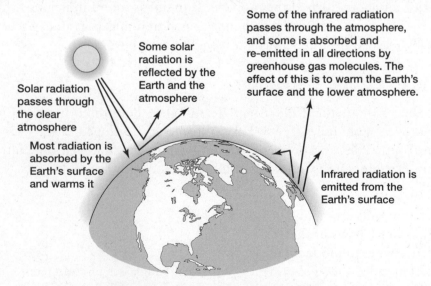

Figure 11.3 The greenhouse effect

Greenhouse Gases

Greenhouse Gas	Average Time in Troposphere (Years)	Relative Warming Potential (CO_2 = 1)	Source
Carbon dioxide (CO_2)	100	1	Burning oil, coal, plants, deforestation, cellular respiration
Carbon tetrachloride (CCl_4)	45	1,500	Cleaning solvent
Chlorofluorocarbons (CFCs)	15 (100 in stratosphere)	1,000–8,000	Air conditioners, refrigerators, foam products, insulation
Halons	65	6,000	Fire extinguishers
Hydrochlorofluorocarbons (HCFCs)	10–400	500–2,000	Air conditioners, refrigerators, foam products, insulation
Hydrofluorocarbons (HFCs)	15–400	150–13,000	Air conditioners, refrigerators, foam products, insulation
Methane (CH_4)	15	25	Rice cultivation, enteric fermentation, production of coal, natural gas leaks
Nitrous oxide (N_2O)	115	300	Burning fossil fuels, fertilizers, livestock wastes, plastic manufacturing
Sulfur hexafluoride (SF_6)	3,200	24,000	Electrical industry as a replacement for PCBs
Tropospheric Ozone (O_3)	Variable	3,000	Combustion of fossil fuels

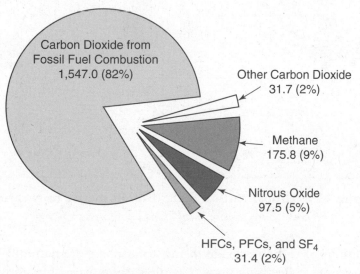

Figure 11.4 U.S. anthropogenic greenhouse gas emissions (2001)
(Million Metric Tons of Carbon Equivalent)

Levels of several important greenhouse gases have increased by about 25% since large-scale industrialization began around 150 years ago. During the past 20 years, about three-quarters of human-made carbon dioxide emissions were from burning fossil fuels. In the United States, greenhouse gas emissions come mostly from energy use. These are driven largely by economic growth, fuel used for electricity generation, and weather patterns affecting heating and cooling needs. Energy-related carbon dioxide emissions, resulting from petroleum and natural gas, represent 82% of total U.S. anthropogenic (caused by humans) greenhouse gas emissions.

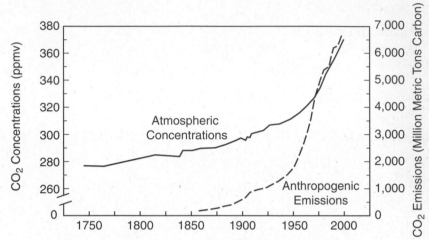

Figure 11.5 Trends in atmospheric CO$_2$ concentrations
Source: Oak Ridge National Laboratory

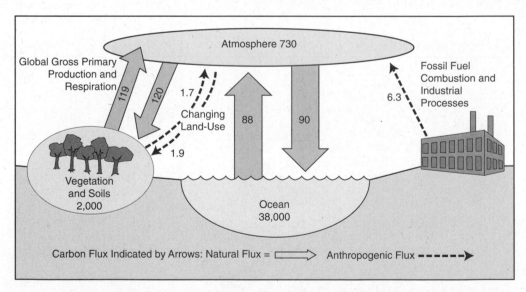

Figure 11.6 Global carbon cycle (billion metric tons carbon)
Source: Intergovernmental Panel on Climate Change

Concentrations of carbon dioxide in the atmosphere are naturally regulated by numerous processes collectively known as the carbon cycle. The movement (flux) of carbon between the atmosphere and the land and oceans is dominated by natural processes, such as plant photosynthesis. Although these natural processes can absorb some of the net 6.1 billion metric tons of anthropogenic carbon dioxide emissions produced each year (measured in carbon equivalent terms), an estimated 3.2 billion metric tons is added to the atmosphere annually. Earth's positive imbalance between emissions and absorption results in the continuing growth in greenhouse gases in the atmosphere.

Impacts and Consequences of Global Warming

Global warming affects the weather, the economy, and numerous other aspects of life.

ACIDIFICATION

The oceans currently absorb 1 metric ton of carbon dioxide per person per year. Increased carbon dioxide absorption of oceans will lower the pH of seawater. This adversely affects corals, plankton, organisms with shells, and reproduction rates as eggs and sperm are exposed to higher levels of acid.

CHANGES IN TROPOSPHERIC WEATHER PATTERNS

Air temperatures today average 5°F to 9°F (3°C to 5°C) warmer than they were before the Industrial Revolution. Historic increases in air temperature averaged less than 2°F (1°C) per 1,000 years. Higher temperatures result in higher amounts of rainfall due to higher rates of evaporation. Worldwide, hurricanes of category 4 or 5 have risen from 20% of all hurricanes in the 1970s to 35% in the 1990s. Precipitation due to hurricanes in the United States has increased 7% during the 20th century. More rainfall increases erosion, which then leads to higher rates of desertification due to deforestation. This then leads to losses in biodiversity as some species are forced out of their habitat. El Niño and La Niña patterns and their frequencies have also changed.

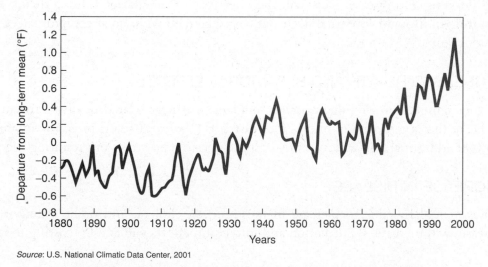

Source: U.S. National Climatic Data Center, 2001

Figure 11.7 Global temperature changes (1880–2000)

DISPLACEMENT OF PEOPLE

The United Nations estimates that by the year 2050, 150 million people will need to be relocated worldwide. This will occur due to the effects of coastal flooding, shoreline erosion, and agricultural disruption.

ECOLOGICAL PRODUCTIVITY

Satellite photos have shown that productivity in the Northern Hemisphere has increased since 1982. However, biomass increases due to warmer temperatures reaches a certain point—the point where limiting factors of water and nutrients curb future productivity increases. In the tropics, plants increase productivity more so than trees (which are carbon sinks). With higher percentages of plants due to increased temperatures and carbon dioxide concentrations, the rates of decomposition increase because plants are shorter lived. As a result, more carbon enters the carbon cycle.

FOREST FIRES

Boreal forest fires in North America used to average 2.5 million acres (10,000 sq km). They now average 7 million acres (28,000 sq km). Forest management practices may also be contributing to the increase.

GLACIER MELTING

Total surface area of glaciers worldwide has decreased by 50% since the end of the 19th century. Temperatures of the Antarctic Southern Ocean rose 0.31°F (0.17°C) between the 1950s and the 1980s. Glacier melting causes landslides, flash floods, glacial lake overflow, and increased variation in water flows into rivers. Hindu Kush and Himalayan glacier melts are reliable water sources for many people in China, India, and much of Asia. Global warming initially increases water flow, causing flooding and disease. Flow will then decrease as the glacier volume dwindles, resulting in drought. Eventual decreases in glacial melt will also affect hydroelectric production.

INCREASED HEALTH AND BEHAVIORAL EFFECTS

Higher temperatures result in higher incidences of heat-related deaths. Estimates indicate that a temperature increase of just 2°F (1°C) will result in approximately 25,000 additional homicides in the United States due to stress and resulting rage.

INCREASE IN DISEASE

Rates of malaria (due to increase in mosquitoes), cholera, and other waterborne diseases will increase. Remediation and mitigation efforts will end up costing more.

INCREASED PROPERTY LOSS

Weather-related disasters have increased 3-fold since the 1960s. Insurance payouts have increased 15-fold (adjusted for inflation) during this same time period. Much of this can be attributed to people moving to vulnerable coastal areas.

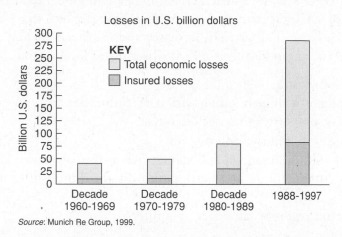

Losses in U.S. billion dollars

KEY
☐ Total economic losses
■ Insured losses

Source: Munich Re Group, 1999.

Figure 11.8 Weather and flood catastrophes since 1960

LOSS IN ECONOMIC DEVELOPMENT

Money that was earmarked for education, improved health care, reduced hunger, and improved sanitation and fresh water supplies, will instead be spent on mitigating the effects of global warming.

LOSS OF BIODIVERSITY

Arctic fauna will be most affected. The food webs of polar bears that depend on ice flows, birds, and marine mammals will be negatively impacted. Many refugee species currently have shifted their ranges toward the poles, averaging 4 miles (6 km) per decade. Bird migrations are averaging over two days earlier per decade. Grasses have become established in Antarctica for the first time. Many species of fish and krill that require cooler waters will be negatively impacted. Decreased glacier melt will impact migratory fish, such as salmon, that need sufficient river flow.

RELEASES OF METHANE FROM HYDRATES
IN COASTAL SEDIMENTS

Methane hydrate (methane clathrate) is a form of water ice that contains methane within its crystal structure. Extremely large deposits of this resource have been discovered in ocean sediments.

RELEASES OF METHANE FROM THAWING PERMAFROST REGIONS

Thawing of permafrost would increase bacterial levels in the soil and eventually lead to higher releases of methane. Estimates of melting of permafrost peat bogs in Siberia could release as much as 70,000 million metric tons of methane (a greenhouse gas) within the next few decades.

RISE IN SEA LEVEL

Sea levels have risen 400 feet (120 m) since the peak of the last ice age (18,000 years ago). From 3,000 years ago to the start of the Industrial Revolution, the rate of sea level rise averaged 0.1 to 0.2 mm per year. Since 1900, sea level has risen about 3 mm per year (over a 10-fold increase). An increase in global temperatures of 3°F to 8°F (1.5°C to 4.5°C) is estimated to lead to an increase of 6 to 37 inches (15 cm to 95 cm) in sea level. If all glaciers, ice caps, and ice sheets melted on Earth, the sea level would rise about 225 feet (69 m). Rises in sea level would:

- Increase coastal erosion
- Create higher storm surge flooding with coastal inundation
- Increase loss of property and coastal habitats
- Cause losses in fish and shellfish catches
- Cause loss of cultural resources and values such as tourism and recreation
- Cause losses in agriculture and aquaculture due to diminishing soil and water quality
- Result in the intrusion of salt water in aquifers.

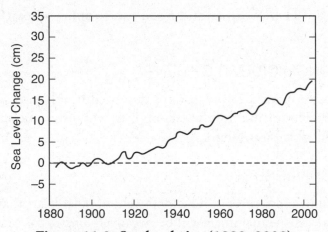

Figure 11.9 Sea level rise (1880–2000)

SLOWING OR SHUTDOWN OF THERMOHALINE CIRCULATION

Melting of the glaciers in Greenland would shift the salt water–freshwater balance in the North Atlantic. This would result in a decrease of heavier saline waters sinking than in traditional ocean circulation patterns. This would have significant effects on the fishing industry. Localized cooling in the North Atlantic brought about through the reduction of thermohaline circulation currents (North Atlantic drift) could result in much colder temperatures in Great Britain and Scandinavia.

Reducing Climate Change

World carbon dioxide emissions are expected to increase by 2% annually between 2001 and 2025. Much of the increase in these emissions is expected to occur in the developing world, such as China and India, where emerging economies fuel economic development with fossil energy. The United States was surpassed by China in 2007 in being the largest emitter of greenhouse gases. Developing countries' emissions are expected to grow by 3% annually between 2001 and 2025 and surpass emissions of industrialized countries by 2018.

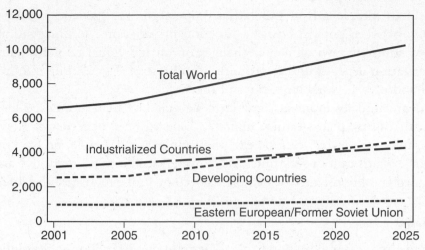

Figure 11.10 World carbon dioxide emissions by region, 2001–2025 (million metric tons of carbon equivalent)
Source: Energy Information Administration

The United States produces about 25% of global carbon dioxide emissions from burning fossil fuels. This is due primarily to a robust economy and 85% of the U.S. energy needs being met through burning fossil fuels.

To stabilize the current global warming crisis would require:

1. A decrease in methane emissions by 8%

2. A decrease in nitrous oxide emissions by 50%

3. A decrease in carbon dioxide emissions by up to 80%

Six methods can be used to reduce dramatic climatic changes brought on by global warming.

1. Increase the efficiency of cars.

2. Move to more renewable sources of energy (wind, solar, geothermal, etc.).

3. Find chemical substitutes that do not impact global warming.

4. Slow down the rate of deforestation and encourage reforestation.

5. Reduce dependence on inorganic, nitrogen-based fertilizers and utilize conservation tillage techniques.

6. Support treaties and protocols that require reductions in greenhouse gas emissions.

LOSS OF BIODIVERSITY

Information on habitat destruction needs to be compared with past habitat conditions. Long-term history of habitat conditions can be obtained from fossil records, ice core samples, tree ring analysis, and the analysis of pollen. Organisms can cope with habitat destruction by migration, adaptation, and acclimatization. Migration depends on the magnitude of degradation, the rate of degradation, the organism's ability to migrate, access routes or corridors, and the proximity and availability of suitable new habitats. Adaptation is the ability to survive due to changing environmental conditions. Adaptation depends on the magnitude and rate of degradation, birth rate, length of generation, population size, genetic variability, and gene flow between populations as a function of variation. Acclimatization is the ability to adjust to environmental changes on an individual or population level. Acclimatization depends on the magnitude and rate of degradation and the physiological and/or behavioral limitations of the species.

Plants are initially more susceptible to habitat loss than animals. This occurs for several reasons: plants cannot migrate; dispersal rates of seeds are slow events (for example, spruce trees can increase their range about 1 mile, or 1.6 km, every 100 years); plants cannot seek nutrients or water; seedlings must survive and grow in degraded conditions; and stressed plants become prone to disease and infestation.

Overuse

Worldwide, more than 3 million fishing boats remove 70 million to 90 million tons of fish and shellfish from the oceans each year. Of the world's marine fish stocks, 70% are fully exploited, overfished, or depleted. Twenty-million metric tons of bycatch (fish and shellfish not sought after) are destroyed each year and represents one-fourth of all catch taken from the sea. Around 80,000 whales, dolphins, seals, and other marine mammals perish as bycatch each year. Shrimp trawlers throw back 5.2 pounds (2.4 kg) of marine life that will eventually die for every pound (0.5 kg) of shrimp they catch. Overall, this amounts to almost 3 billion pounds (1.4 billion kg) of fish destroyed annually by the shrimp industry.

Pollution

Pollution results from human activities such as urban sprawl, transportation, and industry. More significantly in terms of wildlife and biodiversity, human activity expands the effects of pollution into areas where environmental quality may not yet have been severely compromised. Industrial and transportation sources release pollutants into the air, water, and soil that are toxic to most species and degrade their habitats. In addition, light and noise associated with human activity often have negative effects on wildlife behavior and natural cycles.

Pollutants have devastating effects on wildlife when they are released into the soil and water. They affect an animal's endocrine, reproductive, and immune systems. Wildlife can be exposed to pollutants through skin absorption, the animals or plants they eat, and the water they drink. Amphibians and other aquatic species are especially vulnerable to pollutants in streams, rivers, and lakes.

Plants or wildlife (especially species with thin, moist skin such as amphibians) can inhale or absorb air pollutants, causing health problems. Air pollution also contaminates water and soil through acid rain. Sulfur dioxide, a main component of acid rain, can damage plant communities by impairing photosynthesis processes. Plants weakened by acid rain may become vulnerable to root rot, insect damage, and disease, causing serious damage to plant communities and forest ecosystems.

Noise can affect wildlife behavior and physiology. Noise can also cause chronic stress, increased heart rates, metabolism and hormone imbalance, and nervous system stimulation. These responses may cause energy loss, food intake reduction, an avoidance and abandonment of habitat, and even injury or death. Noise will often flush birds from their nests, causing broken eggs, injured young, or exposure to predators. Finally, birdsongs and calls that are used to mate and establish territories may be disrupted by excessive human noise pollution.

Developed areas produce artificial light that causes problems for wildlife that depend on the light from the moon and stars to navigate. Streetlights, neon signs, parking lots, and late-night golf driving ranges may potentially keep wildlife from moving, nesting, or foraging near urban areas.

Introduced Species

Invasive or exotic species are animals and plants that are transported to any area where they do not naturally live. The spread of nonnative species has emerged in recent years as one of the most serious threats to biodiversity. It has undermined the ecological integrity of many native habitats and pushed some rare species to the edge of extinction. Some introduced species simply outcompete native plants and animals for space, food, or water. Others may also fundamentally alter natural disturbance regimes and other ecological processes, making it difficult or impossible for native species to survive. About 15% of the estimated 6,000 nonnative plant and animal species in the United States cause severe economic or ecological impacts. Exotic species have been implicated in the decline of approximately 40% of the species listed for protection under the federal Endangered Species Act.

A major marine source is marine ballast. Every 60 seconds, ships discharge 40,000 gallons (150,000 L) of ballast water that contains foreign plant and animal species into U.S. harbors. Often these plants and animals grow at uncontrolled rates because they have no natural predators in these new locations. These introduced species often become pests and crowd out native plants and animals. Over 250 invasive species of plants and animals are found in San Francisco Bay alone. Common examples of invasive species include zebra mussels, tumbleweed, kudzu, the mongoose, and gypsy moths.

Endangered and Extinct Species

Since 1500 C.E., 816 species have become extinct, 103 of them since 1800—a rate 50 times greater than the natural background rate. In the next 25 years, extinction rates are expected to rise as high as 25%. According to the Nature Conservancy, about one-third of all U.S. plant and animal species are at risk of becoming extinct. Mammals listed as "endangered" rose from 484 in 1996 to 520 in 2000, with primates increasing from 13 to 19. Endangered birds increased from 403 species to 503 species. Endangered freshwater fish more than doubled—from 10 species to 24 species in four years. One-fourth of all mammals and reptiles, one-fifth of all amphibians, one-eighth of all birds, and one-sixth of all conifers are in some manner endangered or are threatened to the point of extinction.

Maintenance Through Conservation

Maintaining and protecting wildlife consists of three major approaches:

- **Species approach**—Protecting *endangered species* through legislation.
- **Ecosystem approach**—Preserving balanced *ecosystems*.
- **Wildlife management approach**—Managing *game species* for sustained yield through international treaties to protect migrating species, improving wildlife habitats, regulating hunting and fishing, creating harvest quotas, and developing population management plans.

Biodiversity can be protected by:

1. Properly designing and updating laws that legally protect endangered and threatened species (such as the Endangered Species Act)

2. Protecting the habitats of endangered species through private or governmental land trusts

3. Reintroducing species into suitable habitats

4. Managing habitats and monitoring land use

5. Establishing breeding programs for endangered or threatened species

6. Creating and expanding wildlife sanctuaries

7. Restoring compromised ecosystems

8. Reducing nonnative and invasive species

RELEVANT LAWS AND TREATIES

Multiple-Use Act (1960): Directed that the national forests be managed for timber, watershed, range, outdoor recreation, wildlife, and fish purposes.

The Convention on International Trade in Endangered Species of Wild Fauna and Flora (CITES) (1963): An international agreement between governments to ensure that international trade in wild animals and plants did not threaten their survival.

Marine Mammal Protection Act (1972): Established federal responsibility to conserve marine mammals.

Endangered Species Act (1973): Provided a program for the conservation of threatened and endangered plants and animals and the habitats in which they are found.

QUICK REVIEW CHECKLIST

- [ ] **Stratospheric Ozone**
    - [ ] ultraviolet radiation
        - [ ] UVA
        - [ ] UVB
        - [ ] UVC
    - [ ] causes of ozone depletion
    - [ ] effects of ozone depletion
    - [ ] strategies for reducing ozone depletion
    - [ ] relevant laws and treaties
        - [ ] Montreal Protocol (1987)
        - [ ] London (1990)
        - [ ] Copenhagen (1992)

QUICK REVIEW CHECKLIST (continued)

- ☐ **Global Warming**
  - ☐ greenhouse gases
    - ☐ carbon dioxide
    - ☐ methane
    - ☐ nitrous oxide
    - ☐ HFC, CFC, HCFC, SF_6
  - ☐ impacts and consequences of global warming
    - ☐ acidification
    - ☐ changes in tropospheric weather patterns
    - ☐ displacement of people
    - ☐ ecological productivity
    - ☐ forest fires
    - ☐ glacier melting
    - ☐ health and behavioral effects
    - ☐ disease
    - ☐ property loss
    - ☐ economic development
    - ☐ biodiversity
    - ☐ methane hydrates in coastal sediments
    - ☐ thawing of permafrost and release of methane
    - ☐ rise in sea level
    - ☐ effect on thermohaline circulation

- ☐ **Reducing Climate Change**

- ☐ **Loss of Biodiversity**

- ☐ **Overuse**

- ☐ **Pollution**

- ☐ **Introduced Species**

- ☐ **Endangered and Extinct Species**

- ☐ **Conservation**
  - ☐ species approach
  - ☐ ecosystem approach
  - ☐ wildlife management approach
  - ☐ specific measures to protect biodiversity

- ☐ **Relevant Laws and Treaties**
  - ☐ Multiple-use Act (1960)
  - ☐ Convention on International Trade in Endangered Species of Wild Fauna and Flora (CITES)—1963
  - ☐ Marine Mammal Protection Act (1972)
  - ☐ Endangered Species Act (1973)

MULTIPLE-CHOICE QUESTIONS

1. Which of the following represents the greatest contribution of methane emission to the atmosphere?

   (A) Enteric fermentation or flatulence from animals
   (B) Coal mining
   (C) Landfills
   (D) Rice cultivation
   (E) Burning of biomass

2. Ozone depletion reactions that occur in the stratosphere are facilitated by

   (A) NO_2^-
   (B) NH_3
   (C) NH_4^+
   (D) N_2O
   (E) NO_3^-

3. In addition to absorbing harmful solar rays, how do ozone molecules help to stabilize the upper atmosphere?

   (A) They release heat to the surroundings.
   (B) They create a buoyant lid on the atmosphere.
   (C) They create a warm layer of atmosphere that keeps the lower atmosphere from mixing with space.
   (D) All of the above are correct.
   (E) None of the above are correct.

4. The bromine released from methyl bromide is about 40 times more damaging to the ozone layer than chlorine on a molecule of chlorofluoro-carbon. Under the Montreal Protocol, methyl bromide in developing countries will be phased out in 2005. What is methyl bromide used for?

   (A) Sterilizing soil in fields and greenhouses
   (B) Killing pests on fruits, vegetables, and grain before export
   (C) Fumigating soils
   (D) Killing termites in buildings
   (E) All of the above

5. Rising sea levels due to global warming would be responsible for all of the following EXCEPT

   (A) destruction of coastal wetlands
   (B) beach erosion
   (C) increased damage due to storms and floods
   (D) increased salinity of estuaries and aquifers
   (E) All of the above

6. True statements about global warming include which of the following?

    I. Average carbon dioxide levels in the atmosphere today are the highest they have ever been in Earth's history.
    II. Average global air temperatures today are the highest they have ever been in Earth's history.
    III. The increases in average global air temperatures are equally distributed across the Earth's surface.

    (A) I only
    (B) II only
    (C) I and II
    (D) III only
    (E) All choices are false

7. One of the reasons the vortex winds in the Antarctic are important in the formation of the hole in the ozone layer is

    (A) they prevent warm, ozone-rich air from mixing with cold, ozone-depleted air
    (B) they quickly mix ozone-depleted air with ozone-rich air
    (C) they harbor vast quantities of N_2O
    (D) they bring in moist, warm air, which accelerates the ozone-forming process
    (E) None of the above

8. Although the Montreal Protocol curtailed production of ozone-depleting substances, the peak concentration of chemicals in the stratosphere is only now being reached. When do scientists expect a recovery in the ozone levels in the stratosphere to occur?

    (A) Immediately
    (B) Within 5 years
    (C) Within 20 years
    (D) Within 50 years
    (E) In about 100 years

9. Over the past 1 million years of Earth's history, the average trend in Earth's temperature would best be described as:

    (A) very large fluctuations, from periods of extreme heat to periods of extreme cold
    (B) very little change, if any, fairly uniform and constant temperature
    (C) a general cooling trend
    (D) a general warming trend
    (E) a number of fluctuations varying by a few degrees

10. The agency responsible for the identification and listing of endangered species is the

    (A) Forest Service
    (B) Agriculture Department
    (C) National Park Service
    (D) Fish and Wildlife Service
    (E) Endangered Species Department of the Interior

11. A treaty that controls international trades in endangered species is known as (the)
    (A) Endangered Species Act
    (B) CITES
    (C) International Treaty on Endangered Species
    (D) Lacey Act
    (E) Federal Preserve System

12. Managing game species for sustained yields would be consistent with what conservation approach?

    (A) Wildlife management approach
    (B) Species approach
    (C) Ecosystem approach
    (D) Sustainable yield approach
    (E) Holistic approach

13. A certain insect was causing extensive damage to local crops. The farmers, who were environmentally conscious and did not want to use pesticides, decided to introduce another insect into their fields that studies have shown would prey on the pest insect. Before any action is taken, the farmers should consider (the)

    (A) principle of natural balance
    (B) principle of unforeseen events
    (C) Murphy's law
    (D) law of supply and demand
    (E) precautionary principle

14. Which of the following is the biggest threat to wildlife preserves?

    (A) Hunters
    (B) Poachers
    (C) Global warming
    (D) Invasive species
    (E) Tourists

15. A certain species of plant is placed on the threatened species list. Several years later it is placed on the endangered species list. This is an example of

    (A) a negative-negative feedback loop
    (B) a positive-negative feedback loop
    (C) a negative-positive feedback loop
    (D) a negative-feedback loop
    (E) a positive-feedback loop

16. The specific form of radiation largely responsible for the formation of ozone in the stratosphere is
    (A) UVA
    (B) UVB
    (C) UVC
    (D) infrared
    (E) gamma rays

17. Which of the following is NOT an effect caused by increased levels of ultraviolet radiation reaching Earth?

    (A) Warming of the stratosphere
    (B) Cooling of the stratosphere
    (C) Increased genetic damage
    (D) Reduction in immunity
    (E) Reduction in plant productivity

18. Which of the following gases is NOT considered a greenhouse gas, responsible for global warming?

    (A) SO_2
    (B) N_2O
    (C) H_2O
    (D) SF_6
    (E) CH_4

19. Which of the following effects would result from the shutdown or slowdown of the thermohaline circulation pattern?

    (A) A warmer Scandinavia and Great Britain
    (B) Freshwater fish moving into the open ocean
    (C) A colder Scandinavia and Great Britain
    (D) A saltier ocean
    (E) A drier Scandinavia and Great Britain

20. The largest number of species are being exterminated per year in

    (A) grasslands
    (B) deserts
    (C) forests
    (D) tropical rain forests
    (E) the tundra

FREE-RESPONSE QUESTION

Part (a): 3 points
Part (b): 4 points
Part (c): 3 points

Total: 10 points

The following charts show global temperature changes and carbon dioxide emissions.

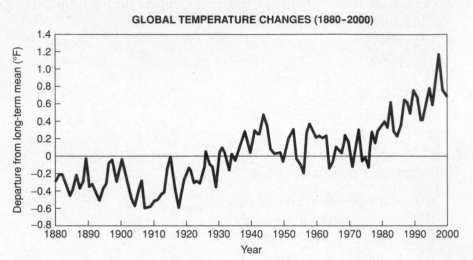

Source: U.S. National Climatic Data Center, 2001

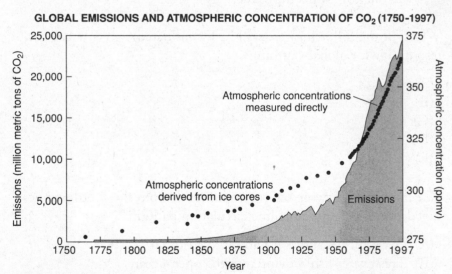

Source: Carbon Dioxide Information Analysis Center, 2001

(a) Describe global warming.

   (i)   What role do naturally occurring atmospheric gases play in global warming?

   (ii) Describe how a certain degree of global warming is necessary for life to exist on Earth.

   (iii) How have atmospheric concentrations of carbon dioxide (CO_2) gas changed since the Industrial Revolution?

(b) What factors may be increasing global temperatures?
    (i)   Compare natural contributions of CO_2 to the atmosphere vs. release of CO_2 through human activities.
    (ii)   Name and describe TWO other gases besides CO_2 that contribute to global warming?
(c) What are the environmental consequences of global warming?
    (i)   How have global mean temperatures changed in the last 200 years?
    (ii)   How have the changes in global mean temperatures in (i) affected weather patterns?
    (iii) List TWO consequences to the environment of increases in global air temperature.

MULTIPLE-CHOICE ANSWERS AND EXPLANATIONS

1. **(C)** Since 1800, there has been a 150% increase in methane concentrations in the atmosphere compared with a 30% increase in carbon dioxide. Methane is about 30 times more effective in contributing to global warming than carbon dioxide.

2. **(D)** Nitrous oxide is responsible for about 7% of the anthropogenic greenhouse gases and stays in the atmosphere for about 120 years. The concentration of nitrous oxide in the atmosphere has increased about 15% since the Industrial Revolution. It has an ozone-depleting potential comparable with many HCFCs. The main source of nitrous oxide are inorganic fertilizers and industrial processes. Natural sources of nitrous oxide arise from biological processes within the soil and oceans.

3. **(D)** Solar energy that is absorbed by ozone molecules and is partly turned into heat creates a warm region in the stratosphere. This creates a stable air mass that resists sinking and mixing with the lower atmosphere, effectively forming a barrier. In the ozone layer, temperature increases with height, creating a stable and buoyant air mass that keeps an effective lid on the lower atmosphere.

4. **(E)** No explanation needed.

5. **(E)** No explanation needed.

6. **(E)** Earth's primitive forests first appeared around 300 million years ago during the Carboniferous Period. Before then, the atmosphere held far more CO_2 but concentrations declined throughout the Carboniferous Period as plants flourished and absorbed more and more CO_2 from the atmosphere through photosynthesis, creating carbon sinks (coal, oil, etc.). During the Carboniferous Period, the atmosphere became greatly depleted of CO_2 (declining from about 2500 ppm to 350 ppm) so that by the end of the Carboniferous Period the atmosphere was less favorable to plant life and plant growth slowed. Today, CO_2 concentrations are approximately 380 ppm (0.038% of our atmosphere). The Arctic is feeling the effects of increases in average global air temperatures the most. Average temperatures in Alaska, western Canada, and eastern Russia are rising at twice the rate of the global average.

7. **(A)** Ozone depletion follows an annual cycle that corresponds to the amount of light that reaches the Antarctic. The cycle begins every year around June when vortex winds develop in the Antarctic. Cold temperatures pro-

duced by these winds create polar stratospheric clouds that capture floating chlorofluorocarbons (CFCs) and other ozone-depleting compounds. For the next two months, a reaction occurs on the cloud surface that frees the chlorine in the CFCs but keeps it contained within the vortex. In September, sunlight returns to the Antarctic and triggers a chemical reaction, causing chlorine to convert ozone to oxygen gas. November brings a breakdown in the vortex and allows the ozone-rich air to combine with the thinning ozone. Wind currents carry this mixture over the southern hemisphere.

8. **(E)** Concentrations of ozone-depleting chlorofluorocarbons (CFCs) have leveled off in the stratosphere and have actually begun to decline in the lower atmosphere. However, the largest Antarctic ozone hole ever recorded occurred in 2000. A CFC molecule can take about 8 years after being released at ground level to reach the stratosphere. Decades may pass until it is converted by sunlight into a form that depletes ozone.

9. **(E)** The mean surface temperature of the planet has been warming at a rate of 0.2°C per decade for the past 30 years. The global mean temperature is now within 1°C of the maximum for the past million years. The last time Earth was this warm was about 3 million years ago when sea level was about 25 meters higher than today. If carbon dioxide emissions are not curbed, global temperatures are likely to rise 2 to 3°C by 2100.

10. **(D)** The Fish and Wildlife Service, in the Department of the Interior, and the National Oceanic and Atmospheric Administration (NOAA) in the Department of Commerce, share responsibility for administration of the Endangered Species Act. An endangered species is one that is in danger of extinction throughout all or a significant portion of its range. A threatened species is one that is likely to become endangered in the foreseeable future.

11. **(B)** CITES (the Convention on International Trade in Endangered Species) is an international agreement between governments. Its aim is to ensure that international trade in specimens of wild animals and plants does not threaten their survival.

12. **(A)** The strength of the traditional wildlife management approach is that it explicitly uses and enhances natural processes to perpetuate populations.

13. **(E)** The precautionary principle states that if the consequences of an action are unknown but are judged to have some potential for major or irreversible negative consequences, that action should be avoided. The concept includes risk prevention, cost effectiveness, ethical responsibilities toward maintaining the integrity of natural biological systems, and risk assessment. It is not the risk that must be avoided but the potential risk that must be prevented.

14. **(C)** All choices but (C) can be dealt with on a local level through specific enforcement and management practices. Global warming is an issue that affects all ecosystems and must be solved on a global scale, requiring international cooperation.

15. **(E)** A positive-feedback loop occurs in a situation in which a change in a certain direction (toward extinction in this case) causes the system to change in the same direction.

16. **(C)** Ozone is produced by oxygen and sunlight in the UVC wavelength range (<240 nm). In the atmosphere, this reaction works only at higher altitudes where there is adequate high-energy UV penetration (>10 km). The atomic oxygen so formed can combine with oxygen gas (O_2) to form ozone (O_3).

17. **(A)** The stratosphere has been cooling over the past three decades. The stratosphere contains the ozone layer, which absorbs sunlight and heats the stratosphere. This long-term cooling trend is generally accepted to result from the loss of the ozone layer as a result of human-made influences. However, the cooling trend is not uniform like ozone loss but, rather, broken into a series of jumps or discontinuities most likely associated with major volcanic eruptions that inject aerosols into the stratosphere. The aerosols also absorb sunlight and heat from the stratosphere, thus temporarily offsetting the cooling trend from ozone loss.

18. **(A)** Sulfur dioxide (SO_2) contributes to acid rain, not global warming.

19. **(C)** There is speculation that global warming could melt glaciers in Greenland, increasing the amount of freshwater in the North Sea. This disruption in balance between salt water and freshwater could theoretically slow down or shut down thermohaline circulation that is responsible for the North Atlantic Drift (a section of the Gulf Stream) that currently stabilizes temperatures in Great Britain and Scandinavia.

20. **(D)** Deforestation in the tropics in order to convert the land to agricultural purposes and cattle grazing is occurring at unprecedented levels. The tropics contain the highest biodiversity anywhere on Earth.

FREE-RESPONSE ANSWER

(a) Energy from the sun drives Earth's weather and climate and heats Earth's surface. In turn, Earth radiates energy back into space. Natural atmospheric greenhouse gases such as water vapor, carbon dioxide, methane, and nitrous oxide trap some of the outgoing energy similar to the glass panels of a greenhouse. Without the greenhouse effect, much of the heat reaching Earth would escape into space. Life as we know it, could not exist. However, Earth's climate is predicted to change due to human activities that have caused these natural gas concentrations to increase dramatically. According to the graph, since the beginning of the Industrial Revolution, atmospheric concentrations of carbon dioxide have increased nearly 30%. In addition, methane concentrations have more than doubled, and nitrous oxide concentrations have increased about 15%. Not all gases contribute to global warming equally. As a reference point, if the global warming potential of carbon dioxide gas is given as a 1, then methane is 20 times more effective in trapping heat energy, and nitrous oxide is over 300 times more effective.

Notable points:

Connection with sun as energy driver.

Energy hitting Earth from the sun is absorbed and reradiated back into space.

Some gases prevent energy from radiating back into space.

Not all gases trap heat equally.

Greenhouse effect is necessary for life on Earth.

Both natural and human-made gases cause the greenhouse effect.

Carbon dioxide is the gas most responsible for the greenhouse effect.

Increase in production of CO_2 is primary factor in greenhouse effect.

How CO_2 is produced.

Comparison of CO_2 levels today as compared with years past.

Mentioning one other greenhouse gas such as methane, water vapor, sulfur hexafluoride, or nitrous oxide.

(b) Scientists generally believe that the combustion of fossil fuels and other human activities are the primary reason for the increased concentration of carbon dioxide. Plant respiration and the decomposition of organic matter release more than 10 times the carbon dioxide released through human activities. However, these releases have generally been in balance during the centuries leading up to the Industrial Revolution, with carbon dioxide being absorbed by plants both terrestrial and oceanic. What has changed in the last few hundred years is the additional release of carbon dioxide by human activities. Fossil fuels burned to run cars and trucks, heat homes and businesses, and power factories are responsible for about 98% of U.S. carbon dioxide emissions, 24% of methane emissions, and 18% of nitrous oxide emissions. Increased agriculture, deforestation, landfills, industrial production, and mining also contribute a significant share of emissions.

In 1997, the United States emitted about one-fifth of total greenhouse gases. By 2100, in the absence of emissions control policies, carbon dioxide concentrations are projected to be 30%–150% higher than today's levels. Water vapor is the most abundant greenhouse gas. It occurs naturally and makes up about two-thirds of the natural greenhouse effect. Other gases that accelerate the greenhouse effect include nitrous oxide, hydrofluorocarbons, perfluorocarbons, and sulfur hexafluoride. Since preindustrial times, atmospheric concentrations of nitrous oxide have increased by 17%, carbon dioxide by 31%, and methane by 151%. Scientists have confirmed that this is primarily due to human activity.

—Decreased snow cover

—Floating ice

—Rise in sea level

—Increased precipitation due to warmer temperatures

—Increased surface temperatures

—Decreased soil moisture in some areas

—Increase in storm intensities

—Increase in rates of disease

—Increase in heatstroke and other heat-associated effects

—Increased flooding in some areas

—Increased droughts in some areas

(c) According to the graph, global mean surface temperatures have increased 0.5°F to 1.0°F since the late 1800s. The 20th century's 10 warmest years all occurred in the last 15 years. The snow cover in the Northern Hemisphere and floating ice in the Arctic Ocean have decreased. Globally, sea level has risen 4 to 8 inches in the last 100 years. Worldwide precipitation over land has increased by about 1% (warmer temperatures usually cause greater amounts of water to evaporate). The frequency of extreme rainfall events has increased throughout much of the United States. Increasing concentrations of greenhouse gases are likely to accelerate the rate of climatic change. Scientists expect that the average global surface temperature could rise 2°F to 10°F in the next century, with significant regional variation. Evaporation will increase as the climate warms, which will increase average global precipitation. Soil moisture is likely to decline in many regions, and intense rainstorms are likely to become more frequent. Sea levels are likely to rise 2 feet along most of the U.S. coasts. A few degrees of warming will increase the chances of more frequent and severe heat waves, which can cause more heat-related death and illness. Greater heat results in increased air pollution as well as damaged crops and depleted water resources. Warming is likely to allow tropical diseases, such as malaria, to spread northward in some areas of the world. It will also intensify Earth's hydrological cycle. Both evaporation and precipitation will increase. Some areas will receive more rain, while other areas will be drier. At the same time, extreme events like floods and droughts are likely to become more frequent. Warming will cause glaciers to melt and oceans to expand. Projections state that sea levels will rise between 4 inches and 3 feet over the next century, threatening low-lying coastal areas.

PRACTICE EXAMS

Practice Exam 1

With Answers and Analysis

SECTION I (MULTIPLE-CHOICE QUESTIONS)

Time: 90 minutes

100 questions

60% of total grade

No calculators allowed

This section consists of 100 multiple-choice questions. Mark your answers carefully on the answer sheet.

General Instructions

Do not open this booklet until you are told to do so by the proctor.

Be sure to write your answers for Section I on the separate answer sheet. Use the test booklet for your scratch work or notes. Remember, though, that no credit will be given for work, notes, or answers written only in the test booklet. Once you have selected an answer, thoroughly blacken the corresponding circle on the answer sheet. To change an answer, erase your previous mark completely, and then record your new answer. Mark only one answer for each question.

Example   **Sample Answer**

The Pacific is   Ⓐ Ⓑ ● Ⓓ Ⓔ

    (A) a river
    (B) a lake
    (C) an ocean
    (D) a sea
    (E) a gulf

There is no penalty for wrong answers on the multiple-choice section, so you should answer all multiple-choice questions. Even if you have no idea of the correct answer, you should try to eliminate any obvious incorrect choices, and then guess.

Because it is not expected that all test takers will complete this section, do not spend too much time on difficult questions. First answer the questions you can answer readily. Then, if you have time, return to the difficult questions later. Do not get stuck on one question. Work quickly but accurately. Use your time effectively.

Answer Sheet

PRACTICE EXAM 1

1 Ⓐ Ⓑ Ⓒ Ⓓ Ⓔ	26 Ⓐ Ⓑ Ⓒ Ⓓ Ⓔ	51 Ⓐ Ⓑ Ⓒ Ⓓ Ⓔ	76 Ⓐ Ⓑ Ⓒ Ⓓ Ⓔ
2 Ⓐ Ⓑ Ⓒ Ⓓ Ⓔ	27 Ⓐ Ⓑ Ⓒ Ⓓ Ⓔ	52 Ⓐ Ⓑ Ⓒ Ⓓ Ⓔ	77 Ⓐ Ⓑ Ⓒ Ⓓ Ⓔ
3 Ⓐ Ⓑ Ⓒ Ⓓ Ⓔ	28 Ⓐ Ⓑ Ⓒ Ⓓ Ⓔ	53 Ⓐ Ⓑ Ⓒ Ⓓ Ⓔ	78 Ⓐ Ⓑ Ⓒ Ⓓ Ⓔ
4 Ⓐ Ⓑ Ⓒ Ⓓ Ⓔ	29 Ⓐ Ⓑ Ⓒ Ⓓ Ⓔ	54 Ⓐ Ⓑ Ⓒ Ⓓ Ⓔ	79 Ⓐ Ⓑ Ⓒ Ⓓ Ⓔ
5 Ⓐ Ⓑ Ⓒ Ⓓ Ⓔ	30 Ⓐ Ⓑ Ⓒ Ⓓ Ⓔ	55 Ⓐ Ⓑ Ⓒ Ⓓ Ⓔ	80 Ⓐ Ⓑ Ⓒ Ⓓ Ⓔ
6 Ⓐ Ⓑ Ⓒ Ⓓ Ⓔ	31 Ⓐ Ⓑ Ⓒ Ⓓ Ⓔ	56 Ⓐ Ⓑ Ⓒ Ⓓ Ⓔ	81 Ⓐ Ⓑ Ⓒ Ⓓ Ⓔ
7 Ⓐ Ⓑ Ⓒ Ⓓ Ⓔ	32 Ⓐ Ⓑ Ⓒ Ⓓ Ⓔ	57 Ⓐ Ⓑ Ⓒ Ⓓ Ⓔ	82 Ⓐ Ⓑ Ⓒ Ⓓ Ⓔ
8 Ⓐ Ⓑ Ⓒ Ⓓ Ⓔ	33 Ⓐ Ⓑ Ⓒ Ⓓ Ⓔ	58 Ⓐ Ⓑ Ⓒ Ⓓ Ⓔ	83 Ⓐ Ⓑ Ⓒ Ⓓ Ⓔ
9 Ⓐ Ⓑ Ⓒ Ⓓ Ⓔ	34 Ⓐ Ⓑ Ⓒ Ⓓ Ⓔ	59 Ⓐ Ⓑ Ⓒ Ⓓ Ⓔ	84 Ⓐ Ⓑ Ⓒ Ⓓ Ⓔ
10 Ⓐ Ⓑ Ⓒ Ⓓ Ⓔ	35 Ⓐ Ⓑ Ⓒ Ⓓ Ⓔ	60 Ⓐ Ⓑ Ⓒ Ⓓ Ⓔ	85 Ⓐ Ⓑ Ⓒ Ⓓ Ⓔ
11 Ⓐ Ⓑ Ⓒ Ⓓ Ⓔ	36 Ⓐ Ⓑ Ⓒ Ⓓ Ⓔ	61 Ⓐ Ⓑ Ⓒ Ⓓ Ⓔ	86 Ⓐ Ⓑ Ⓒ Ⓓ Ⓔ
12 Ⓐ Ⓑ Ⓒ Ⓓ Ⓔ	37 Ⓐ Ⓑ Ⓒ Ⓓ Ⓔ	62 Ⓐ Ⓑ Ⓒ Ⓓ Ⓔ	87 Ⓐ Ⓑ Ⓒ Ⓓ Ⓔ
13 Ⓐ Ⓑ Ⓒ Ⓓ Ⓔ	38 Ⓐ Ⓑ Ⓒ Ⓓ Ⓔ	63 Ⓐ Ⓑ Ⓒ Ⓓ Ⓔ	88 Ⓐ Ⓑ Ⓒ Ⓓ Ⓔ
14 Ⓐ Ⓑ Ⓒ Ⓓ Ⓔ	39 Ⓐ Ⓑ Ⓒ Ⓓ Ⓔ	64 Ⓐ Ⓑ Ⓒ Ⓓ Ⓔ	89 Ⓐ Ⓑ Ⓒ Ⓓ Ⓔ
15 Ⓐ Ⓑ Ⓒ Ⓓ Ⓔ	40 Ⓐ Ⓑ Ⓒ Ⓓ Ⓔ	65 Ⓐ Ⓑ Ⓒ Ⓓ Ⓔ	90 Ⓐ Ⓑ Ⓒ Ⓓ Ⓔ
16 Ⓐ Ⓑ Ⓒ Ⓓ Ⓔ	41 Ⓐ Ⓑ Ⓒ Ⓓ Ⓔ	66 Ⓐ Ⓑ Ⓒ Ⓓ Ⓔ	91 Ⓐ Ⓑ Ⓒ Ⓓ Ⓔ
17 Ⓐ Ⓑ Ⓒ Ⓓ Ⓔ	42 Ⓐ Ⓑ Ⓒ Ⓓ Ⓔ	67 Ⓐ Ⓑ Ⓒ Ⓓ Ⓔ	92 Ⓐ Ⓑ Ⓒ Ⓓ Ⓔ
18 Ⓐ Ⓑ Ⓒ Ⓓ Ⓔ	43 Ⓐ Ⓑ Ⓒ Ⓓ Ⓔ	68 Ⓐ Ⓑ Ⓒ Ⓓ Ⓔ	93 Ⓐ Ⓑ Ⓒ Ⓓ Ⓔ
19 Ⓐ Ⓑ Ⓒ Ⓓ Ⓔ	44 Ⓐ Ⓑ Ⓒ Ⓓ Ⓔ	69 Ⓐ Ⓑ Ⓒ Ⓓ Ⓔ	94 Ⓐ Ⓑ Ⓒ Ⓓ Ⓔ
20 Ⓐ Ⓑ Ⓒ Ⓓ Ⓔ	45 Ⓐ Ⓑ Ⓒ Ⓓ Ⓔ	70 Ⓐ Ⓑ Ⓒ Ⓓ Ⓔ	95 Ⓐ Ⓑ Ⓒ Ⓓ Ⓔ
21 Ⓐ Ⓑ Ⓒ Ⓓ Ⓔ	46 Ⓐ Ⓑ Ⓒ Ⓓ Ⓔ	71 Ⓐ Ⓑ Ⓒ Ⓓ Ⓔ	96 Ⓐ Ⓑ Ⓒ Ⓓ Ⓔ
22 Ⓐ Ⓑ Ⓒ Ⓓ Ⓔ	47 Ⓐ Ⓑ Ⓒ Ⓓ Ⓔ	72 Ⓐ Ⓑ Ⓒ Ⓓ Ⓔ	97 Ⓐ Ⓑ Ⓒ Ⓓ Ⓔ
23 Ⓐ Ⓑ Ⓒ Ⓓ Ⓔ	48 Ⓐ Ⓑ Ⓒ Ⓓ Ⓔ	73 Ⓐ Ⓑ Ⓒ Ⓓ Ⓔ	98 Ⓐ Ⓑ Ⓒ Ⓓ Ⓔ
24 Ⓐ Ⓑ Ⓒ Ⓓ Ⓔ	49 Ⓐ Ⓑ Ⓒ Ⓓ Ⓔ	74 Ⓐ Ⓑ Ⓒ Ⓓ Ⓔ	99 Ⓐ Ⓑ Ⓒ Ⓓ Ⓔ
25 Ⓐ Ⓑ Ⓒ Ⓓ Ⓔ	50 Ⓐ Ⓑ Ⓒ Ⓓ Ⓔ	75 Ⓐ Ⓑ Ⓒ Ⓓ Ⓔ	100 Ⓐ Ⓑ Ⓒ Ⓓ Ⓔ

Directions: For each question or statement, select the one lettered choice that is the best answer and fill in the corresponding circle on the answer sheet.

1. Which of the following would be most likely to increase competition among the members of a squirrel population in a given area?

    (A) An epidemic of rabies within the squirrel population
    (B) An increase in the number of hawk predators
    (C) An increase in the reproduction of squirrels
    (D) An increase in temperature
    (E) An increase in the food supply

2. Approximately how many years ago did life first appear on Earth?

    (A) 1 million
    (B) 500 million
    (C) 1 billion
    (D) 3.5 billion
    (E) 5 billion

3. Which one of the following statements is FALSE?

    (A) The greenhouse effect is a natural process that makes life on Earth possible with 98% of total global greenhouse gas emissions being from natural sources (mostly water vapor) and 2% from human-made sources.
    (B) The United States is the number one contributor to global warming.
    (C) The Kyoto Protocol would have allowed the United States to increase its greenhouse gas emissions—primarily carbon dioxide (CO_2), methane (CH_4), and nitrous oxide (N_2O)—by only 2% per year based on 1990 levels.
    (D) The effects of global warming on weather patterns may lead to adverse human health impacts.
    (E) Global warming may increase the incidence of many infectious diseases.

4. Which of the following would be an external cost?

    (A) The cost of steel in making a refrigerator
    (B) The cost of running a refrigerator for one month
    (C) The cost of labor in producing refrigerators
    (D) The taxes paid by consumers in purchasing refrigerators
    (E) The costs associated with health care when the refrigerator leaks refrigerant into the atmosphere

5. In which stage of the nitrogen cycle do soil bacteria convert ammonium ions (NH_4^+) into nitrate ions (NO_3^-); a form of nitrogen that can be used by plants?

   (A) Nitrogen fixation
   (B) Nitrification
   (C) Assimilation
   (D) Ammonification
   (E) Denitrification

6. Which of the following is NOT an example of environmental mitigation?

   (A) Promoting sound land use planning, based on known hazards
   (B) Relocating or elevating structures out of the floodplain
   (C) Constructing living snow fences
   (D) Organizing a beach cleanup
   (E) Developing, adopting, and enforcing effective building codes and standards

7. Which of the following statements regarding an El Niño is FALSE?

   (A) Depression of the thermocline occurs, which cuts off cold water upwelling.
   (B) A change in atmospheric pressures occurs and is associated with changing ocean water temperatures.
   (C) El Niño affects weather patterns globally.
   (D) An increase in greenhouse gases may increase the incidents of El Niños.
   (E) Northeast and southeast trade winds increase.

8. Most of the Earth's freshwater supply is found in

   (A) lakes
   (B) ice caps and glaciers
   (C) aquifers
   (D) estuaries
   (E) rivers

9. Most municipal solid wastes in the United States consist of

   (A) yard wastes
   (B) food wastes
   (C) plastic
   (D) paper
   (E) glass

10. Rising sea levels due to global warming would be responsible for all of the following EXCEPT

    (A) destruction of coastal wetlands
    (B) beach erosion
    (C) increases due to storm and flood damage
    (D) increased salinity of estuaries and aquifers
    (E) all would be the result of rising sea level

11. Which of the following characteristics are NOT typical of a ground fire?

    I. Fire smolders and/or creeps slowly through the litter and humus layers, consuming all or most of the organic cover, and exposing mineral soil or underlying rock.
    II. Burns the upper litter layer and small branches that lie on or near the ground. Usually move rapidly through an area, and do not consume all the organic layer.
    III. Release considerable amounts of nutrients from the burned fuels, destroy many small organisms and fungi that live in the humus and organic layers, consume seed stored in the litter, and kill roots in all but deep soil layers.

    (A) I only
    (B) II only
    (C) III only
    (D) I and II
    (E) I and III

12. Place the following economic activities in order, starting with those activities closest to natural resources and ending with those furthest away.

    I. Use raw materials to produce or manufacture something new and more valuable.
    II. Professions that process, administer, and disseminate information (e.g., computer engineers, professors, and lawyers).
    III. Agriculture, fishing, hunting, herding, forestry, and mining.
    IV. Include all activities that amount to doing service for others (e.g., doctors, teachers, and secretaries).

    (A) I, II, III, IV
    (B) I, III, IV, II
    (C) III, I, II, IV
    (D) III, I, IV, II
    (E) II, IV, I, III

13. Most of the municipal trash floating in the ocean is composed of

    (A) plastic
    (B) paper
    (C) wood
    (D) metal cans
    (E) yard wastes

14. Most of Earth's mass is found in this region, which is composed of iron, magnesium, aluminum, and silicon-oxygen compounds. At over 1800°F (1000°C), most of this region is solid but the upper third is more plasticlike in nature. Which region is being described?

    (A) Troposphere
    (B) Lithosphere
    (C) Crust
    (D) Mantle
    (E) Core

15. Which of the following statements regarding coral reefs is FALSE?

    (A) Modern reefs can be as much as 2.5 million years old.
    (B) Coral reefs capture about half of all the calcium flowing into the ocean every year, fixing it into calcium carbonate rock at very high rates.
    (C) Coral reefs store large amounts organic carbon and are very effective sinks for carbon dioxide from the atmosphere.
    (D) Coral reefs are among the most biologically diverse ecosystems on the planet.
    (E) Coral reefs are among the most endangered ecosystems on Earth.

16. Which of the following strategies to control pollution would incur the greatest governmental cost?

    (A) Green taxes
    (B) Government subsidies for reducing pollution
    (C) Regulation
    (D) Charging a user fee
    (E) Tradable pollution rights

17. In terms of annual production, which two crops listed below had the greatest success during The Green Revolution (1967–1978)?

    (A) maize and corn
    (B) rice and corn
    (C) wheat and rice
    (D) wheat and maize
    (E) soybean and rice

18. In 1989, the *Exxon Valdez* spilled 10.8 million gallons of crude oil into Prince William Sound in Alaska. What happened to most of the oil?

    (A) It was cleaned up by Exxon.
    (B) It eventually evaporated into the air.
    (C) It sank into the ground.
    (D) It biodegraded and photolyzed.
    (E) It dispersed into the water column.

19. Which of the following contributes LEAST to speciation?

    (A) Sexual reproduction
    (B) Asexual reproduction
    (C) Selection
    (D) Variation
    (E) Isolation

20. Which Act's primary goal is to protect human health and the environment from the potential hazards of waste disposal and calls for conservation of energy and natural resources, reduction in waste generated, and environmentally sound waste management practices?

    (A) RCRA
    (B) FIFRA
    (C) CERCLA
    (D) OSHA
    (E) FEMA

21. One of the earliest sites that utilized Superfund resources was

    (A) Bhopal, India
    (B) Love Canal, New York
    (C) Prince William Sound, Alaska
    (D) Chernobyl, Ukraine
    (E) Donora, Pennsylvania

22. Which growth curve best represents the effects of environmental resistance acting on a sustainable population?

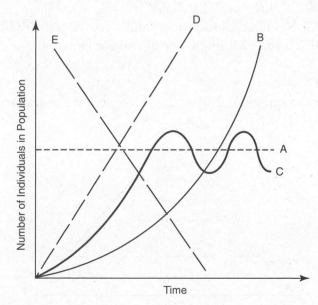

    (A) A
    (B) B
    (C) C
    (D) D
    (E) E

23. The location where two tectonic plates slide apart from each other with the space that was created being filled with molten magma from below, such as the Mid-Atlantic Ridge, the East Pacific Rise, and the East African Great Rift Valley, are known as

   (A) divergent boundaries
   (B) convergent boundaries
   (C) transform boundaries
   (D) tectonic boundaries
   (E) lithospheric boundaries

24. Radioactive materials, lead, arsenic, mercury, nickel, and benzene are all pollutants released from what type of electricity generating plant?

   (A) Hydroelectric
   (B) Solar
   (C) Coal-burning
   (D) Nuclear
   (E) Natural gas

25. On Michigan's Keweenaw Peninsula, copper mills discharged an estimated 200 million tons of copper-contaminated waste directly into Torch Lake, reducing its volume by 20% and leaving a toxic threat to fish and anyone who eats the fish. Which law listed below would address the damage that has been done at Torch Lake?

   (A) 1872 Mining Act
   (B) 1920 Mineral Leasing Act
   (C) 1980 Comprehensive Environmental Response, Compensation, and Liability Act (CERCLA)
   (D) 1976 Resource Conservation and Recovery Act (RCRA)
   (E) 1977 Surface Mining Control and Reclamation Act

Questions 26–27
Base your answers to questions 26 and 27 on the following diagram.

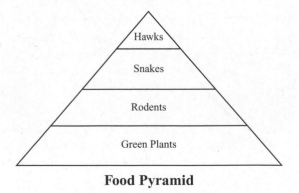

Food Pyramid

26. The greatest amount of energy present in this pyramid is found at the level of the

    (A) hawks
    (B) snakes
    (C) rodents
    (D) green plants
    (E) decomposers

27. The pyramid implies that in order to live and grow, 1,000 kilograms of snakes would require

    (A) less than 1,000 kilograms of green plants
    (B) 1,000 kilograms of rodents
    (C) more than 1,000 kilograms of rodents
    (D) no rodents
    (E) less than 1,000 kilograms of hawks

28. The type of planting in which an agricultural crop is grown simultaneously with a long-term tree crop to provide annual income while the tree crop matures is known as

    (A) crop rotation
    (B) alley cropping
    (C) monocropping
    (D sequential cropping
    (E) intercropping

29. If a city with a population of 100,000 experiences 4,000 births, 3,000 deaths, 500 immigrants, and 200 emigrants within the course of one year, what is the net annual percentage growth rate?

    (A) 0.3%
    (B) 1.3%
    (C) 13%
    (D) 101.3%
    (E) 130%

30. The annual productivity of any ecosystem is greater than the annual increase in biomass of the herbivores in the ecosystem because

    (A) plants convert energy input into biomass more efficiently than animals
    (B) there are always more animals than plants in any ecosystem
    (C) plants have a greater longevity than animals
    (D) during each energy transformation, some energy is lost
    (E) animals convert energy input into biomass more efficiently than plants

Questions 31–33

Following is a diagram showing the relationships that exist in an arid ecosystem. Base your answers to questions 31 through 33 on the diagram and your knowledge of environmental science.

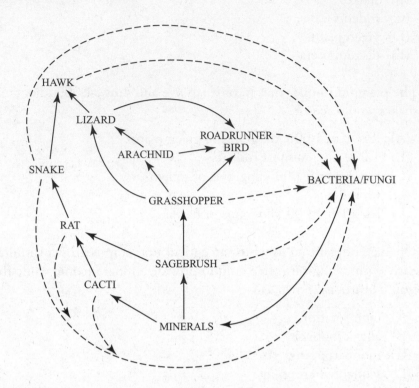

31. The snake is acting as a

    (A) producer
    (B) primary consumer
    (C) secondary consumer
    (D) autotroph
    (E) secondary producer

32. Between which two organisms would there MOST LIKELY be the greatest competition?

    (A) Rat and snake
    (B) Lizard and arachnid
    (C) Rat and roadrunner
    (D) Grasshopper and bacteria/fungi
    (E) Arachnid and roadrunner

33. In the diagram, which statement correctly describes the role of bacteria/ fungi?

   (A) The bacteria/fungi convert radiant energy into chemical energy.
   (B) The bacteria/fungi directly provide a source of nutrition for animals.
   (C) The bacteria/fungi are saprophytic agents restoring inorganic material to the environment.
   (D) The bacteria/fungi convert atmospheric nitrogen into minerals and are found in the nodules of cacti.
   (E) The bacteria/fungi consume live plants and animals.

34. When resources are scarce,

   (A) prices go down
   (B) recycling is not profitable
   (C) investment and potential profits decrease
   (D) there is an impetus for conservation
   (E) there is little competition to discover new or substitute products

35. Examine the three age-structure diagrams below:

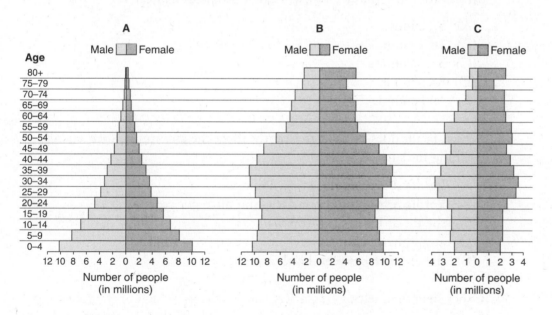

   Which of the age structure diagrams above would be typical for a country experiencing a rapid rate of population growth?

   (A) A
   (B) B
   (C) C
   (D) B and C
   (E) None of the above

36. The annual amount of incoming solar energy varies considerably from tropical to polar latitudes with the polar regions radiating away more thermal energy than they absorb from the Sun in the course of a year. The primary reason that the polar regions are not becoming progressively colder each year is because

    (A) large areas of upwelling in the polar seas keep heat circulating in the region
    (B) as ice melts, it releases its heat energy to the surroundings
    (C) the extensive cloud cover in the polar regions acts as a thermal blanket keeping whatever heat there is from escaping
    (D) underground "hot spots" in the polar seas keep the ocean temperatures in the area fairly stable
    (E) global heat energy is constantly being circulated through both ocean and air currents

37. Approximately five pounds of carbon is released into the atmosphere in the form of carbon dioxide for every gallon of gasoline that is burned. Two cars are making a 500 mile trip. Car A gets 15 miles to the gallon and car B gets 30 miles to the gallon. Approximately how much more carbon (in the form of CO_2) will car A produce than car B?

    (A) 5 pounds
    (B) 16.7 pounds
    (C) 33.3 pounds
    (D) 83 pounds
    (E) 100 pounds

38. Which factor does NOT significantly affect the amount of solar energy reaching the surface of Earth?

    (A) Earth's rotation once every 24 hours
    (B) Earth's revolution around the Sun once per year
    (C) the tilt of Earth's axis (23.5°)
    (D) atmospheric conditions
    (E) the distance between Earth and the Sun

39. Other than the melting of glaciers and ice sheets, which of the following factors has made the largest contribution to the global rise in sea level over the past 100 years?

    (A) Urbanization and its impact on estuaries
    (B) Melting of sea ice
    (C) Increased river runoff
    (D) Warming of ocean surface waters
    (E) Increase in rainfall

40. A chain is dragged across the seafloor, pulling a huge net behind it. A single pass of this net can remove up to a quarter of seafloor life. Repeated passes can remove nearly all seafloor life, including sessile animals and plants plus many species of fish and marine invertebrates. This type of fishing is known as

    (A) bottom trawling or dredging
    (B) chain-fishing
    (C) scraping
    (D) scoop netting
    (E) drag-lining

41. Which of the following items should NOT be placed in a compost pile?

    I.   Chemically treated wood products
    II.   Pet feces
    III. Manure
    IV.   Pernicious weeds
    V.   Bones

    (A) II
    (B) III
    (C) IV
    (D) I, II, IV, V
    (E) I, II, III, IV, V

42. Two-thirds of Iceland's energy sources come from clean, renewable hydro-electric and geothermal sources. Research in Iceland is currently underway in developing hydrogen fuel cells. Iceland is an example of a country that is practicing

    (A) sustainability
    (B) remediation
    (C) conservation
    (D) preservation
    (E) mitigation

43. An electrical power plant that uses X joules of energy derived from natural gas can generate a maximum of Y joules of electrical energy within the same amount of time. Which of the following is always true?

    (A) $X = Y$ due to the Law of Conservation of Energy.
    (B) $X < Y$ due to the First Law of Thermodynamics.
    (C) $X > Y$ due to the Second Law of Thermodynamics.
    (D) $X < Y$ due to the Second Law of Thermodynamics.
    (E) Depending upon the efficiency of the power plant, X could be equal to Y.

44. Which of the following statements are TRUE?

   I. The annual fluctuation of air temperature on land masses influenced by polar cells is greater than the change in temperature occurring in a 24-hour cycle.

   II. In land masses influenced by polar cells, precipitation rather than temperature is the critical factor in plant distribution and soil development.

   III. Land masses influenced primarily by Ferrel cells have defined seasons with strong annual cycles of temperature and precipitation.

   IV. Land masses in equatorial regions primarily influenced by Hadley cells are characterized by low humidity and little precipitation.

   V. Subtropical land masses primarily influenced by Hadley cells are characterized by high relative humidity and tropical forests.

   (A) I and III
   (B) I, II, and IV
   (C) II and III
   (D) III and V
   (E) I, II, IV, and V

45. As urban environments become denser, noise pollution is becoming a major environmental issue as people deal with noise generated from flight paths, freeways, work environments, and neighborhoods. Which of the following is a TRUE statement?

   (A) Loud sound is not dangerous as long as you do not feel any pain in your ears.
   (B) Hearing loss after sound exposure is temporary.
   (C) Hearing loss is caused mostly by aging.
   (D) Loud sound damages only your hearing.
   (E) If you have a hearing loss already, you still have to protect your hearing.

46. What is meant by the term "enriched" uranium?

   (A) pure uranium, with no other elements present
   (B) all nuclei are U-238 in the sample
   (C) uranium that has been rinsed in heavy water to enrich it
   (D) uranium that has a higher proportion of U-235 nuclei than normal
   (E) uranium that has had plutonium added to it

47. Which of the following is NOT a benefit associated with integrated pest management?

   (A) More reliable and effective pest control
   (B) Reduction in the use of the most hazardous pesticides
   (C) Lessening the chance of pesticide resistance developing
   (D) Total elimination of pest species
   (E) All choices are benefits of integrated pest management

48. Which of the following statements about the role of carbon dioxide (CO_2) in the carbon cycle are TRUE?

    I.   Carbon dioxide is produced during photosynthesis
    II. Carbon dioxide concentration in the atmosphere decreases when trees are cut down and the trees decay
    III. The primary non-anthropomorphic source of carbon dioxide is outgassing from the Earth's interior

    (A) I only
    (B) II only
    (C) III only
    (D) II and III only
    (E) I, II, and III

Questions 49–50 refer to the following air pollutants

    (A) Nitrogen dioxide (NO_2)
    (B) Peroxyacl nitrates (PANs)
    (C) Volatile organic compounds (VOCs)
    (D) Ozone (O_3)
    (E) Particulates (PM_{10})

49. Powerful respiratory and eye irritants present in photochemical smog. They are secondary air pollutants, not directly emitted as exhaust from power plants or internal combustion engines, and formed from other pollutants by chemical reactions in the atmosphere.

50. Commonly found in paints and solvents. Examples include benzene, acetone, and formaldehyde.

51. Most commercial fish are caught in which ocean?

    (A) Atlantic
    (B) Indian
    (C) Arctic
    (D) Southern
    (E) Pacific

52. Why is the bioaccumulation of harmful chemicals especially destructive in species such as salmon?

    (A) Salmon migrate long distances, allowing them to spread harmful chemicals into many different ecosystems.
    (B) Salmon are tertiary consumers and are at the top of the food pyramid.
    (C) Salmon are a keystone species, meaning they are "key" in the health of the ecosystem(s) they inhabit.
    (D) Salmon are an increasingly endangered species.
    (E) All of the above are true.

53. Characteristics typical of an oligotrophic lake include which of the following?

    I.   High dissolved oxygen content
    II. High primary productivity
    III. Clear water

    (A) I only
    (B) II only
    (C) III only
    (D) I and III only
    (E) I, II, and III

54. Which federal agency listed below does NOT manage designated federal wilderness areas in the United States?

    (A) National Park Service
    (B) Forest Service
    (C) Bureau of Land Management
    (D) Fish and Wildlife Service
    (E) All share management

55. The greatest environmental impact to using compact fluorescent lightbulbs (CFL) is that they

    (A) are not energy efficient
    (B) contain mercury
    (C) take much longer to start than incandescent lightbulbs
    (D) are more expensive compared to incandescent lightbulbs
    (E) All of the above

56. A compact fluorescent lightbulb (CFL) used for lighting has an efficiency rating of 10%. If for every 10.00 joule of electrical energy consumed by the bulb, which of the following is produced?

    (A) 0.90 joules of light energy
    (B) 1.00 joule of light energy
    (C) 9.00 joules of light energy
    (D) 9.90 joules of heat energy
    (E) 9.90 joules of light energy

Questions 57–58

In 1940, ranchers introduced cattle into an area. The graph below shows the effect of cattle ranching on the populations of two organisms present in the area before the introduction of the cattle. Base your answers to questions 57 and 58 on the graph and on your knowledge of environmental science.

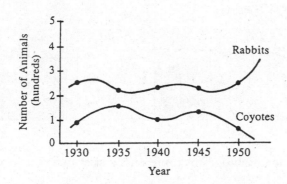

57. The most probable reason for the increase in the rabbit population after 1950 was

    (A) more food became available to the rabbits
    (B) the coyote population declined drastically
    (C) the cattle created a more favorable environment for the rabbits
    (D) the coyotes and cattle competed for the same food
    (E) the coyote population increased

58. If the interrelationship of rabbits and coyotes was once in balance, what is the most probable explanation for the decline of the coyotes?

    (A) Mutations
    (B) Starvation
    (C) Disease
    (D) Increase in reproductive rate
    (E) Removal by human beings

Questions 59–60

Questions 59 and 60 refer to the following graphs of temperature and rainfall for six major ecosystems. A year's temperature from January through December (the line) and rainfall pattern (the shaded area) of each ecosystem are shown.

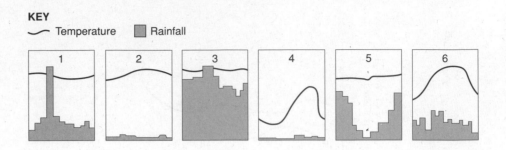

59. Which of the climatograms represents a savanna?

    (A) 1

    (B) 2

    (C) 3

    (D) 5

    (E) 6

60. Which represents a tundra?

    (A) 1

    (B) 2

    (C) 3

    (D) 4

    (E) 5

Question 61

Examine the timber cutting cycle below for Question 61.

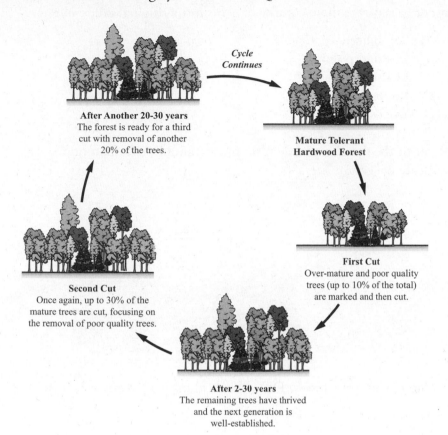

Cycle Continues

After Another 20-30 years
The forest is ready for a third cut with removal of another 20% of the trees.

Mature Tolerant Hardwood Forest

First Cut
Over-mature and poor quality trees (up to 10% of the total) are marked and then cut.

Second Cut
Once again, up to 30% of the mature trees are cut, focusing on the removal of poor quality trees.

After 2-30 years
The remaining trees have thrived and the next generation is well-established.

61. Which form of timber harvesting is represented above?

   (A) Clear-cutting
   (B) Shelterwood cutting
   (C) Selective cutting
   (D) Seed tree harvesting
   (E) None of the above

62. Rank the following biomes in order of most productive to least productive, as measured by biomass produced per acre.

   I. Desert
   II. Tropical rain forests
   III. Tundra
   IV. Grassland

   (A) I, II, III, IV
   (B) IV, III, II, I
   (C) III, I, IV, II
   (D) II, III, IV, I
   (E) II, IV, III, I

63. Kerosene, gasoline, motor oil, asphalt, tar, waxes, and diesel fuel all come from crude oil. Refineries take advantage of what physical property in order to separate these components from the original crude oil?

    (A) Solubility
    (B) Freezing point
    (C) Density
    (D) Boiling point
    (E) Viscosity

64. Refer to the data below taken from a stream. The Roman numerals indicate collection sites.

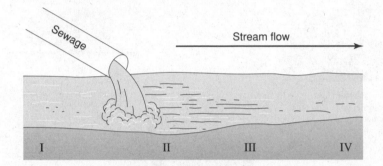

    Where would the lowest DO (dissolved oxygen) content be expected?

    (A) I
    (B) II
    (C) III
    (D) IV
    (E) Dissolved oxygen would not be affected by sewage effluent. Therefore, DO would be equal at all points.

65. The theory that great disasters serve to maintain a population and its food supply balance was initially proposed by

    (A) Darwin
    (B) Wallace
    (C) Hardy and Weinberg
    (D) Malthus
    (E) Lyell

Questions 66–67

The following graph shows survival rates for five animal populations. When survival curves are calculated, the following assumptions are made:

    I. All individuals of a given population are the same age.
    II. No new individuals enter the population.
    III. No individuals leave the population.

These curves show the relationship of the number of individuals in a population to units of physiological life span. Base your answers to questions 66 and 67 on the graph and on your knowledge of environmental science.

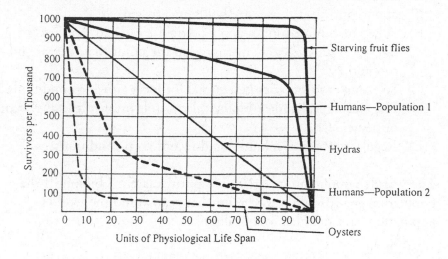

66. According to the data, it can be assumed that

    (A) fruit flies live longer than humans
    (B) oysters outlive fruit flies
    (C) the population of hydras is steadily declining
    (D) the life span of human populations is related to that of oysters
    (E) there is a high mortality rate among young oysters

67. The survival curves indicate that

    (A) starving fruit flies live out their full life span
    (B) human populations are more vulnerable than hydras
    (C) human population 2 has a greater rate of survival than human population 1
    (D) the hydra has a longer life span than the oyster
    (E) fruit flies die directly after pupation

68. The average requirement for drinking water per person per day is approximately

    (A) 1 pint
    (B) 1 quart
    (C) ½ gallon
    (D) 1 gallon
    (E) 3 gallons

69. Which of the following are NOT principles of Integrated Pest Management (IPM)?

    (A) Establishing acceptable pest levels, called action thresholds, and apply controls if those thresholds are crossed.
    (B) When insects are found, apply pesticides early so that insect biological life cycles are disrupted to the point that they are unable to multiply.
    (C) Selecting crop varieties best suited for local growing conditions.
    (D) Use mechanical and/or biological controls prior to the application of pesticides.
    (E) Regularly observe, monitor, and record crop conditions.

70. The world's population in 2010 was approximately 7 billion. If the population growth rate was 2%, in what year would the world's population have doubled to 14 billion?

    (A) 2020
    (B) 2045
    (C) 2090
    (D) 2100
    (E) 2110

71. In 1900 the amount of carbon dioxide gas released into the atmosphere by human activity was estimated to be 250 million metric tons per year. By the year 2000, this amount had increased to just over 350 million metric tons per year. What is the approximate percent increase in carbon dioxide concentration from 1900 to 2000?

    (A) 20%
    (B) 40%
    (C) 80%
    (D) 120%
    (E) 150%

72. Which of the following is NOT an acceptable mitigation technique used to reverse the process of desertification?

    (A) Fixating the soil through the use of shelter belts, woodlots, and windbreaks
    (B) Hyper-fertilizing the soil
    (C) Encourage large scale cultivation of the land to hold the soil in place
    (D) Reforestation
    (E) Provisioning of water

73. Which of the following statements is NOT consistent with "The Tragedy of the Commons" by Garret Hardin?

    (A) We will always add one too many cows to the village commons, destroying it.
    (B) The destruction of the commons will not be stopped by shame, moral admonitions, or cultural mores anywhere nearly so effectively as it will be by the will of the people expressed as a protective mandate, in other words, by government.
    (C) The "Tragedy of the Commons" is a modern phenomenon. Humans were not capable of doing too much damage until the population exceeded certain numbers and their technological tools became powerful beyond a certain point.
    (D) A free-market economy, based on capitalism, does not contribute to the "Tragedy of the Commons."
    (E) We will always opt for an immediate benefit at the expense of less-tangible values such as the availability of a resource to future generations.

74. The most common method of disposing of municipal solid wastes in the United States is

    (A) incineration
    (B) ocean dumping
    (C) sanitary landfills
    (D) recycling
    (E) exporting

75. Place the following events in sequential order

    I.   Atmospheric CO_2 increases
    II. Warmer Ocean
    III. Warmer Atmosphere
    IV. Less CO_2 uptake by the oceans

    (A) I → II → III → IV
    (B) II → IV → I → III
    (C) IV → II → I → III
    (D) II → III → I → IV
    (E) III → II → I → IV

76. A new wide-range pesticide was being tested for efficacy on five species of insects. Which of the graphs below represents the insect species that would have the greatest potential over time for developing resistance to the pesticide?

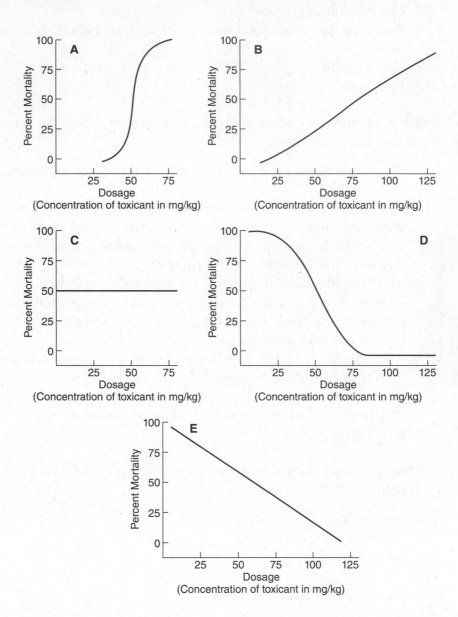

(A) A
(B) B
(C) C
(D) D
(E) E

77. The densest populations of most organisms that live in the ocean are found near the surface. The most probable explanation is that

    (A) the surface is less polluted
    (B) the bottom contains radioactive material
    (C) salt water has more minerals than freshwater
    (D) the light intensity that reaches the ocean decreases with increasing depth
    (E) the largest primary consumers are found near the surface

78. Of the following sources of pollution, which would NOT be classified as a point source of pollution?

    I.   Sulfur oxides released from an electrical generating plant
    II. Oil, grease, and toxic chemicals showing up in a stream
    III. Cyanide leaking from a heap leach pile at an abandoned gold mine site
    IV. Diesel exhaust soot coming from trucks on the interstate

    (A) I and III
    (B) I and IV
    (C) II and IV
    (D) I, III, and IV
    (E) I, II, III, and IV

79. Certain volcanoes are built almost entirely of fluid lava flows that pour out in all directions from a central summit vent or groups of vents. They build a broad, gently sloping, dome-shaped cone. These cones are built up slowly by the accretion of thousands of highly fluid basalt lava flows that spread widely over great distances and then cool as thin, gently, dipping sheets. These types of volcanoes are known as

    (A) Lava domes
    (B) Composite volcanoes
    (C) Cinder cones
    (D) Shield volcanoes
    (E) Stratovolcanoes

80. Of the causes of preventable deaths in the United States listed below, which one causes the MOST deaths per year?

    (A) AIDS
    (B) Illegal drug use
    (C) Alcohol use
    (D) Smoking
    (D) Motor vehicle accidents

Questions 81–83 refer to the locations marked by letters in the world map below.

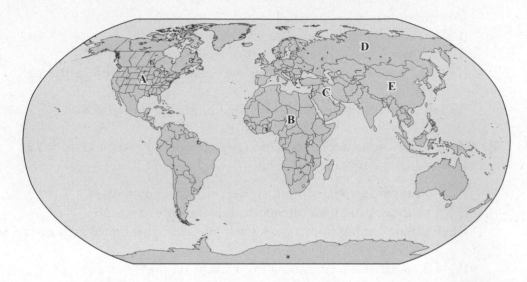

81. The location with the greatest oil reserves.

82. The area with the greatest coal reserves.

83. The area with the greatest natural gas reserves.

84. Which pair of compounds listed below reacts with H_2O to produce acid rain?

   (A) NH_3 and SO_2
   (B) CO and SO_2
   (C) CO_2 and H_2O_2
   (D) SO_3 and NO_3
   (E) SO_2 and NO_x

85. If current population trends continue, which regions of the world will experience the greatest population growth in the next 25 years?

   I.   Central and South America
   II. Africa
   III. Asia

   (A) I only
   (B) II only
   (C) III only
   (D) I and II
   (E) II and III

86. One of the greatest successes of the Endangered Species Act has been the

    (A) passenger pigeon
    (B) whooping crane
    (C) bald eagle
    (D) condor
    (E) auk

87. If global temperature warmed for any reason, atmospheric water vapor would increase due to evaporation. This would increase the greenhouse effect and thereby further raise the temperature. As a result, the ice caps would melt back, making the planet less reflective so that it would warm further. This process is an example of

    (A) positive coupling
    (B) negative coupling
    (C) synergistic feedback
    (D) positive-feedback loop
    (E) negative-feedback loop

88. The most abundant non-anthropogenic greenhouse gas is

    (A) water vapor
    (B) carbon dioxide
    (C) nitrogen
    (D) methane
    (E) tropospheric ozone

89. What is the most frequent cause of beach pollution?

    (A) Polluted runoff and storm water
    (B) Sewage spills from treatment plants
    (C) Oil spills
    (D) Ships dumping their holding tanks into coastal waters
    (E) People leaving their trash on the beach

90. Atmospheric carbon dioxide levels

    (A) are about 10% higher than they were at the time of the Industrial Revolution
    (B) are about 25% higher than they were at the time of the Industrial Revolution
    (C) are about the same as they were at the time of the Industrial Revolution
    (D) are slightly lower than they were at the time of the Industrial Revolution
    (E) are significantly lower than they were at the time of the Industrial Revolution

Question 91

For question 91 use the following information: A scientific study took ice core samples to measure the concentration of carbon dioxide that was present in the atmosphere for the last 1,000 years. Their findings are shown below:

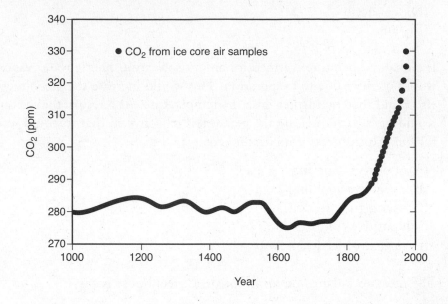

91. Which of the following mathematical setups could be used to determine the approximate percentage increase in carbon dioxide concentration over the last 1,000 years (use the year 1000 as the base year for comparison)?

(A) $\dfrac{330 \text{ ppm} - 280 \text{ ppm}}{280 \text{ ppm}} \times 100\%$

(B) $\dfrac{330 \text{ ppm} + 280 \text{ ppm}}{2} \times 100\%$

(C) $\dfrac{330 \text{ ppm} - 280 \text{ ppm}}{50 \text{ ppm}} \times 100\%$

(D) $\dfrac{330 \text{ ppm} + 280 \text{ ppm}}{330 \text{ ppm}} \times 100\%$

(E) $\dfrac{330 \text{ ppm} + 280 \text{ ppm}}{50 \text{ ppm}} \times 100\%$

92. The major sink for phosphorus is

(A) marine sediments
(B) atmospheric gases
(C) seawater
(D) plants
(E) animals

93. A large agricultural company that manufactures pesticides had developed a new insecticide to kill a certain species of aphid that was damaging citrus crops. After repeated testing using rats, the results are presented below. Which of the following statements listed below is the most accurate statement regarding this insecticide?

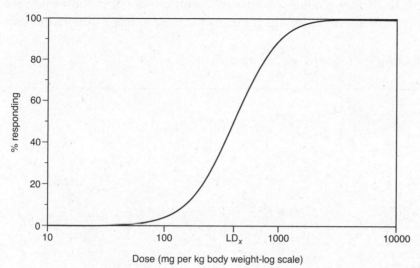

(A) Any aphid receiving 400 mg of this insecticide will die.
(B) For every 100 rats exposed to 400 mg of this insecticide, 50 will die.
(C) For every one kilogram of aphids receiving 400 mg of this insecticide, 50% of them will die.
(D) Out of 100 rats each receiving a dose of 400 mg of this insecticide per kilogram of body weight, 50 will die.
(E) Out of 100 people exposed to 400 mg of this insecticide, 50 will become acutely ill and die.

94. Which of the following would NOT be a likely location for seismic activity?

(A) Along mid-oceanic ridges
(B) Faults associated with volcanic activity
(C) Boundaries between oceanic and continental plates
(D) Interior of continental plates
(E) Boundaries between continental plates

95. Which of the following statements is correct for the third stage of the demographic transition model?

    (A) Birthrate increasing, death rate falling, total population increasing
    (B) Birthrate low, death rate low, total population high and constant
    (C) Birthrate falling, death rate high, total population increasing
    (D) Birthrate falling, death rate falling, total population increasing
    (E) Birthrate high, death rate low, total population high and constant

96. Examine the following weather map.

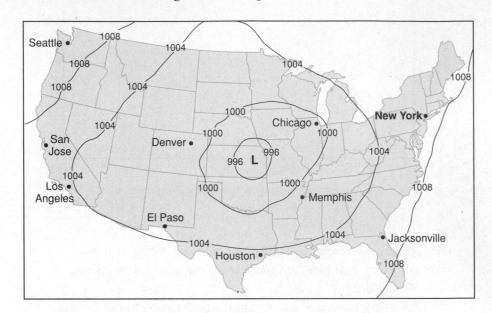

    Which of the following would be TRUE?

    (A) It is likely to be fair weather in the Midwest.
    (B) It is likely to be raining in the Midwest.
    (C) It is likely to be raining in the Northeast.
    (D) Rain would be expected in the western United States.
    (E) Not enough information is provided.

97. The concentration of H^+ ions in a solution with a pH value of 3 is how many times as great as the concentration of H^+ ions in a solution with a pH of 6?

    (A) 2
    (B) 3
    (C) 100
    (D) 1,000
    (E) 10,000

98. Causes of sick building syndrome include all of the following EXCEPT

    (A) radon and asbestos
    (B) chemical contaminants from indoor sources
    (C) chemical contaminants from outdoor sources
    (D) biological contaminants
    (E) inadequate ventilation

99. Which of the following statements is FALSE?

    (A) Evidence exists of a dose-response relationship between nonmela-noma skin cancer and cumulative exposure to UVB radiation.
    (B) Individuals, usually those living in areas with limited sunlight and long, dark winters, may suffer severe photo-allergies to the UVB in sunlight.
    (C) Increased absorption of UVB triggers a thickening of the superficial skin layers and an increase in skin pigmentation.
    (D) There is a relationship between skin cancer prevalence and increases in ultraviolet radiation due to the depletion of tropospheric ozone.
    (E) Acute exposure to UVB causes sunburn, and chronic exposure results in loss of elasticity and increased skin aging.

100. Of the following choices listed below, which constitutes the greatest percent of global freshwater use?

    (A) Domestic use other than drinking (cooking, flushing toilets, showering, etc.)
    (B) Use in energy production
    (C) Agriculture
    (D) Industry
    (E) Drinking

SECTION II (FREE-RESPONSE QUESTIONS)

Time: 90 minutes

No calculators allowed

4 questions

> **Directions:** Answer all four questions, which are weighted equally. The suggested time is about 22 minutes for answering each question. Write all your answers on the pages following the questions in the pink booklet. Where calculations are required, clearly show how you arrived at your answer. Where explanation or discussion is required, support your answers with relevant information and/or specific examples.

1. The environmental impact of washing a load of clothes in an electric washing machine is different than washing the same clothes by hand. Use the information below to answer the questions that follow. Show your calculations.

   Assume the following:

   1. All of the clothes can be washed in one load in the washing machine.

   2. The water entering the water heater is 60°F.

   3. The water leaving the water heater is 130°F.

   4. The electric washing machine uses 20 gallons of water. It uses 110 volts of electricity at an average of 1,500 watts for 30 minutes.

   5. Washing the clothes by hand requires 35 gallons of hot water.

   Other information:

   1 gallon of water = 8 pounds
   1 Btu = amount of energy required to raise the temperature of 1 pound of water by 1°F
   1 kilowatt-hour = 3,400 Btus

   (a) Calculate the total amount of energy (in Btus) to wash the clothes using the washing machine.
   (b) Calculate the total amount of energy (in Btus) to wash the clothes by hand.
   (c) Discuss the economic and environmental costs and benefits of using a washing machine in terms of

       (i)   its manufacture and disposal
       (ii)   selecting one and purchasing it (specifically, how can consumers compare various appliances in terms of their energy use)
       (iii)   steps consumers can take to reduce its environmental impact

2. An AP Environmental Science class did an investigation on competition. Part I of the investigation focused on intraspecific competition to assess the effect of growth among radish plants at different population densities. Part II of the investigation focused on the relative competitiveness of two species of plants (radish and wheat) when they were planted together. The results are presented below:

Part I: Intraspecific Competition Among Radish Plants

Seeds per Pot	Total Biomass per Pot (g)
1	5.0
10	70.0
20	75.0

Part II: Interspecific Competition Between Radish and Wheat Plants

Seeds per Pot	Total Biomass per Pot (g)
1 radish	5.0
1 wheat	3.0
10 radish	50.0
10 wheat	25.0
20 radish	75.0
20 wheat	40.0

(a) Discuss the results of Part I of the investigation.

    (i)   At what population density was the biomass per plant highest?

    (ii)   Identify and describe two resources that may have been limited.

    (iii)   Discuss the results obtained from the class for Part I in terms of two biological laws or principles.

(b) Discuss the results of Part II of the investigation.

    (i)   Which plant was most affected by the competition between the two species?

    (ii)   Describe TWO possible reasons why the plant chosen in (i) above may have been more successful.

    (iii)   Discuss the results obtained from the class for Part II in terms of two biological laws or principles.

3. Examine the age-structure diagrams of Sweden and Kenya below, and answer the following questions.

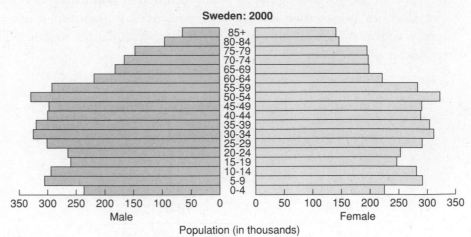

Sweden: 2000

Population (in thousands)

Source: U.S. Census Bureau, International Data Base.

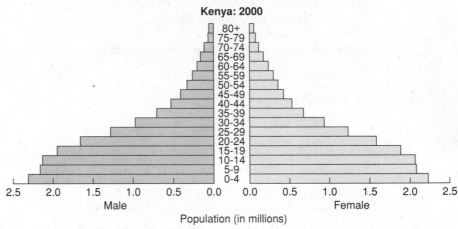

Kenya: 2000

Population (in millions)

Source: U.S. Census Bureau, International Data Base.

(a) Compare and contrast the two age structure diagrams in terms of two population dynamics—birthrate and death rate.

(b) What factors affect birthrates and death rates?

(c) Discuss methods that have been employed in another country to curb population growth.

4. Pesticides have become the most widely used form of pest management and are a controversial topic in environmental science.

(a) Explain what a pesticide is.

    (i) Describe TWO major categories of pesticides. For example: Insecticide—kills insects and other arthropods. (Do NOT use insecticide as one of your categories.)

    (ii) Identify and discuss TWO positive effects of pesticide use.

    (iii) Identify and discuss TWO negative effects of pesticide use.

(b) Discuss TWO alternatives to the use of pesticides.

(c) Name and describe ONE U.S. federal law *OR* ONE international treaty that focuses on the use of pesticides.

ANSWER KEY

Practice Test 1

Section I (Multiple-Choice Questions)

1. C	26. D	51. E	76. B
2. D	27. C	52. C	77. D
3. C	28. B	53. D	78. C
4. E	29. B	54. E	79. D
5. B	30. D	55. B	80. D
6. D	31. C	56. B	81. C
7. E	32. B	57. B	82. A
8. B	33. C	58. E	83. D
9. D	34. D	59. A	84. E
10. E	35. A	60. D	85. E
11. B	36. E	61. C	86. C
12. D	37. D	62. E	87. D
13. A	38. E	63. D	88. A
14. D	39. D	64. C	89. A
15. C	40. A	65. D	90. B
16. C	41. D	66. E	91. A
17. C	42. A	67. A	92. A
18. D	43. C	68. C	93. D
19. B	44. A	69. B	94. D
20. A	45. E	70. B	95. D
21. B	46. D	71. B	96. B
22. C	47. D	72. C	97. D
23. A	48. C	73. D	98. A
24. C	49. B	74. C	99. D
25. C	50. C	75. B	100. C

PREDICT YOUR SCORE ON THE APES EXAM

Place a check mark (✔) next to the multiple-choice questions you got correct on page 469. Then fill in the blanks below to predict your overall score on the APES exam. Essay questions are not used in this prediction as they require subjective grading. You can also use this page to determine your areas of weakness. For example, if you got 5 out of 5 questions correct on the topic The Earth, but only 2 out of 5 questions correct on the topic The Atmosphere, spend some more time reviewing The Atmosphere.

Unit I EARTH SYSTEMS AND RESOURCES (10–15%)

Chapter 1 The Earth
(#2, 14, 23, 79, 94)   _____ correct/5 = _____%

Chapter 2 The Atmosphere
(#7, 36, 38, 44, 96)   _____ correct/5 = _____%

Chapter 3 Global Water Resources and Use
(#8, 39, 53, 68, 100)   _____ correct/5 = _____%

Unit II THE LIVING WORLD (10–15%)

Chapter 4 Ecosystems
(#1, 15, 19, 22, 26, 27, 30, 31, 32, 33, 59, 60)   _____ correct/12 = _____%

Chapter 5 Natural Biogeochemical Cycles
(#5, 48, 92)   _____ correct/3 = _____%

Unit III POPULATIONS (10–15%)

Chapter 6 Populations
(#29, 35, 57, 58, 65, 66, 67, 70, 85, 95)   _____ correct/10 = _____%

Unit IV LAND AND WATER USE (10–15%)

Chapter 7 Land and Water Use
(#6, 11, 17, 25, 28, 40, 47, 51, 54, 61, 69, 72, 73, 76)   _____ correct/14 = _____%

Unit V ENERGY RESOURCES AND CONSUMPTION (10–15%)

Chapter 8 Energy
(#24, 42, 43, 46, 55, 56, 63, 81, 82, 83)   _____ correct/10 = _____%

Unit VI POLLUTION (25–30%)

Chapter 9 Pollution
(#9, 13, 16, 18, 20, 21, 37, 41, 45, 49,
50, 64, 74, 78, 84, 89, 97, 98)   _____ correct/18 = _____%

Chapter 10 Impacts on the Human
Environment
(#4, 12, 34, 52, 80, 93, 99)   _____ correct/7 = _____%

Unit VII GLOBAL CHANGE (10–15%)

Chapter 11 Stratospheric Ozone and
Global Warming
(#3, 10, 62, 71, 75, 77, 86, 87, 88,
90, 91)   _____ correct/11 = _____%

Total Number Correct _____ / 100 = _____%

PREDICTED AP SCORE*	
Less than 50 correct:	1 or 2 (not passing)
50–60 correct:	3 on the APES exam
61–75 correct:	4 on the APES exam
76+ correct:	5 on the APES exam

*Please note this is a rough estimate and is not intended to be an indicator of an actual AP score.

MULTIPLE-CHOICE EXPLANATIONS

1. **(C)** An increase in the population of squirrels would increase the competition for food and space.

2. **(D)** Approximately 3.5 billion years ago, the earliest life appeared on Earth, possibly derived from self-reproducing RNA molecules. DNA molecules eventually evolved and the first genomes soon developed inside enclosed membranes, which provided a stable physical and chemical environment conducive to their replication.

3. **(C)** For (C) to be true, it would have read, "The Kyoto Protocol would have required the United States to *reduce* its greenhouse gas emissions—primarily carbon dioxide (CO_2), methane (CH_4), and nitrous oxide (N_2O)—to 7% below 1990 levels by the year 2012."

4. **(E)** External costs are the costs that are borne by people other than the producer of a product.

5. **(B)** Nitrogen is the fourth most abundant element in living things, being a major constituent of proteins and nucleic acids. Ammonia is produced by the breakdown of these organic sources of nitrogen when organisms die. Nitrification is the process by which this ammonia is converted to nitrites (NO_2^-) by bacteria of the genus *Nitrosomonas* and then to nitrates (NO_3^-) by bacteria of the genus *Nitrobacter*.

6. **(D)** Mitigation involves taking steps to lessen risk by lowering the probability of a risk event's occurrence or reducing its effect should it occur. Organizing a beach cleanup is remediation—reacting after the beach has been polluted.

7. **(E)** The easterly trade winds are driven by a surface pressure pattern of higher pressure in the eastern Pacific and lower pressure in the west. When this pressure gradient weakens, so do the trade winds. The weakened trade winds allow warmer water from the western Pacific to surge eastward leading to a buildup of warm surface water and a sinking of the thermocline in the eastern Pacific. The deeper thermocline limits the amount of nutrient-rich deep water tapped by upwelling processes. These nutrients are vital for sustaining the large fish populations normally found in the region and any reduction in the supply of nutrients means a reduction in the fish population. Convective clouds and heavy rains are fueled by increased buoyancy of the lower atmosphere resulting from heating by the warmer waters below. As the warmer water shifts eastward, so do the clouds and thunderstorms associated with it, resulting in dry conditioning in Indonesia and Australia, while more flood-like conditions exist in Peru and Ecuador. The air-sea interaction that occurs during an El Niño event feed off of each other. As the pressure falls in the east and rises in the west, the surface pressure gradient is reduced and the trade winds weaken. This allows more warm surface water to flow eastward, which brings with it more rain, which leads to a further decrease of pressure in the east because the latent condensation warms the air.

8. **(B)** Refer to page 135. Of the total freshwater on Earth, over 68% is locked up in ice and glaciers. However, as ice and glaciers melt, this number will change significantly. Another 30% of freshwater is in the ground. Rivers are the source of most of the fresh surface water people use, but they only constitute about 0.0002% of the total freshwater on Earth.

9. **(D)** About 38% of municipal solid waste (before recycling) by weight is paper and paper products. Papermaking has an effect on the environment in how and where raw materials are acquired and processed and its impact on waste disposal. About 90% of paper is made of wood and accounts for about 35% of felled trees. Trees grown specifically for paper production account for 16% of all trees commercially grown and 9% of old growth forests. The manufacture and use of recycled paper products results in 35% less water pollution and 74% less air pollution than producing paper from trees. The average per capita paper use worldwide was 110 pounds (50 kg). Recycling 1 ton (0.91 m.t) of paper saves 17 mature trees, 7,000 gallons (26 m^3) of water, 3 cubic yards (2.3 m^3) of landfill space, 2 barrels of oil (84 US gal or 320 l), and 4,100 kilowatt-hours (15 GJ) of electricity—enough energy to power the average American home for six months. Packaging is the single largest category of paper use at 41% of all paper used. Around 115 billion sheets of paper are used annually for personal computers while the average web user prints 28 pages daily.

10. **(E)** Sea level is rising worldwide and is caused by both natural and human factors. It is predicted that within 100 years, there will be a net loss of 17–43% of coastal wetlands due to rising sea levels.

11. **(B)** Ground fires generally kill large and small trees because of the long and high temperature heat pulse generated. They release considerable amounts of nutrients from the burned fuels, destroy many small organisms and fungi that live in the humus and organic layers, consume seed stored in the litter, and kill roots in all but deep soil layers. They increase the chance of surface flow and erosion on slopes, and leave a baked and hardened seedbed that may prevent rapid revegetation. Increased surface runoff across the exposed surface may carry away ash and dissolved nutrients, making conditions even less favorable for plant growth.

12. **(D)** Primary economic activities (III) are at the beginning of the production cycle where humans are in closest contact with resources and the environment. Primary economic activities are located at the site of the natural resources being exploited. In many developing nations, approximately 3/4 of the labor force engages in subsistence farming or herding. By contrast, in highly developed countries only a small fraction of the labor force is directly employed in agriculture (less than 3% in the U.S.).

   Secondary economic activities (I) use raw materials to produce or manufacture something new and more valuable. Examples of secondary activities include manufacturing, processing, producing power, and construction. Secondary economic activities are located either at the resource site or in close proximity to the market for the manufactured/processed good. Location depends upon whether the raw material or finished product costs more to ship. The major share of global secondary manufacturing activity is found within a relatively small number of major industrial concentrations. Rather than manufacturing/producing within its own country, richer nations often "set up shop" in developing nations because costs are significantly cheaper.

   Tertiary economic activities (IV) include all activities that amount to doing services for others. Doctors, teachers, and secretaries provide personal and professional services. Restaurant staff, store clerks, and hotel personnel provide retail and wholesale services.

Quaternary economic activities (II) are not connected to resources, access to a market, or the environment. Rather, they include professions that process, administer, and disseminate information. Computer engineers, professors, and lawyers serve as examples of white-collar professionals who specialize in the collection and manipulation of information. With vast advancements in technology, quaternary economic activities could potentially exist anywhere. However, typically they exist in nations that have access to research centers, universities, efficient transportation and communication networks, and a pool of highly trained, skilled, flexible workers. Quaternary economic activities loom large in highly advanced, developed societies.

13. **(A)** Plastic makes up 90% of all trash floating in the oceans, enough that, in some areas, plastic outweighs plankton by a ratio of 6 to 1. A circular pattern of currents, called the North Pacific Subtropical Gyre, has corralled an enormous vortex of floating garbage, often referred to as the Great Pacific Garbage Patch. About 80% of the debris in the Great Pacific Garbage Patch, which ranges from bottles and fishing gear to toothbrushes and packaging scraps, came from land.

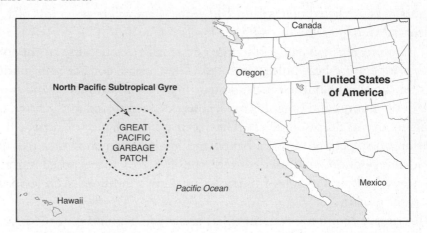

14. **(D)** Refer to Figure 1.3 (page 78).

15. **(C)** Coral reefs are among the most ancient of ecosystem types, dating back to the Mesozoic era some 225 million years ago. The release of carbon dioxide from coral reefs is very small (probably less than 100 million tons of carbon per year) relative to emissions due to fossil fuel combustion (about 5.7 billion tons of carbon per year). Coral reefs store very little organic carbon and are not very effective sinks for carbon dioxide from the atmosphere. Forests are more effective sinks for atmospheric carbon. Although tropical rain forests contain more species than coral reefs, reefs contain more phyla than rain forests. Covering less than 0.2% of the ocean floor, coral reefs contain perhaps 1/4 of all marine species. Despite their limited area, coral reefs may be home to up to 25% of the fish catch of developing countries or 10% of the total amount of fish caught globally for human consumption as food. Coral reefs in 93 of the 109 countries containing them have been damaged or destroyed by human activities. In addition, human impacts may have directly or indirectly caused the death of 5–10% of the world's living reefs. If the pace of destruction is maintained, another 60% could be lost in the next 20 to 40 years. The most important short-term threats to coral reefs are sedimentation (from poor land

use such as clear-cutting on steep slopes and other activities such as dredging, eutrophication (overfertilization and sewage pollution), and destructive fishing methods (dynamiting and overharvesting).

16. **(C)** Green taxes are taxes levied by the government on industries for each unit of pollution and are a source of governmental income. Government subsidies for reducing pollution are limited when industries surpass a break-even point or optimum level of pollution—the point at which cleanup costs exceed the harmful costs of pollution. Regulation is a command-and-control governmental approach that incurs costs to enact and enforce laws, set standards, regulate and monitor potentially harmful activities, and prosecute violators. Furthermore, regulation often focuses on cleanup instead of prevention, discourages innovation by mandating prescribed pollution control strategies, and is often unrealistic with the realities of a competitive global business environment. Charging a user fee provides income to the government by charging industries to utilize a natural resource. Trading pollution or resource use rights occurs between companies. Permits are allocated by the government for certain levels of pollution, and companies are free to trade unused pollution allocations. Once permits are sold or auctioned by the government, further financial impacts occur between the companies, not between the companies and the government. Permits often allow the largest and most financially secure companies to pollute the most, may concentrate pollutants at the most-polluting sites, and may not create economic incentives to reduce pollution since pollution levels are simply moved, not reduced.

17. **(C)** The Green Revolution refers to a series of research, development, and technology transfer initiatives, occurring between the 1940s and the late 1970s, that increased agriculture production around the world. The crops developed during the Green Revolution were high yield varieties, which were bred specifically to respond to fertilizers and produce an increased amount of grain per acre planted. In the 1940s, research began in Mexico that developed new disease-resistant, high-yield varieties of wheat. By combining new wheat varieties with new mechanized agricultural technologies, Mexico was able to produce more wheat than was needed by its own citizens, leading to its becoming an exporter of wheat by the 1960s. Prior to the use of these varieties, the country was importing almost half of its wheat supply. Due to the success of the Green Revolution in Mexico, its technologies spread worldwide in the 1950s and 1960s. The United States, for instance, imported about half of its wheat in the 1940s but after using Green Revolution technologies, it became self-sufficient in the 1950s and became an exporter by the 1960s.

India was on the brink of mass famine in the early 1960s because of its rapidly growing population. Agricultural research resulted in a new variety of rice, IR8, which produced more grain per plant when grown with irrigation and fertilizers. Today, India is one of the world's leading rice producers and growing of IR8 rice has spread throughout Asia.

18. **(D)** According to a 1992 study by the National Oceanographic and Atmospheric Administration, 50% of the spilled oil underwent biodegradation and photolysis (chemical decomposition by the action of radiant electromagnetic energy, especially light). Cleanup crews recovered about 14% of the oil, and approximately 13% sunk to the seafloor. About 2% (some 216,000 gallons) remained on the beaches.

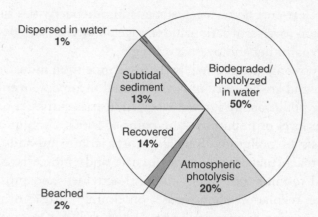

19. **(B)** Asexual reproduction produces organisms that are genetically identical to the parent. Speciation is the result of genetic variability. There are several types of asexual reproduction. Fission is the simplest form of asexual reproduction and involves the division of a single organism into two complete organisms, each genetically identical to the other and to the parent. A similar form of asexual reproduction is regeneration, in which an entire organism may be generated from a part of its parent. Budding occurs when a group of self-supportive cells sprouts from and then detaches from the parent organism.

20. **(A)** The Resource Conservation and Recovery Act (RCRA) of 1976 addresses comprehensive management of nonhazardous and hazardous solid waste, sets minimal standards for all waste disposal facilities and for hazardous wastes, and regulates treatment, storage, and transport.

21. **(B)** In 1980, Congress passed the Superfund statute providing broad authorities both to respond to chemical emergencies and to clean up toxic waste sites for long-term protection.

22. **(C)** Environmental resistance or limiting factors consists of all factors in an environment that limit a population's ability to increase in numbers. Predation, competition for resources, disease, limited food and space, etc., all work to hold a population in check. Environmental resistance can be either density-dependent or density-independent. Factors that are density-dependent are stronger when a population has a higher density (more crowded). Examples would include predation, parasitism, disease, and competition for space or food. Density-independent factors (usually abiotic) will kill organisms—whether they are crowded or not. Examples would include floods, storms, earthquakes, fire, etc. In nature, biotic potential and environmental resistance work together to level out population numbers to an amount that can be supported by the environment. When environmental resistance "pushes down" on J curve growth, the curve levels into what is known as an S curve (or sigmoid curve) and reflects a balanced community.

23. **(A)** Refer to "Plate Tectonics" in Chapter 1.

24. **(C)** The Environmental Protection Agency (EPA) estimates that the emissions to the atmosphere from coal-burning power plants contain 84 of the 187 hazardous air pollutants identified by the EPA as posing a threat to human health and the environment. Coal-fired power plants in the United States release 386,000 tons of hazardous air pollutants into the atmosphere each year and account for 40% of all hazardous air pollutant point sources, more than any other point source category. Coal-burning power plants are the largest

point source category for release of hydrochloric acid, mercury, and arsenic and are a major source of several criteria air pollutants such as sulfur dioxide, oxides of nitrogen, and particulate matter.

25. **(C)** Also known as Superfund, it is a law designed to clean up sites contaminated with hazardous substances. The law authorized the Environmental Protection Agency (EPA) to identify parties responsible for contamination of sites and compel the parties to clean up the sites. Where responsible parties cannot be found, the EPA is authorized to clean up sites itself, using a special trust fund. CERCLA authorizes two kinds of response actions: (1) Removal actions. These are typically short-term response actions, where actions may be taken to address releases or threatened releases requiring prompt response and (2) Remedial actions. These are usually long-term response actions. Remedial actions seek to permanently and significantly reduce the risks associated with releases or threats of releases of hazardous substances that are serious. Choice (E) addresses coal mining.

26. **(D)** Green plants are the producers that can store enough energy to provide the basis upon which a community is built. The least amount of energy is found at the level of the hawks.

27. **(C)** Snakes feed on rodents. At each trophic level, energy is lost. Therefore the snakes must consume more than their biomass to survive.

28. **(B)** Alley cropping is used to enhance or diversify farm products, reduce surface water runoff and erosion, improve utilization of nutrients, reduce wind erosion, modify the microclimate for improved crop production, and improve wildlife habitat. Hardwood trees, like walnut, oak, ash, and pecan, are favored species in alley cropping systems and can potentially provide high-value lumber. Nut crops can be another intermediate product. Common examples of alley cropping plantings include wheat, corn, soybeans, or hay planted in between rows of black walnut or pecan trees.

29. **(B)** The population had grown by 1,300 (4,000 births – 3,000 deaths + 500 immigrants – 200 emigrants = 1,300).

$$\text{Net annual growth rate} = \frac{1,300}{100,000} \times 100\% = 1.3\%$$

30. **(D)** Less energy is available at each trophic level because energy is lost by organisms through respiration and incomplete digestion of food sources. Therefore, fewer herbivores can be supported by the vegetative material.

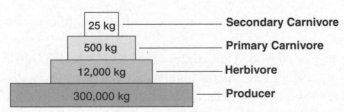

31. **(C)** Secondary consumers are carnivores that feed upon the flesh of other animals (for example, a snake eating a rat).

32. **(B)** Both lizards and arachnids eat grasshoppers. Competition is the struggle between different species for the same resources.

33. **(C)** Saprophytic agents gain nourishment from dead organic matter. They are the organisms of decay. Bacteria and fungi are saprophytes.

34. **(D)** When resources are scarce, the price goes up (law of supply and demand). The increase in prices causes people to conserve resources and use less because they are saving money.

35. **(A)** Diagram A, also known as an expansive pyramid, shows a broad base, indicating a high proportion of children, a rapid rate of population growth, and a low proportion of older people. A steady upward narrowing shows that more people die at each higher age band. This type of pyramid indicates a population in which there is a high birth rate, a high death rate, and a short life expectancy. This is the typical pattern for less economically developed countries, due to little access to and incentive to use birth control, negative environmental factors (e.g., lack of clean water), and poor access to health care.

36. **(E)** The thermohaline circulation plays an important role in supplying heat to the polar regions, and thus in regulating the amount of sea ice in these regions, although poleward heat transport outside the tropics is considerably larger in the atmosphere than in the ocean. Insofar as the thermohaline circulation governs the rate at which deep waters are exposed to the surface, it may also play an important role in determining the concentration of carbon dioxide in the atmosphere.

37. **(D)** Car A travels 500 miles at 15 miles to the gallon and therefore uses about 500/15 = 33.3 gallons of gasoline. Car B travels the same 500 miles but uses about 500/30 = 16.7 gallons of gasoline. Car A uses 33.3 − 16.7 = 16.6 more gallons of gasoline than car B. If each gallon of gasoline that is burned contributes 5 pounds of carbon (in the form of CO_2) to the atmosphere, then car A will contribute 5 × 16.6 = 83 *more* pounds of carbon than car B.

38. **(E)** Earth is actually closest to the sun during the Northern Hemisphere winter.

39. **(D)** As the ocean warms, it expands and sea level rises, accounting for about one-third of the approximately 8 inches (20 cm) sea level rise seen in the past 100 years. Water released by melting glaciers and ice sheets accounts for the other two-thirds of sea level rise.

40. **(A)** Besides the effects already listed, additional effects include:
    - Flattens the ocean bottom, filling in holes, leveling humps, and knocking down protruding organisms, all of which reduce biodiversity
    - Initiates erosion, causing long-term sedimentation problems
    - Changes the microhabitat, affecting primary productivity
    - Damages or kills both commercially harvested species and noncommercial species
    - Unlike clear-cutting in forests, the effects are not visible, thereby not getting much attention

41. **(D)** Pressure-treated wood (sometimes called CCA), which usually has a greenish tint to it, contains arsenic, a highly toxic element, as well as chromium and copper. Dog and cat feces may carry diseases that can infect humans. Morning glory, sheep sorrel, ivy, several kinds of grasses, and some other plants can resprout from their roots and/or stems in the compost pile. Bones (and the fat and marrow) are very attractive to pests such as rats. In addition, fatty food wastes can be very slow to break down because the fat can exclude the air that composting microbes need to do their work. Manure, which is defined as barnyard or stable dung often containing discarded animal bedding, typically contains large amounts of nitrogen (the fresher the manure, the more nitrogen

it contains) and is considered a green ingredient. Fresh manures can heat a compost pile quickly and will accelerate the decomposition of woody materials, autumn leaves, and other browns.

42. **(A)** Sustainability is a concept long recognized and utilized by many cultures. It results from recognition of the need for a harmonious existence between the environment, society, and economy. Sustainability focuses on improving the quality of life for all people without increasing the use of natural resources beyond the capacity of the environment to supply them indefinitely. In order for hydrogen to be a true, long-term, renewable alternative to fossil fuels (it runs more efficiently than gasoline but it costs twice to three times as much to produce), it will need to be produced with a clean, low-cost electricity source such as hydroelectric power. Most oil-reliant countries simply do not have access to vast amounts of clean electricity, but Iceland and Norway do.

43. **(C)** In a fossil fuel power plant, the chemical energy stored in chemical bonds in the fossil fuels (such as coal, fuel oil, or natural gas) and oxygen in the air is converted successively into thermal energy (heat), mechanical energy (spinning turbines), and finally electrical energy for continuous use and distribution across a wide geographic area. Each of these processes is less than 100% efficient, with energy lost (usually as heat) at each stage.—The Second Law of Thermodynamics states that the quality of a particular amount of energy— i.e., the amount of work or action that it can do—diminishes each time this energy is used and is true for all forms of energy (mechanical, chemical, etc.)

44. **(A)** If you missed this question, review Hadley, Ferrel, and polar cells in Chapter 2. In land masses influenced by polar cells, temperature rather than precipitation is the critical factor in plant distribution and soil development. Land masses in equatorial regions primarily influenced by Hadley cells are characterized by high humidity and lots of precipitation (e.g., tropical rain forests). Subtropical land masses primarily influenced by Hadley cells are characterized by low relative humidity and deserts.

45. **(E)** The threshold for pain is at about 120 to 140 dB, but sound begins to damage hearing when it is above 85 dB. Some of the hearing loss after exposure to excessive noise will be permanent. Indication of damage is ringing and noise in the ears (called tinnitus) after sound exposure. Research shows that cumulative exposure to loud sounds, not age, is the major cause of hearing loss.

46. **(D)** Enriched uranium is uranium whose uranium-235 content has been increased through the process of isotope separation. Natural uranium consists mostly of the U-238 isotope, with about 0.72% by weight as U-235, the only isotope existing in nature in any appreciable amount that is fissionable by thermal neutrons. Enriched uranium is a critical component for both nuclear power generation (electricity) and military nuclear weapons. The International Atomic Energy Agency attempts to monitor and control enriched uranium supplies and processes in its efforts to ensure nuclear power generation safety and to curb nuclear weapons proliferation.

47. **(D)** Integrated pest management (IPM) is a broad based ecological approach to agricultural pest control that integrates pesticides/herbicides into a management system incorporating a range of practices for economic control of a pest. In IPM, the purpose is to prevent infestation, to observe patterns of infestation when they occur, and to intervene (without poisons) when necessary. An IPM system is designed around six basic components: (1) acceptable pest levels;

(2) preventive cultural practices; (3) monitoring; (4) mechanical controls; (5) biological controls; and (6) responsible pesticide use.

48. **(C)** Carbon dioxide is produced during cellular respiration, not photosynthesis. When trees (natural sinks for carbon) are cut down, the carbon in the tree is sequestered (remains) until decay processes begin, at which time, some of the carbon is released back into the environment as CO_2. The primary source of CO_2 is outgassing from the Earth's interior at mid-ocean ridges, hot-spot volcanoes, and volcanic arcs. Much of the CO_2 released at subduction zones is derived from the metamorphism of carbonate rocks subducting with the ocean crust. Much of the overall outgassing of CO_2, especially at mid-ocean ridges and hot-spot volcanoes, was stored in the mantle when the Earth formed. Some of the outgassed carbon remains as CO_2 in the atmosphere, some is dissolved in the oceans, some carbon is held as biomass in living or dead and decaying organisms, and some is bound in carbonate rocks. Carbon is removed into long-term storage by burial of sedimentary strata, especially coal and shale that store organic carbon from undecayed biomass and carbonate rocks such as limestone also known as calcium carbonate—$CaCO_3$.

49. **(B)** Peroxyacyl nitrates, or PANs, are powerful respiratory and eye irritants present in photochemical smog. PANs are both toxic and irritating, as they dissolve more readily in water than ozone. They cause eye irritation at concentrations of only a few parts per billion. At higher concentrations they cause extensive damage to vegetation. PANs are mutagenic and can be a factor causing skin cancer. PANs are classified as secondary pollutants as they are not directly emitted as exhaust from power plants or internal combustion engines, but they are formed from other pollutants by chemical reactions in the atmosphere. Since they dissociate quite slowly in the atmosphere, PANs are able to transport NO_x and other unstable compounds far away from their urban and industrial origins and form tropospheric ozone.

50. **(C)** Volatile organic compounds (VOCs) are emitted as gases from certain solids or liquids with high vapor pressures (evaporate easily). Concentrations of many VOCs are often up to ten times higher indoors than outdoors. Examples of VOCs include paints and lacquers, paint strippers, cleaning supplies, pesticides, building materials and furnishings, office equipment such as copiers and printers, glues, and markers.

51. **(E)** Oceans occupy 71% of the Earth's surface. They are divided into five major oceans, which in decreasing order of size are: the Pacific Ocean, Atlantic Ocean, Indian Ocean, Southern Ocean, and Arctic Ocean. Over 70% of the world catch from the sea comes from the Pacific Ocean.

Ocean	Amount of Fish Caught (Million tons)	% Fish Caught
Pacific	83	71
Atlantic	24	20
Indian	10	9
Southern (Antarctic)	0.147	0.1
Arctic	0	0
Overall	116	100%

52. **(C)** Salmon are inseparable from their freshwater, saltwater, and estuarine ecosystems. They are extremely sensitive to changes in water quality, changes in river flow, water turbidity, and temperature. Juvenile salmon feed on freshwater invertebrates that are also indicators of water quality. Generally, the more pristine, diverse, and productive the freshwater ecosystem is, the healthier the salmon stocks. Salmon bring large amounts of marine nutrients upstream to the headwaters of otherwise low productivity rivers. Salmon carcasses are the primary food for aquatic invertebrates and fish, as well as terrestrial fauna ranging from marine mammals to birds—eagles, ducks, and songbirds—to terrestrial mammals, especially bears and humans. Salmon and other anadromous fish bring biomass and nutrients (nitrogen, phosphorus, carbon, and micronutrients) from the sea into freshwater and terrestrial ecosystems.

53. **(D)** Oligotrophic lakes contain very low concentrations of nutrients required for plant growth and thus the overall productivity of these lakes is low. Only a small quantity of organic matter is present; e.g., phytoplankton, zooplankton, algae, aquatic weeds, bacteria, and fish. With so little production of organic matter, there is very little accumulation of organic sediment on the bottom and the water is clear. They are seldom in good agricultural areas since water runoff is low in nutrients.

54. **(E)** (1) National Park Service (Interior Department) provides for the use and enjoyment of the parks by people and to preserve the land in its original state. It manages 13% of federal lands and 40% of the acreage within the National Wilderness Preservation System. (2) The Forest Service (Department of Agriculture) manages public lands in national forests and grasslands. It manages 30% of federal lands and 33% of the acreage within the National Wilderness Preservation System. (3) Bureau of Land Management (Interior Department) initially managed range lands for grazing, oil and gas development, and mining. Their role expanded to include multiple use resources such as wildlife, watersheds, recreation, wilderness, and other conservation values with the passage of the Federal Land Policy and Management Act in 1976. It manages 42% of federal lands and 7% of the acreage within the National Wilderness Preservation System. (4) The Fish and Wildlife Service (Interior Department) administers a national network of lands and waters for the conservation, management, and, where appropriate, restoration of the fish, wildlife, and plant resources and their habitats within the United States. It manages 15% of federal lands and 18% of the acreage within the National Wilderness Preservation System.

55. **(B)** CFLs, like all fluorescent lightbulbs, contain mercury as vapor inside the glass tubing. Most CFLs contain 3–5 mg per bulb, with the bulbs labeled "eco-friendly" containing as little as 1 mg. Because mercury is poisonous, even these small amounts are a concern for landfills and waste incinerators where the mercury from lightbulbs may be released and contribute to air and water pollution. In 2008 the U.S. Environmental Protection Agency (EPA) published a data sheet stating that the net system emission of mercury for CFL lighting was lower than for incandescent lighting of comparable lumen output. This was based on the average rate of mercury emission for electricity production from a coal-fed power plant and the average estimated escape of mercury from a CFL put into a landfill. In the United States, the EPA estimated that if all 270 million compact fluorescent lightbulbs sold in 2007 were sent to landfill

sites, that this would represent around 0.13 metric tons, or 0.1% of all U.S. emissions of mercury, which was 104 metric tons.

56. **(B)** Lighting efficiency ranges of 9–11% for CFLs and 1.9–2.6%, for incandescent lightbulbs. Because of their higher efficacy, CFLs use between one-quarter to one-third of the power of an equivalent incandescent lightbulb. About 50%–70% of the world's total lighting market sales are incandescent. Replacing incandescent lighting with CFLs would save 2.5% of the world's yearly electricity consumption. Since CFLs use much less energy than incandescent lightbulbs, a phase-out of incandescent lightbulbs would result in less CO_2 being emitted into the atmosphere. The efficiency rating is calculated by comparing the amount of energy input to the amount of energy output (work accomplished). Efficiency is usually given as a percentage and can be computed with the following formula:

$$\frac{\text{Useful output}}{\text{Energy input}} = \text{efficiency rating (\textit{in decimal})}$$

Useful output = 10.0 joules × 0.10
Useful output = 1 joule of light and therefore 9 joules of heat energy (wasted)

57. **(B)** The most probable explanation for the increase in the rabbit population after 1950 was that the coyote population declined drastically. The relationship indicated by the graph is one of predator-prey. The coyotes prey upon rabbits, keeping the population in check.

58. **(E)** The most probable explanation for the decline of the coyotes is removal by humans. Since the decline in coyotes occurred with cattle introduction and since cattle and coyotes do not compete for the same food, the individuals that introduced the cattle must have interfered with the coyote population. Because coyotes are predators, they were perceived as dangerous to the cattle and were hunted and poisoned by humans. Attempts to control coyotes by poisoning may deplete the numbers of their natural prey and lead to increasing attacks by coyotes on farm animals.

59. **(A)** Savannas are warm year-round with a prolonged dry season and scattered trees. The environment is intermediate between grassland and forest. An extended dry season followed by a rainy season occurs in Australia; Central, Eastern, and South Africa; India; Madagascar; central South America; Southeast Asia; and Thailand. Savannas consist of grasslands with stands of deciduous shrubs and trees that do not grow more than 30 meters high. Trees and shrubs generally shed leaves during the dry season, which reduces the need for water. Food is limited during the dry season so that many animals migrate during this season. Soils are rich in nutrients. Savannas contain large herds of grazing animals and browsing animals that provide resources for predators.

60. **(D)** The tundra is located at 60° north latitude and farther north. The weather is influenced by the polar cell. Alpine tundra is located in mountainous areas, above the tree line, with well-drained soil and where dominant animals are small rodents and insects. Arctic tundra is frozen treeless plains, low rainfall, low average temperatures (summers average <10°C), and many bogs and ponds. Frozen ground prevents drainage. The growing season lasts 50–60 days. Tundra is found in Alaska, Canada, Europe, Greenland, and Russia. Dominant vegetation includes flowering dwarf shrubs, grasses, lichens, mosses, and sedges. The soil has few nutrients due to low vegetation and little

decomposition. There are between 60 to 100 frost-free days per year. Arctic tundra is higher latitude than alpine tundra.

61. **(C)** Selective cutting is used for the majority of shade-tolerant hardwood forests. About every 20 to 30 years, individual mature and declining (diseased or unhealthy) trees are cut. The growth rate and quality of the remaining trees improves, and young trees of the shade-tolerant species become established in the mostly-shaded understory. Selection cutting imitates minor natural disturbances like wind and disease, and perpetuates an all-aged tolerant hardwood forest.

62. **(E)** Swamps and marshes are the most productive biomes, producing the most biomass per year, while tropical rain forests have the most standing biomass. Extreme deserts are the least-productive biomes. Lakes and streams are equivalent to extreme deserts for having the least standing biomass.

63. **(D)** The boiling point of a crude oil component or fraction, which is the temperature at which it evaporates, is dependent on the length of the carbon chain in the molecule. Those fractions with shorter chains (such as gasoline) evaporate more easily than those with longer chains (such as waxes).

64. **(C)** At the point of discharge, there is a sudden increase in the amount of toxins, suspended solids, and dissolved organic compounds. The water becomes unsuitable for any human use. Aerobic bacteria increase rapidly, reducing the organic pollutants but using up dissolved oxygen. As the oxygen level falls, anaerobic bacteria multiply, resulting in an unpleasant smell or stench. Eventually, as their food supply is used up, the decomposers reduce and algae thrive, reoxygenating the water. Fish and other animal life reappear, and the stream returns to its previous condition.

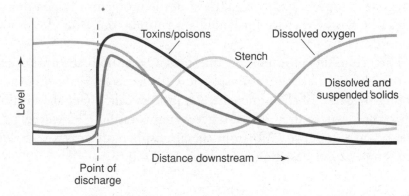

65. **(D)** Thomas Malthus recognized that once the carrying capacity of an area was exceeded, organisms would die of starvation. Darwin's theory of evolution based on natural selection may have been influenced by Malthus's concept.

66. **(E)** Note that only 10% of the population of young oysters reaches the 20th unit of life span.

67. **(A)** Note that almost all of the fruit flies reach the 90th unit of life span before the entire population dies.

68. **(C)** On a cool, inactive day, the average man loses about 12 eight-ounce cups of water but consumes only about 9 cups of water (about half of that from the water in fruits, vegetables, and other solid foods).

69. **(B)** Integrated pest management (IPM) is a broad based ecological approach to agricultural pest control that integrates pesticides/herbicides into a manage-

ment system incorporating a range of practices for economic control of a pest. In IPM, one attempts to prevent infestation, to observe patterns of infestation when they occur, and to intervene when necessary. Synthetic pesticides are generally only used as required and only at specific times in a pest's life cycle.

70. **(B)** To calculate doubling time, divide the growth rate into the number 70. Thus a growth rate of 2% (0.02) will cause a population to double in number in 35 years (70 ÷ 2 = 35). 2010 + 35 years = 2045.

71. **(B)** 350 − 250 = 100   100 / 250 = 0.40   0.40 × 100% = 40%

72. **(C)** Desertification is the degradation of land in any dryland. Caused by a variety of factors, such as climate change and human activities, desertification is a significant global environmental problem. Drylands occupy approximately 40% of Earth's land area and are home to more than 2 billion people, and it has been estimated that some 10–20% of drylands are already degraded. The most common cause of desertification is the overcultivation of desert lands. Overcultivation causes the nutrients in the soil to be depleted faster than they are restored. Furthermore, improper irrigation practices result in salinated soils and the depletion of aquifers.

73. **(D)** A pure capitalistic economy, in which financial gain is the primary societal motivator, leads to always taking just one more. Be careful of the double negative in the question.

74. **(C)** Industrial wastes of unknown content are often commingled with domestic wastes in sanitary landfills. Groundwater infiltration and contamination of water supplies with toxic chemicals have recently led to more active control of landfills and industrial waste disposal. Careful management of sanitary landfills, such as providing for leachate and runoff treatment as well as daily coverage with topsoil, has stopped most of the problems of open dumping. In many areas, however, space for landfills is running out, and alternatives must be found.

75. **(B)** The oceans are an important sink for CO_2 through absorption of the gas into the water surface. As atmospheric CO_2 levels increase, it increases the warming potential of the atmosphere, a process called global warming. If air temperatures warm, they increase ocean temperatures. However, the ability of the ocean to remove CO_2 from the atmosphere decreases with increasing ocean temperatures based on principles of solubility.

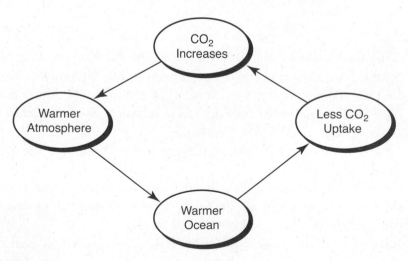

76. **(B)** The slope of the dose-response curves gives a good indication of how a target population will respond to the pesticide. When all members of the population react in a similar way, their dose-response curve is quite steep (Choice A) and the population is said to be fairly homogeneous. On the other hand, if some members of the population are much more sensitive to the pesticide than others, the population is said to be more heterogeneous and the dose-response curve is flatter (Choice B). Populations that are more heterogeneous or diverse tend to survive better through natural selection in a changing environment.

77. **(D)** The depth at which plankton can exist depends on the penetration of sunlight. Sunlight provides the energy for photosynthesis. Since the phytoplankton is abundant near the surface, the region of sunlight penetration, the consumers are also found in this region.

78. **(C)** A point source of pollution is a single, identifiable, localized source of air, water, thermal, or noise or light pollution and is generally considered to be fixed (immobile).

79. **(D)** Shield volcanoes are built almost entirely of fluid lava flows. Flow after flow pours out in all directions from a central summit vent, or group of vents, building a broad, gently sloping cone with a flat, domed shape. They are built up slowly by the accumulation of thousands of flows of highly fluid basaltic lava that spread widely over great distances and then cool as thin, gently dipping sheets. Examples of shield volcanoes include those found in the Hawaiian Island chain, Galapagos Islands, Iceland, and East Africa.

80. **(D)** More preventable deaths in the United States are caused each year by tobacco use than by all deaths from AIDS, illegal drug use, alcohol use, motor vehicle injuries, suicides, and murders combined; however, obesity and its effects are dramatically increasing. Cigarette smoking causes about 1 of every 5 deaths in the United States each year. On average, adults who smoke cigarettes die 14 years earlier than nonsmokers. Based on current cigarette smoking patterns, an estimated 25 million Americans who are alive today will die prematurely from smoking-related illnesses, including 5 million people younger than 18 years of age.

81. **(C)** Countries in the Middle East own 56% of the world's proven oil reserves. A 2008 U.S. Geological Survey estimates that areas north of the Arctic Circle have 13% of the expected undiscovered oil in the world. See Figure 8.10, page 316 to see a list of the world's oil reserves.

82. **(A)** The United States still has the world's largest coal reserves with a slightly more than one-quarter of the total (28%). Russia is second with 18%, and China is third with 13%. Existing supplies are estimated to last for almost 200 years at current rates of consumption. Coal provides 44% of the world's electricity and 27% of its overall energy. The figures for the U.S. are very similar at 48% of electricity and 21% overall. China generates 80% of its electricity from coal and is actually importing coal, despite its vast reserves. Estimates are that 86% of the incremental demand for coal over the next twenty years will come from China and India. See Figure 8.9, page 315 to see a list of the world's coal reserves.

83. **(D)** As of 2009, proven gas reserves are dominated by three countries: Russia (24%), Iran (16%), and Turkmenistan (15%). Due to constant announcements of shale gas recoverable reserves, as well as drilling in Central Asia,

South America, and Africa, deepwater drilling, estimates are undergoing frequent updates. See Figure 8.11, page 316 to see a list of the world's natural gas reserves.

84. **(E)** Chemical formulas involved in producing acid rain include:

(i) $H_2O_{(l)} + CO_{2(g)} \rightleftharpoons H_2CO_{3(aq)}$

(ii) SO_2: $S_{(s)} + O_{2(g)} \rightarrow SO_{2(g)}$

The $SO_{2(g)}$ combines with water to produce sulfurous acid:

$$H_2O_{(l)} + SO_{2(g)} \rightleftharpoons H_2SO_{3(g)}.$$

Sulfur dioxide is however not readily oxidized to sulfur trioxide in dry, clean air. Water droplets and dust particles, however, catalyse the reaction between O_2 and SO_2 in the air producing sulfur trioxide, SO_3. This dissolves in water and produces sulfuric acid, which is a much stronger acid:

$$SO_{2(g)} + \tfrac{1}{2}O_{2(g)} \rightarrow SO_{3(g)} \qquad H_2O_{(l)} + SO_{3(g)} \rightarrow H_2SO_{4(aq)}$$

This can cause considerable damage to buildings, vegetation, and fish populations by destroying fish eggs.

(iii) Sources of NO_x are more widespread. At temperatures over 2370°F (1300°C), nitrogen combines with oxygen to form nitrogen monoxide:

$$N_{2(g)} + O_{2(g)} \rightarrow 2NO_{(g)}$$

These high temperatures can be achieved by: (i) the internal combustion engine; and (ii) lightning in the atmosphere. The nitrogen monoxide slowly combines with oxygen to form soluble nitrogen dioxide gas:

$$2NO_{(g)} + O_{2(g)} \rightarrow 2NO_{2(g)}$$

Nitrogen dioxide readily dissolves in water producing a mixture of nitric and nitrous acids:

$$2NO_{2(g)} + H_2O_{(l)} \rightarrow HNO_{3(aq)} + HNO_{2(g)}$$

85. **(E)** Between 1999 and the start of 2012 when the world's population increased from 6 billion to 7 billion people, the Asian population, which represents 60% of the current world population, grew by an estimated 579 million people making up about 57% of that increase. The African population meanwhile contributed 28% to the population increase.

86. **(C)** From a population of tens of thousands in the 19th century, the bald eagle had declined to only 417 pairs in the lower 48 states by 1963. By 1994, after 20 years of protection through the Endangered Species Act, the population had grown to more than 4,000 breeding pairs.

87. **(D)** Couplings are one-way linkages in which one component of a system affects another component. In positive coupling between components *A* and *B*, a change in *A* causes a change of the same sign in *B*. In negative coupling, a change in *A* causes a change of the opposing sign in *B*. Two or more couplings acting in sequence form a closed loop. In a positive-feedback loop, a positive or negative change in one of the components of the system is amplified by the sequence of couplings. In a negative-feedback loop, the change is reduced in amplitude.

88. **(A)** Non-anthropogenic means not caused by humans. When the choices are ranked by their contribution to the greenhouse effect, they are: (1) water vapor, which contributes 36–72%; (2) carbon dioxide, which contributes 9–26%; (3) methane, which contributes 4–9%, and (4) tropospheric ozone, which contributes 3–7%. Pound for pound, ozone is about 3,000 times stron-

ger as a greenhouse gas than CO_2. Even though there is much less ozone at middle altitudes than CO_2, its impact is considerable, with ozone trapping up to one-third as much heat as CO_2. Nitrogen is not a greenhouse gas.

89. **(A)** In 2000, beach pollution prompted at least 11,270 closings and swimming advisories in the United States, twice the number that occurred in 1999. The increase was due largely to improved and increased monitoring and reporting. The most frequent pollution sources are polluted runoff and storm water, which led to more than 4,102 closings in 2000.

90. **(B)** Atmospheric carbon dioxide levels are rising rapidly. Currently, they are 25% above where they stood before the Industrial Revolution. Earth's atmosphere now contains some 200 gigatons (GT) more carbon than it did two centuries ago.

91. **(A)** % change = ((new value – original value) / original value) × 100

92. **(A)** Marine sediments contain an estimated 4×10^9 Tg (1 Tg = 10^{12} grams with an estimated turnover time of 2×10^8 years). Turnover time is the time it takes for a complete cycle to occur within a system or the ratio of the mass of a reservoir to the rate of its removal from that reservoir.

93. **(D)** The median lethal dose, LD_{50} of a toxin, radiation, or pathogen is the dose required to kill half the members of a tested population after a specified test duration. LD_{50} figures are frequently used as a general indicator of a substance's acute toxicity. An LD_{50} level determined for rats cannot be interpreted as the LD_{50} level for insects or humans.

94. **(D)** In (Λ) activity is low, and it occurs at very shallow depths. The point is that the lithosphere is very thin and weak at these boundaries, so the strain cannot build up enough to cause large earthquakes. The San Andreas fault is a good example of (B) in which two mature plates are scraping by one another. The friction between the plates can be so great that very large strains can build up before they are periodically relieved by large earthquakes. In (C) one plate is thrust or subducted under the other plate so that a deep ocean trench is produced. In (E) shallow earthquakes are associated with high mountain ranges where intense compression is taking place. In (D) the interiors of the plates themselves are largely free of large earthquakes, that is, they are aseismic.

95. **(D)** In stage three of the demographic stage model, birthrates fall due to access to contraception resulting in smaller family sizes, increases in wages, urbanization, a reduction in subsistence agriculture, an increase in the status and education of women, a reduction in the value of children's work, an increase in parental investment in the education of children and other social changes, and population growth rates begin to decrease. Although birthrates are declining, the population is still increasing. The death rate continues to fall from stage two due to greater access to health care, smaller family sizes, and lower childhood mortality rates. Examples of countries in stage three include Mexico, the Philippines, Indonesia, and India.

96. **(B)** Differences in air pressure help cause winds and affect air masses. They are also factors in the formation of storms such as thunderstorms, tornadoes, and hurricanes. Differences in air pressure are shown on a weather map with lines called isobars. The weather map illustrates isobars marking areas of high and low pressure. High-pressure areas generally have dry, good weather, and areas of low pressure have precipitation. On the weather map, the only area of low pressure is centered in the Midwest.

97. **(D)** The pH scale is logarithmic, and as a result, each whole pH value below 7 is ten times more acidic than the next higher value.

98. **(A)** SBS (sick-building syndrome) and BRI (building-related illness) are associated with acute or immediate health problems. Radon and asbestos cause long-term diseases that occur years after exposure and are therefore not considered to be among the causes of sick buildings. Indicators of SBS include headache; eye, nose, or throat irritation; dry cough; dry or itchy skin; dizziness and nausea; difficulty in concentrating; fatigue; and sensitivity to odors.

99. **(D)** Tropospheric ozone would be ozone found in the air that we breathe, generally produced by burning fossil fuels. No relationship has been found that skin cancer is increased by decreases in smog.

100. **(C)** Agriculture accounts for 92% of all freshwater use globally. Specifically, water-intensive cereal grains like wheat, rice, and corn account for 27%; meat production 22%; and dairy 7%. China, India, and the United States are responsible for nearly 38% of global water consumption. The United States, which has a much smaller population than China or India, led the world in per capita consumption of freshwater: 2842 m^3 each year, compared with the global average of 1385 m^3 per year.

FREE-RESPONSE EXPLANATIONS

Question 1

(a) 5 points maximum

Restatement: Total amount of energy (in Btus) to wash the clothes using the washing machine.

Mass of water:

$$20 \text{ gallons } H_2O \times \frac{8 \text{ pounds}}{1 \text{ gallon } H_2O} = 160 \text{ pounds } H_2O \quad \text{(1 point)}$$

Energy to heat water:

$$160 \text{ pounds } H_2O \times \frac{1 \text{ Btu/}°F}{1 \text{ pound } H_2O} \times (130°F - 60°F) = 11{,}200 \text{ Btu} \quad \text{(1 point)}$$

Energy to run washing machine (kWh):

$$1500 \text{ Watts} \times \frac{1 \text{ kW}}{1000 \text{ Watts}} \times 30 \text{ min.} \times \frac{1 \text{ hr.}}{60 \text{ min.}} = 0.75 \text{ kWh} \quad \text{(1 point)}$$

Energy to run washing machine (Btus):

$$0.75 \text{ kWh} \times \frac{3{,}400 \text{ Btu}}{1 \text{ kWh}} = 2{,}550 \text{ Btu} \quad \text{(1 point)}$$

Total energy for washing machine:

$$11{,}200 \text{ Btu} + 2{,}550 \text{ Btu} = \textbf{13{,}750 Btu} \quad \text{(1 point)}$$

(b) 2 points maximum

Restatement: Total amount of energy (in Btus) to wash clothes by hand.

$$35 \text{ gallons } H_2O \times \frac{8 \text{ pounds}}{1 \text{ gallon } H_2O} = 280 \text{ pounds } H_2O \quad \text{(1 point)}$$

Energy to heat water:

$$280 \text{ pounds } H_2O \times \frac{1 \text{ Btu/}°F}{1 \text{ pound } H_2O} \times (130°F - 60°F) = \textbf{19{,}600 Btu} \quad \text{(1 point)}$$

NOTE:

1. If you do NOT show calculations, no points are awarded.
2. No penalty assessed if you do not show units. However, you risk setting up the problem incorrectly if you do not show units so that they cancel properly.
3. If your setup is correct but you make an arithmetic error, no penalty.

(c) 3 points maximum

Restatement: Environmental impact of washing clothes.

NOTE: There are no points for just listing ideas. Each idea MUST be explained. The following are ideas that you could use to write your paragraph(s). Take these ideas and create an outline of the order in which you wish to answer them. You do NOT need to use all ideas. Before you begin, decide on the format of how you wish to answer your question (pros versus cons, chart format with explanations within the chart, compare and contrast, etc.).

(i) Restatement: Discuss the economic and environmental costs and benefits of using a washing machine in terms of its manufacture and disposal. 1 point

- Manufacturing washing machines provides jobs in mining, smelting, designing, engineering, manufacturing, transportation, administration, advertising, repair, and sales.
- Use of natural resources in the manufacture and distribution of washing machines. Examples: use of renewable or less polluting energy sources in manufacturing; use of less polluting methods of transportation.
- Advantages of repairing washing machines rather than discarding them. Discarding them creates landfill issues. Recycling of metal parts and packaging material.

(ii) Restatement: Discuss the economic and environmental costs and benefits of selecting one and purchasing it (specifically, how can consumers compare various appliances in terms of their energy use). 1 point

- Energy efficiency of different models. The U.S. Department of Energy and the U.S. Protection Agency have joined with appliance manufacturers to institute the "Energy Star" program. Appliances displaying an Energy Star label have been certified to significantly exceed the federal efficiency standards.
- Choosing a machine that uses the fewest gallons of water per pound of clothes and one that has high, medium, and low water level controls and an automatic cold rinse cycle.
- Consider high efficiency (HE) washing machines. Advantages of HE washing machines include:

  – A traditional washing machine will use 40 to 47 gallons (151 to 178 liters) of water per cycle, while high efficiency washing machines use 11 to 32 gallons (42 to 121 liters) of water per cycle.

– Energy savings with high efficiency washers are estimated at 50% to 60% per each load. Much of the energy savings afforded by high efficiency washing machines are a result of the significant reduction in hot water they require.

– The horizontal drums utilized in a high efficiency washing machine spin at a much faster rate than other machines. This allows more water to be extracted from the clothes during the spin cycle. Consequently, clothes contain less moisture at the end of the wash and require less time and energy to dry.

– A high efficiency washing machine will use two to four clean rinses per cycle reducing levels of detergent residue left on clothing as well as improving cleaning efficiency by not having clothes sitting in dirty water.

– The tumbling motion in a high efficiency washing machine causes clothes to circulate freely resulting in a more effective cleaning process as well as less wear and tear on garments. The tumble motion is gentler with less stress and pulling on fabric than the agitation motion.

– Tumbling and increased circulation of items in the drum requires that a high efficiency detergent be used in these machines. High efficiency detergents have fewer suds, requiring less water to then rinse away.

(iii) Discuss the economic and environmental costs and benefits of using a washing machine and other appliances in terms of steps consumers can take to reduce its environmental impact. 1 point

- Use appliances during off-peak hours
- Use biodegradable detergents that use minimal amounts of phosphates
- Pre-soak heavily soiled clothes
- Try to use only with full loads
- Use as low a water temperature for the washing cycle as will provide satisfactory results
- Always use a cold rinse cycle
- Follow maintenance schedule and instructions found in owner's manual

Question 2

(a) (i) 1 point maximum

Restatement: Biomass as a function of population density

To determine the optimum population density that produced the greatest biomass would require *dividing the total biomass for each planting by the total amount of seeds planted* per pot. This would provide the average biomass and produce the following results:

Seeds per Pot	Average Biomass (g)
1	5.0
10	7.0
20	3.8

From the data table, it appears that *10 radish seeds per pot produced the largest average biomass.* When graphed, the results look like:

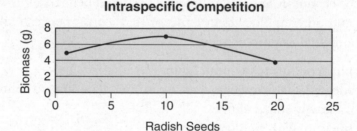

(a) (ii) 2 points maximum

Restatement: Limited resources

The maximum biomass was achieved at 10 seeds per pot. After that, as population density increased, biomass decreased. Factors that may have limited biomass might have included:

1. *Competition for soil nutrients.* As root density increased, less nutrients would have been available for growth.
2. *Competition for light.* As the density increased, less light would have been available for smaller seedlings.
3. *Competition for water.* Given a fixed amount of water provided, as plant density increased, less water would have been available for additional seedlings.

(a) (iii) 2 points maximum

Restatement: Results obtained from the class for Part I in terms of biological laws or principles

The effect of intraspecific competition in plant populations is usually examined by planting the species over a range of densities. The most common result is that a point is reached where the mean weight per plant decreases as density increases, so that the maximum yield approaches some constant value. This result is called the *law of constant yield.* The maximum plant productivity of a particular environment is called the *carrying capacity.* In this case, the carrying capacity was reached when the biomass reached 7.0 grams for the size of the pot. Environmental variables (nutrients, space, water, and light) that restrict the realized niche are called limiting factors. *Liebig's law of the minimum* states that an organism is most limited by the essential factor that is in least supply. In terms of *survivorship,* the radish seeds represent Type III characteristics that include large amounts of seeds being produced with few surviving, small size invaders of disturbed environments, and rapid growth.

(b) (i) 1 point maximum

Restatement: Plant species most affected by competition

To determine which plant species was most negatively affected by interspecific competition would require *dividing the total biomass per pot by the total number of seeds per pot to determine average biomass.* The results are provided below:

Seeds per Pot	Average Biomass (g)
1 radish	5.0
1 wheat	3.0
10 radish	5.0
10 wheat	2.5
20 radish	3.8
20 wheat	2.0

From the table, it appears that the *wheat seedlings were negatively impacted by the presence of the radish seeds.* When graphed, the results are:

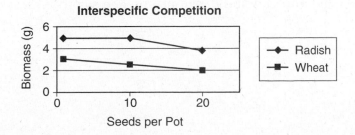

(b) (ii) 2 points maximum

Restatement: Possible reasons why the plant chosen in (b) (i) may have been more successful

Two different species of plants were grown in the *same* medium. *Nutrient requirements may have been different* between the two species. For example, the amount and ratios of minerals contained in the potting soil may have met the metabolic requirements of the radish plants more than the wheat seedlings. *Water and light availability* (either too much or too little) may also have affected outcome. *Differences in growth patterns* (radish may sprout earlier than wheat) may have existed. In this case, the radish seedlings may have *sprouted earlier* and established a population that was taking up a fixed amount of nutrients at a faster rate or had established a canopy that decreased the light available for the wheat seedlings. Simultaneous to the interspecific competition was intraspecific competition. Not only were radish seedlings in competition with wheat seedlings, they were also in competition with other radish seedlings for limited nutrients.

(c) (iii) 2 points maximum

Restatement: Results obtained from the class for Part II in terms of biological laws or principles

In Part II, plant density was held constant in a substitutive or replacement experimental design in which the total density of both species was kept constant while the relative densities were varied (1, 10, and 20). This approach allows investigation of the effects of interspecific competition from the effects of increasing overall plant density on growth or production of a species. However, it requires first quantifying the background effect of intraspecific competition on growth of each species individually. Such an experiment has three possible outcomes. First, one species prospers at the expense of the other (competitive exclusion). Second, one species outperforms the other but only when in higher proportion (coexistence). Third, the two species have no measurable effect on each other (no competition). The latter would be the null hypothesis (H_o) by which the class would judge whether or not one of the other two scenarios happened. Another scenario, which was not tested for, could have been instability—that is, two species are in a constant state of dynamic tension where at one time one species dominates and at other times the other species dominates. Different species of plants are able to coexist within the same biome through resource partitioning, which functions through evolution of different metabolic pathways, having different tolerances to shade, taking up water and nutrients at different depths, and so on.

Question 3

(a) 4 points maximum

List any two characteristics from the column labeled "Sweden" and any two characteristics from the column labeled "Kenya."

Restatement: Given two age-structure diagrams, Sweden and Kenya for 2000, compare and contrast the diagrams in terms of population dynamics.

Age structure diagrams are basically divided into three major age categories:

- Prereproductive (0–15 years old)
- Reproductive (16–45 years old)
- Postreproductive (46 years old–death)

Population Characteristics

	Affected By	Sweden	Kenya
Birth Rate	• Importance of children as a part of the labor force • Urbanization • Cost of raising and educating children • Educational and employment opportunities for women • Infant mortality rate • Average age at marriage • Pensions • Abortions • Birth control • Religious beliefs	• Population has nearly equal proportions of prereproductive and reproductive individuals. • Little growth over a long period of time will produce a population with about equal numbers of people in all age groups. • Children not required or necessary to support parents. • Availability and acceptance of birth control.	• Population has pyramid–shaped age structures, with large numbers of prereproductive individuals. • Population momentum results from large numbers of prereproductive children becoming reproductive within short period of time. • High population rate due to high birth mortality rates. • Children viewed as status symbol. • Resistance to birth control.
Death Rate	• Increased food supply • Better nutrition • Improved medical and public health technology • Improvements in sanitation and personal hygiene • Safer water supplies	• Elderly survive longer due to advances in medical technology and availability. • Social welfare programs ensure that elderly are taken care of.	• Elderly do not survive due to lack of available medical technology. • Disease (for example, malaria or AIDS) and lack of nutritious food decreases life span.

(b) 4 points maximum

Restatement: Factors that affect both birth and death rates

List any four characteristics from the column labeled "Affected By."

See preceding chart.

(c) 2 points maximum

Restatement: Methods that have been employed by another country to curb population growth

List any two of the six methods mentioned.

China: Between 1958 and 1962, an estimated 30 million people died from famine in China. Since then, China has made good progress in trying to feed its people and bring its population growth under control. Much of this reduced population growth was brought about by a drop in the birth rate from 32 to 18 per 1,000 between 1972 and 1985. China instituted one of the most rigorous population control programs in the world at an estimated cost of about $1 per person. Some features of the program included:

1. Strong encouragement for couples to postpone marriage.
2. Providing married couples with free access to sterilization, contraceptives, and abortion.
3. Giving couples who sign pledges to have no more than one child economic rewards such as salary bonuses, extra food, larger pensions, better housing, free medical care and school tuition for their child, and preferential treatment in employment when the child grows up.
4. Requiring those who break the pledge to return all benefits.
5. Exerting pressure on women pregnant with a third child to have abortions.
6. Requiring one of the parents in a two-child family to be sterilized.

Question 4

(a) 1 point maximum (1 point for correct explanation)

Restatement: Definition of a pesticide

A pesticide is any substance or mixture of substances intended for preventing, destroying, repelling, or mitigating any pest. Pests can be insects, rodents or other animals, unwanted plants (weeds), fungi, or microorganisms such as bacteria or viruses.

(i) 2 points maximum (1 point for each correct category of pesticide and description)

Describe TWO major categories of pesticides. For example: Insecticide—kills insects and other arthropods. (Do NOT use insecticide as one of your categories.)

Algicides	Control algae in lakes, canals, swimming pools, water tanks, and other sites.
Antifouling agents	Kill or repel organisms that attach to underwater surfaces, such as boat bottoms.
Antimicrobials	Kill microorganisms (such as bacteria and viruses).
Attractants	Attract pests (for example, to lure an insect or rodent to a trap). Food is not considered a pesticide when used as an attractant.
Biocides	Kill microorganisms.
Defoliants	Cause leaves or other foliage to drop from a plant, usually to facilitate harvest.
Desiccants	Promote drying of living tissues, such as unwanted plant tops.
Disinfectants and sanitizers	Kill or inactivate disease-producing microorganisms on inanimate objects.
Fungicides	Kill fungi (including blights, mildews, molds, and rusts).
Fumigants	Produce gas or vapor intended to destroy pests in buildings or soil.
Herbicides	Kill weeds and other plants that grow where they are not wanted.
Insect growth regulators	Disrupt the molting, maturing from pupal stage to adult, or other life processes of insects.
Insecticides	Kill insects and other arthropods.

Miticides (acaricides)	Kill mites that feed on plants and animals.
Microbial pesticides	Microorganisms that kill, inhibit, or outcompete pests, including insects or other microorganisms.
Molluscicides	Kill snails and slugs.
Nematicides	Kill nematodes (microscopic, wormlike organisms that feed on plant roots).
Ovicides	Kill eggs of insects and mites.
Pheromones	Biochemicals used to disrupt the mating behavior of insects.
Plant growth regulators	Substances (excluding fertilizers or other plant nutrients) that alter the expected growth, flowering, or reproduction rate of plants.
Repellents	Repel pests, including insects (such as mosquitoes) and birds.
Rodenticides	Control rats, mice, and other rodents.

(ii) 2 points maximum (1 point for each correct positive effect and explanation)

Restatement: Two positive effects of pesticide use. Identify and discuss TWO positive effects of pesticide use.

(1) Plants are directly and indirectly humankind's main source of food. They are attacked by tens of thousands of diseases caused by viruses, bacteria, fungi, and other organisms. There are over 30,000 kinds of weeds competing with crops worldwide; thousands of nematode species reduce crop vigor; and some 10,000 species of insects devour crops. It is estimated that one-third of the world's food crop is destroyed by these pests annually. *Pesticides increase the world food supply.*

(2) There are an estimated 300–500 million cases of malaria per year. The majority of these occur in Africa. The vast majority of the estimated 1 million annual deaths from the disease occur among children and mainly among poor African children. Malaria is above all a disease of the poor, impacting at least three times more greatly on the poor than any other disease. Africa's GDP would be up to $100 billion greater if malaria had been eliminated years ago. Mosquitoes have been estimated to be responsible for half of all human deaths due to transmission of disease. *Pesticides improve human health by destroying disease-carrying organisms* (West Nile virus, encephalitis, African sleeping sickness, malaria, yellow fever, plague, etc.).

(iii) 2 points maximum (1 point for each correct negative effect and explanation)

Restatement: Two negative effects of pesticide use. Identify and discuss TWO negative effects of pesticide use.

(1) If a pesticide is continually applied to a population of the pest species, most susceptible individuals will be killed, leaving only resistant individuals. These resistant individuals breed and multiply. Eventually a high proportion of the individuals from that pest species are now resistant to the pesticide. We have simply *caused pest populations with a higher tolerance for poisons to survive and breed*. More toxic pesticides in turn are developed and utilized.

(2) *Pesticides can accumulate in living organisms.* An example of accumulation is the uptake of a water-insoluble pesticide, such as chlordane, by a creature living in water. Since this pesticide is stored in the organism, the pesticide accumulates and increases over time. If this organism is eaten by an organism higher in the food chain that can also store this pesticide, levels can reach higher values in the higher organism than is present in the water in which it lives. Levels in fish, for example, can be tens to hundreds of thousands of times greater than ambient water levels of the same pesticide. This type of accumulation is called bioaccumulation. In this regard, it should be remembered that humans are at the top of the food chain and so may be the most vulnerable to bioaccumulation.

(b) 2 points maximum (1 point for each correct alternative and explanation)

Restatement: Two alternatives to the use of pesticides. Discuss TWO alternatives to the use of pesticides.

GROWING PEST-RESISTANT CROPS

When landscaping a yard or planning a garden, choose plant varieties that are native to the region and climate. Hearty, native plants resist disease and infestation, and they often use less water.

CROP ROTATION

Plant rotation and interplanting prevent the buildup and spread of pests in one area or among specific plant types.

BENEFICIAL INSECTS AND ANIMALS

Protect and encourage the presence of insect-feeding birds, bats, spiders, praying mantises, ladybugs, predatory mites, parasitic flies, and wasps. Beneficial insect species can often be purchased in volume.

PHEROMONES

Pheromones are chemical signals produced by animals to communicate with others of the same species. In insects, they consist of highly specific perfumes, generally derivatives of natural fatty acids closely related to the aromas of fruit. They are non-toxic. Pheromones may be used to attract insects to traps or to deter insects from laying eggs. However, the most widespread and effective application of pheromones is for mating disruption.

(c) 1 point maximum. (1 point for naming a correct U.S. federal law or international treaty along with a correct description.) Note: Credit will be awarded for choosing *any* applicable U.S. federal law or international treaty that focuses on the use of pesticides (e.g., Clean Water Act; Resource Conservation and Recovery Act; Comprehensive Environmental Response, Compensation, and Liability Act (Superfund); etc.).

Restatement: Name and description of one U.S. federal law **OR** one international treaty that focuses on the use of pesticides.

The U. S. federal government first regulated pesticides when Congress passed the Insecticide Act of 1910. This law was intended to protect farmers from adulterated or misbranded products. Congress broadened the federal government's control of pesticides by passing the original Federal Insecticide, Fungicide and Rodenticide Act (FIFRA) of 1947. FIFRA required the Department of Agriculture to register all pesticides prior to their introduction in interstate commerce. A 1964 amendment authorized the secretary of agriculture to refuse registration to pesticides that were unsafe or ineffective and to remove them from the market. In 1970, Congress transferred the administration of FIFRA to the newly created Environmental Protection Agency (EPA). This was the initiation of a shift in the focus of federal policy from the control of pesticides for reasonably safe use in agricultural production to control of pesticides for reduction of unreasonable risks to humans and the environment. This new policy focus was expanded by the passage of the Federal Environmental Pesticide Control Act of 1972 (FEPCA) that amended FIFRA by specifying methods and standards of control in greater detail. In general, there has been a shift toward greater emphasis on minimizing risks associated with toxicity and environmental degradation and away from pesticide efficacy issues. Under FIFRA, no one may sell, distribute, or use a pesticide unless it is registered by the EPA. Registration includes approval by the EPA of the pesticide's label, which must give detailed instructions for its safe use. The EPA must classify each pesticide as either general use, restricted use, or both. General-use pesticides may be applied by anyone. However, restricted-use pesticides may be applied only by certified applicators or persons working under the direct supervision of a certified applicator. Because there are only limited data for new chemicals, most pesticides are initially classified as restricted use. Applicators are certified by a state if the state operates a certification program approved by the EPA.

Practice Exam 2

With Answers and Analysis

SECTION I (MULTIPLE-CHOICE QUESTIONS)

Time: 90 minutes

100 questions

60% of total grade

No calculators allowed

This section consists of 100 multiple-choice questions. Mark your answers carefully on the answer sheet.

General Instructions

Do not open this booklet until you are told to do so by the proctor.

Be sure to write your answers for Section I on the separate answer sheet. Use the test booklet for your scratch work or notes. Remember, though, that no credit will be given for work, notes, or answers written only in the test booklet. Once you have selected an answer, thoroughly blacken the corresponding circle on the answer sheet. To change an answer, erase your previous mark completely, and then record your new answer. Mark only one answer for each question.

Example   **Sample Answer**

The Pacific is   Ⓐ Ⓑ ● Ⓓ Ⓔ

      (A) a river
      (B) a lake
      (C) an ocean
      (D) a sea
      (E) a gulf

There is no penalty for wrong answers on the multiple-choice section, so you should answer all multiple-choice questions. Even if you have no idea of the correct answer, you should try to eliminate any obvious incorrect choices, and then guess.

Because it is not expected that all test takers will complete this section, do not spend too much time on difficult questions. First answer the questions you can answer readily. Then, if you have time, return to the difficult questions later. Do not get stuck on one question. Work quickly but accurately. Use your time effectively.

Answer Sheet

PRACTICE EXAM 2

1 Ⓐ Ⓑ Ⓒ Ⓓ Ⓔ	26 Ⓐ Ⓑ Ⓒ Ⓓ Ⓔ	51 Ⓐ Ⓑ Ⓒ Ⓓ Ⓔ	76 Ⓐ Ⓑ Ⓒ Ⓓ Ⓔ
2 Ⓐ Ⓑ Ⓒ Ⓓ Ⓔ	27 Ⓐ Ⓑ Ⓒ Ⓓ Ⓔ	52 Ⓐ Ⓑ Ⓒ Ⓓ Ⓔ	77 Ⓐ Ⓑ Ⓒ Ⓓ Ⓔ
3 Ⓐ Ⓑ Ⓒ Ⓓ Ⓔ	28 Ⓐ Ⓑ Ⓒ Ⓓ Ⓔ	53 Ⓐ Ⓑ Ⓒ Ⓓ Ⓔ	78 Ⓐ Ⓑ Ⓒ Ⓓ Ⓔ
4 Ⓐ Ⓑ Ⓒ Ⓓ Ⓔ	29 Ⓐ Ⓑ Ⓒ Ⓓ Ⓔ	54 Ⓐ Ⓑ Ⓒ Ⓓ Ⓔ	79 Ⓐ Ⓑ Ⓒ Ⓓ Ⓔ
5 Ⓐ Ⓑ Ⓒ Ⓓ Ⓔ	30 Ⓐ Ⓑ Ⓒ Ⓓ Ⓔ	55 Ⓐ Ⓑ Ⓒ Ⓓ Ⓔ	80 Ⓐ Ⓑ Ⓒ Ⓓ Ⓔ
6 Ⓐ Ⓑ Ⓒ Ⓓ Ⓔ	31 Ⓐ Ⓑ Ⓒ Ⓓ Ⓔ	56 Ⓐ Ⓑ Ⓒ Ⓓ Ⓔ	81 Ⓐ Ⓑ Ⓒ Ⓓ Ⓔ
7 Ⓐ Ⓑ Ⓒ Ⓓ Ⓔ	32 Ⓐ Ⓑ Ⓒ Ⓓ Ⓔ	57 Ⓐ Ⓑ Ⓒ Ⓓ Ⓔ	82 Ⓐ Ⓑ Ⓒ Ⓓ Ⓔ
8 Ⓐ Ⓑ Ⓒ Ⓓ Ⓔ	33 Ⓐ Ⓑ Ⓒ Ⓓ Ⓔ	58 Ⓐ Ⓑ Ⓒ Ⓓ Ⓔ	83 Ⓐ Ⓑ Ⓒ Ⓓ Ⓔ
9 Ⓐ Ⓑ Ⓒ Ⓓ Ⓔ	34 Ⓐ Ⓑ Ⓒ Ⓓ Ⓔ	59 Ⓐ Ⓑ Ⓒ Ⓓ Ⓔ	84 Ⓐ Ⓑ Ⓒ Ⓓ Ⓔ
10 Ⓐ Ⓑ Ⓒ Ⓓ Ⓔ	35 Ⓐ Ⓑ Ⓒ Ⓓ Ⓔ	60 Ⓐ Ⓑ Ⓒ Ⓓ Ⓔ	85 Ⓐ Ⓑ Ⓒ Ⓓ Ⓔ
11 Ⓐ Ⓑ Ⓒ Ⓓ Ⓔ	36 Ⓐ Ⓑ Ⓒ Ⓓ Ⓔ	61 Ⓐ Ⓑ Ⓒ Ⓓ Ⓔ	86 Ⓐ Ⓑ Ⓒ Ⓓ Ⓔ
12 Ⓐ Ⓑ Ⓒ Ⓓ Ⓔ	37 Ⓐ Ⓑ Ⓒ Ⓓ Ⓔ	62 Ⓐ Ⓑ Ⓒ Ⓓ Ⓔ	87 Ⓐ Ⓑ Ⓒ Ⓓ Ⓔ
13 Ⓐ Ⓑ Ⓒ Ⓓ Ⓔ	38 Ⓐ Ⓑ Ⓒ Ⓓ Ⓔ	63 Ⓐ Ⓑ Ⓒ Ⓓ Ⓔ	88 Ⓐ Ⓑ Ⓒ Ⓓ Ⓔ
14 Ⓐ Ⓑ Ⓒ Ⓓ Ⓔ	39 Ⓐ Ⓑ Ⓒ Ⓓ Ⓔ	64 Ⓐ Ⓑ Ⓒ Ⓓ Ⓔ	89 Ⓐ Ⓑ Ⓒ Ⓓ Ⓔ
15 Ⓐ Ⓑ Ⓒ Ⓓ Ⓔ	40 Ⓐ Ⓑ Ⓒ Ⓓ Ⓔ	65 Ⓐ Ⓑ Ⓒ Ⓓ Ⓔ	90 Ⓐ Ⓑ Ⓒ Ⓓ Ⓔ
16 Ⓐ Ⓑ Ⓒ Ⓓ Ⓔ	41 Ⓐ Ⓑ Ⓒ Ⓓ Ⓔ	66 Ⓐ Ⓑ Ⓒ Ⓓ Ⓔ	91 Ⓐ Ⓑ Ⓒ Ⓓ Ⓔ
17 Ⓐ Ⓑ Ⓒ Ⓓ Ⓔ	42 Ⓐ Ⓑ Ⓒ Ⓓ Ⓔ	67 Ⓐ Ⓑ Ⓒ Ⓓ Ⓔ	92 Ⓐ Ⓑ Ⓒ Ⓓ Ⓔ
18 Ⓐ Ⓑ Ⓒ Ⓓ Ⓔ	43 Ⓐ Ⓑ Ⓒ Ⓓ Ⓔ	68 Ⓐ Ⓑ Ⓒ Ⓓ Ⓔ	93 Ⓐ Ⓑ Ⓒ Ⓓ Ⓔ
19 Ⓐ Ⓑ Ⓒ Ⓓ Ⓔ	44 Ⓐ Ⓑ Ⓒ Ⓓ Ⓔ	69 Ⓐ Ⓑ Ⓒ Ⓓ Ⓔ	94 Ⓐ Ⓑ Ⓒ Ⓓ Ⓔ
20 Ⓐ Ⓑ Ⓒ Ⓓ Ⓔ	45 Ⓐ Ⓑ Ⓒ Ⓓ Ⓔ	70 Ⓐ Ⓑ Ⓒ Ⓓ Ⓔ	95 Ⓐ Ⓑ Ⓒ Ⓓ Ⓔ
21 Ⓐ Ⓑ Ⓒ Ⓓ Ⓔ	46 Ⓐ Ⓑ Ⓒ Ⓓ Ⓔ	71 Ⓐ Ⓑ Ⓒ Ⓓ Ⓔ	96 Ⓐ Ⓑ Ⓒ Ⓓ Ⓔ
22 Ⓐ Ⓑ Ⓒ Ⓓ Ⓔ	47 Ⓐ Ⓑ Ⓒ Ⓓ Ⓔ	72 Ⓐ Ⓑ Ⓒ Ⓓ Ⓔ	97 Ⓐ Ⓑ Ⓒ Ⓓ Ⓔ
23 Ⓐ Ⓑ Ⓒ Ⓓ Ⓔ	48 Ⓐ Ⓑ Ⓒ Ⓓ Ⓔ	73 Ⓐ Ⓑ Ⓒ Ⓓ Ⓔ	98 Ⓐ Ⓑ Ⓒ Ⓓ Ⓔ
24 Ⓐ Ⓑ Ⓒ Ⓓ Ⓔ	49 Ⓐ Ⓑ Ⓒ Ⓓ Ⓔ	74 Ⓐ Ⓑ Ⓒ Ⓓ Ⓔ	99 Ⓐ Ⓑ Ⓒ Ⓓ Ⓔ
25 Ⓐ Ⓑ Ⓒ Ⓓ Ⓔ	50 Ⓐ Ⓑ Ⓒ Ⓓ Ⓔ	75 Ⓐ Ⓑ Ⓒ Ⓓ Ⓔ	100 Ⓐ Ⓑ Ⓒ Ⓓ Ⓔ

Directions: For each question or statement, select the one lettered choice that is the best answer and fill in the corresponding circle on the answer sheet.

1. The diagram below represents a phylogenetic tree of the evolution of even-toed ungulates.

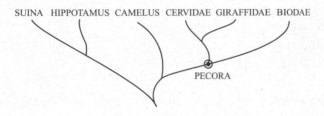

   The most likely explanation for the branching pattern seen in the circled region is that

   (A) environmental changes caused extinction
   (B) inbreeding led to speciation
   (C) no speciation occurred
   (D) speciation was influenced by environmental change
   (E) only the best-adapted organisms survived from generation to generation

2. Two lightbulbs are for sale—a 15-watt compact fluorescent light (CFL) and a 60-watt incandescent. You know that a 15-watt compact fluorescent lightbulb will produce the same amount of light as a 60-watt incandescent lightbulb. If electricity costs $0.10 per kWh and you run each lightbulb for 8,000 hours, how much money will you save in the cost of electricity by buying the compact fluorescent lightbulb?

   (A) $4.00
   (B) $8.00
   (C) $12.00
   (D) $36.00
   (E) $48.00

3. Winds are primarily caused by

   (A) differences in air pressure
   (B) the Coriolis effect
   (C) ocean currents
   (D) seasons
   (E) the Earth's rotation on its axis

4. Which of the following processes does NOT occur within current catalytic converters?

   I. Conversion of nitrogen oxides to nitrogen and oxygen
  II. Removal of carbon dioxide
 III. Conversion of unburned hydrocarbons to carbon dioxide and water

(A) I only
(B) II only
(C) III only
(D) I and II
(E) I and III

5. You and a partner run an automobile salvage yard where you offer used automobile parts to customers, offering them substantial savings over buying new parts. Which of the following auto parts in your salvage yard would pose the greatest risk to stratospheric ozone depletion?

(A) Tires, should they catch on fire.
(B) Oil, should it leak from the crank case and enter the groundwater.
(C) Air conditioners, if they should leak Freon™.
(D) Leaking gasoline, should it catch on fire.
(E) Heavy metals from batteries such as lead should it enter the food web.

6. Suppose that the ecological efficiency at each trophic level of a particular ecosystem is 20%. If the green plants of the ecosystem capture 100 units of energy, about _____ units of energy will be available to support herbivores, and about _____ units of energy will be available to support primary carnivores.

(A) 120, 140
(B) 120, 240
(C) 20, 2
(D) 20, 4
(E) 20, 1

7. The water table is at the

(A) top of the zone of saturation
(B) bottom of the zone of saturation
(C) top of the zone of aeration
(D) bottom of the zone of aeration
(E) middle of the zone of infiltration

8. A soil test report recommends 8 pounds of 8-0-24 fertilizer per 1,000 square feet. How much phosphorus does it recommend if the area planted is equal to 10,000 square feet?

   (A) 0 pounds
   (B) 8 pounds
   (C) 24 pounds
   (D) 80 pounds
   (E) 240 pounds

9. Today, most of the world's energy comes from

   (A) natural gas, coal, and oil
   (B) oil, wood, and hydroelectric
   (C) hydroelectric, solar, and biomass
   (D) coal, oil, and nuclear
   (E) natural gas, hydroelectric, and oil

10. An AP Environmental Science class conducted an experiment to illustrate the principles of Thomas Malthus. On day 1, three male and three female fruit flies were placed in a flat-bottom flask that contained a cornmeal/banana medium. No other flies were added or removed during the course of this experiment. The students counted the number of flies in the flask each week. The graph shows the results that the class obtained after 55 days.

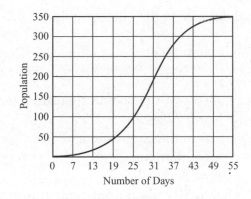

The rate of reproduction is equal to the rate of death on day

   (A) 1
   (B) 25
   (C) 43
   (D) 55
   (E) 1 and 55

11. The concept of net primary productivity

    (A) is the rate at which producers manufacture chemical energy through photosynthesis

    (B) is the rate at which producers use chemical energy through respiration

    (C) is the rate of photosynthesis plus the rate of respiration

    (D) can be thought of as the basic food source for decomposers in an ecosystem

    (E) is usually reported as the energy output of an area of producers over a given time period

12. Which of the following is NOT a unit of energy?

    (A) Joule

    (B) Calorie

    (C) Watt

    (D) Kilowatt-hour

    (E) Btu

13. Which of the following is NOT a phenomenon associated with La Niña?

    (A) Unusually cold ocean temperatures in the eastern equatorial Pacific

    (B) Wetter-than-normal conditions across the Pacific Northwest

    (C) Dryer and warmer-than-normal conditions in the southern states

    (D) Warmer-than-normal winter temperatures in the southeastern United States

    (E) Substantial decrease in the number of hurricanes

14. Which of the following is NOT a possible cause/effect of increasing ocean temperatures?

    (A) A significant increase in the ocean circulation that transports warm water to the North Atlantic

    (B) Large reductions in the Greenland and West Antarctic ice sheets

    (C) Accelerated global warming

    (D) Decreases in upwelling

    (E) Releases of terrestrial carbon from permafrost regions and methane from hydrates in coastal sediments

15. Which of the following would NOT be a chemical property of a persistent organic pollutant such as DDT?

    I. Highly soluble in water

    II. High molecular masses

    III. Usually contain a halogen like chlorine, bromine, or fluorine

    (A) I only

    (B) II only

    (C) III only

    (D) I and II

    (E) II and III

16. The geologic time scale was constructed based upon

    I. fossil records
    II. theory of superposition
    III. global correlation of strata or layers of rocks

    (A) I only
    (B) II
    (C) III
    (D) I and II
    (E) I, II, and III

17. Which biome, found primarily in the eastern United States, central Europe, and eastern Asia, is home to some of the world's largest cities and has probably endured the impact of humans more than any other biome?

    (A) Desert
    (B) Coniferous forest
    (C) Temperate deciduous forest
    (D) Grassland
    (E) Chaparral

18. How does the great ocean conveyor belt moderate the Earth's climate?

    I. It brings more precipitation to the lower latitudes
    II. It brings heat from tropical regions to northern latitudes
    III. It brings cold air from the polar regions to the tropics

    (A) I only
    (B) II only
    (C) III only
    (D) I and II
    (E) II and III

19. An agricultural consequence of higher CO_2 levels in the atmosphere for most crops is:

    I. Decreased nitrogen levels in the crop and their seeds
    II. Increased nitrogen levels in the crop and their seeds
    III. Larger crop yields

    (A) I only
    (B) II only
    (C) III only
    (D) I and III
    (E) II and III

20. Cars, trucks, and buses account for _____ of U.S. greenhouse gas emissions.

    (A) less than 5%
    (B) between 10% and 20%
    (C) between 20% and 33%
    (D) between 35% and 75%
    (E) more than 75%

21. The amount of the environment necessary to produce the goods and services necessary to support a particular lifestyle is known as

    (A) a resource partition
    (B) an ecological footprint
    (C) the per capita index requirement
    (D) the lifestyle index
    (E) commons

22. Which of the organisms listed below are uniquely sensitive to air pollution, making them valuable as early warning indicators of reduced air quality?

    (A) Algae
    (B) Fungus
    (C) Lichen
    (D) Phytoplankton
    (E) Humans

23. Which of the following threats to biodiversity would fall under the category of the introduction of an exotic or invasive species?

    I. Reintroducing black-footed ferrets into Wyoming
    II. Sea lampreys swimming up the Erie Canal to enter the Great Lakes
    III. Bringing wolves into Yellowstone National Park

    (A) I only
    (B) II only
    (C) III only
    (D) I and III
    (E) II and III

24. Which act listed below set criteria for municipal solid waste landfills and prohibited the open dumping of solid wastes?

    (A) CERCLA—Comprehensive Environmental Response, Compensation, and Liability Act (Superfund)
    (B) TOSCA—Toxic Substances Control Act
    (C) RCRA—Resource Conservation and Recovery Act
    (D) Clean Water Act
    (E) None of the above

25. The greatest threat to global biodiversity is

    (A) introduction of invasive species
    (B) poaching
    (C) pollution
    (D) emerging viruses
    (E) deforestation

26. Certain volcanoes have a bowl-shaped crater at the summit and grow to only about a thousand feet. They are usually made of piles of lava, not ash. During the eruption, blobs of lava are blown into the air and break into small fragments that fall around the opening to the volcano. Parícutin in Mexico and the middle of Crater Lake, Oregon, are examples. These are called

    (A) cinder cones
    (B) shield volcanoes
    (C) composite volcanoes
    (D) mud volcanoes
    (E) spatter cones

27. Which U.S. executive agency, commission, service, or department listed below is involved in regulations and protection of endangered species?

    I. Department of the Interior
    II. Fish and Wildlife Service
    III. Environmental Protection Agency

    (A) I only
    (B) II only
    (C) III only
    (D) I and II
    (E) I, II, and III

28. Which of the following is NOT a method used to disinfect municipal water supplies?

    (A) Using chlorine or chlorine compounds
    (B) Using ultraviolet light
    (C) Using ozone
    (D) Using fluorine or fluoride compounds
    (E) Using hydrogen peroxide

29. Excavating and hauling soil off-site to an approved soil disposal/treatment facility would be an example of

    (A) sustainability
    (B) remediation
    (C) conservation
    (D) preservation
    (E) mitigation

Question 30 refers to the locations marked by letters on the world map below.

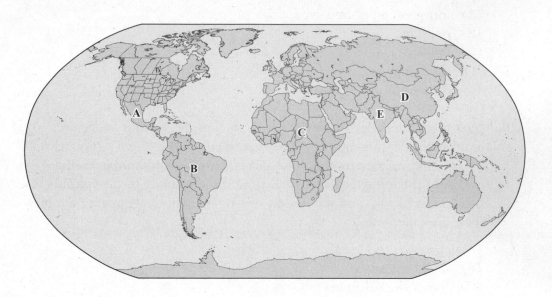

30. The location where fertility rates are highest.

    (A) A
    (B) B
    (C) C
    (D) D
    (E) E

31. Wood in developing countries is primarily used for

    (A) construction
    (B) making furniture
    (C) wood pulp to make paper products
    (D) making cardboard
    (E) cooking and heating

Questions 32–36

Select from the following locations.

    (A) Bhopal, India
    (B) Chernobyl, Ukraine
    (C) Love Canal, New York
    (D) Minamata Bay, Japan
    (E) Three Mile Island, Pennsylvania

32. Site of a hazardous chemical dumping ground over which homes and a school were built.

33. Site of mercury poisoning.

34. The most serious commercial nuclear accident in U.S. history.

35. Leakage of poisonous gases from a pesticide manufacturing plant.

36. Nuclear power plant accident that released 30 to 40 times the radiation of the atomic bombs dropped on Hiroshima and Nagasaki.

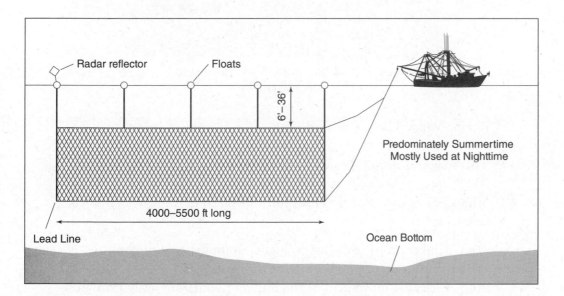

37. The type of fishing seen in the diagram above would be best described as

    (A) bottom trawling
    (B) longline fishing
    (C) drift gill net
    (D) angling
    (E) cast netting

Practice Exam 2

Questions 38–39 refer to the layers of the Earth's atmosphere as shown below.

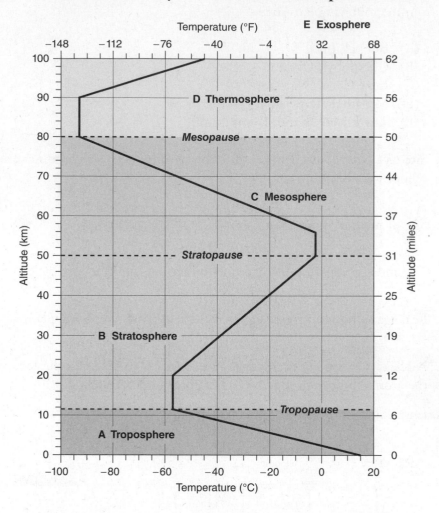

38. Region where UVC is filtered out.

39. This region is mostly heated by transfer of energy from the surface.

40. Stratospheric ozone depletion is most likely to result in which of the following?

    (A) Higher crop yields due to higher amounts of sunlight
    (B) Disruption of photosynthesis in plants
    (C) Increased movement of the human population away from areas influenced by the hole in the ozone
    (D) Less clouds in the sky
    (E) Warmer temperatures

41. Viability is the capacity of living organisms to live, develop, or germinate under favorable conditions. Which of the following factors decreases a population's viability?

    I. Specialized niche
    II. Few competitors
    III. Ability to migrate

    (A) I only
    (B) II only
    (C) III only
    (D) I and III
    (E) II and III

42. Most of the world's electronic wastes end up in what country?

    (A) United States
    (B) India
    (C) Mexico
    (D) China
    (E) South Korea

43. Which one of the following is a secondary sewage treatment process?

    (A) Lagooning
    (B) Filter (oxidizing) beds
    (C) Screening
    (D) Nutrient removal
    (E) Constructed wetlands

44. The largest user of freshwater worldwide is

    (A) mining
    (B) irrigation
    (C) industry
    (D) home use
    (E) production of electrical power

45. Choose the statement that is FALSE.

    (A) Domestic fruits and vegetables are less likely to have pesticide residues than imported ones.
    (B) Cancer may not be the primary risk from chronic, long-term exposure to pesticides.
    (C) When the EPA looks at a pesticide to decide whether to register it for use in the United States, its primary concern is to ensure that there is no significant human health or environmental risk presented by the chemical.
    (D) The federal government does not prohibit the use of pesticides known to cause cancer.
    (E) Washing and peeling fruits and vegetables does not remove all or most pesticide residues.

46. Of the choices listed, cap-and-trade policies have historically been used in controlling

   (A) overfishing
   (B) dumping trash into the open sea
   (C) carbon dioxide emissions
   (D) the storage of nuclear wastes
   (E) the release of dioxin and other pollutants into groundwater systems

Questions 47 and 48 refer to the following laboratory investigation.

An APES class was doing field research using a mark-recapture technique to estimate the population size of a particular species of butterfly. The size of the field was exactly 2 hectares (ha) or 20,000 square meters. Initially, the class caught and marked 150 of these butterflies in the field and then released them. Later, the class recaptured 100 of this species of butterfly, of which 20 were marked.

47. What is the estimate of the population size of this species of butterfly?

   (A) 13
   (B) 30
   (C) 750
   (D) 1,500
   (E) 3,000

48. What was the population density of the butterflies?

   (A) 188 butterflies per ha
   (B) 375 butterflies per ha
   (C) 750 butterflies per ha
   (D) 1,500 butterflies per ha
   (E) 3,000 butterflies per ha

49. An APES class went on a field trip into a coniferous forest. They discovered a very large section of land that had been completely logged. There were just stumps where large coniferous trees had once stood. There was also very little animal life in the area. Which method of logging had most likely been used in this section of land?

   (A) Strip cutting
   (B) Clear cutting
   (C) Seed tree cutting
   (D) Shelterwood cutting
   (E) Selective cutting

50. You have been placed in charge of rebuilding a salmon population in a river basin that contains a hydroelectric dam. Which of the following remediation techniques would NOT be effective?

    (A) Reduce silt runoff
    (B) Build fish ladders
    (C) Decrease water flow from the dam
    (D) Release juvenile salmon from hatcheries
    (E) Use trucks and barges to transport salmon around the dam

51. Which one of the following proposals would NOT increase the sustainability of ocean fisheries management?

    (A) Establish fishing quotas based on past harvests.
    (B) Set quotas for fisheries well below their estimated maximum sustainable yields.
    (C) Sharply reduce fishing subsidies.
    (D) Shift the burden of proof to the fishing industry to show that their operations are sustainable.
    (E) Strengthen integrated coastal management programs.

52. The most abundant element in the Earth's crust is

    (A) silicon
    (B) aluminum
    (C) oxygen
    (D) hydrogen
    (E) carbon

53. Smog levels in large, urban cities are generally highest during the

    (A) summer
    (B) spring
    (C) fall
    (D) winter
    (E) season or time of year does not matter

54. In general, parasites tend to

    (A) become more virulent as they live within the host
    (B) destroy the host completely
    (C) become deactivated as they live within the host
    (D) be only mildly pathogenic
    (E) require large amounts of oxygen

55. The population of a country in 1994 was 200 million. Its rate of growth was 1.2%. Assuming that the rate of growth remains unchanged and all other factors remain constant, in what year will the population of the country reach 400 million?

   (A) 2004
   (B) 2024
   (C) 2040
   (D) 2054
   (E) 2104

56. Which of the following contributes LEAST to acid deposition?

   (A) Sulfur dioxide
   (B) Ammonia
   (C) Nitrogen oxides
   (D) Lead
   (E) Ozone

57. The circulation of air in Hadley cells results in

   (A) low pressure and rainfall at the equator
   (B) high pressure and rainfall at the equator
   (C) low pressure and dry conditions at about 30° north and south of the equator
   (D) high pressure and wet conditions at about 30° north and south of the equator
   (E) both (A) and (C)

58. All of the following are characteristics of *K*-strategists EXCEPT

   (A) mature slowly
   (B) low juvenile mortality rate
   (C) niche generalists
   (D) Type I or II survivorship curve
   (E) intraspecific competition due to density-dependent limiting factors

59. If a city of population 100,000 experiences 1,000 births, 600 deaths, 500 immigrants, and 100 emigrants in the course of a year, what is its net annual percentage growth rate?

   (A) 0.4%
   (B) 0.8%
   (C) 1.6%
   (D) 3.2%
   (E) 8%

Question 60 refers to the diagram below.

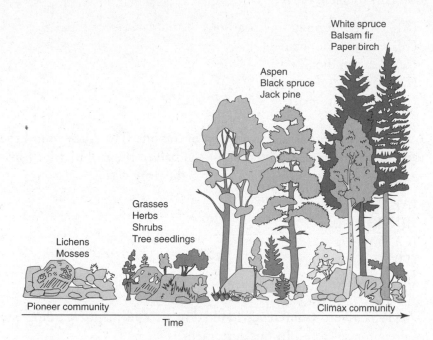

White spruce
Balsam fir
Paper birch

Aspen
Black spruce
Jack pine

Grasses
Herbs
Shrubs
Tree seedlings

Lichens
Mosses

Pioneer community   Climax community

Time

60. The greatest species diversity would be found in

   (A) the pioneer community represented by the lichens and mosses.
   (B) the community composed primarily of grasses, herbs, shrubs, and tree seedlings.
   (C) the community composed primarily of aspen, black spruce, and jack pine.
   (D) the community composed primarily of white spruce, balsam fir, and paper birch.
   (E) all communities equally.

61. A new road connecting a planned community to an existing urban area was needed due to high traffic volume on the existing roadway. The least expensive option was to build the road through a forested area owned by the county. An environmental impact study was conducted and the developers agreed to the following conditions in exchange for the contract: (1) use selective cutting and clearing practices; (2) replace or restore forested areas that will be affected during the construction of the new highway; (3) preserve as much existing vegetation as possible during the construction of the new highway; and (4) the developer would purchase a similar amount of privately held land and place it in conservation easements. This trade-off approach to addressing an environmental issue is known as

   (A) sustainability
   (B) remediation
   (C) preservation
   (D) restoration
   (E) mitigation

62. Which mobile source pollutant cannot be currently controlled by emission control technology?

    (A) Ozone-forming hydrocarbons
    (B) Carbon monoxide
    (C) Carbon dioxide
    (D) Air toxics
    (E) Particulate matter

63. A new cancer drug was being tested on rabbits. The study found that it took 400 milligrams of the drug to kill half of the rabbits whose average weight was 4 kilograms. The LD_{50} for the drug was

    (A) 0.01%
    (B) 0.1 g/kg
    (C) 50 mg/kg
    (D) 10 mg/kg
    (E) 100 g/kg

64. The 1997 Kyoto Conference resulted in an agreement regarding emissions of greenhouse gasses. In this agreement,

    (A) all countries would be subject to the same amount of reductions in their emissions using metric tons as the international standard.
    (B) all countries would be subject to the same percentage reduction in their emissions.
    (C) only the underdeveloped countries would be subject to a reduction in their emissions.
    (D) the United States would be exempt from any mandated reductions.
    (E) the developed countries would set goals for the percentage reduction of their emissions.

65. The largest contaminant (by weight and volume) of inland surface waters such as lakes, rivers, and streams in the United States is

    (A) sediment
    (B) organic wastes
    (C) pathogenic organisms
    (D) heavy metals
    (E) oil

66. Currently, the United States recycles about what percentage of the municipal solid waste it generates?

    (A) 3%
    (B) 15%
    (C) 35%
    (D) 50%
    (E) 75%

Questions 67, 68, and 69 refer to the following diagram of a heavy water moderated nuclear reactor.

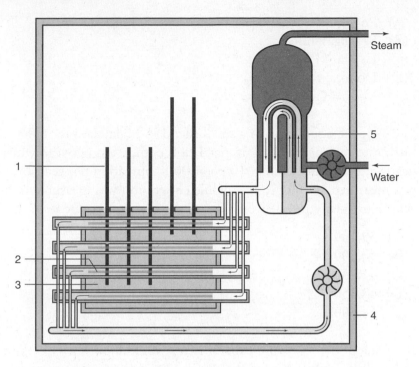

67. "1" in the diagram above represents the

    (A) control rods
    (B) moderator
    (C) fuel rods
    (D) concrete shields
    (E) condensers

68. "3" in the diagram above represents the

    (A) control rods
    (B) moderator
    (C) fuel rods
    (D) concrete shield
    (E) heat exchanger

69. Which one of the statements below is TRUE regarding the moderator and the control rods in a moderated nuclear reactor?

    (A) The moderator and control rods absorb neutrons.
    (B) The moderator and control rods slow the neutrons down.
    (C) The moderator slows the neutrons down, while the control rods absorb the neutrons.
    (D) The control rods slow the neutrons down, while the moderator absorbs the neutrons.
    (E) The moderator slows the neutrons down, while the control rods speed up the neutrons.

70. Which of the cities listed below currently has the HIGHEST level of air pollution?

    (A) Los Angeles, California
    (B) Beijing, China
    (C) London, England
    (D) Donora, Pennsylvania
    (E) Mexico City, Mexico

71. In 1995, the population of a small island in Malaysia was 40,000. The birth rate was measured at 35 per 1,000 population per year, while the death rate was measured at 10 per 1,000 population per year. Immigration was measured at 100 per year, while emigration was measured at 50 per year. How many people would be on the island after one year?

    (A) 39,100
    (B) 40,000
    (C) 41,050
    (D) 42,150
    (E) 44,500

72. In which of the following pairs of items would biodiversity be more likely to be LESS in the first area than in the second?

    (A) savanna, taiga
    (B) large lake, small lake
    (C) temperate area, the Arctic
    (D) temperate area, tropical area
    (E) intertidal zone, benthic zone

73. Which choice listed below makes up 60% of the world's human food energy intake?

    (A) Meat, fish, and milk or milk products
    (B) Rice, corn (maize), and wheat
    (C) Millet, sorghum, roots, and tubers
    (D) Rice and fish
    (E) Beans, rice, corn

74. Among adults, which of the following represents the most preventable cause of death?

    (A) Cardiovascular disease
    (B) AIDS
    (C) Alcoholism
    (D) Use of tobacco
    (E) Traffic accidents

75. The process in which ammonia is oxidized to nitrite (NO_2^-) and nitrate (NO_3^-), the forms most usable by plants, through the action of *Nitrosomonas* and *Nitrobacter* bacteria is known as

    (A) nitrogen fixation
    (B) nitrification
    (C) assimilation
    (D) ammonification
    (E) denitrification

76. Which of the following sections of the Earth contains most of the Earth's mass, is mostly solid, and is primarily composed of iron, magnesium, aluminum, and silicon-oxygen compounds?

    (A) Continental crust
    (B) Oceanic crust
    (C) Core
    (D) Moho
    (E) Mantle

77. Examine the following graph, which shows the predator-prey relationship between hares and lynxes.

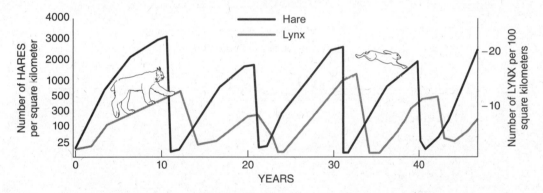

The population cycles of the snowshoe hare and its predator, the lynx, reveal that

    (A) the prey population is controlled by predators alone
    (B) hares and lynxes are so mutually dependent that each species cannot survive without the other
    (C) the relationship is primarily independent; in other words, the number of hares does not have any effect on the number of lynxes and vice versa.
    (D) both hare and lynx populations are regulated mainly by abiotic factors
    (E) the hare population is *r*-selected and the lynx population is *K*-selected

78. "We can burn coal to produce electricity to operate a refrigerator" is an example of the _____ and "If we burn coal to produce electricity to operate a refrigerator, we lose a great deal of energy in the form of heat" is an example of the _____

    (A) first law of thermodynamics, first law of thermodynamics
    (B) second law of thermodynamics, first law of thermodynamics
    (C) first law of thermodynamics, second law of thermodynamics
    (D) first law of thermodynamics, third law of thermodynamics
    (E) third law of thermodynamics, first law of thermodynamics

79. Refer to the following age-structure diagram:

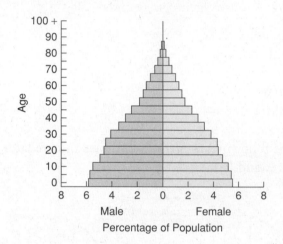

    The age-structure diagram above would be typical for what country?

    (A) United States
    (B) Canada
    (C) Mexico
    (D) Germany
    (E) Japan

80. Why is territoriality an adaptive behavior for songbirds maintaining populations at or near their carrying capacity?

    (A) Because songbirds expend a tremendous amount of energy defending territories, they spend less time feeding their young and fledgling mortality increases.
    (B) Only the fittest males defend territories, and they attract the fittest females; therefore, the best genes are conveyed to the next generation.
    (C) Songbird males defend territories commensurate with the size from which they can derive adequate resources for themselves, their mates, and their chicks.
    (D) Many individuals are killed in the ritualistic conflicts that go along with territorial defense.
    (E) Songbirds make improvements to the territories they inhabit so that they can all enjoy larger clutches and successfully fledged chicks.

81. Butterflies and moths both feed on flowers. Butterflies feed during the day, and moths feed at night. This is an example of

    (A) *r*-strategy
    (B) *K*-strategy
    (C) resource partitioning
    (D) commensalism
    (E) mutualism

82. It costs a copper smelter $200 to reduce its emissions by 1 ton and $250 for an additional ton. It costs an electric utility $100 to reduce its emissions by 1 ton and $150 for an additional ton. What is the cheapest way of reducing total emissions by 2 tons?

    (A) Legislate that each firm must reduce emissions by two tons.
    (B) Charge both firms $251 for every ton they emit.
    (C) Allow each firm to buy a permit to pollute that costs $151.
    (D) File an injunction to halt production until the firms reduce emissions by 2 tons.
    (E) None of the above is correct.

83. Which of the following organisms listed below would be MOST at risk for accumulating fat soluble pesticides?

    (A) Aquatic plants
    (B) Cattle
    (C) Hawks
    (D) Protozoa
    (E) Bees

84. Which of the following examples does/do NOT demonstrate a negative feedback loop?

    (A) Increased technology in agricultural science produces more food resources, resulting in a higher birth rate.
    (B) Frequent large fires can increase atmospheric greenhouse gas concentrations, causing more warming and drought, and leading to more fires, which reduce the trees available to store carbon.
    (C) A thermostat working to keep a home at 68°F during the winter.
    (D) A nuclear chain reaction.
    (E) A, B, and D.

85. Demographic transition leads to stabilizing population growth and is generally characterized as having four separate stages. Place the following stages in the proper order as they would most likely occur.

  I. Birthrates equal mortality rates, and zero population growth is achieved. Birthrates and death rates are both relatively low, and the standard of living is much higher than during the earlier periods. In some countries, birthrates may actually fall below mortality rates and result in net losses in population.

  II. Living conditions are severe, medical care is poor or nonexistent, and the food supply is limited due to poor agricultural techniques, poor preservation, and pestilence. Birthrates are high to replace individuals lost through high mortality rates. The net result is little population growth.

  III. Urbanization decreases the economic incentives for large families. The cost of supporting an urban family grows, and parents are more actively discouraged from having large families. Educational and work opportunities for women decrease birth rates. Obtaining food is not a major focus of the day. Leisure time is available, and retirement safety nets are in place, reducing the need for extra children to support parents. In response to these economic pressures, the birthrate starts to drop, ultimately coming close to the death rate.

  IV. Occurs after the start of industrialization. Standards of hygiene and more modern medical techniques begin to drive the death rate down, leading to a significant upward trend in population size. Mortality rates drop as a result of advances in medical care, improved sanitation, cleaner water supplies, vaccination, and higher levels of education. The net result is a rapid increase in population.

  (A) I, II, III, IV
  (B) IV, III, II, I
  (C) I, IV, II, III
  (D) II, IV, III, I
  (E) III, I, II, IV

86. The concentration of which gas can be reduced by preventing forest depletion?

  (A) Carbon dioxide
  (B) Nitrous oxide
  (C) Oxygen
  (D) Methane
  (E) CFCs

87. Heap leaching could be a process used in the extraction of

    (A) copper
    (B) nickel
    (C) gold
    (D) uranium
    (E) All of the above

88. After a recent storm, an APES class took a field trip to a storm drain out-let entering the Pacific Ocean at Ballona Creek, in southern California. They carefully collected water samples and brought the samples back to the lab. Alpha group took 100.00 mL of the collected water and filtered it through a 1.2 μm Millipore glass fiber filter. The filter was carefully transferred to a premassed stainless steel crucible and placed into a 105°C oven for 24 hours. The following is a hypothetical set of data from alpha group:

    Weight of crucible + filter + residue after 24 hrs at 105°C = 100.000 g
    Weight of crucible + filter = 80.000 g

    What is the total suspended solid amount measured in mg · L^{-1}?

    (A) $(80.000/100.00) \times 100\%$

    (B) $100.00 - 80.00$

    (C) $\dfrac{(100.00 - 80.00) \times 1{,}000 \times 1{,}000}{100.00}$

    (D) $\dfrac{(100.00 - 80.00) \times 1{,}000}{100}$

    (E) $\dfrac{(100.00 + 80.00) \times 100}{1{,}000}$

89. If a plant stores 1,000 units of energy from the sun, and a field mouse eats the plant and is then eaten by a snake, who is then eaten by a bird, who is then eaten by a carnivore, how much of the original 1,000 units of energy will be available to the carnivore?

    (A) 90
    (B) 9
    (C) 1
    (D) 0.9
    (E) 0.1

90. Which of the following is an advantage of using green manure?

    I. Leguminous green manures such as clover contain nitrogen-fixing symbiotic bacteria in root nodules that fix atmospheric nitrogen in a form that plants can use.

    II. It increases the percentage of organic matter (biomass) in the soil, thereby improving water retention, aeration, and other soil characteristics.

    III. The root systems of some varieties of green manure grow deep in the soil and bring up nutrient resources unavailable to shallower-rooted crops.

    (A) I
    (B) II
    (C) III
    (D) I and III
    (E) I, II, and III

91. Which is probably the principal source of nitrates and phosphates?

    (A) The water cycle
    (B) Nitrogen fixation of lighting
    (C) Bacterial decay
    (D) Changes in environmental temperature
    (E) Changes in light intensity

92. Ocean water temperatures fluctuate less than air temperatures over land. The primary reason for this phenomenon is

    (A) land absorbs more heat than water
    (B) winds distribute heat that builds up over the land
    (C) there is more water on Earth than land
    (D) the high heat capacity of water
    (E) water both cools down and heats up faster than land

93. Which of the following pollutants does NOT occur naturally in nature?

    (A) Nitrous oxide
    (B) Radon
    (C) Sulfur dioxide
    (D) Formaldehyde
    (E) All pollutants listed above occur naturally in nature

94. Which of the following sequences correctly lists the different wave arrivals from first to last during an earthquake?

    (A) P waves then S waves and then finally surface waves
    (B) Surface waves then P waves and then finally S waves
    (C) P waves then surface waves and then finally S waves
    (D) S waves then P waves and then finally surface waves
    (E) Surface waves then S waves and then finally P waves

95. Harmful effects of increased UV radiation on Earth's surface include all of the following EXCEPT

    (A) reduction in crop production
    (B) reduction in the growth of phytoplankton and its cumulative effect on food webs
    (C) cooling of the stratosphere
    (D) warming of the stratosphere
    (E) increases in sunburns and damage to the skin

96. Which of the following choices shows the correct order of events that might occur in the process of primary succession?

    (A) Grasses → small bushes → small herbaceous plants → lichen → conifers → long-lived hardwoods → short-lived hardwoods → bare rock
    (B) Bare rock → mosses → grasses → small herbaceous plants → small bushes → conifers → short-lived hardwoods → long-lived hardwoods
    (C) Long-lived hardwoods → short-lived hardwoods → conifers → small bushes → small herbaceous plants → grasses → bare rock
    (D) Bare rock → grasses → mosses → small herbaceous plants → small bushes → conifers → short-lived hardwoods → long-lived hardwoods
    (E) Conifers → bare rock → long-lived hardwoods → small herbaceous plants → lichen → grasses → small bushes → short-lived hardwoods

97. Which of the following indoor pollutants would NOT be contributed by carpeting?

    (A) Formaldehyde
    (B) Styrene
    (C) Mold
    (D) Methylene chloride
    (E) Mites

98. Which of the following groups would be most likely to exhibit uniform dispersion?

    (A) Red squirrels, which actively defend territories
    (B) Cattails, which grow primarily at edges of lakes and streams
    (C) Dwarf mistletoes, which parasitize particular species of forest tree
    (D) Moths in a city at night
    (E) Lake trout, which seek out deep water

99. All of the following are correct statements about the regulation of populations EXCEPT

(A) a logistic equation reflects the effect of density-dependent factors, which can ultimately stabilize a population around the carrying capacity

(B) density-independent factors have a greater effect as a population's density increases

(C) high densities in a population may cause physiological changes that inhibit reproduction

(D) because of the overlapping nature of population-regulating factors, it is often difficult to determine their cause-and-effect relationships precisely

(E) the occurrence of population cycles in some populations may be the result of crowding or lag times in the response to density-dependent factors

100. Which of the following energy sources has the lowest quality?

(A) High-velocity water flow
(B) Fuelwood
(C) Food
(D) Dispersed geothermal energy
(E) Saudi Arabian oil deposits

SECTION II (FREE-RESPONSE QUESTIONS)

Time: 90 minutes

No calculators allowed

4 questions

Directions: Answer all four questions, which are weighted equally. The suggested time is about 22 minutes for answering each question. Write all your answers on the pages following the questions in the pink booklet. Where calculations are required, clearly show how you arrived at your answer. Where explanation or discussion is required, support your answers with relevant information and/or specific examples.

1. A family is building a new home in Buffalo, New York. Buffalo experiences severe winters. Assume the following.

   • The house has 4,000 square feet.
   • 100,000 Btus of heat per square foot are required to heat the house for the winter.
   • Natural gas sells for $5.00 per thousand cubic feet.
   • 1 cubic foot of natural gas supplies 1,000 Btus of heat energy.
   • 1 kilowatt-hour of electricity supplies 10,000 Btus of heat energy.
   • Electricity costs $50 per 500 kWh.

   (a) Calculate the following, showing all the steps of your calculations, including units.

       (i)   The number of cubic feet of natural gas required to heat the house for the winter.
       (ii) The cost of heating the house using natural gas.
       (iii) The cost of heating the house using electricity.

   (b) The homeowners are discussing with their architect the possibility of using either active or passive solar design to reduce their heating costs.

       (i)   Define "active solar systems" and describe ONE method of how they are used in heating a home.
       (ii) Define "passive solar systems" and describe ONE method of how they are used in heating a home.
       (iii) Identify and describe ONE environmental benefit *or* ONE disadvantage of using solar power systems to heat buildings.

   (c) The homeowners wish to incorporate "green design" into their new home.

       (i)   Define "green design."
       (ii) Describe ONE example of "green design" architecture.

2.

Legal Notice

**Initial Public
Offering of
Common Stock**

The Fremont Seafood Company, headquartered in New Orleans, Louisiana, is offering 5,000,000 shares of common stock at $3.00 per share to investors for the purpose of raising capital to construct commercial aquafarms in the Mississippi Delta area to commercially raise shrimp, clams, and salmon. This is a fantastic offer to the right individuals who see aquafarming as a solution to world hunger and the ever dwindling supplies of catching these species in the open ocean. No guarantee of return on investment is implied. For further information on this investment opportunity, contact L.D. Breckenridge, Ltd. of Shreveport, LA.

(a) Define "aquafarming."

   (i) Describe TWO advantages of aquafarming over traditional wild harvesting.

   (ii) Describe TWO negative environmental impacts of aquafarming.

(b) Describe TWO methods that can be employed in aquaculture to lessen the environmental impact.

(c) How is raising and harvesting kelp and bivalve mollusks a more sustainable method of aquafarming than raising and harvesting higher trophic order fish such as salmon?

(d) The newspaper announcement claims that aquafarming is the answer to world hunger. Give TWO examples of how this statement may be contrary to environmental sustainability.

3.   The diagrams below show the growth in the hole in the strato-
      spheric ozone layer over the Antarctic over the last 30 years.

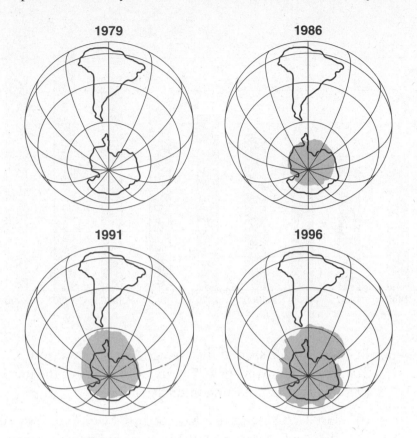

(a) Describe the role and importance of stratospheric ozone to life on
    Earth.

(b) Suggest ONE possible reason for the appearance of the hole in the
    ozone layer, which was first observed in the 1980s.

(c) Ultraviolet (UV) radiation occurs in three forms, known as UVA,
    UVB, and UVC.

   (i)   Describe at least ONE characteristic of EACH form of ultraviolet
         radiation.
   (ii) Describe the effects that increased UV radiation would have on:
         (a) Human health
         (b) Terrestrial ecosystems
         (c) Marine ecosystems

(d) Identify and describe ONE alternative to ozone-destroying chemical
    compounds.

(e) Identify and briefly describe ONE international treaty that addresses
    the release of chemical compounds that destroy stratospheric ozone.

4. The chart below shows the average American life span for the past 160 years.

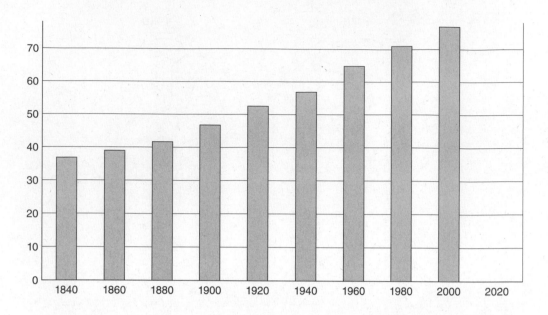

(a) In 1840, the life span of the average American was just 37 years. Today, it is approximately 77 years, with much of the increase in average life span occurring in the last 50 years.

  (i) List TWO events that have occurred within the last 100 years that could account for the increase in human life span.

  (ii) Choose ONE of the events you selected in (i) above and describe in detail its role in increasing average human life span.

(b) Currently, about 3.3 billion people—half of the world's population—are at risk of malaria. Every year, this leads to about 250 million malaria cases and nearly 1 million deaths, with people living in the poorest countries being the most vulnerable. Malaria is especially serious in Africa, where 20% of childhood deaths are caused by the disease (i.e., every 30 seconds a child dies from the disease).

  (i) Explain how malaria is transmitted through the human population.

  (ii) Identify TWO environmental factors that contribute to the emergence of malaria and explain how those factors influence the increase in the incidence of the disease.

  (iii) Traditionally, the spread of malaria was controlled by the use of pesticides such as DDT. However, DDT and other pesticides often have negative environmental impacts. A promising alternative to the use of pesticides is biological control. Describe biological control and provide ONE biological control method for controlling the spread of the disease.

ANSWER KEY

Practice Test 2

Section I (Multiple-Choice Questions)

1. D	26. A	51. A	76. E
2. D	27. E	52. C	77. B
3. A	28. D	53. A	78. C
4. B	29. B	54. D	79. C
5. C	30. C	55. D	80. C
6. D	31. E	56. D	81. C
7. A	32. C	57. A	82. C
8. A	33. D	58. C	83. C
9. A	34. E	59. B	84. E
10. E	35. A	60. D	85. D
11. E	36. B	61. E	86. A
12. C	37. C	62. C	87. E
13. E	38. B	63. B	88. C
14. A	39. A	64. E	89. E
15. A	40. B	65. A	90. E
16. E	41. A	66. C	91. C
17. C	42. D	67. A	92. D
18. B	43. B	68. B	93. E
19. D	44. B	69. C	94. A
20. C	45. A	70. B	95. D
21. B	46. C	71. C	96. B
22. C	47. C	72. D	97. D
23. B	48. B	73. B	98. A
24. C	49. B	74. D	99. B
25. E	50. C	75. B	100. D

PREDICT YOUR SCORE ON THE APES EXAM

Place a check mark (✔) next to the multiple-choice questions you got correct on page 533. Then fill in the blanks below to predict your overall score on the APES exam. Essay questions are not used in this prediction as they require subjective grading. You can also use this page to determine your areas of weakness. For example, if you got 5 out of 5 questions correct on the topic The Earth, but only 2 out of 5 questions correct on the topic The Atmosphere, spend some more time reviewing The Atmosphere.

Unit I EARTH SYSTEMS AND RESOURCES (10–15%)

Chapter 1 The Earth
(#16, 26, 52, 76, 94)   _____ correct/5 = _____%

Chapter 2 The Atmosphere
(#3, 13, 38, 39, 57)   _____ correct/5 = _____%

Chapter 3 Global Water Resources and Use
(#7, 18, 44, 92)   _____ correct/4 = _____%

Unit II THE LIVING WORLD (10–15%)

Chapter 4 Ecosystems
(#1, 6, 11, 17, 54, 58, 60, 80, 81, 89, 96, 98)   _____ correct/12 = _____%

Chapter 5 Natural Biogeochemical Cycles
(#8, 75, 91)   _____ correct/3 = _____%

Unit III POPULATIONS (10–15%)

Chapter 6 Populations
(#10, 30, 41, 47, 48, 55, 59, 77, 79, 85, 99)   _____ correct/11 = _____%

Unit IV LAND AND WATER USE (10–15%)

Chapter 7 Land and Water Use
(#15, 19, 31, 35, 37, 45, 49, 51, 61, 73, 84, 86, 87, 90)   _____ correct/14 = _____%

Practice Exam 2

Unit V ENERGY RESOURCES AND CONSUMPTION (10–15%)

Chapter 8 Energy
(#2, 9, 12, 34, 36, 50, 67, 68, 69, 78, 100)

_____ correct/11 = _____%

Unit VI POLLUTION (25–30%)

Chapter 9 Pollution
(#4, 20, 22, 24, 28, 32, 33, 43, 53, 56, 62, 65, 66, 70, 83, 88, 93, 97)

_____ correct/18 = _____%

Chapter 10 Impacts on the Human Environment
(#21, 29, 42, 46, 63, 74, 82)

_____ correct/7 = _____%

Unit VII GLOBAL CHANGE (10–15%)

Chapter 11 Stratospheric Ozone and Global Warming
(#5, 14, 23, 25, 27, 40, 64, 71, 72, 95)

_____ correct/10 = _____%

Total Number Correct _____ / 100 = _____%

PREDICTED AP SCORE*

Less than 50 correct:	1 or 2 (not passing)
50–60 correct:	3 on the APES exam
61–75 correct:	4 on the APES exam
76+ correct:	5 on the APES exam

*Please note this is a rough estimate and is not intended to be an indicator of an actual AP score.

Practice Exam 2

MULTIPLE-CHOICE EXPLANATIONS

1. **(D)** Speciation occurs when environmental factors change the composition of the gene pool.

2. **(D)** Incandescent: $\dfrac{60 \text{ Watt}}{1} \times \dfrac{\$0.10}{1,000 \text{ Watt} \cdot \text{hr}} \times \dfrac{8,000 \text{ hr}}{1} = \$48.00$

   Compact Fluorescent: $\dfrac{15 \text{ Watt}}{1} \times \dfrac{\$0.10}{1,000 \text{ Watt} \cdot \text{hr}} \times \dfrac{8,000 \text{ hr}}{1} = \$12.00$

   Therefore, the saving is $48.00 − $12.00 = $36.00

3. **(A)** Wind is primarily caused by the uneven heating of Earth's surface; i.e., the equator receives more solar radiation than the poles. This uneven heating results in differences in air pressure and sets convection currents (winds) in motion.

4. **(B)** The three reactions that occur in catalytic converters are:
   (a) Reduction of nitrogen oxides to nitrogen and oxygen:
   $$NO_x \rightarrow O_2 + N_2$$
   (b) Oxidation of carbon monoxide to carbon dioxide:
   $$CO + O_2 \rightarrow CO_2$$
   (c) Oxidation of unburned hydrocarbons to carbon dioxide and water:
   $$C_xH_{2x} + O_2 \rightarrow CO_2 + H_2O$$

   Although catalytic converters are effective at removing hydrocarbons and other harmful emissions, they do not reduce the emission of carbon dioxide produced when fossil fuels are burnt. Additionally, the U.S. Environmental Protection Agency (EPA) has stated catalytic converters are a significant and growing cause of global warming, because of their release of nitrous oxide (N_2O), a greenhouse gas over 300 times more potent than carbon dioxide. The EPA states that motor vehicles contribute approximately 50% of nitrous oxide emissions, and nitrous oxide makes up 7% of greenhouse gases.

5. **(C)** Air conditioners that contain chlorine-fluorine based refrigerants are known as CFCs (chloro-fluorocarbons). One chlorine atom released from a CFC can ultimately destroy over 100,000 stratospheric ozone molecules.

6. **(D)** 100 units of energy are found in the green plants. $100 \times 0.20 = 20$ units available for herbivores. Of the 20 units now available, $20 \times 0.20 = 4$ units are left for the primary carnivores.

7. **(A)** The water table is the upper surface of an area filled with groundwater, separating the zone of aeration (the subsurface region of soil and rocks in which the pores are filled with air and usually some water) from the zone of saturation (the subsurface region in which the pores are filled only with water). Water tables rise and fall with seasonal moisture, water absorption by vegetation, and the withdrawal of groundwater from wells, among other factors. See Figure 3.7 on page 140.

8. **(A)** The three numbers on the side of the fertilizer bag refer to the amount of nitrogen, phosphorus, and potassium that the fertilizer contains. The rest of the bag contains minor nutrients and filler material. Since the number representing phosphorus is 0, no phosphorus is required.

9. **(A)** Notice that all three forms of energy are nonrenewable sources derived from fossil fuels. Oil is the primary energy source for the world today with the United States at approximately 40% dependency on this single source. Coal and natural gas are each around 22% dependency in the United States and the world.

10. **(E)** Wherever on this graph the slope of the line is zero (horizontal), there is no population growth; i.e., the rate of reproduction is equal to the rate of death.

11. **(E)** Primary productivity is the amount of biomass produced through photosynthesis per unit area per time by plants. Gross primary productivity is the total energy fixed by plants through photosynthesis. A portion of the energy of gross primary productivity is used by plants for respiration. Respiration provides a plant with the energy needed for various activities. Subtracting respiration from gross primary productivity gives net primary productivity, which represents the rate of production of biomass that is available for consumption by heterotrophic organisms.

12. **(C)** A watt is a unit of power.

13. **(E)** The effects of La Niña are opposite to those of El Niño. A La Niña effect may be defined as a drop in average sea-surface temperatures to more than 0.7°F (0.4°C) below normal, lasting at least six months, across parts of the eastern tropical Pacific. When La Niña forms, the hurricane season is affected as the cooling water creates dramatic changes in the upper-level air currents that play a major role in storm development. During La Niña, high-level westerly winds either weaken or shift to come from the east, allowing *more* storms to develop.

14. **(A)** In order to balance the excess heating near the equator and cooling at the poles of Earth, both atmosphere and ocean transport heat from low to high latitudes. Warmer surface water is cooled at high latitudes, releasing heat to the atmosphere, which is then radiated away to space. This heat engine operates to reduce equator-to-pole temperature differences and is a prime moderating mechanism for climate on Earth.

15. **(A)** An important chemical property of persistent organic pollutants is their lipid (oil or fat) solubility, which results in their ability to pass through biological phospholipid membranes and bioaccumulate in the fatty tissues of living organisms.

16. **(E)** The geologic time scale is a system describing the timing and relationships between events that have occurred throughout Earth's history. The identification of strata or rock layers by the fossils they contained enabled geologists to correlate strata between continents. If two strata (however far apart or different in composition) contained the same fossils, it was likely they had been laid down at the same time. The principle of superposition states that a sedimentary rock layer in an undisturbed sequence is younger than the one beneath it and older than the one above it. This principle allows sedimentary layers to be viewed as a form of vertical time line, a partial or complete record of the time elapsed from deposition of the lowest layer to deposition of the highest bed.

17. **(C)** Temperate deciduous forests have warm summers and cold winters. Deciduous trees escape these winters by losing their leaves. Typical mammals are bears, badgers, squirrels, woodchucks, insectivores, rodents, wolves, wildcats, and deer. These forests are rich in birds. The climate that is suitable for temperate deciduous forests is most suited for humans—hence forest destruction.

18. **(B)** The great ocean conveyor belt transfers warm water from the Pacific Ocean to the Atlantic as a shallow current and returns cold water from the Atlantic to the Pacific as a deep current that flows further south. As it passes Europe, the surface water evaporates and the ocean water cools, releasing heat to the atmosphere. This release of heat is largely responsible for the relatively warm temperatures enjoyed by western Europe. As the water becomes colder, it increases in salinity and becomes dense, sinking thousands of feet below the surface. The deep water slowly travels south through the oceanic abyss, eventually mixing upward to the surface in different parts of the world up to 1,000 years later. However, global climate changes could alter, or even halt, the current as we know it today. As the Earth heats up, there could be an increase in precipitation and a melting of freshwater ice in the Arctic Ocean (when saltwater freezes it leaves the salt behind), which would flow into the Atlantic Ocean. This additional freshwater could dilute the Atlantic Gulf Stream to the point where it would not continue to sink into the depths of the ocean.

19. **(D)** Crops generally have higher yields when more CO_2 is available. However, while crops may be more productive, the resulting crop will generally be of lower nutritional quality. Nutritional quality declines because while the plants produce more seeds under higher CO_2 levels, the seeds contain less nitrogen. Under the rising CO_2 scenario, livestock and humans would have to increase their intake of plants to compensate for the loss. In a recent study, specific plants grown at higher CO_2 levels had 19% more flowers; 16% more seeds; 4% greater individual seed weight; 25% greater total seed, and a 14% lower concentration of nitrogen in the seeds than those grown at current levels of atmospheric CO_2. On the flip side, legumes increased the amount of nitrogen they take in under higher than normal CO_2 concentration. Changes in the number of flowers, fruits, and seeds and their nutritional quality could have far-reaching consequences as changes in the amount of nutrients in seeds could affect reproductive success and seedling survival. Such changes could also have long-term effects on ecosystem functioning.

20. **(C)** Automobiles and other forms of transportation are responsible for approximately one-third of human-made nitrogen oxides and volatile organic compound emissions, one-fifth of particulate emissions, two-thirds of carbon monoxide emissions, and less than 5% of sulfur dioxide emissions.

21. **(B)** The ecological footprint has emerged as the world's premier measure of humans' demand on nature. It measures how much land and water area a human population requires to produce the resource it consumes and to absorb its carbon dioxide emissions. It currently takes the Earth one year and six months to regenerate what we use in a year.

22. **(C)** Lichens are organisms formed by the mutualistic combination of an alga and a fungus. Lacking roots, stems, and leaves, lichens can grow almost anywhere, but rely on nutrients they accumulate from the air. Lichens appear to function like a natural filter, accumulating airborne pollutants as they are deposited on the lichen surface. Scientists have used them as biomonitors for many years, including an effort to estimate the amount of nuclear fallout from the Chernobyl meltdown in the late 1980s. Using lichens to reflect air pollution levels eliminates the need for installation and maintenance of expensive

air sampling equipment that collects airborne particulates using filters, which are later removed and analyzed in the lab.

23. **(B)** It is thought that improvements to the Erie Canal in 1919 allowed sea lampreys to spread from Lake Ontario to Lake Erie, and eventually spread to Lake Michigan, Lake Huron, and Lake Superior, where it decimated indigenous fish populations in the 1930s and 1940s. Sea lampreys have created a problem with their aggressive parasitism on key predator species and game fish, such as lake trout. The lake trout is considered an apex predator, which means that the entire system relies on its presence to be diverse and healthy. With the removal of an apex predator from a system, the entire system is affected. The sea lamprey is an aggressive predator by nature, which gives it a competitive advantage in a lake system where it has no predators and its prey lacks defenses against it. Lamprey introduction along with poor unsustainable fishing practices caused the lake trout populations to decline drastically. This resulted in the relationship between predators and prey in the Great Lakes' ecosystem becoming unbalanced. Control efforts and research include electric current, chemical lampricides, physical barriers, control through genetic research into the sea lamprey's immune system, and pheromones. Reintroducing animals into a habitat that they once were plentiful in is not an example of introducing an invasive species.

24. **(C)** The Resource Conservation and Recovery Act (RCRA) gives the Environmental Protection Agency (EPA) the authority to control hazardous waste from the "cradle-to-grave." This includes the generation, transportation, treatment, storage, and disposal of hazardous waste. RCRA also sets forth a framework for the management of nonhazardous solid wastes. The 1986 amendments to RCRA enabled the EPA to address environmental problems that could result from underground tanks storing petroleum and other hazardous substances. The Federal Hazardous and Solid Waste Amendments are the 1984 amendments to RCRA that focused on waste minimization and phasing out land disposal of hazardous waste.

25. **(E)** Scientists have identified nearly 2 million individual species, and more than 9 million more species may yet remain undiscovered (the majority of which will be insects). The greatest of all threats to Earth's biodiversity, however, is deforestation. While deforestation threatens ecosystems across the globe, it's particularly destructive to tropical rain forests. In terms of Earth's biodiversity, rain forests are hugely important; though they cover only 7% of the Earth, they house more than half the world's species. Through logging, mining, and farming, humans destroy approximately 2% of the Earth's rain forests every year, often damaging the soil so badly in the process that the forest has a difficult time recovering. In recent history, deforestation has led to approximately 36% of all extinctions, and as the habitat loss accelerates, that number is bound to increase. However, recently in Brazil, satellite imagery revealed that the rate of deforestation fell by 49% compared to the previous year, due in part to stricter environmental regulations and increased enforcement. Recent studies have also shown that as a country's economic conditions improve, its deforestation rate slows considerably as the indigenous populations rely less on the rain forest's resources for survival.

26. **(A)** Cinder cones are one of the most common types of volcanoes. A steep, conical hill of volcanic fragments called cinders accumulates around a vent. The rock fragments, often called cinders, are glassy and contain numerous gas bubbles "frozen" into place as magma explodes into the air and then cools quickly. Cinder cones range in size from tens to hundreds of meters tall and usually occur in groups.

27. **(E)** The U.S. Fish and Wildlife Service is a bureau within the Department of the Interior. As the principal federal partner responsible for administering the Endangered Species Act (ESA), the Fish and Wildlife Service takes the lead in recovering and conserving imperiled species by fostering partnerships, employing scientific research, and developing a workforce of conservation leaders. The Environmental Protection Agency's Endangered Species Protection Program (ESPP) helps promote the recovery of listed species. The ESPP is a program designed to determine whether pesticide use in a certain geographic area may affect any listed species.

28. **(D)** In many areas, fluoride (F^-) is added to water after the disinfection process with the goal of preventing tooth decay, not to disinfect the water. The U.S. Centers for Disease Control and Prevention states that the addition of fluoride to drinking water supplies is "one of 10 great public health achievements of the 20th century." Some areas have excessive levels of natural fluoride in the source water and excessive levels of fluoride can be toxic or cause undesirable cosmetic effects such as staining of teeth. Public opposition to fluoridation has existed since its initiation in the 1940s and stems from perceived safety concerns.

29. **(B)** Remediation technologies are those that render harmful or hazardous substances harmless after they enter the environment.

30. **(C)** Refer to the map below.

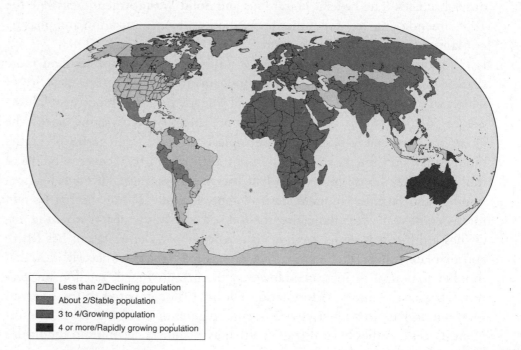

Less than 2/Declining population
About 2/Stable population
3 to 4/Growing population
4 or more/Rapidly growing population

31. **(E)** For the poor in developing countries (urban and rural) wood is usually the principal source of energy for cooking food and for keeping warm. In these countries an estimated 86% of all the wood consumed annually is used as fuel. As populations have grown, this dependence on wood has led inexorably to destruction of the forests. Wood fuels account for two-thirds of all energy sources used in Africa and one-third in Asia. This compares with the 0.3% of total energy use in developed countries. In developing countries, the principal noncommercial fuels other than wood are animal dung and crop residues.

32. **(C)** During the 1940s and 1950s, the Hooker Chemical Company dumped approximately 21,000 tons of organic solvents, acids, and pesticides as well as their by-products, many of them carcinogenic (cancer causing) or teratogenic (creating birth defects), into an abandoned canal in New York State (near Niagara Falls). A school and homes were built over the site. Chemicals began to leak from the ground and cause illness. Since the disaster, various levels of government have spent around $250 million (Superfund) and 20 years cleaning up the site with much of the waste still buried there. New York State has since rebuilt homes in the area at reduced prices to attract new residents.

33. **(D)** From 1932 to 1968, Chisso Corporation (a petrochemical and plastics manufacturer) dumped an estimated 27 tons of mercury compounds into Minamata Bay, Japan. Thousands of people, whose normal diet included fish from the bay, unexpectedly developed symptoms of methyl mercury poisoning. The illness became known as Minamata Disease. Victims were diagnosed as having a degeneration of their nervous systems, numbness occurring in their limbs and lips, their speech becoming slurred, and their vision being constricted; 12,615 people have been officially recognized as patients affected by mercury.

34. **(E)** On March 28, 1979, a minor malfunction occurred in the system that fed water to the steam generators at the Three Mile Island Nuclear Generating Station near Harrisburg, Pennsylvania. This event eventually led to the most serious commercial nuclear accident in U.S. history and caused fundamental changes in the way nuclear power plants were operated and regulated. Despite the severity of the damage, no injuries due to radiation occurred. Eleven days after the events of Three Mile Island, the movie *The China Syndrome* was released—a film about a nuclear accident.

35. **(A)** On the night of December 2–3, 1984, 40 tons of cyanide and other lethal gases began spewing from Union Carbide Corporation's pesticide factory in Bhopal, India. Over half a million people were exposed to the deadly gases. The gases burned the tissues of the eyes and lungs, crossed into the bloodstream, and damaged almost every system in the body. With an estimated 10–15 people continuing to die each month, the number of deaths to date is put at close to 20,000. Today more than 120,000 people are still in need of urgent medical attention.

36. **(B)** On April 26, 1986, a reactor exploded in the town of Chernobyl in the Ukraine and released 30 to 40 times the radioactivity of the atomic bombs dropped on Hiroshima and Nagasaki. Hundreds of thousands of Ukrainians, Russians, and Belorussians had to abandon entire cities and settlements within a 20-mile zone of extreme contamination. Some 3 million people are still living in contaminated areas.

37. **(C)** Drift netting is a fishing technique in which nets, called drift nets, are allowed to drift free in a sea or lake. Usually a drift net is a gill net with floats attached to a rope along the top of the net, and weights attached to another rope along the foot of the net. With gill drift nets, fish try to swim through certain-sized mesh openings but are unable to squeeze through swimming forward. Once in this position, they are prevented from backing out due to the tendency of their gills to become entangled in the net. Drift nets can range in length from 100 feet (30 m) to 2.5 miles (4 km). Nets of up to 30 miles (50 km) have been set in recent times.

38. **(B)** The ozone layer is a layer in Earth's atmosphere that contains relatively high concentrations of ozone (O_3). This layer absorbs 93–99% of the sun's high-frequency ultraviolet light, which is potentially damaging to life on earth. More than 91% of the ozone in Earth's atmosphere is present here. It is mainly located in the lower portion of the stratosphere approximately 42,650–65,620 feet (13–20 km) above Earth, though the thickness varies seasonally and geographically.

39. **(A)** The troposphere begins at the surface of the Earth and extends to between 23,000 feet (7 km) at the poles to 56,000 feet (17 km) at the equator, with some variation due to weather. The troposphere is mostly heated by transfer of energy from the surface, so on average the lowest part of the troposphere is warmest, and temperature decreases with altitude, promoting vertical mixing. The troposphere contains approximately 80% of the mass of the atmosphere.

40. **(B)** Stratospheric ozone depletion describes two distinct but related phenomena observed since the late 1970s: a steady decline of about 4% per decade in the total volume of ozone in the Earth's stratosphere (the ozone layer), and a much larger springtime decrease in stratospheric ozone over Earth's polar regions ("ozone hole"). Effects of decreases in stratospheric ozone resulting in increased UV radiation reaching the Earth include: (a) a 6% to 12% reduction in the growth rate of phytoplankton. An increase in UV radiation also induces DNA damage and DNA synthesis delay in phytoplankton; (b) microorganisms (zooplankton) that feed on phytoplankton are affected if the DNA composition of phytoplankton changes; (c) due to the decreased number of phytoplankton, which is the basis of the food chain in the ocean, krill face a shortage of food, which in turn is the main source of food for various birds and whales in the Antarctic region; (d) increases in UV radiation affects the growth of leaves in plants observed by a reduction in leaf elongation and a reduction in leaf area; and (e) increased UV radiation causes a decrease in photosynthetic activity (photoinhibition).

41. **(A)** Organisms adapted to generalized niches (generalists) are those organisms capable of surviving within a wide range of environmental circumstances with multiple food sources. An example of a generalist would be mice, which can adapt to practically any environment and consume a variety of different seeds, grains, and nuts. Should one food source become scarce, organisms that live in generalized niches have the ability to switch to another. The downside of living in a generalized niche is competition from other species competing for the same resources. Organisms that live in specialized niches on the other hand are not adapted to a wide range of environmental circumstances and food sources. An example of an animal living in a specialized niche would be

the koala, which lives in eucalyptus trees and exclusively consumes eucalyptus leaves. Should anything affect the eucalyptus trees, the viability of the koala population is threatened. The advantage of living in a specialized niche is that there is little interspecific competition for the same resource. Generalists tend to evolve somewhat more quickly than specialists, being put under greater evolutionary pressures.

42. **(D)** China is the dominant recipient of the world's electronic waste (e-waste), with an estimated one billion tons of electronic waste being shipped there each year, mostly from the United States, Canada, and Japan. About 90% of e-waste from the United States is exported to China and Nigeria. E-waste recycling operations are extremely toxic and are usually conducted without protective clothing and with almost 90% of workers suffering from neurological, digestive abnormalities, or skin diseases and many developing breathing problems. Besides skin contact with toxic materials including heavy metals, workers burn plastics coatings to separate them from metals, resulting in inhalation of poisonous gases. Workers also use highly corrosive and dangerous cyanide (heap leaching) and acid baths along riverbanks, which eventually seeps into the groundwater to extract gold from microchips. Studies of China e-waste facilities have shown lead and copper were 371 and 115 times higher, respectively, than established human exposure safety limits.

43. **(B)** Settled sewage liquor is spread onto the surface of a trickling filter (oxidizing) bed, a deep bed made up of coal, limestone chips, or specially fabricated plastic media. Such media must have high surface areas to support the biofilms that form. The sewage liquor is distributed through perforated rotating arms radiating from a central pivot. The distributed sewage liquor trickles through the bed and is collected in drains at the base. These drains also provide a source of air, which percolates up through the bed, keeping it aerobic. Biological films of bacteria, protozoa, and fungi form on the media's surfaces and eat or otherwise reduce the organic content. This biofilm is grazed by insect larvae and worms, which help maintain an optimal thickness. Screening is a primary sewage treatment process. Lagooning, nutrient removal, and constructed wetlands are tertiary sewage treatment processes.

44. **(B)** Almost 60% of all the world's freshwater withdrawals go toward irrigation purposes. Rice production uses the most water; soybeans and oats use the least. Producing electrical power is also a major use of water in the United States. In 1995, 189,700 million gallons of water each day were used to produce electricity—to cool the power-producing equipment.

45. **(A)** In (A), a 1999 study by *Consumer Reports* found that two-thirds of domestic produce had more toxic pesticide residues than those products that were imported. In (B), risks to the human immune, reproductive, and endocrine systems, as well as neurotoxicity, may be equally or even more significant than cancer. (C) is true as written. The legal standard for registration set down by the Federal Insecticide, Fungicide, and Rodenticide Act (FIFRA) is a risk-benefit standard. The EPA must register pesticides if they do not pose "unreasonable risk to man or the environment, taking into account the economic, social and environmental costs and benefits of the use of any pesticide." In (D), 12 of the 26 most widely used pesticides in the United States are classified as possible or probable carcinogens by the EPA based on studies of laboratory

animals. In (E), a study found carcinogens, neurotoxins, and pesticides that disrupt the endocrine or reproductive system in fruits and vegetables that had been washed, peeled, and prepared for consumption. The foods most likely to be contaminated were (in declining order) peaches, apples, celery, potatoes, grapes, and oranges.

46. **(C)** Emissions trading (also known as cap and trade) is an approach used to control pollution by providing economic incentives for achieving reductions in emissions of pollutants. There are active trading programs in several air pollutants. For greenhouse gases, the largest is the European Union Emission Trading Scheme. In the United States there is a national market to reduce acid rain, as well as several regional markets in nitrogen oxides.

47. **(C)** To get the estimate of the population size N, multiply the number marked in the first catch, M_1, by the total number caught in the second catch, C, and divide that by the number of marked recaptures in the second catch, M_2:

$$N = (M_1 \times C) / M_2 = (150 \times 100) / 20 = 750$$

48. **(B)** Population density is calculated as population size divided by area: 750 butterflies / 2 hectares = 375 butterflies per hectare.

49. **(B)** Clear-cutting removes *all* trees from an area in a single cutting. Seed-tree cutting occurs when loggers harvest nearly all of a stand's trees in one cutting but leave a few uniformly distributed seed-producing trees to regenerate the stand. Shelterwood cutting removes all mature trees in an area in two or three cuttings over a period of time. Selective cutting occurs when intermediate-aged or mature trees in an uneven-aged forest are cut singly or in small groups.

50. **(C)** Dams create a series of lakes, slowing the current and delaying downstream migration. The delay interferes with internal biological changes that enable the young salmon to survive in saltwater. In addition, the slow water exposes them to predators and disease. To increase salmon populations, one should release extra water from dams to wash juvenile salmon downstream.

51. **(A)** Today, 3 million fishing boats operate and are greatly depleting the supply of fish and other aquatic life-forms. Over the past 40 years, fishing quotas have more than tripled. In 1950, 20 million tons of fish and marine products were harvested. By 1990, this amount had increased to 100 million tons per year. The depletion of fish stocks has led to overfishing in all oceans and other bodies of water. Past catches were generally higher than those of today due to overfishing. Therefore, to base today's harvest limits on harvest numbers that were probably higher in the past would only accelerate depletion of current fishing stocks.

52. **(C)**

Element	Approximate % by weight
Oxygen	46.6
Silicon	27.7
Aluminum	8.1
Iron	5.0
Calcium	3.6
Sodium	2.8
Potassium	2.6
Magnesium	2.1
All others	1.5

53. **(A)** Smog is a type of air pollution derived from vehicular emission from internal combustion engines and industrial fumes that react in the atmosphere with sunlight to form secondary pollutants that also combine with the primary emissions to form photochemical smog. It is produced by the chemical reaction of sunlight, nitrogen oxides, and volatile organic compounds in the atmosphere. Air pollutants produced during the formation of photochemical smog can include nitrogen oxides (NO_x), peroxyacyl nitrates (PANs), ozone, and volatile organic compounds, all of which are usually highly reactive and oxidizing. It is present in all modern cities, but it is more common in cities with sunny, warm, dry climates and a large number of motor vehicles. Because it travels with the wind, it can affect sparsely populated areas as well. Since there is more sunlight during the summer, photochemical smog is more common during the summer months.

54. **(D)** Virulence is the harm that parasites and diseases cause to their host (e.g., parasite-induced host mortality or reduced fecundity). Parasite virulence is, in general, proportional to the degree that the parasite exploits the host. Parasite offspring are produced by exploiting the host; therefore, some virulence is inevitable. However, too-strong host exploitation leads to high virulence that jeopardizes survival of the host and the parasite itself. Thus, there should be an optimal level of host exploitation and virulence by the parasite.

55. **(D)** To find the doubling time of a population at any given annual rate of growth, divide 72 by the annual growth rate (in this case 1.2): $72 \div 1.2 = 60$ years. $1994 + 60 = 2054$.

56. **(D)** In the United States, roughly two-thirds of all SO_2 and one-fourth of all NO_x come from burning of fossil fuels, especially coal, in electric power plants. Ammonia (NH_3) plays a double role in acidification. First, it neutralizes in the atmosphere to a large extent the acid formed by oxidation of sulfur dioxide and nitrogen oxides, to form particulate ammonium (NH_4^+). Ammonia (NH_3) as such is not an acid but a weak base. However, it does react in the air with strong acids like sulfuric acid or nitric acid, forming slightly acidic ammonium salts, $(NH_4)_2SO_4$ and NH_4NO_3. They are less volatile, form particles, and sink in the end to the ground or rain out. When NH_4^+ is deposited and enters the soil, nitrification can occur. The hydrogen ions from the atmospheric acid that was neutralized by NH_3 in the atmosphere are released and additional acid is formed:

$$NH_4^+ + 2O_2 \rightarrow 2H^+ + NO_3^- + H_2O$$

As a result, NH_4^+ deposition and subsequent nitrification leads directly to soil acidification. Normal rain has a slightly acidic pH of about 5.2, because carbon dioxide and water in the air react together to form carbonic acid, a weak acid (pH 5.6 in distilled water): $H_2O_{(l)} + CO_{2(g)} \rightarrow H_2CO_{3(aq)}$. Carbonic acid then can ionize in water, forming low concentrations of hydronium and carbonate ions: $2H_2O_{(l)} + H_2CO_{3\ (aq)} \rightarrow CO_3^{2-}{}_{(aq)} + 2H_3O^+{}_{(aq)}$. Ozone ($O_3$) oxidizes nitrous oxide (NO) to nitrogen dioxide: $O_{3(g)} + NO_{(g)} \rightarrow NO_{2(g)} + O_{2(g)}$. Nitrogen dioxide can then react with oxygen gas to form nitric acid and nitrous acid, both contributors to acid rain: $2NO_{2(g)} + H_2O_{(g)} \rightarrow HNO_{3(l)} + HNO_{2(l)}$. Lead does not contribute to the formation of acid rain.

57. **(A)** Large-scale circulations develop in Earth's atmosphere due to uneven heating of its surface by the sun's rays. Daytime solar heating is greatest near Earth's equator, where incoming sunlight is nearly perpendicular to the ground. Near the poles, heat lost to space by radiation exceeds the heat gained from sunlight, so air near the poles is losing heat. Conversely, heat gained from sunlight near the equator exceeds heat losses, so air near the equator is gaining heat. The heated air near the equator expands and rises, while the cooled air near the poles contracts and sinks. Rising air creates low pressure at the equator. Air cools as it rises, causing water vapor to condense (rain) as the air cools with increasing altitude. As an air mass cools, it increases in density and descends back to the surface in the subtropics, creating high pressure.

58. **(C)** See the table in Chapter 6, "Populations" that shows differences between *r*-strategists and *K*-strategists.

59. **(B)**

$$\frac{(\text{births} + \text{immigrants}) - (\text{deaths} + \text{emigrants})}{\text{starting population}} \times 100\%$$

$$= \text{net annual percentage growth rate}$$

$$\frac{(1{,}000 + 500) - (600 + 100)}{100{,}000} \times 100\% = 0.8\%$$

60. **(D)** Climax communities are characterized by: stability, high species diversity, low competitive interaction, limited niche overlap, large body size, few offspring per year, one reproductive cycle per year, and *K*-selective species.

61. **(E)** Environmental mitigation is the process of addressing damage to the environment generally caused by public works projects. Environmental mitigation is used to describe projects or programs intended to offset known impacts to an existing natural resource, such as a forest, stream, wetland, or endangered species. Environmental mitigation typically involves a trading system: Debits are recorded when a natural resource has been destroyed or severely impaired, and credits are given when a natural resource has been deemed to be improved or preserved. Actions taken to avoid or minimize environmental damage are considered the most preferable method of mitigation. Potential environmental mitigation activities may include minimizing a proposed activity; restoring temporary impacts; precautionary and/or abatement measures to reduce construction impacts; and providing a suitable replacement or substitute environmental resource of equivalent or greater value.

62. **(C)** Carbon dioxide is the ultimate result of perfect combustion of any carbon-based fuel. The only ways to reduce carbon dioxide emissions are to make vehicles more fuel efficient and/or drive less, to use a noncarbon fuel such as hydrogen, or to use a green fuel such as ethanol that is produced from crops that absorb carbon dioxide as they grow.

63. **(B)** The median lethal dose, LD_{50}, of a toxic substance is the dose required to kill half the members of a tested population after a specified test duration and is frequently used as a general indicator of a substance's acute toxicity.

$$\frac{400 \, \cancel{\text{mg}}}{4 \, \text{kg}} \times \frac{1 \, \text{g}}{1{,}000 \, \cancel{\text{mg}}} = 0.1 \, \text{g/kg}$$

64. **(E)** The Kyoto Protocol is aimed at reducing global warming. The Protocol was initially adopted in 1997 in Kyoto, Japan, and entered into force in 2005. The United States did not agree to the Protocol, and in 2011, Canada withdrew. The Kyoto Protocol contains mandatory aims for the countries that have signed it. The Protocol commits Annex I countries (developed countries and countries in economic transition) to individual, legally-binding commitments on the reduction of their greenhouse gas emissions. The general target that the developed countries have to meet is to reduce their greenhouse gas emissions by approximately 5% below their 1990 levels between 2008–2012. The Kyoto Protocol allows for flexibility in terms of the methods countries could use to meet their gas reduction commitments. Such methods include: (1) compensating for emissions by increasing the number of a country's carbon sinks; (2) trading of emission allowances between countries; (3) promote environmentally-friendly foreign investments from industrialized countries into developing countries; and (4) allow developed countries to sponsor research to decrease emission levels in countries of economic transition. In exchange for the developed country's investment, the host country provides the investor with emission reduction units, also known as carbon credits. The developed economies can afterwards use their carbon credits towards meeting their emission-reduction requirements.

65. **(A)** Sediment is the largest contaminant of surface water by weight and volume in the United States, and is identified as the leading pollution problem in rivers and streams and the fourth leading problem in lakes. Sediment in surface water is largely a result of soil erosion, which is influenced by soil properties and agricultural practices. Sediment buildup reduces the useful life of reservoirs, can clog irrigation canals, block navigation channels, and increase dredging costs. By raising streambeds and burying streamside wetlands, sediment increases the probability and severity of floods. Suspended sediment can increase the cost of water treatment for municipal and industrial water uses. Sediment can also destroy or degrade aquatic wildlife habitat, reducing diversity and damaging commercial and recreational fisheries.

66. **(C)** Municipal Solid Waste (MSW)—more commonly known as trash or garbage—consists of everyday items we use and then throw away, such as product packaging, grass clippings, furniture, clothing, bottles, food scraps, newspapers, appliances, paint, and batteries. In 2010, Americans generated about 250 million tons of trash and recycled and composted over 85 million tons of this material, equivalent to a 34% recycling rate. On average, Americans recycled and composted 1.5 pounds from the 4.43 pounds of MSW generated per person per day.

67. **(A)** Control rods regulate the number of neutrons in the core of a nuclear reactor and so control the rate of the reaction. They are plates or tubes holding material, such as cadmium or boron, that absorb neutrons.

68. **(B)** A moderator is a medium that reduces the speed of fast neutrons, thereby turning them into thermal neutrons capable of sustaining a nuclear chain reaction. Commonly used moderators include regular (light) water (roughly 75% of the world's reactors), solid graphite (20% of reactors), and heavy water (5% of reactors).

69. **(C)** A moderator is a substance, such as water or graphite, that is used in a nuclear reactor to decrease the speed of fast neutrons and increase the likelihood of fission. The reactor control system requires the movement of neutron-absorbing rods (control rods) in the reactor under carefully controlled conditions. They must be arranged to increase reactivity (increase neutron population) slowly and under good control. They must be capable of reducing reactivity, both rapidly and slowly.

70. **(B)** Satellite imaging of the concentrations of PM_{10} air particulates (μg per m^3) from NASA show that cities in China have the highest air pollution concentrations in the world. The World Health Organization (WHO) upper safety level of PM_{10} is 20 μg per m^3. The city with the highest average PM_{10} concentration in the world is Ahvaz, Iran, with a concentration of 372 μg per m^3.

71. **(C)** $N_1 = N_0 + B - D + I - E$

    $N_1 = 40,000 + 35(40) - 10(40) + 100 - 50$

    $N_1 = 41,050$

72. **(D)** Biodiversity is the degree of variation of life forms with a given species, ecosystem, or biome and is a measure of the health of ecosystems. In terrestrial habitats, tropical and temperate regions typically support a large variety of different species whereas polar regions with climatic conditions not being optimal for producers, support fewer species. Biodiversity is not evenly distributed; rather it varies greatly across the globe as well as within regions. Among other factors, the diversity of all living things (biota) depends on temperature, precipitation, altitude, soils, geography, and the presence of other species. Generally, there is an increase in biodiversity from the poles to the tropics. Thus localities at lower latitudes have more species than localities at higher latitudes.

73. **(B)** Of more than 50,000 edible plant species in the world, only a few hundred contribute significantly to food supplies. Just fifteen crop plants provide 90% of the world's food energy intake, with three—rice, maize, and wheat—making up two-thirds of this. These three are the staples of over 4 billion people. Roots and tubers are important staples for over 1 billion people in the developing world. They account for roughly 40% of the food eaten by half the population of sub-Saharan Africa. They are high in carbohydrates, calcium, and vitamin C, but low in protein. One example, cassava has become one of the developing world's most important staples providing a basic diet for around 500 million people, and plantings are increasing faster than for any other crop. Cassava's starchy roots produce more food energy per unit of land than any other staple crop. Nutritionally, the cassava is comparable to potatoes, except that it has twice the fiber content and a higher level of potassium.

74. **(D)** Everyday, 3,000 Americans under the age of 18 become regular smokers, and a third of them will eventually die of nicotine-related causes. Two out of three 12 to 17 year olds who smoked nicotine in the last year show signs of addiction. Everyday, over 1,000 Americans die as a result of nicotine addition. In 1900, 4 billion cigarettes were produced in the United States. By the year 2000, the number had increased to 720 billion.

75. **(B)** Nitrification is a microbial process by which reduced nitrogen compounds (primarily ammonia) are sequentially oxidized to nitrite and nitrate.

The nitrification process is primarily accomplished by two groups of autotrophic nitrifying bacteria that can build organic molecules using energy obtained from inorganic sources, in this case ammonia or nitrite. In the first step of nitrification, ammonia-oxidizing bacteria (*Nitrosomonas*) oxidize ammonia to nitrite $NH_3 + O_2 \rightarrow NO_2^- + 3H^+ + 2e^-$. In the second step of the process, nitrite-oxidizing bacteria (*Nitrobacter*) oxidize nitrite to nitrate $NO_2^- + H_2O \rightarrow NO_3^- + 2H^+ + 2e^-$.

76. **(E)** The mantle is the thick layer of hot, solid rock between the crust and the molten iron core. The mantle makes up the bulk of the Earth, accounting for two-thirds of its mass. The mantle starts about 19 miles (30 km) down and is about 1,800 miles (2,900 km) thick.

77. **(B)** The lynx and hare populations have a predator-prey relationship. Disease, food supply, and other predators are variables in this complex relationship. The flux in this cyclic relationship is what allows the ecosystem dynamic to work. Without flux, vegetation wouldn't have a chance to recover from the hare population's continuous eating, and without vegetation, the hare population could no longer exist in its habitat, and therefore neither could the lynx population that depends upon the hare population for food. Every ten years or so, the hares' reproduction rate increases. As more hares are born, they eat more of their food supply. They eat so much food that they are forced to supplement their diet with less desirable and nutritious food. As the hare population grows, the lynx population begins to increase in response. Because there are so many hares, other predators opportunistically begin to hunt them along with the lynxes. The hares' less nutritious and varied diet begins to have an effect; the hares begin to die due to illness and disease. Fewer hares are born because there is less food. The hare population begins to go into a steep decline. Therefore, the lynx population also begins to decline. Some lynxes starve and others die due to disease. Both the lynx and hare populations have fewer offspring, and this decrease in population gives the vegetation a chance to recover. Once there is enough vegetation for the hares to begin to increase their population, the whole cycle begins again.

78. **(C)** The first law of thermodynamics states that energy can be changed from one form to another but it cannot be created or destroyed. The total amount of energy and matter in the universe remains constant, merely changing from one form to another. The second law of thermodynamics states that in all energy exchanges, if no energy enters or leaves the system, the potential energy of the state will always be less than that of the initial state. This is also commonly referred to as entropy.

79. **(C)** Less-developed countries typically have a large proportion of their population in the pre-reproductive age category.

80. **(C)** The term *territory* refers to any area that an animal of a particular species consistently defends against members of its own species (and occasionally against animals of different species). Animals that defend territories in this way are referred to as territorial. For a songbird to expend energy defending a territory larger than what is required to derive adequate resources would not be energy-efficient. To defend a territory smaller than what is required to derive adequate resources puts the songbird and the clutch in jeopardy.

81. **(C)** Although communities are variable and dynamic in both space and time, the interactions between species lead to patterns of community structure

that are characteristic of particular community types. For example, North American forests have vertical layers—canopy, midstory, and understory—that are composed of different life forms: trees, shrubs, herbs, and so on. Midwestern prairies have species that are active in the spring and fall (cool-season species) and others that are active in midsummer (warm-season species). In the northeast, many communities have some species that bloom in spring, some in summer, and some in fall. These other structures are thought to be a result of resource partitioning. This evolutionary strategy allows species that are potential competitors for a resource (space, light, pollinators) to coexist by specializing in different aspects of the resource.

82. **(C)** Selling pollution permits is essentially the same as charging each firm for every ton that they emit. Essentially, it is charging them in advance. If the pollution permit costs more than abatement, then they will abate. If it costs less, they will buy the permit and continue to pollute. In (A), the copper smelter would have to spend $450 and the electric utility would have to spend $250. In (B), the minimum each company would pay would be $251. In (C), each firm would be charged $151. In (D), halting production of an entire plant would be prohibitive.

83. **(C)** Of the organisms listed, the hawks occupy the highest trophic level as carnivorous consumers. Biomagnification, also known as bioamplification or biological magnification, is the increase in concentration of a substance that occurs in a food chain as a consequence of: (a) persistence (can't be broken down by environmental processes); (b) food chain energetics; and/or (c) low (or nonexistent) rate of internal degradation/excretion of the substance (often due to water insolubility). Lipid, (lipophilic) or fat soluble substances cannot be diluted, broken down, or excreted in urine, a water-based medium, and so accumulate in fatty tissues of an organism if the organism lacks enzymes to degrade them. When eaten by another organism, fats are absorbed in the gut, carrying the substance, which then accumulates in the fats of the predator. Since at each level of the food chain there is a lot of energy loss, a predator must consume much prey, including all of their lipophilic substances.

84. **(E)** Negative feedback causes the initial change to be reduced, slowing down change and helping to regulate the system and keep it in balance. If it is cold outside, the internal temperature of the house eventually drops as cold air seeps in through the walls. When the temperature drops below the point at which the thermostat is set, the thermostat turns on the furnace. As the temperature within the house rises, the thermostat again senses this change and turns off the furnace when the internal temperature reaches the pre-set point. Choices A, B, and D represent positive feedback loops.

85. **(D)** Refer to "Demographic Transition" in Chapter 6.

86. **(A)** Carbon dioxide and nitrous oxide levels are also linked to industry, automobile usage, and the use of fossil fuels to generate power at electrical plants. Nitrous oxide emissions can also be reduced by decreasing the amount of nitrogen-based fertilizers.

87. **(E)** Heap leaching is an industrial mining process that is used to extract copper, nickel, gold, and uranium, and other compounds from ore. The advantage of heap leaching is its relatively low operational costs and the ability to extract valuable mineral resources from what otherwise would be low grade ores. The

mined ore is usually crushed into small chunks and heaped on an impermeable plastic and/or clay lined leach pad where it can be irrigated with a leach solution to dissolve the valuable metals. The environmental consequences of the heap leaching processes are cyanide leaks and infiltration of cyanide and other toxins into the water supply. The production of one gold ring through the heap leaching method can generate up to 20 tons of waste material.

88. **(C)** Solids refer to matter suspended or dissolved in water or wastewater. Solids may affect water or effluent quality in a number of ways. Water with high dissolved solids is generally of inferior palatability and may cause health problems. Highly mineralized waters are unsuitable for many industrial applications. High suspended solids content can also be detrimental to aquatic plants and animals by limiting light and deteriorating habitat. Total dissolved solids are the amount of filterable solids in a water sample. To calculate total suspended solids:

Let A = weight of crucible + filter + residue after 24 hrs at 105°C (mg)
Let B = weight of crucible + filter (mg)

$$\text{Total suspended solids} = \frac{(A-B) \times 1{,}000 \text{ mL/L}}{\text{sample volume (mL)}} \times \frac{1{,}000 \text{ mg}}{g}$$

$$= \frac{(1{,}000 \text{ g} - 80.00 \text{ g}) \times 1{,}000 \text{ mL/L}}{100.00 \text{ mL}} \times \frac{1{,}000 \text{ mg}}{g}$$

89. **(E)** In a food chain, only about 10% of the energy is transferred from one level to the next. The other 90% is used for respiration, growth, digestion, escaping from predators, maintaining body heat, reproduction, etc. Plant (1,000) → mouse (100 available) → snake (10 available) → bird (1 available) → carnivore (0.1 available).

90. **(E)** A green manure is a type of cover crop grown primarily to add nutrients and organic matter to the soil. Typically, a green manure crop is grown for a specific period of time, and then plowed under and incorporated into the soil while green or shortly after flowering. Green manure crops are commonly associated with organic agriculture, and are considered essential for annual cropping systems that wish to be sustainable. In addition to the advantages covered in the question, green manures also function in weed suppression and prevention of soil erosion. Traditionally, the practice of using green manure can be traced back to the fallow cycle of crop rotation, which was used to allow soils to recover.

91. **(C)** Phosphates and nitrates are required for photosynthesis and vary in concentration due to biological activity. In surface waters, where plants are actively involved in the process of photosynthesis, nitrates and phosphates can be in short supply, limiting the amount of biological activity that can take place. The cycling of materials (in this case, nitrates and phosphates) is the function of organisms of decay. Microscopic bacteria in seawater can contain up to 1,000,000 bacterial cells per cubic centimeter.

92. **(D)** Ocean temperatures increase more slowly than land temperatures because of the larger effective heat capacity of the oceans and because the oceans lose

more heat by evaporation. Heat capacity tells you how much heat you can put in before the temperature has risen by 1 degree. If something has a large heat capacity, then more heat can be absorbed before it rises in temperature by 1 degree. The heat capacity of ocean water is about four times that of air. Land temperatures have increased about twice as fast as ocean temperatures (0.25°C per decade for land vs. 0.13°C per decade for oceans). The Northern Hemisphere warms faster than the Southern Hemisphere because there is more land in the Northern Hemisphere.

93. **(E)** Nitrous oxide is emitted by bacteria in soils and oceans and has 300 times more impact as a greenhouse gas than carbon dioxide. Nitrous oxide is the fourth largest contributor to greenhouse gases ranked behind water vapor, carbon dioxide, and methane.

Radon (Rn) is a radioactive element and occurs naturally as the decay product of uranium and thorium. Radon sticks to dust particles in the air. If contaminated dust is inhaled, these particles can stick to the airways of the lung and increase the risk of developing lung cancer. Radon is responsible for the majority of the public exposure to radiation. Radon gas from natural sources can accumulate in buildings, especially in confined areas such as attics and basements. It can also be found in some spring waters and hot springs. According to the Environmental Protection Agency (EPA), radon is the second most frequent cause of lung cancer, after cigarette smoking, causing 21,000 lung cancer deaths per year in the United States.

Sulfur dioxide (SO_2) is a poisonous gas with a pungent, irritating smell that is naturally released by volcanoes. Further oxidation of SO_2, usually in the presence of a catalyst such as NO_2, forms H_2SO_4, and thus acid rain. Sulfur dioxide emissions are also a precursor to particulates in the atmosphere.

Formaldehyde (CH_2O) is found in plants, fruits, vegetables, animals (including humans), and seafood. The highest concentrations of formaldehyde are found in dried shiitake mushrooms (up to 400 mg formaldehyde per kg of mushroom). Formaldehyde is essential in human metabolism and is required for the synthesis of DNA and amino acids. Human blood contains ~2.5 µg of formaldehyde per ml of blood.

94. **(A)** Primary waves (P-waves) travel faster than other waves through the Earth and arrive at seismograph stations first hence the name "Primary." These waves can travel through any type of material, including fluids, and can travel at nearly twice the speed of S waves. Secondary waves (S-waves) arrive at seismograph stations after the faster moving P waves during an earthquake and displace the ground perpendicular to the direction of propagation. S waves can travel only through solids. S waves are about 60% slower than P waves. Surface waves are analogous to water waves and travel along the Earth's surface. Because of their low frequency, long duration, and large amplitude, they can be the most destructive type of seismic wave. They are called surface waves because they diminish as they get further from the surface.

95. **(D)** The more ozone in a given parcel of the stratosphere, the more heat it retains. Ozone generates heat in the stratosphere, both by absorbing the sun's ultraviolet radiation and by absorbing upwelling infrared radiation from the lower atmosphere (troposphere). Consequently, decreased ozone in the stratosphere results in lower stratospheric temperatures and increased UV radiation

reaching the surface of Earth. Observations show that over recent decades, the mid to upper stratosphere (from 30 to 50 km above Earth's surface) has cooled by 2°F to 11°F (1°C to 6°C). This stratospheric cooling has taken place at the same time that greenhouse gas amounts in the lower atmosphere (troposphere) have risen.

96. **(B)** In primary succession, which occurs in virtually a lifeless area (e.g., area below a retreating glacier), pioneer species like lichen, algae, and fungus, as well as other abiotic factors like wind and water, start to change or create conditions better suited for vascular plant growth. These changes include accumulation of organic matter in litter or humic layer, alteration of soil nutrients, and change in pH or water content of soil. These pioneer plants are then dominated and often replaced by plants better adapted to less austere conditions, such as grasses and shrubs that are able to live in thin, mineral-based soils. The structure of the plants themselves can also alter the community. For example, when larger species like trees mature, they produce shade on the developing forest floor, which tends to exclude light-requiring species. Shade-tolerant species will then invade the area.

97. **(D)** Most indoor air pollution experts agree that carpet should be avoided whenever feasible. The reason for this is that carpet is made up of some 120 different chemicals, many of which can cause health problems. Once installed, carpet can collect dust and even lead (tracked in from shoes) and can grow mold and dust mites. Methylene chloride is given off by paint thinners and paint strippers. Methylene chloride has a fairly long atmospheric half-life, 3 to 4 months, indicating the fairly long persistence typical of transported pollutants.

98. **(A)** Uniform distribution means that organisms of a population are generally equally spaced apart. In most situations, a natural uniform dispersion occurs when organisms that comprise a population compete for a common resource. In (A), red squirrels might be found anywhere within their geographic territory, defending it. In (B), cattails would be found clumped in only one area (near the water). In (C), dwarf mistletoe would only be found where a particular species of forest tree is growing. In (D), moths would have a higher density near lighted areas rather than in darker areas, as most moths are attracted by light. In (E), the lake trout would be found more in the deeper areas of the water.

99. **(B)** A density-independent factor is one where the effect of the factor on the size of the population is independent of and does not depend upon the original density or size of the population. The effect of weather is an example of a density-independent factor. A severe storm and flood coming through an area can just as easily wipe out a large population as a small one.

100. **(D)** High-quality energy is capable of performing a large amount of work, while low-quality energy is capable of performing less work. Energy always changes from high to low quality when work is performed. During the change, some energy is lost in the form of heat, which cannot do work (second law of thermodynamics). The amount of energy lost as heat is often as high as 90% of the total energy involved. The reason that (D) is the answer is because of the word "dispersed." Dispersed energy is not concentrated, therefore it is of low quality. An analogy would be ore deposits. A rich gold mine has a lot of gold in concentrated form. A stream might also have a lot of gold (maybe even more than the mine). However, if there are only a few small nuggets every few hundred feet, it is not as rich.

FREE-RESPONSE EXPLANATIONS

Question 1

(a) 3 points maximum

(i) 1 point

Restatement: Number of cubic feet of natural gas required to heat the house for the winter.

$$4{,}000 \text{ \sout{square feet}} \times \frac{100{,}000 \text{ Btus}}{1 \text{ \sout{square foot}}} = \textbf{400{,}000{,}000 Btus}$$

(ii) 1 point

Restatement: Cost of heating the home for one winter using natural gas.

$$400{,}000{,}000 \text{ \sout{Btus}} \times \frac{1 \text{ \sout{cubic foot natural gas}}}{1{,}000 \text{ \sout{Btus}}} \times \frac{\$5.00}{1{,}000 \text{ \sout{cubic feet}}} = \textbf{\$2{,}000}$$

(iii) 1 point

Restatement: Cost of heating the home for one winter using electricity.

$$400{,}000{,}000 \text{ \sout{Btus}} \times \frac{1 \text{ \sout{kWh}}}{10{,}000 \text{ \sout{Btus}}} \times \frac{\$50}{500 \text{ \sout{kWh}}} = \textbf{\$4{,}000}$$

NOTE:
1. If you do NOT show calculations, no points are awarded.
2. No penalty assessed if you do not show units. However, you risk setting up the problem incorrectly if you do not show units so that they cancel properly.
3. If your setup is correct but you make an arithmetic error, no penalty is assessed.

NOTE: For Parts (b) and (c), there are no points for just listing ideas. Each idea MUST be explained. The following are ideas that you could use to write your paragraph(s). Take these ideas, and create an outline of the order in which you wish to answer them. You do NOT need to use all ideas. Before you begin, decide on the format of how you wish to answer your question (pros versus cons, chart format with explanations within the chart, compare and contrast, etc.).

(b) 4 points maximum

> (i) (1 point definition) In active solar heating applications, heat from the sun is collected, stored, and used primarily for domestic hot water and space heating. The reason the system is called active is because pumps and fans are used to transfer the captured heat to an area where it can be stored or used. The main components of an active solar system are the collectors, the collector controls, the storage tank, and the distribution system.

Active Solar System (1 point) Choose ideas from the list below:

- Active liquid solar systems heat water or an antifreeze solution in a collector. Liquid solar collectors are most appropriate for central heating. Flat-plate collectors are the most common. In the collector, a heat transfer fluid such as a water or antifreeze absorbs the solar heat. At the appropriate time, a controller operates a circulating pump to move the fluid through the collector. The heated liquid flows to either a storage tank or a heat exchanger for immediate use.

- Air collectors produce heat earlier and later in the day than liquid systems. Therefore, air systems may produce more usable energy over a heating season than a liquid system of the same size. Solar air collectors have a black metal plate for absorbing heat, which in turn heats air in the collector. A fan then blows this heated air into the house. Air collectors can be installed on a roof or on a south-facing exterior wall. These systems are easier and less expensive to install than a central heating system. They do not have a dedicated storage system or extensive ductwork. The floors, walls, and furniture will absorb some of the solar heat, which will help keep the room warm for a few hours after sunset. Masonry walls and tile floors will also provide more thermal mass and thus provide heat for longer periods. A well-insulated house will make a solar room air heater more efficient.

> (ii) (1 point definition) In passive solar building design, windows, walls, and floors are made to collect, store, and distribute solar energy in the form of heat in the winter and reject solar heat in the summer. This is called passive solar design or climatic design because, unlike active solar heating systems, it doesn't involve the use of mechanical and electrical devices. The key to designing a passive solar building is to best take advantage of the local climate. Elements to be considered include window placement and glazing type, thermal insulation, thermal mass, and shading.

Passive Solar System (1 point definition) Choose ideas from the list below:

- There are two basic approaches to passive solar systems. First, direct gain—solar energy is transmitted through south-facing windows. Works best when the south window area is double-glazed and the building has considerable thermal mass in the form of concrete floors and masonry walls. Second, indirect gain in which a storage mass collects and stores heat directly from the sun and then transfers the heat to the living space(s).

(iii) Choose ONE idea from the list below: (1 point)

Advantages

- Reduces the use of fossil fuels and their emission of greenhouse gases.
- Solar energy is a renewable energy resource.
- The financial costs of solar systems are falling as technology develops.
- Fossil fuels, being a nonrenewable energy source, are running out. As they become more scarce, prices will rise, making solar energy more cost effective in the future.
- Suitable for remote areas that are not connected to energy grids or pipelines.
- Zero risk of indoor pollution such as carbon monoxide.

Disadvantages

- Higher initial cost of equipment than conventional heating systems.
- Clouds may reduce effectiveness.
- A solar energy installation requires a large area for the system to be efficient in providing a source of electricity. This may be a disadvantage in areas where space is short, or expensive.
- The location of solar panels can affect performance, due to possible obstructions from the surrounding buildings or landscape.

(c) 3 points maximum

(i) (1 point definition): A green building focuses on a whole-system approach, including energy conservation, resource-efficient building techniques and materials, indoor air quality, water conservation, and designs that minimize waste while utilizing recycled materials. Green buildings are a product of a good design that minimizes a building's energy needs while reducing construction and maintenance costs over the life cycle of a building.

(ii) (2 points) Choose any TWO ideas from the following:

- Solar collectors for space heating.
- Solar collectors for water heating.
- Photovoltaics to supply electrical energy.
- Hybrid systems that incorporate more than one power source such as wind and solar.
- Use of energy efficient (Energy Star) appliances.
- Products made from environmentally sustainable materials.
- Products that do not contain toxins (ex: PVC pipes, ozone-depleting chemicals, formaldehyde in plywood, paints and stains with VOCs).
- Products that reduce the environmental impact on building operations (ex: new energy saving thermostats, newer landscape irrigation systems that only activate based on soil moisture content).
- Products that remove or warn of indoor pollution hazards (ex: carbon monoxide detectors, air filtration systems, water purifying systems).
- Homes that meet or exceed insulation requirements.
- Green landscaping—landscaping that provides shade during the summer and allows sunlight to warm the house during winter and the use of plants that do not require large amounts of water.

Question 2

(a) Define "aquafarming" (1 point)

Aquafarming is the commercial farming of freshwater and saltwater fish, mollusks, crustaceans, and aquatic plants. Also known as aquaculture, it involves cultivating aquatic populations under controlled conditions.

(i) Describe TWO advantages of aquafarming over traditional wild harvesting. (2 points)

In aquaculture, the life cycle of organisms occurs under controlled conditions. Advantages of having control over the life cycle of organisms include: (1) more intensive farming is possible, which often results in higher yields and greater profits; (2) more uniformity in the product since environmental conditions are controlled and managed, which results in less waste and higher profits; (3) predator control; (4) the ability to accelerate growth and maturation by controlling the climate, especially on farms located in more temperate zones; and (5) most traditional expenses and variables inherent to wild harvesting (the costs of boats, crews, nets, weather conditions, searching for areas with enough of the species that can be captured to be profitable, etc.) are minimized or eliminated.

(ii) Describe TWO negative environmental impacts of aquafarming. (2 points)

Fish waste is organic and composed of nutrients necessary in all components of aquatic food webs. Aquaculture often produces much higher-than-normal fish waste concentrations, as the habitat is confined. The waste collects on the ocean bottom, damaging or eliminating bottom-dwelling life. Waste can also decrease dissolved oxygen levels in the water column, putting further pressure on other organisms. Waste products from aquafarming are often discharged untreated directly into the surrounding aquatic environment and frequently contain antibiotics and pesticides.

Growers often supply their animals with antibiotics to prevent disease, which can accelerate the evolution of bacterial resistance.

Other acceptable answers include:
- *Fish can escape from coastal pens, where they can interbreed with their wild counterparts, diluting wild genetic stocks.*
- *Escaped fish can become invasive, outcompeting native species.*
- *Aquaculture is becoming a significant threat to coastal systems; e.g., about 20% of mangrove forests worldwide have been destroyed since 1980, partly due to shrimp farming.*

(b) Describe TWO methods that can be employed in aquaculture to lessen the environmental impact. (2 points)

Onshore recirculating aquaculture facilities using polyculture techniques and properly sited facilities (e.g., offshore areas with strong currents) can minimize the negative environmental effects.

Other acceptable methods include:
- *Formulate coastal aquaculture development and management plans.*
- *Formulate integrated coastal zone management plans.*
- *Assess the capacity of the local ecosystem to sustain aquaculture development with minimal ecological change, and establish a permit system based on the local ecosystem's capacity for aquafarming.*
- *Establish guidelines governing the use of wetlands and mangrove forests.*
- *Establish guidelines for the use of bioactive compounds (pesticides, hormones, pharmaceuticals, herbicides, etc.)*
- *Assess and evaluate the true consequences of transfers and introduction of exotic organisms.*
- *Regulate discharges from land-based aquaculture through the enforcement of effluent standards.*
- *Establish quality control measures for aquaculture products.*
- *Apply incentives and deterrents to reduce environmental degradation from aquaculture activities.*
- *Monitor water quality using established protocols for any signs of ecological change.*

(c) How is raising and harvesting kelp and bivalve mollusks a more sustainable method of aquafarming than raising and harvesting higher trophic order fish such as salmon? (1 point)

Raising seaweed and filter-feeding bivalve mollusks, such as oysters, clams, mussels, and scallops, has a very low impact on the environment and may even be environmentally restorative, as these filter-feeders filter pollutants and excessive nutrients from the water, often improving water quality. Kelp extract nutrients such as inorganic nitrogen and phosphorus directly from the water, while filter-feeding mollusks can extract nutrients as they feed on particulates such as phytoplankton and detritus.

(d) The newspaper announcement claims that aquafarming is the answer to world hunger. Give TWO examples of how this statement may be contrary to environmental sustainability. (2 points)

Salmon farming currently involves a high demand for wild forage fish for feed, as well as their by-products—fish meal and fish oil. As carnivores high on the food chain, salmon require a lot of protein, and farmed salmon consume more protein than they produce; e.g., each pound of farmed salmon requires up to 6 pounds (2 kg) of wild fish. About 75% of the world's monitored fisheries are already near to or have exceeded their maximum sustainable yield. The industrial-scale extraction of wild forage fish for salmon farming also impacts the survivability of the wild predator fish that rely on them for food.

Question 3

(a) Describe the role and importance of stratospheric ozone to life on Earth. (1 point)

The ozone (O_3) layer, located in the lower portion of the stratosphere, absorbs up to 99% of the sun's high-frequency ultraviolet radiation, which is damaging to life on Earth. About 90% of the atmospheric ozone resides in a layer approximately 6–30 miles (10–50 km) above the Earth's surface, in the region of the atmosphere known as the stratosphere. This stratospheric ozone is commonly referred to as the "ozone layer." The remaining ozone is in the lower region of the atmosphere, the troposphere, which extends from the Earth's surface up to about 6 miles (10 km). Stratospheric ozone plays a beneficial role by absorbing most of the biologically damaging ultraviolet sunlight (UVB and UC) before it reaches the Earth's surface. The absorption of ultraviolet radiation by ozone in this zone creates a source of heat in the stratosphere that increases with altitude. Ozone thus plays a key role in the temperature structure of the Earth's atmosphere. Without the filtering action of the ozone layer, more of the sun's UVB and UVC radiation would penetrate the atmosphere and reach the Earth's surface.

(b) Suggest ONE possible reason for the appearance of the hole in the ozone layer, which was first observed in the 1980s. (1 point)

Scientific evidence has shown that human-produced chemicals are most likely responsible for the observed depletion of the ozone layer. CFCs (chlorofluorocarbons) were the first mass-produced chemical compounds shown to destroy ozone. CFCs were primarily used in refrigeration and air-conditioning (e.g., Freon) and in the dry cleaning industry (e.g., carbon tetrachloride). Later, halocarbons, chemical compounds similar to CFCs but which contain bromine, were also shown to destroy ozone molecules. Halocarbons were used in foam blowing, soil fumigants and pesticides (e.g., methyl bromide), fire retardants and extinguishers, and as a solvent in producing circuit boards (e.g., methyl chloroform).

(c) Ultraviolet (UV) radiation occurs in three forms, known as UVA, UVB, and UVC.

   (i) Describe at least ONE characteristic of EACH form of ultraviolet radiation. (3 points)

   The three types of UV radiation are classified according to their wavelength. They differ in their biological activity and the extent to which they can penetrate the skin; i.e., the shorter the wavelength, the more harmful the UV radiation. However, shorter wavelength UV radiation is less able to penetrate the skin. Short-wavelength UVC is the most damaging type of UV radiation. However, it is completely filtered by the atmosphere and does not reach the Earth's surface. Medium-wavelength UVB is very biologically active but cannot penetrate beyond the superficial skin layers. Most solar UVB is filtered by the atmosphere. The relatively long-wavelength UVA accounts for approximately 95% of the UV radiation reaching the Earth's surface.

(ii) Describe the effects that increased UV radiation would have on:

(a) Human health (1 point)

Changes in the skin's DNA due to UVA and UVB rays can cause serious, long-term skin damage. UVA and UVB radiation can penetrate into the deeper layers of the skin and is responsible for the immediate tanning effect. Furthermore, it also contributes to skin aging and wrinkling, and recent studies suggest that it may also enhance the development of skin cancers. One effect of UV exposure is that it advances the signs of aging. Premature wrinkling is common in people who have been exposed to the sun over long periods of time, as are age spots and uneven complexions. UV radiation can also cause cataracts and weaken the immune system.

(b) Terrestrial ecosystems (1 point)

Excessive exposure to UV radiation can cause cancers in animals and damage their eyesight. Increase UV exposure can harm DNA and proteins, and affect organisms in their developmental stages. These direct effects may lead to indirect effects, such as decreased primary productivity, changes in biodiversity, decreased nitrogen uptake by microorganisms, and reduced capacity for oceans to fix carbon dioxide. Research on the effects of increased UVB exposure in higher trophic levels has shown reduced reproductive capacity, growth, and survival rates. Experiments on certain food crops (e.g., rice and soybeans) have shown lower crop yields when exposed to higher levels of UVB radiation. The plants minimize their exposure to increased UV radiation by limiting the surface area of their foliage, which in turn impairs growth.

(c) Marine ecosystems (1 point)

Phytoplankton, which are located at the base of the aquatic food pyramid, account for approximately 30% of the world's intake of animal protein. Phytoplankton productivity is restricted to the upper layer of the water, where sufficient light is available. A small increase in UVB exposure brought about by less stratospheric ozone could significantly reduce the size of plankton populations, affecting the environment in several ways: (1) with less organic matter in the upper layers of the water, UV radiation can penetrate deeper into the water and affect more complex plants and animals living there; (2) UV radiation directly damages animals during their early development; (3) pollution of the water by toxic substances may synergistically magnify the adverse effects of UV radiation, working its way up the food chain; (4) less plankton means less food for the animals that prey on them and a reduction in fish stocks already depleted by overfishing; (5) decreased bacterial and plankton activity may lead to an increase in dissolved organic matter in ocean waters, as assimilation of dissolved organic matter is reduced. Cyanobacteria, organisms important in nitrogen fixation, are also at risk. Cyanobacteria transform dissolved nitrogen in ocean water to nitrates and other forms that are accessible by higher plants; (6) a decrease in phytoplankton growth reduces the uptake of carbon dioxide by the oceans, thus leaving more CO_2 in the atmospheric reservoir. Increased atmospheric CO_2 has implications for global warming; and (7) decreased amounts of plankton causes a decrease in the amount of dimethyl sulfide (DMS) they release, an important source of cloud condensation nuclei.

(d) Identify and describe ONE alternative to ozone-destroying chemical compounds. (1 point)

Compounds containing C-H bonds (HCFCs) have been designed to replace chlorofluorocarbons. These compounds are more reactive and less likely to survive long enough in the atmosphere to reach the stratosphere, where they would affect the ozone layer. While less damaging than CFCs, HCFCs also have a significant negative impact on the ozone layer. HCFCs are also being phased out.

(e) Identify and briefly describe ONE international treaty that addresses the release of chemical compounds that destroy stratospheric ozone. (1 point)

The 1987 Montreal Protocol on Substances that Deplete the Ozone Layer was an international treaty designed to protect the ozone layer by phasing out the production of a number of substances, especially chlorofluorocarbons (CFCs), believed to be responsible for ozone depletion. Stratospheric ozone depletion can be expected to continue (but at a slower pace) because of CFCs used by nations that have not banned them, and because of gases that are already in the stratosphere. CFCs have a very long atmospheric lifetime, ranging from 50 to more than 100 years, so the complete recovery of the ozone layer is expected to require several lifetimes.

Question 4

(a) (i) 2 points maximum (1 point for each correct event)

Restatement: Two possible events that have occurred within the last 100 years that can account for the increase in human life span.

Since 1900, the average life span of persons living in the United States has increased by more than 30 years, with most of this gain attributable to advances in public health. The three advances in public health that have had the greatest impact on world health and human life span have been the availability of clean water, improvements in sanitation, and the development of vaccines.

(ii) 1 point maximum (1 point for a correct and accurate description of one event listed above)

Restatement: Describe how public sanitation increased average human life span.

At the turn of the 20th century, it was a common practice to dispose of garbage, industrial wastes, and raw sewage by dumping them into waterways. Few municipalities treated wastewater because it was widely believed that running water purified itself. Typhoid, dysentery, and diarrhea were the most common waterborne diseases and were also the third leading cause of death in the United States at that time. As a result of disinfection of public drinking water and improved sanitation methods, the major waterborne diseases have all but ceased to exist in the United States. Worldwide, the median reduction in deaths from water-related diseases is approximately 70% among people with access to potable water and proper sanitation. Yet waterborne diseases continue to be major killers in less-developed countries, causing half of all deaths of children in poor countries.

(b) (i) 1 point maximum (1 point for a correct explanation of how malaria is transmitted)

Restatement: How malaria is transmitted through the human population.

Malaria is naturally transmitted by the bite of a female *Anopheles* mosquito. When this species of mosquito bites an infected person, a small amount of blood is taken, which contains malaria parasites (*Plasmodium*). These parasites develop within the mosquito, and about one week later, when the mosquito takes its next blood meal, the parasites are injected with the mosquito's saliva into the person being bitten. After a period of between two weeks and several months (occasionally years) in the human liver, the malaria parasites start to multiply within red blood cells, causing symptoms that include fever and headache. In severe cases, the disease worsens, leading to coma and death.

(ii) 4 points maximum (1 point for each correct environmental factor, maximum of 2 points; 1 point for each correct explanation of how each factor influenced the increase of the disease, maximum of 2 points)

Restatement: Two environmental factors that contribute to the emergence of malaria and how those factors influence the increase in the incidence of the disease.

Environmental factors that can contribute to the emergence of malaria include:

1. A decrease in the population of mosquito predators, which can increase the mosquito population and the rate of transmission.
2. Genetic resistance to pesticides, which can also increase the mosquito population and the rate of transmission.
3. Changes in the climate (e.g., global warming), which can increase the number of suitable habitats, resulting in increased rates of transmission.
4. Changes in the current habitats (e.g., agriculture, logging), which can increase the number of breeding sites.
5. An increase in the population density, which allows for a greater opportunity for transmission.
6. The emergence of *Plasmodia* strains that are resistant to anti-malarial drugs, which can then lead to an increase in the incidence and transmission of malaria.

(iii) 2 points maximum (1 point for a correct description of biological control and 1 point for a correct method for controlling the spread of malaria)

Restatement: Description of biological control and an example of one biological control method used for controlling the spread of the disease.

Biological control is the reduction of pest populations by natural enemies and typically involves an active human role. It is a method of controlling pests that relies on predation, parasitism, or other natural mechanisms and can be an important component of integrated pest management programs. Effective biocontrol agents that can be used to decrease the incidence of malaria include predatory fish that feed on mosquito larvae; other insects, such as dragonfly nymphs, that consume mosquito larvae in the breeding waters; adult dragonflies that eat adult mosquitoes; other mosquito species that prey on the *Anopheles* mosquito; predatory crustaceans; birds; bats; lizards; and frogs. Microbial pathogens that can be used to target and control *Anopheles* mosquitoes include viruses, bacteria, fungi, protozoa, nematodes, and microsporidia. Dead spores of varieties of the natural soil bacterium Bt (*Bacillus thuringiensis*) can be used to interfere with the digestive systems of *Anopheles* larvae and can be dispersed by hand or dropped by air over large areas.

Index

How to Use the CD-ROM

The software is not installed on your computer; it runs directly from the CD-ROM. Barron's CD-ROM includes an "autorun" feature that automatically launches the application when the CD is inserted into the CD-ROM drive. In the unlikely event that the autorun feature is disabled, follow the manual launching instructions below.

Windows®

1. Click on the Start button and choose "My Computer."
2. Double-click on the CD-ROM drive, which is named **AP_Environmental_Science.exe.**
3. Double-click **AP_Environmental_Science.exe** to launch the program.

MAC®

1. Double-click the CD-ROM icon.
2. Double-click the **AP_Environmental_Science** icon to start the program.

SYSTEM REQUIREMENTS

Microsoft® Windows®
Intel Pentium II 450 MHz,
AMD Athlon 600 MHz or faster processor
(or equivalent).
Memory: 128MB of RAM.
Graphics Memory: 128MB.
Color Display: 1024 × 768
Platforms:
Windows 7, Windows Vista®, Windows XP

MAC®
Intel Core™ Duo
1.33GHz or faster processor.
Memory: 256MB of RAM.
Graphics Memory: 128MB.
Color Display: 1024 × 768
Platforms:
Mac OS 10.4 or higher.